D1268702

CHILTON'S
TOTAL CAR CARE REPAIR MANUAL

CHEVROLET ASTRO
GMC SAFARI
1985-90
REPAIR MANUAL

President, Chilton Enterprises	David S. Loewith
Senior Vice President	Ronald A. Hoxter
Publisher and Editor-In-Chief	Kerry A. Freeman, S.A.E.
Managing Editors	Peter M. Conti, Jr. □ W. Calvin Settle, Jr., S.A.E.
Assistant Managing Editor	Nick D'Andrea
Senior Editors	Debra Gaffney □ Ken Grabowski, A.S.E., S.A.E.
	Michael L. Grady □ Richard J. Rivele, S.A.E.
	Richard T. Smith □ Jim Taylor
	Ron Webb
Director of Manufacturing	Mike D'Imperio
Editor	James B. Steele

CHILTON BOOK COMPANY

*ONE OF THE DIVERSIFIED PUBLISHING COMPANIES,
A PART OF CAPITAL CITIES/ABC, INC.*

Manufactured in USA
© 1990 Chilton Book Company
Chilton Way, Radnor, PA 19089
ISBN 0–8019–8056–9
Library of Congress Catalog Card No. 90–055433
4567890123 3210987654

Contents

Contents

SAFETY NOTICE

Proper service and repair procedures are vital to the safe, reliable operation of all motor vehicles, as well as the personal safety of those performing repairs. This manual outlines procedures for servicing and repairing vehicles using safe, effective methods. The procedures contain many NOTES, CAUTIONS and WARNINGS which should be followed along with standard safety procedures to eliminate the possibility of personal injury or improper service which could damage the vehicle or compromise its safety.

It is important to note that the repair procedures and techniques, tools and parts for servicing motor vehicles, as well as the skill and experience of the individual performing the work vary widely. It is not possible to anticipate all of the conceivable ways or conditions under which vehicles may be serviced, or to provide cautions as to all of the possible hazards that may result. Standard and accepted safety precautions and equipment should be used when handling toxic or flammable fluids, and safety goggles or other protection should be used during cutting, grinding, chiseling, prying, or any other process that can cause material removal or projectiles.

Some procedures require the use of tools specially designed for a specific purpose. Before substituting another tool or procedure, you must be completely satisfied that neither your personal safety, nor the performance of the vehicle will be endangered

Although information in this manual is based on industry sources and is complete as possible at the time of publication, the possibility exists that some car manufacturers made later changes which could not be included here. While striving for total accuracy, Chilton Book Company cannot assume responsibility for any errors, changes or omissions that may occur in the compilation of this data.

PART NUMBERS

Part numbers listed in this reference are not recommendations by Chilton for any product by brand name. They are references that can be used with interchange manuals and aftermarket supplier catalogs to locate each brand supplier's discrete part number.

SPECIAL TOOLS

Special tools are recommended by the vehicle manufacturer to perform their specific job. Use has been kept to a minimum, but where absolutely necessary, they are referred to in the text by the part number of the tool manufacturer. These tools can be purchased under the appropriate part number, from your Chevrolet or GMC dealer or regional distributor or an equivalent tool can be purchased locally from a tool supplier or parts outlet. Before substituting any tool for the recommended one, read the SAFETY NOTICE at the top of this page.

ACKNOWLEDGMENTS

The Chilton Book Company expresses its appreciation to Chevrolet Motor Division, General Motors Corporation, Detroit, Michigan for their generous assistance.

General Information and Maintenance

1

QUICK REFERENCE INDEX

GENERAL INDEX

HOW TO USE THIS BOOK

Chilton's Repair & Tune-Up Guide for the Chevrolet Astro and GMC Safari Vans is intended to help you learn more about the inner working of your vehicle and save you money in it's upkeep and operation.

The first two Sections will be the most used, since they contain maintenance and tune-up information and procedures. Studies have shown that a properly tuned and maintained van can get at least 10% better gas mileage than an out-of-tune van. The other Sections deal with the more complex systems of your van. Operating systems from engine through brakes are covered to the extent that the average do-it-yourselfer becomes mechanically involved. This book will not explain such things as rebuilding the differential for the simple reason that the expertise required and the investment in special tools make this task uneconomical. It will give you detailed instructions to help you change your own brake pads and shoes, replace spark plugs, do many more jobs that will save you money, give you personal satisfaction and help you avoid expensive problems.

A secondary purpose of this book is a reference for owners who want to understand their van and/or their mechanics better. In this case, no tools at all are required.

Before removing any bolts, read through the entire procedure. This will give you the overall view of what tools and supplies will be required. There is nothing more frustrating that having to walk to the bus stop on Monday morning because you were short one bolt on Sunday afternoon. So read ahead and plan ahead. Each operation should be approached logically and all procedures thoroughly understood before attempting any work.

All Sections contain adjustments, maintenance, removal/installation and repair or overhaul procedures. When repair is not considered practical, we tell you how to remove the part and then how to install the new or rebuilt replacement. In this way, you at least save the labor costs. Backyard repair of such components as the alternator is just not practical.

Two basic mechanic's rules should be mentioned: One, whenever the left side of the vehicle or engine is referred to, it is meant to specify the driver's side of the vehicle. Conversely, the right side of the vehicle means the passenger's side. Secondly, most screws and bolts are removed by turning them counterclockwise and/or tightened by turning them clockwise.

Safety is always the most important rule. Constantly be aware of the dangers involved in working on an automobile and take the proper precautions. (See the section in this Section, Servicing Your Vehicle Safely and the SAFETY NOTICE on the acknowledgment page).

Pay attention to the instructions provided. There are 3 common mistakes in mechanical work:

1. Incorrect order of assembly, disassembly or adjustment. When taking something apart or putting it together, doing things in the wrong order usually costs extra time, however, it CAN break something. Read the entire procedure before beginning the disassembly. Do everything in the order in which the instructions say you should do it, even if you can't immediately see a reason for it. When you're taking something apart that is very intricate (for example, a carburetor), you might want to draw a picture of how it looks when assembled at one point, in order to make sure you get everything back in its proper position. (We will supply exploded views whenever possible). When making adjustments, especially tune-up adjustments, do them in order. Often, one adjustment affects another and you cannot expect satisfactory results unless each adjustment is made only when it cannot be changed by any other.

2. Overtorquing (or undertorquing). While it is more common for overtorquing to cause damage, undertorquing can cause a fastener to vibrate loose causing serious damage. Especially, when dealing with aluminum parts, pay attention to torque specifications and utilize a torque wrench in assembly. If a torque figure is not available, remember that if you are using the right tool to do the job, you will probably not have to strain yourself to get a fastener tight enough. The pitch of most threads is so slight that the tension you put on the wrench will be multiplied many, many times in actual force on what you are tightening. A good example of how critical torque is can be seen in the case of spark plug installation, especially where you are putting the plug into an aluminum cylinder head. Too little torque can fail to crush the gasket, causing leakage of combustion gases and consequent overheating of the plug and engine parts. Too much torque can damage the threads or distort the plug, which changes the spark gap.

NOTE: There are many commercial products available for ensuring that fasteners won't come loose, even if they are not torqued just right (a very common brand is Loctite®). If you're worried about getting something together tight enough to hold but loose enough to avoid mechanical damage during assembly, one of these products might offer substantial insurance. Read the label on the package and make sure the product is compatible with the materials, fluids and etc. involved before choosing one.

3. Crossthreading occurs when a part such as a bolt is screwed into a nut or casting at the wrong angle and forced. Crossthreading is more likely to occur if access is difficult. It helps to clean and lubricate the fasteners, then start threading with the part to be installed going straight in. Start the bolt, spark plug and etc. with your fingers. If you encounter resistance, unscrew the part and start over again at a different angle until it can be inserted and turned several turns without much effort. Keep in mind that many parts, especially spark plugs, use tapered threads so that gentle turning will automatically bring the part you're threading to the proper angle if you don't force it or resist a change in angle. Don't put a wrench on the part until it's been turned a couple of turns by hand. If you suddenly encounter resistance, and the part has not been seated fully, don't force it. Pull it back out and make sure it's clean and threading properly.

NOTE: Always take your time and be patient, once you have some experience working on your vehicle, it will become an enjoyable hobby.

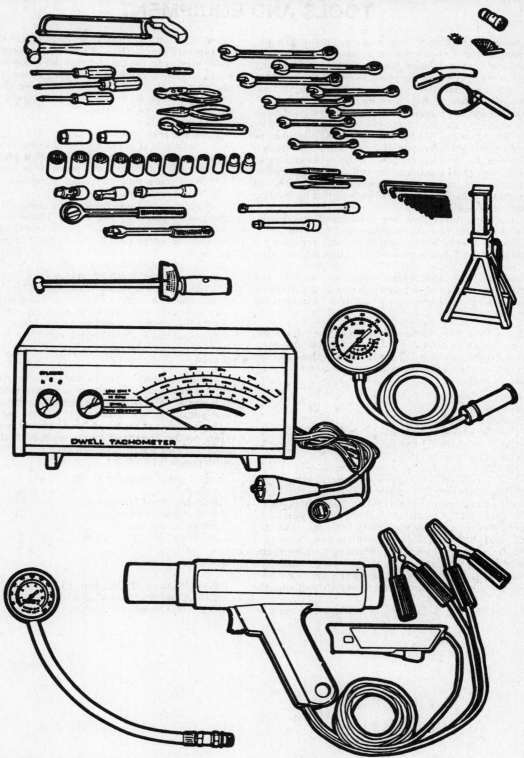

You need only a basic assortment of hand tools for most maintenance and repair jobs

TOOLS AND EQUIPMENT

Naturally, without the proper tools and equipment, it is impossible to properly service your vehicle. It would be impossible to catalog each tool that you would need to perform each or any operation in this book. It would also be unwise for the amateur to rush out and buy an expensive set of tools on the theory that he may need one or more of them at sometime.

The best approach is to proceed slowly, gathering a good quality set of tools that are used most frequently. Don't be misled by the low cost of bargain tools. It is far better to spend a little more for better quality. Forged wrenches, 6- or 12-point sockets and fine tooth ratchets are by far preferable to their less expensive counterparts. As any good mechanic can tell you, there are few worse experiences than trying to work on a vehicle with bad tools. Your monetary savings will be far outweighed by frustration and mangled knuckles.

Begin accumulating tools that are used most frequently; those associated with routine maintenance and tune-up.

In addition to the normal assortment of screwdrivers and pliers you should have the following tools for routine maintenance jobs:

1. SAE (or Metric) or SAE/Metric wrenches—sockets and combination open end/box end wrenches in sizes from $\frac{1}{8}$–$\frac{3}{4}$ in. and 6–19mm and a spark plug socket ($\frac{13}{16}$ in. or $\frac{5}{8}$ in. depending on plug type).

NOTE: If possible, buy various length socket drive extensions. One break in this department is that the metric sockets available in the U.S. will all fit the ratchet handles and extensions you may already have ($\frac{1}{4}$ in., $\frac{3}{8}$ in. and $\frac{1}{2}$ in. drive).

2. Jackstands, for support
3. Oil filter wrench
4. Oil filler spout, for pouring oil
5. Grease gun, for chassis lubrication
6. Hydrometer, for checking the battery
7. A container for draining oil
8. Many rags for wiping up the inevitable mess.

In addition to the above items there are several others that are not absolutely necessary but handy to have around. These include oil dry, a transmission funnel and an usual supply of lubricants, antifreeze and fluids, although these can be purchased as needed. This is a basic list for routine maintenance but only your personal needs and desires can accurately determine your list of tools. If you are serious about maintaining your own vehicle, then a floor jack is as necessary as a spark plug socket. The greatly increased utility, strength and safety of a hydraulic floor jack makes it pay for itself many times over throughout the years.

The second list of tools is for tune-ups. While the tools involved here are slightly more sophisticated, they need not be outrageously expensive. There are several inexpensive tach/dwell meters on the market that are every bit as good for the average mechanic as an expensive professional model. Just be sure that it goes to at least 1,200–1,500 rpm on the tach scale and that it works on 4-, 6- or 8-cylinder engines. A basic list of tune-up equipment could include:

1. Tach/dwell meter.
2. Spark plug wrench.
3. Timing light (a DC light that works from the vehicle's battery is best, although an AC light that plugs into 110V house current will suffice at some sacrifice in brightness).
4. Wire spark plug gauge/adjusting tools.
5. Set of feeler gauges.

In addition to these basic tools, there are several other tools and gauges you may find useful. These include:

1. A compression gauge. The screw-in type is slower to use but eliminates the possibility of a faulty reading due to escaping pressure.
2. A manifold vacuum gauge.
3. A test light, volt/ohm meter.
4. An induction meter. This is used for determining whether or not there is current in a wire. These are handy for use if a wire is broken somewhere in a wiring harness.

As a final note, you will probably find a torque wrench necessary for all but the most basic work. The beam type models are perfectly adequate, although the newer click type are more precise.

NOTE: Special tools are occasionally necessary to perform a specific job or are recommended to make a job easier. Their use has been kept to a minimum. When a special tool is indicated, it will be referred to by manufacturer's part number, and, where possible, an illustration of the tool will be provided so that an equivalent tool may be used. A list of tool manufacturers and their addresses follows:

In the United States, contact:

Service Tool Division
Kent-Moore Corporation
29784 Little Mack
Roseville, MI 48066-2298

In Canada, contact:

Kent-Moore of Canada, Ltd.
2395 Cawthra Mississauga
Ontario, Canada L5A 3P2.

SERVICING YOUR VEHICLE SAFELY

It is virtually impossible to anticipate all of the hazards involved with automotive maintenance and service but care and common sense will prevent most accidents.

The rules of safety for mechanics range from "do not smoke around gasoline," to "use the proper tool for the job." The trick to avoiding injuries is to develop safe work habits and take every possible precaution.

Do's

• Do keep a fire extinguisher and first aid kit within easy reach.

• Do wear safety glasses or goggles when cutting, drilling, grinding or prying, even if you have 20/20 vision. If you wear glasses for the sake of vision, then they should be made of hardened glass that can serve also as safety glasses or wear safety goggles over your regular glasses.

• Do shield your eyes whenever you work around the battery. Batteries contain sulphuric acid. In case of contact with the eyes or skin, flush the area with water or a mixture of water and baking soda, then get medical attention immediately.

• Do use safety stands for any under vehicle service. Jacks are for raising the vehicle. Safety stands are for making sure the vehicle stays raised until you want it to come down. Whenever the vehicle is raised, block the wheels remaining on the ground and set the parking brake.

• Do use adequate ventilation when working with any chemicals. Like carbon monoxide, the asbestos dust resulting from brake lining wear can be poisonous in sufficient quantities.

• Do disconnect the negative battery cable when working on the electrical system. The primary ignition system can contain up to 40,000 volts.

• Do follow the manufacturer's directions whenever working with potentially hazardous materials. Both brake fluid and antifreeze are poisonous if taken internally.

• Do properly maintain your tools. Loose hammer heads, mushroomed punches/chisels, frayed or poorly grounded electrical cords, excessively worn screwdrivers, spread wrenches (open end), cracked sockets, slipping ratchets and/or faulty droplight sockets cause accidents.

• Do use the proper size and type of tool for the job being done.

• Do when possible, pull on a wrench handle rather than push on it and adjust your stance to prevent a fall.

• Do be sure that adjustable wrenches are tightly adjusted on the nut or bolt and pulled so that the face is on the side of the fixed jaw.

• Do select a wrench or socket that fits the nut or bolt. The wrench or socket should sit straight, not cocked.

• Do strike squarely with a hammer — avoid glancing blows.

• Do set the parking brake and block the drive wheels if the work requires that the engine be running.

Dont's

• Don't run an engine in a garage or anywhere else without proper ventilation — EVER! Carbon monoxide is poisonous. It

Always support the car securely with jackstands; never use cinder blocks or tire changing jacks

takes a long time to leave the body and can build up a deadly supply of it in your system by simply breathing in a little every day. You may not realize you are slowly poisoning yourself. Always use power vents, windows, fans or open the garage doors.

• Don't work around moving parts while wearing a necktie or other loose clothing. Short sleeves are much safer than long, loose sleeves and hard-toed shoes with neoprene soles protect your toes and give a better grip on slippery surfaces. Jewelry such as watches, fancy belt buckles, beads or body adornment or any kind is not safe working around a vehicle. Long hair should be hidden under a hat or cap.

• Don't use pockets for tool boxes. A fall or bump can drive a screwdriver deep into your body. Even a wiping cloth hanging from the back pocket can wrap around a spinning shaft or fan.

• Don't smoke when working around gasoline, cleaning solvent or other flammable material.

• Don't smoke when working around the battery. When the battery is being charged, it gives off explosive hydrogen gas.

• Don't use gasoline to wash your hands. There are excellent soaps available. Gasoline may contain lead, and lead can enter the body through a cut, accumulating in the body until you are very ill. Gasoline also removes all the natural oils from the skin so that bone dry hands will suck up oil and grease.

• Don't service the air conditioning system unless you are equipped with the necessary tools and training. The refrigerant, R-12, is extremely cold and when exposed to the air, will instantly freeze any surface it comes in contact with, including your eyes. Although the refrigerant is normally non-toxic, R-12 becomes a deadly poisonous gas in the presence of an open flame. One good whiff of the vapors from burning refrigerant can be fatal.

HISTORY

In 1985, the Astro and Safari Vans were born, it is an in-between van; smaller than the conventional Chevy/GMC vans but larger than the minivans. It is a rear wheel drive vehicle with a wide range of power trains available. The 1990 model year offers an All Wheel Drive version as an option.

Due to the vast array of the state-of-the-art design, engineering, manufacturing and assembly technologies, this model makes available the widest variety of window, seating and equipment options ever offered on compact vans.

MODEL IDENTIFICATION

Four engines are available:

- 2.5L (151 cu. in.) L4, TBI (Throttle Body Injection) (1985–90)
- 4.3L (262 cu. in.) V6, 4-bbl. carburetor (1985)
- 4.3L (262 cu. in.) V6, TBI (Throttle Body Injection) (1986–90)
- 4.3L HO (262 cu. in.) V6, TBI (Throttle Body Injection) (1990)

In 1987, the 2.5L and 4.3L engines were redesigned to incorporate a single serpentine drivebelt, replacing the conventional multiple V-belts. This new system features an automatic belt tensioner, which eliminates the need for belt adjustment throughout the life of the vehicle and increases the expected belt life to 100,000 miles.

Two models are offered: One designed for cargo hauling and the other for passengers. Both are distinguished by a wind tunnel tuned shape which produces a 0.38 aerodynamic drag coefficient—lower than any other small van and lower than many current model passenger vehicles.

The independent front suspension incorporates unequal length A-arms with coil springs. The rear suspension features the first truck use of corrosion free, single leaf fiberglass springs, which are 54 lbs. lighter than a pair of conventional steel springs.

A choice of transmissions is available: The MR2, 76mm 4-speed manual (base), the MH3/ML3, 77mm 5-speed manual (optional) and the MD8, Turbo Hydra-Matic 700-R4 4-speed automatic.

In 1990, an option of full-time All Wheel Drive (AWD) was offered with the 4.3L engine and 4L60 (700-4R) transmission. The power is transmitted through a planetary gear set in the transfer case to the rear axle.

Two fuel tanks are available: A 17 gal. (standard) and a 27 gal. (optional). The fuel economy is expected to be low-to-mid 20's for city driving and low-to-mid 30's for highway driving. The combination of a 4-cyl. engine and a 27 gal. tank may approach the 900 mile driving range.

The manufacturing time is reduced by the introduction of the Single Piece construction approach, whereby, a few large stampings to replace the many small ones. The Astro and Safari boasts of the most extensive corrosion protection of any Chevy truck EVER, which includes: The widest use of 2-sided galvanized steel, a full underbody hot-melt wax spray and seven layers of exterior finish.

Rear wheel anti-lock brakes were introduced in 1989 and four wheel anti-lock brakes were introduced in 1990. Both systems are electronically controlled to help prevent tire skid under various road conditions.

Depending upon the equipment, the Astro and Safari's capable of towing up to 5,000 lbs. (1985–86) and up to 6,000 lbs. (1987–90).

SERIAL NUMBER IDENTIFICATION

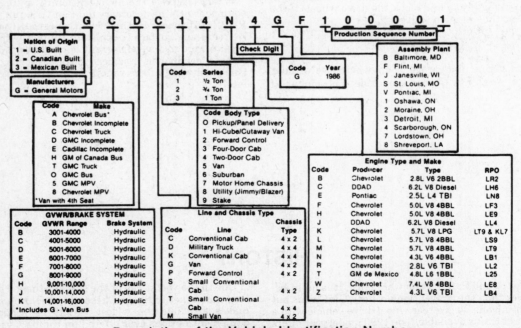

Description of the Vehicle Identification Number

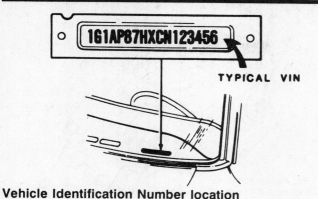

TYPICAL VIN

Vehicle Identification Number location

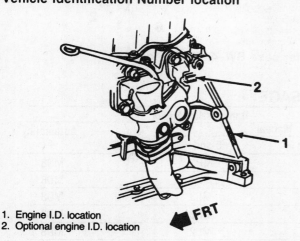

1. Engine I.D. location
2. Optional engine I.D. location

FRT

FRT

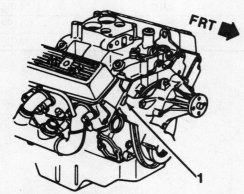

Location of the Engine Identification Number — 2.5L and the 4.3L engine

Vehicle

The vehicle serial number plate is located on the top left side of the instrument panel and can be viewed through the windshield, it identifies the body style, model year, assembly plant, engine usage and production number.

Engine

The 2.5L engine identification numbers are stamped on the left side of the rear engine block flange; the 4.3L engine identification numbers are stamped on a pad of the engine block which is located at the lower front edge of the right side cylinder head. The eighth digit of the serial number identifies the engine used in the vehicle.

Manual Transmission

The transmission serial numbers are located on the front right side of the main housing.

Automatic Transmission

The Turbo Hydra-Matic 700-R4, 4-spd automatic transmission serial numbers are located on the rear right side of the transmission case, above the oil pan.

Drive Axle

All Astro and Safari Vans have the drive axle serial number located on the forward side of the right axle tube. The two or three letter prefix in the serial number identifies the drive axle gear ratio.

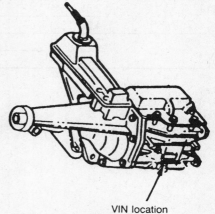

VIN location

Manual transmission VIN location

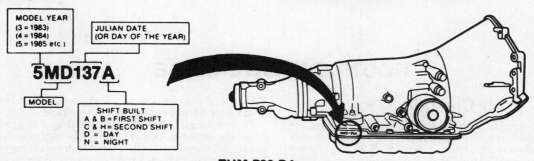

MODEL YEAR
(3 = 1983)
(4 = 1984)
(5 = 1985 etc.)

JULIAN DATE
(OR DAY OF THE YEAR)

5MD137A

MODEL

SHIFT BUILT
A & B = FIRST SHIFT
C & H = SECOND SHIFT
D = DAY
N = NIGHT

THM 700-R4
Location and description of the THM-R4 transmission serial number

Transfer Case

The All Wheel Drive transfer case identification is located on a tag bolted to the bottom of the front output flange.

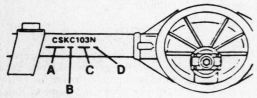

A. Axle code
B. 7½" (1900 mm) Chevrolet St. Catherines
C. Day built
D. Shift (D = Day, N = Night)

Location and description of the drive axle serial number

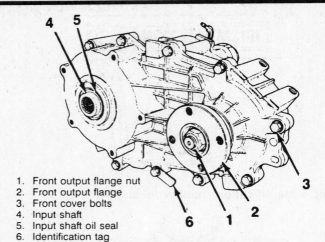

1. Front output flange nut
2. Front output flange
3. Front cover bolts
4. Input shaft
5. Input shaft oil seal
6. Identification tag

Transfer case BW–4472 VIN location

TRANSMISSION USAGE

Years	Engine L (cu. in.)	Transmission Model		Automatic ③
		Manual		
		4-spd. ①	5-spd. ②	
1985	2.5L (151)	MR2	MH3	MD8
	4.3L (262)	MR2	MH3	MD8
1986–87	2.5L (151)	MR2	ML3	MD8
	4.3L (262)	MR2	MH3	MD8
1988–89	2.5L (151)	—	ML2	MD8
	4.3L (262)	—	MH3	MD8
1990	2.5L (151)	—	—	MD8
	4.3L (262)	—	—	MD8

① 76 mm
② 77 mm
③ THM 700-R4 (4L60)

ROUTINE MAINTENANCE

Air Cleaner

An air cleaner is used to keep airborne dirt and dust out of the air flowing through the engine. This material, if allowed to enter the engine, would form an abrasive compound in conjunction with the engine oil and drastically shorten engine life. For this reason, you should never run the engine without the air cleaner in place except for a very brief period in diagnosing a problem.

You should also be sure to use the proper replacement part to avoid poor fit and consequent air leakage.

Proper maintenance is important since a clogged air filter will allow somewhat more dirt to enter the engine and, past a certain point, will enrich the fuel/air mixture, causing poor fuel economy, a drastic increase in emissions and even serious damage to the catalytic converter system.

The air cleaner consists of a metal housing with a replaceable

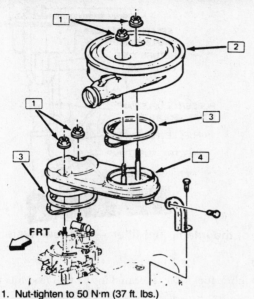

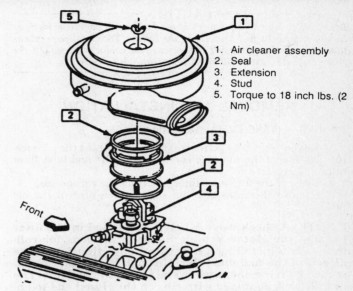

1. Air cleaner assembly
2. Seal
3. Extension
4. Stud
5. Torque to 18 inch lbs. (2 Nm)

Air cleaner assembly — 1988–90 4.3L engine

1. Nut-tighten to 50 N·m (37 ft. lbs.)
2. Air cleaner
3. Seal-remove paper if new seal
4. Adapter

View of the air cleaner assemblies used on the 1986–87 2.5L and 4.3L engines

paper filter and the necessary hoses connecting it to the crankcase ventilation system. The air cleaner cover is held by two nuts on all models. The factory recommends that the filter be replaced once every 30,000 miles. Inspection and replacement should come more often when the vehicle is operated under dusty conditions. To check the effectiveness of your paper element, remove the air cleaner assembly, if the idle speed increases noticeably, the element is restricting airflow and should be replaced.

REMOVAL AND INSTALLATION

1. Remove the air cleaner top nuts and lift off the top.
2. Remove the filter from inside the filter housing.
3. Clean the inside of the air cleaner housing before reinstalling the air filter.
4. To install, use a new filter and reverse the removal procedures. Torque the nuts to 37 ft. lbs. (49 Nm). 18 inch lbs. (2 Nm) for the single wing nut.

Fuel Filter

There are three types of fuel filters used: The internal (1985 4.3L carbureted models), the inline and the in-tank.

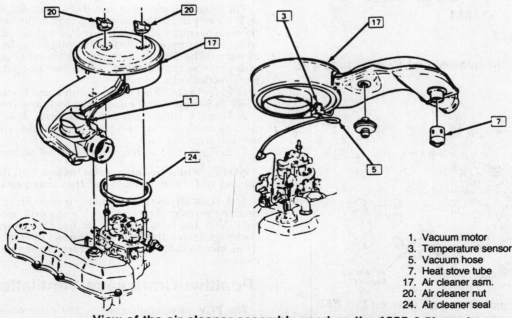

1. Vacuum motor
3. Temperature sensor
5. Vacuum hose
7. Heat stove tube
17. Air cleaner asm.
20. Air cleaner nut
24. Air cleaner seal

View of the air cleaner assembly used on the 1985 2.5L engine

---

CAUTION

Before removing any component of the fuel system on TBI models, be sure to reduce the fuel pressure in the system. The pressure regulator contains an orifice in the fuel system; when the engine is turned Off, the pressure in the system will bleed down within a few minutes.

REMOVAL AND INSTALLATION

Internal — 1985 Carbureted models

1. Disconnect the negative (−) battery cable. At the carburetor, disconnect the fuel line connection at the fuel inlet filter nut.
2. Remove the fuel inlet filter nut from the carburetor.
3. Remove the filter and the spring, then discard the old filter.

NOTE: A check valve MUST be installed in the filter to meet the Motor Vehicle Safety Standards for rollover. When installing a new filter, pay attention to the direction the fuel must flow through it; it MUST be installed with the check valve end facing the fuel line. The new filter is equipped with ribs on the closed end to ensure that it will not be installed incorrectly unless it is forced.

4. Install the spring and the new filter/check valve assembly into the carburetor inlet, followed by the fuel inlet nut. Torque the nut to 18 ft. lbs. (25 Nm). Install the fuel line and tighten the connection. Start the engine and check for leaks. Connect the negative battery cable.

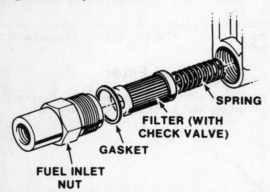

Exploded view of the internal fuel filter — 1985 4.3L carburetor

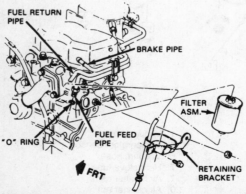

Exploded view of the inline fuel filter on the 2.5L engine — 4.3L engine is similar

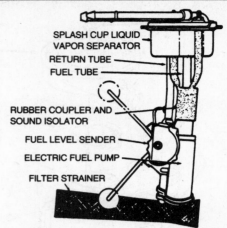

View of the intank fuel filter — TBI fuel systems

Inline

The inline fuel filter is located in the fuel feed line under the hood.

NOTE: If the engine was just turned Off, allow it to rest a few minutes to give the fuel system time to bleed down.

1. Disconnect the negative (−) battery cable. Using two wrenches (one for backup), remove the fuel lines from the filter.
2. Loosen the filter-to-bracket bolt, remove the filter and discard it.

NOTE: When installing a new filter, pay attention to the direction the fuel must flow through it.

3. Install the new filter into the bracket, then install new O-rings and the fuel lines. Using two wrenches, torque the fuel lines-to-filter to 22 ft. lbs. (30 Nm).
4. Connect the negative battery cable.
5. Start the engine and check for leaks.

Intank

The intank filter is constructed of woven plastic and is located on the lower end of the fuel pickup tube in the fuel tank. The filter prevents dirt and water from entering the fuel system; water will enter the system if the filter becomes completely submerged in water. The filter is normally self cleaning and requires no maintenance; should this filter become clogged, the fuel tank must be flushed.

1. Refer to the "Fuel Tank, Removal and Installation" procedures in Section 5 and remove the fuel tank from the vehicle.
2. Using a drift punch and a hammer, drive the fuel lever sending unit's cam lock ring counterclockwise, the lift the sending unit from the tank.
3. Remove the fuel filter from the fuel pump and clean it.

NOTE: When installing the intank fuel filter, be careful not to fold or twist it for this may restrict the flow.

4. **To install**, use a new sending unit-to-fuel tank O-ring and reverse the removal procedures. Using a drift punch and a hammer, drive the cam lock ring, of the fuel lever sending unit, clockwise. Install the fuel tank, connect the fuel lines and electrical wire to the sending unit. Start the engine and check for leaks.

Positive Crankcase Ventilation (PCV)

The PCV valve is attached to the valve cover by a rubber grommet and connected to the intake manifold through a venti-

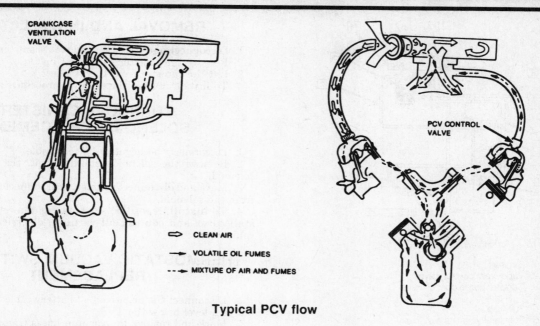

Typical PCV flow

lation hose. Replace the PCV valve and the PCV filter (located in the air cleaner) every 30,000 miles.

REMOVAL AND INSTALLATION

1. Pull the PCV from the valve cover grommet and disconnect it from the ventilation hose(s).
2. Inspect the valve for operation: (1) Shake it to see if the valve is free; (2) Blow through it (air will pass in one direction only).

NOTE: When replacing the PCV valve, it is recommended to use a new one.

3. To install, reverse the removal procedures.

Evaporative Canister

To limit gasoline vapor discharge into the air, this system is designed to trap fuel vapors, which normally escape from the fuel tank and the intake manifold. Vapor arrest is accomplished through the use of the charcoal canister. This canister absorbs fuel vapors and stores them until they can be removed to be burned in the engine. Removal of the vapors from the canister to the engine is accomplished by a canister mounted purge valve (2.5L TBI and 4.3L carbureted engines), the throttle valve position (2.5L and 4.3L TBI engines), a thermostatic vacuum (TVS) switch (4.3L carbureted engines, non-Calif.) or a computer controlled canister purge solenoid (4.3L carbureted engines, Calif.).

In addition to the modifications and the canister, the fuel tank requires a non-vented gas cap. The domed fuel tank positions a vent high enough above the fuel to keep the vent pipe in the vapor at all times. The single vent pipe is routed directly to the canister. From the canister, the vapors are routed to the intake system, where they will be burned during normal combustion.

SERVICING

Every 30,000 miles or 24 months, check all fuel, vapor lines and hoses for proper hookup, routing and condition. If equipped, check that the bowl vent and purge valves work properly. Remove the canister and check for cracks or damage, then replace (if necessary).

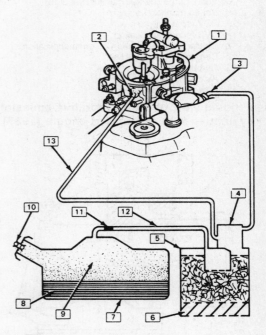

1. TBI
2. Canister purge port
3. Vacuum signal
4. Purge valve
5. Vapor storage canister
6. Purge air
7. Fuel tank
8. Fuel
9. Vapor
10. Pressure-vacuum relief gas cap
11. Vent restricter
12. Fuel tank vent
13. Purge line

Cross-sectional view of the evaporative emission control system — 2.5L TBI engine

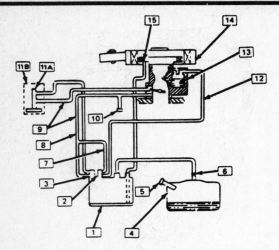

1. Canister
2. Vapor vent control valve
3. Canister purge control valve
4. Fuel tank
5. Fuel cap
6. Fuel tank vent line restriction
7. Vacuum signal for bowl vent valve
8. Vapor purge line (full manifold vacuum)
9. Ported manifold vacuum
10. PCV valve
11A. TVS-federal application
11B. Electric purge solenoid-California application
12. Carburetor bowl vent line
13. Carburetor
14. Air cleaner
15. Fuel vapor canister vent

Cross-sectional view of the evaporative emission control system — 4.3L carbureted engine (1985)

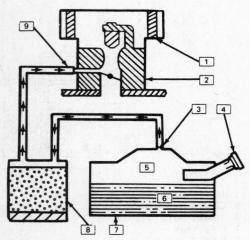

1. Air cleaner
2. T.B.I. unit
3. Restrictor
4. Press-vacuum relief gas cap
5. Vapor
6. Fuel
7. Fuel tank
8. Charcoal canister
9. Purge

Cross-sectional view of the evaporative emission control system — 1986 and later 4.3L TBI engine

REMOVAL AND INSTALLATION

1. Disconnect and mark the charcoal canister vent hoses.
2. Remove the canister-to-bracket bolt.
3. Lift the canister from the bracket.
4. To install, reverse the removal procedures.

CHARCOAL CANISTER SOLENOID REPLACEMENT

1. Disconnect the negative battery cable.
2. Remove the solenoid retaining bolt, the cover and the solenoid.
3. Mark and disconnect the electrical connector and the hoses from the solenoid.
4. **To install**, reposition solenoid, tighten retaining bolt, install cover and connect all vacuum, electrical and battery connections.

THERMOSTATIC VACUUM SWITCH (TVS) REPLACEMENT

1. Disconnect the negative (−) battery cable. Drain the coolant to a level below the TVS.
2. Mark and remove the vacuum hoses from the TVS.
3. Remove the TVS and check it. To check it, perform the following procedures:
    a. Allow the switch to cool below the calibration temperature.
    b. Connect a vacuum gauge(s) to the output port(s), apply vacuum equal to the amount listed on the valve or switch base.
    c. Place the switch base in a container of water, then heat the water above the calibration temperature.

NOTE: Leakage of up to 2 in.Hg in 2 minutes is allowable and does not mean a defective part.

    d. If the operation is satisfactory, reinstall the valve; if it is defective, replace it with a new one.
4. Apply soft setting sealant to the valve threads (DO NOT apply sealant to the end of the valve) and install the valve. Torque the valve to 120 inch lbs. (14 Nm), then turn it clockwise to align it with the hoses.
5. Reinstall the vacuum hoses. Refill the cooling system and connect the negative battery cable.

FILTER REPLACEMENT

The filter is in the bottom of the carbon canister which is located in the engine compartment should be replaced every 30,000 miles or 24 months.
1. Refer to the "Charcoal Canister, Removal and Installation" procedures, in this section and remove the canister from it's bracket.
2. At the bottom of the canister, grasp the filter with your fingers and pull it out.
3. To install, use a new filter and reverse the removal procedures.

Battery

MAINTENANCE-FREE BATTERIES

All Astro and Safari Vans have a Maintenance-Free battery as standard equipment, eliminating the need for fluid level checks and the possibility of specific gravity tests. Nevertheless, the battery does require some attention.
Once a year, the battery terminals and the cable clamps

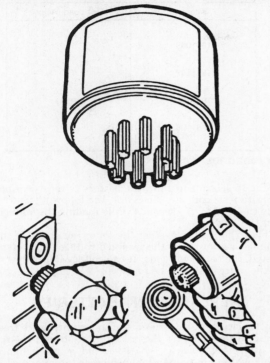

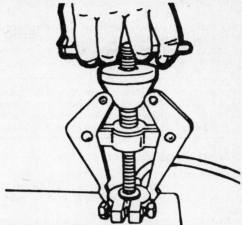

Use a puller to remove the battery cable

A special cleaning tool is available for cleaning the side terminals and clamps

Battery

Baking soda

Cleaning the battery with baking soda and water

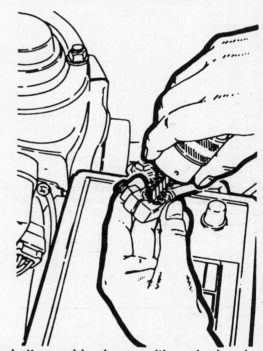

Clean battery cable clamps with a wire brush

connection and inhibit either starting or charging. Special tools are available for cleaning the side terminal clamps and terminals.

Before installing the cables, loosen the battery holddown clamp, remove the battery and check the battery tray. Clear it of any debris and check it for soundness. Rust should be wire brushed away and the metal given a coat of anti-rust paint. Replace the battery and tighten the holddown clamp securely but be careful not to overtighten, which will crack the battery case.

NOTE: Batteries can be cleaned using a solution of baking soda and water. Surface coatings on battery cases can actually conduct electricity which will cause a slight voltage drain, so make sure the battery case is clean.

After the clamps and terminals are clean, reinstall the cables, negative cable last. Give the clamps and terminals a thin exter-

should be cleaned. Remove the side terminal bolts and the cables, negative cable first. Clean the cable clamps and the battery terminals with a wire brush until all corrosion, grease, etc. is removed and the metal is shiny. It is especially important to clean the inside of the clamp thoroughly, since a small deposit of foreign material or oxidation there will prevent a sound electrical

nal coat of nonmetallic grease after installation, to retard corrosion.

Check the cables at the same time that the terminals are cleaned. If the cable insulation is cracked, broken or the ends are frayed, the cable should be replaced with a new one of the same length and gauge.

CAUTION

Keep flames or sparks away from the battery. It gives off explosive hydrogen gas. The battery electrolyte contains sulphuric acid. If you should get any on your skin or in your eyes, flush the affected areas with plenty of clear water. If it lands in your eyes, seek medical help immediately.

Testing the Maintenance Free Battery

Maintenance free batteries, do not require normal attention as far as fluid level checks are concerned. However, the terminals require periodic cleaning, which should be performed at least once a year.

The sealed top battery cannot be checked for charge in the normal manner, since there is no provision for access to the electrolyte. To check the condition of the battery:

1. If the indicator eye on top of the battery is dark, the battery has enough fluid. If the eye is light, the electrolyte fluid is too low and the battery must be replaced.

2. If a green dot appears in the middle of the eye, the battery is sufficiently charged. Proceed to Step 4. If no green dot is visible, charge the battery as in Step 3.

3. Charge the battery at this rate:

NOTE: **DO NOT charge the battery for more than 50 amp-hours. If the green dot appears or if the electrolyte squirts out of the vent hole, stop the charge and proceed to Step 4.**

It may be necessary to tip the battery from side-to-side to get the green dot to appear after charging.

WARNING: **When charging the battery, the electrical system and control unit can be quickly damaged by improper connections, high output battery chargers or incorrect service procedures.**

4. Connect a battery load tester and a voltmeter across the battery terminals (the battery cables should be disconnected from the battery). Apply a 300 amp load to the battery for 15 seconds to remove the surface charge. Remove the load.

Charging Rate Amps	Time
75	40 min
50	1 hr
25	2 hr
10	5 hr

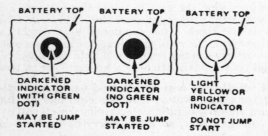

BATTERY TOP — BATTERY TOP — BATTERY TOP

DARKENED INDICATOR (WITH GREEN DOT) — DARKENED INDICATOR (NO GREEN DOT) — LIGHT YELLOW OR BRIGHT INDICATOR

MAY BE JUMP STARTED — MAY BE JUMP STARTED — DO NOT JUMP START

Maintenance-free batteries contain their own built in hydrometer

Battery	Test Load (Amps)
1981099	150
1981102	170
1981104	250
1981108	370

Battery load test values

5. Wait 15 seconds to allow the battery to recover. Apply the appropriate test load, as specified in the following chart:

Apply the load for 15 seconds while reading the voltage. Disconnect the load.

6. Check the results against the following chart. If the battery voltage is at or above the specified voltage for the temperature listed, the battery is good. It the voltage falls below what's listed, the battery should be replaced.

REPLACEMENT BATTERIES

Many replacement batteries are of the maintenance free type. For these batteries, follow the procedures above. If the replacement battery you have purchased is not a maintenance free type, follow these easy maintenance procedures:

Check the battery fluid level at least once a month, more often in hot weather or during extended periods of travel. The electrolyte level should be up to the bottom of the split ring in each cell. If the level is low, add water. Distilled water is good for this purpose, but ordinary tap water can be used.

At least once a year, check the specific gravity of the battery with a hydrometer. It should be between 1.20–1.26 in.Hg on the hydrometer's scale. Most importantly, all the cells should read approximately the same. If one or more cells read significantly lower than the others, it's an indication that these low cells are shorting out. Replace the battery.

If water is added during freezing weather, the vehicle should be driven several miles to allow the electrolyte and water to mix. Otherwise the battery could freeze.

Filling the Battery

Batteries should be checked for proper electrolyte level at least once a month or more frequently. Keep a close eye on any cell or cells that are unusually low or seem to constantly need water—this may indicate a battery on its last legs, a leak, or a problem with the charging system.

Top up each cell to the bottom of the split ring, or, if the battery has no split ring, about 9.5mm (⅜ in.) above the tops of the plates. Use distilled water where available, or ordinary tap water, if the water in your area isn't too hard. Hard water contains minerals that may slowly damage the plates of your battery.

CABLES AND CLAMPS

Twice a year, the battery terminal posts and the cable clamps should be cleaned. Loosen the clamp bolts (you may have to brush off any corrosion with a baking soda and water solution if they are really messy) and remove the cables, negative cable first. On batteries with posts on top, the use of a battery clamp puller is recommended. It is easy to break off a battery terminal if a clamp gets stuck without the puller. These pullers are inexpensive and available in most auto parts stores or auto departments. Side terminal battery cables are secured with a bolt.

The best tool for battery clamp and terminal maintenance is a battery terminal brush. This inexpensive tool has a female ended wire brush for cleaning terminals, and a male ended wire brush inside for cleaning the insides of battery clamps. When using this tool, make sure you get both the terminal posts and the insides of the clamps nice and shiny. Any oxidation, corrosion or foreign material will prevent a sound electrical connection and inhibit either starting or charging. If your battery has side terminals, there is also a cleaning tool available for these.

Before installing the cables, remove the battery holddown clamp or strap and remove the battery. Inspect the battery casing for leaks or cracks (which unfortunately can only be fixed by buying a new battery). Check the battery tray, wash it off with warm soapy water, rinse and dry. Any rust on the tray should be sanded away, and the tray given at least two coats of a quality anti-rust paint. Replace the battery, and install the holddown clamp or strap, but do not overtighten.

Reinstall your clean battery cables, negative cable last. Tighten the cables on the terminal posts snugly; do not overtighten. Wipe a thin coat of petroleum jelly or grease all over the outsides of the clamps. This will help to inhibit corrosion.

Finally, check the battery cables themselves. If the insulation of the cables is cracked or broken, or if the ends are frayed, replace the cable with a new cable of the same length or gauge.

──────────── CAUTION ────────────

Batteries give off hydrogen gas, which is explosive. DO NOT SMOKE around the battery! The battery electrolyte contains sulfuric acid. If you should splash any into your eyes or skin, flush with plenty of clear water and get immediate medical help.

BATTERY CHARGING AND REPLACEMENT

Charging a battery is best done by the slow charging method (often called trickle charging), with a low amperage charger. Quick charging a battery can actually "cook" the battery, damaging the plates inside and decreasing the life of the battery drastically. Any charging should be done in a well ventilated area away from the possibility of sparks or flame. The cell caps

ESTIMATED TEMPERATURE	MINIMUM VOLTAGE
70° F. (21° C.)	9.6
50° F. (10° C.)	9.4
30° F. (0° C.)	9.1
15° F. (−10° C.)	8.8
0° F. (−18° C.)	8.5
0° F. (BELOW: −18° C.)	8.0

Temperature versus voltage drop

(not found on maintenance-free batteries) should be unscrewed from their cells, but not removed.

If the battery must be quick-charged, check the cell voltages and the color of the electrolyte a few minutes after the charge is started. If cell voltages are not uniform or if the electrolyte is discolored with brown sediment, stop the quick charging in favor of a trickle charge. A common indicator of an overcharged battery is the frequent need to add water to the battery.

Belts

INSPECTION

Check the drive belt(s) every 15,000 miles/12 months (heavy usage) or 30,000 miles/24 months (light usage) for evidence of wear such as cracking, fraying and incorrect tension. Determine the belt tension at a point halfway between the pulleys by pressing on the belt with moderate thumb pressure. The belt should deflect about 6mm (¼ in.) over a 178–254mm (7–10 in.) span, or 13mm (½ in.) over a 330–406mm (13–16 in.) span, at this point. If the deflection is found to be too much or too little, perform the tension adjustments.

ADJUSTING TENSION

1985–86 V-belt

NOTE: The following procedures require the use of GM Belt Tension Gauge No. BT–33–95–ACBN (regular V-belts) or BT–33–97M (poly V-belts).

1. If the belt is cold, operate the engine (at idle speed) for 15 minutes; the belt will seat itself in the pulleys allowing the belt fibers to relax or stretch. If the belt is hot, allow it to cool, until it is warm to the touch.

NOTE: A used belt is one that has been rotated at least one complete revolution on the pulleys. This begins the belt seating process and it must never be tensioned to the new belt specifications.

2. Loosen the component-to-mounting bracket bolts.
3. Using a GM Belt Tension Gauge No. BT–33–95–ACBN (standard V-belts) or BT–33–97M (poly V-belts), place the tension gauge at the center of the belt between the longest span.
4. Applying belt tension pressure on the component, adjust the drive belt tension to the correct specifications.
5. While holding the correct tension on the component, tighten the component-to-mounting bracket bolt.
6. When the belt tension is correct, remove the tension gauge.

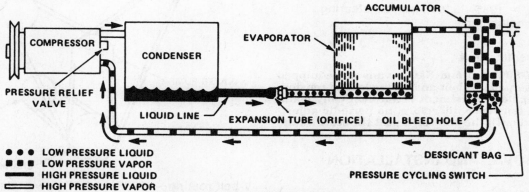

● ● ● LOW PRESSURE LIQUID
▬ ▬ LOW PRESSURE VAPOR
▬▬▬ HIGH PRESSURE LIQUID
═══ HIGH PRESSURE VAPOR

Air conditioning system

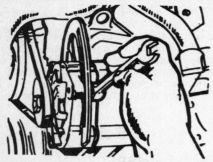

To adjust belt tension or to replace belts, first loosen the component's mounting and adjusting bolts slightly

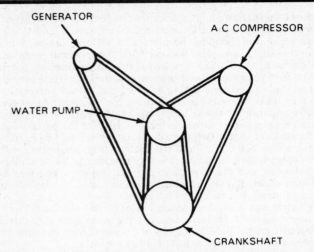

V-belt routing — 1985–86 2.5L manual steering, with air conditioning

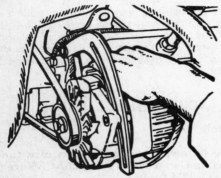

Pull outward on the component and tighten the mounting bolts

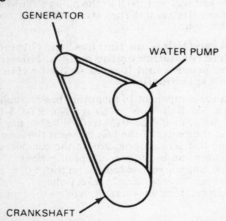

V-belt routing — 1985–86 2.5L manual steering, without air conditioning

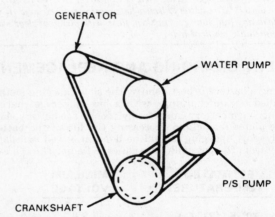

V-belt routing — 1985–86 2.5L power steering, without air conditioning

1987–90 Serpentine Belt

NOTE: 1987–90 Astro and Safari vans are equipped with a single serpentine belt and spring loaded tensioner. The proper belt adjustment is automatically maintained by the tensioner, therefore, no periodic adjustment is needed until the pointer is past the scale on the tensioner.

REMOVAL AND INSTALLATION

V-belt

1. Loosen the component-to-mounting bracket bolts.

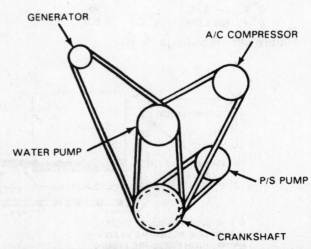

V-belt routing — 1985–86 2.5L power steering, with air conditioning

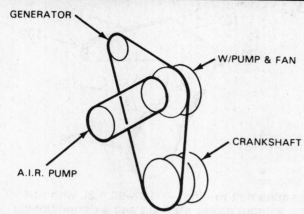

V-belt routing — 1985–86 4.3L manual steering, without air conditioning

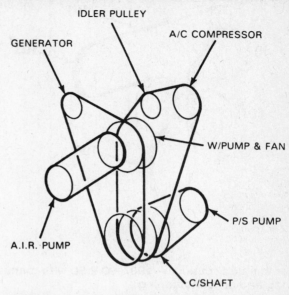

V-belt routing — 1985–86 4.3L power steering, with air conditioning

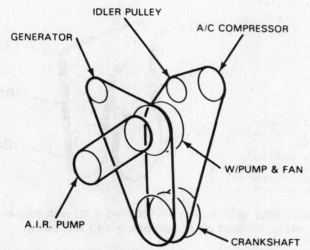

V-belt routing — 1985–86 4.3L manual steering, with air conditioning

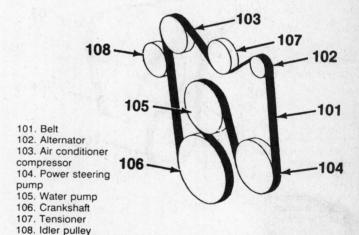

101. Belt
102. Alternator
103. Air conditioner compressor
104. Power steering pump
105. Water pump
106. Crankshaft
107. Tensioner
108. Idler pulley

Serpentine belt routing — 1987 4.3L without AIR pump. All others similar to 1988–90

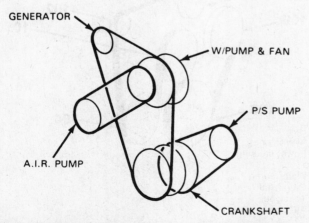

V-belt routing — 1985–86 4.3L power steering, without air conditioning

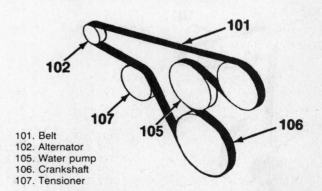

101. Belt
102. Alternator
105. Water pump
106. Crankshaft
107. Tensioner

Serpentine belt routing — 1987–90 2.5L without power steering and air conditioning

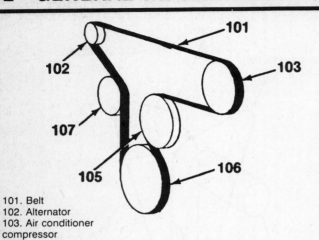

101. Belt
102. Alternator
103. Air conditioner compressor
105. Water pump
106. Crankshaft
107. Tensioner

Serpentine belt routing — 1987–90 2.5L with manual steering and air conditioning

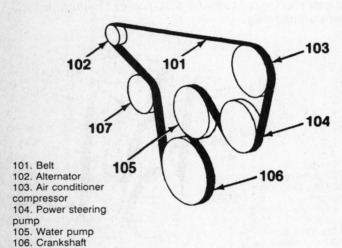

101. Belt
102. Alternator
103. Air conditioner compressor
104. Power steering pump
105. Water pump
106. Crankshaft
107. Tensioner

Serpentine belt routing — 1987–90 2.5L with power steering and air conditioning

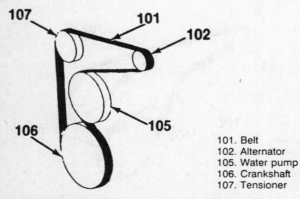

101. Belt
102. Alternator
105. Water pump
106. Crankshaft
107. Tensioner

Serpentine belt routing — 1987–90 4.3L without power steering, air conditioning or AIR pump

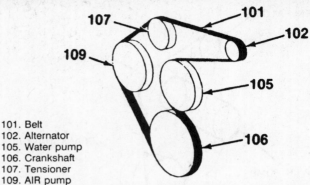

101. Belt
102. Alternator
105. Water pump
106. Crankshaft
107. Tensioner
109. AIR pump

Serpentine belt routing — 1987–90 4.3L with AIR pump, without power steering and air conditioning

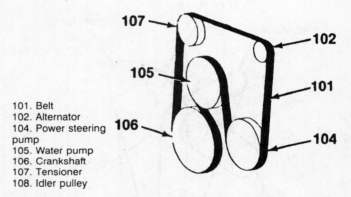

101. Belt
102. Alternator
104. Power steering pump
105. Water pump
106. Crankshaft
107. Tensioner
108. Idler pulley

Serpentine belt routing — 1987–90 4.3L with power steering, without air conditioning and AIR pump

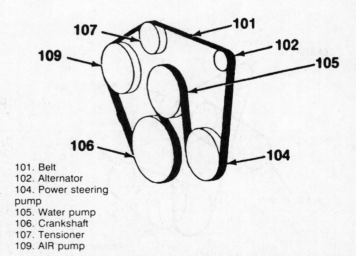

101. Belt
102. Alternator
104. Power steering pump
105. Water pump
106. Crankshaft
107. Tensioner
109. AIR pump

Serpentine belt routing — 1987–90 4.3L with power steering and AIR pump, without air conditioning

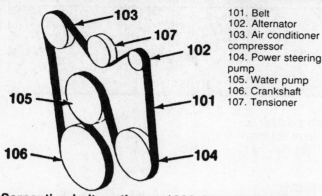

101. Belt
102. Alternator
103. Air conditioner compressor
104. Power steering pump
105. Water pump
106. Crankshaft
107. Tensioner

Serpentine belt routing — 1988–90 4.3L with power steering and air conditioning, without AIR pump

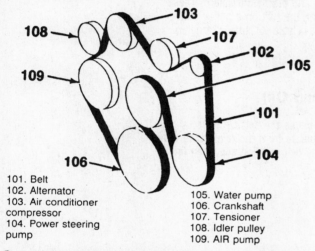

101. Belt
102. Alternator
103. Air conditioner compressor
104. Power steering pump
105. Water pump
106. Crankshaft
107. Tensioner
108. Idler pulley
109. AIR pump

Serpentine belt routing — 1987–90 4.3L with power steering, air conditioning and AIR pump

2. Rotate the component to relieve the tension on the drive belt.

3. Slip the drive belt from the component pulley and remove it from the engine.

NOTE: If the engine uses more than one belt, it may be necessary to remove other belts that are in front of the one being removed.

4. To install, reverse the removal procedures. Adjust the component drive belt tension to specifications.

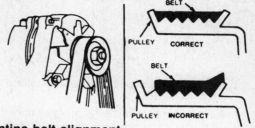

Serpentine belt alignment

1987–90 Serpentine Belt

1. Insert a ½ in. breaker bar into the tensioner pulley.
2. Rotate the tensioner to the left (counterclockwise) and remove the belt.

To install:

1. Route the belt over all the pulleys except the water pump. Refer to the "Serpentine Belt" routing illustrations in this section.
2. Rotate the tensioner pulley to the left (counterclockwise).
3. Install the belt over the water pump and check to see if the correct V-groove tracking is around each pulley.

WARNING: Improper V-groove tracking will cause the belt to fail in a short period of time.

Hoses

The upper/lower radiator hoses and all heater hoses should be checked for deterioration, leaks and loose hose clamps every 15,000 miles or 12 months.

REMOVAL AND INSTALLATION

1. Drain the cooling system.
2. Loosen the hose clamps at each end of the hose.
3. Working the hose back and forth, slide it off it's connection and then install a new hose, if necessary.

NOTE: When replacing the heater hoses, maintain a 38mm (1½ in.) clearance between the hose clip-to-upper control arm and between the rear overhead heater core lines-to-exhaust pipe.

4. To install, reverse the removal procedures.

NOTE: Draw the hoses tight to prevent sagging or rubbing against other components; route the hoses through the clamps as installed originally. Always make sure that the hose clamps are beyond the component bead and placed in the center of the clamping surface before tightening them.

BELT TENSION SPECIFICATIONS

Years	Engine	Tensioning	Alternator	Power Steering	Air Cond.	A.I.R. Pump
1985–86	2.5L	Before Operating The Engine (New Belt)	②	146 Lb.	169 Lb.	—
		After Operating The Engine (Old Belt) ①		67 Lb.	90 Lb.	
	4.3L	Before Operating The Engine (New Belt)	135 Lb.	146 Lb.	169 Lb.	146 Lb.
		After Operating The Engine (Old Belt) ①	67 Lb.	67 Lb.	90 Lb.	67 Lb.
1987–90		Serpentine Belt—Automatically Adjusted				

① At no time should belt exceed "After Operating The Engine" tension. Tension to be checked within 15 minutes after operating the engine. For belts driving more than one adjustable accessory, use highest tension specified. Any tensioning of replacement belts or the retensioning of previously installed but unrun belts, must adhere to above specifications (maximums prior to engine operation and minimums after engine operation). Any re-tensioning of previously run belt must be set to the "After Operating The Engine" specification.

② Generator belt with C60 air conditioning (new belt) 169 Lb.; old belt 90 Lb.
Generator belt with C41 heater (new belt) 146 Lb.; old belt 67 Lb.

HOW TO SPOT WORN V-BELTS

V–Belts are vital to efficient engine operation—they drive the fan, water pump and other accessories. They require little maintenance (occasional tightening) but they will not last forever. Slipping or failure of the V–belt will lead to overheating. If your V–belt looks like any of these, it should be replaced.

Cracking or Weathering

This belt has deep cracks, which cause it to flex. Too much flexing leads to heat build–up and premature failure. These cracks can be caused by using the belt on a pulley that is too small. Notched belts are available for small diameter pulleys.

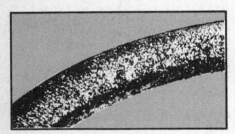

Softening (Grease and Oil)

Oil and grease on a belt can cause the belt's rubber compounds to soften and separate from the reinforcing cords that hold the belt together. The belt will first slip, then finally fail altogether.

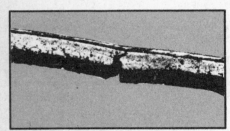

Glazing

Glazing is caused by a belt that is slipping. A slipping belt can cause a run-down battery, erratic power steering, overheating or poor accessory performance. The more the belt slips, the more glazing will be built up on the surface of the belt. The more the belt is glazed, the more it will slip. If the glazing is light, tighten the belt.

Worn Cover

The cover of this belt is worn off and is peeling away. The reinforcing cords will begin to wear and the belt will shortly break. When the belt cover wears in spots or has a rough jagged appearance, check the pulley grooves for roughness.

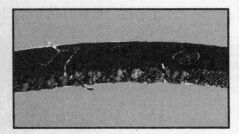

Separation

This belt is on the verge of breaking and leaving you stranded. The layers of the belt are separating and the reinforcing cords are exposed. It's just a matter of time before it breaks completely.

HOW TO SPOT BAD HOSES

Both the upper and lower radiator hoses are called upon to perform difficult jobs in an inhospitable environment. They are subject to nearly 18 psi at under hood temperatures often over 280°F, and must circulate nearly 7500 gallons of coolant an hour—3 good reasons to have good hoses.

Swollen Hose

A good test for any hose is to feel it for soft or spongy spots. Frequently these will appear as swollen areas of the hose. The most likely cause is oil soaking. This hose could burst at any time, when hot or under pressure.

Cracked Hose

Cracked hoses can usually be seen but feel the hoses to be sure they have not hardened; a prime cause of cracking. This hose has cracked down to the reinforcing cords and could split at any of the cracks.

Frayed Hose End (Due to Weak Clamp)

Weakened clamps frequently are the cause of hose and cooling system failure. The connection between the pipe and hose has deteriorated enough to allow coolant to escape when the engine is hot.

Debris In Cooling System

Debris, rust and scale in the cooling system can cause the inside of a hose to weaken. This can usually be felt on the outside of the hose as soft or thinner areas.

AIR CONDITIONING

General Servicing Procedures

The most important aspect of air conditioning service is the maintenance of a pure and adequate charge of refrigerant in the system. A refrigeration system cannot function properly if a significant percentage of the charge is lost. Leaks are common because the severe vibration encountered in an automobile can easily cause a sufficient cracking or loosening of the air conditioning fittings; as a result, the extreme operating pressures of the system force refrigerant out.

The problem can be understood by considering what happens to the system as it is operated with a continuous leak. Because the expansion valve regulates the flow of refrigerant to the evaporator, the level of refrigerant there is fairly constant. The receiver/drier stores any excess of refrigerant, and so a loss will first appear there as a reduction in the level of liquid. As this level nears the bottom of the vessel, some refrigerant vapor bubbles will begin to appear in the stream of liquid supplied to the expansion valve. This vapor decreases the capacity of the expansion valve very little as the valve opens to compensate for its presence. As the quantity of liquid in the condenser decreases, the operating pressure will drop there and throughout the high side of the system. As the R-12 continues to be expelled, the pressure available to force the liquid through the expansion valve will continue to decrease, and, eventually, the valve's orifice will prove to be too much of a restriction for adequate flow even with the needle fully withdrawn.

At this point, low side pressure will start to drop, and severe reduction in cooling capacity, marked by freeze-up of the evaporator coil, will result. Eventually, the operating pressure of the evaporator will be lower than the pressure of the atmosphere surrounding it, and air will be drawn into the system wherever there are leaks in the low side.

Because all atmospheric air contains at least some moisture, water will enter the system and mix with the R-12 and the oil. Trace amounts of moisture will cause sludging of the oil, and corrosion of the system. Saturation and clogging of the filter/drier, and freezing of the expansion valve orifice will eventually result. As air fills the system to a greater and greater extent, it will interfere more and more with the normal flows of refrigerant and heat.

From this description, it should be obvious that much of the repairman's time will be spent detecting leaks, repairing them, and then restoring the purity and quantity of the refrigerant charge. A list of general precautions that should be observed while doing this follows:

1. Keep all tools as clean and dry as possible.

2. Thoroughly purge the service gauges and hoses of air and moisture before connecting them to the system. Keep them capped when not in use.

3. Thoroughly clean any refrigerant fitting before disconnecting it, in order to minimize the entrance of dirt into the system.

4. Plan any operation that requires opening the system beforehand, in order to minimize the length of time it will be exposed to open air. Cap or seal the open ends to minimize the entrance of foreign material.

5. When adding oil, pour it through an extremely clean and dry tube or funnel. Keep the oil capped whenever possible. Do not use oil that has not been kept tightly sealed.

6. Use only refrigerant 12. Purchase refrigerant intended for use in only automatic air conditioning systems. Avoid the use of refrigerant 12 that may be packaged for another use, such as cleaning, or powering a horn, as it is impure.

7. Completely evacuate any system that has been opened to replace a component, or that has leaked sufficiently to draw in moisture and air. This requires evacuating air and moisture with a good vacuum pump for at least one hour.

If a system has been open for a considerable length of time it may be advisable to evacuate the system for up to 12 hours (overnight).

8. Use a wrench on both halves of a fitting that is to be disconnected, so as to avoid placing torque on any of the refrigerant lines.

9. When overhauling a compressor, pour some of the oil into a clean glass and inspect it. If there is evidence of dirt or metal particles, or both, flush all refrigerant components with clean refrigerant before evacuating and recharging the system. In addition, if metal particles are present, the compressor should be replaced.

10. Schrader valves may leak only when under full operating pressure. Therefore, if leakage is suspected but cannot be located, operate the system with a full charge of refrigerant and look for leaks from all Schrader valves. Replace any faulty valves.

Additional Preventive Maintenance Checks

ANTIFREEZE

In order to prevent heater core freeze-up during air conditioning operation, it is necessary to maintain permanent type antifreeze protection of +15°F (−9°C), or lower. A reading of −15°F (−26°C) is ideal since this protection also supplies sufficient corrosion inhibitors for the protection of the engine cooling system.

NOTE: The same antifreeze should not be used longer than the manufacturer specifies.

RADIATOR CAP

For efficient operation of an air conditioned truck's cooling system, the radiator cap should have a holding pressure which meets manufacturer's specifications. A cap which fails to hold these pressures should be replaced.

CONDENSER

Any obstruction of or damage to the condenser configuration will restrict the air flow which is essential to its efficient operation. It is therefore a good rule to keep this unit clean and in proper physical shape.

NOTE: Bug screens are regarded as obstructions.

CONDENSATION DRAIN TUBE

This single molded drain tube expels the condensation, which accumulates on the bottom of the evaporator housing, into the engine compartment. If this tube is obstructed, the air conditioning performance can be restricted and condensation buildup can spill over onto the vehicle's floor.

SAFETY WARNINGS

Because of the importance of the necessary safety precautions that must be exercised when working with air conditioning systems and R-12 refrigerant, a recap of the safety precautions are outlined.

● Avoid contact with a charged refrigeration system, even when working on another part of the air conditioning system or vehicle. If a heavy tool comes into contact with a section of copper tubing or a heat exchanger, it can easily cause the relatively soft material to rupture.

● When it is necessary to apply force to a fitting which contains refrigerant, as when checking that all system couplings are securely tightened, use a wrench on both parts of the fitting involved, if possible. This will avoid putting torque on the refrigerant tubing. It is advisable, when possible, to use tube or line wrenches when tightening these flare nut fittings.

• DO NOT attempt to discharge the system by merely loosening a fitting or removing the service valve caps and cracking these valves. Precise control is possible only when using the service gauges. Place a rag under the open end of the center charging hose while discharging the system to catch any drops of liquid that might escape. Wear protective gloves when connecting or disconnecting service gauge hoses.

• Discharge the system only in a well ventilated area, as high concentrations of the gas can exclude oxygen and act as an anaesthetic. When leak testing or soldering, this is particularly important, as toxic gas is formed when R-12 contacts any flame.

• Never start a system without first verifying that both service valves are back-seated (if equipped) and that all fittings throughout the system are snugly connected.

• Avoid applying heat to any refrigerant line or storage vessel. Charging may be aided by using water heated to less than 125° (52°C) to warm the refrigerant container. Never allow a refrigerant storage container to sit out in the sun or near any other heat source, such as a radiator.

• **Always wear safety goggles when working on a system to protect the eyes.** If refrigerant contacts the eyes, it is advisable in all cases to see a physician as soon as possible.

• Frostbite from liquid refrigerant should be treated by first gradually warming the area with cool water and then gently applying petroleum jelly. A physician should be consulted.

• Always keep the refrigerant drum fittings capped when not in use. Avoid any sudden shock to the drum, which might occur from dropping it or from banging a heavy tool against it. Never carry a drum in the passenger compartment of a vehicle.

• Always completely discharge the system before painting the vehicle (if the paint is to be baked on), or before welding anywhere near the refrigerant lines.

NOTE: Any repair work to an air conditioning system should be left to a professional. DO NOT, under any circumstances, attempt to loosen or tighten any fittings or perform any work other than that outlined here.

SYSTEM INSPECTIONS

Checking For Oil Leaks

Refrigerant leaks show up as oily areas on the various components because the compressor oil is transported around the entire system along with the refrigerant. Look for oily spots on all the hoses and lines, especially on the hose and tubing connections. If there are oily deposits, the system may have a leak, have it checked by a qualified repairman.

NOTE: A small area of oil on the front of the compressor is normal and no cause for alarm.

Checking The Compressor Belt

Refer to the Drive Belts section in this Section. After 1987, the serpentine belt is adjusted automatically by a spring loaded tensioner.

Keep The Condenser Clear

Periodically inspect the front of the condenser for bent fins or foreign material (dirt, buts, leaves, etc.). If any cooling fins are bent, straighten them carefully with needlenose pliers. You can remove any debris with a stiff bristle brush or hose.

Operate The Air Conditioning System Periodically

A lot of air conditioning problems can be avoided by simply running the air conditioner at least once a week regardless of the season. Simply let the system run for at least 5 minutes a week (even in the winter) and you'll keep the internal parts lubricated as well as preventing the hoses from hardening.

Refrigerant Level Check

The CCOT (cycling clutch orifice tube) air conditioning system does not have a refrigerant sight glass as does early model vehicles. A set of manifold gauges will have to be connected to determine the refrigerant level.

1. With the manifold gauges connected as shown in the "Manifold Gauge Connection" illustration in this section. Start the engine and run the air conditioning system, look at the gauge pressures . If the air conditioner is working properly, the pressures will fall within the specifications shown in the "Air Conditioning Performance" chart in this section.

2. Cycle the air conditioner ON and OFF to make sure what you are seeing is clear pressures. Turn the system OFF and watch the manifold gauges. If there is refrigerant in the system, you'll see the low side pressure rise and the high side fall during the off cycle. If you observe good pressures when the system is running and the air flow from the unit in the vehicle is delivering cold air, everything is OK.

3. If you observe low high and low side pressures while the system is operating, the system may be low on refrigerant.

Leak Testing the System

There are several methods of detecting leaks in an air conditioning system; among them, the two most popular are (1) halide leak detection or the open flame method and (2) electronic leak detection.

The halide leak detection is a torch like device which produces a yellow-green color when refrigerant is introduced into the flame at the burner. A purple or violet color indicates the presence of large amounts of refrigerant at the burner.

An electronic leak detector is a small portable electronic device with an extended probe. With the unit activated the probe is passed along those components of the system which contain refrigerant. If a leak is detected, the unit will sound an alarm signal or activate a display signal depending on the manufacturer's design. It is advisable to follow the manufacturer's instructions as the design and function of the detection may vary significantly.

— **CAUTION** —

Caution should be taken to operate either type of detector in well ventilated areas, so as to reduce the chance of personal injury, which may result from coming in contact with poisonous gases produced when R-12 is exposed to flame or electric spark.

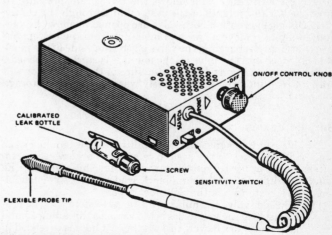

Electronic leak detector

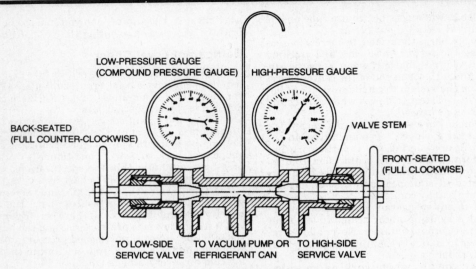

LOW-PRESSURE GAUGE
(COMPOUND PRESSURE GAUGE)   HIGH-PRESSURE GAUGE

VALVE STEM

BACK-SEATED
(FULL COUNTER-CLOCKWISE)

FRONT-SEATED
(FULL CLOCKWISE)

TO LOW-SIDE
SERVICE VALVE

TO VACUUM PUMP OR
REFRIGERANT CAN

TO HIGH-SIDE
SERVICE VALVE

Typical manifold gauge set

GAUGE SETS

Most of the service work performed in air conditioning requires the use of a set of two gauges, one for the high (head) pressure side of the system, the other for the low (suction) side.

The low side gauge records both pressure and vacuum. Vacuum readings are calibrated from 0–30 in.Hg, and the pressure graduations read from 0–60 psi.

The high side gauge measures pressure from 0–300 psi.

Both gauges are threaded into a manifold that contains two hand shut-off valves. Proper manipulation of these valves and the use of the attached test hoses allow the user to perform the following services:

1. Test high and low side pressures.
2. Remove air, moisture and/or contaminated refrigerant.
3. Purge the system of refrigerant.
4. Charge the system with refrigerant.

The manifold valves are designed so they have no direct effect on the gauge readings but serve only to provide for or cut off the flow of refrigerant through the manifold. During all testing and hook-up operations, the valves are kept in a Closed position to avoid disturbing the refrigeration system. The valves are Opened ONLY to purge, evacuate or charge the system.

When purging the system, the center hose is uncapped at the lower end and both valves are cracked (Opened) slightly **(engine NOT running)**. This allows the refrigerant pressure to force the entire contents of the system out through the center hose. During evacuation both valves are opened to allow the vacuum pump to remove all air and moisture from the system before charging. Recharging, the valve on the high side of the manifold is Closed and the valve on the low side is cracked (Opened). Under these conditions, the low pressure in the evaporator will draw refrigerant from the relatively warm refrigerant storage container into the system.

Service Valves

For the user to diagnose an air conditioning system he or she must gain entrance to the system in order to observe the pressures. There are two types of terminals for this purpose, the hand shut off type and the familiar Schrader valve. All Astro/Safari CCOT systems use the Schrader type.

The Schrader valve is similar to a tire valve stem and the process of connecting the test hoses is the same as threading a hand pump outlet hose to a bicycle tire. As the test hose is threaded to the service port the valve core is depressed, allowing the refrig-

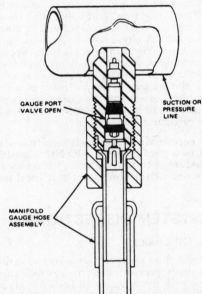

GAUGE PORT
VALVE OPEN

SUCTION OR
PRESSURE
LINE

MANIFOLD
GAUGE HOSE
ASSEMBLY

Manifold gauge hose connected to the Schrader type service port

erant to enter the test hose outlet. Removal of the test hose automatically closes the system.

— CAUTION —

Do NOT remove the gauge hoses while the engine is running. Always turn the engine OFF and allow the system to stabilize before removing the test gauge hoses.

Extreme caution must be observed when removing test hoses from the Schrader valves as some refrigerant will normally escape, usually under high pressure; observe safety precautions.

Using The Manifold Gauges

The following are step-by-step procedures to guide the user to the correct gauge usage.

— CAUTION —

Wear goggles or face shield during all testing operations.

1. Engine NOT running.

In Front Of Condenser

Relative Humidity (%)	Air Temp. C°	Air Temp. F°	Evaporator Pressure	Engine Speed (rpm)	Discharge Air Temp. C°	Discharge Air Temp. F°	High Pressure kPa	High Pressure psi
20	21	70	29.5	2000	4	40	1034.25	150
	27	80	29.5		7	44	1310.05	190
	32	90	30.0		9	48	1689.27	245
	38	100	31.0		14	57	2102.97	305
30	21	70	29.5	2000	6	42	1034.25	150
	27	80	30.0		8	47	1413.47	205
	32	90	31.0		11	51	1827.17	265
	38	100	32.0		16	61	2240.87	325
40	21	70	29.5	2000	7	45	1137.67	165
	27	80	30.0		9	49	1432.42	215
	32	90	32.0		13	55	1930.60	280
	38	100	39.0		18	65	2378.77	345
50	21	70	30.0	2000	8	47	1241.10	180
	27	80	32.0		12	53	1620.32	235
	32	90	34.0		15	59	2034.02	295
	38	100	40.0		21	69	2413.25	350
60	21	70	30.0	2000	9	48	1241.10	180
	27	80	33.0		13	56	1654.80	240
	32	90	36.0		17	63	2068.50	300
	38	100	43.0		23	73	2482.20	360
70	21	70	30.0	2000	10	50	1275.57	185
	27	80	34.0		14	58	1689.27	245
	32	90	38.0		18	65	2102.97	305
	38	100	44.0		24	75	2516.67	365
80	21	70	30.0	2000	10	50	1310.05	190
	27	80	34.0		15	59	1723.75	250
	32	90	39.0		19	67	2137.45	310
90	21	70	30.0	2000	10	50	1379.00	200
	27	80	36.0		17	62	1827.17	265
	32	90	42.0		22	71	2275.35	330

Air conditioning performance chart

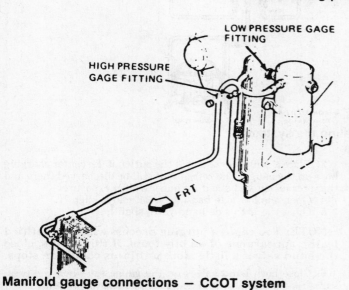

HIGH PRESSURE GAGE FITTING

LOW PRESSURE GAGE FITTING

FRT

Manifold gauge connections — CCOT system

2. Remove the caps from the high and low side service ports. Make sure both gauge valves are closed.

3. Connect the low side test hose to the service valve at the accumulator (large aluminum can).

3. Attach the high side test hose to the service valve that leads to the condenser.

4. Start the engine and allow it to warm-up. All testing and charging of the system should be done after the engine and system has reached normal operating temperatures (except when using certain the charging stations).

5. Adjust the air conditioner controls to **Max. cold**.

6. Observe the gauge readings.

When the gauges are not being used it is a good idea to:

a. Attach both ends of the high and low service hoses to the manifold, if extra outlets are present on the manifold or plug them (if not).

b. If the air and moisture have gotten into the gauges, purge the hoses by supplying refrigerant under pressure to the center hose with both gauge valves open and all openings unplugged. Crack each hose slightly at the manifold end of the valve until refrigerant comes out. This will purge the air from the gauge hoses.

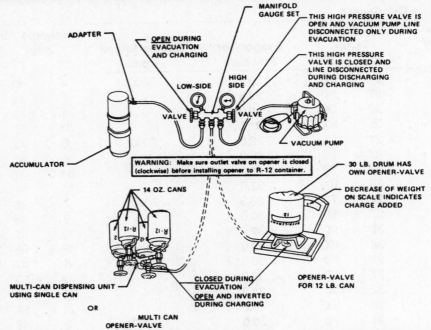

Typical gauge connections for discharge, evacuation and charging the system

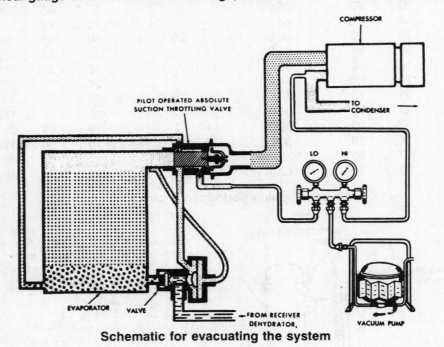

Schematic for evacuating the system

DISCHARGING THE SYSTEM

------ CAUTION ------

Be sure to perform the operation in a well ventilated area.

When it is necessary to remove (purge) the refrigerant pressurized in the system, follow this procedure:

1. Operate the air conditioner for at least 10 minutes. Turn the engine or air conditioning system OFF.
2. Attach the gauges.

3. Place a container or rag at the outlet of the center charging hose on the gauge. The refrigerant will be discharged there and this precaution will avoid its uncontrolled exposure.
4. Open the low side hand valve on gauge slightly.
5. Open the high side hand valve slightly.

NOTE: Too rapid a purging process will be identified by the appearance of an oily foam. If this occurs, close the hand valves a little more until this condition stops.

6. Close both hand valves on the gauge set when the pressures read **0** and all the refrigerant has left the system.

Evacuating the System

Before charging any system it is necessary to purge the refrigerant and draw out the trapped moisture with a suitable vacuum pump. Failure to do so will result in ineffective charging and possible damage to the system.

Use this hook-up for the proper evacuation procedure:

1. Connect both service gauge hoses to the high and low service outlets.

2. Open the high and low side hand valves on the gauge manifold.

3. Install the center charging hose of the gauge set to the vacuum pump.

4. Operate the vacuum pump for at least one hour. If the system has been subjected to open conditions for a prolonged period of time, it may be necessary to "pump the system down" overnight. Refer to the System Sweep procedure.

NOTE: If the low pressure gauge does not show at least 28 in.Hg within 5 minutes, check the system for a leak or loose gauge connectors.

5. Close the hand valves on the gauge manifold.

6. Turn Off the pump.

7. Observe the low pressure gauge to determine if the vacuum is holding. A vacuum drop may indicate a leak.

System Sweep

An efficient vacuum pump can remove all the air contained in a contaminated air conditioning system very quickly, because of its vapor state. Moisture, however, is far more difficult to remove because the vacuum must force the liquid to evaporate before it will be able to be removed from the system. If the system has become severely contaminated, as it might become after all the charge was lost in conjunction with vehicle accident damage, moisture removal is extremely time consuming. A vacuum pump could remove all of the moisture only if it were operated for 12 hours or more.

Under these conditions, sweeping the system with refrigerant will speed the process of moisture removal considerably. To sweep, follow the following procedure:

1. Connect the vacuum pump to the gauges, operate it until the vacuum ceases to increase, then continue the operation for ten more minutes.

2. Charge the system with 50% of its rated refrigerant capacity.

3. Operate the system at fast idle for ten minutes.

4. Discharge the system.

5. Repeat (twice) the process of charging to 50% capacity, running the system for ten minutes, then discharging it for a total of three sweeps.

6. Replace the drier (accumulator).

7. Pump the system down as in Step 1.

8. Add oil if needed and charge the system.

CHARGING

CAUTION

Never attempt to charge the system by opening the high pressure gauge control while the compressor is operating. The compressor accumulating pressure can burst the refrigerant container, causing serious personal injuries.

To check the system, start the engine, operate the air conditioning controls on Max. for approximately five minutes to stabilize the system. The room temperature should be above 70°F (21°C).

1. If the compressor clutch is engaged, the compressor discharge line is warm and the compressor inlet line is cool; the system has a full charge of refrigerant.

2. If the compressor clutch is engaged and there is no significant temperature difference between the compressor inlet and discharge lines; the system is empty or nearly empty. By having the gauge set attached to the system, a measurement can be taken. If the gauge reads less than 25 psi, the low pressure cutoff protection switch has failed.

3. If the compressor clutch is disengaged, the clutch is defective, the clutch circuit is open or the system is out of refrigerant. By-pass the low pressure cut-off switch momentarily to determine the cause.

CAUTION

DO NOT operate the vehicle engine any longer than necessary with the condenser airflow blocked. This blocking action also blocks the cooling system radiator and will cause the system to overheat rapidly.

When the system is low on refrigerant, a leak is present or the system was not properly charged. Use a leak detector to locate the problem area, then repair it. If no leakage is found, evacuate and charge the system to capacity.

ADDING REFRIGERANT OIL

1. Adding oil to the air conditioning system should take place AFTER discharge and BEFORE evacuation.

NOTE: Refrigerant oil can be purchased in 4 oz. pressurized cans similar to the 14 oz. disposable R-12 cans. Also, raw refrigerant oil can be purchased in unpressurized bulk form (qts). The raw oil can be poured in an open suction tube as recommended in the procedures following or injected into the system with a compressor oil injector part No. 8–J7605–03 or equivalent.

2. Remove the suction hose at the accumulator outlet pipe connection.

3. Pour the correct amount of new refrigerant oil 525 viscosity into the hose and then reconnect the hose to the pipe. Evacuate and recharged the system as outlined in the "Recharging" section in this section.

4. When removing air conditioning components for service, an amount of refrigerant oil will be lost and have to be replaced. Refer to the following list for proper component oil specifications. Use 525 viscosity refrigerant oil.

5. Always drain and measure old and new compressors, if less than 1 oz. is drained — add 2 oz. to the empty new compressor. If more than 1 oz. is drained, add the same amount that was drained to the new compressor.

NOTE: New compressors are shipped with about 8 oz. of refrigerant oil. This is too much oil if the system components are full also. Drain the new compressor and add specified amount.

- COMPRESSOR: 1 oz.
- ACCUMULATOR (new): 3.5 oz.
- EVAPORATOR: 3 oz.
- CONDENSER: 1 oz.
- TOTAL SYSTEM: 8.5 oz.

Troubleshooting Basic Air Conditioning Problems

Problem	Cause	Solution
There's little or no air coming from the vents (and you're sure it's on)	• The A/C fuse is blown • Broken or loose wires or connections • The on/off switch is defective	• Check and/or replace fuse • Check and/or repair connections • Replace switch
The air coming from the vents is not cool enough	• Windows and air vent wings open • The compressor belt is slipping • Heater is on • Condenser is clogged with debris • Refrigerant has escaped through a leak in the system • Receiver/drier is plugged	• Close windows and vent wings • Tighten or replace compressor belt • Shut heater off • Clean the condenser • Check system • Service system
The air has an odor	• Vacuum system is disrupted • Odor producing substances on the evaporator case • Condensation has collected in the bottom of the evaporator housing	• Have the system checked/repaired • Clean the evaporator case • Clean the evaporator housing drains
System is noisy or vibrating	• Compressor belt or mountings loose • Air in the system	• Tighten or replace belt; tighten mounting bolts • Have the system serviced

Sight glass condition
  Constant bubbles, foam or oil streaks
  Clear sight glass, but no cold air
  Clear sight glass, but air is cold
  Clouded with milky fluid
	• Undercharged system
	• No refrigerant at all
	• System is OK
	• Receiver drier is leaking dessicant
		• Charge the system
		• Check and charge the system
		• Have system checked

Large difference in temperature of lines	• System undercharged	• Charge and leak test the system
Compressor noise	• Broken valves • Overcharged • Incorrect oil level • Piston slap • Broken rings • Drive belt pulley bolts are loose	• Replace the valve plate • Discharge, evacuate and install the correct charge • Isolate the compressor and check the oil level. Correct as necessary. • Replace the compressor • Replace the compressor • Tighten with the correct torque specification
Excessive vibration	• Incorrect belt tension • Clutch loose • Overcharged • Pulley is misaligned	• Adjust the belt tension • Tighten the clutch • Discharge, evacuate and install the correct charge • Align the pulley
Condensation dripping in the passenger compartment	• Drain hose plugged or improperly positioned • Insulation removed or improperly installed	• Clean the drain hose and check for proper installation • Replace the insulation on the expansion valve and hoses

Troubleshooting Basic Air Conditioning Problems (cont.)

Problem	Cause	Solution
Frozen evaporator coil	• Faulty thermostat • Thermostat capillary tube improperly installed • Thermostat not adjusted properly	• Replace the thermostat • Install the capillary tube correctly • Adjust the thermostat
Low side low—high side low	• System refrigerant is low • Expansion valve is restricted	• Evacuate, leak test and charge the system • Replace the expansion valve
Low side high—high side low	• Internal leak in the compressor—worn	• Remove the compressor cylinder head and inspect the compressor. Replace the valve plate assembly if necessary. If the compressor pistons, rings or
Low side high—high side low (cont.)		cylinders are excessively worn or scored replace the compressor
	• Cylinder head gasket is leaking • Expansion valve is defective • Drive belt slipping	• Install a replacement cylinder head gasket • Replace the expansion valve • Adjust the belt tension
Low side high—high side high	• Condenser fins obstructed • Air in the system • Expansion valve is defective • Loose or worn fan belts	• Clean the condenser fins • Evacuate, leak test and charge the system • Replace the expansion valve • Adjust or replace the belts as necessary
Low side low—high side high	• Expansion valve is defective • Restriction in the refrigerant hose	• Replace the expansion valve • Check the hose for kinks—replace if necessary
Low side low—high side high	• Restriction in the receiver/drier • Restriction in the condenser	• Replace the receiver/drier • Replace the condenser
Low side and high normal (inadequate cooling)	• Air in the system • Moisture in the system	• Evacuate, leak test and charge the system • Evacuate, leak test and charge the system

Windshield Wipers

Intense heat from the sun, snow and ice, road oils and the chemicals used in windshield washer solvents combine to deteriorate the rubber wiper refills. The refills should be replaced about twice a year or whenever the blades begin to streak or chatter.

For maximum effectiveness and longest element life, the windshield and wiper blades should be kept clean. Dirt, tree sap, road tar and so on will cause streaking, smearing and blade deterioration if left on the glass. It is advisable to wash the windshield carefully with a commercial glass cleaner at least once a month. Wipe off the rubber blades with the wet rag afterwards. Do not attempt to move the wipers by hand; damage to the motor and drive mechanism will result.

If the blades are found to be cracked, broken or torn, they should be replaced immediately. Replacement intervals will vary with usage, although ozone deterioration usually limits blade life to about one year. If the wiper pattern is smeared or streaked, or if the blade chatters across the glass, the elements should be replaced. It is easiest and most sensible to replace the elements in pairs.

There are basically three different types of refills, which differ in their method of replacement. One type has two release but-

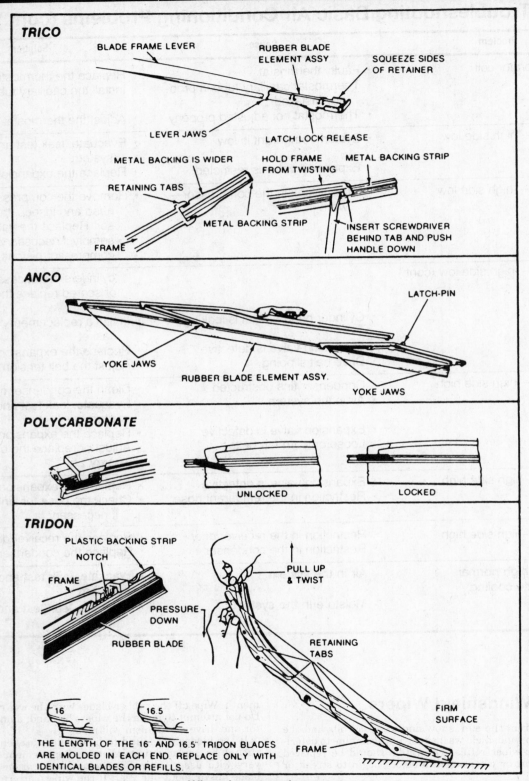

TRICO

BLADE FRAME LEVER

RUBBER BLADE ELEMENT ASSY

SQUEEZE SIDES OF RETAINER

LEVER JAWS

LATCH LOCK RELEASE

METAL BACKING IS WIDER

HOLD FRAME FROM TWISTING

METAL BACKING STRIP

RETAINING TABS

METAL BACKING STRIP

FRAME

INSERT SCREWDRIVER BEHIND TAB AND PUSH HANDLE DOWN

ANCO

LATCH-PIN

YOKE JAWS

RUBBER BLADE ELEMENT ASSY.

YOKE JAWS

POLYCARBONATE

UNLOCKED

LOCKED

TRIDON

PLASTIC BACKING STRIP

NOTCH

FRAME

PULL UP & TWIST

PRESSURE DOWN

RUBBER BLADE

RETAINING TABS

16   16.5

FIRM SURFACE

FRAME

THE LENGTH OF THE 16" AND 16.5" TRIDON BLADES ARE MOLDED IN EACH END. REPLACE ONLY WITH IDENTICAL BLADES OR REFILLS.

Wiper insert replacement

tons, approximately ⅓ of the way up from the ends of the blade frame. Pushing the buttons down releases a lock and allows the rubber filler to be removed from the frame. The new blade slides back into the frame and locks in place.

The second type of refill has two metal tabs which are unlocked by squeezing them together. The rubber blade can then be withdrawn from the frame jaws. A new refill is installed by inserting the refill into the front frame jaws and sliding it rearward to engage the remaining frame jaws. There are usually four jaws. Be certain when installing that the refill is engaged in all of them. At the end of its travel, the tabs will lock into place on the front jaws of the wiper blade frame.

The third type is a refill made from polycarbonate. The refill has a simple locking device at one end which flexes downward out of the groove into which the jaws of the holder fit, allowing easy release. By sliding the new refill through all the jaws and pushing through the slight resistance when it reaches the end of its travel, the refill will lock into position.

Regardless of the type of refill used, make sure that all of the frame jaws are engaged as the refill is pushed into place and locked. The metal blade holder and frame will scratch the glass if allowed to touch it.

WIPER REFILL REPLACEMENT

Normally, if the wipers are not cleaning the windshield properly, only the refill has to be replaced. The blade and arm usually require replacement only in the event of damage. It is only necessary (except on Tridon® refills) to remove the arm or the blade to replace the refill (rubber part), though you may have to position the arm higher on the glass. You can do this by turning the ignition switch on and operating the wipers. When they are positioned where they are accessible, turn the ignition switch off.

There are several types of refills and your vehicle could have any kind, since aftermarket blades and arms may not use exactly the same type refill as the original equipment.

The original equipment wiper elements can be replaced as follows:

1. Lift the wiper arm off the glass.
2. Depress the release lever on the center bridge and remove the blade from the arm.
3. Lift the tab and pinch the end bridge to release it from the center bridge.
4. Slide the end bridge from the wiper blade and the wiper blade from the opposite end bridge.
5. Install a new element and be sure the tab on the end bridge

is down to lock the element in place. Check each release point for positive engagement.

Tires

TIRE ROTATION

Tire wear can be equalized by switching the position of the tire about every 6000 miles. Including a conventional spare in the rotation pattern can give up to 20% more tire life.

—————————— CAUTION ——————————
DO NOT include the new Space Saver® or temporary spare tires in the rotation pattern.

There are certain exceptions to tire rotation, however. Studded snow tires should not be rotated and radials should be kept on the same side of the vehicle (maintain the same direction of rotation). The belts on radial tires get set in a pattern. If the direction of rotation is reversed, it can cause rough ride and vibration.

NOTE: When radials or studded snows are taken off the vehicle, mark them, so you can maintain the same direction of rotation.

TIRE INFLATION

The inflation is the most ignored item of auto maintenance. Gasoline mileage can drop as much as 0.8% for every 1 pound per square inch (psi) of under inflation.

Two items should be a permanent fixture in every glove compartment: a tire pressure gauge and a tread depth gauge. Check the tire air pressure (including the spare) regularly with a pocket type gauge. Kicking the tires won't tell you a thing and the gauge on the service station air hose is notoriously inaccurate.

The tire pressures recommended for your vehicle are usually found on the glove box door or in the owner's manual. Ideally, inflation pressure should be checked when the tires are cool. When the air becomes heated it expands and the pressure increases. Every 10° rise (or drop) in temperature means a difference of 1 psi, which also explains why the tire appears to lose air on a very cold night. When it is impossible to check the tires cold, allow for pressure build-up due to heat. If the hot pressure exceeds the cold pressure by more than 15 psi, reduce your speed, load or both. Otherwise internal heat is created in the

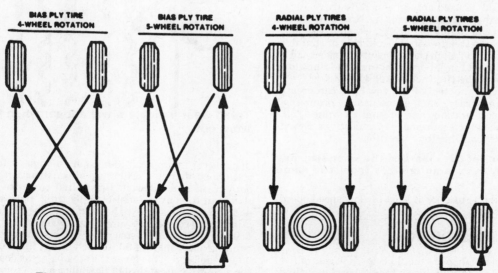

Tire rotation diagrams; note that radials should not be cross-switched

tire. When the heat approaches the temperature at which the tire was cured, during manufacture, the tread can separate from the body.

CAUTION

Never counteract excessive pressure build-up by bleeding off air pressure (letting some air out). This will only further raise the tire operating temperature.

Before starting a long trip with lots of luggage, you can add about 2–4 psi to the tires to make them run cooler but never exceed the maximum inflation pressure on the side of the tire.

TREAD DEPTH

All tires have 8 built-in tread wear indicator bars that show up as 13mm (½ in.) wide smooth bands across the tire when 1.5mm (¹/₁₆ in.) of tread remains. The appearance of tread wear indicators means that the tires should be replaced. In fact, many states have laws prohibiting the use of tires with less than 1.5mm (¹/₁₆ in.) tread.

You can check your own tread depth with an inexpensive gauge or by using a Lincoln head penny. Slip the Lincoln penny into several into several tread grooves. If you can see the top of Lincoln's head in 2 adjacent grooves, the tires have less than 1.5mm (¹/₁₆ in.) tread left and should be replaced. You can measure snow tires in the same manner by using the tails side of the Lincoln penny. If you can see the top of the Lincoln memorial, it's time to replace the snow tires.

TIRE USAGE

The tires on your van were selected to provide the best all around performance for normal operation when inflated as specified. Oversize tires (Load Range D) will not increase the maximum carrying capacity of the vehicle, although they will provide an extra margin of tread life. Be sure to check overall height before using larger size tires which may cause interference with suspension components or wheel wells. When replacing conventional tire sizes with other tire size designations, be sure to check the manufacturer's recommendations. Interchangeability is not always possible because of differences in load ratings, tire dimensions, wheel well clearances, and rim size. Also due to differences in handling characteristics, 70 Series and 60 Series tires should be used only in pairs on the same axle. Radial tires should be used only in sets of four.

The wheels must be the correct width for the tire. Tire dealers have charts of tire and rim compatibility. A mismatch can cause sloppy handling and rapid tread wear. The old rule of thumb is that the tread width should match the rim width (inside bead to inside bead) within 25mm (1 in.). For radial tires, the rim width should be 80% or less of the tire (not tread) width.

The height (mounted diameter) of the new tires can greatly change speedometer accuracy, engine speed at a given road speed, fuel mileage, acceleration, and ground clearance. Tire manufacturers furnish full measurement specifications. Speedometer drive gears are available for correction.

NOTE: Dimensions of tires marked the same size may vary significantly, even among tires from the same manufacturer.

The spare tire should be usable, at least for low speed operation, with the new tires.

TIRE DESIGN

For maximum satisfaction, tires should be used in sets of five. Mixing or different types (radial, bias/belted, fiberglass belted) should be avoided. Conventional bias tires are constructed so

Tread depth can be checked with and inexpensive gauge

A penny works as well as anything for checking tire tread depth; when you can see the top of Lincoln's head, it's time for a new tire

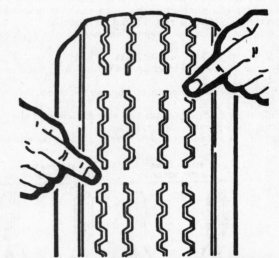

Tread wear indicators will appear when the tire is worn out

that the cords run bead-to-bead at an angle. Alternate plies run at an opposite angle. This type of construction gives rigidity to both tread and sidewall. Bias/belted tires are similar in construction to conventional bias ply tires. Belts run at an angle and also at a 90° angle to the bead, as in the radial tire. Tread life is improved considerably over the conventional bias tire. The radial tire differs in construction, but instead of the carcass plies running at an angle of 90° to each other, they run at an angle of 90° to the bead. This gives the tread a great deal of rigidity and the sidewall a great deal of flexibility and accounts for the characteristic bulge associated with radial tires.

HOW TO READ TIRE WEAR

The way your tires wear is a good indicator of other parts of your car. Abnormal wear patterns are often caused by the need for simple tire maintenance, or for front end alignment.

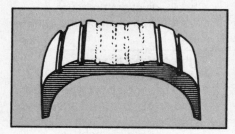

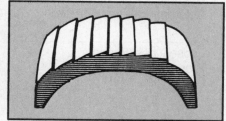

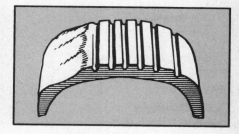

Over-Inflation

Excessive wear at the center of the tread indicates that the air pressure in the tire is consistently too high. The tire is riding on the center of the tread and wearing it prematurely. Occasionally, this wear pattern can result from outrageously wide tires on narrow rims. The cure for this is to replace either the tires or the wheels.

Feathering

Feathering is a condition when the edge of each tread rib develops a slightly rounded edge on one side and a sharp edge on the other. By running your hand over the tire, you can usually feel the sharper edges before you'll be able to see them. The most common causes of feathering are incorrect toe–in setting or deteriorated bushings in the front suspension.

Cupping

Cups or scalloped dips appearing around the edge of the tread almost always indicate worn (sometimes bent) suspension parts. Adjustment of wheel alignment alone will seldom cure the problem. Any worn component that connects the wheel to the vehicle can cause this type of wear. Occasionally, wheels that are out of balance will wear like this, but wheel imbalance usually shows up as bald spots between the outside edges and center of the tread.

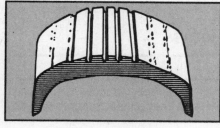

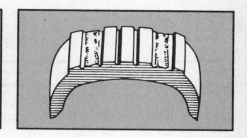

Under-Inflation

This type of wear usually results from consistent under–inflation. When a tire is under inflated, there is too much contact with the road by the outer threads, which wear prematurely. When this type of wear occurs, and the tire pressure is known to be consistently correct, a bent or worn steering component or the need for wheel alignment could be indicated.

One Side Wear

When an inner or outer rib wears faster than the rest of the tire, the need for wheel alignment is indicated. There is excessive camber in the front suspension, causing the wheel to lean too much, putting excessive load on one side of the tire. Misalignment could also be due to sagging springs, worn ball joints, or worn control arm bushings. Be sure the vehicle is loaded the way it's normally driven when you have the wheels aligned.

Second-Rib Wear

Second-rib wear is normally found only in radial tires, and appears where the steel belts end in relation to the tread. Normally, it can be kept to a minimum by paying careful attention to tire pressure and frequently rotation the tires. This is often considered normal wear but excessive amounts indicate that the tires are too wide for the wheels.

Troubleshooting Basic Wheel Problems

Problem	Cause	Solution
The car's front end vibrates at high speed	• The wheels are out of balance • Wheels are out of alignment	• Have wheels balanced • Have wheel alignment checked/adjusted
Car pulls to either side	• Wheels are out of alignment • Unequal tire pressure • Different size tires or wheels	• Have wheel alignment checked/adjusted • Check/adjust tire pressure • Change tires or wheels to same size
The car's wheel(s) wobbles	• Loose wheel lug nuts • Wheels out of balance • Damaged wheel • Wheels are out of alignment • Worn or damaged ball joint • Excessive play in the steering linkage (usually due to worn parts) • Defective shock absorber	• Tighten wheel lug nuts • Have tires balanced • Raise car and spin the wheel. If the wheel is bent, it should be replaced • Have wheel alignment checked/adjusted • Check ball joints • Check steering linkage • Check shock absorbers
Tires wear unevenly or prematurely	• Incorrect wheel size • Wheels are out of balance • Wheels are out of alignment	• Check if wheel and tire size are compatible • Have wheels balanced • Have wheel alignment checked/adjusted

Troubleshooting Basic Tire Problems

Problem	Cause	Solution
The car's front end vibrates at high speeds and the steering wheel shakes	• Wheels out of balance • Front end needs aligning	• Have wheels balanced • Have front end alignment checked
The car pulls to one side while cruising	• Unequal tire pressure (car will usually pull to the low side) • Mismatched tires • Front end needs aligning	• Check/adjust tire pressure • Be sure tires are of the same type and size • Have front end alignment checked
Abnormal, excessive or uneven tire wear See "How to Read Tire Wear"	• Infrequent tire rotation • Improper tire pressure • Sudden stops/starts or high speed on curves	• Rotate tires more frequently to equalize wear • Check/adjust pressure • Correct driving habits
Tire squeals	• Improper tire pressure • Front end needs aligning	• Check/adjust tire pressure • Have front end alignment checked

Tire Size Comparison Chart

| "Letter" sizes | | | Inch Sizes | Metric-inch Sizes | | |
"60 Series"	"70 Series"	"78 Series"	1965–77	"60 Series"	"70 Series"	"80 Series"
		Y78-12	5.50-12, 5.60-12 6.00-12	165/60-12	165/70-12	155-12
		W78-13	5.20-13	165/60-13	145/70-13	135-13
		Y78-13	5.60-13	175/60-13	155/70-13	145-13
			6.15-13	185/60-13	165/70-13	155-13, P155/80-13
A60-13	A70-13	A78-13	6.40-13	195/60-13	175/70-13	165-13
B60-13	B70-13	B78-13	6.70-13	205/60-13	185/70-13	175-13
			6.90-13			
C60-13	C70-13	C78-13	7.00-13	215/60-13	195/70-13	
D60-13	D70-13	D78-13	7.25-13			185-13
E60-13	E70-13	E78-13	7.75-13			
						195-13
			5.20-14	165/60-14	145/70-14	135-14
			5.60-14	175/60-14	155/70-14	145-14
			5.90-14			
A60-14	A70-14	A78-14	6.15-14	185/60-14	165/70-14	155-14
	B70-14	B78-14	6.45-14	195/60-14	175/70-14	165-14
	C70-14	C78-14	6.95-14	205/60-14	185/70-14	175-14
D60-14	D70-14	D78-14				
E60-14	E70-14	E78-14	7.35-14	215/60-14	195/70-14	185-14
F60-14	F70-14	F78-14, F83-14	7.75-14	225/60-14	200/70-14	195-14
G60-14	G70-14	G77-14, G78-14	8.25-14	235/60-14	205/70-14	205-14
H60-14	H70-14	H78-14	8.55-14	245/60-14	215/70-14	215-14
J60-14	J70-14	J78-14	8.85-14	255/60-14	225/70-14	225-14
L60-14	L70-14		9.15-14	265/60-14	235/70-14	
	A70-15	A78-15	5.60-15	185/60-15	165/70-15	155-15
B60-15	B70-15	B78-15	6.35-15	195/60-15	175/70-15	165-15
C60-15	C70-15	C78-15	6.85-15	205/60-15	185/70-15	175-15
	D70-15	D78-15				
E60-15	E70-15	E78-15	7.35-15	215/60-15	195/70-15	185-15
F60-15	F70-15	F78-15	7.75-15	225/60-15	205/70-15	195-15
G60-15	G70-15	G78-15	8.15-15/8.25-15	235/60-15	215/70-15	205-15
H60-15	H70-15	H78-15	8.45-15/8.55-15	245/60-15	225/70-15	215-15
J60-15	J70-15	J78-15	8.85-15/8.90-15	255/60-15	235/70-15	225-15
	K70-15		9.00-15	265/60-15	245/70-15	230-15
L60-15	L70-15	L78-15, L84-15	9.15-15			235-15
	M70-15	M78-15				255-15
		N78-15				

NOTE: Every size tire is not listed and many size comaprisons are approximate, based on load ratings. Wider tires than those supplied new with the vehicle should always be checked for clearance

All General Motors vehicles are capable of using radial tires and they are the recommended type for all years. If they are used, tire sizes and wheel diameters should be selected to maintain ground clearance and tire load capacity equivalent to the minimum specified tire. Radial tires should always be used in sets of five, but in an emergency radial tires can be used with caution on the rear axle only. If this is done, both tires on the rear should be of radial design.

NOTE: Radial tires should never be used on only the front axle.

TIRE STORAGE

Store the tires at proper inflation pressures if they are mounted on wheels. All tires should be kept in a cool, dry place. If they are stored in the garage or basement, DO NOT let them stand on a concrete floor, set them on strips of wood.

ALUMINUM WHEELS

——— CAUTION ———

If your vehicle has aluminum wheels, be very careful when using any type of cleaner on either the wheels or the tires. Read the label on the package of the cleaner to make sure that it will not damage aluminum.

TIRE INFLATION

Factory installed wheels and tires are designed to handle loads up to and including their rated load capacity when inflated to the recommended inflation pressures. Correct tire pressures and driving techniques have an important influence on tire life. Heavy cornering, excessively rapid acceleration and unnecessary braking increase tire wear. Underinflated tires can cause handling problems, poor fuel economy, shortened tire life and tire overloading.

Maximum axle load must never exceed the value shown on the side of the tire. The inflation pressure should never exceed 35 psi (standard tires) or 60 psi (compact tire).

FLUIDS AND LUBRICANTS

Engine Oil and Fuel

OIL

Use ONLY SF/CC, SF/CD, SG/CC or SG/CD rated oils of the recommended viscosity. Under the classification system developed by the American Petroleum Institute, the SG rating designates the highest quality oil for use in passenger vehicles. In addition, Chevrolet recommends the use of an SG/Energy Conserving oil. Oils labeled Energy Conserving (or Saving), Fuel (Gas or Gasoline) Saving, etc. are recommended due to their superior lubricating qualities (less friction—easier engine operation) and fuel saving characteristics. Pick your oil viscosity with regard to the anticipated temperatures during the period before your next oil change. Using the accompanying chart, choose the oil viscosity for the lowest expected temperature. You will be assured of easy cold starting and sufficient engine protection.

FUEL

NOTE: Some fuel additives contain chemicals that can damage the catalytic converter and/or oxygen sensor. Read all of the labels carefully before using any additive in the engine or fuel system.

Fuel should be selected for the brand and octane which performs best with your engine. Judge a gasoline by its ability to prevent pinging, it's engine starting capabilities (cold and hot) and general all weather performance. As far as the octane rating is concerned, refer to the General Engine Specifications chart in Section 3 to find your engine and its compression ratio.

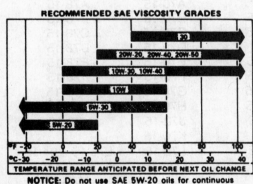

NOTICE: Do not use SAE 5W-20 oils for continuous high-speed driving.

Oil viscosity chart; multi-viscosity oils offer greater temperature latitude

If the compression ratio is 9.0:1 or lower, in most cases a regular unleaded grade of gasoline can be used. If the compression ratio is 9.0:1–9.3:1, use a premium grade of unleaded fuel.

NOTE: Your van's engine fuel requirement can change with time, due to carbon buildup, which changes the compression ratio. If your van's engine knocks, pings or runs on, switch to a higher grade of fuel (if possible) and check the ignition timing. Sometimes changing brands of gasoline will cure the problem. If it is necessary to retard the timing from specifications, don't

change it more than a two degrees. Retarded timing will reduce the power output and the fuel mileage, plus it will increase the engine temperature.

Engine

The mileage figures given in your owner's manual are the Chevrolet recommended intervals for oil and filter changes assuming average driving. If your Astro or Safari Van is being used under dusty, polluted or off-road conditions, change the oil and filter sooner than specified. The same thing goes for vehicles driven in stop-and-go traffic or only for short distances.

Always drain the oil after the engine has been running long enough to bring it to operating temperature. Hot oil will flow easier and more contaminants will be removed along with the oil than if it were drained cold. You will need a large capacity drain pan, which you can purchase at any store that sells automotive parts. Another necessity is a container for the used oil. You will find that plastic bottles, such as those used for bleach or fabric softener, make excellent storage jugs.

NOTE: Dispose of used oil ONLY by finding a service station or facility which accepts used oil for recycling.

Chevrolet recommends changing both the oil and filter during the first oil change and the filter every other oil change thereafter. For the small price of an oil filter, it's cheap insurance to replace the filter at every oil change. One of the larger filter manufacturers points out in it's advertisements that not changing the filter leaves one quart of dirty oil in the engine. This claim is true and should be kept in mind when changing your oil.

SYNTHETIC OIL

There are excellent synthetic and fuel-efficient oils available that, under the right circumstances, can help provide better fuel mileage and better engine protection. However, these advantages come at a price, which can be three or four times the cost per quart of conventional motor oils.

Before pouring any synthetic oils into your vehicle's engine, you should consider the condition of the engine and the type of driving you do. Also, check the manufacturer's warranty conditions regarding the use of synthetics.

Generally, it is best to avoid the use of synthetic oil in both brand new and older, high mileage engines. New engines require a proper break-in, and the synthetics are so slippery that they can prevent this. Most manufacturers recommend that you wait at least 5,000 miles before switching to a synthetic oil. Conversely, older engines are looser and tend to use more oil. Synthetics will slip past worn parts more readily than regular oil, and will be used up faster. If your truck already leaks and/or uses oil (due to worn parts and bad seals or gaskets), it will leak and use more with a slippery synthetic inside.

Consider your type of driving. If most of your accumulated mileage is on the highway at higher, steadier speeds, a synthetic oil will reduce friction and probably help deliver fuel mileage. Under such ideal highway conditions, the oil change interval can be extended, as long as the oil filter will operate effectively for the extended life of the oil. If the filter can't do its job for this extended period, dirt and sludge will build up in your engine's crankcase, sump, oil pump and lines, no matter what type of oil is used. If using synthetic oil in this manner, you should continue to change the oil filter at the recommended intervals.

Trucks used under harder, stop-and-go, short hop circumstances should always be serviced more frequently, and for these trucks, synthetic oil may not be a wise investment. Because of the necessary shorter change interval needed for this type of driving, you cannot take advantage of the long recommended change interval of most synthetic oils.

Finally, most synthetic oil are not compatible with conventional oils and cannot be added to them. This means you should

The oil level is checked with the dipstick

The oil level should be between the "ADD" and "FULL" marks on the dipstick

always carry a couple of quarts of synthetic oil with you while on a long trip, as not all service stations carry this oil.

OIL LEVEL CHECK

The engine oil level is checked with the dipstick.

NOTE: The oil should be checked before the engine is started or 5 minutes after the engine has been shut OFF. This gives the oil time to drain back to the oil pan and prevents an inaccurate oil level reading.

Remove the dipstick from its tube, wipe it clean and insert it back into the tube. Remove it again and observe the oil level. It should be maintained between the Full and Add marks without going above Full or below Add.

--------- CAUTION ---------
DO NOT overfill the crankcase. It may result in oil-fouled spark plugs, oil leaks caused by oil seal failure or engine damage due to foaming of the oil.

OIL AND FILTER CHANGE

1. Operate the engine until it reaches normal operating temperature.
2. Raise and support the front of the vehicle jackstands.
3. Slide a drain pan of at least 6 quarts capacity under the oil pan.
4. Loosen the drain plug. Turn it out by hand by keeping an inward pressure on the plug as you unscrew it. Oil won't escape past the threads and you can remove it without being burned by hot oil.

NOTE: Dispose of the waste oil properly. Do not pollute the environment. Avoid prolonged skin contact with used oil directly or from oil-saturated clothing.

5. Allow the oil to drain completely and then install the drain plug. Do not overtighten the plug or you'll be buying a new pan or a trick replacement plug for damaged threads.
6. Using a strap wrench, remove the oil filter. Keep in mind that it's holding about one quart of dirty, hot oil.
7. Empty the old filter into the drain pan and dispose of the filter.
8. Using a clean rag, wipe off the filter adapter on the engine block. Be sure that the rag does not leave any lint which could clog an oil passage.

The oil drain plug is located at the lowest point of the oil pan

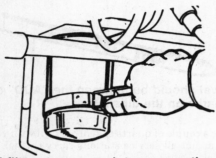

Use an oil filter strap wrench to remove the oil filter; install the new filter by hand

Apply a thin film of clean oil to the new gasket to prevent it from tearing upon installation

9. Coat the rubber gasket on the filter with fresh oil. Spin it onto the engine by hand. When the gasket touches the adapter surface give it another ½–¾ turn; no more or you'll squash the gasket and cause it to leak.
10. Refill the engine with the correct amount of new oil. See the Capacities chart at the end of this Section.
11. Crank the engine over several times and then start it. If the oil pressure gauge shows zero, shut the engine Off and find out what's wrong.
12. If the oil pressure is OK and there are no leaks, shut the engine Off and lower the vehicle.
13. Wait a few minutes and check the oil level. Add oil, as necessary, to bring the level up to the **FULL** mark.

Manual Transmission

FLUID RECOMMENDATIONS

Fill the main transmission housing with API GL5 SAE-80W90 Gear Oil (4-speed), multipurpose gear lubricant or Dexron®II (5-speed) automatic transmission fluid.

LEVEL CHECK

Remove the filler plug from the passenger's side of the transmission (the upper plug if the transmission has two plugs). The

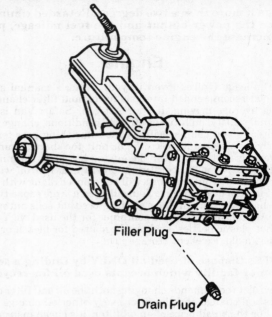

Manual transmission fill and drain plugs

oil should be level with the bottom edge of the filler hole. This should be checked at least once every 6,000 miles and more often if any leakage or seepage is observed.

DRAIN AND REFILL

Under normal conditions, the transmission fluid should not be changed.
1. Raise and support the vehicle on jackstands.
2. Place a fluid catch pan under the transmission.
3. Remove the bottom plug and drain the fluid.
4. Install the bottom plug and refill the transmission housing.

Automatic Transmission

FLUID RECOMMENDATIONS

When adding fluid or refilling the transmission, use Dexron®II automatic transmission fluid.

LEVEL CHECK

Before checking the fluid level of the transmission, drive the vehicle for at least 15 miles to warm the fluid.
1. Place the vehicle on a level surface, apply the parking brake and block the front wheels.
2. Start the engine and move the selector through each range, then place it in **PARK**.

NOTE: When moving the selector through each range, DO NOT race the engine.

3. With the engine running at a low idle, remove the transmission's dipstick to check the fluid level.
4. The level should be at the Full Hot mark of the dipstick. If not, add fluid.

—— CAUTION ——
DO NOT overfill the transmission, damage to the seals could occur. Use Dexron®II automatic transmission fluid. One pint raises the level from Add to Full.

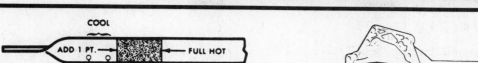

Automatic transmission dipstick marks; the proper level is within the shaded area

Add automatic transmission fluid through the dipstick tube

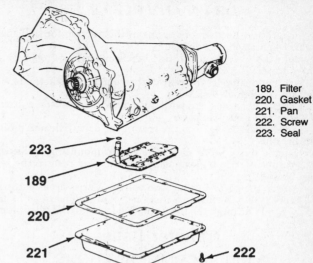

189. Filter
220. Gasket
221. Pan
222. Screw
223. Seal

Exploded view of the transmission oil and filter

DRAIN AND REFILL

The vehicle should be driven 15 miles to warm the transmission fluid before the pan is removed.

NOTE: The fluid should be drained while the transmission is warm.

1. Raise and support the front of vehicle on jackstands.
2. Place a drain pan under the transmission pan.
3. Remove the pan bolts from the front and the sides, then loosen the rear bolts 4 turns.
4. Using a small pry bar, pry the pan from the transmission. This will allow the pan to partially drain. Remove the remaining pan bolts and lower the pan from the transmission.

NOTE: If the transmission fluid is dark or has a burnt smell, transmission damage is indicated. Have the transmission checked professionally.

5. Empty the pan, remove the gasket material and clean with a solvent.
6. Using a putty knife, clean gasket mounting surfaces.
7. To install the oil pan, use a new gasket and sealant, then reverse the removal procedures. Torque the pan bolts to 69 inch. lbs. (11 Nm) in a criss-cross pattern.
8. Using Dexron®II automatic transmission fluid, add it through the filler tube. See the Capacities Chart to determine the proper amount of fluid to be added.

— CAUTION —

DO NOT OVERFILL the transmission. Foaming of the fluid and subsequent transmission damage due to slippage will result.

9. With the gearshift lever in **PARK**, start the engine and let it idle. DO NOT race the engine.
10. Apply the parking brake and move the gearshift lever through each position. Return the lever to **PARK** and check the fluid level with the engine idling. The level should be between the two dimples on the dipstick, about 6mm (¼ in.) below the ADD mark. Add fluid, if necessary.
11. Check the fluid level after the vehicle has been driven enough to thoroughly warm the transmission.

PAN AND FILTER SERVICE

1. Refer to the Drain and Refill procedures in this section and remove the oil pan.

2. Remove the screen and the filter from the valve body.
3. Install a new filter using a new gasket or O-ring.

NOTE: If the transmission uses a filter having a fully exposed screen, it may be cleaned and reused.

4. To install the oil pan, use a new gasket and sealant, then reverse the removal procedures. Torque the pan bolts to 8 inch lbs. (11 Nm) in a crisscross pattern. Refill the transmission.

Drive Axle (Front and Rear)

Several axle ratios are available, with the 190.5mm (7½ in.) ring gear rear axle, to be used with various powertrain applications.

FLUID RECOMMENDATIONS

Standard Axle

Always use SAE–80W or SAE 80W–90 GL5. Drain and refill the differential at first oil fill, then at every other oil fill.

Locking Axle

— CAUTION —

Never use standard differential lubricant in a Positraction® differential.

Always use GM Rear Axle Fluid No. 1052271. Before refilling the rear axle, add 4 ounces of GM Fluid No. 1052358 (limit-slip additive). Drain and refill the differential at first oil fill, then at every other oil fill.

LEVEL CHECK

The lubricant level should be checked at each chassis lubrication and maintained at the bottom of the filler plug hole.

1. Raise and support the vehicle on jackstands; be sure that the vehicle is level.
2. Remove the filler plug, located at the passenger side of the differential carrier.
3. Check the fluid level, it should be level with the bottom of the filler plug hole, add fluid (if necessary).
4. Replace the filler plug and torque to 27 ft. lbs. (37 Nm).

DRAIN AND REFILL

Refer to Fluid Recommendations in this section for information on when to change the fluid.

1. Run the vehicle until the lubricant reaches operating temperature.

2. Raise and support the rear of the vehicle on jackstands; be sure that the vehicle is level.

3. Using a floor jack, support the drive axle. Position a drain pan under the rear axle cover.

4. Remove the cover from the rear of the drive axle and drain the lubricant.

5. Using a putty knife, clean the gasket mounting surfaces.

6. **To install**, use a new gasket, sealant and reverse the removal procedures.

7. Torque the cover-to-rear axle bolts in a criss-cross pattern to 20 ft. lbs. (27 Nm). Using a suction gun or a squeeze bulb, install the fluids through the filler plug hole. Install the filler plug.

Transfer Case

FLUID RECOMMENDATIONS

Always use Dexron®II automatic transmission fluid. Inspect the transfer case level at first oil fill, then at every other oil fill.

LEVEL CHECK

Check the fluid level by removing the fill plug located on the rear side of the case housing.

DRAIN AND REFILL

Refer to Fluid Recommendations in this section for information on when to change the fluid.

1. Run the vehicle until the lubricant reaches operating temperature.

2. Raise and support the vehicle on jackstands; be sure that the vehicle is level.

3. Position a drain pan under the transfer case.

4. Remove the drain plug from the rear of the case housing and drain the lubricant.

5. **To install**, remove the fill plug and replace the drain plug. Torque the drain and fill plugs to 20 ft. lbs. (27 Nm).

6. Fill the transfer case with Dexron®II automatic transmission fluid until the level reaches the fill plug hole. Coat the plug threads with pipe sealant or equivalent. Install the fill plug and torque to 20 ft. lbs. (27 Nm).

Cooling System

At least once every 2 years or 30,000 miles, the engine cooling system should be inspected, flushed and refilled with fresh coolant. If the coolant is left in the system too long, it loses its ability to prevent rust and corrosion. If the coolant has too much water, it won't protect against freezing.

FLUID RECOMMENDATIONS

Using a good quality of ethylene glycol antifreeze (one that will not effect aluminum), mix it with water until a 50–50 antifreeze solution is attained. Colder climates require more antifreeze to prevent freezing. Refer to the chart on the back of the antifreeze container.

LEVEL CHECK

NOTE: When checking the coolant level, the radiator cap does not have to be removed, simply check the coolant recovery tank.

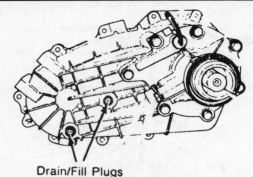

Drain/Fill Plugs

Transfer case fluid plugs

Check the coolant recovery bottle (see through plastic bottle). With the engine Cold, the coolant should be at the ADD mark (recovery tank ¼ full). With the engine warm, the coolant should be at the FULL mark (recovery tank ½ full). If necessary, add fluid to the recovery bottle.

DRAIN AND REFILL

───── CAUTION ─────

When draining the coolant, keep in mind that cats and dogs are attracted by the ethylene glycol antifreeze, and are quite likely to drink any that is left in an uncovered container or in puddles on the ground. This will prove fatal in sufficient quantity. Always drain the coolant into a sealable container. Coolant should be reused unless it is contaminated or several years old. To avoid injuries from scalding fluid and steam, DO NOT remove the radiator cap while the engine and radiator are still HOT.

1. When the engine is cool, remove the radiator cap using the following procedures.

   a. Slowly rotate the cap counterclockwise to the detent.

   b. If any residual pressure is present, WAIT until the hissing noise stops.

   c. After the hissing noise has ceased, press down on the cap and continue rotating it counterclockwise to remove it.

2. Place a fluid catch pan under the radiator, open the radiator drain valve and the engine drain plugs, then drain the coolant.

3. Close the drain valve and install the engine drain plugs.

4. Empty the coolant reservoir and flush it.

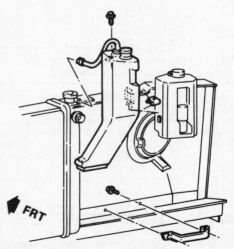

FRT

View of the radiator recovery tank

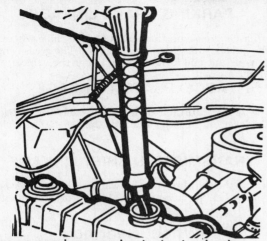

You can use an inexpensive tester to check antifreeze protection

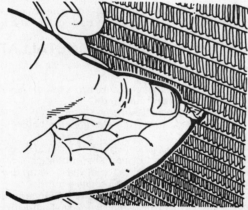

Clean the front of the radiator of any bugs, leaves, or other debris at every yearly coolant change

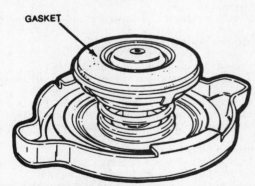

Check the condition of the radiator cap gasket

5. Using the correct mixture of antifreeze, fill the radiator to the bottom of the filler neck and the coolant tank to the FULL mark.

6. Install the radiator cap (make sure that the arrows align with the overflow tube).

7. Run the engine until it reaches the operating temperatures, allow it to cool, then check the fluid level and add fluid (if necessary).

FLUSHING AND CLEANING THE SYSTEM

1. Refer to the Drain and Refill procedures in this section, then drain the cooling system.

2. Close the drain valve and install the engine drain plugs, then add sufficient water to the cooling system.

3. Run the engine, then drain and refill the system. Perform this procedure several times, until the fluid (drained from the system) is clear.

4. Empty the coolant reservoir and flush it.

5. Using the correct mixture of antifreeze, fill the radiator to the bottom of the filler neck and the coolant tank to the FULL mark.

6. Install the radiator cap (make sure that the arrows align with the overflow tube).

Master Cylinder

FLUID RECOMMENDATIONS

Use only heavy-duty DOT-3 brake fluid.

LEVEL CHECK

The brake fluid level should be inspected every 6 months.

1. Remove the master cylinder reservoir caps.

2. The fluid should be 6mm (¼ in.) from top of the reservoir, if necessary, add fluid.

3. Replace the reservoir caps.

Hydraulic Clutch

NOTE: The clutch master cylinder is mounted on the firewall next to the brake master cylinder.

FLUID RECOMMENDATIONS

Use only heavy duty DOT-3 brake fluid.

LEVEL CHECK

The hydraulic clutch reservoir should be checked at least every 6 months. Fill to the line on the reservoir.

Power Steering Pump

The power steering pump reservoir is located at the front left side of the engine.

FLUID RECOMMENDATIONS

Use GM Power Steering Fluid No. 1050017 or equivalent.

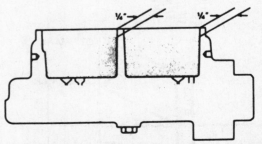

The fluid level in the master cylinder reservoir should be within ¼ inch of the top edge

NOTE: Avoid using automatic transmission fluid in the power steering unit, except in an emergency.

LEVEL CHECK

The power steering fluid should be checked at least every 6 months. There is a Cold and a Hot mark on the dipstick. The fluid should be checked when the engine is warm and turned OFF. If necessary, add fluid to the power steering pump reservoir.

NOTE: On models equipped with a remote reservoir, the fluid level should be 13–25mm (½–1 in.) from the top when the wheels are turned to the extreme left position.

Steering Gear

FLUID RECOMMENDATIONS

Use GM steering gear lubricant No. 1052182 or equivalent.

LEVEL CHECK

The steering lubricant should be checked every 6 months or 7,500 miles.

Chassis Greasing

Chassis greasing should be performed every 6 months or 7,500 miles, it can be performed with a commercial pressurized grease gun or at home by using a hand operated grease gun. Wipe the grease fittings clean before greasing in order to prevent the possibility of forcing any dirt into the component.

Body Lubrication

HOOD LATCH AND HINGES

Clean the latch surfaces and apply clean engine oil to the latch pilot bolts and the spring anchor. Use the engine oil to lubricate the hood hinges as well. Use a chassis grease to lubricate all the pivot points in the latch release mechanism.

DOOR HINGES

The gas tank filler door, the front doors and rear door hinges should be wiped clean and lubricated with clean engine oil. Silicone spray also works well on these parts but must be applied more often. The door lock cylinders can be lubricated easily with a shot of GM silicone spray No. 1052276 or one of the many dry penetrating lubricants commercially available.

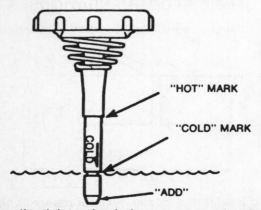

"HOT" MARK

"COLD" MARK

"ADD"

Use the dipstick to check the power steering fluid

PARKING BRAKE LINKAGE

Use chassis grease on the parking brake cable where it contacts the guides, links, levers and pulleys. The grease should be a water resistant one for durability under the vehicle.

ACCELERATOR LINKAGE

Lubricate the throttle body lever, the cable and the accelerator pedal lever (at the support inside the vehicle) with clean engine oil.

TRANSMISSION SHIFT LINKAGE

Lubricate the shift linkage with water resistant chassis grease which meets GM specification No. 6031M or equivalent.

Wheel Bearings

Once every 30,000 miles, clean and repack wheel bearings with a GM Wheel Bearing Grease No. 1051344 or equivalent. Use only enough grease to completely coat the rollers. Remove any excess grease from the exposed surface of the hub and seal.

REMOVAL, PACKING AND INSTALLATION

2-Wheel Drive

Before handling the bearings, there are a few things that you should remember to do and not to do.
Remember to DO the following:
- Remove all outside dirt from the housing before exposing the bearing.
- Treat a used bearing as gently as you would a new one.
- Work with clean tools in clean surroundings.
- Use clean, dry canvas gloves, or at least clean, dry hands.
- Clean solvents and flushing fluids are a must.
- Use clean paper when laying out the bearings to dry.
- Protect disassembled bearings from rust and dirt. Cover them up.
- Use clean rags to wipe bearings.
- Keep the bearings in oil-proof paper when they are to be stored or are not in use.
- Clean the inside of the housing before replacing the bearing.

Do NOT do the following:
- Don't work in dirty surroundings.
- Don't use dirty, chipped or damaged tools.
- Try not to work on wooden work benches or use wooden mallets.
- Don't handle bearings with dirty or moist hands.
- Do not use gasoline for cleaning; use a safe solvent.
- Do not spin-dry bearings with compressed air. They will be damaged.
- Do not spin dirty bearings.
- Avoid using cotton waste or dirty cloths to wipe bearings.
- Try not to scratch or nick bearing surfaces.
- Do not allow the bearing to come in contact with dirt or rust at any time.

NOTE: The following procedures are made easier with the use of GM tools No. J–29117, J–8092, J–8850, J–8457 and J–9746–02 or their equivalents.

1. Raise and support the front of the vehicle on jackstands.
2. Remove the tire/wheel assembly.
3. Remove the caliper-to-steering knuckle bolts and the caliper from the steering knuckle. Using a wire, support the caliper from the vehicle; DO NOT disconnect the brake line.
4. From the hub/disc assembly, remove the dust cap, the cot-

ter pin, the spindle nut, the thrust washer and the outer bearing.

5. Grasping the hub/disc assembly firmly, pull the assembly from the axle spindle.

6. Using a small pry bar, pry the grease seal from the rear of the hub/disc assembly, then remove the inner bearing.

NOTE: DO NOT remove the bearing races from the hub, unless they show signs of damage.

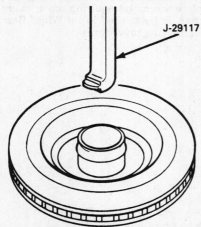

J-29117

Removing the front wheel bearing races from the hub/disc assembly — Two wheel drive

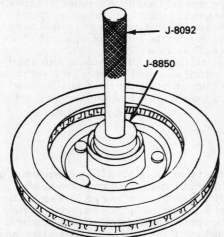

J-8092

J-8850

Installing the inner wheel bearing race to the hub/disc assembly — Two wheel drive

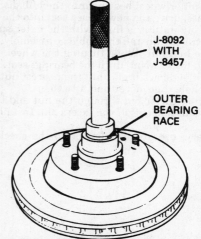

J-8092
WITH
J-8457

OUTER
BEARING
RACE

Installing the outer wheel bearing race to the hub/disc assembly — Two wheel drive

7. If it is necessary to remove the wheel bearing races, use the GM front bearing race removal tool No. J–29117 to drive the races from the hub/disc assembly.

8. Using solvent, clean the grease from all of the parts, then blow them dry with compressed air.

9. Inspect all of the parts for scoring, pitting or cracking, replace the parts (if necessary).

10. If the bearing races were removed, perform the following procedures to the install the them:

a. Using grease, lightly lubricate the inside of the hub/disc assembly.

b. Using the GM seal installation tools No. J–8092 and J–8850, drive the inner bearing race into the hub/disc assembly until it seats.

NOTE: When installing the bearing races, be sure to support the hub/disc assembly with GM tool No. J–9746–02.

c. Using the GM seal installation tools No. J–8092 and J–8457, drive the outer race into the hub/disc assembly until it seats.

11. Using wheel bearing grease, lubricate the bearings, the races and the spindle; be sure to place a gob of grease (inside the hub/disc assembly) between the races to provide an ample supply of lubricant.

NOTE: To lubricate each bearing, place a gob of grease in the palm of the hand, then roll the bearing through the grease until it is well lubricated.

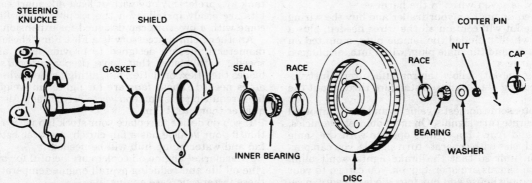

STEERING
KNUCKLE

SHIELD

COTTER PIN

NUT

CAP

GASKET

SEAL

RACE

RACE

BEARING

INNER BEARING

WASHER

DISC

Exploded view of the front wheel hub/bearing assembly — Two wheel drive

12. Place the inner wheel bearing into the hub/disc assembly. Using a flat plate, drive the new grease seal into the rear of the hub/disc assembly until it is flush with the outer surface.

13. Onto the spindle, install the hub/disc assembly, the thrust washer and the hub nut. While turning the wheel, torque the hub nut to 16 ft. lbs. (21 Nm) until the bearings seat. Loosen the nut, retighten it and back it off until the nearest nut slot aligns with a spindle hole (not more than a ½ turn).

14. Install a new cotter pin through the nut and the spindle, then bend the ends and cut off the excess pin. Install the grease cap.

15. If necessary, use a dial indicator to the check the rotor endplay. The endplay should be 0.025–0.127mm (0.001–0.005 in.); if not, readjust the hub/disc assembly.

16. Install the caliper onto the steering knuckle and torque the bolts to 37 ft. lbs. (49 Nm). Road test the vehicle.

All Wheel Drive

The all wheel drive front wheel bearings are the sealed type that require no periodic adjusting or repacking. The bearing and hub is a one piece assembly requiring replacement if the bearings are defective. Refer to the "Front Wheel Bearing" section in Section 8 for bearing procedures.

TRAILER TOWING

Astro and Safari vans are popular as trailer towing vehicles. Their strong construction and variety of power train combinations make them ideal for towing campers, boat trailers and utility trailers.

Factory trailer towing packages are available on most vans. However, if you are installing a trailer hitch and wiring on your vehicle, there are a few things you ought to know.

General Recommendations

Wiring

Wiring the vehicle for towing is fairly easy. There are a number of good wiring kits available and these should be used, rather than trying to design your own. All trailers will need brake lights, turn signals, tail lights and side marker lights. Most states require extra marker lights for overwide trailers. Also, most states have recently required back-up lights for trailers, and most trailer manufacturers have been building trailers with back-up lights for several years.

Additionally, some Class I, most Class II and just about all Class III trailers will have electric brakes.

Add to this number an accessories wire, to operate the trailer internal equipment or to charge the trailer's battery, and you can have as many as seven wires in the harness.

Determine the equipment on your trailer and buy the wiring kit necessary. The kit will contain all the wires needed, plus a plug adapter set which included the female plug, mounted on the bumper or hitch, and the male plug, wired into, or plugged into the trailer harness.

When installing the kit, follow the manufacturer's instructions. The color coding of the wires is standard throughout the industry.

One point to note: some domestic vehicles and most imported vehicles, have separate turn signals. On most domestic vehicles, the brake lights and rear turn signals operate with the same bulb. For those vehicles with separate turn signals, you can purchase an isolation unit so that the brake lights won't blink whenever the turn signals are operated, or, you can go to your local electronics supply house and buy four diodes to wire in series with the brake and turn signal bulbs. Diodes will isolate the brake and turn signals. The choice is yours. The isolation units are simple and quick to install, but far more expensive than the diodes. The diodes, however, require more work to install properly, since they require the cutting of each bulb's wire and soldering in place of the diode.

One, final point, the best kits are those with a spring loaded cover on the vehicle mounted socket. This cover prevents dirt and moisture from corroding the terminals. Never let the vehicle socket hang loosely; always mount it securely to the bumper or hitch.

Cooling

ENGINE

One of the most common, if not THE most common, problems associated with trailer towing is engine overheating.

With factory installed trailer towing packages, a heavy duty cooling system is usually included. Heavy duty cooling systems are available as optional equipment on most vans, with or without a trailer package. If you have one of these extra capacity systems, you shouldn't have overheating problems.

If you have a standard cooling system, without an expansion tank, you'll definitely need to get an aftermarket expansion tank kit, preferably one with at least a 2 quart capacity. These kits are easily installed on the radiator's overflow hose, and come with a pressure cap designed for expansion tanks.

Another helpful accessory is a Flex Fan. These fan are large diameter units are designed to provide more airflow at low speeds, with blades that have deeply cupped surfaces. The blades then flex, or flatten out, at high speed, when less cooling air is needed. These fans are far lighter in weight than stock fans, requiring less horsepower to drive them. Also, they are far quieter than stock fans.

If you do decide to replace your stock fan with a flex fan, note that if your vehicle has a fan clutch, a spacer between the flex fan and water pump hub will be needed.

Aftermarket engine oil coolers are helpful for prolonging engine oil life and reducing overall engine temperatures. Both of these factors increase engine life.

While not absolutely necessary in towing Class I and some

Class II trailers, they are recommended for heavier Class II and all Class III towing.

Engine oil cooler systems consist of an adapter, screwed on in place of the oil filter, a remote filter mounting and a multi-tube, a finned heat exchanger, which is mounted in front of the radiator or air conditioning condenser.

TRANSMISSION

An automatic transmission is usually recommended for trailer towing. Modern automatics have proven reliable and, of course, easy to operate, in trailer towing.

The increased load of a trailer, however, causes an increase in the temperature of the automatic transmission fluid. Heat is the worst enemy of an automatic transmission. As the temperature of the fluid increases, the life of the fluid decreases.

It is essential, therefore, that you install an automatic transmission cooler.

The cooler, which consists of a multi-tube, finned heat exchanger, is usually installed in front of the radiator or air conditioning compressor, and hooked inline with the transmission cooler tank inlet line. Follow the cooler manufacturer's installation instructions.

Select a cooler of at least adequate capacity, based upon the combined gross weights of the van and trailer.

Cooler manufacturers recommend that you use an aftermarket cooler in addition to, and not instead of, the present cooling tank in your vans radiator. If you do want to use it in place of the radiator cooling tank, get a cooler at least two sizes larger than normally necessary.

One note: transmission cooler can, sometimes, cause slow or harsh shifting in the transmission during cold weather, until the fluid has a chance to come up to normal operating temperature. Some coolers can be purchased with or retrofitted with a temperature bypass valve which will allow fluid flow through the cooler only when the fluid has reached operating temperature, or above.

Trailer and Hitch Weight Limits

Trailer Weight

Trailer weight is the first, and most important, factor in determining whether or not your vehicle is suitable for towing the trailer you have in mind. The horsepower-to-weight ratio should be calculated. The basic standard is a ratio of 35:1. That is, 35 lbs. of GVW for every horsepower.

To calculate this ratio, multiply you engine's rated horsepower by 35, then subtract the weight of the vehicle, including passengers and luggage. The resulting figure is the ideal maximum trailer weight that you can tow. One point to consider: a numerically higher axle ratio can offset what appears to be a low trailer weight. If the weight of the trailer that you have in mind is somewhat higher than the weight you just calculated, you might consider changing your rear axle ratio to compensate.

Hitch Weight

There are three kinds of hitches: bumper mounted, frame mounted and load equalizing.

Bumper mounted hitches are those which attach solely to the vehicle's bumper. Many states prohibit towing with this type of hitch, when it attaches to the vehicle's stock bumper, since it subjects the bumper to stresses for which it was not designed. Aftermarket rear step bumpers, designed for trailer towing, are acceptable for use with bumper mounted hitches.

Frame mounted hitches can be of the type which bolts to two or more points on the frame, plus the bumper, or just to several points on the frame. Frame mounted hitches can also be of the tongue type, for Class I towing, or, of the receiver type, for classes II and III.

Load equalizing hitches are usually used for large trailers. Most equalizing hitches are welded in place, they use equalizing bars and chains to level the vehicle after the trailer is connected.

The bolt-on hitches are the most common, since they are relatively easy to install.

Check the gross weight rating of your trailer. Tongue weight is usually figured as 10% of gross trailer weight. Therefore, a trailer with a maximum gross weight of 2,000 lbs. will have a maximum tongue weight of 200 lbs. Class I trailers fall into this category. Class II trailers are those with a gross weight rating of 2,000–3,500 lbs., while Class III trailers fall into the 3,500–6,000 lbs. category. Class IV trailers are those over 6,000 lbs. and are for use with fifth wheel trucks, only.

When you've determined the hitch that you'll need, follow the manufacturer's installation instructions, exactly, especially when it comes to fastener torques. The hitch will subjected to a lot of stress and good hitches come with hardened bolts. Never substitute an inferior bolt for a hardened bolt.

PUSHING AND TOWING

DO NOT push or tow your Astro or Safari Van to start it. Unusually high catalytic converter and exhaust system temperatures may result, which under extreme conditions may ignite the interior floor covering material above the converter.

Astro and Safari Vans may be towed at speeds up to 35 mph and distances not over 50 miles with the driveshaft in place, if no engine/driveline damage is present. If engine/driveline damage is known or suspected, the driveshaft should be disconnected before towing.

To be sure that no damage will occur to your vehicle, consult any GM dealer or professional tow truck service for towing instructions.

NOTE: To avoid damage to the fiberglass springs when raising the vehicle, DO NOT allow the lifting equipment to come into contact with the springs.

JUMP STARTING

JUMP STARTING A DEAD BATTERY

The chemical reaction in a battery produces explosive hydrogen gas. This is the safe way to jump start a dead battery, reducing the chances of an accidental spark that could cause an explosion.

Jump Starting Precautions

1. Be sure both batteries are of the same voltage.
2. Be sure both batteries are of the same polarity (have the same grounded terminal).
3. Be sure the vehicles are not touching.
4. Be sure the vent cap holes are not obstructed.
5. Do not smoke or allow sparks around the battery.
6. In cold weather, check for frozen electrolyte in the battery. Do not jump start a frozen battery.
7. Do not allow electrolyte on your skin or clothing.
8. Be sure the electrolyte is not frozen.

CAUTION: Make certin that the ignition key, in the vehicle with the dead battery, is in the OFF position. Connecting cables to vehicles with on-board computers will result in computer destruction if the key is not in the OFF position.

Jump Starting Procedure

1. Determine voltages of the two batteries; they must be the same.
2. Bring the starting vehicle close (they must not touch) so that the batteries can be reached easily.
3. Turn off all accessories and both engines. Put both vehicles in Neutral or Park and set the handbrake.
4. Cover the cell caps with a rag—do not cover terminals.
5. If the terminals on the run-down battery are heavily corroded, clean them.
6. Identify the positive and negative posts on both batteries and connect the cables in the order shown.
7. Start the engine of the starting vehicle and run it at fast idle. Try to start the car with the dead battery. Crank it for no more than 10 seconds at a time and let it cool for 20 seconds in between tries.
8. If it doesn't start in 3 tries, there is something else wrong.
9. Disconnect the cables in the reverse order.
10. Replace the cell covers and dispose of the rags.

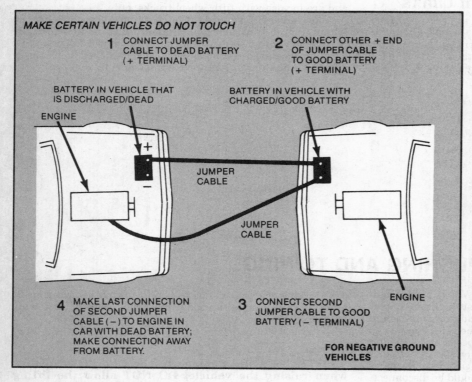

MAKE CERTAIN VEHICLES DO NOT TOUCH

1 CONNECT JUMPER CABLE TO DEAD BATTERY (+ TERMINAL)

2 CONNECT OTHER + END OF JUMPER CABLE TO GOOD BATTERY (+ TERMINAL)

BATTERY IN VEHICLE THAT IS DISCHARGED/DEAD

BATTERY IN VEHICLE WITH CHARGED/GOOD BATTERY

ENGINE

JUMPER CABLE

JUMPER CABLE

ENGINE

4 MAKE LAST CONNECTION OF SECOND JUMPER CABLE (−) TO ENGINE IN CAR WITH DEAD BATTERY; MAKE CONNECTION AWAY FROM BATTERY.

3 CONNECT SECOND JUMPER CABLE TO GOOD BATTERY (− TERMINAL)

FOR NEGATIVE GROUND VEHICLES

Side terminal batteries occasionally pose a problem when connecting jumper cables. There frequently isn't enough room to clamp the cables without touching sheet metal. Side terminal adaptors are available to alleviate this problem and should be removed after use

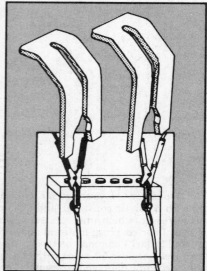

The following procedure is recommended by the manufacturer. Be sure that the booster battery is a 12 volt with a negative ground.

------ CAUTION ------

DO NOT attempt this procedure on a frozen battery, it will probably explode. DO NOT attempt it on a sealed Delco Freedom battery showing a light color in the charge indicator. Be certain to observe the correct polarity connections. Failure to do so will result in almost immediate alternator and regulator destruction. Never allow the jumper cable ends to touch each other.

1. Position the 2 vehicles so that they are not touching. Set the parking brake and place the transmission in Park (AT) or in Neutral (MT). Turn Off the lights, heater and other electrical loads.
2. Remove the vent caps from both the booster and discharged battery. Lay a cloth over the open vent cells of each battery. This is not necessary on batteries equipped with sponge type flame arrestor caps and it is not possible on sealed Freedom batteries.
3. Attach one cable to the positive (+) terminal of the booster battery and the other end to the positive terminal of the discharged battery.

4. Attach one end of the remaining cable to the negative (–) terminal of the booster battery and the other end to the alternator bracket, about 457mm (18 in.) from the discharged battery. DO NOT attach to the negative terminal of discharged batteries.
5. Start the engine of the vehicle with the booster battery. Start the engine of the vehicle with the discharged battery. If the engine will no start, disconnect the batteries as soon as possible. If this is not done, the two batteries will soon reach a state of equilibrium, with both too weak to start any engine. This will not be a problem if the engine of the booster vehicle is kept running fast enough. Lengthy cranking can overheat and damage the starter.
6. Reverse the above steps to disconnect the booster and discharged batteries. Be certain to remove the negative connections first.
7. Dispose of the cloths, for they may have battery acid on them.

------ CAUTION ------

The use of any "hot shot" type of jumper system in excess of 12 volts can damage the electronic control units or cause the discharged battery to explode.

JACKING

The jack supplied with the Astro and Safari van is meant for changing tires; it is not meant to support a vehicle while you crawl under it and work. Whenever it is necessary to get under a vehicle to perform service operations, always be sure that it is adequately supported, preferably by jackstands at the proper points. Always block the wheels when changing tires.

If the van is equipped with a Positraction® rear axle, DO NOT run the engine for any reason with one rear wheel off the ground. Power will be transmitted through the rear wheel remaining on the ground, possibly causing the vehicle to drive itself off the jack.

Some of the service operations in this book require that one or both ends of the vehicle be raised and supported safely. The best arrangement for this, of course, is a grease pit or a vehicle lift but these items are seldom found in the home garage. However, small hydraulic, screw or scissors jacks are satisfactory for raising the vehicle.

Heavy wooden blocks or adjustable jackstands should be used to support the vehicle while it is being worked on. Drive-on trestles or ramps are also a handy and a safe way to raise the vehicle,

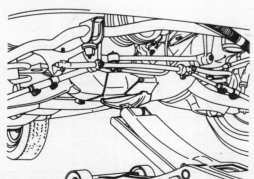

Using the crossmember to lift the front the the vehicle

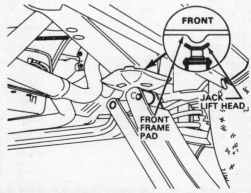

Using the front frame pad to lift the side of the vehicle

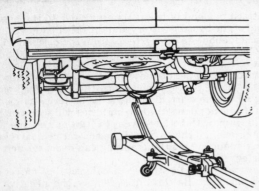

Using the rear axle to lift the rear of the vehicle

assuming their capacity is adequate. These can be bought or constructed from suitable heavy timbers or steel.

In any case, it is always best to spend a little extra time to make sure that your van is lifted and supported safely.

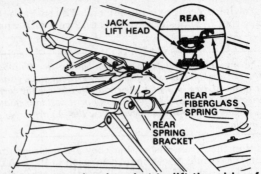

Using the rear spring bracket to lift the side of the vehicle

——— CAUTION ———

Concrete blocks are not recommended. They may crumble if the load is not evenly distributed. Boxes and milk crates of any description MUST not be used. Shake the vehicle a few times to make sure the jackstands are securely supporting the weight before crawling under.

Maintenance Intervals
Schedule I ①

Item No.	To Be Serviced	When to Perform Miles or Months, Whichever Occurs First Miles (000)	The services shown in this schedule up to 48,000 miles are to be performed after 48,000 miles at the same intervals														
			3	6	9	12	15	18	21	24	27	30	33	36	39	42	45	48
1	Engine Oil and Oil filter Change	Every 3,000 Miles or 3 Months	•	•	•	•	•	•	•	•	•	•	•	•	•	•	•	•
2	Chassis Lubrication	Every oil change	•	•	•	•	•	•	•	•	•	•	•	•	•	•	•	•
3	Carburetor Choke and Hose Inspection	At 6,000 Miles, then at 30,000 Miles		•								•				•		
4	Carburetor or T.B.I. Mounting Bolt Torque Check			•								•						
5	Engine Idle Speed Adjustment			•								•						
6	Engine Accessory Drive Belts Inspection	Every 12 Months or 15,000 Miles						•				•					•	
7	Cooling System Service	Every 24 Months or 30,000 Miles										•						
8	Front Wheel Bearing Repack	Every 15,000 Miles						•				•				•		
9	Transmission Service	15,000 Miles						•				•						
10	Vacuum Advance System Inspection	Check at 6,000 Miles, then at 30,000 Miles, and at 45,000 Miles		•								•				•		
11	Spark Plugs and Wire Service	Every 30,000 Miles										•						
12	PCV System Inspection	Every 30,000 Miles										•						
13	EGR System Check	Every 30,000 Miles										•						
14	Air Cleaner and PCV Filter Replacement	Every 30,000 Miles										•						
15	Engine Timing Check	Every 30,000 Miles										•						
16	Fuel Tank, Cap and Lines Inspection	Every 12 Months or 15,000 Miles						•				•				•		
17	Early Fuel Evaporation System Inspection	At 6,000 Miles then at 30,000 Miles		•								•						
18	Evaporative Control System Inspection	At 30,000 Miles										•						
19	Fuel Filter Replacement	Every 15,000 Miles						•				•				•		
20	Valve Lash Adjustment	Every 15,000 Miles						•				•				•		
21	Thermostatically Controlled Air Cleaner Inspection	Every 30,000 Miles																

Maintenance interval – schedule I

Maintenance Intervals (cont.)
Schedule II ②

Item No.	To Be Serviced	When to Perform Miles or Months, Whichever Occurs First Miles (000)	The services shown in this schedule up to 60,000 miles are to be performed after 60,000 miles at the same intervals							
			7.5	15	22.5	30	37.5	45	52.5	60
1	Engine Oil Change	Every 7,500 Miles or 12 Months	●	●	●	●	●	●	●	●
	Oil Filter Change	At First and Every Other Oil Change or 12 Months	●		●		●		●	
2	Chassis Lubrication	Every oil change	●	●	●	●	●	●	●	●
3	Carburetor Choke and Hoses Inspection	At 6 Months or 7,500 Miles and at 60,000 Miles	●		●					●
4	Carburetor or T.B.I. Mounting Bolt Torque Check	At 6 Months or 7,500 Miles and at 60,000 Miles	●							●
5	Engine Idle Speed Adjustment	At 6 Months or 7,500 Miles and at 60,000 Miles	●							●
6	Engine Accessory Drive Belts Inspection	Every 24 Months or 30,000 Miles				●				●
7	Cooling System Service	Every 24 Months or 30,000 Miles				●				●
8	Front Wheel Bearing Repack	Every 30,000 Miles				●				●
9	Transmission Service	30,000 miles				●				●
10	Vacuum Advance System Inspection	Check at 6 Months or 7,500 Miles, then at 30,000 Miles, and then at 15,000 Mile intervals.	●			●		●		●
11	Spark Plugs and Wire Service	Every 30,000 Miles				●				●
12	PCV System Inspection	Every 30,000 Miles				●				●
13	EGR System Check	Every 30,000 Miles				●				●
14	Air Cleaner and PCV Filter Replacement	Every 30,000 Miles				●				●
15	Engine Timing Check	Every 30,000 Miles				●				●
16	Fuel Tank, Cap and Lines Inspection	Every 24 Months 30,000 Miles				●				●
17	Early Fuel Evaporation System Inspection	At 7,500 Miles and at 30,000 Miles than at 30,000 Mile intervals.	●			●				●
18	Evaporative Control System Inspection	Every 30,000 Miles				●				●
19	Fuel Filter Replacement	Every 30,000 Miles				●				●
20	Valve Lash Adjustment	Every 15,000 Miles		●		●		●		●
21	Thermostatically Controlled Air Cleaner Inspection	Every 30,000 Miles				●				●

① Severe service ② Normal service

Maintenance interval — schedule II

CAPACITIES CHART

Years	VIN	Engine No. Cyl. (cu. in.)	Crankcase Includes Filter (qt)	Transmission (pts)			Drive Axle (pts)	Fuel ③ Tank (gal)	Cooling ② System (qt)	
				4-sp	5-sp	Auto			w/AC	wo/AC
1985	E	4-151	3.0	5	4.4	10 ①	4.0	17/27	10.0	10.0
	N	6-262	5.0	5	4.4	10 ①	4.0	17/27	13.5	13.5
1986	E	4-151	3.0	5	4.4	10 ①	4.0	17/27	10.0	10.0
	Z	6-262	5.0	5	4.4	10 ①	4.0	17/27	13.5	13.5
1987	E	4-151	3.0	5	4.4	10 ①	4.0	17/27	10.0	10.0
	Z	6-262	5.0	5	4.4	10 ①	4.0	17/27	13.5	13.5
1988	E	4-151	3.0	5	4.4	10 ①	4.0	17/27	10.0	10.0
	Z	6-262	5.0	5	4.4	10 ①	4.0	17/27	13.5	13.5
1989	E	4-151	3.0	—	4.4	10 ①	4.0	17/27	10.0	10.0
	Z	6-262	5.0	—	4.4	10 ①	4.0	17/27	13.5	13.5
1990	E	4-151	3.5	—	—	10 ①	4.0	27	10.0	10.0
	Z	6-262	5.0	—	—	10 ①	4.0	27	13.5	13.5
	B	6-262	5.0	—	—	10 ①	4.0	27	13.5	13.5

① 23 pts: overhaul
② If equipped with rear heater, add 2.84 qts.
③ Figures divided by a slash are: std/opt

Engine Performance and Tune-Up 2

QUICK REFERENCE INDEX

GENERAL INDEX

TUNE-UP SPECIFICATIONS

Years	VIN	Engine No. Cyl. (cu. in.)	Spark Plugs Type	Gap (in.)	Ignition Timing (deg.) Man. Trans.	Auto. Trans.	Idle Speed Man. Trans.	Auto. Trans.	Valve Clearance In.	Exh.
1985	E	4-151	R43TSX	0.060	②	②	②	②	③	③
	N	6-262	R43CTS	0.040	②	②	②	②	①	①
1986	E	4-151	R43TSX	0.060	②	②	②	②	③	③
	Z	6-262	R43CTS	0.040	②	②	②	②	①	①
1987	E	4-151	R43TSX	0.060	②	②	②	②	④	④
	Z	6-262	R43CTS	0.040	②	②	②	②	①	①
1988	E	4-151	R43TSX	0.060 ②	②	②	②	②	⑤	⑤
	Z	6-262	R43CTS	0.040 ②	②	②	②	②	①	①
1989	E	4-151	R43TS6	0.060	②	②	②	②	⑤	⑤
	Z	6-262	CR43TS	0.035	②	②	②	②	①	①
1990	E	4-151	R43TS6	0.060	—	②	—	②	⑤	⑤
	Z	6-262	CR43TS	0.035	—	②	—	②	①	①
	B ⑥	6-262	CR43TS	0.035	—	②	—	②	①	①

① One turn down from zero lash
② Refer to underhood specifications
③ Torque bolts to 20 ft. lbs. (27 Nm)
④ Torque bolts to 24 ft. lbs. (32 Nm)
⑤ Torque bolts to 22 ft. lbs. (30 Nm)
④ High Output Engine

Troubleshooting Engine Performance

Problem	Cause	Solution
Hard starting (engine cranks normally)	• Binding linkage, choke valve or choke piston	• Repair as necessary
	• Restricted choke vacuum diaphragm	• Clean passages
	• Improper fuel level	• Adjust float level
	• Dirty, worn or faulty needle valve and seat	• Repair as necessary
	• Float sticking	• Repair as necessary
	• Faulty fuel pump	• Replace fuel pump
	• Incorrect choke cover adjustment	• Adjust choke cover
	• Inadequate choke unloader adjustment	• Adjust choke unloader
	• Faulty ignition coil	• Test and replace as necessary
	• Improper spark plug gap	• Adjust gap
	• Incorrect ignition timing	• Adjust timing
	• Incorrect valve timing	• Check valve timing; repair as necessary
Rough idle or stalling	• Incorrect curb or fast idle speed	• Adjust curb or fast idle speed
	• Incorrect ignition timing	• Adjust timing to specification
	• Improper feedback system operation	• Refer to Chapter 4
	• Improper fast idle cam adjustment	• Adjust fast idle cam
	• Faulty EGR valve operation	• Test EGR system and replace as necessary
	• Faulty PCV valve air flow	• Test PCV valve and replace as necessary

Troubleshooting Engine Performance (cont.)

Problem	Cause	Solution
Rough idle or stalling	• Choke binding	• Locate and eliminate binding condition
	• Faulty TAC vacuum motor or valve	• Repair as necessary
	• Air leak into manifold vacuum	• Inspect manifold vacuum connections and repair as necessary
	• Improper fuel level	• Adjust fuel level
	• Faulty distributor rotor or cap	• Replace rotor or cap
	• Improperly seated valves	• Test cylinder compression, repair as necessary
	• Incorrect ignition wiring	• Inspect wiring and correct as necessary
	• Faulty ignition coil	• Test coil and replace as necessary
	• Restricted air vent or idle passages	• Clean passages
	• Restricted air cleaner	• Clean or replace air cleaner filler element
	• Faulty choke vacuum diaphragm	• Repair as necessary
Faulty low-speed operation	• Restricted idle transfer slots	• Clean transfer slots
	• Restricted idle air vents and passages	• Clean air vents and passages
	• Restricted air cleaner	• Clean or replace air cleaner filter element
	• Improper fuel level	• Adjust fuel level
	• Faulty spark plugs	• Clean or replace spark plugs
	• Dirty, corroded, or loose ignition secondary circuit wire connections	• Clean or tighten secondary circuit wire connections
	• Improper feedback system operation	• Refer to Chapter 4
	• Faulty ignition coil high voltage wire	• Replace ignition coil high voltage wire
	• Faulty distributor cap	• Replace cap
Faulty acceleration	• Improper accelerator pump stroke	• Adjust accelerator pump stroke
	• Incorrect ignition timing	• Adjust timing
	• Inoperative pump discharge check ball or needle	• Clean or replace as necessary
	• Worn or damaged pump diaphragm or piston	• Replace diaphragm or piston
	• Leaking carburetor main body cover gasket	• Replace gasket
	• Engine cold and choke set too lean	• Adjust choke cover
	• Improper metering rod adjustment (BBD Model carburetor)	• Adjust metering rod
	• Faulty spark plug(s)	• Clean or replace spark plug(s)
	• Improperly seated valves	• Test cylinder compression, repair as necessary
	• Faulty ignition coil	• Test coil and replace as necessary
	• Improper feedback system operation	• Refer to Chapter 4

Troubleshooting Engine Performance

Problem	Cause	Solution
Faulty high speed operation	• Incorrect ignition timing	• Adjust timing
	• Faulty distributor centrifugal advance mechanism	• Check centrifugal advance mechanism and repair as necessary
	• Faulty distributor vacuum advance mechanism	• Check vacuum advance mechanism and repair as necessary
	• Low fuel pump volume	• Replace fuel pump
	• Wrong spark plug air gap or wrong plug	• Adjust air gap or install correct plug
	• Faulty choke operation	• Adjust choke cover
	• Partially restricted exhaust manifold, exhaust pipe, catalytic converter, muffler, or tailpipe	• Eliminate restriction
	• Restricted vacuum passages	• Clean passages
	• Improper size or restricted main jet	• Clean or replace as necessary
	• Restricted air cleaner	• Clean or replace filter element as necessary
	• Faulty distributor rotor or cap	• Replace rotor or cap
	• Faulty ignition coil	• Test coil and replace as necessary
	• Improperly seated valve(s)	• Test cylinder compression, repair as necessary
	• Faulty valve spring(s)	• Inspect and test valve spring tension, replace as necessary
	• Incorrect valve timing	• Check valve timing and repair as necessary
	• Intake manifold restricted	• Remove restriction or replace manifold
	• Worn distributor shaft	• Replace shaft
	• Improper feedback system operation	• Refer to Chapter 4
Misfire at all speeds	• Faulty spark plug(s)	• Clean or replace spark plug(s)
	• Faulty spark plug wire(s)	• Replace as necessary
	• Faulty distributor cap or rotor	• Replace cap or rotor
	• Faulty ignition coil	• Test coil and replace as necessary
	• Primary ignition circuit shorted or open intermittently	• Troubleshoot primary circuit and repair as necessary
	• Improperly seated valve(s)	• Test cylinder compression, repair as necessary
	• Faulty hydraulic tappet(s)	• Clean or replace tappet(s)
	• Improper feedback system operation	• Refer to Chapter 4
	• Faulty valve spring(s)	• Inspect and test valve spring tension, repair as necessary
	• Worn camshaft lobes	• Replace camshaft
	• Air leak into manifold	• Check manifold vacuum and repair as necessary
	• Improper carburetor adjustment	• Adjust carburetor
	• Fuel pump volume or pressure low	• Replace fuel pump
	• Blown cylinder head gasket	• Replace gasket
	• Intake or exhaust manifold passage(s) restricted	• Pass chain through passage(s) and repair as necessary
	• Incorrect trigger wheel installed in distributor	• Install correct trigger wheel

Troubleshooting Engine Performance (cont.)

Problem	Cause	Solution
Power not up to normal	• Incorrect ignition timing • Faulty distributor rotor • Trigger wheel loose on shaft • Incorrect spark plug gap • Faulty fuel pump • Incorrect valve timing • Faulty ignition coil • Faulty ignition wires • Improperly seated valves • Blown cylinder head gasket • Leaking piston rings • Worn distributor shaft • Improper feedback system operation	• Adjust timing • Replace rotor • Reposition or replace trigger wheel • Adjust gap • Replace fuel pump • Check valve timing and repair as necessary • Test coil and replace as necessary • Test wires and replace as necessary • Test cylinder compression and repair as necessary • Replace gasket • Test compression and repair as necessary • Replace shaft • Refer to Chapter 4
Intake backfire	• Improper ignition timing • Faulty accelerator pump discharge • Defective EGR CTO valve • Defective TAC vacuum motor or valve • Lean air/fuel mixture	• Adjust timing • Repair as necessary • Replace EGR CTO valve • Repair as necessary • Check float level or manifold vacuum for air leak. Remove sediment from bowl
Exhaust backfire	• Air leak into manifold vacuum • Faulty air injection diverter valve • Exhaust leak	• Check manifold vacuum and repair as necessary • Test diverter valve and replace as necessary • Locate and eliminate leak
Ping or spark knock	• Incorrect ignition timing • Distributor centrifugal or vacuum advance malfunction • Excessive combustion chamber deposits • Air leak into manifold vacuum • Excessively high compression • Fuel octane rating excessively low • Sharp edges in combustion chamber • EGR valve not functioning properly	• Adjust timing • Inspect advance mechanism and repair as necessary • Remove with combustion chamber cleaner • Check manifold vacuum and repair as necessary • Test compression and repair as necessary • Try alternate fuel source • Grind smooth • Test EGR system and replace as necessary
Surging (at cruising to top speeds)	• Low carburetor fuel level • Low fuel pump pressure or volume • Metering rod(s) not adjusted properly (BBD Model Carburetor) • Improper PCV valve air flow	• Adjust fuel level • Replace fuel pump • Adjust metering rod • Test PCV valve and replace as necessary

Troubleshooting Engine Performance (cont.)

Problem	Cause	Solution
Surging (at cruising to top speeds)	• Air leak into manifold vacuum	• Check manifold vacuum and repair as necessary
	• Incorrect spark advance	• Test and replace as necessary
	• Restricted main jet(s)	• Clean main jet(s)
	• Undersize main jet(s)	• Replace main jet(s)
	• Restricted air vents	• Clean air vents
	• Restricted fuel filter	• Replace fuel filter
	• Restricted air cleaner	• Clean or replace air cleaner filter element
	• EGR valve not functioning properly	• Test EGR system and replace as necessary
	• Improper feedback system operation	• Refer to Chapter 4

TUNE-UP PROCEDURES

In order to extract the full measure of performance and economy from your engine it is essential that it is properly tuned at regular intervals. A regular tune-up will keep your Van's engine running smoothly and will prevent the annoying breakdowns and poor performance associated with an untuned engine.

A complete tune-up should be performed every 30,000 miles. This interval should be halved if the vehicle is operated under severe conditions such as trailer towing, prolonged idling, start-and-stop driving, or if starting or running problems are noticed. It is assumed that the routine maintenance described in Section 1 has been kept up, as this will have a decided effect on the results of a tune-up. All of the applicable steps of a tune-up should be followed in order, as the result is a cumulative one.

If the specifications on the underhood tune-up sticker in the engine compartment disagree with the Tune-Up Specifications chart in this Section, the figures on the sticker must be used. The sticker often reflects changes made during the production run.

Spark Plugs

Normally, a set of spark plugs requires replacement about every 20,000–30,000 miles on vehicles equipped with an High Energy Ignition (HEI) system. Any vehicle which is subjected to severe conditions will need more frequent plug replacement.

Under normal operation, the plug gap increases about 0.025mm (0.001 in.) for every 1,000–2,000 miles. As the gap increases, the plug's voltage requirement also increases. It requires a greater voltage to jump the wider gap and about 2–3 times as much voltage to fire a plug at high speeds than at idle.

When you are removing the spark plugs, work on one at a time. Don't start by removing the plug wires all at once, for unless you number them, they may become mixed up. Take a minute before you begin and number the wires with tape. The best location for numbering the wires is near the distributor cap.

REMOVAL

When removing the spark plugs, work on one at a time. Don't start by removing the plug wire all at once because unless you number them, they're going to get mixed up. On some models though, it will be more convenient for you to remove all of the wires before you start to work on the plugs. If this is necessary, take a minute before you begin and number the wires with tape before you take them off. The time you spend here will pay off later on.

1. Twist the spark plug boot ½ turn and remove the boot from the plug. You may also use a plug wire removal tool designed especially for this purpose. *DO NOT pull on the wire itself.* When the wire has been removed, take a wire brush and clean the area around the plug. Make sure that all the grime is removed so that none will enter the cylinder after the plug has been removed.

2. Remove the plug using the proper size socket, extensions and universals as necessary.

3. If removing the plug is difficult, drip some penetrating oil (Liquid Wrench®, WD-40® or etc.) on the plug threads, allow it to work, then remove the plug. Also, be sure that the socket is straight on the plug, especially on those hard to reach plugs.

Diagnosis of Spark Plugs

Problem	Possible Cause	Correction
Brown to grayish-tan deposits and slight electrode wear.	• Normal wear.	• Clean, regap, reinstall.
Dry, fluffy black carbon deposits.	• Poor ignition output.	• Check distributor to coil connections.
Wet, oily deposits with very little electrode wear.	• "Break-in" of new or recently overhauled engine. • Excessive valve stem guide clearances. • Worn intake valve seals.	• Degrease, clean and reinstall the plugs. • Refer to Section 3. • Replace the seals.
Red, brown, yellow and white colored coatings on the insulator. Engine misses intermittently under severe operating conditions.	• By-products of combustion.	• Clean, regap, and reinstall. If heavily coated, replace.
Colored coatings heavily deposited on the portion of the plug projecting into the chamber and on the side facing the intake valve.	• Leaking seals if condition is found in only one or two cylinders.	• Check the seals. Replace if necessary. Clean, regap, and reinstall the plugs.
Shiny yellow glaze coating on the insulator.	• Melted by-products of combustion.	• Avoid sudden acceleration with wide-open throttle after long periods of low speed driving. Replace the plugs.
Burned or blistered insulator tips and badly eroded electrodes.	• Overheating.	• Check the cooling system. • Check for sticking heat riser valves. Refer to Section 1. • Lean air-fuel mixture. • Check the heat range of the plugs. May be too hot. • Check ignition timing. May be over-advanced. • Check the torque value of the plugs to ensure good plug-engine seat contact.
Broken or cracked insulator tips.	• Heat shock from sudden rise in tip temperature under severe operating conditions. Improper gapping of plugs.	• Replace the plugs. Gap correctly.

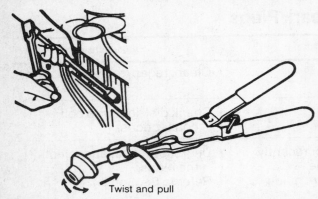

Twist and pull

Remove the spark plugs with a ratchet and long extension. Use special pliers to remove the boots and wire from the spark plug

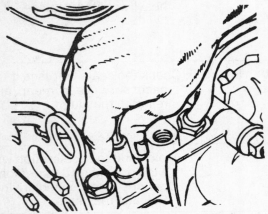

Twist and pull on the rubber boot to remove the spark plug wires; pull on the wire itself

INSPECTION

Check the plugs for deposits and wear. If they are not going to be replaced, clean the plugs thoroughly. Remember that any kind of deposit will decrease the efficiency of the plug. Plugs can be cleaned on a spark plug cleaning machine, which can sometimes be found in service stations or you can do an acceptable job of cleaning with a stiff brush. If the plugs are cleaned, the electrodes must be filed flat. Use an ignition points file, not an emery board or the like, which will leave deposits. The electrodes must be filed perfectly flat with sharp edges; rounded edges reduce the spark plug voltage by as much as 50%.

Check the spark plug gap before installation. The ground electrode (the L-shaped one connected to the body of the plug) must be parallel to the center electrode and the specified size wire gauge (see Tune-Up Specifications) should pass through the gap with a slight drag. Always check the gap on the new plugs, they are not always set correctly at the factory. DO NOT use a flat feeler gauge when measuring the gap, because the reading will be inaccurate.

Wire gapping tools usually have a bending tool attached. Use that to adjust the side electrode until the proper distance is obtained. **Absolutely, never bend the center electrode.** Also, be careful not to bend the side electrode too far or too often; it may weaken and break off within the engine, requiring removal of the cylinder head to retrieve it.

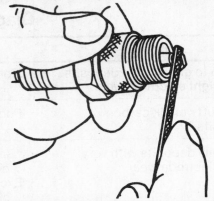

Plugs that are in good condition can be filed and re-used

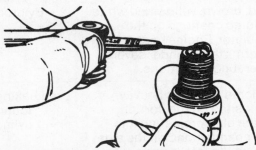

Always use a wire gauge to check the electrode gap

Adjust the electrode gap by bending the side electrode

INSTALLATION

1. Lubricate the threads of the spark plugs with a drop of oil. Install the plugs and tighten them hand tight. Take care not to crossthread them.

2. Tighten the spark plugs with the socket. DO NOT apply the same amount of force you would use for a bolt; just snug them in. If a torque wrench is available, tighten to 11–15 ft. lbs. (14–20 Nm).

3. Install the wire on their respective plugs. Make sure the wires are firmly connected, you will be able to feel them click into place.

Spark Plug Wires

Every 15,000 miles, visually inspect the spark plug cables for burns, cuts or breaks in the insulation. Check the spark plug boots and the nipples on the distributor cap and coil. Replace any damaged wiring.

Every 30,000 miles or so, the resistance of the wires should be

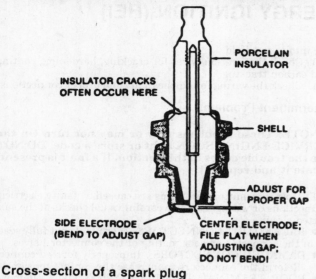

PORCELAIN INSULATOR

INSULATOR CRACKS OFTEN OCCUR HERE

SHELL

ADJUST FOR PROPER GAP

SIDE ELECTRODE (BEND TO ADJUST GAP)

CENTER ELECTRODE; FILE FLAT WHEN ADJUSTING GAP; DO NOT BEND!

Cross-section of a spark plug

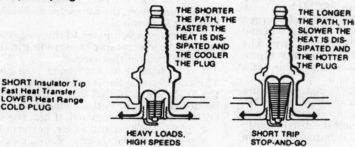

THE SHORTER THE PATH, THE FASTER THE HEAT IS DISSIPATED AND THE COOLER THE PLUG

THE LONGER THE PATH, THE SLOWER THE HEAT IS DISSIPATED AND THE HOTTER THE PLUG

SHORT Insulator Tip Fast Heat Transfer LOWER Heat Range COLD PLUG

HEAVY LOADS, HIGH SPEEDS

SHORT TRIP STOP-AND-GO

LONG Insulator Tip Slow Heat Transfer HIGHER Heat Range HOT PLUG

Spark plug heat range

checked with an ohmmeter. Wires with excessive resistance will cause misfiring and may make the engine difficult to start in damp weather. Generally, the useful life of the cables is 30,000–45,000 miles.

To check the resistance, remove the distributor cap, leaving the wires in place. Connect one lead of an ohmmeter to an electrode within the cap; connect the other lead to the corresponding spark plug terminal (remove it from the spark plug for this test). Replace any wire which shows a resistance over $30,000\Omega$. Generally speaking, however, resistance should not be over $25,000\Omega$, and $30,000\Omega$ must be considered the outer limit of acceptability.

It should be remembered that resistance is also a function of length; the longer the wire the greater the resistance. Thus, if the wires on your van are longer than the factory originals, resistance will be higher, quite possibly outside these limits.

When installing a new set of spark plug wires, replace the wires one at a time so there will be no mixup. Start by replacing the longest cable first. Install the boot firmly over the spark plug. Route the wire exactly the same as the original. Insert the distributor end of the wire firmly into the distributor cap tower, then seat the boot over the tower. Repeat the process for each wire.

FIRING ORDERS

NOTE: To avoid confusion, remove and tag the wires one at a time, for replacement.

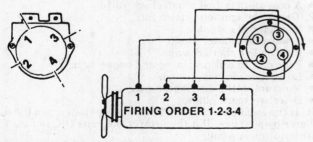

FIRING ORDER 1-2-3-4

Pontiac built (2.5L) 151–4 cylinder engine; Engine firing order: 1–3–4–2; Distributor rotation: clockwise.

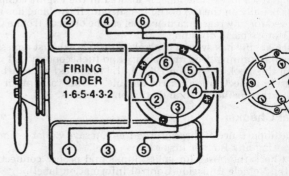

FIRING ORDER 1-6-5-4-3-2

Chevrolet built (4.3L) 262–V6 engine; Engine firing order: 1–6–5–4–3–2; Distributor rotation: clockwise

GM DELCO-REMY HIGH ENERGY IGNITION (HEI)

General Information

The High Energy Ignition distributor is used on most engines. The ignition coil is either mounted to the top of the distributor cap or is externally mounted on the engine, having a secondary circuit high tension wire connecting the coil to the distributor cap and interconnecting primary wiring as part of the engine harness.

The High Energy Ignition distributor is equipped to aid in spark timing changes, necessary for Emissions, Economy and performance. This system is called the Electronic Spark Timing Control (EST). The HEI distributors use a magnetic pick-up assembly, located inside the distributor containing a permanent magnet, a pole piece with internal teeth and a pick-up coil. When the teeth of the rotating timer core and pole piece align, an induced voltage in the pick-up coil signals the electronic module to open the coil primary circuit. As the primary current decreases, a high voltage is induced in the secondary windings of the ignition coil, directing a spark through the rotor and high voltage leads to fire the spark plugs. The dwell period is automatically controlled by the electronic control module (ECM) and is increased with increasing engine rpm. The HEI System features a longer spark duration which is instrumental in firing lean and EGR (Exhaust Gas Recirculation) diluted fuel/air mixtures. The condenser (capacitor) located within the HEI distributor is provided for noise (static) suppression purposes only and is not a regularly replaced ignition system component.

All spark timing changes in the HEI (EST) distributors are done electronically by the Electronic Control Module (ECM), which monitors information from the various engine sensors, computes the desired spark timing and signals the distributor to change the timing accordingly. With this distributor, no vacuum or centrifugal advances are used.

Troubleshooting

NOTE: **An accurate diagnosis is the first step to problem solution and repair. For several of the following steps, a HEI spark tester, tool ST-125, which has a spring clip to attach it to ground. Use of this tool is recommended, as there is more control of the high energy spark and less chance of being shocked. If a tachometer is connected to the TACH terminal on the distributor, disconnect it before proceeding with this test.**

Driveability problems that occur in your vehicle may become very frustrating and difficult to diagnose. An adequate understanding of the vehicles electronic control system will be needed to troubleshoot and repair an intermittent or on going problem.

The vehicles Emission Control Information label contains important information pertaining to emission specifications and setting procedures. The label is located in the engine compartment, usually on the top of the fan shroud. If the label has been removed for any reason, a new label can be ordered from a General Motors parts division.

Each engine has system controls to reduce exhaust emissions while maintaining good driveability and fuel economy. All vehicles in this book except the 1985 4.3L (49 states) with carburetor use an Electronic Control Module (ECM) to monitor and control the air/fuel ratio and ignition functions.

Initial Checks

The importance of these procedures can save valuable time by preventing any further inspections.
1. Check the hoses for splits, kinks and proper connections (see the Vehicle Emission Control Information label).
2. Inspect for air leaks at the throttle body or carburetor and the intake manifold.
3. Check the ignition wires for cracking, hardening, routing and carbon tracking.
4. Check the wiring for pinches, cuts and proper connections.

Intermittent Problems

NOTE: **These problems may or may not turn On the SERVICE ENGINE SOON light or store a code. DO NOT use the trouble codes in this section. If a fault is present, locate it and repair it.**

1. Most intermittent problems are caused by faulty electrical connections or wiring. Perform careful visual checks of the suspected circuits for:
   - BACKED OUT CONNECTORS – Terminals not fully seated in the connector or poor mating of the connector halves.
   - DAMAGED CONNECTORS – Improperly formed connectors. Reform the connectors to increase the contact tension.
   - POOR TERMINAL TO WIRE CONNECTION – Remove the terminal from the connector and check the condition of the wire to the terminal.
2. Connect a voltmeter to the suspected circuit and drive it around. An abnormal voltage reading in the circuit may indicate the problem is in that circuit.
3. The trouble memory code may be lost. Disconnect the Throttle Position Sensor (TPS) and curb idle the engine until the SERVICE ENGINE SOON light turns On. Code 22 should be stored and kept in the memory when the ignition is turned Off (for at least 10 seconds); if not, the ECM is faulty.
4. If the problem still exists, perform the following checks:
   - A sharp electrical surge occurs, usually when a faulty component is operated, such as: a relay, an Electronic Control Module (ECM) driven solenoid or a switch.
   - The improper installation of optional equipment, such as: a two-way radio, lights or etc.
   - Electronic Spark Timing (EST) wires may be too close to the spark plug wires, the distributor wires, the distributor housing, the coil and/or the alternator. Be sure that the distributor ground wire is grounded well.
   - The secondary ignition may be shorted to ground.
   - The Electronic Control Module (ECM) power wire may be grounded.

Hard Starting

The engine cranks OK but will not start for a long period of time, it eventually runs or it may start and immediately dies.
1. Check the fuel system for:
   - Water in the fuel.
   - Poor fuel pressure.
   - A sticking or binding Throttle Position Sensor (TPS).
   - A bad fuel pump relay.
   - A poor in-tank fuel pump check valve.
2. Check the ignition system for:
   - Ignition coil output.
   - A worn distributor shaft.
   - Bare and/or shorted wires.
   - Poor pickup coil resistance and connections.
   - Loose ignition coil ground.
   - Moisture in the distributor cap.
   - Defective spark plugs.
3. If the engine starts, then immediately stalls, open the distributor by-pass line. If it then starts and runs OK, replace the distributor pickup coil.
4. If the engine is hard to start, at normal operating temperature, check the ECM.

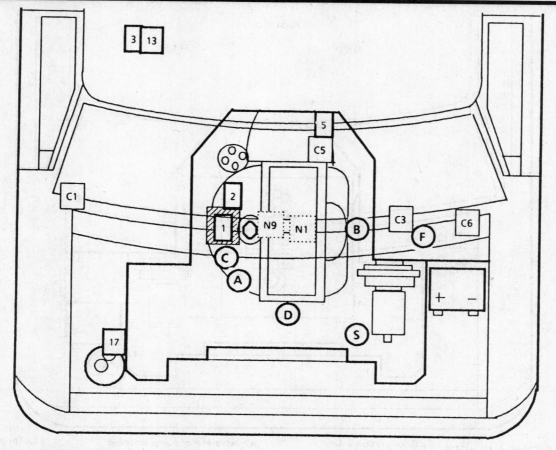

COMPUTER HARNESS

- **C1** Electronic Control Module (ECM)
- **C2** ALCL diagnostic connector
- **C3** "CHECK ENGINE" light
- **C5** ECM harness ground
- **C6** Fuse panel
- **C8** Fuel pump test connector

CONTROLLED DEVICES

- **1** Fuel injector
- **2** Idle air control motor
- **3** Fuel pump relay
- **5** Trans. Conv. Clutch connector
- **13** A/C compressor relay

⬡ Exhaust Gas Recirculation valve

INFORMATION SENSORS

- **A** Manifold pressure (M.A.P.)
- **B** Exhaust oxygen
- **C** Throttle position
- **D** Coolant temperature
- **F** Vehicle speed

NOT ECM CONNECTED

- **N1** Crankcase vent (PCV) valve
- **N9** Exhaust Gas Recirculation valve
- **N17** Fuel vapor canister

Electronic control components — 1985 2.5L TBI engine

Surge and/or Chuggle

At normal speed, with no change in the accelerator pedal position, the engine speeds up and slows down, inspect the following:

- Vehicle Speed Sensor (VSS) using the ALCL diagnostic connector.
- Exhaust Gas Recirculation (EGR) system if the problem is intermittent at idle.
- Ignition timing (see the Vehicle Emission Control Information label).
- Inline fuel filter for restrictions.
- Fuel pressure.
- Alternator output voltage, it must between 9–16V.
- Oxygen sensor.
- Spark plugs, distributor cap and ignition wire condition.
- Transmission Convertor Clutch (TCC) operation.

Lack of Power (Sluggish)

When the accelerator is pushed part way down, there is little or no increase in speed or power.

1. Compare your vehicles performance with a similar one.
2. Check and/or replace the air cleaner.
3. Check the following equipment:
- Ignition timing (see Vehicle Emission Control Information label).
- Fuel system for a plugged fuel filter, poor fuel pressure and/or contaminated fuel.
- Poor Electronic Control Module (ECM) grounds.
- Exhaust Gas Recirculation (EGR) valve being open or partly open all of the time.
- Alternator output voltage, it must between 9–16V.
- Valve timing.
- Engine compression.

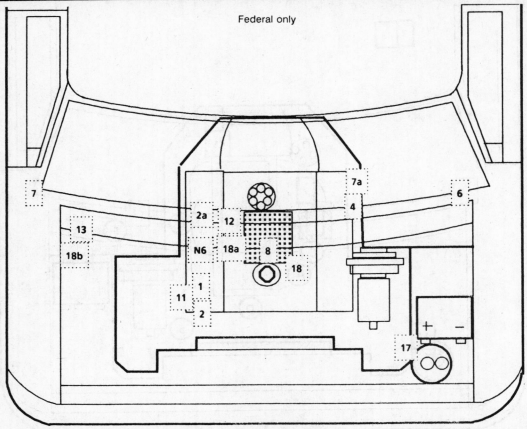

Federal only

EMISSIONS DEVICES

1 Crankcase vent valve (PCV)	3 Deceleration valve	8 Accelerator pump solenoid	18a Throttle kicker solenoid
2 Air injection pump	4 EFE valve	12 EGR solenoid	18b Throttle kicker relay
2a Air injection divert valve	6 Fuse panel	13 Distributor thermal vacuum switch	Exhaust Gas Recirculation valve
	7 Electronic Spark Control module	17 Fuel vapor canister	
	7a ESC knock sensor	18 Throttle kicker	

Electronic control components — 1985 4.3L carbureted engine (Federal)

● Worn camshaft lobes.

4. To inspect the exhaust system, perform the following procedures with the engine at normal operating temperatures:

a. Using a vacuum gauge, connect it to an intake manifold port.

b. Disconnect the EGR solenoid electrical connector or connect the EGR valve directly to a vacuum source bypassing any switches or solenoids.

c. Operate the engine at 1000 rpm and record the vacuum reading.

d. Slowly increase the engine speed to 2500 rpm, hold the speed at 2500 rpm and record the vacuum reading.

NOTE: If the vacuum reading, taken at 2500 rpm, decreases more than 3 inches from the one taken at 1000 rpm, the exhaust system should be inspected for restrictions

e. Disconnect the exhaust pipe from the engine and repeat the Steps 4c and 4d.

NOTE: If the reading still drops more than 3 inches, check the valve timing.

Detonation/Spark Knock

The engine makes a sharp metallic knocks, which range from mild to severe pings, usually worse under acceleration.

1. If a heating problem is noticed, check for:

a. Low engine coolant.

b. A loose water pump drive belt.

c. Restricted air or water flow through the radiator.

2. For other than heating problems, check for:

a. Poor quality fuel (low octane rating).

b. Correct Progammable Read Only Memory (PROM) unit.

c. THERMAC may be staying closed.

d. Ignition timing (see the Vehicle Emission Control Information label).

e. Low fuel pressure.

f. Exhaust Gas Recirculation (EGR) valve may be closed.

g. Transmission for proper shifting points and operation of the Transmission Convertor Clutch (TCC).

h. Incorrect engine parts, such as: camshaft, cylinder head(s), pistons and etc.

3. If the problem persists, obtain a can of engine (carbon) cleaner and follow the instructions on the can.

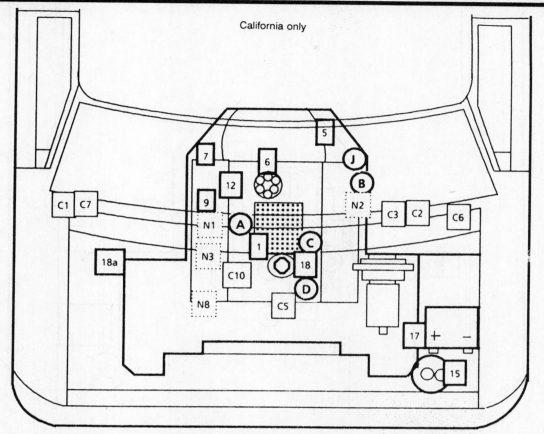

California only

COMPUTER HARNESS
- C1 Electronic Control Module (ECM)
- C2 ALCL diagnostic connector
- C3 "CHECK ENGINE" light
- C5 ECM harness ground
- C6 Fuse panel
- C7 "C.E." lamp driver
- C10 Diagnostic dwell connector

ECM CONTROLLED
- 1 Mixture control solenoid
- 5 Trans. Conv. Clutch connector
- 6 Electronic Spark Timing
- 7 Electronic Spark Control module
- 9 Air injection divert solenoid
- 10 Throttle kicker relay
- 12 Exhaust Gas Recirculation solenoid
- 17a Fuel vapor canister
- 17 Fuel vapor canister solenoid
- 18 Throttle kicker
- 18a Throttle kicker solenoid
- ⬡ Exhaust Gas Recirculation valve

INFORMATION SENSORS
- A Manifold differential pressure
- B Exhaust oxygen
- C Throttle position
- D Coolant temperature
- J ESC knock

EMISSION SYSTEMS
(NOT ECM CONTROLLED)
- N1 Crankcase vent valve (PCV)
- N2 EFE valve
- N3 Deceleration valve
- N8 Air injection pump

Electronic control components — 1985 4.3L carbureted engine (California)

Hesitation or Stumble

This condition is a momentary lack of response when accelerating, which can occur at all speeds but usually when trying to make the vehicle move from a stop sign; it may cause the vehicle to stall, if severe enough.

To check the systems, perform the following checks:
- Low fuel pressure.
- Water in fuel.
- Binding or sticking Throttle Position Sensor (TPS).
- Ignition timing (see Vehicle Emission Control Information label).
- Alternator output, it must be between 9–16V.
- An ungrounded in the High Energy Ignition (HEI) system.
- Non-working emissions canister purge.
- Non-working Exhaust Gas Recirculation (EGR) valve.

Misses or Cuts Out

This condition is a steady pulsation or jerking which follows the engine speed, it is usually more pronounced as the engine increases speed. At low speed or idle, the exhaust has a steady spitting sound.

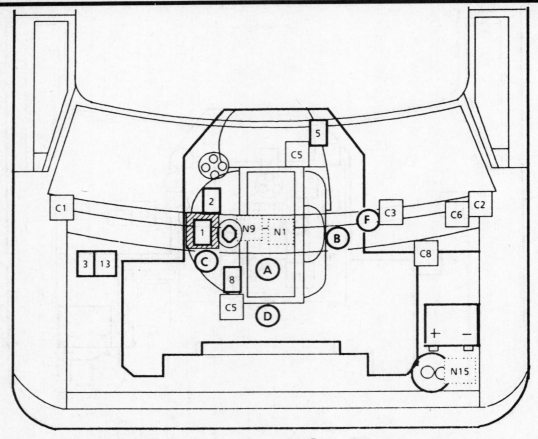

COMPUTER HARNESS ☐ CONTROLLED DEVICES ☐ INFORMATION SENSORS ○

C1 Electronic Control Module (ECM)	**1** Fuel injector	**A** Manifold pressure (M.A.P.)
C2 ALCL diagnostic connector	**2** Idle air control motor	**B** Exhaust oxygen
C3 "SERVICE ENGINE SOON" light	**3** Fuel pump relay	**C** Throttle position
C5 ECM harness ground	**5** Trans. Conv. Clutch connector	**D** Coolant temperature
C6 Fuse panel	**8** Oil pressure switch	**F** Vehicle speed
C8 Fuel pump test connector	**13** A/C compressor relay	

NOT ECM CONNECTED
N1 Crankcase vent (PCV) valve
N9 Exhaust Gas Recirculation valve
N15 Fuel vapor canister

Electronic control components — 1986–87 2.5L TBI engine

1. To check for a missing cylinder, perform the following procedures:

   a. Disconnect the electrical connector from the Idle Air Control (IAC) motor.

   b. Start the engine.

   c. Using insulated pliers, remove one spark plug wire at a time and check for an rpm drop. If no drop is noticed, check the spark plugs for cracks, wear, improper gap, burned electrodes and/or heavy deposits.

   NOTE: If a drop of 50 rpm is recorded between the cylinders, replace the IAC electrical connector and proceed to the Rough, Unstable or Incorrect Idle, Stalling section.

2. Using an ohmmeter, over 30,000Ω, check the spark plug wires and replace them, if necessary.

3. Using the Spark Tester tool No. J–26792 or equivalent, check the ignition coil's primary and secondary voltages.

4. Check the fuel system for a plugged fuel filter, water in the fuel and/or low fuel pump pressure.

5. Inspect the ignition timing (see the Vehicle Emission Control Information label).

6. Perform a compression check on the engine; if the compression is low, repair as necessary.

7. Inspect the distributor cap and rotor for dust, cracks, burns, moisture and etc. Using a fine water mist, spray the cap and plug wires to check for shorts.

8. Remove the rocker arm covers and inspect for bent pushrods, worn rocker arms, broken valve springs and/or worn camshaft lobes.

Poor Fuel Economy

By performing an actual road test, it is determined that the fuel economy is lower than some other actual road test on the same vehicle.

To determine the reason for the poor fuel economy, inspect the following items:

1. The engine thermostat for the wrong heat range or a faulty (always open) part.

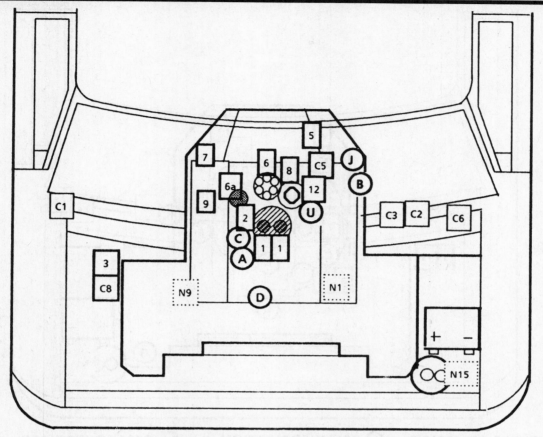

COMPUTER HARNESS

C1 Electronic Control Module
C2 ALCL diagnostic connector
C3 "SERVICE ENGINE SOON" light
C5 ECM harness ground
C6 Fuse panel
C8 Fuel pump test connector

NOT ECM CONNECTED

N1 Crankcase vent valve (PCV)
N9 Air Pump
N15 Fuel Vapor Canister

ECM CONTROLLED

1   Fuel injector
2   Idle air control motor
3   Fuel pump relay
5   Trans. Conv. Clutch connector
6   EST distributor
6a Remote ignition coil
7   Electronic Spark Control module
8   Oil pressure switch
9   Electric Air Control solenoid

INFORMATION SENSORS

A   Manifold Absolute Pressure
    (attached to air cleaner)
B   Exhaust oxygen
C   Throttle position
D   Coolant temperature
F   Vehicle speed
J   ESC knock
U   EGR temp. diagnostic switch

12 Exh. Gas Recirc. vacuum solenoid

Electronic control components — 1986–87 4.3L TBI engine

2. The fuel system for low fuel pressure.
3. The ignition timing (see the Vehicle Emission Control Information label).
4. The Transmission Convertor Clutch (TCC) for proper operation.

Rough, Unstable or Incorrect Idle, Stalling

In this condition, the engine idles unevenly, it may shake (if bad enough) and/or may stall.

To determine the reason(s) for poor operation, inspect the following items:

1. The ignition timing (see the Vehicle Emission Control Informations label).
2. The Park/Neutral (P/N) switch, if equipped with an AT.

3. A leaking fuel injector.
4. A fuel injector operating too rich or lean.

If rough idle occurs ONLY when the engine is Hot, perform the additional checks:

1. To check for vacuum leaks, perform the following checks:
   a. Using the GM Plug tool No. J–33047 or equivalent, block the idle air passage.
   b. If the engine speed is higher than 650 rpm with the throttle closed, locate and correct the vacuum leak, such as: A disconnected Thermac or cruise control hose.
2. The Park/Neutral (P/N) switch, if equipped with an AT.
3. The Throttle Position Switch (TPS) may be sticking or binding, causing the throttle to remain open.
4. Exhaust Gas Recirculation (EGR) system — if it is on while

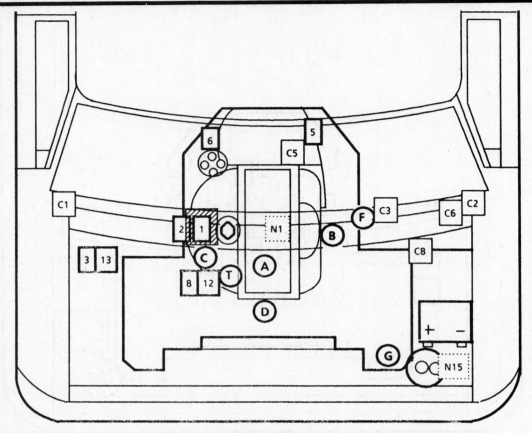

COMPUTER COMMAND CONTROL

C1　Electronic Control Module (E.C.M.)
C2　ALDL diagnostic connector
C3　"SERVICE ENGINE SOON" light
C5　ECM harness ground
C6　Fuse panel
C8　Fuel pump test connector

EMISSION COMPONENTS (NOT ECM CONTROLLED)

N1　Crankcase vent (PCV) valve
N15　Fuel vapor canister

ECM INFORMATION SENSORS

A　Manifold pressure (M.A.P.)
B　Exhaust oxygen
C　Throttle position (T.P.S.)
D　Coolant temperature
F　Vehicle speed (V.S.S.)
G　Power Steering Pressure
T　Manifold Air Temperature (M.A.T.)

ECM CONTROLLED COMPONENTS

1　Fuel injector
2　Idle air control
3　Fuel pump relay
5　Transmission Converter Clutch Connector
6　Electronic Spark Timing Distributor (E.S.T.)
8　Oil pressure switch
12　Exhaust Gas Recirculation Vacuum Solenoid
13　A/C relay

Electronic control components — 1988–90 2.5L TBI engine

the engine is idling, roughness, stalling and hard starting will occur.

5. Battery cables and ground straps—dirty and loose battery connections will cause erratic voltage, which will cause the Idle Air Control (IAC) valve to change its position, resulting in poor idle quality. The IAC valve will not move if the system voltage is below 9V or greater than 17.8V.

6. Power Steering system—the ECM should compensate for power steering loads; if the signal is lost, the vehicle will be difficult to park and steer with heavy loads.

7. Manifold Absolute Pressure (MAP) sensor—idle the engine and disconnect the electrical connector from the sensor, if the idle improves, substitute a known GOOD sensor and recheck.

8. The Air Conditioning (A/C) compressor and relay, also, the refrigerant pressure may be too high or have a faulty cycling switch.

9. The Positive Crankcase Ventilation (PCV) valve—place your finger over the end and release it several times, if the valve does not snap back, replace it.

10. Perform a cylinder compression check and compare the results, then repair as necessary.

11. Oxygen sensor—inspect it for sensor contamination (white, powdery coating) and high electrical conductivity; as a result, the ECM will reduce the amount of fuel to the engine.

12. Air Management system—check for intermittent air to the ports while in the Closed Loop operation (4.3L engines).

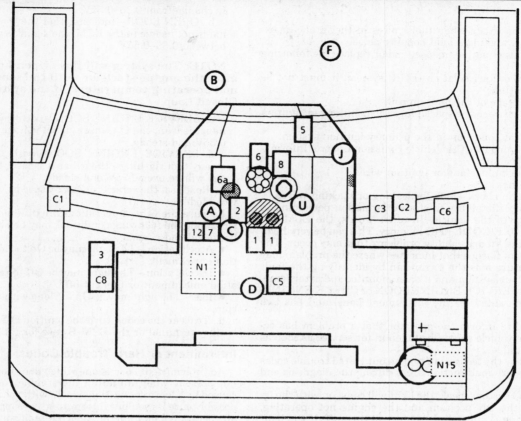

COMPUTER COMMAND CONTROL

C1 Electronic Control Module (E.C.M.)
C2 ALDL diagnostic connector
C3 "SERVICE ENGINE SOON" light
C5 ECM harness ground
C6 Fuse panel
C8 Fuel pump test connector

EMISSION COMPONENTS (NOT ECM CONTROLLED)

N1 Crankcase vent valve (PCV)
N15 Fuel Vapor Canister

ECM INFORMATION SENSORS

A Manifold Absolute Pressure (M.A.P.)
B Exhaust oxygen
C Throttle position (T.P.S.)
D Coolant temperature
F Vehicle speed (V.S.S.)
J Electronic Spark Control Knock (E.S.C.)

ECM CONTROLLED COMPONENTS

1 Fuel injector
2 Idle air control
3 Fuel pump relay
5 Transmission Converter Clutch Connector
6 Electronic Spark Timing Distributor (E.S.T.)
6a Remote ignition coil
7 Electronic Spark Control module (E.S.C.)
8 Oil pressure switch
12 Exhaust Gas Recirculation Vacuum Solenoid

Electronic control components — 1988–90 4.3L TBI engine

Abnormal Emissions (Odors)

To correct abnormal emissions, inspect or test the following items, for:
1. Excessive CO and HC emissions (odors), plus, any thing that will make the engine run rich.
2. Incorrect ignition timing (see the Vehicle Emission Control Information label).
3. Loading of the fuel emissions canister.
4. Stuck or blocked Positive Crankcase Ventilation (PCV) valve.
5. Condition of the spark plugs, ignition wires and distributor cap.
6. Lead contamination of the Catalytic Converter.

Dieseling

This condition exists when the ignition key is turned Off and the engine continues to run roughly. If the engine runs smoothly, check and/or adjust the ignition switch.

NOTE: The only way to prevent the engine from dieseling is to eliminate fuel leakage to the cylinders.

To remedy this situation, turn the ignition switch On, to energize the fuel pump, then check the fuel injector(s) and the throttle body for fuel leakage. If necessary, repair or replace the leaking items.

Backfire

This condition exists when fuel ignites in the intake or exhaust manifold, making a loud popping noise.

To correct this situation, inspect and/or replace the following items:

- Exhaust Gas Recirculation (EGR) system, it must not be open all of the time.
- Output voltage of the ignition coil.
- Crossfire between the spark plugs (distributor cap, ignition wires).
- Intermittent condition in the primary ignition system.
- Ignition timing (see the Vehicle Emission Control Information label).
- Faulty spark plugs and/or ignition wires.
- Valve timing.
- Compression check—look for leaking or sticking valves.

The ECM has the ability to store information pertaining to the driveability of the vehicle. In other words, the ECM can store a **TROUBLE CODE** in its memory. This can be very helpful in diagnosing an driveability problems that may occur. The code is a series of flashes that indicates where the problem may exist. This feature aids the technician by identifying the fault via a trouble code system and a dash mounted indicator lamp, marked either SERVICE ENGINE SOON or CHECK ENGINE. The lamp is mounted on the instrument panel and has two functions:

1. It is used to inform the operator that a problem has occurred and the vehicle should be taken in for service as soon as reasonably possible.

2. It is used by the technician to read out stored trouble codes in order to localize malfunction areas during the diagnosis and repair phases.

As a bulb and system check, the light will come on with the ignition key in the ON position and the engine not operating. When the engine is started, the light will turn off. If the light does not turn off, the self diagnostic system has detected a problem in the system. If the problem goes away, the light will go out, in most cases after ten second, but a trouble code will be set in the ECM's memory.

Non-Scan Diagnostic Checks

The following is an explanation of the NON-SCAN diagnostic circuit check:

1. With engine stopped, the ignition turned On and a steady SERVICE ENGINE SOON light On, at the instrument panel, indicates that there is battery and ignition voltage to the ECM.

2. Connect a jumper wire between the terminals **A** to **B** of the ALCL diagnostic connector (located beneath the instrument panel), the following instrument panel display will occur:

   a. The ECM will cause the SERVICE ENGINE SOON lamp to flash a Code 12, which indicates that the ECM diagnostics are working.

   b. The Code 12 will flash three times, followed by any other trouble codes that are stored in its memory.

   c. Each additional code will flash three times, starting with the lowest code, then the cycle will start over again with the Code 12.

   d. If there are no other codes, the Code 12 will flash continuously until the jumper wire is disconnected or the engine is started.

3. Record all of the stored codes, except Code 12, then consult the service shop.

4. The Field Service Mode may be helpful in the diagnosis, depending on the severity of the problem. With the diagnostic terminal grounded and the engine running, the ECM will respond to the O_2 sensor signal voltage and use the SERVICE ENGINE SOON light to display the following information:

   a. CLOSED LOOP—confirms that the O_2 sensor signal is being used by the ECM to control the fuel delivery and that the system is working normally; the signal voltage will quick-ly change from 0.35–0.55V.

   b. OPEN LOOP—indicates that the O_2 sensor voltage signal is not usable to the ECM; the signal is at a constant value between 0.35–0.55V.

NOTE: The system will flash Open Loop for ½–2 min. after the engine starts or until the sensor reaches normal operating temperature; if the system fails to go to Closed Loop.

   c. SERVICE ENGINE SOON—with this light Off, the exhaust is lean; the O_2 sensor signal voltage will remain under 0.35V and steady.

   d. SERVICE ENGINE SOON—with this light On and steady (not flashing), the exhaust is rich; the O_2 sensor voltage will be over 0.55V and steady.

5. Road test the vehicle, at steady speeds, using the Field Service Mode.

Because the vehicle operations are different in the Field Service Mode the following conditions may be observed and should be considered normal:

- Acceleration—The light may be On too long due to acceleration enrichment.
- Deceleration—The light may be Off too long due to deceleration enleanment or fuel cut-off.
- Idle—The light may be On too long with the idle below 1200 rpm.

6. To clear the codes, turn the ignition Off and disconnect the battery terminal or the ECM **B** fuse for ten seconds.

Intermittent or Hard Trouble Codes

An intermittent code is one which does not reset itself and is not present when initiating the trouble codes. It is often be caused by a loose connection which, with vehicle movement, can possibly cure its self but intermittently reappear. A hard code is an operational malfunction which remains in the ECM memory and will be presented when calling for the trouble code display.

The Electronic Control Module (ECM) is actually a computer. It uses numerous sensors to look at many engine operating conditions. It has been programmed to know what certain sensor readings should be under most all operating conditions and if the sensor readings are not what the ECM thinks it should be, the ECM will turn on the SERVICE ENGINE SOON or CHECK ENGINE indicator light and will store a trouble code in its memory. When called up, the trouble code directs the technician to examine a particular circuit in order to locate and repair the trouble code setting defect.

Assembly Line Communication Link (ALCL)

In order to access the ECM to provide the trouble codes stored in its memory, the Assembly Line Communication Link (also known as the Assembly Line Diagnostic Link or ALDL) is used.

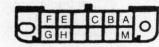

- A. Ground
- B. Diagnostic terminal
- C. AIR pump, if used
- E. Serial data (V6/V8)
- F. Torque converter clutch, if used
- G. Fuel pump
- H. Brake sense speed input
- M. Serial data (L4)

1987–90 ALDL (assembly line diagnostic link) located under the right side instrument panel

NOTE: This connector is utilized at the assembly plant to insure the engine is operating properly before the vehicle is shipped.

Terminal **B** of the diagnostic connector is the diagnostic ter-

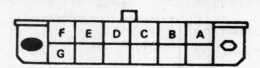

A. Ground
B. Diagnostic terminal
C. AIR pump, if used
D. C.E. lamp
E. Serial data
F. Torque converter clutch, if used
G. Fuel pump (EFI)

1985–86 ALCL (assembly line communication link) located under the right side instrument panel

minal and it can be connected to terminal **A**, or ground, to enter the diagnostic mode, or the field service mode on fuel injection models. Use a small jumper wire connected from terminal **A** to terminal **B**.

ENTERING DIAGNOSTIC MODE

If the diagnostic terminal is grounded with the ignition in the ON position and the engine stopped, the system will enter the diagnostic mode. In this mode, the ECM will accomplish the following:

1. The ECM will display a code 12 by flashing the SERVICE ENGINE SOON or CHECK ENGINE light, which indicates the system is working. A code 12 consists of one flash, followed by a short pause, then two flashes in quick succession.

a. This code will be flashed three times. If no other codes are stored, code 12 will continue to flash until the diagnostic terminal is disconnected from the ground circuit.

b. On a carbureted engine, the engine should not be started with the diagnostic terminal grounded, because it may continue to flash a code 12 with the engine running. Also, if the test terminal is grounded after the engine is running any stored codes will flash, but code 12 will flash only if there is a problem with the distributor reference signal.

c. On fuel injected engines, codes can only be obtained with the engine stopped. Grounding the diagnostic terminal with the engine running activates the FIELD SERVICE MODE.

2. The ECM will display any stored codes by flashing the SERVICE ENGINE SOON or CHECK ENGINE light. Each code will be flashed three times, then code 12 will be flashed again.

a. On carbureted engines, if a trouble code is displayed, the memory is cleared, then the engine is operated to see if the code is a hard or intermittent failure.

b. If the code represents a hard failure, a diagnostic code chart is used to locate the area of the failure.

c. If an intermittent failure is determined, the problem circuits can be examined physically for reasons of failure.

d. On fuel injected engines, if a trouble code is displayed, a diagnostic code chart is used to locate the area of failure.

3. The ECM will energize all controlled relays and solenoids that are involved in the current engine operation.

a. On carbureted engines, the ISC motor, if equipped, will move back and forth and the mixture control solenoid will be pulsed for 25 seconds or until the engine is started, which ever occurs first.

b. On fuel injected engines, the IAC valve is moved back and forth or is fully extended, depending upon the engine family.

Field Service Mode
FUEL INJECTION MODELS

If the diagnostic terminal is grounded with the engine operating, the system will enter the Field Service Mode. In this mode, the SERVICE ENGINE SOON or CHECK ENGINE indicator light will show whether the system is in Open or Closed Loop operation.

When in the Open Loop mode, the indicator light will flash two and one half times per second.

When in the Closed Loop Mode, the indicator light will flash once every second. Also, in Closed Loop, the light will stay out most of the time if the system is too lean. The light will stay on most of the time is the system is too rich. In either case, the Field Service Mode Check, which is part of the diagnostic circuit check, will direct the technician to the fault area.

While in the Field Service Mode, the ECM will be in the following mode:
1. The distributor will have a fixed spark advance.
2. New trouble codes cannot be stored in the ECM.
3. The closed loop timer is bypassed.

Trouble Codes

The trouble codes indicate problems in the following areas:

1. CODE 12 – No Distributor Reference Signal to the ECM. This code is not stored in the memory and will only flash while the fault is present. Normal code with the ignition switch in the ON position and the engine not operating. This code is used to tell you that the system is working properly.

2. CODE 13 – Oxygen Sensor circuit. The engine must be operated up to four minutes at part throttle, under road conditions, before this code will set.

3. CODE 14 – Shorted Coolant Sensor circuit. The engine must run five minutes before this code will set.

4. CODE 15 – Open Coolant Sensor circuit. The engine must run five minutes before this code will set.

5. CODE 21 – Throttle Position Sensor (TPS) circuit voltage high (open circuit or misadjusted TPS). The engine must operate ten seconds, at specified curb idle speed before this code will set.

6. CODE 22 – Throttle Position Sensor (TPS) circuit voltage low (grounded circuit or misadjusted TPS). The engine must run twenty seconds at specified curb idle speed.

7. CODE 23 – (1985–87) Mixture Control Solenoid circuit open or grounded. (1988–90) Manifold Air Temperature low temperature indication.

8. CODE 24 – Vehicle Speed Sensor (VSS) circuit. The vehicle must operate up to two minutes, at road speed before this code will set.

9. CODE 25 – (1988–90) Manifold Air Temperature high temperature indication.

10. CODE 32 – (1985–87) Barometric Pressure Sensor (BARO) circuit low. (1988–90) Exhaust Gas Recirculation vacuum switch shorted, switch not closed after the ECM has commanded for a specific time period or EGR solenoid in open.

11. CODE 33 – (1988–90) Manifold Absolute Pressure low vacuum.

12. CODE 34 – Vacuum Sensor or Manifold Absolute Pressure (MAP) circuit. The engine must be operated up to two minutes, at the specified curb idle before this code will set.

13. CODE 35 – Idle Speed Control (ISC) switch circuit shorted. Up to 70% TPS for over five seconds.

14. CODE 41 – (1985–87) No Distributor Reference Signal to the ECM at specified engine vacuum. This code will store in the memory.

15. CODE 42 – Electronic Spark Timing (EST) bypass circuit or EST circuit grounded or open.

16. CODE 43 – Electronic Spark Control (ESC) retard signal for too long of a time. Will cause retard in EST signal.

17. CODE 44 – Lean Exhaust Indication. The engine must operate for two minutes, in the closed loop mode and at part throttle before this code will set.

18. CODE 45 – Rich Exhaust Indication. The engine must operate for two minutes, in closed loop mode and at part throttle before this code will set.

19. CODE 51 – Faulty or improperly installed calibration unit (PROM), MEM-CAL, OR ECM. It takes up to 30 seconds before this code will set.

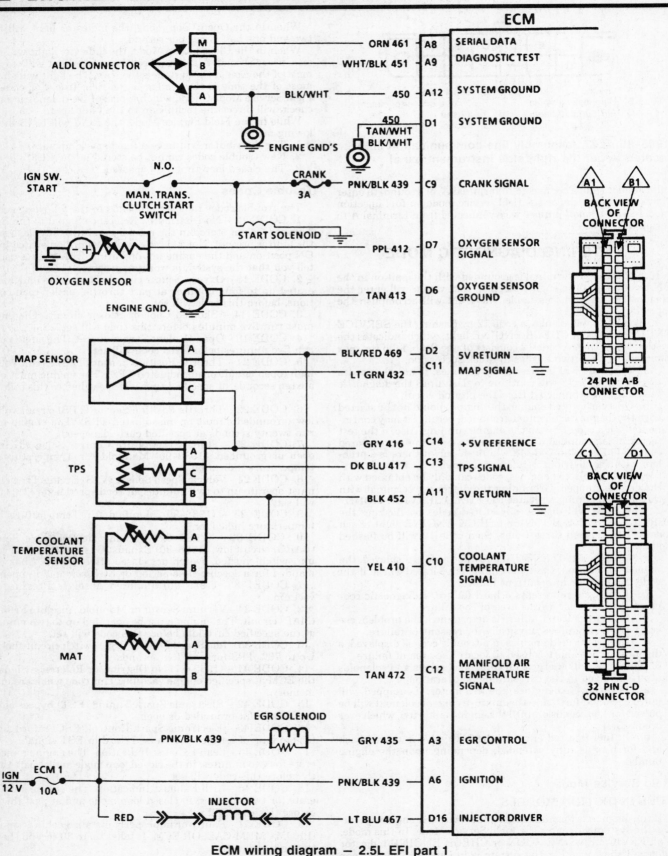

ECM wiring diagram — 2.5L EFI part 1

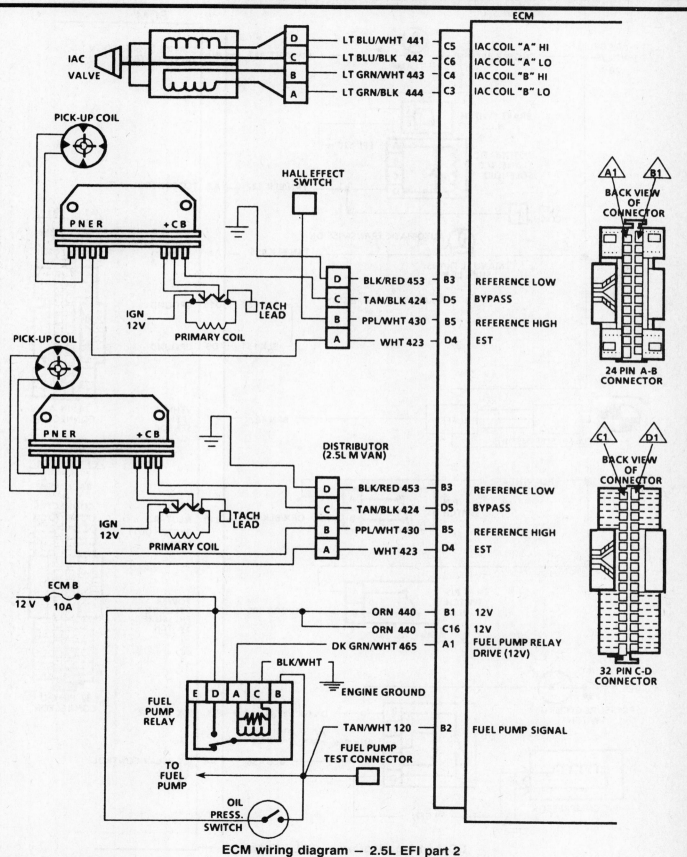

ECM wiring diagram — 2.5L EFI part 2

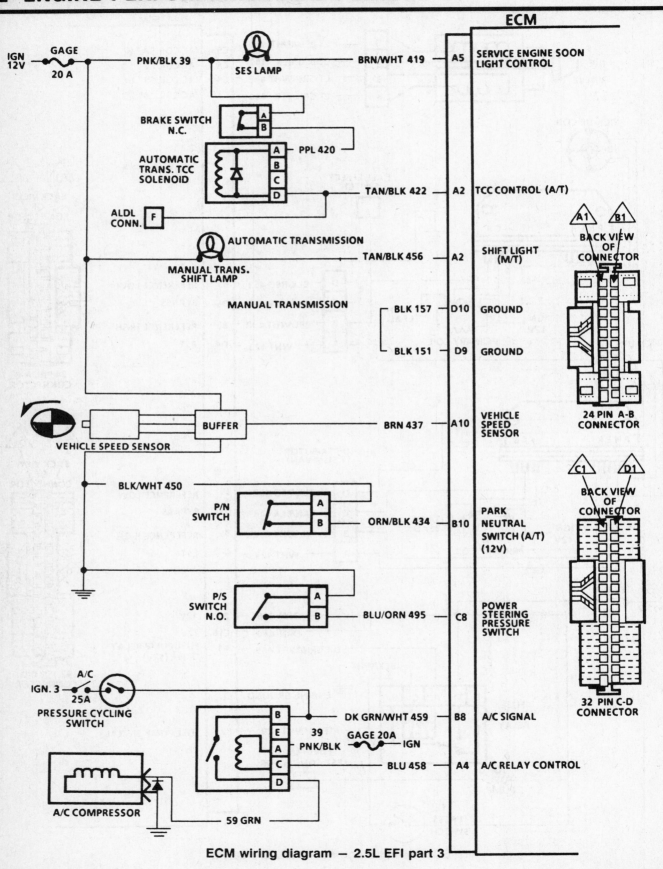

ECM wiring diagram — 2.5L EFI part 3

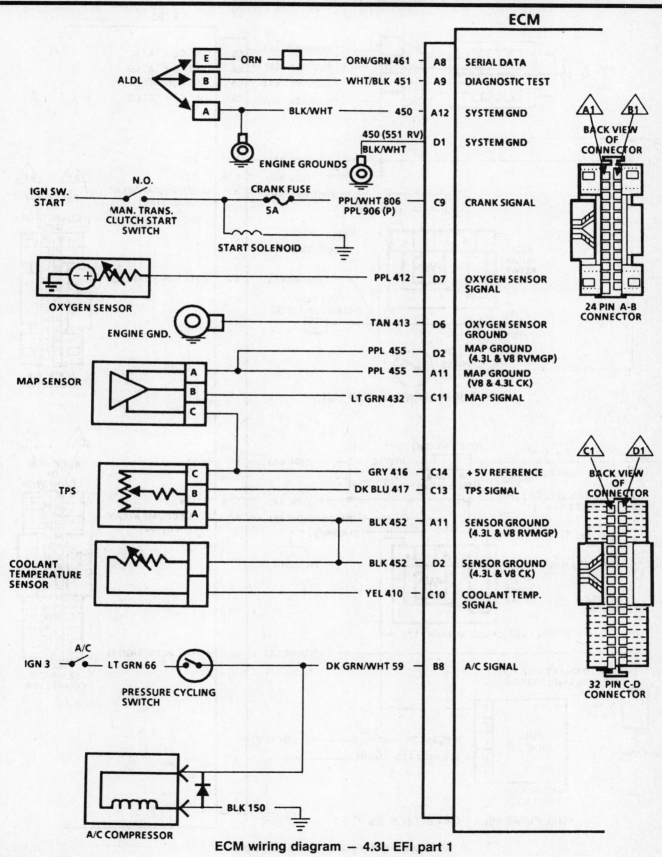

ECM wiring diagram — 4.3L EFI part 1

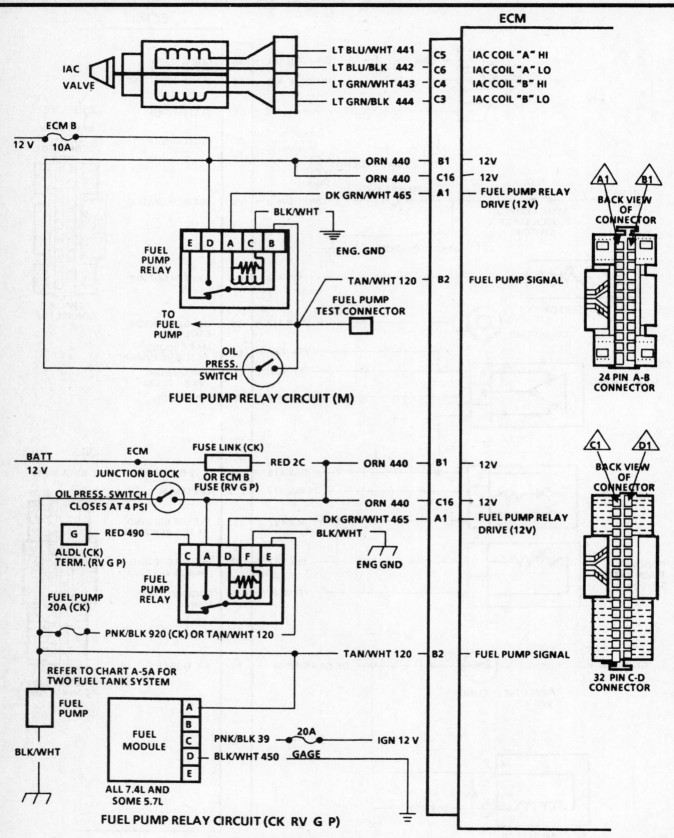

ECM wiring diagram — 4.3L EFI part 2

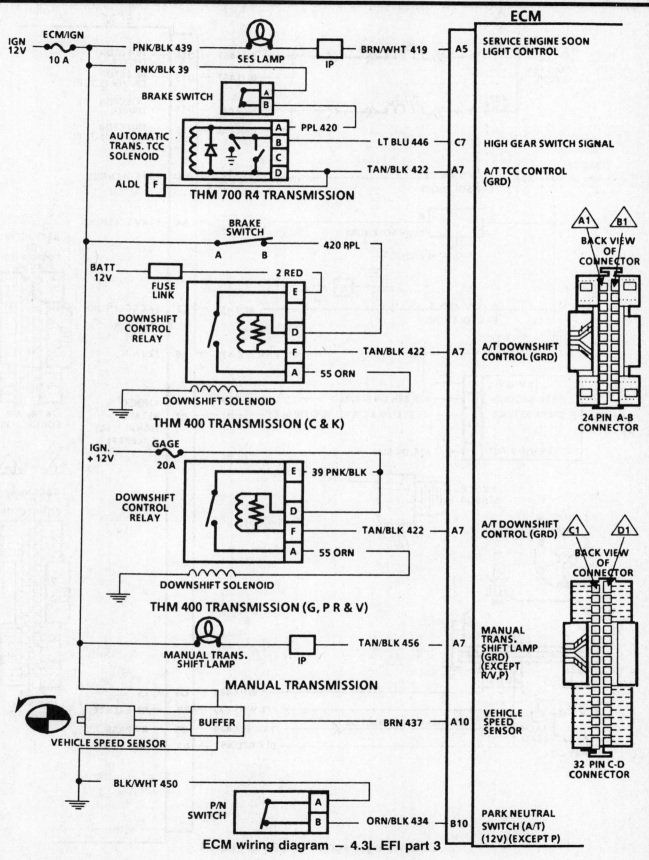

ECM wiring diagram – 4.3L EFI part 3

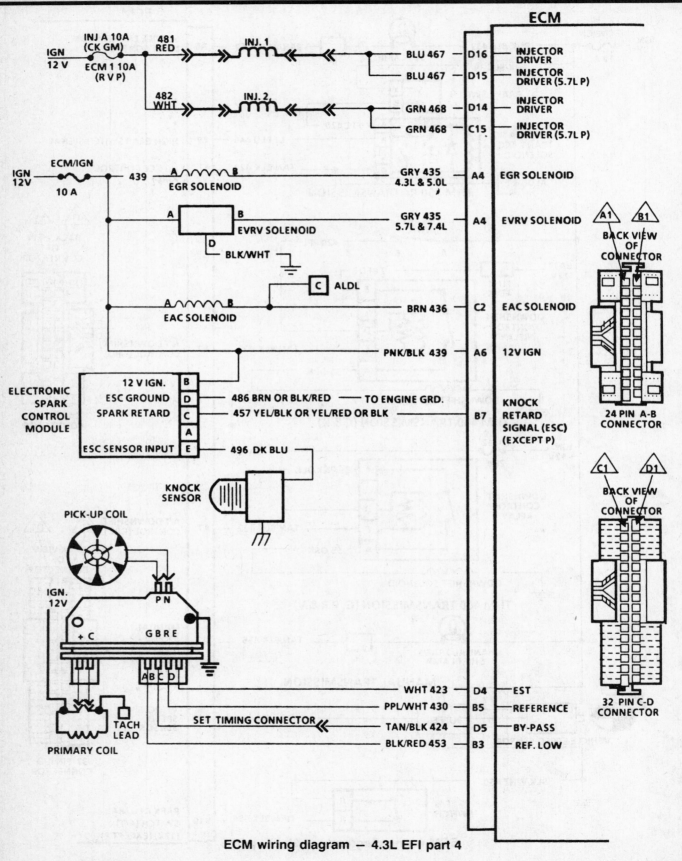

ECM wiring diagram — 4.3L EFI part 4

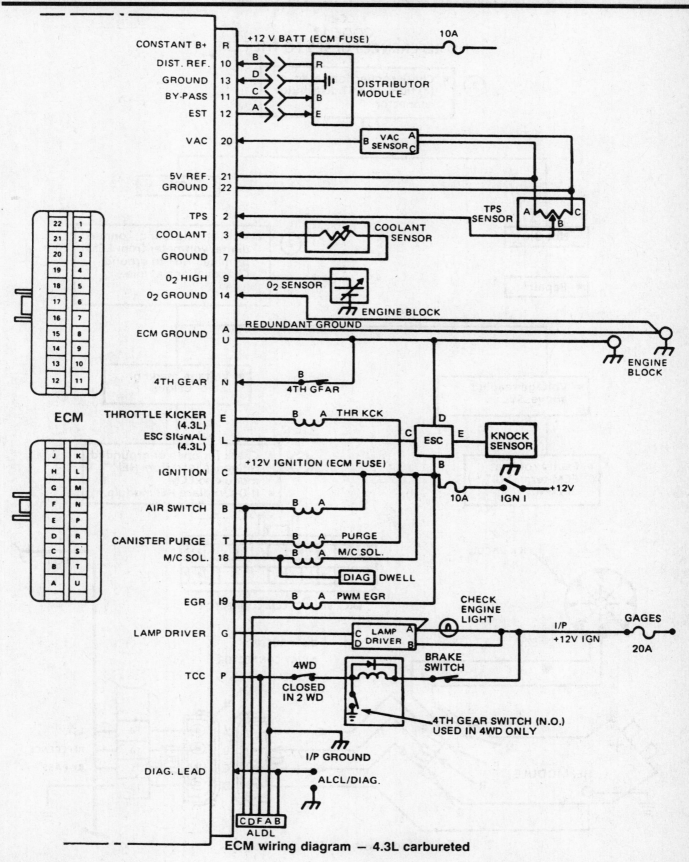

ECM wiring diagram — 4.3L carbureted

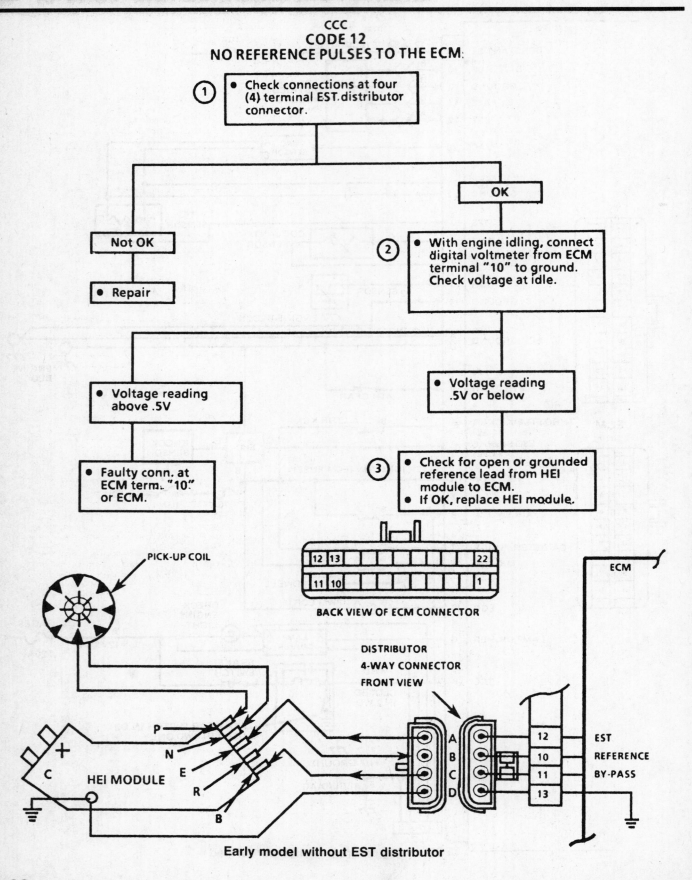

CCC
CODE 12
NO REFERENCE PULSES TO THE ECM:

① • Check connections at four (4) terminal EST distributor connector.

OK

Not OK

② • With engine idling, connect digital voltmeter from ECM terminal "10" to ground. Check voltage at idle.

• Repair

• Voltage reading above .5V

• Voltage reading .5V or below

• Faulty conn. at ECM term. "10" or ECM.

③ • Check for open or grounded reference lead from HEI module to ECM.
• If OK, replace HEI module.

PICK-UP COIL

| 12 | 13 | | | | | | | | | 22 |
| 11 | 10 | | | | | | | | | 1 |

BACK VIEW OF ECM CONNECTOR

ECM

DISTRIBUTOR
4-WAY CONNECTOR
FRONT VIEW

P
N
E
R
B

C

HEI MODULE

A
B
C
D

12	EST
10	REFERENCE
11	BY-PASS
13	

Early model without EST distributor

CODE 13
(OPEN OXYGEN SENSOR CIRCUIT)

Check for sticking or misadjusted throttle position sensor. If 13 and 21 are displayed, go to 21 first.

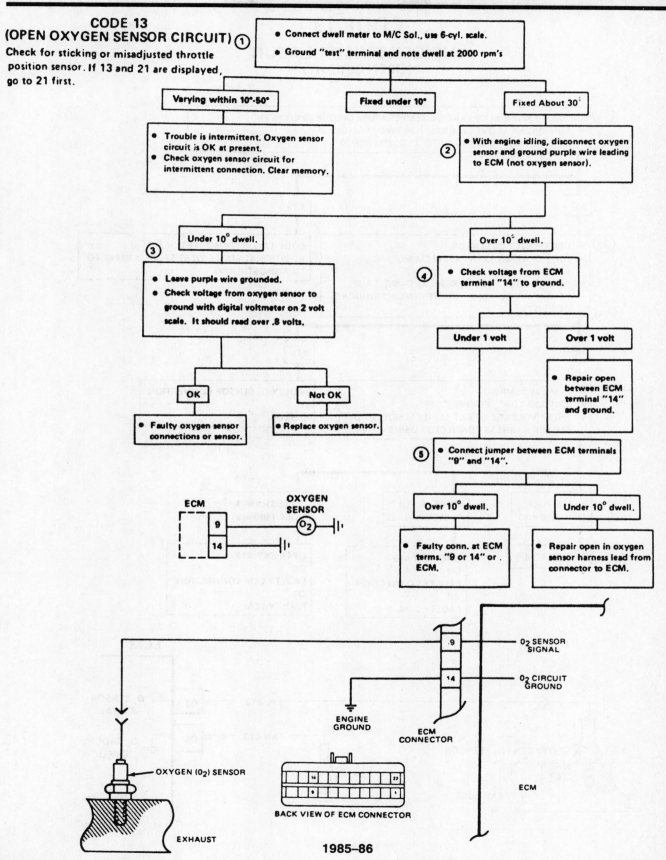

①
- Connect dwell meter to M/C Sol., use 6-cyl. scale.
- Ground "test" terminal and note dwell at 2000 rpm's

Varying within 10°-50°
- Trouble is intermittent. Oxygen sensor circuit is OK at present.
- Check oxygen sensor circuit for intermittent connection. Clear memory.

Fixed under 10°

Fixed About 30°
②
- With engine idling, disconnect oxygen sensor and ground purple wire leading to ECM (not oxygen sensor).

Under 10° dwell.
③
- Leave purple wire grounded.
- Check voltage from oxygen sensor to ground with digital voltmeter on 2 volt scale. It should read over .8 volts.

OK
- Faulty oxygen sensor connections or sensor.

Not OK
- Replace oxygen sensor.

Over 10° dwell.
④
- Check voltage from ECM terminal "14" to ground.

Under 1 volt

Over 1 volt
- Repair open between ECM terminal "14" and ground.

⑤
- Connect jumper between ECM terminals "9" and "14".

Over 10° dwell.
- Faulty conn. at ECM terms. "9 or 14" or ECM.

Under 10° dwell.
- Repair open in oxygen sensor harness lead from connector to ECM.

ECM 9 14 — **OXYGEN SENSOR** O₂

O₂ SENSOR SIGNAL — .9
O₂ CIRCUIT GROUND — 14
ENGINE GROUND
ECM CONNECTOR
ECM

OXYGEN (O₂) SENSOR
EXHAUST

BACK VIEW OF ECM CONNECTOR

1985–86

CODE 13

OXYGEN SENSOR CIRCUIT
(OPEN CIRCUIT)

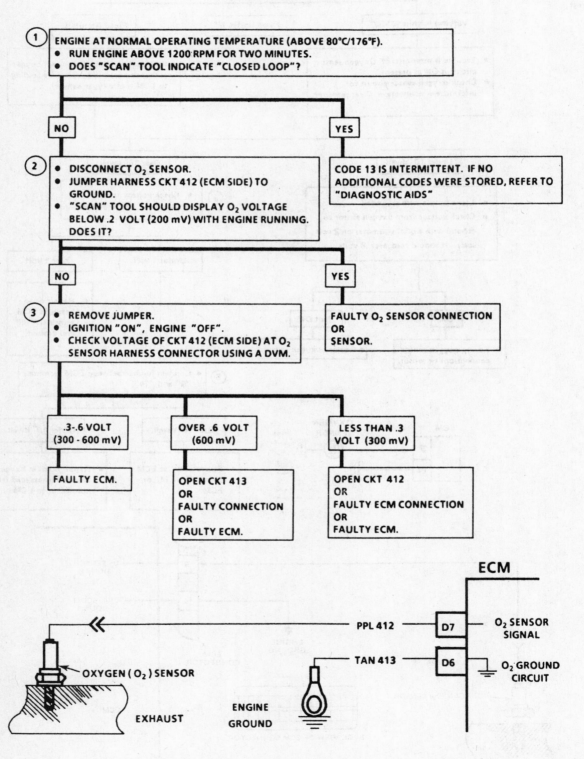

1
- ENGINE AT NORMAL OPERATING TEMPERATURE (ABOVE 80°C/176°F).
- RUN ENGINE ABOVE 1200 RPM FOR TWO MINUTES.
- DOES "SCAN" TOOL INDICATE "CLOSED LOOP"?

NO   **YES**

2
- DISCONNECT O_2 SENSOR.
- JUMPER HARNESS CKT 412 (ECM SIDE) TO GROUND.
- "SCAN" TOOL SHOULD DISPLAY O_2 VOLTAGE BELOW .2 VOLT (200 mV) WITH ENGINE RUNNING. DOES IT?

CODE 13 IS INTERMITTENT. IF NO ADDITIONAL CODES WERE STORED, REFER TO "DIAGNOSTIC AIDS"

NO   **YES**

3
- REMOVE JUMPER.
- IGNITION "ON", ENGINE "OFF".
- CHECK VOLTAGE OF CKT 412 (ECM SIDE) AT O_2 SENSOR HARNESS CONNECTOR USING A DVM.

FAULTY O_2 SENSOR CONNECTION OR SENSOR.

.3-.6 VOLT (300 - 600 mV)	OVER .6 VOLT (600 mV)	LESS THAN .3 VOLT (300 mV)
FAULTY ECM.	OPEN CKT 413 OR FAULTY CONNECTION OR FAULTY ECM.	OPEN CKT 412 OR FAULTY ECM CONNECTION OR FAULTY ECM.

ECM

PPL 412 — D7 — O_2 SENSOR SIGNAL

TAN 413 — D6 — O_2 GROUND CIRCUIT

OXYGEN (O_2) SENSOR

EXHAUST

ENGINE GROUND

1987–90

CODE 14
SHORTED COOLANT SENSOR CIRCUIT
If the engine hot light is 'on", check for overheating condition first.

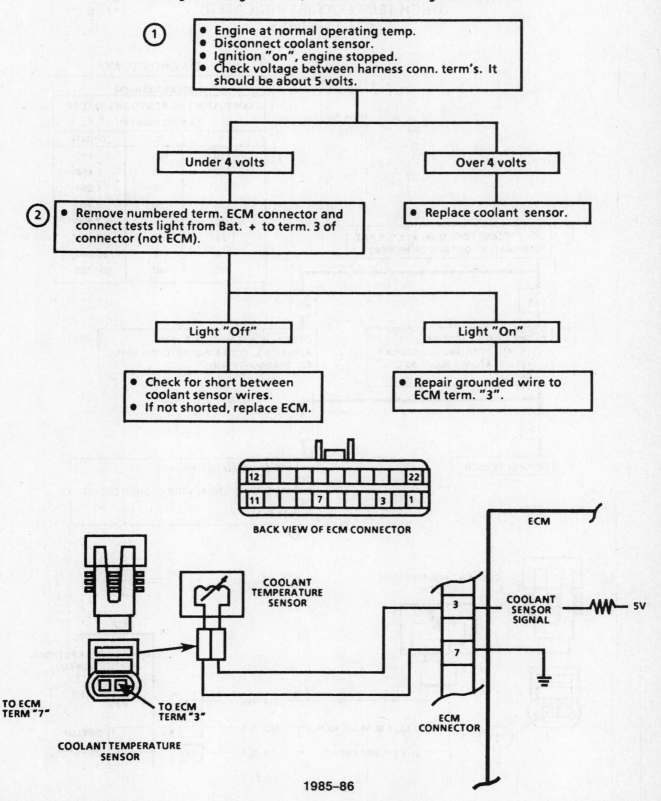

① ● Engine at normal operating temp.
● Disconnect coolant sensor.
● Ignition "on", engine stopped.
● Check voltage between harness conn. term's. It should be about 5 volts.

Under 4 volts

Over 4 volts

② ● Remove numbered term. ECM connector and connect tests light from Bat. + to term. 3 of connector (not ECM).

● Replace coolant sensor.

Light "Off"

Light "On"

● Check for short between coolant sensor wires.
● If not shorted, replace ECM.

● Repair grounded wire to ECM term. "3".

```
12                      22
11        7        3  1
```

BACK VIEW OF ECM CONNECTOR

COOLANT TEMPERATURE SENSOR

ECM

3

COOLANT SENSOR SIGNAL — 5V

7

TO ECM TERM "7"

TO ECM TERM "3"

ECM CONNECTOR

COOLANT TEMPERATURE SENSOR

1985-86

CODE 14
COOLANT TEMPERATURE SENSOR CIRCUIT
(HIGH TEMPERATURE INDICATED)
ALL ENGINES

DIAGNOSTIC AID

COOLANT SENSOR		
TEMPERATURE VS. RESISTANCE VALUES		
(APPROXIMATE)		
°F	°C	OHMS
210	100	185
160	70	450
100	38	1,800
70	20	3,400
40	4	7,500
20	-7	13,500
0	-18	25,000
-40	-40	100,700

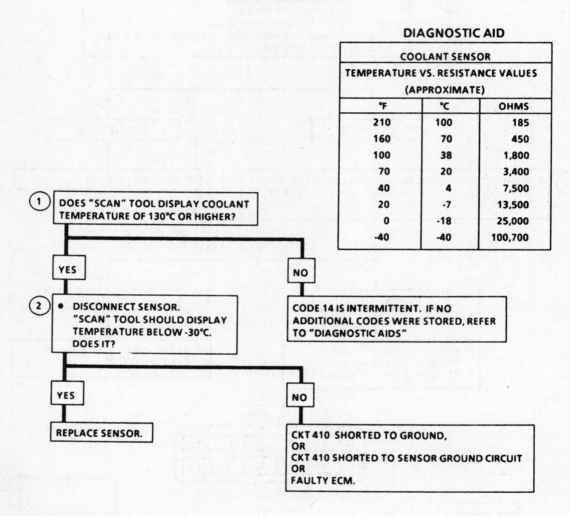

1. DOES "SCAN" TOOL DISPLAY COOLANT TEMPERATURE OF 130°C OR HIGHER?

YES

NO

2. • DISCONNECT SENSOR. "SCAN" TOOL SHOULD DISPLAY TEMPERATURE BELOW -30°C. DOES IT?

CODE 14 IS INTERMITTENT. IF NO ADDITIONAL CODES WERE STORED, REFER TO "DIAGNOSTIC AIDS"

YES

NO

REPLACE SENSOR.

CKT 410 SHORTED TO GROUND, OR
CKT 410 SHORTED TO SENSOR GROUND CIRCUIT OR
FAULTY ECM.

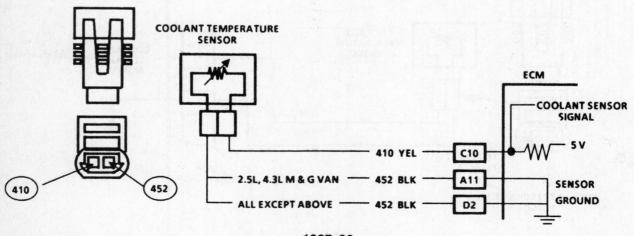

1987-90

CODE 15
OPEN COOLANT SENSOR CIRCUIT

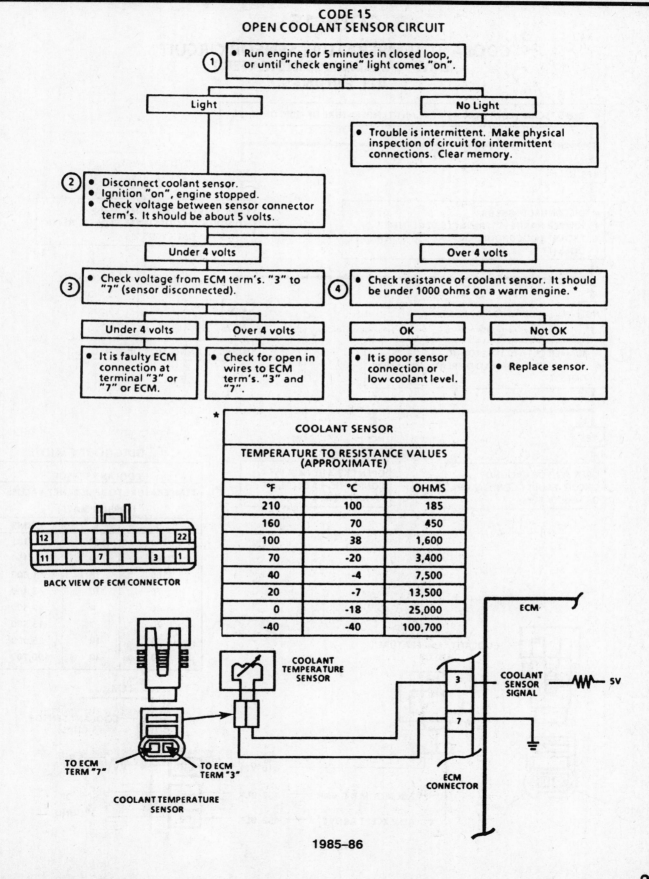

COOLANT SENSOR		
TEMPERATURE TO RESISTANCE VALUES (APPROXIMATE)		
°F	°C	OHMS
210	100	185
160	70	450
100	38	1,600
70	-20	3,400
40	-4	7,500
20	-7	13,500
0	-18	25,000
-40	-40	100,700

1985–86

CODE 15

COOLANT TEMPERATURE SENSOR CIRCUIT
(LOW TEMPERATURE INDICATED)
ALL ENGINES

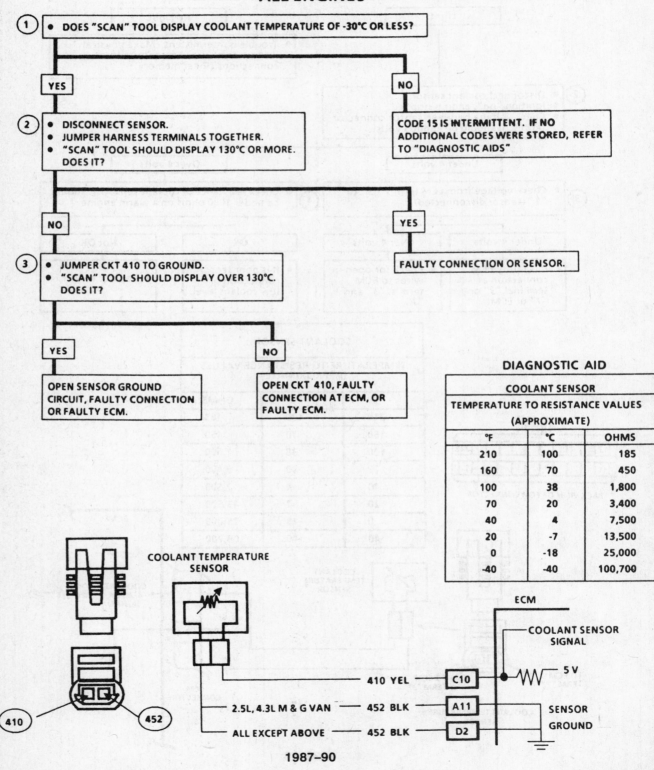

①
- DOES "SCAN" TOOL DISPLAY COOLANT TEMPERATURE OF -30°C OR LESS?

YES

②
- DISCONNECT SENSOR.
- JUMPER HARNESS TERMINALS TOGETHER.
- "SCAN" TOOL SHOULD DISPLAY 130°C OR MORE. DOES IT?

NO

CODE 15 IS INTERMITTENT. IF NO ADDITIONAL CODES WERE STORED, REFER TO "DIAGNOSTIC AIDS"

NO

③
- JUMPER CKT 410 TO GROUND.
- "SCAN" TOOL SHOULD DISPLAY OVER 130°C. DOES IT?

YES

FAULTY CONNECTION OR SENSOR.

YES

OPEN SENSOR GROUND CIRCUIT, FAULTY CONNECTION OR FAULTY ECM.

NO

OPEN CKT 410, FAULTY CONNECTION AT ECM, OR FAULTY ECM.

DIAGNOSTIC AID

COOLANT SENSOR		
TEMPERATURE TO RESISTANCE VALUES (APPROXIMATE)		
°F	°C	OHMS
210	100	185
160	70	450
100	38	1,800
70	20	3,400
40	4	7,500
20	-7	13,500
0	-18	25,000
-40	-40	100,700

COOLANT TEMPERATURE SENSOR

ECM

COOLANT SENSOR SIGNAL

5 V

410 YEL — C10

2.5L, 4.3L M & G VAN — 452 BLK — A11

ALL EXCEPT ABOVE — 452 BLK — D2

SENSOR GROUND

410   452

1987-90

CODE 21
OPEN TPS CIRCUIT OR MISADJUSTED
Check for stuck or misadjusted TPS
Repair as necessary. If OK, proceed:

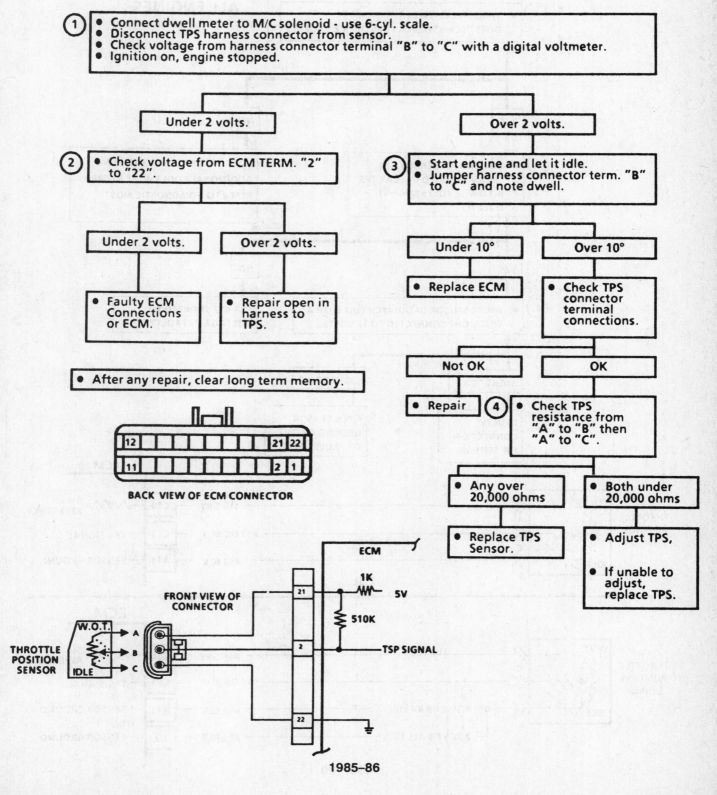

(1)
- Connect dwell meter to M/C solenoid - use 6-cyl. scale.
- Disconnect TPS harness connector from sensor.
- Check voltage from harness connector terminal "B" to "C" with a digital voltmeter.
- Ignition on, engine stopped.

Under 2 volts.

Over 2 volts.

(2)
- Check voltage from ECM TERM. "2" to "22".

(3)
- Start engine and let it idle.
- Jumper harness connector term. "B" to "C" and note dwell.

Under 2 volts.

Over 2 volts.

- Faulty ECM Connections or ECM.

- Repair open in harness to TPS.

Under 10°

Over 10°

- Replace ECM

- Check TPS connector terminal connections.

- After any repair, clear long term memory.

Not OK

OK

- Repair

(4)
- Check TPS resistance from "A" to "B" then "A" to "C".

12 21 22
11 2 1

BACK VIEW OF ECM CONNECTOR

- Any over 20,000 ohms

- Both under 20,000 ohms

- Replace TPS Sensor.

- Adjust TPS,
- If unable to adjust, replace TPS.

ECM

1K

5V

FRONT VIEW OF CONNECTOR

510K

W.O.T.

A

THROTTLE POSITION SENSOR

B

C

IDLE

21

2

TSP SIGNAL

22

1985–86

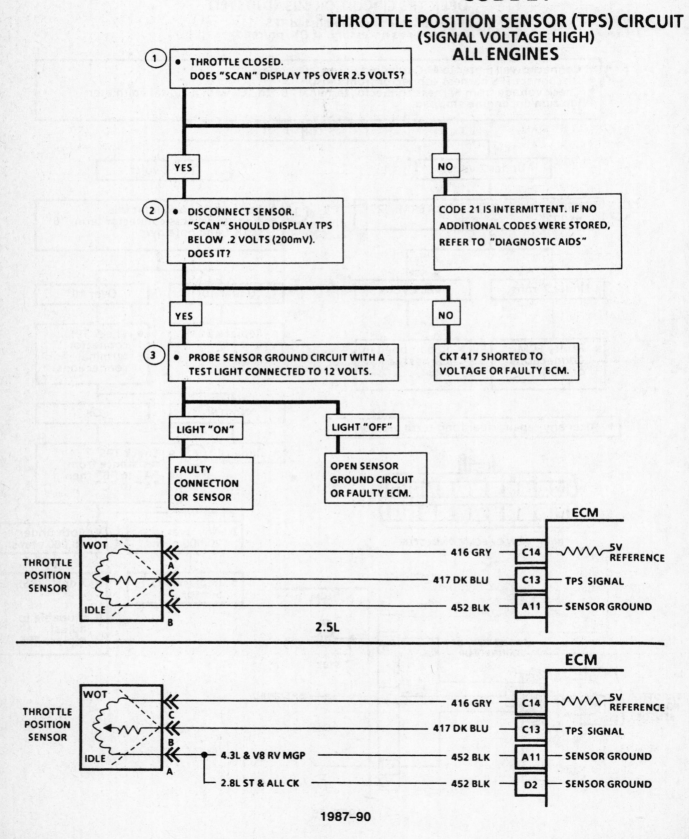

CODE 21
THROTTLE POSITION SENSOR (TPS) CIRCUIT
(SIGNAL VOLTAGE HIGH)
ALL ENGINES

1. • THROTTLE CLOSED.
   DOES "SCAN" DISPLAY TPS OVER 2.5 VOLTS?

YES

NO

2. • DISCONNECT SENSOR.
   "SCAN" SHOULD DISPLAY TPS BELOW .2 VOLTS (200mV). DOES IT?

CODE 21 IS INTERMITTENT. IF NO ADDITIONAL CODES WERE STORED, REFER TO "DIAGNOSTIC AIDS"

YES

NO

3. • PROBE SENSOR GROUND CIRCUIT WITH A TEST LIGHT CONNECTED TO 12 VOLTS.

CKT 417 SHORTED TO VOLTAGE OR FAULTY ECM.

LIGHT "ON"

LIGHT "OFF"

FAULTY CONNECTION OR SENSOR

OPEN SENSOR GROUND CIRCUIT OR FAULTY ECM.

THROTTLE POSITION SENSOR

WOT
IDLE

	ECM
416 GRY	C14 — 5V REFERENCE
417 DK BLU	C13 — TPS SIGNAL
452 BLK	A11 — SENSOR GROUND

2.5L

THROTTLE POSITION SENSOR

WOT
IDLE

	ECM
416 GRY	C14 — 5V REFERENCE
417 DK BLU	C13 — TPS SIGNAL
4.3L & V8 RV MGP — 452 BLK	A11 — SENSOR GROUND
2.8L ST & ALL CK — 452 BLK	D2 — SENSOR GROUND

1987–90

CODE 22
THROTTLE POSITION SENSOR (TPS) CIRCUIT
(SIGNAL VOLTAGE LOW)
ALL ENGINES

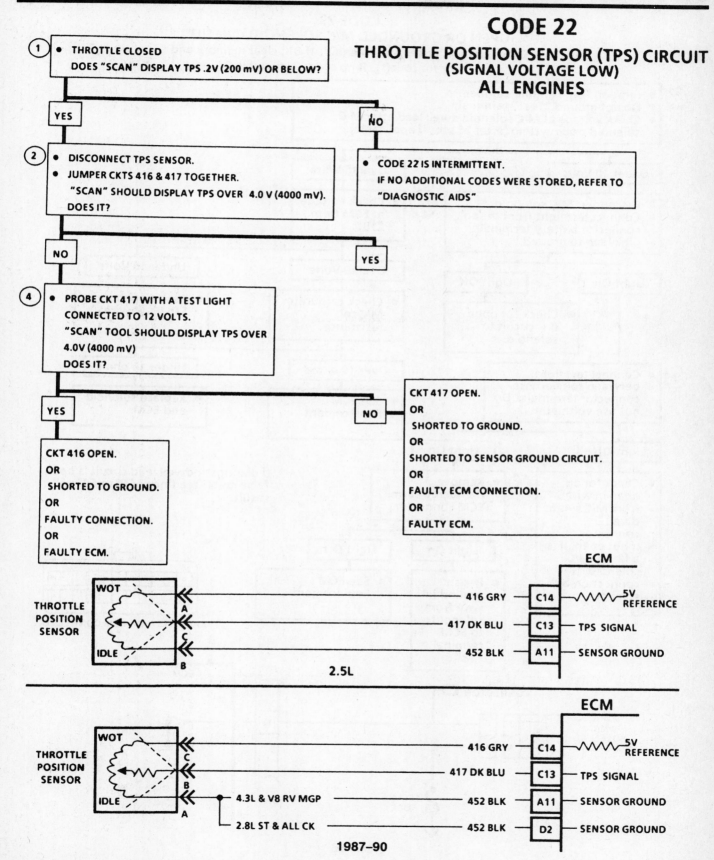

1
- THROTTLE CLOSED
  DOES "SCAN" DISPLAY TPS .2V (200 mV) OR BELOW?

YES

NO

2
- DISCONNECT TPS SENSOR.
- JUMPER CKTS 416 & 417 TOGETHER.
  "SCAN" SHOULD DISPLAY TPS OVER 4.0 V (4000 mV).
  DOES IT?

- CODE 22 IS INTERMITTENT.
  IF NO ADDITIONAL CODES WERE STORED, REFER TO "DIAGNOSTIC AIDS"

NO

YES

4
- PROBE CKT 417 WITH A TEST LIGHT CONNECTED TO 12 VOLTS.
  "SCAN" TOOL SHOULD DISPLAY TPS OVER 4.0V (4000 mV)
  DOES IT?

YES

NO

CKT 417 OPEN.
OR
SHORTED TO GROUND.
OR
SHORTED TO SENSOR GROUND CIRCUIT.
OR
FAULTY ECM CONNECTION.
OR
FAULTY ECM.

CKT 416 OPEN.
OR
SHORTED TO GROUND.
OR
FAULTY CONNECTION.
OR
FAULTY ECM.

THROTTLE POSITION SENSOR

WOT

IDLE

A
C
B

416 GRY — C14 — 5V REFERENCE
417 DK BLU — C13 — TPS SIGNAL
452 BLK — A11 — SENSOR GROUND

ECM

2.5L

THROTTLE POSITION SENSOR

WOT

IDLE

C
B
A

416 GRY — C14 — 5V REFERENCE
417 DK BLU — C13 — TPS SIGNAL
4.3L & V8 RV MGP — 452 BLK — A11 — SENSOR GROUND
2.8L ST & ALL CK — 452 BLK — D2 — SENSOR GROUND

ECM

1987–90

CODE 23
OPEN OR GROUNDED M/C SOLENOID CIRCUIT
Check connections at M/C solenoid. If OK, clear memory and
recheck for code(s). If no code 23, circuit is OK.

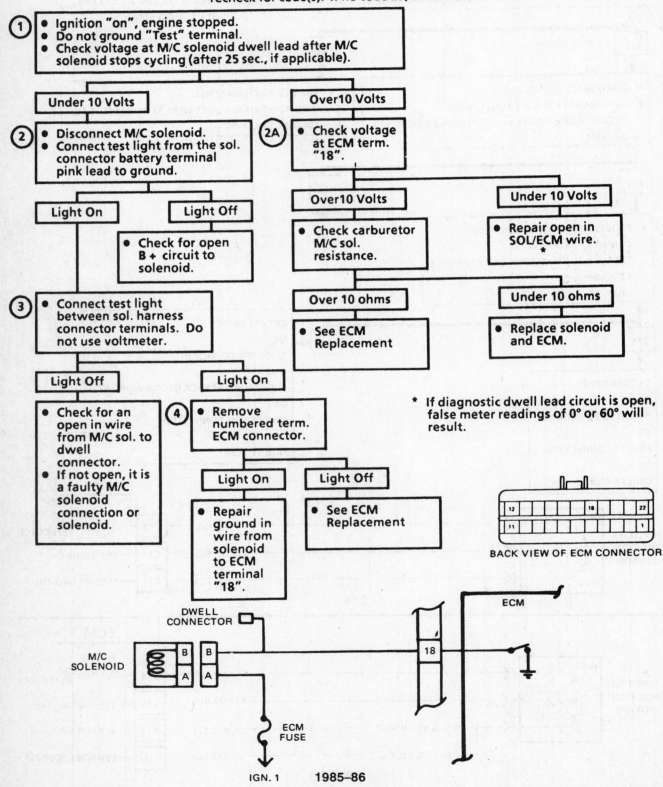

1
- Ignition "on", engine stopped.
- Do not ground "Test" terminal.
- Check voltage at M/C solenoid dwell lead after M/C solenoid stops cycling (after 25 sec., if applicable).

Under 10 Volts

Over 10 Volts

2
- Disconnect M/C solenoid.
- Connect test light from the sol. connector battery terminal pink lead to ground.

2A
- Check voltage at ECM term. "18".

Light On

Light Off
- Check for open B + circuit to solenoid.

Over 10 Volts
- Check carburetor M/C sol. resistance.

Under 10 Volts
- Repair open in SOL/ECM wire. *

Over 10 ohms
- See ECM Replacement

Under 10 ohms
- Replace solenoid and ECM.

3
- Connect test light between sol. harness connector terminals. Do not use voltmeter.

Light Off
- Check for an open in wire from M/C sol. to dwell connector.
- If not open, it is a faulty M/C solenoid connection or solenoid.

Light On

4
- Remove numbered term. ECM connector.

Light On
- Repair ground in wire from solenoid to ECM terminal "18".

Light Off
- See ECM Replacement

* If diagnostic dwell lead circuit is open, false meter readings of 0° or 60° will result.

BACK VIEW OF ECM CONNECTOR

DWELL CONNECTOR

M/C SOLENOID

ECM

18

ECM FUSE

IGN. 1   1985–86

CODE 23
MANIFOLD AIR TEMPERATURE (MAT) SENSOR CIRCUIT
(LOW TEMPERATURE INDICATED)
2.5L ENGINE

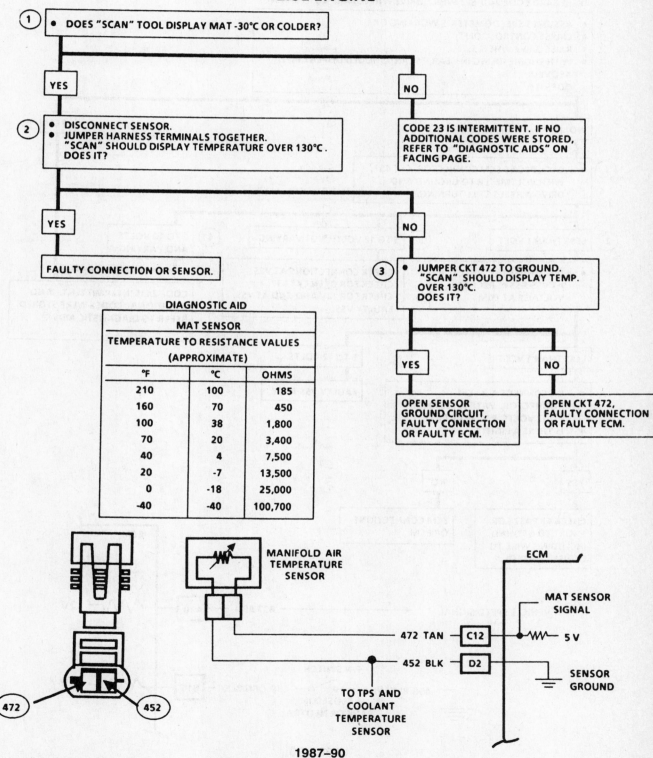

1 • DOES "SCAN" TOOL DISPLAY MAT -30°C OR COLDER?

YES

NO

2 • DISCONNECT SENSOR.
• JUMPER HARNESS TERMINALS TOGETHER. "SCAN" SHOULD DISPLAY TEMPERATURE OVER 130°C. DOES IT?

CODE 23 IS INTERMITTENT. IF NO ADDITIONAL CODES WERE STORED, REFER TO "DIAGNOSTIC AIDS" ON FACING PAGE.

YES

NO

FAULTY CONNECTION OR SENSOR.

3 • JUMPER CKT 472 TO GROUND. "SCAN" SHOULD DISPLAY TEMP. OVER 130°C. DOES IT?

YES

NO

OPEN SENSOR GROUND CIRCUIT, FAULTY CONNECTION OR FAULTY ECM.

OPEN CKT 472, FAULTY CONNECTION OR FAULTY ECM.

DIAGNOSTIC AID

MAT SENSOR		
TEMPERATURE TO RESISTANCE VALUES (APPROXIMATE)		
°F	°C	OHMS
210	100	185
160	70	450
100	38	1,800
70	20	3,400
40	4	7,500
20	-7	13,500
0	-18	25,000
-40	-40	100,700

MANIFOLD AIR TEMPERATURE SENSOR

ECM

MAT SENSOR SIGNAL

472 TAN — C12 — 5 V

452 BLK — D2

SENSOR GROUND

472

452

TO TPS AND COOLANT TEMPERATURE SENSOR

1987–90

CODE 24

VSS CIRCUIT FAULT
ALL ENGINES

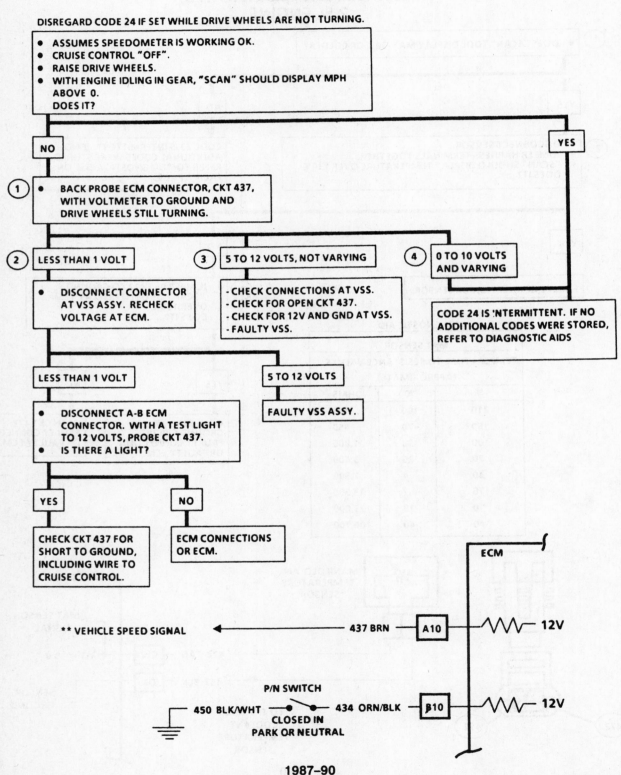

DISREGARD CODE 24 IF SET WHILE DRIVE WHEELS ARE NOT TURNING.

- ASSUMES SPEEDOMETER IS WORKING OK.
- CRUISE CONTROL "OFF".
- RAISE DRIVE WHEELS.
- WITH ENGINE IDLING IN GEAR, "SCAN" SHOULD DISPLAY MPH ABOVE 0.
  DOES IT?

NO

YES

① • BACK PROBE ECM CONNECTOR, CKT 437, WITH VOLTMETER TO GROUND AND DRIVE WHEELS STILL TURNING.

② **LESS THAN 1 VOLT**

③ **5 TO 12 VOLTS, NOT VARYING**

④ **0 TO 10 VOLTS AND VARYING**

• DISCONNECT CONNECTOR AT VSS ASSY. RECHECK VOLTAGE AT ECM.

- CHECK CONNECTIONS AT VSS.
- CHECK FOR OPEN CKT 437.
- CHECK FOR 12V AND GND AT VSS.
- FAULTY VSS.

CODE 24 IS INTERMITTENT. IF NO ADDITIONAL CODES WERE STORED, REFER TO DIAGNOSTIC AIDS

LESS THAN 1 VOLT

5 TO 12 VOLTS

• DISCONNECT A-B ECM CONNECTOR. WITH A TEST LIGHT TO 12 VOLTS, PROBE CKT 437.
• IS THERE A LIGHT?

FAULTY VSS ASSY.

YES

NO

CHECK CKT 437 FOR SHORT TO GROUND, INCLUDING WIRE TO CRUISE CONTROL.

ECM CONNECTIONS OR ECM.

ECM

** VEHICLE SPEED SIGNAL ◄── 437 BRN ── A10 ──/\/\── 12V

P/N SWITCH

450 BLK/WHT ──•⟋ •── 434 ORN/BLK ── B10 ──/\/\── 12V
CLOSED IN
PARK OR NEUTRAL

1987–90

CODE 25
MANIFOLD AIR TEMPERATURE (MAT) SENSOR
CIRCUIT
(HIGH TEMPERATURE INDICATED)
ALL ENGINES

DIAGNOSTIC AID		
MAT SENSOR		
TEMPERATURE TO RESISTANCE VALUES		
(APPROXIMATE)		
°F	°C	OHMS
210	100	185
160	70	450
100	38	1,800
70	20	3,400
40	4	7,500
20	-7	13,500
0	-18	25,000
-40	-40	100,700

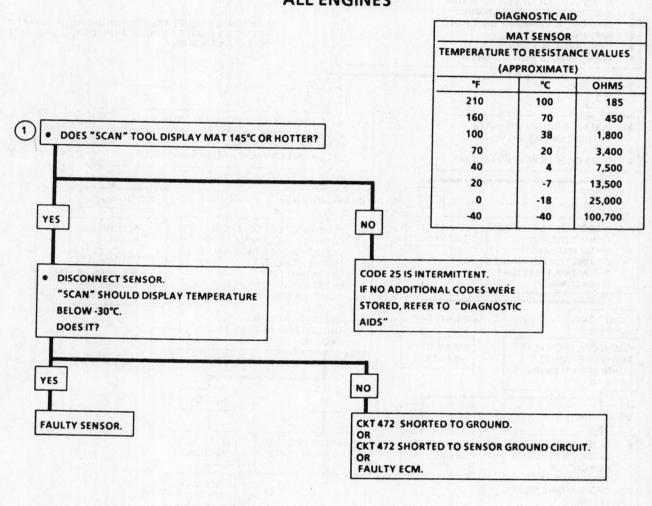

① • DOES "SCAN" TOOL DISPLAY MAT 145°C OR HOTTER?

YES

NO

• DISCONNECT SENSOR.
"SCAN" SHOULD DISPLAY TEMPERATURE
BELOW -30°C.
DOES IT?

CODE 25 IS INTERMITTENT.
IF NO ADDITIONAL CODES WERE
STORED, REFER TO "DIAGNOSTIC
AIDS"

YES

NO

FAULTY SENSOR.

CKT 472 SHORTED TO GROUND.
OR
CKT 472 SHORTED TO SENSOR GROUND CIRCUIT.
OR
FAULTY ECM.

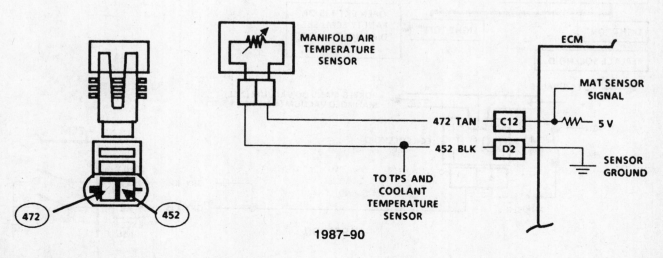

MANIFOLD AIR
TEMPERATURE
SENSOR

ECM

MAT SENSOR
SIGNAL

472 TAN — C12 — 5 V

452 BLK — D2

SENSOR
GROUND

TO TPS AND
COOLANT
TEMPERATURE
SENSOR

472   452

1987–90

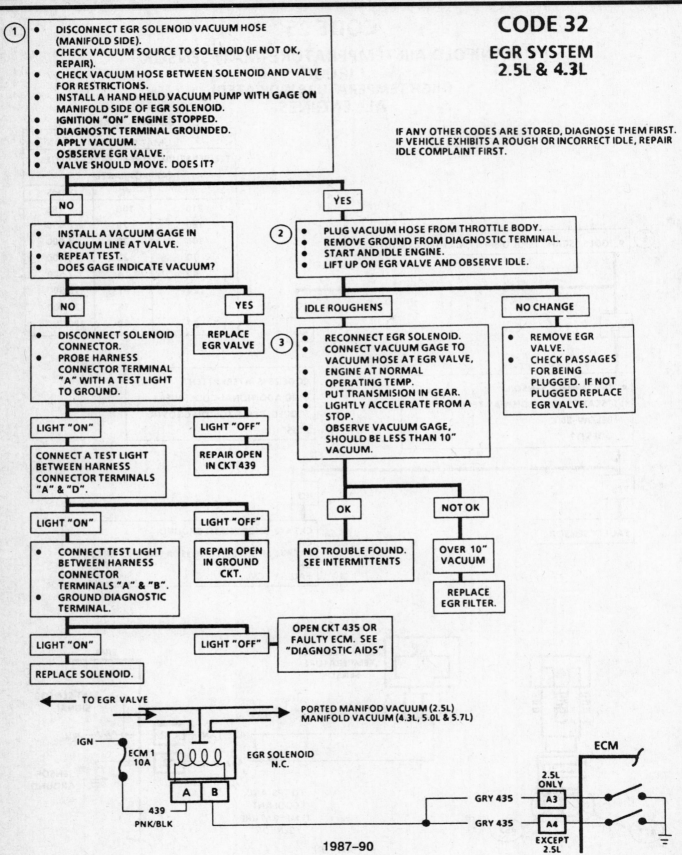

① • DISCONNECT EGR SOLENOID VACUUM HOSE (MANIFOLD SIDE).
• CHECK VACUUM SOURCE TO SOLENOID (IF NOT OK, REPAIR).
• CHECK VACUUM HOSE BETWEEN SOLENOID AND VALVE FOR RESTRICTIONS.
• INSTALL A HAND HELD VACUUM PUMP WITH GAGE ON MANIFOLD SIDE OF EGR SOLENOID.
• IGNITION "ON" ENGINE STOPPED.
• DIAGNOSTIC TERMINAL GROUNDED.
• APPLY VACUUM.
• OSBSERVE EGR VALVE.
• VALVE SHOULD MOVE. DOES IT?

CODE 32

EGR SYSTEM
2.5L & 4.3L

IF ANY OTHER CODES ARE STORED, DIAGNOSE THEM FIRST.
IF VEHICLE EXHIBITS A ROUGH OR INCORRECT IDLE, REPAIR IDLE COMPLAINT FIRST.

NO

• INSTALL A VACUUM GAGE IN VACUUM LINE AT VALVE.
• REPEAT TEST.
• DOES GAGE INDICATE VACUUM?

YES

② • PLUG VACUUM HOSE FROM THROTTLE BODY.
• REMOVE GROUND FROM DIAGNOSTIC TERMINAL.
• START AND IDLE ENGINE.
• LIFT UP ON EGR VALVE AND OBSERVE IDLE.

NO

• DISCONNECT SOLENOID CONNECTOR.
• PROBE HARNESS CONNECTOR TERMINAL "A" WITH A TEST LIGHT TO GROUND.

YES

REPLACE EGR VALVE

IDLE ROUGHENS

③ • RECONNECT EGR SOLENOID.
• CONNECT VACUUM GAGE TO VACUUM HOSE AT EGR VALVE, ENGINE AT NORMAL OPERATING TEMP.
• PUT TRANSMISION IN GEAR.
• LIGHTLY ACCELERATE FROM A STOP.
• OBSERVE VACUUM GAGE, SHOULD BE LESS THAN 10" VACUUM.

NO CHANGE

• REMOVE EGR VALVE.
• CHECK PASSAGES FOR BEING PLUGGED. IF NOT PLUGGED REPLACE EGR VALVE.

LIGHT "ON"

CONNECT A TEST LIGHT BETWEEN HARNESS CONNECTOR TERMINALS "A" & "D".

LIGHT "OFF"

REPAIR OPEN IN CKT 439

LIGHT "ON"

• CONNECT TEST LIGHT BETWEEN HARNESS CONNECTOR TERMINALS "A" & "B".
• GROUND DIAGNOSTIC TERMINAL.

LIGHT "OFF"

REPAIR OPEN IN GROUND CKT.

OK

NO TROUBLE FOUND. SEE INTERMITTENTS

NOT OK

OVER 10" VACUUM

REPLACE EGR FILTER.

LIGHT "ON"

REPLACE SOLENOID.

LIGHT "OFF"

OPEN CKT 435 OR FAULTY ECM. SEE "DIAGNOSTIC AIDS"

TO EGR VALVE

PORTED MANIFOD VACUUM (2.5L)
MANIFOLD VACUUM (4.3L, 5.0L & 5.7L)

IGN

ECM 1
10A

EGR SOLENOID
N.C.

A B

439
PNK/BLK

ECM

2.5L ONLY

GRY 435   A3

GRY 435   A4

EXCEPT 2.5L

1987–90

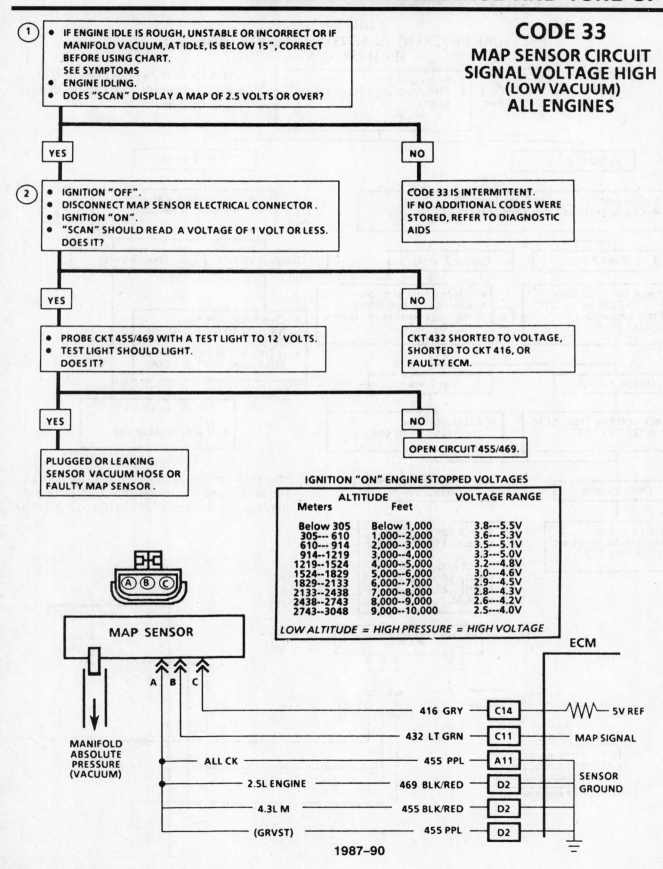

CODE 33
MAP SENSOR CIRCUIT SIGNAL VOLTAGE HIGH (LOW VACUUM) ALL ENGINES

1
- IF ENGINE IDLE IS ROUGH, UNSTABLE OR INCORRECT OR IF MANIFOLD VACUUM, AT IDLE, IS BELOW 15", CORRECT BEFORE USING CHART. SEE SYMPTOMS
- ENGINE IDLING.
- DOES "SCAN" DISPLAY A MAP OF 2.5 VOLTS OR OVER?

YES　　　　　　　　　　　　**NO**

2
- IGNITION "OFF".
- DISCONNECT MAP SENSOR ELECTRICAL CONNECTOR.
- IGNITION "ON".
- "SCAN" SHOULD READ A VOLTAGE OF 1 VOLT OR LESS. DOES IT?

CODE 33 IS INTERMITTENT. IF NO ADDITIONAL CODES WERE STORED, REFER TO DIAGNOSTIC AIDS

YES　　　　　　　　　　　　**NO**

- PROBE CKT 455/469 WITH A TEST LIGHT TO 12 VOLTS.
- TEST LIGHT SHOULD LIGHT. DOES IT?

CKT 432 SHORTED TO VOLTAGE, SHORTED TO CKT 416, OR FAULTY ECM.

YES　　　　　　　　　　　　**NO**

PLUGGED OR LEAKING SENSOR VACUUM HOSE OR FAULTY MAP SENSOR.

OPEN CIRCUIT 455/469.

IGNITION "ON" ENGINE STOPPED VOLTAGES

ALTITUDE		VOLTAGE RANGE
Meters	Feet	
Below 305	Below 1,000	3.8---5.5V
305--- 610	1,000--2,000	3.6---5.3V
610--- 914	2,000--3,000	3.5---5.1V
914--1219	3,000--4,000	3.3---5.0V
1219--1524	4,000--5,000	3.2---4.8V
1524--1829	5,000--6,000	3.0---4.6V
1829--2133	6,000--7,000	2.9---4.5V
2133--2438	7,000--8,000	2.8---4.3V
2438--2743	8,000--9,000	2.6---4.2V
2743--3048	9,000--10,000	2.5---4.0V

LOW ALTITUDE = HIGH PRESSURE = HIGH VOLTAGE

MAP SENSOR

(A) (B) (C)

A　B　C

MANIFOLD ABSOLUTE PRESSURE (VACUUM)

ECM

416 GRY	C14	5V REF
432 LT GRN	C11	MAP SIGNAL
ALL CK — 455 PPL	A11	
2.5L ENGINE — 469 BLK/RED	D2	SENSOR GROUND
4.3L M — 455 BLK/RED	D2	
(GRVST) — 455 PPL	D2	

1987–90

CODE 34
PRESSURE DIFFERENTIAL SENSOR (VAC) VOLTAGE TOO
HIGH OR LOW

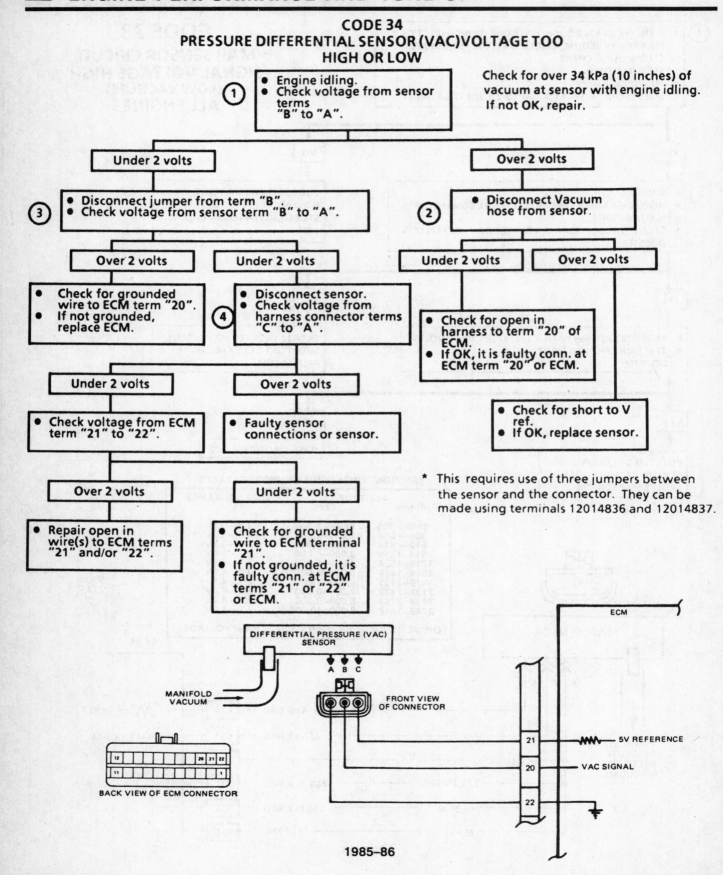

① • Engine idling.
• Check voltage from sensor terms "B" to "A".

Check for over 34 kPa (10 inches) of vacuum at sensor with engine idling. If not OK, repair.

Under 2 volts

Over 2 volts

③ • Disconnect jumper from term "B".
• Check voltage from sensor term "B" to "A".

② • Disconnect Vacuum hose from sensor.

Over 2 volts

Under 2 volts

Under 2 volts

Over 2 volts

• Check for grounded wire to ECM term "20".
• If not grounded, replace ECM.

④ • Disconnect sensor.
• Check voltage from harness connector terms "C" to "A".

• Check for open in harness to term "20" of ECM.
• If OK, it is faulty conn. at ECM term "20" or ECM.

Under 2 volts

Over 2 volts

• Check voltage from ECM term "21" to "22".

• Faulty sensor connections or sensor.

• Check for short to V ref.
• If OK, replace sensor.

Over 2 volts

Under 2 volts

• Repair open in wire(s) to ECM terms "21" and/or "22".

• Check for grounded wire to ECM terminal "21".
• If not grounded, it is faulty conn. at ECM terms "21" or "22" or ECM.

* This requires use of three jumpers between the sensor and the connector. They can be made using terminals 12014836 and 12014837.

DIFFERENTIAL PRESSURE (VAC) SENSOR

A B C

MANIFOLD VACUUM

FRONT VIEW OF CONNECTOR

ECM

BACK VIEW OF ECM CONNECTOR

12 20 21 22
11   1

21 — 5V REFERENCE
20 — VAC SIGNAL
22

1985–86

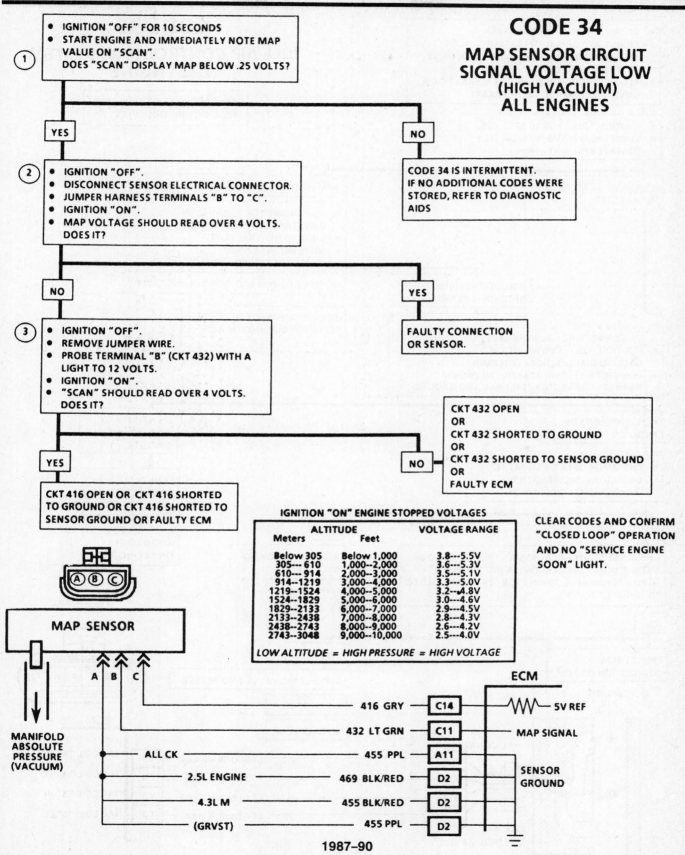

CODE 34

MAP SENSOR CIRCUIT
SIGNAL VOLTAGE LOW
(HIGH VACUUM)
ALL ENGINES

1
- IGNITION "OFF" FOR 10 SECONDS
- START ENGINE AND IMMEDIATELY NOTE MAP VALUE ON "SCAN".
  DOES "SCAN" DISPLAY MAP BELOW .25 VOLTS?

YES

NO

CODE 34 IS INTERMITTENT.
IF NO ADDITIONAL CODES WERE STORED, REFER TO DIAGNOSTIC AIDS

2
- IGNITION "OFF".
- DISCONNECT SENSOR ELECTRICAL CONNECTOR.
- JUMPER HARNESS TERMINALS "B" TO "C".
- IGNITION "ON".
- MAP VOLTAGE SHOULD READ OVER 4 VOLTS. DOES IT?

NO

YES

FAULTY CONNECTION OR SENSOR.

3
- IGNITION "OFF".
- REMOVE JUMPER WIRE.
- PROBE TERMINAL "B" (CKT 432) WITH A LIGHT TO 12 VOLTS.
- IGNITION "ON".
- "SCAN" SHOULD READ OVER 4 VOLTS. DOES IT?

NO

CKT 432 OPEN
OR
CKT 432 SHORTED TO GROUND
OR
CKT 432 SHORTED TO SENSOR GROUND
OR
FAULTY ECM

YES

CKT 416 OPEN OR CKT 416 SHORTED TO GROUND OR CKT 416 SHORTED TO SENSOR GROUND OR FAULTY ECM

CLEAR CODES AND CONFIRM "CLOSED LOOP" OPERATION AND NO "SERVICE ENGINE SOON" LIGHT.

IGNITION "ON" ENGINE STOPPED VOLTAGES

ALTITUDE		VOLTAGE RANGE
Meters	Feet	
Below 305	Below 1,000	3.8---5.5V
305--- 610	1,000--2,000	3.6---5.3V
610--- 914	2,000--3,000	3.5---5.1V
914--1219	3,000--4,000	3.3---5.0V
1219--1524	4,000--5,000	3.2---4.8V
1524--1829	5,000--6,000	3.0---4.6V
1829--2133	6,000--7,000	2.9---4.5V
2133--2438	7,000--8,000	2.8---4.3V
2438--2743	8,000--9,000	2.6---4.2V
2743--3048	9,000--10,000	2.5---4.0V

LOW ALTITUDE = HIGH PRESSURE = HIGH VOLTAGE

A B C

MAP SENSOR

MANIFOLD ABSOLUTE PRESSURE (VACUUM)

A B C

ECM

	416 GRY	C14	5V REF
	432 LT GRN	C11	MAP SIGNAL
ALL CK	455 PPL	A11	SENSOR GROUND
2.5L ENGINE	469 BLK/RED	D2	
4.3L M	455 BLK/RED	D2	
(GRVST)	455 PPL	D2	

1987-90

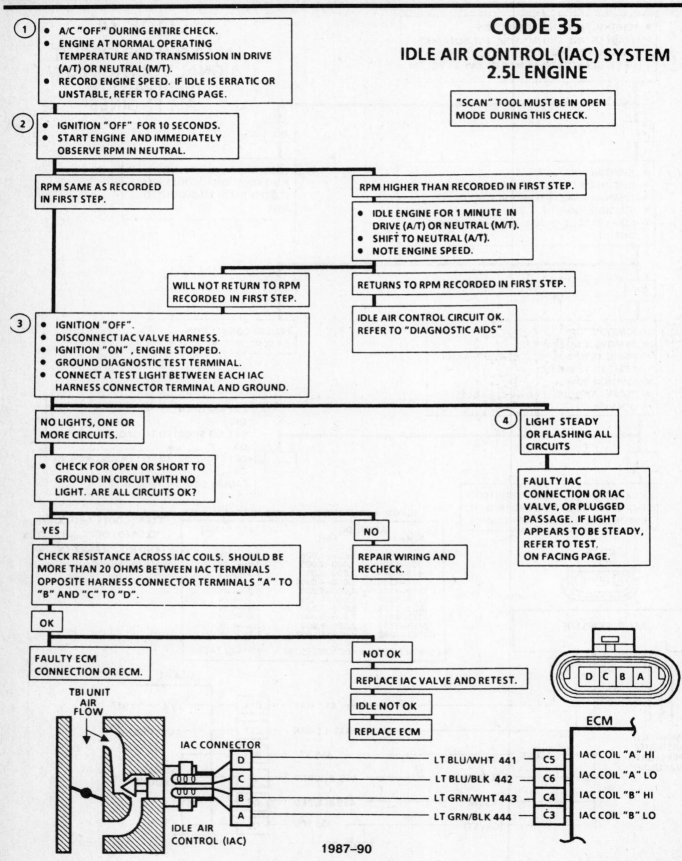

**① **
- A/C "OFF" DURING ENTIRE CHECK.
- ENGINE AT NORMAL OPERATING TEMPERATURE AND TRANSMISSION IN DRIVE (A/T) OR NEUTRAL (M/T).
- RECORD ENGINE SPEED. IF IDLE IS ERRATIC OR UNSTABLE, REFER TO FACING PAGE.

CODE 35
IDLE AIR CONTROL (IAC) SYSTEM
2.5L ENGINE

"SCAN" TOOL MUST BE IN OPEN MODE DURING THIS CHECK.

**② **
- IGNITION "OFF" FOR 10 SECONDS.
- START ENGINE AND IMMEDIATELY OBSERVE RPM IN NEUTRAL.

RPM SAME AS RECORDED IN FIRST STEP.

RPM HIGHER THAN RECORDED IN FIRST STEP.

- IDLE ENGINE FOR 1 MINUTE IN DRIVE (A/T) OR NEUTRAL (M/T).
- SHIFT TO NEUTRAL (A/T).
- NOTE ENGINE SPEED.

WILL NOT RETURN TO RPM RECORDED IN FIRST STEP.

RETURNS TO RPM RECORDED IN FIRST STEP.

IDLE AIR CONTROL CIRCUIT OK. REFER TO "DIAGNOSTIC AIDS"

**③ **
- IGNITION "OFF".
- DISCONNECT IAC VALVE HARNESS.
- IGNITION "ON", ENGINE STOPPED.
- GROUND DIAGNOSTIC TEST TERMINAL.
- CONNECT A TEST LIGHT BETWEEN EACH IAC HARNESS CONNECTOR TERMINAL AND GROUND.

NO LIGHTS, ONE OR MORE CIRCUITS.

**④ ** LIGHT STEADY OR FLASHING ALL CIRCUITS

- CHECK FOR OPEN OR SHORT TO GROUND IN CIRCUIT WITH NO LIGHT. ARE ALL CIRCUITS OK?

FAULTY IAC CONNECTION OR IAC VALVE, OR PLUGGED PASSAGE. IF LIGHT APPEARS TO BE STEADY, REFER TO TEST, ON FACING PAGE.

YES

NO

CHECK RESISTANCE ACROSS IAC COILS. SHOULD BE MORE THAN 20 OHMS BETWEEN IAC TERMINALS OPPOSITE HARNESS CONNECTOR TERMINALS "A" TO "B" AND "C" TO "D".

REPAIR WIRING AND RECHECK.

OK

FAULTY ECM CONNECTION OR ECM.

NOT OK

REPLACE IAC VALVE AND RETEST.

IDLE NOT OK

REPLACE ECM

TBI UNIT AIR FLOW

IAC CONNECTOR

IDLE AIR CONTROL (IAC)

ECM

D	LT BLU/WHT 441	C5	IAC COIL "A" HI
C	LT BLU/BLK 442	C6	IAC COIL "A" LO
B	LT GRN/WHT 443	C4	IAC COIL "B" HI
A	LT GRN/BLK 444	C3	IAC COIL "B" LO

D C B A

1987–90

CODE 41
NO DISTRIBUTOR REFERENCE SIGNAL

If vacuum has been applied to MAP or VAC sensors with the key 'ON' engine not running, a false Code 41 could be set.

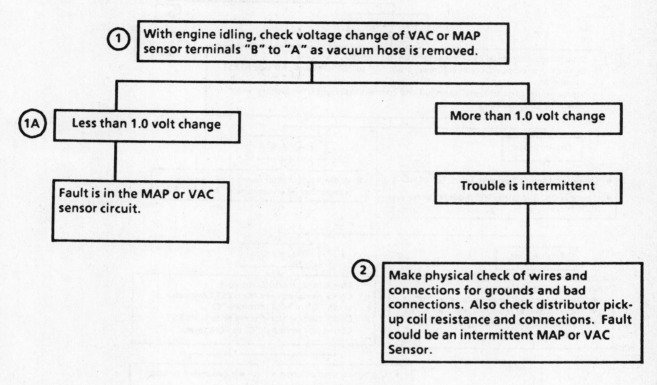

① With engine idling, check voltage change of VAC or MAP sensor terminals "B" to "A" as vacuum hose is removed.

1A Less than 1.0 volt change

Fault is in the MAP or VAC sensor circuit.

More than 1.0 volt change

Trouble is intermittent

② Make physical check of wires and connections for grounds and bad connections. Also check distributor pick-up coil resistance and connections. Fault could be an intermittent MAP or VAC Sensor.

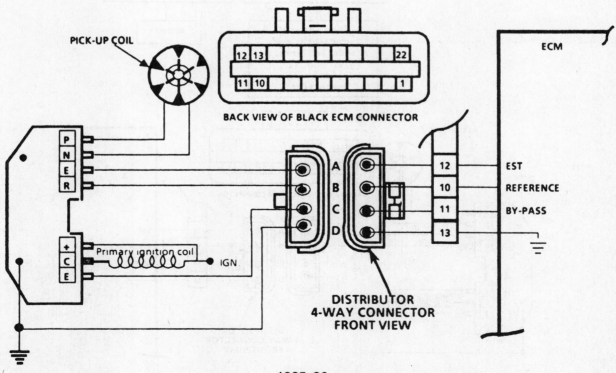

PICK-UP COIL

ECM

12 13   22
11 10   1

BACK VIEW OF BLACK ECM CONNECTOR

P
N
E
R

A
B
C
D

12   EST
10   REFERENCE
11   BY-PASS
13

+
C
E

Primary ignition coil   IGN

**DISTRIBUTOR
4-WAY CONNECTOR
FRONT VIEW**

1985–86

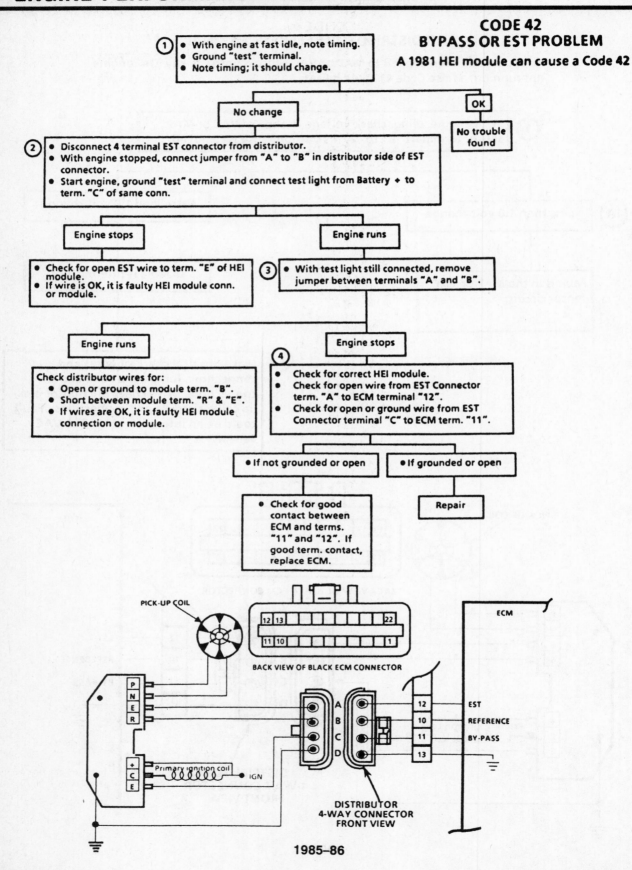

CODE 42
BYPASS OR EST PROBLEM
A 1981 HEI module can cause a Code 42

①
- With engine at fast idle, note timing.
- Ground "test" terminal.
- Note timing; it should change.

No change

OK

No trouble found

②
- Disconnect 4 terminal EST connector from distributor.
- With engine stopped, connect jumper from "A" to "B" in distributor side of EST connector.
- Start engine, ground "test" terminal and connect test light from Battery + to term. "C" of same conn.

Engine stops

- Check for open EST wire to term. "E" of HEI module.
- If wire is OK, it is faulty HEI module conn. or module.

Engine runs

③
- With test light still connected, remove jumper between terminals "A" and "B".

Engine runs

Check distributor wires for:
- Open or ground to module term. "B".
- Short between module term. "R" & "E".
- If wires are OK, it is faulty HEI module connection or module.

Engine stops

④
- Check for correct HEI module.
- Check for open wire from EST Connector term. "A" to ECM terminal "12".
- Check for open or ground wire from EST Connector terminal "C" to ECM term. "11".

• If not grounded or open

• If grounded or open

- Check for good contact between ECM and terms. "11" and "12". If good term. contact, replace ECM.

Repair

PICK-UP COIL

12 13   22
11 10   1

BACK VIEW OF BLACK ECM CONNECTOR

ECM

P
N
E
R

A — 12 — EST
B — 10 — REFERENCE
C — 11 — BY-PASS
D — 13

+
C
E

Primary ignition coil — IGN

DISTRIBUTOR
4-WAY CONNECTOR
FRONT VIEW

1985–86

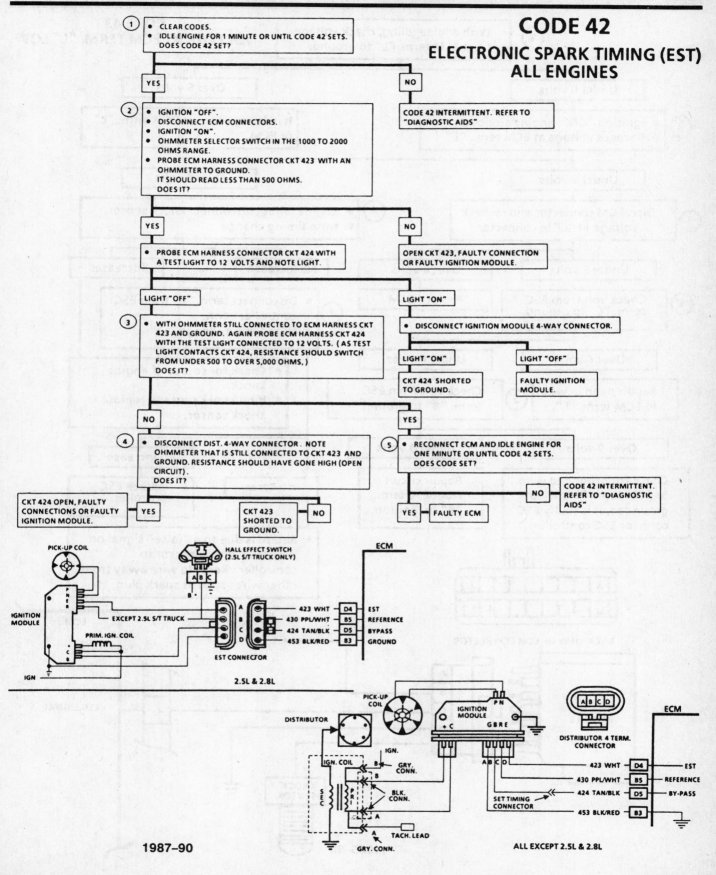

CODE 42
ELECTRONIC SPARK TIMING (EST)
ALL ENGINES

1
- CLEAR CODES.
- IDLE ENGINE FOR 1 MINUTE OR UNTIL CODE 42 SETS. DOES CODE 42 SET?

YES

NO → CODE 42 INTERMITTENT. REFER TO "DIAGNOSTIC AIDS"

2
- IGNITION "OFF".
- DISCONNECT ECM CONNECTORS.
- IGNITION "ON".
- OHMMETER SELECTOR SWITCH IN THE 1000 TO 2000 OHMS RANGE.
- PROBE ECM HARNESS CONNECTOR CKT 423 WITH AN OHMMETER TO GROUND. IT SHOULD READ LESS THAN 500 OHMS. DOES IT?

YES

NO → OPEN CKT 423, FAULTY CONNECTION OR FAULTY IGNITION MODULE.

- PROBE ECM HARNESS CONNECTOR CKT 424 WITH A TEST LIGHT TO 12 VOLTS AND NOTE LIGHT.

LIGHT "OFF"

LIGHT "ON"
- DISCONNECT IGNITION MODULE 4-WAY CONNECTOR.

LIGHT "ON" → CKT 424 SHORTED TO GROUND.

LIGHT "OFF" → FAULTY IGNITION MODULE.

3
- WITH OHMMETER STILL CONNECTED TO ECM HARNESS CKT 423 AND GROUND. AGAIN PROBE ECM HARNESS CKT 424 WITH THE TEST LIGHT CONNECTED TO 12 VOLTS. (AS TEST LIGHT CONTACTS CKT 424, RESISTANCE SHOULD SWITCH FROM UNDER 500 TO OVER 5,000 OHMS.) DOES IT?

NO

YES

4
- DISCONNECT DIST. 4-WAY CONNECTOR. NOTE OHMMETER THAT IS STILL CONNECTED TO CKT 423 AND GROUND. RESISTANCE SHOULD HAVE GONE HIGH (OPEN CIRCUIT). DOES IT?

CKT 424 OPEN, FAULTY CONNECTIONS OR FAULTY IGNITION MODULE. ← YES

NO → CKT 423 SHORTED TO GROUND.

5
- RECONNECT ECM AND IDLE ENGINE FOR ONE MINUTE OR UNTIL CODE 42 SETS. DOES CODE SET?

YES → FAULTY ECM

NO → CODE 42 INTERMITTENT. REFER TO "DIAGNOSTIC AIDS"

PICK-UP COIL

HALL EFFECT SWITCH (2.5L S/T TRUCK ONLY)

ECM

IGNITION MODULE

EXCEPT 2.5L S/T TRUCK

PRIM. IGN. COIL

EST CONNECTOR

IGN

A	423 WHT	D4	EST
B	430 PPL/WHT	B5	REFERENCE
C	424 TAN/BLK	D5	BYPASS
D	453 BLK/RED	B3	GROUND

2.5L & 2.8L

DISTRIBUTOR

PICK-UP COIL

IGNITION MODULE

IGN. COIL

GRY. CONN.

BLK. CONN.

TACH. LEAD

GRY. CONN.

DISTRIBUTOR 4 TERM. CONNECTOR

ECM

SET TIMING CONNECTOR

	423 WHT	D4	EST
	430 PPL/WHT	B5	REFERENCE
	424 TAN/BLK	D5	BY-PASS
	453 BLK/RED	B3	

1987–90

ALL EXCEPT 2.5L & 2.8L

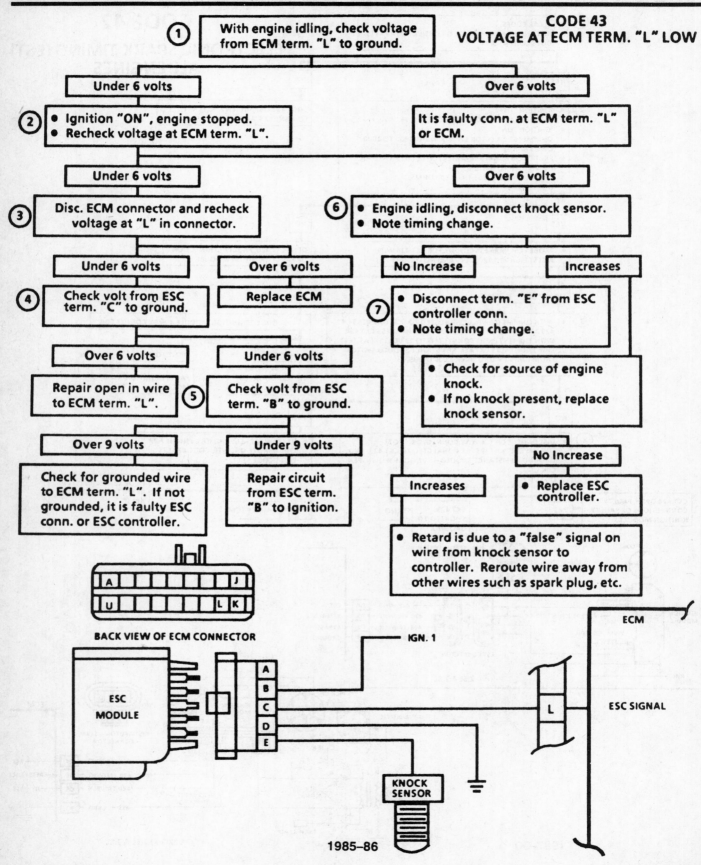

**CODE 43
VOLTAGE AT ECM TERM. "L" LOW**

① With engine idling, check voltage from ECM term. "L" to ground.

Under 6 volts

② • Ignition "ON", engine stopped.
• Recheck voltage at ECM term. "L".

Under 6 volts

③ Disc. ECM connector and recheck voltage at "L" in connector.

Under 6 volts

④ Check volt from ESC term. "C" to ground.

Over 6 volts

Repair open in wire to ECM term. "L".

Over 9 volts

Check for grounded wire to ECM term. "L". If not grounded, it is faulty ESC conn. or ESC controller.

Over 6 volts

Replace ECM

Under 6 volts

⑤ Check volt from ESC term. "B" to ground.

Under 9 volts

Repair circuit from ESC term. "B" to Ignition.

Over 6 volts

It is faulty conn. at ECM term. "L" or ECM.

Over 6 volts

⑥ • Engine idling, disconnect knock sensor.
• Note timing change.

No Increase

Increases

⑦ • Disconnect term. "E" from ESC controller conn.
• Note timing change.

• Check for source of engine knock.
• If no knock present, replace knock sensor.

No Increase

• Replace ESC controller.

Increases

• Retard is due to a "false" signal on wire from knock sensor to controller. Reroute wire away from other wires such as spark plug, etc.

A J
U L K

BACK VIEW OF ECM CONNECTOR

ESC MODULE

IGN. 1

A
B
C
D
E

L

ECM

ESC SIGNAL

KNOCK SENSOR

1985–86

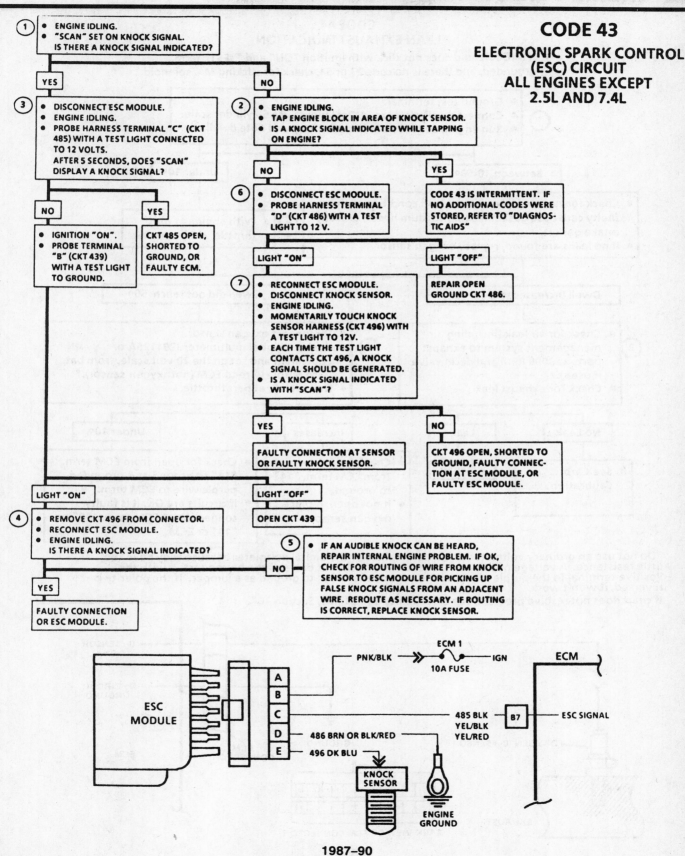

CODE 43

ELECTRONIC SPARK CONTROL (ESC) CIRCUIT ALL ENGINES EXCEPT 2.5L AND 7.4L

1.
- ENGINE IDLING.
- "SCAN" SET ON KNOCK SIGNAL. IS THERE A KNOCK SIGNAL INDICATED?

YES / **NO**

2.
- ENGINE IDLING.
- TAP ENGINE BLOCK IN AREA OF KNOCK SENSOR. IS A KNOCK SIGNAL INDICATED WHILE TAPPING ON ENGINE?

3.
- DISCONNECT ESC MODULE.
- ENGINE IDLING.
- PROBE HARNESS TERMINAL "C" (CKT 485) WITH A TEST LIGHT CONNECTED TO 12 VOLTS. AFTER 5 SECONDS, DOES "SCAN" DISPLAY A KNOCK SIGNAL?

NO / **YES**

NO

YES
CODE 43 IS INTERMITTENT. IF NO ADDITIONAL CODES WERE STORED, REFER TO "DIAGNOSTIC AIDS"

6.
- DISCONNECT ESC MODULE.
- PROBE HARNESS TERMINAL "D" (CKT 486) WITH A TEST LIGHT TO 12 V.

- IGNITION "ON".
- PROBE TERMINAL "B" (CKT 439) WITH A TEST LIGHT TO GROUND.

CKT 485 OPEN, SHORTED TO GROUND, OR FAULTY ECM.

LIGHT "ON" / **LIGHT "OFF"**

REPAIR OPEN GROUND CKT 486.

7.
- RECONNECT ESC MODULE.
- DISCONNECT KNOCK SENSOR.
- ENGINE IDLING.
- MOMENTARILY TOUCH KNOCK SENSOR HARNESS (CKT 496) WITH A TEST LIGHT TO 12V.
- EACH TIME THE TEST LIGHT CONTACTS CKT 496, A KNOCK SIGNAL SHOULD BE GENERATED.
- IS A KNOCK SIGNAL INDICATED WITH "SCAN"?

YES / **NO**

FAULTY CONNECTION AT SENSOR OR FAULTY KNOCK SENSOR.

CKT 496 OPEN, SHORTED TO GROUND, FAULTY CONNECTION AT ESC MODULE, OR FAULTY ESC MODULE.

LIGHT "ON" / **LIGHT "OFF"**

OPEN CKT 439

4.
- REMOVE CKT 496 FROM CONNECTOR.
- RECONNECT ESC MODULE.
- ENGINE IDLING. IS THERE A KNOCK SIGNAL INDICATED?

5.
NO
IF AN AUDIBLE KNOCK CAN BE HEARD, REPAIR INTERNAL ENGINE PROBLEM. IF OK, CHECK FOR ROUTING OF WIRE FROM KNOCK SENSOR TO ESC MODULE FOR PICKING UP FALSE KNOCK SIGNALS FROM AN ADJACENT WIRE. REROUTE AS NECESSARY. IF ROUTING IS CORRECT, REPLACE KNOCK SENSOR.

YES
FAULTY CONNECTION OR ESC MODULE.

ESC MODULE

A
B — PNK/BLK → ECM 1 10A FUSE → IGN — ECM
C — 485 BLK YEL/BLK YEL/RED — B7 — ESC SIGNAL
D — 486 BRN OR BLK/RED
E — 496 DK BLU

KNOCK SENSOR

ENGINE GROUND

1987-90

CODE 44
LEAN EXHAUST INDICATION

- If M/C solenoid does not click with ignition "ON" and "TEST" term. grounded, and there is no code 23 or 54, check for sticking M/C solenoid.

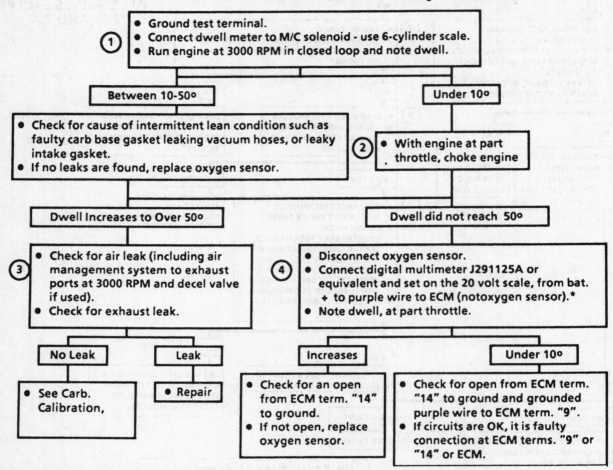

①
- Ground test terminal.
- Connect dwell meter to M/C solenoid - use 6-cylinder scale.
- Run engine at 3000 RPM in closed loop and note dwell.

Between 10-50°

- Check for cause of intermittent lean condition such as faulty carb base gasket leaking vacuum hoses, or leaky intake gasket.
- If no leaks are found, replace oxygen sensor.

Under 10°

②
- With engine at part throttle, choke engine

Dwell Increases to Over 50°

Dwell did not reach 50°

③
- Check for air leak (including air management system to exhaust ports at 3000 RPM and decel valve if used).
- Check for exhaust leak.

④
- Disconnect oxygen sensor.
- Connect digital multimeter J291125A or equivalent and set on the 20 volt scale, from bat. + to purple wire to ECM (notoxygen sensor).*
- Note dwell, at part throttle.

No Leak

- See Carb. Calibration,

Leak

- Repair

Increases

- Check for an open from ECM term. "14" to ground.
- If not open, replace oxygen sensor.

Under 10°

- Check for open from ECM term. "14" to ground and grounded purple wire to ECM term. "9".
- If circuits are OK, it is faulty connection at ECM terms. "9" or "14" or ECM.

*Do not use an ordinary voltmeter or jumper in place of the digital voltmeter because they have too little resistance. A voltage of 1.0V to 1.7V (such as a flashlight battery) can be connected with the Positive terminal to the purple wire and the negative terminal to ground as a jumper. If the polarity is reversed, it won't work.

If chart does not resolve problem, see Driveability Symptoms, Section "B".

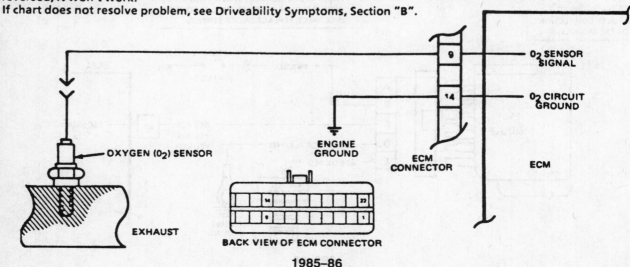

OXYGEN (O₂) SENSOR

EXHAUST

ENGINE GROUND

BACK VIEW OF ECM CONNECTOR

9 — O₂ SENSOR SIGNAL

14 — O₂ CIRCUIT GROUND

ECM CONNECTOR

ECM

1985–86

CODE 44
LEAN EXHAUST INDICATED
ALL ENGINES

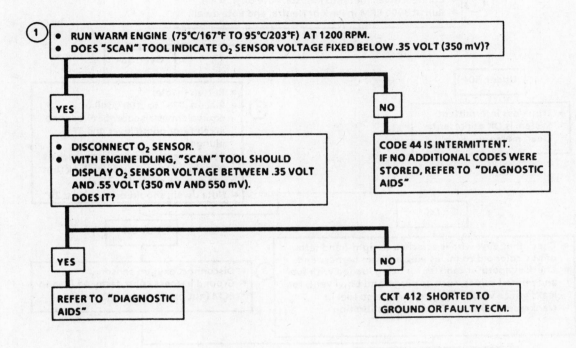

①
- RUN WARM ENGINE (75°C/167°F TO 95°C/203°F) AT 1200 RPM.
- DOES "SCAN" TOOL INDICATE O_2 SENSOR VOLTAGE FIXED BELOW .35 VOLT (350 mV)?

YES
- DISCONNECT O_2 SENSOR.
- WITH ENGINE IDLING, "SCAN" TOOL SHOULD DISPLAY O_2 SENSOR VOLTAGE BETWEEN .35 VOLT AND .55 VOLT (350 mV AND 550 mV). DOES IT?

NO
CODE 44 IS INTERMITTENT. IF NO ADDITIONAL CODES WERE STORED, REFER TO "DIAGNOSTIC AIDS"

YES
REFER TO "DIAGNOSTIC AIDS"

NO
CKT 412 SHORTED TO GROUND OR FAULTY ECM.

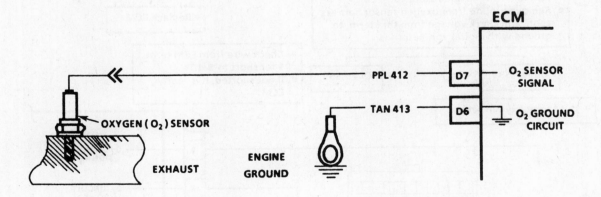

ECM

OXYGEN (O_2) SENSOR

EXHAUST

ENGINE GROUND

PPL 412 — D7 — O_2 SENSOR SIGNAL

TAN 413 — D6 — O_2 GROUND CIRCUIT

1987–90

CODE 45
RICH EXHAUST INDICATION

If M/C solenoid does not click with ign. "ON" and 'TEST' term. grounded, and there is no Code 23 or 54, check for sticking M/C solenoid.

If Code 54 is present, go to Chart 54 first.

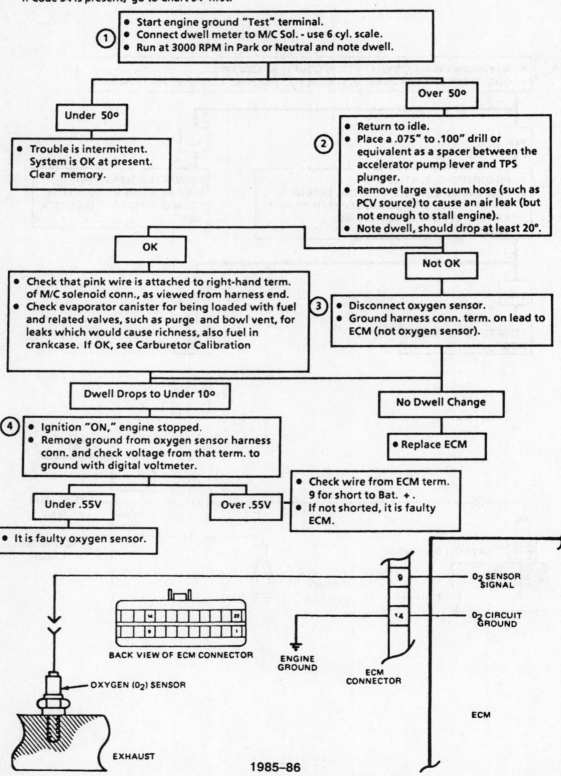

1
- Start engine ground "Test" terminal.
- Connect dwell meter to M/C Sol. - use 6 cyl. scale.
- Run at 3000 RPM in Park or Neutral and note dwell.

Under 50°
- Trouble is intermittent. System is OK at present. Clear memory.

Over 50°

2
- Return to idle.
- Place a .075" to .100" drill or equivalent as a spacer between the accelerator pump lever and TPS plunger.
- Remove large vacuum hose (such as PCV source) to cause an air leak (but not enough to stall engine).
- Note dwell, should drop at least 20°.

OK
- Check that pink wire is attached to right-hand term. of M/C solenoid conn., as viewed from harness end.
- Check evaporator canister for being loaded with fuel and related valves, such as purge and bowl vent, for leaks which would cause richness, also fuel in crankcase. If OK, see Carburetor Calibration

Not OK

3
- Disconnect oxygen sensor.
- Ground harness conn. term. on lead to ECM (not oxygen sensor).

Dwell Drops to Under 10°

4
- Ignition "ON," engine stopped.
- Remove ground from oxygen sensor harness conn. and check voltage from that term. to ground with digital voltmeter.

No Dwell Change
- Replace ECM

Under .55V
- It is faulty oxygen sensor.

Over .55V
- Check wire from ECM term. 9 for short to Bat. +.
- If not shorted, it is faulty ECM.

BACK VIEW OF ECM CONNECTOR

OXYGEN (0₂) SENSOR

ENGINE GROUND

ECM CONNECTOR

O₂ SENSOR SIGNAL

O₂ CIRCUIT GROUND

9

14

ECM

EXHAUST

1985-86

CODE 45
RICH EXHAUST INDICATED
ALL ENGINES

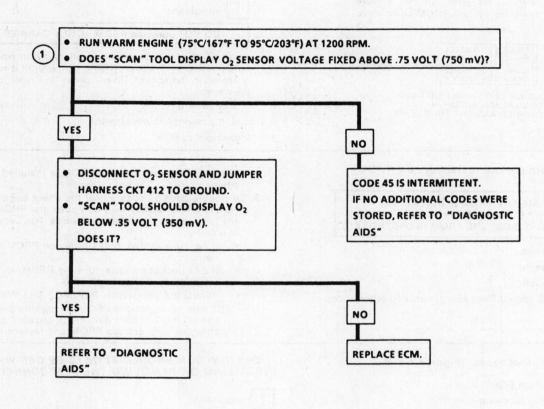

①
- RUN WARM ENGINE (75°C/167°F TO 95°C/203°F) AT 1200 RPM.
- DOES "SCAN" TOOL DISPLAY O₂ SENSOR VOLTAGE FIXED ABOVE .75 VOLT (750 mV)?

YES
- DISCONNECT O₂ SENSOR AND JUMPER HARNESS CKT 412 TO GROUND.
- "SCAN" TOOL SHOULD DISPLAY O₂ BELOW .35 VOLT (350 mV). DOES IT?

NO
CODE 45 IS INTERMITTENT. IF NO ADDITIONAL CODES WERE STORED, REFER TO "DIAGNOSTIC AIDS"

YES
REFER TO "DIAGNOSTIC AIDS"

NO
REPLACE ECM.

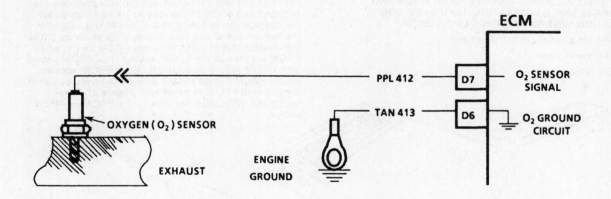

ECM

PPL 412 — D7 — O₂ SENSOR SIGNAL

TAN 413 — D6 — O₂ GROUND CIRCUIT

OXYGEN (O₂) SENSOR

EXHAUST

ENGINE GROUND

1987-90

CODE 51
PROM PROBLEM

Check that all pins are fully inserted in the socket. If OK, replace PROM and recheck, if problem not corrected, replace ECM.

Inspect (Figure 3)

For correct indexing of reference end of the PROM carrier and carefully set aside. Do not remove PROM from carrier to confirm PROM correctness.

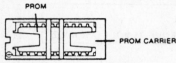

PROM

PROM CARRIER

NOTCH IN PROM REFERENCED TO SMALLER NOTCH IN CARRIER AND THE PIN #1 END.

Figure 3

Install or Connect (Figures 1 and 3)

1. PROM in PROM socket

Important

' DO NOT press on PROM - ONLY CARRIER.

Small notch of carrier should be aligned with small notch in socket. Press on PROM carrier until it is firmly seated in the socket. Do not press on PROM; only the carrier.

2. Access cover on ECM
3. ECM in passenger compartment
4. Connectors to ECM

Important (Before installing new PROM)

ANYTIME THE PROM IS INSTALLED BACKWARDS AND THE IGNITION SWITCH IS TURNED ON, THE PROM IS DESTROYED.

Functional Check

1. Turn ignition on
2. Enter diagnostics
   A. Code 12 should flash four times. (No other codes present.) This indicates the PROM is installed properly.
   B. If trouble code 51 occurs or if the check engine light is on constantly with no codes, the PROM is not fully seated. installed backwards, has bent pins, or is faulty.
   - If not fully seated, press firmly on PROM carrier.
   - If it is necessary to remove the PROM, follow instructions in steps "A" & "B."
   - If installed backwards, REPLACE THE PROM.
   - If pins bend, remove PROM, straighten pins, and reinstall. If bent pins break or crack during straightening, discard PROM and replace it.

Remove or Disconnect (Figures 1 and 2)

1. Connectors from ECM
2. ECM mounting hardware

Important

ELECTRONIC CONTROL MODULE (ECM) MOUNTING HARDWARE NOT ILLUSTRATED. HARDWARE CONFIGURATION WILL VARY WITH CAR DIVISION.

3. ECM from passenger compartment
4. ECM access cover
5. PROM removal

THE IGNITION SHOULD ALWAYS BE OFF WHEN INSTALLING OR REMOVING THE ECM CONNECTORS

Important

Using the rocker-type PROM removal tool, engage one end of the PROM carrier with the hook end of the tool. Press on the vertical bar end of the tool and rock the engaged end of the PROM carrier up as far as possible. Engage the opposite end of the PROM carrier in the same manner and rock this end up as far as possible. Repeat this process until the PROM carrier and PROM are free of the PROM socket. The PROM carrier with PROM in it should lift off of the PROM socket easily. PROM carrier should only be removed by using the pictured PROM removal tool (Figure 2). Other methods could cause damage to the PROM or PROM socket.

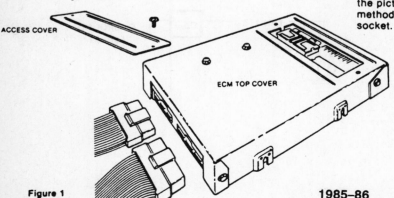

ACCESS COVER

ECM TOP COVER

Figure 1

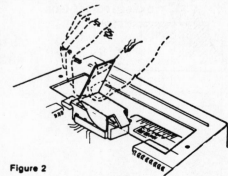

1985–86   Figure 2

CODE 54

FUEL PUMP CIRCUIT
(LOW VOLTAGE)

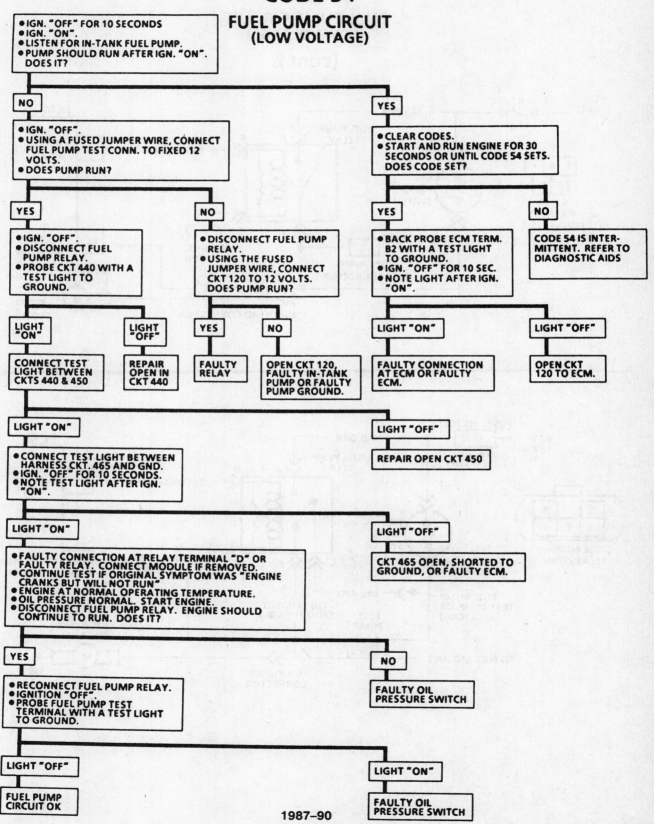

1987-90

CODE 54

FUEL PUMP CIRCUIT
(LOW VOLTAGE)

(cont.)

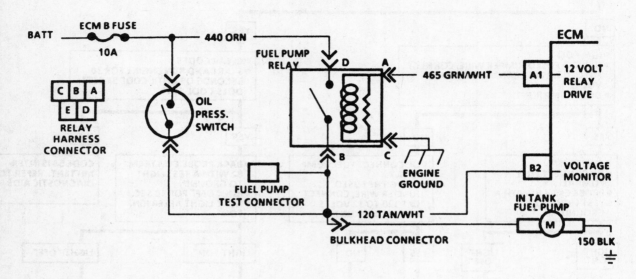

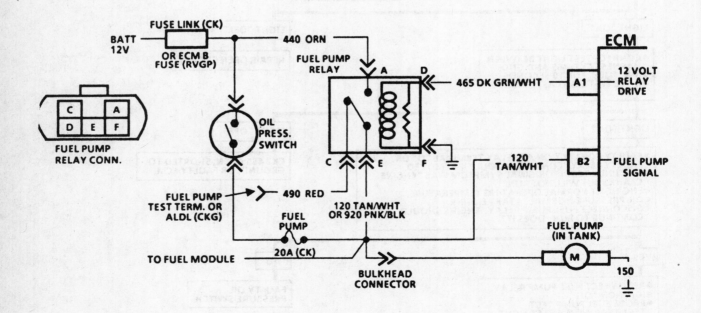

1987-90

CODE 54

CONSTANT HIGH VOLTAGE FROM M/C SOLENOID-TO-ECM

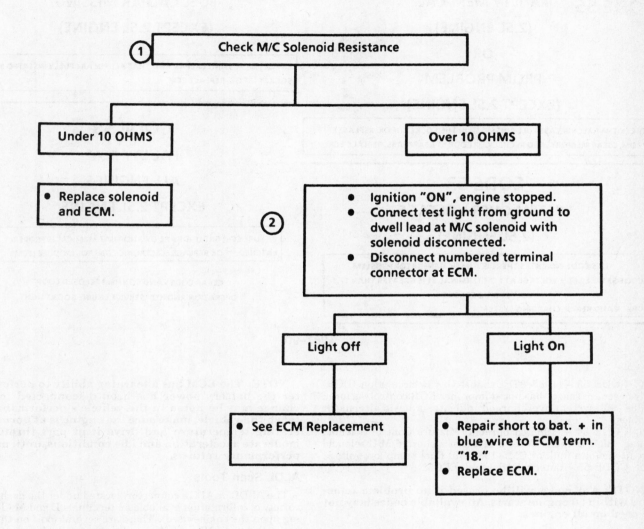

① **Check M/C Solenoid Resistance**

Under 10 OHMS

- **Replace solenoid and ECM.**

Over 10 OHMS

②
- **Ignition "ON", engine stopped.**
- **Connect test light from ground to dwell lead at M/C solenoid with solenoid disconnected.**
- **Disconnect numbered terminal connector at ECM.**

Light Off

- **See ECM Replacement**

Light On

- **Repair short to bat. + in blue wire to ECM term. "18."**
- **Replace ECM.**

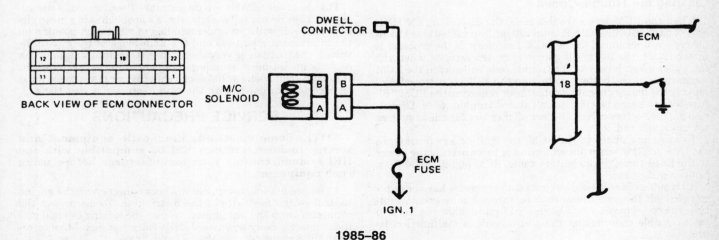

BACK VIEW OF ECM CONNECTOR

M/C SOLENOID

DWELL CONNECTOR

ECM FUSE

IGN. 1

ECM

1985–86

CODE 51
CODE 52
CODE 53
CODE 55

CODE 51

FAULTY MEM-CAL

(2.5L ENGINE)

OR

PROM PROBLEM

(EXCEPT 2.5L ENGINE)

CHECK THAT ALL PINS ARE FULLY INSERTED IN THE SOCKET. IF OK, REPLACE PROM, CLEAR MEMORY, AND RECHECK. IF CODE 51 REAPPEARS, REPLACE ECM.

CODE 53

SYSTEM OVER VOLTAGE

(2.5L ENGINE)

THIS CODE INDICATES THERE IS A BASIC GENERATOR PROBLEM.
- CODE 53 WILL SET IF VOLTAGE AT ECM TERMINAL B1 IS GREATER THAN 17.1 VOLTS FOR 2 SECONDS.
- CHECK AND REPAIR CHARGING SYSTEM.

CODE 52

FUEL CALPAK MISSING

(EXCEPT 2.5L ENGINE)

CHECK FOR MISSING CALPAK AND THAT ALL PIN ARE FULLY INSERTED IN THE SOCKET - IF OK, REPLACE ECM.

CODE 55

FAULTY ECM

ALL ENGINES

EXCEPT 2.5L ENGINE

BE SURE ECM GROUNDS ARE OK AND THAT MEM-CAL IS PROPERLY LATCHED. IF OK REPLACE ELECTRONIC CONTROL MODULE (ECM).

CLEAR CODES AND CONFIRM "CLOSED LOOP" OPERATION AND NO "SERVICE ENGINE SOON" LIGHT.

1987–90

20. CODE 53 – (1985–87) Exhaust Gas Recirculation (EGR) valve vacuum sensor has noted improper EGR control vacuum. (1988–90) system overcharged indicates a basic alternator problem.

21. CODE 54 – (1985 carbureted) Mixture Control Solenoid voltage high at the ECM as a result of a shorted M/C solenoid circuit and/or a faulty ECM. (1986–90) Fuel pump low voltage

22. CODE 55 – (later models) faulty ECM

NOTE: Any codes will be erased if no problem re-occurs within 50 engine starts. All available codes may not be used on all engines.

Clearing the Trouble Codes

When the ECM sets a trouble code, the SERVICE ENGINE SOON or CHECK ENGINE lamp will be illuminated and a trouble code will be stored in the ECM's memory. If the problem is intermittent, the light will go out after ten seconds when the fault goes away, however, the trouble code will stay in the ECM memory until the battery voltage to the ECM is removed. Removing the battery negative cable for or removing the ECM "B" fuse for ten seconds will clear all stored trouble codes. Disconnecting the battery cable will clear all memory functions such as the clock and radio.

To prevent damage to the ECM, the ignition key must be in the OFF position when disconnecting or reconnecting the power to the ECM through the battery cable, ECM pigtail, ECM fuse, jumper cables, etc.

All trouble codes should be cleared after repairs have been accomplished. In some cases, such as through a diagnostic routine, the codes may have to be cleared first to allow the ECM to set a trouble code during the test, should a malfunction be present.

NOTE: The ECM has a learning ability to perform after the battery power has been disconnected to it. A change may be noted in the vehicle's performance. To teach the vehicle, make sure the engine is at normal operating temperature and drive it at part throttle, at moderate acceleration and idle conditions, until normal performance returns.

ALDL Scan Tools

The ALDL or ALCL connector, located under the dash, has a variety of information available on terminals **E** and **M** (depending upon the engine used). There are several tools on the market, called "SCAN" units for reading the available information.

The use of the SCAN tools do not make the diagnostics unnecessary. They do not tell exactly where a problem is in a given circuit. However, with an understanding of what each position on the instrument measures and the knowledge of the circuit involved, the tool can be very useful in getting information which could be more time consuming to get with outer test equipment. It must be emphasized that each type scanner instrument must be used in accordance with the manufacturers instructions.

SERVICE PRECAUTIONS

NOTE: Some electronic diagnostic equipment and service tachometers may not be compatible with the HEI system, consult your manufacturer before using such equipment.

1. Before making compression checks, disconnect the engine control switch feed wire at the distributor. To disconnect the connector from the distributor, release the locking tab and pull the connector body downward; NEVER use a metal tool to release the locking tab, for the tab may break off.

2. The distributor needs no periodic lubrication, for the engine lubrication system lubricates the lower bushing and an oil reservoir lubricates the upper bushing.

3. The tachometer (TACH) terminal is located next to the engine control switch (BAT) connector on the distributor cap.

NOTE: NEVER allow the tachometer terminal to touch ground, for damage to the module, ECM and/or the coil may result.

4. Since there are no points in the ignition system, NO manual dwell adjustment is necessary or possible.

5. The material used in the construction of the spark plug wires is very soft and pliable. These wires can withstand high heat and carry a higher voltage. It is very important that the wires be routed correctly, for they are highly susceptible to scuffing and/or cutting.

NOTE: When removing a spark plug wire, be sure to twist the boot and then pull on it to remove it. Do NOT pull on the wire to remove it.

Ignition Timing

NOTE: The following procedure requires the use of a distributor wrench and a timing light. When using a timing light, be sure to consult the manufacturer's recommendations for installation and usage.

ADJUSTMENT

1. Refer to the ignition timing specifications, listed on the Vehicle Emissions Control Information label, located on the radiator support panel and follow the instructions.

2. Using a timing light, connect it to the engine by performing the following procedures:

    a. If using a non-inductive type, connect an adapter between the No. 1 spark plug and the spark plug wire; DO NOT puncture the spark plug wire, for this will cause a voltage leak.

    b. If using an inductive type, clamp it around the No. 1 spark plug wire.

    c. If using a magnetic type, place the probe in the connector located near the damper pulley; this type must be used with special electronic timing equipment.

3. At the 4-terminal EST connector of the distributor, disconnect the black/tan wire connector, about 152mm (6 in.) from the distributor.

4. Start the engine aim the timing light at the timing mark on the damper pulley; a line on the damper pulley will align the timing mark. If necessary (to adjust the timing), loosen the distributor holddown clamp and slowly turn the distributor slightly to align the marks. When the alignment is correct, tighten the holddown bolt.

5. Turn the engine Off, remove the timing light and reconnect the black/tan wire (if disconnected) of the distributor.

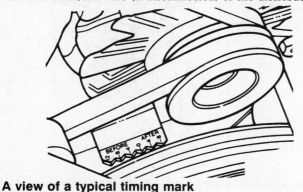

A view of a typical timing mark

Valve Lash

The engines described in this book utilize a hydraulic valve lifter system to obtain zero lash. No adjustment is necessary. An initial adjustment is required anytime that the lifters are removed or the valve train is disturbed.

ADJUSTMENT

2.5L L4 Engine

1. Refer to the Rocker Arm Cover, Removal and Installation procedures in Section 3 and remove the rocker arm cover.

2. Rotate the crankshaft until the mark on the damper pulley aligns with the **0** mark on the timing plate and the No. 1 cylinder is on the compression stroke.

NOTE: To determine if the No. 1 cylinder is on the compression stroke, shake the rocker arms of the No. 1 cylinder, if they move the cylinder is on the compression stroke, if they don't move the cylinder is on the exhaust stroke. If the cylinder is on the exhaust stroke, it will be necessary to rotate the crankshaft one full revolution.

3. With the engine on the compression stroke, adjust the exhaust valves of cylinders No. 1 & 3 and the intake valves of cylinders No. 1 & 2.

4. To adjust the valves, torque the rocker arm studs to the specified torque:
- 1985–86: 20 ft. lbs. (28 Nm).
- 1987: 24 ft. lbs. (32 Nm).
- 1988–90: 22 ft. lbs. (30 Nm).

5. Rotate the crankshaft one complete revolution and align the mark on the damper pulley with the **0** mark on the timing plate.

6. With the engine on the compression stroke, adjust the exhaust valves of cylinders No. 2 & 4 and the intake valves of cylinders No. 3 & 4 to the specified torque.

7. To complete the installation, use new valve cover gaskets and install the rocker arm cover.

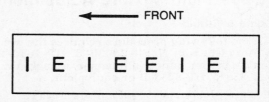

Valve arrangement of the 2.5L, 4-cyl Pontiac built engine (E-exhaust; I-intake)

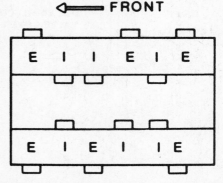

Valve arrangement of the 4.3L, V6 Chevrolet built engine (E-exhaust; I-intake)

4.3L V6 Engine

1. Refer to the Rocker Arm Cover, Removal and Installation procedures in Section 3 and remove the rocker arm cover.

2. Rotate the crankshaft until the mark on the damper pulley aligns with the **0** mark on the timing plate and the No. 1 cylinder is on the compression stroke.

NOTE: To determine if the No. 1 cylinder is on the compression stroke, shake the rocker arms of the No. 1 cylinder, if they move the cylinder is on the compression stroke, if they don't move the cylinder is on the exhaust stroke. If the cylinder is on the exhaust stroke, it will be necessary to rotate the crankshaft one full revolution.

3. With the engine on the compression stroke, adjust the exhaust valves of cylinders No. 1, 5 & 6 and the intake valves of cylinders No. 1, 2 & 3.

4. To adjust the valves, perform the following procedures:

   a. Back out the adjusting nut until lash can be felt at the pushrod.

   b. While rotating the pushrod, turn the adjusting nut inward until all of the lash is removed.

   c. When the play has disappeared, turn the adjusting nut inward one additional turns.

5. Rotate the crankshaft one complete revolution and align the mark on the damper pulley with the **0** mark on the timing plate.

6. With the engine on the compression stroke, adjust the exhaust valves of cylinders No. 2, 3 & 4 and the intake valves of cylinders No. 4, 5 & 6.

7. To adjust the valves, perform the following procedures:

   a. Back out the adjusting nut until lash can be felt at the pushrod.

   b. While rotating the pushrod, turn the adjusting nut inward until all of the lash is removed.

   c. When the play has disappeared, turn the adjusting nut inward one additional turns.

8. To complete the installation, use new valve cover gaskets and install the rocker arm cover.

Idle Speed and Mixture Adjustments

4.3L Engine w/4-bbl.

NOTE: The following procedure requires the use of a dwell meter, GM tool No. J–29030–B, BT–7610–B or equivalent, a center punch, a hammer, a hacksaw, GM tool No. J–33815, BT–8253–B or equivalent.

The idle air bleed valve and the idle mixture needles are sealed with hardened plugs, to protect the factory settings. These settings are not to be tampered with, except for, cleaning, part replacement or if the carburetor is the cause of trouble.

1. If necessary to remove the idle air bleed cover, perform the following procedures:

   a. Remove the air cleaner and the gasket.

   b. Using masking tape or equivalent, cover the internal bowl vents and the air inlets to the idle air bleed valve.

   c. Carefully drill out the idle air bleed cover pop rivet heads.

   d. Using a drift and a small hammer, drive out the remaining portions of the rivet shanks.

   e. Remove/discard the idle air bleed cover and the masking tape used to cover the vents and the air passages.

2. To set the idle air bleed valve, perform the following procedures:

   a. Using the GM tool No. J–33815, BT–8253–B or equivalent, position it in the throttle side D-shaped hole in the air horn casting. The tool's upper end should be positioned over the open cavity next to the idle air bleed valve.

   b. Holding the gauging tool down slightly, so that the solenoid plunger is against the solenoid stop, adjust the idle air bleed valve so that the gauging tool will pivot over and just contact the top of the valve.

3. Using a new idle air bleed cover and pop rivets, install the cover to the air horn casting.

4. If necessary to adjust the idle mixture needle screws, perform the following procedures to remove the hardened steel plugs:

   a. Refer to the Carburetor, Removal and Installation procedures in Section 5 and remove the carburetor from the engine.

   b. Invert the carburetor and drain the fuel from the float bowl.

   c. Position the carburetor, in the inverted position, in a holding fixture to gain access to the idle mixture needle plugs.

NOTE: When positioning the carburetor, be careful not to damage the linkage, the tubes and other parts protruding from the air horn.

   d. Using a hacksaw, make two parallel cuts into the throttle body; cut on each side of the locator points beneath the idle mixture needle plugs.

   e. Using a punch and a hammer, drive the casting segment toward the hardened plug, be sure to drive out the plug.

   f. Repeat this process for the other plug.

1. Tool contacting valve
2. Guide
3. Idle air bleed valve
4. Gaging tool—J-33815-2/BT8253B (1.756″ high)
5. Plunger against stop

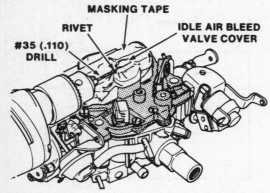

Removing the idle air bleed cover — 4.3L 4-bbl carburetor

MASKING TAPE
RIVET
#35 (.110) DRILL
IDLE AIR BLEED VALVE COVER

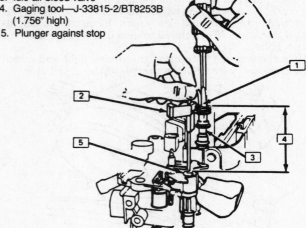

Positioning the idle air valve — 4.3L 4-bbl carburetor

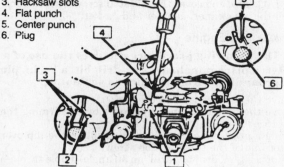

1. Recessed idle mixture needle and plug locations
2. Locator points
3. Hacksaw slots
4. Flat punch
5. Center punch
6. Plug

Removing the idle needle plugs — 4.3L 4-bbl carburetor

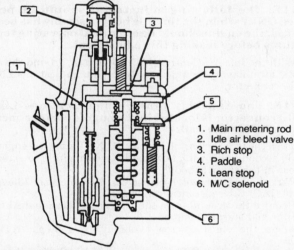

1. Main metering rod
2. Idle air bleed valve
3. Rich stop
4. Paddle
5. Lean stop
6. M/C solenoid

Cross-sectional view of the mixture control solenoid — 4.3L 4-bbl carburetor

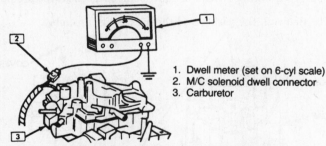

1. Dwell meter (set on 6-cyl scale)
2. M/C solenoid dwell connector
3. Carburetor

Connecting the dwell meter to the M/C electrical connector — 4.3L 4-bbl carburetor

5. Using the GM tool No. J–29030–B, BT–7610–B or equivalent, turn the idle mixture needle screws clockwise until they are lightly seated, then turn them counterclockwise 3 turns.

6. Using a new carburetor-to-intake manifold gasket, install the carburetor onto the engine, DO NOT install the air cleaner or gasket.

7. Disconnect the vacuum hose-to-canister purge valve and plug it. At the carburetor, disconnect the electrical connector from the Mixture Control (M/C) solenoid.

8. Using a dwell meter, connect it to the M/C solenoid electrical connector and set it on the 6-cyl. scale.

9. Start the engine and allow it to reach normal operating temperatures.

10. Place the transmission in Drive (AT) or Neutral (MT), then adjust the idle mixture needle screws, in ⅛ turn increments, until the dwell reading varies within the 25–35° range (be as close to 30° as possible). If the reading is too low, turn the idle mixture needle screws counterclockwise. If the reading is too high, turn the idle mixture needle screws clockwise.

NOTE: Be sure to allow the engine to stabilize between adjustments.

11. After the adjustment is complete, seal the idle mixture screw openings with silicone sealant, this will prevent any further adjustment of the idle mixture screws and prevent any fuel vapor loss.

12. Adjust the curb idle speed, if necessary.

13. Check and/or adjust the fast idle speed by referring information on the Vehicle Emission Control Information Label in the engine compartment.

1985–87 2.5L EFI Engine

NOTE: The following procedures require the use a tachometer, GM tool No. J–33047 or equivalent, GM Torx® Bit No. 20, silicone sealant, a $^5/_{32}$ in. drill bit, a prick punch and a $^1/_{16}$ in. pin punch.

The throttle stop screw, used in regulating the minimum idle speed, is adjusted at the factory and is not necessary to perform. This adjustment should be performed ONLY when the throttle body has been replaced.

NOTE: The replacement of the complete throttle body assembly will have the minimum idle adjusted at the factory.

1. Remove the air cleaner and the gasket. Be sure to plug the THERMAC vacuum port (air cleaner vacuum line-to-throttle body) on the throttle body.

2. Remove the throttle valve cable from the throttle control bracket to provide access to the minimum air adjustment screw.

3. Using the manufacturer's instructions, connect a tachometer to the engine.

4. Remove the electrical connector from the Idle Air Control (IAC) valve, located on the throttle body.

5. To remove the throttle stop screw cover, perform the following procedures:

 a. Using a prick punch, mark the housing at the top over the center line of the throttle stop screw.

 b. Using a $^5/_{32}$ in. drill bit, drill (on an angle) a hole through the casting to the hardened cover.

 c. Using a $^1/_{16}$ in. pin punch, place it through the hole and drive out the cover to expose the throttle stop screw.

6. Place the transmission in Park (AT) or Neutral (MT), start the engine and allow the idle speed to stabilize.

7. Using the GM tool No. J–33047 or equivalent, install it into the idle air passage of the throttle body; be sure that the tool is fully seated in the opening and no air leaks exist.

8. Using the GM Torx® Bit No. 20, turn the throttle stop screw until the engine speed is 475–525 rpm (AT in Park or Neutral) or 750–800 rpm (MT in Neutral).

9. With the idle speed adjusted, stop the engine, remove the tool No. J–33047 from the throttle body.

10. Reconnect the Idle Air Control (IAC) electrical connector.

11. Using silicone sealant or equivalent, cover the throttle stop screw.

12. Reinstall the gasket and the air cleaner assembly.

1988–90 2.5L
1988–90 4.3L with EFI

Before performing this check, there should be no codes displayed, idle air control system has been checked and ignition timing is correct.

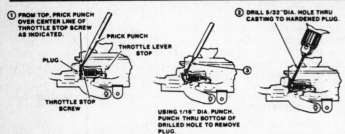

Removing the throttle stop screw cover from the throttle body

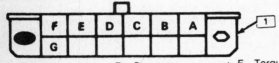

A. Ground
B. Diagnostic terminal
C. AIR pump, if used
D. Computer command control lamp
E. Serial data
F. Torque converter clutch, if used
G. Fuel pump (EFI)

ALCL connector terminal identification

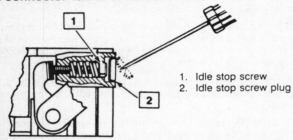

1. Idle stop screw
2. Idle stop screw plug

Removing the throttle stop screw cover from the throttle body — late model 2.5L engine

1. **CONTROLLED IDLE SPEED CHECK:** set the parking brake and block the wheels.
2. Connect a SCAN tool to the ALDL connector with the tool in the OPEN MODE.
3. Start the engine and bring it to normal operating temperature.
4. Check for correct state of Park/Neutral switch on the SCAN tool.
5. If the idle and IAC counts are not within specifications:
- 2.5L MT in **NEUTRAL** 800 rpm, 5–20 IAC valve counts and in the closed loop.
- 2.5L AT in **DRIVE** 750 rpm, 5–20 IAC valve counts and in the closed loop.
- 4.3L MT in **NEUTRAL** 500–550 rpm, 2–12 IAC valve counts and in the closed loop.
- 4.3L AT in **DRIVE** 500–550 rpm, 10–25 IAC valve counts and in the closed loop.
6. **MINIMUM IDLE AIR RATE CHECK:** check the controlled idle speed and perform the idle air control system check first.
7. With the IAC valve connected, ground the diagnostic **A** and **B** terminals of the ALDL connector.
8. Turn ON the ignition with engine NOT running, wait for ten seconds to allow the IAC valve to stabilize. Remove the ground from the ALDL and disconnect the IAC valve.
9. Connect the SCAN tool to the ALDL connector and place in the open mode. If a SCAN tool is not available, connect a tachometer to the engine.
10. Start the engine and allow to stabilize.
11. Check the rpm using the specifications.
12. If the minimum idle rate is not within specifications perform the following:
a. Remove the idle stop screw plug by piercing it with an awl, then apply leverage to remove the plug.

b. Adjust the screw to the specified rpm.
c. Turn the engine OFF, disconnect the SCAN tool, reconnect the IAC valve and cover the idle stop screw with silicone
13. Install the air cleaner, adapter and gasket.

1985–87 4.3L EFI Engine

NOTE: The following procedure requires the use of a tachometer, a prick punch, a $5/32$ in. drill bit, a $1/16$ in. pin punch, a grounding wire and silicone sealant.

1. Remove the air cleaner and the gasket.
2. Remove the throttle stop screw cover by performing the following procedures:
a. Using a prick punch, mark the housing at the top over the center line of the throttle stop screw.
b. Using a $5/32$ in. drill bit, drill (on an angle) a hole through the casting to the hardened cover.
c. Using a $1/16$ in. pin punch, place it through the hole and drive out the cover to expose the throttle stop screw.

NOTE: The following adjustment should be performed ONLY when the throttle body assembly has been replaced; the engine should be at normal operating temperatures before making this adjustment.

3. With the Idle Air Control (IAC) connected, ground the diagnostic terminal of the Assembly Line Communications Link (ALCL) connector.

NOTE: The Assembly Line Communications Link (ALCL) connector is located in the engine compartment on the left side firewall.

4. Turn the ignition switch On but DO NOT start the engine. Wait 30 seconds, this will allow the IAC valve pintle to extend and seat in the throttle body.
5. With the ignition switch turned On, disconnect the Idle Air Control (IAC) valve electrical connector.
6. Remove the ground from the Diagnostic Terminal ALCL connector and start the engine.
7. Adjust the idle stop screw to obtain 400–450 rpm (AT in Drive).
8. Turn the ignition Off and reconnect the IAC valve electrical connector.
9. Using silicone sealant or equivalent, cover the throttle stop screw.
10. Reinstall the gasket and the air cleaner assembly.

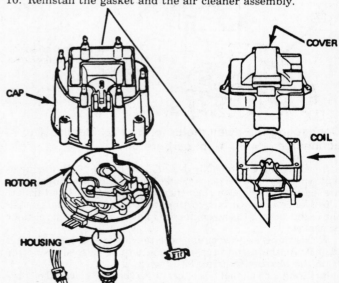

Removing the internal ignition coil — 4.3L 4-bbl engine

Engine and Engine Overhaul

3

QUICK REFERENCE INDEX

GENERAL INDEX

ENGINE ELECTRICAL

The engine electrical system can be broken down into three separate and distinct systems:
1. The ignition system.
2. The charging system.
3. The starting system.

BATTERY AND STARTING SYSTEM

Basic Operating Principles

The battery is the first link in the chain of mechanisms which work together to provide cranking of the automobile engine. In most modern vans, the battery is a lead/acid electrochemical device consisting of six 2v subsections connected in series so the unit is capable of producing approximately 12v of electrical pressure. Each subsection, or cell, consists of a series of positive and negative plates held a short distance apart in a solution of sulfuric acid and water. The two types of plates are of dissimilar metals. This causes a chemical reaction to be set up, and it is this reaction which produces current flow from the battery when its positive and negative terminals are connected to an electrical appliance such as a lamp or motor. The continued transfer of electrons would eventually convert the sulfuric acid in the electrolyte to water, and make the two plates identical in chemical composition. As electrical energy is removed from the battery, its voltage output tends to drop. Thus, measuring battery voltage and battery electrolyte composition are two ways of checking the ability of the unit to supply power. During the starting of the engine, electrical energy is removed from the battery. However, if the charging circuit is in good condition and the operating conditions are normal, the power removed from the battery will be replaced by the generator (or alternator) which will force electrons back through the battery, reversing the normal flow, and restoring the battery to its original chemical state.

The battery and starting motor are linked by very heavy electrical cables designed to minimize resistance to the flow of current. Generally, the major power supply cable that leaves the battery goes directly to the starter, while other electrical system needs are supplied by a smaller cable. During starter operation, power flows from the battery to the starter and is grounded through the van's frame and the battery's negative ground strap.

The starting motor is a specially designed, direct current electric motor capable of producing a very great amount of power for its size. One thing that allows the motor to produce a great deal of power is its tremendous rotating speed. It drives the engine through a tiny pinion gear (attached to the starter's armature), which drives the very large flywheel ring gear at a greatly reduced speed. Another factor allowing it to produce so much power is that only intermittent operation is required of it. This, little allowance for air circulation is required, and the windings can be built into a very small space.

The starter solenoid is a magnetic device which employs the small current supplied by the starting switch circuit of the ignition switch. This magnetic action moves a plunger which mechanically engages the starter and electrically closes the heavy switch which connects it to the battery. The starting switch circuit consists of the starting switch contained within the ignition switch, a transmission neutral safety switch or clutch pedal switch, and the wiring necessary to connect these in series with the starter solenoid or relay.

A pinion, which is a small gear, is mounted to a one-way drive clutch. This clutch is splined to the starter armature shaft. When the ignition switch is moved to the **start** position, the solenoid plunger slides the pinion toward the flywheel ring gear via a collar and spring. If the teeth on the pinion and flywheel match properly, the pinion will engage the flywheel immediately. If the gear teeth butt one another, the spring will be com-

pressed and will force the gears to mesh as soon as the starter turns far enough to allow them to do so. As the solenoid plunger reaches the end of its travel, it closes the contacts that connect the battery and starter and then the engine is cranked.

As soon as the engine starts, the flywheel ring gear begins turning fast enough to drive the pinion at an extremely high rate of speed. At this point, the one-way clutch begins allowing the pinion to spin faster than the starter shaft so that the starter will not operate at excessive speed. When the ignition switch is released from the starter position, the solenoid is de-energized, and a spring contained within the solenoid assembly pulls the gear out of mesh and interrupts the current flow to the starter.

Some starter employ a separate relay, mounted away from the starter, to switch the motor and solenoid current on and off. The relay thus replaces the solenoid electrical switch, buy does not eliminate the need for a solenoid mounted on the starter used to mechanically engage the starter drive gears. The relay is used to reduce the amount of current the starting switch must carry.

THE CHARGING SYSTEM

Basic Operating Principles

The automobile charging system provides electrical power for operation of the vehicle's ignition and starting systems and all the electrical accessories. The battery services as an electrical surge or storage tank, storing (in chemical form) the energy originally produced by the engine driven generator. The system also provides a means of regulating generator output to protect the battery from being overcharged and to avoid excessive voltage to the accessories.

The storage battery is a chemical device incorporating parallel lead plates in a tank containing a sulfuric acid/water solution. Adjacent plates are slightly dissimilar, and the chemical reaction of the two dissimilar plates produces electrical energy when the battery is connected to a load such as the starter motor. The chemical reaction is reversible, so that when the generator is producing a voltage (electrical pressure) greater than that produced by the battery, electricity is forced into the battery, and the battery is returned to its fully charged state.

The vehicle's generator is driven mechanically, through V-belts, by the engine crankshaft. It consists of two coils of fine wire, one stationary (the stator), and one movable (the rotor). The rotor may also be known as the armature, and consists of fine wire wrapped around an iron core which is mounted on a shaft. The electricity which flows through the two coils of wire (provided initially by the battery in some cases) creates an intense magnetic field around both rotor and stator, and the interaction between the two fields creates voltage, allowing the generator to power the accessories and charge the battery.

There are two types of generators: the earlier is the direct current (DC) type. The current produced by the DC generator is generated in the armature and carried off the spinning armature by stationary brushes contacting the commutator. The commutator is a series of smooth metal contact plates on the end of the armature. The commutator is a series of smooth metal contact plates on the end of the armature. The commutator plates, which are separated from one another by a very short gap, are connected to the armature circuits so that current will flow in one directions only in the wires carrying the generator output. The generator stator consists of two stationary coils of wire which draw some of the output current of the generator to form a powerful magnetic field and create the interaction of fields which generates the voltage. The generator field is wired in series with the regulator.

Newer automobiles use alternating current generators or alternators, because they are more efficient, can be rotated at higher speeds, and have fewer brush problems. In an alternator, the field rotates while all the current produced passes only through the stator winding. The brushes bear against continuous slip rings rather than a commutator. This causes the current produced to periodically reverse the direction of its flow. Diodes (electrical one-way switches) block the flow of current from traveling in the wrong direction. A series of diodes is wired together to permit the alternating flow of the stator to be converted to a pulsating, but unidirectional flow at the alternator output. The alternator's field is wired in series with the voltage regulator.

The regulator consists of several circuits. Each circuit has a core, or magnetic coil of wire, which operates a switch. Each switch is connected to ground through one or more resistors. The coil of wire responds directly to system voltage. When the voltage reaches the required level, the magnetic field created by the winding of wire closes the switch and inserts a resistance into the generator field circuit, thus reducing the output. The contacts of the switch cycle open and close many times each second to precisely control voltage.

While alternators are self-limiting as far as maximum current is concerned, DC generators employ a current regulating circuit which responds directly to the total amount of current flowing through the generator circuit rather than to the output voltage. The current regulator is similar to the voltage regulator except that all system current must flow through the energizing coil on its way to the various accessories.

High Energy Ignition (HEI) System

The HEI system operates in basically the same manner as the conventional ignition system, with the exception of the type of switching device used. A toothed iron timer core is mounted on the distributor shaft which rotates inside of an electronic pole piece. The pole piece has internal teeth (corresponding to those on the timer core) which contains a permanent magnet and pick-up coil (not to be confused with the ignition coil). The pole piece senses the magnetic field of the timer core teeth and sends a signal to the ignition module which electronically controls the primary coil voltage. The ignition coil operates in basically the same manner as a conventional ignition coil (though the ignition coils DO NOT interchange).

NOTE: The HEI systems uses a capacitor within the distributor which is primarily used for radio interference purposes.

None of the electrical components used in the HEI systems are adjustable. If a component is found to be defective, it must be replaced.

PRECAUTIONS

Before troubleshooting the systems, it might be a good idea to take note of the following precautions:

Timing Light Use

Inductive pick-up timing lights are the best kind to use. Timing lights which connect between the spark plug and the spark plug wire occasionally give false readings.

Some engines incorporate a magnetic timing probe terminal (at the damper pulley) for use of special electronic timing equipment. Refer to the manufacturer's instructions when using this equipment.

Spark Plug Wires

The plug wires are of a different construction than conventional wires. When replacing them, make sure to use the correct wires, since conventional wires won't carry the higher voltage. Also, handle them carefully to avoid cracking or splitting them and never pierce them.

Tachometer Use

Not all tachometers will operate or indicate correctly. While some tachometers may give a reading, this does not necessarily mean the reading is correct. In addition, some tachometers connect differently than others. If you can't figure out whether or not your tachometer will work on your vehicle, check with the tachometer manufacturer.

System Testers

Instruments designed specifically for testing the HEI system are available from several tool manufacturers. Some of these will even test the module.

Ignition Coil

The ignition coil on the 2.5L engine, is located on the right rear side of the engine; on the 4.3L (1985) engine, it is located on top of the distributor cap; on the 4.3L (1986–90) engine, it is located on intake manifold to the right side of the distributor.

TESTING

NOTE: The following procedures require the use of an ohmmeter.

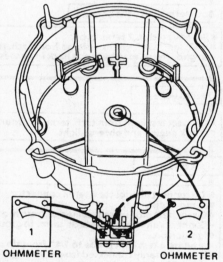

Testing the internal ignition coil — 4.3L 4-bbl engine

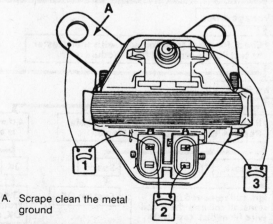

A. Scrape clean the metal ground

Testing the external ignition coil for the 2.5L and 4.3L TBI engine.

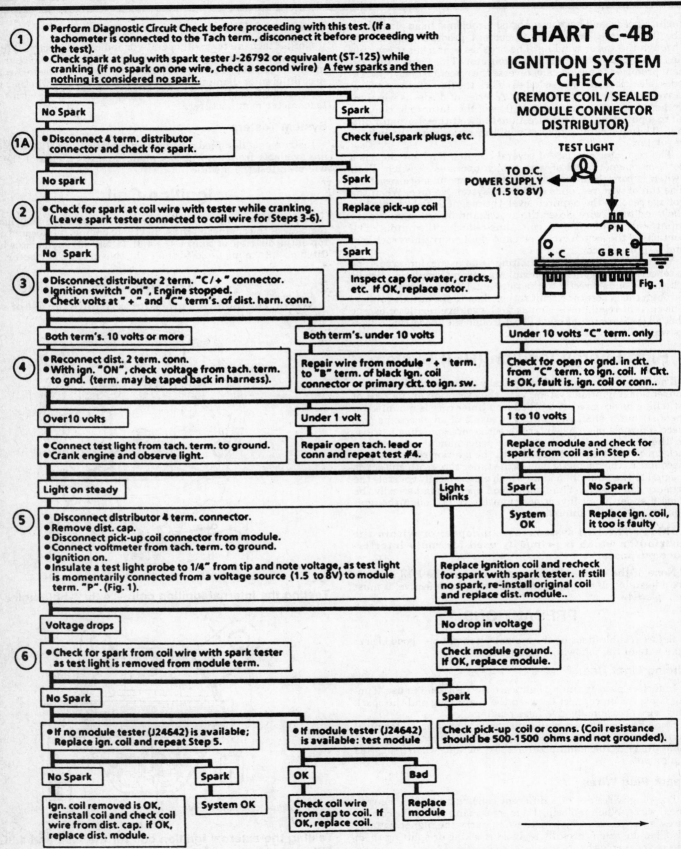

CHART C-4B

IGNITION SYSTEM CHECK

(REMOTE COIL / SEALED MODULE CONNECTOR DISTRIBUTOR)

(1)
- Perform Diagnostic Circuit Check before proceeding with this test. (If a tachometer is connected to the Tach term., disconnect it before proceeding with the test).
- Check spark at plug with spark tester J-26792 or equivalent (ST-125) while cranking (if no spark on one wire, check a second wire) A few sparks and then nothing is considered no spark.

No Spark	Spark

(1A)
- Disconnect 4 term. distributor connector and check for spark.

Check fuel, spark plugs, etc.

No spark	Spark

(2)
- Check for spark at coil wire with tester while cranking. (Leave spark tester connected to coil wire for Steps 3-6).

Replace pick-up coil

No Spark	Spark

(3)
- Disconnect distributor 2 term. "C/+" connector.
- Ignition switch "on", Engine stopped.
- Check volts at " + " and "C" term's. of dist. harn. conn.

Inspect cap for water, cracks, etc. If OK, replace rotor.

Both term's. 10 volts or more	Both term's. under 10 volts	Under 10 volts "C" term. only

(4)
- Reconnect dist. 2 term. conn.
- With ign. "ON", check voltage from tach. term. to gnd. (term. may be taped back in harness).

Repair wire from module " + " term. to "B" term. of black ign. coil connector or primary ckt. to ign. sw.

Check for open or gnd. in ckt. from "C" term. to ign. coil. If Ckt. is OK, fault is. ign. coil or conn..

Over 10 volts	Under 1 volt	1 to 10 volts

(5)
- Connect test light from tach. term. to ground.
- Crank engine and observe light.

Repair open tach. lead or conn and repeat test #4.

Replace module and check for spark from coil as in Step 6.

Light on steady		Light blinks	Spark	No Spark

(5)
- Disconnect distributor 4 term. connector.
- Remove dist. cap.
- Disconnect pick-up coil connector from module.
- Connect voltmeter from tach. term. to ground.
- Ignition on.
- Insulate a test light probe to 1/4" from tip and note voltage, as test light is momentarily connected from a voltage source (1.5 to 8V) to module term. "P". (Fig. 1).

System OK

Replace ign. coil, it too is faulty

Replace ignition coil and recheck for spark with spark tester. If still no spark, re-install original coil and replace dist. module..

Voltage drops	No drop in voltage

(6)
- Check for spark from coil wire with spark tester as test light is removed from module term.

Check module ground. If OK, replace module.

No Spark	Spark

- If no module tester (J24642) is available; Replace ign. coil and repeat Step 5.

- If module tester (J24642) is available: test module

Check pick-up coil or conns. (Coil resistance should be 500-1500 ohms and not grounded).

No Spark	Spark	OK	Bad

Ign. coil removed is OK, reinstall coil and check coil wire from dist. cap. if OK, replace dist. module.

System OK

Check coil wire from cap to coil. If OK, replace coil.

Replace module

Diagnosis chart and wiring schematic — 2.5L TBI engine

CHART C-4B

IGNITION SYSTEM CHECK
(REMOTE COIL / SEALED MODULE CONNECTOR DISTRIBUTOR)
(cont.)

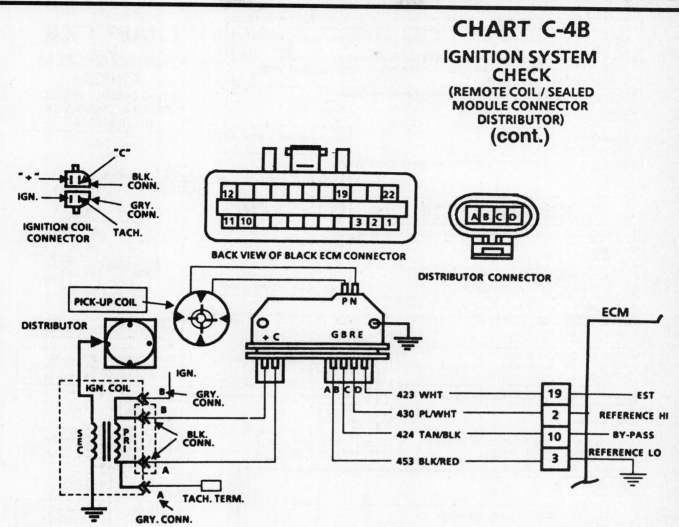

2.5L Engine

For this procedure, the ignition coil may be removed from the engine or simply remove the electrical connectors and test it on the engine.

1. Using an ohmmeter (on the high scale), connect the probes between the primary (low voltage) terminal and coil ground; the reading should be very high or infinity, if not, replace the coil.

2. Using an ohmmeter (on the low scale), connect the probes between both primary (low voltage) terminals; the reading should be very low or zero, if not, replace the coil.

3. Using an ohmmeter (on the high scale), connect the probes between a primary (low voltage) terminal and the secondary (high voltage) terminal; the reading should be high (not infinite), if not, replace the coil.

4.3L Carbureted Engine — 1985

To test the ignition coil, the distributor cap must be removed from the distributor.

1. Remove the electrical connector from the distributor cap and the distributor cap from the distributor. Place the distributor cap on a workbench in the inverted position.

2. Using an ohmmeter (on the low scale), connect the probes between the primary (low voltage) terminals; the reading should be low or nearly zero, if not, replace the coil.

3. Using an ohmmeter (on the high scale), connect the probes between a primary (low voltage) terminal and the secondary (center terminal or high voltage) terminal; the reading should be high (not infinite), if not, replace the coil.

4.3L TBI Engine — 1986–90

For this procedure, the ignition coil may be removed from the engine or simply remove the electrical connectors and test it on the engine.

1. Using an ohmmeter (on the high scale), connect the probes between the primary (low voltage) terminal and coil ground; the reading should be very high or infinity, if not, replace the coil.

2. Using an ohmmeter (on the low scale), connect the probes between both primary (low voltage) terminals; the reading should be very low or zero, if not, replace the coil.

3. Using an ohmmeter (on the high scale), connect the probes between a primary (low voltage) terminal and the secondary (high voltage) terminal; the reading should be high (not infinite), if not, replace the coil.

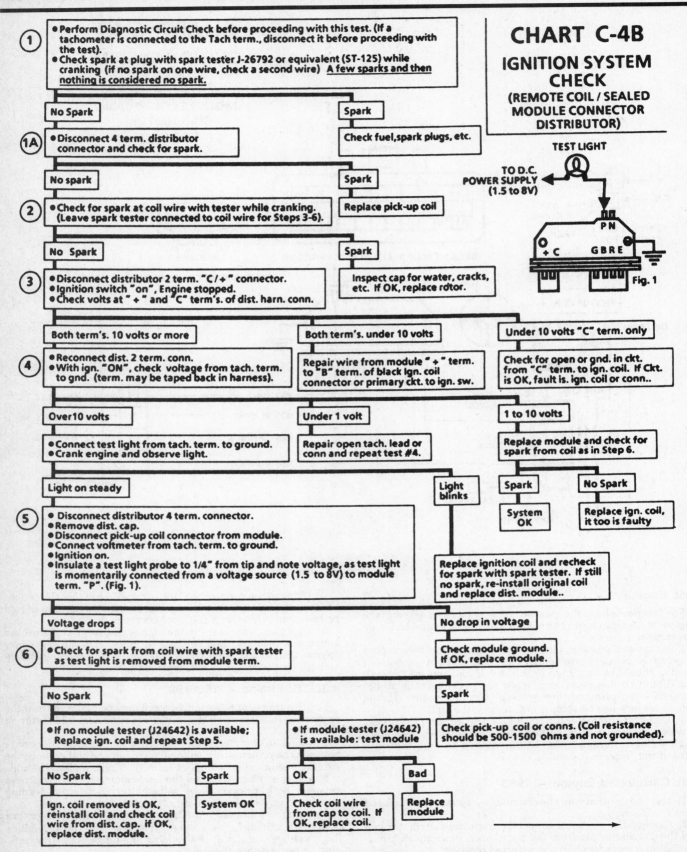

① • Perform Diagnostic Circuit Check before proceeding with this test. (If a tachometer is connected to the Tach term., disconnect it before proceeding with the test).
• Check spark at plug with spark tester J-26792 or equivalent (ST-125) while cranking (if no spark on one wire, check a second wire) A few sparks and then nothing is considered no spark.

CHART C-4B

IGNITION SYSTEM CHECK
(REMOTE COIL / SEALED MODULE CONNECTOR DISTRIBUTOR)

No Spark | Spark

①A • Disconnect 4 term. distributor connector and check for spark. | Check fuel, spark plugs, etc.

No spark | Spark

② • Check for spark at coil wire with tester while cranking. (Leave spark tester connected to coil wire for Steps 3-6). | Replace pick-up coil

No Spark | Spark

③ • Disconnect distributor 2 term. "C/+" connector.
• Ignition switch "on", Engine stopped.
• Check volts at " + " and "C" term's of dist. harn. conn. | Inspect cap for water, cracks, etc. If OK, replace rotor.

Both term's. 10 volts or more | Both term's. under 10 volts | Under 10 volts "C" term. only

④ • Reconnect dist. 2 term. conn.
• With ign. "ON", check voltage from tach. term. to gnd. (term. may be taped back in harness). | Repair wire from module " + " term. to "B" term. of black ign. coil connector or primary ckt. to ign. sw. | Check for open or gnd. in ckt. from "C" term. to ign. coil. If Ckt. is OK, fault is. ign. coil or conn..

Over10 volts | Under 1 volt | 1 to 10 volts

• Connect test light from tach. term. to ground.
• Crank engine and observe light. | Repair open tach. lead or conn and repeat test #4. | Replace module and check for spark from coil as in Step 6.

Light on steady | Light blinks | Spark | No Spark

⑤ • Disconnect distributor 4 term. connector.
• Remove dist. cap.
• Disconnect pick-up coil connector from module.
• Connect voltmeter from tach. term. to ground.
• Ignition on.
• Insulate a test light probe to 1/4″ from tip and note voltage, as test light is momentarily connected from a voltage source (1.5 to 8V) to module term. "P". (Fig. 1). | | System OK | Replace ign. coil, it too is faulty

Replace ignition coil and recheck for spark with spark tester. If still no spark, re-install original coil and replace dist. module..

Voltage drops | No drop in voltage

⑥ • Check for spark from coil wire with spark tester as test light is removed from module term. | Check module ground. If OK, replace module.

No Spark | Spark

• If no module tester (J24642) is available; Replace ign. coil and repeat Step 5. | • If module tester (J24642) is available: test module | Check pick-up coil or conns. (Coil resistance should be 500-1500 ohms and not grounded).

No Spark | Spark | OK | Bad

Ign. coil removed is OK, reinstall coil and check coil wire from dist. cap. if OK, replace dist. module. | System OK | Check coil wire from cap to coil. If OK, replace coil. | Replace module

Diagnosis chart and wiring schematic — 4.3L TBI engine

CHART C-4B
IGNITION SYSTEM CHECK

(REMOTE COIL / SEALED MODULE CONNECTOR DISTRIBUTOR)
(cont.)

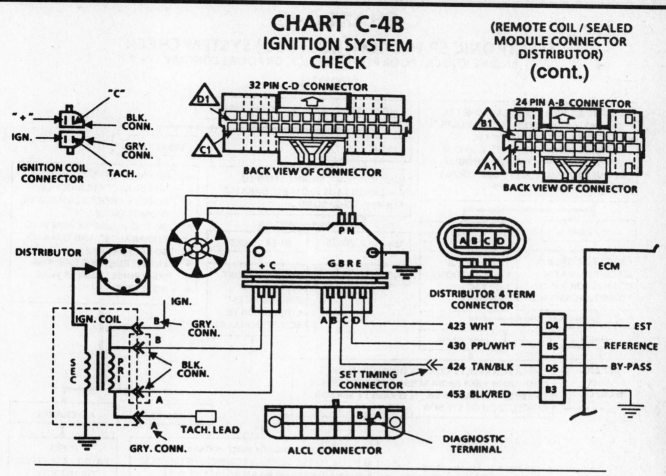

CHART C-5

ELECTRONIC SPARK CONTROL (ESC) SYSTEM CHECK
ENGINE KNOCK, POOR PERFORMANCE, OR POOR ECONOMY

4.3L ENGINE
FUEL INJECTION (TBI)

THIS CHART SHOULD BE USED AFTER ALL OTHER CAUSES OF SPARK KNOCK HAVE BEEN CHECKED. I.E., TIMING, EGR, ENGINE TEMPERATURE OR EXCESSIVE ENGINE NOISE, ETC.

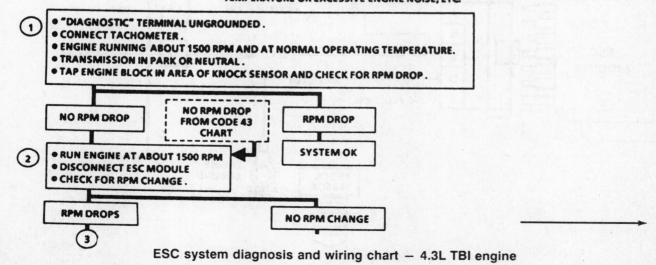

ESC system diagnosis and wiring chart — 4.3L TBI engine

CHART C - 5

ELECTRONIC SPARK CONTROL (ESC) SYSTEM CHECK
ENGINE KNOCK , POOR PERFORMANCE, OR POOR ECONOMY
(cont.)

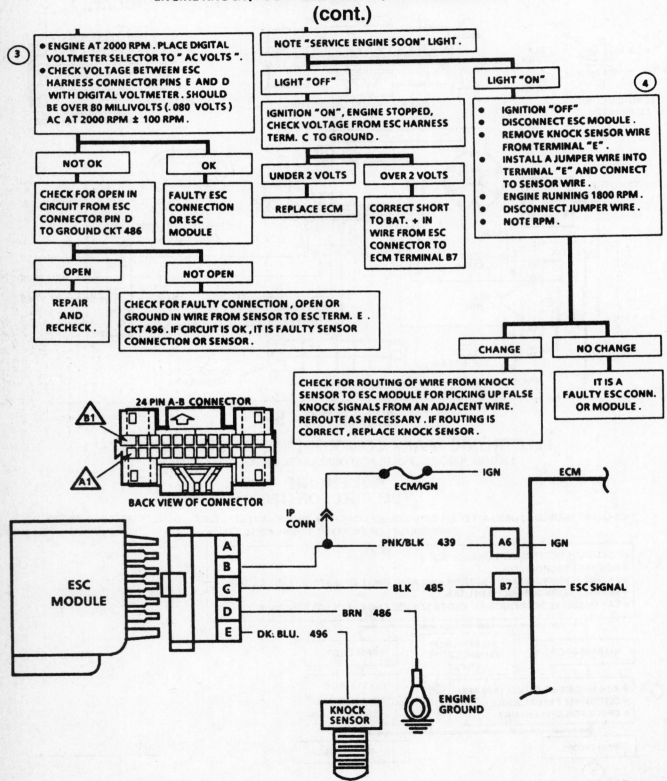

③
- ENGINE AT 2000 RPM . PLACE DIGITAL VOLTMETER SELECTOR TO " AC VOLTS ".
- CHECK VOLTAGE BETWEEN ESC HARNESS CONNECTOR PINS E AND D WITH DIGITAL VOLTMETER . SHOULD BE OVER 80 MILLIVOLTS (.080 VOLTS) AC AT 2000 RPM ± 100 RPM .

NOTE "SERVICE ENGINE SOON" LIGHT .

LIGHT "OFF"

IGNITION "ON", ENGINE STOPPED, CHECK VOLTAGE FROM ESC HARNESS TERM. C TO GROUND .

LIGHT "ON" ④

- IGNITION "OFF"
- DISCONNECT ESC MODULE .
- REMOVE KNOCK SENSOR WIRE FROM TERMINAL "E" .
- INSTALL A JUMPER WIRE INTO TERMINAL "E" AND CONNECT TO SENSOR WIRE .
- ENGINE RUNNING 1800 RPM .
- DISCONNECT JUMPER WIRE .
- NOTE RPM .

NOT OK

OK

UNDER 2 VOLTS

OVER 2 VOLTS

CHECK FOR OPEN IN CIRCUIT FROM ESC CONNECTOR PIN D TO GROUND CKT 486

FAULTY ESC CONNECTION OR ESC MODULE

REPLACE ECM

CORRECT SHORT TO BAT. + IN WIRE FROM ESC CONNECTOR TO ECM TERMINAL B7

OPEN

NOT OPEN

REPAIR AND RECHECK .

CHECK FOR FAULTY CONNECTION , OPEN OR GROUND IN WIRE FROM SENSOR TO ESC TERM. E . CKT 496 . IF CIRCUIT IS OK , IT IS FAULTY SENSOR CONNECTION OR SENSOR .

CHANGE

NO CHANGE

CHECK FOR ROUTING OF WIRE FROM KNOCK SENSOR TO ESC MODULE FOR PICKING UP FALSE KNOCK SIGNALS FROM AN ADJACENT WIRE. REROUTE AS NECESSARY . IF ROUTING IS CORRECT , REPLACE KNOCK SENSOR .

IT IS A FAULTY ESC CONN. OR MODULE .

B1

24 PIN A-B CONNECTOR

A1

BACK VIEW OF CONNECTOR

ESC MODULE

A
B
C
D
E

IGN
ECM/IGN

IP CONN

ECM

PNK/BLK   439   A6   IGN

BLK   485   B7   ESC SIGNAL

BRN   486

DK: BLU.   496

KNOCK SENSOR

ENGINE GROUND

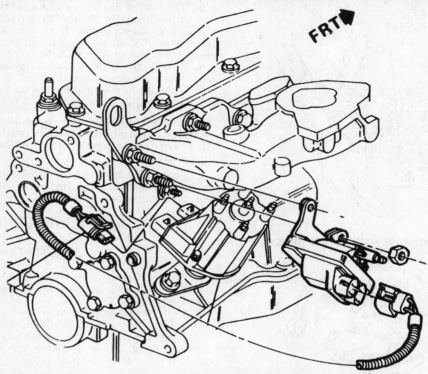

Removing the external ignition coil — 2.5L TBI engine — 4.3L TBI engine similar

REMOVAL AND INSTALLATION

2.5L Engine

The ignition coil is located near the cylinder head at the right rear side of the engine. The coil is located under the intake manifold on the later model 2.5L engines.

1. Disconnect the negative battery terminal and remove the console cover.

2. At the ignition coil, disconnect the ignition switch-to-coil wire and the distributor-to-coil wires.

3. Remove the coil-to-engine nuts/bolts and the coil from the engine.

4. If necessary, test or replace the ignition coil.

5. To install, mount the coil onto the engine, torque the nuts to 20 ft. lbs. (27 Nm) and reconnect all coil and battery connectors.

4.3L Carbureted Engine — 1985

The ignition coil is located in the top of the distributor which is positioned at the top rear of the engine.

1. Disconnect the negative battery terminal and remove the console cover from inside the vehicle.

2. At the ignition coil, on top of the distributor, disconnect the electrical connector and remove the spark plug wire retainer.

3. Remove the coil cover-to-distributor cap screws and the cover. Mark the coil terminals for installation purposes.

4. Remove the coil-to-distributor cap screws and the coil from the cap.

5. If necessary, test or replace the coil.

6. To install, position the high tension button and seal and coil into the cap.

7. Insert the terminals into the proper cap locations. Install the coil cover and spark plug retainer. Reconnect the coil and battery terminals.

4.3L TBI Engine — 1986–90

The ignition coil is located, on top of the intake manifold, next to the distributor.

1. Disconnect the negative battery terminal and remove the console cover inside the vehicle.

2. Disconnect the engine control switch and tachometer terminals from the ignition coil.

3. Disconnect the ignition coil-to-distributor lead wire from the coil.

4. Remove the coil bracket/coil assembly-to-engine bracket nuts and the assembly from the engine.

5. If necessary, test or replace the coil.

6. If necessary to remove the coil from the bracket, perform the following procedures:

    a. Using a drill, drill out the coil-to-bracket rivets.

    b. Using a center punch, drive the rivets from the coil-to-bracket assembly.

    c. Remove the coil from the coil bracket.

To install:

1. Install the coil to the bracket with two screws, position the coil on the engine and torque the nuts to 20 ft. lbs. (27 Nm).

2. Connect the coil connectors and negative battery cable. Install the console cover.

Ignition Module

The ignition modules are located inside the distributor; they may be replaced without removing the distributor from the engine.

REMOVAL AND INSTALLATION

1. Disconnect the negative battery terminal and remove the console cover.

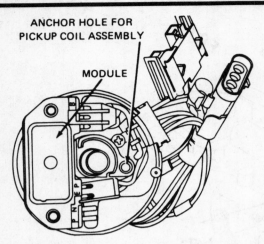

Replacing the ignition module — 2.5L distributor

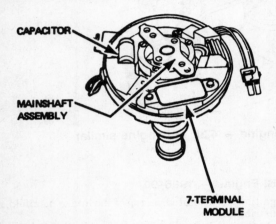

Replacing the ignition module — 4.3L distributor

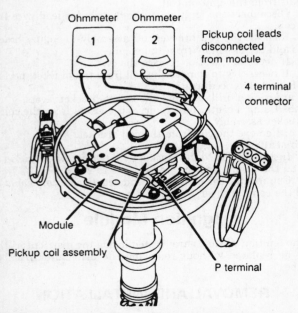

Testing the pickup coil — 1985 4.3L carbureted

2. Remove the distributor cap and the rotor.

3. If the flange, of the distributor shaft is positioned above the module, place a socket on the crankshaft pulley bolt and rotate the crankshaft (turning the distributor shaft) to provide clearance to the ignition module.

4. Remove the ignition module-to-distributor bolts, lift the module and disconnect the electrical connectors from it.

5. If the module is suspected as being defective, take it to a module testing machine and have it tested.

NOTE: When replacing the module, sure to coat the module-to-distributor surface with silicone lubricant (dielectric compound) that will provide heat dissipation.

6. **To install,** apply silicone lubricant to the module mounting area of the distributor. Install the rotor, the distributor cap and the negative battery terminal.

Pickup Coil

TESTING

1. With the ignition key **OFF**, remove the console cover, distributor cap, rotor and disconnect the pickup coil-to-module wire harness.

2. Connect an ohmmeter from the distributor housing to one pickup lead. The reading should be infinite at all times.

3. Connect an ohmmeter to both pickup coil wire terminals. The reading should be steady at one value within 500–1500 ohms. If not replace the pickup coil.

REMOVAL AND INSTALLATION

1. Disconnect the negative (−) battery cable.

2. Remove the distributor cap and rotor. Do NOT remove the spark plug wires from the cap.

3. Mark the distributor housing, position of rotor and relationship from the distributor housing-to-engine block for installation purposes.

4. Remove the distributor clamp and remove the distributor from the engine. Refer to the Distributor procedures in this Section for assistance.

5. Place the distributor in a vise and mark the distributor shaft and gear so they can be reassembled in the same position.

6. Drive out the roll pin and remove the gear and shaft from the distributor.

7. Remove the attaching screws, magnetic shield, retaining ring, pickup coil and pole piece.

To install:

1. Install the pole piece, pickup coil, retaining ring, magnetic shield and retaining screws.

2. Install the gear and shaft to the distributor. Drive in the roll pin.

3. Install the distributor and clamp to the marked position. Refer to the Distributor procedures in this Section for assistance.

4. Install the distributor cap and rotor.

5. Connect the negative (−) battery cable.

6. Adjust the timing to specifications.

Distributor

REMOVAL AND INSTALLATION

Engine Not Rotated

This condition exists if the engine has not been rotated with the distributor removed.

1. Disconnect the negative battery terminal from the battery and remove the console cover.

2. Tag and disconnect the electrical connector(s) from the distributor.

3. Remove the distributor cap (DO NOT remove the spark plug wires) from the distributor and move it aside.

4. Using a crayon or chalk, make locating marks (for installation purposes) on the rotor, the ignition module, the distributor housing and the engine block.

5. Loosen and remove the distributor clamp bolt and clamp, then lift the distributor from the engine.

NOTE: Noting the relative position of the rotor and the module alignment marks, make a second mark on the rotor to align it with the one mark on the module.

To install:

1. Install a new O-ring on the distributor housing.

2. Align the second mark on the rotor with the mark on the module, then install the distributor, taking care to align the mark on the housing with the one on the engine.

NOTE: It may be necessary to lift the distributor and turn the rotor slightly to align the gears and the oil pump driveshaft. The crankshaft may have to moved very slightly to engage the oil pump driveshaft with the distributor. Do NOT force the distributor into the engine with the distributor clamp.

3. With the respective marks aligned, install the clamp and bolt finger tight.

4. Install and secure the distributor cap.

5. Connect the electrical connector(s) to the distributor.

6. Connect a timing light to the engine (following the manufacturer's instructions). Start the engine, then check and/or adjust the timing.

Follow the timing instructions on the emission label in the engine compartment or the "Ignition Timing" procedures in Section 2.

7. Turn the engine Off, tighten the distributor clamp bolt and remove the timing light.

Engine Rotated

This condition exists when the engine has been rotated with the distributor removed.

1. Disconnect the negative battery terminal from the battery and remove the console cover.

2. Tag and disconnect the electrical connector(s) from the distributor.

3. Remove the distributor cap (DO NOT remove the ignition wires) from the distributor and move it aside.

4. Using a crayon or chalk, make locating marks (for installation purposes) on the rotor, the ignition module, the distributor housing and the engine.

5. Loosen and remove the distributor clamp bolt and clamp, then lift the distributor from the engine.

NOTE: Noting the relative position of the rotor and the module alignment marks, make a second mark on the rotor to align it with the one mark on the module.

To install:

6. Install a new O-ring on the distributor housing.

7. Rotate the crankshaft to position the No. 1 cylinder on the TDC of it's compression stroke. This may be determined by inserting a rag into the No. 1 spark plug hole and slowly turn the engine crankshaft. When the timing mark on the crankshaft pulley aligns with the **0** mark on the timing scale and the rag is blown out by the compression, the No. 1 piston is at top-dead-center (TDC).

8. Turn the rotor so that it will point to the No. 1 terminal of the distributor cap.

9. Install the distributor into the engine block. It may be necessary to turn the rotor, a little in either direction, in order to engage the gears.

10. Tap the starter a few times to ensure that the oil pump shaft is mated to the distributor shaft.

11. Bring the engine to No. 1 TDC again and check to see that the rotor is indeed pointing toward the No. 1 terminal of the cap.

12. With the respective marks aligned, install the clamp and bolt finger tight.

13. Install and secure the distributor cap.

14. Connect the electrical connector(s) to the distributor.

15. Connect a timing light to the engine (following the manufacturer's instructions). Start the engine, then check and/or adjust the timing.

16. Turn the engine Off, tighten the distributor clamp bolt and remove the timing light.

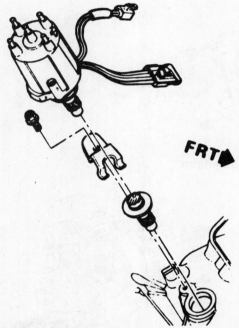

Removing the distributor — 2.5L engine

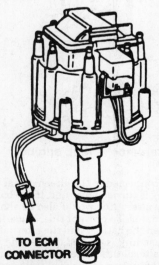

View of the HEI distributor — 4.3L engine

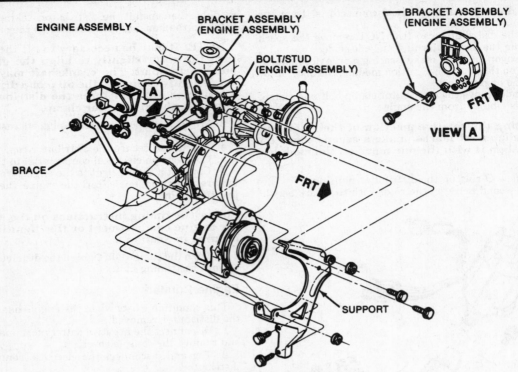

View of the alternator — 2.5L engine

Alternator

The alternator charging system is a negative (−) ground system which consists of an alternator, a regulator, a charge indicator, a storage battery and wiring connecting the components, and fuse link wire.

The alternator is belt-driven from the engine. Energy is supplied from the alternator/regulator system to the rotating field through two brushes to two slip-rings. The slip-rings are mounted on the rotor shaft and are connected to the field coil. This energy supplied to the rotating field from the battery is called excitation current and is used to initially energize the field to begin the generation of electricity. Once the alternator starts to generate electricity, the excitation current comes from its own output rather than the battery.

The alternator produces power in the form of alternating current. The alternating current is rectified by 6 diodes into direct current. The direct current is used to charge the battery and power the rest of the electrical system.

When the ignition key is turned on, current flows from the battery, through the charging system indicator light on the instrument panel, to the voltage regulator, and to the alternator. Since the alternator is not producing any current, the alternator warning light comes on. When the engine is started, the alternator begins to produce current and turns the alternator light off. As the alternator turns and produces current, the current is divided in two ways: part to the battery to charge the battery and power the electrical components of the vehicle, and part is returned to the alternator to enable it to increase its output. In this situation, the alternator is receiving current from the battery and from itself. A voltage regulator is wired into the current supply to the alternator to prevent it from receiving too much current which would cause it to put out too much current. Conversely, if the voltage regulator does not allow the alternator to receive enough current, the battery will not be fully charged and will eventually go dead.

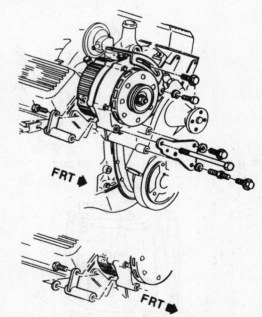

View of the alternator — 4.3L engine

The battery is connected to the alternator at all times, whether the ignition key is turned on or not. If the battery were shorted to ground, the alternator would also be shorted. This would damage the alternator. To prevent this, a fuse link is installed in the wiring between the battery and the alternator. If the battery is shorted, the fuse link is melted, protecting the alternator.

In 1986, the alternators experienced engineering changes, which are: The elimination of the diode trio and the reduction of the external wiring connectors from three-to-two wires.

NOTE: The new alternators are not serviceable and no periodic maintenance is required.

ALTERNATOR PRECAUTIONS

Observing these precautions will ensure safe handling of the electrical system components and will avoid damage to the vehicle's electrical system:

1. Be absolutely sure of the polarity of a booster battery before making connections. Connect the cables positive-to-positive and negative-to-negative. If jump starting, connect the positive cables first and the last connection to a ground on the body of the booster vehicle, so that arcing cannot ignite the hydrogen gas that may have accumulated near the battery. Even a momentary connection of a booster battery with polarity reserved may damage the alternator diodes.
2. Disconnect both vehicle battery cables before attempting to charge the battery.
3. Never ground the alternator output or battery terminal. Be cautious when using metal tools around a battery to avoid creating a short circuit between the terminals.
4. Never run an alternator without a load unless the field circuit (1985) is disconnected.
5. Never attempt to polarize an alternator.
6. Never disconnect any electrical components with the ignition switch turned **On.**

CHARGING SYSTEM TROUBLESHOOTING

There are many possible ways in which the charging system can malfunction. Often the source of a problem is difficult to diagnose, requiring special equipment and a good deal of experience. This is usually not the case, however, where the charging system fails completely and causes the dash board warning light to come on or the battery to become dead. To troubleshoot a complete system failure only two pieces of equipment are needed: a test light, to determine that current is reaching a certain point; and a current indicator (ammeter), to determine the direction of the current flow and its measurement in amps.

This test works under three assumptions:
1. The battery is known to be good and fully charged.
2. The alternator belt is in good condition and adjusted to the proper tension.
3. All connections in the system are clean and tight.

NOTE: In order for the current indicator to give a valid reading, the truck must be equipped with battery cables which are of the same gauge size and quality as original equipment battery cables.

1. Turn off all electrical components on the truck.
2. Make sure the doors of the truck are closed.
3. If the truck is equipped with a clock, disconnect the clock by removing the lead wire from the rear of the clock.
4. Disconnect the positive battery cable from the battery and connect the ground wire on a test light to the disconnected positive battery cable.
5. Touch the probe end of the test light to the positive battery post. The test light should not light. If the test light does light, there is a short or open circuit on the truck.
6. Disconnect the voltage regulator wiring harness connector at the voltage regulator.
7. Turn on the ignition key.
8. Connect the wire on a test light to a good ground (engine bolt).
9. Touch the probe end of a test light to the ignition wire connector into the voltage regulator wiring connector. This wire corresponds to the **I** terminal on the regulator. If the test light goes on, the charging system warning light circuit is complete. If the test light does not come on and the warning light on the instrument panel is on, either the resistor wire, which is parallel with the warning light, or the wiring to the voltage regulator, is defective. If the test light does not come on and the warning light is not on, either the bulb is defective or the power supply wire form the battery through the ignition switch to the bulb has an open circuit. Connect the wiring harness to the regulator.

10. Examine the fuse link wire in the wiring harness from the starter relay to the alternator. If the insulation on the wire is cracked or split, the fuse link may be melted.
11. Connect a test light to the fuse link by attaching the ground wire on the test light to an engine bolt and touching the probe end of the light to the bottom of the fuse link wire where it splices into the alternator output wire. If the bulb in the test light does not light, the fuse link is melted.
12. Start the engine and place a current indicator on the positive battery cable.
13. Turn off all electrical accessories and make sure the doors are closed. If the charging system is working properly, the gauge will show a draw of less than 5 amps. If the system is not working properly, the gauge will show a draw of more than 5 amps. A charge moves the needle toward the battery, a draw moves the needle away from the battery. Turn the engine off.
14. Disconnect the wiring harness from the voltage regulator at the regulator at the regulator connector.
15. Connect a male spade terminal (solderless connector) to each end of a jumper wire.
16. Insert one end of the wire into the wiring harness connector which corresponds to the **A** terminal on the regulator.
17. Insert the other end of the wire into the wiring harness connector which corresponds to the **F** terminal on the regulator.
18. Position the connector with the jumper wire installed so that it cannot contact any metal surface under the hood.
19. Position a current indicator gauge on the positive battery cable. Have an assistant start the engine. Observe the reading on the current indicator. Have your assistant slowly raise the speed of the engine to about 2,000 rpm or until the current indicator needle stops moving, whichever comes first. Do not run the engine for more than a short period of time in this condition. If the wiring harness connector or jumper wire becomes excessively hot during this test, turn off the engine and check for a grounded wire in the regulator wiring harness. If the current indicator shows a charge of about three amps less than the output of the alternator, the alternator is working properly. If the previous tests showed a draw, the voltage regulator is defective. If the gauge does not show the proper charging rate, the alternator is defective.

PRELIMINARY CHARGING SYSTEM TESTS

1. If you suspect a defect in your charging system, first perform these general checks before going on to more specific tests.
2. Check the condition of the alternator belt and tighten it if necessary.
3. Clean the battery cable connections at the battery. Make sure the connections between the battery wires and the battery clamps are good. Reconnect the negative terminal only and proceed to the next step.
4. With the key off, insert a test light between the positive terminal on the battery and the disconnected positive battery terminal clamp. If the test light comes on, there is a short in the electrical system of the truck. The short must be repaired before proceeding. If the light does not come on, proceed to the next step.

NOTE: If the truck is equipped with an electric shock, the clock must be disconnected.

5. Check the charging system wiring for any obvious breaks or shorts.
6. Check the battery to make sure it is fully charged and in good condition.

CHARGING SYSTEM OPERATIONAL TEST

NOTE: You will need a current indicator to perform this test. If the current indicator is to give an accurate reading, the battery cables must be the same gauge and length as the original equipment.

1. With the engine running and all electrical systems turned off, place a current indicator over the positive battery cable.

2. If a charge of roughly five amps is recorded, the charging system is working. If a draw of about five amps is recorded, the system is not working. The needle moves toward the battery when a charge condition is indicated, and away from the battery when a draw condition is indicated.

3. If a draw is indicated, proceed with further testing. If an excessive charge (10–15 amps) is indicated, the regulator may be at fault.

OUTPUT TEST

1. You will need an ammeter for this test.
2. Disconnect the battery ground cable.
3. Disconnect the wire from the battery terminal on the alternator.
4. Connect the ammeter negative lead to the battery terminal wire removed in step three, and connect the ammeter positive lead to the battery terminal on the alternator.
5. Reconnect the battery ground cable and turn on all electrical accessories. If the battery is fully charged, disconnect the coil wire and bump the starter a few times to partially discharge it.
6. Start the engine and run it until you obtain a maximum current reading on the ammeter.
7. If the current is not within ten amps of the rated output of the alternator, the alternator is working properly. If the current is not within ten amps, insert a screwdriver in the test hole in the end frame of the alternator and ground the tab in the test hole against the side of the hole.
8. If the current is now within ten amps of the rated output, remove the alternator and have the voltage regulator replaced. If it is still below ten amps of rated output, have the alternator repaired.

REMOVAL AND INSTALLATION

NOTE: The following procedures require the use of GM Belt Tension Gauge No. BT–33–95–ACBN for regular V-belts, or BT–33–97M for serpentine belts. The belt should deflect about 6mm (¼ in.) over a 178–254mm (7–

10 in.) span, or 13mm (½ in.) over a 330–406mm (13–16 in.) span at this point.

1. Disconnect the negative battery terminal from the battery.
2. Remove the top radiator hose bracket from the radiator.
3. Remove the wiring harness that is clamped to the radiator core support.
4. Remove the upper fan support-to-radiator support bolts and the fan support.
5. Label and disconnect the alternator's electrical connectors.
6. Remove the alternator brace bolt and the drive belt.
7. Support the alternator, then remove the mounting bolts and the unit from the vehicle.

To install:
1. Install the alternator and adjust the drive belt tension. Torque the top mounting bolt as follows:
- 2.5L to 20 ft. lbs. (27 Nm)
- 4.3L to 18.4 ft. lbs. (25 Nm)
Lower mounting bolt as follows:
- 2.5L to 37 ft. lbs. (50 Nm)
- 4.3L to 35 ft. lbs. (47 Nm)
2. Reconnect the negative battery terminal.
3. To adjust the drive belt, perform the following procedures:
   a. If the belt is cold, operate the engine (at idle speed) for 15 minutes; the belt will seat itself in the pulleys allowing the belt fibers to relax or stretch. If the belt is hot, allow it to cool, until it is warm to the touch.

NOTE: A used belt is one that has been rotated at least one complete revolution on the pulleys. This begins the belt seating process and it must never be tensioned to the new belt specifications.

   b. Loosen the component-to-mounting bracket bolts.
   c. Using a GM Belt Tension Gauge No. BT–33–95–ACBN (standard V-belts) or BT–33–97M (poly V-belts), place the tension gauge at the center of the belt between the longest span.
   d. Applying belt tension pressure on the component, adjust the drive belt tension to the correct specifications.
   e. While holding the correct tension on the component, tighten the component-to-mounting bracket bolt.
   f. When the belt tension is correct, remove the tension gauge.

Regulator

The voltage regulators are sealed units mounted within the alternator body and are are nonadjustable.

REMOVAL AND INSTALLATION

1985 Models

NOTE: This procedure is to be performed with the alternator removed from the vehicle. The new alternators, 1986 and later models, are non-serviceable.

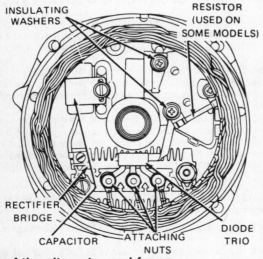

View of the alternator end frame

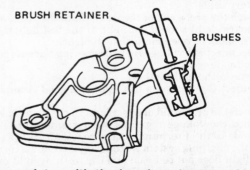

Voltage regulator with the brushes depressed

Troubleshooting Basic Charging System Problems

Problem	Cause	Solution
Noisy alternator	• Loose mountings • Loose drive pulley • Worn bearings • Brush noise • Internal circuits shorted (High pitched whine)	• Tighten mounting bolts • Tighten pulley • Replace alternator • Replace alternator • Replace alternator
Squeal when starting engine or accelerating	• Glazed or loose belt	• Replace or adjust belt
Indicator light remains on or ammeter indicates discharge (engine running)	• Broken fan belt • Broken or disconnected wires • Internal alternator problems • Defective voltage regulator	• Install belt • Repair or connect wiring • Replace alternator • Replace voltage regulator
Car light bulbs continually burn out—battery needs water continually	• Alternator/regulator overcharging	• Replace voltage regulator/alternator
Car lights flare on acceleration	• Battery low • Internal alternator/regulator problems	• Charge or replace battery • Replace alternator/regulator
Low voltage output (alternator light flickers continually or ammeter needle wanders)	• Loose or worn belt • Dirty or corroded connections • Internal alternator/regulator problems	• Replace or adjust belt • Clean or replace connections • Replace alternator or regulator

1. Mark scribe lines on the end-frames to make the reassembly easier.

2. Remove the 4 through-bolts and separate the drive end-frame assembly from the rectifier end-frame assembly.

3. Remove the 3 diode trio attaching nuts and the 3 regulator attaching screws.

4. Remove the diode trio and the regulator from the end frame.

NOTE: Before installing the regulator, push the brushes into the brush holder and install a brush retainer or a tooth pick to hold the brushes in place.

5. To install the regulator, reverse the removal procedures. After the alternator is assembled, remove the brush retainer.

VOLTAGE ADJUSTMENT

The voltage regulator is electronic and is housed within the alternator. Adjustment of the regulator is not possible. Should replacement of the regulator become necessary, the alternator must be disassembled.

Battery

The battery is mounted in front, left side of the engine compartment. It is a non-tamperable type with side mounted terminals.

REMOVAL AND INSTALLATION

1. Disconnect the negative battery terminal, then the positive battery terminal.

2. Remove the battery holddown retainer.

3. Remove the battery from the vehicle.

4. Inspect the battery, the cables and the battery carrier for damage.

5. Clean any rust or corrosion from the terminals, tray or body with baking soda and water. Remove the rust and repaint with a rust preventative paint.

6. **To install,** place the battery in the tray using a battery carrying strap. Torque the battery retainer to 11 ft. lbs. (15 Nm) and the top bar to 8 ft. lbs. (11 Nm).

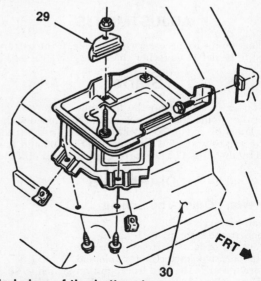

Exploded view of the battery tray

ALTERNATOR AND REGULATOR SPECIFICATIONS

| Years | Engine No. Cyl. (cu. in.) | Alternator | | | Series | Rotation | Type |
		Field Current @ 12v (amps)	Output (amps)	Regulated Volts @ 75°F			
1985	4-151	4.0-5.0	30	12	10-SI	CW	100
	6-262	4.0-4.6	57	12	15-SI	CW	100
1986	4-151	5.4-6.4	85 ①	12	CS-130	CW	100
	6-262	5.4-6.4	85 ①	12	CS-130	CW	100
1987	4-151	4.8-5.7	85	12	CS-130	CW	100
	6-262	4.8-5.7	85 ①	12	CS-130	CW	100
1988–90	4-151	6.0-7.5	95	12	CS-130	CW	100
	6-262	4.8-5.7	85 ①	12	CS-130	CW	100

① Heavy duty-100 amps

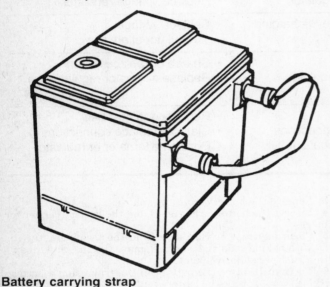

Battery carrying strap

ADJUSTMENTS

No adjustments are necessary or possible. If the battery is determined to be defective (other than charging), discard it.

Starter

The starter is located on the left side (2.5L) or right side (4.3L) of the engine. The 1985–87 2.5L is equipped with a 5MT starter. The 4.3L is equipped with a 10MT. In the model year 1988, the names of the 5MT changed to SD–200 and the 10MT changed to the SD–300. The starters are basically still the same.

DIAGNOSIS

Starter Won't Crank The Engine

1. Dead battery.
2. Open starter circuit, such as:
   a. Broken or loose battery cables.
   b. Inoperative starter motor solenoid.
   c. Broken or loose wire from ignition switch to solenoid.
   d. Poor solenoid or starter ground.
   e. Bad ignition switch.
3. Defective starter internal circuit, such as:
   a. Dirty or burnt commutator.
   b. Stuck, worn or broken brushes.
   c. Open or shorted armature.
   d. Open or grounded fields.
4. Starter motor mechanical faults, such as:
   a. Jammed armature end bearings.
   b. Bad bearings, allowing armature to rub fields.
   c. Bent shaft.
   d. Broken starter housing.
   e. Bad starter drive mechanism.
   f. Bad starter drive or flywheel-driven gear.
5. Engine hard or impossible to crank, such as:
   a. Hydrostatic lock, water in combustion chamber.
   b. Crankshaft seizing in bearings.
   c. Piston or ring seizing.
   d. Bent or broken connecting rod.
   e. Seizing of connecting rod bearings.
   f. Flywheel jammed or broken.

Starter Spins Freely, Won't Engage

1. Sticking or broken drive mechanism.
2. Damaged ring gear.

SHIMMING THE STARTER

Starter noise during cranking and after the engine fires is often a result of too much or too little distance between the starter pinion gear and the flywheel. A high pitched whine during cranking (before the engine fires) can be caused by the pinion and flywheel being too far apart. Likewise, a whine after the engine starts (as the key is released) is often a result of the pinion-flywheel relationship being too close. In both cases flywheel damage can occur. Shims are available in 0.015 in. sizes to properly adjust the starter on its mount. You will also need a flywheel turning tool, available at most auto parts stores or from any auto tool store or salesperson.

If your truck's starter emits the above noises, follow the shimming procedure below:

1. Disconnect the negative battery cable.
2. Remove the flywheel inspection cover on the bottom of the bellhousing.
3. Using the flywheel turning tool, turn the flywheel and examine the flywheel teeth. If damage is evident, the flywheel should be replaced.
4. Insert a screwdriver into the small hole in the bottom of the starter and move the starter pinion and clutch assembly so

the pinion and flywheel teeth mesh. If necessary, rotate the flywheel so that a pinion tooth is directly in the center of the two flywheel teeth and on the centerline of the two gears, as shown in the accompanying illustration.

5. Check the pinion-to-flywheel clearance by using a 0.5mm (0.020 in.) wire gauge (a spark plug wire gauge may work here, or you can make your own). Make sure you center the pinion tooth between the flywheel teeth and the gauge—NOT in the corners, as you may get a false reading. If the clearance is under this minimum, shim the starter away from the flywheel by adding shim(s) one at a time to the starter mount. Check clearance after adding each shim.

6. If the clearance is a good deal over 0.5mm (0.020 in.) — in the vicinity of 1.3mm (0.050 in.) plus, shim the starter towards the flywheel. Broken or severely mangled flywheel teeth are also a good indicator that the clearance here is too great. Shimming the starter towards the flywheel is done by adding shims to the outboard starter mounting pad only. Check the clearance after each shim is added. A shim of 0.015 in. at this location will decrease the clearance about 0.010 in.

REMOVAL AND INSTALLATION

1. Disconnect the negative battery cable.
2. Raise and support the front of the vehicle on jackstands.
3. If equipped, remove any starter braces or shields that may be in the way.
4. Disconnect the electrical connectors from the starter solenoid.
5. Remove the starter-to-engine bolts, nuts, washers and shims. Allow the starter to drop, then remove it from the engine.

NOTE: Be sure to keep the shims in order so that they may be reinstalled in the same order.

To install:
1. Install the starter, shims and bolts. Torque the starter-to-engine bolts to 31 ft. lbs. (42 Nm) for the 2.5L and 28 ft. lbs. (38 Nm) for the 4.3L. Connect the wires to the starter solenoid and the negative battery cable.
2. Install any braces or shields if so equipped. Start the engine and check for proper operation.

SOLENOID REPLACEMENT

1. Refer to the Starter, Removal and Installation procedures in this section and remove the starter, then place it on a workbench.
2. Remove the screw and the washer from the motor connector strap terminal.
3. Remove the two solenoid retaining screws.
4. Twist the solenoid housing clockwise to remove the flange key from the keyway in the housing, then remove the housing.
To install:
1. Place the return spring on the plunger and place the solenoid body on the drive housing. Turn it counterclockwise to engage the flange key.
2. Place the two retaining screws in position, then install the screw and washer which secures the strap terminal. Install the unit on the starter.

OVERHAUL

Drive Replacement

1. Disconnect the field coil straps from the solenoid.
2. Remove the through-bolts, then separate the commutator end-frame, the field frame assembly, the drive housing and the armature assembly, from each other.
3. Slide the two piece thrust collar off the end of the armature shaft.
4. Slide a suitably sized metal cylinder, such as a standard ½ in. (12.7mm) pipe coupling or an old pinion, onto the shaft so that the end of the coupling or pinion butts against the edge of the pinion retainer.
5. Support the lower end of the armature securely on a soft surface, such as a wooden block and tap the end of the coupling or pinion, driving the retainer towards the armature end of the snaping.
6. Using a pair of pliers, remove the snaping from the groove in the armature shaft. Then, slide the retainer and the starter drive from the shaft.
7. To assemble, lubricate the drive end of the armature shaft with silicone lubricant and slide the starter drive onto the shaft *with the pinion facing outward*. Slide the retainer onto the shaft *with the cupped surface facing outward*.
8. Again, support the armature on a soft surface, with the pinion at the upper end. Center the snaping on top of the shaft (use a new snaping if the original was damaged during removal). Gently place a block of wood flat on top of the snaping, so as not to move it from a centered position. Tap the wooden block with a hammer in order to force the snaping around the shaft. Then, slide the ring down into the snaping groove.

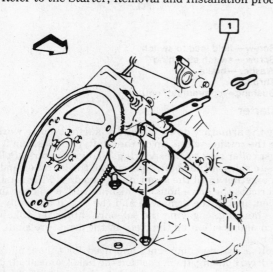

Replacing the starter — 4.3L engine

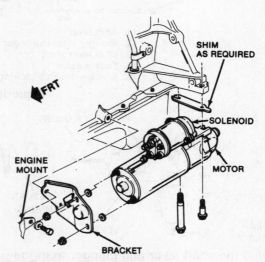

Replacing the starter — 2.5L engine

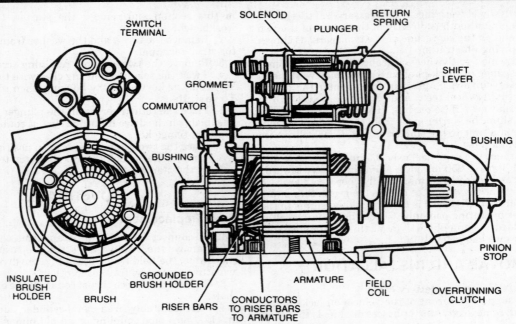

Cross-sectional view — 5MT starter

1. Frame—commutator end
2. Brush and holder pkg.
3. Brush
4. Brush holder
5. Housing—drive end
6. Frame and field asm.
7. Solenoid switch
8. Armature
9. Drive asm.
10. Plunger

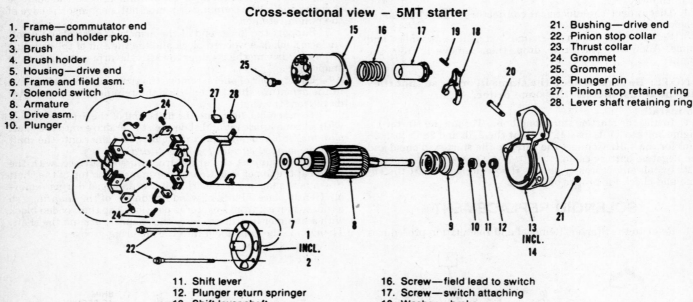

11. Shift lever
12. Plunger return springer
13. Shift lever shaft
14. Lock washer
15. Screw—brush attaching

16. Screw—field lead to switch
17. Screw—switch attaching
18. Washer—brake
19. Thru bolt
20. Bushing—commutator end

21. Bushing—drive end
22. Pinion stop collar
23. Thrust collar
24. Grommet
25. Grommet
26. Plunger pin
27. Pinion stop retainer ring
28. Lever shaft retaining ring

Exploded view of the starter

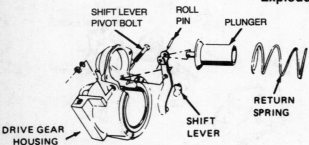

Removing the shaft lever and plunger from the starter

9. Lay the armature down flat on the surface you're working on. Slide the retainer close, up on the shaft, then position it and the thrust collar next to the snapring. Using two pairs of pliers, on opposite sides of the shaft, squeeze the thrust collar and the retainer together until the snapring is forced into the retainer.

10. Lubricate the drive housing bushing with a silicone lubricant. Then, install the armature and the clutch assembly into the drive housing, engaging the solenoid shift lever yoke with the clutch and positioning the front of the armature shaft into the bushing.

11. Apply a sealing compound, approved for this application onto the drive housing, then, position the field frame around the armature's shaft and against the drive housing. *Work slowly and carefully to prevent damaging the starter brushes.*

12. Lubricate the bushing in the commutator end-frame with a silicone lubricant, place the leather brake washer onto the armature shaft and then slide the commutator end-frame over the shaft and into position against the field frame. Line up the bolt holes, then install and tighten the through-bolts.

13. Reconnect the field coil straps to the **Motor** terminal of the solenoid.

NOTE: **If replacement of the starter drive fails to cure the improper engagement of the starter pinion to flywheel, there are probably defective parts in the solenoid and/or the shift lever. The best procedure would probably be to take the assembly to a shop where a pinion clearance check can be made by energizing the solenoid on a test bench. If the pinion clearance is incorrect, disassemble the solenoid and the shift lever, then inspect and replace the worn parts.**

Brush Replacement

1. Disassemble the starter by following Steps 1 and 2 of the Drive Replacement procedure, above.

2. Replace the brushes, one at a time, to avoid having to mark the wiring. For each brush, remove the brush holding screw and the old brush, then position the new brush in the same direction (large end toward the center of the field frame), position the wire connector on top of the brush, line up the holes and reinstall the screw. Make sure the screw is snug enough to ensure good contact.

3. Reassemble the starter according to Steps 10–13, above.

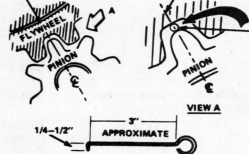

Snapring installation

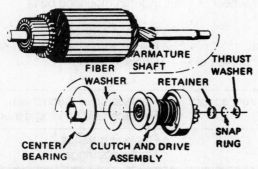

Use a piece of pipe to drive to drive the retainer toward the snapring

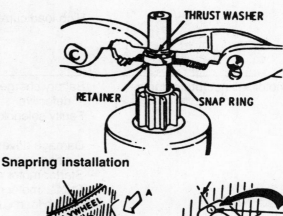

Flywheel-to-pinion clearance

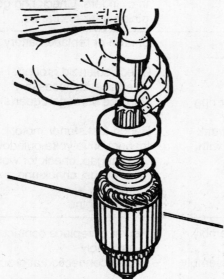

Starter and drive assembly removed

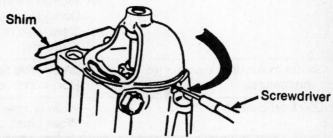

Engaging the starter to check pinion clearance

STARTER SPECIFICATIONS

Years	Engine No. Cyl. (cu. in.)	Series	Type	No-Load Test		
				Amps	Volts	RPM
1985–88	4-151	5 MT	101	50–75	10	6,000–11,900
	6-262	10 MT	101	70–110	10	6,500–11,700
1989–90	4-151	SD-200	—	50–75	10	6,000–11,900
	6-262	SD-300	—	70–110	10	6,500–11,700

Troubleshooting Basic Starting System Problems

Problem	Cause	Solution
Starter motor rotates engine slowly	• Battery charge low or battery defective	• Charge or replace battery
	• Defective circuit between battery and starter motor	• Clean and tighten, or replace cables
	• Low load current	• Bench-test starter motor. Inspect for worn brushes and weak brush springs.
	• High load current	• Bench-test starter motor. Check engine for friction, drag or coolant in cylinders. Check ring gear-to-pinion gear clearance.
Starter motor will not rotate engine	• Battery charge low or battery defective	• Charge or replace battery
	• Faulty solenoid	• Check solenoid ground. Repair or replace as necessary.
	• Damage drive pinion gear or ring gear	• Replace damaged gear(s)
	• Starter motor engagement weak	• Bench-test starter motor
	• Starter motor rotates slowly with high load current	• Inspect drive yoke pull-down and point gap, check for worn end bushings, ch›ck ring gear clearance
	• Engine seized	• Repair engine
Starter motor drive will not engage (solenoid known to be good)	• Defective contact point assembly	• Repair or replace contact point assembly
	• Inadequate contact point assembly ground	• Repair connection at ground screw
	• Defective hold-in coil	• Replace field winding assembly
Starter motor drive will not disengage	• Starter motor loose on flywheel housing	• Tighten mounting bolts
	• Worn drive end busing	• Replace bushing
	• Damaged ring gear teeth	• Replace ring gear or driveplate
	• Drive yoke return spring broken or missing	• Replace spring
Starter motor drive disengages prematurely	• Weak drive assembly thrust spring	• Replace drive mechanism
	• Hold-in coil defective	• Replace field winding assembly
Low load current	• Worn brushes	• Replace brushes
	• Weak brush springs	• Replace springs

Standard Torque Specifications and Fastener Markings

In the absence of specific torques, the following chart can be used as a guide to the maximum safe torque of a particular size/grade of fastener.

- There is no torque difference for fine or coarse threads.
- Torque values are based on clean, dry threads. Reduce the value by 10% if threads are oiled prior to assembly.
- The torque required for aluminum components or fasteners is considerably less.

U.S. Bolts

SAE Grade Number	1 or 2			5			6 or 7		
Number of lines always 2 less than the grade number.									
Bolt Size (Inches)—(Thread)	Maximum Torque			Maximum Torque			Maximum Torque		
	Ft./Lbs.	Kgm	Nm	Ft./Lbs.	Kgm	Nm	Ft./Lbs.	Kgm	Nm
¼ — 20	5	0.7	6.8	8	1.1	10.8	10	1.4	13.5
— 28	6	0.8	8.1	10	1.4	13.6			
⁵/₁₆ — 18	11	1.5	14.9	17	2.3	23.0	19	2.6	25.8
— 24	13	1.8	17.6	19	2.6	25.7			
⅜ — 16	18	2.5	24.4	31	4.3	42.0	34	4.7	46.0
— 24	20	2.75	27.1	35	4.8	47.5			
⁷/₁₆ — 14	28	3.8	37.0	49	6.8	66.4	55	7.6	74.5
— 20	30	4.2	40.7	55	7.6	74.5			
½ — 13	39	5.4	52.8	75	10.4	101.7	85	11.75	115.2
— 20	41	5.7	55.6	85	11.7	115.2			
⁹/₁₆ — 12	51	7.0	69.2	110	15.2	149.1	120	16.6	162.7
— 18	55	7.6	74.5	120	16.6	162.7			
⅝ — 11	83	11.5	112.5	150	20.7	203.3	167	23.0	226.5
— 18	95	13.1	128.8	170	23.5	230.5			
¾ — 10	105	14.5	142.3	270	37.3	366.0	280	38.7	379.6
— 16	115	15.9	155.9	295	40.8	400.0			
⅞ — 9	160	22.1	216.9	395	54.6	535.5	440	60.9	596.5
— 14	175	24.2	237.2	435	60.1	589.7			
1 — 8	236	32.5	318.6	590	81.6	799.9	660	91.3	894.8
— 14	250	34.6	338.9	660	91.3	849.8			

Metric Bolts

Relative Strength Marking	4.6, 4.8			8.8		
Bolt Markings						
Bolt Size Thread Size x Pitch (mm)	Maximum Torque			Maximum Torque		
	Ft./Lbs.	Kgm	Nm	Ft./Lbs.	Kgm	Nm
6 x 1.0	2–3	.2–.4	3–4	3–6	.4–.8	5–8
8 x 1.25	6–8	.8–1	8–12	9–14	1.2–1.9	13–19
10 x 1.25	12–17	1.5–2.3	16–23	20–29	2.7–4.0	27–39
12 x 1.25	21–32	2.9–4.4	29–43	35–53	4.8–7.3	47–72
14 x 1.5	35–52	4.8–7.1	48–70	57–85	7.8–11.7	77–110
16 x 1.5	51–77	7.0–10.6	67–100	90–120	12.4–16.5	130–160
18 x 1.5	74–110	10.2–15.1	100–150	130–170	17.9–23.4	180–230
20 x 1.5	110–140	15.1–19.3	150–190	190–240	26.2–46.9	160–320
22 x 1.5	150–190	22.0–26.2	200–260	250–320	34.5–44.1	340–430
24 x 1.5	190–240	26.2–46.9	260–320	310–410	42.7–56.5	420–550

ENGINE MECHANICAL

Description

Two engines and three fuel systems are used to power your Astro/Safari Van, they are: Pontiac built 2.5L (151 cu. in.) EFI for 1985–90, Chevy built 4.3L (262 cu. in.) 4-bbl for 1985 and 4.3L (262 cu. in.) EFI for 1986–90.

On the 1985, 2.5L EFI engine, the cylinder head and engine block are both constructed of cast iron. The valve guides are integral with the cylinder head and the rocker arms are retained by individual threaded shoulder bolts. Hydraulic roller lifters are incorporated to reduce the friction between the valve lifters and the camshaft lobes.

On the 1986–90, 2.5L EFI engine, a few changes appeared, such as: (1) the pistons were replaced with hypereutectic types (pistons embedded with silicone nodules in the walls to reduce the cylinder wall friction), (2) a reduced weight, high efficiency alternator and (3) a variable ratio air conditioning compressor.

The 4.3L engine, utilizes a 4-bbl (for 1985) or an EFI system (for 1986–87) and the use of swirl chamber heads (to increase power and fuel efficiency). The engine block and cylinder heads are constructed of cast iron. Other major features are: a wider oil pan flange, raised rails inside the cylinder heads (to improve oil return control), machined rocker cover seal surfaces, a trough along the rocker cover rails (to channel oil away from the gasket) and even distribution of the clamping loads, to make this engine one of the most leak-resistant on the road today.

In 1986, the 4.3L EFI engine began using a new one-piece rear crankshaft seal, lighter engine oil, remachined camshaft lobes and new poly-vee alternator drive belts.

In 1987, the 4.3L EFI engine began using roller valve lifters instead of the standard flat bottom lifters. The roller lifter is still hydraulic requiring no valve adjustment. The roller lifter incorporates a roller that rides along the cam lobe reducing friction and component wear. A roller lifter restrictor and retainer is needed to keep the lifter from turning in the bore while the engine is running. All 2.5L EFI engines incorporate the roller lifter configuration.

Engine Overhaul Tips

Most engine overhaul procedures are fairly standard. In addition to specific parts replacement procedures and complete specifications for your individual engine, this Section also is a guide to accept rebuilding procedures. Examples of standard rebuilding practice are shown and should be used along with specific details concerning your particular engine.

Competent and accurate machine shop services will ensure maximum performance, reliability and engine life.

On most instances it is more profitable for the do-it-yourself mechanic to remove, clean and inspect the component(s), buy the necessary parts and deliver these to a shop for actual machine work.

On the other hand, much of the rebuilding work (crankshaft, block, bearings, piston rods, and other components) is well within the scope of the do-it-yourself mechanic.

TOOLS

The tools required for an engine overhaul or parts replacement will depend on the depth of your involvement. With a few exceptions, they will be the tools found in a mechanic's tool kit (see Section 1). More in-depth work will require any or all of the following:

- A dial indicator (reading in thousandths) mounted on a universal base
- Micrometers and telescope gauges
- Jaw and screw-type pullers

- Scraper
- Valve spring compressor
- Ring groove cleaner
- Piston ring expander and compressor
- Ridge reamer
- Cylinder hone or glaze breaker
- Plastigage®
- Engine stand

Use of most of these tools is illustrated in this Section. Many can be rented for a one-time use from a local parts jobber or tool supply house specializing in automotive work.

Occasionally, the use of special tools is called for. See the information on Special Tools and Safety Notice in the front of this book before substituting another tool.

INSPECTION TECHNIQUES

Procedures and specifications are given in this Section for inspecting, cleaning and assessing the wear limits of most major components. Other procedures such as Magnaflux® and Zyglo® can be used to locate material flaws and stress cracks. Magnaflux® is a magnetic process applicable only to ferrous materials. The Zyglo® process coats the material with a fluorescent dye penetrant and can be used on any material. Check for suspected surface cracks can be more readily made using spot check dye. The dye is sprayed onto the suspected area, wiped off and the area sprayed with a developer. Cracks will show up brightly.

OVERHAUL TIPS

Aluminum has become extremely popular for use in engines, due to its low weight. Observe the following precautions when handling aluminum parts:

- Never hot tank aluminum parts (the caustic hot tank solution will eat the aluminum.
- Remove all aluminum parts (identification tag, etc.) from engine parts prior to the tanking.
- Always coat threads lightly with engine oil or anti-seize compounds before installation, to prevent seizure.
- Never over-torque bolts or spark plugs especially in aluminum for you may strip the threads.

Stripped threads in any component can be repaired using any of several commercial repair kits (Heli-Coil®, Microdot®, Keenserts®, etc.).

When assembling the engine, any parts that will have frictional contact must be prelubed to provide lubrication at initial start-up. Any product specifically formulated for this purpose can be used, but engine oil is not recommended as a prelube.

When semi-permanent (locked, but removable) installation of bolts or nuts is desired, threads should be cleaned and coated with Loctite® or other similar, commercial non-hardening sealant.

REPAIRING DAMAGED THREADS

Several methods of repairing damaged threads are available. Heli-Coil® (shown here), Keenserts® and Microdot® are among the most widely used. All involve basically the same principle—drilling out stripped threads, tapping the hole and installing a prewound insert—making welding, plugging and oversize fasteners unnecessary.

Two types of thread repair inserts are usually supplied—a standard type for most Inch Coarse, Inch Fine, Metric Course and Metric Fine thread sizes and a spark lug type to fit most spark plug port sizes. Consult the individual manufacturer's catalog to determine exact applications. Typical thread repair kits will contain a selection of prewound threaded inserts, a tap (corresponding to the outside diameter threads of the insert) and an installation tool. Spark plug inserts usually differ because they require a tap equipped with pilot threads and a combined reamer/tap section. Most manufacturers also supply blister-packed thread repair inserts separately in addition to a master kit containing a variety of taps and inserts plus installation tools.

Before effecting a repair to a threaded hole, remove any snapped, broken or damaged bolts or studs. Penetrating oil can be used to free frozen threads; the offending item can be removed with locking pliers or with a screw or stud extractor. After the hole is clear, the thread can be repaired, as follows:

Checking Engine Compression

A noticeable lack of engine power, excessive oil consumption and/or poor fuel mileage measured over an extended period are all indicators of internal engine wear. Worn piston rings, scored or worn cylinder bores, blown head gaskets, sticking or burnt valves and worn valve seats are all possible culprits here. A check of each cylinder's compression will help you locate the problems.

As mentioned in the Tools and Equipment part of Section 1, a screw-in type compression gauge is more accurate that the type you simply hold against the spark plug hole, although it takes slightly longer to use. It's worth it to obtain a more accurate reading. Follow the procedures below.

1. Warm up the engine to normal operating temperature.
2. Remove all spark plugs.
3. Disconnect the high tension lead from the ignition coil.
4. Fully open the throttle, either by operating the carburetor throttle linkage by hand or by having an assistant floor the accelerator pedal.
5. Screw the compression gauge into the No. 1 spark plug hole until the fitting is snug.

NOTE: Be careful not to crossthread the plug hole. On aluminum cylinder heads use extra care, as the threads in these heads are easily ruined.

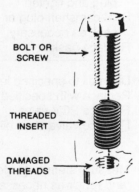

Damaged bolt holes can be repaired with thread repair inserts

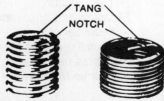

Standard thread repair insert (left) and spark plug thread insert (right)

6. Ask an assistant to depress the accelerator pedal fully on both carbureted and fuel injected vehicles. Then, while reading the compression gauge, ask the assistant to crank the engine two or three times in short bursts using the ignition switch.

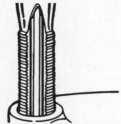

With the tap supplied, tap the hole to receive the thread insert. Keep the tap well oiled and back it out frequently to avoid clogging the threads

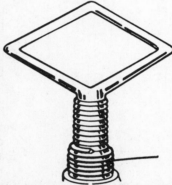

Screw the threaded insert onto the installation tool until the tang engages the slot. Screw the insert into the tapped hole until it is ¼–½ turn below the top surface. After installation, break off the tang with a hammer and punch

Drill out the damaged threads with the specified drill bit. Drill completely through the hole or to the bottom of a blind hole

The screw-in type compression gauge is more accurate

Troubleshooting Engine Mechanical Problems

Problem	Cause	Solution
External oil leaks	• Fuel pump gasket broken or improperly seated	• Replace gasket
	• Cylinder head cover RTV sealant broken or improperly seated	• Replace sealant; inspect cylinder head cover sealant flange and cylinder head sealant surface for distortion and cracks
	• Oil filler cap leaking or missing	• Replace cap
	• Oil filter gasket broken or improperly seated	• Replace oil filter
	• Oil pan side gasket broken, improperly seated or opening in RTV sealant	• Replace gasket or repair opening in sealant; inspect oil pan gasket flange for distortion
	• Oil pan front oil seal broken or improperly seated	• Replace seal; inspect timing case cover and oil pan seal flange for distortion
	• Oil pan rear oil seal broken or improperly seated	• Replace seal; inspect oil pan rear oil seal flange; inspect rear main bearing cap for cracks, plugged oil return channels, or distortion in seal groove
	• Timing case cover oil seal broken or improperly seated	• Replace seal
	• Excess oil pressure because of restricted PCV valve	• Replace PCV valve
	• Oil pan drain plug loose or has stripped threads	• Repair as necessary and tighten
	• Rear oil gallery plug loose	• Use appropriate sealant on gallery plug and tighten
	• Rear camshaft plug loose or improperly seated	• Seat camshaft plug or replace and seal, as necessary
	• Distributor base gasket damaged	• Replace gasket
Excessive oil consumption	• Oil level too high	• Drain oil to specified level
	• Oil with wrong viscosity being used	• Replace with specified oil
	• PCV valve stuck closed	• Replace PCV valve
	• Valve stem oil deflectors (or seals) are damaged, missing, or incorrect type	• Replace valve stem oil deflectors
	• Valve stems or valve guides worn	• Measure stem-to-guide clearance and repair as necessary
	• Poorly fitted or missing valve cover baffles	• Replace valve cover
	• Piston rings broken or missing	• Replace broken or missing rings
	• Scuffed piston	• Replace piston
	• Incorrect piston ring gap	• Measure ring gap, repair as necessary
	• Piston rings sticking or excessively loose in grooves	• Measure ring side clearance, repair as necessary
	• Compression rings installed upside down	• Repair as necessary
	• Cylinder walls worn, scored, or glazed	• Repair as necessary

Troubleshooting Engine Mechanical Problems (cont.)

Problem	Cause	Solution
	• Piston ring gaps not properly staggered	• Repair as necessary
	• Excessive main or connecting rod bearing clearance	• Measure bearing clearance, repair as necessary
No oil pressure	• Low oil level	• Add oil to correct level
	• Oil pressure gauge, warning lamp or sending unit inaccurate	• Replace oil pressure gauge or warning lamp
	• Oil pump malfunction	• Replace oil pump
	• Oil pressure relief valve sticking	• Remove and inspect oil pressure relief valve assembly
	• Oil passages on pressure side of pump obstructed	• Inspect oil passages for obstruction
	• Oil pickup screen or tube obstructed	• Inspect oil pickup for obstruction
	• Loose oil inlet tube	• Tighten or seal inlet tube
Low oil pressure	• Low oil level	• Add oil to correct level
	• Inaccurate gauge, warning lamp or sending unit	• Replace oil pressure gauge or warning lamp
	• Oil excessively thin because of dilution, poor quality, or improper grade	• Drain and refill crankcase with recommended oil
	• Excessive oil temperature	• Correct cause of overheating engine
	• Oil pressure relief spring weak or sticking	• Remove and inspect oil pressure relief valve assembly
	• Oil inlet tube and screen assembly has restriction or air leak	• Remove and inspect oil inlet tube and screen assembly. (Fill inlet tube with lacquer thinner to locate leaks.)
	• Excessive oil pump clearance	• Measure clearances
	• Excessive main, rod, or camshaft bearing clearance	• Measure bearing clearances, repair as necessary
High oil pressure	• Improper oil viscosity	• Drain and refill crankcase with correct viscosity oil
	• Oil pressure gauge or sending unit inaccurate	• Replace oil pressure gauge
	• Oil pressure relief valve sticking closed	• Remove and inspect oil pressure relief valve assembly
Main bearing noise	• Insufficient oil supply	• Inspect for low oil level and low oil pressure
	• Main bearing clearance excessive	• Measure main bearing clearance, repair as necessary
	• Bearing insert missing	• Replace missing insert
	• Crankshaft end play excessive	• Measure end play, repair as necessary
	• Improperly tightened main bearing cap bolts	• Tighten bolts with specified torque
	• Loose flywheel or drive plate	• Tighten flywheel or drive plate attaching bolts
	• Loose or damaged vibration damper	• Repair as necessary

Troubleshooting Engine Mechanical Problems (cont.)

Problem	Cause	Solution
Connecting rod bearing noise	• Insufficient oil supply	• Inspect for low oil level and low oil pressure
	• Carbon build-up on piston	• Remove carbon from piston crown
	• Bearing clearance excessive or bearing missing	• Measure clearance, repair as necessary
	• Crankshaft connecting rod journal out-of-round	• Measure journal dimensions, repair or replace as necessary
	• Misaligned connecting rod or cap	• Repair as necessary
	• Connecting rod bolts tightened improperly	• Tighten bolts with specified torque
Piston noise	• Piston-to-cylinder wall clearance excessive (scuffed piston)	• Measure clearance and examine piston
	• Cylinder walls excessively tapered or out-of-round	• Measure cylinder wall dimensions, rebore cylinder
	• Piston ring broken	• Replace all rings on piston
	• Loose or seized piston pin	• Measure piston-to-pin clearance, repair as necessary
	• Connecting rods misaligned	• Measure rod alignment, straighten or replace
	• Piston ring side clearance excessively loose or tight	• Measure ring side clearance, repair as necessary
	• Carbon build-up on piston is excessive	• Remove carbon from piston
Valve actuating component noise	• Insufficient oil supply	• Check for: (a) Low oil level (b) Low oil pressure (c) Plugged push rods (d) Wrong hydraulic tappets (e) Restricted oil gallery (f) Excessive tappet to bore clearance
	• Push rods worn or bent	• Replace worn or bent push rods
	• Rocker arms or pivots worn	• Replace worn rocker arms or pivots
	• Foreign objects or chips in hydraulic tappets	• Clean tappets
	• Excessive tappet leak-down	• Replace valve tappet
	• Tappet face worn	• Replace tappet; inspect corresponding cam lobe for wear
	• Broken or cocked valve springs	• Properly seat cocked springs; replace broken springs
	• Stem-to-guide clearance excessive	• Measure stem-to-guide clearance, repair as required
	• Valve bent	• Replace valve
	• Loose rocker arms	• Tighten bolts with specified torque
	• Valve seat runout excessive	• Regrind valve seat/valves
	• Missing valve lock	• Install valve lock
	• Push rod rubbing or contacting cylinder head	• Remove cylinder head and remove obstruction in head
	• Excessive engine oil (four-cylinder engine)	• Correct oil level

Troubleshooting the Cooling System

Problem	Cause	Solution
High temperature gauge indication—overheating	• Coolant level low • Fan belt loose • Radiator hose(s) collapsed • Radiator airflow blocked • Faulty radiator cap • Ignition timing incorrect • Idle speed low • Air trapped in cooling system • Heavy traffic driving • Incorrect cooling system component(s) installed • Faulty thermostat • Water pump shaft broken or impeller loose • Radiator tubes clogged • Cooling system clogged • Casting flash in cooling passages • Brakes dragging • Excessive engine friction • Antifreeze concentration over 68% • Missing air seals • Faulty gauge or sending unit • Loss of coolant flow caused by leakage or foaming • Viscous fan drive failed	• Replenish coolant • Adjust fan belt tension • Replace hose(s) • Remove restriction (bug screen, fog lamps, etc.) • Replace radiator cap • Adjust ignition timing • Adjust idle speed • Purge air • Operate at fast idle in neutral intermittently to cool engine • Install proper component(s) • Replace thermostat • Replace water pump • Flush radiator • Flush system • Repair or replace as necessary. Flash may be visible by removing cooling system components or removing core plugs. • Repair brakes • Repair engine • Lower antifreeze concentration percentage • Replace air seals • Repair or replace faulty component • Repair or replace leaking component, replace coolant • Replace unit
Low temperature indication—undercooling	• Thermostat stuck open • Faulty gauge or sending unit	• Replace thermostat • Repair or replace faulty component
Coolant loss—boilover	• Overfilled cooling system • Quick shutdown after hard (hot) run • Air in system resulting in occasional "burping" of coolant • Insufficient antifreeze allowing coolant boiling point to be too low • Antifreeze deteriorated because of age or contamination • Leaks due to loose hose clamps, loose nuts, bolts, drain plugs, faulty hoses, or defective radiator	• Reduce coolant level to proper specification • Allow engine to run at fast idle prior to shutdown • Purge system • Add antifreeze to raise boiling point • Replace coolant • Pressure test system to locate source of leak(s) then repair as necessary

Troubleshooting the Cooling System (cont.)

Problem	Cause	Solution
Coolant loss—boilover	• Faulty head gasket • Cracked head, manifold, or block • Faulty radiator cap	• Replace head gasket • Replace as necessary • Replace cap
Coolant entry into crankcase or cylinder(s)	• Faulty head gasket • Crack in head, manifold or block	• Replace head gasket • Replace as necessary
Coolant recovery system inoperative	• Coolant level low • Leak in system • Pressure cap not tight or seal missing, or leaking • Pressure cap defective • Overflow tube clogged or leaking • Recovery bottle vent restricted	• Replenish coolant to FULL mark • Pressure test to isolate leak and repair as necessary • Repair as necessary • Replace cap • Repair as necessary • Remove restriction
Noise	• Fan contacting shroud • Loose water pump impeller • Glazed fan belt • Loose fan belt • Rough surface on drive pulley • Water pump bearing worn • Belt alignment	• Reposition shroud and inspect engine mounts • Replace pump • Apply silicone or replace belt • Adjust fan belt tension • Replace pulley • Remove belt to isolate. Replace pump. • Check pulley alignment. Repair as necessary.
No coolant flow through heater core	• Restricted return inlet in water pump • Heater hose collapsed or restricted • Restricted heater core • Restricted outlet in thermostat housing • Intake manifold bypass hole in cylinder head restricted • Faulty heater control valve • Intake manifold coolant passage restricted	• Remove restriction • Remove restriction or replace hose • Remove restriction or replace core • Remove flash or restriction • Remove restriction • Replace valve • Remove restriction or replace intake manifold

NOTE: *Immediately after shutdown, the engine enters a condition known as heat soak. This is caused by the cooling system being inoperative while engine temperature is still high. If coolant temperature rises above boiling point, expansion and pressure may push some coolant out of the radiator overflow tube. If this does not occur frequently it is considered normal.*

Troubleshooting the Serpentine Drive Belt

Problem	Cause	Solution
Tension sheeting fabric failure (woven fabric on outside circumference of belt has cracked or separated from body of belt)	• Grooved or backside idler pulley diameters are less than minimum recommended • Tension sheeting contacting (rubbing) stationary object • Excessive heat causing woven fabric to age • Tension sheeting splice has fractured	• Replace pulley(s) not conforming to specification • Correct rubbing condition • Replace belt • Replace belt

Troubleshooting the Serpentine Drive Belt (cont.)

Problem	Cause	Solution
Noise (objectional squeal, squeak, or rumble is heard or felt while drive belt is in operation)	• Belt slippage • Bearing noise • Belt misalignment • Belt-to-pulley mismatch • Driven component inducing vibration • System resonant frequency inducing vibration	• Adjust belt • Locate and repair • Align belt/pulley(s) • Install correct belt • Locate defective driven component and repair • Vary belt tension within specifications. Replace belt.
Rib chunking (one or more ribs has separated from belt body)	• Foreign objects imbedded in pulley grooves • Installation damage • Drive loads in excess of design specifications • Insufficient internal belt adhesion	• Remove foreign objects from pulley grooves • Replace belt • Adjust belt tension • Replace belt
Rib or belt wear (belt ribs contact bottom of pulley grooves)	• Pulley(s) misaligned • Mismatch of belt and pulley groove widths • Abrasive environment • Rusted pulley(s) • Sharp or jagged pulley groove tips • Rubber deteriorated	• Align pulley(s) • Replace belt • Replace belt • Clean rust from pulley(s) • Replace pulley • Replace belt
Longitudinal belt cracking (cracks between two ribs)	• Belt has mistracked from pulley groove • Pulley groove tip has worn away rubber-to-tensile member	• Replace belt • Replace belt
Belt slips	• Belt slipping because of insufficient tension • Belt or pulley subjected to substance (belt dressing, oil, ethylene glycol) that has reduced friction • Driven component bearing failure • Belt glazed and hardened from heat and excessive slippage	• Adjust tension • Replace belt and clean pulleys • Replace faulty component bearing • Replace belt
"Groove jumping" (belt does not maintain correct position on pulley, or turns over and/or runs off pulleys)	• Insufficient belt tension • Pulley(s) not within design tolerance • Foreign object(s) in grooves • Excessive belt speed • Pulley misalignment • Belt-to-pulley profile mismatched • Belt cordline is distorted	• Adjust belt tension • Replace pulley(s) • Remove foreign objects from grooves • Avoid excessive engine acceleration • Align pulley(s) • Install correct belt • Replace belt

Troubleshooting the Serpentine Drive Belt (cont.)

Problem	Cause	Solution
Belt broken (Note: identify and correct problem before replacement belt is installed)	• Excessive tension	• Replace belt and adjust tension to specification
	• Tensile members damaged during belt installation	• Replace belt
	• Belt turnover	• Replace belt
	• Severe pulley misalignment	• Align pulley(s)
	• Bracket, pulley, or bearing failure	• Replace defective component and belt
Cord edge failure (tensile member exposed at edges of belt or separated from belt body)	• Excessive tension	• Adjust belt tension
	• Drive pulley misalignment	• Align pulley
	• Belt contacting stationary object	• Correct as necessary
	• Pulley irregularities	• Replace pulley
	• Improper pulley construction	• Replace pulley
	• Insufficient adhesion between tensile member and rubber matrix	• Replace belt and adjust tension to specifications
Sporadic rib cracking (multiple cracks in belt ribs at random intervals)	• Ribbed pulley(s) diameter less than minimum specification	• Replace pulley(s)
	• Backside bend flat pulley(s) diameter less than minimum	• Replace pulley(s)
	• Excessive heat condition causing rubber to harden	• Correct heat condition as necessary
	• Excessive belt thickness	• Replace belt
	• Belt overcured	• Replace belt
	• Excessive tension	• Adjust belt tension

7. Read the compression gauge at the end of each series of cranks, and record the highest of these readings. Repeat this procedure for each of the engine's cylinders. Compare the highest reading of each cylinder to the compression pressure specification in the "Tune-Up Specifications" chart in Section 2. The specs in this chart are maximum values.

NOTE: A cylinder's compression pressure should not be below 100 psi (689 kPa). Usually acceptable if it is not less than 80 percent of maximum. The difference between each cylinder should be no more than 12–14 pounds.

8. If a cylinder is unusually low, pour a tablespoon of clean engine oil into the cylinder through the spark plug hole and repeat the compression test. If the compression rises after adding the oil, it appears that the cylinder's piston rings or bore are damaged or worn. If the pressure remains low, the valves may not be seating properly (a valve job is needed), or the head gasket may be blown near that cylinder. If compression in any two adjacent cylinders is low and if the addition of oil does not help

the compression, there is leakage past the head gasket. Oil and coolant water in the combustion chamber can result from this problem. There may be evidence of water droplets on the engine dipstick when a head gasket has blown.

NORMAL - Compression builds up quickly and evenly to the specified compression on each cylinder.

PISTON RINGS - Compression low on the first stroke, then tends to build up on the following strokes, but does not reach normal. This reading should be tested with the addition of a few shots of engine oil into the cylinder. If the compression increases considerably, the rings are leaking compression.

VALVES - Low on the first stroke, does not tend to build up on following strokes. This reading will stay around the same with a few shots of engine oil in the cylinder.

HEAD GASKET - The compression reading is low between two adjacent cylinders. The head gasket between the two cylinders may be blown. If there is signs of white smoke coming from the exhaust while the engine is running may indicate water leaking into the cylinder and being converted into steam. Check around the cylinder head-to-cylinder block area for signs of coolant and oil leakage, indicating a leaking head gasket.

GENERAL ENGINE SPECIFICATIONS

Years	VIN	Engine No. Cyl. (cu. in.)	Fuel System Type	SAE Net Horsepower @ rpm	SAE Net Torque ft. lb. @ rpm	Bore × Stroke	Comp. Ratio	Oil Press. (psi.) @2000 rpm
1985–87	E	4-151	TBI	98 @ 4400	134 @ 3200	4.000 × 3.000	9.0:1	36–41
1985	N	6-262	4-bbl	150 @ 4000	225 @ 2400	4.000 × 3.480	9.3:1	30–35
1986–87	Z	6-262	TBI	150 @ 4000	230 @ 2400	4.000 × 3.480	9.3:1	30–35
1988–90	E	4-151	TBI	92 @ 4400	134 @ 3200	4.000 × 3.000	8.3:1	36–41
	Z	6-262	TBI	145 @ 4000	230 @ 2400	4.000 × 3.480	9.3:1	30–35
	B ①	6-262	TBI	170 @ 4000	235 @ 2400	4.000 × 3.480	9.3:1	30–35

TBI: Throttle Body Injection
① 262 (4.3L) High Output

VALVE SPECIFICATIONS

Year	VIN	Engine No. Cyl. (cu. in.)	Seat Angle (deg)	Face Angle (deg)	Spring Test Pressure (lbs. @ in.)	Spring Installed Height (in.)	Stem to Guide Clearance (in.) Intake	Stem to Guide Clearance (in.) Exhaust	Stem Diameter (in.) Intake	Stem Diameter (in.) Exhaust
1985	N	6-262	46	45	③	1.72 ④	0.0010–0.0027	0.0010–0.0027	N/A	N/A
1985–87	E	4-151	46	45	①	1.69	0.0010–0.0027	②	0.342–0.343	0.342–0.343
1986–87	Z	6-262	46	45	③	1.72 ④	0.0010–0.0027	0.0010–0.0027	NA	NA
1988–90	E	4-151	46	45	⑤	1.44	0.0010–0.0025	0.0013–0.0030	0.3133–0.3138	0.3128–0.3135
	Z	6-262	46	45	③	1.72 ④	0.0010–0.0027	0.0010–0.0027	NA	NA
	B ⑥									

NA: Information not available
① 78–86 @ 1.66—Closed
170–180 @ 1.26—Open
② 0.0010–0.0027—Top
0.0020–0.0037—Bottom
③ 76–84 @ 1.70—Closed
④ ± 1/32
⑤ 71–78 @ 1.44—Closed
150–170 @ 1.04 Open
⑥ 1990 6-262 High Output

CRANKSHAFT AND CONNECTING ROD SPECIFICATIONS

All specifications in inches

Years	VIN	Engine No. Cyl. (cu. in.)	Crankshaft Main Bearing Journal Dia.	Crankshaft Main Bearing Oil Clearance	Crankshaft Shaft End Play	Crankshaft Thrust on No.	Connecting Rod Journal Dia.	Connecting Rod Oil Clearance	Connecting Rod Side Clearance
1985	N	6-262	①	②	0.002–0.006	4	2.2487–2.2497	0.0010–0.0032	0.007–0.015
1985–87	E	4-151	2.300	0.0005–0.0022	0.0035–0.0085	5	2.0000	0.0005–0.0026	0.006–0.022
1986–87	Z	6-262	①	②	0.002–0.006	4	2.2487–2.2497	0.0013–0.0035	0.006–0.014
1988–90	E	4-151	2.300	0.0005–0.0022	0.0035–0.0085	5	2.0000	0.0005–0.0026	0.006–0.022
	Z B ③	6-262	①	②	0.002–0.006	4	2.2487–2.2497	0.0013–0.0035	0.006–0.014

① No. 1—2.4484–2.4493
No. 2 & 3—2.4481–2.4490
No. 4—2.4479–2.4488
② No. 1—0.0008–0.0020
No. 2 & 3—0.0011–0.0023
No. 4—0.0017–0.0032
③ 1990 6-262 High Output

PISTON AND RING SPECIFICATIONS

All specifications in inches

Years	VIN	Engine No. Cyl. (cu. in.)	Ring Gap			Ring Side Clearance			Piston Clearance
			#1 Compr.	#2 Compr.	Oil Control	#1 Compr.	#2 Compr.	Oil Control	
1985	E	4-151	0.0100–0.0220	0.0100–0.0270	0.0150–0.0550	0.0015–0.0030	0.0015–0.0030	—	①
1986–87	E	4-151	0.0100–0.0200	0.0100–0.0200	0.0200–0.0600	0.002–0.003	0.001–0.003	0.002–0.006	0.0014–0.0022②
1985	N	6-262	0.0100–0.0200	0.0100–0.0250	0.0150–0.0550	0.0012–0.0032	0.0012–0.0032	0.002–0.007	0.00025–0.00035
1986–87	Z	6-262	0.0100–0.0200	0.0100–0.0250	0.0150–0.0550	0.0012–0.0032	0.0012–0.0032	0.002–0.007	0.00025–0.00035
1988	E	4-151	0.0100–0.0200	0.0100–0.0250	0.0150–0.0550	0.0012–0.0032	0.0012–0.0032	0.002–0.007	0.0007–0.0017
1989–90	E	4-151	0.0100–0.0200	0.0100–0.0200	0.0200–0.0600	0.002–0.003	0.001–0.003	0.015–0.055	0.00098–0.0022
1988–90	Z B③	6-262	0.0100–0.0200	0.0100–0.0250	0.0150–0.0550	0.0012–0.0032	0.0012–0.0032	0.002–0.007	0.0007–0.0017

① 0.0025–0.0033 (Top)
　0.0017–0.0041 (Bottom)
② Measured 1.8 inch down from top of piston
③ 1990 6-262 High Output

TORQUE SPECIFICATIONS

All specifications in ft. lbs.

Years	VIN	Engine No. Cyl. (cu. in.)	Cyl. Head	Conn. Rod	Main Bearing	Crankshaft Damper	Flywheel	Manifold	
								Intake	Exhaust
1985	E	4-151	92	32	70	160	44	29	44
1986–87	E	4-151	90	32	70	160	①	②	③
1985	N	6-262	65	45	70	60	55–75	30	20
1986–87	Z	6-262	65	45	75	70	75	36	③
1988	E	4-151	④	32	70	160	①	25	36
1989–90	E	4–151	④	30	65	160	①	25	36
1988–90	Z B⑤	6-262	65	45	80	70	75	35	③

① 55 ft. lbs.—Automatic
　65 ft. lbs.—Manual
② Refer to the Manifold Installation procedures for the correct torquing procedures.
③ 26 ft. lbs.—Center two bolts
　20 ft. lbs.—All other bolts
④ Torque all bolts in sequence to 18 ft. lbs. (25 Nm). Then, torque in sequence, all bolts (except number 9) to 26 ft. lbs. (35 Nm). Torque number 9 to 18 ft. lbs. (25 Nm). Then torque all bolts an additional 90 degrees (¼ turn) in sequence.
⑤ 1990 6–262 High Output

CAMSHAFT SPECIFICATIONS

All specifications in inches.

Years	VIN	Engine No. Cyl. (cu. in.)	Journal Diameter					Bearing Clearance	Elevation		End Play
			1	2	3	4	5		Int.	Exh.	
1985–87	E	4-151	1.869	1.869	1.869	—	—	0.0007–0.0027	0.398	0.398	0.0015–0.0050
1985	N	6-262	1.868–1.869	1.868–1.869	1.868–1.869	1.868–1.869	—	N.A.	0.355–0.359	0.388–0.392	0.004–0.012

CAMSHAFT SPECIFICATIONS

All specifications in inches.

Years	VIN	Engine No. Cyl. (cu. in.)	Journal Diameter					Bearing Clearance	Elevation		End Play
			1	2	3	4	5		Int.	Exh.	
1986–87	Z	6-262	1.868–1.869	1.868–1.869	1.868–1.869	1.868–1.869	—	N.A.	0.355–0.359	0.388–0.392	0.004–0.012
1988	E	4-151	1.869	1.869	1.869	—	—	0.0007–0.0027	0.398	0.398	0.0015–0.0050
1989–90	E	4-151	1.869	1.869	1.869	—	—	0.0007–0.0027	0.232	0.232	0.0015–0.0050
1988–90	Z B ①	6-262	1.868–1.869	1.868–1.869	1.868–1.869	1.868–1.869	—	NA	0.357	0.390	0.004–0.012

N.A.—Not available
① 1990 6-262 High Output

Engine

REMOVAL AND INSTALLATION

2.5L Engine

— **CAUTION** —

Before removing any component of the fuel system (TBI models), be sure to reduce the fuel pressure in the system. The pressure regulator (TBI models) contains an orifice in the fuel system; when the engine is turned Off, the pressure in the system will bleed down within a few minutes.

1. Disconnect the negative battery cable from the battery.
2. From inside the vehicle, remove the engine cover.
3. Place a drain pan under the radiator, open the drain cock and drain the cooling system; be sure to save the cooling fluid for reuse.

— **CAUTION** —

When draining the coolant, keep in mind that cats and dogs are attracted by the ethylene glycol antifreeze, and are quite likely to drink any that is left in an uncovered container or in puddles on the ground. This will prove fatal in sufficient quantity. Always drain the coolant into a sealable container. Coolant should be reused unless it is contaminated or several years old.

4. Remove the headlight bezel and grille.
5. Remove the lower radiator close out panel and the radiator support brace.
6. Remove the lower tie bar, the cross braces and the hood latch assembly.
7. Remove the radiator hoses, then disconnect and plug the transmission-to-radiator oil cooler lines (if equipped).
8. Remove the radiator filler panels, then the radiator and the fan shroud as an assembly.
9. At the bulkhead connector, disconnect the engine electrical harness. Disconnect the electrical harness from the Electronic Control Module (ECM) and pull it through the bulkhead.
10. Remove the heater hoses from the heater core.
11. Disconnect the accelerator, the cruise control and the detent (if equipped) cables. Disconnect the ground cable from the cylinder head.
12. Remove the oil filler neck and the thermostat housing from the engine.
13. Remove the purge hose from the charcoal canister, then the air cleaner and adapter from the carburetor or throttle body. Disconnect the fuel hoses from the throttle body.
14. Raise and support the front of the vehicle on jackstands.

15. Disconnect the exhaust pipe from the exhaust manifold. Remove the flywheel cover from the bellhousing.
16. Disconnect the electrical harness from the transmission and the frame, then the electrical connectors from the starter.
17. Remove the starter-to-engine bolts and the starter from the engine.
18. Remove the through bolts from the engine mounts and install an engine lifting device to the engine.
19. Remove the bellhousing-to-engine bolts, then lower the vehicle. Using a floor jack, support the transmission.
20. Using an engine lifting device, lift the engine, separate it from the transmission and remove it from the vehicle.

To install:

1. Using an engine lifting device, lift the engine, connect it to the transmission and install it in the vehicle.
2. Install the bellhousing-to-engine bolts, torque to 32 ft. lbs. (44 Nm) then lower the vehicle. Using a floor jack, support the transmission.
3. Install the through bolts to the engine mounts and remove an engine lifting device from the engine.
4. Install the starter-to-engine bolts and starter.
5. Connect the electrical harness to the transmission and the frame, then the electrical connectors to the starter.
6. Connect the exhaust pipe to the exhaust manifold. Install the flywheel cover to the bellhousing.
7. Raise and support the front of the vehicle on jackstands.
8. Install the purge hose to the charcoal canister, then the air cleaner and adapter to the carburetor or throttle body. Connect the fuel hoses to the throttle body.
9. Install the oil filler neck and the thermostat housing to the engine.
10. Connect the accelerator, the cruise control and the detent (if equipped) cables. Connect the ground cable to the cylinder head.
11. Install the heater hoses to the heater core.
12. At the bulkhead connector, connect the engine electrical harness. Connect the electrical harness to the Electronic Control Module (ECM).
13. Install the radiator, filler panels and the fan shroud as an assembly.
14. Install the radiator hoses, then connect the transmission-to-radiator oil cooler lines (if equipped).
15. Install the lower tie bar, the cross braces and the hood latch assembly.
16. Install the lower radiator close out panel and the radiator support brace.
17. Install the headlight bezel and grille.
18. Refill the cooling system.

19. From inside the vehicle, install the engine cover.

20. Connect the negative battery cable to the battery.

21. Start the engine and check for fluid leaks and proper operation.

NOTE: All engine fasteners are important parts that may affect the performance of the components and systems, they could result in major repair expense. If replacement becomes necessary, they MUST BE replaced with the same part number or equivalent part. Use specific torque values when assembling the parts, to assure proper retention.

4.3L Engine

———————— CAUTION ————————

To reduce the risk of fire and personal injury, it is necessary to relieve the fuel system pressure before servicing any fuel system component. If this procedure is not performed, fuel may be sprayed out of the connection under pressure. Always keep a dry chemical (Class B) fire extinguisher near the work area. Relieve the pressure on the fuel system before disconnecting any fuel line connection.

1. Disconnect the negative battery cable from the battery.

2. Place a pan under the radiator, open the drain cock and drain the engine coolant.

———————— CAUTION ————————

When draining the coolant, keep in mind that cats and dogs are attracted by the ethylene glycol antifreeze, and are quite likely to drink any that is left in an uncovered container or in puddles on the ground. This will prove fatal in sufficient quantity. Always drain the coolant into a sealable container. Coolant should be reused unless it is contaminated or several years old.

3. Raise and support the front of the vehicle on jackstands.

4. Disconnect the exhaust pipes from the exhaust manifolds.

5. At the flywheel cover, remove the strut rods, then the flywheel cover from the bellhousing. If equipped with an automatic transmission, mark the torque converter-to-flywheel position, then disconnect the torque converter from the flywheel.

6. Disconnect the electrical connectors from the starter, then remove the starter from the engine. Disconnect the electrical harness and connectors from the transmission and the frame.

7. Remove the oil filter and the lower fan shroud bolts. Disconnect the fuel hoses from the frame.

8. From the radiator, disconnect the lower transmission oil cooler line (if used) and the lower engine oil cooler line (if used).

9. Remove the through bolts of the engine-to-frame mounts, then remove the jackstands and lower the vehicle.

10. Remove the headlight bezels and the grille. At the radiator, remove the lower close-out panel, the support brace and the core support cross brace, then remove the lower tie-bar and the hood latch mechanism.

11. At the firewall, remove the master cylinder.

12. From the radiator, remove the upper fan shroud, the upper radiator core support, the filler panels and the radiator.

NOTE: Before removing the radiator, be sure to discharge the air conditioning system (if equipped).

13. From inside the vehicle, remove the engine cover and the right side kick panel.

14. From the air conditioning system, remove the rear compressor brace, the hose from the accumulator, then the compressor (with the bracket) and the accumulator.

15. Remove the power steering pump (DO NOT disconnect the pressure hoses) and move it aside.

16. Disconnect the vacuum hoses from the intake manifold. Disconnect the electrical harness connector from the bulkhead and the Electronic Control Module (ECM); push the electrical harness connector through the bulkhead.

17. Remove the distributor cap, the fuel line(s) from the carbu-

retor or throttle body and the diverter valve (if equipped).

18. Remove the transmission dipstick tube, the heater hose(s) from the heater core, the horn and the Air Injector Reactor (AIR) check valves.

19. Using and engine lifting device, attach it to the engine.

20. Using a floor jack, raise and support the transmission, then remove the bellhousing-to-engine bolts.

21. Raise the engine, disconnect it from the bellhousing and remove it from the vehicle.

To install:

NOTE: All engine fasteners are important parts that may affect the performance of the components and systems, they could result in major repair expense. If replacement becomes necessary, they MUST BE replaced with the same part number or equivalent part. Use specific torque values when assembling the parts, to assure proper retention.

1. Place the engine on a lifting device and lower the engine into the vehicle, connect it to the bellhousing.

2. Using a floor jack, raise and support the transmission, then install the bellhousing-to-engine bolts.

3. Remove the engine lifting device.

4. Install the transmission dipstick tube, the heater hose(s) to the heater core, the horn and the Air Injector Reactor (AIR) check valves.

5. Install the distributor cap, the fuel line(s) to the carburetor or throttle body and the diverter valve (if equipped).

6. Connect the vacuum hoses to the intake manifold. Connect the electrical harness connector to the bulkhead and the Electronic Control Module (ECM).

7. Install the power steering pump.

8. To the air conditioning system, install the rear compressor brace, the hose to the accumulator, then the compressor (with the bracket) and the accumulator.

9. From inside the vehicle, install the engine cover and the right side kick panel.

10. To the radiator, install the upper fan shroud, the upper radiator core support, the filler panels and the radiator.

11. At the firewall, install the master cylinder.

12. Install the headlight bezels and the grille. At the radiator, install the lower close-out panel, the support brace and the core support cross brace, then install the lower tie-bar and the hood latch mechanism.

13. Install the through bolts of the engine-to-frame mounts, then and lower the vehicle.

14. From the radiator, connect the lower transmission oil cooler line (if used) and the lower engine oil cooler line (if used).

15. Install a new oil filter and the lower fan shroud bolts. Connect the fuel hoses to the frame.

16. Connect the electrical connectors to the starter after installing the starter to the engine. Connect the electrical harness and connectors to the transmission and the frame.

17. If equipped with an automatic transmission, note the torque converter-to-flywheel position, then connect the torque converter to the flywheel at the marked position. At the flywheel cover, install the strut rods, then the flywheel cover to the bellhousing.

18. Connect the exhaust pipes to the exhaust manifolds.

19. Refill the engine with coolant and oil.

20. Connect the negative battery cable to the battery.

21. Start the engine and check for leaks and proper operation.

Pushrod Side Cover

REMOVAL AND INSTALLATION

2.5L Engine

The pushrod side cover is located on the right side of the engine and must be removed to service the valve lifters.

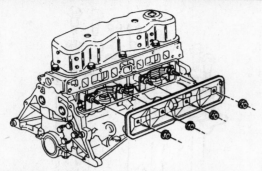

Replacing the side cover — 2.5L engine

1. Disconnect the negative battery cable from the battery.
2. Remove the alternator and the bracket from the engine.
3. Place a pan under the radiator, open the drain cock and drain the cooling system. Remove the intake manifold-to-engine brace.

——— CAUTION ———

When draining the coolant, keep in mind that cats and dogs are attracted by the ethylene glycol antifreeze, and are quite likely to drink any that is left in an uncovered container or in puddles on the ground. This will prove fatal in sufficient quantity. Always drain the coolant into a sealable container. Coolant should be reused unless it is contaminated or several years old.

4. Remove the lower radiator and heater hoses.
5. Disconnect the electrical connector from the oil sender and the wiring harness from around the pushrod side cover. Remove the wiring harness brackets from the pushrod cover.
6. Remove the side cover-to-engine nuts and the side cover.
7. Using a putty knife, clean the gasket mounting surfaces.

NOTE: Use a solvent to clean the oil and grease from the gasket mounting surfaces.

To install:
1. Install the side cover-to-engine with a new gasket and torque the nuts to 120 inch lbs. (14 Nm).
2. Connect the electrical connector to the oil sender and the wiring harness to the pushrod side cover.
3. Install the lower radiator and heater hoses.
4. Install the intake manifold-to-engine brace.
5. Refill the engine with coolant.
6. Install the alternator and the bracket to the engine.
7. Connect the negative battery cable to the battery.
8. Start the engine and check for leaks.

Rocker Arm Cover

REMOVAL AND INSTALLATION

2.5L Engine

1. Disconnect the negative battery cable from the battery.
2. Remove the air cleaner.
3. Disconnect the Positive Crankcase Ventilation (PCV) valve hose, the ignition wires from the rocker arm cover.
4. Remove the Exhaust Gas Recirculation (EGR) valve.
5. From the intake stud, label and disconnect the vacuum hoses.
6. Remove the rocker arm cover-to-cylinder head bolts and the cover.
7. Using a putty knife, clean the gasket mounting surface.

NOTE: Be sure to use solvent to remove any oil or grease that may remain on the sealing surfaces.

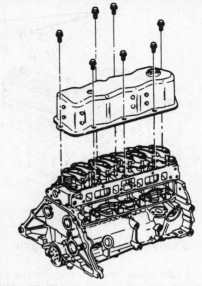

Removing the valve cover — 2.5L engine

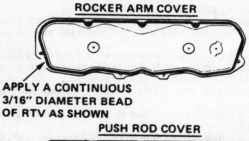

ROCKER ARM COVER

APPLY A CONTINUOUS 3/16" DIAMETER BEAD OF RTV AS SHOWN

PUSH ROD COVER

APPLY A CONTINUOUS 3/16" DIAMETER BEAD OF RTV AS SHOWN

Applying RTV sealant to the valve and the pushrod side cover gaskets — 2.5L engine

To install:
1. Using a new gasket, a 3/16 in. (4.7mm) continuous bead of RTV sealant, install the rocker arm cover and torque to 84 inch lbs. (10 Nm).
2. To the intake stud, connect the vacuum hoses.
3. Install the Exhaust Gas Recirculation (EGR) valve.
4. Connect the Positive Crankcase Ventilation (PCV) valve hose, the ignition wires to the rocker arm cover.
5. Install the air cleaner.
6. Connect the negative battery cable to the battery.
7. Start the engine and check for leaks.

4.3L Engine
RIGHT SIDE

1. Disconnect the negative battery cable from the battery.
2. Remove the air cleaner. Disconnect the Air Injection Reaction (AIR) hoses from the diverter valve, then the diverter valve bracket from the intake manifold.

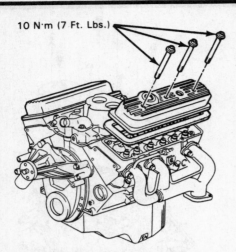

10 N·m (7 Ft. Lbs.)

Installing the valve cover — 4.3L engine

3. From the alternator bracket, remove the engine oil filler tube and the transmission (if equipped with an automatic transmission) oil filler tube.

4. From the valve cover, remove the Positive Crankcase Ventilation (PCV) valve.

5. From the back side of the right cylinder head, remove the AIR pipe-to-cylinder head bolts and move the pipe (hose) out of the way.

6. Remove the ignition wires from the valve cover and the distributor cap (with the wires attached), then move the cap out of the way.

7. Remove the valve cover-to-cylinder head bolts and the cover.

8. Using a putty knife, clean the gasket mounting surfaces.

To install:

1. Using a new gasket, install the rocker cover and torque to 84 inch lbs. (10 Nm).

2. Install the ignition wires to the valve cover and the distributor cap.

3. To the back side of the right cylinder head, install the AIR pipe-to-cylinder head bolts.

4. To the rocker cover, install the Positive Crankcase Ventilation (PCV) valve.

5. To the alternator bracket, install the engine oil filler tube and the transmission (if equipped with an automatic transmission) oil filler tube.

6. Install the air cleaner. Connect the Air Injection Reaction (AIR) hoses to the diverter valve.

7. Connect the negative battery cable to the battery.

8. Start the engine and check for leaks.

LEFT SIDE

1. Disconnect the negative battery cable from the battery.

2. Remove the air cleaner.

NOTE: If equipped with a carburetor, remove the vacuum pipe from the carburetor.

3. Disconnect the electrical harness from the rocker arm cover and any vacuum hoses (if necessary).

4. Disconnect the accelerator and the detent cables from the carburetor/throttle body, then remove the mounting brackets from the intake manifold.

5. Remove the valve cover-to-cylinder head bolts and the cover.

6. Using a putty knife, clean the gasket mounting surfaces.

To install:

1. Using a new gasket, torque the rocker cover-to-cylinder head bolts to 84 inch lbs. (10 Nm).

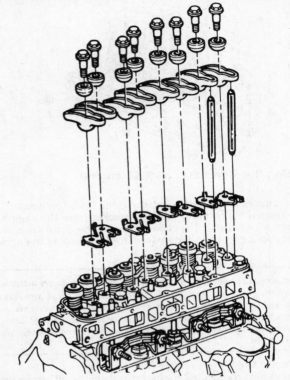

Exploded view of the rocker arm assembly — 2.5L engine

2. Connect and install the mounting bracket, accelerator and the detent cables to the carburetor/throttle body.

3. Connect the electrical harness to the rocker arm cover and any vacuum hoses (if necessary).

4. Install the air cleaner.

5. Connect the negative battery cable to the battery.

6. Start the engine and check for leaks.

Rocker Arms

The rocker arm opens and closes the valves through a very simple ball pivot type operation.

REMOVAL AND INSTALLATION

2.5L Engine

1. Refer to the Valve Cover, Removal and Installation procedures in this section and remove the valve cover.

2. Using a socket wrench, remove the rocker arm bolts, the ball washer and the rocker arm.

NOTE: If only the pushrod is to be removed, back off the rocker arm bolt, swing the rocker arm aside and remove the pushrod. When removing more than assembly, at the same time, be sure to keep them in order for reassembly purposes.

3. Inspect the rocker arms and ball washers for scoring and/or other damage, replace them (if necessary).

NOTE: If replacing worn components with new ones, be sure to coat the new parts with Molykote® before installation.

To install:

1. Install the pushrod guide if removed.

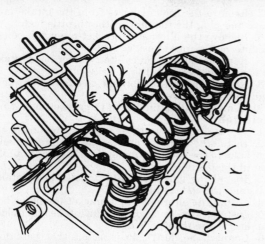

Removing the rocker arm assemblies — 4.3L engine

2. Install the ball washer, rocker arms and bolts. Torque the rocker arm-to-cylinder head bolts to 22 ft. lbs. (30 Nm) with the camshaft on the base circle during torquing; DO NOT overtighten.

3. Install the rocker arm cover and torque the bolts to 84 inch lbs. (10 Nm).

4. Start the engine, the check for oil leaks and engine operation.

4.3L Engine

1. Refer to the Valve Cover, Removal and Installation procedures in this section and remove the valve covers.

2. Using a socket wrench remove the rocker arm-to-cylinder head nuts, the ball washers, the rocker arms and the pushrods (if necessary).

3. Inspect the parts for excessive wear and/or damage, then replace any parts (if necessary).

NOTE: If replacing any parts with new ones, coat the new parts with Molykote®.

To install:

1. Install the rocker arm ball pivot and nut.

2. To prepare the engine for valve adjustment, rotate the crankshaft until the mark on the damper pulley aligns with the **0** mark on the timing plate and the No. 1 cylinder is on the compression stroke.

NOTE: To determine if the No. 1 cylinder is on the compression stroke, shake the rocker arms of the No. 1 cylinder, if they move, the cylinder is on the compression stroke; if they don't move, the cylinder is on the exhaust stroke. If the cylinder is on the exhaust stroke, it will be necessary to rotate the crankshaft one full revolution.

3. With the engine on the compression stroke, adjust the exhaust valves of cylinders No. 1, 5 & 6 and the intake valves of cylinders No. 1, 2 & 3, by performing the following procedures:

   a. Back out the adjusting nut until lash can be felt at the pushrod.

   b. While rotating the pushrod, turn the adjusting nut inward until all of the lash is removed.

   c. When the play has disappeared, turn the adjusting nut inward one additional turn.

4. Rotate the crankshaft one complete revolution and align the mark on the damper pulley with the **0** mark on the timing plate.

5. With the engine on the compression stroke, adjust the exhaust valves of cylinders No. 2, 3 & 4 and the intake valves of

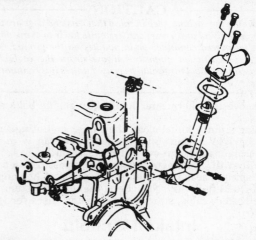

Exploded view of the thermostat and housing — 2.5L engine

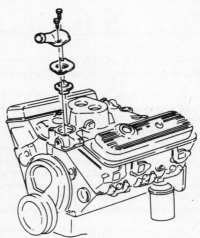

Exploded view of the thermostat and housing — 4.3L engine

cylinders No. 4, 5 & 6, by performing the following procedures:

   a. Back out the adjusting nut until lash can be felt at the pushrod.

   b. While rotating the pushrod, turn the adjusting nut inward until all of the lash is removed.

   c. When the play has disappeared, turn the adjusting nut inward one additional turn.

6. Install the rocker arm cover and torque the bolts 84 inch lbs. (10 Nm).

7. Start the engine, then check for oil leaks and engine operation.

Thermostat

The thermostat is located inside the thermostat housing, which is attached to the front of the cylinder head (2.5L) or to the front of the intake manifold (4.3L).

REMOVAL AND INSTALLATION

1. Disconnect the negative battery cable from the battery.

2. Place a catch pan under the radiator, open the drain cock and drain the cooling system.

CAUTION

When draining the coolant, keep in mind that cats and dogs are attracted by the ethylene glycol antifreeze, and are quite likely to drink any that is left in an uncovered container or in puddles on the ground. This will prove fatal in sufficient quantity. Always drain the coolant into a sealable container. Coolant should be reused unless it is contaminated or several years old.

---

3. Remove the thermostat housing-to-engine bolts and the thermostat.

4. Using a putty knife, clean the gasket mounting surfaces.

5. Using RTV sealant or equivalent, place an ⅛ in. (3mm) bead of sealant in the groove of the water outlet.

6. **To install,** use a new thermostat (if possible), a new gasket and silicone sealer. Torque the thermostat housing-to-engine bolts to 21 ft. lbs. (28 Nm). Refill the cooling system. Reconnect the battery cable, start the engine and check for leaks.

Intake Manifold

REMOVAL AND INSTALLATION

2.5L Engine

The intake manifold is located on the right side of the cylinder head.

CAUTION

Relieve the pressure on the fuel system before disconnecting any fuel line connection!

---

1. Disconnect the negative battery cable from the battery.

2. Place a catch pan under the radiator, open the drain cock and drain the cooling fluid.

CAUTION

When draining the coolant, keep in mind that cats and dogs are attracted by the ethylene glycol antifreeze, and are quite likely to drink any that is left in an uncovered container or in puddles on the ground. This will prove fatal in sufficient quantity. Always drain the coolant into a sealable container. Coolant should be reused unless it is contaminated or several years old.

---

3. Remove the air cleaner assembly. Label and disconnect the vacuum hoses from the exhaust manifold, thermostat housing and etc.

4. Label and disconnect the electrical connectors that may be in the way. Disconnect the accelerator, the cruise control and TV cables.

5. Remove the coolant hoses from the intake manifold. Remove and plug the fuel line at the throttle body.

6. Remove the alternator bracket-to-engine bolts and move the alternator/bracket aside.

7. Remove the ignition coil-to-cylinder head/intake manifold bolts and the coil from the engine.

8. Remove the intake manifold-to-engine bolts and the manifold from the engine.

9. Using a putty knife, clean the gasket mounting surfaces.

To install:

1. Use a new gasket and sealant on some bolts.

2. Install the manifold and torque the intake manifold-to-engine bolts to the specification in the "Intake Manifold" illustration in this section.

3. Install the ignition coil-to-cylinder head/intake manifold bolts and the coil to the engine.

4. Install the alternator and bracket-to-engine bolts.

5. Install the coolant hoses to the intake manifold. Install the fuel line at the throttle body.

6. Connect the electrical connectors that were disconnected. Connect the accelerator, the cruise control and TV cables.

7. Install the air cleaner assembly. Connect the vacuum hoses to the exhaust manifold, thermostat housing and etc.

8. Refill the engine with coolant.

9. Connect the negative battery cable to the battery.

10. Start the engine and check for leaks.

4.3L Engine

The intake manifold is located between the cylinder heads.

CAUTION

If equipped with an EFI system, relieve the pressure on the fuel system before disconnecting any fuel line connection!

---

1. Disconnect the negative battery cable from the battery.

2. Remove the air cleaner. Disconnect the Electronic Spark Control (ESC) electrical connector. Remove the distributor.

3. Place a catch pan under the radiator, open the drain cock and drain the cooling fluid.

CAUTION

When draining the coolant, keep in mind that cats and dogs are attracted by the ethylene glycol antifreeze, and are quite likely to drink any that is left in an uncovered container or in puddles on the ground. This will prove fatal in sufficient quantity. Always drain the coolant into a sealable container. Coolant should be reused unless it is contaminated or several years old.

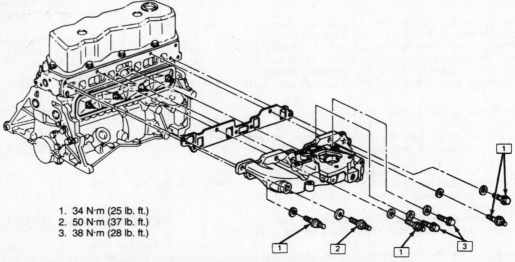

1. 34 N·m (25 lb. ft.)
2. 50 N·m (37 lb. ft.)
3. 38 N·m (28 lb. ft.)

Installing and torquing the intake manifold — 2.5L engine

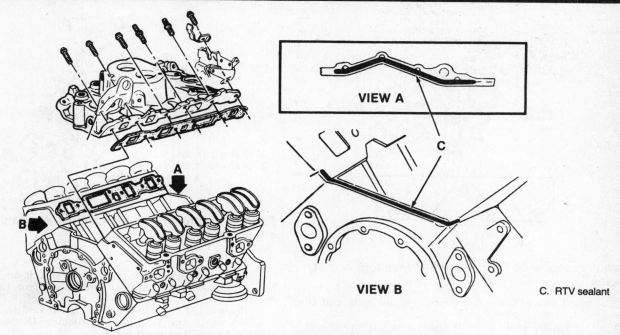

VIEW A

VIEW B

C. RTV sealant

Installing the intake manifold and applying sealant — 4.3L engine

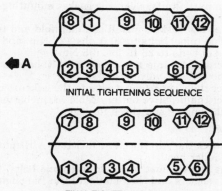

INITIAL TIGHTENING SEQUENCE

FINAL TIGHTENING SEQUENCE

Torquing sequence of the intake manifold — 4.3L engine

4. Disconnect the accelerator and the transmission detent (if equipped) cables.

5. Remove the rear brace from the air conditioning compressor, then the engine and the transmission oil filler (if equipped) tube(s) from the alternator bracket.

6. Remove the air conditioning compressor belt idler (if equipped) from the alternator bracket, then the alternator bracket.

7. From the carburetor or throttle body, remove the fuel hoses, the vacuum lines and the electrical connectors.

8. Remove the Air Injection Reactor (AIR) hoses and brackets.

9. Remove the heater hose from the intake manifold.

10. Remove the intake manifold-to-cylinder head bolts and the intake manifold from the engine.

11. Using a putty knife, clean the gasket mounting surfaces, the carbon deposits from the exhaust/EGR passages and the scale/deposits from the coolant passages.

12. Using the Magnaflux® or equivalent process, inspect the intake manifold for cracks.

To install:

1. Use new gaskets and RTV sealant (apply a 3/16 in. (4.7mm) bead to the front and rear manifold seals). Torque the intake manifold-to-cylinder head bolts/studs (in sequence) to 36 ft. lbs. (49 Nm).

2. Connect the heater hose to the intake manifold.

3. Install the Air Injection Reactor (AIR) hoses and brackets.

4. To the carburetor or throttle body, install the fuel hoses, the vacuum lines and the electrical connectors.

5. Install the air conditioning compressor belt idler (if equipped) to the alternator bracket, then the alternator bracket.

6. Install the rear brace to the air conditioning compressor, then the engine and the transmission oil filler (if equipped) tube(s) to the alternator bracket.

7. Connect the accelerator and the transmission detent (if equipped) cables.

8. Refill the engine with cooling fluid.

9. Install the distributor and adjust the timing as outlined in Section 2. Install the air cleaner. Connect the Electronic Spark Control (ESC) electrical connector.

10. Connect the negative battery cable to the battery.

11. Start the engine and check for leaks.

Exhaust Manifold

REMOVAL AND INSTALLATION

2.5L Engine

The exhaust manifold is located on the left side of the engine.

1. Disconnect the negative battery cable from the battery.

2. If equipped, remove the Thermac heat stove pipe from the exhaust manifold.

3. At the air conditioning compressor, remove the drive belt, the compressor (lay it aside) and the rear adjusting bracket.

4. Raise and support the front of the vehicle on jackstands.

5. Disconnect the exhaust pipe from the exhaust manifold, then lower the vehicle.

6. Remove the air cleaner and disconnect the electrical connector from the oxygen sensor.

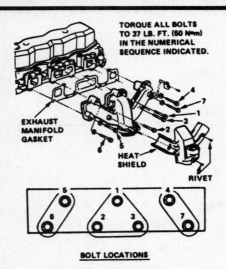

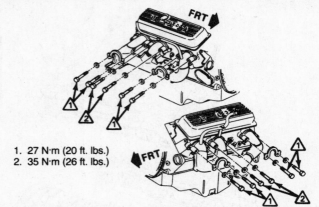

1. 27 N·m (20 ft. lbs.)
2. 35 N·m (26 ft. lbs.)

Torquing sequence for the exhaust manifold — 2.5L engine (1986–87)

Torquing sequence for the exhaust manifold — 2.5L engine

7. Remove the exhaust manifold-to-engine bolts and the manifold from the engine.

8. Using a putty knife, clean the gasket mounting surfaces.

To install:

1. Use a new gasket. Install the manifold and torque in sequence to 37 ft. lbs. (50 Nm) for 1985 models, or 44 ft. lbs. (60 Nm) for 1986–90 models.

2. Install the air cleaner and connect the electrical connector to the oxygen sensor.

3. Connect the exhaust pipe to the exhaust manifold, then lower the vehicle.

4. At the air conditioning compressor, install the compressor, drive belt and the rear adjusting bracket.

5. If equipped, install the Thermac heat stove pipe to the exhaust manifold.

6. Connect the negative battery cable to the battery.

7. Start the engine and check for leaks.

4.3L Engine
RIGHT SIDE

1. Disconnect the negative battery cable from the battery.

2. Raise and support the front of the vehicle on jackstands.

3. Disconnect the right exhaust pipe from the exhaust manifold.

4. Remove the jackstands and lower the vehicle.

5. Disconnect the Air Injection Reactor (AIR) hose from the check valve and the diverter valve.

6. Remove the exhaust manifold-to-engine bolts, the washers, the tab washers and the manifold from the engine.

7. Using a putty knife, clean the gasket mounting surfaces.

To install:

1. Using a new gasket, install the manifold and torque the outer manifold (pipe) bolts to 20 ft. lbs. (27 Nm) and the inner manifold (pipe) bolts to 26 ft. lbs. (35 Nm).

2. Connect the Air Injection Reactor (AIR) hose to the check valve and the diverter valve.

3. Connect the right exhaust pipe to the exhaust manifold.

4. Connect the negative battery cable to the battery.

5. Start the engine and check for leaks.

LEFT SIDE

1. Disconnect the Air Injection Reactor (AIR) pipe bracket from the cylinder head.

2. Remove the exhaust manifold-to-engine bolts, the washers, the tab washers and the manifold from the engine.

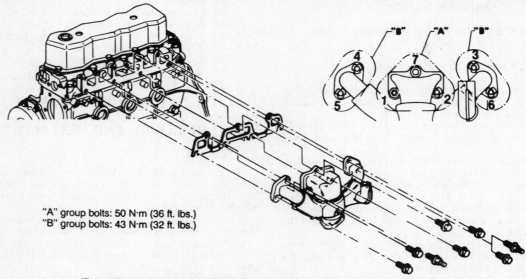

"A" group bolts: 50 N·m (36 ft. lbs.)
"B" group bolts: 43 N·m (32 ft. lbs.)

Torquing sequence for the exhaust manifold — 4.3L engine

NOTE: If equipped with a heat shield, remove it.

3. Using a putty knife, clean the gasket mounting surfaces.

To install:

1. Use a new gasket. Install the manifold and torque the outer manifold (pipe) bolts to 20 ft. lbs. (27 Nm) and the inner manifold (pipe) bolts to 26 ft. lbs. (35 Nm).

2. Connect the Air Injection Reactor (AIR) pipe bracket to the cylinder head.

3. Raise and safely support the vehicle with jackstands.

4. Connect the left exhaust pipe to the exhaust manifold.

5. Lower the vehicle.

6. Connect the negative battery cable to the battery.

7. Start the engine and check for leaks.

Air Conditioning Compressor

REMOVAL AND INSTALLATION

2.5L Engine

1. Refer to, Discharging The Air Conditioning System in Section 1 and discharge the air conditioning system.

2. Disconnect the negative battery cable from the battery.

3. Disconnect the electrical connectors from the compressor.

4. At the rear of the compressor, remove the bracket from the exhaust manifold.

5. Remove the compressor-to-front bracket bolts, the drive belt and the compressor from the vehicle.

To install:

1. Install the compressor and torque the compressor-to-front bracket bolts to 22 ft. lbs. (30 Nm) and the compressor-to-rear bracket bolts to 18 ft. lbs. (25 Nm).

2. Refer to the, Drive Belt Adjusting procedures in Section 1 and adjust the air conditioning drive belt.

3. Refer to, Charging The Air Conditioning System in Section 1, evacuate and charge the air conditioning system.

4. Connect the negative battery cable and start the engine to check for proper operation.

4.3L Engine

1. Refer to, Discharging The Air Conditioning System in Section 1 and discharge the air conditioning system.

2. Disconnect the negative battery cable from the battery.

3. Disconnect the electrical connectors from the compressor.

4. From the rear of the compressor, remove the intake manifold-to-compressor support bracket.

NOTE: If the engine is equipped with a carburetor, disconnect the vacuum brake from the carburetor for access.

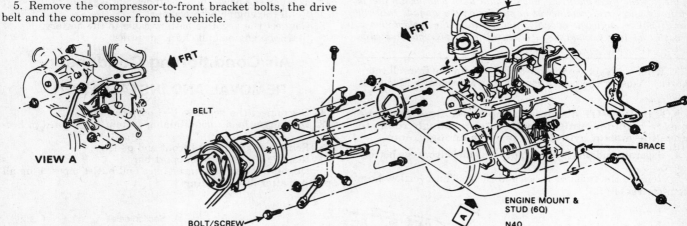

Exploded view of the air conditioning compressor and mounting brackets — 2.5L engine

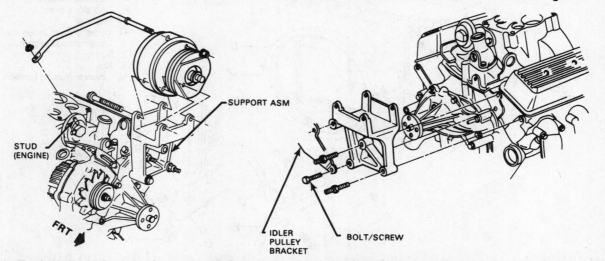

Exploded view of the air conditioning compressor and mounting brackets — 4.3L engine

5. Remove the drive belt idler bracket-to-intake manifold bolts, the drive belt and the bracket from the vehicle.

6. Remove the compressor-to-mounting bracket bolts and the compressor from the vehicle.

To install:

1. Install the compressor and torque the compressor-to-front bracket bolts to 25 ft. lbs. (34 Nm), the idler belt-to-engine bracket bolts to 16 ft. lbs. (22 Nm) and the compressor support bracket bolts to 61 ft. lbs. (83 Nm).

2. Refer to the, Drive Belt Adjusting procedures in Section 1 and adjust the air conditioning drive belt.

3. Refer to, Charging The Air Conditioning System in Section 1, evacuate and recharge the air conditioning system.

4. Connect the negative battery cable and start the engine to check performance.

Radiator

REMOVAL AND INSTALLATION

1. Disconnect the negative battery cable from the battery.

2. Place a catch pan under the radiator, open the drain cock and drain the cooling system.

CAUTION

When draining the coolant, keep in mind that cats and dogs are attracted by the ethylene glycol antifreeze, and are quite likely to drink any that is left in an uncovered container or in puddles on the ground. This will prove fatal in sufficient quantity. Always drain the coolant into a sealable container. Coolant should be reused unless it is contaminated or several years old.

3. Remove the brake master cylinder from the firewall (non-power brakes) or the power booster (power brakes) and move it aside.

NOTE: DO NOT disconnect the brake lines from the master cylinder, unless there is not enough room to move the master cylinder to provide enough room.

4. Separate and remove the upper fan shield from the bottom shield.

5. Remove the radiator hoses and the coolant overflow hose from the radiator.

6. If equipped with transmission and/or engine oil cooler lines, perform the following procedures:

   a. Disconnect the upper transmission-to-radiator and/or the upper engine-to-radiator lines from the radiator.

   b. Raise and support the front of the vehicle on jackstands.

   c. Disconnect the lower transmission-to-radiator and/or the lower engine-to-radiator lines from the radiator.

7. Remove the radiator mounting bolts and the radiator from the vehicle.

8. Inspect the radiator for leaks or physical damage, then repair (if necessary).

NOTE: The radiator is constructed of aluminum, if repairs are necessary, it should be taken to a radiator repair shop.

To install:

1. Install the radiator and torque all of the fasteners to 18 ft. lbs. (25 Nm).

2. Connect the lower transmission-to-radiator and/or the lower engine-to-radiator lines to the radiator.

3. Connect the upper transmission-to-radiator and/or the upper engine-to-radiator lines to the radiator.

4. Install the upper fan shield to the bottom shield.

5. Install the radiator hoses and the coolant overflow hose to the radiator.

6. Install the brake master cylinder to the firewall (non-power brakes) or the power booster (power brakes).

7. Refill the engine with coolant.

8. Connect the negative battery cable to the battery.

9. Start the engine and check for leaks.

Air Conditioning Condenser

REMOVAL AND INSTALLATION

1. Disconnect the negative (−) battery cable.

2. Discharge the air conditioning system as outlined in Section 1.

3. Remove the grille and front end panel.

4. Remove the radiator support bar.

5. Disconnect the condenser inlet and outlet pipes. Plug all openings after disconnecting.

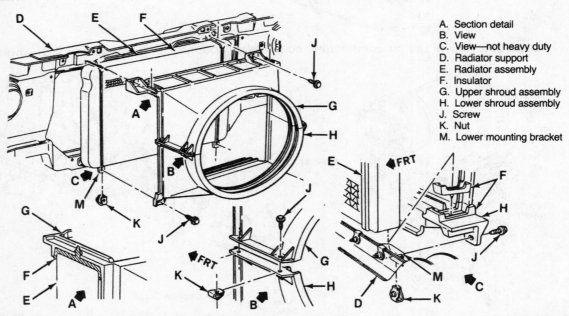

A. Section detail
B. View
C. View—not heavy duty
D. Radiator support
E. Radiator assembly
F. Insulator
G. Upper shroud assembly
H. Lower shroud assembly
J. Screw
K. Nut
M. Lower mounting bracket

Exploded view of the radiator and fan shroud assembly — 2.5L engine shown, 4.3L engine similar

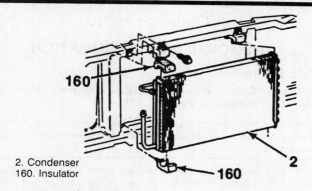

2. Condenser
160. Insulator

Air conditioning condenser

6. Remove the insulator retaining bolts and condenser.
To install:
1. Install the condenser and torque the retaining bolts to 20 ft. lbs. (27 Nm).

2. Unplug and connect the refrigerant pipes.
3. Install the radiator support bar, grille and front end panel.
4. Flush, evacuate and charge the air conditioning system as outlined in Section 1.

Cooling Fan

REMOVAL AND INSTALLATION

1. Disconnect the negative (−) battery cable.
2. Remove the upper fan shroud.
3. Remove the fan to fan clutch attaching bolts or nuts.
4. Remove the fan clutch-to-water pump bolts or nuts and remove the fan clutch.
To install:
1. Install the fan and clutch. Torque the bolts or nuts to 18 ft. lbs. (24 Nm).
2. Install the upper fan shroud.
3. Start the engine and check operation.

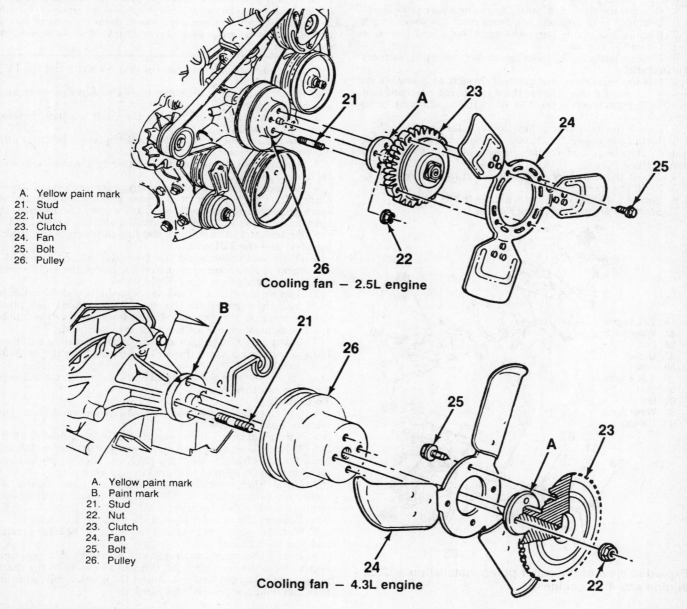

A. Yellow paint mark
21. Stud
22. Nut
23. Clutch
24. Fan
25. Bolt
26. Pulley

Cooling fan — 2.5L engine

A. Yellow paint mark
B. Paint mark
21. Stud
22. Nut
23. Clutch
24. Fan
25. Bolt
26. Pulley

Cooling fan — 4.3L engine

Water Pump

REMOVAL AND INSTALLATION

1. Disconnect the negative battery cable from the battery.
2. Place a catch pan under the radiator, open the drain cock and drain the cooling system.

— CAUTION —

When draining the coolant, keep in mind that cats and dogs are attracted by the ethylene glycol antifreeze, and are quite likely to drink any that is left in an uncovered container or in puddles on the ground. This will prove fatal in sufficient quantity. Always drain the coolant into a sealable container. Coolant should be reused unless it is contaminated or several years old.

3. At the front of the engine, loosen the accessory drive belt adjustments and remove the belts.
4. Remove the upper fan shroud. Remove the fan/clutch assembly-to-water pump bolts and the fan/clutch assembly from the water pump pulley.
5. Remove the drive belt pulley from the water pump.
6. Remove the clamps and the hoses from the water pump.
7. Remove the water pump-to-engine bolts and the water pump from the engine.
8. Using a putty knife, clean the gasket mounting surfaces.
To install:
1. Use new gasket(s), coat the bolt threads with sealant and install the water pump. Torque the water pump-to-engine bolts to 17 ft. lbs. (25 Nm) for the 2.5L or 22 ft. lbs. (29 Nm) for the 4.3L.
2. Install the drive belt pulley to the water pump.
3. Install the upper fan shroud, the fan/clutch assembly-to-water pump bolts and the fan/clutch assembly to the water pump pulley.
4. Adjust the accessory drive belt as outlined in Section 1.
5. Refill the cooling system.
6. Connect the negative battery cable to the battery.
7. Start the engine and check for leaks.

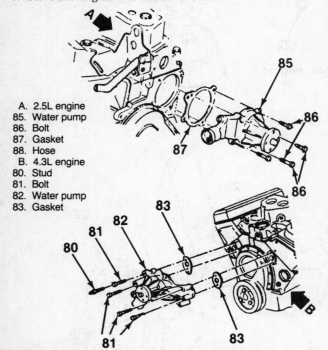

A. 2.5L engine
85. Water pump
86. Bolt
87. Gasket
88. Hose
B. 4.3L engine
80. Stud
81. Bolt
82. Water pump
83. Gasket

Exploded view of the water pump installation — 2.5L engine and 4.3L engine

Cylinder Head

REMOVAL AND INSTALLATION

2.5L Engine

NOTE: Before disassembling the engine, make sure that it is overnight cold.

— CAUTION —

Relieve the pressure on the fuel system before disconnecting any fuel line connection!

1. Disconnect the negative battery cable. Refer to the Rocker Arm Cover, Removal and Installation in this section and remove the rocker arm cover.
2. Place a catch pan under the radiator, open the drain cock and drain the cooling system.

— CAUTION —

When draining the coolant, keep in mind that cats and dogs are attracted by the ethylene glycol antifreeze, and are quite likely to drink any that is left in an uncovered container or in puddles on the ground. This will prove fatal in sufficient quantity. Always drain the coolant into a sealable container. Coolant should be reused unless it is contaminated or several years old.

3. Disconnect the accelerator, the cruise control and the TVS cables, if equipped.
4. From the intake manifold, remove the water pump bypass and heater hoses.
5. From the alternator, remove the front and rear braces, then move it aside.
6. Disconnect the air conditioning compressor brackets and move the compressor aside.
7. Remove the thermostat housing-to-cylinder head bolts and the housing from the engine.
8. Remove the ground cable and any necessary electrical connectors from the cylinder head. Disconnect the wires from the spark plugs and the oxygen sensor. Disconnect and remove the ignition coil from the intake manifold and the cylinder head.
9. Remove the vacuum lines and fuel hoses from the intake manifold and the TBI unit.
10. Disconnect the exhaust pipe from the exhaust manifold.
11. Remove the rocker arm nuts, the washers, the rocker arms and the pushrods from the cylinder head.
12. Remove the cylinder head-to-engine bolts and the cylinder head from the engine (with the manifolds attached), then place the assembly on a workbench. If necessary, remove the intake and the exhaust manifolds from the cylinder head.
13. Using a putty knife, clean the gasket mounting surfaces. Using a wire brush, clean the carbon deposits from the combustion chambers.
14. Inspect the cylinder head and block for cracks, nicks, heavy scratches or other damage.
To install:
1. Use new gaskets, sealant (where necessary) and install the cylinder head onto the block.
2. Torque all the cylinder head bolts (in sequence) to 18 ft. lbs. (25 Nm). Then torque all bolts (except #9) to 26 ft. lbs. (35 Nm). Torque #9 bolt to 18 ft. lbs. (25 Nm). Then torque all bolts an additional 90 degrees (¼ turn) in sequence.
3. Install the pushrods rocker arms and nuts. Torque all rocker arm bolts to 22 ft. lbs. (30 Nm) with the camshaft lobe on the base circle for each rocker arm.
4. Connect the exhaust pipe to the exhaust manifold.
5. Install the vacuum lines and fuel hoses to the intake manifold and the TBI unit.
6. Install the ground cable and any necessary electrical connectors from the cylinder head. Connect the wires to the spark plugs and the oxygen sensor. Connect the ignition coil to the intake manifold and the cylinder head.

7. Install the thermostat housing-to-cylinder head bolts and the housing to the engine.

8. Connect the air conditioning compressor brackets.

9. To the alternator, install the front and rear braces.

10. To the intake manifold, install the water pump bypass and heater hoses.

11. Connect the accelerator, the cruise control and the TVS cables, if equipped.

12. Refill the engine with coolant.

13. Refer to the Rocker Arm Cover, Removal and Installation in this section and install the rocker arm cover.

14. Start the engine and check for leaks and proper operation.

4.3L Engine

> ### CAUTION
>
> *If equipped with an EFI system, relieve the pressure on the fuel system before disconnecting any fuel line connection.*

1. Refer to the Rocker Arm, Removal and Installation, the Intake Manifold, Removal and Installation and the Exhaust Manifold, Removal and Installation procedures in this section, then remove the rocker arms, the intake manifold and the exhaust manifold (depending on which cylinder head is being removed) from the engine.

2. Remove the cylinder head bolts, the cylinder head(s) and the gasket(s) (discard the gasket).

3. Using a putty knife, clean the gasket mounting surfaces.

4. Inspect the cylinder head and block for cracks, nicks, heavy scratches or other damage.

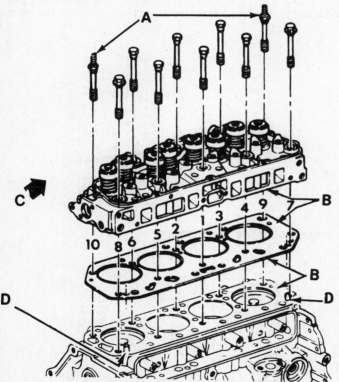

A. Apply sealing compound to threads on these bolts
B. Mounting surfaces of block asm., head asm. and both sides of gasket must be free of oil and foreign material
C. Forward
D. Dowel pins

Cylinder head installation and torquing sequence — 2.5L engine

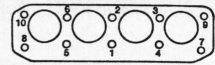

Cylinder head torque sequence — 2.5L engine

To install:

1. Use new gasket(s), sealant (where necessary) and install the cylinder head onto the block. The head gasket is installed with the bead up.

NOTE: If a steel head gasket is used, coat both sides of the gasket (thinly and evenly) with sealer. Clean the bolt threads, apply sealing compound No. 1052080 or equivalent and install the bolts finger tight.

2. Torque the head bolts in three steps, in sequence. The first step to 25 ft. lbs. (34 Nm), the second step to 45 ft. lbs. (61 Nm) and the late step to 65 ft. lbs. (88 Nm).

3. Install the pushrods, rocker arms and nuts. Adjust the valves as outlined below:

4. Rotate the crankshaft until the mark on the damper pulley aligns with the **0** mark on the timing plate and the No. 1 cylinder is on the compression stroke.

NOTE: To determine if the No. 1 cylinder is on the compression stroke, shake the rocker arms of the No. 1 cylinder, if they move the cylinder is on the compression stroke, if they don't move the cylinder is on the exhaust stroke. If the cylinder is on the exhaust stroke, it will be necessary to rotate the crankshaft one full revolution.

5. With the engine on the compression stroke, adjust the exhaust valves of cylinders No. 1, 5 & 6 and the intake valves of cylinders No. 1, 2 & 3.

6. To adjust the valves, perform the following procedures:

a. Back out the adjusting nut until lash can be felt at the pushrod.

b. While rotating the pushrod, turn the adjusting nut inward until all of the lash is removed.

c. When the play has disappeared, turn the adjusting nut inward one additional turns.

7. Rotate the crankshaft one complete revolution and align the mark on the damper pulley with the **0** mark on the timing plate.

8. With the engine on the compression stroke, adjust the exhaust valves of cylinders No. 2, 3 & 4 and the intake valves of cylinders No. 4, 5 & 6.

9. To adjust the valves, perform the following procedures:

a. Back out the adjusting nut until lash can be felt at the pushrod.

b. While rotating the pushrod, turn the adjusting nut inward until all of the lash is removed.

c. When the play has disappeared, turn the adjusting nut inward one additional turns.

10. Refer to the Rocker Arm cover, Removal and Installation, the Intake Manifold, Removal and Installation and the Exhaust Manifold, Removal and Installation procedures in this section, then install the intake manifold and the exhaust manifold (depending on which cylinder head is being removed) from the engine. Install the rocker arm covers.

11. Change the oil and filter, refill the engine with clean coolant, connect the negative battery cable, start the engine, check for leaks and proper operation.

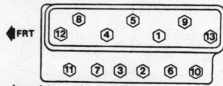

Cylinder head torquing sequence — 4.3L engine

CLEANING AND INSPECTION

1. Refer to the Valves, Removal and Installation procedures in this section and remove the valve assemblies from the cylinder head.

2. Using a small wire power brush, clean the carbon from the combustion chambers and the valve ports.

3. Inspect the cylinder head for cracks in the exhaust ports, combustion chambers or external cracks to the water chamber.

4. Thoroughly clean the valve guides using a suitable wire bore brush.

NOTE: Excessive valve stem-to-bore clearance will cause excessive oil consumption and may cause valve breakage. Insufficient clearance will result in noisy and sticky functioning of the valve and disturb engine smoothness.

5. Measure the valve stem clearance as follows:

   a. Clamp a dial indicator on one side of the cylinder head rocker arm cover gasket rail.

   b. Locate the indicator so that movement of the valve stem from side to side (crosswise to the head) will cause a direct movement of the indicator stem. The indicator stem must contact the side of the valve stem just above the valve guide.

   c. Prop the valve head about $1/16$ in. (1.5mm) off the valve seat.

   d. Move the stem of the valve from side to side using light pressure to obtain a clearance reading. If the clearance exceeds specifications, it will be necessary to ream (for oversize valves) or knurl (raise the bore for original valves) the valve guides.

6. Inspect the rocker arm studs for wear or damage.

7. Install a dial micrometer into the valve guide and check the valve seat for concentricity.

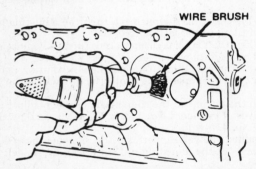

Remove the carbon from the cylinder head with a wire brush and electric drill

Measuring the valve stem clearance

Check the cylinder head for warpage

RESURFACING

1. Using a straightedge, check the cylinder head for warpage.

2. If warpage exceeds 0.003 in. (0.076mm) in a 6 in. (152mm) span, or 0.006 in. (0.152mm) over the total length, the cylinder head must be resurfaced. Resurfacing can be performed at most machine shops.

NOTE: When resurfacing the cylinder head(s), the intake manifold mounting position is altered and must be corrected by machining a proportionate amount from the intake manifold flange.

Valves

REMOVAL AND INSTALLATION

1. Refer to the Cylinder Head, Removal and Installation procedures in this section and remove the cylinder head.

2. Using a C-Type spring compressor, compress the valve springs, then remove the valve keepers, the cap (2.5L) or rotor

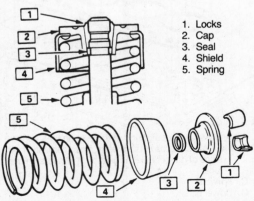

Compressing the valve spring — typical

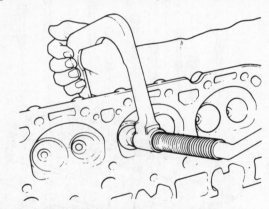

1. Locks
2. Cap
3. Seal
4. Shield
5. Spring

Exploded view of the valve components — 2.5L engine

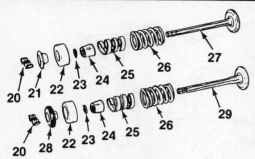

20.	Valve keeper
21.	Cap
22.	Shield
23.	O-ring seal
24.	Seal
25.	Damper
26.	Spring
27.	Intake valve
28.	Rotator
29.	Exhaust valve

Exploded view of the valve components — 4.3L engine

(4.3L), the O-ring seal, the shield, damper (4.3L), valve stem seal (4.3L) and the spring.

3. Remove the valve(s) from the cylinder head.

NOTE: If removing all of the valves at one time, be sure to keep them in order for reinstallation purposes.

4. Using a bench mounted wire brush, clean all of the deposits from the valve faces and stems. Using a small drill mounted wire brush, clean the deposits from the combustion chambers.

5. Inspect the valves, the valve seats and the valve guides for damage or wear; replace or re-machine the damaged parts or items. Reface the valve(s) and valve seat(s) or lap the valve into the cylinder head.

6. To install, lubricate the parts being installed, use new seals on the valves, new gaskets and reverse the removal procedures. Adjust the valves. Refill the cooling system. Start the engine and check the timing. Inspect the cooling system and the fuel system for leaks.

INSPECTION

Inspect the valve faces and seats (in the head) for pits, burned spots and other evidence of poor seating. If a valve face is in such bad shape that the head of the valve must be ground, in order to true up the face, discard the valve, because the sharp edge will run too hot. The correct angle for valve faces is 45° degrees. We recommend the refacing be performed by a reputable machine shop.

Check the valve stem for scoring and burned spots. If not noticeably scored or damaged, clean the valve stem with solvent to remove all gum and varnish. Clean the valve guides using solvent and an expanding wire-type valve guide cleaner. If you have access to a dial indicator for measuring valve stem-to-guide clearance, mount it so that the stem of the indicator is at 90° degrees to the valve stem and as close to the valve guide as possible. Move the valve off its seat, then measure the valve guide-to-stem clearance by rocking the stem back and forth to actuate the dial indicator. Measure the valve stem diameter using a micrometer, and compare to specifications to determine whether the stem or guide wear is responsible for the excess clearance. If a dial indicator and micrometer are not available to you, take the cylinder head and valves to a reputable machine shop for inspection.

Some of the engines covered in this guide are equipped with valve rotators, which double as valve spring caps. In normal operation the rotators put a certain degree of wear on the tip of the valve stem; this wear appears as concentric rings on the stem tip. However, if the rotator is not working properly, the wear may appear as straight notches or **X** patterns across the valve stem tip. Whenever the valves are removed from the cylinder head, the tips should be inspected for improper pattern, which could indicate valve rotator problems. Valve stem tips will have to be ground flat if the rotator problems are severe.

FOR DIMENSIONS, REFER TO SPECIFICATIONS

CHECK FOR BENT STEM

DIAMETER

VALVE FACE ANGLE

1/32" MINIMUM

THIS LINE PARALLEL WITH VALVE HEAD

Critical valve dimensions

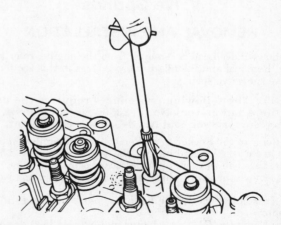

Using an expandable wire type cleaner to clean the valve guides

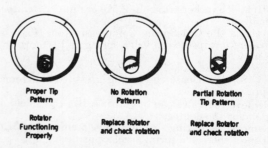

Proper Tip Pattern — Rotator Functioning Properly

No Rotation Pattern — Replace Rotator and check rotation

Partial Rotation Tip Pattern — Replace Rotator and check rotation

Using and "X" to check the valve stem wear

REFACING

NOTE: All valve grinding operations should be performed by a qualified machine shop; only the valve lapping operation is recommended to be performed by the inexperienced mechanic.

Valve Lapping

When valve faces and seats have been refaced and/or recut, or if they are determined to be in good condition, the valves MUST BE lapped in to ensure efficient sealing when the valve closes against the seat.

1. Invert the cylinder head so that the combustion chambers are facing upward.

2. Lightly lubricate the valve stems with clean engine oil and coat the valve seats with valve grinding compound. Install the valves in the cylinder head as numbered.

3. Attach the suction cup of a valve lapping tool to a valve head. You will probably have to moisten the cup to securely attach the tool to the valve.

4. Rotate the tool between the palms, changing position and lifting the tool often to prevent grooving. Lap the valve until a smooth polished seat is evident (you may have to add a bit more compound after some lapping is done).

5. Remove the valve and tool, then remove ALL traces of the grinding compound with a solvent-soaked rag or rinse the head with solvent.

NOTE: Valve lapping can also be done by fastening a suction cup to a piece of drill rod in a hand egg-beater type drill. Proceed as above, using the drill as a lapping tool. Due to the higher speeds involved when using the hand drill, care must be exercised to avoid grooving the seat. Lift the tool and change direction of rotation often.

Valve Springs

REMOVAL AND INSTALLATION

If the cylinder head is removed from the engine, refer to the Valve, Removal and Installation procedures in this section and remove the valve spring.

NOTE: The following procedures requires the use of GM Air Adapter tool No. J–23590 or equivalent, and Spring Compressor tool No. J–5892 or equivalent.

1. Refer to the Rocker Arm, Removal and Installation procedures in this section and remove the rocker arm bolts (2.5L) or nuts (4.3L), the washers and the rocker arms.

2. Remove the spark plugs from the cylinders being worked on.

3. To remove the valve keepers, perform the following procedures:

   a. Using the GM Air Adapter tool No. J–23590 or equivalent, install it into the spark plug hole.

   b. Apply compressed air to the cylinder to hold the valves in place.

   c. Install a rocker arm bolt (2.5L) or nut (4.3L) into the cylinder head.

   d. Using the GM Spring Compressor tool No. J–5892 or equivalent, compress the valve spring and remove the valve keepers.

   e. Carefully release the spring pressure and remove the compressor tool.

4. Remove the valve cap or rotor (4.3L), the shield and the spring and/or the damper (4.3L).

5. Remove the O-ring seal and valve stem seal (4.3L).

6. Inspect the valve spring, replace as necessary.

7. Lubricate the parts with engine oil, then install a new O-

Lapping the valves by hand

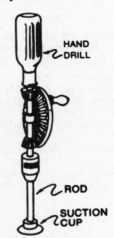

Home made valve lapping tool

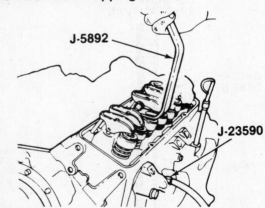

Removing the valve keepers from the valve assemblies

ring seal and valve stem seal (4.3L) onto each valve stem.

8. To complete the installation, adjust the valves and reverse the removal procedures. Start the engine, then check and/or adjust the timing.

INSPECTION

1. Position the valve spring on a flat, clean surface next to a square.

2. Measure the height of the spring and rotate it against the

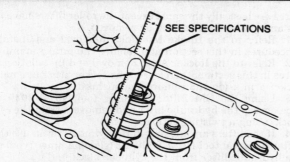

Measuring the installed height of the valve spring

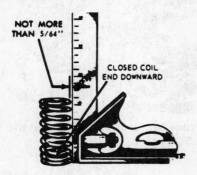

Checking the pressure of the valve spring

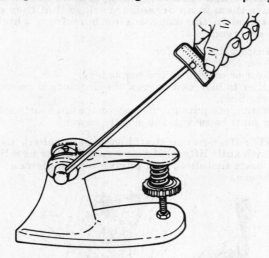

Check the valve spring free length and squareness

engine of the square to measure the distortion (out-of-roundness). If the spring height varies between the springs by more than $\frac{1}{16}$ in. (1.5mm), replace the spring.

3. Using a valve spring tester, check the spring pressure at the installed and compressed height.

Valve Seats

The valve seats are cast into the cylinder head(s) and cannot be replaced; the seats can be machined during a valve job to provide optimum sealing between the valve and the seat.

The seating services should be performed by a professional machine shop which has the specialized knowledge and tools necessary to perform the service.

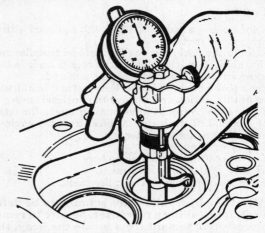

Have the valve seat concentricity checked at a machine shop

Valve Guides

The engines covered in this guide use integral valves guides; that is, they are a part of the cylinder head and cannot be replaced. The guides can, however, be reamed oversize if they are found to be worn past an acceptable limit. Occasionally, a valve guide bore will be oversize as manufactured. These are marked on the inboard side of the cylinder heads on the machined surface just above the intake manifold.

If the guides must be reamed (this service is available at most machine shops), then valves with oversize stems must be fitted. Valves are usually available in 0.001 in. (0.0254mm), 0.003 in. (0.0762mm) and 0.005 in. (0.127mm) stem oversizes. Valve guides which are not excessively worn or distorted may, in some cases, be knurled rather than reamed. Knurling is a process in which the metal on the valve guide bore is displaced and raised, thereby reducing clearance. Knurling also provides excellent oil control. The option of knurling rather than reaming valve guides should be discussed with a reputable machinist or engine specialist.

Valve Lifters

In 1987, the 4.3L EFI engine began using roller valve lifters instead of the standard flat bottom lifters. The roller lifter is still hydraulic requiring no valve adjustment. The roller lifter incorporates a roller that rides along the cam lobe reducing friction and component wear. A roller lifter restrictor and retainer is needed to keep the lifter from turning in the bore while the engine is running. All 2.5L EFI engines incorporate the roller lifter configuration.

REMOVAL AND INSTALLATION

NOTE: Valve lifters and pushrods should be kept in order so they can be reinstalled in their original position.

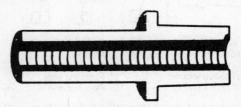

Cutaway of a knurled valve guide

2.5L Engine

This engine uses a hydraulic lifter with equipped with a roller to reduce engine friction.

1. Refer to the Rocker Arm, Removal and Installation procedures in this section, then loosen the rocker arms bolts, move the rocker arms aside and remove the pushrods.
2. Refer to the Pushrod Cover, Removal and Installation procedures in this section and remove the pushrod cover.
3. Remove the hydraulic lifter retainer studs, the retainer(s) and the guides. Lift the hydraulic lifter from the engine block.
4. Inspect the hydraulic lifter for:
- Wear or scuffing.
- Wear or scuffing in the engine bore.
- Freedom of the roller movement.
- Flat spots or pitting on the roller surface.

NOTE: If the hydraulic lifter is found to be defective, replace it. If installing a new lifter, be sure to remove all of the protective sealant from inside the body, then lubricate it and the roller with engine oil.

To install:

1. Use new gaskets, sealant and install the lifters. Torque the lifter retainer-to-engine studs to 96 inch lbs. (11 Nm).
2. Install the pushrods and reposition the rocker arms. Adjust the valve lash as outlined in this Section or Section 2.
3. Install the pushrod cover as outlined in this Section.
4. Start the engine, establish normal operating temperature and check for leaks.

4.3L Engine
1985–86

This engine uses a hydraulic lifter without a cam roller. The 1987 and later engines use roller lifters. The removal procedures are basically the same except the roller lifters have retainers and guides that have to be removed.

1. Refer to the Intake Manifold, Removal and Installation procedures in this section and remove the intake manifold.
2. Refer to the Rocker Arm, Removal and Installation procedures in this section, then loosen the rocker arm nuts, move the rocker arm aside and remove the pushrods.
3. Using the GM Lifter Remover tool No. J–3049 (pliers type), grasp the hydraulic lifter and remove it from the cylinder block, using a twisting action.
4. If the lifters are sticking in the cylinder block, use the GM Lifter Removal tool No. J–9290–01 (slide hammer type) to pull the hydraulic lifter from the cylinder block.

NOTE: When removing the hydraulic lifters, be sure to place them in an organizer rack so that they may be reinstalled in the same engine bore from which they were removed.

5. Inspect the lifters for:
- Wear or scuffing.
- Wear or scuffing in the engine bore.
- Lifter to bore clearance; if the clearance is excessive, replace the lifter.
- Worn spots, pitting or damage on the lifter surface; the lifter foot must be smooth and slightly convex.

NOTE: If a new camshaft has been installed, install all new hydraulic lifters. If a new camshaft or new lifter(s) have been installed, add engine oil supplement to the crankcase.

Using GM tool No. J–3049 to remove the hydraulic lifters — 4.3L engine

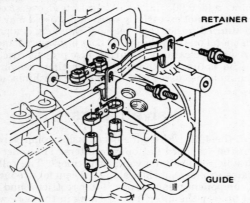

Exploded view of the hydraulic lifter-to-engine assembly — 2.5L engine

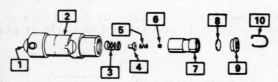

1. Roller
2. Lifter body
3. Plunger spring
4. Ball check retainer
5. Ball check spring
6. Ball check
7. Plunger
8. Oil metering valve
9. Push rod seat
10. Retainer ring

Exploded view of the hydraulic roller lifter — 2.5L engine and the 1987–90 4.3L engine

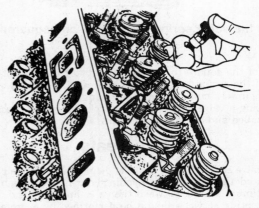

Using GM tool No. J–9290–01 to remove the hydraulic lifters — 4.3L engine

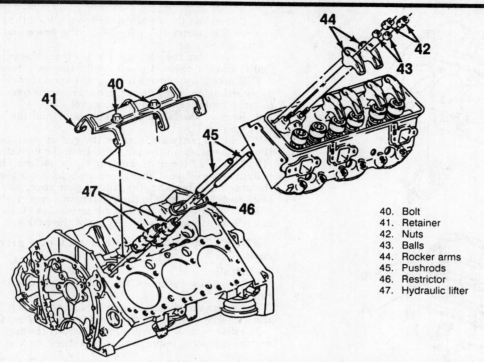

40. Bolt
41. Retainer
42. Nuts
43. Balls
44. Rocker arms
45. Pushrods
46. Restrictor
47. Hydraulic lifter

Exploded view of the hydraulic lifter-to-engine assembly — 4.3L engine

To install:

1. Use new gaskets, sealant and install the lifter into their bore, as removed, if using the old ones.

2. Refer to the Rocker Arm, Removal and Installation procedures in this section, then adjust the rocker arms.

3. Refer to the Intake Manifold, Removal and Installation procedures in this section and install the intake manifold.

4. Install the rocker arm covers, fill the engine with oil and coolant, start the engine and check for leaks. Establish normal operating temperature.

Rocker Stud

REPLACEMENT

NOTE: **The following tools will be necessary for this procedure: Rocker stud replacement tool J–5802–01, Reamer J–5715 (0.003 in. os) or Reamer J–6036 (0.013 in. os) and Installer J–6880, or their equivalents.**

1. Remove the rocker cover.

2. Remove the rocker arm.

3. Place the tool over the stud. Install the nut and flat washer.

4. Tighten the nut to remove the stud.

To install:

5. Using one of the reamers, ream the stud hole as necessary.

6. Coat the lower end of the new stud with SAE 80W–90 gear oil.

7. Using the installing tool, install the new stud. The stud is properly installed when the tool bottoms on the cylinder head.

8. Install the rocker arm(s) and adjust the valves.

9. Install the cover.

Oil Pan

REMOVAL AND INSTALLATION

1. Disconnect the negative battery cable from the battery.

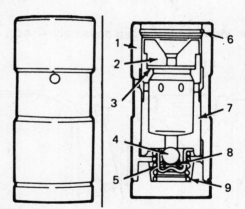

1. Lifter body
2. Pushrod seat
3. Metering valve
4. Check ball
5. Check ball retainer
6. Pushrod seat retainer
7. Plunger
8. Check ball spring
9. Plunger spring

Exploded view of the non-roller hydraulic lifter — before 1987 4.3L engine

2. Raise and support the front of the vehicle on jackstands.

3. Position a catch pan under the crankcase and drain the oil from the engine.

CAUTION

The EPA warns that prolonged contact with used engine oil may cause a number of skin disorders, including cancer! You should make every effort to minimize your exposure to used engine oil. Protective gloves should be worn when changing the oil. Wash your hands and any other exposed skin areas as soon as possible after exposure to used engine oil. Soap and water, or waterless hand cleaner should be used.

4. Remove the strut rods. Remove the flywheel/torque convertor dust cover from the bellhousing.

5. Disconnect the electrical connectors from the starter, then remove the starter-to-engine bolts, the brace and the starter from the vehicle.

6. Disconnect the exhaust pipe(s) from the exhaust manifold(s) and the exhaust pipe-to-catalytic converter hanger(s).

7. If necessary, remove the engine mount through bolts, then using an engine lifting device, raise the engine (enough) in order to make room for the oil pan removal.

8. Remove the oil pan-to-engine bolts and the oil pan from the engine.

9. Using a putty knife, clean the gasket mounting surfaces. Using solvent, clean the excess oil from the mounting surfaces.

10. On the 2.5L engine, apply a $\frac{3}{16}$ in. (4.7mm) bead of RTV sealant to the oil pan flange (keep the bead inside the bolt holes), the rear main bearing, the timing gear cover and the engine block sealing surface. On the 4.3L engine, apply a small amount of RTV sealant to the front and rear corners of the oil pan; too much sealant may prevent sealing of the gasket.

NOTE: The 4.3L engine uses a one piece oil pan gasket.

To install:

1. Use a new gasket (4.3L), RTV sealant and install the oil pan.

2. Torque the oil pan-to-engine bolts to 96 inch lbs. (11 Nm) and the oil pan-to-engine nuts to 14 ft. lbs. (20 Nm) for the 4.3L.

3. Fill the crankcase with fresh oil. Start the engine, establish normal operating temperatures and check for leaks.

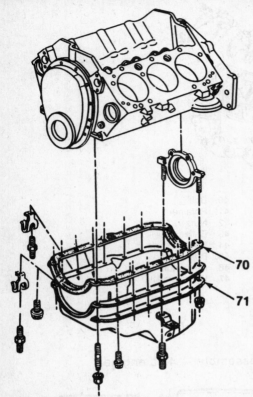

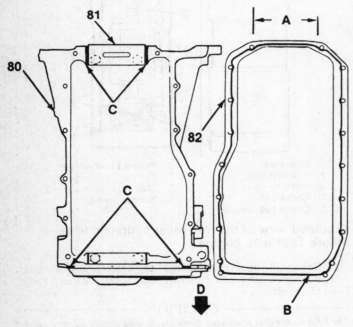

Exploded view of the oil pan assembly — 4.3L engine

A. 10 mm (⅜-inch) wide x 5 mm (³/₁₆-inch) thick
B. 5 mm (³/₁₆-inch) wide x 3 mm (⅛-inch) thick
C. 3 mm (⅛-inch) bead in areas shown
D. Front of engine
80. Block
81. Rear main bearing cap
82. Oil pan

Appling RTV sealant to the oil pan — 2.5L engine

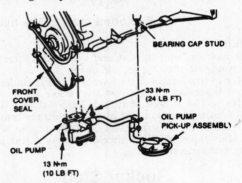

View of the oil pump — 2.5L engine

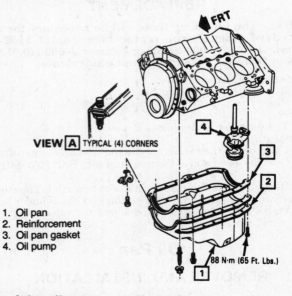

1. Oil pan
2. Reinforcement
3. Oil pan gasket
4. Oil pump

View of the oil pump — 4.3L engine

Oil Pump

REMOVAL AND INSTALLATION

1. Refer to the Oil Pan, Removal and Installation procedures in this section and remove the oil pan.

2. Remove the oil pump-to-rear main bearing cap bolts, the pump and the extension shaft.

To install:

1. Assemble the oil pump and the extension shaft into the rear main bearing cap; be sure to align the slot (on top of the extension shaft) with the drive tang (on the lower end of the distributor driveshaft).

2. Torque the oil pump-to-bearing cap bolts to 22 ft. lbs. (30 Nm) for the 2.5L or 65 ft. lbs. (88 Nm) for the 4.3L.

3. Refill the crankcase with fresh oil. Start the engine, establish normal operating temperatures and check for leaks.

OVERHAUL

1. Remove the pump cover-to-pump screws and the cover.

2. Mark the gear teeth so that they may be reassembled in the same position.

3. Separate the idler gear, the drive gear and the shaft from the pump body.

4. Remove the retaining pin from the pressure valve, then separate the valve and the related parts.

5. If the pickup screen and the pipe assembly need replacing, place the pump in a soft-jawed vise and remove the pipe from the pump. Do not disturb the pickup screen on the pipe; it is serviced as an assembly.

NOTE: If the pickup screen and pipe assembly have been removed from the pump, it should be replaced with a new one.

6. Wash all of the parts in solvent, blow dry with compressed air.

7. Inspect the parts for cracks, damage or excessive wear.

NOTE: If the pump gears or body are damaged, replace the entire pump assembly.

8. Check the drive gear shaft-to-body for looseness, the pump cover for wear (which would permit leaks past the end gears), the pickup screen/pipe assembly for damage and the pressure regulator for fit.

9. If any of the parts are defective, replace any parts that may be defective.

To assemble:

1. Torque the pump cover-to-pump body screws to 84 inch lbs. (10 Nm).

2. Refill the crankcase with fresh oil.

NOTE: Pack the inside of the pump completely with petroleum jelly. DO NOT use engine oil. The pump MUST be primed this way or it will not produce any oil pressure when the engine is started.

Crankshaft Pulley, Damper and Oil Seal

REMOVAL AND INSTALLATION

2.5L Engine

NOTE: The following procedure requires the use of the GM Seal Installer/Centering tool No. J–34995 or equivalent.

1. Disconnect the negative battery cable from the battery.

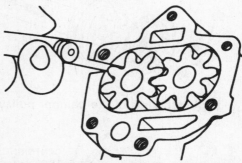

1. Shaft extension
2. Pump body
3. Drive gear and shaft
4. Idler gear
5. Pump cover
6. Pressure regulator valve
7. Pressure regulator spring
8. Retaining pin
9. Screws
10. Pickup screen and pipe

Exploded view of the oil pump

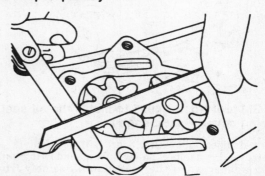

Measuring the clearance between the oil pump gears and the oil pump body

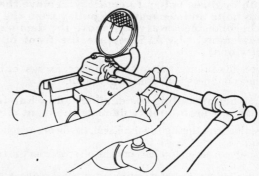

Measure the oil pump end clearance with a feeler gauge and straightedge

Install the oil pump screen by tapping lightly

2. If equipped, remove the power steering fluid reservoir from the radiator shroud.

3. Remove the upper fan shroud. Loosen and remove the ac-

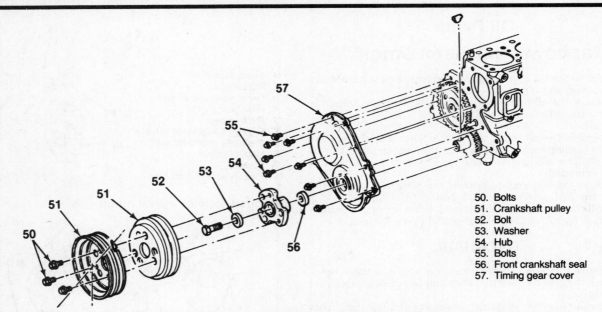

Exploded view of the damper pulley/hub assembly and the timing cover — 2.5L engine

50. Bolts
51. Crankshaft pulley
52. Bolt
53. Washer
54. Hub
55. Bolts
56. Front crankshaft seal
57. Timing gear cover

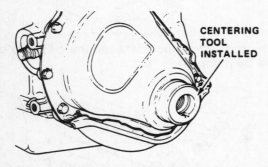

Using GM tool No. J–34995 to install the oil seal into the timing cover — 2.5L engine

cessory-to-damper pulley drive belts.

4. Remove the damper pulley/hub assembly-to-crankshaft bolt and washer, then the pulley/hub assembly from the crankshaft.

NOTE: The damper pulley is connected to the damper pulley hub by three bolts; if necessary, remove the pulley-to-hub bolts and separate the pulley from the hub. When it becomes necessary to remove the damper pulley/hub assembly, ALWAYS replace the front oil seal with a new one.

5. Inspect the damper hub (oil seal surface) for rust or burrs; remove the roughness with fine emery cloth.

NOTE: When installing the damper pulley hub to the crankshaft, be careful not to damage the front oil seal.

6. To replace the timing cover oil seal, perform the following procedures:

   a. Using a medium pry bar, pry the oil seal from the timing cover.

   b. Using the GM Seal Installer/Centering tool No. J–34995 or equivalent, install the new oil seal into the timing cover, then remove the tool from the timing cover.

To install:

1. Install the damper hub, lubricate the it with engine oil, align it onto the keyway and push onto crankshaft. Torque the

damper pulley hub-to-crankshaft bolt to 160 ft. lbs. (217 Nm).

2. Install the drive belts and adjust the belt tension.

3. Install the upper fan shroud.

4. If equipped, install the power steering fluid reservoir to the radiator shroud.

5. Connect the negative battery cable to the battery.

6. Start the engine, check for leaks and proper operation.

4.3L Engine

NOTE: The following procedure requires the use of GM Torsional Damper Puller/Installer tool No. J–23523–E or equivalent, and the GM Seal Installer tool No. J–23042 or equivalent.

1. Disconnect the negative battery cable from the battery.

2. Loosen and remove the accessory-to-damper pulley drive belts.

3. Remove the drive belt pulley-to-damper bolts and the pulley from the damper. Remove the damper-to-crankshaft bolt.

4. Using the GM Torsional Damper Puller/Installer tool No. J–23523–E or equivalent, connect it to the damper and remove it from the crankshaft.

NOTE: When performing this operation, ALWAYS replace the front oil seal with a new one.

5. To replace the oil seal to the timing cover, perform the following procedures:

   a. Using a medium pry bar, pry the oil seal from the timing cover.

   b. Coat the lips of the new seal with engine oil.

   c. Using the GM Seal Installer tool No. J–23042 or equivalent, install the new oil seal into the timing cover, then remove the tool from the timing cover.

6. Inspect the damper (oil seal surface) for rust or burrs; remove the roughness with fine emery cloth.

To install:

NOTE: When installing the damper onto the crankshaft, be careful not to damage the front oil seal.

1. Lubricate the hub with engine oil, align it with the keyway and install it onto the crankshaft. Using the GM Torsional Damper Puller/Installer tool No. J–23523–E or equivalent, connect it to the damper and press it onto the crankshaft.

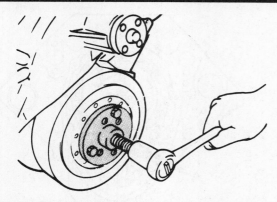

Using GM tool No. J–23523 to remove the damper from the crankshaft — 4.3L engine

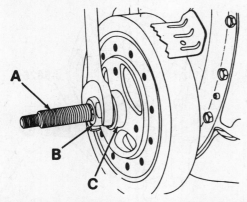

Using GM tool No. J–23523 to press the damper onto the crankshaft — 4.3L engine

2. Torque the damper pulley hub-to-crankshaft bolt to 70 ft. lbs. (95 Nm).
3. Install the drive belts and adjust the belt tension.
4. Start the engine, check for leaks and normal operation.

Timing Cover and Oil Seal

REMOVAL AND INSTALLATION

2.5L Engine

NOTE: **The following procedure requires the use of the GM Seal Installer/Centering tool No. J–34995 or equivalent.**

1. Disconnect the negative (−) battery cable. Refer to the Crankshaft Pulley, Damper and Oil Seal, Removal and Installation procedures in this section and remove the damper from the crankshaft.
2. Remove the fan and the pulley.
3. Remove the alternator and the brackets from the front of the engine.
4. Remove the lower radiator hose clamp at the water pump.
5. Remove the timing cover-to-oil pan bolts, the timing cover-to-engine bolts and the cover from the engine.
6. Using a medium pry bar, pry the oil seal from the timing cover.
7. Using a putty knife, clean the gasket mounting surfaces. The clean the surface with solvent to remove all traces of oil and grease.

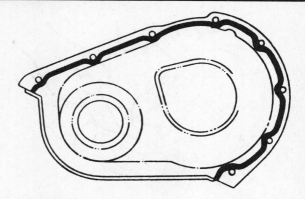

Applying RTV sealer to the timing gear cover

NOTE: **The timing cover can become distorted very easily, so be careful when cleaning the gasket surface.**

To install:
1. Apply engine oil to the lips of the new oil seal. Using the GM Seal Installer/Centering tool No. J–34995 or equivalent, install the new oil seal into the timing cover; leave the tool installed in the timing cover.
2. Using RTV sealant or equivalent, apply a ¼ in. (6mm) wide bead to the timing cover mounting surface and a ⅜ in. (9.5mm) wide bead to the oil pan at the timing cover sealing surface.
3. Install the timing cover onto the engine and partially tighten the bolts.
4. First, torque the timing cover-to-engine bolts to 90 inch lbs. (11 Nm); secondly, torque the timing cover-to-oil pan bolts to 90 inch lbs. (11 Nm). Remove the Seal Installer/Centering tool No. J–34995 or equivalent, from the timing cover.
5. Install and torque the damper pulley hub-to-crankshaft bolt to 160 ft. lbs. (217 Nm).
6. Adjust the drive belt(s) tension. Refill the cooling system (if necessary) and the power steering reservoir (if equipped).
7. Connect the negative battery cable, start the engine and check for leaks.

4.3L Engine

NOTE: **The following procedure requires the use of GM Torsional Damper Puller/Installer tool No. J–23523–E or equivalent, and the GM Seal Installer tool No. J–23042 or equivalent.**

1. Disconnect the negative (−) battery cable. Refer to the Crankshaft Pulley, Damper and Oil Seal, Removal and Installation procedures in this section and remove the damper from the crankshaft.
2. Place a catch pan under the radiator, open the drain cock and drain the cooling system.

——————— CAUTION ———————
When draining the coolant, keep in mind that cats and dogs are attracted by the ethylene glycol antifreeze, and are quite likely to drink any that is left in an uncovered container or in puddles on the ground. This will prove fatal in sufficient quantity. Always drain the coolant into a sealable container. Coolant should be reused unless it is contaminated or several years old.
————————————————————————

3. Remove the timing cover-to-engine bolts and the cover from the engine.
4. Using a putty knife, clean the gasket mounting surfaces. Using solvent and a rag, clean the oil and grease from the gasket mounting surfaces.
5. Inspect the timing cover for distortion and damage, if necessary, replace it.

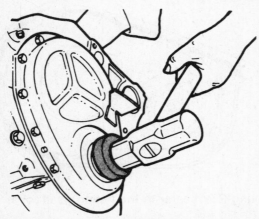

Using GM tool No. J–23042 to install the oil seal into the timing cover, either installed or removed from the engine — 4.3L engine

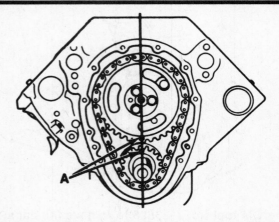

Aligning the timing gear sprockets — 4.3L engine

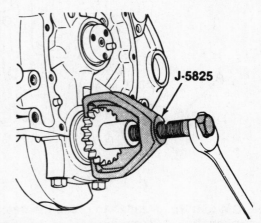

Removing the crankshaft sprocket — 4.3L engine

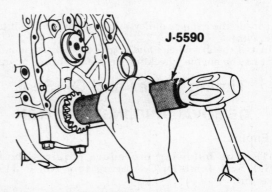

Installing the crankshaft sprocket — 4.3L engine

6. To replace the oil seal in the timing cover, perform the following procedures:

a. Using a medium pry bar, pry the oil seal from the timing cover.

b. Coat the lips of the new oil seal with engine oil.

NOTE: The oil seal is installed with the open end of the seal lips facing toward the inside of the engine.

c. Using the GM Seal Installer tool No. J–23042 or equivalent, drive the new oil seal into the timing cover.

To install:

1. Use a new gasket, apply an ⅛ in. (3mm) bead of sealant (to hold the gasket in place), then align the cover with the dowels and install the cover finger tight. Torque the timing cover-to-engine bolts to 92 inch lbs. (11 Nm).

NOTE: When torquing the timing cover bolts, tighten them alternately and evenly, while evenly pressing on the cover.

2. Using the GM Torsional Damper Puller/Installer tool No. J–23523–E or equivalent, torque the damper pulley hub-to-crankshaft bolt to 70 ft. lbs. (95 Nm).

3. Install the drive belts and adjust the belt tension. Refill the cooling system.

4. Connect the negative battery cable, start the engine and check for leaks.

Timing Chain

REMOVAL AND INSTALLATION

4.3L Engine

NOTE: The following procedure requires the use of GM Crankshaft Sprocket Puller tool No. J–5825 or equivalent, and GM Crankshaft Sprocket Installer tool No. J–5590 or equivalent.

1. Disconnect the negative (−) battery cable. Refer to the Timing Cover, Removal and Installation procedures in this section and remove the timing cover.

2. Rotate the crankshaft until the marks on the timing chain sprockets are facing each other.

3. Remove the camshaft sprocket-to-camshaft bolts, the camshaft sprocket and timing chain from the camshaft.

NOTE: If difficulty is experienced in removing the camshaft sprocket, tap it at the lower edge with a mallet.

4. Inspect the timing chain, the camshaft sprocket and the crankshaft sprocket for wear, then replace them (if necessary).

5. If necessary to remove and install the crankshaft sprocket, perform the following procedures:

a. Using the GM Crankshaft Sprocket Puller tool No. J–5825 or equivalent, pull the crankshaft sprocket from the crankshaft.

b. Remove the the woodruff key.

To install:

1. Place the woodruff key into the crankshaft groove and align the crankshaft sprocket with the key.

2. Using the GM Crankshaft Sprocket Installer tool No. J–5590 or equivalent, and a hammer, drive the crankshaft sprocket onto the crankshaft until it seats.

3. To install the camshaft sprocket, position the timing chain onto the sprockets, align the sprockets (timing marks facing one another), then the camshaft sprocket onto the camshaft and the camshaft sprocket bolts. Torque the camshaft sprocket-to-camshaft bolts to 18 ft. lbs. (25 Nm).

4. Install the timing cover as outlined earlier in this section.

5. Refill the cooling system, connect the negative battery cable, start the engine and check for leaks.

Timing Gears

REMOVAL AND INSTALLATION

2.5L Engine

The timing gear is pressed onto the camshaft. To remove or install the timing gear, an arbor press must be used.

NOTE: The following procedure requires the use of an arbor press, a press plate, the GM Gear Removal tool No. J–971 or equivalent, the GM Gear Installation tool No. J–21474-13, J–21795-1 or equivalent.

1. Disconnect the negative (–) battery cable. Refer to the Camshaft, Removal and Installation procedures in this section and remove the camshaft from the engine.

2. Using an arbor press, a press plate and the GM Gear Removal tool No. J–971 or equivalent, press the timing gear from the camshaft.

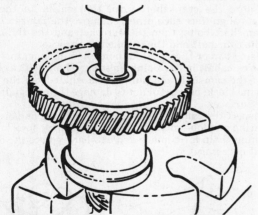

Removing the timing gear from the crankshaft — 2.5L engine

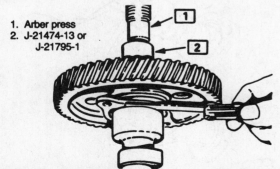

1. Arber press
2. J-21474-13 or J-21795-1

Installing the timing gear onto the camshaft — 2.5L engine

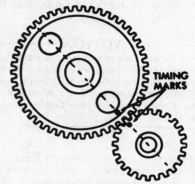

Aligning the timing gear marks — 2.5L engine

Removing the camshaft-to-engine thrust plate bolts — 2.5L engine

NOTE: When pressing the timing gear from the camshaft, be certain that the position of the press plate does not contact the woodruff key.

To install:

1. Position the press plate to support the camshaft at the back of the front journal. Place the gear spacer ring and the thrust plate over the end of the camshaft, then install the woodruff key. Press the timing gear onto the camshaft, until it bottoms against the gear spacer ring.

NOTE: The end clearance of the thrust plate should be 0.0015–0.005 in. (0.038–0.127mm). If less than 0.0015 in. (0.038mm), replace the spacer ring; if more than 0.005 in. (0.127mm), replace the thrust plate.

2. Align the marks on the timing gears, install the timing cover, pulleys and adjust the accessory drive belts.

3. Connect the negative battery cable, start the engine and check operation.

Camshaft

REMOVAL AND INSTALLATION

2.5L Engine

1. Disconnect the negative (–) battery cable. Refer to the Pushrod Cover, Removal and Installation and the Valve Lifters, Removal and Installation procedures in this section, then remove the pushrods and the valve lifters from the engine.

NOTE: When removing the pushrods and the valve lifters, be sure to keep them in order for reassembly purposes.

2. Place a catch pan under the radiator, open the drain cock and drain the cooling system.

CAUTION

When draining the coolant, keep in mind that cats and dogs are attracted by the ethylene glycol antifreeze, and are quite likely to drink any that is left in an uncovered container or in puddles on the ground. This will prove fatal in sufficient quantity. Always drain the coolant into a sealable container. Coolant should be reused unless it is contaminated or several years old.

---

3. Remove the power steering reservoir from the fan shroud, then the upper fan shroud, the radiator. Remove the grille, the headlight bezel and the bumper filler panel.

4. Remove the accessory drive belts, the cooling fan and the water pump pulley.

5. If equipped with air conditioning, disconnect the condenser baffles and the condenser, then raise the condenser and block it aside.

6. Remove the crankshaft drive belt pulley and the damper hub. Remove the timing gear cover-to-engine bolts and the cover.

7. Label and disconnect the distributor electrical connectors, then the holddown bolt and the distributor from the engine. Remove the oil pump driveshaft.

8. Label and disconnect the vacuum lines from the intake manifold and the thermostat housing, then remove the Exhaust Gas Recirculation (EGR) valve from the intake manifold.

9. Remove the camshaft thrust plate-to-engine bolts. While supporting the camshaft (to prevent damaging the bearing or lobe surfaces), remove it from the front of the engine.

10. Inspect the camshaft for scratches, pitting and/or wear on the bearing and lobe surfaces. Check the timing gear teeth for damage.

To install:

1. Lubricate all of the parts with engine oil and install the camshaft carefully so not to damage the cam bearings. Torque the camshaft thrust plate-to-engine bolts to 90 inch lbs. (11 Nm).

2. Connect the vacuum lines to the intake manifold and the thermostat housing, then install the Exhaust Gas Recirculation (EGR) valve to the intake manifold.

3. Install the oil pump driveshaft.

4. Install the distributor, adjust the timing and connect the distributor electrical connectors.

5. Install the timing gear cover-to-engine bolts and the cover. Install the crankshaft drive belt pulley and the damper hub.

6. If equipped with air conditioning, connect the condenser baffles and the condenser.

7. Install the accessory drive belts, the cooling fan and the water pump pulley.

8. Install the power steering reservoir to the fan shroud, then the upper fan shroud, the radiator. Install the grille, the headlight bezel and the bumper filler panel.

9. Connect the negative (−) battery cable. Refer to the Pushrod Cover, Removal and Installation and the Valve Lifters, Removal and Installation procedures in this section, then install the pushrods and the valve lifters to the engine.

10. Refill the engine with coolant, connect the negative battery cable, start the engine and check for leaks.

4.3L Engine

NOTE: The following procedure requires the use of the GM Torsional Damper Puller/Installer tool No. J–23523–E or equivalent.

1. Disconnect the negative (−) battery cable. Refer to the Valve Lifters, Removal and Installation procedures in this section and remove the valve lifters from the engine.

NOTE: When removing the pushrods and the valve lifters, be sure to keep them in order for reassembly purposes.

2. Place a catch pan under the radiator, open the drain cock and drain the cooling system. Remove the radiator.

CAUTION

When draining the coolant, keep in mind that cats and dogs are attracted by the ethylene glycol antifreeze, and are quite likely to drink any that is left in an uncovered container or in puddles on the ground. This will prove fatal in sufficient quantity. Always drain the coolant into a sealable container. Coolant should be reused unless it is contaminated or several years old.

---

3. Loosen and remove the accessory drive belts from the crankshaft pulley.

4. If equipped, remove the power steering pump and move it aside; DO NOT disconnect the pressure hoses.

5. Remove the Air Injection Reactor (AIR) pump/bracket, the fan and the water pump pulley.

6. Disconnect the electrical connectors, then remove the alternator mounting bracket from the water pump.

7. Remove the water pump-to-engine bolts and the pump from the engine.

8. To remove the damper hub, perform the following procedures:

   a. Remove the drive belt pulley-to-damper bolts and the pulley from the damper.

   b. Remove the damper-to-crankshaft bolt.

   c. Using the GM Torsional Damper Puller/Installer tool No. J–23523–E or equivalent, connect it to the damper and remove it from the crankshaft.

9. Remove the timing cover-to-engine bolts and the cover from the engine.

10. Rotate the crankshaft until the marks on the timing sprockets align (face each other). Remove the camshaft sprocket-to-camshaft bolts, then the sprocket and the timing chain from the camshaft and the crankshaft sprocket.

11. Using two or three, $\frac{5}{16}$ in. bolts, 4–5 in. long, install them into the camshaft holes. Using these camshaft bolts as handles, support the camshaft and pull the camshaft from the front of the engine block; be careful not to damage the camshaft bearing or lobe surfaces.

12. Inspect the camshaft for scratches, pitting and/or wear on the bearing and lobe surfaces. Check the timing sprockets teeth and timing chain for damage and/or wear, replace the damaged parts (if necessary).

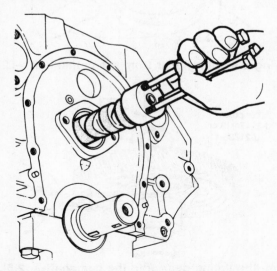

Replacing the camshaft – 4.3L engine

To install:

1. Lubricate the parts with engine oil and install the camshaft carefully not to damage the cam bearings.

2. With the timing chain installed on the sprockets, realign the timing mark (on the sprockets) and install the camshaft sprocket to the camshaft. Torque the camshaft sprocket-to-camshaft bolts to 18 ft. lbs. (25 Nm).

3. Use new gaskets, sealant (if necessary) and Install the timing gear cover as outlined in this Section.

4. Install and adjust the drive belt tensions.

5. Connect the negative battery cable.

6. Refill the cooling system, start the engine, allow it to reach normal operating temperatures and check for leaks.

7. Check and/or adjust the engine timing.

INSPECTION

Using solvent, degrease the camshaft and clean out all of the oil holes. Visually inspect the cam lobes and bearing journals for excessive wear. If a lobe is questionable, check all of the lobes as indicated. If a journal or lobe is worn, the camshaft MUST BE reground or replaced.

NOTE: If a journal is worn, there is a good chance that the bushings are worn and need replacement.

If the lobes and journals appear intact, place the front and rear journals in V-blocks and rest a dial indicator on the center journal. Rotate the camshaft to check the straightness. If deviation exceeds 0.001 in. (0.0254mm), replace the camshaft.

Check the camshaft lobes with a micrometer, by measuring the lobes from the nose to the base and again at 90° (see illustration). The lobe lift is determined by subtracting the second measurement from the first. If all of the exhaust and intake lobes are not identical, the camshaft must be reground or replace.

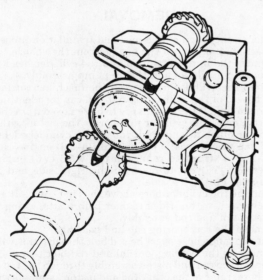

Check the camshaft for straightness

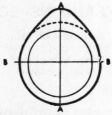

Camshaft lobe measurement

Camshaft Bearings

REMOVAL AND INSTALLATION

2.5L Engine

NOTE: The following procedure requires the use of the GM Camshaft Bushing Removal/Installation Adapter tool No. J–21437–1 or equivalent, and GM Camshaft Bushing Removal/Installation Handle tool No. J–21054–1 or equivalent.

1. Refer to the Engine, Removal and Installation procedures in this section and remove the engine from the vehicle and secure it onto a work stand.

2. Refer to the Camshaft, Removal and Installation and the Oil Pan, Removal and Installation procedures in this section and remove the camshaft and the oil pan from the engine.

3. Remove the flywheel-to-crankshaft bolts and the flywheel from the engine.

4. Using a blunt tool, drive the camshaft expansion plug from the rear of the engine.

5. Using the GM Camshaft Bushing Removal/Installation Adapter tool No. J–21437–1 or equivalent and a hammer, drive the front camshaft bearing toward the rear and the rear camshaft bearing toward the front of the engine.

6. Install the GM Camshaft Bushing Removal/Installation Handle tool No. J–21054–1 or equivalent, onto the GM Camshaft Bushing Removal/Installation Adapter tool No. J–21437–1 or equivalent, and drive the center camshaft bearing toward the rear of the engine.

To install:

1. Position the bearing on the tool(s) and tighten the end bolt to draw the bearing into its seat. Make sure that the oil holes are lined up and free from obstructions.

NOTE: The front bearing MUST BE driven to approximately ⅛ in. (3mm) behind the front of the cylinder block; BE SURE that the oil hole-to-timing gear oil nozzle is uncovered.

2. Install the camshaft being careful not to damage the new bearings.

3. Adjust the valves as outlined in the ''Valve Lash'' procedures in Section 2.

4. Refill the cooling system and the crankcase. Start the engine, allow it to reach normal operating temperatures and check for leaks.

4.3L Engine

To perform this procedure, it is recommended to remove the engine from the vehicle.

NOTE: The following procedure requires the use of the GM Camshaft Bearing Remover/Installer tool No. J–6098 or equivalent.

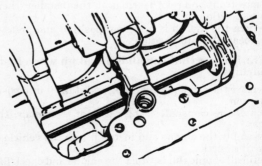

Replacing the camshaft bearings — 2.5L engine

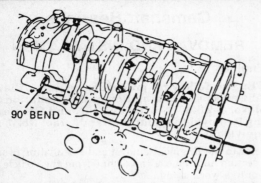

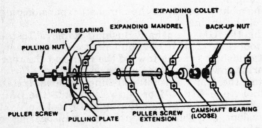

Aligning the camshaft bearing oil holes with a piece of wire bent to a 90 degree angle. The holes MUST be in alignment

Replacing the camshaft bearings, using GM tool No. J–6098 – 4.3L engine

1. Refer to the Camshaft, Removal and Installation and the Crankshaft, Removal and Installation procedures in this section and remove the camshaft and the crankshaft from the engine; leave the cylinder heads attached and the pistons in place.

NOTE: Before removing the crankshaft, tape the threads of the connecting rod bolts to prevent damage to the crankshaft. Fasten the connecting rods against the sides of the engine, so that they will not be in the way while replacing the camshaft bearings.

2. Drive the camshaft rear plug from the block.
3. Assemble the GM Camshaft Bearing Remover/Installer tool No. J–6098 or equivalent, using it's shoulder, on the bearing to be removed.
4. Gradually, tighten the puller nut until the bearing is removed. Remove the remaining bearings, leaving the front and the rear for last.
5. To remove the front and rear bearing, reverse the position of the tool, so as to press the bearings toward the center of the block.

To install:
1. Install the new bearings, leave the tool in this position, pilot the new front and rear bearings on the installer, then press them into position.
2. Return the tool to it's original position and press the remaining bearings into position.

NOTE: Ensure that the oil holes align when installing the bearings.

3. Replace the camshaft rear plug and stake it into position to aid retention.
4. Install the camshaft using care not to damage the cam bearings.
5. Assembly the engine and install it into the vehicle as outlined in this Section.
6. Refill all engine fluids, start the engine and check for proper operation.

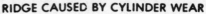

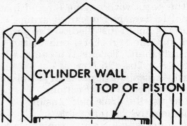

Remove the ridge from the cylinder bore

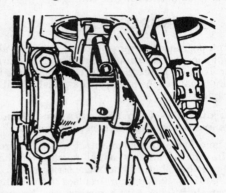

Push the piston out with a hammer handle

Pistons and Connecting Rods

REMOVAL

1. Refer to the Engine, Removal and Installation procedures in this section and remove the engine from the vehicle.
2. Remove the intake manifold and the cylinder head(s).
3. Remove the oil pan and the oil pump assembly.
4. Stamp the cylinder number on the machined surfaces of the bolt bosses of the connecting rod and cap for identification when reinstalling. If the pistons are to be removed from the connecting rod, mark the cylinder number on the piston with a silver pencil or quick drying paint for proper cylinder identification and cap to rod location. The 2.5L (4–cyl) engine is numbered 1–2–3–4 (front-to-rear); on the 4.3L (V6) engine, is numbered 1–3–5 (front-to-rear) on the right side and 2–4–6 (front-to-rear) on the left side.
5. Examine the cylinder bore above the ring travel. If a ridge exists, remove it with a ridge reamer before attempting to remove the piston and rod assembly.
6. Remove the rod bearing cap and bearing.
7. Install a guide hose over the rod bolt threads; this will prevent damage to the bearing journal and rod bolt threads.
8. Remove the rod and piston assembly through the top of the cylinder bore; remove the other rod and piston assemblies in the same manner.

CLEANING AND INSPECTION

Using a piston ring expanding tool, remove the piston rings from the pistons; any other method (screwdriver blades, pliers, etc.) usually results in the rings being bent, scratched or distorted and/or the piston itself being damaged.

Pistons

Clean the varnish from the piston skirts and pins with a cleaning solvent. DO NOT WIRE BRUSH ANY PART OF THE

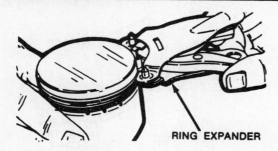

Remove the piston rings

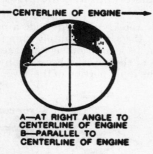

Clean the piston ring grooves

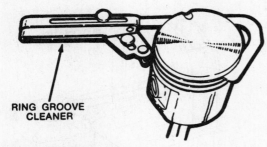

Cylinder bore measuring points

PISTON. Clean the ring grooves with a groove cleaner and make sure that the oil ring holes and slots are clean.

--- CAUTION ---

Do NOT use any solvent that will damage aluminum parts. Some hot tank solutions will dissolve aluminum.

Inspect the piston for cracked ring lands, scuffed or damaged skirts, eroded areas at the top of the piston. Replace the pistons that are damaged or show signs of excessive wear.

Inspect the grooves for nicks of burrs that might cause the rings to hang up.

Measure the piston skirt (across the center line of the piston pin) and check the piston clearance.

Connecting Rods

Wash the connecting rods in cleaning solvent and dry with compressed air. Check for twisted or bent rods and inspect for nicks or cracks. Replace the connecting rods that are damaged.

Cylinder Bores

Using a telescoping gauge or an inside micrometer, measure the diameter of the cylinder bore, perpendicular (90°) to the piston pin, at 2½ in. (63.5mm) below the surface of the cylinder block. The difference between the two measurements is the piston clearance.

Measuring the cylinder bore with a dial indicator

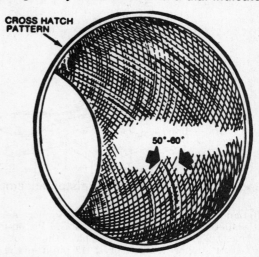

Correct cylinder bore honing pattern

If the clearance is within specifications or slightly below (after the cylinders have been bored or honed), finish honing is all that is necessary, If the clearance is excessive, try to obtain a slightly larger piston to bring the clearance within specifications. If this is not possible obtain the first oversize piston and hone the cylinder or (if necessary) bore the cylinder to size. Generally, if the cylinder bore is tapered more than 0.005 in. (0.127mm) or is out-of-round more than 0.003 in. (0.0762mm), it is advisable to rebore for the smallest possible oversize piston and rings. After measuring, mark the pistons with a felt-tip pen for reference and for assembly.

NOTE: Boring of the cylinder block should be performed by a reputable machine shop with the proper equipment. In some cases, clean-up honing can be done with the cylinder block in the vehicle, but most excessive honing and all cylinder boring MUST BE done with the block stripped and removed from the vehicle.

PISTON PIN REPLACEMENT

NOTE: The following procedure requires the use of the GM Fixture/Support Assembly tool No. J–24086–20 or equivalent, the GM Piston Pin Removal tool No. J–24086–8 or equivalent, and the GM Piston Pin Installation tool No. J–24086–9 or equivalent.

Use care at all times when handling and servicing the connecting rods and pistons. To prevent possible damage to these units, DO NOT clamp the rod or piston in a vise since they may become distorted. DO NOT allow the pistons to strike one another, against hard objects or bench surfaces, since distortion of the piston contour or nicks in the soft aluminum material may result.

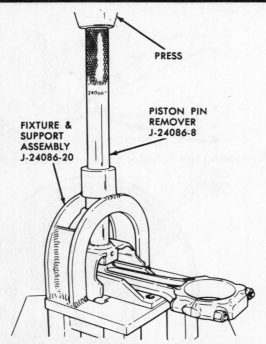

Removing the piston pin from the piston assembly

1. Using an arbor press, the GM Fixture/Support Assembly tool No. J–24086–20 or equivalent, and the GM Piston Pin Removal tool No. J–24086–8 or equivalent, place the piston assembly in the fixture/support tool and press the pin from the piston assembly.

NOTE: The piston and the piston pin are a matched set which are not serviced separately.

2. Using solvent, wash the varnish and oil from the parts, then inspect the parts for scuffing or wear.

3. Using a micrometer, measure the diameter of the piston pin. Using a inside micrometer or a dial bore gauge, measure the diameter of the piston bore.

NOTE: If the piston pin-to-piston clearance is in excess of 0.001 in. (0.0254mm), replace the piston and piston pin assembly.

4. Before installation, lubricate the piston pin and the piston bore with engine oil.

5. To install the piston pin into the piston assembly, use an arbor press, the GM Fixture/Support Assembly tool No. J–24086–20 or equivalent, and the GM Piston Pin Installation tool No. J–24086–9 or equivalent, then press the piston pin into the piston/connecting rod assembly.

NOTE: When installing the piston pin into the piston/connecting rod assembly and the installation tool bottoms onto the support assembly, DO NOT exceed 5000 lbs. of pressure for structural damage may occur to the tool.

6. After installing the piston pin, make sure that the piston has freedom of movement with the piston pin. The piston/connecting rod assembly is ready for installation into the engine block.

PISTON RING REPLACEMENT AND SIDE CLEARANCE MEASUREMENT

Check the pistons to see that the ring grooves and oil return

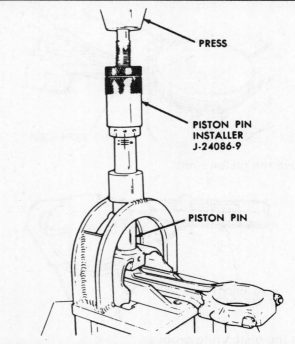

Installing the piston pin into the piston assembly

holes have been properly cleaned. Slide a piston ring into its groove and check the side clearance with a feeler gauge. Make sure the feeler gauge is inserted between the ring and its lower land (lower edge of the groove), because any wear that occurs forms a step at the inner portion of the lower land. If the piston

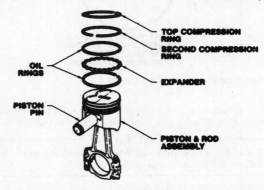

Exploded view of the piston and ring assembly

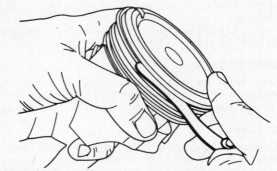

Using a feeler gauge to check the ring side clearances

grooves have been worn to the extent that relatively high steps exist on the lower land, the piston should be replaced, because these will interfere with the operation of the new rings and ring clearances will be excessive. Piston rings are not furnished in oversize widths to compensate for ring groove wear.

Install the rings on the piston, bottom ring first, using a piston ring expander. There is a high risk of breaking or distorting the rings and/or scratching the piston, if the rings are installed by hand or other means.

Position the rings on the piston as illustrated; spacing of the various piston ring gaps is crucial to the proper oil retention and cylinder wear. When installing the new rings, refer to the installation diagram furnished with the new parts.

CHECKING RING END GAP

The piston ring end gap should be checked while the rings are removed from the pistons. Incorrect end gap indicates that the wrong size rings are being used; *ring breakage could result.*

1. Compress the new piston ring into a cylinder (one at a time).

2. Squirt some clean oil into the cylinder so that the ring and the top 2 in. (51mm) of the cylinder wall are coated.

3. Using an inverted piston, push the ring approximately 1 in. (25.4mm) below the top of the cylinder.

4. Using a feeler gauge, measure the ring gap and compare it to the Ring Gap chart in this Section. Carefully remove the ring from the cylinder.

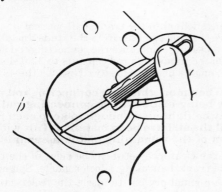

ROD BEARING REPLACEMENT

Replacement bearings are available in standard size and undersize (for reground crankshafts). Connecting rod-to-crankshaft bearing clearance is checked using Plastigage® at either the top or the bottom of each crank journal. The Plastigage® has a range of 0.001–0.003 in. (0.0254–0.0762mm).

1. Remove the rod cap with the bearing shell. Completely clean the bearing shell and the crank journal, blow any oil from the oil hole in the crankshaft; place the Plastigage® lengthwise along the bottom center of the lower bearing shell, then install the cap with the shell and torque the bolt or nuts to specification. DO NOT turn the crankshaft with the Plastigage® on the bearing.

2. Remove the bearing cap with the shell. The flattened Plastigage® will be found sticking to either the bearing shell or the crank journal. DO NOT remove it yet.

3. Use the scale printed on the Plastigage® envelope to measure the flattened material at its widest point. The number within the scale which most closely corresponds to the width of the Plastigage® indicates the bearing clearance in thousandths of an inch.

4. Check the specifications chart in this Section for the desired clearance. It is advisable to install a new bearing if the clearance exceeds 0.003 in. (0.0762mm); however, if the bearing

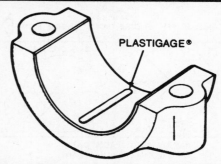

Plastigage® installed on the lower bearing shell

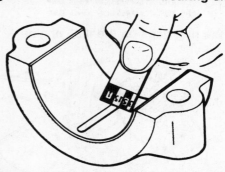

Measure the Plastigage® to determine bearing (rod or main clearance)

is in good condition and is not being checked because of bearing noise, bearing replacement is not necessary.

5. If you are installing new bearings, try a standard size, then each undersize in order until one is found that is within the specified limits when checked for clearance with Plastigage®; each undersize shell has its size stamped on it.

6. When the proper size shell is found, clean off the Plastigage®, oil the bearing thoroughly, reinstall the cap with its shell and torque the rod bolt nuts to specifications.

NOTE: With the proper bearing selected and the nuts torqued, it should be possible to move the connecting rod back and forth freely on the crank journal as allowed by the specified connecting rod end clearance. If the rod cannot be moved, either the rod bearing is too far undersize or the rod is misaligned.

INSTALLATION

Position the rings on the piston as illustrated; *spacing of the various piston ring gaps is crucial to proper oil retention and even cylinder wear.* When installing new rings, refer to the installation diagram furnished with the new parts.

Install the connecting rod to the piston, making sure that the piston installation notches and marks (if any) on the connecting rod are in proper relation to one another.

1. Make sure that the connecting rod big-end bearings (including the end cap) are of the correct size and properly installed.

2. Fit rubber hoses over the connecting rod bolts to protect the crankshaft journals, as in the Piston Removal procedure. Lubricate the connecting rod bearings with clean engine oil.

3. Using the ring compressor, compress the rings around the piston head. Insert the piston assembly into the cylinder, so that the notch (on top of the piston) faces the front of the engine.

4. From beneath the engine, coat each crank journal with clean oil. Using a hammer handle, drive the connecting rod/piston assembly into the cylinder bore. Align the connecting rod

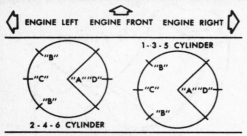

"A" OIL RING SPACER GAP
(Tang in Hole or Slot within Arc)
"B" OIL RING RAIL GAPS
"C" 2ND COMPRESSION RING GAP
"D" TOP COMPRESSION RING GAP

Locating the ring gaps on the 4.3L engine — the 2.5L engine is similar

Install the piston ring compressor, then tap the piston into the cylinder bore. Make sure that the piston front marks are correctly positioned to the front of the engine when installing

Install the pistons with the notch facing the front of the engine

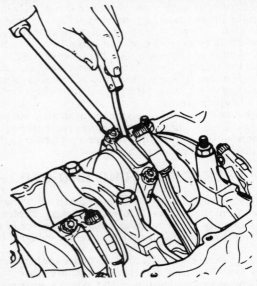

Check the connecting rod side clearance with a feeler gauge. Use a small pry bar to carefully spread the rods to the specified clearance

(with bearing shell) onto the crankshaft journal.

5. Remove the rubber hoses from the studs. Install the bearing cap (with bearing shell) onto the connecting rod and the cap nuts. Torque the connecting rod cap nuts to 32 ft. lbs. (43 Nm) for the 2.5L engine or 45 ft. lbs. (61 Nm) for the 4.3L engine.

NOTE: When more than one connecting rod/piston assembly are being installed, the connecting rod cap nuts should only be tightened enough to keep each rod in position until the all have been installed. This will ease the installation of the remaining piston assemblies.

6. Check the clearance between the sides of the connecting rods and the crankshaft using a feeler gauge. Spread the rods slightly with a small pry bar to insert the feeler gauge. If the clearance is below the minimum tolerance, the rod may be machined to provide adequate clearance. If the clearance is excessive, substitute an unworn rod and recheck. If clearance is still outside specifications, the crankshaft must be welded and reground or replaced.

7. To complete the installation, reverse the removal procedures. Refill the cooling system. Refill the engine crankcase. Start the engine, allow it to reach normal operating temperatures and check for leaks.

Engine Block Heater and Freeze Plugs

REMOVAL AND INSTALLATION

--- CAUTION ---

Removing the block heater or freeze plug may cause personal injury if the engine is not completely cooled down. Even after the radiator has been drained, there will be engine coolant still in the block. Use care when removing assembly from the block.

NOTE: To remove an engine freeze plug or block heater, accessories may have to be removed, such as the starter motor, motor mount, etc. Remove an obstruction before attempting to remove the freeze plug.

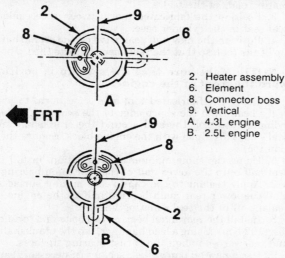

2. Heater assembly
6. Element
8. Connector boss
9. Vertical
A. 4.3L engine
B. 2.5L engine

Engine block heater — located in the freeze plug hole in engine block

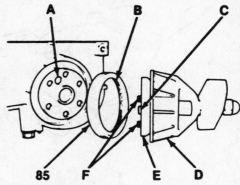

A. Alignment hole in crankshaft
B. Dust lip
C. Dowel pin
D. Collar
E. Mandrel
F. Screws
85. Crankshaft rear oil seal

Using GM tool No. J–34924 or equivalent, to install the rear oil seal — 2.5L engine

1. Disconnect the negative (−) battery cable.
2. **To remove the block heater,** drain the engine coolant, disconnect the electrical connector, loosen the retaining screw and remove the heater from the block.

────────── CAUTION ──────────
When draining the coolant, keep in mind that cats and dogs are attracted by the ethylene glycol antifreeze, and are quite likely to drink any that is left in an uncovered container or in puddles on the ground. This will prove fatal in sufficient quantity. Always drain the coolant into a sealable container. Coolant should be reused unless it is contaminated or several years old.
───────────────────────────────

3. **To remove the freeze plug,** drain the engine coolant, drive chisel through the plug and pry outward. Or drill an ⅛ in. hole into the plug and use a dent puller to remove the freeze plug.

To install:

1. To install the block heater, coat the O-ring with engine oil and clean the block mating surface free of rust and corrosion. Install the heater and tighten the retaining screw. Connect the electrical and negative battery cable.
2. To install the freeze plug, coat the new plug with silicone sealer and clean the block mating surface free of rust and corrosion. Using a deep socket the size of the interior of the plug, drive the plug into the block until the plug lip is flush with the cylinder block. Run silicone sealer around the mating area.
3. Fill the engine with coolant and check for leaks.

Rear Main Oil Seal

REMOVAL AND INSTALLATION

2.5L Engine

The rear main oil seal is a one piece unit. It can be removed or installed without removing the oil pan or the crankshaft.

NOTE: The following procedure requires the use of the GM Oil Seal Installation tool No. J–34924 or equivalent.

1. Disconnect the negative (−) battery cable. Refer to the Transmission, Removal and Installation procedures in Section 7 and remove the transmission from the vehicle.
2. If equipped with a manual transmission, remove the clutch

assembly, the flywheel-to-crankshaft bolts and the flywheel from the crankshaft.
3. Using a small prybar, pry the oil seal from the rear of the crankshaft.

NOTE: When removing the oil seal, be careful not to damage the crankshaft sealing surface.

4. To install the new oil seal into the rear retainer, perform the following procedures:
   a. Using new engine oil, lubricate the inner and outer diameter of the seal.
   b. Using the GM Oil Seal Installation tool No. J–34924 or equivalent, install the new oil seal onto it, position the assembly against the crankshaft.
   c. Align the dowel with the alignment hole in the crankshaft and thread the attaching screws into the tapped holes in the crankshaft.
   d. Using a screwdriver, tighten the screws securely; this will ensure that the seal is installed squarely over the crankshaft.
   e. Turn the handle until it bottoms and remove the installation tool.
5. To complete the installation, install the flywheel, the clutch assembly and the transmission. Torque the flywheel-to-crankshaft bolts to 55 ft. lbs. (75 Nm) and the bellhousing-to-engine bolts to 46 ft. lbs. (63 Nm).

4.3L Engine — 1985

1. Refer to the Oil Pan, Removal and Installation procedures in this section and remove the oil pan from the engine.
2. Remove the oil pump and the rear main bearing cap.
3. Using a small pry bar, pry the oil seal from the rear main bearing cap.
4. Using a small hammer and a brass pin punch, drive the top half of the oil seal from the rear main bearing. Drive it out far enough, so it may be removed with a pair of pliers.
5. Using a non-abrasive cleaner, clean the rear main bearing cap and the crankshaft.

To install:

1. Fabricate an oil seal installation tool from 0.004 in. (0.01mm) shim stock, shape the end to ½ in. (12.7mm) long by ¹¹⁄₆₄ in. (4.4mm) wide.
2. Coat the new oil seal with engine oil; DO NOT coat the

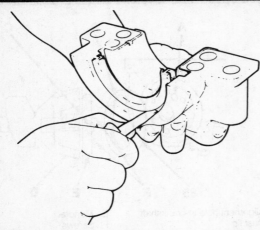

Removing the lower half of the rear main oil seal from the rear bearing cap — 4.3L engine (1985)

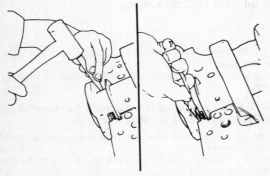

Removing the upper half of the rear main oil seal from the engine block — 4.3L engine (1985)

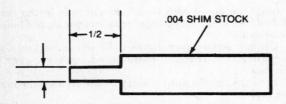

Dimensions for making a rear main oil seal installation tool — 4.3L engine (1985)

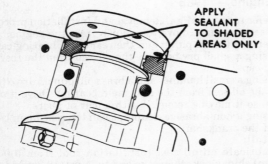

Applying RTV sealant to the rear main oil seal halves — 4.3L engine (1985)

mating ends of the seal.

3. Position the fabricated tool between the crankshaft and seal seat in the cylinder case.

4. Position the new half seal between the crankshaft and the tip of the tool, so that the seal bead contacts the tip of the tool.

NOTE: Make sure that the seal lip is positioned toward the front of the engine.

5. Using the fabricated tool as a shoe horn, to protect the seal's bead from the sharp edge of the seal seat surface in the cylinder case, roll the seal around the crankshaft. When the seal's ends are flush with the engine block, remove the installation tool.

6. Using the same manner of installation, install the lower seal half onto the lower half of the rear main bearing cap.

7. Apply sealant to the cap-to-case mating surfaces and install the lower rear main bearing half to the engine; keep the sealant off of the seal's mating line.

8. Install the rear main bearing cap bolts and torque to 75 ft. lbs. (102 Nm). Using a lead hammer, tap the crankshaft forward and rearward, to align the thrust bearing surfaces.

9. Use a new oil pan gasket, sealant (if necessary) and install the oil pan.

10. Refill the crankcase with clean engine oil and connect the negative battery cable.

11. Start the engine, allow it to reach normal operating temperatures and check for leaks.

4.3L Engine — 1986 and Later

NOTE: The following procedure requires the use of the GM Oil Seal Installation tool No. J–35621 or equivalent.

1. Refer to the Transmission, Removal and Installation procedures in Section 7 and remove the transmission from the vehicle.

2. If equipped with a manual transmission, remove the clutch assembly, the flywheel-to-crankshaft bolts and the flywheel from the crankshaft.

3. Using a small prybar, insert it into the notches provided in the oil seal retainer and pry the oil seal from the retainer.

NOTE: When removing the oil seal from the retainer, be careful not to nick the crankshaft sealing surface.

To install:

1. Install the new oil seal into the rear retainer, perform the following procedures:

   a. Using engine oil, lubricate the inner and outer diameter of the seal.

   b. Using the GM Oil Seal Installation tool No. J–35621, install the new oil seal onto it, position the assembly against the crankshaft and thread the attaching screws into the tapped holes in the crankshaft.

   c. Using a screwdriver, tighten the screws securely; this will ensure that the seal is installed squarely over the crankshaft.

   d. Turn the handle until it bottoms and remove the installation tool.

2. Install the flywheel, the clutch assembly and the transmission. Torque the flywheel-to-crankshaft bolts to 75 ft. lbs. (102 Nm) and the bellhousing-to-engine bolts to 46 ft. lbs. (63 Nm) for carburetor models or 55 ft. lbs. (75 Nm) for throttle body models.

Crankshaft and Main Bearings

REMOVAL AND INSTALLATION

NOTE: The following procedure requires the use of the GM Guide Tool Set No. J–6305–11 (2.5L engine), J–5239 (4.3L engine) or equivalent.

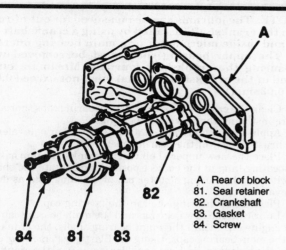

A. Rear of block
81. Seal retainer
82. Crankshaft
83. Gasket
84. Screw

Exploded view of the rear oil seal — 4.3L engine (1986–present)

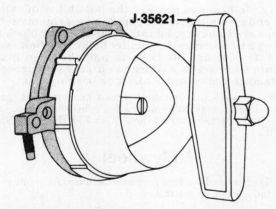

Using the oil seal installation tool No. J–35621 to install the new oil seal — 4.3L engine

1. Refer to the Engine, Removal and Installation procedures in this section and remove the engine from the vehicle.
2. If equipped with a flywheel, remove it and mount the engine onto a workstand.
3. Disconnect the spark plug wires from the plugs, then remove the spark plugs.
4. Remove the drive belt pulley from the damper hub, the damper hub-to-crankshaft bolt, the damper hub from the crankshaft and the timing cover from the engine.

NOTE: After removing the damper hub from the crankshaft, be sure to remove the woodruff key from the crankshaft. When removing the damper hub from the crankshaft, the oil seal should be replaced.

5. Rotate the crankshaft, until the timing marks on the timing gears (2.5L engine) or sprockets (4.3L engine) align with each other, then remove the timing gear (2.5L) or timing chain/sprocket (4.3L) from the crankshaft.

NOTE: After removing the timing gear or sprocket from the crankshaft, be sure to remove the woodruff key from the crankshaft.

6. Place a catch pan under the engine, remove the oil pan plug and drain the oil into the pan. Invert the engine and remove the oil pan from the engine.

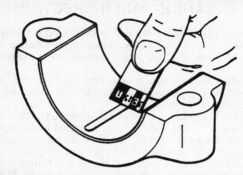

Measure the main bearing clearance by comparing the flattened strip to the Plastigage® scale as shown

— CAUTION —

The EPA warns that prolonged contact with used engine oil may cause a number of skin disorders, including cancer! You should make every effort to minimize your exposure to used engine oil. Protective gloves should be worn when changing the oil. Wash your hands and any other exposed skin areas as soon as possible after exposure to used engine oil. Soap and water, or waterless hand cleaner should be used.

NOTE: If working on the 4.3L engine, remove the oil pump.

7. Inspect the connecting rods and bearing caps for identification marks (numbers); if there are none, mark them for reassembly purposes.
8. Remove the connecting rod nuts and caps, then store them in the order of removal. Using the GM Guide Tool Set No. J–6305–11 (2.5L engine), J–5239 (4.3L engine) or equivalent, install them on the connecting rod studs and push the connecting rods into the block. Remove the bearing shells from the connecting rod and the bearing cap.

NOTE: When installing the guide tool set onto the connecting rod studs, position the long tool so that it may be used to push the connecting rod up into the bore.

9. Check the main bearing caps for identification marks (if not identified, mark them). Remove the main bearing caps and store them in order, for reassembly purposes; the caps must be reinstalled in their original position.
10. Remove the crankshaft, the main bearing inserts and the rear main oil seal (2.5L), the rear main oil shell sections (4.3L, 1985) or the rear main oil seal/retainer (4.3L, 1986 and later).

NOTE: When removing the bearing shells, it is recommended to replace them with new ones.

11. Using solvent, clean all of the parts for inspection purposes. If necessary, replace any part that may be questionable.
To install:
1. Use new bearing shell inserts and check the bearing clearances using the Plastigage® method.

NOTE: If necessary, deliver the crankshaft to an automotive machine shop, have the crankshaft journals ground and new bearing shells matched.

2. Lubricate all of the parts and oil seals with assembly lube or clean engine oil.
3. Use new gaskets (sealant if necessary) and install the oil pump pickup and oil pan. Torque the main bearing cap-to-engine bolts to 70 ft. lbs. (95 Nm) for the 2.5L or 75 ft. lbs. (102 Nm) for the 4.3L.
4. Refill the cooling system (with the saved coolant) and the crankcase (with new oil). Connect the negative battery cable, start the engine, allow it to reach normal operating temperatures and check for leaks.

CLEANING AND INSPECTION

1. Remove the bearing cap and wipe the oil from the crankshaft journal and outer/inner surfaces of the bearing shell.

2. Place a piece of Plastigage® material in the center of the bearing.

3. Reinstall the bearing cap and bearing. Lubricate the main bearing bolts with engine oil, install the bolts and torque them to specifications.

4. Remove the bearing caps and determine the bearing clearance by comparing the width of the flattened Plastigage® material at its widest point with the graduations on the gaging material container. The number within the graduation on the envelope indicates the clearance in millimeters or thousandths of an inch. If the clearance is greater than allowed. REPLACE BOTH BEARING SHELLS AS A SET. Recheck the clearance after replacing the shells. Refer to the Main Bearing Replacement in this section.

MAIN BEARING REPLACEMENT

Main bearing clearances must be corrected by the use of selective upper and lower shells. UNDER NO CIRCUMSTANCES should the use of shims behind the shells to compensate for wear be attempted. To install the main bearing shells, proceed as follows:

1. Refer to the Oil Pan, Removal and Installation procedures in this section and remove the oil pan.

2. Loosen all of the main bearing cap bolts.

3. Remove the bearing cap bolts, the caps and the lower bearing shell.

4. Insert a flattened cotter pin or a roll out pin in the oil passage hole in the crankshaft, then rotate the crankshaft in the direction opposite to the cranking rotation. The pin will contact the upper shell and roll it out.

5. The main bearing journals should be checked for roughness and wear. Slight roughness may be removed with a fine grit polishing cloth, saturated with engine oil. Burrs may be removed with a fine oil stone. If the journals are scored or ridged, the crankshaft must be replaced.

NOTE: The journals can be measured for out-of-round with the crankshaft installed by using a crankshaft caliper and inside micrometer or a main bearing micrometer. The upper bearing shell must be removed when measuring the crankshaft journals. Maximum out-of-round of the crankshaft journal must not exceed 0.0015 in. (0.038mm).

6. Clean the crankshaft journals and bearing caps thoroughly before installing the new main bearings.

7. Apply special lubricant, GM No. 1050169 or equivalent, to the thrust flanges of the bearing shells.

8. Place the new upper shell on the crankshaft journal with the locating tang in the correct position and rotate the shaft to turn it into place using a cotter pin or a roll out pin as during removal.

9. Place a new bearing shell in the bearing cap.

10. Lubricate the new bearings and the main bearing cap bolts with engine oil. Install the main bearing shells, the crankshaft and the main bearing caps. Using the Plastigage® method, check the bearing clearances. Using a feeler gauge, pry the crankshaft forward and rearward, then check for the crankshaft (thrust bearing) end play.

NOTE: In order to prevent the possibility of cylinder block and/or main bearing cap damage, the main bearing caps are to be tapped into their cylinder block cavity, using a brass or leather mallet before the bolts are installed. Do not use the bolts to pull the main bearing caps into their seats. Failure to observe this procedure may damage the cylinder block or bearing cap.

11. To complete the installation, use new oil seals, gaskets (sealant, if necessary). Torque the main bearing cap-to-engine bolts to 70 ft. lbs. (95 Nm) for the 2.5L or 75 ft. lbs. (102 Nm) for the 4.3L.

Flywheel

The flywheel and the ring gear are machined from one piece of metal and cannot be separated.

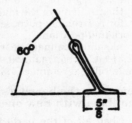

Fabricate a roll-out pin as illustrated, if necessary

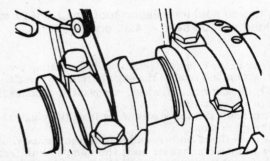

Use a feeler gauge to check the crankshaft endplay during assembly

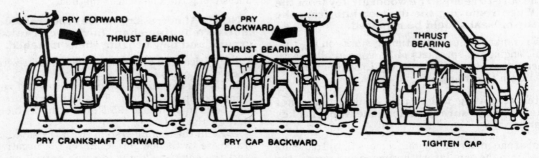

Align the thrust bearing as illustrated. Torque the caps to specifications

REMOVAL AND INSTALLATION

NOTE: The following procedure requires the use of the GM Clutch Disc Aligner tool No. J–33169 or equivalent.

1. Refer to the Manual Transmission, Removal and Installation procedures in Section 7 and remove the transmission from the bellhousing.

2. Remove the slave cylinder-to-bellhousing bolts and move the slave cylinder aside; DO NOT disconnect the hydraulic line from the cylinder.

3. Remove the bellhousing-to-engine bolts and the bellhousing from the engine. When removing the bellhousing, slide the clutch fork from the ball stud.

NOTE: The clutch fork ball stud is threaded into the bellhousing and can easily be replaced, if necessary.

4. Using the GM Clutch Disc Aligner tool No. J–33169 or equivalent, position it in the pilot bushing (to support the clutch disc).

5. Inspect the flywheel/pressure plate assembly for match marks (a stamped or a painted **X** mark); if no mark exists, mark the flywheel and the pressure plate.

6. Loosen the clutch-to-flywheel bolts, evenly (one turn at a time), until the spring tension is relieved, then remove the retaining bolts, the pressure plate and the clutch assembly.

7. Remove the flywheel-to-crankshaft bolts and the flywheel from the engine.

8. Clean the clutch disc (use a stiff brush), the pressure plate and the flywheel of all dirt, oil and grease. Inspect the flywheel, the pressure plate and the clutch disc for scoring, cracks, heat checking and/or other defects.

NOTE: When the flywheel is removed, it is a good idea to replace the rear main oil seal, the pilot bushing and/or the clutch plate (if necessary).

To install:

1. Align flywheel with the crankshaft, then torque the flywheel-to-crankshaft bolts to 55–75 ft. lbs. (74–102 Nm) for the 2.5L or 48–62 ft. lbs. (67–85 Nm) for the 4.3L.

2. Using the GM Clutch Disc Aligner tool No. J–33169 or equivalent, position it in the pilot bushing (to support the clutch disc), then assemble the clutch disc (the damper springs facing the transmission), the pressure plate and the retaining bolts onto the flywheel.

NOTE: When installing the pressure plate onto the flywheel, be sure to align the X marks.

3. Tighten the pressure plate-to-flywheel bolts gradually and evenly (to prevent clutch plate distortion) to 15–22 ft. lbs. (20–29 Nm) for the 2.5L or 25–35 ft. lbs. (34–48 Nm) for the 4.3L, then remove the alignment tool.

4. Lubricate the pilot bushing and the clutch release lever. Torque the bellhousing-to-engine bolts to 11–15 ft. lbs. (15–21 Nm), the transmission-to-bellhousing bolts to 25 ft. lbs. (34 Nm) and the clutch slave cylinder-to-bellhousing bolts to 10–15 ft. lbs. (14–21 Nm).

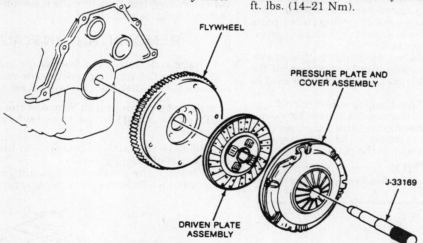

FLYWHEEL

PRESSURE PLATE AND COVER ASSEMBLY

J-33169

DRIVEN PLATE ASSEMBLY

Replacing the flywheel and clutch assembly

EXHAUST SYSTEM

Safety

For a number of different reasons, exhaust system work can be the most dangerous type of work you can do on your van. Always observe the following precautions:

• Support the van extra securely. Not only will you often be working directly under it, but you'll frequently be using a lot of force, such as heavy hammer blows to dislodge rusted parts. This can cause an improperly supported van to shift and possibly fall.

● Wear goggles. Exhaust system parts are always rusty. Metal chips can be dislodged, even when you're only turning rusted bolts. Attempting to pry pipes apart with a chisel makes chips fly even more frequently. Gloves are also recommended to protect against rusty chips and sharp, jagged edges.

● If you're using a cutting torch, keep it at a great distance from either the fuel tank or lines. Stop frequently and check the temperature of fuel and brake lines or the tank. Even slight heat can expand or vaporize the fuel, resulting in accumulated vapor or a liquid leak near your torch.

● Watch where your hammer blows fall. You could easily tap a brake or fuel line when you hit an exhaust system part with a glancing blow. Inspect all lines and hoses in the work area before driving the van.

— CAUTION —

Be very careful when working on or near the catalytic converter. External temperatures can reach 1500°F (815°C) and more, causing severe burns. Removal or installation should be performed only on a cold exhaust system.

Special Tools

A number of special exhaust system tools can be rented from auto supply houses or local stores that rent special equipment. A common one is a tail pipe expander, designed to enable you to join pipes of identical diameter.

It may also be quite helpful to use solvents designed to loosen rusted bolts or flanges. Soaking rusted hardware the night before you do the job can speed the work of freeing rusted parts considerably. Remember that these solvents are often flammable. Apply them only after the parts are cool.

Two types of pipe connections are used on the exhaust system, they are: the ball joint (to allow angular movement for alignment purposes) and the slip joint. No gaskets are used in the entire system.

The system is supported by free hanging rubber mountings which permit some movement of the exhaust system but do not allow the transfer of noise and vibration into the passenger compartment. Any noise vibrations or rattles in the exhaust system are usually caused by misalignment of the parts.

— CAUTION —

Before performing any operation on the exhaust system, be sure to allow it to cool down.

Front Pipe

REMOVAL AND INSTALLATION

1. Raise and support the front of the vehicle on jackstands.
2. Remove the front pipe(s)-to-manifold(s) nuts and separate (pry, if necessary) the front pipe (ball joint) from the exhaust manifold(s).
3. At the catalytic converter, loosen the front pipe-to-converter clamp nuts, slide the clamp away from converter and separate the front pipe from the converter.

NOTE: Use a twisting motion to separate the front pipe-to-converter slip joint connection. If the front pipe cannot be removed from the catalytic converter, use a hammer (to loosen the connection) or wedge tool separate the connection.

4. Inspect the pipe for holes, damage or deterioration; if necessary, replace the front pipe.
5. **To install,** lubricate the front pipe-to-manifold(s) studs/nuts and the front pipe-to-converter clamp threads, then torque the clamps to 20 ft. lbs. (27 Nm).
6. Start the engine and check for exhaust leaks.

Catalytic Converter

The catalytic converter is an emission control device added to the exhaust system to reduce the emission of hydrocarbon and carbon monoxide pollutants.

REMOVAL AND INSTALLATION

1. Raise and support the front of the vehicle on jackstands.
2. Remove the catalytic converter-to-muffler stud nuts and separate the muffler from the converter.

NOTE: The connection between the converter and the muffler is a ball joint type, which can be easily separated.

3. Remove the catalytic converter-to-front pipe clamp nuts and move the clamp forward.
4. Remove the converter-to-mounting bracket bolts (if equipped), then twist the converter to separate it from the front pipe.

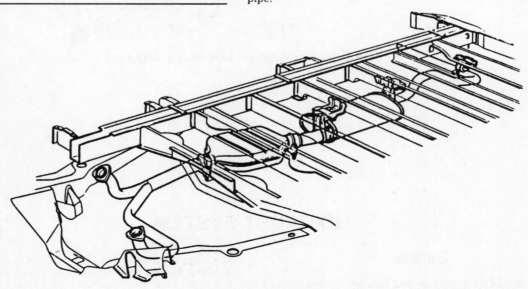

View of the exhaust system with the 4.3L engine — 2.5L engine equipped vehicle is similar

5. Inspect the condition of the catalytic converter for physical damage, replace it, if necessary.

NOTE: When installing the catalytic converter, be sure that it is installed with adequate clearance from the floor pan, to prevent overheating of the vehicle floor.

6. **To install,** align the components and reverse the removal procedures; be careful not to damage the pipe sealing surfaces when tightening the retaining clamps. Torque the clamps to 20 ft. lbs. (27 Nm).

7. Start the engine and check for exhaust leaks.

Muffler

NOTE: The following procedure requires the use of GM Sealing Compound No. 1051249 or equivalent. When replacing the muffler, always replace the tail pipe.

REMOVAL AND INSTALLATION

1. Refer to the Tail Pipe, Removal and Installation procedures in this section and remove the tail pipe from the vehicle.
2. Loosen and move the catalytic converter-to-muffler clamp or remove the catalytic converter-to-muffler flange bolts and separate the items.
3. Remove the muffler-to-mounting bracket bolts and lower the muffler from the vehicle.
4. **To install,** coat the slip joints with GM Sealing Compound No. 1051249 or equivalent and loosely install the components onto the vehicle.
5. After aligning the components, torque the connecting bolts and clamps to 20 ft. lbs. (27 Nm).

NOTE: When torquing the exhaust system connectors, be careful not to tighten the pipe clamps too tight, for deformation of the pipes may occur.

6. Start the engine and check for exhaust leaks.

Tail Pipe

NOTE: The following procedure requires the use of GM Sealing Compound No. 1051249 or equivalent.

REMOVAL AND INSTALLATION

NOTE: Normally, when the tail pipe requires replacement, the muffler should be replaced also.

1. Raise and support the rear of the vehicle on jackstands.
2. Remove the tail pipe-to-muffler clamp, then slide the clamp rearward.
3. Remove the tail pipe-to-mounting bracket clamp.
4. Using a twisting motion, remove the tail pipe from the muffler.

NOTE: If removal of the tail pipe difficult, use a hammer to free the pipe from the muffler.

5. Inspect the tail pipe for holes of physical damage.
6. **To install,** use a new tail pipe (if necessary), a new muffler (if necessary), apply GM Sealing Compound No. 1051249 or equivalent to the slip joint(s), lubricate the pipe clamp threads with engine oil, loosely assemble the exhaust system, then final torque the components to 20 ft. lbs. (27 Nm).
7. Start the engine and check for exhaust leaks.

TROUBLESHOOTING

Engine Speed Oscillates at Idle

When the engine idle speed will not remain constant, replace or repair the following items or systems, as necessary:
- A faulty fuel pump.
- A leaky Exhaust Gas Recirculation (EGR) valve.
- A blown head gasket.
- A worn camshaft.
- Worn timing gears, chain or sprockets.
- Leaking intake manifold-to-engine gasket.
- A blocked Positive Crankcase Ventilation (PCV) valve.
- Overheating of the cooling system.

Low Power Output of Engine

When the engine power output is below normal, replace or repair the following items or systems, as necessary:
- Overheating of the cooling system.
- Leaks in the vacuum system.
- Leaking of the fuel pump or hoses.
- Unadjusted valve timing.
- A blown head gasket.
- A slipping clutch disc or unadjusted pedal.
- Excessive piston-to-bore clearance.
- A worn camshaft.
- Sticking valve(s) or weak valve spring(s).
- A poorly operating diverter valve.
- A faulty pressure regulator valve (Auto. Trans.).
- Low fluid level (Auto. Trans.).

Poor High Speed Operation

When the engine cannot maintain high speed operations, replace or repair the following items or systems, as necessary:
- A faulty fuel pump producing low fuel volume.
- A restriction in the intake manifold.
- A worn distributor shaft.
- Unadjusted valve timing.
- Leaking valves or worn valve springs.

Poor Acceleration

When the engine experiences poor acceleration characteristics, replace or repair the following items or systems, as necessary:
- Incorrect ignition timing.
- Poorly seated valves.
- Improperly adjusted accelerator pump stroke (carburetor equipped).
- Worn accelerator pump diaphragm or piston (carburetor equipped).

Backfire — Intake Manifold

When the engine backfires through the intake manifold, replace or repair the following items or systems, as necessary:
- Incorrect ignition timing.
- Incorrect operation of the choke (carburetor equipped).
- Choke setting (initial clearance) too large (carburetor equipped).
- Defective Exhaust Gas Recirculation (EGR) valve.
- A very lean air/fuel mixture (carburetor equipped).

Backfire — Exhaust Manifold

When the engine backfires through the exhaust manifold, replace or repair the following items or systems, as necessary:
- Leaks in the vacuum hose system.
- Leaks in the exhaust system.
- Faulty choke adjustments or operation (carburetor equipped).
- Faulty vacuum diverter valve.

Engine Detonation (Dieseling)

When the engine operates beyond the controlled limits, replace or repair the following items or systems, as necessary:

- Faulty ignition electrical system components.
- The ignition timing may be too far advanced.
- Inoperative Exhaust Gas Recirculation (EGR) valve.
- Inoperative Positive Crankcase Ventilation (PCV) valve.
- Faulty or loose spark plugs.
- Clogged fuel delivery system.
- Sticking, leaking or broken valves.
- Excessive deposits in the combustion chambers.
- Leaks in the vacuum system.

Excessive Oil Leakage

When large amounts of oil are noticed under the engine after each operation, replace or repair the following items or systems, as necessary:
- Damaged or broken oil filter gasket.
- Leaking oil pressure sending switch.
- Worn rear main oil seal gasket.
- Worn front main oil seal gasket.
- Damaged or broken fuel pump gasket (mechanical pump).
- Damaged or loose valve cover gasket.
- Damaged oil pan gasket or bent oil pan.
- Improperly seated oil pan drain plug.
- Broken timing chain cover gasket.
- Blocked camshaft bearing drain hole.

Heavy Oil Consumption

When the engine is burning large amounts of oil, replace or repair the following items or systems, as necessary:
- The engine oil level may be to high.
- The engine oil may be to thin.
- Wrong size of piston rings.
- Clogged piston ring grooves or oil return slots.
- Insufficient tension of the piston rings.
- Piston rings may be sticking in the grooves.
- Excessively worn piston ring grooves.
- Reversed (upside-down) compression rings.
- Non-staggered piston ring gaps.
- Improper Positive Crankcase Ventilation (PCV) valve operation.
- Damaged valve O-ring seals.
- Restricted oil drain back holes.
- Worn valve stem or guides.
- Damaged valve stem oil deflectors.
- Too long intake gasket dowels.
- Mismatched rail and expander of the oil ring.
- Excessive clearance of the main and connecting rods.
- Scored or worn cylinder walls.

Negative Oil Pressure

When the engine presents no oil pressure, replace or repair the following items or systems, as necessary:
- Low oil level in the crankcase.
- Broken oil pressure gauge or sender.
- Blocked oil pump passages.
- Blocked oil pickup screen or tube.
- Malfunctioning oil pump.
- Sticking oil pressure relief valve.
- Leakage of the internal oil passages.
- Worn (loose) camshaft bearings.

Low Oil Pressure

When the engine presents low oil pressure, replace or repair the following items or systems, as necessary:
- Low oil level in the crankcase.
- Blocked oil pickup screen or tube.
- Malfunctioning or excessive clearance of the oil pump.
- Sticking oil pressure relief valve.
- Very thin engine oil.
- Worn (loose) main, rod or camshaft bearings.

High Oil Pressure

When the engine presents high oil pressure, replace or repair the following items or systems, as necessary:
- Sticking (closed) oil pressure relief valve.
- Wrong grade of oil.
- Faulty oil pressure gauge or sender.

Knocking Main Bearings

When the main bearings are constantly making noise, replace or repair the following items or systems, as necessary:
- Oval shaped crankshaft journals.
- Loose torque converter or flywheel mounting bolts.
- Loose damper pulley hub.
- Excessive clearance of the main bearings.
- Excessive belt tension.
- Low oil supply to the main bearings.
- Extreme crankshaft end play.

Knocking Connecting Rods

When the connecting rod bearings are constantly making noise, replace or repair the following items or systems, as necessary:
- Misaligned connecting rod or cap.
- Missing bearing shell or excessive bearing clearance.
- Incorrectly torqued connecting rod bolts.
- Connecting rod journal of the crankshaft is out-of-round.

Knocking Pistons and Rings

When the pistons and/rings are constantly making noise, replace or repair the following items or systems, as necessary:
- Misaligned connecting rods.
- Out-of-round or tapered cylinder bore.
- Loose or tight ring side clearance.
- Build-up of carbon on the piston(s).
- Piston-to-cylinder bore clearance is excessive.
- Broken piston rings.
- Loose or seized piston pin(s).

Knocking Valve Train

When the valve train is constantly making noise, replace or repair the following items or systems, as necessary:
- Retighten any loose rocker arms.
- Remove any dirt or chips in the valve lifters.
- Excessive valve stem-to-guide clearance.
- Remove restrictions from valve lifter oil holes.
- Incorrect valve lifter may be installed in the engine.
- Valve lock(s) may be missing.
- Valve lifter check ball may be faulty.
- Valve lifter leak down may be excessive.
- Rocker arm nut may be reversed (installed upside-down).
- Camshaft lobes may be excessively worn.
- Bent or worn pushrods.
- Excessively worn bridged pivots or rocker arms.
- Cocked or broken valve springs.
- Bent valve(s).
- Worn valve lifter face(s).
- Damaged lifter plunger or pushrod seat.

Knocking Valves

When the valves are constantly noisy, replace or repair the following items or systems, as necessary:
- Unadjusted valve lash.
- Valve springs may be broken.
- Pushrods may be bent.
- Camshaft lobes may be excessively worn.
- Dirty or worn valve lifters.
- Valve guides may be worn.
- Valve seat or face runout may be excessive.
- Loose rocker arm studs.

Emission 4 *Controls*

QUICK REFERENCE INDEX

GENERAL INDEX

EMISSION CONTROLS

The exhaust emission control systems used on the Astro/Safari engines perform a specific function to lower exhaust emissions while maintaining good fuel economy and driveability.

Computer Command Control

The ECM (electronic control module) controls fuel delivery, ignition timing, air management, exhaust gas recirculation and engagement of the torque converter clutch.

Fuel Control System

The ECM controls the air/fuel delivery to the combustion chamber by controlling the fuel flow through the carburetor or fuel injectors.

Evaporative Emission Control

This system uses a charcoal canister which stores fuel vapor from the fuel tank. The vapor is consumed in the normal combustion process when the engine is running and stored in the canister when not running.

Ignition/Electronic Spark Timing (EST)

This system is controlled by the ECM. It controls ignition timing depending on engine performance. This system is located in the distributor assembly.

Electronic Spark Control (ESC)

This system uses a knock sensor in connection with the ECM. The system will allow the engine to have maximum spark advance without spark knock.

Exhaust Gas Recirculation (EGR)

The EGR system uses a valve to feed a small amount of exhaust gas back into the intake manifold to control formation of NOx and is controlled by the ECM.

Transmission Converter Clutch (TCC)

The TCC is ECM controlled and is used on all engines with the Turbo Hydra-Matic 700R4 automatic transmission. This system reduces slippage losses in the torque converter by coupling the engine flywheel to the output shaft of the transmission.

Positive Crankcase Ventilation (PCV)

The system passes crankcase vapors into the intake manifold to be burned in the combustion chamber. This system is not controlled by the ECM.

Air Management

This system provides additional oxygen to the exhaust gases to continue the combustion process. The oxygen is injected into the exhaust manifold by the uses of an air pump.

Thermostatic Air Cleaner

The THERMAC system regulates heated air through the air cleaner to provide uniform inlet air temperature to increase cold engine driveability.

Crankcase Ventilation System

OPERATION

The crankcase vapors are drawn into the intake manifold to be burned in the combustion chambers, instead of merely venting the crankcase vapors into the atmosphere. An added benefit to engines equipped with this system is that the engine oil will tend to stay cleaner for a longer period of time; therefore, if you notice that the oil in your engine becomes dirty very easily, check the functioning of the PCV valve. Engines which use a PCV system are calibrated to run richer, to compensate for the added air which accompanies the crankcase vapors to the combustion chambers. If the PCV valve or line is clogged, the engine idle will tend to be rough due to the excessively rich mixture. Maintenance is covered in Section 1.

TESTING

NOTE: Inspect the PCV system hose(s) and connections at each tune-up and replace any deteriorated hos-

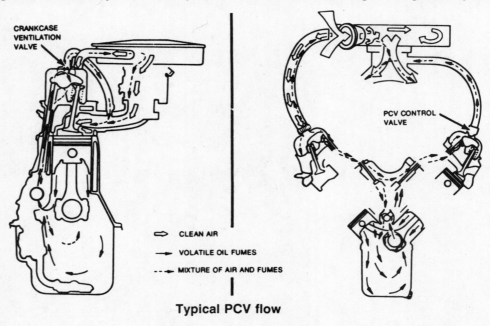

CRANKCASE VENTILATION VALVE

PCV CONTROL VALVE

⇨ CLEAN AIR
→ VOLATILE OIL FUMES
--→ MIXTURE OF AIR AND FUMES

Typical PCV flow

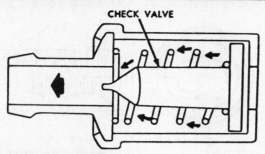

Cross section of a PCV valve

es. **Check the PCV valve at every tune-up and replace it at 30,000 mile intervals.**

1. Remove the PCV valve from the rocker arm cover.
2. Operate the engine at idle speed.
3. Place your thumb over the end of the valve to check for vacuum. If no vacuum exists, check the valve, the hoses or the manifold port for a plugged condition.
4. Remove the valve from the hose(s), then shake it and listen for a rattling of the check needle (inside the valve); the rattle means the valve is working. If no rattle is heard, replace the valve.

REMOVAL AND INSTALLATION

1. Pull the PCV valve from the rocker arm cover grommet.
2. Remove the hose(s) from the PCV valve.
3. Shake the valve to make sure that it is not plugged.
4. To install, reverse the removal procedures.

Evaporative Emission Controls (EEC)

OPERATION

The EEC system is designed to reduce the amount of escaping

1. TBI
2. Canister purge port
3. Vacuum signal
4. Purge valve
5. Vapor storage canister
6. Purge air
7. Fuel tank
8. Fuel
9. Vapor
10. Pressure-vacuum relief gas cap
11. Vent restricter
12. Fuel tank vent
13. Purge line

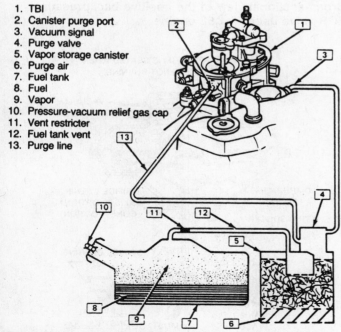

Evaporative Emission Control (EEC) system — 2.5L engine

gasoline vapors into the atmosphere. Fuel vapors are directed through lines to a canister containing an activated charcoal filter; unburned fuel vapor is trapped here until the engine is started. When the engine is started, the canister is purged by air drawn in by the manifold vacuum. The air/fuel vapor mixture is drawn into the engine and burned.

On the 4.3L carburetor models (Calif.), depending upon various conditions of operation, the ECM will either energize or de-energize the solenoid. When the solenoid is energized, vacuum is not available to draw fuel vapors from the canister; when de-energized, vacuum draws the canister vapors into the intake tract of the engine.

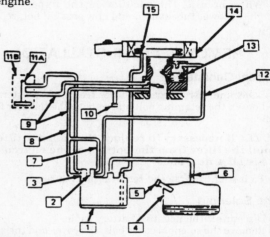

1. Canister
2. Vapor vent control valve
3. Canister purge control valve
4. Fuel tank
5. Fuel cap
6. Fuel tank vent line restriction
7. Vacuum signal for bowl vent valve
8. Vapor purge line (full manifold vacuum)
9. Ported manifold vacuum
10. PCV valve
11A. TVS-federal application
11B. Electric purge solenoid-California application
12. Carburetor bowl vent line
13. Carburetor
14. Air cleaner
15. Fuel vapor canister vent

Cross-sectional view of the evaporative emission control system — 4.3L engine carbureted engine (1985)

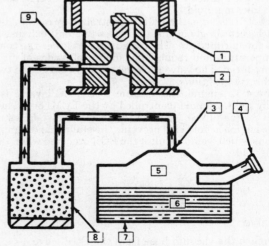

1. Air cleaner
2. T.B.I. unit
3. Restrictor
4. Press-vacuum relief gas cap
5. Vapor
6. Fuel
7. Fuel tank
8. Charcoal canister
9. Purge

Cross-sectional view of the evaporative emission control system — 4.3L TBI engine (1986–90)

TESTING

Charcoal Canister

2.5L AND 4.3L (1985)

1. Remove the lower tube of the canister (purge valve) and install a short length of tube, then try to blow through it (little or no air should pass).
2. Using a vacuum source, apply 15 in.Hg to the upper tube of the canister (purge valve). The diaphragm should hold the vacuum for at least 20 seconds, if not replace the canister.
3. While holding the vacuum on the upper tube, blow through the lower tube (air should now pass); if not, replace the canister.

REMOVAL AND INSTALLATION

Charcoal Canister

1. Label and disconnect the hoses from the canister.
2. Loosen the retaining bolt and remove the canister from the vehicle.

NOTE: If necessary to replace the canister filter, simply pull the filter from the bottom of the charcoal filter and install a new one.

3. To install, reverse the removal procedures.

Purge Solenoid

1. Disconnect the negative battery cable.
2. Remove the solenoid cover bolt, the cover and the solenoid.
3. Disconnect the electrical connector and the hoses from the solenoid.
4. To install, reverse the removal procedures.

Exhaust Gas Recirculation (EGR) System

OPERATION

All engines are equipped with an exhaust gas recirculation (EGR) system. This system consists of a metering valve, a vacuum line to the intake manifold and cast-in exhaust gas passages in the intake manifold.

On the 2.5L engine, the EGR is controlled by manifold vacuum which accordingly opens and closes to admit exhaust gases into the fuel/air mixture. The exhaust gases lower the combustion temperature and reduce the amount of oxides of nitrogen (NOx) produced. The valve is closed at idle between the two extreme throttle positions.

On the 4.3L engine, the vacuum to the EGR valve is controlled by EGR solenoid (controlled by the ECM) or a Thermal Vacuum Switch (TVS). Vacuum to the EGR valve is restricted until the engine is hot. This prevents the stalling and lumpy idle conditions which would result if the EGR occurred when the engine was cold.

TESTING

EGR Valve

1. Remove the vacuum hose from the EGR valve.
2. Using a vacuum source, connect it to the EGR valve hose fitting and apply 10 in.Hg; the valve should lift off of its seat, if not, replace the EGR valve.
3. Clean the carbon deposits from the valve and intake manifold. With the valve removed, run the engine for 3–5 seconds to blow the carbon out of the intake manifold.

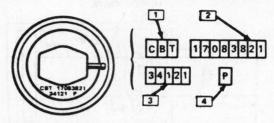

1. Assembly plant code
2. Part number
3. Date built
4. Look here for letter
   P = postive back pressure
   N = negative back pressure
   Blank = ported valve

Explanation of the EGR valve serial numbers

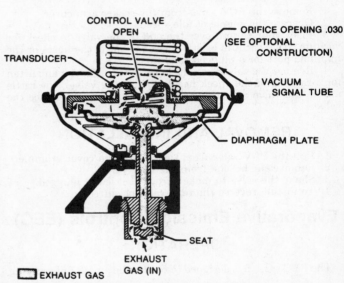

Cross-sectional view of the positive backpressure EGR valve used — 2.5L engine

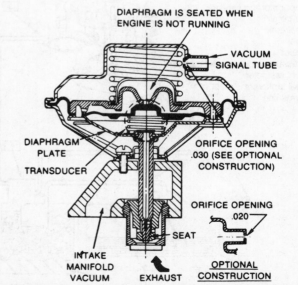

Cross-sectional view of the negative backpressure EGR valve used — 4.3L engine

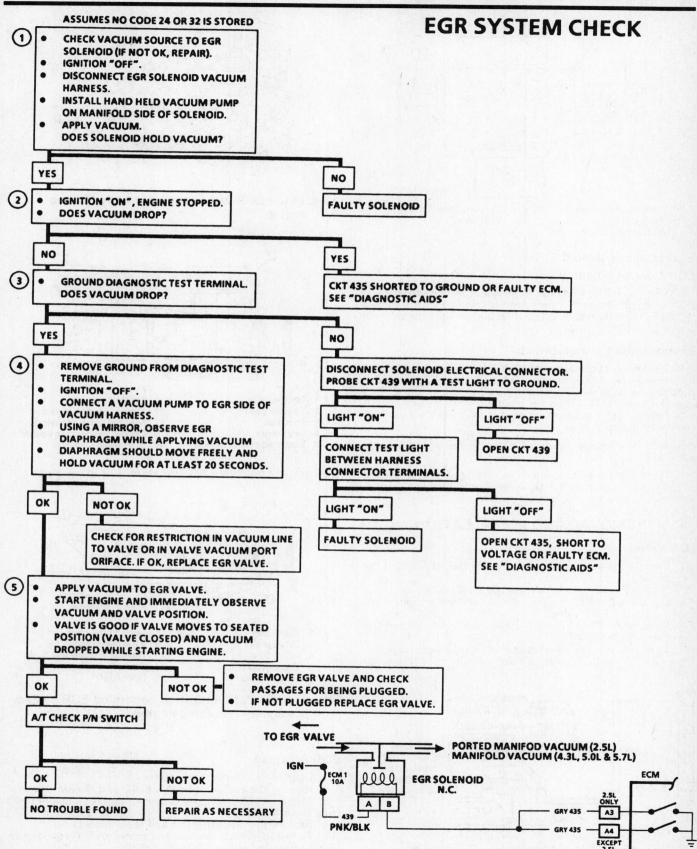

ASSUMES NO CODE 24 OR 32 IS STORED

①
- CHECK VACUUM SOURCE TO EGR SOLENOID (IF NOT OK, REPAIR).
- IGNITION "OFF".
- DISCONNECT EGR SOLENOID VACUUM HARNESS.
- INSTALL HAND HELD VACUUM PUMP ON MANIFOLD SIDE OF SOLENOID.
- APPLY VACUUM.
  DOES SOLENOID HOLD VACUUM?

YES

NO

FAULTY SOLENOID

②
- IGNITION "ON", ENGINE STOPPED.
- DOES VACUUM DROP?

NO

YES

③
- GROUND DIAGNOSTIC TEST TERMINAL. DOES VACUUM DROP?

CKT 435 SHORTED TO GROUND OR FAULTY ECM. SEE "DIAGNOSTIC AIDS"

YES

NO

④
- REMOVE GROUND FROM DIAGNOSTIC TEST TERMINAL.
- IGNITION "OFF".
- CONNECT A VACUUM PUMP TO EGR SIDE OF VACUUM HARNESS.
- USING A MIRROR, OBSERVE EGR DIAPHRAGM WHILE APPLYING VACUUM
- DIAPHRAGM SHOULD MOVE FREELY AND HOLD VACUUM FOR AT LEAST 20 SECONDS.

DISCONNECT SOLENOID ELECTRICAL CONNECTOR. PROBE CKT 439 WITH A TEST LIGHT TO GROUND.

LIGHT "ON"

LIGHT "OFF"

CONNECT TEST LIGHT BETWEEN HARNESS CONNECTOR TERMINALS.

OPEN CKT 439

OK

NOT OK

LIGHT "ON"

LIGHT "OFF"

CHECK FOR RESTRICTION IN VACUUM LINE TO VALVE OR IN VALVE VACUUM PORT ORIFACE. IF OK, REPLACE EGR VALVE.

FAULTY SOLENOID

OPEN CKT 435, SHORT TO VOLTAGE OR FAULTY ECM. SEE "DIAGNOSTIC AIDS"

⑤
- APPLY VACUUM TO EGR VALVE.
- START ENGINE AND IMMEDIATELY OBSERVE VACUUM AND VALVE POSITION.
- VALVE IS GOOD IF VALVE MOVES TO SEATED POSITION (VALVE CLOSED) AND VACUUM DROPPED WHILE STARTING ENGINE.

OK

NOT OK
- REMOVE EGR VALVE AND CHECK PASSAGES FOR BEING PLUGGED.
- IF NOT PLUGGED REPLACE EGR VALVE.

A/T CHECK P/N SWITCH

TO EGR VALVE

PORTED MANIFOD VACUUM (2.5L)
MANIFOLD VACUUM (4.3L, 5.0L & 5.7L)

IGN

ECM 1
10A

EGR SOLENOID
N.C.

OK

NOT OK

NO TROUBLE FOUND

REPAIR AS NECESSARY

A   B

439
PNK/BLK

ECM

2.5L
ONLY
A3

GRY 435

GRY 435

A4
EXCEPT
2.5L

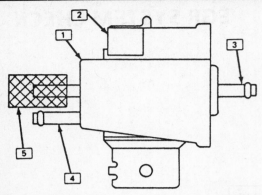

1. EGR control solenoid
2. Electrical connector
3. Vacuum connector from source
4. Vacuum connector to EGR valve
5. Vent

EGR control solenoid

EGR Control Solenoid

1. Disconnect the electrical connector from the solenoid.
2. Using an ohmmeter, measure the solenoid's resistance, it should be more than 20Ω. If less than 20Ω, replace the solenoid and/or possibly the ECM.

Thermostatic Vacuum Switch

If the thermostatic vacuum switch is not working, a Code 32 will store in the ECM memory and a "Service Engine Soon" lamp will light on the instrument panel.
1. Remove the TVS from the engine.
2. Using a vacuum gauge, connect it to one of the hose connections and apply 10 in.Hg.

NOTE: A vacuum drop of 2 in.Hg in 2 minutes is allowable.

3. Place the tip of the switch in boiling water. When the switch reaches 195°F (91°C), the valve should open and the vacuum will drop; if not, replace the switch.

REMOVAL AND INSTALLATION

EGR Valve

1. Remove the engine cover (from inside the vehicle) and the air cleaner.
2. Detach the vacuum hose from the EGR valve.
3. On the 4.3L EFI engine, disconnect the temperature switch from the EGR valve.
4. Remove the EGR valve-to-intake manifold bolts and the valve from the manifold.
5. To install, use a new gasket and reverse the removal procedures. Torque the EGR valve-to-manifold bolts to 14 ft. lbs. (20 Nm).

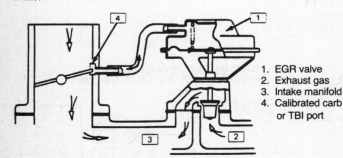

1. EGR valve
2. Exhaust gas
3. Intake manifold
4. Calibrated carb or TBI port

View of the EGR valve operation — 2.5L engine

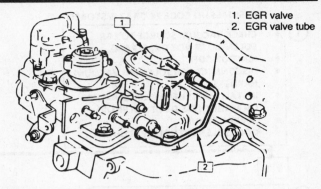

1. EGR valve
2. EGR valve tube

View of the EGR valve-to-throttle body hookup — 2.5L engine

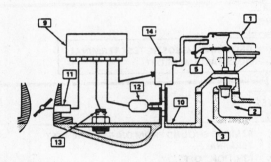

1. EGR valve
2. Exhaust gas
3. Intake air
5. Diaphragm
9. Electronic control module
10. Manifold vacuum
11. Throttle position sensor
12. Manifold pressure sensor
13. Coolant temperature sensor
14. EGR control solenoid

Electronic controlled EGR system — 4.3L engine

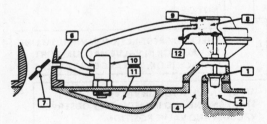

1. EGR valve
2. Exhaust gas
4. Intake flow
6. Vacuum port
7. Throttle valve
8. Vacuum chamber
9. Valve return spring
10. Thermal vacuum switch
11. Coolant
12. Diaphragm

Thermostatic Vacuum Switch controlled EGR system — 4.3L engine carbureted engine

EGR Solenoid

1. Disconnect the negative battery cable.
2. Remove the engine cover (1986–87) and the air cleaner.
3. Disconnect the electrical connector and the vacuum hoses from the solenoid.
4. Remove the mounting nut and the solenoid.
5. To install, reverse the removal procedures. Torque the solenoid mounting nut to 17 ft. lbs. (25 Nm).

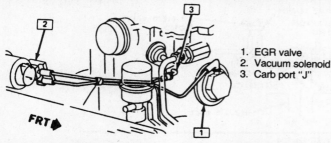

1. EGR valve
2. Vacuum solenoid
3. Carb port "J"

View of the EGR solenoid — 4.3L engine carbureted

Thermostatic Vacuum Switch (TVS)
4.3L Carbureted Engine

The thermostatic vacuum switch, is installed on the front left side of the intake manifold.

1. Drain the radiator to a level below the Thermostatic Vacuum Switch (TVS).

―――――― CAUTION ――――――

When draining the coolant, keep in mind that cats and dogs are attracted by the ethylene glycol antifreeze, and are quite likely to drink any that is left in an uncovered container or in puddles on the ground. This will prove fatal in sufficient quantity. Always drain the coolant into a sealable container. Coolant should be reused unless it is contaminated or several years old.

2. Disconnect the vacuum hoses from the switch.
3. Remove the switch from the engine.
4. To install, apply soft sealant to the threaded portion of the new switch and reverse the removal procedure. Torque the TVS to 120 inch lbs. (14 Nm). Refill the cooling system, start the engine and check for leaks.

RESETTING

To clear the codes stored in the ECM, turn the ignition Off and disconnect the negative battery terminal or the ECM **B** fuse for ten seconds.

Thermostatic Air Cleaner (THERMAC)

OPERATION

This system is designed to improve driveability and exhaust

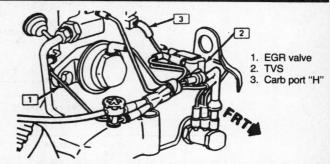

1. EGR valve
2. TVS
3. Carb port "H"

View of the EGR Thermostatic Vacuum Switch — 4.3L engine

emissions when the engine is cold. Components added to the basic air cleaner assembly include a temperature sensor (connected to a manifold vacuum source), a vacuum diaphragm motor (connected to the temperature sensor) and an inlet damper door (installed in the air cleaner inlet snorkel). Additional components of the system include an exhaust manifold mounted heat stove and a hot air duct running from the heat source to the underside of the air cleaner snorkel.

When the engine is cold, the temperature sensor allows vacuum to pass through to the vacuum diaphragm motor. The vacuum acting on the vacuum motor causes the motor to close the damper door, which prohibits the introduction of cold, outside air to the air cleaner. The intake vacuum then pulls hot air, generated by the exhaust manifold, through the hot air duct and into the air cleaner. This heated air supply helps to more effectively vaporize the fuel mixture entering the engine. As the engine warms, the temperature sensor bleeds off vacuum to the vacuum motor, allowing the damper door to gradually open.

The usual problems with this system are leaking vacuum lines (which prevent proper operation of the sensor and/or motor); torn or rusted through hot air ducts and/or rusted through heat stoves (either condition will allow the introduction of too much cold air to the air cleaner). Visually check and replace these items as necessary. Should the system still fail to operate properly, disconnect the vacuum line from the vacuum motor and apply at least 7 in.Hg of vacuum directly to the motor from an outside vacuum source; the damper door should close. If the door does not close, either the vacuum motor is defective or the damper door and/or linkage is binding. If the door closes, but then gradually opens (with a steady vacuum source), the vacuum motor is defective.

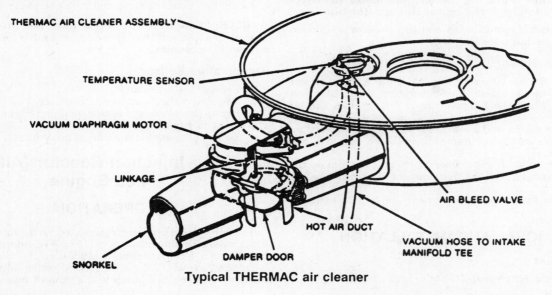

THERMAC AIR CLEANER ASSEMBLY

TEMPERATURE SENSOR

VACUUM DIAPHRAGM MOTOR

LINKAGE

SNORKEL

DAMPER DOOR

HOT AIR DUCT

AIR BLEED VALVE

VACUUM HOSE TO INTAKE MANIFOLD TEE

Typical THERMAC air cleaner

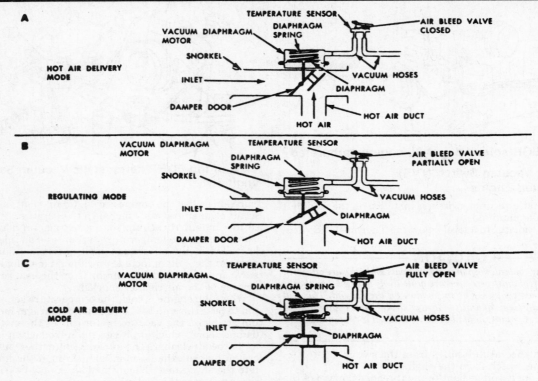

Schematic of the vacuum motor operation

TESTING

Vacuum Motor

1. With the engine Off, disconnect the hose from the vacuum diaphragm motor.
2. Using a vacuum source, apply 7 in.Hg to the vacuum motor; the door should close and block off the outside air, completely.
3. Bend the vacuum hose (to trap the vacuum in the motor) and make sure that the door stays closed; if not, replace the vacuum motor.

NOTE: Before replacing the vacuum motor (if defective), be sure to check the motor linkage, for binding.

4. If the vacuum motor is OK and the problem still exists, check the temperature sensor.

Temperature Sensor

1. Remove the air cleaner cover and place a thermometer near the temperature sensor; the temperature MUST BE below 86°F (30°C). When the temperature is OK, replace the air cleaner.
2. Start the engine and allow it to idle. Watch the vacuum motor door, it should close immediately (if the engine is cool enough).
3. When the vacuum motor door starts to open, remove the air cleaner cover and read the thermometer, it should be about 131°F (55°C).
4. If the door does not respond correctly, replace the temperature sensor.

REMOVAL AND INSTALLATION

Vacuum Motor

1. Remove the air cleaner.

2. Disconnect the vacuum hose from the motor.
3. Using a ⅛ in. drill bit, drill out the spot welds, then enlarge as necessary to remove the retaining strap.
4. Remove the retaining strap.
5. Lift up the motor and cock it to one side to unhook the motor linkage at the control damper assembly.
6. Install the new vacuum motor as follows:
   a. Using a $^7/_{64}$ in. drill bit, drill a hole in the snorkel tube at the center of the vacuum motor retaining strap.
   b. Insert the vacuum motor linkage into the control damper assembly.
   c. Use the motor retaining strap and a sheet metal screw to secure the retaining strap and motor to the snorkel tube.

NOTE: Make sure the screw does not interfere with the operation of the damper assembly; shorten the screw, if necessary.

Temperature Sensor

1. Remove the air cleaner.
2. Disconnect the hoses from the sensor.
3. Pry up the tabs on the sensor retaining clip and remove the clip and sensor from the air cleaner.
4. To install, reverse the removal procedures.

Air Injection Reactor (AIR)
4.3L Engine

OPERATION

The AIR system uses an air pump, a diverter valve (1985 Federal), an electric air control valve (1985–87 California), air check valves and a deceleration valve (1985).

On the Federal (1985) models, the diverter valve, directs the air flow from the AIR pump to the exhaust manifolds (during

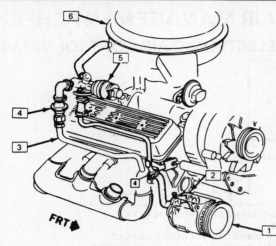

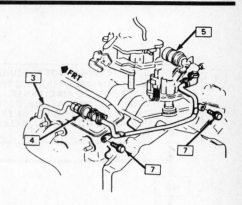

1. Air pump
2. Adapter and seal—tighten screws to 25 N·m (18 ft. lbs)
3. Air injection pipe—tighten nuts to 28 N·m (20 ft. lbs.)
4. Check valve—tighten to 85 N·m (26 ft. lbs.)
5. Diverter valve or EAC valve
6. Air cleaner
7. Bolt—tighten to 34 N·m (25 ft. lbs.)

View of the AIR Injection Reaction system — 4.3L engine

normal operation) and away from the exhaust manifolds (during engine deceleration).

On the California (1985–87) models, the Electronic Control Module (ECM) operates the electric air control valve which directs the air flow to the engine exhaust manifold ports or the the air cleaner. When the engine is cold or in wide-open throttle, the ECM energizes the solenoid to direct the air flow into the exhaust manifold check valves. When the engine warms, operating at high speeds or deceleration, the ECM de-energizes the electric air control valve, changing the air flow from the exhaust manifold to the air cleaner. The diversion of the air flow to the air cleaner acts as a silencer.

A check valve, on each side of the engine, prevents back flow of the exhaust gases into the air pump, if there is an exhaust backfire or pump drive belt failure.

The deceleration valve helps to prevent backfiring during periods of high vacuum (deceleration) by allowing large quantities of air to flow into the intake manifold.

TESTING

Air Injection Pump

1. Check for proper drive belt tension.
2. Make sure that the pump is not seized.
3. Remove the air hoses, accelerate the engine to 1,500 rpm and check for air flow from the hose outlets.

Check Valves

1. Disconnect the hose from the valve and unscrew the valve from the injection manifold assembly.
2. Blow into each side of the valve: air should pass only in one direction; if air passes through the valve in both directions, replace the valve. Check each valve in the same manner.

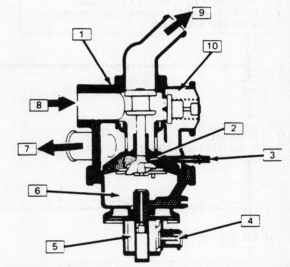

1. Electric air control (EAC) valve
2. Decel timing assembly
3. Manifold vacuum signal tube
4. Electrical terminal
5. EAC solenoid
6. Decel timing chamber
7. Air to air cleaner
8. Air from air pump
9. Air to exhaust ports or manifold
10. Pressure relief assembly

Cross-sectional view of the electric air control valve — 4.3L engine (1986–90)

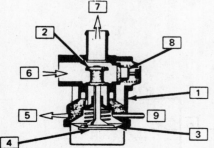

1. Standard diverter valve
2. Metering valve
3. Diaphragm
4. Timing valve
5. Vent
6. Pump air inlet
7. Exhaust port outlet
8. Relief valve
9. Vacuum signal tube

Cross-sectional view of the diverter valve — 4.3L engine (1985)

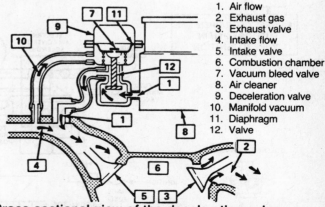

1. Air flow
2. Exhaust gas
3. Exhaust valve
4. Intake flow
5. Intake valve
6. Combustion chamber
7. Vacuum bleed valve
8. Air cleaner
9. Deceleration valve
10. Manifold vacuum
11. Diaphragm
12. Valve

Cross-sectional view of the deceleration valve — 4.3L engine (1985)

AIR MANAGEMENT CHECK
(ELECTRONIC AIR CONTROL VALVE)

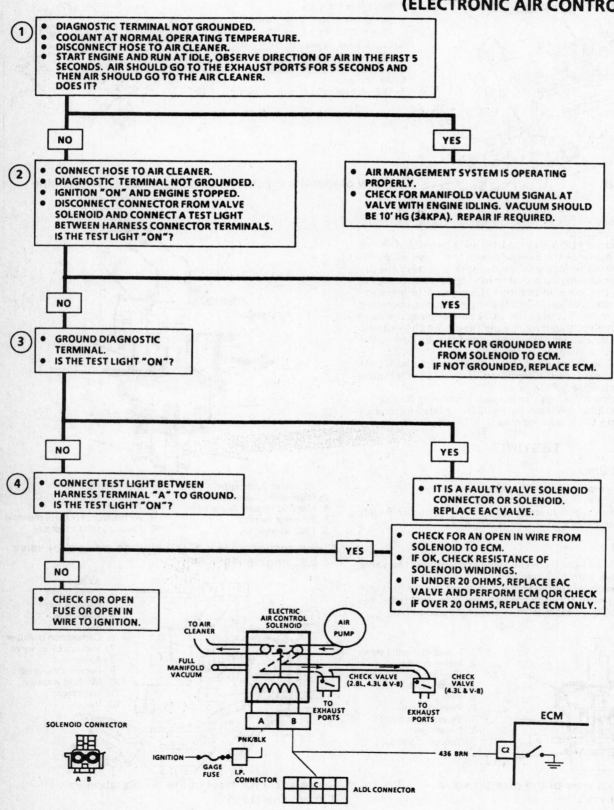

1
- DIAGNOSTIC TERMINAL NOT GROUNDED.
- COOLANT AT NORMAL OPERATING TEMPERATURE.
- DISCONNECT HOSE TO AIR CLEANER.
- START ENGINE AND RUN AT IDLE, OBSERVE DIRECTION OF AIR IN THE FIRST 5 SECONDS. AIR SHOULD GO TO THE EXHAUST PORTS FOR 5 SECONDS AND THEN AIR SHOULD GO TO THE AIR CLEANER.
  DOES IT?

NO

YES

2
- CONNECT HOSE TO AIR CLEANER.
- DIAGNOSTIC TERMINAL NOT GROUNDED.
- IGNITION "ON" AND ENGINE STOPPED.
- DISCONNECT CONNECTOR FROM VALVE SOLENOID AND CONNECT A TEST LIGHT BETWEEN HARNESS CONNECTOR TERMINALS. IS THE TEST LIGHT "ON"?

- AIR MANAGEMENT SYSTEM IS OPERATING PROPERLY.
- CHECK FOR MANIFOLD VACUUM SIGNAL AT VALVE WITH ENGINE IDLING. VACUUM SHOULD BE 10' HG (34KPA). REPAIR IF REQUIRED.

NO

YES

3
- GROUND DIAGNOSTIC TERMINAL.
- IS THE TEST LIGHT "ON"?

- CHECK FOR GROUNDED WIRE FROM SOLENOID TO ECM.
- IF NOT GROUNDED, REPLACE ECM.

NO

YES

4
- CONNECT TEST LIGHT BETWEEN HARNESS TERMINAL "A" TO GROUND.
- IS THE TEST LIGHT "ON"?

- IT IS A FAULTY VALVE SOLENOID CONNECTOR OR SOLENOID. REPLACE EAC VALVE.

YES

- CHECK FOR AN OPEN IN WIRE FROM SOLENOID TO ECM.
- IF OK, CHECK RESISTANCE OF SOLENOID WINDINGS.
- IF UNDER 20 OHMS, REPLACE EAC VALVE AND PERFORM ECM QDR CHECK
- IF OVER 20 OHMS, REPLACE ECM ONLY.

NO

- CHECK FOR OPEN FUSE OR OPEN IN WIRE TO IGNITION.

Diverter Valve

The diverter valve will act like the electric air control valve, except, that it is not controlled by an ECM. Air is directed to the exhaust ports, unless there is a sudden rise of manifold vacuum due to throttle deceleration.

Electric Air Control Valve

1. Perform the following inspection checks:
   a. The engine coolant must be at operating temperatures.
   b. Disconnect the air cleaner-to-electric air control valve hose.
   c. Start the engine and operate it at idle (under 2000 rpm). Within the first 5 seconds, the air should be directed to the exhaust ports and then change to the air cleaner.
   d. If the system checks OK, the electric air control valve is working.
2. If inspections in Step 1 were not satisfactory, perform the following procedures:
   a. Turn the engine Off but allow the ignition switch to remain On.
   b. Reconnect the air cleaner-to-electric air control valve hose.
   c. Disconnect the electrical connector from the electric air control valve solenoid and connect a test light between the harness connector terminals.
   d. If the test light is On, check for a ground between the solenoid-to-ECM wire (Circuit 436) or replace the ECM (if not grounded).
3. If the test light is Off, perform the following procedures:
   a. Using a jumper wire, connect it between the ECM diagnostic (C2) terminal and ground.
   b. If the test light turns On, replace the electric air control valve.
   c. Remove the jumper wire.
4. If the test light still remains Off, perform the following procedures:
   a. Connect one probe of the test light to terminal **A** of the solenoid's connector and the other probe to a ground.
   b. If the light still remains Off, check for a blown fuse or an broken ignition (pink) wire.
5. If the light turns On, check for the following problems:
   a. A broken solenoid-to-ECM (Circuit 436) wire or check the solenoid's resistance of the air control valve.
   b. If the resistance of the solenoid is above 20Ω, replace the ECM.
   c. If the resistance of the solenoid is below 20Ω, replace the electric air control valve and the ECM.

Deceleration Valve

1. Install a tachometer to the engine and allow the engine to establish normal operating temperatures.
2. Remove the air cleaner and plug the air cleaner vacuum hose(s).
3. Operate the engine at idle speed, then remove the deceleration valve-to-intake manifold (diaphragm) hose.
4. Reconnect the hose and listen for a noticeable air flow (hiss) through the air cleaner-to-deceleration valve hose; there should also be a noticeable drop in idle speed.
5. If the air flow does not continue for at least one second or the engine speed does not drop, check the hoses (of the deceleration valve) for restrictions or leaks.
6. If no restrictions are found, replace the deceleration valve.

REMOVAL AND INSTALLATION

Air Injection Pump

1. Compress the drive belt to keep the pump pulley from turning, then loosen the pump pulley bolts.
2. Loosen the pump-to-mounting brackets, release the ten-

sion on the drive belt and remove the drive belt.
3. Unscrew the mounting bolts and then remove the pump pulley.
4. If necessary, use a pair of needle nose pliers to pull the fan filter from the hub.
5. Remove the hoses, the vacuum lines, the electrical connectors (if equipped) and the air control or diverter valve.
6. Unscrew the pump mounting bolts and then remove the pump.
To install:
1. Install the pump and torque the pump pulley bolts to 90 inch lbs. (10 Nm) and the pump-to-bracket nuts/bolts to 25 ft. lbs. (34 Nm). Adjust the drive belt tension after installation.
2. Connect all hoses and electrical connectors.

Check Valve(s)

1. Remove the clamp and disconnect the hose from the valve.
2. Unscrew the valve from the air injection pipe.
3. To test the valve(s), air should pass only in one direction.
4. To install, reverse the removal procedures.

Air Control Valve

1. Disconnect the negative battery cable.
2. Disconnect the air inlet and outlet hoses from the valve.
3. Disconnect the electrical connector (if equipped) and the vacuum hoses at the valve. Remove the electric air control or the diverter valve.
4. To install, reverse the removal procedures. For California models, check the system operation.

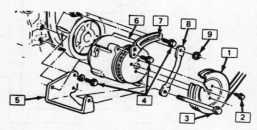

1. Pulley
2. Bolt—tighten to 10 N·m (90 in. lbs.)
3. Bolt—tighten to 45 N·m (32 ft. lbs.)
4. Bolt—tighten to 84 N·m (25 ft. lbs.)
5. Support
6. Air pump
7. Bracket
8. Brace
9. Nut—tighten to 34 N·m (25 ft. lbs.)

Exploded view of the air pump assembly — 4.3L engine

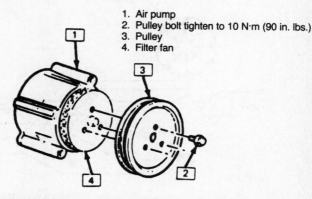

1. Air pump
2. Pulley bolt tighten to 10 N·m (90 in. lbs.)
3. Pulley
4. Filter fan

Removing the air filter from the air pump — 4.3L engine

1. Bracket
2. Deceleration valve
3. Bolt—tighten to 3.5 N·m (30 in. lbs.)

Removing the deceleration valve — 4.3L engine

Air Switching Valve

The switching valve is replaced in basically the same manner as the control valve.

Deceleration Valve

1. Remove the vacuum hoses from the valve.
2. Remove the deceleration valve-to-engine bracket screws.
3. Remove the deceleration valve.
4. To install, reverse the removal procedures. Torque the deceleration valve-to-engine bracket screws to 30 inch lbs. (4 Nm).

Electronic Spark Timing (EST) System

The EST system does not have vacuum or mechanical spark advance mechanisms, as these functions are controlled electronically by the distributor module assembly and the ECM of the computer emissions system.

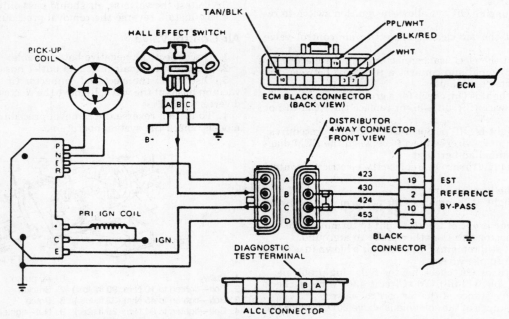

Schematic of the electronic spark timing system — 2.5L engine (1985)

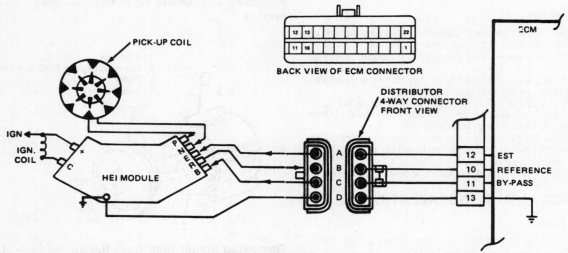

Schematic of the electronic spark timing system — 4.3L engine (1985)

The purpose of the EST system is to precisely adjust the spark timing according to specific engine operating conditions, as sensed by the various monitoring devices of the computer emissions system.

Because the EST system is directly tied into the computer emissions system, service, testing and repair should be performed by a qualified, professional technician.

For further EST system information, refer to the Electronic Spark Control (ESC) System in this section.

Electronic Spark Control (ESC) System

OPERATION

Since varying octane levels of gasoline can cause detonation (spark knock) in an engine, causing piston and ring rattle or vibration, the ESC system has been added to the engine to remedy the knocking situation by retarding the spark timing by as much as 20°; this allows the engine to maximize the spark advance to improve the fuel economy and driveability.

A sensor is mounted on the left side of the block (near the cylinders) to detect the knock and send the information to the Electronic Spark Control (ESC) module. The ESC module sends a signal to the Electronic Control Module (ECM) which adjusts the Electronic Spark Timing (EST) to reduce the spark knock. If no signal is received from the ESC sensor, the ECM provides normal spark advance.

Loss of the signal, through a bad ESC sensor, ESC module or a poor ground, will cause the engine to operate sluggishly and cause a Code 43 (to be set).

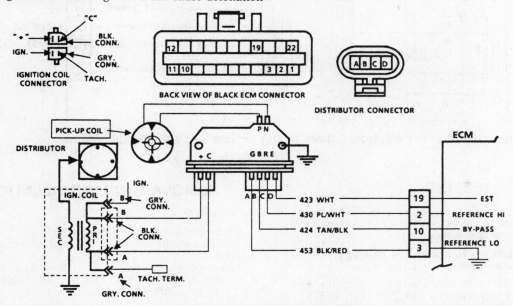

Schematic of the electronic spark timing system — 2.5L engine (1986–90)

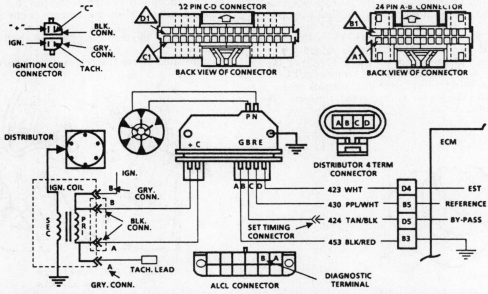

Schematic of the electronic spark timing system — 4.3L engine (1986–87)

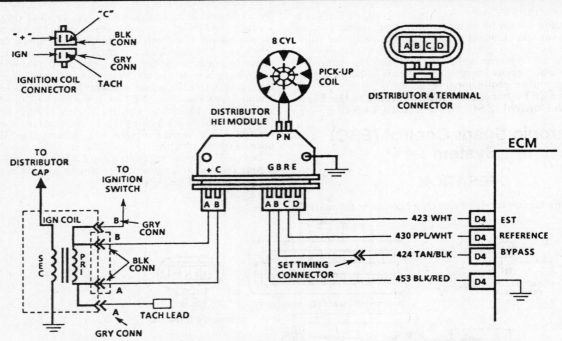

Schematic of the electronic spark timing system — 1988–90 4.3L engine

TESTING

1. With the engine operating at 1,500 rpm, the transmission in Neutral or Park, tap on the engine block in the area of the knock sensor, the engine rpm should drop.

NOTE: If the speed does not drop, the timing is not retarding or it is retarded all of the time.

2. Disconnect the ESC module connector (the engine rpm should drop); after 4 seconds, the "CHECK ENGINE" or "SERVICE ENGINE SOON" light should turn ON and the Code 43 will be stored.

3. Using a digital voltmeter (set on the low AC scale), check the knock sensor voltage; low or no voltage will indicate an open circuit at terminal **E** or a bad sensor.

4. Check the CHECK ENGINE light and the Code 43 in the ESC system. If no light turns ON, the ECM is not retarding the engine spark for there may be voltage on the **L** (1985) or **B7** (1986–90) terminal or the ECM may be faulty, replace the ECM.

5. Disconnect the electrical connector from the knock sensor; if the rpm increases with the sensor disconnected, the sensor is bad and should be replaced.

REMOVAL AND INSTALLATION

Knock Sensor

1. Disconnect the negative battery cable.
2. Disconnect the electrical harness connector from the knock sensor.
3. Remove the knock sensor from the engine block.
4. To install, apply Teflon® tape to the threads and reverse the removal procedures.

ESC Module

The ESC module is located at the top rear of the engine.
1. Disconnect the electrical harness connector from the ESC module.
2. Remove the mounting screws and the ESC module from the vehicle.
3. To install, reverse the removal procedures.

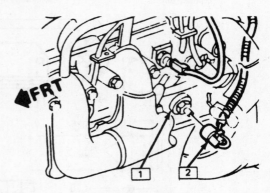

1. ESC knock sensor
2. Harness connector

Location of the knock sensor — 4.3L engine

View of the knock sensor — 4.3L engine

IGNITION SYSTEM CHECK
(REMOTE COIL / SEALED MODULE CONNECTOR DISTRIBUTOR)
ALL ENGINES

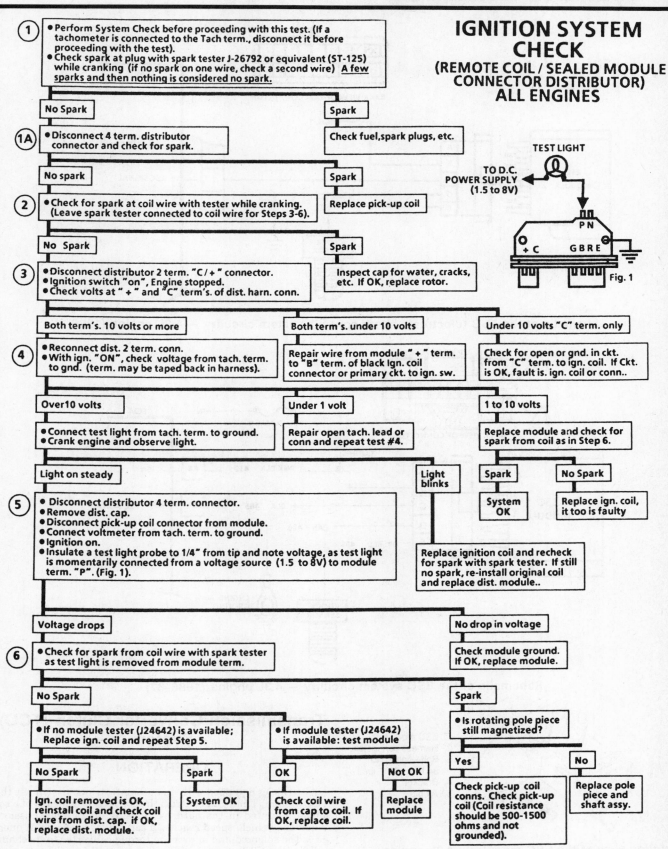

1
- Perform System Check before proceeding with this test. (If a tachometer is connected to the Tach term., disconnect it before proceeding with the test).
- Check spark at plug with spark tester J-26792 or equivalent (ST-125) while cranking (if no spark on one wire, check a second wire) A few sparks and then nothing is considered no spark.

No Spark	Spark

1A
- Disconnect 4 term. distributor connector and check for spark.

Spark → Check fuel, spark plugs, etc.

No spark	Spark

2
- Check for spark at coil wire with tester while cranking. (Leave spark tester connected to coil wire for Steps 3-6).

Spark → Replace pick-up coil

No Spark	Spark

3
- Disconnect distributor 2 term. "C/+" connector.
- Ignition switch "on", Engine stopped.
- Check volts at "+" and "C" term's. of dist. harn. conn.

Spark → Inspect cap for water, cracks, etc. If OK, replace rotor.

TEST LIGHT

TO D.C. POWER SUPPLY (1.5 to 8V)

P N
O +C G B R E
Fig. 1

Both term's. 10 volts or more	Both term's. under 10 volts	Under 10 volts "C" term. only

4
- Reconnect dist. 2 term. conn.
- With ign. "ON", check voltage from tach. term. to gnd. (term. may be taped back in harness).

Repair wire from module "+" term. to "B" term. of black Ign. coil connector or primary ckt. to ign. sw.

Check for open or gnd. in ckt. from "C" term. to ign. coil. If Ckt. is OK, fault is. ign. coil or conn..

Over 10 volts	Under 1 volt	1 to 10 volts

- Connect test light from tach. term. to ground.
- Crank engine and observe light.

Repair open tach. lead or conn and repeat test #4.

Replace module and check for spark from coil as in Step 6.

Light on steady		Light blinks	Spark	No Spark

System OK | Replace ign. coil, it too is faulty

5
- Disconnect distributor 4 term. connector.
- Remove dist. cap.
- Disconnect pick-up coil connector from module.
- Connect voltmeter from tach. term. to ground.
- Ignition on.
- Insulate a test light probe to 1/4" from tip and note voltage, as test light is momentarily connected from a voltage source (1.5 to 8V) to module term. "P". (Fig. 1).

Replace ignition coil and recheck for spark with spark tester. If still no spark, re-install original coil and replace dist. module..

Voltage drops	No drop in voltage

Check module ground. If OK, replace module.

6
- Check for spark from coil wire with spark tester as test light is removed from module term.

No Spark	Spark

- If no module tester (J24642) is available; Replace ign. coil and repeat Step 5.

- If module tester (J24642) is available: test module

- Is rotating pole piece still magnetized?

No Spark	Spark	OK	Not OK	Yes	No

Ign. coil removed is OK, reinstall coil and check coil wire from dist. cap. if OK, replace dist. module.

System OK

Check coil wire from cap to coil. If OK, replace coil.

Replace module

Check pick-up coil conns. Check pick-up coil (Coil resistance should be 500-1500 ohms and not grounded).

Replace pole piece and shaft assy.

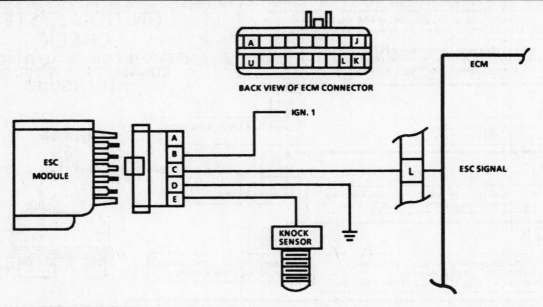

Schematic of the ESC (electronic spark control) system circuitry — 4.3L engine (1985)

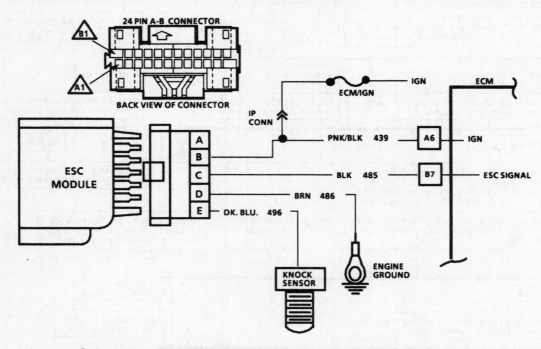

Schematic of the ESC system circuitry — 4.3L engine (1986–87)

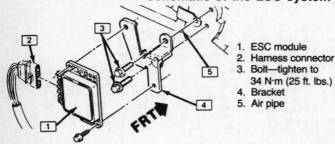

Exploded view of the ESC module — 4.3L engine

1. ESC module
2. Harness connector
3. Bolt—tighten to 34 N·m (25 ft. lbs.)
4. Bracket
5. Air pipe

Transmission Converter Clutch (TCC) System

OPERATION

All vehicles equipped with an automatic transmission use the TCC system. The ECM controls the converter by means of a solenoid mounted in the outdrive housing of the transmission. When the vehicle speed reaches a certain level, the ECM energizes the solenoid and allows the torque converter to mechanically couple the transmission to the engine. When the operating

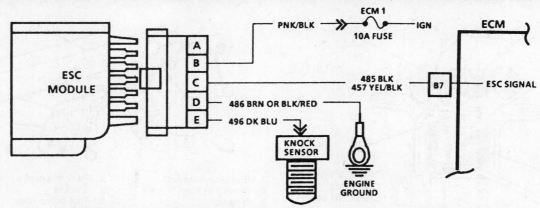

Schematic of the electronic spark control system — 1988–90 4.3L engine

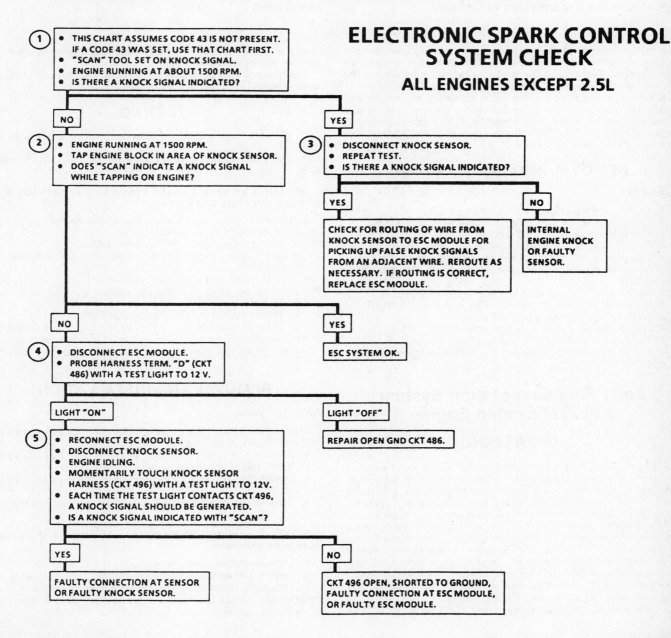

ELECTRONIC SPARK CONTROL SYSTEM CHECK

ALL ENGINES EXCEPT 2.5L

1.
- THIS CHART ASSUMES CODE 43 IS NOT PRESENT. IF A CODE 43 WAS SET, USE THAT CHART FIRST.
- "SCAN" TOOL SET ON KNOCK SIGNAL.
- ENGINE RUNNING AT ABOUT 1500 RPM.
- IS THERE A KNOCK SIGNAL INDICATED?

NO

2.
- ENGINE RUNNING AT 1500 RPM.
- TAP ENGINE BLOCK IN AREA OF KNOCK SENSOR.
- DOES "SCAN" INDICATE A KNOCK SIGNAL WHILE TAPPING ON ENGINE?

YES

3.
- DISCONNECT KNOCK SENSOR.
- REPEAT TEST.
- IS THERE A KNOCK SIGNAL INDICATED?

YES

CHECK FOR ROUTING OF WIRE FROM KNOCK SENSOR TO ESC MODULE FOR PICKING UP FALSE KNOCK SIGNALS FROM AN ADJACENT WIRE. REROUTE AS NECESSARY. IF ROUTING IS CORRECT, REPLACE ESC MODULE.

NO

INTERNAL ENGINE KNOCK OR FAULTY SENSOR.

NO

4.
- DISCONNECT ESC MODULE.
- PROBE HARNESS TERM. "D" (CKT 486) WITH A TEST LIGHT TO 12 V.

YES

ESC SYSTEM OK.

LIGHT "ON"

5.
- RECONNECT ESC MODULE.
- DISCONNECT KNOCK SENSOR.
- ENGINE IDLING.
- MOMENTARILY TOUCH KNOCK SENSOR HARNESS (CKT 496) WITH A TEST LIGHT TO 12V.
- EACH TIME THE TEST LIGHT CONTACTS CKT 496, A KNOCK SIGNAL SHOULD BE GENERATED.
- IS A KNOCK SIGNAL INDICATED WITH "SCAN"?

LIGHT "OFF"

REPAIR OPEN GND CKT 486.

YES

FAULTY CONNECTION AT SENSOR OR FAULTY KNOCK SENSOR.

NO

CKT 496 OPEN, SHORTED TO GROUND, FAULTY CONNECTION AT ESC MODULE, OR FAULTY ESC MODULE.

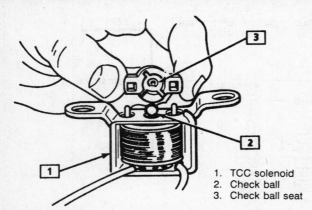

1. TCC solenoid
2. Check ball
3. Check ball seat

Torque converter clutch solenoid — automatic trans. Located in the transmission valve body

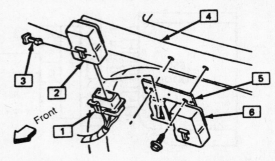

1. Electrical connector
2. Downshift control relay
3. Retainer
4. Plenum panel (firewall)
5. Bracket
6. Fuel pump relay

Downshift control relay — located next to the fuel pump relay

conditions indicate that the transmission should operate as a normal fluid coupled transmission, the ECM will de-energize the solenoid. Depressing the brake pedal will also return the transmission to normal automatic operation.

If the converter clutch is applied at all times, the engine will stall immediately. If the converter clutch does not apply, fuel economy may be lower than expected. If the 4th gear switch does not operate, the TCC will not apply at the right time, engagement may be in any gear.

REMOVAL AND INSTALLATION

Automatic

1. Disconnect the negative (−) battery cable.
2. Raise the vehicle and safely support with jackstands.
3. Drain the transmission fluid.
4. Remove the transmission oil pan and gasket.
5. Disconnect the electrical connector and remove two solenoid retaining screws. Remove the solenoid with the check ball.
To install:
1. Install the solenoid with the check ball in place.
2. Torque the retaining screws to 84 inch lbs. (10 Nm).
3. Connect the electrical connector.
4. Install the oil pan with a new gasket.
5. Torque the pan bolts to 144 inch lbs. (15 Nm).
6. Lower the vehicle, connect the battery cable and check operation.

Early Fuel Evaporation System 4.3L Carbureted Engine

OPERATION

The early fuel evaporation system provides a rapid heating source to the engine induction system during cold driveaway conditions, thus, providing quick fuel evaporation and more uniform fuel distribution. When reducing the length of carburetor choking time, the exhaust emissions are also reduced.

The system consists of a valve and a vacuum actuator which increases the exhaust gas flow under the intake manifold during cold operation. The valve, located under the left exhaust manifold, is operated by a vacuum actuator which is controlled by a Thermal Vacuum Switch (TVS), mounted on the front of the intake manifold. Applying vacuum to the actuator, closes the valve, causing the intake manifold to heat up.

As the coolant temperature increases, the TVS turns Off the

vacuum to the actuator, thereby, causing the valve to open; the engine now operates normally.

Operational checks should be made at normal maintenance intervals.

TESTING

1. With the engine Cold, observe the position of the actuator arm.
2. Start the engine and observe the movement of the actuator arm.

NOTE: The arm should move in toward the diaphragm, to close the valve.

3. With the valve closed, allow the engine to warm, then observe the position of the valve:
    a. If the valve Opens, the system is OK.
    b. If the valve stays Closed, replace the Thermal Vacuum Switch (TVS).
4. If the valve did not Close, disconnect the vacuum hose from the valve, start the engine (engine running Cold) and check the vacuum:
    a. If no vacuum is felt, replace the TVS.
    b. If vacuum is felt, try to move the valve arm to check for freeness. If the arm moves freely, replace the actuator valve; if the arm does not move, lubricate it or replace the actuator valve.

REMOVAL AND INSTALLATION

Actuator Valve

The actuator valve is located between the left exhaust manifold and the exhaust pipe.
1. Remove the vacuum hose from the actuator of the valve.
2. Raise and support the vehicle on jackstands.
3. Remove the exhaust pipe-to-manifold nuts and the tension springs.
4. Remove the lower right hand exhaust (crossover) pipe and seal.

NOTE: It may not be necessary to remove the crossover pipe entirely.

5. Remove the actuator valve.
6. Inspect the actuator valve and replace it, if necessary.
7. To install, use new seals, gaskets and reverse the removal procedures. Torque the exhaust manifold-to-exhaust pipe nuts to 15 ft. lbs. (20 Nm).

TORQUE CONVERTER CLUTCH (TCC)
(ELECTRICAL DIAGNOSIS)
2.5L ENGINES

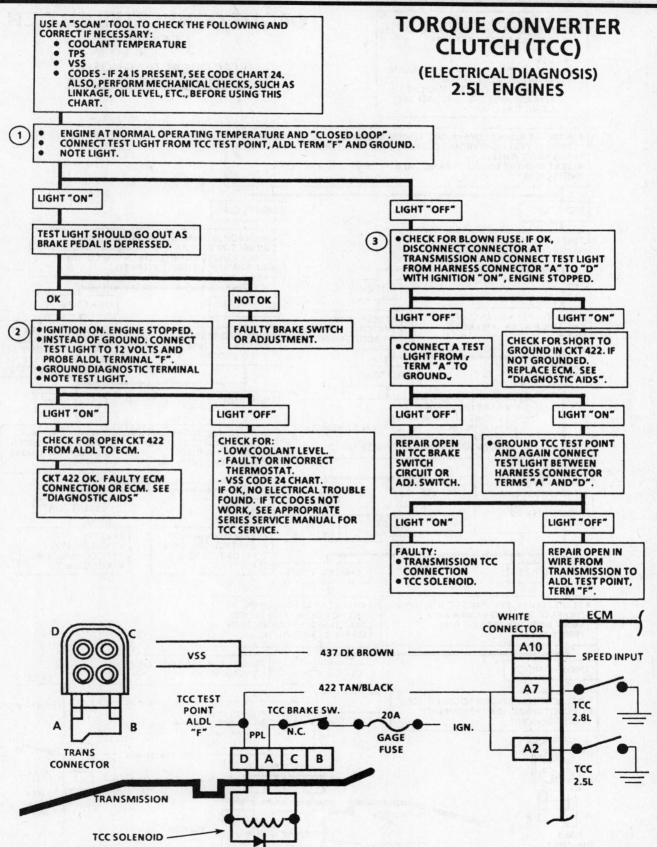

USE A "SCAN" TOOL TO CHECK THE FOLLOWING AND CORRECT IF NECESSARY:
- COOLANT TEMPERATURE
- TPS
- VSS
- CODES - IF 24 IS PRESENT, SEE CODE CHART 24. ALSO, PERFORM MECHANICAL CHECKS, SUCH AS LINKAGE, OIL LEVEL, ETC., BEFORE USING THIS CHART.

1
- ENGINE AT NORMAL OPERATING TEMPERATURE AND "CLOSED LOOP".
- CONNECT TEST LIGHT FROM TCC TEST POINT, ALDL TERM "F" AND GROUND.
- NOTE LIGHT.

LIGHT "ON"

TEST LIGHT SHOULD GO OUT AS BRAKE PEDAL IS DEPRESSED.

OK

2
- IGNITION ON. ENGINE STOPPED.
- INSTEAD OF GROUND. CONNECT TEST LIGHT TO 12 VOLTS AND PROBE ALDL TERMINAL "F".
- GROUND DIAGNOSTIC TERMINAL
- NOTE TEST LIGHT.

LIGHT "ON"

CHECK FOR OPEN CKT 422 FROM ALDL TO ECM.

CKT 422 OK. FAULTY ECM CONNECTION OR ECM. SEE "DIAGNOSTIC AIDS"

LIGHT "OFF"

CHECK FOR:
- LOW COOLANT LEVEL.
- FAULTY OR INCORRECT THERMOSTAT.
- VSS CODE 24 CHART.
IF OK, NO ELECTRICAL TROUBLE FOUND. IF TCC DOES NOT WORK, SEE APPROPRIATE SERIES SERVICE MANUAL FOR TCC SERVICE.

NOT OK

FAULTY BRAKE SWITCH OR ADJUSTMENT.

LIGHT "OFF"

3
- CHECK FOR BLOWN FUSE. IF OK, DISCONNECT CONNECTOR AT TRANSMISSION AND CONNECT TEST LIGHT FROM HARNESS CONNECTOR "A" TO "D" WITH IGNITION "ON", ENGINE STOPPED.

LIGHT "OFF"

- CONNECT A TEST LIGHT FROM , TERM "A" TO GROUND.

LIGHT "OFF"

REPAIR OPEN IN TCC BRAKE SWITCH CIRCUIT OR ADJ. SWITCH.

LIGHT "ON"

CHECK FOR SHORT TO GROUND IN CKT 422. IF NOT GROUNDED. REPLACE ECM. SEE "DIAGNOSTIC AIDS".

LIGHT "ON"

- GROUND TCC TEST POINT AND AGAIN CONNECT TEST LIGHT BETWEEN HARNESS CONNECTOR TERMS "A" AND "D".

LIGHT "ON"

FAULTY:
- TRANSMISSION TCC CONNECTION.
- TCC SOLENOID.

LIGHT "OFF"

REPAIR OPEN IN WIRE FROM TRANSMISSION TO ALDL TEST POINT, TERM "F".

D C
A B
TRANS CONNECTOR

VSS —— 437 DK BROWN ——

WHITE CONNECTOR

A10 — SPEED INPUT

422 TAN/BLACK —— A7

TCC 2.8L

TCC TEST POINT ALDL "F" PPL TCC BRAKE SW. N.C. 20A GAGE FUSE IGN.

D A C B

A2

TCC 2.5L

ECM

TRANSMISSION

TCC SOLENOID

TORQUE CONVERTER CLUTCH (TCC)
(ELECTRICAL DIAGNOSIS)
4.3L (UNDER 8500 GVW)

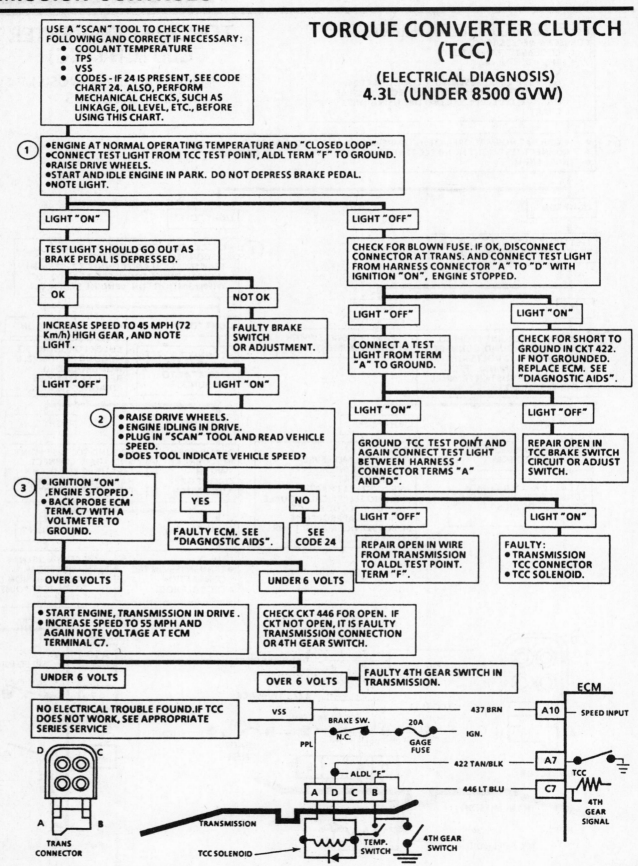

USE A "SCAN" TOOL TO CHECK THE FOLLOWING AND CORRECT IF NECESSARY:
- COOLANT TEMPERATURE
- TPS
- VSS
- CODES - IF 24 IS PRESENT, SEE CODE CHART 24. ALSO, PERFORM MECHANICAL CHECKS, SUCH AS LINKAGE, OIL LEVEL, ETC., BEFORE USING THIS CHART.

1
- ENGINE AT NORMAL OPERATING TEMPERATURE AND "CLOSED LOOP".
- CONNECT TEST LIGHT FROM TCC TEST POINT, ALDL TERM "F" TO GROUND.
- RAISE DRIVE WHEELS.
- START AND IDLE ENGINE IN PARK. DO NOT DEPRESS BRAKE PEDAL.
- NOTE LIGHT.

LIGHT "ON"

TEST LIGHT SHOULD GO OUT AS BRAKE PEDAL IS DEPRESSED.

OK

INCREASE SPEED TO 45 MPH (72 Km/h) HIGH GEAR, AND NOTE LIGHT.

NOT OK

FAULTY BRAKE SWITCH OR ADJUSTMENT.

LIGHT "OFF"

LIGHT "ON"

2
- RAISE DRIVE WHEELS.
- ENGINE IDLING IN DRIVE.
- PLUG IN "SCAN" TOOL AND READ VEHICLE SPEED.
- DOES TOOL INDICATE VEHICLE SPEED?

3
- IGNITION "ON", ENGINE STOPPED.
- BACK PROBE ECM TERM. C7 WITH A VOLTMETER TO GROUND.

YES

FAULTY ECM. SEE "DIAGNOSTIC AIDS".

NO

SEE CODE 24

OVER 6 VOLTS

- START ENGINE, TRANSMISSION IN DRIVE.
- INCREASE SPEED TO 55 MPH AND AGAIN NOTE VOLTAGE AT ECM TERMINAL C7.

UNDER 6 VOLTS

CHECK CKT 446 FOR OPEN. IF CKT NOT OPEN, IT IS FAULTY TRANSMISSION CONNECTION OR 4TH GEAR SWITCH.

UNDER 6 VOLTS

NO ELECTRICAL TROUBLE FOUND. IF TCC DOES NOT WORK, SEE APPROPRIATE SERIES SERVICE

OVER 6 VOLTS

FAULTY 4TH GEAR SWITCH IN TRANSMISSION.

LIGHT "OFF"

CHECK FOR BLOWN FUSE. IF OK, DISCONNECT CONNECTOR AT TRANS. AND CONNECT TEST LIGHT FROM HARNESS CONNECTOR "A" TO "D" WITH IGNITION "ON", ENGINE STOPPED.

LIGHT "OFF"

CONNECT A TEST LIGHT FROM TERM "A" TO GROUND.

LIGHT "ON"

CHECK FOR SHORT TO GROUND IN CKT 422. IF NOT GROUNDED. REPLACE ECM. SEE "DIAGNOSTIC AIDS".

LIGHT "ON"

GROUND TCC TEST POINT AND AGAIN CONNECT TEST LIGHT BETWEEN HARNESS CONNECTOR TERMS "A" AND "D".

LIGHT "OFF"

REPAIR OPEN IN TCC BRAKE SWITCH CIRCUIT OR ADJUST SWITCH.

LIGHT "OFF"

REPAIR OPEN IN WIRE FROM TRANSMISSION TO ALDL TEST POINT. TERM "F".

LIGHT "ON"

FAULTY:
- TRANSMISSION TCC CONNECTOR
- TCC SOLENOID.

VSS

BRAKE SW. N.C.   20A GAGE FUSE   IGN.

437 BRN — A10 — SPEED INPUT

PPL

422 TAN/BLK — A7

ALDL "F"

446 LT BLU — C7

A D C B

TRANSMISSION

TCC SOLENOID

TEMP. SWITCH   4TH GEAR SWITCH

ECM

TCC

4TH GEAR SIGNAL

D C
A B

TRANS CONNECTOR

MANUAL TRANSMISSION SHIFT LIGHT CHECK
VEHICLES BELOW 8500 GVW ONLY

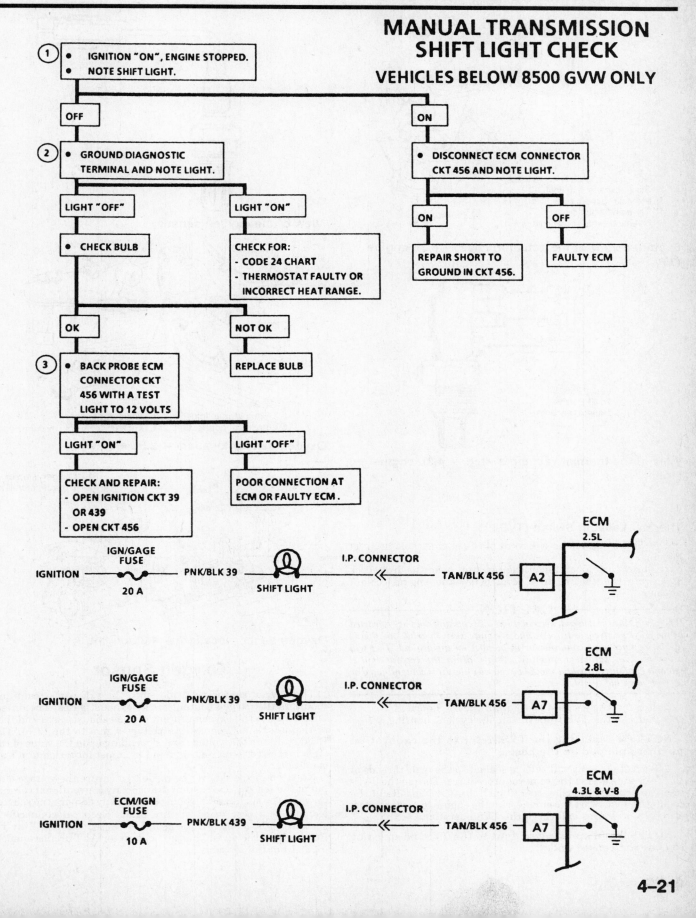

1
- IGNITION "ON", ENGINE STOPPED.
- NOTE SHIFT LIGHT.

OFF

ON

2
- GROUND DIAGNOSTIC TERMINAL AND NOTE LIGHT.

- DISCONNECT ECM CONNECTOR CKT 456 AND NOTE LIGHT.

LIGHT "OFF"

LIGHT "ON"

ON

OFF

- CHECK BULB

CHECK FOR:
- CODE 24 CHART
- THERMOSTAT FAULTY OR INCORRECT HEAT RANGE.

REPAIR SHORT TO GROUND IN CKT 456.

FAULTY ECM

OK

NOT OK

3
- BACK PROBE ECM CONNECTOR CKT 456 WITH A TEST LIGHT TO 12 VOLTS

REPLACE BULB

LIGHT "ON"

LIGHT "OFF"

CHECK AND REPAIR:
- OPEN IGNITION CKT 39 OR 439
- OPEN CKT 456

POOR CONNECTION AT ECM OR FAULTY ECM.

IGNITION — IGN/GAGE FUSE 20 A — PNK/BLK 39 — SHIFT LIGHT — I.P. CONNECTOR — TAN/BLK 456 — A2 — ECM 2.5L

IGNITION — IGN/GAGE FUSE 20 A — PNK/BLK 39 — SHIFT LIGHT — I.P. CONNECTOR — TAN/BLK 456 — A7 — ECM 2.8L

IGNITION — ECM/IGN FUSE 10 A — PNK/BLK 439 — SHIFT LIGHT — I.P. CONNECTOR — TAN/BLK 456 — A7 — ECM 4.3L & V-8

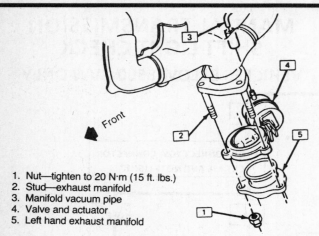

1. Nut—tighten to 20 N·m (15 ft. lbs.)
2. Stud—exhaust manifold
3. Manifold vacuum pipe
4. Valve and actuator
5. Left hand exhaust manifold

Exploded view of the actuator valve — 4.3L engine (1985)

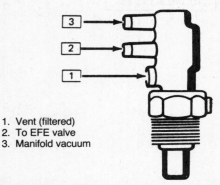

1. Vent (filtered)
2. To EFE valve
3. Manifold vacuum

View of the thermal vacuum switch — 4.3L engine (1985)

Thermal Vacuum Switch (TVS)

The TVS is located on the front of the engine coolant outlet housing.

1. Place a catch pan under the radiator, open the drain cock and drain the coolant to a level below the engine coolant housing.

--- CAUTION ---

When draining the coolant, keep in mind that cats and dogs are attracted by the ethylene glycol antifreeze, and are quite likely to drink any that is left in an uncovered container or in puddles on the ground. This will prove fatal in sufficient quantity. Always drain the coolant into a sealable container. Coolant should be reused unless it is contaminated or several years old.

2. Remove the vacuum hoses from the TVS ports.
3. Remove the TVS from the engine coolant housing.

NOTE: If replacing the TVS, refer to the calibration number stamped on the base.

4. To install, apply soft setting sealant to the male threads of the TVS and reverse the removal procedures. Torque the TVS-to-engine coolant housing to 120 inch lbs. (14 Nm). Refill the cooling system. Start the engine, run the engine to normal operating temperatures and check the TVS operation.

NOTE: When applying sealant to the TVS, be sure not to coat the sensor end.

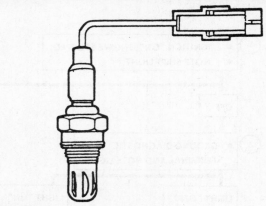

View of the oxygen sensor

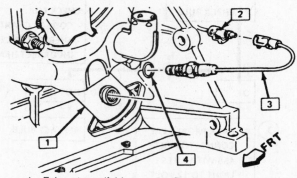

1. Exhaust manifold
2. Electrical connector
3. Oxygen sensor
4. Gasket

Oxygen sensor location — 2.5L engine

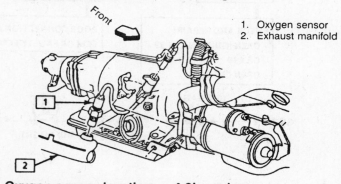

1. Oxygen sensor
2. Exhaust manifold

Oxygen sensor location — 4.3L engine

Oxygen Sensor

The oxygen sensor protrudes into the exhaust stream and monitors the oxygen content of the exhaust gases. The difference between the oxygen content of the exhaust gases and that of the outside air generates a voltage signal to the ECM. The ECM monitors this voltage and, depending upon the value of the signal received, issues a command to adjust for a rich or a lean condition.

No attempt should ever be made to measure the voltage output of the sensor. The current drain of any conventional voltmeter would be such that it would permanently damage the sensor. No jumpers, test leads or any other electrical connections should ever be made to the sensor. Use these tools ONLY on the ECM side of the wiring harness connector AFTER disconnecting it from the sensor.

REMOVAL AND INSTALLATION

The oxygen sensor must be replaced every 30,000 miles (48,000 km). The sensor may be difficult to remove when the engine temperature is below 120°F (48°C). Excessive removal force may damage the threads in the exhaust manifold or pipe; follow the removal procedure carefully.

1. Locate the oxygen sensor.

NOTE: It protrudes from the exhaust manifold on the left side of engine or at the Y-intersection of the exhaust pipe (4.3L – 1985), it looks somewhat like a spark plug.

2. Disconnect the negative (–) battery cable and the electrical connector from the oxygen sensor.
3. Spray a commercial solvent onto the sensor threads and allow it to soak in for at least five minutes.
4. Carefully unscrew and remove the sensor.
5. **To install,** first coat the new sensor's threads with GM anti-seize compound No. 5613695 or equivalent. This is not a conventional anti-seize paste. The use of a regular compound may electrically insulate the sensor, rendering it inoperative. You must coat the threads with an electrically conductive anti-seize compound.
6. Torque the sensor to 30 ft. lbs. (42 Nm). Be careful not to damage the electrical pigtail; check the sensor boot for proper fit and installation.

Computer Command Control (CCC) System

The Computer Command Control (CCC) System is an electronically controlled exhaust emission system that can monitor and control a large number of interrelated emission control systems. It can monitor many engine/vehicle operating conditions and then use the information to control the various engine related systems. The system is thereby making constant adjustments to maintain good vehicle performance under all normal driving conditions while at the same time allowing the catalytic converter to effectively control the emissions of HC, CO and NOx.

OPERATION

Electronic Control Module (ECM)

The Electronic Control Module (ECM) is the control center of the fuel control system. It constantly monitors various information from the sensors and controls the systems that affect the vehicle performance. The ECM has two parts: A Controller (the ECM without the PROM) and a separate calibrator (the PROM). The ECM is located behind the instrument panel's console trim plate.

Programmable Read Only Memory (PROM)

To allow the Controller to be used in many different vehicles, a device called a Calibrator or Programmable Read Only Memory (PROM) is used. The PROM which is located inside the ECM, stores information such as: the vehicle's weight, engine, transmission, axle ratio and many other specifications. Since the PROM stores specific information, it is important that the correct one be used in the right vehicle.

NOTE: Due to the intricacy of the system, it is advised to have a qualified mechanic perform any testing, adjusting or replacement of the system components. System damage may occur if testing is not performed correctly.

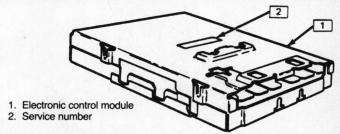

1. Electronic control module
2. Service number

View of the electronic control module (ECM)

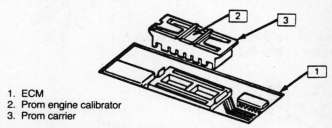

1. ECM
2. Prom engine calibrator
3. Prom carrier

Removing the PROM from the ECM

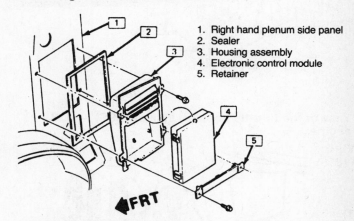

1. Right hand plenum side panel
2. Sealer
3. Housing assembly
4. Electronic control module
5. Retainer

Location of the electronic control (ECM)

Throttle Position Sensor (TPS)

The throttle position sensor is mounted on the throttle body or carburetor and is used to supply throttle position information to the ECM. The ECM memory stores an average of operating conditions with the ideal air/fuel ratios for each of these conditions. When the ECM receives a signal that indicates throttle position change, it immediately shifts to the last remembered set of operating conditions that resulted in an ideal air/fuel ratio control. The memory is continually being updated during normal operations.

TESTING

The throttle position sensor is non-adjustable but a test should be performed ONLY when throttle body parts have been replaced or AFTER the minimum idle speed has been adjusted.

NOTE: The following procedure requires the use of the Digital Voltmeter tool No. J–29125–A or equivalent.

1. Using the Digital Voltmeter tool No. J–29125–A or equivalent, set it on the 0–5.0V scale, then connect the probes to the

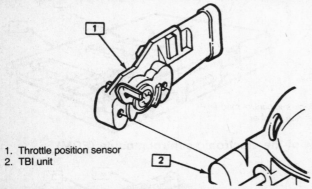

1. Throttle position sensor
2. TBI unit

View of the throttle position sensor (TPS) — 2.5L engine (1985–86)

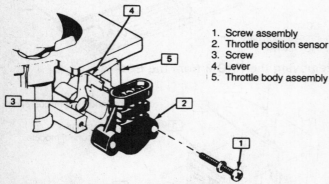

1. Screw assembly
2. Throttle position sensor
3. Screw
4. Lever
5. Throttle body assembly

View of the throttle position sensor (TPS) — 4.3L engine

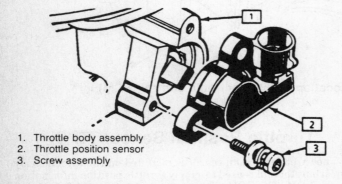

1. Throttle body assembly
2. Throttle position sensor
3. Screw assembly

Throttle position sensor — 1987–90 2.5L engine

center terminal **B** and the outside terminal **C** (2.5L engine) or **A** (4.3L engine).

NOTE: To attach probes to the TPS electrical connector, disconnect the TPS electrical connector, install thin wires into the sockets and reconnect the connector.

2. Turn the ignition switch On (engine stopped).
3. The output voltage should be 1.25V. If the voltage is more that 1.25V, replace the TPS.
4. Remove the voltmeter and the jumper wires.

REMOVAL AND INSTALLATION

1. Remove the air cleaner.
2. Disconnect the electrical connector from the throttle position sensor (TPS).

3. Remove the TPS mounting screws, the lockwashers and the retainers.
4. Remove the TPS sensor.
To install:
1. Make sure that the throttle valve is in the closed position, then install the TPS sensor.

NOTE: Make sure that the TPS pickup lever is located ABOVE the tang on the throttle actuator lever.

2. Lubricate the mounting screws with Loctite® (thread locking compound) No. 262 or equivalent, then torque to 18 inch lbs. (2 Nm).
3. Connect the TPS connector and negative battery cable.
4. Start the engine and check for proper operation.

Manifold Pressure Sensor (MAP)

The manifold pressure sensors, used ONLY on fuel injected engines, are located on the air cleaner side.

OPERATION

The manifold pressure sensor measures the pressure (load and speed) changes in the intake manifold, then converts these changes into voltage output. The voltage changes are sent to the ECM, which analyzes the information to alter the fuel delivery and the ignition timing.

At closed throttle, the MAP sensor produces relatively low MAP output, while at wide-open throttle, it would produce high output. When the pressure inside the intake manifold is equal to the outside pressure, the MAP sensor will produce high output voltage.

NOTE: The manifold absolute pressure is opposite what would measure on a vacuum gauge.

This sensor is also used to measure the barometric pressure (under certain conditions) to adjust for differences in altitude.

The failure of the MAP sensor circuit should set a Code 33 or 34.

TESTING

NOTE: The following procedure requires the use of a Voltmeter and a Vacuum pump.

1. Turn the ignition switch On (engine stopped).
2. Using a voltmeter, set it on the 0–10.0V scale, then attach the probes to the MAP sensor terminals **A** and **B**. Compare the acquired voltage to the voltage/altitude chart for the correct values; if not correct, replace the sensor.
3. Using a vacuum pump, apply 10 in.Hg to the MAP sensor and note the change; it should be 1.2–2.3V less than the initial voltage, (if not) replace the sensor.

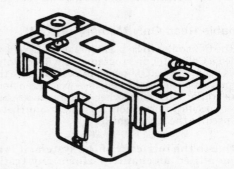

View of the manifold absolute pressure (MAP) sensor — TBI engines

ALTITUDE	VOLTAGE RANGE
BELOW 1,000	**3.8 - 5.5V**
1,000 - 2000	3.6 - 5.3V
3,000 - 4,000	3.3 - 5.0V
4,000 - 5,000	3.2 - 4.8V
5,000 - 6,000	3.0 - 4.6V
6,000 - 7,000'	2.9 - 4.5V
7,000 - 8,000'	2.8 - 4.3V
8,000 - 9,000	2.6 - 4.2V
9,000 - 10,000'	2.5 - 4.0V

Manifold absolute pressure (MAP) chart

4. If no trouble is found, check the vacuum hose for leakage or restriction. If replacing the hose, be sure to use one specifically for MAP sensor use.

REMOVAL AND INSTALLATION

The sensor is located on or near the air cleaner assembly.
1. Remove the sensor-to-throttle body vacuum hose.

2. Disconnect the sensor's electrical connector.
3. Remove the MAP sensor from the air cleaner mounting bracket.
4. To install, reverse the removal procedures.

"Check Engine" or "Service Engine Soon" Light

RESETTING

An amber "CHECK ENGINE" or "SERVICE ENGINE SOON" light is located in the instrument panel to indicate a problem in the computer command control system. The light will come ON when the ignition key is ON. The light should go OFF after the engine has started. If the light blinks or stays ON, a problem may be present in the system. Code 12 is not a fault code, it is a check code to tell that the diagnosis system is working properly.

After the problem has been taken care of, reset the light by removing the battery voltage for 30 seconds. This will remove all stored codes. The ECM "B" fuse or negative battery cable can be used to clear the codes from the memory. Make sure the problem has been taken care of before removing the ECM power. All previous memory will be lost after the ECM power has been disconnected.

VACUUM DIAGRAMS

NOTE: The vacuum hose routing diagrams shown in this manual may not exactly match the diagram for your vehicle. Due to production and emission legislation, the diagrams may have changed midway through a production run. Always refer to the underhood sticker in your vehicle first. Use the vacuum hose diagrams as guides if there is no diagram available.

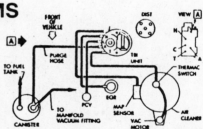

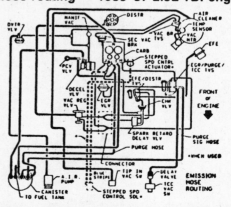

Vacuum hose routing – 1985–87 2.5L TBI engine

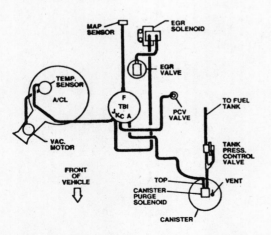

Vacuum hose routing – 1988–90 2.5L TBI engine

Vacuum hose routing – 1985 4.3L carbureted engine (federal)

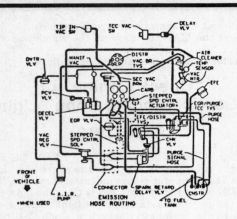

Vacuum hose routing — 1985 4.3L carbureted engine (federal and low altitude)

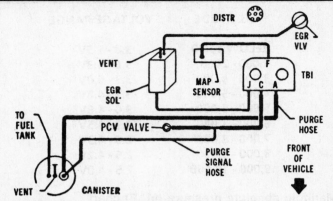

Vacuum hose routing — 1988–90 4.3L TBI engine (federal without AIR pump)

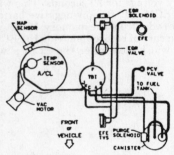

Vacuum hose routing — 1986–88 4.3L TBI engine

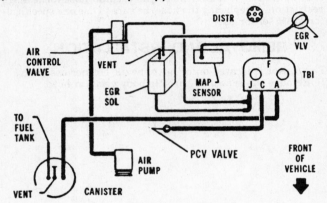

Vacuum hose routing — 1988–90 4.3L TBI engine (federal with AIR pump)

Fuel System

QUICK REFERENCE INDEX

GENERAL INDEX

CARBURETED FUEL SYSTEM

Only the 1985 4.3L engine uses a carburetor.

Mechanical Fuel Pump

The mechanical fuel pump is located on the right front of the engine.

REMOVAL AND INSTALLATION

—————— CAUTION ——————
Before removing any component of the fuel system, be sure to reduce the fuel pressure in the system. Keep a fire extinguisher close by when servicing the fuel system. Place a rag under the fuel line and slowly remove the line from the fitting.

1. Disconnect the negative (−) battery cable, the fuel inlet hose from the fuel pump and the vapor return hose (if equipped).
2. Disconnect the fuel outlet hose from the fuel pump.
3. Remove the fuel pump-to-engine bolts, the fuel pump, the pushrod, the gasket and the mounting plate.
4. Using a putty knife, clean the gasket mounting surfaces.
To install:
1. Use a new gasket with silicone sealer.

2. Install the mounting plate, gasket, pushrod and fuel pump. Torque the mounting bolts to 27 ft. lbs. (38 Nm).
3. Connect the fuel outlet hose to the fuel pump.
4. Connect the fuel inlet hose to the fuel pump and the vapor return hose (if equipped).
5. Connect the negative battery cable, start the engine and check for fuel leaks.

TESTING

Flow Test

1. Remove the fuel pump-to-carburetor line from the carburetor.
2. Place the fuel line into a clean container.
3. Crank the engine; approximately ½ pint of the fuel should be delivered in 15 seconds.
4. If the fuel flow is below minimum, inspect the fuel system for restrictions; if no restrictions are found, replace the fuel pump.

Pressure Test

NOTE: **The following procedure requires the use of a GM Fuel Pressure Gauge tool No. J-29658-A or equivalent.**

Troubleshooting Basic Fuel System Problems

Problem	Cause	Solution
Engine cranks, but won't start (or is hard to start) when cold	• Empty fuel tank • Incorrect starting procedure • Defective fuel pump • No fuel in carburetor • Clogged fuel filter • Engine flooded • Defective choke	• Check for fuel in tank • Follow correct procedure • Check pump output • Check for fuel in the carburetor • Replace fuel filter • Wait 15 minutes; try again • Check choke plate
Engine cranks, but is hard to start (or does not start) when hot— (presence of fuel is assumed)	• Defective choke	• Check choke plate
Rough idle or engine runs rough	• Dirt or moisture in fuel • Clogged air filter • Faulty fuel pump	• Replace fuel filter • Replace air filter • Check fuel pump output
Engine stalls or hesitates on acceleration	• Dirt or moisture in the fuel • Dirty carburetor • Defective fuel pump • Incorrect float level, defective accelerator pump	• Replace fuel filter • Clean the carburetor • Check fuel pump output • Check carburetor
Poor gas mileage	• Clogged air filter • Dirty carburetor • Defective choke, faulty carburetor adjustment	• Replace air filter • Clean carburetor • Check carburetor
Engine is flooded (won't start accompanied by smell of raw fuel)	• Improperly adjusted choke or carburetor	• Wait 15 minutes and try again, without pumping gas pedal • If it won't start, check carburetor

1. Remove the air cleaner, then disconnect and plug the THERMAC vacuum port on the carburetor.
2. Place a rag (to catch excess fuel) under the fuel line-to-carburetor connection. Disconnect the fuel line from the carburetor.

NOTE: When disconnecting the fuel line, use a back-up wrench to hold the fuel nut on the carburetor.

3. Using a GM Fuel Pressure Gauge tool No. J–29658–A or equivalent, install it into the fuel line.
4. Start the engine and observe the fuel pressure, it should be 4–6.5 psi.

NOTE: If the fuel pressure does not meet specifications, inspect the fuel system for restrictions or replace the fuel pump.

5. Stop the engine, relieve the fuel pressure and remove the GM Fuel Pressure Gauge tool No. J–29658–A or equivalent.
6. Install a new fuel line-to-carburetor O-ring or washer. Unplug the THERMAC vacuum port. Start the engine and check for fuel leaks.

Carburetor

ADJUSTMENTS

Idle Speed and Mixture Adjustments

Refer to the Idle Speed and Mixture Adjustment procedures in Section 2 and adjust the idle speed and fuel mixture.

Float and Fuel Level Adjustment

NOTE: The following procedure requires the use of the GM Float Gauge tool No. J–34935, BT–8420–A or equivalent.

1. Remove the air cleaner from the carburetor.
2. With the engine idling and the choke plate in the Wide-Open position, insert the GM Float Gauge tool No. J–34935, BT–8420–A or equivalent, into the vent hole (slot) of the air horn; allow the gauge to float freely.

NOTE: DO NOT press down on the gauge, for flooding or float damage may occur.

3. Observe the mark (on the gauge) that aligns with the top of the air horn; the float setting should be within $\pm \frac{1}{16}$ in. (1.5mm) of the specifications.

NOTE: Incorrect fuel pressure will adversely affect the fuel level.

4. If the float level is not correct, perform the following procedures:
   a. Turn the ignition switch Off.

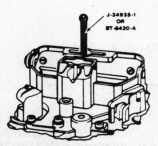

Using the GM float gauge tool No. J–34935–1, BT–8420–A or equivalent, to check the float level

b. Disconnect the fuel line, the throttle linkage and/or any electrical connectors from the top of the carburetor (air horn).
   c. Remove the air horn-to-fuel bowl screws. Lift the air horn from the fuel bowl and discard the gasket.
   d. Bend the float tang (at the needle valve) to the correct specifications.
   e. To install the air horn, use a new fuel bowl gasket, install the air horn and the air horn-to-fuel bowl screws.
   f. Install the throttle linkage and the fuel line.
5. To complete the installation, install the air cleaner. Start the engine and check for fuel leaks.

Air Valve Spring Adjustment

1. Using a $\frac{3}{32}$ in. Allen wrench, loosen the air valve spring lock screw.
2. Turning the tension adjusting screw counterclockwise, open the air valve part way.
3. Turning the tension adjusting screw clockwise, close the air valve, then turn it an additional number of specified turns (see carburetor chart).
4. Tighten the lock screw, then apply Lithium grease to the spring-to-lever contact area.

Choke Coil Lever Adjustment

1. Drill out and remove the choke coil housing cover rivets. Retain the choke housing cover, then remove the thermostatic cover and coil assembly from the choke housing.
2. Place the fast idle cam follower on the high step of the fast idle cam.
3. Close the choke valve by pushing up on the thermostatic coil tang (counterclockwise).
4. Insert a drill or gauge, of the specified size, into the hole in the choke housing. The lower edge of the choke lever should be just touching the side of the gauge.
5. If the choke lever is not touching the side of the gauge, bend the choke rod until you see that it does.

Fast Idle Cam (Choke Rod) Adjustment

NOTE: The following procedure requires the use of the GM Valve Angle Gauge tool No. J–26701, BT–7704 or equivalent.

1. Using a rubber band, attach it between the green tang of the intermediate choke shaft and the air horn housing.
2. Open the throttle and allow the choke valve to close.

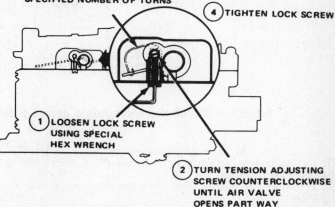

Adjusting the air valve spring — M4ME and E4ME carburetors

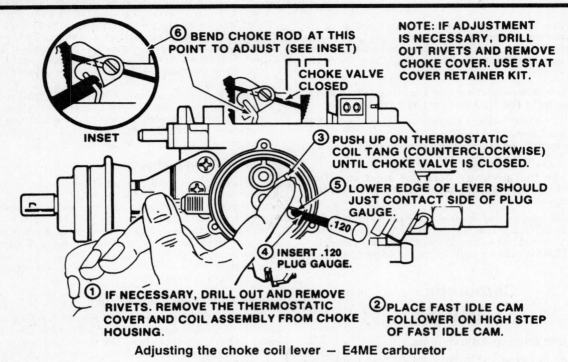

⑥ BEND CHOKE ROD AT THIS POINT TO ADJUST (SEE INSET)

NOTE: IF ADJUSTMENT IS NECESSARY, DRILL OUT RIVETS AND REMOVE CHOKE COVER. USE STAT COVER RETAINER KIT.

CHOKE VALVE CLOSED

INSET

③ PUSH UP ON THERMOSTATIC COIL TANG (COUNTERCLOCKWISE) UNTIL CHOKE VALVE IS CLOSED.

⑤ LOWER EDGE OF LEVER SHOULD JUST CONTACT SIDE OF PLUG GAUGE.

.120

④ INSERT .120 PLUG GAUGE.

① IF NECESSARY, DRILL OUT AND REMOVE RIVETS. REMOVE THE THERMOSTATIC COVER AND COIL ASSEMBLY FROM CHOKE HOUSING.

② PLACE FAST IDLE CAM FOLLOWER ON HIGH STEP OF FAST IDLE CAM.

Adjusting the choke coil lever — E4ME carburetor

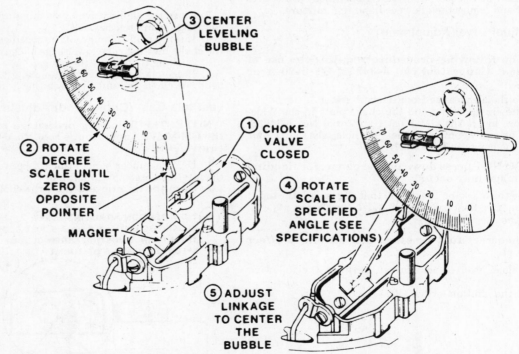

③ CENTER LEVELING BUBBLE

② ROTATE DEGREE SCALE UNTIL ZERO IS OPPOSITE POINTER

MAGNET

① CHOKE VALVE CLOSED

④ ROTATE SCALE TO SPECIFIED ANGLE (SEE SPECIFICATIONS)

⑤ ADJUST LINKAGE TO CENTER THE BUBBLE

Adjusting the choke valve angle gauge tool No. J– 26701, BT-7704 or equivalent

3. Using the GM Valve Angle Gauge tool No. J–26701, BT-7704 or equivalent, attach it to the choke plate, then perform the following procedures:

    a. Rotate the degree scale until the zero is opposite the pointer.

    b. Center the leveling bubble.

    c. Rotate the scale to the specified angle degrees (see carburetor chart).

4. Position the cam follower on the 2nd step (against the rise of the high step) of the fast idle cam.

NOTE: If the cam follower does not contact the cam, adjust the fast idle speed screw. Final fast idle speed adjustment MUST BE performed according to the underhood emission control information label.

① ATTACH RUBBER BAND TO GREEN TANG OF INTERMEDIATE CHOKE SHAFT

② OPEN THROTTLE TO ALLOW CHOKE VALVE TO CLOSE

③ SET UP ANGLE GAGE AND SET ANGLE TO SPECIFICATIONS

④ PLACE CAM FOLLOWER ON SECOND STEP OF CAM, AGAINST RISE OF HIGH STEP. IF CAM FOLLOWER DOES NOT CONTACT CAM, TURN IN FAST IDLE SPEED SCREW ADDITIONAL TURN(S).

NOTICE: FINAL FAST IDLE SPEED ADJUSTMENT MUST BE PERFORMED ACCORDING TO UNDER-HOOD EMISSION CONTROL INFORMATION LABEL.

⑤ ADJUST BY BENDING TANG OF FAST IDLE CAM UNTIL BUBBLE IS CENTERED.

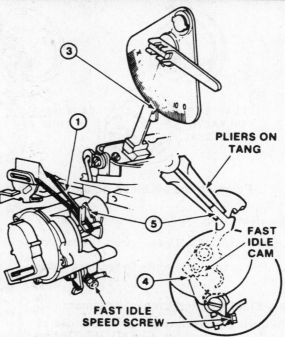

PLIERS ON TANG

FAST IDLE CAM

FAST IDLE SPEED SCREW

Fast idle cam (choke rod) adjustment — E4ME carburetor

① ATTACH RUBBER BAND TO GREEN TANG OF INTERMEDIATE CHOKE SHAFT

② OPEN THROTTLE TO ALLOW CHOKE VALVE TO CLOSE

③ SET UP ANGLE GAGE AND SET TO SPECIFICATION

④ RETRACT VACUUM BREAK PLUNGER USING VACUUM SOURCE, AT LEAST 18" HG. PLUG AIR BLEED HOLES WHERE APPLICABLE

ON QUADRAJETS, AIR VALVE ROD MUST NOT RESTRICT PLUNGER FROM RETRACTING FULLY. IF NECESSARY, BEND ROD (SEE ARROW) TO PERMIT FULL PLUNGER TRAVEL. FINAL ROD CLEARANCE MUST BE SET AFTER VACUUM BREAK SETTING HAS BEEN MADE.

⑤ WITH AT LEAST 18" HG STILL APPLIED, ADJUST SCREW TO CENTER BUBBLE

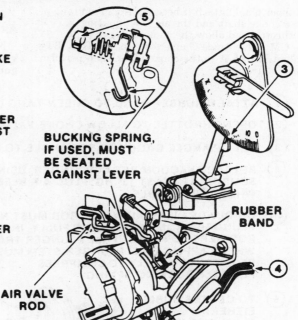

BUCKING SPRING, IF USED, MUST BE SEATED AGAINST LEVER

RUBBER BAND

AIR VALVE ROD

Front (primary side) vacuum break adjustment — E4ME carburetor

5. Center the bubble of the Valve Angle Gauge, by bending the fast idle cam tang.

Front (Primary Side) Vacuum Break Adjustment

NOTE: The following procedure requires the use of the GM Valve Angle Gauge tool No. J–26701, BT–7704 or equivalent.

1. Using a rubber band, attach it between the green tang of the intermediate choke shaft and the air horn housing.
2. Open the throttle and allow the choke valve to close.
3. Using the GM Valve Angle Gauge tool No. J–26701, BT–7704 or equivalent, attach it to the choke plate, then perform the following procedures:
   a. Rotate the degree scale until the zero is opposite the pointer.
   b. Center the leveling bubble.

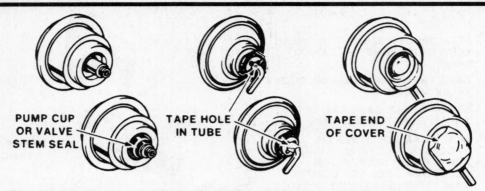

PUMP CUP
OR VALVE
STEM SEAL

TAPE HOLE
IN TUBE

TAPE END
OF COVER

Plugging the air bleed holes of the vacuum break — E4ME carburetor

c. Rotate the scale to the specified angle degrees (see carburetor chart).

4. Apply a vacuum source (18 in.Hg) to retract the vacuum break and plug the air bleed holes.

5. Center the bubble of the Valve Angle Gauge, by turning the adjusting screw.

Rear (Secondary Side) Vacuum Break Adjustment

NOTE: The following procedure requires the use of the GM Valve Angle Gauge tool No. J–26701, BT-7704 or equivalent.

1. Using a rubber band, attach it between the green tang of the intermediate choke shaft and the air horn housing.

2. Open the throttle and allow the choke valve to close.

3. Using the GM Valve Angle Gauge tool No. J–26701, BT-7704 or equivalent, attach it to the choke plate, then perform the following procedures:

a. Rotate the degree scale until the zero is opposite the pointer.

b. Center the leveling bubble.

c. Rotate the scale to the specified angle degrees (see carburetor chart).

4. Apply a vacuum source (18 in.Hg) to retract the vacuum break and plug the air bleed holes.

5. Center the bubble of the Valve Angle Gauge by performing one of the following procedures:

a. Using a 1/8 in. Allen wrench, turn the vacuum break adjusting screw.

b. Using a rod bending tool, support the S-rod and bend the vacuum break rod.

Air Valve Rod Adjustment

NOTE: The following procedure requires the use of an vacuum source (18 in.Hg) and a 0.025 in. (0.6mm) plug gauge.

① ATTACH RUBBER BAND TO GREEN TANG OF INTERMEDIATE CHOKE SHAFT.

② OPEN THROTTLE TO ALLOW CHOKE VALVE TO CLOSE.

③ SET UP ANGLE GAGE AND SET ANGLE TO SPECIFICATION.

④ RETRACT VACUUM BREAK PLUNGER, USING VACUUM SOURCE. AT LEAST 18" HG. PLUG AIR BLEED HOLES WHERE APPLICABLE.

④A ON QUADRAJETS, AIR VALVE ROD MUST NOT RESTRICT PLUNGER FROM RETRACTING FULLY. IF NECESSARY BEND ROD HERE TO PERMIT FULL PLUNGER TRAVEL. WHERE APPLICABLE, PLUNGER STEM MUST BE EXTENDED FULLY TO COMPRESS PLUNGER BUCKING SPRING.

⑤ TO CENTER BUBBLE, EITHER:
A. ADJUST WITH 1/8" HEX WRENCH (VACUUM STILL APPLIED)

-OR-

B. SUPPORT AT "S" AND BEND VACUUM BREAK ROD (VACUUM STILL APPLIED)

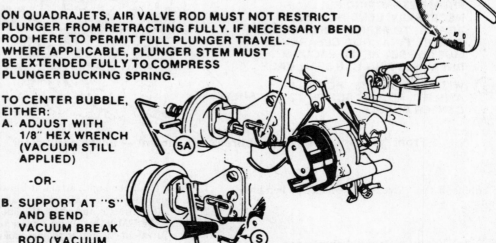

Rear (secondary side) vacuum break adjustment — E4ME carburetor

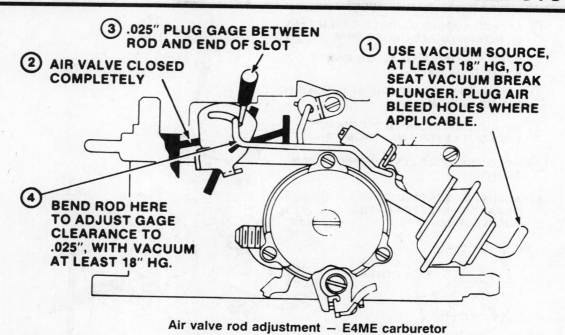

③ .025" PLUG GAGE BETWEEN ROD AND END OF SLOT

② AIR VALVE CLOSED COMPLETELY

① USE VACUUM SOURCE, AT LEAST 18" HG, TO SEAT VACUUM BREAK PLUNGER. PLUG AIR BLEED HOLES WHERE APPLICABLE.

④ BEND ROD HERE TO ADJUST GAGE CLEARANCE TO .025", WITH VACUUM AT LEAST 18" HG.

Air valve rod adjustment — E4ME carburetor

1. Apply a vacuum source (18 in.Hg) to retract the vacuum break and plug the air bleed holes.
2. Open the throttle and allow the choke valve to close.
3. Using a 0.025 in. (0.6mm) plug gauge, position it between the control rod and the slot in the choke valve cam.
4. To adjust, bend (using a bending tool) the air valve rod.

Secondary Lockout Adjustment

NOTE: The following procedure requires the use of a 0.015 in. (0.38mm) plug gauge and a rod bending tool.

1. Pull the choke wide open by pushing out on the choke lever.
2. Open the throttle until the end of the secondary actuating lever is opposite the toe of the lockout lever.

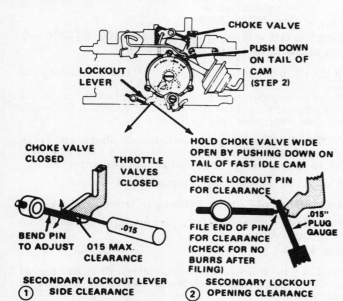

CHOKE VALVE

PUSH DOWN ON TAIL OF CAM (STEP 2)

LOCKOUT LEVER

CHOKE VALVE CLOSED

THROTTLE VALVES CLOSED

BEND PIN TO ADJUST

.015

015 MAX. CLEARANCE

SECONDARY LOCKOUT LEVER ① SIDE CLEARANCE

HOLD CHOKE VALVE WIDE OPEN BY PUSHING DOWN ON TAIL OF FAST IDLE CAM

CHECK LOCKOUT PIN FOR CLEARANCE

FILE END OF PIN FOR CLEARANCE (CHECK FOR NO BURRS AFTER FILING)

.015" PLUG GAUGE

SECONDARY LOCKOUT ② OPENING CLEARANCE

Secondary lockout adjustment — M4ME and E4ME carburetors

3. Measure the clearance between the lockout lever and the secondary lever.
4. Bend the lockout pin until the clearance is in accordance with the proper specifications.

Unloader Adjustment

NOTE: The following procedure requires the use of the GM Valve Angle Gauge tool No. J–26701, BT–7704 or equivalent, a rubber band and a bending tool.

1. Using a rubber band, attach it between the green tang of the intermediate choke shaft and the air horn housing.
2. Open the throttle and allow the choke valve to close.
3. Using the GM Valve Angle Gauge tool No. J–26701, BT–7704 or equivalent, attach it to the choke plate, then perform the following procedures:
   a. Rotate the degree scale until the zero is opposite the pointer.
   b. Center the leveling bubble.
   c. Rotate the scale to the specified angle degrees (see carburetor chart).

NOTE: On a Quadrajet, hold the secondary lockout lever away from the pin.

4. Adjust and hold the throttle lever in the wide-open position.
5. Center the bubble of the Valve Angle Gauge, by bending the fast idle lever tang.

Throttle Position Sensor (TPS)

The throttle position sensor is a position meter, mounted on the carburetor; one end is connected to the ECM and the other to a ground. As the throttle plate opens, the output voltage increases; at wide-open throttle the output voltage is approx. 5V.

NOTE: The following procedure requires the use of GM Adjustment tool No. J–28696 or equivalent, a digital voltmeter tool No. J–29125–A, a drill, a $\frac{5}{64}$ in. drill bit.

1. Disconnect the negative battery cable from the battery.
2. Remove the air cleaner and stuff a clean rag into the intake bore to keep the carburetor clean.

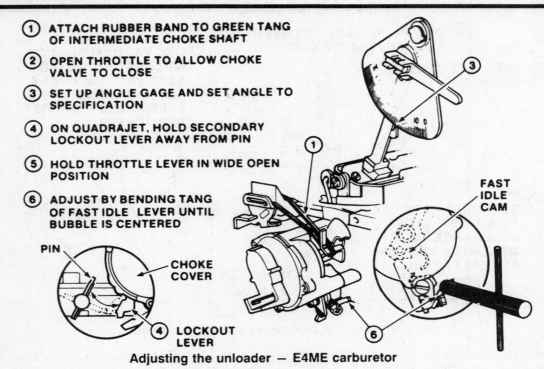

① ATTACH RUBBER BAND TO GREEN TANG OF INTERMEDIATE CHOKE SHAFT

② OPEN THROTTLE TO ALLOW CHOKE VALVE TO CLOSE

③ SET UP ANGLE GAGE AND SET ANGLE TO SPECIFICATION

④ ON QUADRAJET, HOLD SECONDARY LOCKOUT LEVER AWAY FROM PIN

⑤ HOLD THROTTLE LEVER IN WIDE OPEN POSITION

⑥ ADJUST BY BENDING TANG OF FAST IDLE LEVER UNTIL BUBBLE IS CENTERED

Adjusting the unloader — E4ME carburetor

3. To remove the throttle position plug cover, perform the following procedures:

   a. Using a $\frac{5}{64}$ in. drill bit, drill a hole in the aluminum plug covering the throttle position solenoid adjusting screw.

NOTE: When drilling the hole in the aluminum plug, be careful not to damage the adjusting screw head.

   b. Using a No. 8, ½ in. self-tapping screw, install it into the drilled hole.

   c. Using a wide blade screwdriver, pry against the screw head to remove the plug, then discard the plug.

4. Using the GM adjusting tool No. J–28696, BT–7967–A or equivalent, remove the throttle position solenoid adjusting screw.

5. Using the digital voltmeter tool No. J–29125–A or equivalent, connect one probe to the center terminal and the other to the bottom terminal of the throttle position solenoid connector.

6. Turn the ignition switch On with the engine stopped. Install the throttle position solenoid adjustment screw.

7. Using the GM adjusting tool No. J–28696, BT–7967–A or equivalent, install the throttle position solenoid adjusting screw

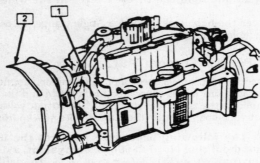

1. Plug (throttle position sensor adjustment screw)
2. Drill

Drilling a hole in the TPS screw cover plug

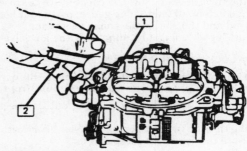

1. TPS adjustment screw
2. Tool—J28696/BT7967A

Using the GM adjusting tool No. J–28696, BT–7967–A or equivalent, to adjust the TPS screw

and turn it to obtain a voltage of 0.255V (air conditioning Off and at curb idle).

8. After the adjustment is complete, install a new throttle position solenoid plug cover; drive the plug in until it flush with the raised pump lever boss on the casting.

NOTE: If a throttle position solenoid plug is not available, apply Delco Threadlock Adhesive X–10® or equivalent, to the screw threads and repeat the adjustment.

9. After adjustment, clear the trouble code memory.

Mixture Control Solenoid (Plunger Travel)

If the dwell is off at 3000 rpm, perform this check and/or adjustment procedure.

CHECKING

NOTE: The following procedure requires the use of the GM Float Gauge tool No. J–34935, BT–8420–A or equivalent.

1. With the engine Off, remove the air cleaner from the carburetor.

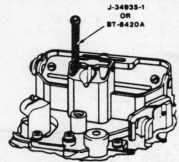

Checking the mixture control solenoid plunger travel — E4ME carburetor

2. Insert the GM Float Gauge tool No. J–34935–1, BT–8420–A or equivalent, into the vertical D-shaped vent hole of the air horn; allow the gauge to touch the solenoid plunger.

NOTE: If difficulty is experienced in inserting the gauge into the hole, it may be necessary to grind some of the material from it.

3. With the gauge released (plunger in the Up position), observe and record the mark (on the gauge) that aligns with the top of the air horn.

4. Press down (lightly) on the gauge until it bottoms, then read and record the mark that aligns with the top of the air horn.

5. Subtract the Up position from the Down position; the difference is the total plunger travel:

   a. If the plunger travel is $\frac{1}{16}$–$\frac{3}{16}$ in. (1.5–4.8mm) and the dwell reading was OK at 3,000 rpm (10°–50°), refer to the Idle Air Bleed Valve Adjustment, located in the Idle Speed and Mixture Adjustment procedures in Section 2.

   b. If the plunger travel is less than $\frac{1}{16}$ in. (1.5mm) or greater than $\frac{3}{16}$ in. (4.8mm) or the dwell reading was Off at 3,000 rpm, adjust the mixture control solenoid plunger travel.

ADJUSTMENT

NOTE: The following procedure requires the use of the GM Mixture Solenoid Gauge tool No. J–33815–1, BT–8253–A or equivalent, and the GM Adjustment tool No. J–28696–10, BT–7928 or equivalent.

1. Disconnect the negative battery terminal from the battery, then the mixture control solenoid, the throttle position sensor and the idle speed solenoid connectors from the carburetor.

2. To remove the air horn, perform the following procedures:

   a. Remove the idle speed solenoid-to-air horn screws and the solenoid.

   b. Remove the choke lever-to-choke shaft screw, rotate the upper choke lever and remove the choke rod from the slot in the lever.

   c. To remove the choke rod from the lower lever (inside the float bowl casting), use a small screwdriver to hold the lower lever outward and twist the rod counterclockwise.

   d. Remove the fuel pump link from the pump lever; DO NOT remove the pump link from the air horn.

   e. From the front of the float bowl, remove the front vacuum break hose from the tube.

   f. Remove the air horn-to-fuel bowl screws and lift the air horn straight up from the float bowl; discard the gasket.

NOTE: When removing the air horn-to-float bowl screws, be sure to remove the 2 countersunk screws located next to the venturi.

3. Remove the solenoid adjustment screw, the rich limit stop,

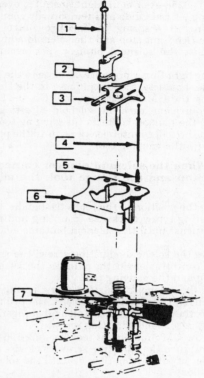

1. Screw—solenoid adjusting (lean mixture)
2. Stop—rich limit
3. Solenoid plunger
4. Rod—primary metering
5. Spring—primary metering rod
6. Insert—float bowl
7. M/C solenoid

Exploded view of the mixture control solenoid assembly — E4ME carburetor

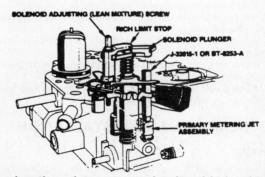

Positioning the mixture control solenoid gauging tool

the mixture control solenoid plunger, the primary metering rods with the springs, the plastic filler block and the mixture control solenoid.

4. Inspect the carburetor for the cause of an incorrect mixture:

   a. Inspect for a worn mixture control solenoid bore or sticking plunger.

   b. Inspect the metering rods for an incorrect part number, sticking condition and improperly installed rods or springs.

   c. Inspect for dirt in the jets.

5. Using the GM Mixture Solenoid Gauging tool No. J–

33815-1, BT–8253–A or equivalent, install it over the throttle side metering jet rod guide and temporarily reinstall the solenoid adjusting screw spring, the mixture control solenoid, the plunger, the rich limit stop and the solenoid adjusting screw.

6. To adjust the solenoid plunger, perform the following procedures:

    a. Using light finger pressure, as close to the plunger shaft as possible, hold the solenoid plunger in the Down position.

    b. Using the GM Adjustment tool No. J–28696–10, BT–7928 or equivalent, turn the solenoid adjusting screw clockwise until the plunger contacts the gauging tool.

    c. Turn the tool counterclockwise until the plunger breaks contact with the gauging tool.

NOTE: When the solenoid plunger contacts both the Solenoid Stop and the Gauge tool, the adjustment is correct.

7. Noting the position of the tool's tee handle, turn the solenoid's adjusting screw clockwise (counting and recording the number of turns) until the solenoid bottoms against the float bowl.

8. Remove the solenoid adjusting screw, the rich limit stop, the mixture control solenoid, the plunger, the solenoid adjusting screw spring and the gauging tool.

9. Install the solenoid adjusting screw spring, the mixture control solenoid, the plastic filler block, the primary metering rods/springs, the mixture control solenoid plunger, the rich limit stop and the solenoid adjusting screw.

10. Using the GM Adjustment tool No. J–28696–10, BT–7928 or equivalent, turn the adjusting screw clockwise (counting the exact number of turns from Step 7) until the solenoid bottoms against the float bowl.

11. To install the air horn, use a new gasket and reverse the removal procedures. Start the engine and check the dwell at 3000 rpm.

12. To set the engine for dwell inspection, perform the following procedures:

    a. Disconnect and plug the vacuum line-to-canister purge valve.

    b. Ground the diagnostic test terminal.

    c. Attach a dwell meter to the engine.

    d. Operate the engine until normal operating temperature is established; the upper radiator hose is Hot.

13. To inspect the dwell, operate the engine at 3,000 rpm and check for the following conditions:

    a. If the dwell is 10–50° the mixture control solenoid adjustment is complete.

    b. If the dwell is greater than 50°, check the carburetor for a rich condition.

    c. If the dwell is less than 10°, check for vacuum leaks or a lean operating carburetor.

REMOVAL AND INSTALLATION

Carburetor

1. Raise the hood. From inside the vehicle, remove the engine cover.

2. Disconnect the negative battery terminal from the battery.

3. Remove the air cleaner and the accelerator linkage.

4. If equipped with an AT, remove the detent cable from the carburetor.

5. Disconnect the cruise control, if equipped.

6. Label and disconnect all of the necessary vacuum lines.

7. Place a shop cloth under the fuel line-to-carburetor connection and disconnect the fuel line from the carburetor; the cloth will catch the excess fuel.

8. Label and disconnect all of the necessary electrical connections.

9. Remove the carburetor-to-intake manifold bolts, the carburetor and the gasket (discard it).

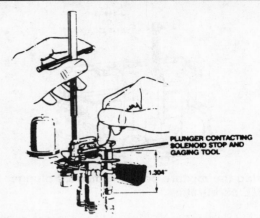

Adjusting the mixture control solenoid screw

To install:

1. Use a new carburetor-to-intake manifold gasket and install the carburetor onto the manifold. Torque the carburetor-to-intake manifold bolts to 84 inch lbs. (9.5 Nm) [long] or 132 inch lbs. (14 Nm) [short].

2. Connect all of the necessary electrical connections.

3. Place a shop cloth under the fuel line-to-carburetor connection and connect the fuel line to the carburetor; the cloth will catch the excess fuel.

4. Connect all of the necessary vacuum lines.

5. Connect the cruise control, if equipped.

6. If equipped with an AT, install the detent cable to the carburetor.

7. Install the accelerator linkage and air cleaner.

8. Connect the negative battery terminal to the battery.

9. Install the engine cover and lower the hood.

10. Start the engine and check for leaks and proper operation.

Throttle Position Sensor (TPS)

1. Disconnect the negative battery terminal from the battery, then the mixture control solenoid, the throttle position sensor and the idle speed solenoid connectors from the carburetor.

2. At the air horn, remove the following items by performing the following procedures:

    a. Remove the idle speed solenoid-to-air horn screws and the solenoid.

    b. Remove the choke lever-to-choke shaft screw, rotate the upper choke lever and remove the choke rod from the slot in the lever.

    c. To remove the choke rod from the lower lever (inside the float bowl casting), use a small screwdriver to hold the lower lever outward and twist the rod counterclockwise.

    d. Remove the fuel pump link from the pump lever; DO NOT remove the pump link from the air horn.

    e. From the front of the float bowl, remove the front vacuum break hose from the tube.

    f. Remove the air horn-to-fuel bowl screws and lift the air horn straight up from the float bowl; discard the gasket.

NOTE: When removing the air horn-to-float bowl screws, be sure to remove the 2 countersunk screws located next to the venturi.

3. To remove the throttle position solenoid from the float bowl, perform the following procedures:

    a. Using a flat tool or a piece of metal, lay it across the float bowl to protect the gasket sealing surface.

    b. Using a small prybar, lightly depress the throttle position solenoid sensor and hold against the spring tension.

    c. Using a small chisel, pry upward (against the bowl staking) to remove the staking.

NOTE: When removing the bowl staking, be sure to apply prying force against the metal piece and not the bowl casting.

d. Pushing up on the bottom of the throttle position solenoid electrical connector, remove it and the connector assembly from the fuel bowl.

To install:

1. Install the throttle position solenoid/connector assembly, align the groove in the electrical connector with the slot in the float bowl casting. Push down on the assembly so that the connector and wires are located below the bowl casting surface; be sure the green throttle position solenoid actuator plunger is aligned in the air horn.

2. Install the air horn, hold the pump plunger assembly down against the return spring tension. Align the pump plunger stem with the hole in the gasket and the gasket over the throttle position solenoid plunger, the solenoid plunger return spring, the metering rods, the solenoid mounting screws and the electrical connector. Use the two dowel locating pins (on the float bowl) to align the gasket.

3. While holding the solenoid metering rod plunger, the air horn gasket and the pump plunger assembly, align the slot in the end of the plunger with the solenoid mounting screw.

4. While lowering the air horn assembly (carefully) onto the float bowl, position the throttle position solenoid adjustment lever of the throttle position solenoid sensor and guide the pump plunger stem through the air horn casting seal.

NOTE: To ease the installation of the air horn onto the float bowl, insert a thin screwdriver between the air horn gasket and the float bowl to raise the throttle position solenoid adjustment lever while positioning it over the throttle position solenoid sensor.

5. Install the air horn-to-float bowl screws and tighten all of the screws evenly, using the torquing sequence.

6. Reconnect all of the vacuum and electrical connectors. Clear the trouble code from the ECM memory. Check and/or adjust the throttle position solenoid voltage.

7. Connect the negative battery cable, start the engine, check for leaks and proper operation.

Mixture Control Solenoid

NOTE: The following procedure requires the use of GM Solenoid Adjusting tool No. J–28696–1 or equivalent.

1. Disconnect the negative battery terminal from the battery, then the mixture control solenoid and the Throttle Position Sensor (TPS) electrical connectors from the carburetor.

2. Remove the air horn, by performing the following procedures:

a. Remove the choke lever-to-choke shaft screw, rotate the

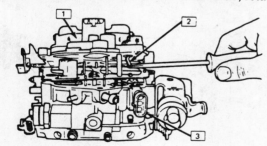

1. Air horn
2. TPS adjustment lever
3. TPS electrical connector

Using a suitable tool to install the air horn onto the float bowl — E4ME carburetor

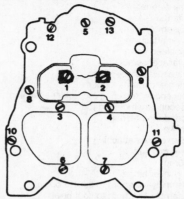

Air horn torquing sequence — E4ME carburetor

upper choke lever and remove the choke rod from the slot in the lever.

b. To remove the choke rod from the lower lever (inside the float bowl casting), use a small screwdriver to hold the lower lever outward and twist the rod counterclockwise.

c. Remove the fuel pump link from the pump lever; DO NOT remove the pump link from the air horn.

d. From the front of the float bowl, remove the front vacuum break hose from the tube.

e. Remove the air horn-to-fuel bowl screws and lift the air horn straight up from the float bowl; discard the gasket.

NOTE: When removing the air horn-to-float bowl screws, be sure to remove the 2 countersunk screws located next to the venturi.

f. Lift the air horn straight up from the float bowl.

3. Using the GM Solenoid Adjusting tool No. J–28696–1 or equivalent, remove the mixture control solenoid adjusting screw.

4. Lift the air horn-to-float bowl gasket from the dowel locating pins and discard it.

5. Remove the plastic filler block from over the float bowl.

6. Lift (carefully) each metering rod from the guided metering jet; be sure to remove the return spring with each rod.

7. Remove the mixture control solenoid-to-float bowl screw, then lift the solenoid and the connector assembly from the float bowl.

NOTE: If a new mixture control solenoid package is being installed, the solenoid and the plunger MUST BE installed as a matched set.

8. When installing the mixture control solenoid, perform the following procedures:

a. Align the solenoid's pin with the hole in the raised boss at the bottom of the float bowl.

b. Align the wires of the solenoid's connector in the bowl slot or the plastic insert (if used).

c. Install the solenoid-to-fuel bowl mounting screw and engage the first six screw threads (to assure proper thread engagement).

9. To complete the installation, use a new gasket and reverse the removal procedures. Calibrate the mixture control solenoid plunger.

Carburetor Overhaul

Efficient carburetion depends greatly on careful cleaning and inspection during overhaul, since dirt, gum, water or varnish in or on the carburetor parts are often responsible for poor performance.

Overhaul your carburetor in a clean, dust-free area. Carefully

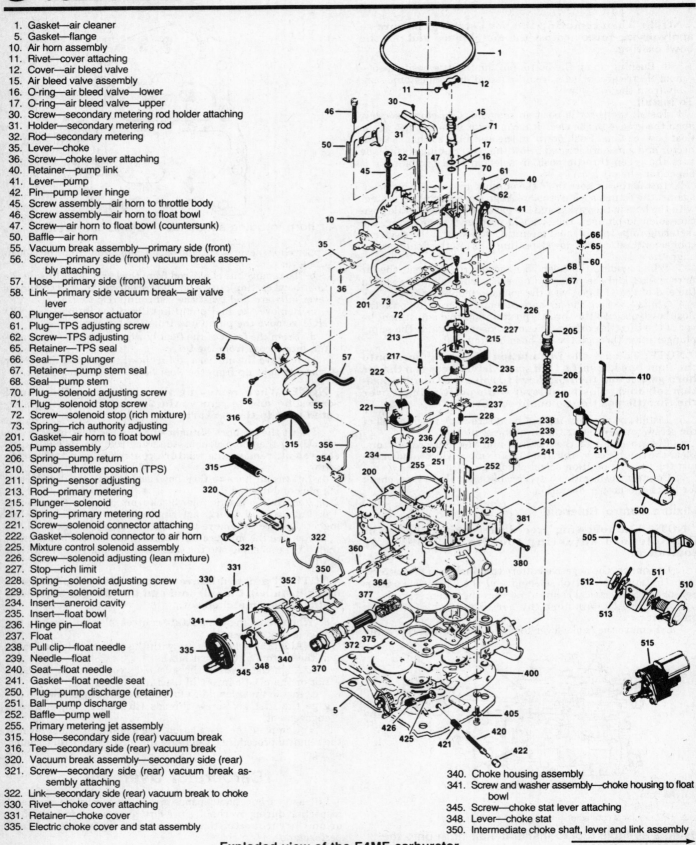

1. Gasket—air cleaner
5. Gasket—flange
10. Air horn assembly
11. Rivet—cover attaching
12. Cover—air bleed valve
15. Air bleed valve assembly
16. O-ring—air bleed valve—lower
17. O-ring—air bleed valve—upper
30. Screw—secondary metering rod holder attaching
31. Holder—secondary metering rod
32. Rod—secondary metering
35. Lever—choke
36. Screw—choke lever attaching
40. Retainer—pump link
41. Lever—pump
42. Pin—pump lever hinge
45. Screw assembly—air horn to throttle body
46. Screw assembly—air horn to float bowl
47. Screw—air horn to float bowl (countersunk)
50. Baffle—air horn
55. Vacuum break assembly—primary side (front)
56. Screw—primary side (front) vacuum break assembly attaching
57. Hose—primary side (front) vacuum break
58. Link—primary side vacuum break—air valve lever
60. Plunger—sensor actuator
61. Plug—TPS adjusting screw
62. Screw—TPS adjusting
65. Retainer—TPS seal
66. Seal—TPS plunger
67. Retainer—pump stem seal
68. Seal—pump stem
70. Plug—solenoid adjusting screw
71. Plug—solenoid stop screw
72. Screw—solenoid stop (rich mixture)
73. Spring—rich authority adjusting
201. Gasket—air horn to float bowl
205. Pump assembly
206. Spring—pump return
210. Sensor—throttle position (TPS)
211. Spring—sensor adjusting
213. Rod—primary metering
215. Plunger—solenoid
217. Spring—primary metering rod
221. Screw—solenoid connector attaching
222. Gasket—solenoid connector to air horn
225. Mixture control solenoid assembly
226. Screw—solenoid adjusting (lean mixture)
227. Stop—rich limit
228. Spring—solenoid adjusting screw
229. Spring—solenoid return
234. Insert—aneroid cavity
235. Insert—float bowl
236. Hinge pin—float
237. Float
238. Pull clip—float needle
239. Needle—float
240. Seat—float needle
241. Gasket—float needle seat
250. Plug—pump discharge (retainer)
251. Ball—pump discharge
252. Baffle—pump well
255. Primary metering jet assembly
315. Hose—secondary side (rear) vacuum break
316. Tee—secondary side (rear) vacuum break
320. Vacuum break assembly—secondary side (rear)
321. Screw—secondary side (rear) vacuum break assembly attaching
322. Link—secondary side (rear) vacuum break to choke
330. Rivet—choke cover attaching
331. Retainer—choke cover
335. Electric choke cover and stat assembly
340. Choke housing assembly
341. Screw and washer assembly—choke housing to float bowl
345. Screw—choke stat lever attaching
348. Lever—choke stat
350. Intermediate choke shaft, lever and link assembly

Exploded view of the E4ME carburetor

352. Fast idle cam assembly
354. Lever—intermediate choke
356. Link—choke
360. Lever—secondary throttle lockout
364. Seal—intermediate choke shaft
370. Nut—fuel inlet
372. Gasket—fuel inlet nut
375. Filter—fuel inlet
377. Spring—fuel filter
380. Screw—throttle stop

381. Spring—throttle stop screw
400. Throttle body assembly
401. Gasket—float bowl to throttle body
405. Screw assembly—float bowl to throttle body
410. Link—pump
420. Needle—idle mixture
421. Spring—idle mixture needle
422. Plug—idle mixture needle
425. Screw—fast idle adjusting

426. Spring—fast idle adjusting screw
500. Solenoid and bracket assembly
501. Screw—bracket attaching
505. Bracket—solenoid
510. Throttle kicker assembly
511. Bracket—throttle kicker
512. Nut—throttle kicker assembly attaching
513. Washer—tab locking
515. Idle speed control assembly

disassemble the carburetor, referring often to the exploded views and directions packaged with the rebuilding kit. Keep all similar and look-alike parts segregated during disassembly and cleaning to avoid accidental interchange during assembly. Make a note of all jet sizes.

When the carburetor is disassembled, wash all parts (except diaphragms, electric choke units, solenoids, pump plunger and any other plastic, leather, fiber or rubber parts) in clean carburetor solvent. DO NOT leave the parts in the solvent any longer than is necessary to sufficiently loosen the deposits. Excessive cleaning may remove the special finish from the float bowl and choke valve bodies, leaving these parts unfit for service. Rinse all parts in clean solvent and blow them dry with compressed air or allow them to air dry. Wipe clean all cork, plastic, leather and fiber parts with a clean, lint-free cloth.

Blow out all passages and jets with compressed air and be sure that there are no restrictions or blockages. Never use wire or similar tools to clean the jets, fuel passages or air bleeds. Clean all jets and valves separately to avoid accidental interchange.

Check all parts for wear or damage. If wear or damage is found, replace the defective parts. Especially check the following:

1. Check the float needle and seat for wear. If wear is found, replace the complete assembly.

2. Check the float hinge pin for wear and the float(s) for dents or distortion. Replace the float if fuel has leaked into it.

3. Check the throttle and choke shaft bores for wear or an out-of-round condition. Damage or wear to the throttle arm, shaft or shaft bore will often require replacement of the throttle body. These parts require a close fitting tolerance; wear may allow air leakage, which could affect starting and idling.

NOTE: Throttle shafts and bushings are not included in overhaul kits. They can be purchased separately.

4. Inspect the idle mixture adjusting needles for burrs or grooves. Any such condition requires replacement of the needle, since you will not be able to obtain a satisfactory idle.

5. Test the accelerator pump check valves. They should pass air one way but not the other. Test for proper seating by blowing and sucking on the valve. Replace the valve check ball and spring as necessary. If the valve is satisfactory, wash the valve parts again to remove breath moisture.

6. Check the bowl cover for warped surfaces with a straightedge.

7. Closely inspect the accelerator pump plunger for wear and damage, replacing as necessary.

8. After the carburetor is assembled, check the choke valve for freedom of operation.

Carburetor overhaul kits are recommended for each overhaul. These kits contain all gaskets and new parts to replace those which deteriorate most rapidly. Failure to replace all parts supplied with the kit (especially gaskets) can result in poor performance later.

Some carburetor manufacturers supply overhaul kits of three basic types: minor repair, major repair and gasket kits. Basically, they contain the following:

Minor Repair Kits:
- All gaskets
- Float needle valve
- All diagrams
- Spring for the pump diaphragm

Major Repair Kits:
- All jets and gaskets
- All diaphragms
- Float needle valve
- Pump ball valve
- Float
- Complete intermediate rod
- Intermediate pump lever
- Some cover holddown screws and washers

Gasket Kits:
- All gaskets

After cleaning and checking all components, reassembly the carburetor, using new parts and referring to the exploded view. When reassembling, make sure that all screws and jets are tight in their seats but DO NOT overtighten, for the tips will be distorted. Tighten all screws gradually, in rotation. DO NOT tighten the needle valves into their seats; uneven jetting will result. Always use new gaskets. Be sure to adjust the float level when reassembling.

DISASSEMBLY

Idle Speed Solenoid Removal

Remove the attaching screws, then remove the Idle Speed Solenoid. The Idle Speed Solenoid should not be immersed in any carburetor cleaner, and should always be removed before complete carburetor overhaul, as carburetor cleaner will damage the internal components.

Idle Mixture Needle Plug Removal

1. Use hacksaw to make two parallel cuts in the throttle body, one on each side of the locator points near one idle mixture needle plug. The distance between the cuts will depend on the size of the punch to be used. Cuts should reach down to the steel plug, but should but extend more than 1/8 in. (3mm) beyond the locator points.

2. Place a flat punch at a point near the ends of the saw marks in the throttle body. Hold the punch at a 45° angle, and drive it into the throttle body until the casting breaks away, exposing the hardened steel plug. The plug will break, rather than remaining intact. Remove all the loose pieces.

3. Repeat the procedure for the other idle mixture needle plug.

Idle Air Bleed Valve Removal

1. Cover internal bowl vents and air inlets to the bleed valve with masking tape.

2. Carefully align a 7/64 in. drill bit on rivet head. Drill only

enough to remove head of each rivet holding the idle air bleed valve cover.

3. Use a suitably sized punch to drive out the remainder of the rivet from the castings. Repeat procedure with other rivet.

—————————— CAUTION ——————————

For the next operation, safety glasses must be worn to protect eyes from possible metal shaving damage.

4. Lift off cover and remove any pieces of rivet still inside tower. Use shop air to blow out any remaining chips.

5. Remove idle air bleed valve from the air horn.

6. Remove and discard O-ring seals from valve. New O-ring seals are required for reassembly. The idle air bleed valve is serviced as a complete assembly only.

Air Horn Removal

1. Remove upper choke lever from the end of choke shaft by removing retaining screw. Rotate upper choke lever to remove choke rod from slot in lever.

2. Remove choke rod from lower lever inside the float bowl casting. Remove rod by holding lower lever outward with small screwdriver and twisting rod counterclockwise.

3. Remove secondary metering rods by removing the small screw in the top of the metering rod hanger. Lift upward on the metering rod hanger until the secondary metering rods are completely out of the air horn. Metering rods may be disassembled from the hanger by rotating the ends out of the holes in the end of the hanger.

4. Remove pump link retainer and remove link from pump lever.

NOTE: Do not attempt to remove the lever, as damage to the air horn could result.

5. Remove front vacuum break hose from tube on float bowl.

6. Remove eleven air horn-to-bowl screws; then remove the two countersunk attaching screws located next to the venturi. If used, remove secondary air baffle deflector from beneath the two center air horn screws.

7. Remove air horn from float bowl by lifting it straight up. The air horn gasket should remain on the float bowl for removal later.

NOTE: When removing air horn from float bowl, use care to prevent damaging the mixture control solenoid connector, Throttle Position Sensor (TPS) adjustment lever, and the small tubes protruding from the air horn. These tubes are permanently pressed into the air horn casting. DO NOT remove them.

8. Remove front vacuum break bracket attaching screws. The vacuum break assembly may now be removed from the air valve dashpot rod, and the dashpot rod from the air valve lever.

NOTE: Do not place vacuum break assembly in carburetor cleaner, as damage to vacuum break will occur.

9. Remove Throttle Position Sensor (TPS) plunger by pushing plunger down through seal in air horn.

10. Remove the throttle position solenoid seal and pump plunger stem seal by inverting air horn and using a small screwdriver to remove staking holding seal retainers in place. Remove and discard retainers and seals.

NOTE: Use care in removing the throttle position solenoid plunger seal retainer and pump plunger stem seal retainer to prevent damage to air horn casting. New seals and retainers are required for reassembly.

11. Invert air horn, and use Tool J-28696-4, BT-7967A, or equivalent, to remove rich mixture stop screw and spring.

12. Use a suitable punch to drive the lean mixture screw plug and rich mixture stop screw plug out of the air horn. Discard the plugs.

13. Further disassembly of the air horn is not required for cleaning purposes.

The choke valve and choke valve screws, the air valves and air valve shaft should not be removed. However, if it is necessary to replace the air valve closing springs or center plastic eccentric cam, a repair kit is available. Instructions for assembly are included in the repair kit.

Float Bowl Disassembly

The following special tools, or their equivalents, will be necessary for this procedure: J-28696-10, BT-7928, J-22769, BT-3006M, J-28696-4, and BT-7928.

1. Remove solenoid metering rod plunger by lifting straight up.

2. Remove air horn gasket by lifting it from the dowel locating pins on float bowl. Discard gasket.

3. Remove pump plunger from pump well.

4. Remove staking holding Throttle Position Sensor (TPS) in bowl as follows:

   a. Lay a flat tool or metal piece across bowl casting to protect gasket sealing surface.

   b. Use a small screwdriver to depress throttle position solenoid sensor lightly and hold against spring tension.

   c. Observing safety precautions, pry upward with a small chisel or equivalent to remove bowl staking, making sure prying force is exerted against the metal piece and not against the bowl casting. Use care not to damage the throttle position solenoid sensor.

   d. Push up from bottom on electrical connector and remove throttle position solenoid and connector assembly from bowl. Use care in removing sensor and connector assembly to prevent damage to this critical electrical part.

   e. Remove spring from bottom of throttle position solenoid well in float bowl.

5. Remove plastic bowl insert from float bowl.

6. Carefully lift each metering rod out of the guided metering jet, checking to be sure the return spring is removed with each metering rod.

NOTE: Use extreme care when handling these critical parts to avoid damage to the metering rod and spring.

7. Remove the mixture control solenoid from the float bowl as follows:

   a. Remove screw attaching solenoid connector to float bowl. Do not remove solenoid connector from float bowl until called for in text.

   b. Use Tool J-28696-10, BT-7928, or equivalent, to remove lean mixture (solenoid) screw. Do not remove plunger return spring or connector and wires from the solenoid body. The mixture control solenoid, with plunger and connector, is only serviced as a complete assembly.

   c. Remove rubber gasket from top of solenoid connector and discard.

   d. Remove solenoid screw tension spring (next to float hanger pin).

8. Remove float assembly and float needle by pulling up on retaining pin. Remove needle and seat and gasket using set remover Tool J-22769, BT-3006M, or equivalent.

9. Remove large mixture control solenoid tension spring from boss on bottom of float bowl located between guided metering jets.

10. If necessary, remove the primary main metering jets using special Tool J-28696-4, BT-7928, or equivalent.

NOTE: Use care installing tool on jet, to prevent damage to the metering rod guide (upper area), and locating tool over vertical float sections on lower area of jet. Also, no attempt should be made to remove the second-

ary metering jets (metering orifice plates). These jets are fixed and, if damaged, entire bowl replacement is required.

11. Remove pump discharge check ball retainer and turn bowl upside down, catching discharge ball as if falls.
12. Remove secondary air baffle, if replaced is required.
13. Remove pump well fill slot baffle only if necessary.

Choke Disassembly

Special tools J–9789–118, BT–30–15, or their equivalents, will be necessary for this procedure.

The tamper-resistant choke cover is used to discourage unnecessary readjustment of the choke thermostatic cover and coil assembly. However, if it is necessary to remove the cover and coil assembly during normal carburetor disassembly for cleaning and normal carburetor disassembly for cleaning and overhaul, the procedures below should be followed.

1. Support float bowl and throttle body, as an assembly, on a suitable holding fixture such as Tool J–9789–118, BT–30–15, or equivalent.
2. Carefully align a $\frac{5}{32}$ in. drill bit on the rivet head and drill only enough to remove the rivet head. Drill the two remaining rivet heads, then use a drift and small hammer to drive the remainder of the rivets out of the choke housing.

NOTE: Use care in drilling to prevent damage to the choke cover or housing.

3. Remove the two conventional retainers, retainer with tab, and choke cover assembly from choke housing.
4. Remove choke housing assembly from float bowl by removing retaining screw and washer inside the choke housing. The complete choke assembly can be removed from the float bowl by sliding outward.
5. Remove secondary throttle valve lock-out lever from float bowl.
6. Remove lower choke lever from inside float bowl cavity by inverting bowl.
7. To disassemble intermediate choke shaft from choke housing, remove coil lever retaining screw at end of shaft inside the choke housing. Remove thermostatic coil lever from flats on intermediate choke shaft.
8. Remove intermediate choke shaft from the choke housing by sliding it outward. The fast idle cam can now be removed from the intermediate choke shaft. Remove the cup seal from the float bowl cleaning purposes. DO NOT ATTEMPT TO REMOVE THE INSERT!
9. Remove fuel inlet nut, gasket, check valve, filter assembly and spring. Discard Check valve filter assembly and gasket.
10. Remove three throttle body-to-bowl attaching screws and lockwashers and remove throttle body assembly.
11. Remove throttle body-to-bowl insulator gasket.

Throttle Body Disassembly

Special tools J–29030–B and BT–7610B, or their equivalents, will be necessary for this procedure.

Place throttle body assembly on carburetor holding fixture to avoid damage to throttle valves.

1. Remove pump rod from the throttle lever by rotating the rod until the tang on the rod aligns with the slot in the lever.
2. Use Tool J–29030–B, BT–7610B, or equivalent, to remove idle mixture needles for thorough throttle body cleaning.
3. Further disassembly of the throttle body is not required for cleaning purposes. The throttle valve screws are permanently staked in place and should not be removed. The throttle body is serviced as a complete assembly.

ASSEMBLY

The following special tools, or their equivalents, will be

necessary for this procedure: J–29030–B, BT–7610B, J–9789–118, BT–30–15, J–23417, BT–6911, J–28696–4, J–22769, BT–3006M, J–33815–1, BT–8253–A, J–28696–10, and BT–7928.

1. Install the lower end of the pump rod in the throttle lever by aligning the tang on the rod with the slot in the lever. The end of the rod should point outward toward the throttle lever.
2. Install idle mixture needles and springs using Tool J–29030–B, BT–7610B, or equivalent. Lightly seat each needle and then turn counterclockwise the number of specified turns, the final idle mixture adjustment is made on the vehicle.
3. If a new float bowl assembly is used, stamp or engrave the model number on the new float bowl. Install new throttle body-to-bowl insulator gasket over two locating dowels on bowl.
4. Install throttle body making certain throttle body is properly located over dowels on float bowl. Install three throttle body-to-bowl screws and lockwashers and tighten evenly and securely.
5. Place carburetor on proper holding fixture such as J–9789–118, BT–30–15 or equivalent.
6. Install fuel inlet filter spring, a new check valve filter assembly, new gasket and inlet nut. Tighten nut to 18 ft. lbs. (24 Nm).

NOTE: When installing a service replacement filter, make sure the filter is the type that includes the check valve to meet government safety standard. New service replacement filters with check valve meet this requirement. When properly installed, the hole in the filter faces toward the inlet nut. Ribs on the closed end of the filter element prevent it from being installed incorrectly, unless forced. Tightening beyond the specified torque can damage the nylon gasket.

7. Install a new cup seal into the insert on the side of the float bowl for the intermediate choke shaft. The lip on the cup seal faces outward.
8. Install the secondary throttle valve lock-out lever on the boss of the float bowl, with the recess hole in the lever facing inward.
9. Install the fast idle cam on the intermediate choke shaft (steps on cam face downward).
10. Carefully install fast idle cam and intermediate choke shaft assembly in the choke housing. Install the thermostatic coil lever on the flats on the intermediate choke shaft. Inside thermostatic choke coil lever is properly aligned when both inside and outside levers face toward the fuel inlet. Install inside lever retaining screw into the end of the intermediate choke shaft.
11. Install lower choke rod (inner) lever into cavity in float bowl.
12. Install choke housing to bowl, sliding intermediate choke shaft into lower (inner) lever. Tool J–23417, BT–6911 or equivalent, can be used to hold the lower choke lever in correct position while installing the choke housing. The intermediate choke shaft lever and fast idle cam are in correct position when the tang on lever is beneath the fast idle cam.
13. Install choke housing retaining screws and washers. Check linkage for freedom of movement. Do not install choke cover and coil assembly until inside coil lever is adjusted.
14. If removed, install air baffle in secondary side of float bowl with notches toward the top. Top edge of baffle must be flush with bowl casting.
15. If removed, install baffle inside of the pump well with slot toward the bottom.
16. Install pump discharge check ball and retainer screw in the passage next to the pump well.
17. If removed, carefully install primary main metering jets in bottom of float bowl using or Tool J–28696–4, BT–7928, equivalent.

NOTE: Use care in installing jets to prevent damage to metering rod guide.

18. Install large mixture control solenoid tension spring over boss on bottom of float bowl.

19. Install needle seat assembly, with gasket, using seat installer J–22769, BT–3006M, or equivalent.

20. To make adjustment easier, carefully bend float arm before assembly.

21. Install float needle onto float arm by sliding float lever under needle pull clip. Proper installation of the needle pull clip is to hook the clip over the edge of the float on the float arm facing the float pontoon.

22. Install float hinge pin into float arm with end of loop of pin facing pump well. Install float assembly by aligning needle in the seat, and float hinge pin into locating channels in float bowl. DO NOT install float needle pull clip into holes in float arm.

23. Make a float level adjustment as necessary.

24. Install mixture control solenoid screw tension spring between raised bosses next to float hanger pin.

25. Install mixture control solenoid and connector assembly as follows:

    a. Install new rubber gasket on top of solenoid connector.

    b. Install solenoid carefully in the float chamber, aligning pin on end of solenoid with hole in raised boss at bottom of bowl. Align solenoid connector wires to fit in slot in bowl.

    c. Install lean mixture (solenoid) screw through hole in solenoid bracket and tension spring in bowl, engaging first six screw threads to assure proper thread engagement.

    d. Install mixture control solenoid gauging Tool J–33815–1, BT–8253–A, or equivalent over the throttle side metering jet rod guide, and temporarily install solenoid plunger.

    e. Holding the solenoid plunger against the Solenoid Stop, use Tool J–28696–10, BT–7928, or equivalent, to turn the lean mixture (solenoid) screw slowly clockwise, until the solenoid plunger just contacts the gauging tool. The adjustment is correct when the solenoid plunger is contacting BOTH the Solenoid Stop and the Gauging Tool.

    f. Remove solenoid plunger and gauging tool.

26. Install connector attaching screw, but DO NOT overtighten, as that could cause damage to the connector.

27. Install Throttle Position Sensor return spring in bottom of well in float bowl.

28. Install Throttle Position Sensor and connector assembly in float bowl by aligning groove in electrical connector with slot in float bowl casting. Push down on connector and sensor assembly so that connector and wires are located below bowl casting surface.

29. Install plastic bowl insert over float valve, pressing downward until properly seated (flush with bowl casting surface).

30. Slide metering rod return spring over metering rod tip until small end of spring stops against shoulder on rod. Carefully install metering rod and spring assembly through holding in plastic bowl insert and gently lower the metering rod into the guided metering jet, until large end of spring seats on the recess on end of jet guide.

CAUTION

Do not force metering rod down in jet. Use extreme care when handling these critical parts to avoid damage to rod and spring. if service replacement metering rods, springs and jets are installed, they must be installed in matched sets.

31. Install pump return spring in pump well.

32. Install pump plunger assembly in pump well.

33. Holding down on pump plunger assembly against return spring tension, install air horn gasket by aligning pump plunger stem with hole in gasket, and aligning holes in gasket over throttle position solenoid plunger, solenoid plunger return spring metering rods, solenoid attaching screw and electrical connector. Position gasket over the two dowel locating pins on the float bowl.

34. Holding down on air horn gasket and pump plunger assembly, install the solenoid-metering rod plunger in the solenoid, aligning slot in end of plunger with solenoid attaching screw. Be sure plunger arms engage top of each metering.

35. If a service replacement Mixture Control Solenoid package is installed, the solenoid and plunger MUST be installed as a matched set.

Air Horn Assembly

The following special tools, or their equivalents, will be necessary for this procdure: J–28696–10, J–2869–4, BT–7967A, J–34935–1, BT–8420A, BT–7928, J–33815–2, and BT–8353B.

1. If removed, install the throttle position solenoid adjustment screw in the air horn using Tool J–28696–10, BT–7967A, or equivalent. Final adjustment of the Throttle Position Sensor is made on the vehicle.

2. Inspect the air valve shaft pin for lubrication. Apply a liberal quantity of lithium base grease to the air valve shaft pin, especially in the area contacted by the air valve spring.

3. Install new pump plunger and throttle position solenoid plunger seals and retainers in air horn casting. The lip on the seal faces outward, away from the air horn mounting surface. Lightly stake seal retainer in three places, choosing locations different from the original stakings.

4. Install rich mixture stop screw and rich authority adjusting spring from bottom side of the air horn. Use Tool J–2869–4, BT–7967A, or equivalent, to bottom the stop screw lightly, then back out ¼ turn. Final adjustment procedure will be covered later in this section.

5. Install throttle position solenoid actuator plunger in the seal.

6. Carefully lower the air horn assembly onto the float bowl while positioning the throttle position solenoid adjustment lever over the throttle position solenoid sensor and guiding pump plunger stem through the seal in the air horn casting. To ease installation, insert a thin screwdriver between the air horn gasket and float bowl to raise the throttle position solenoid adjustment lever, positioning it over the throttle position solenoid sensor.

7. Make sure that the bleed tubes and accelerating well tubes are positioned properly through the holes in the air horn gasket. Do not force the air horn assembly onto the bowl, but lower it lightly into place over the two dowel locating pins.

8. Install two long air horn screws and lockwashers, nine short screws and lockwashers and two countersunk screws located next to the carburetor venturi area. Install secondary air baffle beneath the No. 3 and 4 screws. Tighten all screws evenly and securely.

9. Install air valve rod into slot in the lever on the end of the air valve shaft. Install the other end of the rod in hole in front vacuum break plunger. Install front vacuum break and bracket assembly on the air horn, using two attaching screws. Tighten screw securely. Connect pump link to pump lever and install retainer.

NOTE: Use care installing the roll pin to prevent damage to the pump lever bearing surface and casting bosses.

10. Install two secondary metering rods into the secondary metering rod hanger (upper end of rods point toward each other). Install secondary metering rod holder, with rods, onto air valve cam follower. Install retaining screw and tighten securely. Work air valves up and down several times to make sure they remove freely in both directions.

11. Connect choke rod into lower choke lever inside bowl cavity. Install choke rod in slot in upper choke lever, and position lever on end of choke shaft, making sure flats on end of shaft align

with flats in lever. Install attaching screw and tighten securely. When properly installed, the number on the lever will face outward.

12. Adjust the rich mixture stop screw:

a. Insert external float gauging Tool J–34935–1, BT–8420A, or equivalent, in the vertical D-shaped vent hole in the air horn casting (next to the idle air bleed valve) and allow it to float freely.

b. Read (at eye level) the mark on the gauge, in inches, that lines up with the tip of the air horn casting.

c. Lightly press down on gauge, and again read and record the mark on the gauge that lines up with the top of the air horn casting.

d. Subtract gauge UP dimension, found in Step b, from gauge DOWN dimension, found in Step c, and record the difference in inches. This difference in dimension is the total solenoid plunger travel.

e. Insert Tool J–28696–10, BT–7928, or equivalent, in the access hole in the air horn, and adjust the rich mixture stop screw to obtain 1/8 in. (3mm) total solenoid plunger travel.

13. With the solenoid plunger travel correctly set, install the plugs supplied in the service kit into the air horn to retain the setting and prevent fuel vapor loss:

a. Install the plug, hollow end down, into the access hole to the lean mixture (solenoid) screw and use a suitably sized punch to drive the plug into the air horn until top of plug is even with the lower edge of the hole chamber.

b. In a similar manner, install the plug over the rich mixture screw access hole and drive the plug into place so that the tip of the plug is 1/16 in. (1.5mm) below the surface of the air horn casting.

14. Install the Idle Air Bleed Valve as follows:

a. Lightly coat two new O-ring seals with automatic transmission fluid, to aid in their installation on the idle air bleed valve body. The thick seal goes in the upper groove and the thin seal goes in the lower groove.

b. Install the idle air bleed valve in the air horn, making sure that there is proper thread engagement.

c. Insert idle air bleed valve gauging Tool J–33815–2, BT–8353B, or equivalent, in throttle side D-shaped vent hole of the air horn casting. The upper end of the tool should be positioned over the open cavity next to the idle air bleed valve.

d. Hold the gauging tool down lightly so that the solenoid plunger is against the solenoid stop, then adjust the idle air bleed valve so that the gauging tool will pivot over and just contact the top of the valve.

e. Remove the gauging tool.

f. The final adjustment of the idle air bleed valve is made on the vehicle to obtain idle mixture control.

15. Perform the Air Valve Spring Adjustment and Choke coil Lever Adjustment as previously described.

16. Install the cover and coil assembly in the choke housing, as follows:

a. Place the cam follower on the highest step of the fast idle cam.

b. Install the thermostatic cover and coil assembly in the choke housing, making sure the coil tang engages the inside coil pickup lever. Ground contact for the electric choke is provided by a metal plate located at the rear of the choke cover assembly. DO NOT install a choke cover gasket between the electric choke assembly and the choke housing.

c. A choke cover retainer kit is required to attach the choke cover to the choke housing. Follow the instructions found in the kit and install the proper retainer and rivets using a suitable blind rivet tool.

d. It may be necessary to use an adapter (tube) if the installing tool interferes with the electrical connector tower on the choke cover.

17. Install the hose on the front vacuum brake and on the tube on the float bowl.

18. Position the idle speed solenoid and bracket assembly on the float bowl, retaining it with two large countersunk screws.

19. Perform the Choke Rod-Fast Idle Cam Adjustment, Primary (Front) Vacuum Break Adjustment, Air Valve Rod Adjustment - Front, Unloader Adjustment and the Secondary Lockout Adjustment as previously described.

20. Reinstall the carburetor on the vehicle with a new flange gasket.

FUEL INJECTION SYSTEM

NOTE: This book contains simple testing and service procedures for for your Van's fuel injection system. More comprehensive testing and diagnosis procedures may be found in CHILTON'S GUIDE TO FUEL INJECTION AND FEEDBACK CARBURETORS, book part number 7488, available at your local retailer.

Electric Fuel Pump

The electric fuel pump is attached to the fuel sending unit, located in the fuel tank.

REMOVAL AND INSTALLATION

NOTE: The following procedure requires the use of the GM Fuel Gauge Sending Unit Retaining Cam tool No. J–24187 or equivalent.

———— CAUTION ————

Before removing any component of the fuel system (TBI models), be sure to reduce the fuel pressure in the system. The pressure regulator (TBI models) contains an orifice in the fuel system; when the engine is turned Off, the pressure in the system will bleed down within a few minutes.

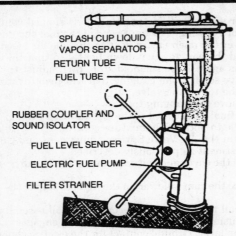

SPLASH CUP LIQUID
VAPOR SEPARATOR
RETURN TUBE
FUEL TUBE

RUBBER COUPLER AND
SOUND ISOLATOR

FUEL LEVEL SENDER
ELECTRIC FUEL PUMP

FILTER STRAINER

TBI fuel pump

1. If the fuel system has been in use, turn the ignition switch Off and allow the system time to reduce the fuel pressure.
2. Disconnect the negative battery terminal from the battery.

NOTE: Be sure to keep a Class B (dry chemical) fire extinguisher nearby.

------------------ CAUTION ------------------
Due to the possibility of fire or explosion, never drain or store gasoline in an open container.

3. Using a hand pump or a siphon hose, drain the gasoline into an approved container.
4. Raise and support the vehicle on jackstands.
5. Support the fuel tank and remove the fuel tank-to-vehicle straps.
6. Lower the tank slightly, then remove the sender unit wires, the hoses and the ground strap.
7. Remove the fuel tank from the vehicle.
8. Using the GM Fuel Gauge Sending Unit Retaining Cam tool No. J–24187 (or equivalent) or a brass drift and a hammer, remove the cam locking ring (fuel sending unit) counterclockwise, then lift the sending unit from the fuel tank.
9. Remove the fuel pump from the fuel sending unit, by performing the following procedures:
   a. Pull the fuel pump up into the mounting tube, while pulling outward (away) from the bottom support.

NOTE: When removing the fuel pump from the sending unit, be careful not to damage the rubber insulator and the strainer.

   b. When the pump assembly is clear of the bottom support, pull it out of the rubber connector.
To install:
1. Inspect the fuel pump hose and bottom sound insulator for signs of deterioration, then replace it, if necessary.
2. Push the fuel pump onto the sending tube.
3. Using a new sending unit-to-fuel tank O-ring, install the sending unit into the fuel tank.

NOTE: When installing the sending unit, be careful not to fold or twist the fuel strainer, for it will restrict the fuel flow.

4. Using the GM Fuel Gauge Sending Unit Retaining Cam tool No. J–24187 (or equivalent) or a brass drift and a hammer, turn the sending unit-to-fuel tank locking ring clockwise.
5. Install the fuel tank, align the insulator strips in install the strap bolts. Torque the inner fuel tank strap-to-vehicle bolts to

26 ft. lbs. (35 Nm) and the outer fuel tank strap-to-vehicle nuts/bolts to 26 ft. lbs. (35 Nm).
6. Connect the fuel lines.
7. Connect the negative battery cable, start the engine and check for leaks.
8. Lower the vehicle.

TESTING AND ADJUSTMENTS

Flow Test

1. Remove the fuel pump-to-throttle body line from the throttle body.
2. Place the fuel line in a clean container.
3. Turn the ignition switch On; approximately ½ pint of the fuel should be delivered in 15 seconds.
4. If the fuel flow is below minimum, inspect the fuel system for restrictions; if no restrictions are found, replace the fuel pump.

Pressure Test

NOTE: The following procedure requires the use of a GM Fuel Pressure Gauge tool No. J–29658–A or equivalent.

1. If equipped with an EFI equipped engine, refer to the Fuel Pressure Relief procedures in this section and relieve the fuel pressure.
2. Remove the air cleaner, then disconnect and plug the THERMAC vacuum port on the throttle body unit.
3. Place a rag (to catch excess fuel) under the fuel line-to-throttle body connection. Disconnect the fuel line from the throttle body.

NOTE: When disconnecting the fuel line, use a back-up wrench to hold the fuel nut on the throttle body.

4. Using a GM Fuel Pressure Gauge tool No. J–29658–A or equivalent, install it into the fuel line.
5. Start the engine and observe the fuel pressure, **the fuel pump pressure should be 9–13 psi (62–90 kPa).**

NOTE: If the fuel pressure does not meet specifications, inspect the fuel system for restrictions or replace the fuel pump.

6. Turn the engine Off, relieve the fuel pressure and remove the GM Fuel Pressure Gauge tool No. J–29658–A or equivalent.
7. Install a new fuel line-to-throttle body O-ring and reverse the removal procedures. Unplug from the THERMAC vacuum port. Start the engine and check for fuel leaks.

Fuel Pump Relay

The fuel pump relay is mounted on the right-side of the engine compartment. Check for loose electrical connections; no other service is possible, except replacement.

REMOVAL AND INSTALLATION

1. Disconnect the negative battery terminal from the battery.
2. Disconnect the relay/electrical connector assembly from the bracket.
3. Pull the fuel pump relay from the electrical connector.

FUEL PRESSURE RELIEF

2.5L Engine

1. From the fuse block, located in the passenger compartment, remove the fuse labeled, Fuel Pump.
2. Start the engine.

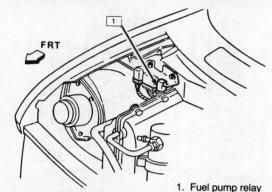

1. Fuel pump relay

Location of the fuel pump relay

NOTE: The engine will start and run, for a short period of time, until the remaining fuel is used up.

3. Engage the starter, a few more times, to relieve any remaining pressure.

4. Turn the ignition switch Off and install the Fuel Pump fuse into the fuse block.

4.3L EFI Engine

Allow the engine to set for 5–10 minutes; this will allow the orifice (in the fuel system) to bleed off the pressure.

Throttle Body

The Model 300 throttle body, used on the 2.5L engine (1985–87), is a single barrel, single injector type. The 1988–90 2.5L engine is equipped with a model 700 single barrel, single injector type. The Model 220 throttle body, used on the 4.3L engine (1986–90), is a dual barrel, twin injector type. The operation of all three types are basically the same.

Both throttle bodies are constantly monitored by the ECM to produce a 14.7:1 air/fuel ratio, which is vital to the catalytic converter operation.

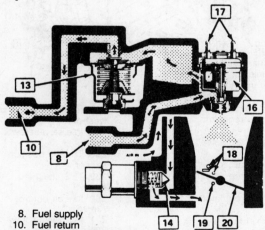

8. Fuel supply
10. Fuel return
13. Pressure regulator (part of fuel meter cover)
14. Idle air control (IAC) valve (shown open)
16. Fuel injector
17. Fuel injector terminals
18. Ported vacuum sources*
19. Manifold vacuum source*
20. Throttle valve

Operation of the TBI unit — model 300

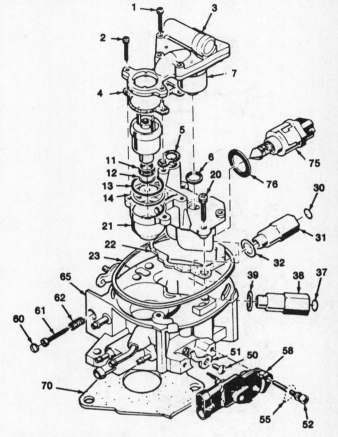

1. Screw & washer assembly—long (3)
2. Screw & washer assembly—short (2)
3. Fuel meter cover assembly
4. Gasket—fuel meter cover
5. Gasket—fuel meter outlet
6. Dust seal—pressure regulator
7. Pressure regulator
11. Filter—fuel injector nozzle
12. Lower "O" ring
13. Upper "O" ring
14. Back-up washer—fuel injector
20. Screw & washer assembly—attaching (3)
21. Fuel meter body assembly
22. Gasket—fuel meter body
23. Gasket—air filter
30. Fuel return line "O" ring
31. Nut—fuel return
32. Gasket—fuel return nut
37. Fuel inlet line "O" ring
38. Nut—fuel inlet
39. Gasket—fuel inlet nut
50. Screw—TPS lever attaching
51. Lever—TPS
52. Screw & washer assembly—attaching
55. Retainer—TPS attaching screw
58. Sensor—throttle position
60. Plug—idle stop screw
61. Screw—throttle stop
62. Spring—throttle stop screw
65. Throttle body assembly
70. Gasket—flange mounting
75. Idle air control assembly
76. Gasket—IAC to throttle body

Exploded view of the Model 300 throttle body — 2.5L engine

REMOVAL AND INSTALLATION

CAUTION

Before removing any component of the fuel system (TBI models), be sure to reduce the fuel pressure in the system. The pressure regulator (TBI models) contains an orifice in the fuel system; when the engine is turned Off, the pressure in the system will bleed down within a few minutes.

1. Refer to the Fuel Pressure Relief procedures in this section and reduce the pressure in the fuel system.

2. Remove the air cleaner. Disconnect the negative battery cable from the battery.

3. Disconnect the electrical connectors from the idle air control valve, the throttle position sensor and the fuel injector(s).

4. Remove the throttle return spring(s), the cruise control (if equipped) and the throttle linkage.

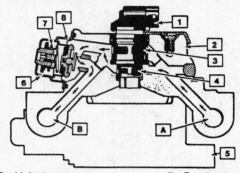

1. Fuel injector
2. Fuel meter assembly
3. Purge filter
4. Inlet filter
5. Throttle body assembly
6. Pressure regulator cover
7. Pressure regulator spring
8. Pressure regulator diaphragm
A. Fuel inlet
B. Fuel outlet

Operation of the TBI unit — model 700

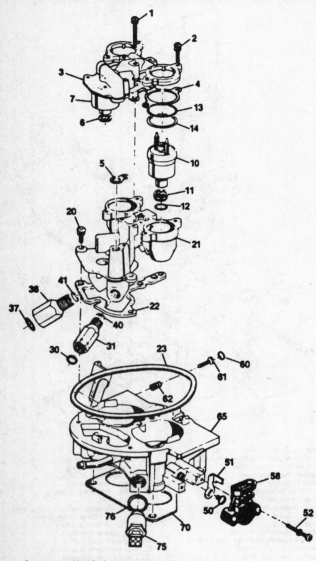

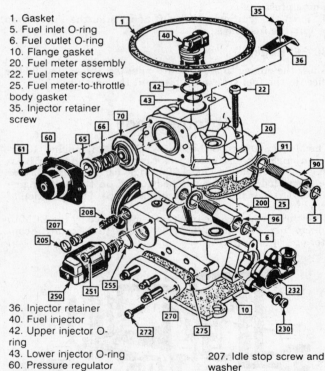

1. Gasket
5. Fuel inlet O-ring
6. Fuel outlet O-ring
10. Flange gasket
20. Fuel meter assembly
22. Fuel meter screws
25. Fuel meter-to-throttle body gasket
35. Injector retainer screw

36. Injector retainer
40. Fuel injector
42. Upper injector O-ring
43. Lower injector O-ring
60. Pressure regulator cover
61. Pressure regulator screw
65. Spring seat
66. Pressure regulator spring
70. Pressure regulator diaphragm
90. Fuel inlet nut
91. Fuel nut seal
96. Fuel outlet nut
200. Throttle body assembly
205. Idle stop screw plug

207. Idle stop screw and washer
208. Idle stop screw spring
230. Throttle position sensor
232. TPS attaching screw
250. Idle air control valve
251. IAC valve screw
255. IAC O-ring
270. Tube module
272. Tube module attaching screw
275. Tube module gasket

1. Screw assembly—fuel meter cover attaching—long
2. Screw assembly—fuel meter cover attaching—short
3. Fuel meter cover assembly
4. Gasket—fuel meter cover
5. Gasket—fuel meter outlet
6. Seal—pressure regulator
7. Pressure regulator
10. Injector—fuel
11. Filter—fuel injector inlet
12. O-ring—fuel injector—lower
13. O-ring—fuel injector—upper
14. Washer—fuel injector
20. Screw assembly—fuel meter body—throttle body attaching
21. Fuel meter body assembly
22. Gasket—throttle body to fuel meter body
23. Gasket—air filter
30. O-ring—fuel return line
31. Nut—fuel outlet
37. O-ring—fuel inlet line
38. Nut—fuel inlet
40. Gasket—fuel outlet nut
41. Gasket—fuel inlet nut
50. Screw—TPS lever attaching
51. Lever—TPS
52. Screw assembly—TPS attaching

58. Sensor—throttle position (TPS)
60. Plug—idle stop screw
61. Screw assembly—idle stop
62. Spring—idle stop screw
65. Throttle body assembly
70. Gasket—flange
75. Valve assembly—idle air control (IAC)
76. Gasket—idle air control valve assembly

Exploded view of the Model 220 throttle body — 4.3L engine

Exploded view of the model 700 throttle body — 2.5L engine

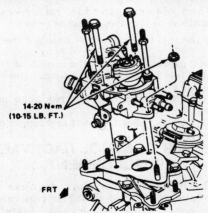

**14-20 N·m
(10-15 LB. FT.)**

FRT

Replacing the throttle body — 2.5L engine (1985–87)

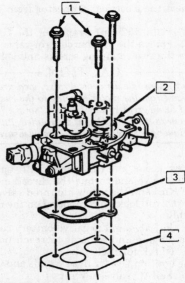

1. Bolt—tighten to 16 N·m (12 ft. lbs.)
2. TBI unit
3. Gasket
4. Engine inlet manifold

Replacing the throttle body — 4.3L engine (1986–90)

5. Label and disconnect the vacuum hoses from the throttle body.
6. Place a rag (to catch the excess fuel) under the fuel line-to-throttle body connection, then disconnect the fuel line from the throttle body.
7. Remove the attaching hardware, the throttle body-to-intake manifold bolts, the throttle body and the gasket.

NOTE: Be sure to place a cloth in the intake manifold to prevent dirt from entering the engine.

8. Using a putty knife (if necessary), clean the gasket mounting surfaces.

To install:
1. Use a new gasket. Install the gasket, throttle body and mounting bolts. Torque the throttle body-to-intake manifold nuts/bolts to 13 ft. lbs. (17 Nm).
2. Connect the fuel lines to the throttle body.
3. Connect the vacuum hoses to the throttle body.
4. Install the throttle return spring(s), the cruise control (if equipped) and the throttle linkage.

5. Depress the accelerator pedal to the floor and release it, to see if the pedal returns freely.
6. Connect the electrical connectors to the idle air control valve, the throttle position sensor and the fuel injector(s).
7. Install the air cleaner. Connect the negative battery cable to the battery.
8. Start the engine, check for leaks and proper operation.

INJECTOR REPLACEMENT

——————— **CAUTION** ———————

When removing the injector(s), be careful not to damage the electrical connector pins (on top of the injector), the injector fuel filter and the nozzle. The fuel injector is serviced as a complete assembly ONLY, it is an electrical component and should not be immersed in any kind of cleaner.

1. Remove the air cleaner. Disconnect the negative battery terminal from the battery.
2. Refer to the Fuel Pressure Relief procedures in this section and relieve the fuel pressure.

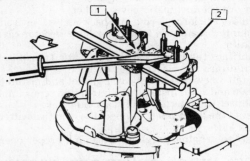

1. Fuel meter cover gasket
2. Removing fuel injector

Using a prybar to remove the fuel injector from the throttle body — 4.3L engine, 2.5L is similar (Model 300 and 220)

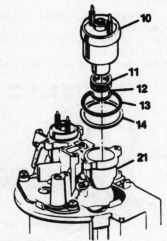

10. Injector—fuel
11. Filter—fuel injector inlet
12. "O" ring—fuel injector—lower
13. "O" ring—fuel injector—upper
14. Washer—fuel injector
21. Fuel meter body assembly

Removing the fuel injector from the throttle body — 4.3L engine, 2.5L is similar

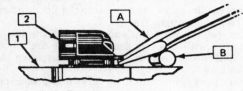

1. Fuel meter body
2. Fuel injector
A. Suitable prybar
B. Fulcrum

Removing the fuel injector — model 700

3. At the injector connector, squeeze the two tabs together and pull it straight up.

4. Remove the fuel meter cover and leave the cover gasket in place.

5. Using a small pry bar or tool No. J–26868, carefully lift the injector until it is free from the fuel meter body.

6. Remove the small O-ring form the nozzle end of the injector. Carefully rotate the injector's fuel filter back-and-forth to remove it from the base of the injector.

7. Discard the fuel meter cover gasket.

8. Remove the large O-ring and back-up washer from the top of the counterbore of the fuel meter body injector cavity.

To install:

1. Lubricate the O-rings with automatic transmission fluid and push it into the fuel injector cavity.

2. Install a new fuel meter cover gasket and install the cover (Model 300 and 220). Install the retainer and screw (Model 700).

3. Connect the injector electrical connector.

4. Install the air cleaner. Connect the negative battery terminal to the battery.

5. Start the engine, check for leaks and proper operation.

FUEL METER COVER REPLACEMENT

NOTE: The fuel meter cover does not have to be removed to replace the single fuel injector for the Model 700 throttle body (1987–90 2.5L engine). For the Model 220 and 300, the fuel meter cover does have to be removed to replace the injector.

1. Remove the air cleaner. Disconnect the negative battery terminal from the battery.

2. At the injector electrical connector, squeeze the two tabs together and pull it straight up.

3. Remove the fuel meter-to-fuel meter body screws and lockwashers.

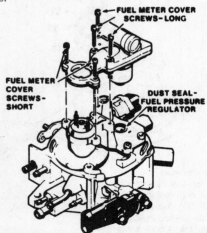

Removing the fuel meter cover from the throttle body — 2.5L engine, 4.3L is similar

NOTE: When removing the fuel meter cover screws, note the location of the two short screws.

4. Remove the fuel meter cover and discard the gasket.

To install:

1. Use a new gasket and install the injector if removed.

2. Install the fuel meter cover and torque the screws to 30 inch lbs. (4.0 Nm).

3. Reconnect the injector electrical connector and negative battery cable.

4. Start the engine, check for leaks and proper operation.

IDLE AIR CONTROL (IAC) VALVE REPLACEMENT

NOTE: The following procedure requires the use of the GM Removal tool No. J–33031 or equivalent.

1. From inside the vehicle, remove the engine cover.

2. Remove the air cleaner. Disconnect the negative battery terminal from the battery.

3. Disconnect the electrical connector from the idle air control valve.

4. Using a 1¼ in. (32mm) wrench or the GM Removal tool No. J–33031, remove the idle air control valve (Model 220 and 300). Remove the two retaining screws and valve (Model 700).

────────── **CAUTION** ──────────

Before installing a new idle air control valve, measure the distance that the valve extends (from the motor housing to the end of the cone); the distance should be no greater than 1⅛ in. (28mm). If it extends to far, damage will occur to the valve when it is installed. Push the valve pintle in slowly with finger pressure until the correct measurement is obtained.

To install:

1. Use a new gasket and the correct IAC replacement valve.

2. Install the valve and torque the thread mounted valve to 13 ft. lbs. (18 Nm) and the screw mounted valve to 28 inch lbs. (3.3 Nm). Use thread locking compound on the retaining screws before assembly.

3. Connect the valve and negative battery cable.

4. Start the engine and allow it to reach normal operating temperatures. Check for fuel leaks.

5. Turn the ignition ON for five seconds and OFF for ten seconds to allow the IAC valve to reset.

6. The vehicle may have to driven a few miles before the IAC valve will return to normal.

NOTE: The ECM will reset the idle speed when the vehicle is driven at 30 mph.

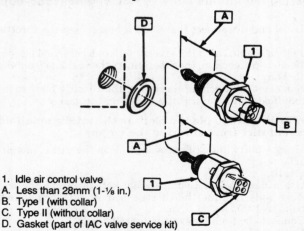

1. Idle air control valve
A. Less than 28mm (1-⅛ in.)
B. Type I (with collar)
C. Type II (without collar)
D. Gasket (part of IAC valve service kit)

Exploded view of the idle air control (IAC) valves — model 220 and 300

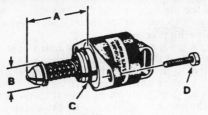

A. Distance of pintle
   extension
B. Diameter of pintle
C. IAC valve O-ring
D. Valve attaching screw

Exploded view of the Idle air control valve — model 700 throttle body

THROTTLE POSITION SENSOR (TPS)

1. Disconnect the negative (−) battery cable. Remove the air cleaner.
2. Disconnect the electrical connector from the throttle position sensor (TPS).
3. Remove the throttle position solenoid mounting screws, the lockwashers and the retainers.
4. Remove the throttle position solenoid sensor.

To install:

1. Make sure that the throttle valve is in the closed position, then install the throttle position solenoid sensor.

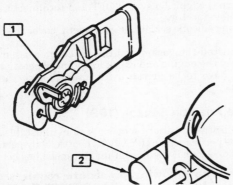

1. Throttle position sensor
2. TBI unit

Exploded view of the throttle position sensor — 2.5L engine model 300

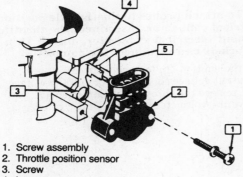

1. Screw assembly
2. Throttle position sensor
3. Screw
4. Lever
5. Throttle body assembly

Exploded view of the throttle position sensor — 4.3L engine

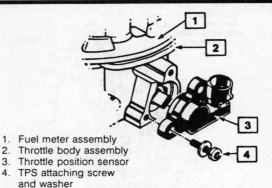

1. Fuel meter assembly
2. Throttle body assembly
3. Throttle position sensor
4. TPS attaching screw
   and washer

Exploded view of the throttle position sensor — 2.5L engine model 700

2. Coat the retaining screws with Loctite® (thread locking compound) No. 262. Install the throttle position solenoid mounting retainers, lockwashers and screws. Torque the screws to 18 inch lbs. (2.0 Nm).
3. Connect the electrical connector to the throttle position sensor.
4. Connect the negative (−) battery cable and install the air cleaner.
5. Start the engine and check for proper operation.

NOTE: Make sure the the throttle position solenoid pickup lever is located ABOVE the tang on the throttle actuator lever.

ADJUSTMENTS

Idle Speed and Mixture Adjustment

2.5L EFI ENGINE

NOTE: The following procedures require the use a tachometer, GM tool No. J–33047, BT–8207 or equivalent, GM Torx® Bit No. 20, silicone sealant, a $^5/_{32}$ in. drill bit, a prick punch and a $^1/_{16}$ in. pin punch.

The throttle stop screw, used in regulating the minimum idle speed, is adjusted at the factory and is not necessary to perform. This adjustment should be performed ONLY when the throttle body has been replaced.

NOTE: The replacement of the complete throttle body assembly will have the minimum idle adjusted at the factory.

1. Remove the air cleaner and the gasket. Be sure to plug the THERMAC vacuum port (air cleaner vacuum line-to-throttle body) on the throttle body.
2. Remove the throttle valve cable from the throttle control bracket to provide access to the minimum air adjustment screw.
3. Using the manufacturer's instructions, connect a tachometer to the engine.
4. Remove the electrical connector from the Idle Air Control (IAC) valve, located on the throttle body.
5. If necessary to remove the throttle stop screw cover, perform the following procedures:
   a. Using a prick punch, mark the housing at the top over the center line of the throttle stop screw.
   b. Using a $^5/_{32}$ in. drill bit, drill (on an angle) a hole through the casting to the hardened cover.
   c. Using a $^1/_{16}$ in. pin punch, place it through the hole and drive out the cover to expose the throttle stop screw.
6. Place the transmission in **PARK** (AT) or **NEUTRAL** (MT), start the engine and allow the idle speed to stabilize.

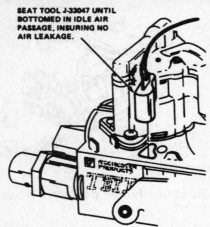

Installing the tool J–33047 to adjust the idle speed — 2.5L engine (model 300 TBI)

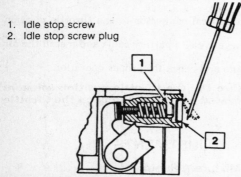

1. Idle stop screw
2. Idle stop screw plug

Removing the idle stop screw plug — 2.5L engine model 700 TBI

7. Using the GM tool No. J–33047, BT–8207 or equivalent, install it into the idle air passage of the throttle body; be sure that the tool is fully seated in the opening and no air leaks exist.

8. Using the GM Torx® Bit No. 20, turn the throttle stop screw until the engine speed is 475–525 rpm (AT in **PARK** or **NEUTRAL**) or 750–800 rpm (MT in **NEUTRAL**).

9. With the idle speed adjusted, stop the engine, remove the tool No. J–33047, BT–8207 or equivalent, from the throttle body.

10. Reconnect the Idle Air Control (IAC) electrical connector.

11. Using silicone sealant or equivalent, cover the throttle stop screw.

12. Reinstall the gasket and the air cleaner assembly.

13. The vehicle may have to be driven a few miles before the IAC valve will stabilize.

4.3L EFI ENGINE

NOTE: **The following procedure requires the use of a tachometer, a prick punch, a $^5/_{32}$ in. drill bit, a $^1/_{16}$ in. pin punch, a grounding wire and silicone sealant.**

1. Remove the air cleaner and the gasket.

2. If necessary to remove the throttle stop screw cover, perform the following procedures:

a. Using a prick punch, mark the housing at the top over the center line of the throttle stop screw.

b. Using a $^5/_{32}$ in. drill bit, drill (on an angle) a hole through the casting to the hardened cover.

c. Using a $^1/_{16}$ in. pin punch, place it through the hole and drive out the cover to expose the throttle stop screw.

NOTE: **The following adjustment should be performed ONLY when the throttle body assembly has been replaced; the engine should be at normal operating temperatures before making this adjustment.**

3. With the Idle Air Control (IAC) connected, ground the diagnostic terminal of the Assembly Line Communications Link (ALCL) connector or (ALDL).

NOTE: **The Assembly Line Communications Link (ALCL) connector or (ALDL) is located in the engine compartment on the left side firewall.**

4. Turn the ignition switch ON, but DO NOT start the engine. Wait 30 seconds, this will allow the IAC valve pintle to extend and seat in the throttle body.

5. With the ignition switch turned ON, disconnect the Idle Air Control (IAC) valve electrical connector.

6. Remove the ground from the Diagnostic Terminal ALCL connector and start the engine.

7. Adjust the idle stop screw to obtain 400–450 rpm (AT in **DRIVE**).

8. Turn the ignition switch OFF and reconnect the IAC valve electrical connector.

9. Using silicone sealant or equivalent, cover the throttle stop screw.

10. Reinstall the gasket and the air cleaner assembly.

11. Start the engine and check for proper operation. The vehicle may have to be driven a few miles before the IAC valve stabilizes.

Throttle Position Sensor (TPS)

The throttle position sensor is non-adjustable but a test should be performed ONLY when throttle body parts have been replaced or AFTER the minimum idle speed has been adjusted.

NOTE: **The following procedure requires the use of the Digital Voltmeter tool No. J–29125–A or equivalent.**

1. Using the Digital Voltmeter tool No. J–29125–A or equivalent, set it on the 0–5.0V scale, then connect the probes to the center terminal **B** and the outside terminal **C** (2.5L engine) or **A** (4.3L engine).

NOTE: **To attach probes to the throttle position solenoid electrical connector, disconnect the throttle position solenoid electrical connector, install thin wires into the sockets and reconnect the connector.**

2. Turn the ignition On (engine stopped).

3. The output voltage should be 1.25V. If the voltage is more that 1.25V, replace the throttle position solenoid.

4. Remove the voltmeter and the jumper wires.

FUEL TANK

The fuel tank is located under the left side, center of the vehicle and is held in place by two metal straps.

REMOVAL AND INSTALLATION

1. Disconnect the negative battery terminal from the battery.

NOTE: Be sure to keep a Class B (dry chemical) fire extinguisher nearby.

—————— **CAUTION** ——————

Due to the possibility of fire or explosion, never drain or store gasoline in an open container.

2. Using a hand pump or a siphon hose, drain the gasoline into an approved container.
3. Raise and support the vehicle on jackstands.
4. Support the fuel tank and remove the fuel tank-to-vehicle straps.
5. Lower the tank slightly, then remove the sender unit wires, the hoses and the ground strap.
6. Remove the fuel tank from the vehicle.

To install:

NOTE: Be sure to connect the sender unit wires and the hoses before final installation of the fuel tank.

1. Align the insulator strips and position the tank into the vehicle. Torque the inner fuel tank strap-to-vehicle bolts to 26 ft. lbs. (35 Nm) and the outer fuel tank strap-to-vehicle nuts/bolts to 26 ft. lbs. (35 Nm).

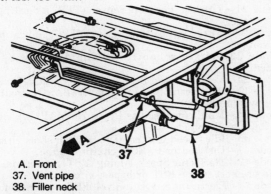

A. Front
37. Vent pipe
38. Filler neck

View of installed fuel tank

2. Make sure all hoses and electrical connectors are secure and properly routed to prevent damage.
3. Lower the vehicle, connect the negative battery cable, start the engine and check for leaks and proper operation.

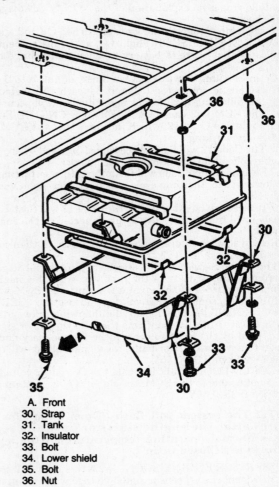

A. Front
30. Strap
31. Tank
32. Insulator
33. Bolt
34. Lower shield
35. Bolt
36. Nut

Exploded view of the fuel tank and accessories

ELECTRONIC ENGINE CONTROLS

Troubleshooting

—————— **CAUTION** ——————

If attempting to do any checking or repair of the electrical system, be very careful, for these systems are VERY delicate and major damage can occur. All work of this nature should be referred to a qualified technician.

All GM dealerships are equipped with a testing tool, known as SCAN (it connects to the ALCL diagnostic connector), which performs quick checks of the sensors and switches that provide information to the Electronic Control Module (ECM). Due to the cost factor, it is not advisable for the do-it-yourselfer to purchase one. Since these troubleshooting procedures will be limited to NON-SCAN procedures, it is advisable to schedule an appointment with a dealership to have the vehicle thoroughly checked.

Understanding the diagnostic checks and using it correctly will reduce the diagnostic time and prevent unnecessary replacement of parts.

Non-Scan Diagnostic Checks

The following is an explanation of the NON-SCAN diagnostic circuit check:

1. With engine stopped, the ignition turned On and a steady "SERVICE ENGINE SOON" light On, at the instrument panel, indicates that there is battery and ignition voltage to the ECM.

2. Connect a jumper wire between the terminals **A** to **B** of the ALCL diagnostic connector (located beneath the instrument panel), the following instrument panel display will occur:

   a. The ECM will cause the "SERVICE ENGINE SOON" lamp to flash a Code 12, which indicates that the ECM diagnostics are working.

   b. The Code 12 will flash three times, followed by any other trouble codes that are stored in its memory.

   c. Each additional code will flash three times, starting with the lowest code, then the cycle will start over again with the Code 12.

   d. If there are no other codes, the Code 12 will flash continuously until the jumper wire is disconnected or the engine is started.

3. Record all of the stored codes, except Code 12, then consult the service shop.

4. The "Field Service Mode" may be helpful in the diagnosis, depending on the severity of the problem. With the diagnostic terminal grounded and the engine running, the ECM will respond to the O$_2$ sensor signal voltage and use the "SERVICE ENGINE SOON" light to display the following information:

   a. CLOSED LOOP—confirms that the O$_2$ sensor signal is being used by the ECM to control the fuel delivery and that the system is working normally; the signal voltage will quickly change from 0.35–0.55V.

   b. OPEN LOOP—indicates that the O$_2$ sensor voltage signal is not usable to the ECM; the signal is at a constant value between 0.35–0.55V.

NOTE: The system will flash "Open Loop" for $\frac{1}{2}$–2 minutes after the engine starts or until the sensor reaches normal operating temperature; if the system fails to go to "Closed Loop".

   c. SERVICE ENGINE SOON—with this light Off, the exhaust is lean; the O$_2$ sensor signal voltage will remain under 0.35V and steady.

   d. SERVICE ENGINE SOON—with this light On and steady (not flashing), the exhaust is rich; the O$_2$ sensor voltage will be over 0.55V and steady.

5. Road test the vehicle, at steady speeds, using the "Field Service Mode".

Because the vehicle operations are different in the "Field Service Mode" the following conditions may be observed and should be considered normal:

- Acceleration—The light may be On too long due to acceleration enrichment.
- Deceleration—The light may be Off too long due to deceleration enleanment or fuel cut-off.
- Idle—The light may be On too long with the idle below 1,200 rpm.

6. To clear the codes, turn the ignition Off and disconnect the battery terminal or the ECM **B** fuse for ten seconds.

ECM CODE DESCRIPTIONS
2.5L EFI Engines

- Code 12—No reference code.

- Code 13—Oxygen sensor circuit open.
- Code 14—Coolant sensor circuit indicating low signal voltage.
- Code 15—Coolant sensor circuit indicating high signal voltage.
- Code 21—Throttle Position Sensor (TPS) indicating high signal voltage.
- Code 22—Throttle Position Sensor (TPS) indicating low signal voltage.
- Code 24—Vehicle Speed Sensor (VSS) defective.
- Code 33—Manifold Absolute Pressure (MAP) sensor indicating high signal voltage.
- Code 34—Manifold Absolute Pressure (MAP) sensor indicating low signal voltage.
- Code 35—Idle Air Control (IAC) valve defective.
- Code 42—Electronic Spark Timing (EST) circuit indicating an open or short in the EST or bypass circuits.
- Code 44—Lean exhaust indicating open oxygen sensor circuit.
- Code 45—Rich exhaust indicating open oxygen sensor circuit.
- Code 51—Programmable Read Only Memory (PROM) unit defective or loose terminals.
- Code 55—Electronic Control Module (ECM) unit defective.

4.3L Engines w/Carburetor

- Code 12—No reference code.
- Code 13—Oxygen sensor circuit open.
- Code 14—Coolant sensor circuit indicating low signal voltage.
- Code 15—Coolant sensor circuit indicating high signal voltage.
- Code 21—Throttle Position Sensor (TPS) indicating high signal voltage.
- Code 22—Throttle Position Sensor (TPS) indicating low signal voltage.
- Code 23—Mixture control solenoid circuit open or grounded.
- Code 24—Vehicle Speed Sensor (VSS) circuit defective.
- Code 32—Barometric Pressure Sensor (BARO) circuit indicating low voltage.
- Code 34—Manifold Absolute Pressure (MAP) sensor indicating low signal voltage.
- Code 35—Idle Speed Control (ISC) switch short circuited.
- Code 41—Distributor-to-ECM circuit open.
- Code 42—Electronic Spark Timing (EST) circuit indicating an open or short in the EST or bypass circuits.
- Code 43—Electronic Spark Control (ESC) system defective.
- Code 44—Lean exhaust indicating open oxygen sensor circuit.
- Code 45—Rich exhaust indicating open oxygen sensor circuit.
- Code 51—Programmable Read Only Memory (PROM) unit defective or loose terminals.
- Code 53—Exhaust Gas Recirculation (EGR) system defective
- Code 54—Mixture control Solenoid shorted and/or faulty ECM.
- Code 55—Electronic Control Module (ECM) unit defective.

4.3L Engine w/Throttle Body

- Code 12—No reference code.
- Code 13—Oxygen sensor circuit open.
- Code 14—Coolant sensor circuit indicating low signal voltage.
- Code 15—Coolant sensor circuit indicating high signal voltage.
- Code 21—Throttle Position Sensor (TPS) indicating high signal voltage.

- Code 22 — Throttle Position Sensor (TPS) indicating low signal voltage.
- Code 24 — Vehicle Speed Sensor (VSS) defective.
- Code 32 — Exhaust Gas Recirculation (EGR) system failure.
- Code 33 — Manifold Absolute Pressure (MAP) sensor indicating high signal voltage.
- Code 34 — Manifold Absolute Pressure (MAP) sensor indicating low signal voltage.
- Code 42 — Electronic Spark Timing (EST) circuit indicating an open or short in the EST or bypass circuits.
- Code 43 — Electronic Spark Control (ESC) system defective.
- Code 44 — Lean exhaust indicating open oxygen sensor circuit.
- Code 45 — Rich exhaust indicating open oxygen sensor circuit.
- Code 51 — Programmable Read Only Memory (PROM) unit defective or loose terminals.
- Code 52 — CALPAK unit defective.
- Code 55 — Electronic Control Module (ECM) unit defective.

DIAGNOSTIC INSPECTION

Initial Checks

The importance of these procedures can save valuable time by preventing any further inspections.

1. Check the hoses for splits, kinks and proper connections (see the Vehicle Emission Control Information label).
2. Inspect for air leaks at the throttle body or carburetor and the intake manifold.
3. Check the ignition wires for cracking, hardening, routing and carbon tracking.
4. Check the wiring for pinches, cuts and proper connections.

Intermittent Problems

NOTE: These problems may or may not turn On the "SERVICE ENGINE SOON" light or store a code. DO NOT use the trouble codes in this section. If a fault is present, locate it and repair it.

1. Most intermittent problems are caused by faulty electrical connections or wiring. Perform careful visual checks of the suspected circuits for:
- BACKED OUT CONNECTORS — Terminals not fully seated in the connector or poor mating of the connector halves.
- DAMAGED CONNECTORS — Improperly formed connectors. Reform the connectors to increase the contact tension.
- POOR TERMINAL TO WIRE CONNECTION — Remove the terminal from the connector and check the condition of the wire to the terminal.

2. Connect a voltmeter to the suspected circuit and drive it around. An abnormal voltage reading in the circuit may indicate the problem is in that circuit.
3. The trouble memory code may be lost. Disconnect the Throttle Position Sensor (TPS) and curb idle the engine until the "SERVICE ENGINE SOON" light turns On. Code 22 should be stored and kept in the memory when the ignition is turned Off (for at least 10 seconds); if not, the ECM is faulty.
4. If the problem still exists, perform the following checks:
- A sharp electrical surge occurs, usually when a faulty component is operated, such as: a relay, an Electronic Control Module (ECM) driven solenoid or a switch.
- The improper installation of optional equipment, such as: A two-way radio, lights or etc.
- Electronic Spark Timing (EST) wires may be too close to the spark plug wires, the distributor wires, the distributor housing, the coil and/or the alternator. Be sure that the distributor ground wire is grounded well.
- The secondary ignition may be shorted to ground.
- The Electronic Control Module (ECM) power wire may be grounded.

Hard Starting

The engine cranks OK but will not start for a long period of time, it eventually runs or it may start and immediately dies.

1. Check the fuel system for:
- Water in the fuel.
- Poor fuel pressure.
- A sticking or binding Throttle Position Sensor (TPS).
- A bad fuel pump relay.
- A poor in-tank fuel pump check valve.
2. Check the ignition system for:
- Ignition coil output.
- A worn distributor shaft.
- Bare and/or shorted wires.
- Poor pickup coil resistance and connections.
- Loose ignition coil ground.
- Moisture in the distributor cap.
- Defective spark plugs.
3. If the engine starts, then immediately stalls, open the distributor by-pass line. If it then starts and runs OK, replace the distributor pickup coil.
4. If the engine is hard to start, at normal operating temperature, check the ECM.

Surge and/or Chuggle

At normal speed, with no change in the accelerator pedal position, the engine speeds up and slows down, inspect the following:
- Vehicle Speed Sensor (VSS) using the ALCL diagnostic connector.
- Exhaust Gas Recirculation (EGR) system if the problem is intermittent at idle.
- Ignition timing (see the Vehicle Emission Control Information label).
- Inline fuel filter for restrictions.
- Fuel pressure.
- Alternator output voltage, it must between 9–16V.
- Oxygen sensor.
- Spark plugs, distributor cap and ignition wire condition.
- Transmission Convertor Clutch (TCC) operation.

Lack of Power (Sluggish)

When the accelerator is pushed part way down, there is little or no increase in speed or power.

1. Compare your vehicles performance with a similar one.
2. Check and/or replace the air cleaner.
3. Check the following equipment:
- Ignition timing (see Vehicle Emission Control Information label).
- Fuel system for a plugged fuel filter, poor fuel pressure and/or contaminated fuel.
- Poor Electronic Control Module (ECM) grounds.
- Exhaust Gas Recirculation (EGR) valve being open or partly open all of the time.
- Alternator output voltage, it must between 9–16V.
- Valve timing.
- Engine compression.
- Worn camshaft lobes.
4. To inspect the exhaust system, perform the following procedures with the engine at normal operating temperatures:
   a. Using a vacuum gauge, connect it to an intake manifold port.
   b. Disconnect the EGR solenoid electrical connector or connect the EGR valve directly to a vacuum source bypassing any switches or solenoids.
   c. Operate the engine at 1,000 rpm and record the vacuum reading.
   d. Slowly increase the engine speed to 2,500 rpm, hold the speed at 2,500 rpm and record the vacuum reading.

NOTE: If the vacuum reading, taken at 2,500 rpm, decreases more than 3 in.Hg from the one taken at 1,000 rpm, the exhaust system should be inspected for restrictions

e. Disconnect the exhaust pipe from the engine and repeat the Steps 4c and 4d.

NOTE: If the reading still drops more than 3 in.Hg, check the valve timing.

Detonation/Spark Knock

The engine makes a sharp metallic knocks, which range from mild to severe pings, usually worse under acceleration.
1. If a heating problem is noticed, check for:
   a. Low engine coolant.
   b. A loose water pump drive belt.
   c. Restricted air or water flow through the radiator.
2. For other than heating problems, check for:
   a. Poor quality fuel (low octane rating).
   b. Correct Programmable Read Only Memory (PROM) unit.
   c. THERMAC may be staying closed.
   d. Ignition timing (see the Vehicle Emission Control Information label).
   e. Low fuel pressure.
   f. Exhaust Gas Recirculation (EGR) valve may be closed.
   g. Transmission for proper shifting points and operation of the Transmission Convertor Clutch (TCC).
   h. Incorrect engine parts, such as: camshaft, cylinder head(s), pistons and etc.
3. If the problem persists, obtain a can of engine (carbon) cleaner and follow the instructions on the can.

Hesitation or Stumble

This condition is a momentary lack of response when accelerating, which can occur at all speeds but usually when trying to make the vehicle move from a stop sign; it may cause the vehicle to stall, if severe enough.

To check the systems, perform the following checks:
• Low fuel pressure.
• Water in fuel.
• Binding or sticking Throttle Position Sensor (TPS).
• Ignition timing (see Vehicle Emission Control Information label).
• Alternator output, it must be between 9–16V.
• An ungrounded in the High Energy Ignition (HEI) system.
• Non-working emissions canister purge.
• Non-working Exhaust Gas Recirculation (EGR) valve.

Misses or Cuts Out

This condition is a steady pulsation or jerking which follows the engine speed, it is usually more pronounced as the engine increases speed. At low speed or idle, the exhaust has a steady spitting sound.
1. To check for a missing cylinder, perform the following procedures:
   a. Disconnect the electrical connector from the Idle Air Control (IAC) motor.
   b. Start the engine.
   c. Using insulated pliers, remove one spark plug wire at a time and check for an rpm drop. If no drop is noticed, check the spark plugs for cracks, wear, improper gap, burned electrodes and/or heavy deposits.

NOTE: If a drop of 50 rpm is recorded between the cylinders, replace the IAC electrical connector and proceed to the "Rough, Unstable or Incorrect Idle, Stalling" section.

2. Using an ohmmeter, over 30,000Ω, check the spark plug wires and replace them, if necessary.
3. Using the Spark Tester tool No. J–26792 or equivalent, check the ignition coil's primary and secondary voltages.
4. Check the fuel system for a plugged fuel filter, water in the fuel and/or low fuel pump pressure.
5. Inspect the ignition timing (see the Vehicle Emission Control Information label).
6. Perform a compression check on the engine; if the compression is low, repair as necessary.
7. Inspect the distributor cap and rotor for dust, cracks, burns, moisture and etc. Using a fine water mist, spray the cap and plug wires to check for shorts.
8. Remove the rocker arm covers and inspect for bent pushrods, worn rocker arms, broken valve springs and/or worn camshaft lobes.

Poor Fuel Economy

By performing an actual road test, it is determined that the fuel economy is lower than some other actual road test on the same vehicle.

To determine the reason for the poor fuel economy, inspect the following items:
1. The engine thermostat for the wrong heat range or a faulty (always open) part.
2. The fuel system for low fuel pressure.
3. The ignition timing (see the Vehicle Emission Control Information label).
4. The Transmission Convertor Clutch (TCC) for proper operation.

Rough, Unstable or Incorrect Idle, Stalling

In this condition, the engine idles unevenly, it may shake (if bad enough) and/or may stall.

To determine the reason(s) for poor operation, inspect the following items:
1. The ignition timing (see the Vehicle Emission Control Informations label).
2. The Park/Neutral (P/N) switch, if equipped with an AT.
3. A leaking fuel injector.
4. A fuel injector operating too rich or lean.

If rough idle occurs ONLY when the engine is Hot, perform the additional checks:
1. To check for vacuum leaks, perform the following checks:
   a. Using the GM Plug tool No. J–33047 or equivalent, block the idle air passage.
   b. If the engine speed is higher than 650 rpm with the throttle closed, locate and correct the vacuum leak, such as: A disconnected Thermac or cruise control hose.
2. The Park/Neutral (P/N) switch, if equipped with an AT.
3. The Throttle Position Switch (TPS) may be sticking or binding, causing the throttle to remain open.
4. Exhaust Gas Recirculation (EGR) system — if it is on while the engine is idling, roughness, stalling and hard starting will occur.
5. Battery cables and ground straps — dirty and loose battery connections will cause erratic voltage, which will cause the Idle Air Control (IAC) valve to change its position, resulting in poor idle quality. The IAC valve will not move if the system voltage is below 9V or greater than 17.8V.
6. Power Steering system — the ECM should compensate for power steering loads; if the signal is lost, the vehicle will be difficult to park and steer with heavy loads.
7. Manifold Absolute Pressure (MAP) sensor — idle the engine and disconnect the electrical connector from the sensor, if the idle improves, substitute a known GOOD sensor and recheck.
8. The air conditioning compressor and relay, also, the refrigerant pressure may be too high or have a faulty cycling switch.

9. The Positive Crankcase Ventilation (PCV) valve—place your finger over the end and release it several times, if the valve does not snap back, replace it.

10. Perform a cylinder compression check and compare the results, then repair as necessary.

11. Oxygen sensor—inspect it for sensor contamination (white, powdery coating) and high electrical conductivity; as a result, the ECM will reduce the amount of fuel to the engine.

12. Air Management system—check for intermittent air to the ports while in the "Closed Loop" operation (4.3L engines).

Abnormal Emissions (Odors)

To correct abnormal emissions, inspect or test the following items, for:

1. Excessive CO and HC emissions (odors), plus, any thing that will make the engine run rich.

2. Incorrect ignition timing (see the Vehicle Emission Control Information label).

3. Loading of the fuel emissions canister.

4. Stuck or blocked Positive Crankcase Ventilation (PCV) valve.

5. Condition of the spark plugs, ignition wires and distributor cap.

6. Lead contamination of the Catalytic Converter.

Dieseling

This condition exists when the ignition switch is turned Off and the engine continues to run roughly. If the engine runs smoothly, check and/or adjust the ignition switch.

NOTE: The only way to prevent the engine from dieseling is to eliminate fuel leakage to the cylinders.

To remedy this situation, turn the ignition switch On, to energize the fuel pump, then check the fuel injector(s) and the throttle body for fuel leakage. If necessary, repair or replace the leaking items.

Backfire

This condition exists when fuel ignites in the intake or exhaust manifold, making a loud popping noise.

To correct this situation, inspect and/or replace the following items:

• Exhaust Gas Recirculation (EGR) system, it must not be open all of the time.

• Output voltage of the ignition coil.

• Crossfire between the spark plugs (distributor cap, ignition wires).

• Intermittent condition in the primary ignition system.

• Ignition timing (see the Vehicle Emission Control Information label).

• Faulty spark plugs and/or ignition wires.

• Valve timing.

• Compression check—look for leaking or sticking valves.

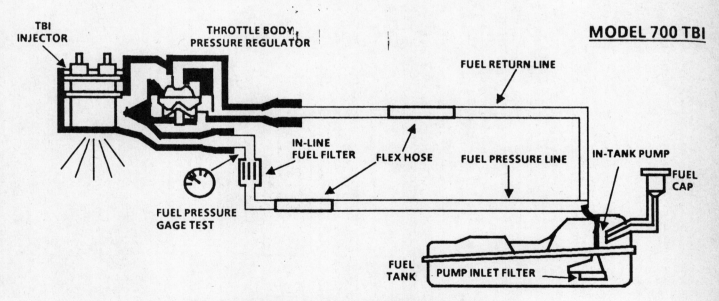

Fuel system pressure test for all fuel injected engines

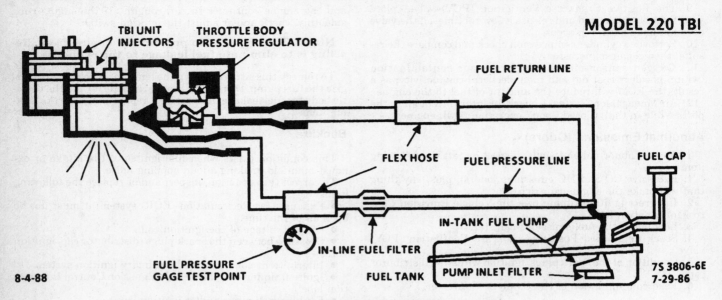

MODEL 220 TBI

TBI UNIT INJECTORS

THROTTLE BODY PRESSURE REGULATOR

FUEL RETURN LINE

FLEX HOSE

FUEL PRESSURE LINE

FUEL CAP

IN-TANK FUEL PUMP

IN-LINE FUEL FILTER

FUEL PRESSURE GAGE TEST POINT

FUEL TANK

PUMP INLET FILTER

8-4-88

7S 3806-6E
7-29-86

Fuel system pressure test for all fuel injected engines

6 Chassis Electrical

QUICK REFERENCE INDEX

GENERAL INDEX

UNDERSTANDING BASIC ELECTRICITY

At the rate which both import and domestic manufacturers are incorporating electronic control systems into their production lines, it won't be long before every new vehicle is equipped with one or more on-board computer. These electronic components (with no moving parts) should theoretically last the life of the vehicle, provided nothing external happens to damage the circuits or memory chips.

While it is true that electronic components should never wear out, in the real world malfunctions do occur. It is also true that any computer-based system is extremely sensitive to electrical voltages and cannot tolerate careless or haphazard testing or service procedures. An inexperienced individual can literally do major damage looking for a minor problem by using the wrong kind of test equipment or connecting test leads or connectors with the ignition switch ON. When selecting test equipment, make sure the manufacturers instructions state that the tester is compatible with whatever type of electronic control system is being serviced. Read all instructions carefully and double check all test points before installing probes or making any test connections.

The following section outlines basic diagnosis techniques for dealing with computerized automotive control systems. Along with a general explanation of the various types of test equipment available to aid in servicing modern electronic automotive systems, basic repair techniques for wiring harnesses and connectors is given. Read the basic information before attempting any repairs or testing on any computerized system, to provide the background of information necessary to avoid the most common and obvious mistakes that can cost both time and money. Although the replacement and testing procedures are simple in themselves, the systems are not, and unless one has a thorough understanding of all components and their function within a particular computerized control system, the logical test sequence these systems demand cannot be followed. Minor malfunctions can make a big difference, so it is important to know how each component affects the operation of the overall electronic system to find the ultimate cause of a problem without replacing good components unnecessarily. It is not enough to use the correct test equipment; the test equipment must be used correctly.

Safety Precautions

──────────── CAUTION ────────────
Whenever working on or around any computer based microprocessor control system, always observe these general precautions to prevent the possibility of personal injury or damage to electronic components.

• Never install or remove battery cables with the key ON or the engine running. Jumper cables should be connected with the key OFF to avoid power surges that can damage electronic control units. Engines equipped with computer controlled systems should avoid both giving and getting jump starts due to the possibility of serious damage to components from arcing in the engine compartment when connections are made with the ignition ON.

• Always remove the battery cables before charging the battery. Never use a high output charger on an installed battery or attempt to use any type of "hot shot" (24 volt) starting aid.

• Exercise care when inserting test probes into connectors to insure good connections without damaging the connector or spreading the pins. Always probe connectors from the rear (wire) side, NOT the pin side, to avoid accidental shorting of terminals during test procedures.

• Never remove or attach wiring harness connectors with the ignition switch ON, especially to an electronic control unit.

• Do not drop any components during service procedures and never apply 12 volts directly to any component (like a solenoid

or relay) unless instructed specifically to do so. Some component electrical windings are designed to safely handle only 4 or 5 volts and can be destroyed in seconds if 12 volts are applied directly to the connector.

• Remove the electronic control unit if the vehicle is to be placed in an environment where temperatures exceed approximately 176°F (80°C), such as a paint spray booth or when arc or gas welding near the control unit location in the car.

ORGANIZED TROUBLESHOOTING

When diagnosing a specific problem, organized troubleshooting is a must. The complexity of a modern automobile demands that you approach any problem in a logical, organized manner. There are certain troubleshooting techniques that are standard:

1. Establish when the problem occurs. Does the problem appear only under certain conditions? Were there any noises, odors, or other unusual symptoms?

2. Isolate the problem area. To do this, make some simple tests and observations; then eliminate the systems that are working properly. Check for obvious problems such as broken wires, dirty connections or split or disconnected vacuum hoses. Always check the obvious before assuming something complicated is the cause.

3. Test for problems systematically to determine the cause once the problem area is isolated. Are all the components functioning properly? Is there power going to electrical switches and motors? Is there vacuum at vacuum switches and/or actuators? Is there a mechanical problem such as bent linkage or loose mounting screws? Doing careful, systematic checks will often turn up most causes on the first inspection without wasting time checking components that have little or no relationship to the problem.

4. Test all repairs after the work is done to make sure that the problem is fixed. Some causes can be traced to more than one component, so a careful verification of repair work is important to pick up additional malfunctions that may cause a problem to reappear or a different problem to arise. A blown fuse, for example, is a simple problem that may require more than another fuse to repair. If you don't look for a problem that caused a fuse to blow, for example, a shorted wire may go undetected.

Experience has shown that most problems tend to be the result of a fairly simple and obvious cause, such as loose or corroded connectors or air leaks in the intake system; making careful inspection of components during testing essential to quick and accurate troubleshooting. Special, hand held computerized testers designed specifically for diagnosing the Computer Command Control system are available from a variety of aftermarket sources, as well as from the vehicle manufacturer, but care should be taken that any test equipment being used is designed to diagnose that particular computer controlled system accurately without damaging the control module (ECM) or components being tested.

NOTE: Pinpointing the exact cause of trouble in an electrical system can sometimes only be accomplished by the use of special test equipment. The following describes commonly used test equipment and explains how to put it to best use in diagnosis. In addition to the information covered below, the manufacturer's instructions booklet provided with the tester should be read and clearly understood before attempting any test procedures.

TEST EQUIPMENT

Jumper Wires

Jumper wires are simple, yet extremely valuable, pieces of

test equipment. Jumper wires are merely wires that are used to bypass sections of a circuit. The simplest type of jumper wire is merely a length of multistrand wire with an alligator clip at each end. Jumper wires are usually fabricated from lengths of standard automotive wire and whatever type of connector (alligator clip, spade connector or pin connector) that is required for the particular vehicle being tested. The well equipped tool box will have several different styles of jumper wires in several different lengths. Some jumper wires are made with three or more terminals coming from a common splice for special purpose testing. In cramped, hard-to-reach areas it is advisable to have insulated boots over the jumper wire terminals in order to prevent accidental grounding, sparks, and possible fire, especially when testing fuel system components.

Jumper wires are used primarily to locate open electrical circuits, on either the ground (−) side of the circuit or on the hot (+) side. If an electrical component fails to operate, connect the jumper wire between the component and a good ground. If the component operates only with the jumper installed, the ground circuit is open. If the ground circuit is good, but the component does not operate, the circuit between the power feed and component is open. You can sometimes connect the jumper wire directly from the battery to the hot terminal of the component, but first make sure the component uses 12 volts in operation. Some electrical components, such as fuel injectors, are designed to operate on about 4 volts and running 12 volts directly to the injector terminals can burn out the wiring. By inserting an inline fuseholder between a set of test leads, a fused jumper wire can be used for bypassing open circuits. Use a 5 amp fuse to provide protection against voltage spikes. When in doubt, use a voltmeter to check the voltage input to the component and measure how much voltage is being applied normally. By moving the jumper wire successively back from the lamp toward the power source, you can isolate the area of the circuit where the open is located. When the component stops functioning, or the power is cut off, the open is in the segment of wire between the jumper and the point previously tested.

─────────────── **CAUTION** ───────────────

Never use jumpers made from wire that is of lighter gauge than used in the circuit under test. If the jumper wire is of too small gauge, it may overheat and possibly melt. Never use jumpers to bypass high resistance loads (such as motors) in a circuit. Bypassing resistances, in effect, creates a short circuit which may, in turn, cause damage and fire. Never use a jumper for anything other than temporary bypassing of components in a circuit.

12 Volt Test Light

The 12 volt test light is used to check circuits and components while electrical current is flowing through them. It is used for voltage and ground tests. Twelve volt test lights come in different styles but all have three main parts; a ground clip, a probe, and a light. The most commonly used 12 volt test lights have pick-type probes. To use a 12 volt test light, connect the ground clip to a good ground and probe wherever necessary with the pick. The pick should be sharp so that it can penetrate wire insulation to make contact with the wire, without making a large hole in the insulation. The wrap-around light is handy in hard to reach areas or where it is difficult to support a wire to push a probe pick into it. To use the wrap around light, hook the wire to be probed with the hook and pull the trigger. A small pick will be forced through the wire insulation into the wire core.

─────────────── **CAUTION** ───────────────

Do not use a test light to probe electronic ignition spark plug or coil wires. Never use a pick-type test light to probe wiring on computer controlled systems unless specifically instructed to do so. Any wire insulation that is pierced by the test light probe should be taped and sealed with silicone after testing.

Like the jumper wire, the 12 volt test light is used to isolate opens in circuits. But, whereas the jumper wire is used to bypass the open to operate the load, the 12 volt test light is used to locate the presence of voltage in a circuit. If the test light glows, you know that there is power up to that point; if the 12 volt test light does not glow when its probe is inserted into the wire or connector, you know that there is an open circuit (no power). Move the test light in successive steps back toward the power source until the light in the handle does glow. When it does glow, the open is between the probe and point previously probed.

NOTE: The test light does not detect that 12 volts (or any particular amount of voltage) is present; it only detects that some voltage is present. It is advisable before using the test light to touch its terminals across the battery posts to make sure the light is operating properly.

Self-Powered Test Light

The self-powered test light usually contains a 1.5 volt penlight battery. One type of self-powered test light is similar in design to the 12 volt test light. This type has both the battery and the light in the handle and pick-type probe tip. The second type has the light toward the open tip, so that the light illuminates the contact point. The self-powered test light is dual purpose piece of test equipment. It can be used to test for either open or short circuits when power is isolated from the circuit (continuity test). A powered test light should not be used on any computer controlled system or component unless specifically instructed to do so. Many engine sensors can be destroyed by even this small amount of voltage applied directly to the terminals.

Open Circuit Testing

To use the self-powered test light to check for open circuits, first isolate the circuit from the vehicle's 12 volt power source by disconnecting the battery or wiring harness connector. Connect the test light ground clip to a good ground and probe sections of the circuit sequentially with the test light. (start from either end of the circuit). If the light is out, the open is between the probe and the circuit ground. If the light is on, the open is between the probe and end of the circuit toward the power source.

Short Circuit Testing

By isolating the circuit both from power and from ground, and using a self-powered test light, you can check for shorts to ground in the circuit. Isolate the circuit from power and ground. Connect the test light ground clip to a good ground and probe any easy-to-reach test point in the circuit. If the light comes on, there is a short somewhere in the circuit. To isolate the short, probe a test point at either end of the isolated circuit (the light should be on). Leave the test light probe connected and open connectors, switches, remove parts, etc., sequentially, until the light goes out. When the light goes out, the short is between the last circuit component opened and the previous circuit opened.

NOTE: The 1.5 volt battery in the test light does not provide much current. A weak battery may not provide enough power to illuminate the test light even when a complete circuit is made (especially if there are high resistances in the circuit). Always make sure that the test battery is strong. To check the battery, briefly touch the ground clip to the probe; if the light glows brightly the battery is strong enough for testing. Never use a self-powered test light to perform checks for opens or shorts when power is applied to the electrical system under test. The 12 volt vehicle power will quickly burn out the 1.5 volt light bulb in the test light.

Voltmeter

A voltmeter is used to measure voltage at any point in a circuit, or to measure the voltage drop across any part of a circuit. It can also be used to check continuity in a wire or circuit by indicating current flow from one end to the other. Voltmeters usually have various scales on the meter dial and a selector switch to allow the selection of different voltages. The voltmeter has a positive and a negative lead. To avoid damage to the meter, always connect the negative lead to the negative (−) side of circuit (to ground or nearest the ground side of the circuit) and connect the positive lead to the positive (+) side of the circuit (to the power source or the nearest power source). Note that the negative voltmeter lead will always be black and that the positive voltmeter will always be some color other than black (usually red). Depending on how the voltmeter is connected into the circuit, it has several uses.

A voltmeter can be connected either in parallel or in series with a circuit and it has a very high resistance to current flow. When connected in parallel, only a small amount of current will flow through the voltmeter current path; the rest will flow through the normal circuit current path and the circuit will work normally. When the voltmeter is connected in series with a circuit, only a small amount of current can flow through the circuit. The circuit will not work properly, but the voltmeter reading will show if the circuit is complete or not.

Available Voltage Measurement

Set the voltmeter selector switch to the 20V position and connect the meter negative lead to the negative post of the battery. Connect the positive meter lead to the positive post of the battery and turn the ignition switch ON to provide a load. Read the voltage on the meter or digital display. A well charged battery should register over 12 volts. If the meter reads below 11.5 volts, the battery power may be insufficient to operate the electrical system properly. This test determines voltage available from the battery and should be the first step in any electrical trouble diagnosis procedure. Many electrical problems, especially on computer controlled systems, can be caused by a low state of charge in the battery. Excessive corrosion at the battery cable terminals can cause a poor contact that will prevent proper charging and full battery current flow.

Normal battery voltage is 12 volts when fully charged. When the battery is supplying current to one or more circuits it is said to be "under load". When everything is off the electrical system is under a "no-load" condition. A fully charged battery may show about 12.5 volts at no load; will drop to 12 volts under medium load; and will drop even lower under heavy load. If the battery is partially discharged the voltage decrease under heavy load may be excessive, even though the battery shows 12 volts or more at no load. When allowed to discharge further, the battery's available voltage under load will decrease more severely. For this reason, it is important that the battery be fully charged during all testing procedures to avoid errors in diagnosis and incorrect test results.

Voltage Drop

When current flows through a resistance, the voltage beyond the resistance is reduced (the larger the current, the greater the reduction in voltage). When no current is flowing, there is no voltage drop because there is no current flow. All points in the circuit which are connected to the power source are at the same voltage as the power source. The total voltage drop always equals the total source voltage. In a long circuit with many connectors, a series of small, unwanted voltage drops due to corrosion at the connectors can add up to a total loss of voltage which impairs the operation of the normal loads in the circuit.

INDIRECT COMPUTATION OF VOLTAGE DROPS

1. Set the voltmeter selector switch to the 20 volt position.
2. Connect the meter negative lead to a good ground.

3. Probe all resistances in the circuit with the positive meter lead.
4. Operate the circuit in all modes and observe the voltage readings.

DIRECT MEASUREMENT OF VOLTAGE DROPS

1. Set the voltmeter switch to the 20 volt position.
2. Connect the voltmeter negative lead to the ground side of the resistance load to be measured.
3. Connect the positive lead to the positive side of the resistance or load to be measured.
4. Read the voltage drop directly on the 20 volt scale.

Too high a voltage indicates too high a resistance. If, for example, a blower motor runs too slowly, you can determine if there is too high a resistance in the resistor pack. By taking voltage drop readings in all parts of the circuit, you can isolate the problem. Too low a voltage drop indicates too low a resistance. If, for example, a blower motor runs too fast in the MED and/or LOW position, the problem can be isolated in the resistor pack by taking voltage drop readings in all parts of the circuit to locate a possibly shorted resistor. The maximum allowable voltage drop under load is critical, especially if there is more than one high resistance problem in a circuit because all voltage drops are cumulative. A small drop is normal due to the resistance of the conductors.

HIGH RESISTANCE TESTING

1. Set the voltmeter selector switch to the 4 volt position.
2. Connect the voltmeter positive lead to the positive post of the battery.
3. Turn on the headlights and heater blower to provide a load.
4. Probe various points in the circuit with the negative voltmeter lead.
5. Read the voltage drop on the 4 volt scale. Some average maximum allowable voltage drops are:
   FUSE PANEL — 7 volts
   IGNITION SWITCH — 5 volts
   HEADLIGHT SWITCH — 7 volts
   IGNITION COIL (+) — 5 volts
   ANY OTHER LOAD — 1.3 volts

NOTE: Voltage drops are all measured while a load is operating; without current flow, there will be no voltage drop.

Ohmmeter

The ohmmeter is designed to read resistance (ohms) in a circuit or component. Although there are several different styles of ohmmeters, all will usually have a selector switch which permits the measurement of different ranges of resistance (usually the selector switch allows the multiplication of the meter reading by 10, 100, 1,000, and 10,000). A calibration knob allows the meter to be set at zero for accurate measurement. Since all ohmmeters are powered by an internal battery (usually 9 volts), the ohmmeter can be used as a self-powered test light. When the ohmmeter is connected, current from the ohmmeter flows through the circuit or component being tested. Since the ohmmeter's internal resistance and voltage are known values, the amount of current flow through the meter depends on the resistance of the circuit or component being tested.

The ohmmeter can be used to perform continuity test for opens or shorts (either by observation of the meter needle or as a self-powered test light), and to read actual resistance in a circuit. It should be noted that the ohmmeter is used to check the resistance of a component or wire while there is no voltage applied to the circuit. Current flow from an outside voltage source (such as the vehicle battery) can damage the ohmmeter, so the circuit or component should be isolated from the vehicle electrical system before any testing is done. Since the ohmmeter uses its own voltage source, either lead can be connected to any test point.

NOTE: When checking diodes or other solid state components, the ohmmeter leads can only be connected one way in order to measure current flow in a single direction. Make sure the positive (+) and negative (−) terminal connections are as described in the test procedures to verify the one-way diode operation.

In using the meter for making continuity checks, do not be concerned with the actual resistance readings. Zero resistance, or any resistance readings, indicate continuity in the circuit. Infinite resistance indicates an open in the circuit. A high resistance reading where there should be none indicates a problem in the circuit. Checks for short circuits are made in the same manner as checks for open circuits except that the circuit must be isolated from both power and normal ground. Infinite resistance indicates no continuity to ground, while zero resistance indicates a dead short to ground.

RESISTANCE MEASUREMENT

The batteries in an ohmmeter will weaken with age and temperature, so the ohmmeter must be calibrated or "zeroed" before taking measurements. To zero the meter, place the selector switch in its lowest range and touch the two ohmmeter leads together. Turn the calibration knob until the meter needle is exactly on zero.

NOTE: All analog (needle) type ohmmeters must be zeroed before use, but some digital ohmmeter models are automatically calibrated when the switch is turned on. Self-calibrating digital ohmmeters do not have an adjusting knob, but its a good idea to check for a zero readout before use by touching the leads together. All computer controlled systems require the use of a digital ohmmeter with at least 10 megohms impedance for testing. Before any test procedures are attempted, make sure the ohmmeter used is compatible with the electrical system or damage to the on-board computer could result.

To measure resistance, first isolate the circuit from the vehicle power source by disconnecting the battery cables or the harness connector. Make sure the key is OFF when disconnecting any components or the battery. Where necessary, also isolate at least one side of the circuit to be checked to avoid reading parallel resistances. Parallel circuit resistances will always give a lower reading than the actual resistance of either of the branches. When measuring the resistance of parallel circuits, the total resistance will always be lower than the smallest resistance in the circuit. Connect the meter leads to both sides of the circuit (wire or component) and read the actual measured ohms on the meter scale. Make sure the selector switch is set to the proper ohm scale for the circuit being tested to avoid misreading the ohmmeter test value.

WARNING: Never use an ohmmeter with power applied to the circuit. Like the self-powered test light, the ohmmeter is designed to operate on its own power supply. The normal 12 volt automotive electrical system current could damage the meter!

Ammeters

An ammeter measures the amount of current flowing through a circuit in units called amperes or amps. Amperes are units of electron flow which indicate how fast the electrons are flowing through the circuit. Since Ohms Law dictates that current flow in a circuit is equal to the circuit voltage divided by the total circuit resistance, increasing voltage also increases the current level (amps). Likewise, any decrease in resistance will increase the amount of amps in a circuit. At normal operating voltage, most circuits have a characteristic amount of amperes, called "current draw" which can be measured using an ammeter. By referring to a specified current draw rating, measuring

the amperes, and comparing the two values, one can determine what is happening within the circuit to aid in diagnosis. An open circuit, for example, will not allow any current to flow so the ammeter reading will be zero. More current flows through a heavily loaded circuit or when the charging system is operating.

An ammeter is always connected in series with the circuit being tested. All of the current that normally flows through the circuit must also flow through the ammeter; if there is any other path for the current to follow, the ammeter reading will not be accurate. The ammeter itself has very little resistance to current flow and therefore will not affect the circuit, but it will measure current draw only when the circuit is closed and electricity is flowing. Excessive current draw can blow fuses and drain the battery, while a reduced current draw can cause motors to run slowly, lights to dim and other components to not operate properly. The ammeter can help diagnose these conditions by locating the cause of the high or low reading.

Multimeters

Different combinations of test meters can be built into a single unit designed for specific tests. Some of the more common combination test devices are known as Volt/Amp testers, Tach/Dwell meters, or Digital Multimeters. The Volt/Amp tester is used for charging system, starting system or battery tests and consists of a voltmeter, an ammeter and a variable resistance carbon pile. The voltmeter will usually have at least two ranges for use with 6, 12 and 24 volt systems. The ammeter also has more than one range for testing various levels of battery loads and starter current draw and the carbon pile can be adjusted to offer different amounts of resistance. The Volt/Amp tester has heavy leads to carry large amounts of current and many later models have an inductive ammeter pickup that clamps around the wire to simplify test connections. On some models, the ammeter also has a zero-center scale to allow testing of charging and starting systems without switching leads or polarity. A digital multimeter is a voltmeter, ammeter and ohmmeter combined in an instrument which gives a digital readout. These are often used when testing solid state circuits because of their high input impedance (usually 10 megohms or more).

The tach/dwell meter combines a tachometer and a dwell (cam angle) meter and is a specialized kind of voltmeter. The tachometer scale is marked to show engine speed in rpm and the dwell scale is marked to show degrees of distributor shaft rotation. In most electronic ignition systems, dwell is determined by the control unit, but the dwell meter can also be used to check the duty cycle (operation) of some electronic engine control systems. Some tach/dwell meters are powered by an internal battery, while others take their power from the car battery in use. The battery powered testers usually require calibration much like an ohmmeter before testing.

Special Test Equipment

A variety of diagnostic tools are available to help troubleshoot and repair computerized engine control systems. The most sophisticated of these devices are the console type engine analyzers that usually occupy a garage service bay, but there are several types of aftermarket electronic testers available that will allow quick circuit tests of the engine control system by plugging directly into a special connector located in the engine compartment or under the dashboard. Several tool and equipment manufacturers offer simple, hand held testers that measure various circuit voltage levels on command to check all system components for proper operation. Although these testers usually cost about $300–500, consider that the average computer control module (or ECM) can cost just as much and the money saved by not replacing perfectly good sensors or components in an attempt to correct a problem could justify the purchase price of a special diagnostic tester the first time it's used.

These computerized testers can allow quick and easy test measurements while the engine is operating or while the car is being driven. In addition, the on-board computer memory can be read to access any stored trouble codes; in effect allowing the computer to tell you where it hurts and aid trouble diagnosis by pinpointing exactly which circuit or component is malfunctioning. In the same manner, repairs can be tested to make sure the problem has been corrected. The biggest advantage these special testers have is their relatively easy hookups that minimize or eliminate the chances of making the wrong connections and getting false voltage readings or damaging the computer accidentally.

NOTE: It should be remembered that these testers check voltage levels in circuits; they don't detect mechanical problems or failed components if the circuit voltage falls within the preprogrammed limits stored in the tester PROM unit. Also, most of the hand held testes are designed to work only on one or two systems made by a specific manufacturer.

A variety of aftermarket testers are available to help diagnose different computerized control systems. Owatonna Tool Company (OTC), for example, markets a device called the OTC Monitor which plugs directly into the assembly line diagnostic link (ALDL). The OTC tester makes diagnosis a simple matter of pressing the correct buttons and, by changing the internal PROM or inserting a different diagnosis cartridge, it will work on any model from full size to subcompact, over a wide range of years. An adapter is supplied with the tester to allow connection to all types of ALDL links, regardless of the number of pin terminals used. By inserting an updated PROM into the OTC tester, it can be easily updated to diagnose any new modifications of computerized control systems.

Wiring Harnesses

The average automobile contains about ½ mile of wiring, with hundreds of individual connections. To protect the many wires from damage and to keep them from becoming a confusing tangle, they are organized into bundles, enclosed in plastic or taped together and called wire harnesses. Different wiring harnesses serve different parts of the vehicle. Individual wires are color coded to help trace them through a harness where sections are hidden from view.

A loose or corroded connection or a replacement wire that is too small for the circuit will add extra resistance and an additional voltage drop to the circuit. A ten percent voltage drop can result in slow or erratic motor operation, for example, even though the circuit is complete. Automotive wiring or circuit conductors can be in any one of three forms:
1. Single strand wire
2. Multistrand wire
3. Printed circuitry

Single strand wire has a solid metal core and is usually used inside such components as alternators, motors, relays and other devices. Multistrand wire has a core made of many small strands of wire twisted together into a single conductor. Most of the wiring in an automotive electrical system is made up of multistrand wire, either as a single conductor or grouped together in a harness. All wiring is color coded on the insulator, either as a solid color or as a colored wire with an identification stripe. A printed circuit is a thin film of copper or other conductor that is printed on an insulator backing. Occasionally, a printed circuit is sandwiched between two sheets of plastic for more protection and flexibility. A complete printed circuit, consisting of conductors, insulating material and connectors for lamps or other components is called a printed circuit board. Printed circuitry is used in place of individual wires or harnesses in places where space is limited, such as behind instrument panels.

Wire Gauge

Since computer controlled automotive electrical systems are

very sensitive to changes in resistance, the selection of properly sized wires is critical when systems are repaired. The wire gauge number is an expression of the cross section area of the conductor. The most common system for expressing wire size is the American Wire Gauge (AWG) system.

Wire cross section area is measured in circular mils. A mil is $\frac{1}{1000}$ in. (0.001 in.); a circular mil is the area of a circle one mil in diameter. For example, a conductor ¼ in. in diameter is 0.250 in. or 250 mils. The circular mil cross section area of the wire is 250 squared (250^2) or 62,500 circular mils. Imported car models usually use metric wire gauge designations, which is simply the cross section area of the conductor in square millimeters (mm^2).

Gauge numbers are assigned to conductors of various cross section areas. As gauge number increases, area decreases and the conductor becomes smaller. A 5 gauge conductor is smaller than a 1 gauge conductor and a 10 gauge is smaller than a 5 gauge. As the cross section area of a conductor decreases, resistance increases and so does the gauge number. A conductor with a higher gauge number will carry less current than a conductor with a lower gauge number.

NOTE: Gauge wire size refers to the size of the conductor, not the size of the complete wire. It is possible to have two wires of the same gauge with different diameters because one may have thicker insulation than the other.

12 volt automotive electrical systems generally use 10, 12, 14, 16 and 18 gauge wire. Main power distribution circuits and larger accessories usually use 10 and 12 gauge wire. Battery cables are usually 4 or 6 gauge, although 1 and 2 gauge wires are occasionally used. Wire length must also be considered when making repairs to a circuit. As conductor length increases, so does resistance. An 18 gauge wire, for example, can carry a 10 amp load for 10 feet without excessive voltage drop; however if a 15 foot wire is required for the same 10 amp load, it must be a 16 gauge wire.

An electrical schematic shows the electrical current paths when a circuit is operating properly. It is essential to understand how a circuit works before trying to figure out why it does not. Schematics break the entire electrical system down into individual circuits and show only one particular circuit. In a schematic, no attempt is made to represent wiring and components as they physically appear on the vehicle; switches and other components are shown as simply as possible. Face views of harness connectors show the cavity or terminal locations in all multi-pin connectors to help locate test points.

If you need to backprobe a connector while it is on the component, the order of the terminals must be mentally reversed. The wire color code can help in this situation, as well as a keyway, lock tab or other reference mark.

NOTE: Some wiring diagrams are included in this book. As trucks have become more complex and available with longer option lists, wiring diagrams have grown in size and complexity. It has become almost impossible to provide a readable reproduction of a wiring diagram in a book this size.

WIRING REPAIR

Soldering is a quick, efficient method of joining metals permanently. Everyone who has the occasion to make wiring repairs should know how to solder. Electrical connections that are soldered are far less likely to come apart and will conduct electricity much better than connections that are only "pig-tailed" together. The most popular (and preferred) method of soldering is with an electrical soldering gun. Soldering irons are available in many sizes and wattage ratings. Irons with higher wattage ratings deliver higher temperatures and recover lost heat faster. A small soldering iron rated for no more than 50 watts is recommended, especially on electrical systems where excess heat can damage the components being soldered.

There are three ingredients necessary for successful soldering; proper flux, good solder and sufficient heat. A soldering flux is necessary to clean the metal of tarnish, prepare it for soldering and to enable the solder to spread into tiny crevices. When soldering, always use a resin flux or resin core solder which is non-corrosive and will not attract moisture once the job is finished. Other types of flux (acid core) will leave a residue that will attract moisture and cause the wires to corrode. Tin is a unique metal with a low melting point. In a molten state, it dissolves and alloys easily with many metals. Solder is made by mixing tin with lead. The most common proportions are 40/60, 50/50 and 60/40, with the percentage of tin listed first. Low priced solders usually contain less tin, making them very difficult for a beginner to use because more heat is required to melt the solder. A common solder is 40/60 which is well suited for all-around general use, but 60/40 melts easier, has more tin for a better joint and is preferred for electrical work.

Soldering Techniques

Successful soldering requires that the metals to be joined be heated to a temperature that will melt the solder – usually 360–460°F (182–238°C). Contrary to popular belief, the purpose of the soldering iron is not to melt the solder itself, but to heat the parts being soldered to a temperature high enough to melt the solder when it is touched to the work. Melting flux-cored solder on the soldering iron will usually destroy the effectiveness of the flux.

NOTE: Soldering tips are made of copper for good heat conductivity, but must be "tinned" regularly for quick transference of heat to the project and to prevent the solder from sticking to the iron. To "tin" the iron, simply heat it and touch the flux-cored solder to the tip; the solder will flow over the hot tip. Wipe the excess off with a clean rag, but be careful as the iron will be hot.

After some use, the tip may become pitted. If so, simply dress the tip smooth with a smooth file and "tin" the tip again. An old saying holds that "metals well cleaned are half soldered." Flux-cored solder will remove oxides but rust, bits of insulation and oil or grease must be removed with a wire brush or emery cloth. For maximum strength in soldered parts, the joint must start off clean and tight. Weak joints will result in gaps too wide for the solder to bridge.

If a separate soldering flux is used, it should be brushed or swabbed on only those areas that are to be soldered. Most solders contain a core of flux and separate fluxing is unnecessary. Hold the work to be soldered firmly. It is best to solder on a wooden board, because a metal vise will only rob the piece to be soldered of heat and make it difficult to melt the solder. Hold the soldering tip with the broadest face against the work to be soldered. Apply solder under the tip close to the work, using enough solder to give a heavy film between the iron and the piece being soldered, while moving slowly and making sure the solder melts properly. Keep the work level or the solder will run to the lowest part and favor the thicker parts, because these require more heat to melt the solder. If the soldering tip overheats (the solder coating on the face of the tip burns up), it should be retinned. Once the soldering is completed, let the soldered joint stand until cool. Tape and seal all soldered wire splices after the repair has cooled.

Wire Harness and Connectors

The on-board computer (ECM) wire harness electrically connects the control unit to the various solenoids, switches and sensors used by the control system. Most connectors in the engine compartment or otherwise exposed to the elements are protected against moisture and dirt which could create oxidation and deposits on the terminals. This protection is important because of the very low voltage and current levels used by the computer and sensors. All connectors have a lock which secures the male and female terminals together, with a secondary lock holding the seal and terminal into the connector. Both terminal locks must be released when disconnecting ECM connectors.

These special connectors are weather-proof and all repairs require the use of a special terminal and the tool required to service it. This tool is used to remove the pin and sleeve terminals. If removal is attempted with an ordinary pick, there is a good chance that the terminal will be bent or deformed. Unlike standard blade type terminals, these terminals cannot be straightened once they are bent. Make certain that the connectors are properly seated and all of the sealing rings in place when connecting leads. On some models, a hinge-type flap provides a backup or secondary locking feature for the terminals. Most secondary locks are used to improve the connector reliability by retaining the terminals if the small terminal lock tangs are not positioned properly.

Molded-on connectors require complete replacement of the connection. This means splicing a new connector assembly into the harness. All splices in on-board computer systems should be soldered to insure proper contact. Use care when probing the connections or replacing terminals in them as it is possible to short between opposite terminals. If this happens to the wrong terminal pair, it is possible to damage certain components. Always use jumper wires between connectors for circuit checking and never probe through weatherproof seals.

Open circuits are often difficult to locate by sight because corrosion or terminal misalignment are hidden by the connectors. Merely wiggling a connector on a sensor or in the wiring harness may correct the open circuit condition. This should always be considered when an open circuit or a failed sensor is indicated. Intermittent problems may also be caused by oxidized or loose connections. When using a circuit tester for diagnosis, always probe connections from the wire side. Be careful not to damage sealed connectors with test probes.

All wiring harnesses should be replaced with identical parts, using the same gauge wire and connectors. When signal wires are spliced into a harness, use wire with high temperature insulation only. With the low voltage and current levels found in the system, it is important that the best possible connection at all wire splices be made by soldering the splices together. It is seldom necessary to replace a complete harness. If replacement is necessary, pay close attention to insure proper harness routing. Secure the harness with suitable plastic wire clamps to prevent vibrations from causing the harness to wear in spots or contact any hot components.

NOTE: Weatherproof connectors cannot be replaced with standard connectors. Instructions are provided with replacement connector and terminal packages. Some wire harnesses have mounting indicators (usually pieces of colored tape) to mark where the harness is to be secured.

In making wiring repairs, it's important that you always replace damaged wires with wires that are the same gauge as the wire being replaced. The heavier the wire, the smaller the gauge number. Wires are color-coded to aid in identification and whenever possible the same color coded wire should be used for replacement. A wire stripping and crimping tool is necessary to install solderless terminal connectors. Test all crimps by pulling on the wires; it should not be possible to pull the wires out of a good crimp.

Wires which are open, exposed or otherwise damaged are repaired by simple splicing. Where possible, if the wiring harness is accessible and the damaged place in the wire can be located, it is best to open the harness and check for all possible damage. In an inaccessible harness, the wire must be bypassed with a new insert, usually taped to the outside of the old harness.

When replacing fusible links, be sure to use fusible link wire, NOT ordinary automotive wire. Make sure the fusible segment is of the same gauge and construction as the one being replaced and double the stripped end when crimping the terminal connector for a good contact. The melted (open) fusible link segment of the wiring harness should be cut off as close to the harness as possible, then a new segment spliced in as described. In the case of a damaged fusible link that feeds two harness wires, the harness connections should be replaced with two fusible link wires so that each circuit will have its own separate protection.

NOTE: Most of the problems caused in the wiring harness are due to bad ground connections. Always check all vehicle ground connections for corrosion or looseness before performing any power feed checks to eliminate the chance of a bad ground affecting the circuit.

Repairing Hard Shell Connectors

Unlike molded connectors, the terminal contacts in hard shell connectors can be replaced. Weatherproof hard-shell connectors with the leads molded into the shell have non-replaceable terminal ends. Replacement usually involves the use of a special terminal removal tool that depress the locking tangs (barbs) on the connector terminal and allow the connector to be removed from the rear of the shell. The connector shell should be replaced if it shows any evidence of burning, melting, cracks, or breaks. Replace individual terminals that are burnt, corroded, distorted or loose.

NOTE: The insulation crimp must be tight to prevent the insulation from sliding back on the wire when the wire is pulled. The insulation must be visibly compressed under the crimp tabs, and the ends of the crimp should be turned in for a firm grip on the insulation.

The wire crimp must be made with all wire strands inside the crimp. The terminal must be fully compressed on the wire strands with the ends of the crimp tabs turned in to make a firm grip on the wire. Check all connections with an ohmmeter to insure a good contact. There should be no measurable resistance between the wire and the terminal when connected.

Mechanical Test Equipment

Vacuum Gauge

Most gauges are graduated in inches of mercury (in.Hg), although a device called a manometer reads vacuum in inches of water (in. H_2O). The normal vacuum reading usually varies between 18 and 22 in.Hg at sea level. To test engine vacuum, the vacuum gauge must be connected to a source of manifold vacuum. Many engines have a plug in the intake manifold which can be removed and replaced with an adapter fitting. Connect the vacuum gauge to the fitting with a suitable rubber hose or, if no manifold plug is available, connect the vacuum gauge to any device using manifold vacuum, such as EGR valves, etc. The vacuum gauge can be used to determine if enough vacuum is reaching a component to allow its actuation.

Hand Vacuum Pump

Small, hand-held vacuum pumps come in a variety of designs. Most have a built-in vacuum gauge and allow the component to be tested without removing it from the vehicle. Operate the pump lever or plunger to apply the correct amount of vacuum required for the test specified in the diagnosis routines. The level of vacuum in inches of Mercury (in.Hg) is indicated on the pump gauge. For some testing, an additional vacuum gauge may be necessary.

Intake manifold vacuum is used to operate various systems and devices on late model vehicles. To correctly diagnose and solve problems in vacuum control systems, a vacuum source is necessary for testing. In some cases, vacuum can be taken from the intake manifold when the engine is running, but vacuum is normally provided by a hand vacuum pump. These hand vacuum pumps have a built-in vacuum gauge that allow testing while the device is still attached to the component. For some tests, an additional vacuum gauge may be necessary.

HEATING AND AIR CONDITIONING

NOTE: Refer to Section 1 for discharging, evacuating and recharging the air conditioning system.

Heater Blower Motor

REMOVAL AND INSTALLATION

Front (Main) Motor

The blower motor is located in the engine compartment on the right side of the firewall.
1. Disconnect the negative battery terminal from the battery.
2. Disconnect the electrical connector from the blower motor.
3. Remove the radiator coolant collecting bottle from the right side of the engine compartment.
4. Remove the windshield washer fluid bottle from the right side of the engine compartment.

5. Remove the blower motor-to-duct housing screws and the blower motor from the vehicle.
6. If necessary, replace the blower motor-to-duct housing gasket.

To install:
1. Install the motor and gasket. Torque the retaining screws to 18 inch lbs. (1.6 Nm).
2. Install the windshield washer fluid bottle to the right side of the engine compartment.
3. Install the radiator coolant collecting bottle to the right side of the engine compartment.
4. Connect the electrical connector to the blower motor.
5. Connect the negative battery terminal from the battery.
6. Check for proper operation.
7. Refill the windshield washer bottle and the radiator coolant collecting bottle.

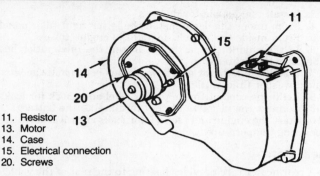

11. Resistor
13. Motor
14. Case
15. Electrical connection
20. Screws

View of the heater blower motor and case

Rear (Overhead) Motor

A rear overhead heater provides heating to the rear of the vehicle. It is located on the left side of the vehicle, in front of the wheel fender and is concealed behind a cover.
1. Disconnect the negative battery terminal from the battery.
2. Remove the cover-to-heater unit and the cover.
3. Disconnect the electrical connector from the blower motor.
4. Remove the blower motor-to-heater housing screws and the blower motor.
5. If necessary, replace the blower motor-to-heater housing gasket.
To install:
1. Use a new gasket (if necessary) and install the motor. Torque the retaining screws to 18 inch lbs. (1.6 Nm).
2. Connect the electrical connector to the blower motor.
3. Install the cover-to-heater unit and the cover.
4. Connect the negative battery terminal to the battery and check operation.

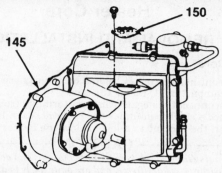

145. Blower motor and evaporator case
150. Resistor

Exploded view of a blower motor resistor — all are similar

Blower Motor Resistor

A blower motor resistor is mounted on top of each blower/heater or blower/evaporator case.

REMOVAL AND INSTALLATION

1. Disconnect the negative battery terminal from the battery.
2. Disconnect the electrical connector from the resistor.
3. Remove the resistor-to-case screws and lift the resistor from the case.
4. **To install,** install the resistor and retaining screws. Connect the electrical connector and negative battery cable.

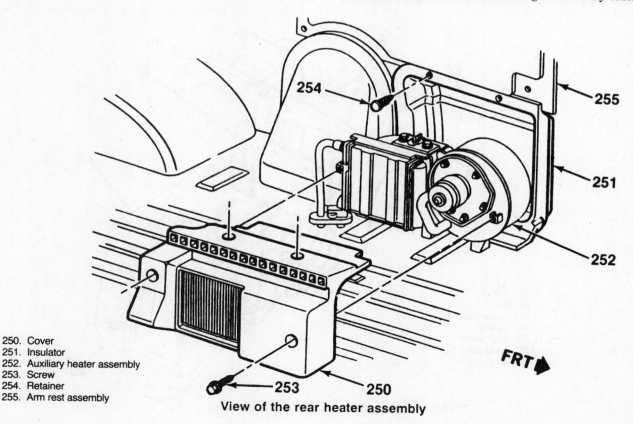

250. Cover
251. Insulator
252. Auxiliary heater assembly
253. Screw
254. Retainer
255. Arm rest assembly

FRT

View of the rear heater assembly

Heater Core

REMOVAL AND INSTALLATION

Front Core

The front heater core is located on the right side of the passenger compartment, under the dash.

1. Disconnect the negative battery terminal from the battery.
2. Place a catch pan under the radiator, open the drain cock and drain the coolant to a level below the heater core.

— CAUTION —

When draining the coolant, keep in mind that cats and dogs are attracted by the ethylene glycol antifreeze, and are quite likely to drink any that is left in an uncovered container or in puddles on the ground. This will prove fatal in sufficient quantity. Always drain the coolant into a sealable container. Coolant should be reused unless it is contaminated or several years old.

3. Remove the radiator overflow coolant bottle and the windshield washer fluid bottle.
4. In the engine compartment, remove the inlet/outlet hose clamps from the heater core. Remove and plug the heater hoses to prevent coolant spillage.
5. From inside the vehicle, remove the engine cover to provide extra room.
6. From under the dash, remove the lower right filler panel.
7. Remove the distributor duct, for extra room.
8. Remove the heater-to-cowl bolts and the heater assembly from the vehicle.
9. Separate the cover plate and the heater core from the heater assembly.

To install:

1. Assemble the cover plate and the heater core to the heater assembly.
2. Install the heater-to-cowl bolts and the heater assembly to the vehicle.

3. Install the distributor duct.
4. From under the dash, install the lower right filler panel.
5. From inside the vehicle, install the engine cover.
6. In the engine compartment, install the inlet/outlet hose clamps to the heater core.
7. Install the radiator overflow coolant bottle and the windshield washer fluid bottle.
8. Refill the coolant to the proper level and check for leaks.
9. Connect the negative battery terminal to the battery.
10. Start the engine and recheck for leaks after it has reached operating temperature.

Rear Core

A rear heater core provides heating to the rear of the vehicle. It is located on the left side of the vehicle, in front of the wheel fender and is concealed behind a cover.

1. Disconnect the negative battery terminal from the battery.
2. Place a catch pan under the radiator, open the drain cock and drain the cooling system.

— CAUTION —

When draining the coolant, keep in mind that cats and dogs are attracted by the ethylene glycol antifreeze, and are quite likely to drink any that is left in an uncovered container or in puddles on the ground. This will prove fatal in sufficient quantity. Always drain the coolant into a sealable container. Coolant should be reused unless it is contaminated or several years old.

3. From under the vehicle (at the rear heating unit), remove the inlet/outlet hose clamps from the heater core. Remove and plug the heater hoses to prevent coolant excess spillage.
4. From inside the vehicle, remove the heating unit cover.
5. Remove the heater core from the blower assembly.
6. Inspect the heater hoses for deterioration, then replace (if necessary).

To install:

1. Install the heater core into the blower assembly. Make

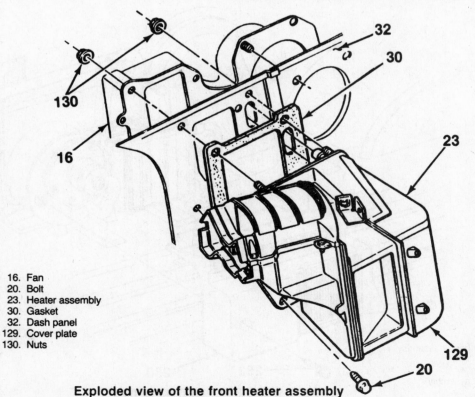

16. Fan
20. Bolt
23. Heater assembly
30. Gasket
32. Dash panel
129. Cover plate
130. Nuts

Exploded view of the front heater assembly

sure all the seals are positioned properly.

2. From inside the vehicle, install the heating unit cover.

3. From under the vehicle (at the rear heating unit), install the inlet/outlet hose clamps to the heater core.

4. Refill the radiator to the proper level.

5. Connect the negative battery terminal to the battery.

6. Start the engine and check for leaks.

Control Assembly

The control assembly is located on the instrument panel to the right side of the steering wheel.

REMOVAL AND INSTALLATION

1. Disconnect the negative battery terminal from the battery.

2. Remove the instrument panel bezel.

3. Remove the control assembly-to-instrument panel screws

and pull the control assembly from the instrument panel.

4. Disconnect the electrical connectors, the control cables and the blower switch from the control assembly.

To install:

1. Install the control assembly after connecting the electrical connectors, the control cables and the blower switch.

2. Install the control assembly-to-instrument panel screws.

3. Install the instrument panel bezel.

4. Connect the negative battery terminal to the battery.

5. Check for proper operation.

Evaporator Blower Motor

REMOVAL AND INSTALLATION

Front System

The blower motor is located in the engine compartment on

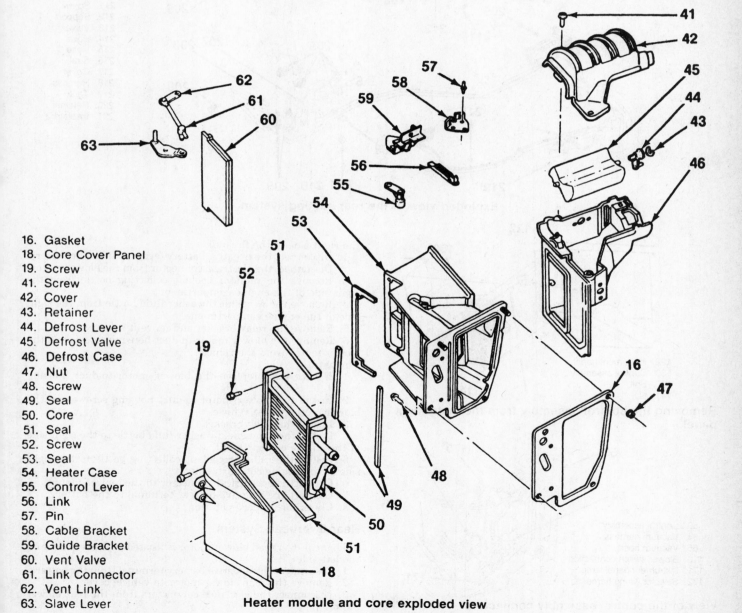

16. Gasket
18. Core Cover Panel
19. Screw
41. Screw
42. Cover
43. Retainer
44. Defrost Lever
45. Defrost Valve
46. Defrost Case
47. Nut
48. Screw
49. Seal
50. Core
51. Seal
52. Screw
53. Seal
54. Heater Case
55. Control Lever
56. Link
57. Pin
58. Cable Bracket
59. Guide Bracket
60. Vent Valve
61. Link Connector
62. Vent Link
63. Slave Lever

Heater module and core exploded view

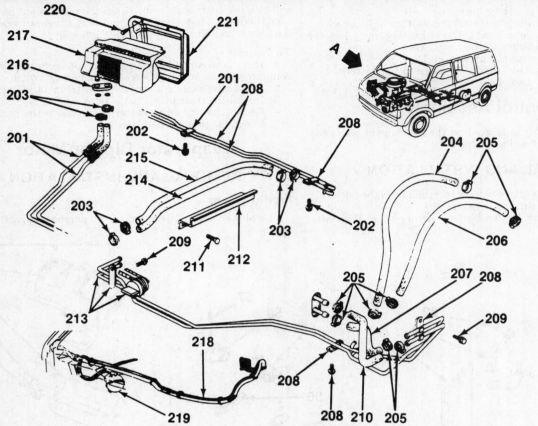

201.	Pipe
202.	Screw
203.	Clamp
204.	Hose
205.	Clamp
206.	Hose
207.	Hose
208.	Bracket
209.	Screw
210.	Hose
211.	Screw
212.	Support
213.	Valve
214.	Hose
215.	Hose
216.	Seal
217.	Cover
218.	Harness
219.	Tank
220.	Retainer
221.	Insulator

Exploded view of the rear heating system

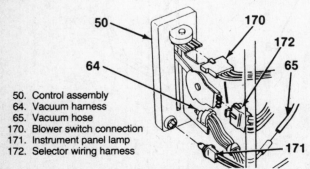

122. Instrument panel
130. Control assembly
140. Bolt
141. Nut

Removing the control assembly from the instrument panel

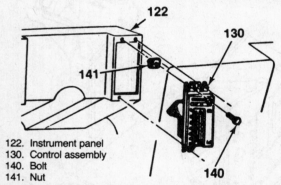

50. Control assembly
64. Vacuum harness
65. Vacuum hose
170. Blower switch connection
171. Instrument panel lamp
172. Selector wiring harness

View of the control assembly connectors

the right side of the firewall.
1. Disconnect the negative battery terminal from the battery.
2. Disconnect the electrical connector from the blower motor.
3. Remove the radiator coolant collecting bottle from the right side of the engine compartment.
4. Remove the windshield washer fluid bottle from the right side of the engine compartment.
5. Remove the relay bracket and move it aside.
6. Remove the blower motor-to-duct housing screws and the blower motor from the vehicle.
To install:
1. If necessary, replace the blower motor-to-duct housing gasket.
2. Install the blower motor-to-duct housing screws and the blower motor to the vehicle.
3. Install the relay bracket.
4. Install the windshield washer fluid bottle to the right side of the engine compartment.
5. Install the radiator coolant collecting bottle to the right side of the engine compartment.
6. Connect the electrical connector to the blower motor.
7. Connect the negative battery terminal to the battery.
8. Check for proper operation.

Rear Overhead System

The rear overhead blower motor is located at the rear door on the left side.
1. Disconnect the negative battery terminal from the battery.
2. Remove the rear blower motor-to-vehicle cover.
3. Disconnect the electrical connectors from the rear blower motor.

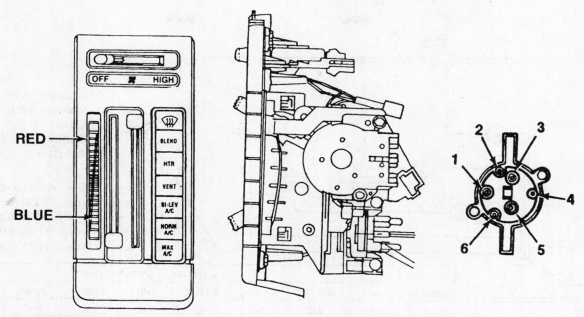

CONNECTION	PORT NO.	SELECT VALVE OPERATING CHART						
		MAX. A/C	NORM A/C	BI-LEVEL	VENT	HTR	BLEND	DEF.
Source	1	Conn. 3,5,6	Conn. 4,5,6	Conn. 4,5	Conn. 4,5,6	Conn. 4	No Conn.	Conn. 2
Def.	2	VENT	VENT	VENT	VENT	VENT	VENT	Conn. 1
REC/OSA	3	Conn. 1,5,6	VENT	VENT	VENT	VENT	VENT	VENT
HTR	4	VENT	Conn. 1,5,6	Conn. 1,5	Conn. 1,5,6	Conn. 1	VENT	VENT
MODE (A/C)	5	Conn. 1,3,6	Conn. 1,4,6	Conn. 1,4	Conn. 1,4,6	VENT	VENT	VENT
MODE (HTR)	6	Conn. 1,3,5	Conn. 1,4,5	VENT	Conn. 1,4,5	VENT	VENT	VENT

BLOWER SWITCH				
	POSITION			
TERM	OFF	M_1	M_2	HI
B +	No Continuity	Conn. To M_1	Conn. To M_2	Conn. To H
H	No Continuity	No Continuity	No Continuity	Conn. to B +
M_1	No Continuity	Conn. To B +	Continuity Optional	No Continuity
M_2	No Continuity	No Continuity	Conn. To B +	Continuity Optional

CONNECTION	TERM NO.	SELECT VALVE OPERATING CHART						
		MAX. A/C	NORM A/C	BI-LEVEL	VENT	HEAT	BLEND	DEFROST
Compressor	1	Conn. 3,5	Conn. 3,5	Conn. 3,5	No Conn.	No Conn.	Conn. 3,5	Conn. 3,5
No Used	2				No Conn.			
B +	3	Conn. 1,5	Conn. 1,5	Conn. 1,5	No Conn.	No Conn.	Conn. 1,5	Conn. 1,5
No Used	4				No Conn.			
Compressor	5	Conn. 1,3	Conn. 1,3	Conn. 1,3	No Conn.	No Conn.	Conn. 1,3	Conn. 1,3

Heater-Air conditioning control unit operation chart

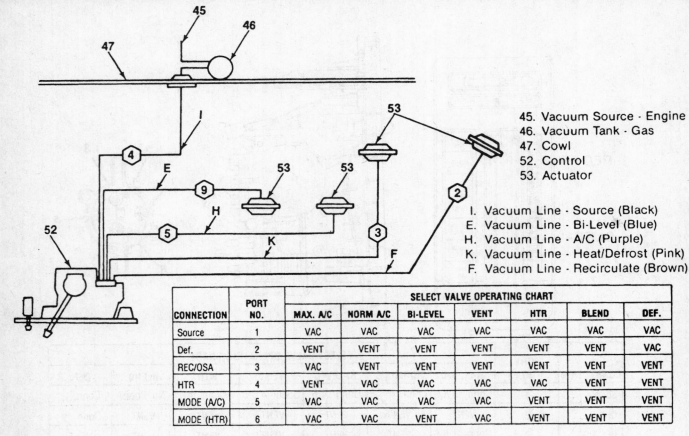

CONNECTION	PORT NO.	SELECT VALVE OPERATING CHART						
		MAX. A/C	NORM A/C	BI-LEVEL	VENT	HTR	BLEND	DEF.
Source	1	VAC	VAC	VAC	VAC	VAC	VAC	VAC
Def.	2	VENT	VENT	VENT	VENT	VENT	VENT	VAC
REC/OSA	3	VAC	VENT	VENT	VENT	VENT	VENT	VENT
HTR	4	VENT	VAC	VAC	VAC	VAC	VENT	VENT
MODE (A/C)	5	VAC	VAC	VAC	VAC	VENT	VENT	VENT
MODE (HTR)	6	VAC	VAC	VENT	VAC	VENT	VENT	VENT

45. Vacuum Source - Engine
46. Vacuum Tank - Gas
47. Cowl
52. Control
53. Actuator

I. Vacuum Line - Source (Black)
E. Vacuum Line - Bi-Level (Blue)
H. Vacuum Line - A/C (Purple)
K. Vacuum Line - Heat/Defrost (Pink)
F. Vacuum Line - Recirculate (Brown)

Heater-Air conditioning vacuum circuit chart

4. Remove the blower motor-to-blower case screws and the blower motor from the vehicle.

To install:

1. Install the blower motor-to-blower case screws and the blower motor to the vehicle.

2. Connect the electrical connectors to the rear blower motor.

3. Install the rear blower motor-to-vehicle cover.

4. Connect the negative battery terminal to the battery.

5. Check for normal operation.

Air Conditioning System Blower Motor Relay

The blower motor relay is located on a bracket attached to the right side of the vehicle, near the blower motor.

REMOVAL AND INSTALLATION

1. Disconnect the negative battery terminal from the battery.

2. Disconnect the electrical connector from the blower motor relay.

3. Remove the blower motor relay bracket-to-vehicle screws, lift the bracket and remove the relay from the bracket.

4. To install, reverse the removal procedures.

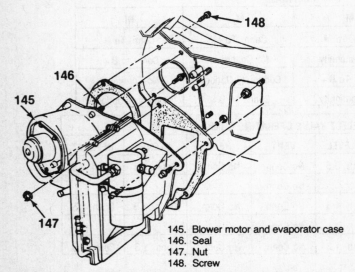

145. Blower motor and evaporator case
146. Seal
147. Nut
148. Screw

Exploded view of the heater blower/evaporator case — front air conditioning system

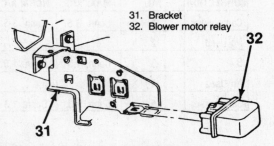

31. Bracket
32. Blower motor relay

Replacing the blower motor relay

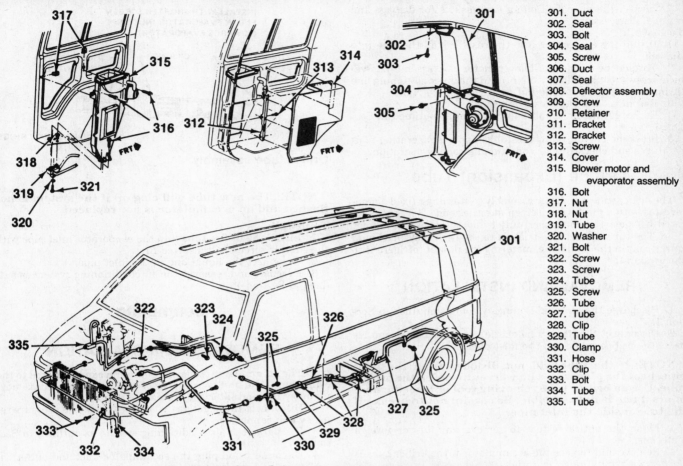

301.	Duct
302.	Seal
303.	Bolt
304.	Seal
305.	Screw
306.	Duct
307.	Seal
308.	Deflector assembly
309.	Screw
310.	Retainer
311.	Bracket
312.	Bracket
313.	Screw
314.	Cover
315.	Blower motor and evaporator assembly
316.	Bolt
317.	Nut
318.	Nut
319.	Tube
320.	Washer
321.	Bolt
322.	Screw
323.	Screw
324.	Tube
325.	Screw
326.	Tube
327.	Tube
328.	Clip
329.	Tube
330.	Clamp
331.	Hose
332.	Clip
333.	Bolt
334.	Tube
335.	Tube

Exploded view of the rear overhead air conditioning unit

Evaporator Core

Two evaporator cores are used, one in the front (engine compartment) and one at the rear (overhead) door. The rear overhead air conditioning system works in conjunction with the front system.

REMOVAL AND INSTALLATION

NOTE: Before removing the evaporator core, the air conditioning system must be discharged. Refer to the air conditioning Discharging procedures in Section 1 and discharge the air conditioning system.

Front System

The front evaporator core is located in the engine compartment on the right side of the firewall inside the heater/evaporator/blower motor case.

1. Disconnect the negative battery terminal from the battery.
2. Remove the radiator coolant collecting bottle and the windshield washer fluid bottle.
3. Disconnect any necessary electrical connectors.
4. Discharge the air conditioning system as outlined in Section 1. Disconnect the air conditioning refrigerant lines from the evaporator.
5. Remove the relay bracket and move it aside.
6. Remove the evaporator/blower case nuts and the case, then separate the evaporator from the case.

To install:
1. Install the evaporator into the case and tighten the retainers.
2. Install the relay bracket.
3. Connect the air conditioning refrigerant lines to the evaporator.
4. Connect any necessary electrical connectors.
5. Install the radiator coolant collecting bottle and the windshield washer fluid bottle.
6. Connect the negative battery terminal to the battery.
7. Evacuate and recharge the air conditioning system as outlined in Section 1.
8. Start the engine, allow it establish normal operating temperatures and check the air conditioning cooling operation.

Rear Overhead System

1. Disconnect the negative battery terminal from the battery.
2. Remove the rear evaporator/blower motor-to-vehicle cover.
3. Disconnect the electrical connectors from the rear blower motor and the resistor.
4. Discharge the air conditioning system as outlined in Section 1. From under the left rear of the vehicle, remove the air conditioning line fitting-to-evaporator fitting nut.
5. Remove the evaporator/blower motor case-to-vehicle screws and the case from the vehicle.
6. Separate the air conditioning evaporator from the evaporator/blower motor case assembly.

7. Inspect the air conditioning line gaskets for damage and replace (if necessary).

To install:

1. Install the evaporator into the case. Install the case into the vehicle.

2. Torque the evaporator/blower motor case assembly-to-vehicle screws to 4 inch lbs. (0.5 Nm) and the air conditioning line fitting-to-evaporator fitting nut to 18 ft. lbs. (25 Nm).

3. Reconnect the electrical connectors.

4. Recharge the air conditioning system as outlined in Section 1.

5. Start the engine, allow it establish normal operating temperatures and check the air conditioning cooling operation.

Orifice (Expansion) Tube

The orifice tube is a plastic assembly containing a fixed diameter tube with a mesh filter screen at either end. The tube is located between the condenser outlet and the evaporator inlet tube. The tube acts as a restriction to the high pressure liquid refrigerant in the liquid line, metering the flow of refrigerant to the evaporator.

REMOVAL AND INSTALLATION

1. Discharge the air conditioning system as outlined in Section 1.

2. Disconnect the liquid line at the evaporator inlet and remove the orifice tube from the inlet pipe.

NOTE: If the tube will not dislodge from the inlet pipe, heat the pipe with a hair dryer to loosen the orifice tube. Use an orifice tube removing tool or a needle nose pliers if one is not available. Be careful not to break off the tube inside the inlet pipe.

3. Flush the entire system to remove any dirt or foreign materials.

4. Remove and replace the accumulator if the orifice tube is clogged with any foreign material.

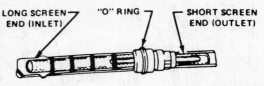

INSTALL WITH SHORTER SCREEN END IN EVAPORATOR INLET PIPE (TOWARDS EVAPORATOR)

LONG SCREEN END (INLET) — "O" RING — SHORT SCREEN END (OUTLET)

USE NEW "O" RINGS

Orifice tube assembly

NOTE: The new tube will clog up if the system is not flushed and an accumulator is not replaced.

To install:

1. Install the orifice tube into the evaporator inlet pipe with the shorter screen end inserted first.

2. Reconnect the liquid line to the inlet pipe.

3. Evacuate and recharge the air conditioning system as outlined in Section 1.

Accumulator

REMOVAL AND INSTALLATION

1. The accumulator is a large aluminum can connected to the evaporator. The unit is in charge of storing refrigerant, removing moisture and filter the system.

2. Disconnect the negative (−) battery cable and pressure relief switch connector.

3. Discharge the air conditioning system as outlined in Section 1.

4. Disconnect and plug the accumulator inlet and outlet.

5. Cap the open lines immediately after removal.

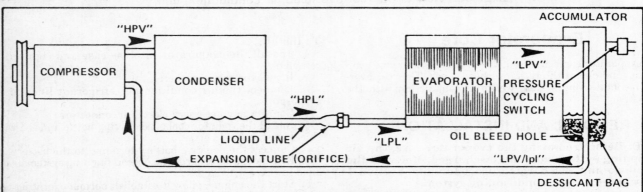

PRESSURE CYCLING SYSTEM

"HPV" — HIGH PRESSURE VAPOR LEAVING COMPRESSOR.

"HPL" — VAPOR IS COOLED DOWN BY CONDENSER AIR FLOW AND LEAVES AS HIGH PRESSURE LIQUID.

"LPL" — ORIFICE METERS THE LIQUID R-12, INTO EVAPORATOR, REDUCING ITS PRESSURE, AND WARM BLOWER AIR ACROSS EVAPORATOR CORE CAUSES BOILING OFF OF LIQUID INTO VAPOR.

"LPV" — LEAVES EVAPORATOR AS LOW PRESSURE VAPOR AND RETURNS WITH THE SMALL AMOUNT OF . . .

"lpl" — . . . LOW PRESSURE LIQUID THAT DIDN'T BOIL OFF COMPLETELY BACK TO THE COMPRESSOR TO BE COMPRESSED AGAIN.

Orifice (expansion) tube location

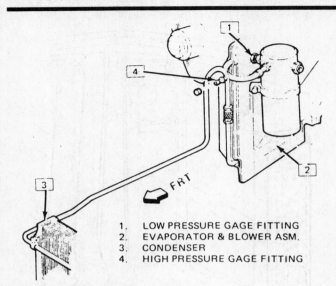

1. LOW PRESSURE GAGE FITTING
2. EVAPORATOR & BLOWER ASM.
3. CONDENSER
4. HIGH PRESSURE GAGE FITTING

Accumulator assembly

6. Remove the accumulator retaining screws and accumulator.
To install:
1. Install 2 fluid oz. (60 ml) of 525 viscosity refrigerant oil into the new accumulator.
2. Install the accumulator with new O-rings.

3. Connect the two pipes to the unit.
4. Evacuate and recharge the system as outlined in chapter 1.

Water Control Valve
Air Conditioning Only

REMOVAL AND INSTALLATION

1. The water control valve is located at the heater core inlet and outlet pipes. The valve is used to shut off hot water flow to the heater core during air conditioning operation.
2. Allow the engine to cool down. Drain the engine coolant into a suitable container.

— **CAUTION** —

When draining the coolant, keep in mind that cats and dogs are attracted by the ethylene glycol antifreeze, and are quite likely to drink any that is left in an uncovered container or in puddles on the ground. This will prove fatal in sufficient quantity. Always drain the coolant into a sealable container. Coolant should be reused unless it is contaminated or several years old.

3. Remove the hose clamps and hoses from the valve and remove the valve from the heater core pipes.

WARNING: Cut the hoses off of the heater core if they will not remove easily. Damage to the heater core may result if the hoses are forced away from the heater core.

4. Install the valve with new hoses and tighten the clamps.
5. Refill the engine with clean coolant.
6. Start the engine and check for proper operation.

RADIO

REMOVAL AND INSTALLATION

1. Disconnect the negative battery terminal from the battery.
2. Remove the instrument panel-to-engine cover assembly.
3. Remove the radio-to-instrument panel bezel.
4. Remove the radio-to-instrument panel fasteners.
5. Pull the radio (slightly) from the instrument, then disconnect the antenna and electrical connectors.
6. Remove the radio from the instrument panel.

To install:
1. Install the radio into the instrument panel after connecting the antenna and electrical connectors.
2. Install the radio-to-instrument panel fasteners.
3. Install the radio-to-instrument panel bezel.
4. Install the instrument panel-to-engine cover assembly.
5. Connect the negative battery terminal to the battery and check operation.

51. Radio receiver
52. Clip bracket
53. Radio bracket
54. Nut
55. Instrument panel
56. Screw

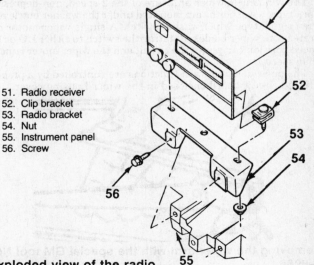

Exploded view of the radio

Dash mounted speaker removal

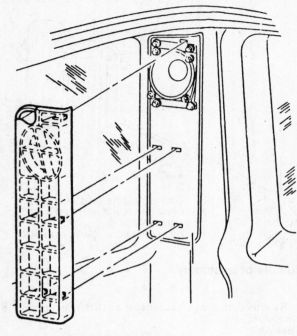

Rear pillar speaker removal

WINDSHIELD WIPERS

The windshield wiper units are of the 2-speed, non-depressed park type, a washer pump mounted under the washer bottle and turn signal type wiper/washer switch. A single wiper motor operates both wiper blades. Rotating the switch to either **LO** or **HI** speed position completes the circuit and the wiper motor runs at that speed.

The pulse/demand wash functions are controlled by a plug-in printed circuit board enclosed in the wiper housing cover.

Removing the wiper arm with the special GM tool No. J–8966

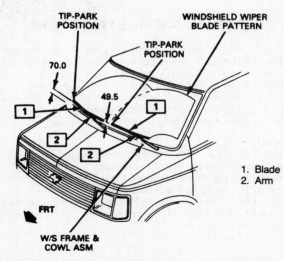

Positioning the wiper arms on the windshield

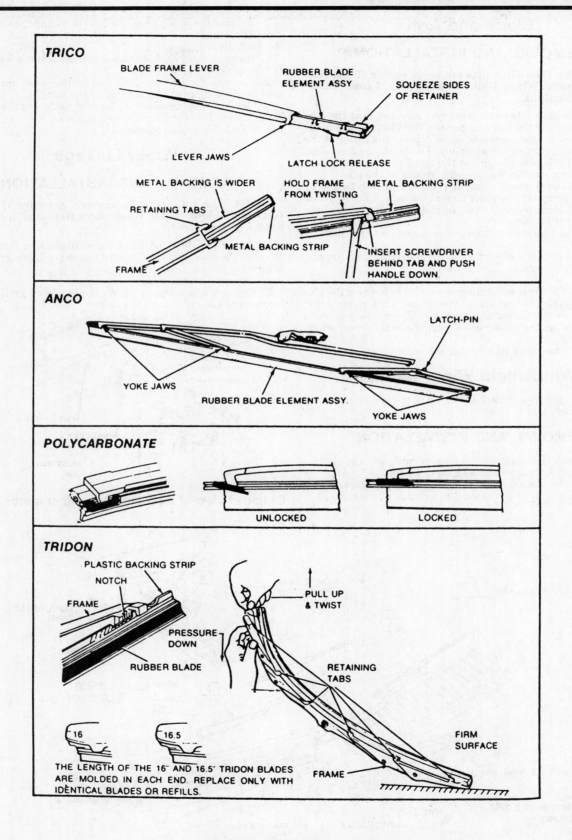

Wiper insert replacement

Blade and Arm

REMOVAL AND INSTALLATION

NOTE: The following procedure is easier if you use GM Windshield Wiper Blade/Arm Removal tool No. J–8966 or equivalent.

If the wiper assembly has a press type release tab at the center, simply depress the tab and remove the blade. If the blade has no release tab, use a screwdriver to depress the spring at the center; this will release the assembly. To install the assembly, position the blade over the pin (at the tip of the arm) and press until the spring retainer engages the groove in the pin.

To remove the element, either depress the release button or squeeze the spring type retainer clip (at the outer end) together and slide the blade element out. To install, slide the new element in until it latches.

1. Insert the tool under the wiper arm and lever the arm off the shaft.
2. Disconnect the washer hose from the arm (if equipped), then remove the arm.

To install:
1. Operate the wiper motor (momentarily) to position the pivot shafts into the Park position. The proper Park position for the arms is with the blades approximately 50mm on the driver's side, or 70mm on the passenger's side, above the lower windshield molding.
2. Connect the water hose and check operation.

Windshield Wiper Motor

The windshield wiper motor is located in the engine compartment on the left side of the cowl.

REMOVAL AND INSTALLATION

1. Disconnect the negative (–) battery cable and the electrical connector from the windshield wiper motor.
2. Remove the transmission link from the wiper motor crank arm by pulling or prying it toward the rear of the vehicle.

3. Remove the wiper motor-to-cowl bolts and the wiper motor from the vehicle.

To install:
1. Install the wiper motor-to-cowl bolts and the wiper motor to the vehicle.
2. Connect the transmission link to the wiper motor crank arm by pushing toward the front of the vehicle.
3. Connect the negative (–) battery cable and the electrical connector to the windshield wiper motor.
4. Check for proper operation.

Wiper Linkage

REMOVAL AND INSTALLATION

NOTE: The following procedure is easier if you use GM Windshield Wiper Blade/Arm Removal tool No. J–8966 or equivalent.

1. Using the GM Windshield Wiper Blade/Arm Removal tool No. J–8966 or equivalent, remove the wiper blade/arm assemblies from the pivot shafts.
2. Remove the antenna.
3. Remove the outside air cowl ventilator grille-to-cowl screws and the grille from the cowl.

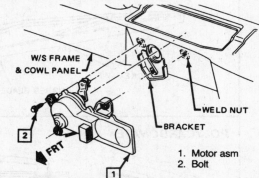

1. Motor asm
2. Bolt

Exploded view of the windshield wiper motor

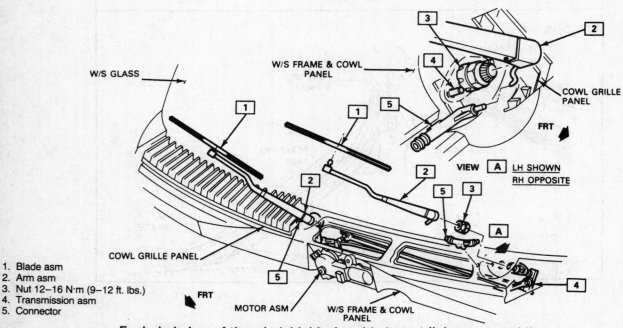

1. Blade asm
2. Arm asm
3. Nut 12–16 N·m (9–12 ft. lbs.)
4. Transmission asm
5. Connector

Exploded view of the windshield wiper blade and linkage assemblies

4. At the center of the cowl, remove the link rod-to-motor drive nut, then disengage the link rod from the pins.

5. Remove the arm transmission pivot shaft assembly-to-cowl nuts.

6. Remove the pivot shaft assembly (with link rod) from the plenum chamber.

To install:

1. Operate the wiper motor (momentarily) to position the pivot shafts into the Park position.

2. Install the pivot shaft assembly (with link rod) to the ple-num chamber.

3. Install the arm transmission pivot shaft assembly-to-cowl nuts.

4. At the center of the cowl, install the link rod-to-motor drive nut.

5. Install the outside air cowl ventilator grille-to-cowl screws and grille to the cowl.

6. Install the antenna.

7. Install the wiper blade/arm assemblies to the pivot shafts. Check for proper operation.

INSTRUMENTS AND SWITCHES

Instrument Cluster

REMOVAL AND INSTALLATION

1. Disconnect the negative battery terminal from the battery.

2. Remove the lower steering column cover-to-instrument panel screws and the cover.

3. Remove the instrument cluster trim plate-to-instrument cluster screws and the panel, then allow the panel to hang to the left side by the wiring.

4. Remove the air conditioning control-to-instrument panel screws and move the control assembly aside.

5. For access, remove the seat alarm assembly from the bracket, on the left side of the instrument panel.

6. Remove the instrument panel cluster-to-instrument panel fasteners and the cluster assembly.

7. Disconnect the speedometer cable, the speed sensor and any other necessary electrical connectors.

To install:

1. Connect the speedometer cable, the speed sensor and any other necessary electrical connectors.

2. Install the instrument panel cluster-to-instrument panel fasteners and the cluster assembly.

3. Install the seat alarm assembly to the bracket, on the left side of the instrument panel.

4. Install the air conditioning control-to-instrument panel screws and the control assembly.

5. Install the instrument cluster trim plate-to-instrument cluster screws and the panel.

6. Install the lower steering column cover-to-instrument panel screws and the cover.

7. Connect the negative battery terminal to the battery and check operation.

Speedometer

REMOVAL AND INSTALLATION

1. Disconnect the negative (–) battery cable.

2. Remove the instrument cluster from the instrument panel as previously outlined in this Section.

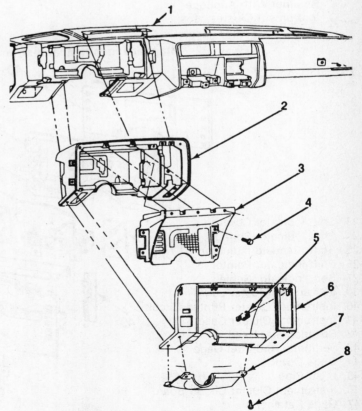

1. Instrument panel upper trim pad
2. Instrument cluster housing
3. Instrument cluster assembly
4. Screw
5. Retainer
6. Instrument panel cluster trim plate
7. Lower steering column trim plate
8. Screw

Exploded view of the instrument cluster and panel

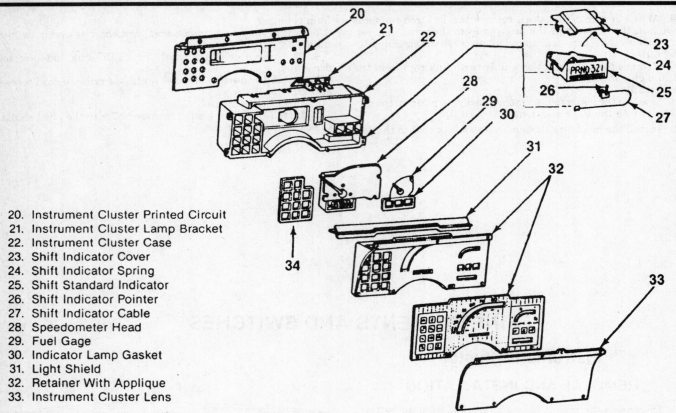

20. Instrument Cluster Printed Circuit
21. Instrument Cluster Lamp Bracket
22. Instrument Cluster Case
23. Shift Indicator Cover
24. Shift Indicator Spring
25. Shift Standard Indicator
26. Shift Indicator Pointer
27. Shift Indicator Cable
28. Speedometer Head
29. Fuel Gage
30. Indicator Lamp Gasket
31. Light Shield
32. Retainer With Applique
33. Instrument Cluster Lens

Standard mechanical instrument cluster exploded view

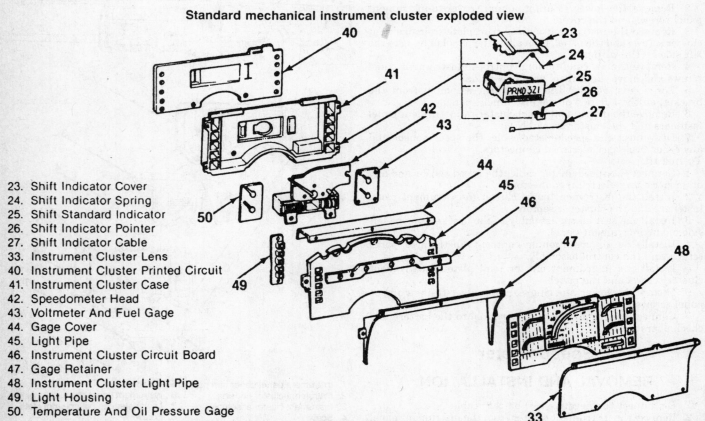

23. Shift Indicator Cover
24. Shift Indicator Spring
25. Shift Standard Indicator
26. Shift Indicator Pointer
27. Shift Indicator Cable
33. Instrument Cluster Lens
40. Instrument Cluster Printed Circuit
41. Instrument Cluster Case
42. Speedometer Head
43. Voltmeter And Fuel Gage
44. Gage Cover
45. Light Pipe
46. Instrument Cluster Circuit Board
47. Gage Retainer
48. Instrument Cluster Light Pipe
49. Light Housing
50. Temperature And Oil Pressure Gage

Optional mechanical instrument cluster exploded view

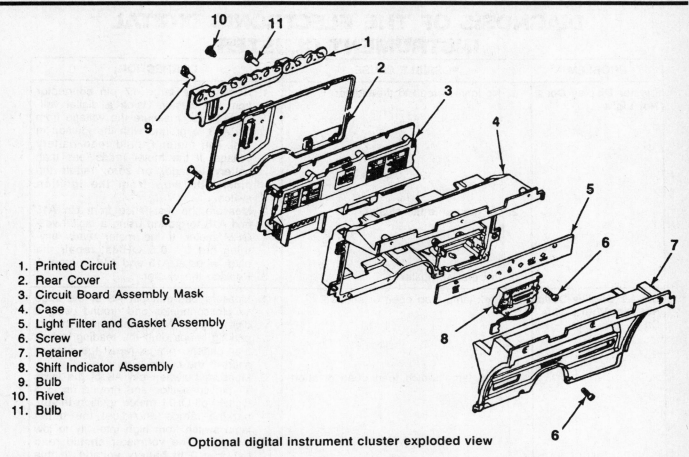

1. Printed Circuit
2. Rear Cover
3. Circuit Board Assembly Mask
4. Case
5. Light Filter and Gasket Assembly
6. Screw
7. Retainer
8. Shift Indicator Assembly
9. Bulb
10. Rivet
11. Bulb

Optional digital instrument cluster exploded view

3. Remove the speedometer head retaining screws and the speedometer.

To install:
1. Install the speedometer head and retaining screws.
2. Install the instrument cluster.
3. Connect the negative battery cable.

Gauges

REMOVAL AND INSTALLATION

1. Disconnect the negative (–) battery cable.
2. Remove the instrument cluster from the instrument panel as previously outlined in this Section.
3. Remove the gauge retaining screws and gauge.

To install:
1. Install the gauge, retaining screws, instrument cluster and negative battery cable.
2. Check for proper operation.

Instrument Panel

REMOVAL AND INSTALLATION

1. Disconnect the negative battery terminal from the battery.
2. Remove the lower steering column cover-to-instrument panel screws and the cover.
3. Remove the lower instrument panel-to-engine cover nuts/bolts and the lower instrument panel-to-dash bolts.
4. Remove the instrument cluster trim plate-to-instrument cluster screws and the panel, then allow the panel to hang to the left side by the wiring.

5. Remove the air conditioning control-to-instrument panel screws and move the control assembly aside.
6. For access, remove the seat alarm assembly from the bracket, on the left side of the instrument panel.
7. Remove the instrument panel cluster-to-instrument panel fasteners and the cluster assembly.
8. Disconnect the speedometer cable, the speed sensor and any other necessary electrical connectors.
9. Remove the instrument panel-to-cowl screws and the instrument panel from the vehicle.

To install:
1. Connect the speedometer cable, the speed sensor and any other necessary electrical connectors.
2. Install the instrument panel-to-cowl screws and the instrument panel to the vehicle.
3. Install the instrument panel cluster-to-instrument panel fasteners and the cluster assembly.
4. Install the seat alarm assembly to the bracket.
5. Install the air conditioning control-to-instrument panel screws.
6. Install the instrument cluster trim plate-to-instrument cluster screws and the panel.
7. Install the lower instrument panel-to-engine cover nuts/bolts and the lower instrument panel-to-dash bolts.
8. Install the lower steering column cover-to-instrument panel screws and the cover.
9. Connect the negative battery terminal to the battery and check for proper operation.

DIAGNOSIS

NOTE: Refer to the diagnostic charts using the wiring diagrams at the end of this Section.

DIAGNOSIS OF THE ELECTRONIC DIGITAL INSTRUMENT CLUSTER

PROBLEM	POSSIBLE CAUSE	CORRECTION
Cluster Display Does Not Light	1. No ignition feed to the cluster.	1. Remove the large 17 pin connector from the cluster. Using a digital volt-OHM meter, measure the voltage from pin A13 to ground with the ignition in run. The meter should read battery voltage. If the meter reads less than battery voltage, or zero, repair the pink/white wire from the ignition switch.
	2. No ground to the cluster.	2. Measure the resistance from pin A15 and A16 to ground using a digital volt-OHM meter. If the meter reads anything but 0 - 0.5 OHMs, repair the black wires at A15 and A16 to ground.
	3. Inoperative cluster	3. Replace the cluster.
Cluster Display Does Not Dim With Lights On	1. Park lamp feed open or shorted.	1. Measure between pin A8 of the large 17 pin connector, and ground using a digital volt-OHM meter. Ignition in run, parking lamps on. If the reading is less than battery voltage, repair the open or short at the brown wire.
	2. Park lamp switch feed open or shorted.	2. Measure between pin A8 of the large 17 pin connector, and ground using a digital volt-OHM meter. Ignition in run, parking lamps on. Adjust the panel lamp switch from high intensity to low intensity. The voltmeter should read between 0 to battery voltage. If this reading is not obtained, repair the gray wire and/or the park lamp switch.
	3. Cluster inoperative.	3. If the previous 2 steps are OK, replace the instrument cluster.
Cluster Display Always Dim	Inoperative cluster.	Replace the cluster.
Cluster Display Does Not Switch Between English and Metric	1. Inoperative cluster control switch or wiring.	1. Disconnect the large 17 pin connector at the cluster. Measure the resistance between pin A2 and ground. The resistance should be zero in one position, and open in the other. If the switch does not respond in this manner, repair the light blue wire from the cluster to the switch, the switch, or the black wire from the switch to ground.
	2. Inoperative cluster.	2. If the switch and wiring are correct, replace the cluster.
Speedometer Inoperative or Inaccurate, Odometer Operates Correctly	Inoperative instrument cluster.	Replace the cluster.
One Or Both Odometers Do Not Operate Properly But The Speedometer Operates Properly	Inoperative instrument cluster.	Replace the cluster.

DIAGNOSIS OF THE ELECTRONIC DIGITAL INSTRUMENT CLUSTER (cont'd)

PROBLEM	POSSIBLE CAUSE	CORRECTION
Speedometer And Odometers Do Not Operate	No vehicle speed sensor signal.	Disconnect the large 17 pin connector from the cluster, and the connector from the digital ratio adapter. Measure the resistance between the wire at pin A1 of the cluster and the wire at pin B of the digital ratio adapter harness. If the resistance is above zero OHMs, and the vehicle speed sensor circuit is working properly, replace the instrument cluster.
Cluster Display Does Not Switch Between Total And Trip Odometer	1. Inoperative cluster control switch or wiring. 2. Inoperative cluster.	1. Disconnect the large 17 pin connector at the cluster. Measure the resistance between pin A3 and ground. The resistance should be zero in one position, and open in the other. If the switch does not respond in this manner repair the light green wire from the cluster to the switch, the switch, or the black wire from the switch to ground. 2. If the switch and wiring are correct, replace the cluster.
Trip Odometer Does Not Reset	1. Inoperative cluster control switch or wiring. 2. Inoperative cluster.	1. Disconnect the large 17 pin connector at the cluster. Measure the resistance between pin A5 and ground. The resistance should be zero in one position, and open in the other. If the switch does not respond in this manner repair the light green/black wire from the cluster to the switch, the switch, or black wire from the switch to ground. 2. If the switch and wiring are correct, replace the cluster.
Fuel Gage Is Inaccurate	Shorts or opens in the wiring from the fuel tank sender, or an inoperative fuel sender unit.	Disconnect the fuel gage sender at the tank and connect one lead of J 33431 to the pink wire and the other to ground. Turn the ignition to the run position, and set the resistance dials of J 33431 to zero OHMs. The fuel gage should read empty. Set the resistance dials to 35 OHMs. The fuel gage should read half full (7 to 8 segments lit). Set the resistance dials to 90 OHMs. The fuel gage should read full. If the gage responds correctly, check the black wire to ground at the fuel sender unit. If the black wire is OK replace the fuel tank sender. If the gage does not respond correctly to the test, check the pink wire from the fuel sender to the cluster. If this wire is OK replace the cluster.
Low Fuel Indicator Does Not Light With Low Fuel Level	Inoperative cluster.	Replace the cluster.

DIAGNOSIS OF THE ELECTRONIC DIGITAL INSTRUMENT CLUSTER (cont'd)

PROBLEM	POSSIBLE CAUSE	CORRECTION
Temperature Gage Is Inaccurate	Shorts or opens in the wiring from the temperature sender, or an inoperative temperature sending unit.	Disconnect the temperature sender and connect one lead of J 33431 to the dark green wire and the other to ground. Turn the ignition to the run position, and set the resistance dials of J 33431 to 1400 OHMs. The temperature gage should read cold. Set the resistance dials to 400 OHMs. The fuel gage should read half (7 to 8 segments lit). Set the resistance dials to zero OHMs. The fuel gage should read hot. If the gage responds correctly, replace the temperature gage sender. If the gage does not respond correctly to the test, check the dark green wire from the temperature sender to the cluster. If this wire is OK, replace the cluster.
Temperature Indicator Does Not Light With The Engine Coolant Overheated	Inoperative cluster.	Replace the instrument cluster.
Oil Pressure Gage Is Inaccurate	Shorts or opens in the wire from the oil pressure sender, or an inoperative oil pressure sending unit.	Disconnect the oil pressure sender and connect one lead of J 33431 to the tan wire and the other to ground. Turn the ignition to the run position, and set the resistance dials of J 33431 to zero OHMs. The oil gage should read low. Set the resistance dials to 35 OHMs. The oil gage should read half (7 to 8 segments lit). Set the resistance dials to 90 OHMs. The oil gage should read high. If the gage responds correctly, replace the oil gage sender. If the gage does not respond correctly to the test, check the tan wire from the oil sender to the cluster. If this wire is OK replace the cluster.
Oil Pressure Indicator Does Not Light	Inoperative cluster.	Replace the instrument cluster.
Voltmeter Is Inaccurate	Short, open or high resistance in the brown wire from the generator.	Measure the voltage between the battery terminals. Then measure the voltage between the brown wire, and a good chassis ground. If the readings are different, repair the brown wire. If the readings are the same, check the black wire for high resistance to ground. If the black wires at the cluster are OK replace the instrument cluster.

DIAGNOSIS OF THE VEHICLE SPEED SENSOR AND DIGITAL RATIO ADAPTOR CONTROLLER

PROBLEM	POSSIBLE CAUSE	CORRECTION
Speedometer And Odometer Are Inaccurate	Incorrect digital ratio adaptor.	Check for the correct digital ratio adapter.

DIAGNOSIS OF THE VEHICLE SPEED SENSOR AND DIGITAL RATIO ADAPTOR CONTROLLER (cont'd)

PROBLEM	POSSIBLE CAUSE	CORRECTION
Speedometer And Odometer Do Not Operate Properly	1. Inoperative digital ratio adapter.	1. Disconnect the digital ratio adapter, and place the ignition in run. Check for voltage between the pink/black wire in the harness and a good chassis ground. If the voltage is less than the battery voltage, check for an open or short in the pink/black wire.
	2. Poor ground path from the digital ratio adapter.	2. Check for voltage between the pink/black wire in the harness and the black/white wire. If the voltage is less than battery voltage, check for an open or short in the black/white wire.
	3. No signal from the vehicle speed sensor.	3. Raise and support the vehicle, start the engine, and place the transmission in drive. Check for AC voltage that changes with the engine rpm between the purple/white wire, and the light green/black wire at the digital ratio adapter. If there is not AC voltage at these wires, check for opens in the purple/white wire and the light green wire. If there are not shorts or opens, replace the vehicle speed sensor.
	4. Inoperative digital ratio adapter (speedometer output).	4. Raise and support, the vehicle start the engine, and place the transmission in drive. Check for AC voltage that changes with the engine RPM, replace the digital ratio adapter.
	5. Inoperative digital ratio adapter (cruise output).	5. Raise and support the vehicle, start the engine, and place the transmission in drive. Check for AC voltage that changes with the engine rpm between the yellow and the black/white wires at the digital ratio adapter connector (connector attached) if AC voltage valves with rpm, replace the digital ratio adapter.
	6. Inoperative instrument cluster.	6. Refer to DIAGNOSIS OF THE ELECTRONIC INSTRUMENT CLUSTER in this section.

DIAGNOSIS OF THE FUEL GAGE

PROBLEM	POSSIBLE CAUSE	CORRECTION
Gage Stays at "E"	1. No fuel. 2. Circuit is grounded.	1. Fill the fuel tank. 2. Disconnect the lead at the fuel tank. The gage should read past the "F". If the gage does not read past the "F", replace the fuel tank sender. If the gage stays at "E", find the ground in the circuit between the gage and the fuel tank.

DIAGNOSIS OF THE FUEL GAGE (cont'd)

PROBLEM	POSSIBLE CAUSE	CORRECTION
Gage Stays at "F" or Beyond	Open circuit between the gage and the sender.	Disconnect the sender lead at the fuel tank. Ground the lead. The fuel gage should read at "E". If the gage reads at "E", replace the sender. If the gage still reads at "F" or beyond, find the open between the gage and the fuel tank.
Gage Reads Wrong	1. Corrosion or a loose connection. 2. Sender. 3. Gage.	1. Clean the terminals. Tighten the terminals. 2. Remove the sender. Test the sender with an ohmmeter. The empty position should read 1 ohm. The one-half full position should read 44 ohms. The full position should read 88 ohms. 3. Disconnect the front body connector. Connect J 24538-A tester to the lead that goes to the gage. Turn the engine control switch ON. If the gage responds accurately, check the wiring between the rear compartment and the front body connector. If the gage reads between one fourth and one half with the J 24538-A set at 90 ohms, remove the gage and check for loose nuts at the gage terminals. Tighten the nuts and replace the gage. If the gage doesn't read according to the J 24538-A settings, replace the gage.

DIAGNOSIS OF THE COOLANT TEMPERATURE GAGE

PROBLEM	POSSIBLE CAUSE	CORRECTION
Gage Does Not Move from "Cold" when the Engine is "Hot"	1. Blown fuse. 2. Open circuit. 3. Sensor.	1. Check fuse and replace if blown. 2&3. Turn engine control switch key "on." Do not start engine. Remove the lead at the sensor unit. Connect the test lamp from the sensor lead to ground. If the lamp glows, then short the sensor lead to ground. Gage should indicate "HOT." If the gage indicates "HOT," check the sensor lead conector on the sensor. If OK, replace the sensor. If the gage indicates "COLD," the gage is stuck. Replace the gage. If the lamp does not glow, check for continuity between the sensor unit terminal at the gage and ground, and between the ignition terminal and ground. Also check the case ground. If all checks "OK," replace the gage. Turn switch "OFF."
Gage Indicates "Hot" with Cold Engine	Shorted or grounded circuit.	Remove the sensor lead at the sensor unit. The gage should swing to "COLD." If the gage does not swing to "COLD," check the sensor unit for an external short. If there is no external short, replace the sensor. If the gage stays "HOT," check for a short circuit in the gage to sensor wiring. If there is no short, replace the gage.

DIAGNOSIS OF THE COOLANT TEMPERATURE GAGE (cont'd)

PROBLEM	POSSIBLE CAUSE	CORRECTION
Gage Reads Low	1. Resistance in the circuit due to corrosion or a loose connection. 2. Sensor.	1. Clean and tighten the terminals and connections in the circuit. Check for resistance in the ground path of the sensor. 2. Remove the lead at the sensor. Measure the resistance with an ohmmeter. At 40 /C (104 /F) the resistance is 1365 ohms. At 125 /C (257 /F) the resistance is 55.1 ohms. If the sensor does not have approximately these values, replace the sensor.
Gage Reads High	1. Sensor. 2. Circuit has a high resistance ground.	1. Measure the sensor's resistance as described in the previous step. 2. Disconnect the sensor lead at the gage and sensor. Check for a high resistance ground with an ohmmeter. Repair the circuit.

DIAGNOSIS OF THE OIL PRESSURE GAGE

PROBLEM	POSSIBLE CAUSE	CORRECTION
Gage Reads at "0"	1. Low oil level. 2. The circuit is grounded between the gage and the sensor. 3. Sensor.	1. Check oil level. Add oil if necessary. 2. Remove the sensor lead at the sensor. The gage should read "80." If the gage stays at "0", remove the sensor lead at the gage. The gage should read "80. " If the gage reads "80", find the ground in the circuit between the gage and the sensor. If the gage reads "0", replace the gage. 3. Remove the sensor lead at the sensor. Connect an ohmmeter to the sensor. With the engine stopped, the resistance should be one ohm. With the engine running, the resistance should be about 44 ohms at 40 psi (275 kPa). If the sensor reads one ohm with the engine running, replace the sensor.
Gage Reads "80" PSI or Above	The sensor circuit has an open.	Disconnect the sensor lead from the sensor. Ground the sensor lead. The gage should read "0" psi. If the gage reads "0" psi, replace the sensor. If the gage stays at "80" psi, find the open in the circuit between the gage and the sensor.
Gage Readings are in Error	Gage.	Remove the sensor lead from the sensor. Connect the J 24538-A Tester to the sensor lead and ground. If the gage responds accurately to the tester, replace the sensor. If the gage does not respond accurately to the tester, replace the gage.

DIAGNOSIS OF THE VOLTMETER

PROBLEM	POSSIBLE CAUSE	CORRECTION
Voltmeter Reads at 9 or Below	1. Discharged battery.	1. Measure the voltage across the battery. Recharge the battery. Read the dash voltmeter with the charger working. The voltage should come up to at least 12 volts. Find and correct the cause of the battery discharging.
	2. High resistance in the voltmeter connections.	2. Clean and tighten the connections.
	3. Voltmeter.	3. Apply 12 volts directly to the voltmeter. If the voltmeter doesn't respond accurately, replace the voltmeter.

DIAGNOSIS OF THE OIL PRESSURE WARNING SYSTEM (MECHANICAL CLUSTER)

PROBLEM	POSSIBLE CAUSE	CORRECTION
Lamp Won't Light with the Engine Not Running and the Ignition Switch Turned to On	1. Lamp bulb is burned out. 2. Open in the switch lead circuit.	1. Check the bulb. Replace the bulb if necessary. 2. Remove the switch lead from the switch. Ground the switch lead. If the lamp does not light, find and correct the open in the circuit. If the lamp does light, replace the switch.

DIAGNOSIS OF THE COOLANT TEMPERATURE WARNING SYSTEM

PROBLEM	POSSIBLE CAUSE	CORRECTION
Lamp Won't Light During Bulb Check	1. Lamp bulb is burned out. 2. Open in the switch lead circuit.	1. Check the bulb. Replace the bulb if necessary. 2. Remove the switch lead from the switch. Ground the switch lead. If the lamp does not light, find and correct the open in the circuit. If the lamp does light, replace the switch.

DIAGNOSIS OF THE BRAKE WARNING SYSTEM

PROBLEM	POSSIBLE CAUSE	CORRECTION
Warning Lamp Won't Light During Bulb Check	1. Lamp bulb is burned out. 2. Open in the circuit.	1. Replace the bulb. 2. Remove the switch lead at the switch. Refer to BRAKES (SEC. 9). Ground the switch lead with a jumper. If the lamp comes on, test the switch. Refer to BRAKES (SEC. 9). If the switch is bad, replace it. Refer to BRAKES (SEC. 9).

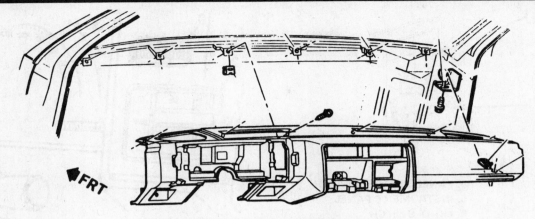

Exploded view of the instrument panel

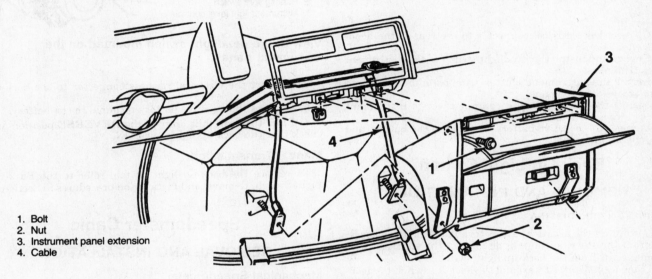

1. Bolt
2. Nut
3. Instrument panel extension
4. Cable

Removing the lower instrument panel

Windshield Wiper Switch

The windshield wiper switch is located on the end of the combination switch, attached to the steering column.

REMOVAL AND INSTALLATION

NOTE: Refer to the Combination Switch, Removal and Installation procedures in Section 8 to replace the combination switch.

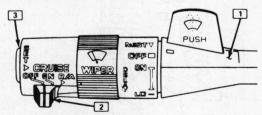

1. Directional signal lever
2. Off/on/resume/accel switch
3. Set/coast switch

View of the combination switch

Headlight Switch

The headlight switch, a push button switch to turn the lights On and Off, is located on the left side of the instrument panel. A rheostat dial, located just above the headlight/parking light switch, is used to control the illumination of the instrument panel.

A dimmer switch (part of the combination switch), to control the **Hi** and **Lo** beam operation, is located on the steering column; the lights are changed by pulling the combination switch lever toward the driver.

REMOVAL AND INSTALLATION

1. Disconnect the negative battery terminal from the battery.
2. Remove the lower steering column cover-to-instrument panel screws and the cover.
3. Remove the instrument cluster trim plate-to-instrument cluster screws and the panel, then allow the panel to hang to the left side by the wiring.
4. Disconnect the electrical connector from the rear of the headlight switch.
5. Disengage and remove the headlight switch from the instrument cluster trim plate.

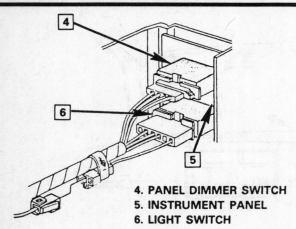

4. PANEL DIMMER SWITCH
5. INSTRUMENT PANEL
6. LIGHT SWITCH

Light and dimmer switch connectors

To install:

1. Connect the electrical connector to the rear of the headlight switch.

2. Engage and install the headlight switch to the instrument cluster trim plate.

3. Install the instrument cluster trim plate-to-instrument cluster screws and the panel.

4. Install the lower steering column cover-to-instrument panel screws and the cover.

5. Connect the negative battery terminal to the battery and check operation.

Back-Up Light Switch

REMOVAL AND INSTALLATION

Automatic Transmission

1. Disconnect the negative battery terminal from the battery.

2. From the steering column, disconnect the electrical harness connector from the back-up light switch.

3. Using a small pry bar, expand the back-up switch-to-steering column retainers and remove the switch from the steering column.

To install:

1. Install the back-up switch-to-steering column retainers to install the switch to the steering column.

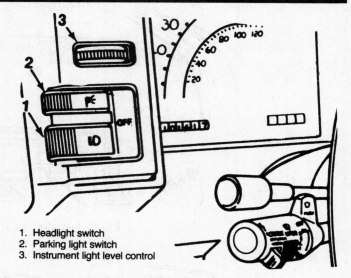

1. Headlight switch
2. Parking light switch
3. Instrument light level control

View of the headlight switch mounted on the instrument panel

2. Connect the electrical harness connector to the back-up light switch.

3. Connect the negative battery terminal to the battery.

4. Place the gear shift lever in the **REVERSE** position and check that the back-up lights turn ON.

Manual Transmission

To replace the back-up light switch, refer to the Back-Up Light Switch, Removal and Installation procedures in Section 7.

Speedometer Cable

REMOVAL AND INSTALLATION

Mechanical Speedometer

1. Refer to the Instrument Cluster, Removal and Installation procedures in this section and remove the instrument cluster.

2. From the rear of the instrument cluster, remove the speedometer cable-to-head fitting.

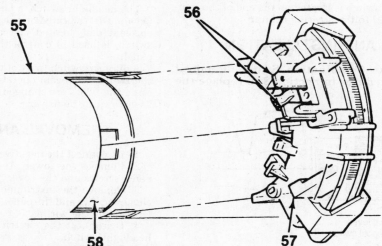

55. Steering column jacket
56. Switch terminals
57. Tangs
58. Shift tube

Removing the backup light switch from the steering column — automatic transmission

DIAGNOSIS OF HEADLAMP SYSTEM

PROBLEM	POSSIBLE CAUSE	CORRECTION
One Headlamp Inoperative or Intermittent	1. Loose connection. 2. Sealed beam unit.	1. Secure the connections to the headlamp including the ground (black wire). 2. Replace the headlamp.
One or More Headlamps are Dim	1. Open ground connection at the headlamp. 2. Black ground wire mislocated in the headlamp connector (three-wire, hi-lo, connector only).	1. Repair the black wire connection between the headlamp and the body ground. 2. Relocate the black wire in the connector.
One or More Headlamps Short Life	Charge circuit problem.	Refer to ENGINE ELECTRICAL (SEC. 3), charging system diagnosis.
All Headlamps Inoperative or Intermittent	1. Loose connection. 2. Dimmer switch. 3. Open wiring — lamp switch to the dimmer switch. 4. Open wiring — lamp switch to the battery. 5. Shorted ground circuit. 6. Switch.	1. Check and secure connections at the dimmer switch and the lamp switch. 2. Check the voltage at the dimmer switch with a test lamp. 3. Check the yellow wire with a test lamp. If the bulb lights at the lamp switch yellow wire terminal but not at the dimmer switch, repair the open wire. 4. Check the red wire terminal at the lamp switch with a test lamp. If the bulb does not light, repair the open red wire circuit to the battery (possible open fusible link). 5. If, after a few minutes operation, the headlamps flicker "ON" and "OFF" and/or a thumping noise can be heard from the lamp switch (circuit breaker opening and closing), repair the short to ground in the circuit between the lamp switch and the headlamps. After repairing the short, check for headlamp flickering after one minute operation. If flickering occurs, the circuit breaker has been damaged and the lamp switch must be replaced. 6. Check the red and yellow wire terminals at the lamp switch with the test lamp. If the bulb lights at the red wire terminal but not at the yellow terminal, replace the lamp switch.
Upper or Lower Beam Will Not Light or Intermittent	1. Open connection or faulty dimmer switch. 2. Short circuit to ground.	1. Check the dimmer switch terminals with a test lamp. If the bulb lights at the light green or tan wire terminals, repair the open wiring between the dimmer switch and the headlamps. If the bulb will not light at either of these terminals, depending upon switch position, replace the dimmer switch. 2. Follow the diagnosis above (all headlamps inoperative or intermittent).

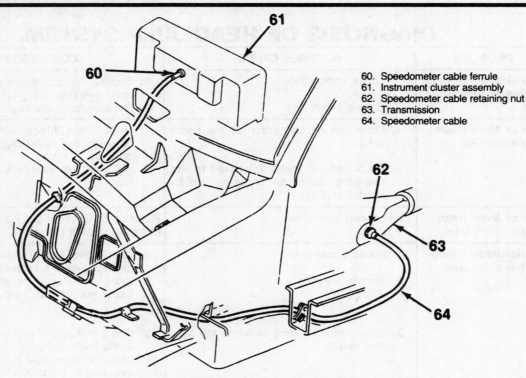

60. Speedometer cable ferrule
61. Instrument cluster assembly
62. Speedometer cable retaining nut
63. Transmission
64. Speedometer cable

View of the speedometer cable routing

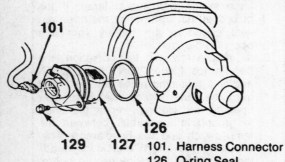

101. Harness Connector
126. O-ring Seal
127. Vehicle Speed Sensor (VSS)
129. Bolt

Electronic vehicle speed sensor — automatic trans

3. If replacing ONLY the speedometer cable core, perform the following procedures:

   a. Disconnect the speedometer casing from the speedometer head.

   b. Pull the speedometer cable core from the speedometer casing.

   c. Using lubricant P/N 6478535 or equivalent, lubricate a new speedometer cable core and install the cable into the casing.

4. If replacing the speedometer cable core and the speedometer cable casing, perform the following procedures:

   a. Disconnect the speedometer cable casing from the speedometer head.

   b. Disconnect the speedometer cable casing from the transmission.

   c. Remove the various speedometer cable/casing retaining clips.

   d. Remove the speedometer cable/casing assembly from the vehicle.

Electronic Speedometer

1. Disconnect the negative (−) battery cable.
2. Raise and safely support the vehicle with jackstands.
3. Disconnect the harness connector at the transmission.
4. Remove the retaining bolt and sensor.
5. Drain the excess fluid into a drain pan.
6. Replace the O-ring seal if damaged.

To install:
1. Install the sensor with a new O-ring. Coat the seal with a film of transmission fluid.
2. Install the bolt and torque to 96 inch lbs. (11 Nm).
3. Connect the harness connector and negative battery cable.
4. Start the engine and allow to reach normal operating temperature.
5. Refill the transmission with fluid to the proper level and check operation.

LIGHTING

Headlights

REMOVAL AND INSTALLATION

NOTE: The following procedure may require the use of the GM Safety Aimer tool No. J-6878-01 or equivalent.

1. Disconnect the negative battery terminal from the battery.
2. Remove the headlight bezel-to-fender screws and the bezel; allow the bezel to hang by the parking/side marker light wires.
3. Remove the headlight retaining-to-fender spring.
4. Remove the headlight retaining ring-to-fender screws and the retaining ring.
5. Disconnect the electrical connector from the headlight and remove the headlight from the vehicle.

To install:

1. Connect the electrical connector to the headlight and install the headlight into the vehicle.
2. Install the headlight retaining ring-to-fender screws and the retaining ring.
3. Install the headlight retaining-to-fender spring.
4. Install the headlight bezel-to-fender screws and the bezel.
5. Connect the negative battery terminal to the battery.
6. Check the headlight operation. Although, adjustment procedures may not be necessary, DO check the aim of the headlight.

NOTE: If necessary to adjust the headlight aim, use the GM Safety Aimer tool No. J-6878-01 or equivalent.

HEADLIGHT AIMING

Horizontal and vertical aiming of each headlight is done by two adjusting screws which move the mounting ring against the tension of the coil spring.

Some state and local authorities have specific requirements

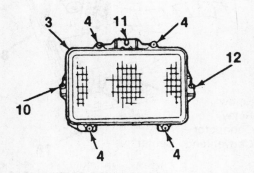

3. Headlamp Retaining Ring
4. Headlamp Retaining Ring Screws
10. Horizontal Adjusting Screw—Right Lamp
11. Vertical Adjusting Screw
12. Horizontal Adjusting Screw—Left Lamp

Headlight aiming

for aiming headlights and these requirements should be followed.

Fog Light

REMOVAL AND INSTALLATION

Remove the fog light electrical connector, retaining bolt and light from the air dam and the bumper.

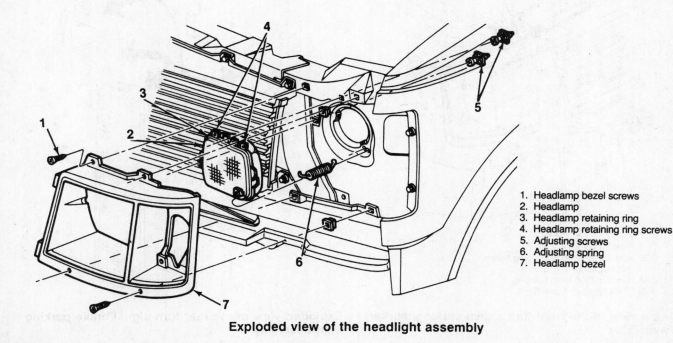

1. Headlamp bezel screws
2. Headlamp
3. Headlamp retaining ring
4. Headlamp retaining ring screws
5. Adjusting screws
6. Adjusting spring
7. Headlamp bezel

Exploded view of the headlight assembly

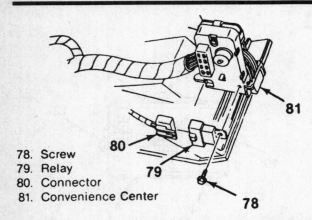

78. Screw
79. Relay
80. Connector
81. Convenience Center

Foglamp relay — located in the convenience center under the instrument panel

Signal and Marker Lights

AIMING

1. Park the truck on level ground, facing, perpendicular to, and about 25 ft. from a flat wall.
2. Remove any stone shields and switch on the fog lights.
3. Loosen the mounting hardware of the lights so you can aim them as follows:
   a. The horizontal distance between the light beams on the wall should be the same as between the lights themselves.
   b. The vertical height of the light beams above the ground should be 4 inches less than the distance between the ground and the center of the lamp lenses.
4. Tighten the mounting hardware.

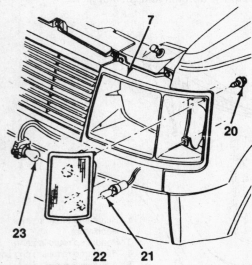

7. Headlamp bezel
20. Combination lamp housing screw
21. Marker lamp
22. Combination lamp housing
23. Park and turn signal lamp

Exploded view of the front turn signal/parking/marker light assembly

REMOVAL AND INSTALLATION

Front Turn Signal and Parking Lights

1. Disconnect the negative battery terminals from the battery.
2. Remove the headlight bezel-to-fender screws and the bezel; allow the bezel to hang by the turn signal/parking/marker light wires.
3. From the rear headlight bezel, remove the turn signal/parking/marker lamp-to-bezel screws and the turn signal/parking/marker lamp.
4. Disconnect the turn signal bulb and the parking/marker bulb from the lamp housing and the housing from the vehicle.
5. To install, use new bulbs (if necessary) and reverse the removal procedures. Check the turn signal and the parking/marker light operations

Rear Turn Signal, Brake and Parking Lights

1. Disconnect the negative battery terminal from the battery.
2. Remove the rear turn signal/brake/parking lamp-to-vehicle screw and the lamp housing from the vehicle.
3. Replace the defective bulb(s).
4. To install, reverse the removal procedures.

License Plate Lamp

REMOVAL AND INSTALLATION

Remove the mounting screws, lamp assembly and light bulb.

30. Stop and turn signal lamp
31. Lamp housing
32. Lamp housing screw
33. Back up lamp
34. Marker lamp
35. Harness grommet

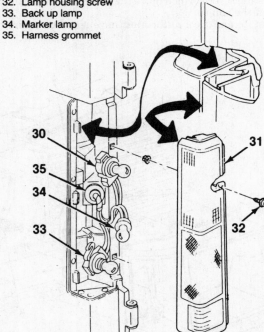

Exploded view of the rear turn signal/brake/parking light assembly

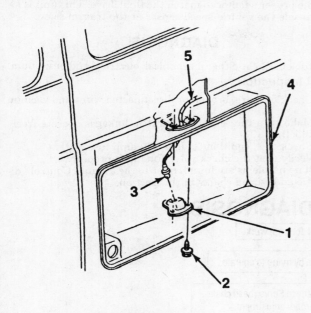

1. Lamp Assembly
2. Bolt
3. Bulb
4. Rear License Plate
   Housing
5. Body Harness

License plate light

Lamp Usage	Quantity	Trade No.	Power Rating at 12.8V, Watts
Headlamps	2	6052	65/55
	2	H6054	65/35
			Candle Power
Dome Lamps	2	211-2	12
Oil Pressure Indicator Lamp[2]	1	194	2
Generator Indicator Lamp	1	168	3
Instrument Cluster Illum.[1]	4	168	3
Instrument Cluster Illum.[2]	8	194	2
Headlamp Beam Indicator Lamp	1	161	1
Park, Signal Lamp	2	2057	32/2
Tail, Stop Lamps	2	2057	32/2
License Lamp	1	194	2
Temperature Indicator Lamp[2]	1	194	2
Service Engine Soon Lamp	1	194	2
Glove Box Lamp	1	194	2
Directional Indicator	2	194	2
Marker Lamps	4	194	2
Brake Warning Indicator Lamp	1	194	2
Back-up Lamp	2	1156	32
Radio Dial Lamp-AM-AM/FM	1	168	3
Heater or A/C Control	1	194	2
Transmission Indicator Dial and Auto. Trans.	1	194	2
Manual Transmission Upshift (4 Cyl.)	1	194	2
Stepwell Lamp	3	212-2	6
Reading Lamp	4	906	6
Safety Belt Warning	1	194	2
Cigarette Lighter Lamp	1	658	1/2
Ashtray Lamp	1	161	1
Beverage Tray Lamp	1	161	1
Headlight Switch Lamp	1	73	.3
Power Mirror Switch Lamp	1	73	.3

[1]With gages only.   [2]Only with indicator cluster.

Light bulb application chart

CRUISE CONTROL

The cruise control system is a speed control system which maintains a desired vehicle speed under normal driving conditions. However, steep grades up or down may cause variations in the selected speed.

The main components of the cruise control system are the mode control switches, controller (module), servo unit, speed sensor, vacuum supply, electrical and vacuum release switches.

To release the system, two release switches are provided. An electrical release switch is mounted on the brake pedal bracket and clutch pedal bracket on the vehicles equipped with manual transmissions. A vacuum release valve is mounted on the brake pedal bracket. The valve vents the trapped vacuum in the servo when the brake pedal is depressed, allowing the servo to return the throttle to idle position.

OPERATION

The controller interprets the position of the servo, position of the mode control switches and the output of the speed sensor. The servo consists of a vacuum tank and an open solenoid valve to vent the diaphragm chamber to atmosphere. The digital ratio adapter is a solid state device that is used to change the signal from the vehicle speed sensor to the a digital signal. The adapter is matched to the final drive of each vehicle and most be replaced

with the proper adapter to match the final drive. This unit is located inside the vehicle speed sensor at the transmission.

DIAGNOSIS

A problem can be either mechanical, electrical and/or vacuum.

Initial Inspection

1. Check for bare, broken or disconnected wires and vacuum hoses.
2. Make sure the servo and throttle linkages operate freely and smoothly.
3. Check the "Ignition/Gauges" 20 amp fuse.
4. Verify that the check valve functions properly.
5. If no problems are found, refer to the "Cruise Control" diagnostic and wiring charts in this section.

CRUISE CONTROL DIAGNOSIS

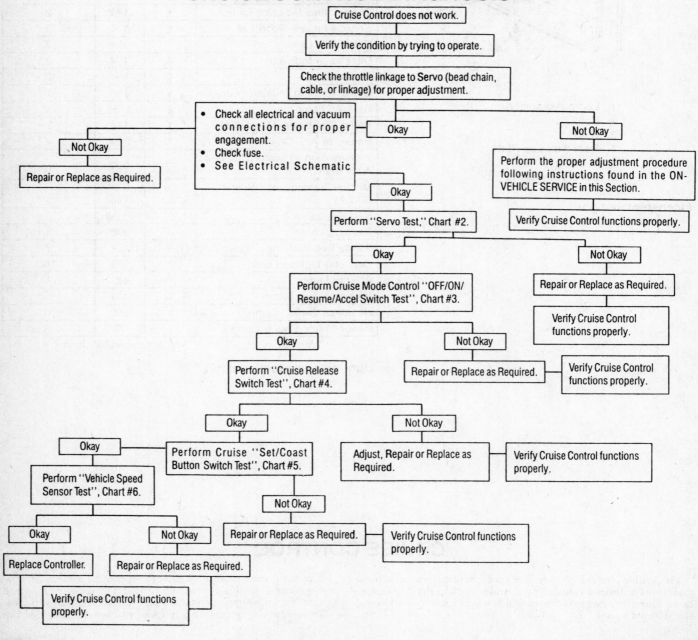

SERVO TEST

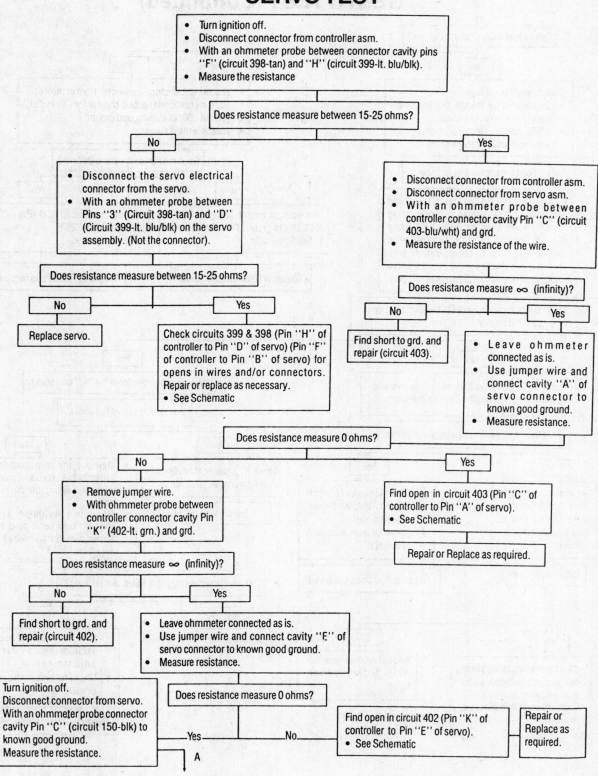

- Turn ignition off.
- Disconnect connector from controller asm.
- With an ohmmeter probe between connector cavity pins "F" (circuit 398-tan) and "H" (circuit 399-lt. blu/blk).
- Measure the resistance

Does resistance measure between 15-25 ohms?

No

Yes

- Disconnect the servo electrical connector from the servo.
- With an ohmmeter probe between Pins "3" (Circuit 398-tan) and "D" (Circuit 399-lt. blu/blk) on the servo assembly. (Not the connector).

- Disconnect connector from controller asm.
- Disconnect connector from servo asm.
- With an ohmmeter probe between controller connector cavity Pin "C" (circuit 403-blu/wht) and grd.
- Measure the resistance of the wire.

Does resistance measure between 15-25 ohms?

Does resistance measure ∞ (infinity)?

No

Yes

Replace servo.

Check circuits 399 & 398 (Pin "H" of controller to Pin "D" of servo) (Pin "F" of controller to Pin "B" of servo) for opens in wires and/or connectors. Repair or replace as necessary.
- See Schematic

No

Yes

Find short to grd. and repair (circuit 403).

- Leave ohmmeter connected as is.
- Use jumper wire and connect cavity "A" of servo connector to known good ground.
- Measure resistance.

Does resistance measure 0 ohms?

No

Yes

- Remove jumper wire.
- With ohmmeter probe between controller connector cavity Pin "K" (402-lt. grn.) and grd.

Find open in circuit 403 (Pin "C" of controller to Pin "A" of servo).
- See Schematic

Repair or Replace as required.

Does resistance measure ∞ (infinity)?

No

Yes

Find short to grd. and repair (circuit 402).

- Leave ohmmeter connected as is.
- Use jumper wire and connect cavity "E" of servo connector to known good ground.
- Measure resistance.

- Turn ignition off.
- Disconnect connector from servo.
- With an ohmmeter probe connector cavity Pin "C" (circuit 150-blk) to known good ground.
- Measure the resistance.

Does resistance measure 0 ohms?

Yes

A

No

Find open in circuit 402 (Pin "K" of controller to Pin "E" of servo).
- See Schematic

Repair or Replace as required.

SERVO TEST (Continued)

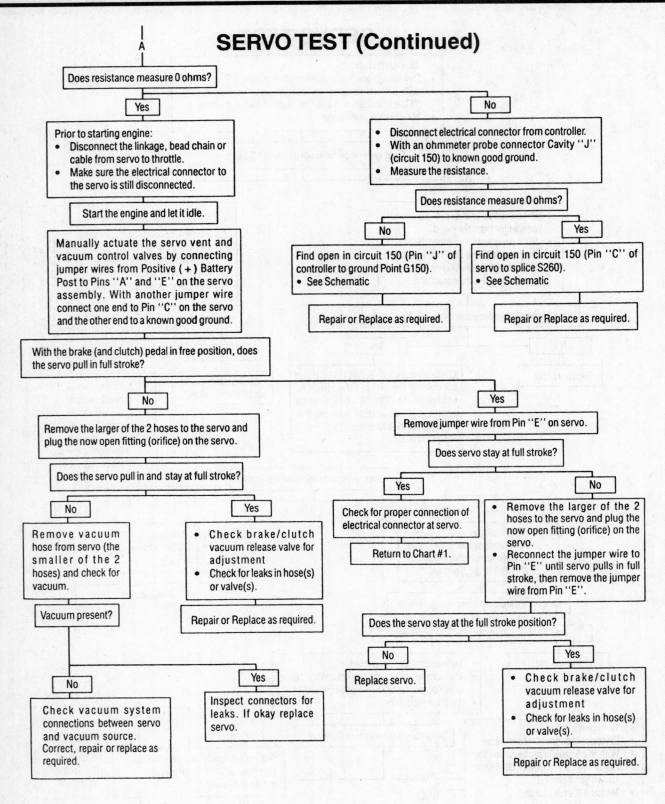

A

Does resistance measure 0 ohms?

Yes

Prior to starting engine:
- Disconnect the linkage, bead chain or cable from servo to throttle.
- Make sure the electrical connector to the servo is still disconnected.

Start the engine and let it idle.

Manually actuate the servo vent and vacuum control valves by connecting jumper wires from Positive (+) Battery Post to Pins "A" and "E" on the servo assembly. With another jumper wire connect one end to Pin "C" on the servo and the other end to a known good ground.

With the brake (and clutch) pedal in free position, does the servo pull in full stroke?

No

Remove the larger of the 2 hoses to the servo and plug the now open fitting (orifice) on the servo.

Does the servo pull in and stay at full stroke?

No

Remove vacuum hose from servo (the smaller of the 2 hoses) and check for vacuum.

Vacuum present?

No

Check vacuum system connections between servo and vacuum source. Correct, repair or replace as required.

Yes

Inspect connectors for leaks. If okay replace servo.

Yes

- Check brake/clutch vacuum release valve for adjustment
- Check for leaks in hose(s) or valve(s).

Repair or Replace as required.

No

- Disconnect electrical connector from controller.
- With an ohmmeter probe connector Cavity "J" (circuit 150) to known good ground.
- Measure the resistance.

Does resistance measure 0 ohms?

No

Find open in circuit 150 (Pin "J" of controller to ground Point G150).
- See Schematic

Repair or Replace as required.

Yes

Find open in circuit 150 (Pin "C" of servo to splice S260).
- See Schematic

Repair or Replace as required.

Yes

Remove jumper wire from Pin "E" on servo.

Does servo stay at full stroke?

Yes

Check for proper connection of electrical connector at servo.

Return to Chart #1.

No

- Remove the larger of the 2 hoses to the servo and plug the now open fitting (orifice) on the servo.
- Reconnect the jumper wire to Pin "E" until servo pulls in full stroke, then remove the jumper wire from Pin "E".

Does the servo stay at the full stroke position?

No

Replace servo.

Yes

- Check brake/clutch vacuum release valve for adjustment
- Check for leaks in hose(s) or valve(s).

Repair or Replace as required.

CRUISE "OFF/ON/RESUME/ACCEL" SWITCH TEST

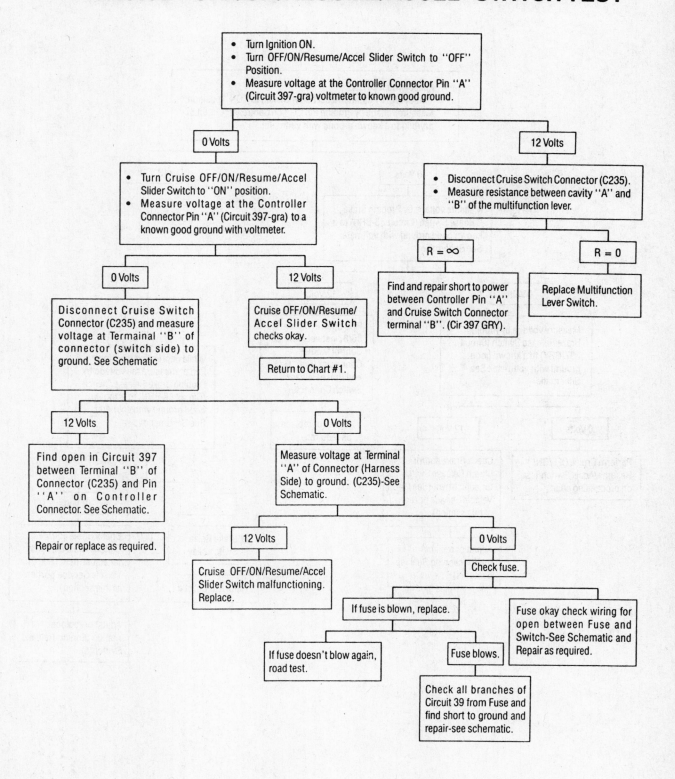

- Turn Ignition ON.
- Turn OFF/ON/Resume/Accel Slider Switch to "OFF" Position.
- Measure voltage at the Controller Connector Pin "A" (Circuit 397-gra) voltmeter to known good ground.

0 Volts

12 Volts

- Turn Cruise OFF/ON/Resume/Accel Slider Switch to "ON" position.
- Measure voltage at the Controller Connector Pin "A" (Circuit 397-gra) to a known good ground with voltmeter.

- Disconnect Cruise Switch Connector (C235).
- Measure resistance between cavity "A" and "B" of the multifunction lever.

0 Volts

12 Volts

R = ∞

R = 0

Disconnect Cruise Switch Connector (C235) and measure voltage at Termainal "B" of connector (switch side) to ground. See Schematic

Cruise OFF/ON/Resume/Accel Slider Switch checks okay.

Find and repair short to power between Controller Pin "A" and Cruise Switch Connector terminal "B". (Cir 397 GRY).

Replace Multifunction Lever Switch.

Return to Chart #1.

12 Volts

0 Volts

Find open in Circuit 397 between Terminal "B" of Connector (C235) and Pin "A" on Controller Connector. See Schematic.

Measure voltage at Terminal "A" of Connector (Harness Side) to ground. (C235)-See Schematic.

Repair or replace as required.

12 Volts

0 Volts

Cruise OFF/ON/Resume/Accel Slider Switch malfunctioning. Replace.

Check fuse.

If fuse is blown, replace.

Fuse okay check wiring for open between Fuse and Switch-See Schematic and Repair as required.

If fuse doesn't blow again, road test.

Fuse blows.

Check all branches of Circuit 39 from Fuse and find short to ground and repair-see schematic.

CRUISE RELEASE SWITCH TEST

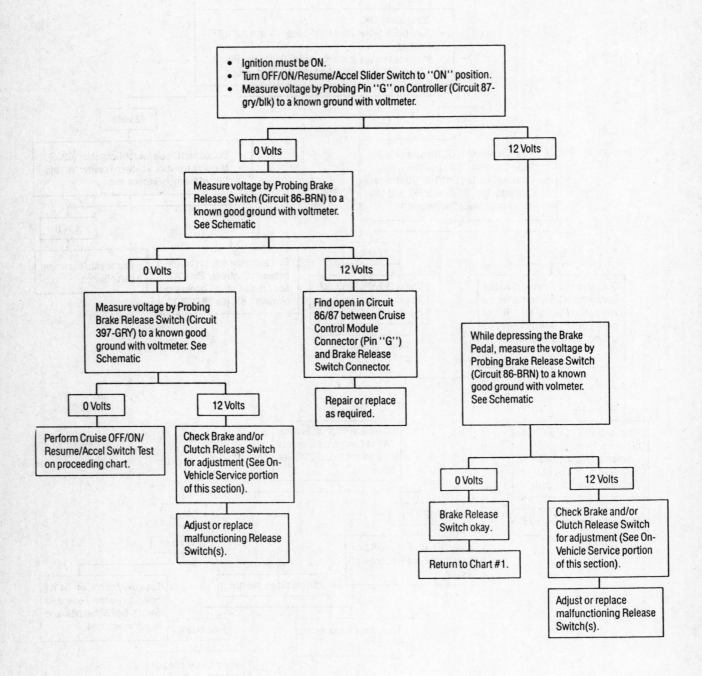

- Ignition must be ON.
- Turn OFF/ON/Resume/Accel Slider Switch to "ON" position.
- Measure voltage by Probing Pin "G" on Controller (Circuit 87-gry/blk) to a known ground with voltmeter.

0 Volts

Measure voltage by Probing Brake Release Switch (Circuit 86-BRN) to a known good ground with voltmeter. See Schematic

0 Volts

Measure voltage by Probing Brake Release Switch (Circuit 397-GRY) to a known good ground with voltmeter. See Schematic

0 Volts

Perform Cruise OFF/ON/Resume/Accel Switch Test on proceeding chart.

12 Volts

Check Brake and/or Clutch Release Switch for adjustment (See On-Vehicle Service portion of this section).

Adjust or replace malfunctioning Release Switch(s).

12 Volts

Find open in Circuit 86/87 between Cruise Control Module Connector (Pin "G") and Brake Release Switch Connector.

Repair or replace as required.

12 Volts

While depressing the Brake Pedal, measure the voltage by Probing Brake Release Switch (Circuit 86-BRN) to a known good ground with volmeter. See Schematic

0 Volts

Brake Release Switch okay.

Return to Chart #1.

12 Volts

Check Brake and/or Clutch Release Switch for adjustment (See On-Vehicle Service portion of this section).

Adjust or replace malfunctioning Release Switch(s).

CRUISE SET/COAST BUTTON SWITCH TEST

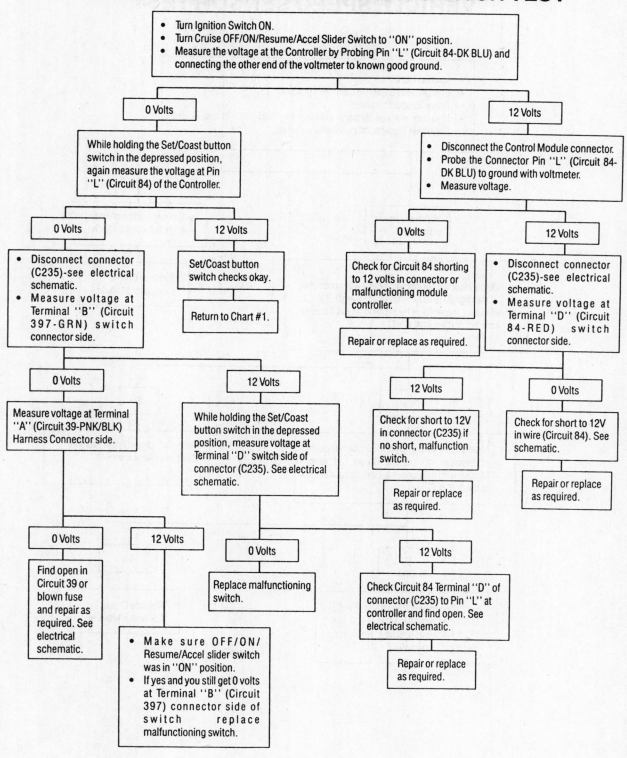

- Turn Ignition Switch ON.
- Turn Cruise OFF/ON/Resume/Accel Slider Switch to "ON" position.
- Measure the voltage at the Controller by Probing Pin "L" (Circuit 84-DK BLU) and connecting the other end of the voltmeter to known good ground.

0 Volts

While holding the Set/Coast button switch in the depressed position, again measure the voltage at Pin "L" (Circuit 84) of the Controller.

0 Volts

- Disconnect connector (C235)-see electrical schematic.
- Measure voltage at Terminal "B" (Circuit 397-GRN) switch connector side.

0 Volts

Measure voltage at Terminal "A" (Circuit 39-PNK/BLK) Harness Connector side.

0 Volts

Find open in Circuit 39 or blown fuse and repair as required. See electrical schematic.

12 Volts

- Make sure OFF/ON/Resume/Accel slider switch was in "ON" position.
- If yes and you still get 0 volts at Terminal "B" (Circuit 397) connector side of switch replace malfunctioning switch.

12 Volts

While holding the Set/Coast button switch in the depressed position, measure voltage at Terminal "D" switch side of connector (C235). See electrical schematic.

0 Volts

Replace malfunctioning switch.

12 Volts

Check Circuit 84 Terminal "D" of connector (C235) to Pin "L" at controller and find open. See electrical schematic.

Repair or replace as required.

12 Volts

Set/Coast button switch checks okay.

Return to Chart #1.

12 Volts

- Disconnect the Control Module connector.
- Probe the Connector Pin "L" (Circuit 84-DK BLU) to ground with voltmeter.
- Measure voltage.

0 Volts

Check for Circuit 84 shorting to 12 volts in connector or malfunctioning module controller.

Repair or replace as required.

12 Volts

Check for short to 12V in connector (C235) if no short, malfunction switch.

Repair or replace as required.

12 Volts

- Disconnect connector (C235)-see electrical schematic.
- Measure voltage at Terminal "D" (Circuit 84-RED) switch connector side.

0 Volts

Check for short to 12V in wire (Circuit 84). See schematic.

Repair or replace as required.

VEHICLE SPEED SENSOR TEST

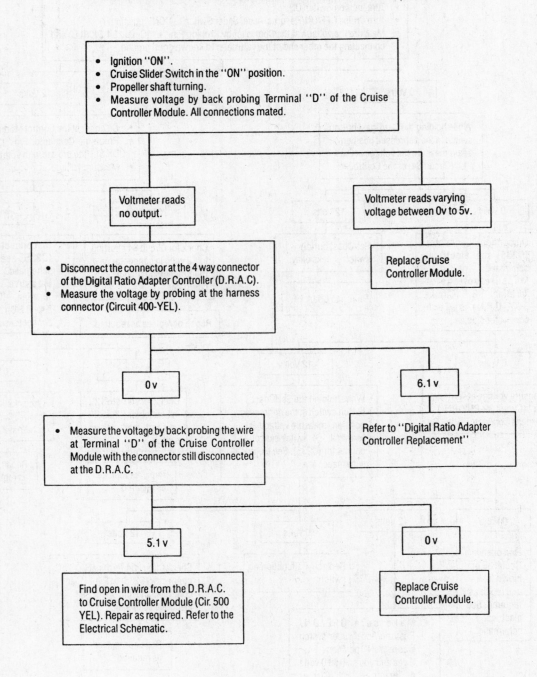

- Ignition "ON".
- Cruise Slider Switch in the "ON" position.
- Propeller shaft turning.
- Measure voltage by back probing Terminal "D" of the Cruise Controller Module. All connections mated.

Voltmeter reads no output.

Voltmeter reads varying voltage between 0v to 5v.

- Disconnect the connector at the 4 way connector of the Digital Ratio Adapter Controller (D.R.A.C.).
- Measure the voltage by probing at the harness connector (Circuit 400-YEL).

Replace Cruise Controller Module.

0 v

6.1 v

- Measure the voltage by back probing the wire at Terminal "D" of the Cruise Controller Module with the connector still disconnected at the D.R.A.C.

Refer to "Digital Ratio Adapter Controller Replacement"

5.1 v

0 v

Find open in wire from the D.R.A.C. to Cruise Controller Module (Cir. 500 YEL). Repair as required. Refer to the Electrical Schematic.

Replace Cruise Controller Module.

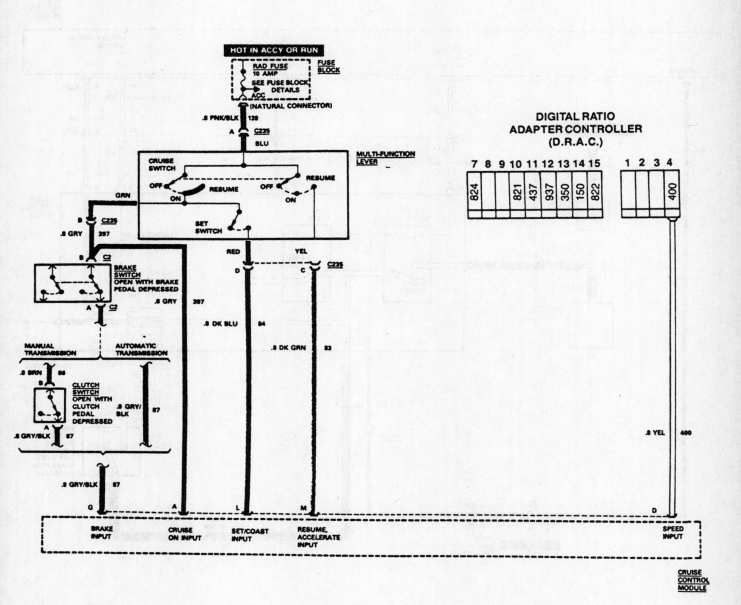

Cruise control wiring schematic

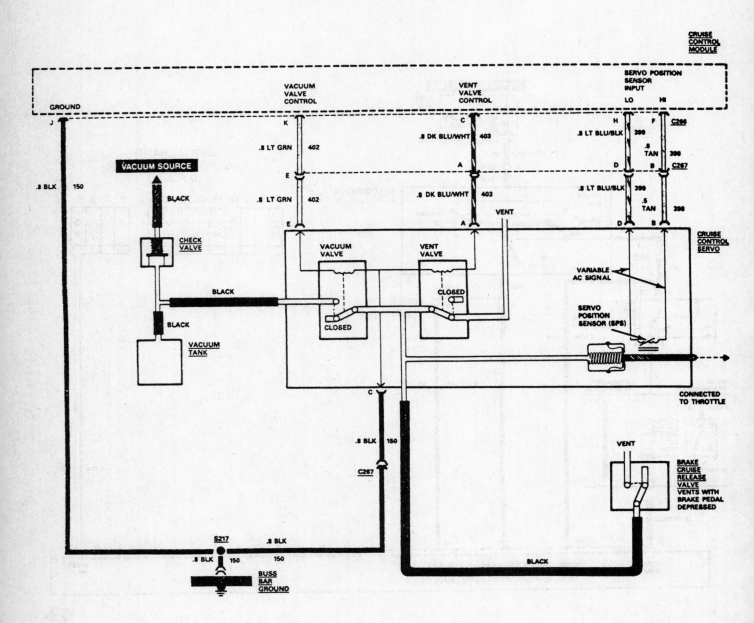

Cruise control wiring schematic

**CONTROL SWITCH
CONTINUNITY CHECK**

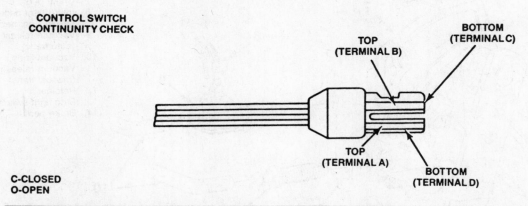

TOP
(TERMINAL B)

BOTTOM
(TERMINAL C)

TOP
(TERMINAL A)

BOTTOM
(TERMINAL D)

C-CLOSED
O-OPEN

SET/COAST (S/C) SW	POSITION SLIDER	C-B	C-D	C-A	B-D	B-A	D-A
NORMAL	OFF	O	O	O	O	O	O
NORMAL	ON	O	O	O	O	C	O
NORMAL	R/A	C	O	C	O	C	O
DEPRESSED	OFF	O	O	O	C	C	O
DEPRESSED	ON	O	O	O	C	C	C
DEPRESSED	R/A	C	C	C	C	C	C

CRUISE CONTROLLER (MODULE) CHECKS AT CONNECTOR
- **IGNITION ON**
- **CONTROLLER DISCONNECTED**

PIN	FUNCTION	VOLTAGE TO GND	RESISTANCE	CONDITIONS
G	BRAKE/CLUTCH INPUT	12V	-	BRAKE (AND CLUTCH) NOT DEPRESSED
		0V	-	BRAKE (AND/OR CLUTCH) DEPRESSED
L	SET/COAST	12V	-	SLIDER SWITCH "ON" - SET/COAST DEPRESSED
		0V	-	SLIDER SWITCH "ON" - SET/COAST NORMAL
		0V	-	SLIDER SWITCH "OFF" - SET/COAST NORMAL
M	RESUME/ ACCEL. INPUT	12V	-	SLIDER SWITCH "R/A" POSITION
		0V	-	SLIDER SWITCH "ON" - SET/COAST DEPRESSED OR NORMAL
		0V	-	SLIDER SWITCH "OFF" - SET/COAST DEPRESSED OR NORMAL
J	GROUND	-	0 Ω	MEASURED TO VEHICLE GROUND
A	ON/OFF INPUT	12V	-	SLIDER SWITCH "ON"
		0V	-	SLIDER SWITCH "OFF" - SET/COAST DEPRESSED OR NORMAL
B	INDICATOR LAMP	12V	-	CRUISE ARMED
F	SPS HIGH	-	15-25 Ω	MEASURED BETWEEN PINS F & H - SERVO CONNECTED
H	SPS LOW	-	∞ Ω	MEASURED BETWEEN PINS F & H - SERVO DISCONNECTED
D	SPEED SIGNAL	-		SEE SPEED SENDER TEST CHART
K	VACUUM VALVE CONTROL	-	30-55 Ω	MEASURED TO GROUND - SERVO CONNECTED
		-	∞ Ω	MEASURED TO GROUND - SERVO NOT CONNECTED
C	VENT VALVE CONTROL	-	30-55 Ω	MEASURED TO GROUND - SERVO CONNECTED
		-	∞ Ω	MEASURED TO GROUND - SERVO NOT CONNECTED

SERVO CHECKS
- **SERVO CONNECTOR DISCONNECTED**
- **MEASURE AT SERVO PINS**

PIN	FUNCTION	RESISTANCE	CONDITIONS
D	SPS HIGH	15-25	MEASURED BETWEEN PINS D AND B
B	SPS LOW	-	(IF MEASURED RESISTANCE IS NOT STATED VALVE, REPLACE SERVO)
A	VENT VALVE	30-55	MEASURED BETWEEN PINS A AND C
		-	(IF MEASURED RESISTANCE IS NOT STATED VALVE, REPLACE SERVO)
E	VACUUM VALVE	30-55	MEASURED BETWEEN PINS E AND C
			(IF MEASURED RESISTANCE IS NOT STATED VALVE, REPLACE SERVO)

Controller, servo and control switch check

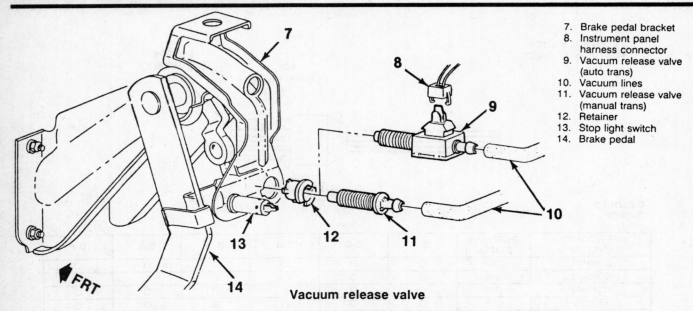

7. Brake pedal bracket
8. Instrument panel harness connector
9. Vacuum release valve (auto trans)
10. Vacuum lines
11. Vacuum release valve (manual trans)
12. Retainer
13. Stop light switch
14. Brake pedal

Vacuum release valve

Vacuum Release Switch

REMOVAL AND INSTALLATION

1. Disconnect the negative (–) battery cable.
2. Disconnect the instrument panel harness and vacuum lines.
3. Turn the retainer counter clockwise to unseal the valve and remove the valve.

To install:
1. Turn the retainer clockwise to seat.
2. Install the release valve until it seats on the retainer with the brake pedal in the depressed position.
3. Note that audible clicks can be heard as the threaded portion of the valve is pushed through the retainer toward the brake pedal.

a. **Release Valve Adjustment:** fully depress the brake pedal with the engine NOT running.
b. Push the vacuum hose side of the valve toward the bracket until the valve bottoms on the retainer.
c. Pull the brake pedal firmly rearward against the pedal stop until no clicking sound can be heard.
d. Release the brake and repeat step C.
4. Connect the vacuum and electrical connectors.
5. Connect the negative battery cable and check operation.

Control Module

REMOVAL AND INSTALLATION

1. Disconnect the negative (–) battery cable.
2. Remove the harness connector.

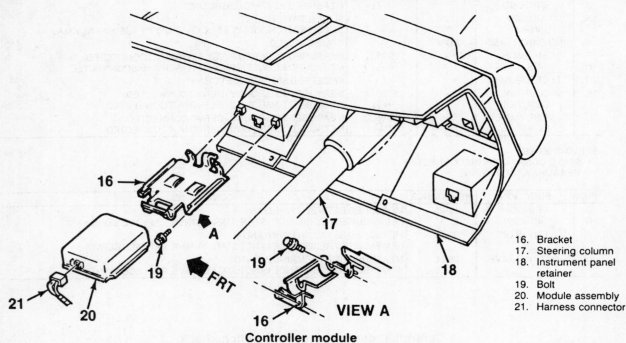

16. Bracket
17. Steering column
18. Instrument panel retainer
19. Bolt
20. Module assembly
21. Harness connector

VIEW A

Controller module

3. Remove the module by prying back the retaining clip on the bracket and sliding the module out.

To install:

1. Install the module and harness connector.
2. Connect the negative battery cable and check operation.

Servo Unit

REMOVAL AND INSTALLATION

1. Disconnect the negative (–) battery cable.
2. Remove the vacuum hoses, retainer, rod-to-throttle shaft, bolts and the servo.

NOTE: Do NOT allow any flexible components to route within two inches near moving parts and throttle linkages. Use plastic tie straps to hold components away from moving parts.

To install:

1. Install the servo, bolts, rod-to-throttle shaft, retainer and vacuum hoses.
2. Connect the negative battery cable and check operation.

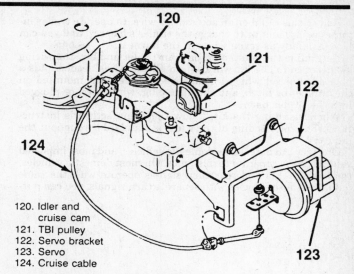

120. Idler and cruise cam
121. TBI pulley
122. Servo bracket
123. Servo
124. Cruise cable

Servo unit — 2.5L engine

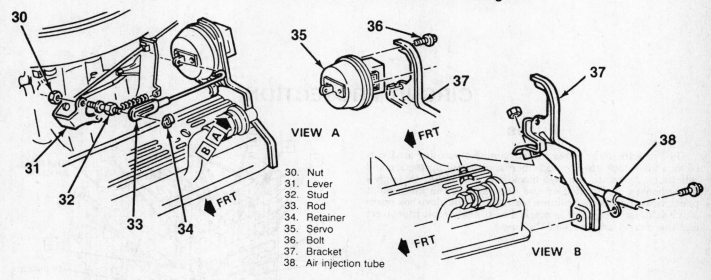

30. Nut
31. Lever
32. Stud
33. Rod
34. Retainer
35. Servo
36. Bolt
37. Bracket
38. Air injection tube

Servo unit — 4.3L engine

TRAILER WIRING

Wiring the van for towing is fairly easy. There are a number of good wiring kits available and these should be used, rather than trying to design your own. All trailers will need brake lights and turn signals as well as tail lights and side marker lights. Most states require extra marker lights for overly wide trailers. Also, most states have recently required back-up lights for trailers, and most trailer manufacturers have been building trailers with back-up lights for several years.

Additionally, some Class I, most Class II and just about all Class III trailers will have electric brakes.

Add to this number an accessories wire, to operate trailer internal equipment or to charge the trailer's battery, and you can have as many as seven wires in the harness.

Determine the equipment on your trailer and buy the wiring kit necessary. The kit will contain all the wires needed, plus a plug adapter set which included the female plug, mounted on the bumper or hitch, and the male plug, wired into, or plugged into the trailer harness.

When installing the kit, follow the manufacturer's instructions. The color coding of the wires is standard throughout the industry.

One point to note: some domestic vehicles, and most imported vehicles, have separate turn signals. On most domestic vehicles, the brake lights and rear turn signals operate with the same bulb. For those vehicles with separate turn signals, you can pur-chase an isolation unit so that the brake lights won't blink whenever the turn signals are operated, or, you can go to your local electronics supply house and buy four diodes to wire in series with the brake and turn signal bulbs. Diodes will isolate the brake and turn signals. The choice is yours. The isolation units are simple and quick to install, but far more expensive than the diodes. The diodes, however, require more work to install properly, since they require the cutting of each bulb's wire and soldering in place of the diode.

One, final point, the best kits are those with a spring loaded cover on the vehicle mounted socket. This cover prevent dirt and moisture from corroding the terminals. Never let the vehicle socket hang loosely; always mount it securely to the bumper or hitch.

CIRCUIT PROTECTION

Fuses

The fuses are of the miniaturized (compact) size and are located on a fuse block, they provide increased circuit protection and reliability. Access to the fuse block is gained either through a swing-down unit (located on the underside of the instrument panel, near the steering column) or through the glove box opening. Each fuse receptacle is marked as to the circuit it protects and the correct amperage of the fuse.

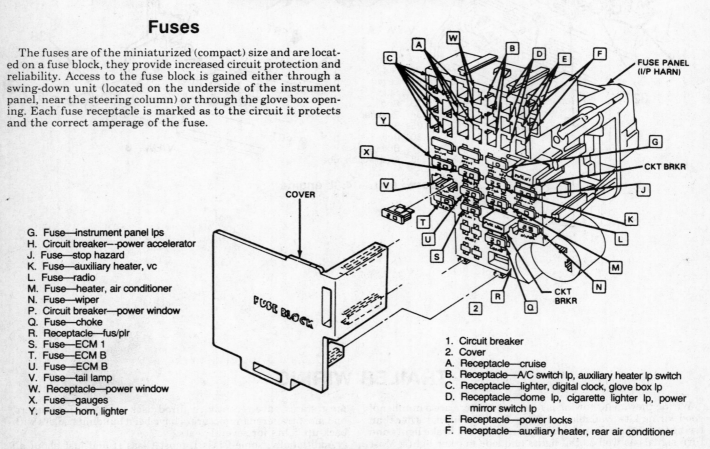

G. Fuse—instrument panel lps
H. Circuit breaker—power accelerator
J. Fuse—stop hazard
K. Fuse—auxiliary heater, vc
L. Fuse—radio
M. Fuse—heater, air conditioner
N. Fuse—wiper
P. Circuit breaker—power window
Q. Fuse—choke
R. Receptacle—fus/plr
S. Fuse—ECM 1
T. Fuse—ECM B
U. Fuse—ECM B
V. Fuse—tail lamp
W. Receptacle—power window
X. Fuse—gauges
Y. Fuse—horn, lighter

1. Circuit breaker
2. Cover
A. Receptacle—cruise
B. Receptacle—A/C switch lp, auxiliary heater lp switch
C. Receptacle—lighter, digital clock, glove box lp
D. Receptacle—dome lp, cigarette lighter lp, power mirror switch lp
E. Receptacle—power locks
F. Receptacle—auxiliary heater, rear air conditioner

View of the fuse block

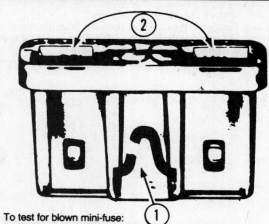

To test for blown mini-fuse:
1. Pull fuse out and check visually
2. With the circuit activated use a test light across the points shown

MINI FUSE COLOR CODES	
RATING	**COLOR**
5 AMP	TAN
10 AMP	RED
20 AMP	YELLOW
25 AMP	WHITE

Blown fuse

REPLACEMENT

1. Pull the fuse from the fuse block.
2. Inspect the fuse element (through the clear plastic body) to the blade terminal for defects.

NOTE: When replacing the fuse, DO NOT use one of a higher amperage.

3. To install, reverse the removal procedures.

Convenience Center

The Convenience Center is a swing-down unit located on the underside of the instrument panel, near the steering column. The swing-down feature provides central location and easy access to buzzers, relays and flasher units. All units are serviced by plug-in replacement.

Fusible Links

In addition to fuses, the wiring harness incorporates fusible links (in the battery feed circuits) to protect the wiring. Fusible links are 4 in. (102mm) sections of copper wire, 4 gauges smaller than the circuit(s) they are protecting, designed to melt under electrical overload. There are four different gauge sizes used. The fusible links are color coded so that they may be installed in their original positions.

REPLACEMENT

● Fusible link A — Rust/silver, powers ECM, located at starter solenoid.
● Fusible link B — Gray/silver, powers air conditioning blower, located at battery connection block.
● Fusible link C — Black/silver, powers fuel pump circuit, located at battery connection block.
● Fusible link D — Black/silver, powers ignition switch, located at battery connection block.

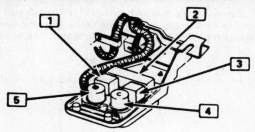

1. Horn relay
2. Seat belt—ignition key—headlight buzzer
3. Choke relay (vacant w/EFI)
4. Hazard flasher
5. Signal flasher

Convenience center and components

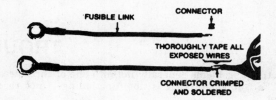

New fusible links are spliced to the wire

● Fusible link E — Rust/silver, powers alternator, located at starter solenoid.
● Fusible link F — Rust/silver, powers alternator (2.5L), located at starter solenoid.
1. Disconnect the negative battery terminal from the battery.
2. Locate the cause of the problem and repair before replacing the link.
3. Locate the burned out link.
4. Strip away the melted insulation and cut the burned link ends from the wire.
5. Strip the wire back ½ in. (12.7mm) to allow soldering of the new link.
6. Using a new fusible link 4 gauges smaller than the protected circuit and approximately 10 in. (254mm) long, solder it into the circuit.

NOTE: Whenever splicing a new wire, always bond the splice with rosin core solder, then cover with electrical tape. Using acid core solder may cause corrosion.

7. Tape and seal all splices with silicone to weatherproof repairs.
8. After taping the wire, tape the electrical harness leaving an exposed 5 in. (127mm) loop of wire.
9. Reconnect the battery.

Circuit Breakers

A circuit breaker is an electrical switch which breaks the circuit in case of an overload. The circuit breaker is located on the lower center of the fuse block. The circuit breaker will remain open until the short or overload condition in the circuit is corrected.

RESETTING

Locate the circuit breaker on the fuse block, then push the circuit breaker in until it locks. If the circuit breaker kicks itself Off again, locate and correct the problem in the electrical circuit.

6 CHASSIS ELECTRICAL

The windshield wiper motor has a self setting circuit breaker built into the motor assembly. This breaker is non-serviceable and requires replacement of the wiper motor unit if defective.

Flashers

The turn signal flasher is mounted under the instrument panel to the right of the steering column.

The hazard flasher is mounted in the convenience center. The convenience center is located to the left of the steering column and at the lower edge of the instrument panel.

TROUBLESHOOTING

Electrical problems generally fall into one of three areas:

1. The component that is not functioning is not receiving current.

2. The component itself is not functioning.

3. The component is not properly grounded. Problems that fall into the first category are by far the most complicated. It is the current supply system to the component which contains all the switches, relays, fuses and etc.

The electrical system can be checked with a test light and a jumper wire. A test light is a device that looks like a pointed screwdriver with a wire attached to it. It has a light bulb inside its handle. A jumper wire is a piece of insulated wire with an alligator clip attached to each end.

If a light bulb is not working, you must follow a systematic plan to determine which of the three causes is the villain.

1. Turn On the switch that controls the inoperable bulb.

2. Disconnect the power supply wire from the bulb.

3. Attach the ground wire on the test light to a good metal ground.

4. Touch the probe end of the test light to the end of the power supply wire that was disconnected from the bulb. If the bulb is receiving current, the test light will turn On.

NOTE: If the bulb is one which works only when the ignition key is turned on (turn signal), make sure the key is turned On.

If the test light does not turn On, then the problem is in the circuit between the battery and the bulb. As mentioned before, this includes all the switches, fuses and relays in the system. The problem is an open circuit between the battery and the bulb. If the fuse is blown and, when replaced, immediately blows again, there is a short circuit in the system which must be located and repaired. If there is a switch in the system, bypass it with a jumper wire. This is done by connecting one end of the jumper wire to the power supply wire into the switch and the other end of the jumper wire to the wire coming out of the switch. If the test light turns On with the jumper wire installed, the switch or whatever was bypassed is defective.

NOTE: Never substitute the jumper wire for the bulb, as the bulb is the component required to use the power from the power source.

5. If the bulb in the test light turns On, the current is getting to the bulb that is not working in the vehicle. This eliminates the first of the three possible causes. Connect the power supply wire and connect a jumper wire from the bulb to a good metal ground. Do this with the switch which controls the bulb turned On and also the ignition switch turned On (if it is required for the light to work). If the bulb works with the jumper wire installed, then it has a bad ground. This is usually caused by the metal area on which the bulb mounts to the vehicle being coated with some type of foreign matter or rust.

6. If neither test located the source of the trouble, then the light bulb itself is defective.

The above test procedures can be applied to any of the components of the chassis electrical system by substituting the component that is not working for the light bulb. Remember that for any electrical system to work, all connections must be clean and tight.

WIRING DIAGRAMS
1985–1986

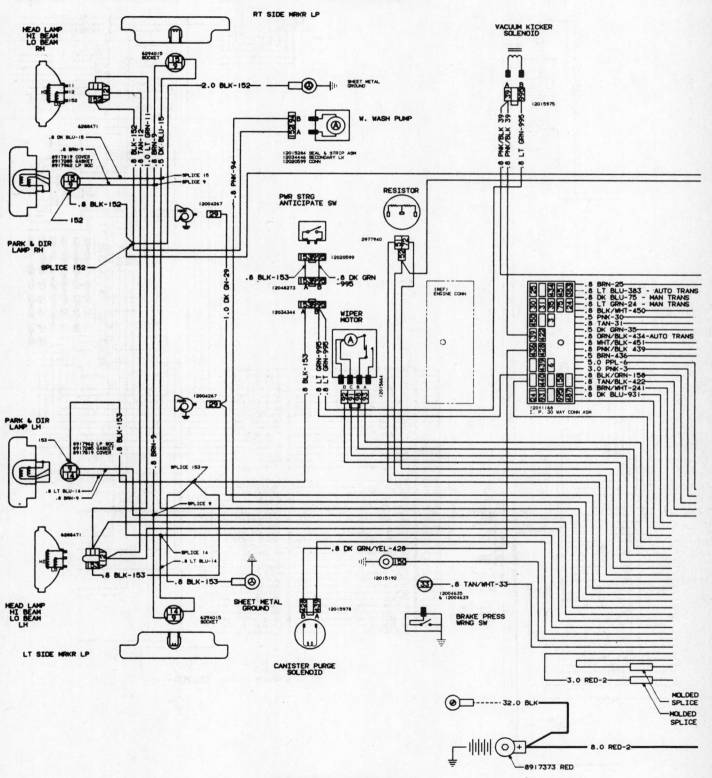

ASTRO VAN 1

1985–1986

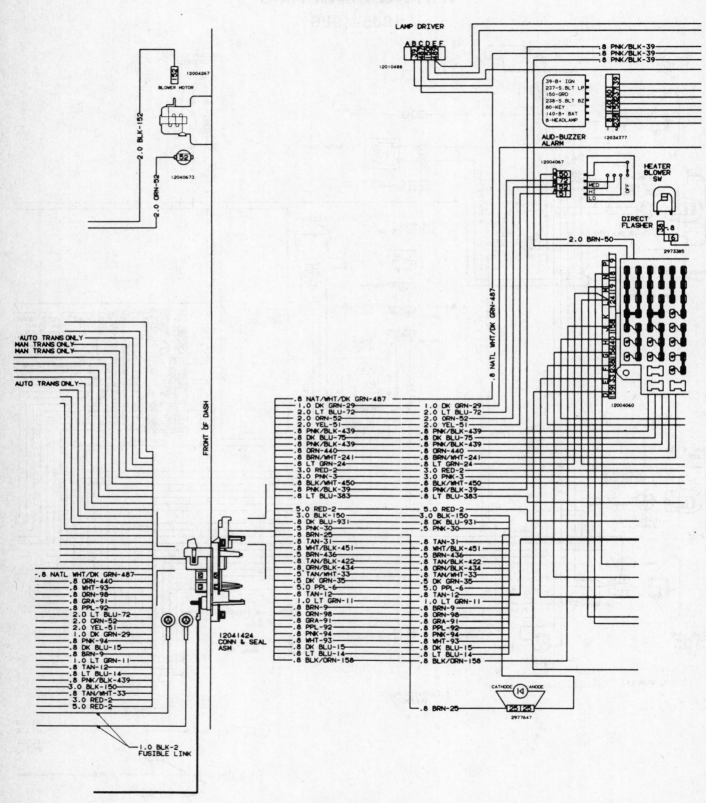

ASTRO VAN 1

1985-1986

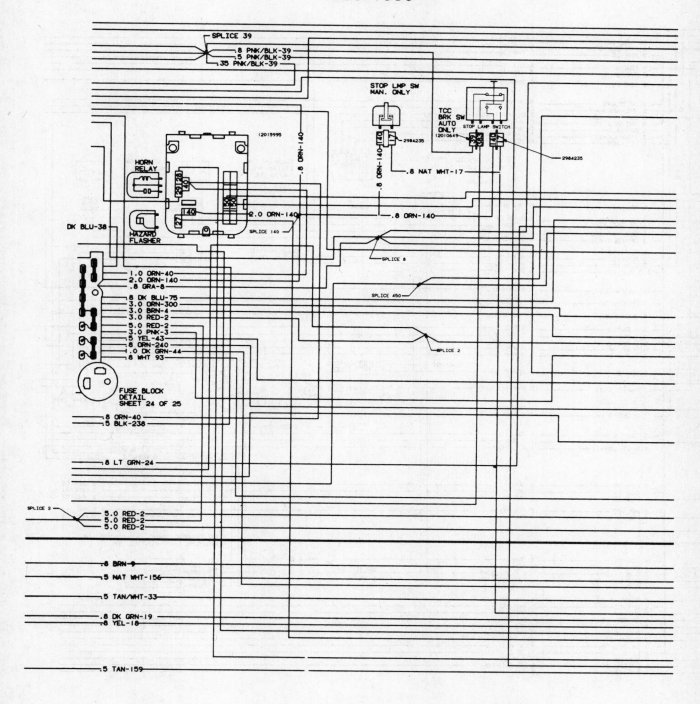

SPLICE 39
.8 PNK/BLK-39
.5 PNK/BLK-39
.35 PNK/BLK-39

STOP LAMP SW
MAN. ONLY

TCC
BRK SW
AUTO
ONLY

STOP LAMP SWITCH

12015995

2984235

2984235

12010649

HORN
RELAY

HAZARD
FLASHER

DK BLU-38

.8 ORN-140

.8 NAT WHT-17

.8 ORN-140

2.0 ORN-140

SPLICE 140

SPLICE 8

SPLICE 450

SPLICE 2

1.0 ORN-40
2.0 ORN-140
.8 GRA-8
.8 DK BLU-75
3.0 ORN-300
3.0 BRN-4
3.0 RED-2
5.0 RED-2
.5 PNK-3
.5 YEL-43
.8 ORN-240
1.0 DK GRN-44
.8 WHT 93

FUSE BLOCK
DETAIL
SHEET 24 OF 25

.8 ORN-40
.5 BLK-238

.8 LT GRN-24

SPLICE 2
5.0 RED-2
5.0 RED-2
5.0 RED-2

.8 BRN-9

.5 NAT WHT-156

.5 TAN/WHT-33

.8 DK GRN-19
.8 YEL-18

.5 TAN-159

CIRCUIT DIAGRAMS 1985
LB1 V6 CALIFORNIA

ASTRO VAN 1

1985–1986

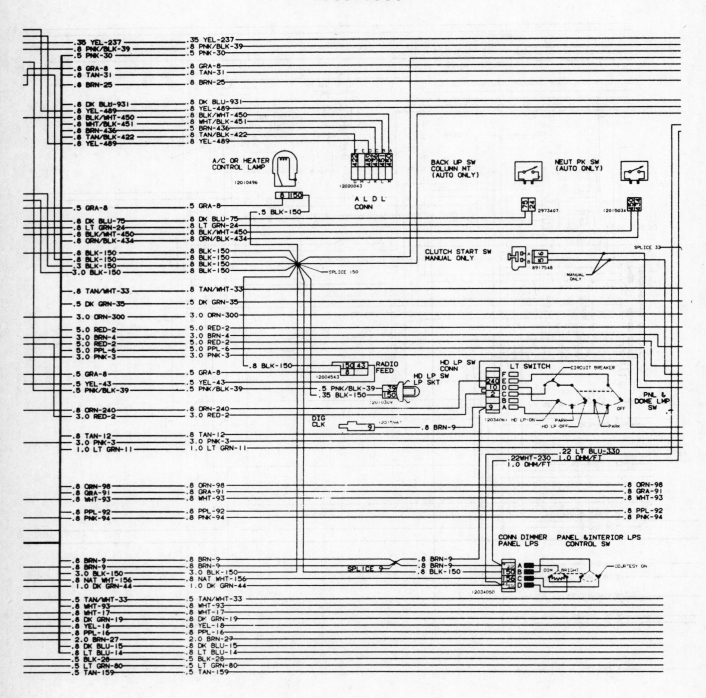

ASTRO VAN 1

1985–1986

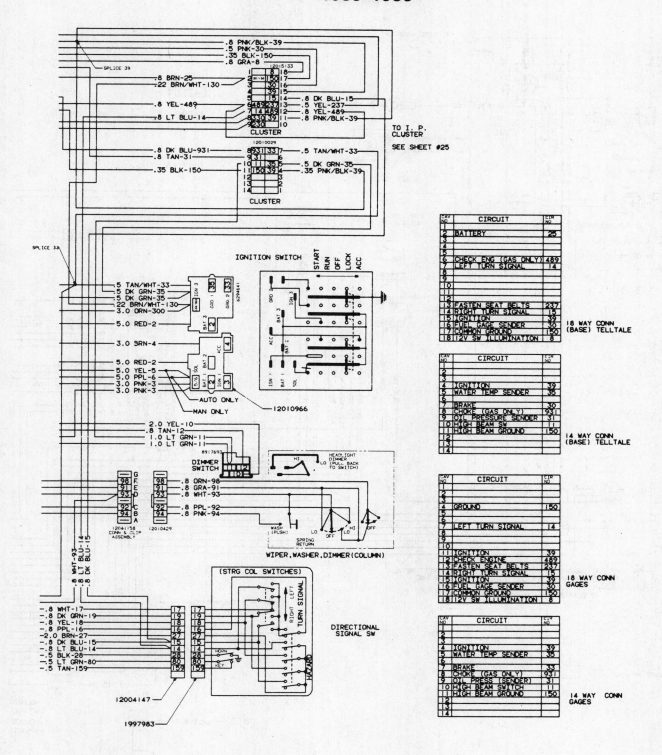

ASTRO VAN 1

1985-1986

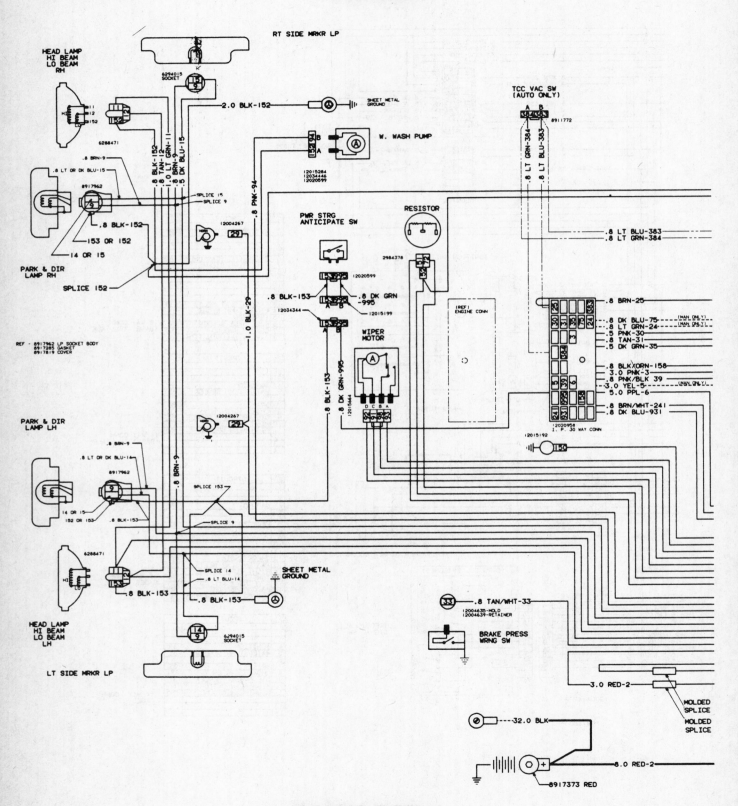

ASTRO VAN 1A

1985-1986

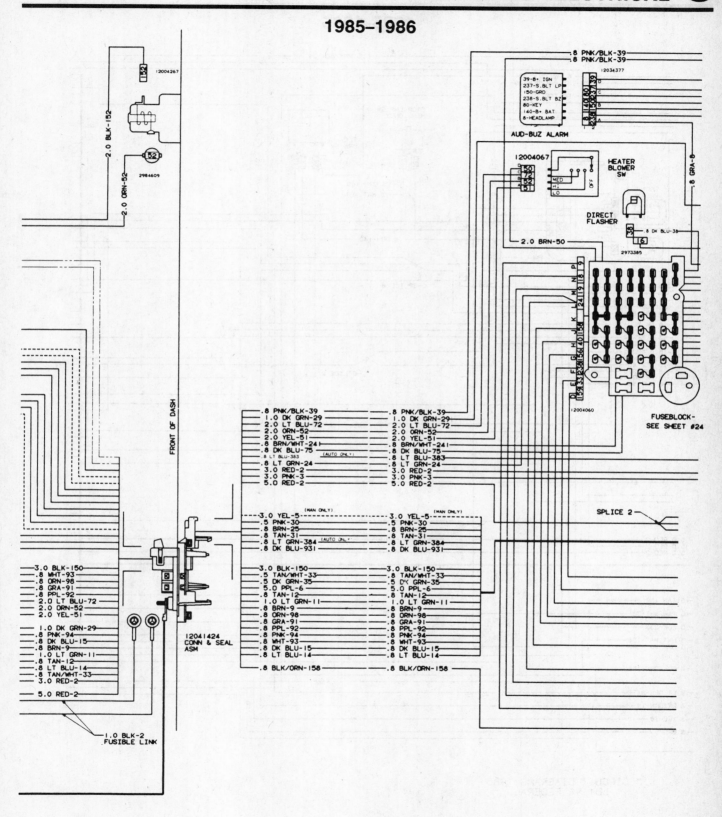

ASTRO VAN 1A

1985–1986

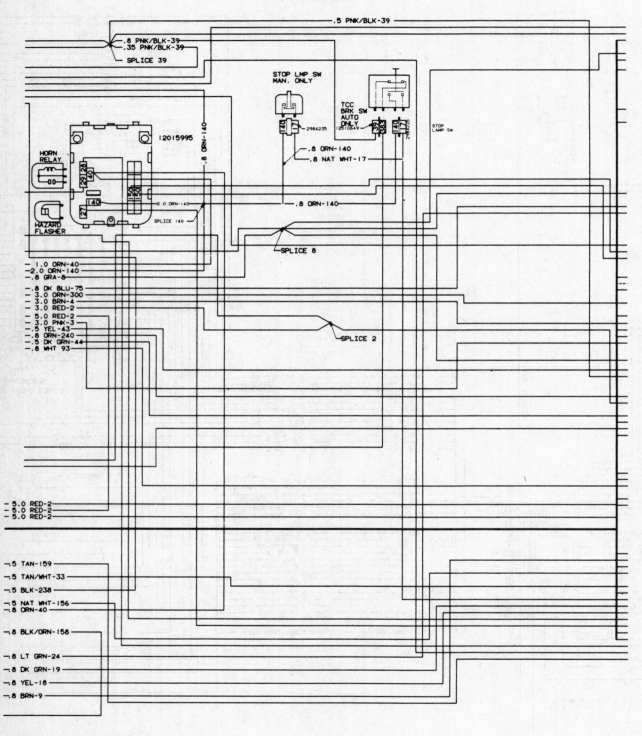

CIRCUIT DIAGRAMS 1985
LBI V6 FEDERAL

ASTRO VAN 1A

1985–1986

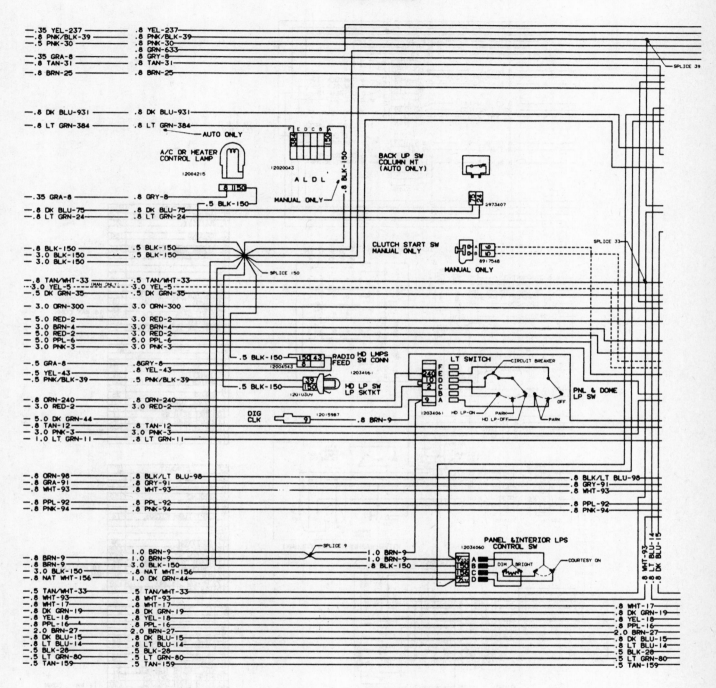

ASTRO VAN 1A

1985–1986

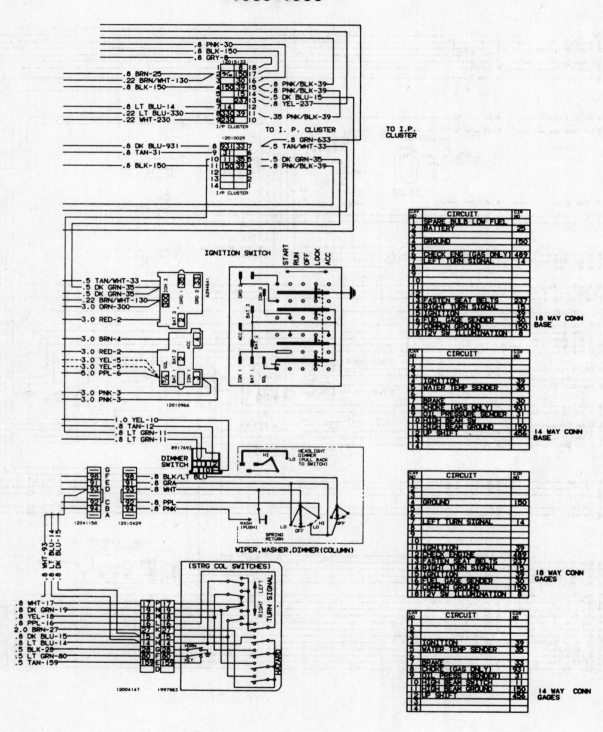

ASTRO VAN 1A

1985–1986

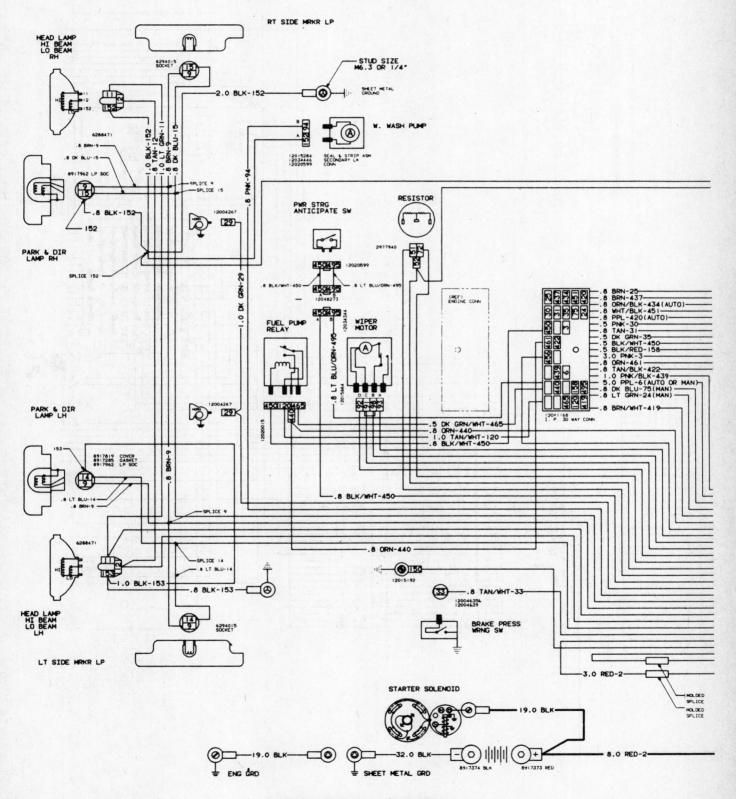

ASTRO VAN 1B

1985–1986

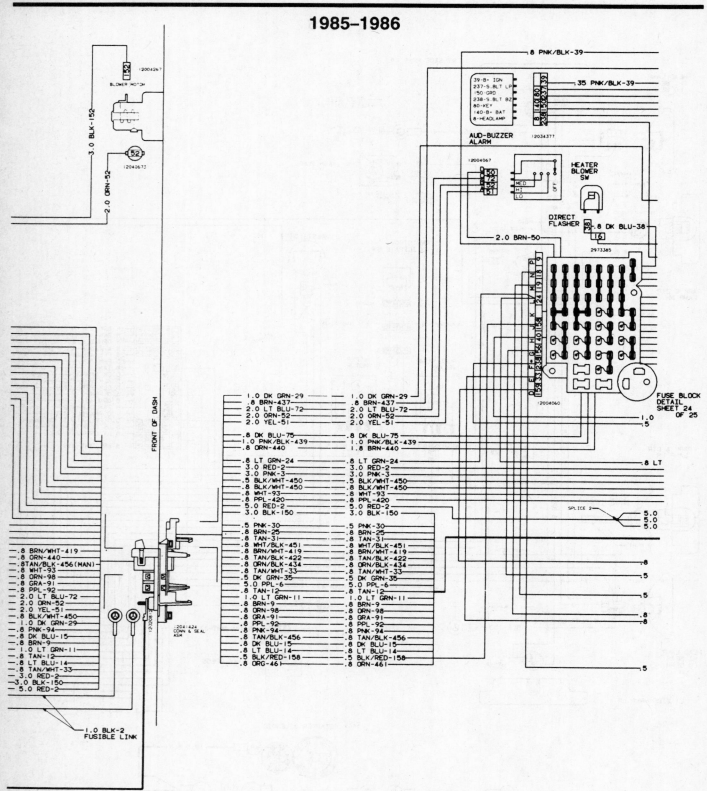

ASTRO VAN 1B

1985–1986

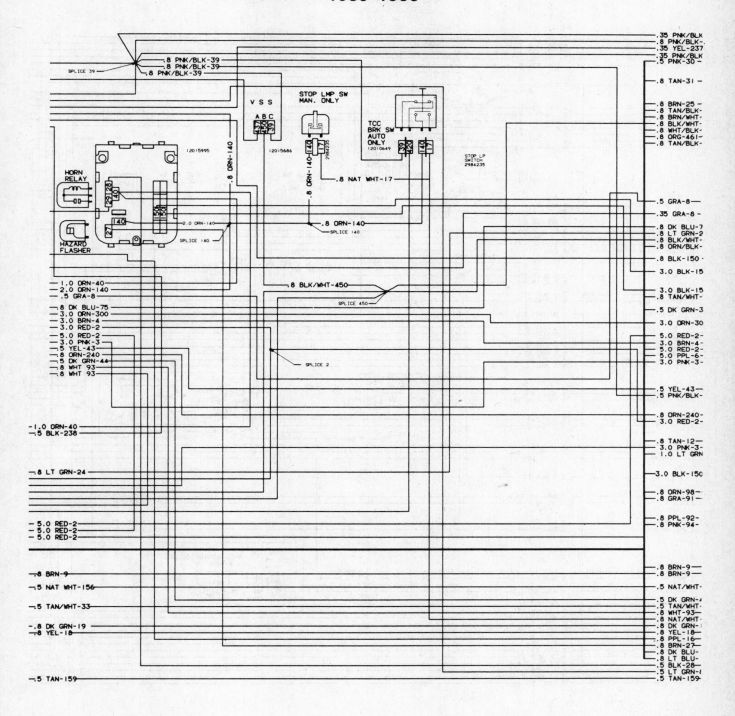

CIRCUIT DIAGRAMS 1985
M VAN I. P. LN8-TBI

ASTRO VAN 1B

1985–1986

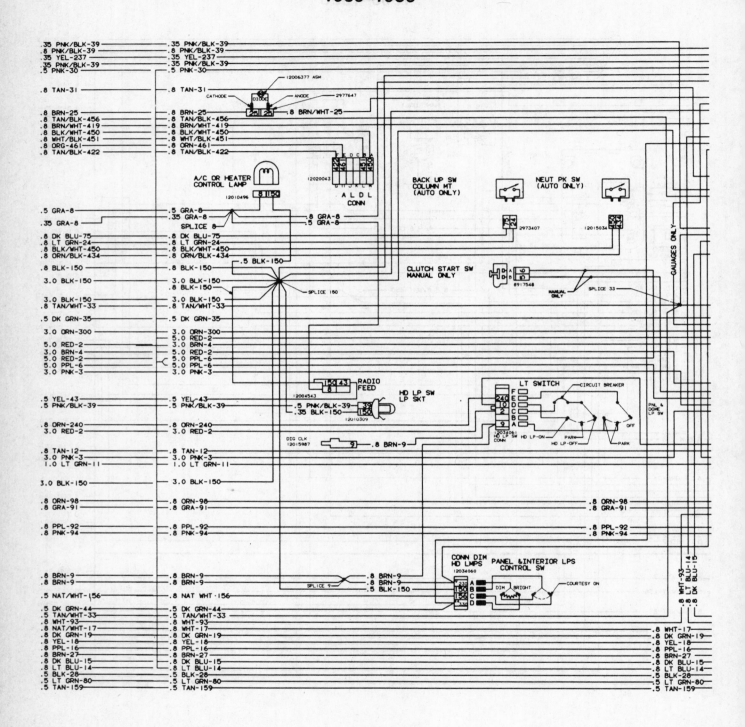

ASTRO VAN 1B

1985–1986

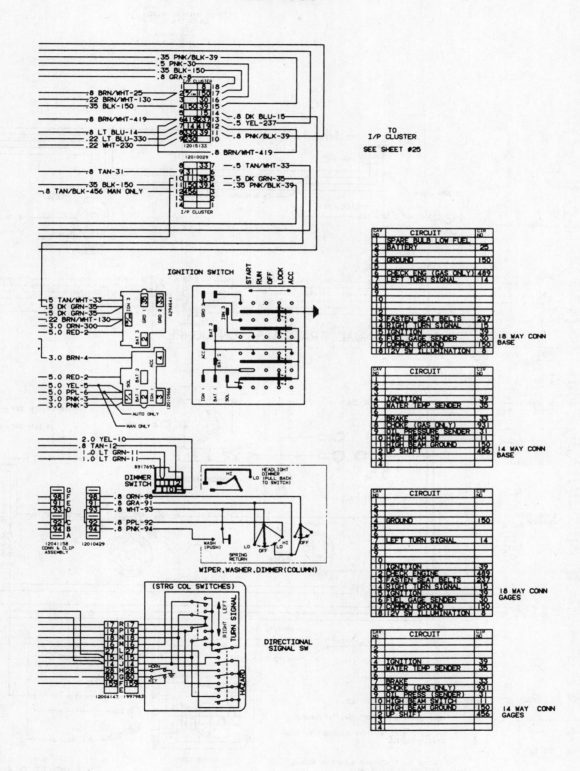

ASTRO VAN 1B

1985–1986

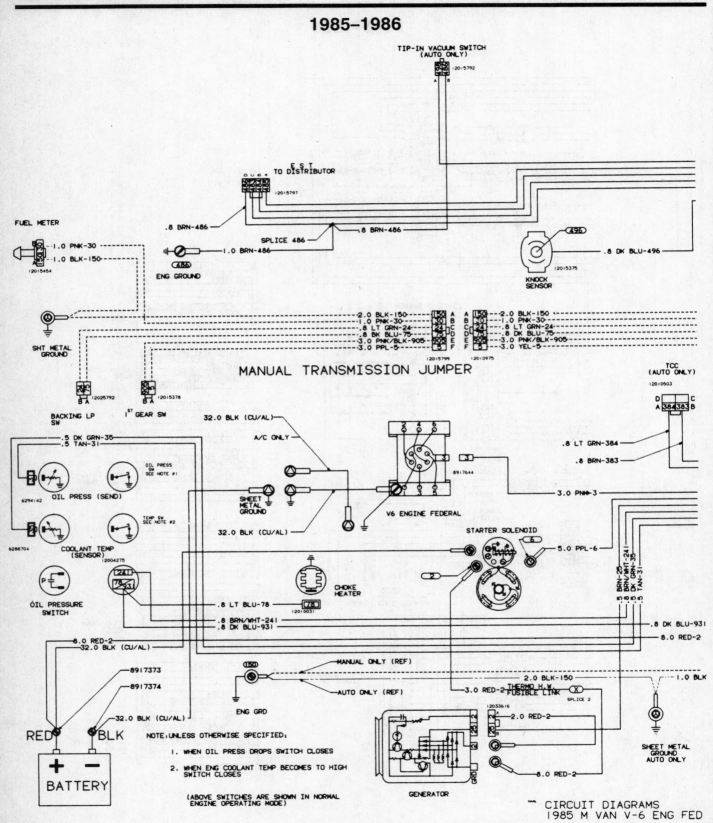

TIP-IN VACUUM SWITCH
(AUTO ONLY)
12015792

E.S.T.
TO DISTRIBUTOR
12015797

FUEL METER

1.0 PNK-30
1.0 BLK-150
12015454

.8 BRN-486

SPLICE 486

1.0 BRN-486

ENG GROUND

.8 BRN-486

KNOCK
SENSOR
12015375

.8 DK BLU-496

SHT METAL
GROUND

2.0 BLK-150 | 150 | A | A | 150 | 2.0 BLK-150
1.0 PNK-30 | 30 | B | B | 30 | 1.0 PNK-30
.8 LT GRN-24 | 24 | C | C | 24 | .8 LT GRN-24
.8 BK BLU-75 | 75 | D | D | 75 | .8 DK BLU-75
3.0 PNK/BLK-905 | 905 | E | E | 905 | 3.0 PNK/BLK-905
3.0 PPL-5 | 5 | F | F | 5 | 3.0 YEL-5
12015799   12010975

MANUAL TRANSMISSION JUMPER

TCC
(AUTO ONLY)
12010503

.8 LT GRN-384
.8 BRN-383

BACKING LP
SW
12025792

1ST GEAR SW
12015378

OIL PRESS
SW
SEE NOTE #1

.5 DK GRN-35
.5 TAN-31

OIL PRESS (SEND)
6294142

32.0 BLK (CU/AL)

A/C ONLY

8917644

V6 ENGINE FEDERAL

3.0 PNK-3

SHEET
METAL
GROUND

TEMP SW
SEE NOTE #2

COOLANT TEMP
(SENSOR)
6288704
12004275

32.0 BLK (CU/AL)

STARTER SOLENOID

5.0 PPL-6

OIL PRESSURE
SWITCH

24
78
931

CHOKE
HEATER

.8 LT BLU-78   12010031

.8 BRN/WHT-241
.8 DK BLU-931

.5 BRN-25
.8 BRN/WHT-241
.5 DK GRN-35
.5 TAN-31

.8 DK BLU-931

8.0 RED-2

6.0 RED-2
32.0 BLK (CU/AL)

8917373
8917374

32.0 BLK (CU/AL)

150

MANUAL ONLY (REF)

AUTO ONLY (REF)

ENG GRD

2.0 BLK-150

3.0 RED-2   THERMO H.W.
FUSIBLE LINK   SPLICE 2

12033616
2.0 RED-2

1.0 BLK

SHEET METAL
GROUND
AUTO ONLY

RED   BLK

+   −

BATTERY

GENERATOR

8.0 RED-2

NOTE: UNLESS OTHERWISE SPECIFIED:

1. WHEN OIL PRESS DROPS SWITCH CLOSES

2. WHEN ENG COOLANT TEMP BECOMES TO HIGH
   SWITCH CLOSES

(ABOVE SWITCHES ARE SHOWN IN NORMAL
ENGINE OPERATING MODE)

CIRCUIT DIAGRAMS
1985 M VAN V-6 ENG FED

ASTRO VAN 1C

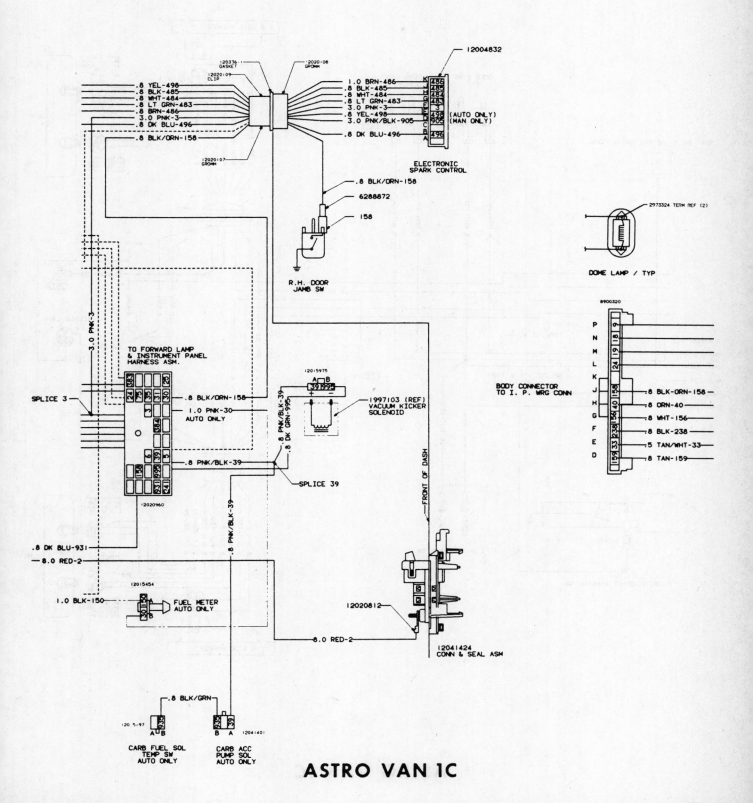

ASTRO VAN 1C

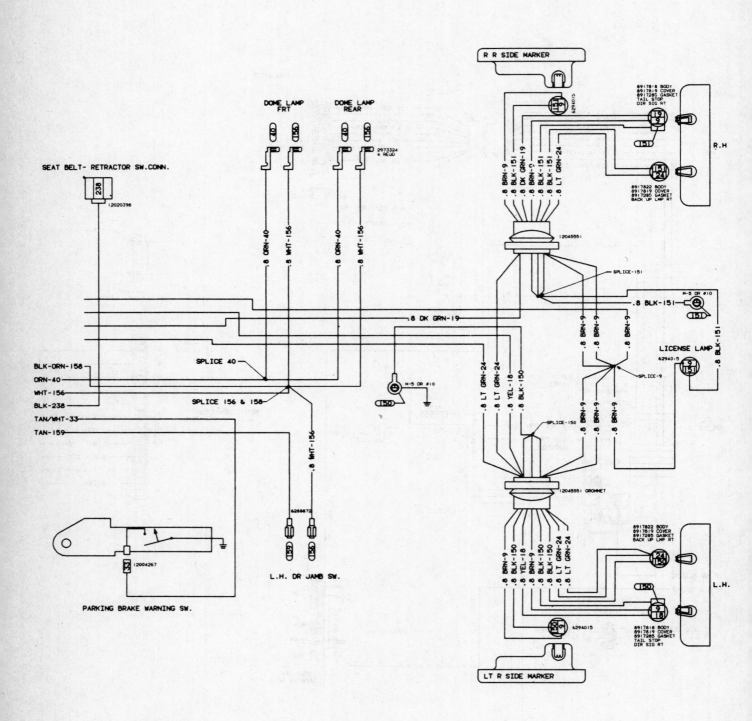

ASTRO VAN 1C

1985-1986

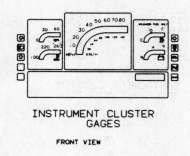

INSTRUMENT CLUSTER
GAGES

FRONT VIEW

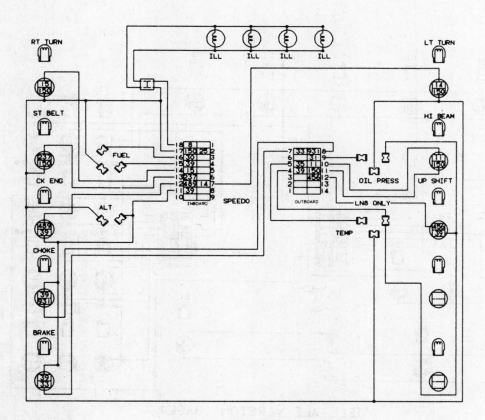

GAGE VERSION

REAR VIEW (OF CIRCUIT)

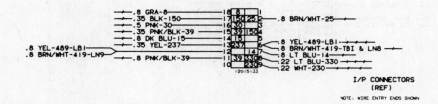

I/P CONNECTORS
(REF)

NOTE: WIRE ENTRY ENDS SHOWN

ASTRO VAN 1C

1985–1986

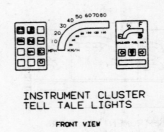

INSTRUMENT CLUSTER
TELL TALE LIGHTS

FRONT VIEW

ILLUMINATION BULBS REQUIRED; 9 WITH AUTOTRANS
8 WITH MAN TRANS

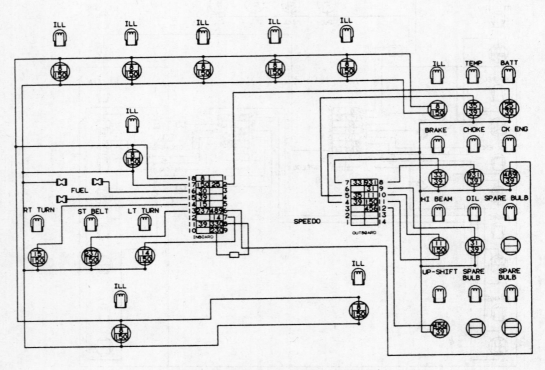

TELLTALE VERSION (BASE)

REAR VIEW (OF CIRCUIT)

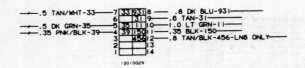

ASTRO VAN 1C

NOTE:

1. WHEN OIL PRESSURE DROPS SWITCH CLOSES.

2. WHEN ENGINE COOLANT TEMP BECOMES TOO HIGH SWITCH CLOSES.

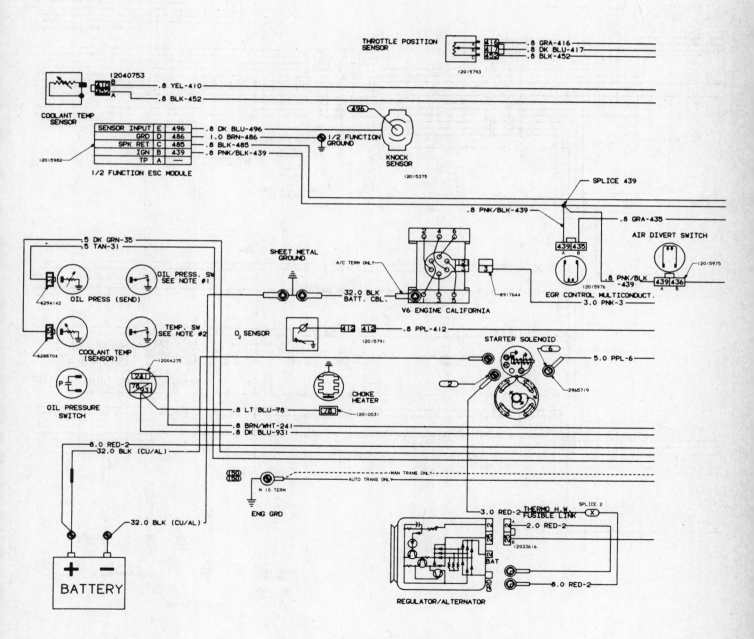

ASTRO VAN 1D

1985–1986

16006834 (REF)
DIFFERENTIAL PRESSURE
(VACUUM) SENSOR

EST
SIG
COND

HEI
REF

E S T

12015797

.8 BLK-452

SPLICE 452 & 453

12015384

.8 GRA-416

.8 BLK-452
.8 DK BLU-417
.8 YEL-410
.8 LT GRN-432
.8 BLK-452
DRAIN WIRE CIR 453
.8 PPL-412
.8 GRA-416
.8 BLK-485
.8 BRN-436
.8 GRA-435

SPLICE 416

1.0 PNK/BLK-439

.8 BLK-452
.8 DK BLU-417
.8 YEL-410
.8 LT GRN-432
.8 BLK-452
DRAIN WIRE SHIELDING CIR 453 & 430
.8 PPL-412
.8 GRA-416
.8 BLK-485
.8 BRN 436
.8 GRA-435
1.0 PNK/BLK-439

SPLICE 439

1.0 PNK/BLK-439 (GXL)

CARB AIR FUEL
SOLENOID

439

411

.8 LT BLU-411

411

12015256

DIAG

CARB FUEL SOL
TEMP SW

.5 BRN-25
.5 TAN-31

.5 BRN-25
.5 TAN-31

.5 DK GRN-35

.5 DK GRN-35

3.0 PNK-3
5.0 PPL-6

3.0 PNK-3
5.0 PPL-6

2.0 BLK-150
1.0 PNK-30
.8 LT GRN-24
.8 DK BLU-75

150 A
30 B
24 C
75 D

A 150
B 30
C 24
D 75

2.0 BLK-150
1.0 PNK-30
.8 LT GRN-24
.8 DK BLU-75

FUEL METER
CONN

12015454

12015797

12010974

MAN TRANS JMPR WIRE

.8 BRN/WHT-241

.8 BRN/WHT-241

8.0 RED-2
2.0 BLK-150

8.0 RED-2
2.0 BLK-150

.8 DK BLU-931

.8 DK BLU-931

2.0 BLK-150

2.0 BLK-150

.8 BLK-150

SHEET METAL
GROUND

MAN TRANS
ONLY

.8 LT GRN-24
.8 DK BLU-75

24

413
450

12015792

TO BACK UP LP SW

ENGINE GROUNDS

413
450

ASTRO VAN 1D

1985–1986

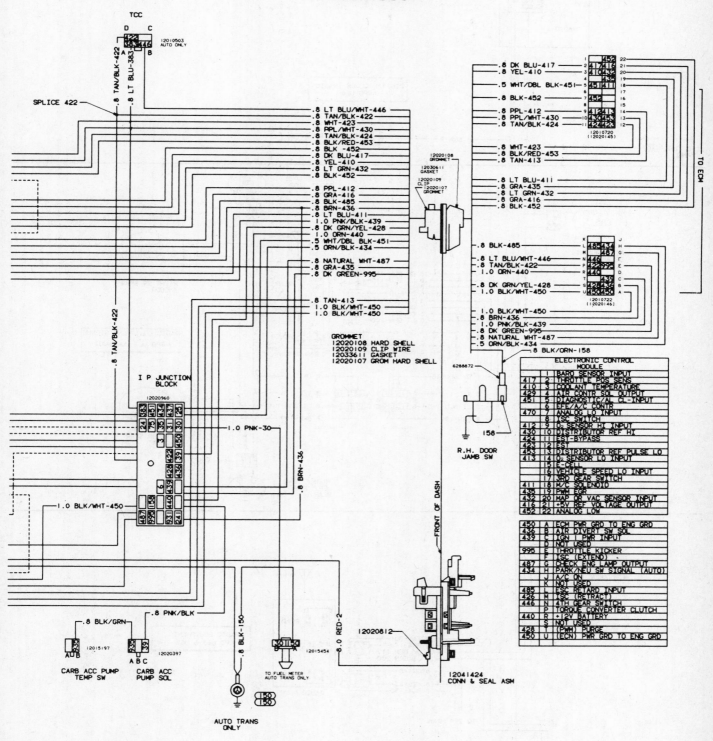

CIRCUIT DIAGRAMS
LBI V6 ENG WRG (CALIF)

ASTRO VAN 1D

1985–1986

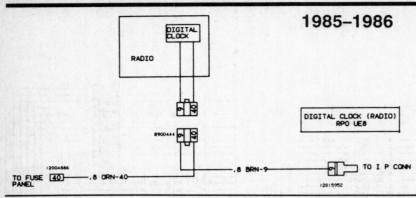

RADIO

DIGITAL CLOCK

DIGITAL CLOCK (RADIO)
RPO UE8

8900444

12004886
TO FUSE PANEL [40] — .8 ORN-40 ———— .8 BRN-9 ———— TO I P CONN
12015752

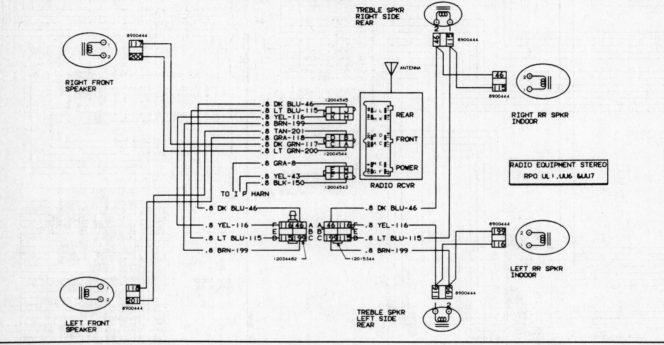

TREBLE SPKR RIGHT SIDE REAR

ANTENNA

RIGHT FRONT SPEAKER

8900444

8900444

RIGHT RR SPKR INDOOR

.8 DK BLU-46   12004545
.8 LT BLU-115
.8 YEL-116
.8 BRN-199
.8 TAN-201
.8 GRA-118
.8 DK GRN-117
.8 LT GRN-200   12004544

REAR

FRONT

.8 GRA-8
.8 YEL-43
.8 BLK-150   12004543

POWER

TO I P HARN

RADIO RCVR

RADIO EQUIPMENT STEREO
RPO UL1, UU6 & UU7

.8 DK BLU-46   .8 DK BLU-46
.8 YEL-116   F   A   .8 YEL-116
.8 LT BLU-115   D   C   .8 LT BLU-115
.8 BRN-199   .8 BRN-199
12034482   12015344

8900444

LEFT RR SPKR INDOOR

LEFT FRONT SPEAKER

8900444

TREBLE SPKR LEFT SIDE REAR

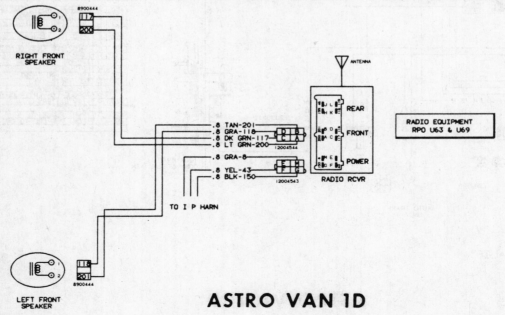

RIGHT FRONT SPEAKER

8900444

ANTENNA

REAR

.8 TAN-201
.8 GRA-118
.8 DK GRN-117
.8 LT GRN-200   12004544

FRONT

.8 GRA-8
.8 YEL-43
.8 BLK-150   12004543

POWER

RADIO RCVR

RADIO EQUIPMENT
RPO U63 & U69

TO I P HARN

LEFT FRONT SPEAKER

8900444

ASTRO VAN 1D

1985–1986

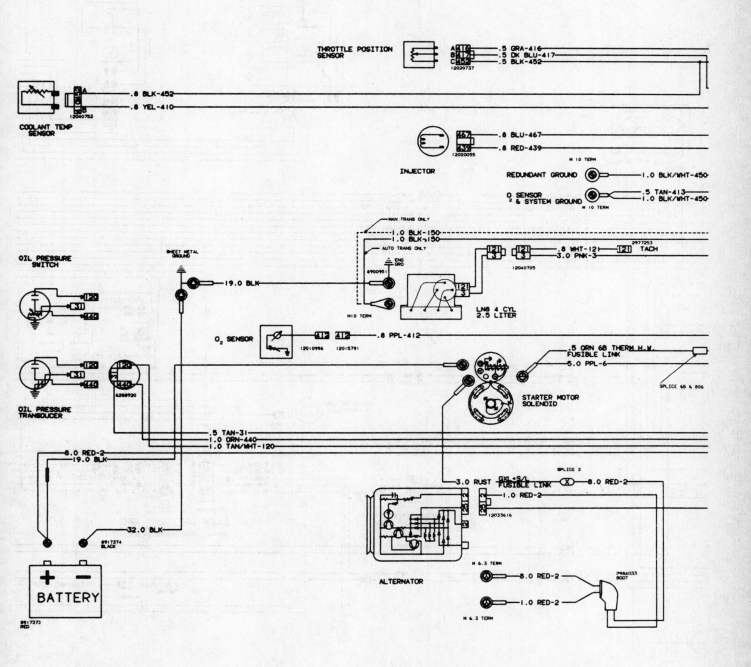

THROTTLE POSITION SENSOR
12020737
A .5 GRA-416
B .5 DK BLU-417
C .5 BLK-452

COOLANT TEMP SENSOR
12040753
A .8 BLK-452
B .8 YEL-410

INJECTOR
12020055
.8 BLU-467
.8 RED-439

REDUNDANT GROUND
M 10 TERM
1.0 BLK/WHT-450

O₂ SENSOR & SYSTEM GROUND
.5 TAN-413
1.0 BLK/WHT-450
M 10 TERM

OIL PRESSURE SWITCH

OIL PRESSURE TRANSDUCER
6200920

SHEET METAL GROUND
19.0 BLK

MAN TRANS ONLY
1.0 BLK-150
1.0 BLK-150
AUTO TRANS ONLY
890095

ENG GRD
M10 TERM

121 3
121 3
.8 WHT-121
3.0 PNK-3
121 TACH
2977253

12040705

LN8 4 CYL 2.5 LITER

O₂ SENSOR
12010996 12015791
412 412 .8 PPL-412

.5 ORN 68 THERM H.W. FUSIBLE LINK
5.0 PPL-6
SPLICE 68 & 806

STARTER MOTOR SOLENOID

.5 TAN-31
1.0 ORN-440
1.0 TAN/WHT-120

8.0 RED-2
19.0 BLK

32.0 BLK
8917374 BLACK

BATTERY
8917373 RED

3.0 RUST
GXL·S/ FUSIBLE LINK
SPLICE 2
8.0 RED-2
1.0 RED-2
12033616

ALTERNATOR

M 6.3 TERM
8.0 RED-2
2484033 BOOT
M 6.3 TERM
1.0 RED-2

ASTRO VAN 1E

1985–1986

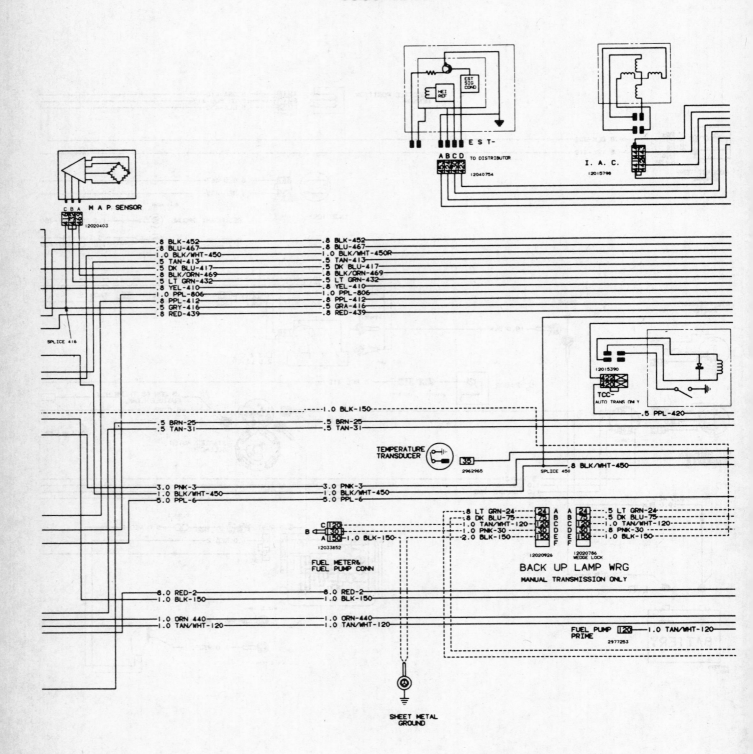

M A P SENSOR

12020403

SPLICE 416

.8 BLK-452
.8 BLU-467
1.0 BLK/WHT-450
.5 TAN-413
.5 DK BLU-417
.8 BLK/ORN-469
.5 LT GRN-432
.8 YEL-410
1.0 PPL-806
.8 PPL-412
.5 GRY-416
.8 RED-439

.8 BLK-452
.8 BLU-467
1.0 BLK/WHT-450R
.5 TAN-413
.5 DK BLU-417
.8 BLK/ORN-469
.5 LT GRN-432
.8 YEL-410
1.0 PPL-806
.8 PPL-412
.5 GRA-416
.8 RED-439

A B C D
TO DISTRIBUTOR
12040754

E S T–

I. A. C.
12015798

12015390

TCC–
AUTO TRANS ONLY

.5 PPL-420

1.0 BLK-150

.5 BRN-25
.5 TAN-31

.5 BRN-25
.5 TAN-31

TEMPERATURE
TRANSDUCER
2962965

35

SPLICE 450
.8 BLK/WHT-450

3.0 PNK-3
1.0 BLK/WHT-450
5.0 PPL-6

3.0 PNK-3
1.0 BLK/WHT-450
5.0 PPL-6

.8 LT GRN-24
.8 DK BLU-75
1.0 TAN/WHT-120
1.0 PNK-30
2.0 BLK-150

24
75
120
30
150

A
B
C
D
E
F

A
B
C
D
E
F

24
75
120
30
150

.5 LT GRN-24
.5 DK BLU-75
1.0 TAN/WHT-120
.8 PNK-30
1.0 BLK-150

C 120
B
A 150
1.0 BLK-150
12033852

FUEL METER&
FUEL PUMP CONN

12020926

12020786
WEDGE LOCK

BACK UP LAMP WRG
MANUAL TRANSMISSION ONLY

8.0 RED-2
1.0 BLK-150

8.0 RED-2
1.0 BLK-150

1.0 ORN 440
1.0 TAN/WHT-120

1.0 ORN-440
1.0 TAN/WHT-120

FUEL PUMP 120
PRIME
2977253
1.0 TAN/WHT-120

SHEET METAL
GROUND

CIRCUIT DIAGRAMS
1985 M VAN 4 CYL TBI

ASTRO VAN 1E

1985–1986

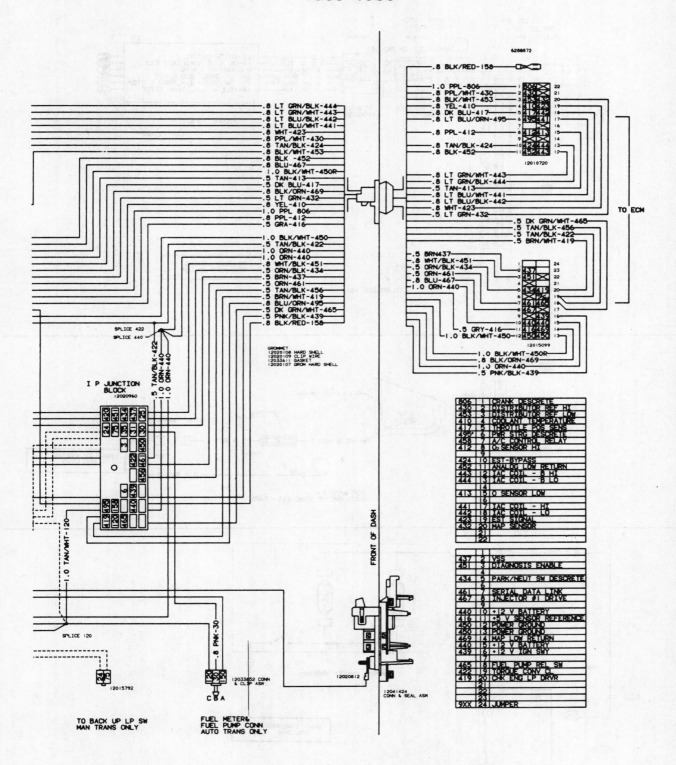

ASTRO VAN 1E

1985-1986

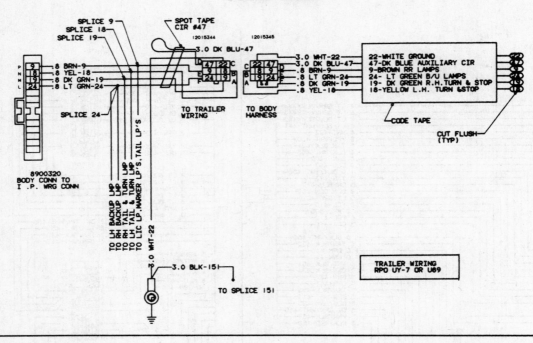

SPLICE 9
SPLICE 18
SPLICE 19

SPOT TAPE
CIR #47

12015344   12015345

3.0 DK BLU-47

P	9	.8 BRN-9
N	18	.8 YEL-18
M	19	.8 DK GRN-19
L	24	.8 LT GRN-24

SPLICE 24

8900320
BODY CONN TO
I.P. WRG CONN

TO TRAILER
WIRING

TO BODY
HARNESS

3.0 WHT-22
3.0 DK BLU-47
.8 BRN-9
.8 LT GRN-24
.8 DK GRN-19
.8 YEL-18

22-WHITE GROUND
47-DK BLUE AUXILIARY CIR
9-BROWN RR LAMPS
24- LT GREEN B/U LAMPS
19- DK GREEN R.H. TURN & STOP
18-YELLOW L.H. TURN & STOP

CODE TAPE

CUT FLUSH
(TYP)

TO LH BACKUP LMP
TO RH BACKUP LMP
TO RH TAIL & TURN LMP
TO LH TAIL & TURN LMP
TO LIC LP.MARKER LP'S.TAIL LP'S

3.0 WHT-22

3.0 BLK-151

TO SPLICE 151

TRAILER WIRING
RPO UY-7 OR U89

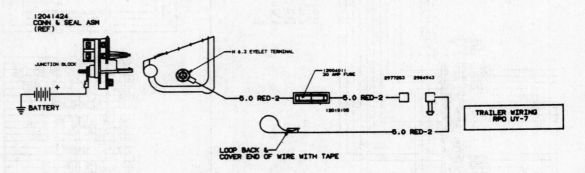

12041424
CONN & SEAL ASM
(REF)

JUNCTION BLOCK

M 6.3 EYELET TERMINAL

BATTERY

12004911
30 AMP FUSE

2977253   2964943

5.0 RED-2   5.0 RED-2

12010105

5.0 RED-2

LOOP BACK &
COVER END OF WIRE WITH TAPE

TRAILER WIRING
RPO UY-7

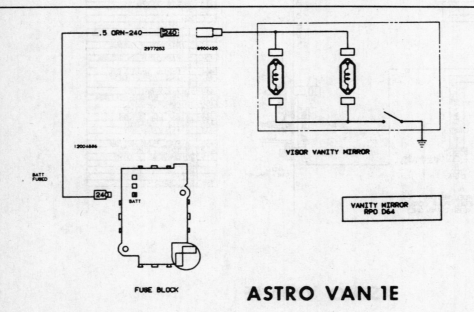

.5 ORN-240   240

2977253   8900420

VISOR VANITY MIRROR

BATT
FUSED

240

BATT

VANITY MIRROR
RPO D64

12004886

FUSE BLOCK

ASTRO VAN 1E

1985-1986

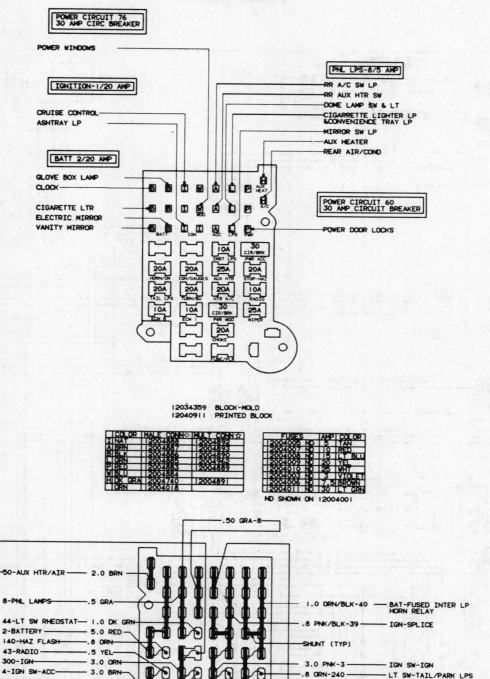

ASTRO VAN 1F

1985–1986

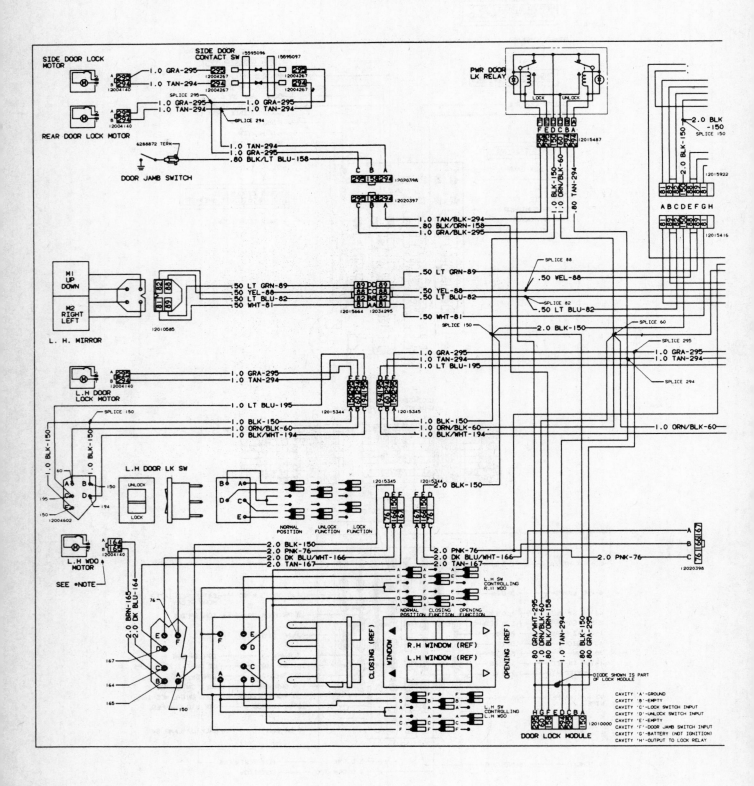

ASTRO VAN 1F

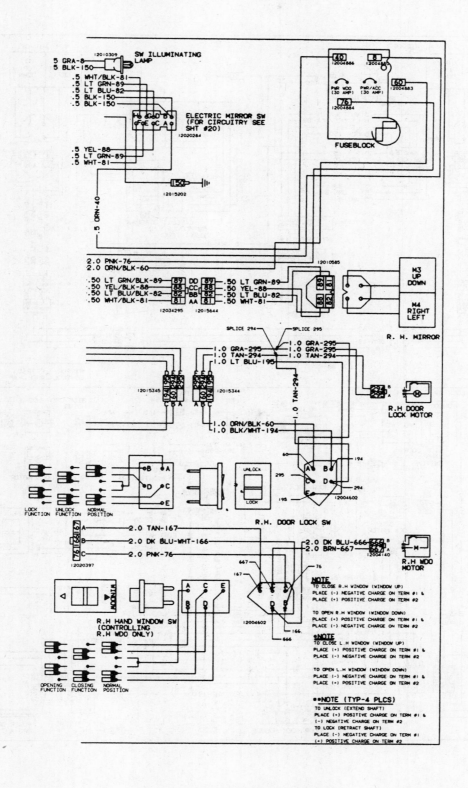

ASTRO VAN 1F

1985–1986

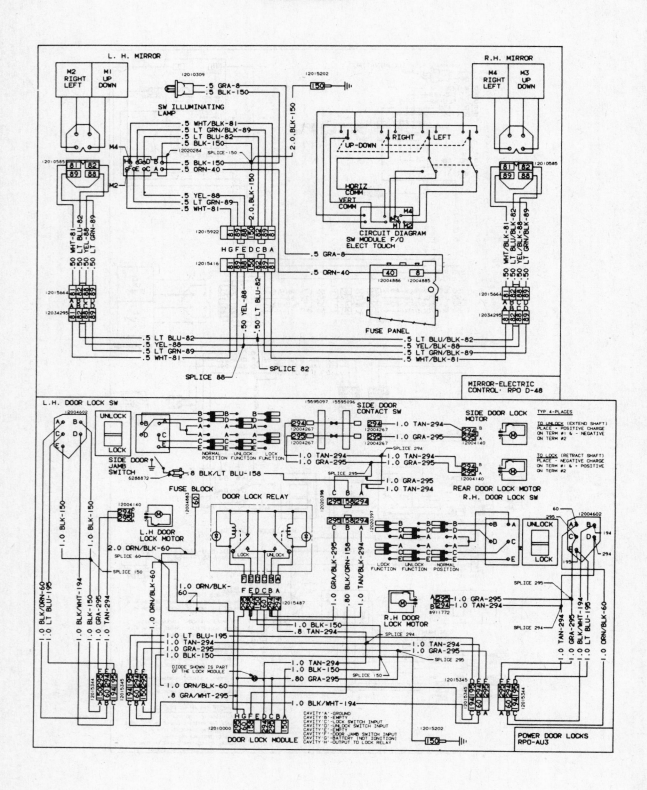

ASTRO VAN 1F

1985-1986

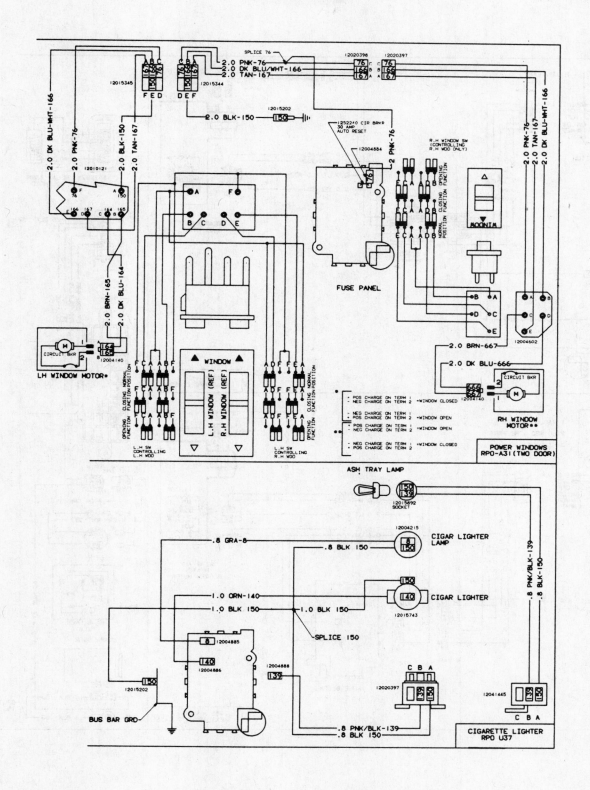

ASTRO VAN 1F

1985–1986

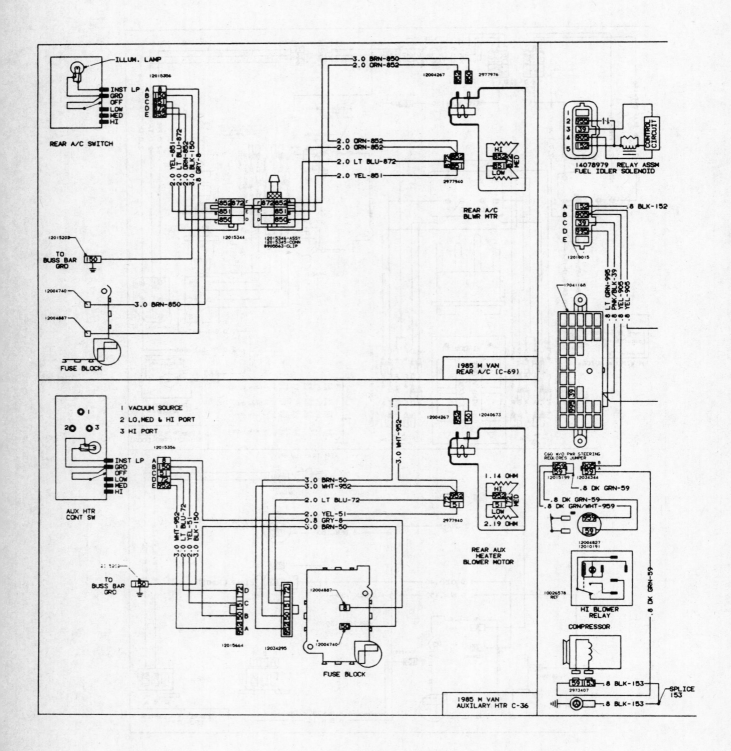

ASTRO VAN 1G

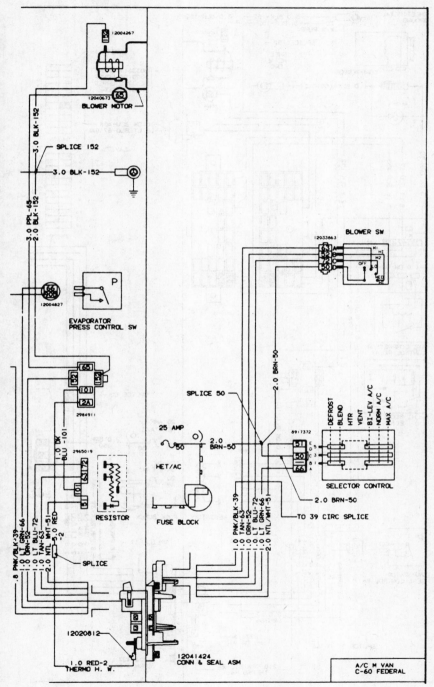

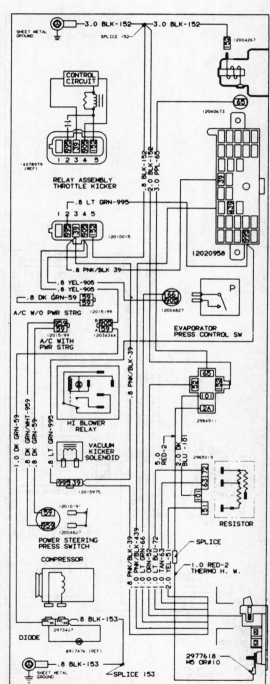

ASTRO VAN 1G

1985–1986

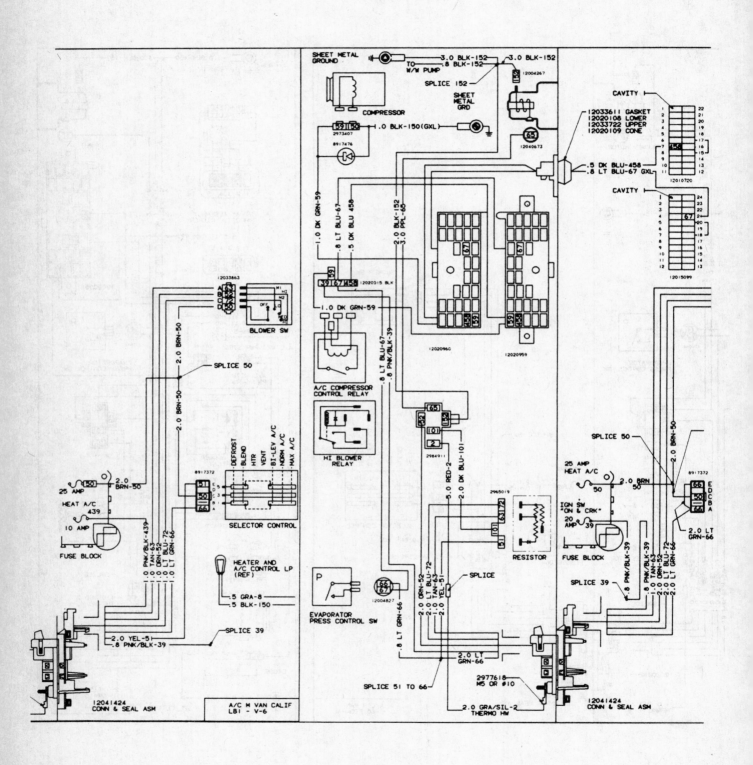

ASTRO VAN 1G

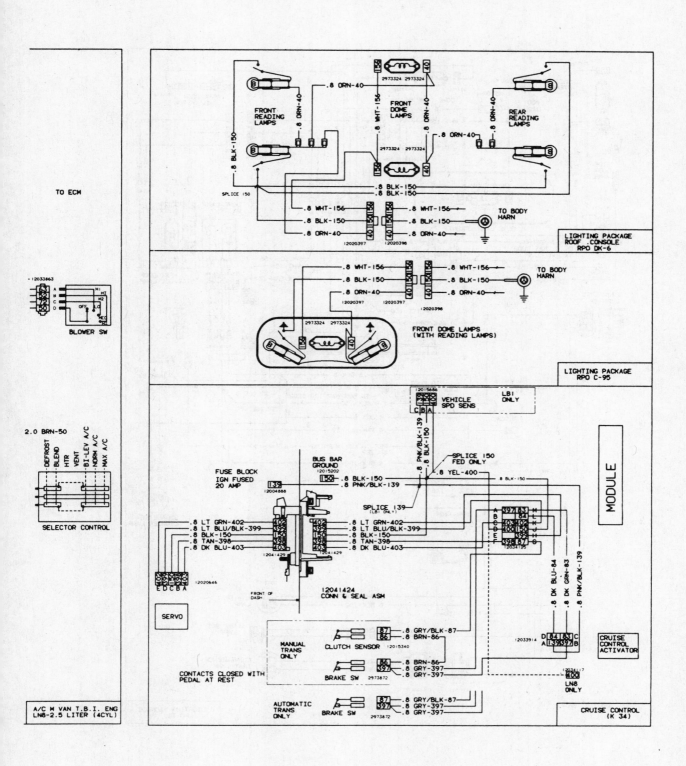

ASTRO VAN 1G

1985–1986

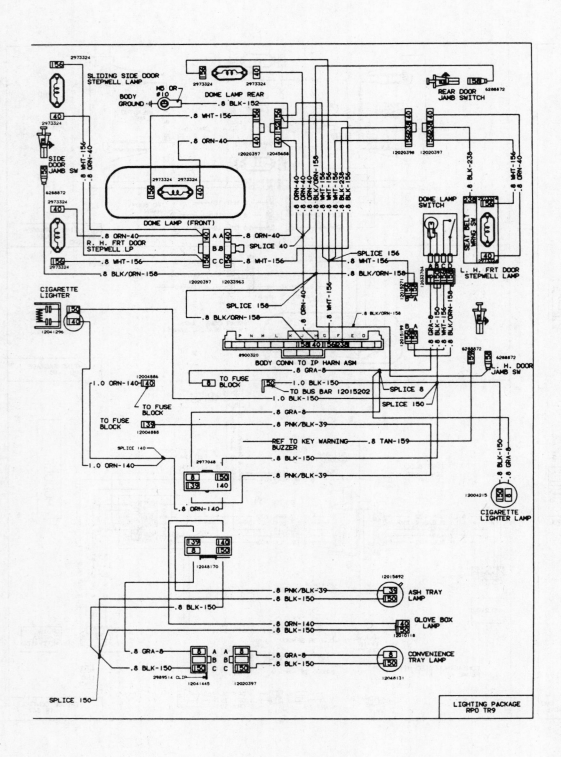

ASTRO VAN 1G

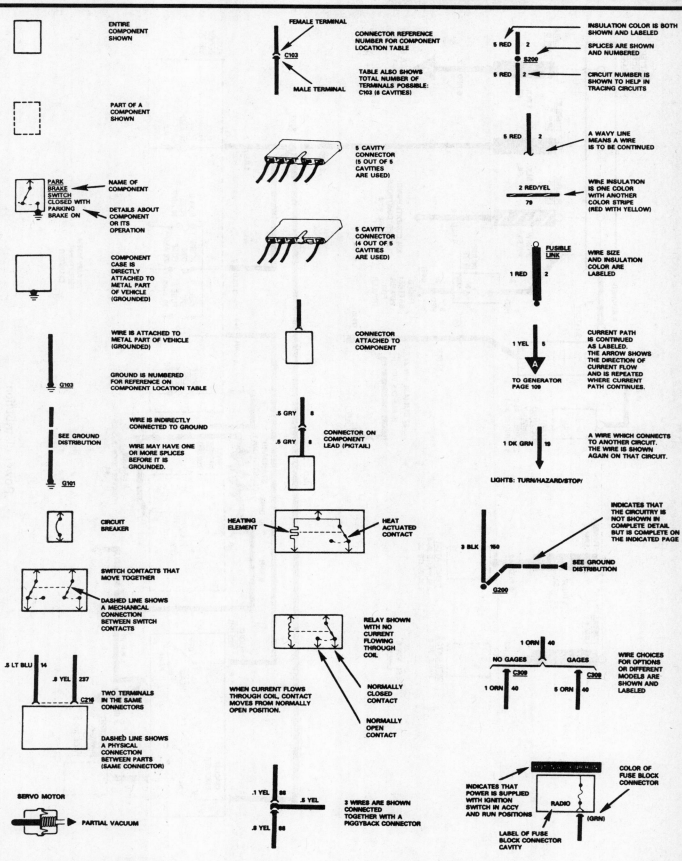

ENTIRE COMPONENT SHOWN

PART OF A COMPONENT SHOWN

PARK BRAKE SWITCH CLOSED WITH PARKING BRAKE ON — NAME OF COMPONENT

DETAILS ABOUT COMPONENT OR ITS OPERATION

COMPONENT CASE IS DIRECTLY ATTACHED TO METAL PART OF VEHICLE (GROUNDED)

WIRE IS ATTACHED TO METAL PART OF VEHICLE (GROUNDED)

G103 — GROUND IS NUMBERED FOR REFERENCE ON COMPONENT LOCATION TABLE

SEE GROUND DISTRIBUTION — WIRE IS INDIRECTLY CONNECTED TO GROUND

G101 — WIRE MAY HAVE ONE OR MORE SPLICES BEFORE IT IS GROUNDED.

CIRCUIT BREAKER

SWITCH CONTACTS THAT MOVE TOGETHER

DASHED LINE SHOWS A MECHANICAL CONNECTION BETWEEN SWITCH CONTACTS

.5 LT BLU 14   .8 YEL 237   C214

TWO TERMINALS IN THE SAME CONNECTORS

DASHED LINE SHOWS A PHYSICAL CONNECTION BETWEEN PARTS (SAME CONNECTOR)

SERVO MOTOR — PARTIAL VACUUM

FEMALE TERMINAL   C103   MALE TERMINAL — CONNECTOR REFERENCE NUMBER FOR COMPONENT LOCATION TABLE

TABLE ALSO SHOWS TOTAL NUMBER OF TERMINALS POSSIBLE: C103 (6 CAVITIES)

5 CAVITY CONNECTOR (5 OUT OF 5 CAVITIES ARE USED)

5 CAVITY CONNECTOR (4 OUT OF 5 CAVITIES ARE USED)

CONNECTOR ATTACHED TO COMPONENT

.5 GRY 8   .5 GRY 8 — CONNECTOR ON COMPONENT LEAD (PIGTAIL)

HEATING ELEMENT   HEAT ACTUATED CONTACT

RELAY SHOWN WITH NO CURRENT FLOWING THROUGH COIL

WHEN CURRENT FLOWS THROUGH COIL, CONTACT MOVES FROM NORMALLY OPEN POSITION.

NORMALLY CLOSED CONTACT

NORMALLY OPEN CONTACT

.1 YEL 88   .5 YEL   .8 YEL 88 — 3 WIRES ARE SHOWN CONNECTED TOGETHER WITH A PIGGYBACK CONNECTOR

5 RED 2   S200   5 RED 2 — INSULATION COLOR IS BOTH SHOWN AND LABELED

SPLICES ARE SHOWN AND NUMBERED

CIRCUIT NUMBER IS SHOWN TO HELP IN TRACING CIRCUITS

5 RED 2 — A WAVY LINE MEANS A WIRE IS TO BE CONTINUED

2 RED/YEL 79 — WIRE INSULATION IS ONE COLOR WITH ANOTHER COLOR STRIPE (RED WITH YELLOW)

FUSIBLE LINK   1 RED 2 — WIRE SIZE AND INSULATION COLOR ARE LABELED

1 YEL 5   A   TO GENERATOR PAGE 109 — CURRENT PATH IS CONTINUED AS LABELED. THE ARROW SHOWS THE DIRECTION OF CURRENT FLOW AND IS REPEATED WHERE CURRENT PATH CONTINUES.

1 DK GRN 19 — A WIRE WHICH CONNECTS TO ANOTHER CIRCUIT. THE WIRE IS SHOWN AGAIN ON THAT CIRCUIT.

LIGHTS: TURN/HAZARD/STOP/

3 BLK 150   G200 — INDICATES THAT THE CIRCUITRY IS NOT SHOWN IN COMPLETE DETAIL BUT IS COMPLETE ON THE INDICATED PAGE

SEE GROUND DISTRIBUTION

1 ORN 40   NO GAGES   C309   GAGES   C309   1 ORN 40   5 ORN 40 — WIRE CHOICES FOR OPTIONS OR DIFFERENT MODELS ARE SHOWN AND LABELED

INDICATES THAT POWER IS SUPPLIED WITH IGNITION SWITCH IN ACCY AND RUN POSITIONS

RADIO   (GRN) — COLOR OF FUSE BLOCK CONNECTOR

LABEL OF FUSE BLOCK CONNECTOR CAVITY

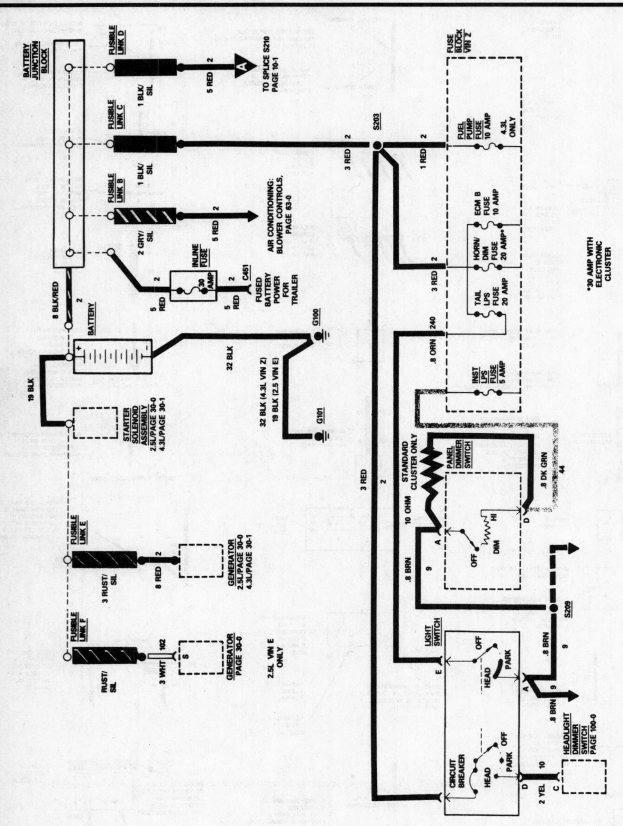

Power distribution

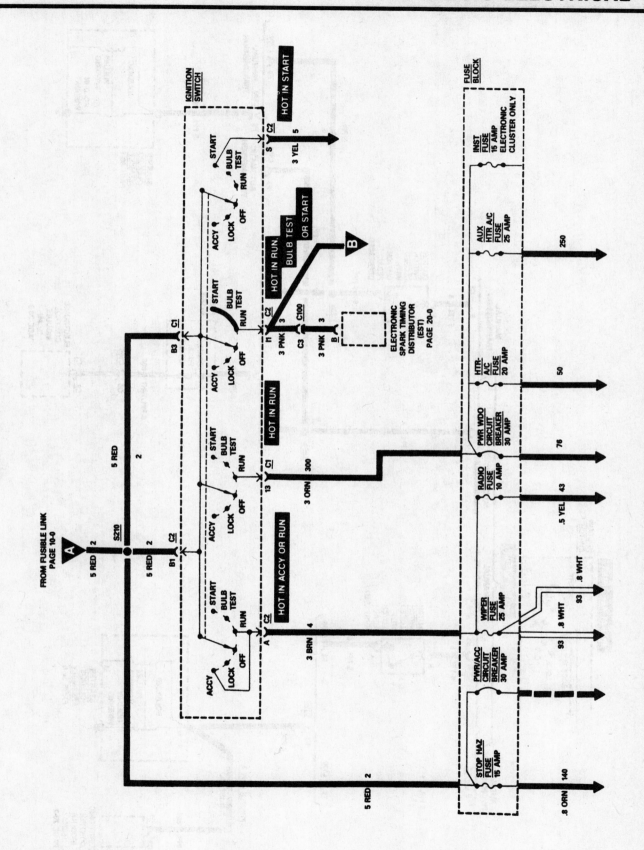

1987–1990

Power distribution

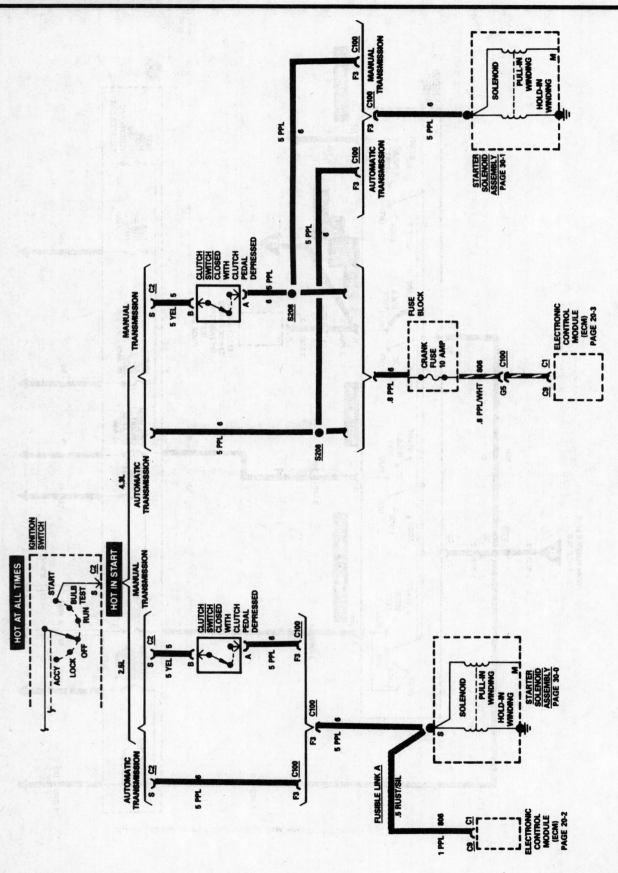

Power distribution

1987–1990

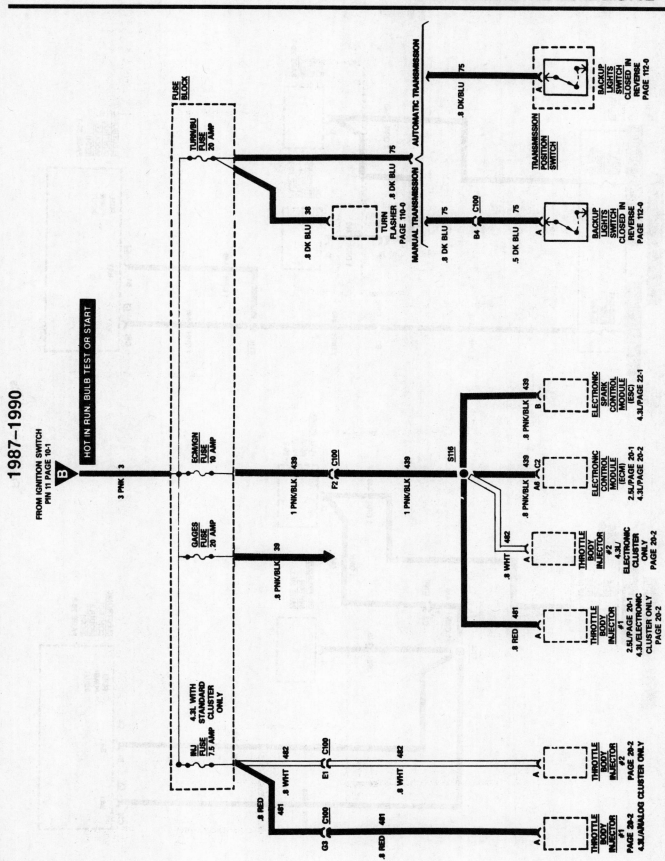

Fuse block details — EFI, ECM, Ignition, Trn/Bu fuse

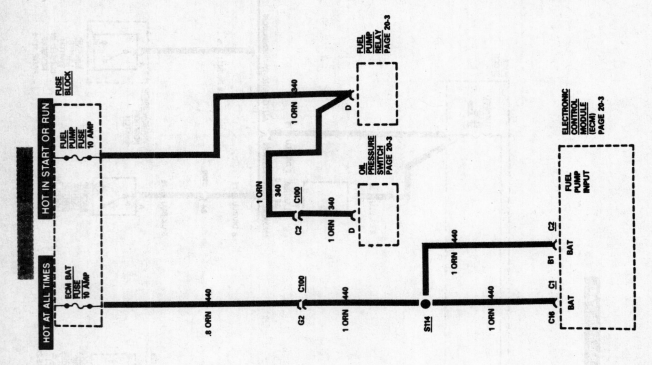

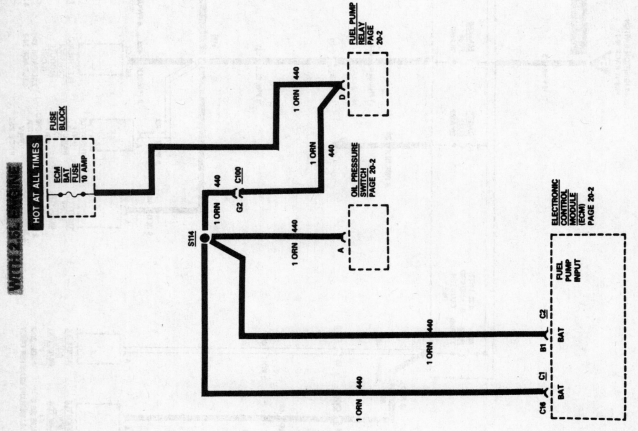

Fuse block details

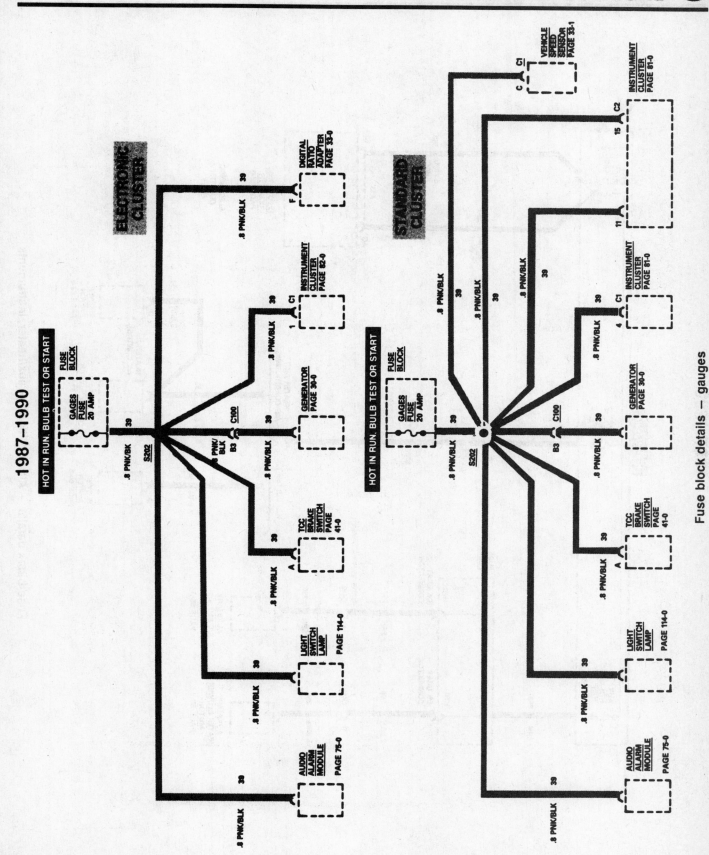

Fuse block details — gauges

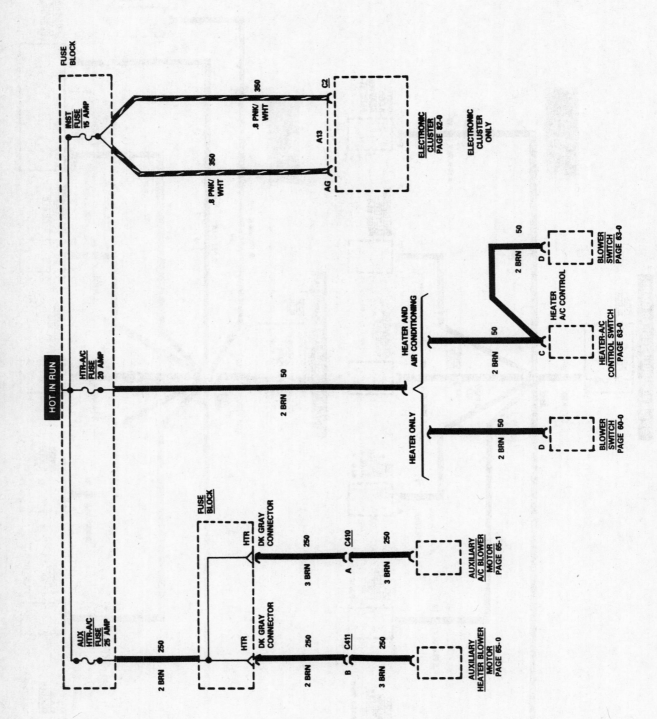

1987–1990

Fuse block details – Air conditioning, aux/heater, instruments

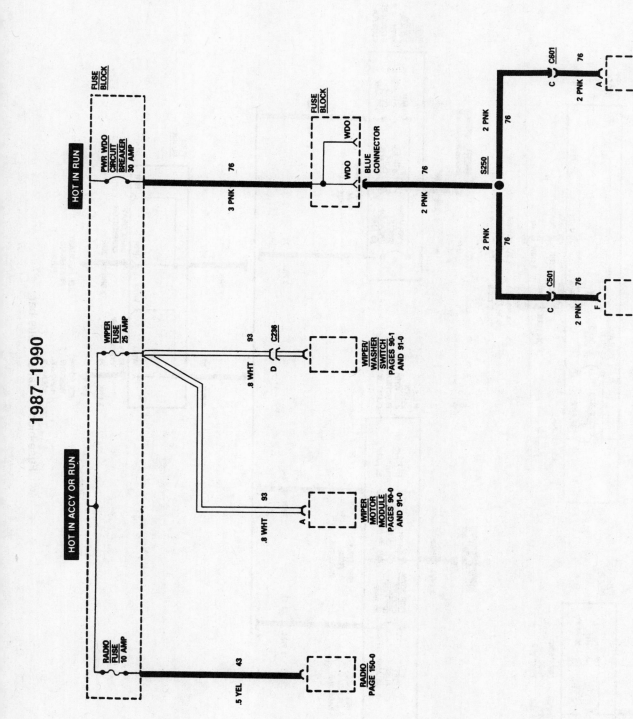

Fuse block details — radio, wiper, power window circuit breaker

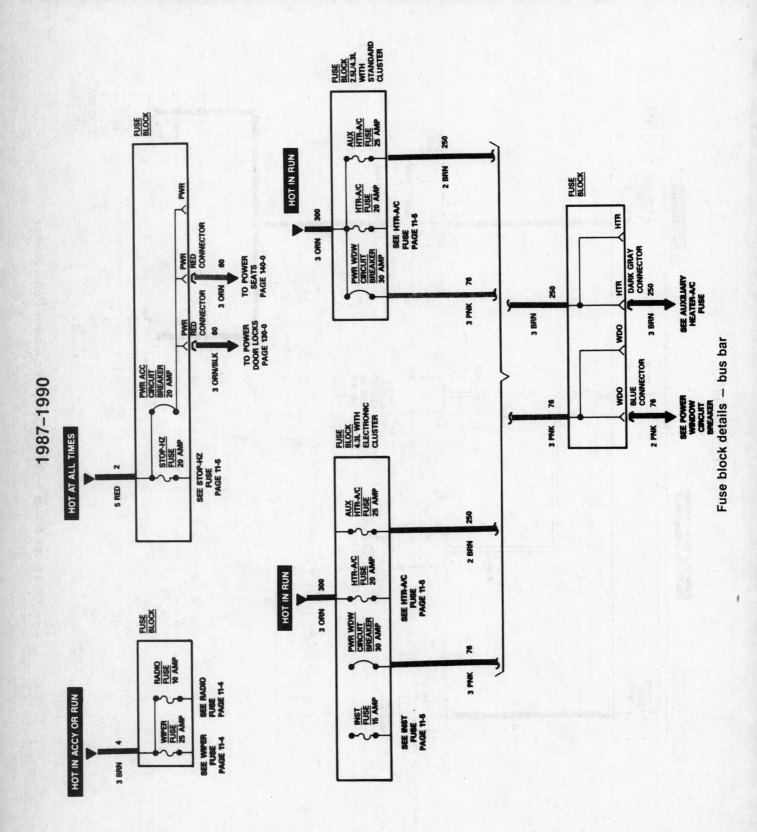

1987-1990

Fuse block details – bus bar

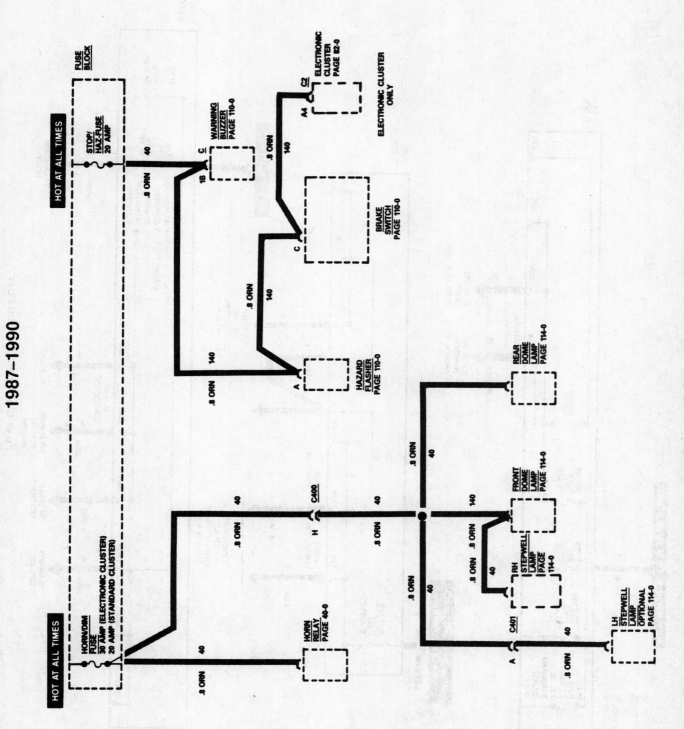

1987–1990

Fuse block details – horn and stop/hazard

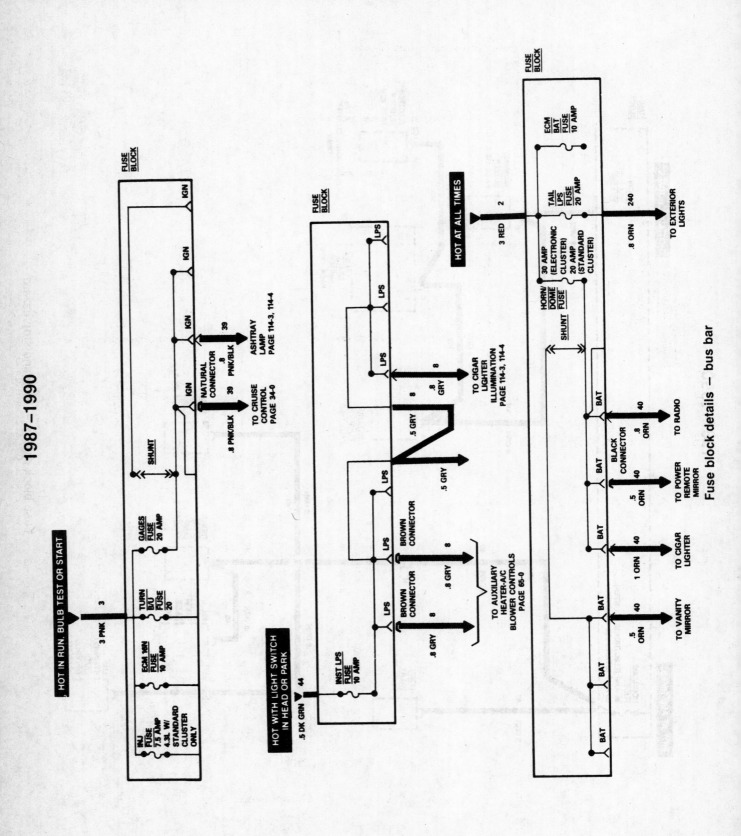

1987–1990

HOT IN RUN. BULB TEST OR START

HOT WITH LIGHT SWITCH IN HEAD OR PARK

HOT AT ALL TIMES

FUSE BLOCK

INJ FUSE 7.5 AMP 4.3L W/ STANDARD CLUSTER ONLY

ECM IGN FUSE 10 AMP

TURN B/U FUSE 20

GAGES FUSE 20 AMP

SHUNT

IGN
IGN
IGN
IGN
IGN

NATURAL CONNECTOR

3 PNK

3

.8 PNK/BLK

39 PNK/BLK

39

ASHTRAY LAMP
PAGE 114-3, 114-4

TO CRUISE CONTROL
PAGE 34-0

FUSE BLOCK

INST LPS FUSE 10 AMP

BROWN CONNECTOR

BROWN CONNECTOR

LPS
LPS
LPS
LPS
LPS
LPS

.5 DK GRN

44

.8 GRY

8

.8 GRY

8

.5 GRY

.5 GRY

8

.8 GRY

8

TO AUXILIARY HEATER-A/C BLOWER CONTROLS
PAGE 65-0

TO CIGAR LIGHTER ILLUMINATION
PAGE 114-3, 114-4

FUSE BLOCK

ECM BAT FUSE 10 AMP

TAIL LPS FUSE 20 AMP

HORN/ DOME FUSE

30 AMP (ELECTRONIC CLUSTER)
20 AMP (STANDARD CLUSTER)

SHUNT

3 RED

2

.8 ORN

240

TO EXTERIOR LIGHTS

BAT
BAT
BAT
BAT
BAT
BAT

BLACK CONNECTOR

.8 ORN

40

TO RADIO

.5 ORN

40

TO POWER REMOTE MIRROR

1 ORN

40

TO CIGAR LIGHTER

.5 ORN

40

TO VANITY MIRROR

Fuse block details – bus bar

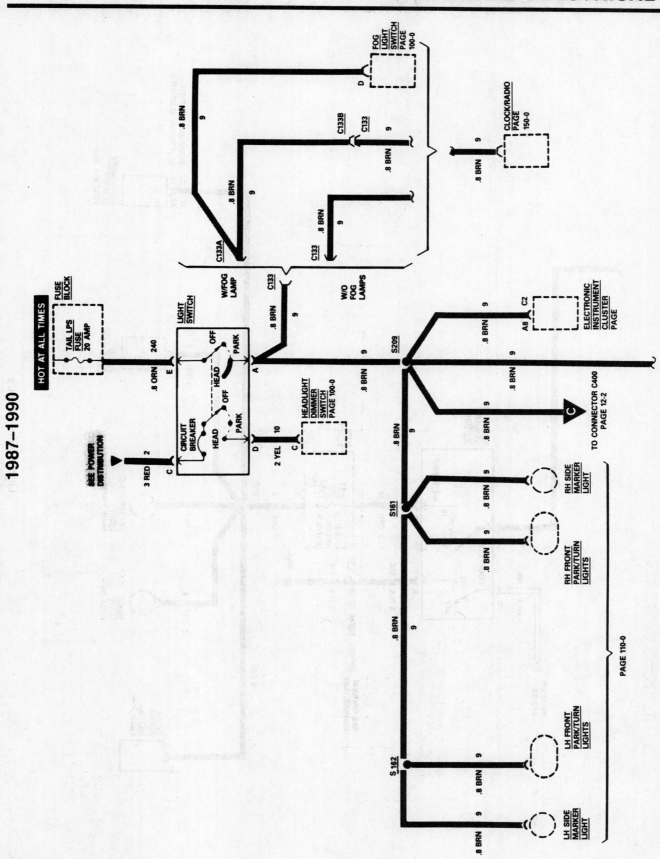

1987–1990

Light switch details

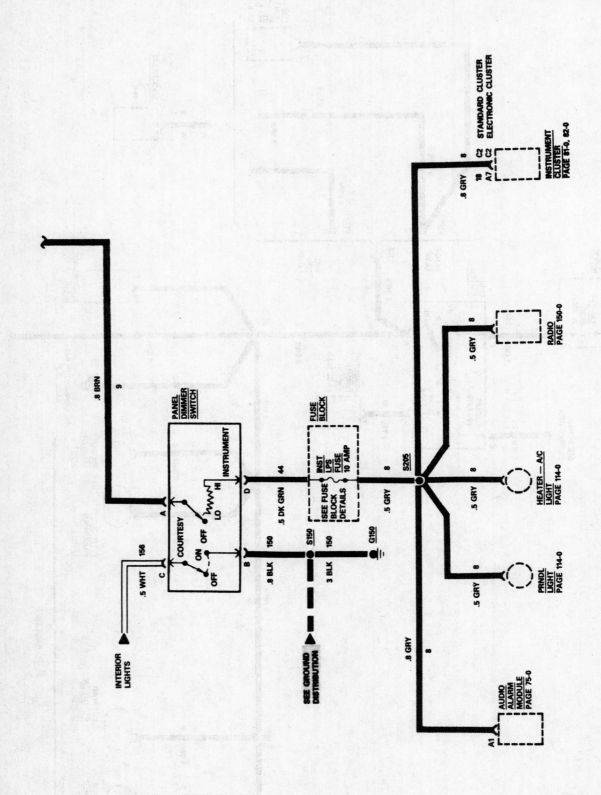

1987–1990

Light switch details

1987–1990

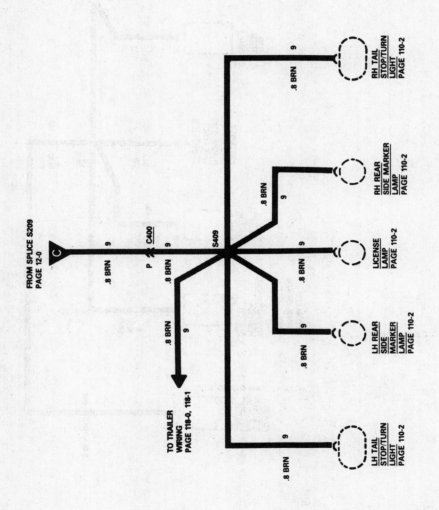

FROM SPLICE S209
PAGE 12-0

.8 BRN
9

P   C400

.8 BRN
9

S409

.8 BRN
9
TO TRAILER
WIRING
PAGE 118-0, 118-1

.8 BRN
9
RH TAIL
STOP/TURN
LIGHT
PAGE 110-2

.8 BRN
9
RH REAR
SIDE MARKER
LAMP
PAGE 110-2

.8 BRN
9
LICENSE
LAMP
PAGE 110-2

.8 BRN
9
LH REAR
SIDE
MARKER
LAMP
PAGE 110-2

.8 BRN
9
LH TAIL
STOP/TURN
LIGHT
PAGE 110-2

Light switch details

1987–1990

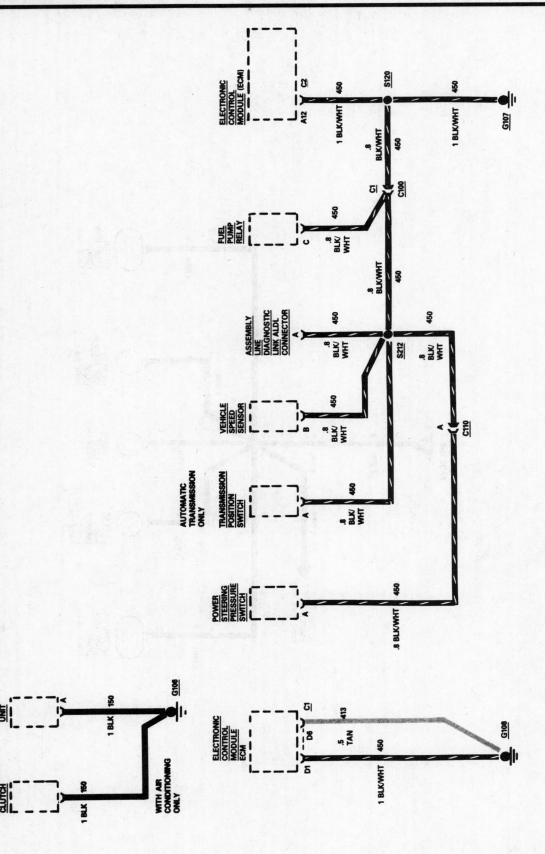

Ground distribution — engine grounds

2.5L VIN E

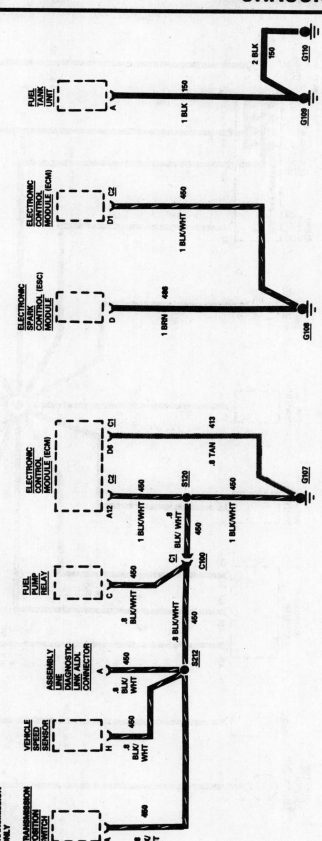

Ground distribution — engine grounds

1987–1990

4.3L VIN Z

1987–1990

4.3L VIN Z, ELECTRONIC CLUSTER

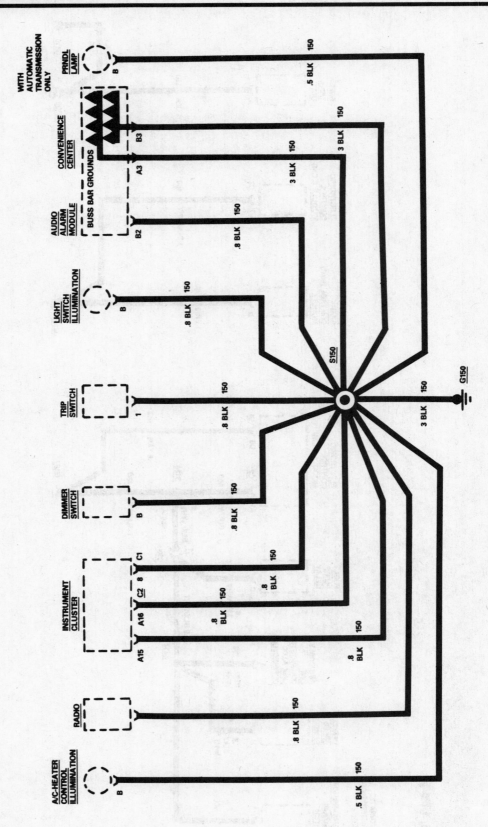

Ground distribution — electronic instrument panel

1987–1990

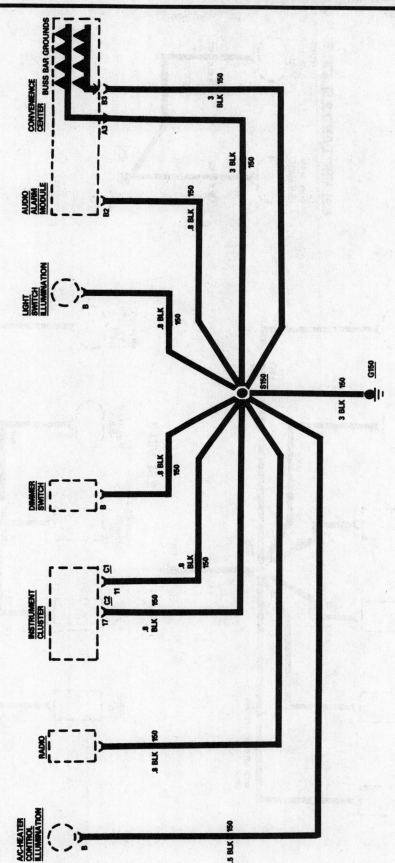

Ground distribution – standard instrument panel

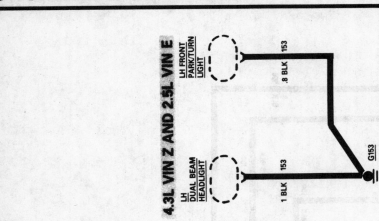

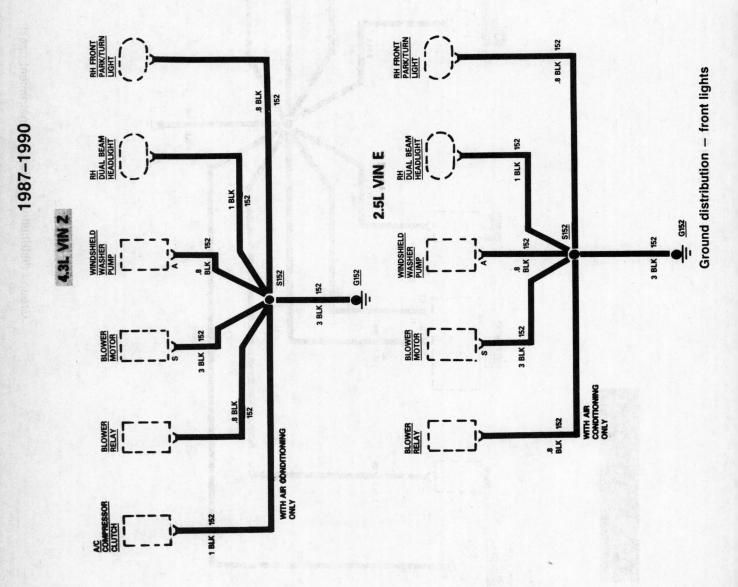

Ground distribution – front lights

1987–1990

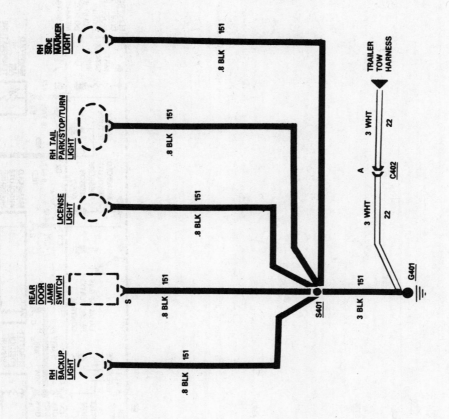

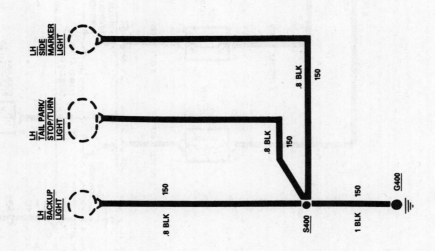

Ground distribution — rear lights

Throttle body injection – 2.5L, engine data sensors and fuel injection

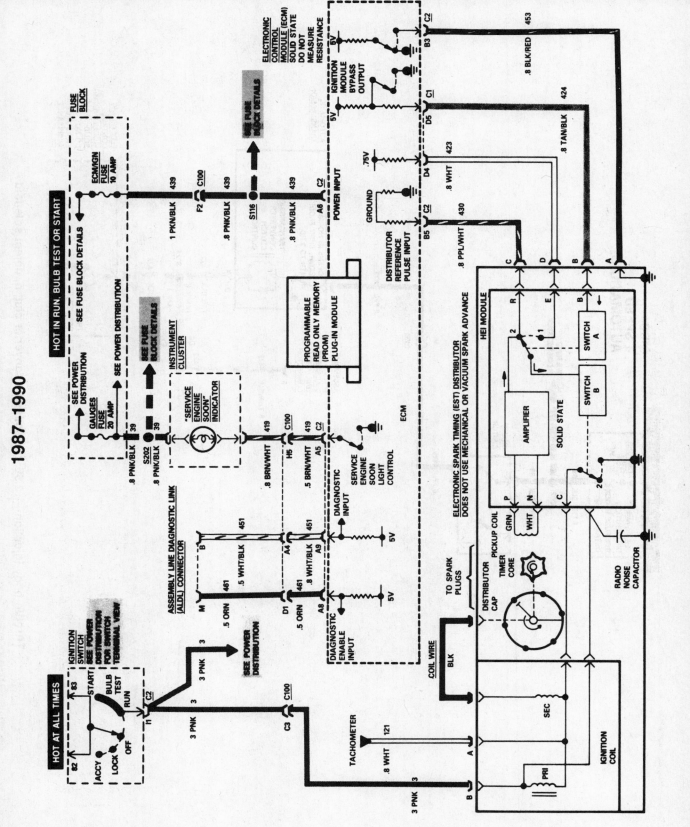

Throttle body injection – 2.5L, ignition and service engine soon light

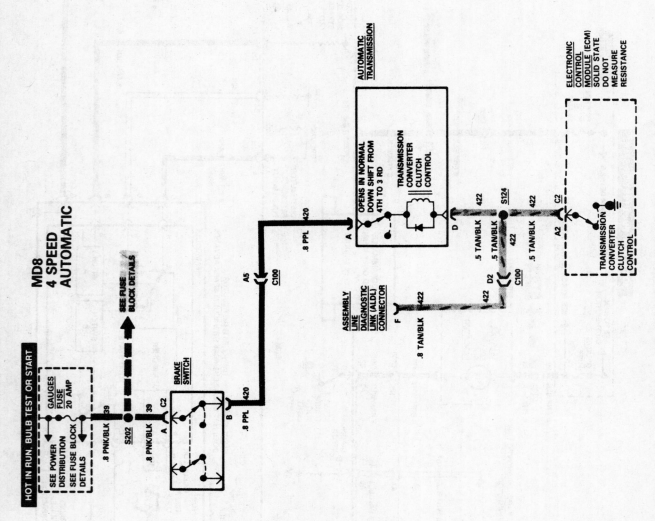

1987–1990

MD8 4 SPEED AUTOMATIC

HOT IN RUN, BULB TEST OR START

SEE POWER DISTRIBUTION

GAUGES FUSE 20 AMP

SEE FUSE BLOCK DETAILS

SEE FUSE BLOCK DETAILS

.8 PNK/BLK 39 S202 39 .8 PNK/BLK A C2

BRAKE SWITCH

B .8 PPL 420

A5 C100

.8 PPL 420

AUTOMATIC TRANSMISSION

A OPENS IN NORMAL DOWN SHIFT FROM 4TH TO 3 RD

TRANSMISSION CONVERTER CLUTCH CONTROL

D

.5 TAN/BLK 422 S124

.5 TAN/BLK 422

.5 TAN/BLK 422 C2 A2

D2 C100

422 .5 TAN/BLK 422

ASSEMBLY LINE DIAGNOSTIC LINK (ALDL) CONNECTOR

F .8 TAN/BLK 422

ELECTRONIC CONTROL MODULE (ECM) SOLID STATE DO NOT MEASURE RESISTANCE

TRANSMISSION CONVERTER CLUTCH CONTROL

Throttle body injection — 2.5L, transmission converter clutch, detent solenoid

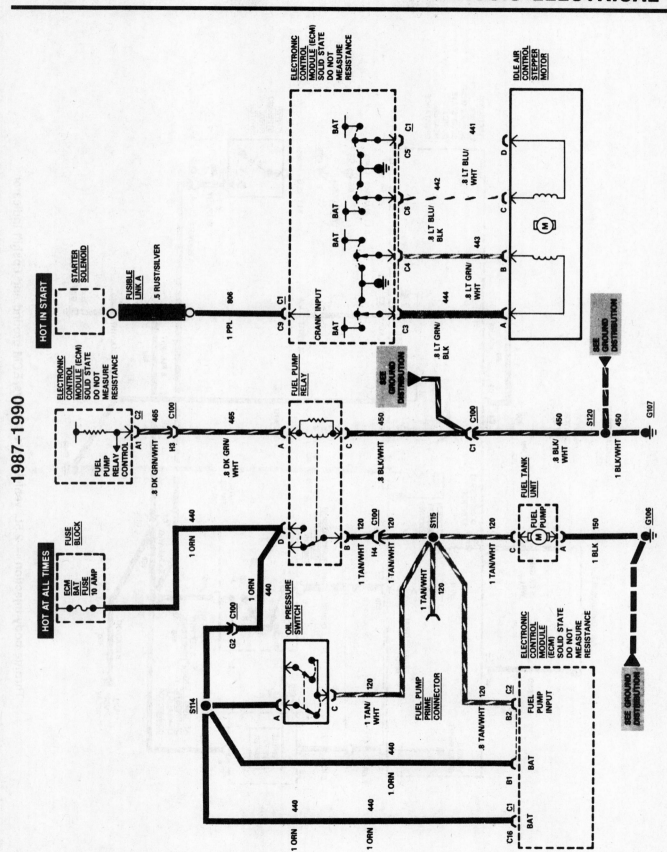

1987–1990

Throttle body injection — 2.5L, fuel pump control and idle air control

1987–1990

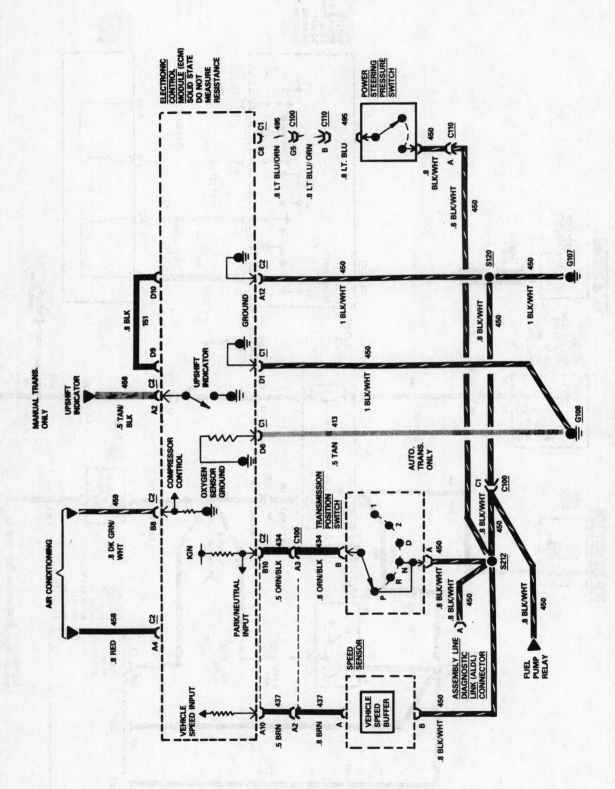

Throttle body injection – 2.5L, vehicle data sensors, ECM ground and upshift indicator

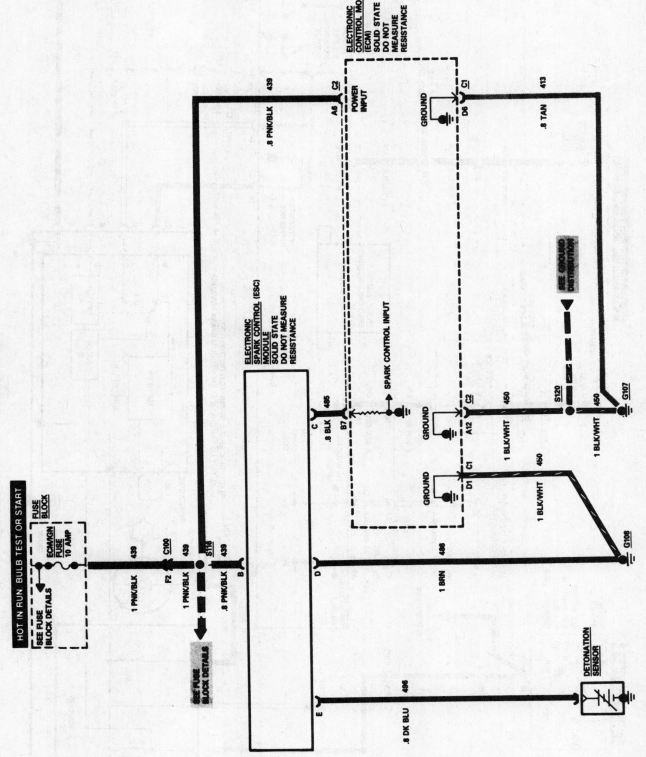

Throttle body injection — 4.3L, spark control

1987–1990

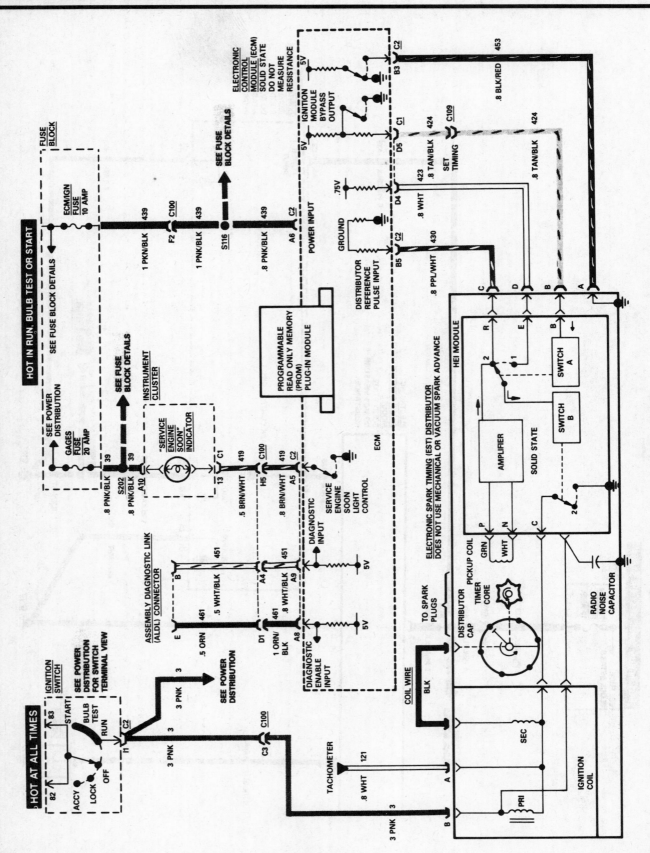

Throttle body injection – 4.3L, ignition and service engine soon indicator

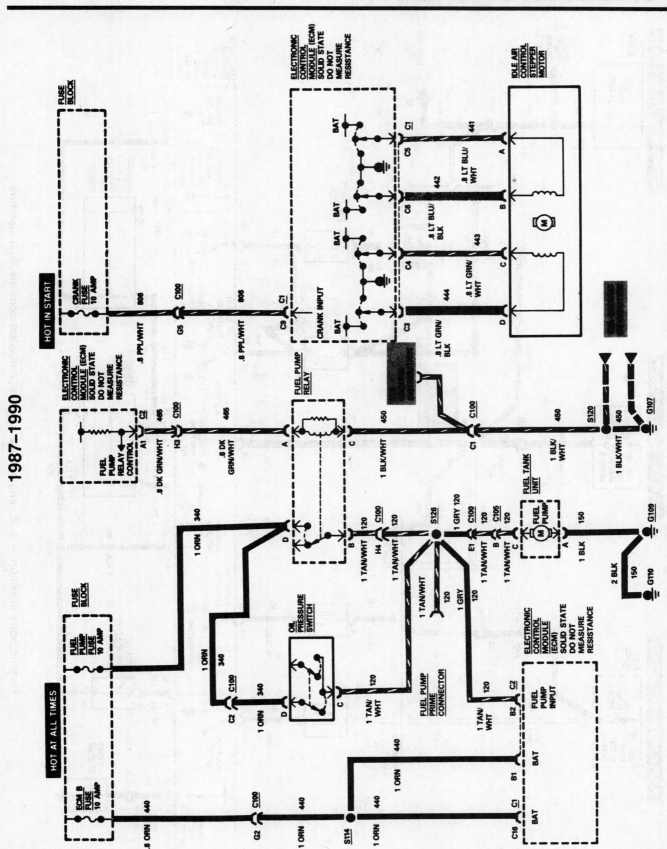

1987-1990

Throttle body injection — 4.3L, fuel pump and idle air control

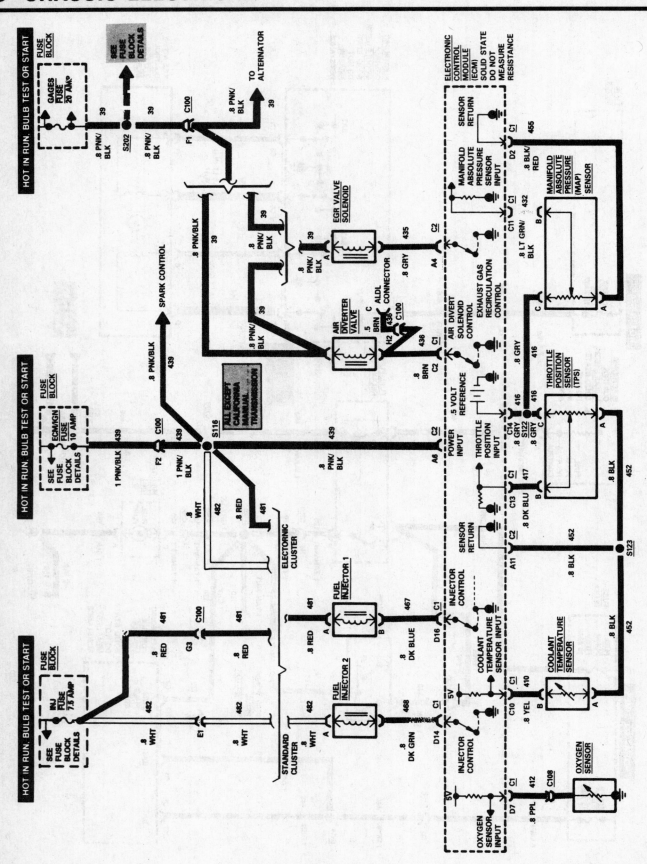

Throttle body injection — 4.3L, engine data sensors, emission controls, fuel injectors

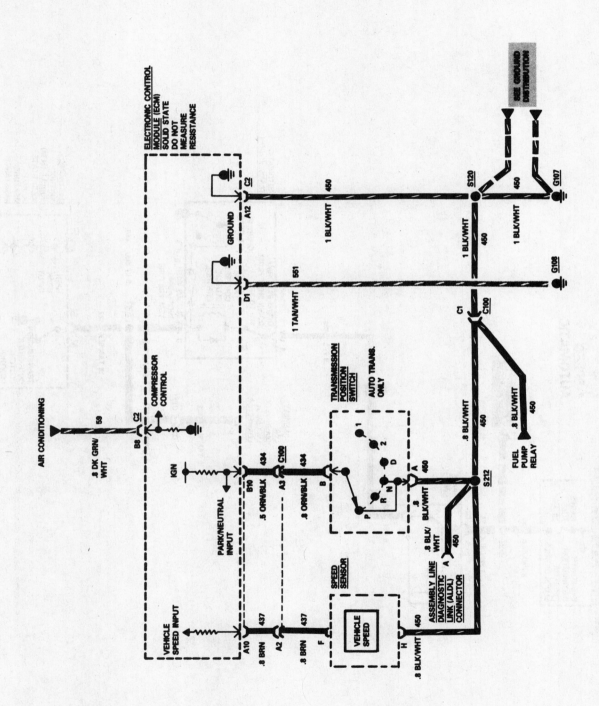

1987–1990

Throttle body injection — 4.3L, vehicle data sensors

1987-1990

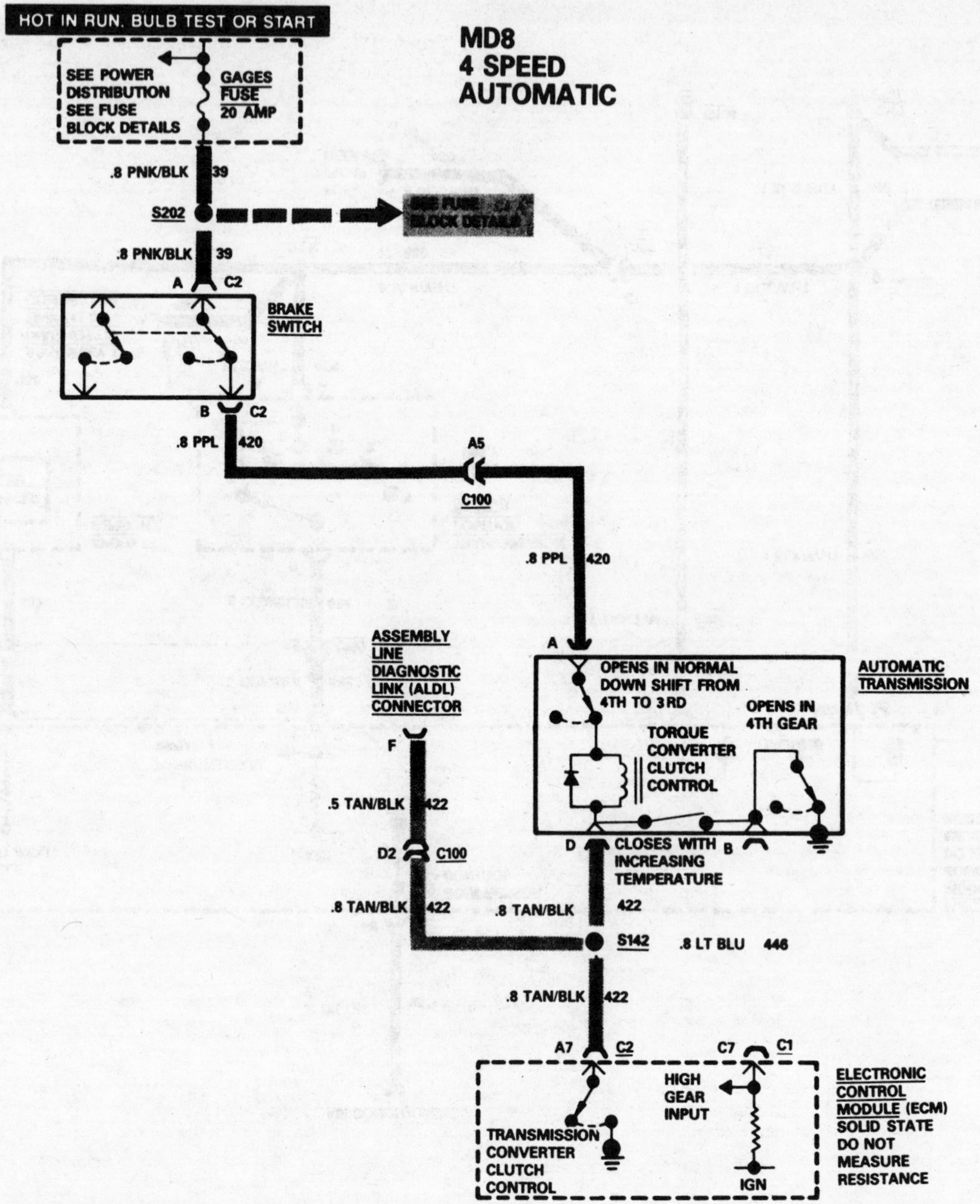

**MD8
4 SPEED
AUTOMATIC**

HOT IN RUN. BULB TEST OR START

SEE POWER
DISTRIBUTION
SEE FUSE
BLOCK DETAILS

GAGES
FUSE
20 AMP

.8 PNK/BLK

39

S202

.8 PNK/BLK

39

C2

A

BRAKE
SWITCH

B

C2

.8 PPL

420

SEE FUSE
BLOCK DETAILS

A5

C100

.8 PPL

420

AUTOMATIC
TRANSMISSION

A

OPENS IN NORMAL
DOWN SHIFT FROM
4TH TO 3RD

OPENS IN
4TH GEAR

TORQUE
CONVERTER
CLUTCH
CONTROL

D

CLOSES WITH B
INCREASING
TEMPERATURE

422

S142

.8 LT BLU

446

ASSEMBLY
LINE
DIAGNOSTIC
LINK (ALDL)
CONNECTOR

F

.5 TAN/BLK

422

D2

C100

.8 TAN/BLK

422

.8 TAN/BLK

.8 TAN/BLK

422

A7

C2

ELECTRONIC
CONTROL
MODULE (ECM)
SOLID STATE
DO NOT
MEASURE
RESISTANCE

C7

C1

HIGH
GEAR
INPUT

IGN

TRANSMISSION
CONVERTER
CLUTCH
CONTROL

Throttle body injection – 4.3L, transmission converter clutch, detent solenoid

HOT IN RUN, BULB TEST OR START

FUSE BLOCK

FUSE BLOCK

GAGES FUSE 20 AMP

SEE FUSE BLOCK DETAILS

SEE FUSE BLOCK DETAILS

SEE POWER DISTRIBUTION

POWER DISTRIBUTION

INSTRUMENT CLUSTER

"VOLTS" INDICATOR

GENERATOR

39

39

25

.8 BRN

C100

25

.5 BRN

A1

G1

39

.8 PNK/BLK

REGULATOR

FIELD (ROTOR)

P

L

F

S

.8 PNK/BLK

.8 PNK/BLK

.8 PNK/BLK

S202

RECTIFIER BRIDGE

BATTERY

STATOR

SEE POWER DISTRIBUTION

A/C BLOWER CONTROLS

5 RED

2

FUSIBLE LINK B

2 GRY/SIL

SEE POWER DISTRIBUTION

3 RED

2

FUSIBLE LINK C

1 BLK/SIL

G101

19 BLK

G100

32 BLK

BATTERY

3 WHT

102

8 RED

2

FUSIBLE LINK F

1 RUST/SIL

FUSIBLE LINK E

3 RUST/SIL

1987–1990

SEE POWER DISTRIBUTION

S210

5 RED

2

FUSIBLE LINK D

1 BLK/SIL

BATTERY JUNCTION BLOCK

2

8 BLK/ RED

1

19 BLK

FLYWHEEL

ENGINE

PLUNGER

DRIVE ASSEMBLY

SHIFT LEVER

RETURN SPRING

B

MOTOR CONTACTS

M

STARTER MOTOR

M

5 RED

2

5 RED

2

IGNITION SWITCH

MANUAL TRANSMISSION

C2

S

5 YEL

B

CLUTCH SWITCH CLOSED WITH CLUTCH PEDAL DEPRESSED

5

A

5 PPL

6

C100

5 PPL

6

F3

5 PPL

6

SOLENOID

HOLD-IN WINDING

PULL-IN WINDING

S

M

START

BULB TEST

RUN

OFF

LOCK

ACCY

C1

B3

B2

C2

FUSIBLE LINK A

.5 RUST/SIL

STARTER SOLENOID ASSEMBLY

1 PPL

806

C9

ELECTRONIC CONTROL MODULE

AUTOMATIC TRANSMISSION

C2

S

5 PPL

6

5 PPL

6

Starter and charging system – 2.5L engine

Starter and charging system – 4.3L engine

1987–1990

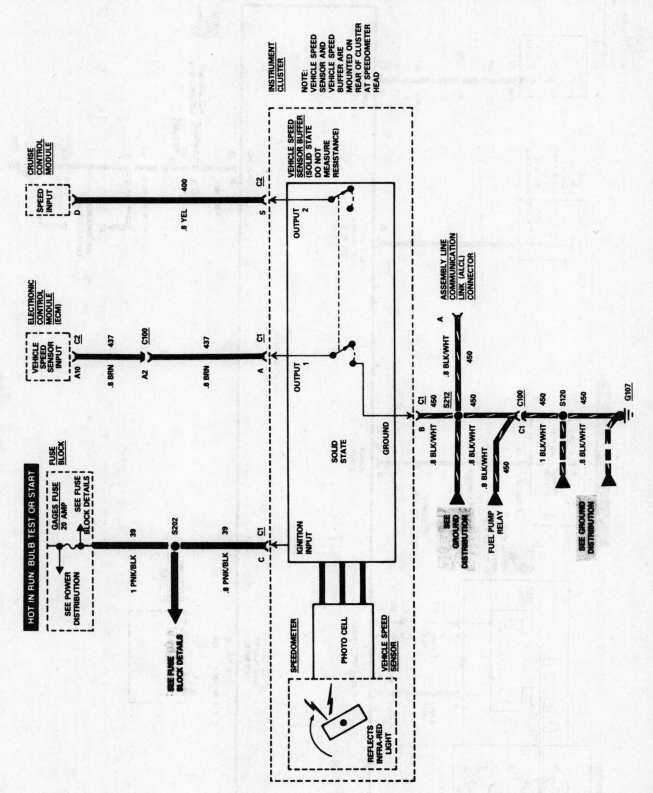

1987-1990

Vehicle speed sensor – standard instrument panel

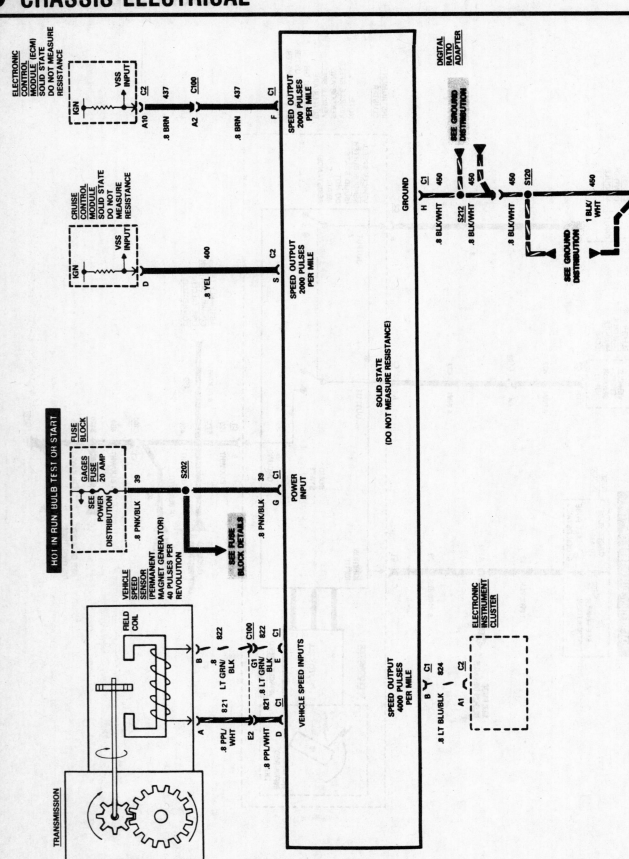

1987–1990

Vehicle speed sensor – electronic instrument panel

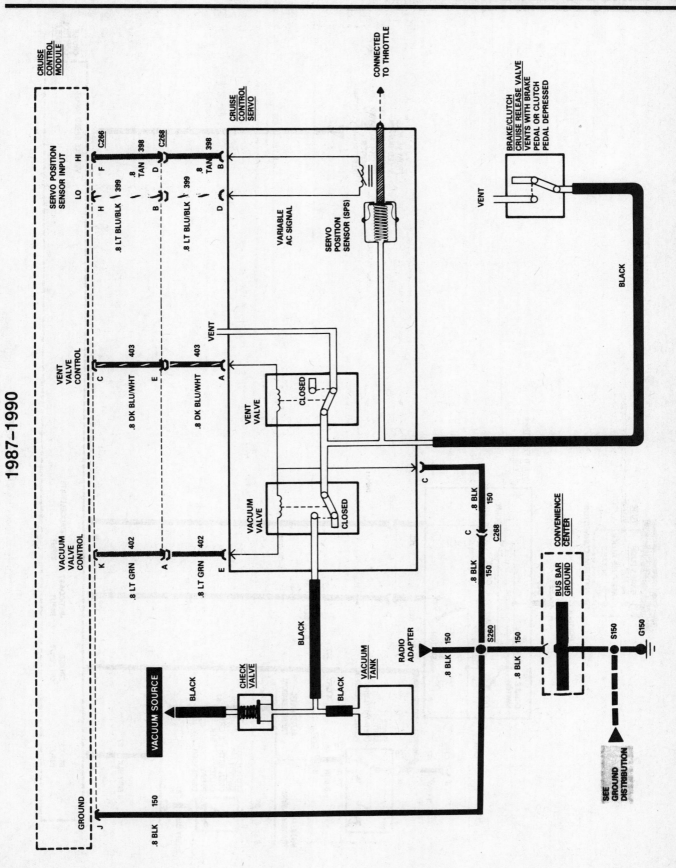

1987–1990

Cruise control

1987–1990

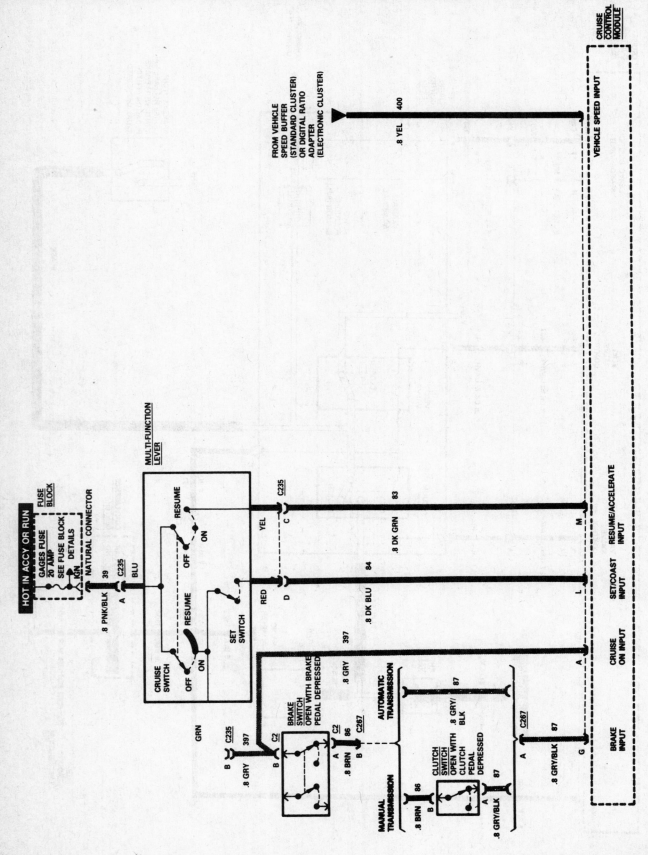

Cruise control

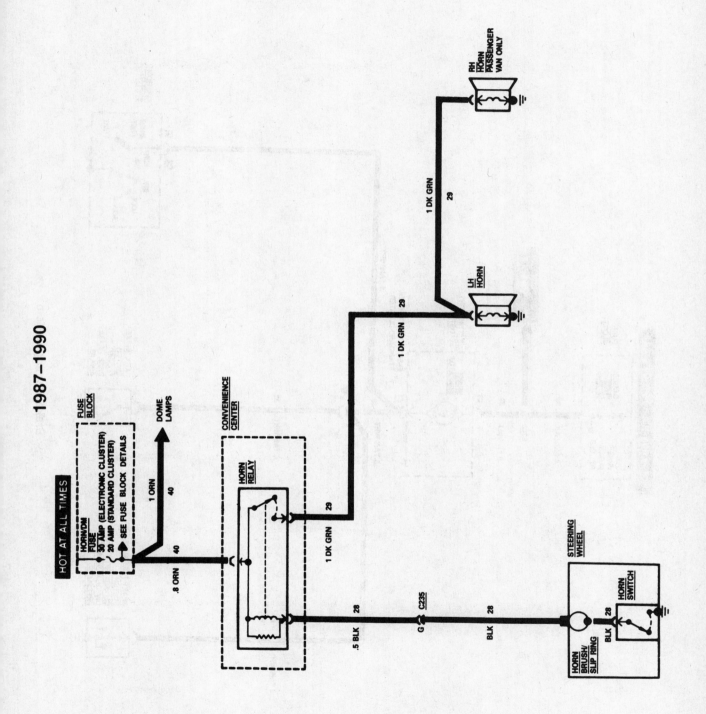

1987–1990

Horns

1987–1990

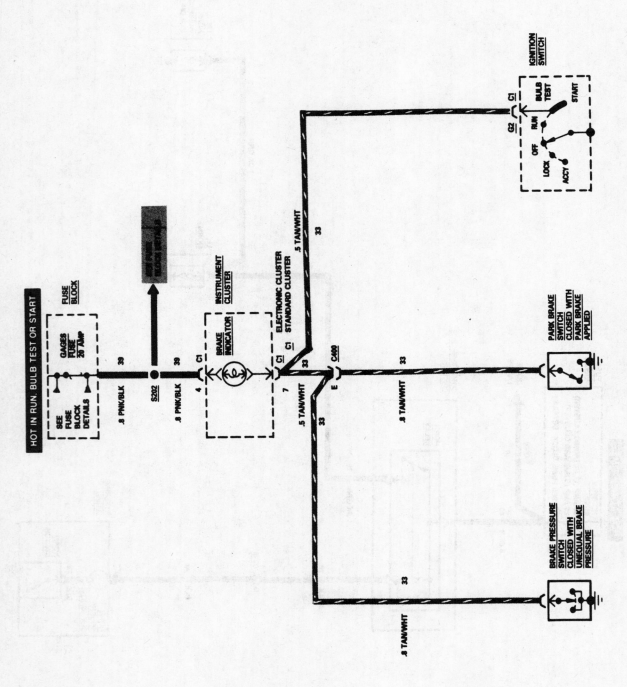

Brake warning system

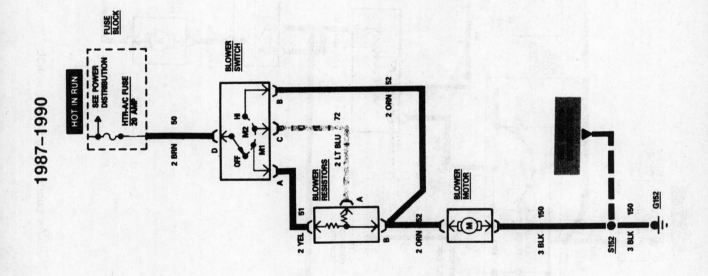

1987–1990

HOT IN RUN

FUSE BLOCK

SEE POWER DISTRIBUTION

HTR-AC FUSE 20 AMP

2 BRN 50

BLOWER SWITCH

D

OFF

M1

M2

HI

A

C

B

2 YEL 51

BLOWER RESISTORS

2 LT BLU 72

A

B

52 2 ORN

2 ORN 52

BLOWER MOTOR

M

3 BLK 150

S152

3 BLK 150

G152

Heater

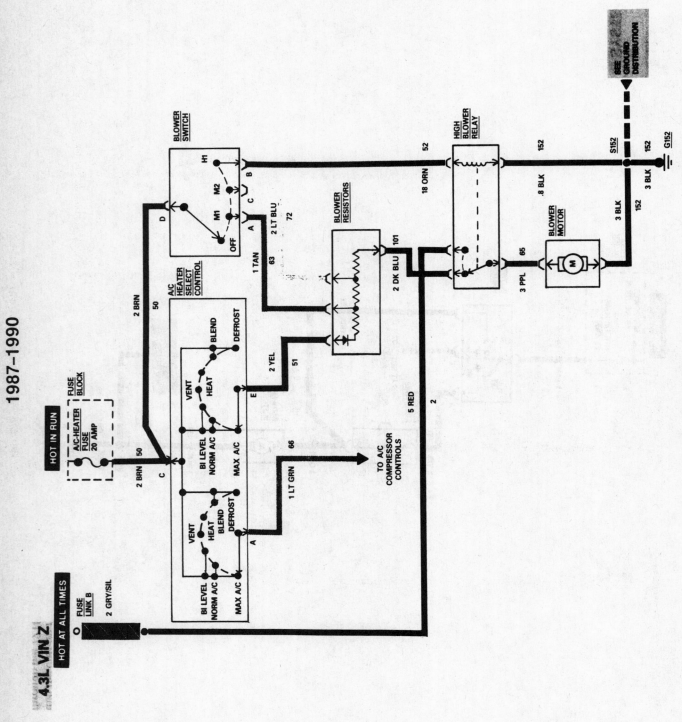

1987–1990

Air conditioning blower — 4.3L

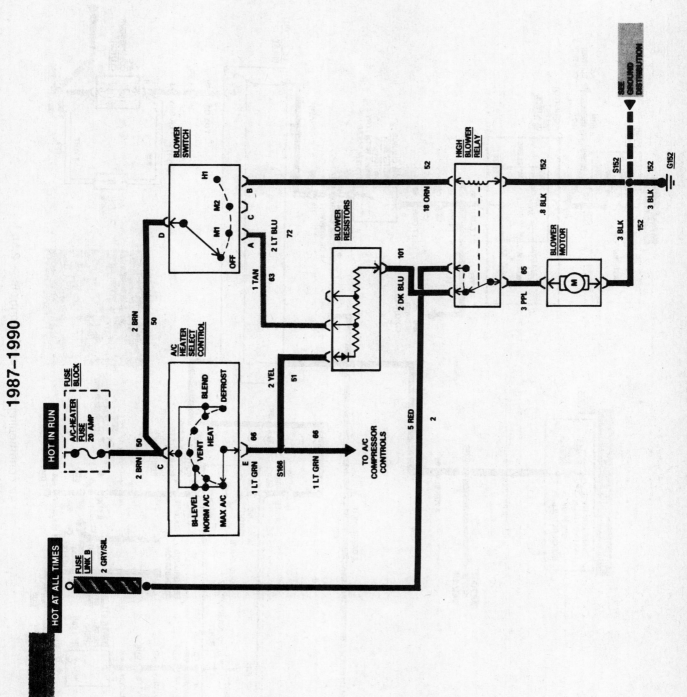

1987–1990

Air conditioning blower controls — 2.5L

1987–1990

2.5L, VIN E

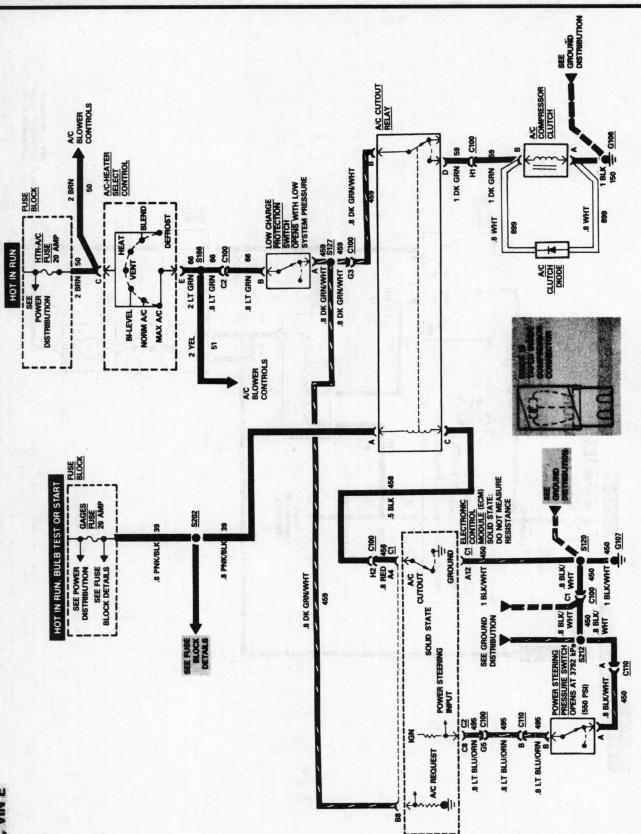

Air conditioning compressor controls – 2.5L

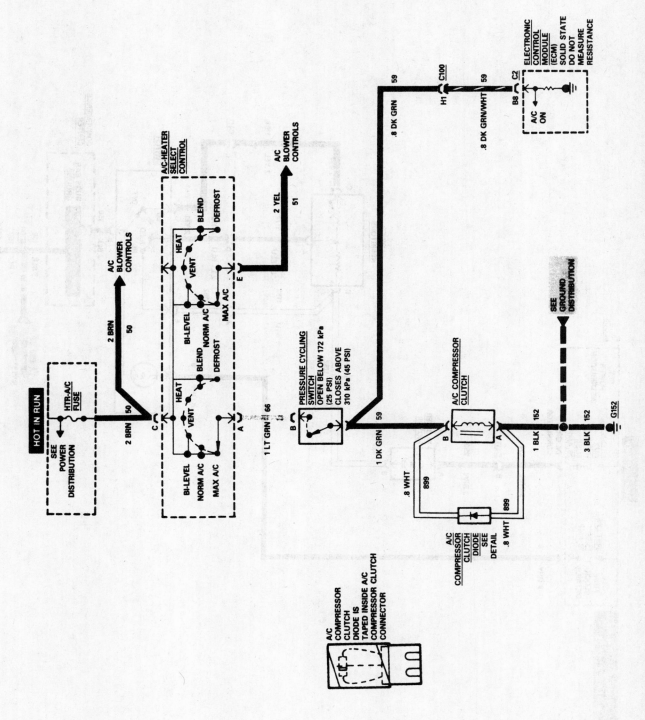

1987-1990

4.3L VIN Z

HOT IN RUN

SEE POWER DISTRIBUTION

HTR-A/C FUSE

A/C BLOWER CONTROLS

A/C-HEATER SELECT CONTROL

BLEND DEFROST
HEAT VENT
BI-LEVEL BLEND DEFROST
NORM A/C
MAX A/C

HEAT VENT
BI-LEVEL
NORM A/C
MAX A/C

A/C BLOWER CONTROLS

2 BRN 50

2 BRN 50

2 BRN 50

C

A

E

2 YEL 51

1 LT GRN 66

PRESSURE CYCLING SWITCH
OPEN BELOW 172 kPa (25 PSI)
CLOSES ABOVE 310 kPa (45 PSI)

B

59

1 DK GRN 59

.8 DK GRN 59

H1 C100

.8 DK GRN/WHT 59

B8 C2

ELECTRONIC CONTROL MODULE (ECM)
SOLID STATE
DO NOT MEASURE RESISTANCE

A/C ON

A/C COMPRESSOR CLUTCH

B A

1 BLK 152

.8 WHT 899

.8 WHT 899

A/C COMPRESSOR CLUTCH DIODE SEE DETAIL

SEE GROUND DISTRIBUTION

3 BLK 152

G152

A/C COMPRESSOR CLUTCH DIODE IS TAPED INSIDE A/C COMPRESSOR CLUTCH CONNECTOR

Air conditioning compressor controls — 4.3L

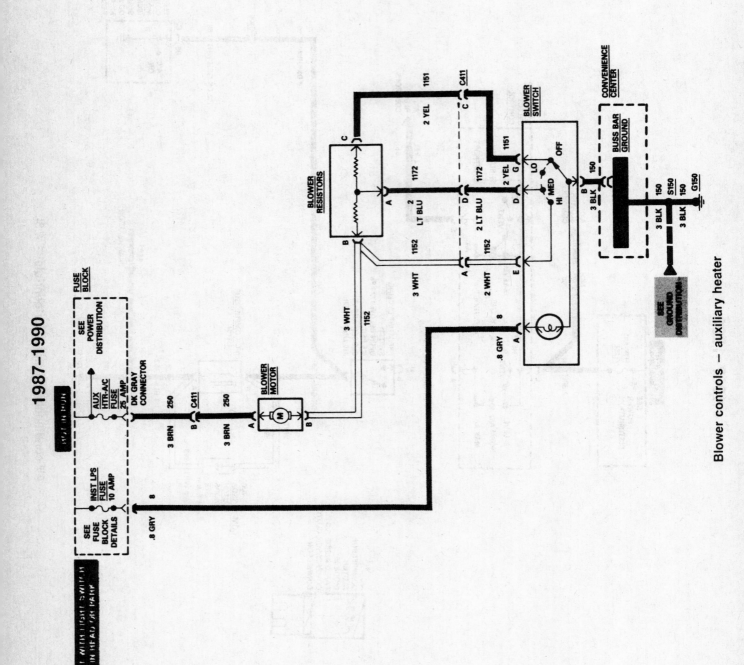

Blower controls – auxiliary heater

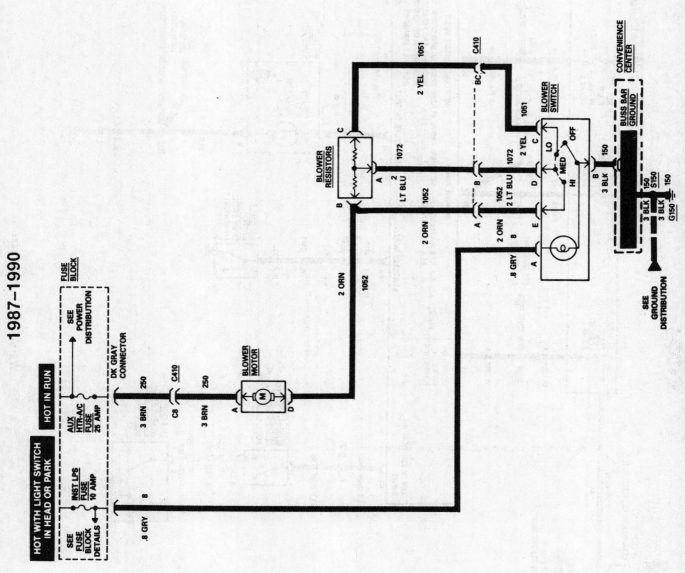

Blower controls — auxiliary Air conditioning

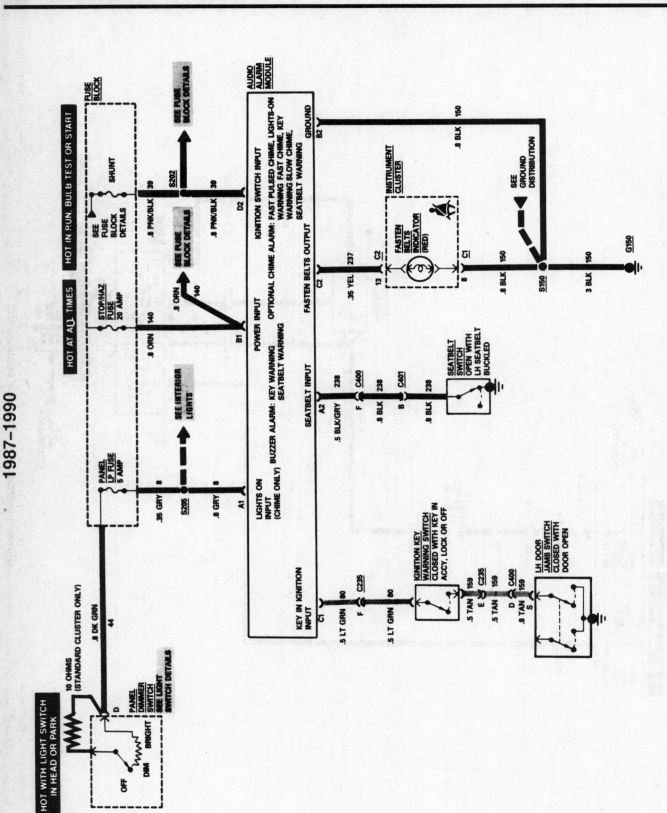

1987–1990

Warnings, chime, buzzer

1987–1990

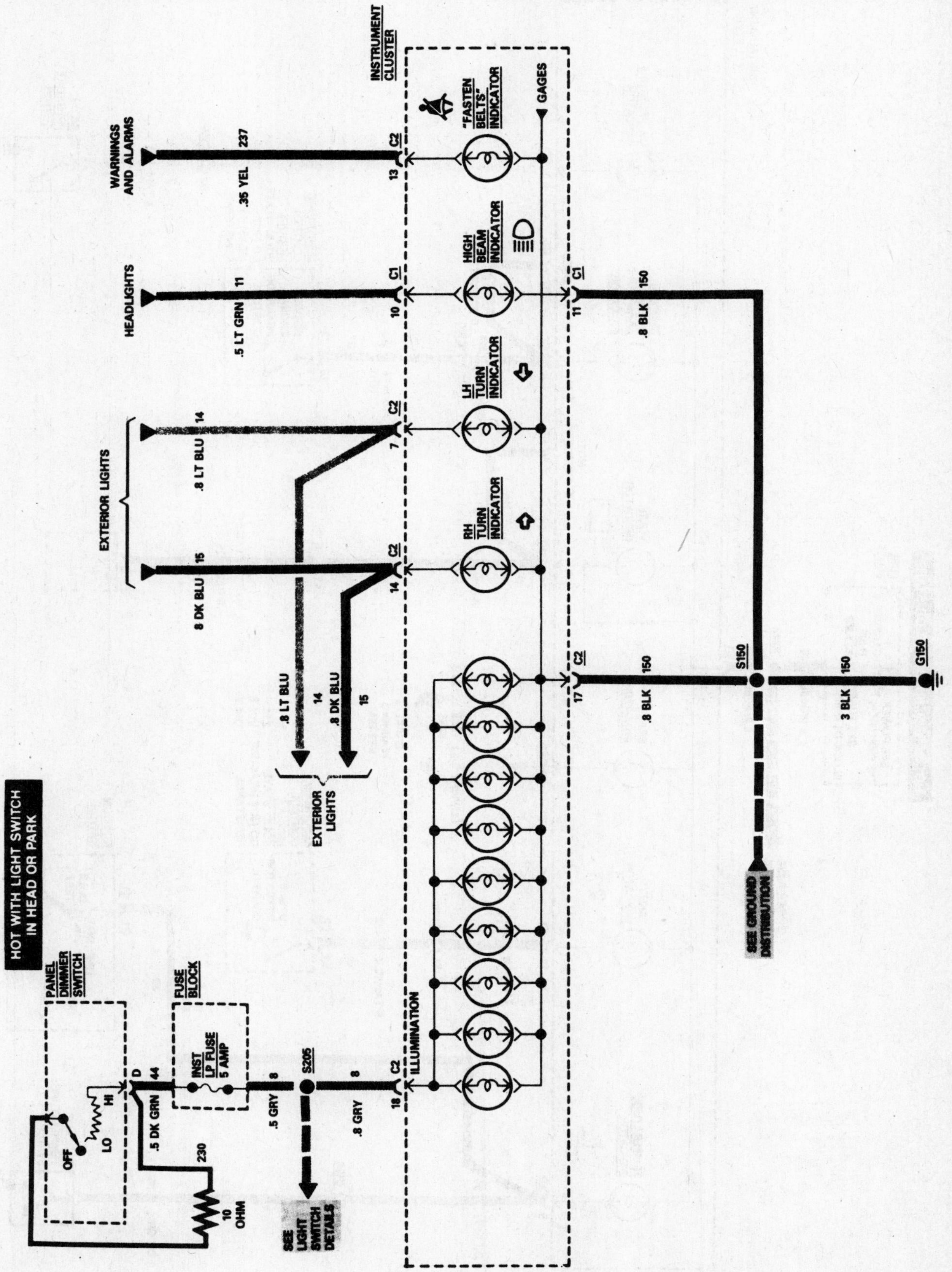

INSTRUMENT CLUSTER

WARNINGS AND ALARMS

237

.35 YEL

13 C2

"FASTEN BELTS" INDICATOR

GAGES

HEADLIGHTS

11

.5 LT GRN

10 C1

HIGH BEAM INDICATOR

11 C1

150

.8 BLK

EXTERIOR LIGHTS

.8 LT BLU 14

7 C2

LH TURN INDICATOR

8 DK BLU 15

14 C2

RH TURN INDICATOR

.8 LT BLU 14

.8 DK BLU 15

EXTERIOR LIGHTS

17 C2

150

.8 BLK

S150

150

3 BLK

G150

SEE GROUND DISTRIBUTION

ILLUMINATION

HOT WITH LIGHT SWITCH IN HEAD OR PARK

PANEL DIMMER SWITCH

OFF LO HI

D 44

.5 DK GRN

230

10 OHM

FUSE BLOCK

INST LP FUSE 5 AMP

8

S205

.5 GRY

.8 GRY

8 C2

18

SEE LIGHT SWITCH DETAILS

Instrument panel — lights, indicators

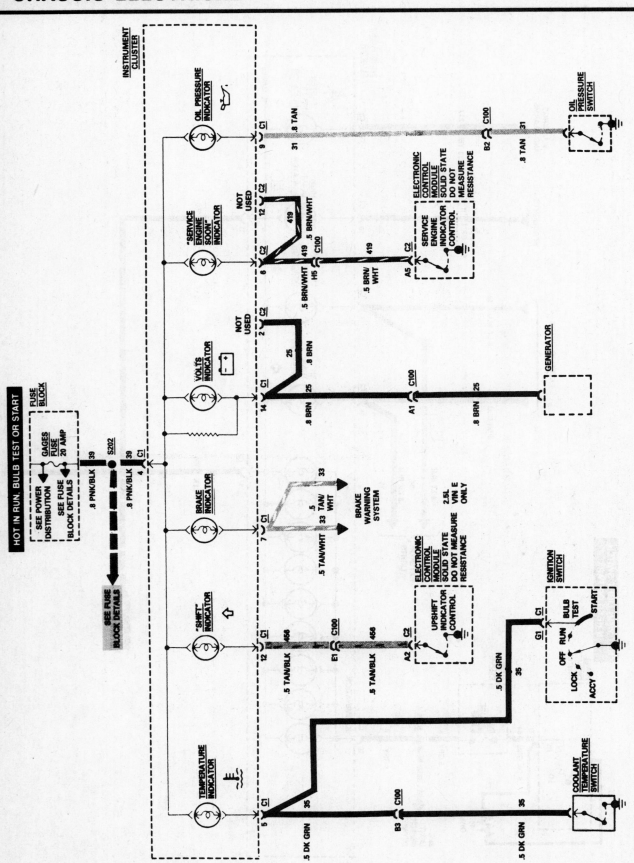

Instrument panel – indicators without gauges

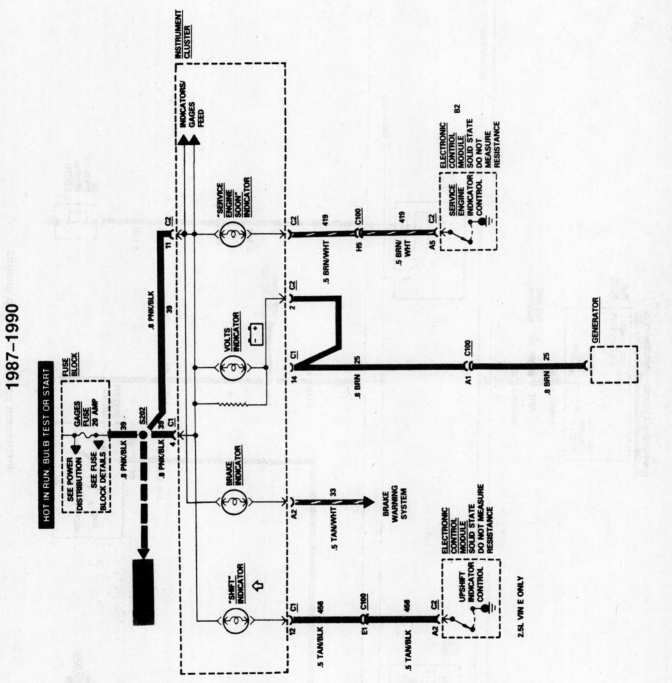

1987–1990

Instrument panel – indicators with gauges

1987–1990

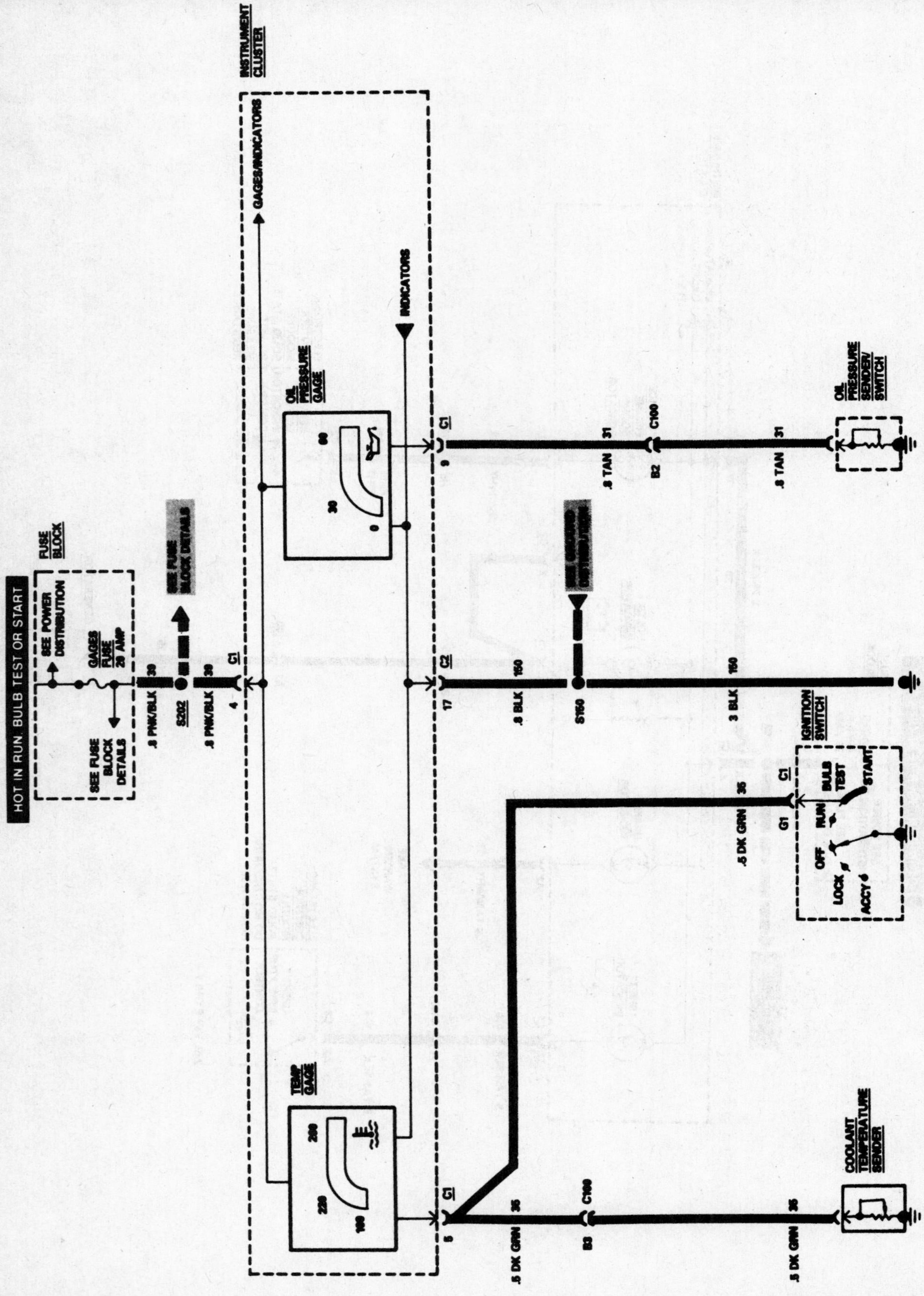

INSTRUMENT CLUSTER

GAGES/INDICATORS

INDICATORS

OIL PRESSURE GAGE

OIL PRESSURE SENDER/SWITCH

80

20

0

G1

9

.8 TAN   31   C100   .8 TAN   31
B2

FUSE BLOCK

SEE FUSE BLOCK DETAILS

SEE POWER DISTRIBUTION

GAGES FUSE 20 AMP

SEE FUSE BLOCK DETAILS

.8 PNK/BLK   30

S202

.8 PNK/BLK   30

G1
4

C2
17   .8 BLK   150   S150   3 BLK   150

C1

.5 DK GRN   35

IGNITION SWITCH

G1   BULB TEST   START

RUN

OFF

LOCK   ACCY

TEMP GAGE

260

220   180

G1
5   .5 DK GRN   35   C100   .5 DK GRN   35
B3

COOLANT TEMPERATURE SENDER

HOT IN RUN, BULB TEST OR START

Instrument panel — oil, temp gauges

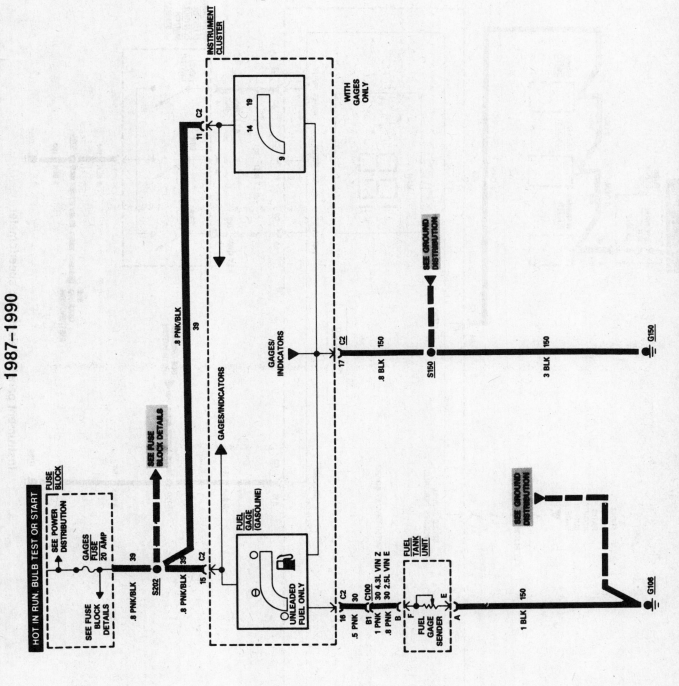

1987-1990

Instrument panel — fuel, voltmeter gauges

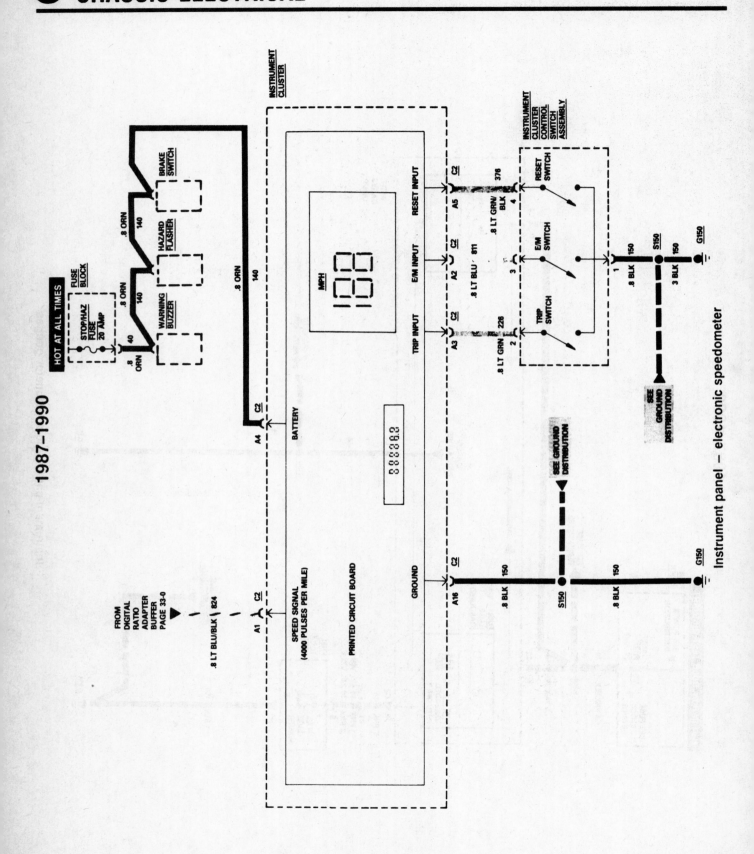

Instrument panel – electronic speedometer

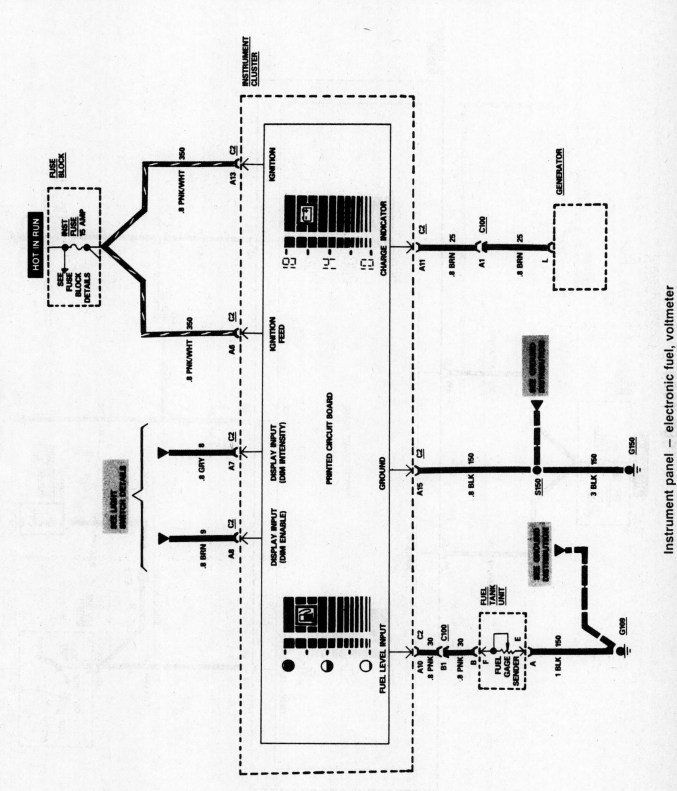

1987–1990

Instrument panel — electronic fuel, voltmeter

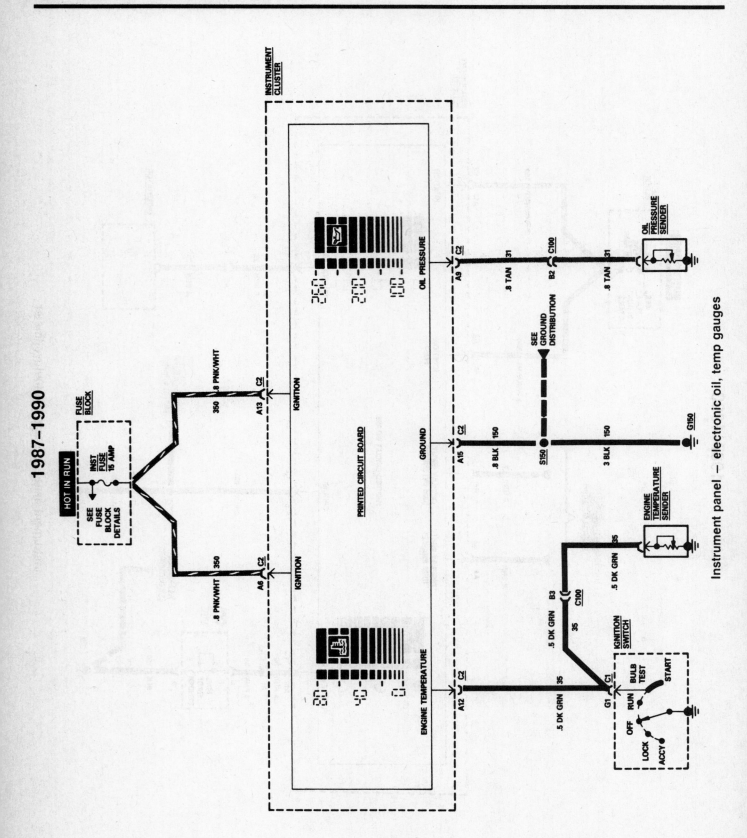

1987-1990

Instrument panel — electronic oil, temp gauges

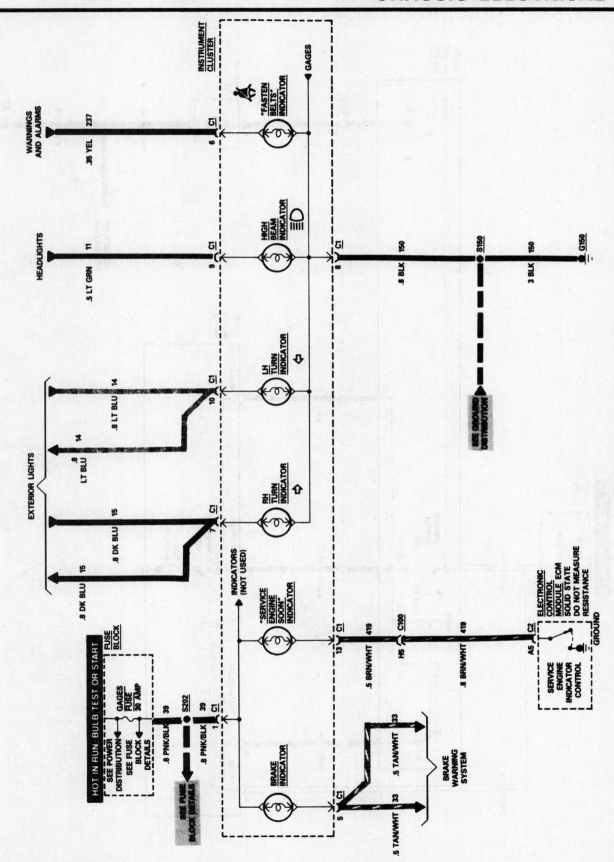

1987–1990

Instrument panel – electronic indicators

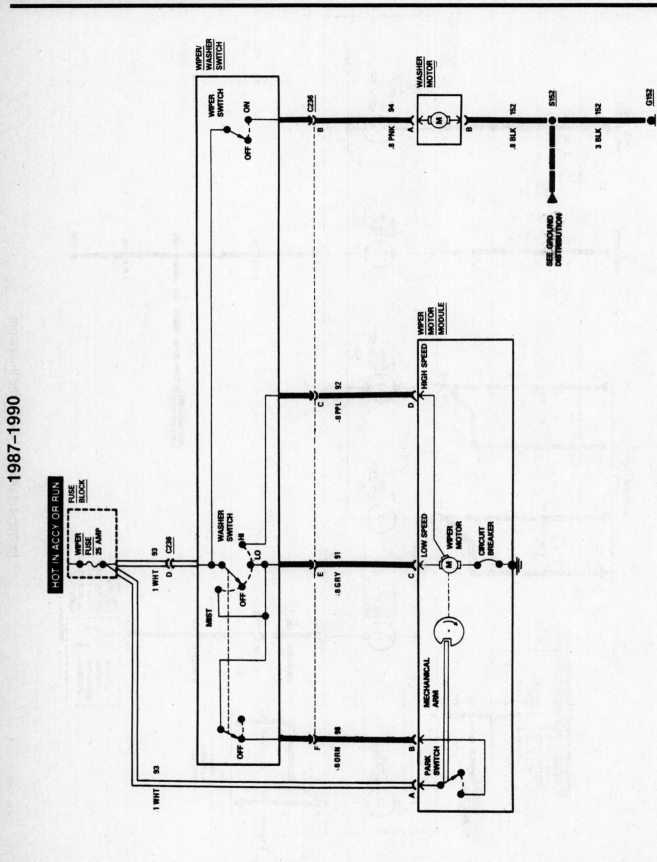

1987–1990

Wiper/washer

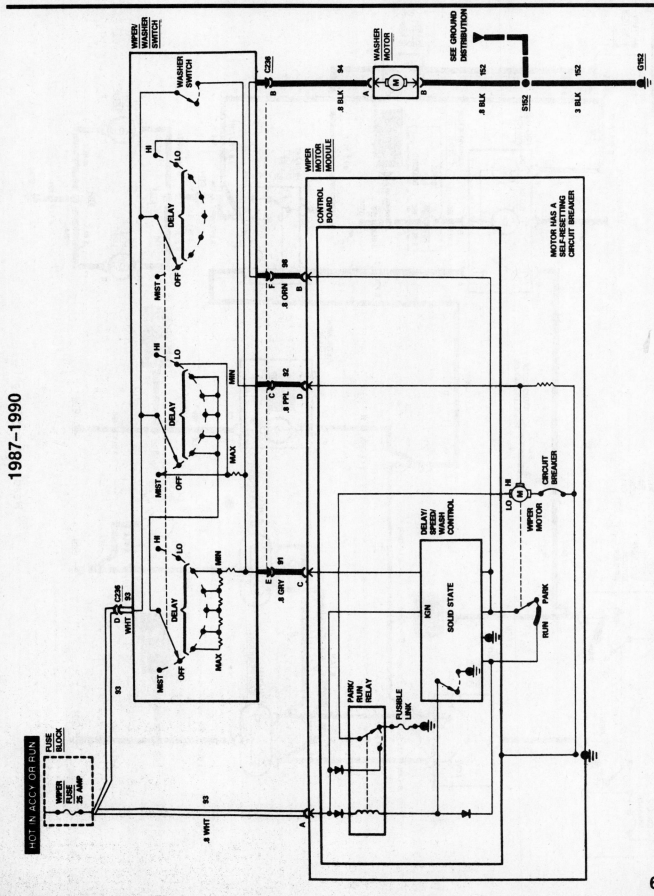

1987–1990

Wiper/washer delay

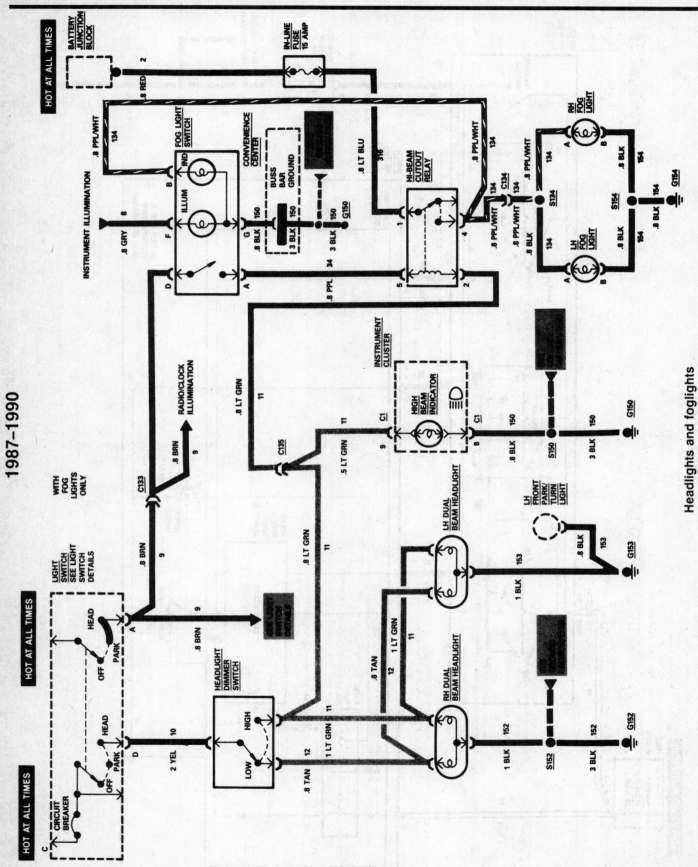

Headlights and foglights

1987-1990

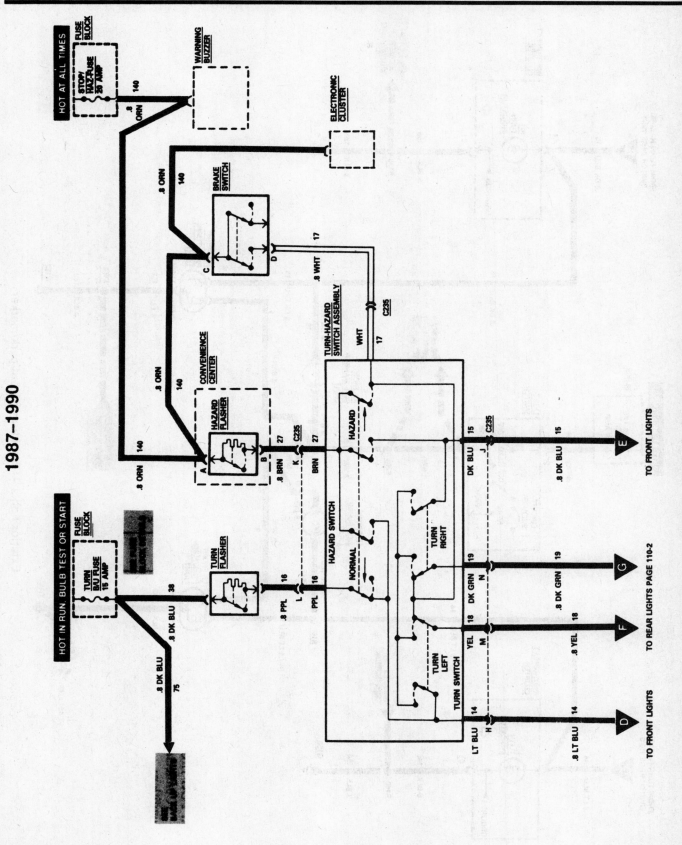

1987–1990

Exterior lights — turn/hazard/stop

Exterior lights — front turn/hazard/park/marker

1987-1990

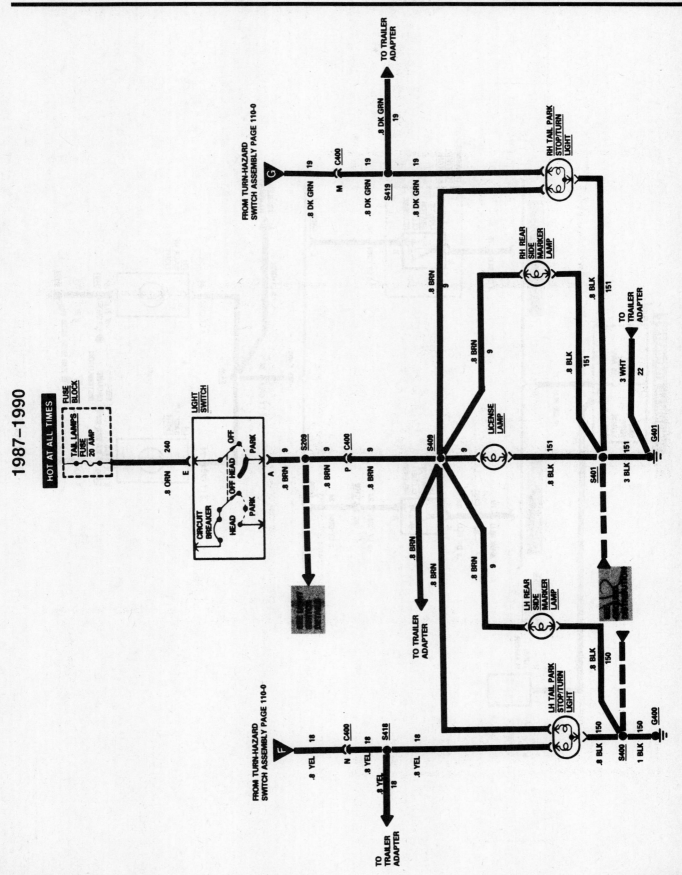

1987–1990

HOT AT ALL TIMES

Exterior lights – tail/stop/turn/license

1987–1990

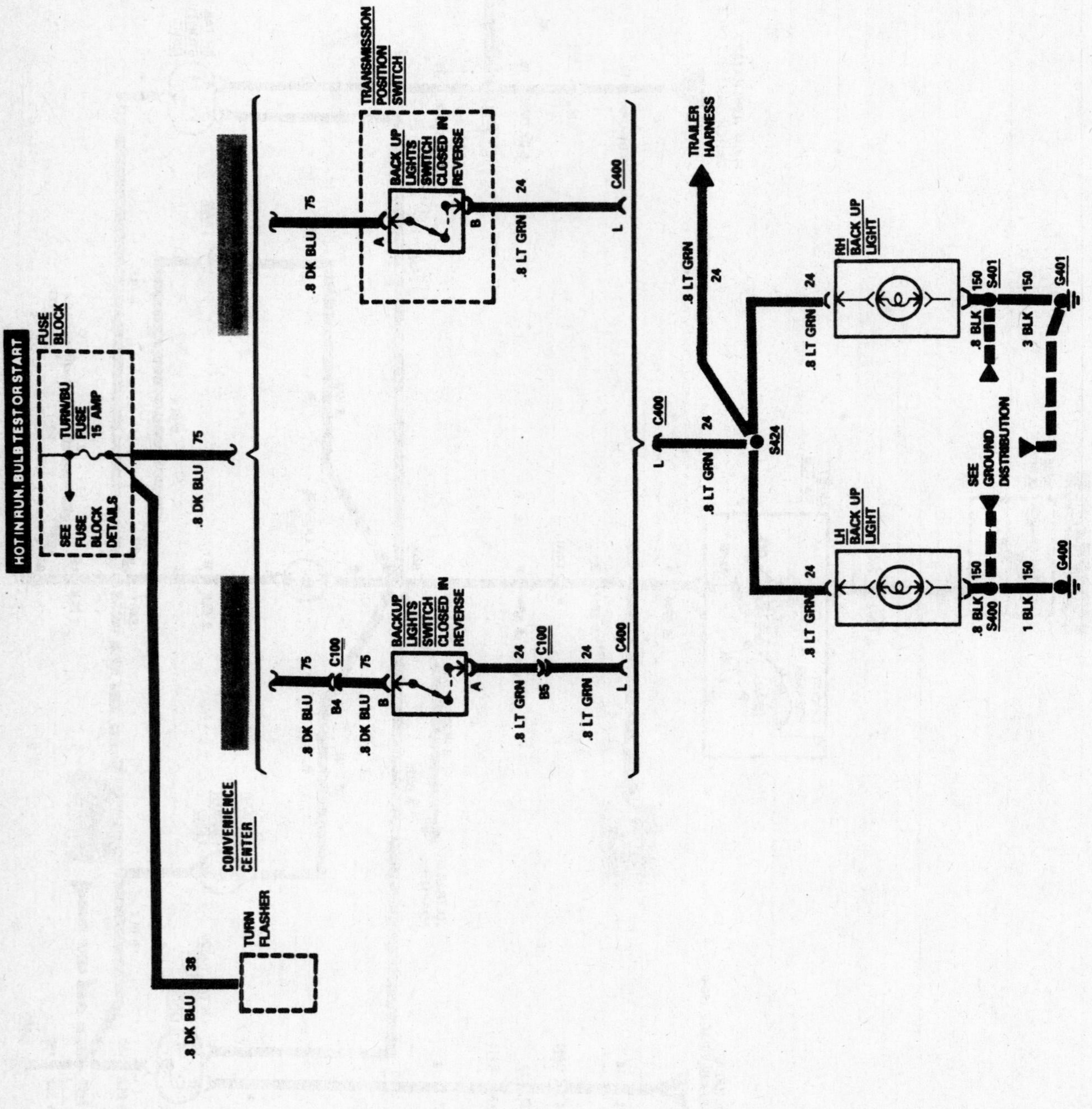

HOT IN RUN, BULB TEST OR START

FUSE BLOCK

SEE FUSE BLOCK DETAILS

TURN/BU FUSE 15 AMP

.8 DK BLU 75

.8 DK BLU 75

CONVENIENCE CENTER

TURN FLASHER

.8 DK BLU 38

TRANSMISSION POSITION SWITCH

BACK UP LIGHTS SWITCH CLOSED IN REVERSE

.8 DK BLU 75

A

B

.8 LT GRN 24

L C400

BACKUP LIGHTS SWITCH CLOSED IN REVERSE

.8 DK BLU 75 C100 B4

.8 DK BLU 75 B

B

A

.8 LT GRN 24 C100 B5

.8 LT GRN 24 L C400

TRAILER HARNESS

.8 LT GRN 24

L C400

.8 LT GRN 24

S424

.8 LT GRN 24

RH BACK UP LIGHT

.8 LT GRN 24

150 S401

.8 BLK 150

G401

3 BLK

SEE GROUND DISTRIBUTION

LH BACK UP LIGHT

.8 LT GRN 24

150 S400

.8 BLK 150

G400

1 BLK

Backup lights

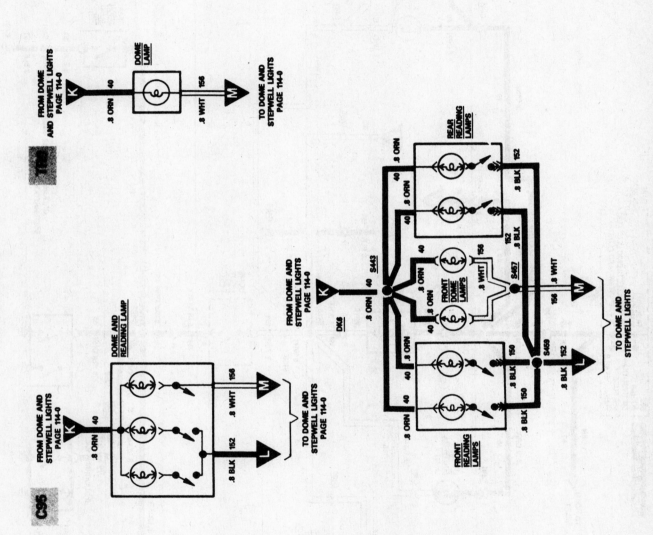

Interior lights – dome reading

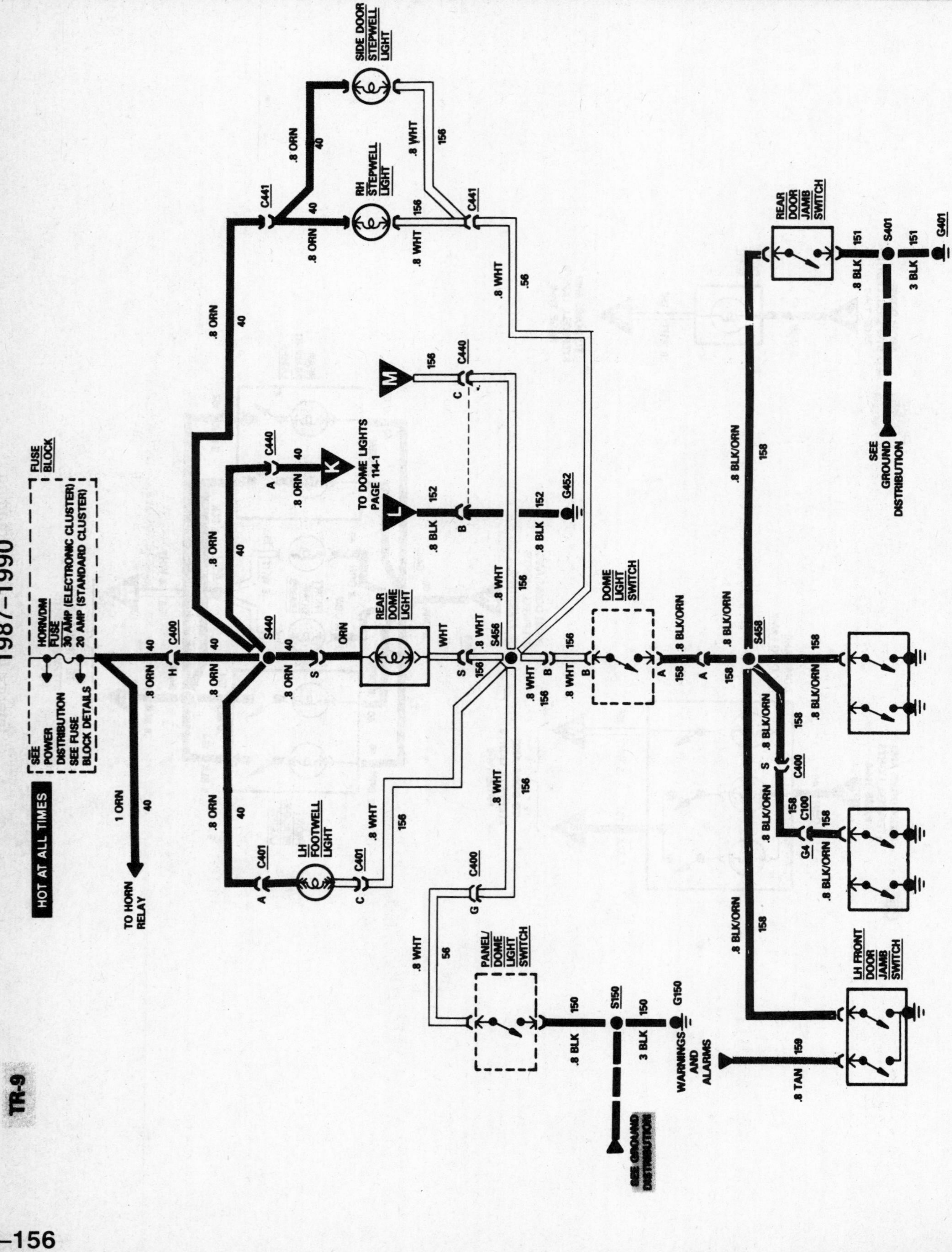

1987-1990

SIDE DOOR STEPWELL LIGHT

RH STEPWELL LIGHT

REAR DOOR JAMB SWITCH

FUSE BLOCK

HORN/DM FUSE
30 AMP (ELECTRONIC CLUSTER)
20 AMP (STANDARD CLUSTER)

SEE POWER DISTRIBUTION

SEE FUSE BLOCK DETAILS

HOT AT ALL TIMES

TO HORN RELAY

TO DOME LIGHTS PAGE 114-1

REAR DOME LIGHT

LH FOOTWELL LIGHT

PANEL/DOME LIGHT SWITCH

DOME LIGHT SWITCH

WARNINGS AND ALARMS

SEE GROUND DISTRIBUTION

SEE GROUND DISTRIBUTION

LH FRONT DOOR JAMB SWITCH

Interior lights – dome/stepwell

TR-9

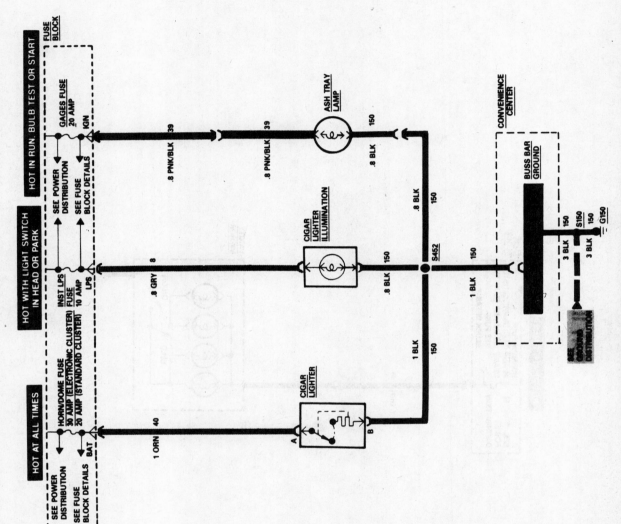

1987–1990

U37

Interior lights — cigar lighter/ash tray

1987–1990

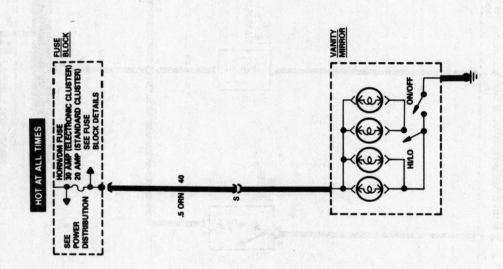

FUSE BLOCK

HOT AT ALL TIMES

HORN/DM FUSE
30 AMP (ELECTRONIC CLUSTER)
20 AMP (STANDARD CLUSTER)
SEE FUSE
BLOCK DETAILS

SEE
POWER
DISTRIBUTION

.5 ORN 40

S

VANITY
MIRROR

ON/OFF

HI/LO

Interior lights — vanity mirror

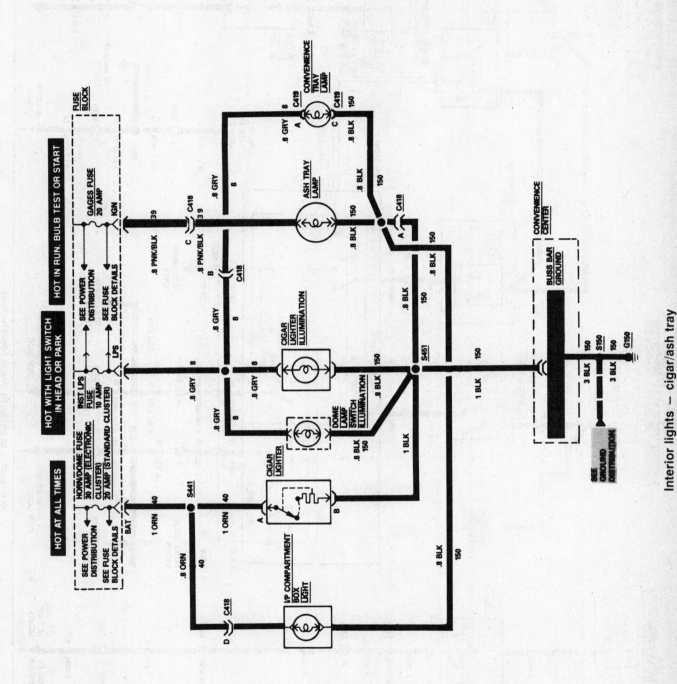

1987–1990

Interior lights — cigar/ash tray

TR9

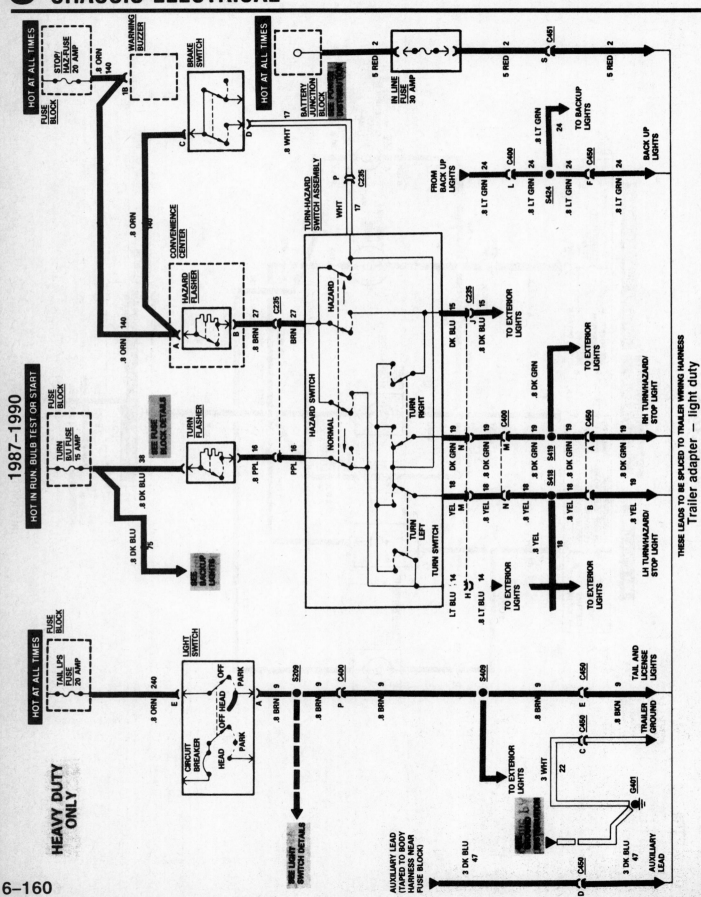

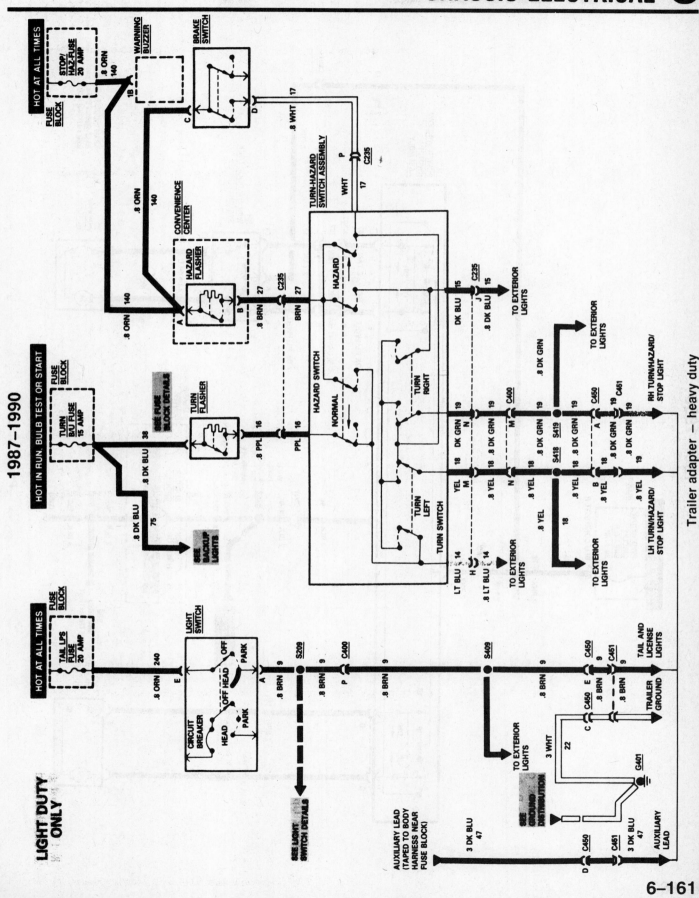

1987-1990

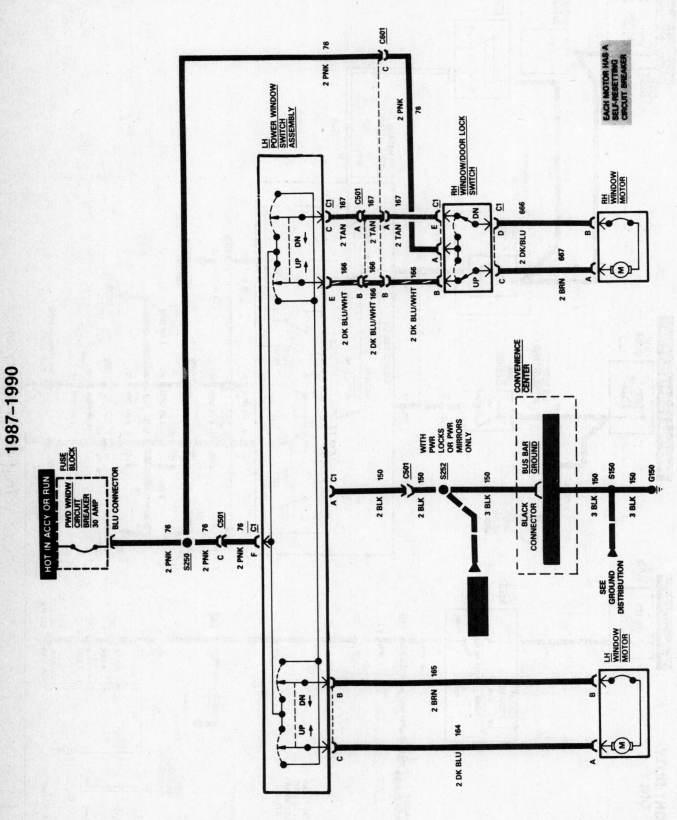

EACH MOTOR HAS A
SELF-RESETTING
CIRCUIT BREAKER

Power windows

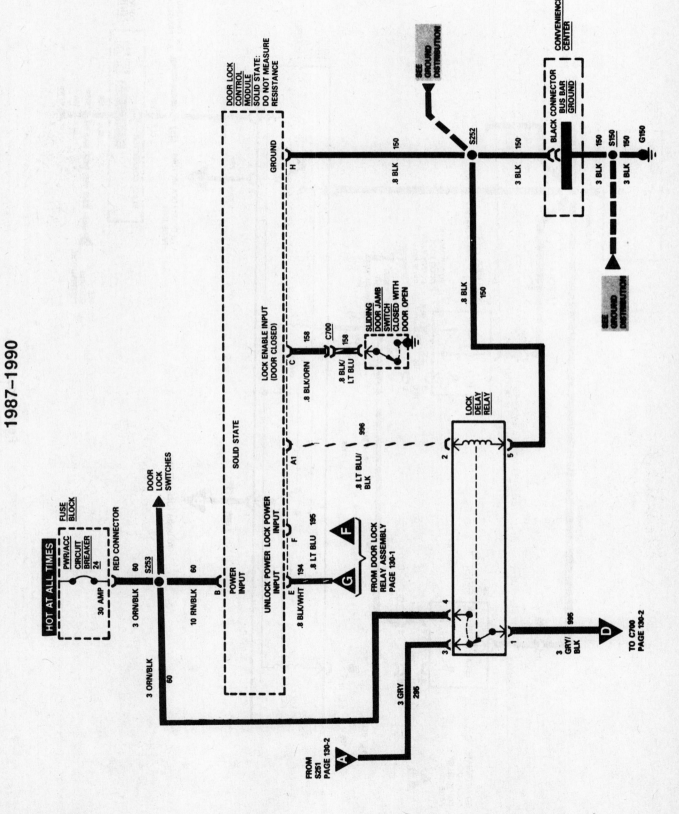

1987–1990

Power door locks

1987–1990

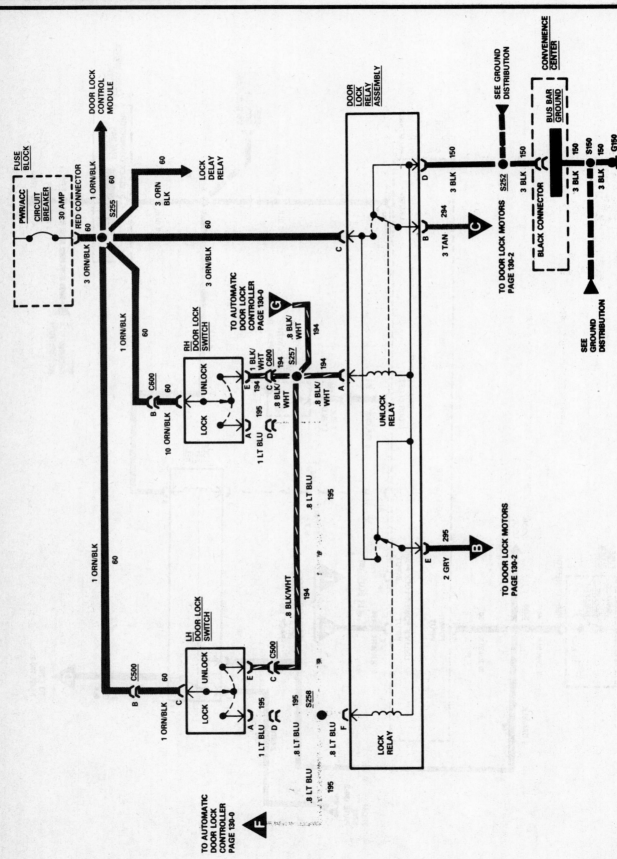

Power door locks

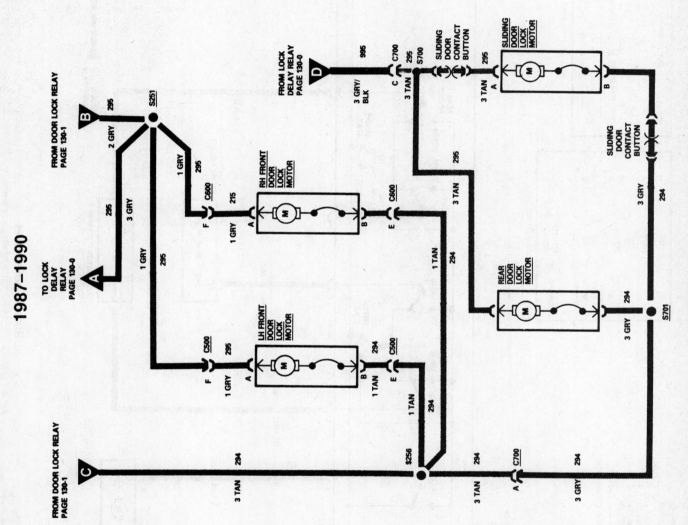

1987–1990

Power door locks

1987-1990

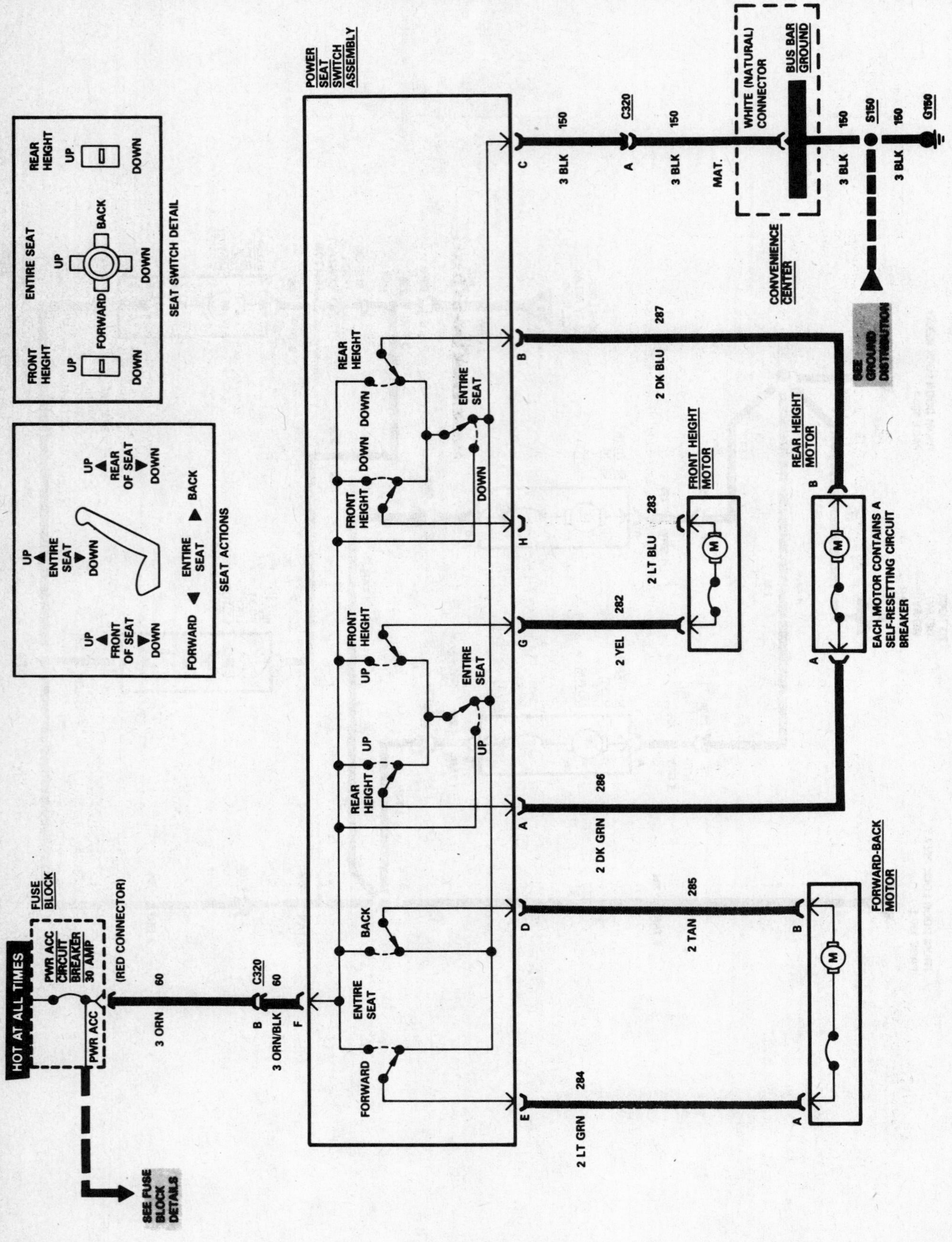

SEAT SWITCH DETAIL

REAR HEIGHT UP DOWN

ENTIRE SEAT UP DOWN BACK FORWARD

FRONT HEIGHT UP DOWN

SEAT ACTIONS

UP ENTIRE SEAT DOWN

UP REAR OF SEAT DOWN

UP FRONT OF SEAT DOWN

UP ENTIRE SEAT DOWN

FORWARD ▼ ENTIRE SEAT ▲ BACK

POWER SEAT SWITCH ASSEMBLY

WHITE (NATURAL) CONNECTOR

BUS BAR GROUND

CONVENIENCE CENTER

SEE GROUND DISTRIBUTION

REAR HEIGHT

ENTIRE SEAT

DOWN DOWN

FRONT HEIGHT

DOWN

C   3 BLK   150   A   3 BLK   150   MAT.   C320   150   3 BLK   S150   3 BLK   150   G150

B   2 DK BLU   287

FRONT HEIGHT MOTOR   REAR HEIGHT MOTOR

H   2 LT BLU   283   M   B

FRONT HEIGHT

ENTIRE SEAT

UP   UP

REAR HEIGHT

G   2 YEL   282   M   A

EACH MOTOR CONTAINS A SELF-RESETTING CIRCUIT BREAKER

A   2 DK GRN   286

BACK

D   2 TAN   285   B   FORWARD-BACK MOTOR

ENTIRE SEAT

FORWARD

FUSE BLOCK

PWR ACC CIRCUIT BREAKER 30 AMP

HOT AT ALL TIMES

(RED CONNECTOR)

PWR ACC

60   3 ORN   C320   60   B   3 ORN/BLK   F

E   2 LT GRN   284   M   A

SEE FUSE BLOCK DETAILS

Six way power seat

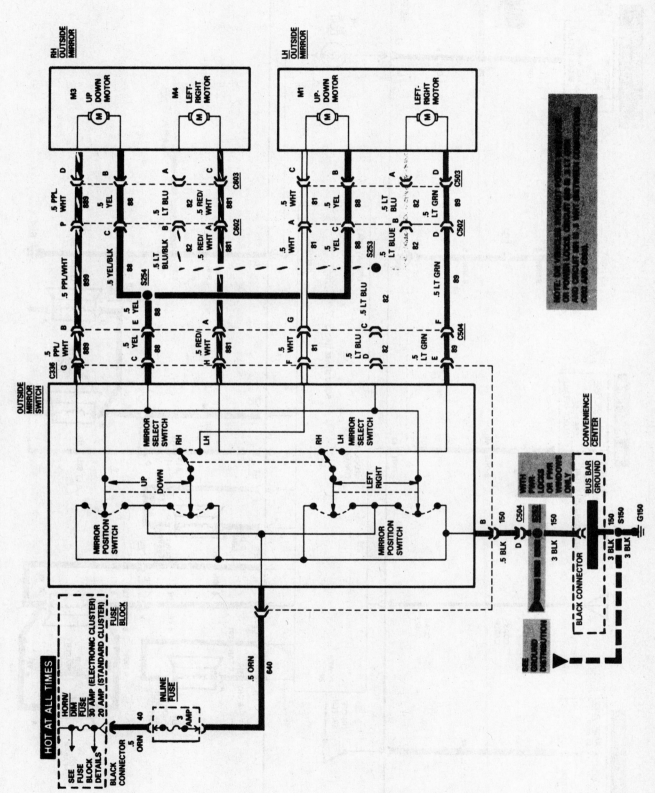

Power remote mirrors

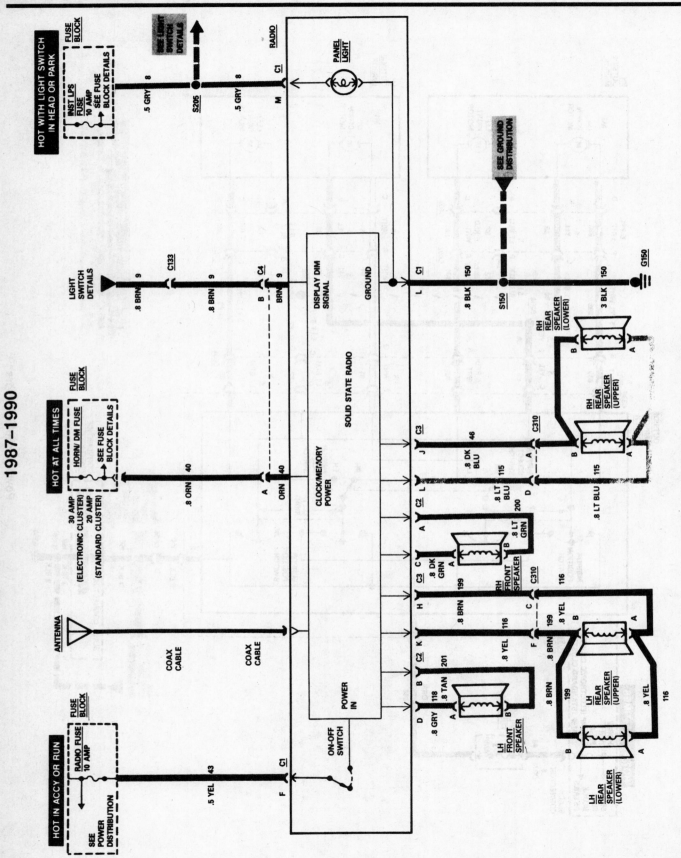

Radio and clock – with cassette

1987–1990

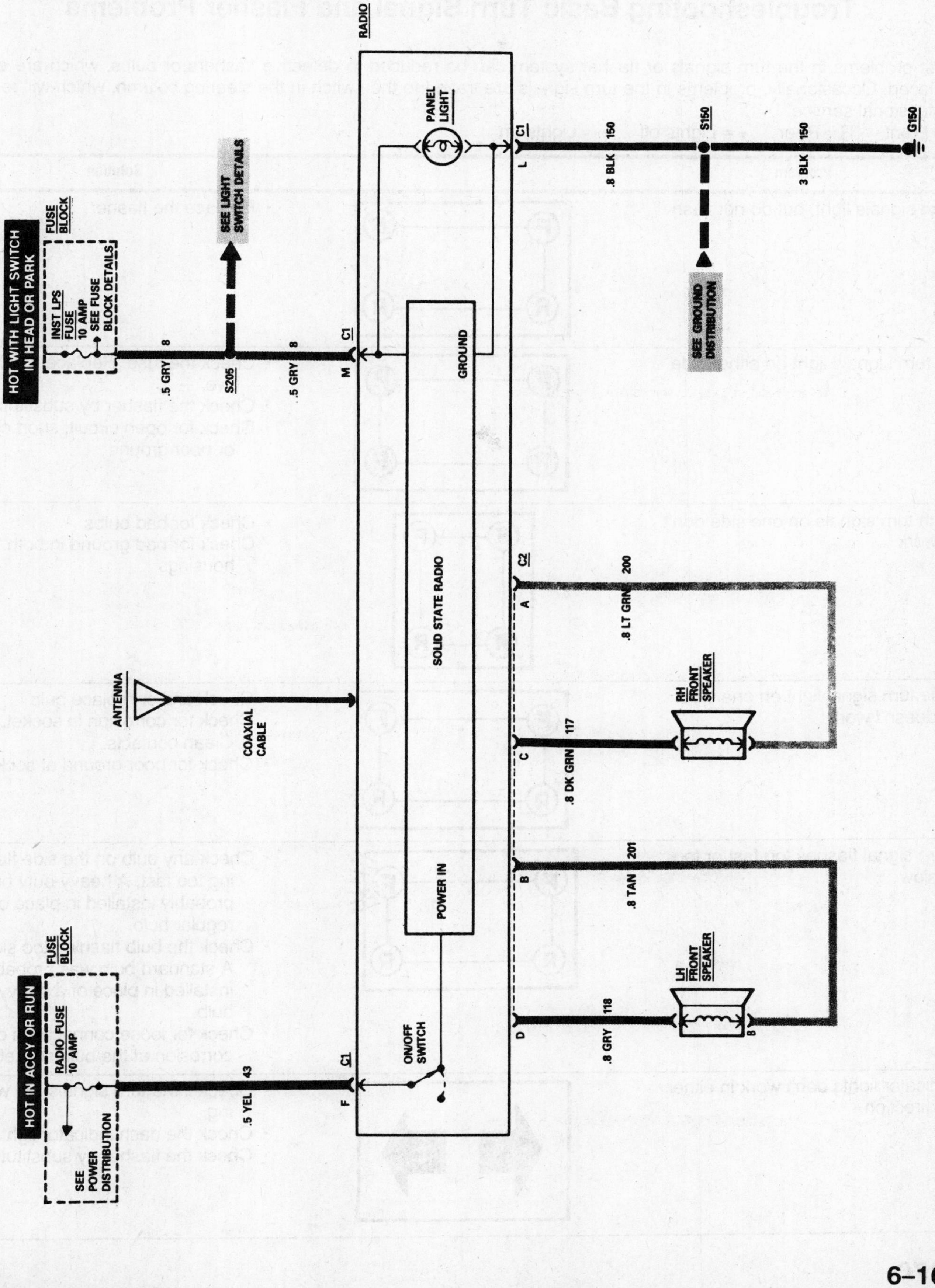

RADIO

PANEL LIGHT

C1
L
.8 BLK 150
S150
3 BLK 150
G150

SEE GROUND DISTRIBUTION

HOT WITH LIGHT SWITCH IN HEAD OR PARK

FUSE BLOCK

INST LPS FUSE 10 AMP SEE FUSE BLOCK DETAILS

SEE LIGHT SWITCH DETAILS

.5 GRY 8
S205
.5 GRY 8
C1
M

SOLID STATE RADIO

GROUND

ANTENNA

COAXIAL CABLE

C2
A
.8 LT GRN 200
RH FRONT SPEAKER

C
.8 DK GRN 117

POWER IN

B
.8 TAN 201
LH FRONT SPEAKER

D
.8 GRY 118

HOT IN ACCY OR RUN

FUSE BLOCK

RADIO FUSE 10 AMP

SEE POWER DISTRIBUTION

.5 YEL 43
C1
F

ON/OFF SWITCH

Radio — without cassette

Troubleshooting Basic Turn Signal and Flasher Problems

Most problems in the turn signals or flasher system can be reduced to defective flashers or bulbs, which are easily replaced. Occasionally, problems in the turn signals are traced to the switch in the steering column, which will require professional service.

F = Front   R = Rear   ● = Lights off   o = Lights on

Problem		Solution
Turn signals light, but do not flash		• Replace the flasher
No turn signals light on either side		• Check the fuse. Replace if defective. • Check the flasher by substitution • Check for open circuit, short circuit or poor ground
Both turn signals on one side don't work		• Check for bad bulbs • Check for bad ground in both housings
One turn signal light on one side doesn't work		• Check and/or replace bulb • Check for corrosion in socket. Clean contacts. • Check for poor ground at socket
Turn signal flashes too fast or too slow		• Check any bulb on the side flashing too fast. A heavy-duty bulb is probably installed in place of a regular bulb. • Check the bulb flashing too slow. A standard bulb was probably installed in place of a heavy-duty bulb. • Check for loose connections or corrosion at the bulb socket
Indicator lights don't work in either direction		• Check if the turn signals are working • Check the dash indicator lights • Check the flasher by substitution

Troubleshooting Basic Turn Signal and Flasher Problems

Problem		Solution

One indicator light doesn't light		· On systems with 1 dash indicator:
		   See if the lights work on the same side. Often the filaments have been reversed in systems combining stoplights with taillights and turn signals.
		   Check the flasher by substitution
		· On systems with 2 indicators:
		   Check the bulbs on the same side
		   Check the indicator light bulb
		   Check the flasher by substitution

Troubleshooting Basic Lighting Problems

Problem	Cause	Solution
Lights		
One or more lights don't work, but others do	· Defective bulb(s) · Blown fuse(s) · Dirty fuse clips or light sockets · Poor ground circuit	· Replace bulb(s) · Replace fuse(s) · Clean connections · Run ground wire from light socket housing to car frame
Lights burn out quickly	· Incorrect voltage regulator setting or defective regulator · Poor battery/alternator connections	· Replace voltage regulator · Check battery/alternator connections
Lights go dim	· Low/discharged battery · Alternator not charging · Corroded sockets or connections · Low voltage output	· Check battery · Check drive belt tension; repair or replace alternator · Clean bulb and socket contacts and connections · Replace voltage regulator
Lights flicker	· Loose connection · Poor ground · Circuit breaker operating (short circuit)	· Tighten all connections · Run ground wire from light housing to car frame · Check connections and look for bare wires
Lights "flare"—Some flare is normal on acceleration—if excessive, see "Lights Burn Out Quickly"	· High voltage setting	· Replace voltage regulator
Lights glare—approaching drivers are blinded	· Lights adjusted too high · Rear springs or shocks sagging · Rear tires soft	· Have headlights aimed · Check rear springs/shocks · Check/correct rear tire pressure

Troubleshooting Basic Lighting Problems

Problem	Cause	Solution
Turn Signals		
Turn signals don't work in either direction	• Blown fuse • Defective flasher • Loose connection	• Replace fuse • Replace flasher • Check/tighten all connections
Right (or left) turn signal only won't work	• Bulb burned out • Right (or left) indicator bulb burned out • Short circuit	• Replace bulb • Check/replace indicator bulb • Check/repair wiring
Flasher rate too slow or too fast	• Incorrect wattage bulb • Incorrect flasher	• Flasher bulb • Replace flasher (use a variable load flasher if you pull a trailer)
Indicator lights do not flash (burn steadily)	• Burned out bulb • Defective flasher	• Replace bulb • Replace flasher
Indicator lights do not light at all	• Burned out indicator bulb • Defective flasher	• Replace indicator bulb • Replace flasher

Troubleshooting Basic Dash Gauge Problems

Problem	Cause	Solution
Coolant Temperature Gauge		
Gauge reads erratically or not at all	• Loose or dirty connections • Defective sending unit • Defective gauge	• Clean/tighten connections • Bi-metal gauge: remove the wire from the sending unit. Ground the wire for an instant. If the gauge registers, replace the sending unit. • Magnetic gauge: disconnect the wire at the sending unit. With ignition ON gauge should register COLD. Ground the wire; gauge should register HOT.
Ammeter Gauge—Turn Headlights ON (do not start engine). Note reaction		
Ammeter shows charge Ammeter shows discharge Ammeter does not move	• Connections reversed on gauge • Ammeter is OK • Loose connections or faulty wiring • Defective gauge	• Reinstall connections • Nothing • Check/correct wiring • Replace gauge
Oil Pressure Gauge		
Gauge does not register or is inaccurate	• On mechanical gauge, Bourdon tube may be bent or kinked • Low oil pressure	• Check tube for kinks or bends preventing oil from reaching the gauge • Remove sending unit. Idle the engine briefly. If no oil flows from sending unit hole, problem is in engine.

Troubleshooting Basic Dash Gauge Problems

Problem	Cause	Solution
Gauge does not register or is inaccurate	• Defective gauge	• Remove the wire from the sending unit and ground it for an instant with the ignition ON. A good gauge will go to the top of the scale.
	• Defective wiring	• Check the wiring to the gauge. If it's OK and the gauge doesn't register when grounded, replace the gauge.
	• Defective sending unit	• If the wiring is OK and the gauge functions when grounded, replace the sending unit

All Gauges

All gauges do not operate	• Blown fuse	• Replace fuse
	• Defective instrument regulator	• Replace instrument voltage regulator
All gauges read low or erratically	• Defective or dirty instrument voltage regulator	• Clean contacts or replace
All gauges pegged	• Loss of ground between instrument voltage regulator and car	• Check ground
	• Defective instrument regulator	• Replace regulator

Warning Lights

Light(s) do not come on when ignition is ON, but engine is not started	• Defective bulb	• Replace bulb
	• Defective wire	• Check wire from light to sending unit
	• Defective sending unit	• Disconnect the wire from the sending unit and ground it. Replace the sending unit if the light comes on with the ignition ON.
Light comes on with engine running	• Problem in individual system	• Check system
	• Defective sending unit	• Check sending unit (see above)

Troubleshooting the Heater

Problem	Cause	Solution
Blower motor will not turn at any speed	• Blown fuse	• Replace fuse
	• Loose connection	• Inspect and tighten
	• Defective ground	• Clean and tighten
	• Faulty switch	• Replace switch
	• Faulty motor	• Replace motor
	• Faulty resistor	• Replace resistor
Blower motor turns at one speed only	• Faulty switch	• Replace switch
	• Faulty resistor	• Replace resistor
Blower motor turns but does not circulate air	• Intake blocked	• Clean intake
	• Fan not secured to the motor shaft	• Tighten security

Troubleshooting the Heater

Problem	Cause	Solution
Heater will not heat	• Coolant does not reach proper temperature • Heater core blocked internally • Heater core air-bound • Blend-air door not in proper position	• Check and replace thermostat if necessary • Flush or replace core if necessary • Purge air from core • Adjust cable
Heater will not defrost	• Control cable adjustment incorrect • Defroster hose damaged	• Adjust control cable • Replace defroster hose

Troubleshooting Basic Windshield Wiper Problems

Problem	Cause	Solution
Electric Wipers		
Wipers do not operate—Wiper motor heats up or hums	• Internal motor defect • Bent or damaged linkage • Arms improperly installed on linking pivots	• Replace motor • Repair or replace linkage • Position linkage in park and reinstall wiper arms
Wipers do not operate—No current to motor	• Fuse or circuit breaker blown • Loose, open or broken wiring • Defective switch • Defective or corroded terminals • No ground circuit for motor or switch	• Replace fuse or circuit breaker • Repair wiring and connections • Replace switch • Replace or clean terminals • Repair ground circuits
Wipers do not operate—Motor runs	• Linkage disconnected or broken	• Connect wiper linkage or replace broken linkage
Vacuum Wipers		
Wipers do not operate	• Control switch or cable inoperative • Loss of engine vacuum to wiper motor (broken hoses, low engine vacuum, defective vacuum/fuel pump) • Linkage broken or disconnected • Defective wiper motor	• Repair or replace switch or cable • Check vacuum lines, engine vacuum and fuel pump • Repair linkage • Replace wiper motor
Wipers stop on engine acceleration	• Leaking vacuum hoses • Dry windshield • Oversize wiper blades • Defective vacuum/fuel pump	• Repair or replace hoses • Wet windshield with washers • Replace with proper size wiper blades • Replace pump

7 Drive Train

QUICK REFERENCE INDEX

GENERAL INDEX

UNDERSTANDING THE MANUAL TRANSMISSION

Because of the way an internal combustion engine breathes, it can produce torque, or twisting force, only within a narrow speed range. Most modern, overhead valve engines must turn at about 2,500 rpm to produce their peak torque. By 4,500 rpm they are producing so little torque that continued increases in engine speed produce no power increases.

The manual transmission and clutch are employed to vary the relationship between engine speed and the speed of the wheels so that adequate engine power can be produced under all circumstances. The clutch allows engine torque to be applied to the transmission input shaft gradually, due to mechanical slippage. The car can, consequently, be started smoothly from a full stop.

The transmission changes the ratio between the rotating speeds of the engine and the wheels by the use of gears. 4-speed or 5-speed transmissions are most common. The lower gears allow full engine power to be applied to the rear wheels during acceleration at low speeds.

The clutch drive plate is a thin disc, the center of which is splined to the transmission input shaft. Both sides of the disc are covered with a layer of material which is similar to brake lining and which is capable of allowing slippage without roughness or excessive noise.

The clutch cover is bolted to the engine flywheel and incorporates a diaphragm spring which provides the pressure to engage the clutch. The cover also houses the pressure plate. The driven disc is sandwiched between the pressure plate and the smooth surface of the flywheel when the clutch pedal is released, thus forcing it to turn at the same speed as the engine crankshaft.

The transmission contains a mainshaft which passes all the way through the transmission, from the clutch to the driveshaft. This shaft is separated at one point, so that front and rear portions can turn at different speeds.

Power is transmitted by a countershaft in the lower gears and reverse. The gears of the countershaft mesh with gears on the mainshaft, allowing power to be carried from one to the other. All the countershaft gears are integral with that shaft, while several of the mainshaft gears can either rotate independently of the shaft or be locked to it. Shifting from one gear to the next causes one of the gears to be freed from rotating with the shaft and locks another to it. Gears are locked and unlocked by internal dog clutches which slide between the center of the gear and the shaft. The forward gears usually employ synchronizers; friction members which smoothly bring gear and shaft to the same speed before the toothed dog clutches are engaged.

MANUAL TRANSMISSION

Identification

Manual transmissions are identified by using the following descriptions:

a. The number of forward gears.
b. The measured distance between the centerlines of the mainshaft and the countergear.

The 4-speed (76mm) transmission is a fully synchronized unit with blocker ring synchronizers and a sliding mesh reverse gear.

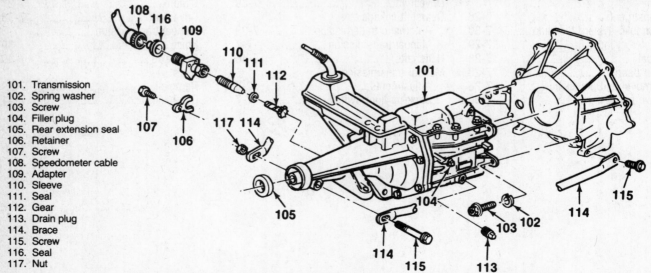

101. Transmission
102. Spring washer
103. Screw
104. Filler plug
105. Rear extension seal
106. Retainer
107. Screw
108. Speedometer cable
109. Adapter
110. Sleeve
111. Seal
112. Gear
113. Drain plug
114. Brace
115. Screw
116. Seal
117. Nut

View of the MH3/ML3, 5-speed transmission — MR2, 4-speed is similar

The transmission case houses the various gears, bearings and shafts, a shift control cover and an extension housing. The floor-mounted gearshift lever assembly is located on top of the extension housing; the shifting mechanism is connected to the shift control cover by adjustable shifting arms. The MR2 model is used in combination with both engines.

The 5-speed (77mm) transmission is a fully synchronized unit with blocker ring synchronizers and a sliding mesh reverse gear. It has an aluminum transmission case that houses the various gears, bearings and an extension housing. The floor-mounted gearshift lever assembly is located on top of the extension housing. The ML3 model, is used with the 2.5L engine; the MH3 model is used with the 4.3L engine.

In 1990, the Astro/Safari van could be ordered with All Wheel Drive as an option. It is only available with an automatic overdrive transmission and the 4.3L engine. The BW-4472 transfer case is an aluminum two piece unit with a chain driven viscous clutch. The All Wheel Drive is automatic and has no external controls.

Adjustment

NOTE: The shifter mechanism, of the 5-speed transmission, does not require adjustment and can be serviced independently.

Troubleshooting the Manual Transmission and Transfer Case

Problem	Cause	Solution
Transmission shifts hard	• Clutch adjustment incorrect • Clutch linkage or cable binding • Shift rail binding	• Adjust clutch • Lubricate or repair as necessary • Check for mispositioned selector arm roll pin, loose cover bolts, worn shift rail bores, worn shift rail, distorted oil seal, or extension housing not aligned with case. Repair as necessary.
	• Internal bind in transmission caused by shift forks, selector plates, or synchronizer assemblies • Clutch housing misalignment	• Remove, dissemble and inspect transmission. Replace worn or damaged components as necessary. • Check runout at rear face of clutch housing
	• Incorrect lubricant • Block rings and/or cone seats worn	• Drain and refill transmission • Blocking ring to gear clutch tooth face clearance must be 0.030 inch or greater. If clearance is correct it may still be necessary to inspect blocking rings and cone seats for excessive wear. Repair as necessary.
Gear clash when shifting from one gear to another	• Clutch adjustment incorrect • Clutch linkage or cable binding • Clutch housing misalignment • Lubricant level low or incorrect lubricant • Gearshift components, or synchronizer assemblies worn or damaged	• Adjust clutch • Lubricate or repair as necessary • Check runout at rear of clutch housing • Drain and refill transmission and check for lubricant leaks if level was low. Repair as necessary. • Remove, disassemble and inspect transmission. Replace worn or damaged components as necessary.

Troubleshooting the Manual Transmission and Transfer Case (cont.)

Problem	Cause	Solution
Transmission noisy	• Lubricant level low or incorrect lubricant	• Drain and refill transmission. If lubricant level was low, check for leaks and repair as necessary.
	• Clutch housing-to-engine, or transmission-to-clutch housing bolts loose	• Check and correct bolt torque as necessary
	• Dirt, chips, foreign material in transmission	• Drain, flush, and refill transmission
	• Gearshift mechanism, transmission gears, or bearing components worn or damaged	• Remove, disassemble and inspect transmission. Replace worn or damaged components as necessary.
	• Clutch housing misalignment	• Check runout at rear face of clutch housing
Jumps out of gear	• Clutch housing misalignment	• Check runout at rear face of clutch housing
	• Gearshift lever loose	• Check lever for worn fork. Tighten loose attaching bolts.
	• Offset lever nylon insert worn or lever attaching nut loose	• Remove gearshift lever and check for loose offset lever nut or worn insert. Repair or replace as necessary.
	• Gearshift mechanism, shift forks, selector plates, interlock plate, selector arm, shift rail, detent plugs, springs or shift cover worn or damaged	• Remove, disassemble and inspect transmission cover assembly. Replace worn or damaged components as necessary.
	• Clutch shaft or roller bearings worn or damaged	• Replace clutch shaft or roller bearings as necessary
Jumps out of gear (cont.)	• Gear teeth worn or tapered, synchronizer assemblies worn or damaged, excessive end play caused by worn thrust washers or output shaft gears	• Remove, disassemble, and inspect transmission. Replace worn or damaged components as necessary.
	• Pilot bushing worn	• Replace pilot bushing
Will not shift into one gear	• Gearshift selector plates, interlock plate, or selector arm, worn, damaged, or incorrectly assembled	• Remove, disassemble, and inspect transmission cover assembly. Repair or replace components as necessary.
	• Shift rail detent plunger worn, spring broken, or plug loose	• Tighten plug or replace worn or damaged components as necessary
	• Gearshift lever worn or damaged	• Replace gearshift lever
	• Synchronizer sleeves or hubs, damaged or worn	• Remove, disassemble and inspect transmission. Replace worn or damaged components.

Troubleshooting the Manual Transmission and Transfer Case (cont.)

Problem	Cause	Solution
Locked in one gear—cannot be shifted out	• Shift rail(s) worn or broken, shifter fork bent, setscrew loose, center detent plug missing or worn	• Inspect and replace worn or damaged parts
	• Broken gear teeth on countershaft gear, clutch shaft, or reverse idler gear	• Inspect and replace damaged part
	Gearshift lever broken or worn, shift mechanism in cover incorrectly assembled or broken, worn damaged gear train components	• Disassemble transmission. Replace damaged parts or assemble correctly.
Transfer case difficult to shift or will not shift into desired range	• Vehicle speed too great to permit shifting	• Stop vehicle and shift into desired range. Or reduce speed to 3–4 km/h (2–3 mph) before attempting to shift.
	• If vehicle was operated for extended period in 4H mode on dry paved surface, driveline torque load may cause difficult shifting	• Stop vehicle, shift transmission to neutral, shift transfer case to 2H mode and operate vehicle in 2H on dry paved surfaces
	• Transfer case external shift linkage binding	• Lubricate or repair or replace linkage, or tighten loose components as necessary
	• Insufficient or incorrect lubricant	• Drain and refill to edge of fill hole with SAE 85W-90 gear lubricant only
	• Internal components binding, worn, or damaged	• Disassemble unit and replace worn or damaged components as necessary
Transfer case noisy in all drive modes	• Insufficient or incorrect lubricant	• Drain and refill to edge of fill hole with SAE 85W-90 gear lubricant only. Check for leaks and repair if necessary. Note: If unit is still noisy after drain and refill, disassembly and inspection may be required to locate source of noise.
Noisy in—or jumps out of four wheel drive low range	• Transfer case not completely engaged in 4L position	• Stop vehicle, shift transfer case in Neutral, then shift back into 4L position
	• Shift linkage loose or binding	• Tighten, lubricate, or repair linkage as necessary
	• Shift fork cracked, inserts worn, or fork is binding on shift rail	• Disassemble unit and repair as necessary
Lubricant leaking from output shaft seals or from vent	• Transfer case overfilled	• Drain to correct level
	• Vent closed or restricted	• Clear or replace vent if necessary

Troubleshooting the Manual Transmission and Transfer Case (cont.)

Problem	Cause	Solution
Lubricant leaking from output shaft seals or from vent (cont.)	• Output shaft seals damaged or installed incorrectly	• Replace seals. Be sure seal lip faces interior of case when installed. Also be sure yoke seal surfaces are not scored or nicked. Remove scores, nicks with fine sandpaper or replace yoke(s) if necessary.
Abnormal tire wear	• Extended operation on dry hard surface (paved) roads in 4H range	• Operate in 2H on hard surface (paved) roads

SHIFTER RODS

4-Speed (MR2)

NOTE: The following procedure requires the use of ¼ in. pin gauge.

1. At each shifting swivel (located on the shifter side cover), loosen the jam nuts on the shifter rods.

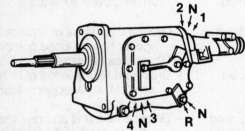

View of the shifting lever positions — MR2, 4-speed transmission

2. From inside the vehicle, place the floor mounted, gear shift lever in the Neutral position.

3. From under the vehicle, place the shifter rods in the Neutral position.

4. Using a ¼ in. pin gauge, position it in the holes of the gear shift control levers.

5. While applying forward pressure (separately) on each shifter rod, tighten the shifter rod jam nuts, located on each side of the shifting swivel.

6. Remove the pin gauge and check the shifting operation. Lubricate the shifting levers.

CLUTCH SWITCH

A clutch switch is located under the instrument panel and attached to the top of the clutch pedal.

1. Disconnect the negative battery terminal from the battery.

2. Remove the lower steering column-to-instrument panel cover.

3. Disconnect the electrical connector from the clutch switch.

120. Shift lever
121. Shift control
122. Retainer
123. Washer
124. Control lever
125. Shift rod, 1st/2nd
126. Shift rod, 3rd/4th
127. Shift rod, rev.
128. Nut
129. Swivel
130. Nut
131. Shift lever
132. Washer
133. Retainer
A. Gage pin hole

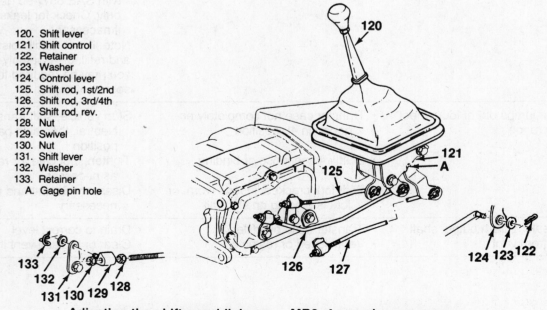

Adjusting the shifter rod linkage — MR2, 4-speed transmission

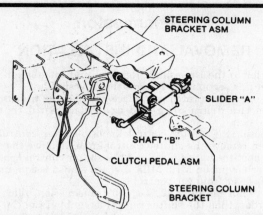

STEERING COLUMN
BRACKET ASM

SLIDER "A"

SHAFT "B"

CLUTCH PEDAL ASM

STEERING COLUMN
BRACKET

Adjusting the clutch (neutral start) switch — manual transmission

NOTE: Be sure to leave any carpets and floor mats (being used in the vehicle) in place, when making the adjustment.

4. At the clutch switch, move the slider (adjuster) to the rear of the clutch switch shaft.
5. Push the clutch pedal to the floor.
6. While holding the clutch pedal to the floor, move the slider down the clutch switch shaft until it stops.

NOTE: When moving the slider down the clutch switch shaft, a clicking noise can be heard.

7. Release the clutch pedal; the adjustment is complete.
8. Reconnect the electrical connector, the hush panel and the negative battery terminal.

Back-up Light Switch

REMOVAL AND INSTALLATION

1. Disconnect the negative battery terminal from the battery.
2. From the left rear of the transmission, disconnect the electrical connector from the back-up light switch.
3. Remove the back-up light switch from the transmission.
To install:
1. Apply thread sealing compound and install the switch. Torque the switch to 17 ft. lbs. (23 Nm). Connect the electrical connector.
2. Place the gear shift lever in the Reverse position and check the back-up lights are turned On.

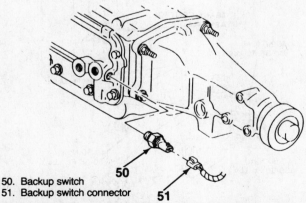

50. Backup switch
51. Backup switch connector

Exploded view of the back-up light switch — manual transmission

Shift Linkage

REMOVAL AND INSTALLATION

4-speed

1. Disconnect the negative (−) battery cable.
2. Raise the vehicle and support with jackstands.
3. Disconnect the shift rods from the control lever.
4. Remove the control mounting bolts and shifter.
5. Lower the vehicle.
6. Remove the shifter knob, boot retaining screws and boot.
7. Pull the shifter assembly from the floor.
To install:
1. Install the shifter assembly into the floor.
2. Install the shifter knob, boot retaining screws and boot.
3. Raise the vehicle and support with jackstands.
4. Install the control mounting bolts and shifter.
5. Connect the shift rods to the control lever.
6. Lower the vehicle.
7. Connect the negative (−) battery cable.

5-speed

1. Disconnect the negative (−) battery cable.
2. Remove the transmission from the vehicle as outlined in this Section.
3. Remove the four dust cover clips, rubber boot and dust cover.
4. Remove the four control base-to-extension housing mounting bolts.
5. Remove the control assembly from the transmission.
To install:
1. Position the control lever into the transmission and install the two bolts to the side of the extension housing.

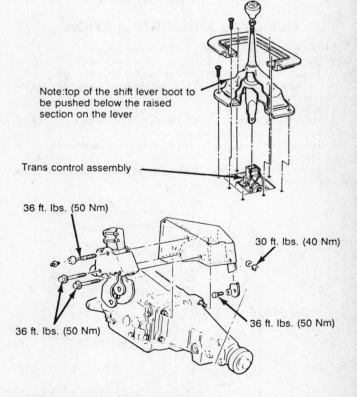

Note: top of the shift lever boot to be pushed below the raised section on the lever

Trans control assembly

36 ft. lbs. (50 Nm)

30 ft. lbs. (40 Nm)

36 ft. lbs. (50 Nm)

36 ft. lbs. (50 Nm)

4-speed manual shifter assembly

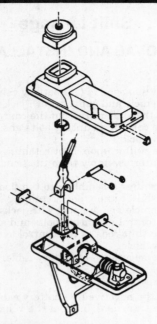

5-speed manual shifter assembly

2. Torque the side bolts to 35 ft. lbs. (47 Nm) and the top bolts to 13 ft. lbs. (17 Nm).

3. Apply a bead of RTV sealer to the groove around the base of the dust cover and install the cover and retaining clips.

4. Install the rubber boot and transmission assembly as outlined in this Section.

Rear Extension Seal

REMOVAL AND INSTALLATION

1. Disconnect the negative (−) battery cable.
2. Raise the vehicle and support with jackstands.
3. Remove the driveshaft as outlined in this Section.
4. Using a suitable prybar, pry the rear seal out of the extension housing.
To install:
5. Coat the outside of the seal with silicone sealer and the lip of the seal with chassis grease.
6. Install the new seal with an extension seal installer or equivalent.
7. Install the driveshaft, lower the vehicle and connect the negative battery cable.

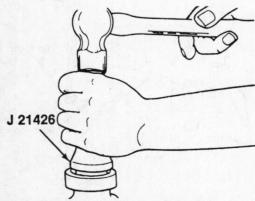

J 21426

Rear extension housing seal installation

Transmission

REMOVAL AND INSTALLATION

1. Refer to the Driveshaft, Removal and Installation procedures in this section and remove the driveshaft.
2. Using a clean catch pan, place it under the transmission, remove the drain plug and drain the fluid from the transmission.
3. Loosen the shifter control knob-to-shifter control lever nut, then remove the shifter control knob. Remove the shifter control boot-to-chassis plate and the shifter control boot.
4. If removing an MH3/ML3, 5-speed transmission, unscrew the shift lever from the control lever.
5. If removing an MR2, 4-speed transmission, remove the shifter rods, then the shifter control assembly from the extension housing.
6. Disconnect the speedometer cable and the seal from the transmission.
7. Disconnect the electrical connector from the transmission.
8. If necessary, disconnect and lower the exhaust pipe(s).
9. Using a transmission jack, place it under and connect it to the transmission, then support it with the jack.
10. Remove the transmission-to-crossmember nuts/bolts and the transmission-to-chassis braces nuts/bolts, then remove the braces and the crossmember.

NOTE: If any spacers are used, make a note of them so that they may be installed in their original position.

11. While supporting the transmission, remove the transmission-to-bellhousing bolts; DO NOT allow it to hang on the input shaft.
12. Move the transmission/jack assembly rearward and remove the transmission from the vehicle.
To install:
1. Using high temperature grease, place a thin coat on the main drive gear splines.
2. Align the transmission's input shaft with the bell housing/clutch assembly and slide the transmission into the clutch assembly.

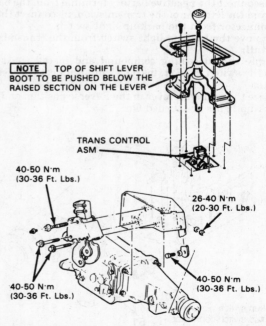

NOTE TOP OF SHIFT LEVER BOOT TO BE PUSHED BELOW THE RAISED SECTION ON THE LEVER

TRANS CONTROL ASM

40-50 N·m (30-36 Ft. Lbs.)

26-40 N·m (20-30 Ft. Lbs.)

40-50 N·m (30-36 Ft. Lbs.)

40-50 N·m (30-36 Ft. Lbs.)

Removing the shift control assembly from the MR2, 4-speed transmission

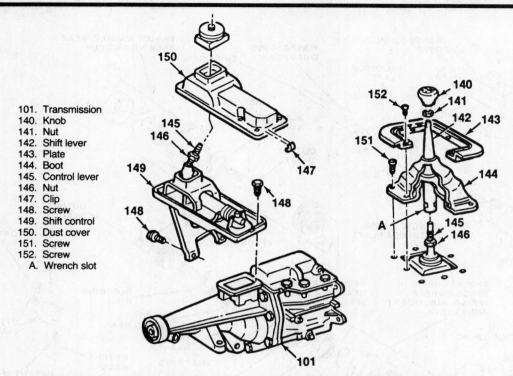

101. Transmission
140. Knob
141. Nut
142. Shift lever
143. Plate
144. Boot
145. Control lever
146. Nut
147. Clip
148. Screw
149. Shift control
150. Dust cover
151. Screw
152. Screw
A. Wrench slot

Removing the shift control lever from the MH3/ML3, 5-speed transmission

NOTE: When installing the transmission, shift the transmission into High gear, then turn the output shaft to align the input shaft splines with the clutch plate.

3. Observe the following torques.
● transmission-to-bellhousing bolts: 50 ft. lbs.
● transmission-to-mount bolts: 40 ft. lbs. for the MR2 or 33 ft. lbs. for the for the MH3/ML3
● crossmember-to-mount bolts: 26 ft. lbs. for the MR2 or 18 ft. lbs. for the MH3/ML3
● crossmember-to-chassis bolts: 37 ft. lbs.
● transmission-to-brace bolts: 26 ft. lbs.
● shifter control assembly-to-extension housing bolts: 23 ft. lbs.
● shifter rod swivel nut: 18 ft. lbs.
● shifter lever nut: 35 ft. lbs.

4-Speed Overhaul

Before Disassembly

Cleanliness is an important factor in the overhaul of the transmission. Before attempting any disassembly operation, the exterior of the transmission should be thoroughly cleaned to prevent the possibility of dirt entering the transmission internal mechanism. During inspection and reassembly, all parts should be thoroughly cleaned with cleaning fluid and then air dried. Wiping cloths or rags should not be used to dry parts. All oil passages should be blown out and checked to make sure that they are not obstructed. Small passages should be checked with tag wire. All parts should be inspected to determine which parts are to be replaced.

TRANSMISSION DISASSEMBLY

1. Remove the drain plug and drain lubricant from transmission.

2. Thoroughly clean the exterior of the transmission assembly.

3. Using a hammer and punch, remove the roll pin that retains the offset lever to shift rail.

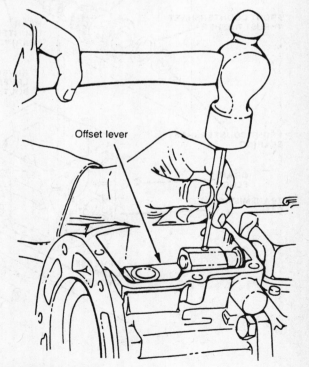

Offset lever

Offset lever roll pin

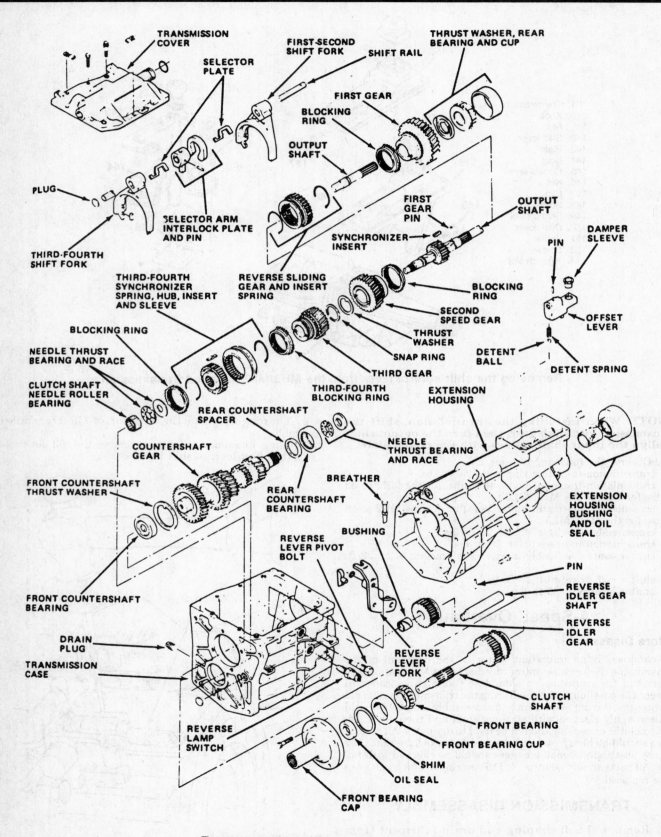

Transmission exploded view — 4-speed

1. Transmission cover
2. Cover to extension O-ring seal
3. Shift shaft
4. 3rd/4th shift fork
5. Shift fork plate
6. Control selector arm
7. Gear selector interlock plate
8. 1st/2nd shift fork
9. Shift fork insert
10. Roll pin
11. Synchronizer spring
12. Reverse sliding gear
13. Output shaft with 1/2 synchronizer
13A. Anti-rattle spring/ball
14. 1/2 synchronizer blocking ring
15. 1st speed gear
16. 1st speed gear thrust washer
17. Rear bearing
18. 5th speed driven gear
19. Snapring
20. Speedometer drive gear
21. Speedometer drive gear clip
22. Mainshaft rear bearing
23. Main drive gear thrust needle bearing
24. Main drive gear gear bearing race
25. 3/4 synchronizer ring
26. 3/4 synchronizer spring
27. 3/4 synchronizer hub
28. 3/4 synchronizer key
29. 3/4 synchronizer sleeve
30. 3rd speed gear
31. Snapring
32. 2nd speed gear thrust washer
33. 2nd speed gear
34. 1/2 synchronizer key
35. 1st speed gear thrust washer retainer pin
36. Counter gear front bearing
37. Counter gear front thrust washer
38. Counter gear
39. Counter gear bearing front spacer
40. Counter gear rear bearing
41. Counter gear bearing rear spacer
42. Snapring
43. 5th speed drive gear
44. 5th synchronizer ring
45. 5th synchronizer key
46. 5th synchronizer hub
47. 5th synchronizer spring
48. 5th synchronizer sleeve
49. 5th synchronizer key retainer
50. 5th synchronizer thrust bearing front race

51. 5th synchronizer needle thrust bearing
52. 5th synchronizer thrust bearing rear race
53. Snapring
54. Transmission oiling funnel
55. Magnet nut
56. Magnet
57. Transmission case
58. Fill and drain plug
59. Reverse lock spring
60. Reverse shift fork
61. Fork roller
62. Reverse fork pin

63. Shift rail pin
64. Rail pin roller
65. 5th and reverse shift rail
66. Shift fork insert
67. Roll pin
68. 5th shift fork
69. 5th and reverse relay lever
70. Reverse relay lever retainer ring
71. Reverse idler gear shaft
72. Reverse idler gear (including bushing)

73. 5th speed shift lever pivot pin
74. Extension ventilator
75. Steel ball
76. Detent spring
77. Control lever boot retainer
78. Control lever boot
79. Control lever boot lower retainer
80. Transmission lever and housing control
81. Shift lever dampener sleeve
82. Offset shift lever
83. Detent and guide plate
84. Extension rear oil seal
85. Extension housing bushing
86. Extension housing
87. Main drive gear
88. Front bearing
89. Bearing adjust shim
90. Drive gear bearing retainer
91. Drive gear bearing oil seal

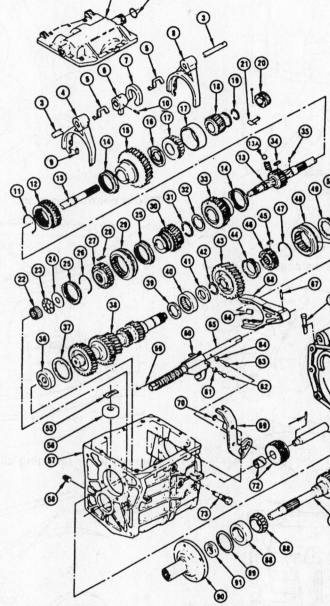

Transmission exploded view — 5-speed

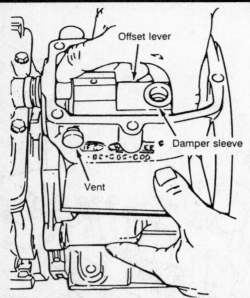

Extension housing-to-transmission case — 4-speed

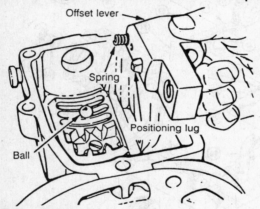

Detent ball and spring — 4-speed

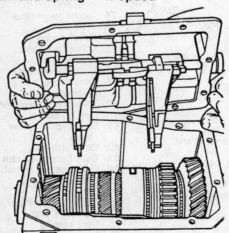

Transmission shift cover — 4-speed

4. Remove the extension housing attaching bolts. Separate the extension housing from the transmission case and remove the housing and offset lever as an assembly.

5. Remove the detent ball and spring from offset lever and remove roll pin from the extension housing or offset lever.

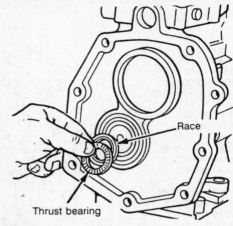

Thrust bearing and race — 4-speed

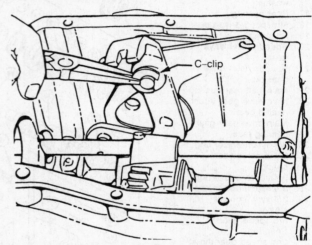

Reverse lever retaining clip — 4-speed

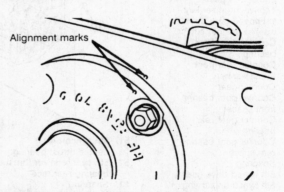

Bearing cap alignment — 4-speed

6. Remove the transmission shift cover attaching bolts. Pry the shift cover loose using the proper tool and remove cover from transmission case.

7. Remove the clip that retains reverse lever to reverse lever pivot bolt.

8. Remove the reverse lever pivot bolt and remove reverse lever and fork as an assembly.

9. Using a hammer and punch, mark position of front bearing cap to transmission case. Remove the front bearing cap bolts and remove bearing cap.

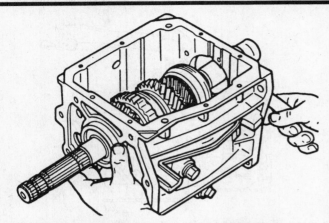

Mainshaft bearing race removal — 4-speed

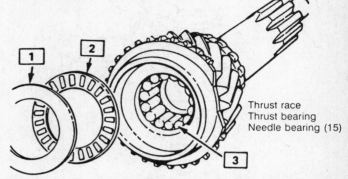

Thrust race
Thrust bearing
Needle bearing (15)

Drive gear roller bearing, thrust bearing and race — 4-speed

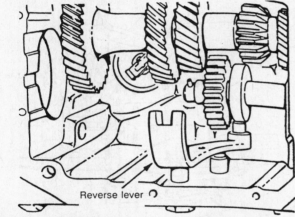

Reverse lever

Reverse lever and shift fork — 4-speed

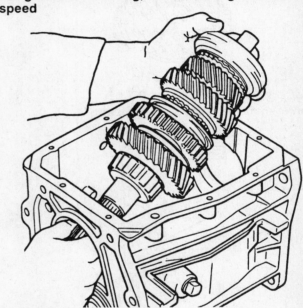

Mainshaft servicing — 4-speed

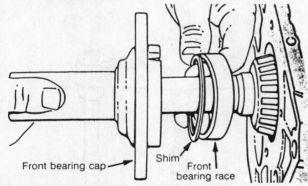

Front bearing cap   Shim   Front bearing race

Drive gear servicing — 4-speed

10. Remove the small retaining and large locating snaprings from front drive gear bearing.

11. Install a bearing puller J-22912–01 or equivalent, on the front bearing and puller J-8433–1 or equivalent, with 2 bolts on end of drive gear and remove and discard bearing. A new bearing must be used when assembling the transmission.

12. Remove the retaining and locating snaprings from rear bearing and mainshaft. Install a puller J-22912–01 or equivalent, on bearing and puller J-8433–1 or equivalent, with 2 bolts (J-33171 or equivalent) on end of mainshaft and remove and discard the used bearing. A new bearing must be used when assembling the transmission.

13. Remove the drive gear from the mainshaft and transmission case.

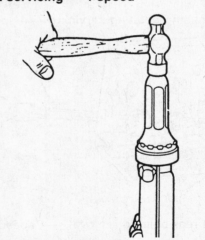

Extension housing seal servicing — 4-speed

14. Remove the mainshaft from transmission case by tipping mainshaft down at the rear and lifting shaft out through shift cover opening.

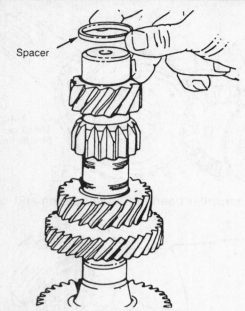

Spacer

Countershaft rear spacer — 4-speed

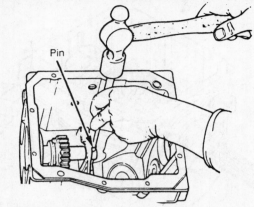

Pin

Reverse idler gear shaft — 4-speed

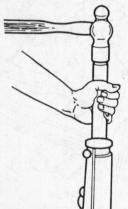

Extension housing bushing servicing — 4-speed

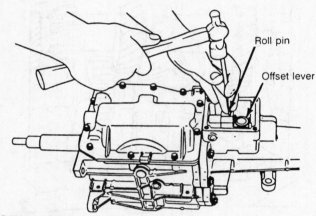

Roll pin

Offset lever

Offset lever roll pin — 5-speed

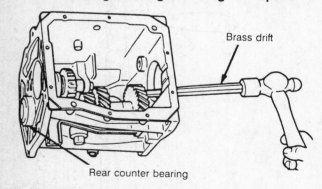

Brass drift

Rear counter bearing

Countershaft rear bearing removal — 4-speed

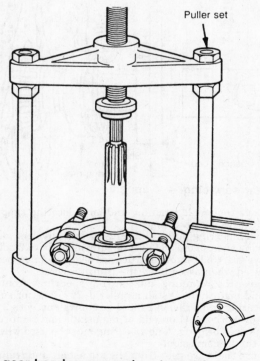

Puller set

Drive gear bearing removal — 4-speed

15. Using a hammer and punch, remove the roll pin retaining the reverse idler gear shift in the transmission case. Remove the idler gear and shaft from the case.

16. Remove the countershaft from rear of case using loading tool J–26624. Remove the countershaft gear and loading tool as an assembly the from case along with thrust washers.

MAINSHAFT

Disassembly

1. Scribe an alignment mark on the 3rd/4th synchronizer hub and sleeve for reassembly. Remove the retaining snapring and remove 3rd/4th synchronizer assembly from the mainshaft.
2. Slide the 3rd gear off mainshaft.
3. Remove the 2nd gear retaining snapring. Remove the tabbed thrust washer, 2nd gear and blocker ring from the mainshaft.
4. Remove the 1st gear thrust washer and roll pin from the mainshaft. Use pliers to remove the roll pin.
5. Remove the 1st gear and blocker ring from mainshaft.
6. Scribe an alignment mark on 1st/2nd synchronizer hub and sleeve for reassembly.
7. Remove the synchronizer springs and keys from 1st/2nd sleeve and remove sleeve from the shaft.

NOTE: Do not attempt to remove the 1st/2nd hub from the mainshaft. The hub and mainshaft are assembled and machined as a unit.

8. Remove the loading tool J–26624 or equivalent, roller bearings, spacers and thrust washers from the countershaft gear.

Inspection

1. Inspect all drive gear bearing rollers for wear.
2. Inspect all gears for excessive wear, chips or cracks and replace any that are worn or damaged.
3. Check the clutch sleeves to see that they slide freely on their hubs.
4. Inspect all synchronizers for wear.

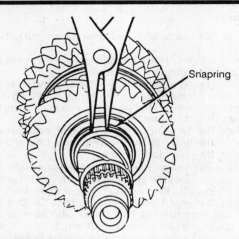

Second gear snapring — 5-speed

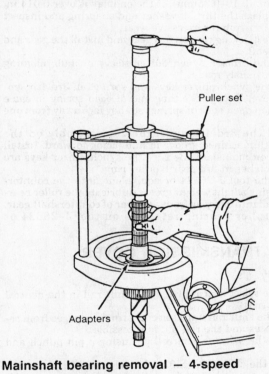

Mainshaft bearing removal — 4-speed

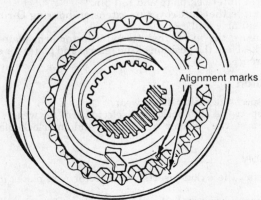

Marking synchronizer assembly — 4-speed

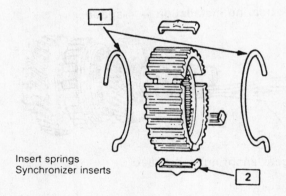

Insert springs
Synchronizer inserts

Synchronizer insert spring — 4-speed

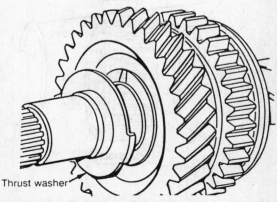

Thrust washer

First gear thrust washer — 4-speed

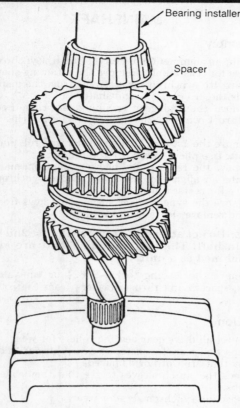

Mainshaft bearing installation — 4-speed

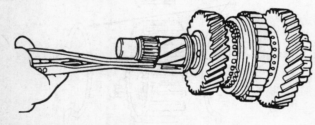

Second gear snapring — 4-speed

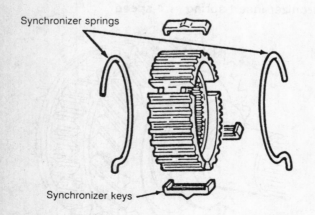

Synchronizer spring installation — 5-speed

Assembly

1. Coat the mainshaft and gear bores with transmission lubricant.

2. Install the 1st/2nd synchronizer sleeve on mainshaft, aligning marks previously made.

3. Install the synchronizer keys and springs into the 1st/2nd synchronizer sleeve. Engage the tang end of springs into the same synchronizer key but position open ends of springs so they face away from one another.

4. Place the blocking ring on 1st gear and install gear and ring on mainshaft. Be sure the synchronizer keys engage notches in 1st gear blocking ring.

5. Install the 1st gear roll pin in the mainshaft.

6. Place the blocking ring on 2nd gear and install gear and ring on mainshaft. Be sure the synchronizer keys engage the notches in 2nd gear blocking ring. Install the 2nd gear thrust washer and snapring on the mainshaft. Be sure the thrust washer tab is engaged in mainshaft notch.

7. Measure the 2nd gear endplay using a feeler gauge. Insert a gauge between gear and thrust washer. The endplay should be 0.004–0.014 in. (0.10–0.35mm). If the endplay is over 0.014 in. (0.35mm), replace the thrust washer and snapring and inspect the synchronizer hub for excessive wear.

8. Place the blocking ring on 3rd gear and install the gear and ring on mainshft.

9. Install the 3rd/4th synchronizer sleeve on hub, aligning the marks previously made.

10. Install the synchronizer keys and springs in 3rd/4th synchronizer sleeve. Engage the tang end of each spring in same key but position open ends of springs so they face away from one another.

11. Install the 3rd/4th synchronizer assembly on the mainshaft with machined groove in hub facing forward. Install the snapring on mainshaft. Be sure the synchronizer keys are engaged in notches in 3rd gear blocker ring.

12. Install the tool J–26624 or equivalent, into the countershaft gear. Using a light weight grease, lubricate the roller bearings and install into bores at front and rear of countershaft gear. Install the roller bearing retainers on tool J–26624 or equivalent.

TRANSMISSION COVER

Disassembly

1. Place the selector arm plates and shift rail in the neutral position (centered).

2. Rotate the shift rail until selector arm disengages from selector arm plates and the roll pin is accessible.

3. Remove the selector arm roll pin using a pin punch and hammer.

4. Remove the shift rail, shift forks, selector arm plates, selector arm, interlock plate and roll pin.

5. Remove the shift cover to extension housing O-ring seal using a suitable tool.

6. Remove the nylon inserts and selector arm plates from shift forks. Note the position of the inserts and plates for assembly reference.

Inspection

1. Inspect the shift rail for wear.
2. Inspect the shift forks and selector arm for wear.
3. Inspect the selector arm plates and interlock plate for wear.

Assembly

1. Install the nylon inserts and selector arm plates in shift forks.

2. If removed, install the shift rail plug. Coat the edges of plug with sealer before installing.

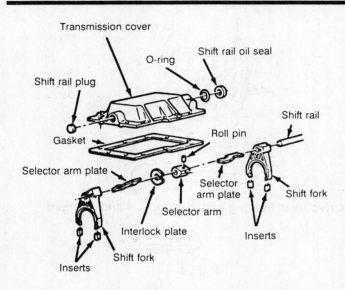

Transmission cover exploded view — 4 and 5-speed

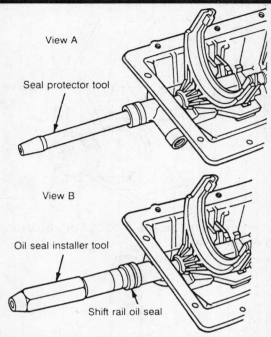

Shift rail oil seal installation — 4 and 5-speed

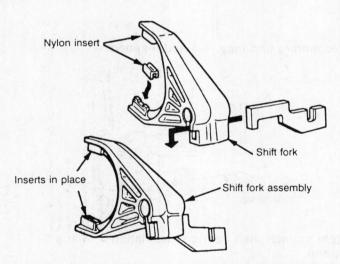

Shift forks and selector arm plates — 4 and 5-speed

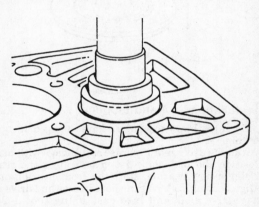

Front countershaft bearing installation — 4 and 5-speed

3. Coat the shift rail and rail bores with light weight grease and insert shift rail in cover. Install the rail until flush with inside edge of cover.

4. Place the 1st/2nd shift fork in cover with fork offset facing rear of cover and push the shift rail through fork. The 1st/2nd shift fork is the larger of the 2 forks.

5. Position the selector arm and C-shaped interlock plate in the cover and insert shift rail through the arm. Widest part of the interlock plate must face away from the cover and selector arm roll pin hole must face downward and toward rear of the cover.

6. Position the 3rd/4th shift fork in cover with fork offset facing rear of the cover. The 3rd/4th shift fork selector arm plate must be under 1st/2nd shift for selector arm plate.

7. Push the shift rail through 3rd/4th shift fork and into front bore in cover.

8. Rotate the shift rail until selector arm plate at the forward end of rail faces away from, but is parallel to the cover.

9. Align the roll pin holes in selector arm and shift rail and install the roll pin. The roll pin must be flush with surface of selector arm to prevent pin from contacting selector arm plates during shifts.

10. Install a new shift cover to extension housing O-ring seal. Coat the O-ring seal with transmission lubricant.

TRANSMISSION ASSEMBLY

1. Coat the countershaft gear thrust washers with petroleum jelly and position washer in the case.

2. Position the countershaft gear in case and install the countershaft from rear of case. Be sure that the thrust washers stay in place during installation of countershaft and gear.

3. Position the reverse idler gear in case with shift lever groove facing rear of case and install the reverse idler shaft from rear of case. Install roll pin in shaft and center pin in shaft.

4. Install the mainshaft assembly into the case. Do not disturb position of the synchronizer assemblies during installation.

5. Install the 4th gear blocking ring in 3rd/4th synchronizer

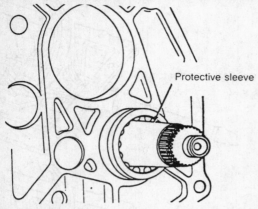

Installing protector sleeve J–33032 or equivalent — 4 and 5-speed

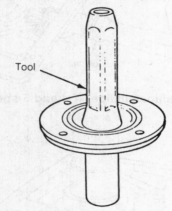

Seal installation — 4 and 5-speed

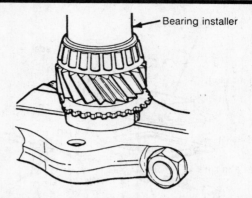

Drive gear bearing installation — 4 and 5-speed

Measuring end play — 4 and 5-speed

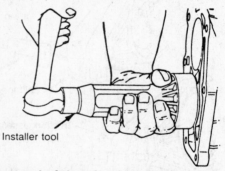

Rear countershaft bearing installation — 4 and 5-speed

sleeve. Be sure the synchronizer keys engaged in notches in blocker ring.

6. Install the drive gear into case and engage with mainshaft.

7. Position the mainshaft 1st gear against the rear of the case. Using a new bearing, start the front bearing onto drive gear. Align bearing with bearing bore in case and drive the bearing onto drive gear and into case using tool J–25234 or equivalent.

8. Install the front bearing retaining and locating snaprings.

9. Apply a 1/8 in. (3mm) diameter bead of RTV sealant, No. 732 or equivalent, on case mating surface of the front bearing cap. Install the bearing cap aligning marks previously made. Apply non-hardening sealer on attaching bolts and install bolts. Torque the bolts to specification.

10. Install the 1st gear thrust washer with oil grove facing 1st gear on mainshaft, aligning the slot in washer with 1st gear roll pin.

11. Using a new bearing, position rear bearing on the mainshaft. Align the bearing with bearing bore in case and drive bearing into case using tool J–25234 or equivalent.

12. Install the locating and retaining snaprings on rear bearing.

13. Install the speedometer gear and retaining clip on mainshaft.

14. Apply non-hardening sealer to the threads of reverse lever pivot bolt and start bolt into case. Engage the reverse lever fork in the reverse idler gear and reverse lever on pivot bolt. Tighten the bolt to specifications and install retaining clip.

15. Rotate the drive gear and mainshaft gear. If blocker rings tend to stick on gears, release the rings by gently prying them off the cones.

16. Apply a 1/8 in. (3mm) diameter bead or RTV sealant, No. 732 or equivalent, on the cover mating surface of transmission. Place the reverse lever in neutral and position cover on case.

17. Install 2 dowel type bolts first to align cover on the case. Install the remaining cover bolts and torque to specifications. The offset lever to shift rail roll pin hole must be in the vertical position after cover installation.

18. Apply a 1/8 in. (3mm) diameter bead of RTV sealant, No. 732 or equivalent, on the extension housing to transmission case mating surface.

19. Place the extension housing over mainshaft to a position where shift rail is in the shift cover opening.

20. Install the detent spring in offset lever. Place the ball in neutral guide plate detent position. Apply pressure on the offset lever, slide offset lever onto shift rail and seat extension housing to transmission case.

21. Install the extension housing retaining bolts. Torque bolts to specifications.

22. Align the hole in offset lever and shift rail and install roll pin.

23. Fill the transmission to its proper level with recommended lubricant.

Extension housing-to-transmission case — 5-speed

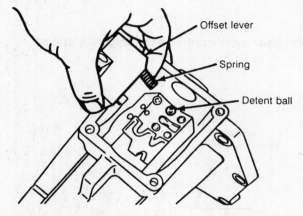

Detent ball and spring — 5-speed

Offset lever

Spring

Detent ball

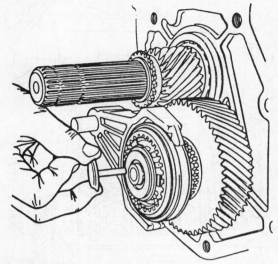

Plastic funnel — 5-speed

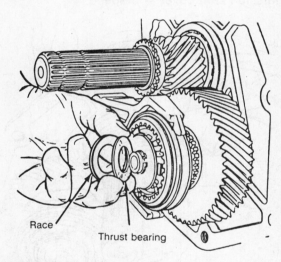

Race

Thrust bearing

Thrust bearing and race — 5 — speed

5-Speed Overhaul

Before Disassembly

Cleanliness is an important factor in the overhaul of the transmission. Before attempting any disassembly operation, the exterior of the transmission should be thoroughly cleaned to prevent the possibility of dirt entering the transmission internal mechanism. During inspection and reassembly, all parts should be thoroughly cleaned with cleaning fluid and then air dried. Wiping cloths or rags should not be used to dry parts. All oil passages should be blown out and checked to make sure that they are not obstructed. Small passages should be checked with tag wire. All parts should be inspected to determine which parts are to be replaced.

CASE DISASSEMBLY

1. Remove the drain plug on transmission case and drain lubricant.
2. Thoroughly clean the exterior of the transmission assembly.
3. Using a pin punch and hammer, remove the roll pin attaching offset lever-to-shift rail.
4. Remove the extension housing to transmission case bolts and remove the housing and offset lever as an assembly. Do not attempt to remove the offset lever while the extension housing

is still bolted in place. The lever has a positioning lug engaged in the housing detent plate which prevents moving the lever far enough for removal.

5. Remove the detent ball and spring from the offset lever and remove the roll pin from the extension housing or offset lever.
6. Remove the plastic funnel, thrust bearing race and thrust bearing from rear of countershaft. The countershaft rear thrust bearing, bearing washer and plastic funnel may be found inside the extension housing.
7. Remove the bolts attaching transmission cover and shift fork assembly and remove cover. Two of the transmission cover attaching bolts are alignment-type dowel bolts. Note the location of these bolts for assembly reference.
8. Using a punch and hammer, drive the roll pin from the 5th gearshift fork while supporting the end of the shaft with a block of wood.

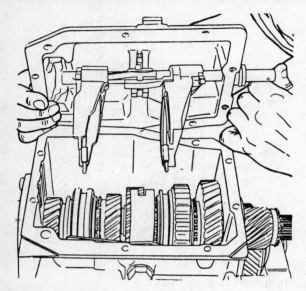

Transmission shift cover — 5-speed

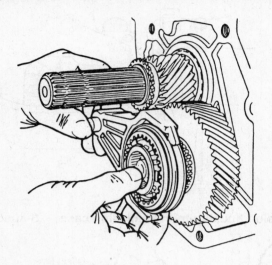

Fifth gear synchronizer servicing — 5-speed

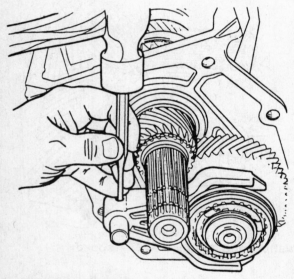

Fifth gear shift fork roll pin — 5-speed

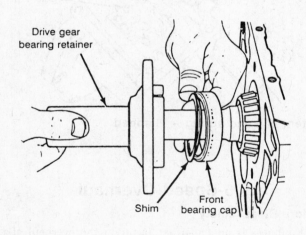

Bearing cap and shims — 5-speed

9. Remove the 5th synchronizer gear snapring, shift fork, 5th gear synchronizer sleeve, blocking ring and 5th speed drive gear from the rear of countershaft.

10. Remove the snapring from the 5th speed driven gear.

11. Using a hammer and punch, mark both bearing caps and case for assembly reference.

12. Remove the front bearing cap bolts and remove front bearing cap. Remove the front bearing race and end play shims from front bearing cap.

13. Rotate the drive gear until flat surface faces counter shaft and remove the drive gear from transmission case.

14. Remove the reverse lever C-clip and pivot bolt.

15. Remove the mainshaft rear bearing race and then tilt mainshaft assembly upward and remove the assembly from transmission case.

16. Unhook the overcenter link spring from front of transmission case.

17. Rotate the 5th gear/reverse shift rail to disengage the rail from reverse lever assembly. Remove the shift rail from rear of transmission case.

18. Remove the reverse lever and fork assembly from transmission case.

19. Using a hammer and punch, the drive roll pin from forward end of reverse idler shaft and remove the reverse idler shaft, rubber O-ring and gear from the transmission case.

20. Remove the rear countershaft snapring and spacer.

21. Insert a brass drift through drive gear opening in front of transmission case and, using an arbor press, carefully press countershaft rearward to remove rear countershaft bearing.

22. Move the countershaft assembly rearward, tilt countershaft upward and remove from the case. Remove the countershaft front thrust washer and rear bearing spacer.

23. Remove the countershaft front bearing from transmission case using an arbor press.

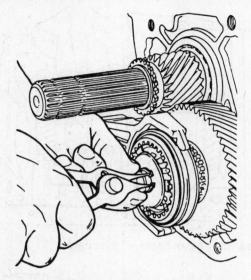

Fifth gear synchronizer snapring — 5-speed

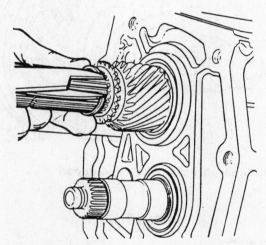

Fifth speed gear snapring — 5-speed

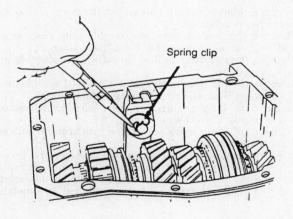

Reverse lever retaining clip — 5-speed

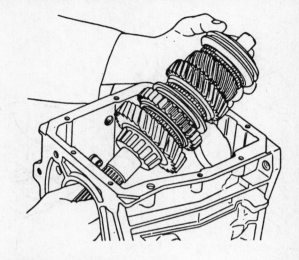

Mainshaft servicing — 5-speed

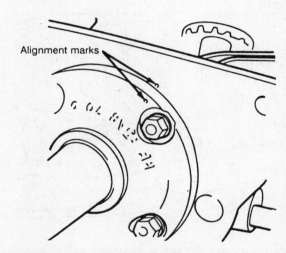

Alignment marks

Bearing cap-to-case alignment — 5-speed

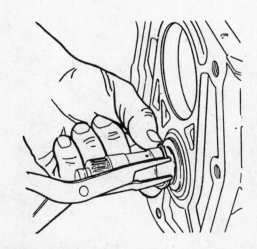

Countershaft snapring and spacer — 5-speed

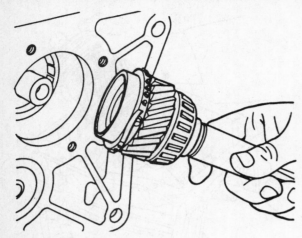

Drive gear servicing — 5-speed

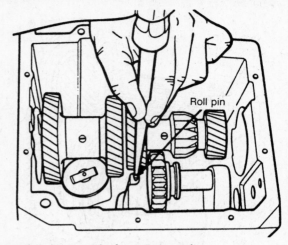

Reverse idler gear shaft — 5-speed

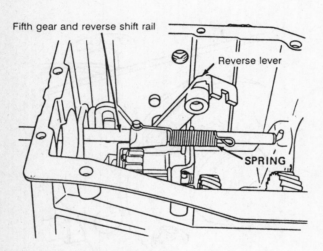

Fifth gear/reverse shift rail — 5-speed

Second gear thrust washer — 4-speed

MAINSHAFT

Disassembly

1. Remove the thrust bearing washer from front end of mainshaft.
2. Scribe a reference mark on the 3rd/4th synchronizer hub and sleeve for reassembly.
3. Remove the 3rd/4th synchronizer blocking ring, sleeve, hub and 3rd gear as an assembly from the mainshaft.
4. Remove the snapring, tabbed thrust washer and 2nd gear from the mainshaft.
5. Remove the 5th gear with tool J–22912–01 or equivalent and arbor press. Slide the rear bearing of mainshaft.
6. Remove the 1st gear thrust washer, roll pin, 1st gear and synchronizer ring from the mainshaft.
7. Scribe a reference mark on 1st/2nd synchronizer hub and sleeve for reassembly.
8. Remove the synchronizer spring and keys from 1st/reverse sliding gear and remove gear from mainshaft hub. Do not attempt to remove the 1st/2nd reverse hub from the mainshaft. The hub and shaft are assembled and machined as a matched set.

Inspection

1. Inspect all drive gear bearing rollers for wear.

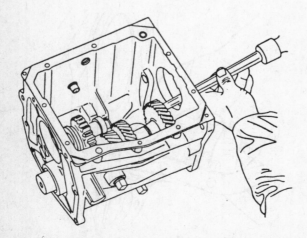

Rear countershaft bearing removal — 5-speed

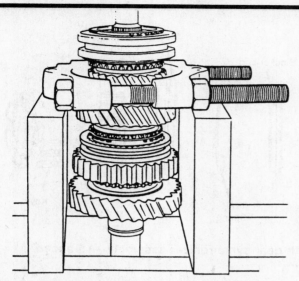

3rd/4th synchronizer removal — 5-speed

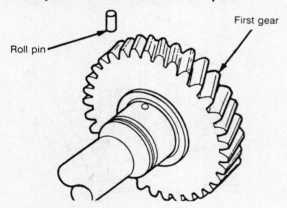

First gear roll pin — 4-speed

2. Inspect all gears for excessive wear, chips or cracks and replace any that are worn or damaged.

3. Check the clutch sleeves to see that they slide freely on their hubs.

4. Inspect all synchronizers for wear.

Assembly

1. Coat the mainshaft and gear bores with transmission lubricant.

2. Install the 1st/2nd synchronizer sleeve on the mainshaft hub aligning marks made at disassembly.

3. Install the 1st/2nd synchronizer keys and springs. Engage the tang end of each spring in same synchronizer key but position open end of springs opposite of each other.

4. Install the blocker ring and 2nd gear on mainshaft. Install the tabbed thrust washer and 2nd gear retaining snapring on the mainshaft. Be sure the washer tab is properly seated in the mainshaft notch.

5. Install the blocker ring and 1st gear on mainshaft. Install the 1st gear roll pin and then 1st gear thrust washer.

6. Slide the rear bearing on mainshaft.

7. Install the 5th speed gear on mainshaft using tool J-22912-01 or equivalent and arbor press. Install the snapring on mainshaft.

8. Install the 3rd gear, 3rd/4th synchronizer assembly and thrust bearing on mainshaft. The synchronizer hub offset must face forward.

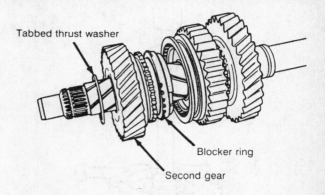

Second gear and thrust washer — 5-speed

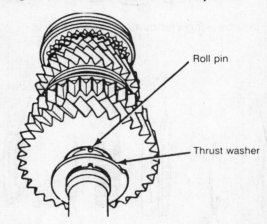

First gear thrust washer and roll pin — 5-speed

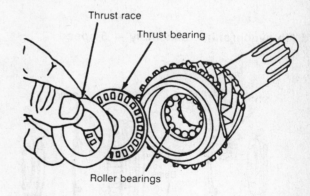

Drive gear thrust bearing and race — 5-speed

DRIVE GEAR

Disassembly

1. Remove the bearing race, thrust bearing and roller bearings from the cavity of drive gear.

2. Using tool J-22912-01 or equivalent and an arbor press, remove the bearing from drive gear.

3. Wash the parts in a cleaning solvent.

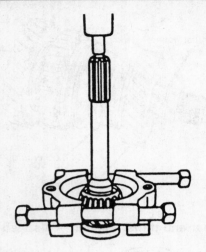

Drive gear bearing removal — 5-speed

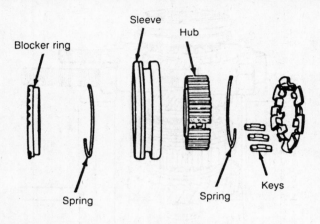

Fifth gear synchronizer assembly — 5-speed

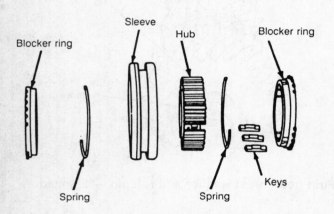

3rd/4th synchronizer assembly — 5-speed

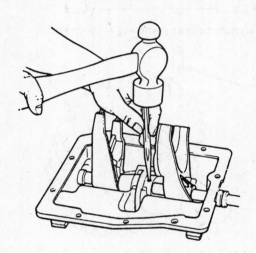

Roll pin removal — 4 and 5-speed

Inspection

1. Inspect the gear teeth for wear.
2. Inspect the drive shaft pilot for wear.

Assembly

1. Using tool J–22912–01 or equivalent with an arbor press, install the bearing on drive gear.
2. Coat the roller bearings and drive gear bearing bore with grease. Install the roller bearings into bore of drive gear.
3. Install the thrust bearing and race in drive gear.

TRANSMISSION COVER

Disassembly

1. Place the selector arm plates and shift rail in the neutral position (centered).
2. Rotate the shift rail until selector arm disengages from selector arm plates and the roll pin is accessible.
3. Remove the selector arm roll pin using a pin punch and hammer.
4. Remove the shift rail, shift forks, selector arm plates, selector arm, interlock plate and roll pin.

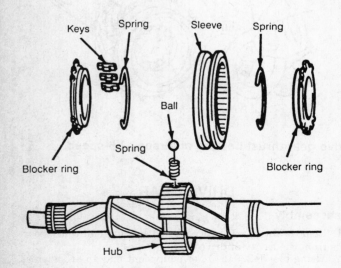

1st/2nd synchronizer assembly — 5-speed

5. Remove the shift cover to extension housing O-ring seal using a suitable tool.

6. Remove the nylon inserts and selector arm plates from shift forks. Note the position of the inserts and plates for assembly reference.

Inspection

1. Inspect the shift rail for wear.
2. Inspect the shift forks and selector arm for wear.
3. Inspect the selector arm plates and interlock plate for wear.

Assembly

1. Install the nylon inserts and selector arm plates in shift forks.

2. If removed, install the shift rail plug. Coat the edges of plug with sealer before installing.

3. Coat the shift rail and rail bores with light weight grease and insert shift rail in cover. Install the rail until flush with inside edge of cover.

4. Place the 1st/2nd shift fork in cover with fork offset facing rear of cover and push the shift rail through fork. The 1st/2nd shift fork is the larger of the 2 forks.

5. Position the selector arm and C-shaped interlock plate in the cover and insert shift rail through the arm. Widest part of the interlock plate must face away from the cover and selector arm roll pin hole must face downward and toward rear of the cover.

6. Position the 3rd/4th shift fork in cover with fork offset facing rear of the cover. The 3rd/4th shift fork selector arm plate must be under 1st/2nd shift for selector arm plate.

7. Push the shift rail through 3rd/4th shift fork and into front bore in cover.

8. Rotate the shift rail until selector arm plate at the forward end of rail faces away from, but is parallel to the cover.

9. Align the roll pin holes in selector arm and shift rail and install the roll pin. The roll pin must be flush with surface of selector arm to prevent pin from contacting selector arm plates during shifts.

10. Install a new shift cover to extension housing O-ring seal. Coat the O-ring seal with transmission lubricant.

TRANSMISSION ASSEMBLY

1. Coat the countershaft front bearing bore with Loctite® 601, or equivalent and install the front countershaft bearing flush with facing of case using an arbor press.

2. Coat the countershaft tabbed thrust washer with grease and install washer so tab engages depression in case.

3. Tip transmission case on end and install the countershaft in front bearing bore.

4. Install the countershaft rear bearing spacer. Coat the countershaft rear bearing with grease and install the bearing using tool J–29895 or equivalent and sleeve J–33032, or its equivalent. The bearing when correctly installed will extend beyond the case surface 0.125 in. (3mm).

5. Position the reverse idler gear in case with shift lever groove facing rear of case and install the reverse idler shaft from rear of case. Install roll pin in idler shaft.

6. Install assembled mainshaft into transmission case. Install the rear mainshaft bearing race in case.

7. Install the drive gear in case and engage in 3rd/4th synchronizer sleeve and blocker ring.

8. Install the front bearing race in front bearing cap. Do not install shims in front bearing cap at this time.

9. Temporarily install the front bearing cap.

10. Install the 5th speed/reverse lever, pivot bolt and retaining clip. Coat pivot bolt threads with non-hardening sealer. Be sure to engage reverse lever fork in reverse idler gear.

11. Install the countershaft rear bearing spacer and retaining snapring.

12. Install the 5th speed gear on countershaft.

13. Insert the 5th speed/reverse rail in rear of case and install into reverse 5th speed lever. Rotate the rail during installation to simplify engagement with lever. Connect the spring to front of case.

14. Position the 5th gear shift fork on 5th gear synchronizer assembly and install synchronizer on countershaft and shift fork on shift rail. Make sure the roll pin hole in shift fork and shift rail are aligned.

15. Support the 5th gear shift rail and fork on a block of wood and install roll pin.

16. Install the thrust race against 5th speed synchronizer hub and install snapring. Install the thrust bearing against race on countershaft. Coat both bearing and race with petroleum jelly.

17. Install the lipped thrust race over needle-type thrust bearing and install plastic funnel into hole in end of countershaft gear.

18. Temporarily install the extension housing and attaching bolts. Turn the transmission case on end and mount a dial indicator on extension housing with indicator on the end of mainshaft.

19. Rotate the mainshaft and "zero" the dial indicator. Pull upward on mainshaft until endplay is removed and record reading. Mainshaft bearings require a preload of 0.001–0.005 in. (0.025–0.127mm) to set preload, select a shim pack measuring 0.001–0.005 in. (0.025–0.127mm) greater than the dial indicator reading recorded.

20. Remove the front bearing cap and front bearing race Install necessary shims to obtain preload and reinstall bearing race.

21. Apply a ⅛ in. (3mm) bead of RTV sealant, No. 732 or equivalent, on case mating surface of front bearing cap. Install the bearing cap aligning marks made during disassembly and torque bolts to specification.

22. Remove the extension housing.

23. Move the shift forks on transmission cover and synchronizer sleeves inside transmission to the neutral position.

24. Apply a ⅛ in. (3mm) bead of RTV sealant, No. 732 or equivalent, or cover mating surface of transmission.

25. Lower the cover onto case while aligning shift forks and synchronizer sleeves. Center the cover and install the 2 dowel bolts. Install remaining bolts and torque to specification. The offset lever to shift rail roll pin hole must be in the vertical position after cover installation.

26. Apply a ⅛ in. (3mm) bead of RTV sealant, No. 732 or equivalent, on extension housing to transmission case mating surface.

27. Install the extension housing over mainshaft and shift rail to a position where shift rail just enters shift cover opening.

28. Install the detent spring into offset lever and place steel ball in neutral guide plate detent. Position the offset lever on steel ball and apply pressure on offset lever and at the time seat extension housing against transmission case.

29. Install the extension housing bolts and torque to specification.

30. Align and install the roll pin in offset lever and shift rail.

31. Fill transmission to its proper level with lubricant.

CLUTCH

Astro/Safari vans use a hydraulic clutch system which consists of a master and a slave cylinder. When pressure is applied to the clutch pedal (pedal depressed), the push rod contacts the plunger and pushes it up the bore of the master cylinder. During the first $\frac{1}{32}$ in. (0.8mm) of movement, the center valve seal closes the port to the fluid reservoir tank and as the plunger continues to move up the bore of the cylinder, the fluid is forced through the outlet line to the slave cylinder mounted on the clutch housing. As fluid is pushed down the pipe from the master cylinder, this in turn forces the piston in the slave cylinder outward. A push rod is connected to the slave cylinder and rides in the pocket of the clutch fork. As the slave cylinder piston moves rearward the push rod forces the clutch fork and the release bearing to disengage the pressure plate from the clutch disc. On the return stroke (pedal released), the plunger moves back as a result of the return pressure of the clutch. Fluid returns to the master cylinder and the final movement of the plunger lifts the valve seal off the seat, allowing an unrestricted flow of fluid between the system and the reservoir.

A piston return spring in the slave cylinder preloads the clutch linkage and assures contact of the release bearing with the clutch release fingers at all times. As the driven disc wears, the diaphragm spring fingers move rearward forcing the release bearing, fork and push rod to move. This movement forces the slave cylinder piston forward in its bore, displacing hydraulic fluid up into the master cylinder reservoir, thereby providing the self-adjusting feature of the hydraulic clutch linkage system.

Before attempting to repair the clutch, transmission, hydraulic system or related linkages for any reason other than an obvious failure, the problem and probable cause should be identified. A large percentage of clutch and manual transmission problems are manifested by shifting difficulties such as high shift effort, gear clash and grinding or transmission blockout. When any of these problems occur, a careful analysis of these difficulties should be made, then the basic checks and adjustments performed before removing the clutch or transmission for repairs. Run the engine at a normal idle with the transmission in Neutral (clutch engaged). Disengage the clutch, wait about 10 seconds and shift the transmission into Reverse (no grinding noise should be heard). A grinding noise indicates incorrect clutch travel, lost motion, clutch misalignment or internal problems such as failed dampers, facings, cushion springs, diaphragm spring fingers, pressure plate drive straps, pivot rings or etc.

Adjustments

Since the hydraulic system provides automatic clutch adjustment, no adjustment of the clutch linkage or pedal height is required.

Clutch Disc and Pressure Plate
REMOVAL AND INSTALLATION

—————— CAUTION ——————
The clutch plate contains asbestos, which has been determined to be a cancer causing agent. Never clean the clutch surfaces with compressed air! Avoid inhaling any dust from any clutch surface! When cleaning clutch surfaces, use a commercially available brake cleaning fluid.

1. Refer to the Transmission, Removal and Installation procedures in this section and remove the transmission from the vehicle.
2. Remove the slave cylinder attaching bolts and the bell housing.

3. Slide the clutch fork from the ball stud and remove the fork from the dust boot.

NOTE: The ball stud is threaded into the clutch housing and can be easily replaced.

4. Install the Clutch Pilot tool No. J–33169 into the clutch plate to support it during removal.
5. The flywheel and clutch cover are marked with X's for correct assembly or white painted letters, if these are not visible, scribe new marks.
6. Gradually loosen the clutch-to-flywheel bolts (one turn at a time) until all of the spring pressure is released.
7. Remove the bolts and the clutch assembly.

NOTE: The clutch pilot bearing is an oil impregnated type bearing pressed into the crankshaft. This bearing requires attention when the clutch is removed from the vehicle, at which time it should be cleaned and inspected for excessive wear or damage and should be replaced (if necessary).

To install:
1. Crank the engine over by hand until the X-mark on the flywheel is on the bottom.
2. Position the clutch disc and pressure plate in the same relative location as removed and support with the clutch pilot tool.

NOTE: The clutch disc is installed with the damper springs and slinger toward the transmission.

3. Rotate the clutch assembly until the X-marks on the flywheel and clutch assembly align. Align the cover bolt holes with those in the flywheel.
4. Install the bolts, then tighten evenly and gradually. Install the remaining bolts. Torque the bolts evenly to 15–22 ft. lbs. (20–29 Nm). Do NOT overtighten.
5. Remove the clutch pilot tool.
6. Lubricate the ball socket on the clutch fork and reinstall on the ball stud.
7. Pack the recess on the inside of the throw out bearing collar and the throw out groove with graphite grease.
8. Install the bell housing and the slave cylinder.
9. Install the throw out bearing on the fork. Lubricate the bearing groove.

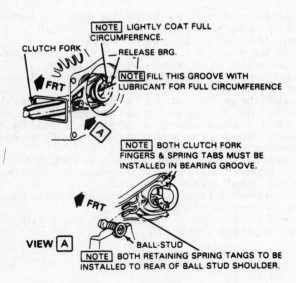

Clutch release bearing lubrication points — typical

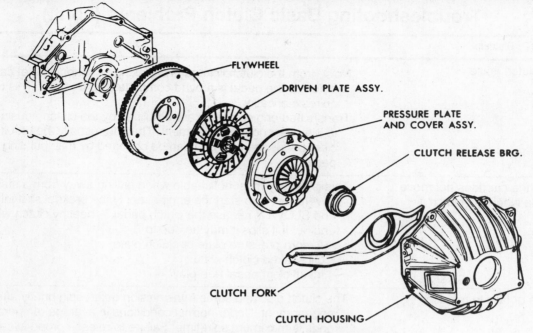

Exploded view of the clutch assembly

1. Clutch cover
2. Fork ball stud
3. Main drive gear bearing retainer
4. Release bearing
5. Diaphragm spring
6. Clutch fork
7. Pressure plate
8. Driven disc
9. Pilot bearing
10. Flywheel

Cross-section view of the clutch assembly

CLUTCH

Troubleshooting Basic Clutch Problems

Problem	Cause
Excessive clutch noise	Throwout bearing noises are more audible at the lower end of pedal travel. The usual causes are: • Riding the clutch • Too little pedal free-play • Lack of bearing lubrication A bad clutch shaft pilot bearing will make a high pitched squeal, when the clutch is disengaged and the transmission is in gear or within the first 2″ of pedal travel. The bearing must be replaced.

Troubleshooting Basic Clutch Problems (cont.)

Problem	Cause
Excessive clutch noise	Noise from the clutch linkage is a clicking or snapping that can be heard or felt as the pedal is moved completely up or down. This usually requires lubrication. Transmitted engine noises are amplified by the clutch housing and heard in the passenger compartment. They are usually the result of insufficient pedal free-play and can be changed by manipulating the clutch pedal.
Clutch slips (the car does not move as it should when the clutch is engaged)	This is usually most noticeable when pulling away from a standing start. A severe test is to start the engine, apply the brakes, shift into high gear and SLOWLY release the clutch pedal. A healthy clutch will stall the engine. If it slips it may be due to: • A worn pressure plate or clutch plate • Oil soaked clutch plate • Insufficient pedal free-play
Clutch drags or fails to release	The clutch disc and some transmission gears spin briefly after clutch disengagement. Under normal conditions in average temperatures, 3 seconds is maximum spin-time. Failure to release properly can be caused by: • Too light transmission lubricant or low lubricant level • Improperly adjusted clutch linkage
Low clutch life	Low clutch life is usually a result of poor driving habits or heavy duty use. Riding the clutch, pulling heavy loads, holding the car on a grade with the clutch instead of the brakes and rapid clutch engagement all contribute to low clutch life.

10. Observe the following torques.
  • pressure plate-to-flywheel bolts: 15–22 ft. lbs. for the 4-speed or 25–35 ft. lbs. for the 5-speed
  • flywheel-to-crankshaft bolts: 60–75 ft. lbs. for the 4-speed or 55–75 ft. lbs. for the 5-speed
  • slave cylinder-to-bellhousing bolts: 10–15 ft. lbs.

NOTE: If replacing an MR2, 4-speed transmission, lubricate and adjust the transmission shift linkages.

Pilot Bearing

REMOVAL AND INSTALLATION

1. Disconnect the negative (−) battery cable.

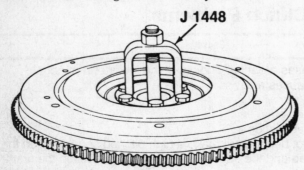

J 1448

Pilot bearing removing tool

2. Remove the transmission, bellhousing and clutch assembly from the vehicle as outlined in this Section.
3. Using a pilot bearing removing tool J–1448, remove the pilot bearing from the crankshaft.
To install:
1. Using a pilot bearing installing tool J–1522, install the new pilot bearing. Lubricate the bearing with chassis grease before installing the transmission.
2. Install the clutch, bellhousing and transmission assembly into the vehicle.
3. Connect the negative battery cable and check operation.

Clutch Pedal

REMOVAL AND INSTALLATION

1. Disconnect the negative (−) battery cable.
2. Remove the hush panel and clutch start switch.
3. Remove the retainer (105), washer and pin.
4. Remove the pushrod, retainer and clutch pedal. Slide a long screw or rod through the bracket while removing the clutch pedal to hold the brake pedal in place.
5. Remove the bushings and spring.
To install:
1. Install a new spring and bushings.
2. Install the clutch pedal while removing the long screw or rod.
3. Install a new retainer, pushrod, pin, washer and retainer.
4. Install the clutch start switch, hush panel and negative battery cable.

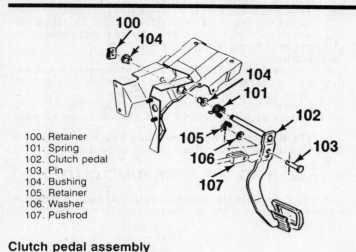

100. Retainer
101. Spring
102. Clutch pedal
103. Pin
104. Bushing
105. Retainer
106. Washer
107. Pushrod

Clutch pedal assembly

5. Lubricate the clutch pedal with chassis grease and adjust the clutch start switch as outlined in this Section under the "Clutch Switch".

Master Cylinder

The clutch master cylinder is located in the engine compartment, on the left side of the firewall, above the steering column.

REMOVAL AND INSTALLATION

1. Disconnect negative battery cable.
2. Remove hush panel from under the dash.
3. Disconnect push rod from clutch pedal.
4. Disconnect hydraulic line from the clutch master cylinder using a flare nut wrench.
5. Remove the master cylinder-to-cowl brace nuts. Remove master cylinder and overhaul (if necessary).
6. Using a putty knife, clean the master cylinder and cowl mounting surfaces.

To install:
1. Install the master cylinder-to-cowl brace nuts and master cylinder.
2. Connect hydraulic line to the clutch master cylinder using a flare nut wrench.
3. Connect push rod to clutch pedal.
4. Install hush panel to the dash.
5. Connect negative battery cable.
6. Torque the master cylinder-to-cowl brace nuts to 10–15 ft. lbs. (14–20 Nm). Fill master cylinder with new hydraulic fluid conforming to Dot 3 specifications.
7. Bleed and check the hydraulic clutch system for leaks.

OVERHAUL

1. Remove the filler cap and drain fluid from the master cylinder.
2. Remove the reservoir and seal from the master cylinder. Pull back the dust cover and remove the snapring.
3. Remove the pushrod assembly. Using a block of wood, tap the master cylinder on it to eject the plunger assembly from the cylinder bore.
4. Remove the seal (carefully) from the front of the plunger assembly, ensuring no damage occurs to the plunger surfaces.
5. From the rear of the plunger assembly, remove the spring, the support, the seal and the shim.
6. Using clean brake fluid, clean all of the parts.

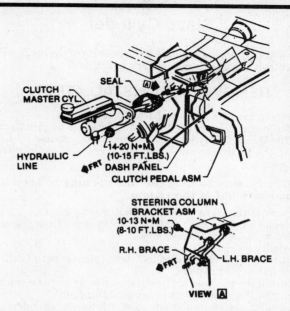

Exploded view of the clutch master cylinder-to-cowl assembly

107. Pushrod
140. Reservoir
144. Master cylinder
220. Seal
222. Support
223. Shim
224. Plunger
225. Seal
226. Seal
227. Snap ring
228. Dust cover
229. Spring

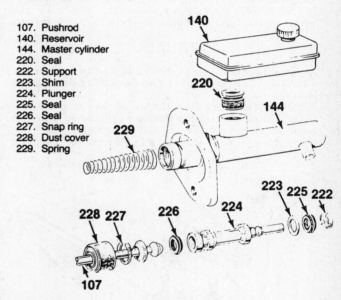

Exploded view of the clutch master cylinder

7. Inspect the cylinder bore and the plunger for ridges, pitting and/or scratches; the dust cover for wear and cracking; replace the parts if any of the conditions exist.

To install:
8. Use new seals, lubricate all of the parts in clean brake fluid, and fit the plunger seal to the plunger.
9. Insert the plunger assembly, valve end leading into the cylinder bore (easing the entrance of the plunger seal).
10. Position the push rod assembly into the cylinder bore, then install a new snapring to retain the push rod. Install dust cover onto the master cylinder. Lubricate the inside of the dust cover with Girling® Rubber Grease or equivalent.

NOTE: Be careful not to use any lubricant that will deteriorate rubber dust covers or seals.

Slave Cylinder

The slave cylinder is located on the left side of the bellhousing and controls the clutch release fork operation.

REMOVAL AND INSTALLATION

1. Disconnect the negative battery cable.
2. Raise and support the front of the vehicle on jackstands.
3. Disconnect the hydraulic line from clutch master cylinder. Remove the hydraulic line-to-chassis screw and the clip from the chassis.

NOTE: Be sure to plug the line opening to keep dirt and moisture out of the system.

4. Remove the slave cylinder-to-bellhousing nuts.
5. Remove the pushrod and the slave cylinder from the vehicle, then overhaul it (if necessary).

To install:
1. Lubricate leading end of the slave cylinder with Girling® Rubber Lube or equivalent.
2. Install the pushrod and the slave cylinder into the vehicle.
3. Install the slave cylinder-to-bellhousing nuts.
4. Connect the hydraulic line to clutch master cylinder.
5. Lower the front of the vehicle.
6. Connect the negative battery cable.
7. Torque the slave cylinder-to-bellhousing nuts to 10–15 ft. lbs. (14–20 Nm). Fill the master cylinder with new brake fluid conforming to Dot 3 specifications. Bleed the hydraulic system.

OVERHAUL

1. Remove the shield, the pushrod and dust cover from the slave cylinder, then inspect the cover for damage or deterioration.
2. Remove the snapring from the end of the cylinder bore.
3. Using a block of wood, tap the slave cylinder on it to eject the plunger, then remove the seal and the spring.
4. Using clean brake fluid, clean all of the parts.

5. Inspect the cylinder bore and the plunger for ridges, pitting and/or scratches, the dust cover for wear and cracking; replace the parts if any of the conditions exist.

To install:
6. Use new seals and lubricate all of the parts in clean brake fluid. Install the spring, the plunger seal and the plunger into the cylinder bore, then install a new snapring.
7. Lubricate the inside of the dust cover with Girling® Rubber Grease or equivalent, then install it into the slave cylinder.

NOTE: Be careful not to use any lubricant that will deteriorate the rubber dust covers or seals.

BLEEDING THE HYDRAULIC CLUTCH

Bleeding air from the hydraulic clutch system is necessary whenever any part of the system has been disconnected or the

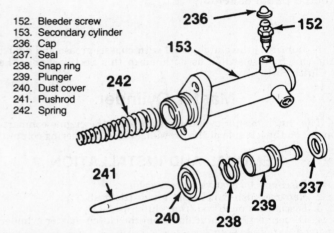

152. Bleeder screw
153. Secondary cylinder
236. Cap
237. Seal
238. Snap ring
239. Plunger
240. Dust cover
241. Pushrod
242. Spring

Exploded view of the clutch slave cylinder

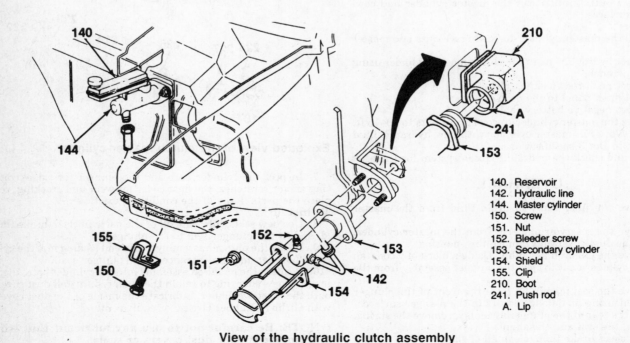

140. Reservoir
142. Hydraulic line
144. Master cylinder
150. Screw
151. Nut
152. Bleeder screw
153. Secondary cylinder
154. Shield
155. Clip
210. Boot
241. Push rod
A. Lip

View of the hydraulic clutch assembly

fluid level (in the reservoir) has been allowed to fall so low, that air has been drawn into the master cylinder.

1. Fill master cylinder reservoir with new brake fluid conforming to Dot 3 specifications.

WARNING: Never, under any circumstances, use fluid which has been bled from a system to fill the reservoir as it may be aerated, have too much moisture content and possibly be contaminated.

2. Raise and support the front of the vehicle on jackstands.
3. Remove the slave cylinder attaching bolts.

4. Hold slave cylinder at approximately 45° with the bleeder at highest point. Fully depress clutch pedal and open the bleeder screw.
5. Close the bleeder screw and release clutch pedal.
6. Repeat the procedure until all of the air is evacuated from the system. Check and refill master cylinder reservoir as required to prevent air from being drawn through the master cylinder.

NOTE: Never release a depressed clutch pedal with the bleeder screw open or air will be drawn into the system.

AUTOMATIC TRANSMISSION

Understanding Automatic Transmissions

The automatic transmission allows engine torque and power to be transmitted to the rear wheels within a narrow range of engine operating speeds. The transmission will allow the engine to turn fast enough to produce plenty of power and torque at very low speeds, while keeping it at a sensible rpm at high vehicle speeds. The transmission performs this job entirely without driver assistance. The transmission uses a light fluid as the medium for the transmission of power. This fluid also works in the operation of various hydraulic control circuits and as a lubricant. Because the transmission fluid performs all of these three functions, trouble within the unit can easily travel from one part to another. For this reason, and because of the complexity and unusual operating principles of the transmission, a very sound understanding of the basic principles of operation will simplify troubleshooting.

THE TORQUE CONVERTER

The torque converter replaces the conventional clutch. It has three functions:
1. It allows the engine to idle with the vehicle at a standstill, even with the transmission in gear.
2. It allows the transmission to shift from range to range smoothly, without requiring that the driver close the throttle during the shift.
3. It multiplies engine torque to an increasing extent as vehicle speed drops and throttle opening is increased. This has the effect of making the transmission more responsive and reduces the amount of shifting required.

The torque converter is a metal case which is shaped like a sphere that has been flattened on opposite sides. It is bolted to the rear end of the engine's crankshaft. Generally, the entire metal case rotates at engine speed and serves as the engine's flywheel.

The case contains three sets of blades. One set is attached directly to the case. This set forms the torus or pump. Another set is directly connected to the output shaft, and forms the turbine.

The third set is mounted on a hub which, in turn, is mounted on a stationary shaft through a one-way clutch. This third set is known as the stator.

A pump, which is driven by the converter hub at engine speed, keeps the torque converter full of transmission fluid at all times. Fluid flows continuously through the unit to provide cooling.

Under low speed acceleration, the torque converter functions as follows:

The torus is turning faster than the turbine. It picks up fluid at the center of the converter and, through centrifugal force, slings it outward. Since the outer edge of the converter moves faster than the portions at the center, the fluid picks up speed.

The fluid then enters the outer edge of the turbine blades. It then travels back toward the center of the converter case along the turbine blades. In impinging upon the turbine blades, the fluid loses the energy picked up in the torus.

If the fluid were now to immediately be returned directly into the torus, both halves of the converter would have to turn at approximately the same speed at all times, and torque input and output would both be the same.

In flowing through the torus and turbine, the fluid picks up two types of flow, or flow in two separate directions. It flows through the turbine blades, and it spins with the engine. The stator, whose blades are stationary when the vehicle is being accelerated at low speeds, converts one type of flow into another. Instead of allowing the fluid to flow straight back into the torus, the stator's curved blades turn the fluid almost 90 degrees toward the direction of rotation of the engine. Thus the fluid does not flow as fast toward the torus, but is already spinning when the torus picks it up. This has the effect of allowing the torus to turn much faster than the turbine. This difference in speed may be compared to the difference in speed between the smaller and larger gears in any gear train. The result is that engine power output is higher, and engine torque is multiplied.

As the speed of the turbine increases, the fluid spins faster and faster in the direction of engine rotation. As a result, the ability of the stator to redirect the fluid flow is reduced. Under cruising conditions, the stator is eventually forced to rotate on its one-way clutch in the direction of engine rotation. Under these conditions, the torque converter begins to behave almost like a solid shaft, with the torus and turbine speeds being almost equal.

THE PLANETARY GEARBOX

The ability of the torque converter to multiply engine torque is limited. Also, the unit tends to be more efficient when the turbine is rotating at relatively high speeds. Therefore, a planetary gearbox is used to carry the power output of the turbine to the driveshaft.

Planetary gears function very similarly to conventional transmission gears. However, their construction is different in that three elements make up one gear system, and, in that all three elements are different from one another. The three elements are: an outer gear that is shaped like a hoop, with teeth cut into the inner surface; a sun gear, mounted on a shaft and located at the very center of the outer gear; and a set of three planet gears, held by pins in a ring-like planet carrier, meshing with both the sun gear and the outer gear. Either the outer gear or the sun gear may be held stationary, providing more than one possible torque multiplication factor for each set of gears. Also, if all three gears are forced to rotate at the same speed, the gearset forms, in effect, a solid shaft.

Most modern automatics use the planetary gears to provide either a single reduction ratio of about 1.8:1, or two reduction gears: a low of about 2.5:1, and an intermediate of about 1.5:1. Bands and clutches are used to hold various portions of the gearsets to the transmission case or to the shaft on which they are mounted. Shifting is accomplished, then, by changing the portion of each planetary gearset which is held to the transmission case or to the shaft.

THE SERVOS AND ACCUMULATORS

The servos are hydraulic pistons and cylinders. They resemble the hydraulic actuators used on many familiar machines, such as bulldozers. Hydraulic fluid enters the cylinder, under pressure, and forces the piston to move to engage the band or clutches.

The accumulators are used to cushion the engagement of the servos. The transmission fluid must pass through the accumulator on the way to the servo. The accumulator housing contains a thin piston which is sprung away from the discharge passage of the accumulator. When fluid passes through the accumulator on the way to the servo, it must move the piston against spring pressure, and this action smooths out the action of the servo.

THE HYDRAULIC CONTROL SYSTEM

The hydraulic pressure used to operate the servos comes from the main transmission oil pump. This fluid is channeled to the various servos through the shift valves. There is generally a manual shift valve which is operated by the transmission selec-

tor lever and an automatic shift valve for each automatic upshift the transmission provides: i.e., 2-speed automatics have a low/high shift valve, while 3-speeds have a 1–2 valve, and a 2–3 valve.

There are two pressures which effect the operation of these valves. One is the governor pressure which is affected by vehicle speed. The other is the modulator pressure which is affected by intake manifold vacuum or throttle position. Governor pressure rises with an increase in vehicle speed, and modulator pressure rises as the throttle is opened wider. By responding to these two pressures, the shift valves cause the upshift points to be delayed with increased throttle opening to make the best use of the engine's power output.

Most transmissions also make use of an auxiliary circuit for downshifting. This circuit may be actuated by the throttle linkage or the vacuum line which actuates the modulator, or by a cable or solenoid. It applies pressure to a special downshift surface on the shift valve or valves.

The transmission modulator also governs the line pressure, used to actuate the servos. In this way, the clutches and bands will be actuated with a force matching the torque output of the engine.

Identification

The THM 700-R4 is a fully automatic transmission which provides 4 forward gears and a reverse gear. The oil pressure and shifting points are controlled by the throttle opening, via a Throttle Valve (TV) cable.

Fluid Pan

REMOVAL AND INSTALLATION

NOTE: The fluid should be drained when the transmission is warm.

1. Raise and support the front of the vehicle with jackstands.
2. Place a drain catch pan under the transmission oil pan.
3. Remove the pan bolts from the front and sides of the pan, then loosen the rear bolts 4 turns.
4. Using a small pry bar, pry the oil pan loose and allow the pan to partially drain. Remove the remaining pan bolts and carefully lower the pan away from the transmission.

NOTE: If the transmission fluid is dark or has a burnt smell, transmission damage may be indicated. Have the transmission checked professionally.

If the pan sticks, carefully tap sideways on the pan with a rubber or plastic mallet to break it loose; DO NOT dent the pan.

5. Empty and wash the pan in solvent, then blow dry with compressed air.

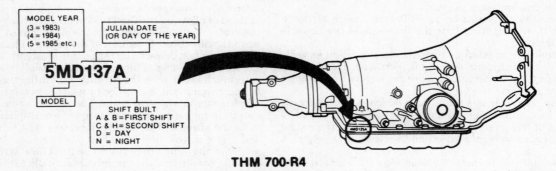

THM 700-R4

Identification of the THM 700-R4 transmission

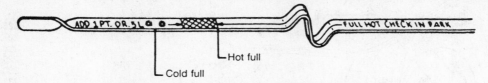

700-4R automatic transmission dipstick

Hot full

Cold full

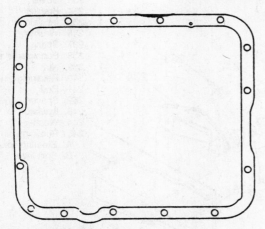

View of the THM 700-R4 oil pan gasket

6. Using a putty knife, clean the gasket mounting surfaces.
To install:

1. Use a new filter, a new gasket and install the pan and bolts finger tight. Torque the pan-to-transmission bolts to 144 inch lbs. in a crisscross pattern. Recheck the bolt torque after all of the bolts have been tightened once. Add Dexron®II automatic transmission fluid through the filler tube.

WARNING: Do not overfill the transmission; foaming of the fluid and subsequent transmission damage due to slippage will result.

2. With the gear selector lever in **PARK**, start the engine and let it idle; DO NOT race the engine.

3. Move the gear selector lever through each position, holding the brakes. Return the lever to **PARK** and check the fluid level with the engine idling. The level should be between the two dimples on the dipstick, about ¼ in. (6mm) below the **ADD** mark. Add fluid, if necessary.

4. Check the fluid level after the vehicle has been driven enough to thoroughly warm the transmission. Details are given under Fluid Level Checks earlier in Section 1. If the transmission is overfilled, the excess must be drained off. Use a suction pump through the fill tube, if necessary.

FILTER SERVICE

1. Refer to the Fluid Pan, Removal and Installation procedures in this section and remove the fluid pan.

2. Remove the transmission filter screws or clips and the filter from the valve body. The filter may have either a fibrous or screen filtering element and is retained by one or two fasteners.

NOTE: If the transmission uses a filter having a fully exposed screen, it may be cleaned and reused.

3. To install, use a new filter, a new gasket and install the fluid pan. Torque the pan-to-transmission bolts to 144 inch lbs. in a crisscross pattern. Recheck the bolt torque after all of the bolts have been tightened once. Add Dexron®II automatic transmission fluid through the filler tube.

Adjustments

SHIFT LINKAGE

1. Firmly apply the parking brake.

2. Raise and support the front of the vehicle on jackstands.

3. At the left side of the transmission, loosen the shift rod swivel-to-equalizer lever nut.

4. Rotate the transmission shift lever clockwise (forward) to the last detent (Park) position, then turn it counterclockwise (rearward) to the rear of the 2nd detent (Neutral) position.

5. At the steering column, place the gear selector lever into the Neutral position.

NOTE: When positioning the gear selector lever, DO NOT use the steering column indicator to find the Neutral position.

6. Tightly, hold the shifting rod (swivel) against the equalizer lever, then torque the adjusting nut to 11 ft. lbs. (14 Nm).

7. Using the gear selector lever (on the steering column), place it in the **PARK** position and check the adjustment. Move the gear selector lever into the various positions; the engine must start in the **PARK** and the **NEUTRAL** positions.

8. If the engine will not start in the **NEUTRAL** and/or **PARK** positions, refer to "Back-Up Light Switch" adjustment in Section 6 and adjust the switch.

― **CAUTION** ―
With the gear selector lever in the PARK position, the parking pawl should engage the rear internal gear lugs or output ring gear lugs to prevent the vehicle from rolling and causing personal injury.

9. Align the gear selector lever indicator, if necessary. Lower the vehicle and release the parking brake.

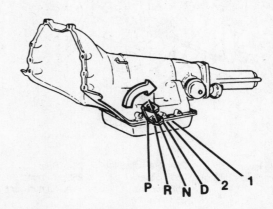

View of the shifting positions — THM 700 — R4

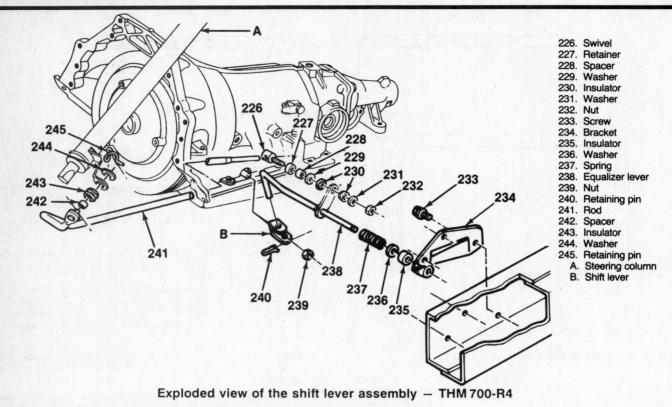

226. Swivel
227. Retainer
228. Spacer
229. Washer
230. Insulator
231. Washer
232. Nut
233. Screw
234. Bracket
235. Insulator
236. Washer
237. Spring
238. Equalizer lever
239. Nut
240. Retaining pin
241. Rod
242. Spacer
243. Insulator
244. Washer
245. Retaining pin
A. Steering column
B. Shift lever

Exploded view of the shift lever assembly — THM 700-R4

THROTTLE VALVE (TV) CABLE

If the TV cable is broken, sticky, misadjusted or incorrect part for the model, the vehicle may exhibit various malfunctions, such as: delayed or full throttle shifts.

Preliminary Checks

1. Inspect and/or correct the transmission fluid level.
2. Make sure that the brakes are not dragging and that the engine is operating correctly.
3. Make sure that the cable is connected at both ends.
4. Make sure that the correct cable is installed.

Adjustment

1. If necessary, remove the air cleaner.
2. If the cable has been removed and installed, check to see that the cable slider is in the zero or the fully adjusted position; if not, perform the following procedures:
   a. Depress and hold the readjust tab.
   b. Move the slider back through the fitting (away from the throttle lever) until it stops against the fitting.
   c. Release the readjust tab.
3. Rotate the throttle lever to the Full Throttle Stop position to obtain a minimum of 1 click.
4. Release the throttle lever.

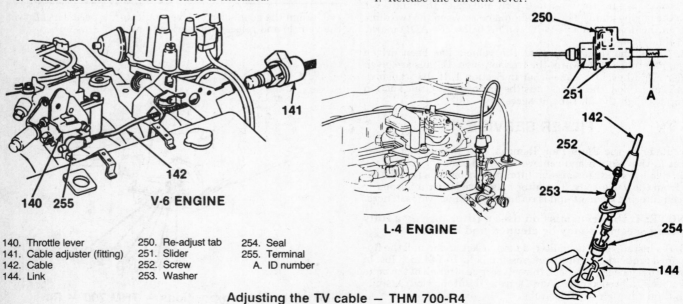

V-6 ENGINE

L-4 ENGINE

140. Throttle lever
141. Cable adjuster (fitting)
142. Cable
144. Link
250. Re-adjust tab
251. Slider
252. Screw
253. Washer
254. Seal
255. Terminal
A. ID number

Adjusting the TV cable — THM 700-R4

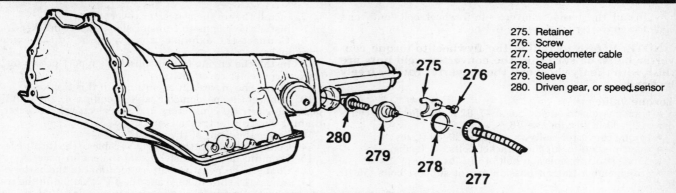

275. Retainer
276. Screw
277. Speedometer cable
278. Seal
279. Sleeve
280. Driven gear, or speed sensor

Exploded view of the speedometer cable assembly — THM 700-R4

Neutral Safety Switch

The Neutral Safety Switch is a part of the Back-Up Light Switch. For the replacement or adjustment procedures, refer to the Back-Up Light Switch, Removal and Installation procedures in Section 6.

Back-up Light Switch

NOTE: The back-up light switch is located on the steering column. To replace the back-up light switch, refer to the Back-Up Light Switch, Removal and Installation procedures in Section 6.

Transmission

REMOVAL AND INSTALLATION

NOTE: The following procedure requires the use of the Torque Converter Holding tool No. J-21366 or equivalent.

1. Refer to the Driveshaft, Removal and Installation procedures in this section and remove the driveshaft.
2. Disconnect the negative battery terminal from the battery.
3. From inside the vehicle, remove the engine cover.
4. Disconnect the Throttle Valve (TV) cable from the throttle lever.
5. Raise and support the front of the vehicle on jackstands.
6. Disconnect the speedometer cable (if equipped), the shift linkage, the electrical connectors and any electrical connector retaining clips from the transmission.
7. Remove the engine-to-transmission support braces (at the torque converter cover) bolts.
8. Disconnect the exhaust crossover pipe from the exhaust manifold(s).
9. Remove the engine-to-transmission support brackets.
10. Remove the torque converter cover, then matchmark the flywheel to the torque converter; matching of the marks will maintain the original balance.
11. Remove the torque converter-to-flywheel bolts/nuts and slide the converter back into the transmission.
12. Using a transmission jack, position it under and secure it to the transmission, then raise the transmission slightly.
13. Remove the crossmember-to-transmission mount bolts and the crossmember-to-frame bolts; if insulators are used, be sure to remove them. Remove the crossmember from the vehicle by moving it rearward.
14. Lower the transmission (slightly), then disconnect the oil cooler lines and the Throttle Valve (TV) cable from it.

NOTE: When disconnecting the oil cooler lines and the TV cable, be sure to plug the openings to keep dirt out of the system.

15. Using a block of wood and a floor jack, place them under the rear of the engine and support it.
16. Using the Torque Converter Holding tool No. J-21366 or equivalent, secure the torque converter to the transmission.
17. Remove the transmission-to-engine bolts and the transmission from the vehicle.

To install:

1. Install the transmission and transmission-to-engine bolts into the vehicle using a transmission jack.
2. Remove the Torque Converter Holding tool No. J-21366 or equivalent.
3. Remove the rear engine support.
4. Lower the transmission (slightly), then connect the oil cooler lines and the Throttle Valve (TV) cable to it.
5. Install the crossmember, crossmember-to-transmission mount bolts and the crossmember-to-frame bolts; if insulators are used, be sure to install them.

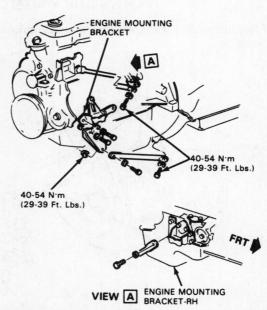

View of the automatic transmission support brackets — 2.5L engine

6. Install the torque converter-to-flywheel bolts/nuts and slide the converter towards the flywheel.

NOTE: Before installing the flywheel-to-torque converter bolts, be sure that the converter weld nuts are flush with the flywheel and the converter rotates freely by hand.

Torque values:

- transmission-to-engine bolts: 47–62 ft. lbs. for the 4-cylinder or 29–39 ft. lbs. for the V6
- torque converter-to-flywheel bolts: 29–39 ft. lbs.
- transmission-to-support bracket bolts: 34 ft. lbs.
- damper-to-transmission bolt: 45 ft. lbs.
- crossmember-to-transmission mount support bolts: 55 ft. lbs.
- transmission mount-to-mount support bolts: 25 ft. lbs.
- crossmember-to-frame bolts: 65 ft. lbs.

7. Install the torque converter cover.
8. Install the engine-to-transmission support brackets.
9. Connect the exhaust crossover pipe to the exhaust manifold(s).
10. Install the engine-to-transmission support braces (at the torque converter cover) bolts.
11. Install the driveshaft as outlined in this Section.
12. Connect the speedometer cable (if equipped), the shift linkage, the electrical connectors and any electrical connector retaining clips to the transmission.
13. Lower the front of the vehicle.
14. Connect the Throttle Valve (TV) cable to the throttle lever.
15. From inside the vehicle, install the engine cover.
16. Connect the negative battery terminal to the battery.
17. Adjust the shift linkage and the TV cable. Refill the transmission with Dexron® II automatic transmission fluid and check for proper performance and operation.

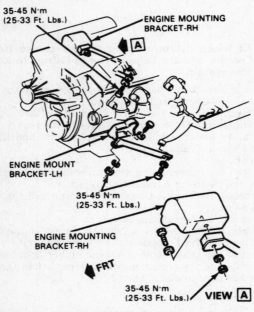

View of the automatic transmission support brackets — 4.3L engine

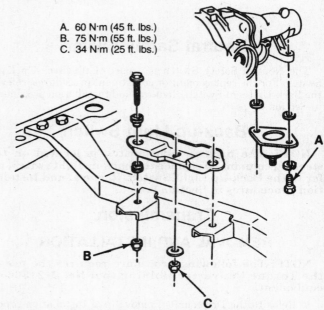

Exploded view of the transmission mount assembly — THM 700-R4

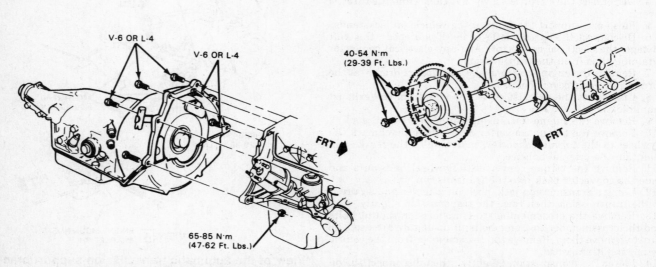

Removing the transmission and flywheel from the engine — THM 700-R4

TRANSFER CASE

Identification

In 1990, the Astro/Safari van could be ordered with All Wheel Drive as an option. It is only available with an automatic overdrive transmission and the 4.3L engine. The BW-4472 transfer case is an aluminum two piece unit with a chain driven viscous clutch. The All Wheel Drive is automatic and has no external controls. The torque is transmitted through the input shaft to the planet carrier assembly. The viscous clutch provides the connection between the gear ring and sun gear shaft. An aluminum tag is attached the under side of the self tapping case bolts.

Front or Rear Shaft Seal

REMOVAL AND INSTALLATION

1. Raise and support the vehicle with jackstands.
2. Mark the driveshaft and flange for installation. Remove the front or rear driveshaft as outlined in this Section.
3. Remove the front output flange nut and washer. Not used on rear.
4. Remove the rubber sealing washer. Not used on rear.
5. Remove the output flange. Not used on rear.
6. Pry out the output oil seal with a suitable pry bar being careful not to damage the seat bore.
To install:
1. Align the water drain hole in the output shaft oil seal with the drain groove in the extension housing. Use a front output seal installer J-37668 or install the front or rear shaft seal.
2. Lubricate seal lips with Dexron®II fluid.
3. Install the front output shaft flange, rubber sealing washer, steel washer and flange nut. Torque the nut to 80 ft. lbs. (108 Nm).
4. Install the driveshaft to the marked location as outlined in this Section.
5. Check the transfer case lubricant by removing the fill plug. If fluid does not spill out of the hole, add Dexron®II automatic transmission fluid to the fill hole until lubricant reaches the top of the hole.
6. Lower the vehicle and check operation.

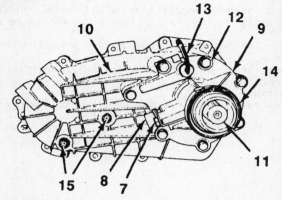

7. Speed sensor bolt
8. Speed sensor
9. Extension housing
10. Rear case half
11. Output shaft assembly
12. Extension housing bolt
13. Breather assembly
14. Output shaft oil seal
15. Drain/fill plugs

Transfer case fill and drain plugs (15)

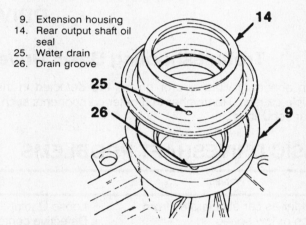

9. Extension housing
14. Rear output shaft oil seal
25. Water drain
26. Drain groove

Extension housing oil seal alignment

9. Extension housing
14. Rear output shaft oil seal

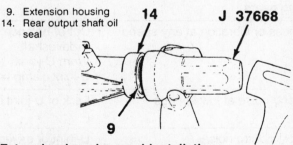

Extension housing seal installation

Transfer Case

REMOVAL AND INSTALLATION

1. Disconnect the negative (−) battery cable.
2. Raise the vehicle and support with jackstands.
3. Drain the oil from the transfer case into a suitable container.

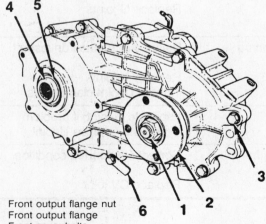

1. Front output flange nut
2. Front output flange
3. Front cover bolts
4. Input shaft
5. Input shaft oil seal
6. Identification tag

BW-4472 transfer case — All wheel drive

4. Remove the front and rear driveshaft as outlined in this Section.

5. Disconnect the breather hose and all electrical connectors.

6. Support the transfer case with a suitable transmission jack.

7. Remove the transfer case support bracket and adapter-to-case bolts.

8. Remove the transfer case mount nuts, transfer case and adapter gasket.

To install:

1. Make sure all gasket surfaces are clean and free of grease or oil.

2. Install a new transfer case-to-adapter gasket with sealer.

3. Install the transfer case to the adapter and torque the bolts to 38 ft. lbs. (52 Nm).

4. Install the support bracket and torque the bolts to 94 ft. lbs. (128 Nm).

5. Connect the electrical connectors and breather hose.

6. Install the front and rear driveshafts as outlined in this Section.

7. Fill the transfer case to the bottom of the fill hole with Dexron®II automatic transmission fluid.

8. Lower the vehicle, connect the negative battery cable and check operation.

DRIVELINE

Troubleshooting Basic Driveshaft and Rear Axle Problems

When abnormal vibrations or noises are detected in the driveshaft area, this chart can be used to help diagnose possible causes. Remember that other components such as wheels, tires, rear axle and suspension can also produce similar conditions.

BASIC DRIVESHAFT PROBLEMS

Problem	Cause	Solution
Shudder as car accelerates from stop or low speed	• Loose U-joint • Defective center bearing	• Replace U-joint • Replace center bearing
Loud clunk in driveshaft when shifting gears	• Worn U-joints	• Replace U-joints
Roughness or vibration at any speed	• Out-of-balance, bent or dented driveshaft • Worn U-joints • U-joint clamp bolts loose	• Balance or replace driveshaft • Replace U-joints • Tighten U-joint clamp bolts
Squeaking noise at low speeds	• Lack of U-joint lubrication	• Lubricate U-joint; if problem persists, replace U-joint
Knock or clicking noise	• U-joint or driveshaft hitting frame tunnel • Worn CV joint	• Correct overloaded condition • Replace CV joint

BASIC REAR AXLE PROBLEMS

First, determine when the noise is most noticeable.

Drive Noise — Produced under vehicle acceleration.

Coast Noise — Produced while the car coast with a closed throttle.

Float Noise — Occurs while maintaining constant car speed (just enough to keep speed constant) on a level road.

Road Noise

Brick or rough surfaced concrete roads produce noises that seem to come from the rear axle. Road noise is usually identical in Drive or Coast and driving on a different type of road will tell whether the road is the problem.

Tire Noise

Tire noises are often mistaken for rear axle problems. Snow treads or unevenly worn tires produce vibrations seeming to originate elsewhere. Temporarily inflating the tire to 40 lbs will significantly alter tire noise, but will have no effect on rear axle noises (which normally cease below about 30 mph).

Engine/Transmission Noise

Determine at what speed the noise is more pronounced, then stop the car in a quiet place. With the transmission in Neutral, run the engine through speeds corresponding to road speeds where the noise was noticed. Noises produced with the car standing still are coming from the engine or transmission.

Front Wheel Bearings

While holding the car speed steady, lightly apply the foot brake; this will often decease bearing noise, as some of the load is taken from the bearing.

Rear Axle Noises

Eliminating other possible sources can narrow the cause to the rear axle, which normally produces noise from worn gears or bearings. Gear noises tend to peak in a narrow speed range, while bearing noises will usually vary in pitch with engine speeds.

NOISE DIAGNOSIS

The Noise Is	Most Probably Produced By
• Identical under Drive or Coast	• Road surface, tires or front wheel bearings
• Different depending on road surface	• Road surface or tires
• Lower as the car speed is lowered	• Tires
• Similar with car standing or moving	• Engine or transmission
• A vibration	• Unbalanced tires, rear wheel bearing, unbalanced driveshaft or worn U-joint
• A knock or click about every 2 tire revolutions	• Rear wheel bearing
• Most pronounced on turns	• Damaged differential gears
• A steady low-pitched whirring or scraping, starting at low speeds	• Damaged or worn pinion bearing
• A chattering vibration on turns	• Wrong differential lubricant or worn clutch plates (limited slip rear axle)
• Noticed only in Drive, Coast or Float conditions	• Worn ring gear and/or pinion gear

The Astro/Safari van's rear driveshaft is of the conventional, open type. Located at either end of the driveshaft is a universal joint (U-joint), which allows the driveshaft to move up and down to match the motion of the front and rear axle. The main problem with the simple U-joint is that as the angle of the shaft increases past three to four degrees, the driven yoke rotates slower or faster than the drive yoke. This problem can be reduced by adding an additional U-joint or incorporate a constant velocity joint.

The front driveshaft uses two constant velocity joints to transfer the power from the transfer case to the front drive axle. The constant velocity joint allows the driveline angle to be adjusted according to the up and down movement of the vehicle without disturbing the power flow.

The rear U-joint (injected nylon or internal snaprings) connects the driveshaft to a slip-jointed yoke. This yoke is internally splined and allows the driveshaft to move in and out on the transmission splines. On the production U-joints, nylon is injected through a small hole in the yoke during manufacture and flows along a circular groove between the U-joint and the yoke, creating a non-metallic snapring.

The rear U-joint is clamped to the rear axle pinion. The rear U-joint is secured in the yoke, using external snaprings (inside the yoke ears). It is attached to the rear axle pinion by use of bolted straps.

Bad U-joints, requiring replacement, will produce a clunking sound when the vehicle is put into gear and when the transmission shifts from gear-to-gear. This is due to worn needle bearings or scored trunnion end possibly caused by improper lubrication during assembly. U-joints require no periodic maintenance and therefore have no lubrication fittings.

A vibration damper is employed as part of the slip joint. This damper cannot be serviced separately from the slip joint; if either component goes bad, the two must be replaced as a unit.

Driveshaft and U-Joints

REMOVAL AND INSTALLATION

Front

1. Disconnect the negative (−) battery cable.
2. Raise the vehicle and support with jackstands.
3. Mark the positions of the driveshaft components related to the driveshaft and flanges. The components must be reassembled in the same position to maintain proper balance.

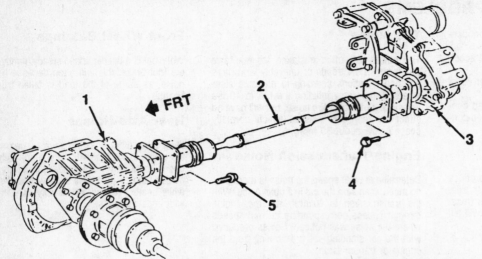

1. Front axle
2. Front driveshaft
3. Transfer case
4. Bolt
5. Bolt

Exploded view of the front driveshaft — All wheel drive

4. Remove the transfer and front axle flanges-to-driveshaft bolts.
5. Pull the driveshaft forward and down to remove.
To install:
1. Inspect the plastic shrouds for cracking or deterioration, replace if necessary.
2. Install the shaft to the reference marks made previously.
3. Install the flange-to-driveshaft bolts and torque the axle flange bolts to 53 ft. lbs. (72 Nm) and the transfer case flange bolts to 92 ft. lbs. (125 Nm).
4. Lower the vehicle and check for proper operation.

Rear

1. Raise and support the rear of the vehicle on jackstands.
2. Using paint, matchmark the relationship of the driveshaft-to-pinion flange.
3. Remove the universal joint-to-rear axle retainers.

NOTE: If the bearing cups are loose, tape them together to prevent dropping or loosing the roller bearings.

4. Remove the driveshaft by sliding it forward, to disengage it from the axle flange, and then rearward, passing it under the axle housing.

NOTE: When removing the driveshaft, DO NOT drop it or allow the universal joints to bend at extreme angles, for this may fracture the plastic injected joints.

5. Inspect the driveshaft splines and surfaces for burrs, damage or wear.
To install:
6. Position the driveshaft into the transmission, align it with the matchmarks on the axle flange. Torque the universal joint-to-pinion flange bolts to 12–17 ft. lbs. (15–25 Nm).

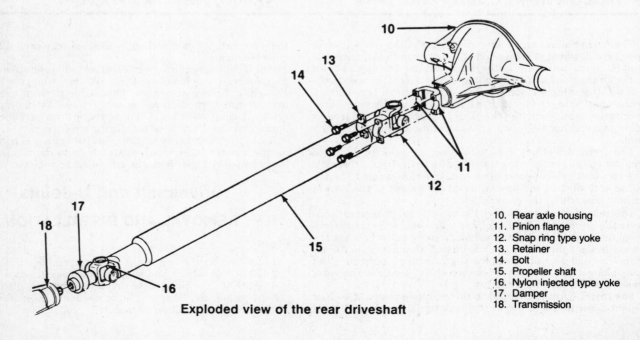

10. Rear axle housing
11. Pinion flange
12. Snap ring type yoke
13. Retainer
14. Bolt
15. Propeller shaft
16. Nylon injected type yoke
17. Damper
18. Transmission

Exploded view of the rear driveshaft

U-JOINT OVERHAUL

Two types of universal joints are used: The front uses an internal snapring (production is plastic injected) and the rear uses an external snapring.

NOTE: The following procedure requires the use of an Arbor Press, the GM Cross Press tool No. J–9522–3 or equivalent, the GM Spacer tool No. J–9522–5 or equivalent, and a 1⅛ in. socket.

Internal Snapring (Front)

1. While supporting the driveshaft, in the horizontal position, position it so that the lower ear of the front universal joint's shaft yoke is supported on a 1⅛ in. socket.

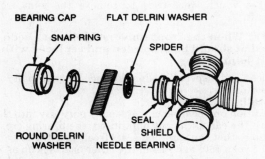

BEARING CAP FLAT DELRIN WASHER
SNAP RING
SPIDER
ROUND DELRIN WASHER NEEDLE BEARING
SEAL SHIELD

Exploded view of the front (replacement) universal joint — internal snapring

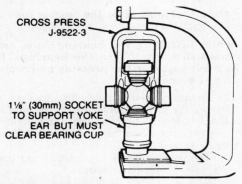

CROSS PRESS J-9522-3

1⅛" (30mm) SOCKET TO SUPPORT YOKE EAR BUT MUST CLEAR BEARING CUP

Removing the universal joint from the driveshaft

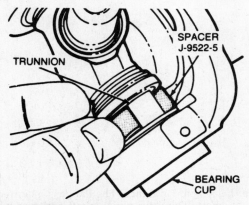

SPACER J-9522-5
TRUNNION
BEARING CUP

Using the GM spacer tool No. J–9522–5 or equivalent, to completely remove the universal joint from the driveshaft

NOTE: DO NOT clamp the driveshaft tube in a vise, for the tube may become damaged.

2. Using the GM Cross Press tool No. J–9522–3 or equivalent, place it on the horizontal bearing cups and press the lower bearing cup out of the yoke ear; the pressing action will shear the plastic retaining ring from the lower bearing cup. If the bearing cup was not completely removed, insert the GM Spacer tool No. J–9522–5 or equivalent, onto the universal joint, then complete the pressing procedure to remove the joint.

3. Rotate the driveshaft and shear the plastic retainer from the opposite side of the yoke.

4. Disengage the slip yoke from the driveshaft.

5. To remove the universal joint from the slip yoke, perform the procedures used in Steps 1–4.

NOTE: When the front universal joint has been disassembled, it must be discarded and replaced with a service kit joint, for the production joint is not equipped with bearing retainer grooves on the bearing cups.

6. Clean (remove any remaining plastic particles) and inspect the slip yoke and driveshaft for damage, wear or burrs.

NOTE: The universal joint service kit includes: A pregreased cross assembly, four bearing cups with seals, needle rollers, washers, four bearing retainers and grease. Make sure that the bearing cup seals are installed to hold the needle bearings in place for handling.

To install:

7. Position one bearing cup assembly part way into the yoke ear (turn the ear to the bottom), insert the bearing cross (into the yoke) so that the trunnion seats freely into the bearing cup. Turn the yoke 180° and install the other bearing cup assembly.

NOTE: When installing the bearing cup assemblies, make sure the trunnions are started straight and true into the bearing cups.

8. Using the arbor press, press the bearing cups onto the cross trunnion, until they seat.

NOTE: While installing the bearing cups, twist the cross trunnion to work it into the bearings. If there seems to be a hangup, stop the pressing and recheck the needle roller alignment.

9. Once the bearing cup retainer grooves have cleared the inside of the yoke, stop the pressing and install the snaprings.

10. If the other bearing cup retainer groove has not cleared the inside of the yoke, use a hammer to aid in the seating procedure.

11. To install the yoke/universal assembly to the driveshaft, perform the Steps 7–10 of this procedure.

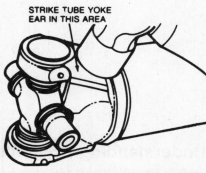

STRIKE TUBE YOKE EAR IN THIS AREA

Tapping the universal joint to seal the retaining rings — internal rings

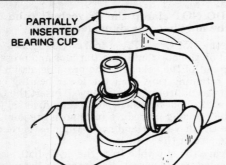

Installing the new universal joint bearing cross into the slip yoke

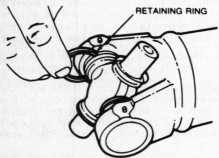

Installing the new universal joint retaining rings — internal rings

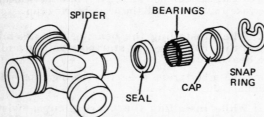

Exploded view of the rear universal joint — external snapring

External Snapring (Rear)

1. Remove the snaprings from inside the yoke ears.

2. While supporting the driveshaft, in the horizontal position, position it so that the lower ear of the front universal joint's shaft yoke is supported on a 1⅛ in. socket.

NOTE: DO NOT clamp the driveshaft tube in a vise, for the tube may become damaged.

3. Using the GM Cross Press tool No. J–9522–3 or equivalent, place it on the horizontal bearing cups and press the lower bearing cup out of the yoke ear. If the bearing cup was not completely removed, insert the GM Spacer tool No. J–9522–5 or equivalent, onto the universal joint, then complete the pressing procedure.

4. Rotate the driveshaft and press the bearing cup from the opposite side of the yoke.

5. Disengage the slip yoke from the driveshaft.

6. To remove the universal joint from the slip yoke, perform Steps 1–4 which were used to remove the joint from the driveshaft.

NOTE: When the front universal joint has been disassembled, it should be discarded and replaced with a service kit joint.

7. Clean and inspect the slip yoke and the driveshaft for damage, wear or burrs.

To install:

8. Position one bearing cup assembly part way into the yoke ear (turn the ear to the bottom), insert the bearing cross (into the yoke) so that the trunnion seats freely into the bearing cup. Turn the yoke 180° and install the other bearing cup assembly.

NOTE: When installing the bearing cup assemblies, make sure the trunnions are started straight and true into the bearing cups.

9. Using the arbor press, press the bearing cups onto the cross trunnion, until they seat.

NOTE: While installing the bearing cups, twist the cross trunnion to work it into the bearings. If there seems to be a hangup, stop the pressing and recheck the needle roller alignment.

10. Once the bearing cup clears the retainer grooves (inside of the yoke ear), stop the pressing and install the snaprings.

11. If the other bearing cup has not cleared the retainer groove (inside the yoke ear), use a hammer and a brass drift punch to aid in the seating procedure.

12. To install the yoke/universal assembly to the driveshaft, perform the Steps 8–11 of this procedure.

REAR AXLE

Understanding Drive Axles

The drive axle is a special type of transmission that reduces the speed of the drive from the engine and transmission and divides the power to the wheels. Power enters the axle from the driveshaft via the companion flange. The flange is mounted on the drive pinion shaft. The drive pinion shaft and gear which carry the power into the differential turn at engine speed. The gear on the end of the pinion shaft drives a large ring gear the axis of rotation of which is 90 degrees away from the of the pinion. The pinion and gear reduce the gear ratio of the axle, and change the direction of rotation to turn the axle shafts which drive both wheels. The axle gear ratio is found by dividing the number of pinion gear teeth into the number of ring gear teeth.

The ring gear drives the differential case. The case provides the two mounting points for the ends of a pinion shaft on which are mounted two pinion gears. The pinion gears drive the two side gears, one of which is located on the inner end of each axle shaft.

By driving the axle shafts through the arrangement, the differential allows the outer drive wheel to turn faster than the inner drive wheel in a turn.

The main drive pinion and the side bearings, which bear the weight of the differential case, are shimmed to provide proper bearing preload, and to position the pinion and ring gears properly.

WARNING: The proper adjustment of the relationship of the ring and pinion gears is critical. It should be attempted only by those with extensive equipment and/or experience.

Limited-slip differentials include clutches which tend to link each axle shaft to the differential case. Clutches may be engaged either by spring action or by pressure produced by the torque on the axles during a turn. During turning on a dry pavement, the effects of the clutches are overcome, and each wheel turns at the required speed. When slippage occurs at either wheel, however, the clutches will transmit some of the power to the wheel which has the greater amount of traction. Because of the presence of clutches, limited-slip units require a special lubricant.

Identification

Two types of rear axles are used: The standard and the locking. The axle is of a semi-floating type, where the vehicle weight is carried on the axle housing. It is designed for use with an open driveline and fiberglass leaf springs. All of the power transmitting parts are enclosed in a Salisbury type axle (a carrier casting with pressed tubes, welded into the carrier). A removable cover at the rear of the housing, allows the axle to be serviced without removing the entire assembly from the vehicle.

The Eaton built (locking) rear axle, equipped with a speed sensitive, multi-disc clutch pack mechanism, locks both wheels together if either wheel spins excessively during slow vehicle operation.

The rear axle identification number is located on the front, right side of the axle tube. See the Rear Axle Specification chart in Section 1 for information on determining the axle ratio, differential type, manufacturer and date built, from the letter codes.

Determining Axle Ratio

An axle ratio is obtained by dividing the number of teeth on the drive pinion gear into the number of teeth on the ring gear.

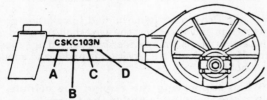

A. Axle code
B. 7½″ (190 mm) Chevrolet St. Catherines
C. Day built
D. Shift (D = Day, N = Night)

View of the rear axle identification number

For instance, on a 4.11:1 ratio, the driveshaft will turn 4.11 times for every turn of the rear wheels.

The most accurate way to determine the axle ratio is to drain the differential, remove the cover and count the number of teeth on the ring and the pinion.

An easier method is raise and support the rear of the vehicle on jackstands. Make a chalk mark on the rear wheel and the driveshaft. Block the front wheels and put the transmission in **NEUTRAL**. Turn the rear wheel one complete revolution and count the number of turns made by the driveshaft. The number of driveshaft rotations is the axle ratio. More accuracy can be obtained by going more than one tire revolution and dividing the result by the number of tire rotations.

The axle ratio is also identified by the axle serial number prefix on the axle; the axle ratios are listed in the dealer's parts books according to the prefix number.

Axle Shaft, Bearing and Seal

REMOVAL AND INSTALLATION

NOTE: The following procedures requires the use of the GM Slide Hammer tool No. J–2619 or equivalent, the GM Adapter tool No. J–2619–4 or equivalent, the GM Axle Bearing Puller tool No. J–22813–01 or equivalent, the GM Axle Shaft Seal Installer tool No. J–33782 or equivalent and the Axle Shaft Bearing Installer tool No. J–34974 or equivalent.

1. Raise and support the rear of the vehicle on jackstands.
2. Remove the rear wheel assemblies and the brake drums.

— CAUTION —

Brake shoes contain asbestos, which has been determined to be a cancer causing agent. Never clean the brake surfaces with compressed air! Avoid inhaling any dust from any brake surface! When cleaning brake surfaces, use a commercially available brake cleaning fluid.

3. Using a wire brush, clean the dirt/rust from around the rear axle cover.
4. Place a catch pan under the differential, then remove the drain plug (if equipped) or rear axle cover and drain the fluid (discard it).
5. At the differential, remove the rear pinion shaft lock bolt and the pinion shaft.
6. Push the axle shaft inward and remove the C-lock from the button end of the axle shaft.
7. Remove the axle shaft from the axle housing, be careful not to damage the oil seal.
8. Using a putty knife, clean the gasket mounting surfaces.

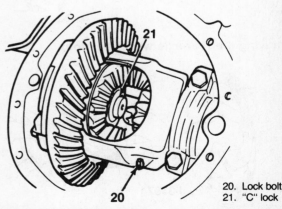

20. Lock bolt
21. "C" lock

View of the rear axle pinion shaft lock bolt and the "C" lock retainer

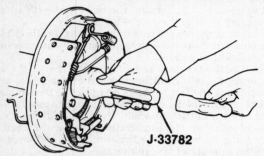

Installing the new oil seal in the axle housing tube

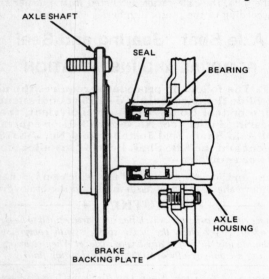

Sectional view of the rear axle, bearing and seal assembly

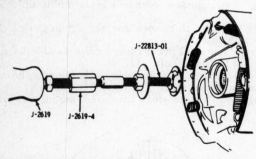

Removing the rear axle wheel bearing

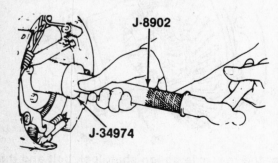

Installing the rear axle wheel bearing

NOTE: It is recommended, when the axle shaft is removed, to replace the oil seal.

9. To replace the oil seal, perform the following procedures:

a. Using a medium pry bar, pry the oil seal from the end of the rear axle housing; DO NOT damage the housing oil seal surface.

b. Clean and inspect the axle tube housing.

c. Using the GM Axle Shaft Seal Installer tool No. J–33782 or equivalent, drive the new seal into the housing until it is flush with the axle tube.

d. Using gear oil, lubricate the new seal lips.

10. If replacing the wheel bearing, perform the following procedures:

a. Using the GM Slide Hammer tool No. J–2619 or equivalent, the GM Adapter tool No. J–2619–4 or equivalent and the GM Axle Bearing Puller tool No. J–22813–01 or equivalent, install the tool assembly so that the tangs engage the outer race of the bearing.

b. Using the action of the slide hammer, pull the wheel bearing from the axle housing.

c. Using solvent, throughly clean the wheel bearing, then blow dry with compressed air. Inspect the wheel bearing for excessive wear or damage, then replace it (if necessary).

d. With a new or the reused bearing, place a blob of heavy grease in the palm of your hand, then work the bearing into the grease until it is thoroughly lubricated.

e. Using the Axle Shaft Bearing Installer tool No. J–34974 or equivalent, drive the bearing into the axle housing until it bottoms against the seat.

To install:

1. Slide the axle shaft into the rear axle housing and engage the splines of the axle shaft with the splines of the rear axle side gear, then install the C-lock retainer on the axle shaft button end.

2. After the C-lock is installed, pull the axle shaft outward to seat the C-lock retainer in the counterbore of the side gears.

NOTE: When installing the axle shaft(s), be careful not to cut the oil seal lips.

3. Install the pinion shaft through the case and the pinions, then install a new pinion shaft lock bolt. Torque the new lock bolt to 25 ft. lbs. (34 Nm).

4. Use a new rear axle cover gasket and install the housing cover. Torque the carrier cover-to-rear axle housing bolts to 20 ft. lbs. (27 Nm).

5. Refill the housing with SAE–80W or SAE 80W–90 GL-5 oil to a level 3/8 in. (10mm) below the filler plug hole.

NOTE: When adding oil to the rear axle, be aware that some locking differentials require the use of a special gear lubricant additive GM No. 1052271.

Axle Housing

REMOVAL AND INSTALLATION

1. Refer to the Driveshaft, Removal and Installation procedures in this section and disconnect the driveshaft from the rear axle housing; the driveshaft may either be removed or supported on a wire. Using a floor jack, position it under and support the rear axle housing.

NOTE: When supporting the rear of the vehicle, be sure to place the jackstands under the frame.

2. Remove the rear wheel assemblies.

3. Remove the shock absorber-to-axle housing nuts/bolts, then swing the shock absorbers away from the axle housing.

4. Disconnect the brake lines from the axle housing clips and the wheel cylinders.

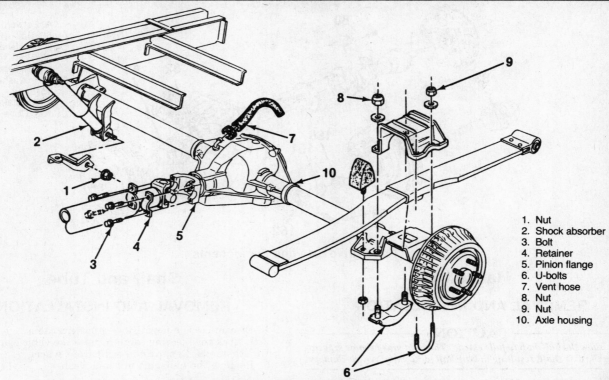

1. Nut
2. Shock absorber
3. Bolt
4. Retainer
5. Pinion flange
6. U-bolts
7. Vent hose
8. Nut
9. Nut
10. Axle housing

Exploded view of the rear axle housing

NOTE: When disconnecting the brake lines from the wheel cylinders, be sure to plug the lines to keep dirt from entering the lines.

5. Disconnect the axle housing-to-spring U-bolt nuts, the U-bolts and the anchor plates.

6. Remove the vent hose from the top of the axle housing.

7. Using the floor jack, lower the axle housing and remove from the vehicle.

To install:

1. Using the floor jack, raise the axle housing to the vehicle.

2. Install the vent hose to the top of the axle housing.

3. Connect the axle housing-to-spring U-bolt nuts, the U-bolts and the anchor plates. Torque the inner U-bolt-to-anchor plate nuts to 41 ft. lbs. (56 Nm), the outer U-bolt-to-anchor

plate nuts to 48 ft. lbs. (65 Nm).

4. Connect the brake lines to the axle housing clips and the wheel cylinders.

5. Install the shock absorber-to-axle housing nuts/bolts. Torque the shock absorber-to-axle housing nuts/bolts to 74 ft. lbs. (101 Nm).

6. Install the rear wheel assemblies.

7. Refer to the Driveshaft, Removal and Installation procedures in this section and connect the driveshaft to the rear axle housing. Torque the driveshaft-to-pinion flange retainer nuts to 27 ft. lbs. (35 Nm).

8. Check and refill the axle housing with SAE–80W or SAE 80W–90 GL-5 oil to a level ⅜ in. (10mm) below the filler plug hole.

9. Bleed the rear brake system as outlined in Section 9.

ALL WHEEL DRIVE FRONT DRIVE AXLE

Identification

The front drive axle uses a conventional ring and pinion gear set to transmit the driving force of the engine to the front wheels. The halfshafts are completely flexible, consisting of an inner and outer constant velocity (CV) joint connected by an axle shaft. The inner CV joint is a TRI-POT design, which can move in and out. The outer CV joint is an RZEPPA design which is also flexible, but can not move in and out.

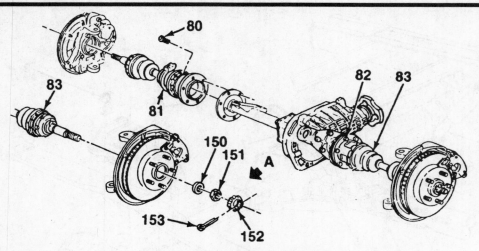

A. Forward
80. Bolt
81. Halfshaft (right)
82. Bolt
83. Halfshaft (left)
150. Washer
151. Nut
152. Retainer
153. Cotter pin

Front drive axle and components

Halfshaft

REMOVAL AND INSTALLATION

CAUTION

Do not allow the halfshaft to fully extend. The joint may become separated from the axle shaft, resulting in halfshaft failure and vehicle damage.

1. Disconnect the negative (−) battery cable.
2. Unlock the steering column so the linkage is free to move.
3. Raise the vehicle and support with jackstands.
4. Remove the front wheel assemblies.
5. Remove the axle nut and washer.

IMPORTANT: Support the lower control arm with a jackstands to release spring tension.

6. Remove the lower shock absorber nut and bolt.
7. Remove the halfshaft flange-to-axle bolts, insert a drift through the opening in the top of the brake caliper into the vanes of the brake rotor. Keep the halfshaft from turning.
8. Use a Posilock® Puller model 110 or equivalent to push the halfshaft through the hub and remove the halfshaft.

To install:
1. Install the halfshaft to the hub, axle washer and nut.
2. Insert a drift through the opening in the top of the brake caliper into the vanes of the brake rotor to keep the halfshaft from turning.
3. Torque the shaft nut to 160–200 ft. lbs. (220–270 Nm).
4. Install the halfshaft-to-axle flange bolts and torque to 60 ft. lbs. (80 Nm).
5. Install the lower shock bolt and nuts and torque to 18 ft. lbs. (25 Nm).
6. Refill the front drive axle if any fluid was lost.
7. Install the wheel assemblies, lower the vehicle, connect the negative battery cable and check for proper operation.

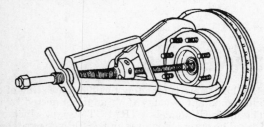

Removing the halfshaft from the hub

Shaft and Tube

REMOVAL AND INSTALLATION

1. Disconnect the negative (−) battery cable.
2. Unlock the steering column, raise the vehicle and support with jackstands. Remove the right front wheel.
3. Remove the halfshaft nut and washer.

IMPORTANT: Support the lower control arm with a jackstand to unload the spring pressure.

5. Remove the lower shock absorber bolt and nut.
6. Remove the output shaft bolts. Insert a drift through the opening in the top of the brake caliper into the vanes of the brake rotor.
7. Keep the shaft from turning and use a posilock Puller Model 110 or equivalent to push the halfshaft through the hub.
8. Remove the right halfshaft.
9. Remove the tube support bracket nuts, carrier bolts, shaft and tube assembly.

To install:
1. Clean the sealing surfaces of the tube and carrier assembly with solvent.
2. Apply a bead of RTV sealer to the carrier sealing surface.
3. Install the shaft, tube and bolts. Torque the bolts to 36 ft. lbs. (48 Nm).
4. Install the support bracket nuts and torque to 55 ft. lbs. (75 Nm).
5. Install the halfshaft, output shaft-to-halfshaft bolts and torque to 60 ft. lbs. (80 Nm).
6. Install the lower shock bolt and nut.
7. Check the differential lubricant and add if necessary. Install the front tire.
8. Remove the jackstands and lower the vehicle.

Output Shaft Seal and Bearing

REMOVAL AND INSTALLATION

Tools needed: slide hammer J–29307, countershaft roller bearing remover J–29369–2, axle tube bearing installer J–33844 and output shaft seal installer J–33893.
1. Disconnect the negative (−) battery cable, raise the vehicle and support with jackstands.
2. Remove the halfshaft and tube assembly as outlined in this section.

Pinion Oil Seal

REMOVAL AND INSTALLATION

1. Disconnect the negative (−) battery cable, raise the vehicle and support with jackstands.
2. Mark the driveshaft and flange. Remove the driveshaft and support out of the way with wire or rope.
3. Mark the nut, washer and flange so during installation the same amount of torque can be provided for the correct amount of bearing preload. Remove the pinion flange nut and washer using a companion flange holder J–8614–01 or equivalent.
4. Place a container under the flange and remove the flange.
5. Remove the oil seal by driving it out of the carrier with a blunt chisel.

To install:
1. Clean all seal surfaces and remove burrs.
2. Install the new seal using an oil seal installer J–33782.
3. Lubricate the seal lip with differential fluid.
4. Install the pinion flange, washer and nut. Torque the nut to previously marked position. Then turn the nut $1/16$ in. (1.5mm) beyond the alignment marks.
5. Install the driveshaft to the marked position and torque the bolts to 55 ft. lbs. (75 Nm).
6. Install the wheels, add differential lubricant, lower the vehicle and check operation.

Differential Assembly

REMOVAL AND INSTALLATION

1. Disconnect the negative (−) battery cable and unlock the steering.
2. Raise the vehicle and support it with jackstands. Remove the front wheels.
3. Mark the positions of the driveshaft and halfshafts.
4. Insert a drift through the opening in the top of the brake caliper into the vanes in the brake rotor to keep the axle from turning.

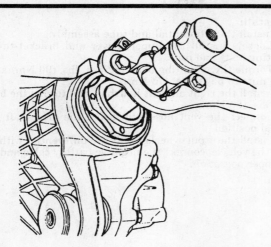

Removing and installing the pinion nut — use same tool to remove the flange

3. Remove the shaft with deflector and retaining ring by striking the inside of the shaft flange with a brass hammer to dislodge the shaft. Pull the shaft out of the seal housing
4. Remove the shaft seal and bearing by using the tools mentioned in the beginning of this procedure.

To install:
1. Lubricate the seal lips, bearings and friction surfaces with axle lubricant before assembly.
2. Install the bearing using the bearing installer.
3. Install the seal.
4. Install the shaft using care not to damage the seal.
5. Install the shaft and tube assembly as outlined in this section.
6. Refill the differential with lubricant.
7. Lower the vehicle and check operation.

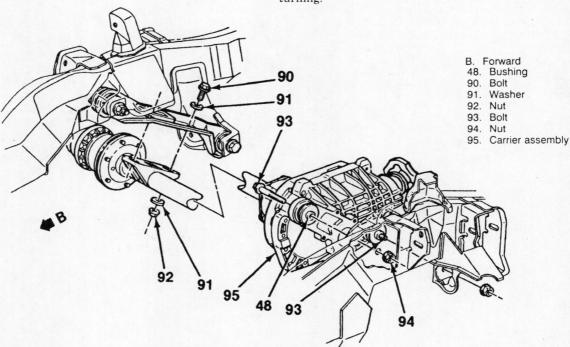

B. Forward
48. Bushing
90. Bolt
91. Washer
92. Nut
93. Bolt
94. Nut
95. Carrier assembly

Differential carrier assembly

5. Disconnect the driveshaft from the differential and fasten out of the way.

6. Disconnect the vent hose and remove the halfshaft-to-output shaft bolts.

7. Remove the tube-to-carrier bolts.

8. Remove the halfshafts and support out of the way with wire. Be careful not to damage the joint boots or CV joints.

9. Remove the axle tube support bracket-to-frame nuts and washers.

10. Remove the upper and lower mounting nuts and bolts.

11. Remove the differential assembly from the vehicle by sliding the entire unit to the right, drop the tube end and twist the carrier to clear the mounting brackets, oil pan and steering linkage.

To install:

1. Install the differential and tube assembly.

2. Loosely install the upper, lower and bracket-to-frame mounting bolts and nuts.

3. Torque the mounting bolts to 65 ft. lbs. (90 Nm) and the frame nuts to 55 ft. lbs. (75 Nm).

4. Install the right and left halfshaft and torque the bolts to 60 ft. lbs. (80 Nm).

5. Connect the vent hose and install the driveshaft to the original position.

6. Install the front wheels, refill the differential with fluid, lower the vehicle, connect the negative battery cable and check for proper operation.

Suspension and Steering

8

2-WHEEL DRIVE FRONT SUSPENSION

The front suspension is designed to allow each wheel to compensate for changes in the road surface without appreciably affecting the opposite wheel. Each wheel is independently connected to the frame by a steering knuckle, ball joint assemblies, and upper and lower control arms. The control arms are specifically designed and positioned to allow the steering knuckles to move in a prescribed three dimensional arc. The front wheels are held in proper relationship to each other by two tie rods which are connected to steering arms on the knuckles and to an intermediate rod.

Coil chassis springs are mounted between the spring housings on the frame and the lower control arms. Ride control is provided by double, direct acting, shock absorbers mounted inside the coil springs and attached to the lower control arms by nuts and bolts. The upper portion of each shock absorber extends through the upper control arm frame bracket and is secured with two grommets, two grommet retainers and a nut.

Side role of the front suspension is controlled by a spring steel stabilizer shaft. It is mounted in rubber bushings which are held to the frame side rails by brackets. The ends of the stabilizer are connected to the lower control arms by link bolts isolated by rubber grommets.

The upper control arm is attached to the upper control arm shaft through isolating rubber bushings. The upper control arm shaft, in turn, is bolted to frame brackets.

A ball joint assembly is riveted to the outer end of the upper control arm. It is preloaded by a rubber spring to insure proper seating of the ball in the socket. The upper ball joint is attached to the steering knuckle by a torque prevailing nut.

The inner ends of the lower control arm have pressed-in bushings. Bolts, passing through the bushings, attach the arm to the frame. The lower ball joint assembly is a press fit in the arm and attaches to the steering knuckle with a torque prevailing nut.

Rubber grease seals are provided at the ball socket assemblies to keep dirt and moisture from entering the joint and damaging the bearing surfaces.

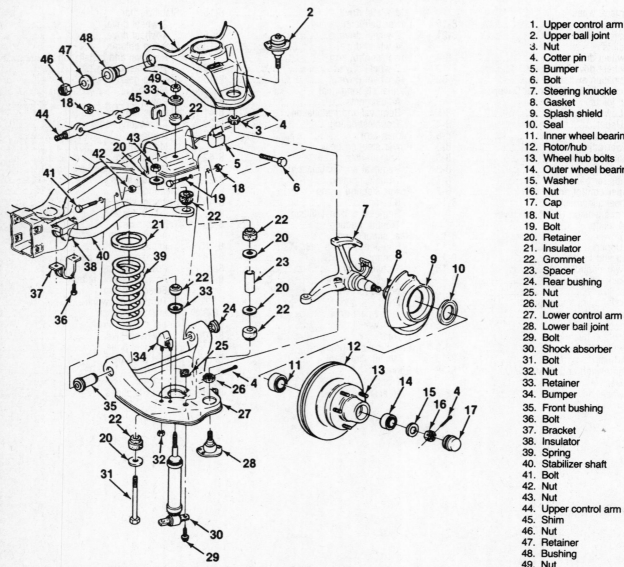

1. Upper control arm
2. Upper ball joint
3. Nut
4. Cotter pin
5. Bumper
6. Bolt
7. Steering knuckle
8. Gasket
9. Splash shield
10. Seal
11. Inner wheel bearing
12. Rotor/hub
13. Wheel hub bolts
14. Outer wheel bearing
15. Washer
16. Nut
17. Cap
18. Nut
19. Bolt
20. Retainer
21. Insulator
22. Grommet
23. Spacer
24. Rear bushing
25. Nut
26. Nut
27. Lower control arm
28. Lower ball joint
29. Bolt
30. Shock absorber
31. Bolt
32. Nut
33. Retainer
34. Bumper
35. Front bushing
36. Bolt
37. Bracket
38. Insulator
39. Spring
40. Stabilizer shaft
41. Bolt
42. Nut
43. Nut
44. Upper control arm shaft
45. Shim
46. Nut
47. Retainer
48. Bushing
49. Nut

Exploded view of the front suspension system — two wheel drive

Coil Springs

REMOVAL AND INSTALLATION

NOTE: The following procedure requires the use of the GM Spring Remover tool No. J–23028 or equivalent.

1. Raise and support the front of the vehicle on jackstands so that the lower control arms hang free.
2. Disconnect the shock absorber-to-lower control arm nuts, then push the shock absorber up into the coil spring.
3. Using the GM Spring Remover tool No. J–23028 or equivalent, secure it to a floor jack, then position the assembly under the lower control arm so that it cradles the inner bushings.
4. Disconnect the stabilizer bar from the lower control arm.
5. Using a safety chain, install it through the coil spring and the lower control arm.

──────── CAUTION ────────

The coil springs are under a considerable amount of tension. Be extremely careful when removing or installing them; they can exert enough force to cause serious injury!

6. Raise the floor jack (with the spring remover tool) to take the tension off of the lower control arm-to-chassis bolts/nuts, then remove the nuts and bolts.

NOTE: When removing the lower control arm-to-chassis bolts/nuts, be sure to remove the rear set first, then the front set.

7. Carefully, lower the floor jack (with the spring remover tool) until the tension is released from the coil spring.

NOTE: When removing the coil spring, DO NOT apply force to the lower control arm or the lower ball joint. Proper maneuvering of the spring will provide easy removal.

8. Before installing the coil spring, position it in the following order:
   a. The coil spring top has a coiled, flat shape with a gripper notch at the end of the coil; the bottom has a coiled, helical shape.
   b. Place the coil spring so that the tape (on the coil) is at the lowest position.
   c. Position the lower end of the coil spring so that it covers part or all of the inspection drain hole. The other drain hole MUST BE partially or completely uncovered.
   d. Place the insulator at the top of the coil spring.

To install:

1. Using the GM Spring Remover tool No. J–23028 floor jack assembly, raise the lower control arm/coil spring assembly using the floor jack and install the lower control arm-to-chassis nuts/bolts.
2. Pull the shock absorber down, then install the shock absorber-to-lower control arm nuts/bolts. Torque the nuts and bolts to 18 ft. lbs. (25 Nm).
3. Lower the front of the vehicle, so that it is resting on its own weight, then torque the lower control arm-to-chassis nuts/bolts to 96 ft. lbs. (128 Nm).
4. Check and/or adjust the front end alignment.

Shock Absorbers

REMOVAL AND INSTALLATION

1. Raise and support the front of the vehicle on jackstands. Remove the wheels.
2. While holding the upper end of the shock absorber (to keep

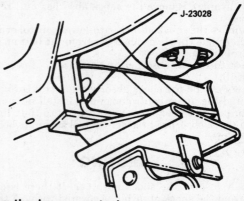

Supporting the lower control arm with the spring removing tool

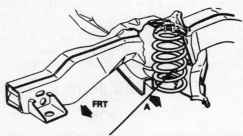

SPRING TO BE INSTALLED WITH TAPE AT LOWEST POSITION. BOTTOM OF SPRING IS COILED HELICAL, AND THE TOP IS COILED FLAT WITH A GRIPPER NOTCH NEAR END OF SPRING COIL.

AFTER ASSEMBLY, END OF SPRING COIL MUST COVER ALL OR PART OF ONE IN-SPECTION DRAIN HOLE. THE OTHER HOLE MUST BE PARTLY EXPOSED OR COM-PLETELY UNCOVERED. ROTATE SPRING AS NECESSARY.

Positioning the coil spring — front suspension, two wheel drive

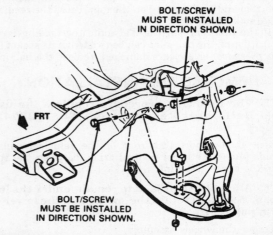

BOLT/SCREW MUST BE INSTALLED IN DIRECTION SHOWN.

BOLT/SCREW MUST BE INSTALLED IN DIRECTION SHOWN.

Replacing the lower control arm — front suspension, two wheel drive

it from turning), remove the shock absorber nut, retainer and grommet.

3. Remove the shock absorber-to-lower control arm nuts and bolts, then slide the shock absorber from the bottom of the lower control arm.

4. Test the shock absorber and replace it, if necessary.

To install:

1. Fully extend the shock absorber, insert it through the coil spring and the upper control arm and install nuts and bolts.

2. Torque the upper shock absorber nut to 15 ft. lbs. (20 Nm) and the shock absorber-to-lower control arm nuts/bolts to 18 ft. lbs. (25 Nm).

TESTING

Visually inspect the shock absorber. If there is evidence of leakage and the shock absorber is covered with oil, the shock is defective and should be replaced.

If there is no sign of excessive leakage (a small amount of weeping is normal) bounce the van at one corner by pressing down on the bumper and releasing it. When you have the van bouncing as much as you can, release the bumper. The van should stop bouncing after the first rebound. If the bouncing continues past the center point of the bounce more than once, the shock absorbers are worn and should be replaced.

Upper Ball Joint

INSPECTION

NOTE: Before performing this inspection, make sure that the wheel bearings are adjusted correctly and that the control arm bushings are in good condition.

1. Raise and support the front of the vehicle by placing jackstands under each lower control arm as close as possible to each lower ball joint.

NOTE: Before performing the upper ball joint replacement, be sure that the vehicle is stable and the lower control arm bumpers are not contacting the frame.

2. Using a dial indicator, position it so that it contacts the wheel rim.

3. To measure the horizontal deflection, perform the following procedures:

    a. Grasp the tire (top and bottom), then pull outward on the top and push inward on the bottom; record the reading on the dial indicator.

    b. Grasp the tire (top and bottom), then pull outward on the bottom and push inward on the top; record the reading on the dial indicator.

    c. If the difference in the dial indicator reading is more than 3.175mm, the ball joint can be twisted in its socket (with finger pressure) or appears damaged, replace the ball joint.

REMOVAL AND INSTALLATION

NOTE: The following procedure requires the use of the GM Ball Joint Remover tool No. J–23742 or equivalent.

1. Raise and support the front of the vehicle by placing jackstands under the lower control arms, between the spring seat and the lower ball joint.

NOTE: Allow the floor jack to remain under the lower control arm seat, to retain the spring and the lower control arm position.

2. Remove the wheels assembly.

3. From the upper ball joint, remove the cotter pin, the nut and the grease fitting.

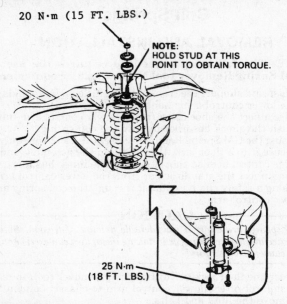

20 N·m (15 FT. LBS.)

NOTE: HOLD STUD AT THIS POINT TO OBTAIN TORQUE.

25 N·m (18 FT. LBS.)

Replacing the shock absorber — front suspension

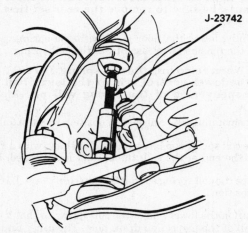

J–23742

Disconnecting the upper ball joint from the upper control arm

4. Using the GM Ball Joint Remover tool No. J–23742 or equivalent, separate the upper ball joint from the steering knuckle. Pull the steering knuckle free of the ball joint after removal.

NOTE: After separating the steering knuckle from the upper ball joint, be sure to support steering knuckle/hub assembly to prevent damaging the brake hose.

5. To remove the upper ball joint from the upper control arm, perform the following procedures:

    a. Using a 3mm drill bit, drill a 6mm deep hole into each rivet.

    b. Using a 13mm drill bit, drill off the rivet heads.

    c. Using a pin punch and the hammer, drive the rivets from the upper ball joint-to-upper control arm assembly and remove the upper ball joint.

To install:

1. Clean and inspect the steering knuckle hole. Replace the steering knuckle, if any out of roundness is noted.

2. Use a new upper ball joint, position the upper ball joint-to-

upper control arm bolts facing upward.

3. Torque the upper ball joint-to-upper control arm bolts to 96 inch lbs. (11 Nm).

4. Seat the upper ball joint into the steering knuckle and install the nut. Torque the upper ball joint-to-steering knuckle nut to 52 ft. lbs. (70 Nm) and the wheel nuts to 90 ft. lbs. (122 Nm).

5. Install a new cotter pin to the lower ball joint stud.

NOTE: When installing the cotter pin to the upper ball joint-to-steering knuckle nut, be sure to turn the castle nut an addition amount to expose the cotter pin hole.

6. Using a grease gun, lubricate the upper ball joint until grease oozes from the grease seal.

7. Inspect and/or adjust the wheel bearing and the front end alignment.

8. Remove the lower control arm support and lower the vehicle.

Lower Ball Joint

INSPECTION

NOTE: Before performing this inspection, make sure that the wheel bearings are adjusted correctly and that the control arm bushings are in good condition.

Visually check the wear indicator; if it is flush or inside the ball joint cover surface, replace the ball joint.

REMOVAL AND INSTALLATION

NOTE: The following procedure requires the use of the GM Ball Joint Remover tool No. J–23742 or equivalent, the GM Ball Joint Remover tool No. J–9519–7 or equivalent, the GM Ball Joint Installer tool No. J–9519–9 or equivalent, and the GM Ball Joint Fixture tool No. J–9519–10 or equivalent.

1. Raise and support the front of the vehicle on jackstands. Remove the wheels.

2. Using a floor jack, place it under the spring seat of the lower control arm, then raise the jack to support the arm.

NOTE: The floor jack MUST remain under the lower control arm, during the removal and installation procedures, to retain the arm and spring positions.

3. Remove the cotter pin (discard it) and the ball joint nut.

4. Using the GM Ball Joint Remover tool No. J–23742 or equivalent, disconnect the lower ball joint from the steering knuckle. Pull the steering knuckle away from the lower control arm, place a block of wood between the frame and the upper control arm; make sure that the brake hose is free of tension.

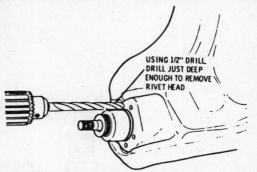

Use a ½ inch drill to drill the upper ball joint rivet heads

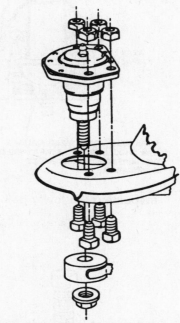

When installing the new upper ball joint, make sure that the nuts are on top

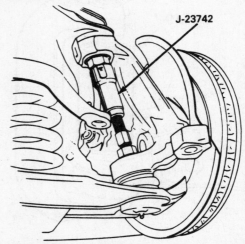

Disconnecting the lower ball joint from the steering knuckle/hub assembly — front suspension, two wheel drive

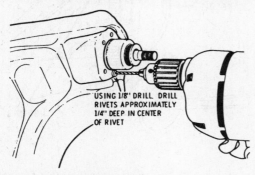

Drill the upper ball joint rivets

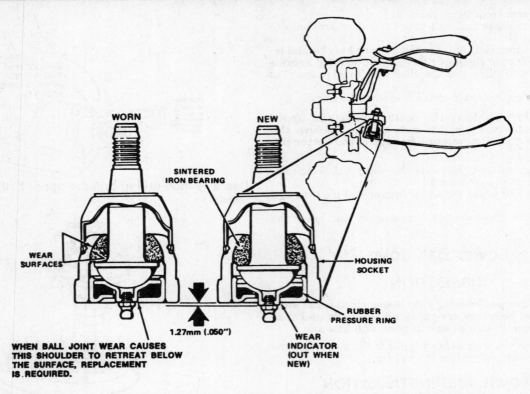

WORN

NEW

SINTERED
IRON BEARING

WEAR
SURFACES

HOUSING
SOCKET

RUBBER
PRESSURE RING

1.27mm (.050")

WEAR
INDICATOR
(OUT WHEN
NEW)

WHEN BALL JOINT WEAR CAUSES
THIS SHOULDER TO RETREAT BELOW
THE SURFACE, REPLACEMENT
IS REQUIRED.

Inspecting the lower ball joint indicator — front suspension, two wheel drive

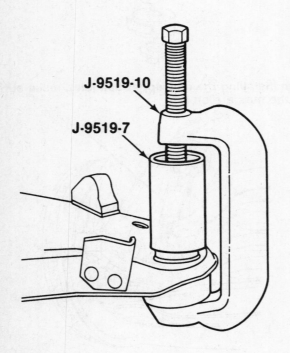

J-9519-10

J-9519-7

Removing the lower ball joint from the lower control
arm — front suspension, two wheel drive

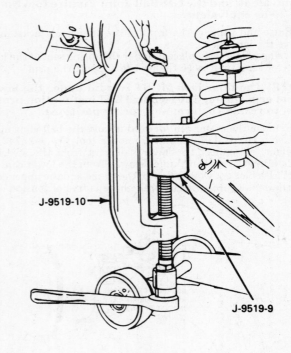

J-9519-10

J-9519-9

Installing the new lower ball joint into the lower
control arm — front suspension, two wheel drive

5. From the lower ball joint, remove the rubber grease seal and the grease fitting.

6. Using the GM Ball Joint Remover tool No. J–9519–7 or equivalent, and the GM Ball Joint Fixture tool No. J–9519–10 or equivalent, remove the lower ball joint from the lower control arm.

To install:

1. Position the new lower ball joint into the lower control arm. Using the GM Ball Joint Installer tool No. J–9519–9 or equivalent, and the GM Ball Joint Fixture tool No. J–9519–10 or equivalent, press the new lower ball joint into the lower control arm.

2. Install the grease fitting and the grease seal onto the lower ball joint; the grease seal MUST BE fully seated on the ball joint and the grease purge hole MUST face inboard.

3. Torque the ball joint-to-steering knuckle nut to 81 ft. lbs. (110 Nm) and the wheel nuts to 90 ft. lbs. (122 Nm).

4. Install a new cotter pin to the lower ball joint stud.

NOTE: When installing the cotter pin to the lower ball joint-to-steering knuckle nut, be sure to turn the castle nut an addition amount to expose the cotter pin hole.

5. Using a grease gun, lubricate the lower ball joint until grease oozes from the grease seal. Inspect and/or adjust the wheel bearing and the front end alignment.

6. Remove the lower control arm support and lower the vehicle.

Stabilizer Bar

REMOVAL AND INSTALLATION

1. Raise and support the front of the vehicle on jackstands. Remove the wheels.

2. Disconnect the stabilizer bar link nuts from the lower control arms.

3. Remove the stabilizer bar-to-frame clamps.

4. Remove the stabilizer bar from the vehicle.

To install:

1. Install the stabilizer bar-to-frame clamps and link nuts.

2. Torque the stabilizer bar link-to-lower control arm bolts to 13 ft. lbs. (18 Nm) and the stabilizer retainer-to-frame bolts to 22 ft. lbs. (29 Nm).

Upper Control Arm

REMOVAL AND INSTALLATION

NOTE: The following procedure requires the use of the GM Ball Joint Remover tool No. J–23742 or equivalent.

1. Raise and support the front of the vehicle by placing jackstands under the lower control arms, between the spring seat and the lower ball joint.

NOTE: Allow the floor jack to remain under the lower control arm seat, to retain the spring and the lower control arm position.

2. Remove the wheels.

3. From the upper ball joint, remove the cotter pin and the ball joint-to-upper control arm nut.

4. Using the GM Ball Joint Remover tool No. J–23742 or equivalent, separate the upper ball joint from the steering knuckle/hub assembly. Pull the steering knuckle free of the ball joint after removal.

NOTE: After separating the steering knuckle from the upper ball joint, be sure to support steering knuckle/hub assembly to prevent damaging the brake hose.

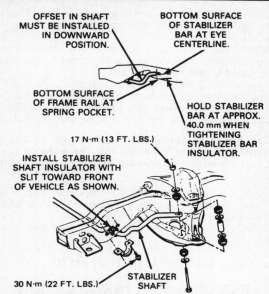

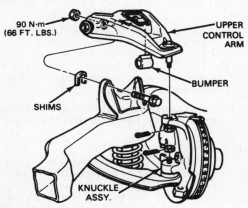

Replacing the stabilizer bar — front suspension, two wheel drive

Removing the upper control arm

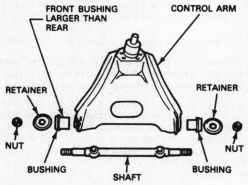

Exploded view of the upper control arm

5. Remove the upper control arm-to-frame nuts and bolts, then lift and remove the upper control arm from the vehicle.

NOTE: Tape the shims together and identify them so that they can be installed in the proper positions from which they were removed.

6. Clean and inspect the steering knuckle hole. Replace the steering knuckle, if any out of roundness is noted.

To install:

1. Attach the upper control arm to the frame, insert the shims in their proper positions, seat the upper ball joint into the steering knuckle and install the nut.

2. Torque the upper control arm-to-frame bolts to 66 ft. lbs. (90 Nm), the upper ball joint-to-steering knuckle nut to 52 ft. lbs. (69 Nm) and the wheel nuts to 90 ft. lbs. (122 Nm).

3. Install a new cotter pin to the upper ball joint stud.

NOTE: When installing the cotter pin to the upper ball joint-to-steering knuckle nut, be sure to turn the castle nut an addition amount to expose the cotter pin hole.

4. Using a grease gun, lubricate the upper ball joint until grease oozes from the grease seal. Inspect and/or adjust the wheel bearing and the front end alignment.

5. Remove the lower control arm support and lower the vehicle.

Lower Control Arm

REMOVAL AND INSTALLATION

NOTE: The following procedure requires the use of the GM Ball Joint Remover tool No. J–23742 or equivalent.

1. Refer to the Coil Spring, Removal and Installation procedures in this section and remove the coil spring.

2. Remove the cotter pin (discard it) and the ball joint nut.

3. Using the GM Ball Joint Remover tool No. J–23742 or equivalent, disconnect the lower ball joint from the steering knuckle and the lower control arm from the vehicle.

NOTE: Place a block of wood between the frame and the upper control arm; make sure that the brake hose is free of tension.

To install:

1. Position the lower ball joint stud into the steering knuckle. Torque the ball joint-to-steering knuckle nut to 81 ft. lbs. (110 Nm).

2. Make sure the spring is secure and install the control arm-to-chassis bolts.

3. Lower the front of the vehicle, so that it is resting on its own weight, then torque the lower control arm-to-chassis nuts/bolts to 96 ft. lbs. (130 Nm) and the wheel nuts to 90 ft. lbs. (122 Nm).

4. Install a new cotter pin to the lower ball joint stud.

NOTE: When installing the cotter pin to the lower ball joint-to-steering knuckle nut, be sure to turn the castle nut an addition amount to expose the cotter pin hole.

5. Using a grease gun, lubricate the lower ball joint until grease oozes from the grease seal. Inspect and/or adjust the wheel bearing and the front end alignment.

6. Pull the shock absorber down, then install the shock absorber-to-lower control arm nuts/bolts. Torque the nuts and bolts to 18 ft. lbs. (25 Nm).

7. Remove the lower control arm support and lower the vehicle.

Knuckle and Spindle

REMOVAL AND INSTALLATION

NOTE: The following procedure requires the use of the GM Tie Rod End Puller tool J–6627 or equivalent, and the GM Ball Joint Remover tool No. J–23742 or equivalent.

1. Siphon some brake fluid from the brake master cylinder.

2. Raise and support the front of the vehicle on jackstands. Remove the wheels.

NOTE: When supporting the vehicle on jackstands, DO NOT place the jackstands directly under the lower control arms for the vehicle may slip off the jackstands during the steering knuckle removal.

3. Remove the brake caliper from the steering knuckle and support it on a wire.

4. Remove the grease cup, the cotter pin, the castle nut and the hub assembly.

5. Remove the splash shield-to-steering knuckle bolts and the shield.

6. At the tie rod end-to-steering knuckle stud, remove the cotter pin and the nut. Using the GM Tie Rod End Puller tool J–6627 or equivalent, separate the tie rod end from the steering knuckle.

7. From the upper and lower ball joint studs, remove the cotter pins and the nuts.

8. Using a floor jack, place it under the spring seat of the lower control arm and support the arm.

9. Using the GM Ball Joint Remover tool No. J–23742 or equivalent, separate the upper ball joint from the steering knuckle.

10. Raise the upper control arm to separate it from the steering knuckle.

11. Using the GM Ball Joint Remover tool No. J–23742 or equivalent, separate the lower ball joint from the steering knuckle, then lift the steering knuckle from the lower control arm.

12. Clean and inspect the steering knuckle and spindle for signs of wear or damage; if necessary, replace the steering knuckle.

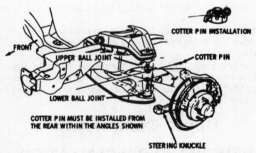

Exploded view of the steering knuckle and cotter pin — front suspension, two wheel drive

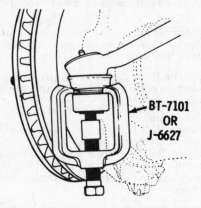

Disconnect the tie rod end from the steering knuckle — front suspension, two wheel drive

To install:

1. To install the steering knuckle, position it onto the lower ball joint stud, then lift the upper control arm to insert the upper ball joint stud into the steering knuckle.

2. Torque the upper ball joint-to-steering knuckle nut to 52 ft. lbs. (69 Nm) and the lower ball joint-to-steering knuckle nut to 81 ft. lbs. (110 Nm). Remove the floor jack from under the lower control arm.

3. Install a new cotter pin into the upper and lower ball joint studs.

NOTE: When installing the cotter pin to the lower ball joint-to-steering knuckle nut, be sure to turn the castle nut an addition amount to expose the cotter pin hole.

4. Torque the tie rod end-to-steering knuckle nut to 30 ft. lbs. (41 Nm), the splash shield-to-steering knuckle bolts to 120 inch lbs. (14 Nm).

5. Have a qualified alignment technician align the front end.

6. Remove the jackstands and lower the vehicle.

7. Refill the brake master cylinder and check operation.

Front Wheel Bearings

REMOVAL

NOTE: The following procedure requires the use of an Arbor Press and the GM Front Outer Race Remover tool No. J–29117 or equivalent, the GM Driver Handle tool No. J–8092 or equivalent, the GM Outer Bearing Outer Race Installer tool No. J–8457 or equivalent, the GM Inner Bearing Outer Race Installer tool No. J–8850 or equivalent, and the GM Bearing Remover tool No. J–9746–02 or equivalent.

Before handling the bearings, there are a few things that you should remember to do and not to do.

Remember to DO the following:

• Remove all outside dirt from the housing before exposing the bearing.

• Treat a used bearing as gently as you would a new one.

• Work with clean tools in clean surroundings.

• Use clean, dry canvas gloves, or at least clean, dry hands.

• Clean solvents and flushing fluids are a must.

• Use clean paper when laying out the bearings to dry.

• Protect disassembled bearings from rust and dirt. Cover them up.

• Use clean rags to wipe bearings.

• Keep the bearings in oil-proof paper when they are to be stored or are not in use.

• Clean the inside of the housing before replacing the bearing.

Do NOT do the following:

• Don't work in dirty surroundings.

• Don't use dirty, chipped or damaged tools.

• Try not to work on wooden work benches or use wooden mallets.

• Don't handle bearings with dirty or moist hands.

• Do not use gasoline for cleaning; use a safe solvent.

• Do not spin-dry bearings with compressed air. They will be damaged.

• Do not spin dirty bearings.

• Avoid using cotton waste or dirty cloths to wipe bearings.

• Try not to scratch or nick bearing surfaces.

• Do not allow the bearing to come in contact with dirt or rust at any time.

1. Raise and support the front of the vehicle on jackstands.

2. Remove the wheel and tire assembly.

3. Remove the brake caliper from the steering knuckle and place a block of wood between the brake pads; using a wire, support the brake caliper (from the vehicle) without disconnecting the brake hose.

--- **CAUTION** ---

Brake shoes contain asbestos, which has been determined to be a cancer causing agent. Never clean the brake surfaces with compressed air! Avoid inhaling any dust from any brake surface! When cleaning brake surfaces, use a commercially available brake cleaning fluid.

4. Remove the dust cap, the cotter pin, the spindle nut, the thrust washer and the outer wheel bearing, then remove the disc/hub/bearing assembly.

NOTE: When removing the disc/hub/bearing assembly, be careful not to drop the wheel bearing.

5. Using a medium pry bar, pry the grease seal from the inner edge of the hub assembly, then remove the inner wheel bearing.

6. Using the GM Front Outer Race Remover tool No. J–29117 or equivalent, and an arbor press, remove the wheel bearing races from the hub assembly.

PACKING

Using solvent, wash all of the parts and check for excessive wear or damage.

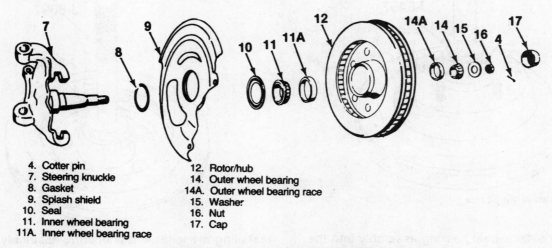

4. Cotter pin
7. Steering knuckle
8. Gasket
9. Splash shield
10. Seal
11. Inner wheel bearing
11A. Inner wheel bearing race
12. Rotor/hub
14. Outer wheel bearing
14A. Outer wheel bearing race
15. Washer
16. Nut
17. Cap

Exploded view of the disc/hub assembly

NOTE: If blow drying the wheel bearings with compressed air, DO NOT spin them, for damage may occur to the bearings.

Pack both wheel bearings using high melting point wheel bearing grease for disc brakes. Ordinary grease will melt and ooze out ruining the pads. Bearings should be packed using a cone-type wheel bearing greaser tool. If one is not available they may be packed by hand. Place a healthy glob of grease in the palm of one hand and force the edge of the bearing into it so that the grease fills the bearing. Do this until the whole bearing is packed.

NOTE: Sodium-based grease is not compatible with lithium-based grease. Read the package labels and be careful not to mix the two types. If there is any doubt as to the type of grease used, completely clean the old grease from the bearing and hub before replacing.

INSTALLATION AND ADJUSTMENT

1. Position the disc/hub assembly (wheel studs facing downward) on the GM Bearing Remover tool No. J–9746–02 or equivalent.
2. Using the GM Driver Handle tool No. J–8092 or equivalent, and the GM Inner Bearing Outer Race Installer tool No. J–8850 or equivalent, press the inner wheel bearing assembly into the rear of the disc/hub assembly until the bearing seats against the shoulder.
3. Using a flat plate, drive a new grease seal into the rear of the disc/hub assembly, then lubricate the lip of the seal.
4. Turn and position the disc/hub assembly (wheel studs facing upward) on the GM Bearing Remover tool No. J–9746–02 or equivalent.
5. Using the GM Driver Handle tool No. J–8092 or equiva-

lent, and the GM Outer Bearing Outer Race Installer tool No. J–8457 or equivalent, press the outer wheel bearing assembly into the front of the disc/hub assembly until the bearing seats against the shoulder.
6. Install the disc/hub assembly, the thrust washer and the nut onto the wheel spindle. While turning the wheel assembly in the forward direction, tighten the spindle nut to 12 ft. lbs. (15 Nm).
7. Loosen the spindle nut, then tighten it again until the slot in the nut aligns with the hole in the spindle, then install a new cotter pin.

NOTE: When the disc/hub assembly is properly adjusted, the end play should be 0.025–0.13mm.

8. After installing the cotter pin, bend the ends against the spindle nut and cut off any excess which will interfere with the dust cap.
9. Lower the vehicle and road test.

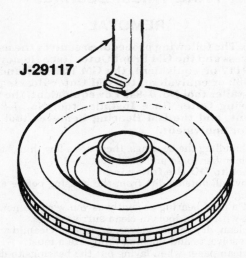

Removing the wheel bearing races from the disc/hub assembly — two wheel drive

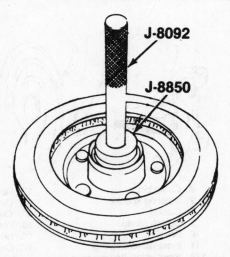

Installing the inner wheel bearing assembly into the disc/hub assembly — two wheel drive

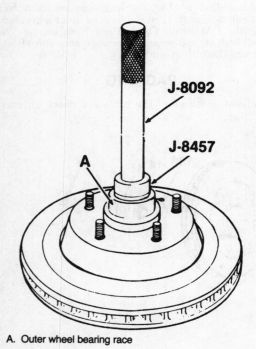

A. Outer wheel bearing race

Installing the outer wheel bearing assembly into the disc/hub assembly — two wheel drive

4-WHEEL DRIVE FRONT SUSPENSION

The All Wheel Drive Astro van front suspension uses a rigidly mounted differential and constant velocity halfshafts. The differential remains stationary while the halfshafts move up and down depending on the road surface.

The upper and lower control arm are of the wishbone configuration as the two wheel drive. The lower control arms are sprung with torsion bars instead of coil springs. The torsion bars are mounted to the frame crossmember and are adjustable to maintain proper vehicle height.

Torsion Bars and Support

REMOVAL AND INSTALLATION

1. Disconnect the negative (−) battery cable.
2. Raise the vehicle and support with jackstands.
3. Mark the adjustment bolt setting on bolt adjusters. Decrease the tension on the adjustment arm using an adjusting tool J–36202.
4. Remove the adjusting bolt and retainer plate.
5. Move the tool aside, slide the torsion bar forward and remove the adjustment arm.
6. Remove the nuts and bolts from the torsion bar support-to-crossmember. Slide the crossmember rearward.
7. Mark the location of the front and rear ends. Mark either left or right because the bars are different.
8. Remove the support crossmember, retainer, spacer and insulator from the crossmember.

To install:

1. Install the insulator, spacer and retainer onto the support crossmember.
2. Install the crossmember onto the frame, rearward of the mounting holes.
3. Make sure the bars are on their respective sides. Slide the crossmember forward until the bars are supported.
4. Install the adjustment arms, crossmember bolts and nuts. Torque the center nut to 18 ft. lbs. (24 Nm) and the edge nuts to 46 ft. lbs. (62 Nm).
5. Install the adjustment retainer plates and bolt.
6. Increase the tension using the unloader tool J–36202.
7. Set the adjuster to the marked position.
8. Release the tension on the bar until the load is taken up by the adjustment bolt and remove the unloader tool.
9. Lower the vehicle and check the "Z" height as outlined in the "Alignment" procedures in this Section.

Shock Absorbers

REMOVAL AND INSTALLATION

1. Raise the vehicle and support with jackstands and remove the front tire.
2. Remove the lower bolt and nut.
3. Collapse the shock, remove the upper bolt, nut and shock absorber.

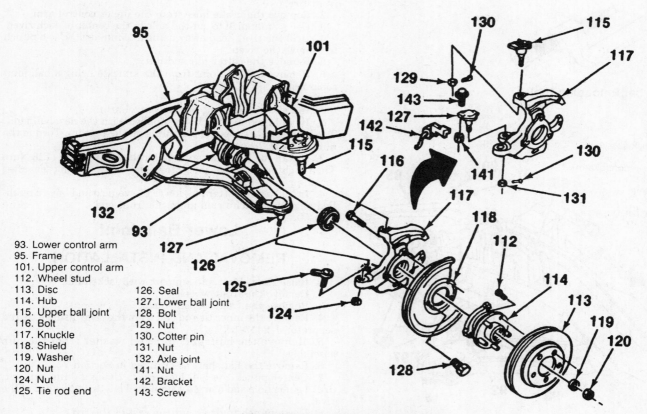

93. Lower control arm
95. Frame
101. Upper control arm
112. Wheel stud
113. Disc
114. Hub
115. Upper ball joint
116. Bolt
117. Knuckle
118. Shield
119. Washer
120. Nut
124. Nut
125. Tie rod end
126. Seal
127. Lower ball joint
128. Bolt
129. Nut
130. Cotter pin
131. Nut
132. Axle joint
141. Nut
142. Bracket
143. Screw

All wheel drive front suspension

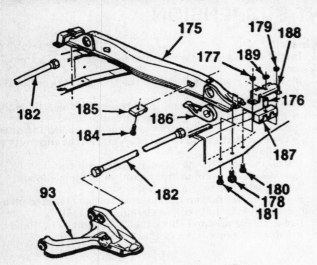

93. Lower control arm
175. Support
176. Spacer
177. Nut
178. Bolt
179. Nut
180. Bolt
181. Bolt

182. Torsion bars
184. Adjusting bolt
185. Retaining plate
186. Adjusting arm
187. Insulator
188. Retainer
189. Nut

Torsion bar and support assembly

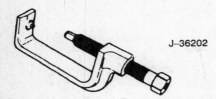

J-36202

Torsion bar unloading tool

90. Nut
91. Shock absorber
92. Nut
93. Lower control arm
94. Bolt
95. Frame
96. Bolt
97. Washer

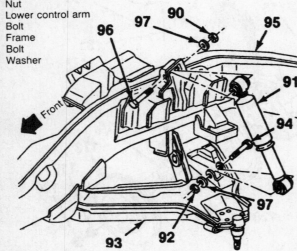

Shock absorber assembly

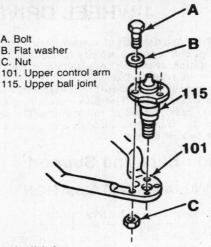

A. Bolt
B. Flat washer
C. Nut
101. Upper control arm
115. Upper ball joint

Upper ball joint

To install:
1. Install the shock, nuts and bolts.
2. Torque the nuts to 66 ft. lbs. (90 Nm).
3. Install the tire and torque the lug nuts to 90 ft. lbs. (122 Nm) and lower the vehicle.

Upper Ball Joint

REMOVAL AND INSTALLATION

1. Raise the vehicle and support with jackstands. Remove the front tire.
2. Remove the brake hose from the upper control arm.
3. Use a 3mm drill to cut the hole in the center of each rivet.
4. Drill the rivet head away using a 13mm drill. Use a punch to remove the rivets.
5. Remove the cotter pin and nut.
6. Remove the ball joint from the knuckle using a ball joint separator.
To install:
1. Install the ball joint to the control arm.
2. Install the nuts and bolts supplied with the new ball joint. The bolt is on the top and the nut is on the bottom. Torque the nuts to 22 ft. lbs. (30 Nm).
3. Install the ball joint nut and torque to 94 ft. lbs. (128 Nm). Then tighten to align the cotter pin. DO NOT loosen after torquing.
4. Install a new cotter pin, lower the vehicle and have a qualified alignment technician align the front end.

Lower Ball Joint

REMOVAL AND INSTALLATION

1. Raise the vehicle and support with jackstands.
2. Remove the front wheels.
3. Remove the front splash shield.
4. Remove the inner tie rod end from the relay using a tie rod separator J-2419-01.
5. Remove the halfshaft nut and washer from the hub assembly.
6. Remove the halfshaft as outlined in Section 7.
7. Center punch the ball joint rivet. Using a 3mm drill bit, drill a guide hole and using a 13mm drill bit, drill the head of the rivet.
8. Use a punch to drive out the rest of the rivet.
9. Remove the ball joint cotter pin.

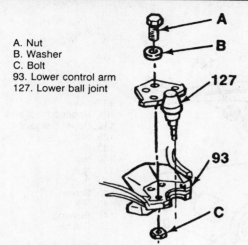

A. Nut
B. Washer
C. Bolt
93. Lower control arm
127. Lower ball joint

Lower ball joint

10. Support the lower control arm with a jackstands to release the torsion bar tension.
11. Remove the ball joint nut.
12. Remove the knuckle from the ball joint using a ball joint separator tool J–29193 and remove the ball joint.
To install:
1. Install the ball joint, bolts, washers and nuts. Torque the nuts to 22 ft. lbs. (30 Nm).
2. Install the joint-to-control arm and nut.
3. Torque the nut to 92 ft. lbs. (125 Nm). Tighten the nut to align the cotter pin hole, but no more than $\frac{1}{6}$ of a turn.
4. Install a new cotter pin and bend over.
5. Load the torsion bar using the loading tool J–36202.
6. Install the halfshaft assembly as outlined in Section 7.

7. Install the inner tie rod end, torque the nut to 35 ft. lbs. (47 Nm) and install a new cotter pin, if so equipped.
8. Install the splash shield, front wheel and lower the vehicle.
9. Have a qualified alignment technician align the front end.

Stabilizer Bar

REMOVAL AND INSTALLATION

NOTE: Keep the right or left suspension components separated and do not interchange.

1. Raise the vehicle and support with jackstands. Remove the front wheels.
2. Remove the nuts, bolts and spacers from the end links.
3. Remove the bolts and clamps from the frame.
4. Remove the bar and insulators.
To install:
1. Install the insulators so that the slits face forward.
2. Install the shaft to the frame and lower control arm.
3. Install the clamps and bolts. Torque the clamp bolts to 12 ft. lbs. (17 Nm).
4. Install the spacers, link bolts and nuts. Torque the nuts to 22 ft. lbs. (30 Nm).
5. Install the front wheels and lower the vehicle.

Upper Control Arm

REMOVAL AND INSTALLATION

1. Raise the vehicle and support with jackstands under the lower control arms.
2. Remove the front wheels and disconnect the negative (−) battery cable.
3. Remove the brake hose from the control arm and tie out of the way.

93. Lower control arm
95. Frame
103. Nut
104. Spacer
105. Bolt
107. Stabilizer shaft
108. Clamp
109. Bolt
110. Insulator

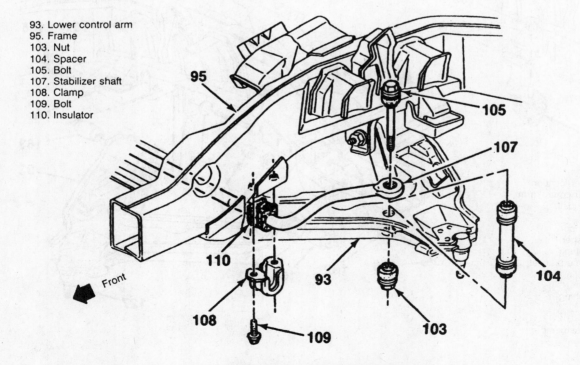

Stabilizer bar and components

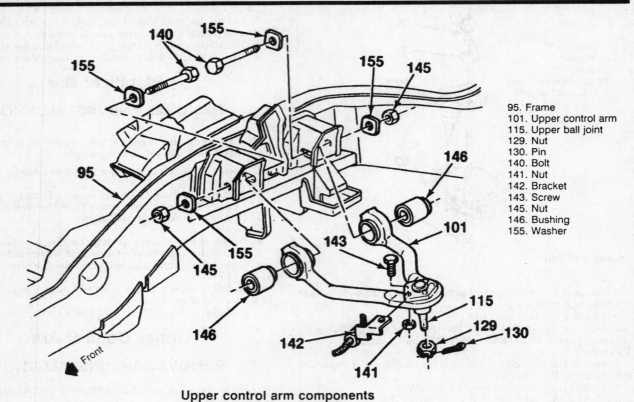

95. Frame
101. Upper control arm
115. Upper ball joint
129. Nut
130. Pin
140. Bolt
141. Nut
142. Bracket
143. Screw
145. Nut
146. Bushing
155. Washer

Upper control arm components

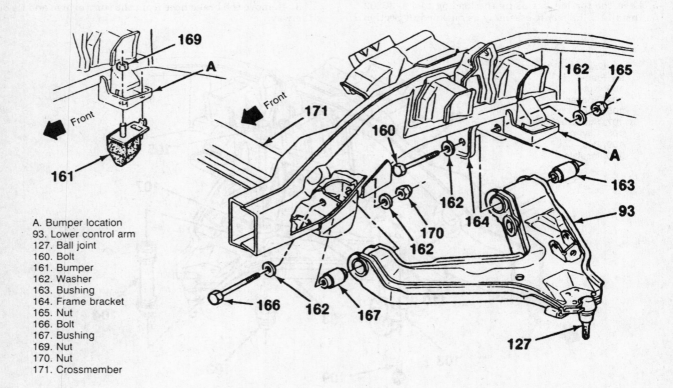

A. Bumper location
93. Lower control arm
127. Ball joint
160. Bolt
161. Bumper
162. Washer
163. Bushing
164. Frame bracket
165. Nut
166. Bolt
167. Bushing
169. Nut
170. Nut
171. Crossmember

Lower control arm components

4. Remove the ball joint cotter pin and nut.

5. Disconnect the control arm from the knuckle using a ball joint separator.

6. Remove the control arm nuts, bolts and washers. Remove the control arm with the bushings.

To install:

1. Install the upper control arm to the frame.

2. Install the bolts and the washers. Make sure the bolt threads are opposed inside the bracket. Do not tighten until the vehicle is on the ground.

3. Install the upper ball joint-to-knuckle.

4. Torque the nut to 94 ft. lbs. (128 Nm) and align the cotter pin slot.

5. Install a new cotter pin and bend over.

6. Install the brake hose and front wheel.

7. Lower the vehicle.

8. Torque the control arm bushing nuts to 88 ft. lbs. (120 Nm) at normal suspension height.

Lower Control Arm

REMOVAL AND INSTALLATION

NOTE: Tools Needed: universal tie rod separator J-24319-01, torsion bar unloader J-36202, lower control arm bushing service kit J-36618 and ball joint C-clamp J-9519-23.

1. Raise the vehicle and support with jackstands.

2. Remove the front wheels.

3. Remove the front splash shield to gain access to the tie rod.

4. Disconnect the stabilizer bar from the control arm.

5. Remove the shock absorber as outlined in this Section.

6. Disconnect the inner tie rod from the relay rod using a tie rod separator.

7. Remove the outer halfshaft nut and washer. Remove the halfshaft from the hub as outlined in Section 7.

8. Unload the torsion bar using the unloading tool J-36202. First, mark the adjuster for installation. Support the lower control arm with jackstands. Loosen the bolt and remove the adjustment arm. Slide the bar forward to remove the adjusting arm.

9. Remove the ball joint cotter pin, nut and ball joint from the control arm using a ball joint separator.

10. Remove the nuts and bolts and lower control arm with the torsion bat assembly.

11. If replacing bushings: unbend the crimps using a punch and remove the bushing using a bushing service kit J-36618-2, J-9519-23, J-36618-4 and J-36618-1.

To install:

1. Install the front bushing using tools J-36618 and J-9519-23. Crimp the bushing after in place.

2. Install the rear bushing using J-36618 and J-9519-23.

3. Install the torsion bar-to-lower control arm and install the assembly into the vehicle. Position the front leg of the lower control arm into the crossmember before installing the rear leg into the frame bracket.

4. Install the halfshaft and torque the bolts to 57 ft. lbs. (78 Nm) and the hub nut to 173 ft. lbs. (235 Nm).

5. Install the control arm bolts with new nuts. Do NOT torque at this time.

6. Install the ball joint-to-knuckle. Torque the nut to 96 ft. lbs. (130 Nm). Install a new cotter pin and bend over.

7. Install the adjuster arm to the marked position.

8. Install the shock absorber.

9. Install the stabilize bar and splash shield.

10. Install the front wheels and lower the vehicle.

11. Torque the lower control arm nuts with the suspension at the correct height to 135 ft. lbs. (185 Nm).

12. Recheck all fasteners for proper torque and installation before road testing.

13. Refill the differential if any fluid was lost.

14. Have a qualified alignment technician align the front end.

Hub, Knuckle and Bearing

REMOVAL AND INSTALLATION

NOTE: Tool Needed: ball joint separator J-36607, or equivalent.

1. Remove ⅔ of the fluid from the brake reservoir.

2. Raise the vehicle and support with jackstands.

3. Remove the front wheels. Place a protective cover over the halfshaft boots.

—————————— CAUTION ——————————

Some brake pads contain asbestos, which has been determined to be a cancer causing agent. Never clean the brake surfaces with compressed air! Avoid inhaling any dust from any brake surface! When cleaning brake surfaces, use a commercially available brake cleaning fluid.

4. Remove the brake caliper as outlined in Section 9. Support the caliper with a piece of wire.

5. Remove the brake disc, halfshaft nut and washer.

6. Remove the tie rod nut and tie rod end using a tie rod separator.

7. Using a puller, remove the hub and bearing assembly.

8. Remove the halfshaft as outlined in this Section.

9. Support the lower control arm with jackstands.

10. Remove the upper ball joint nut and disconnect the joint from the knuckle using a ball joint separator.

11. Remove the lower ball joint nut and disconnect the joint from the knuckle using a ball joint separator.

12. Remove the knuckle from the vehicle.

NOTE: The front wheel bearings are a sealed unit that requires no periodic maintenance or repacking. The hub and bearing has to be replaced as a unit if defective.

To install:

1. If removed, install a new seal into the knuckle using a seal installer J-36605.

2. Install the knuckle to the upper and lower ball joints. Install the nuts and torque to 94 ft. lbs. (128 Nm).

3. Install new cotter pins and bend over.

4. Install the splash shield, if removed.

5. Install the halfshaft.

6. Install the hub and bearing assembly. Torque the bolts to 66 ft. lbs. (90 Nm).

7. Install the tie rod end, nut, torque to 35 ft. lbs. (48 Nm) and install a new cotter pin.

8. Install the halfshaft washer and nut, torque to 173 ft. lbs. (235 Nm).

9. Install the brake disc, caliper and front wheels.

10. Remove the jackstands and lower the vehicle.

11. Refill the brake master cylinder.

12. Recheck all fasteners for proper torque and assembly.

13. Have the front aligned by a qualified alignment technician.

WHEEL ALIGNMENT SPECIFICATIONS

| Years | Model | Caster (deg.) | | Camber (deg.) | | Toe-in (In.) |
		Range	Pref.	Range	Pref.	
1985–87	All	1.7P–3.7P	2.7P	0.14P–1.74P	0.94P	0.05P–0.25P
1988–90	2-wheel drive	2.2P–3.2P	2.7P	0.30P–1.30P	0.80P	0.05P–0.15P
1990	4-wheel drive	2.52P–4.52P	3.52P	0.41P–1.41P	0.91P	0.05P–1.5N

FRONT END ALIGNMENT

NOTE: Aligning the front end should be left to a qualified alignment technician with the special equipment needed to perform an accurate alignment.

Caster

Caster is the tilting of the front steering axis either forward or backward from the vertical. A backward tilt is said to be positive (+) and a forward tilt is said to be negative (−).

Camber

Camber is the inward or outward tilting of the front wheels from the vertical. When the wheels tilt outward at the top, the camber is said to be positive (+). When the wheels tilt inward at the top, the camber is said to be negative (−). The amount of tilt is measured in degrees from the vertical and this measurement is called the camber angle.

Toe-In

Toe-in is the turning in of the front wheels. The actual amount of toe-in is normally only a fraction of a degree. The purpose of toe-in is to ensure parallel rolling of the front wheels. Excessive toe-in or toe-out will cause tire wear.

Trim Height

Measure the trim height at the "Z" dimension. Refer to the Alignment illustration for the All Wheel Drive vehicles. The trim height is an average the the high and lower measurements. The front trim height can be raised or lowered by turning the torsion bar adjusting bolt in or out.

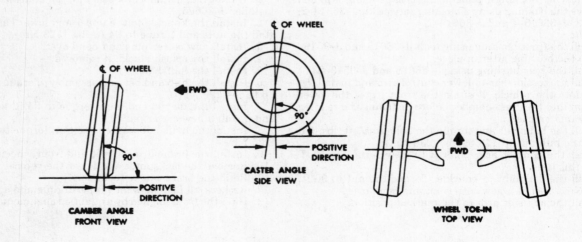

Visual description of the camber, caster and toe-in

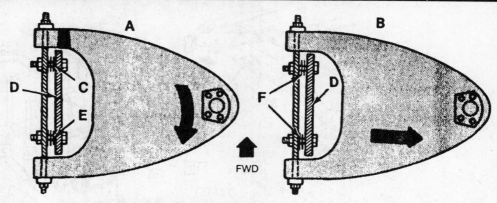

A. Caster
B. Camber
C. Subtract shims here to increase caster
D. Frame
E. Add shims here to increase caster
F. Subtract shims equally to increase camber

FWD

Caster and camber adjustment

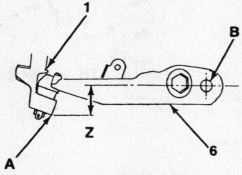

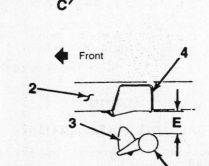

Front

1. Steering knuckle
2. Frame
3. Jounce bumper
4. Axle stop bracket
5. Rear axle
6. Lower control arm
7. Nut
8. Torsion bar support
9. Torsion bar adjustment arm

A. Lower corner of steering knuckle
B. Center line of front lower control arm bolt
C. One revolution changes "Z" height 0.2 inch (6.0mm)
E. D height = 5.31 ± .24 inch (135.0 ± 6.0mm)
Z. Z height = 3.1 ± 0.2 inch (136.0 ± 6.0mm)

All wheel drive front trim height procedure

REAR SUSPENSION

The rear suspension system consists of several major components: The double acting shock absorbers, variable rate single leaf fiberglass springs and various attachment parts. The single leaf fiberglass springs are connected to the frame by a hanger assembly with integral bushings in the front and a shackle assembly with integral bushings in the rear. The shackle assembly, in response to different road and payload conditions, allows the leaf spring to "change its length". The rear axle is connected to both the fiberglass leaf springs and the shock absorbers by various attaching parts.

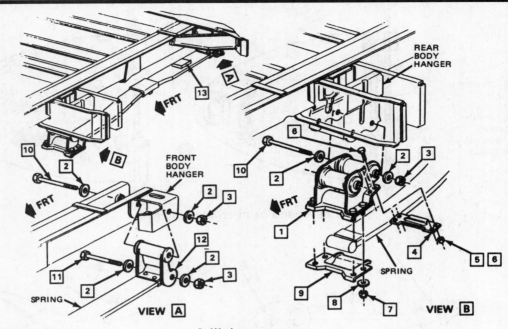

1. Hanger asm
2. Washer
3. Nut 100–120 N·m (74–88 ft. lbs.)
4. Cam asm
5. Nut 15–20 N·m (11–15 ft. lbs.)
6. Bolt 15–20 N·m (11–15 ft. lbs.)
7. Nut 20–30 N·m (15–22 ft. lbs.)
8. Washer
9. Retainer
10. Bolt
11. Bolt
12. Shackle asm
13. Mass damper

Exploded view of the fiberglass rear spring assembly

Leaf Spring

REMOVAL AND INSTALLATION

NOTE: The following procedure requires the use of two jackstands and two floor lifts.

1. Raise and support the rear of the vehicle on jackstands.

NOTE: When supporting the rear of the vehicle, support the axle and the body separately to relieve the load on the rear spring.

2. Remove the wheel and tire assembly.

3. At the rear of the fiberglass spring, loosen (DO NOT remove) the shackle-to-frame bolt and the shackle-to-spring.

4. Remove the shock absorber-to-axle bolt, then separate the shock absorber from the axle.

NOTE: If removing the shock absorber from the right side, it is necessary to remove the parking brake bracket.

5. Remove the axle U-bolt-to-anchor plate nuts, the lower plate-to-anchor plate nuts, the U-bolts and the lower plate, then lower the axle.

NOTE: When lowering the axle, be careful not to let the axle hang on the brake hose.

6. At the front of the fiberglass spring, remove the retainer-to-hanger assembly nuts, the washers and the retainer(s).

7. At the rear of the fiberglass spring, remove the spring-to-shackle nut, washer and bolt. Remove the fiberglass spring from the vehicle.
To install:

1. Attach the spring to the shackle (DO NOT tighten the nuts/bolts), rotate the shackle forward to clear the rear bumper bracket, position the spring into the slot on the hanger and attach the retainer-to-hanger fasteners.

2. Using the axle supports, raise and position the axle housing under the fiberglass spring. Using the U-bolts and the lower plates, connect the axle housing to the spring.

NOTE: When installing the axle housing, be sure that the full weight of the axle is resting on the supports; the fiberglass spring MUST NOT support any of the axle weight.

3. Torque the axle U-bolt-to-spring nuts to 48 ft. lbs. (65 Nm) and the axle lower plate-to-spring nuts to 40 ft. lbs. (54 Nm).

4. To adjust the rear suspension trim height, perform the following:

   a. Raise the axle/spring assembly until the clearance between the top of the axle and the bottom of the frame is 135mm.

NOTE: If the axle supports are not in complete contact with the axle housing and resting firmly on the floor, damage to the spring and axle could result.

   b. Torque the shackle-to-spring nuts/bolts to 81 ft. lbs. (110 Nm) and the retainer-to-hanger assembly nuts to 26 ft. lbs. (34 Nm).

5. Connect the shock absorber to the axle housing, then torque the nut/bolt to 75 ft. lbs. (102 Nm).

NOTE: When installing the shock absorber on the right side, be sure to position the parking brake bracket on the bolt before the nut is installed.

6. Install the wheel assemblies and lower the vehicle.

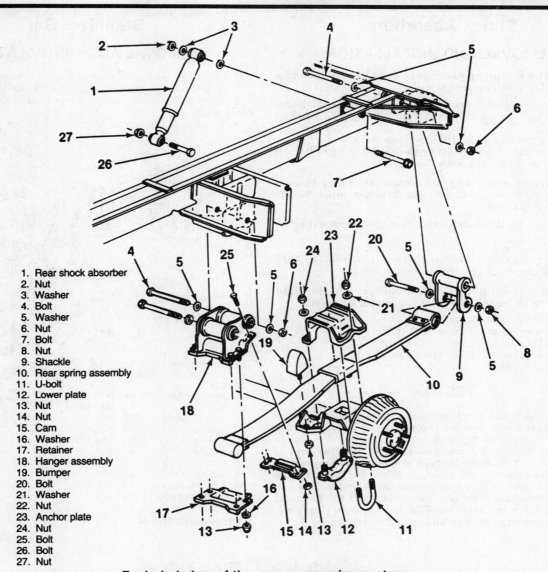

1. Rear shock absorber
2. Nut
3. Washer
4. Bolt
5. Washer
6. Nut
7. Bolt
8. Nut
9. Shackle
10. Rear spring assembly
11. U-bolt
12. Lower plate
13. Nut
14. Nut
15. Cam
16. Washer
17. Retainer
18. Hanger assembly
19. Bumper
20. Bolt
21. Washer
22. Nut
23. Anchor plate
24. Nut
25. Bolt
26. Bolt
27. Nut

Exploded view of the rear suspension system

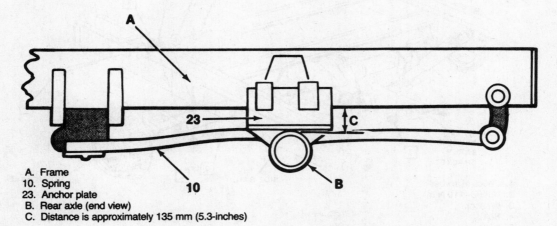

A. Frame
10. Spring
23. Anchor plate
B. Rear axle (end view)
C. Distance is approximately 135 mm (5.3-inches)

Adjusting the rear suspension trim height

Shock Absorbers

REMOVAL AND INSTALLATION

NOTE: The following procedure requires the use of a lifting device and two jackstands.

1. Raise and support the rear of the vehicle on jackstands (positioned under the frame), then support the axle housing independently.
2. Remove the shock absorber-to-frame bolts.
3. Remove the shock absorber-to-axle housing bolts and shock absorber from the vehicle.

NOTE: When removing the shock absorber-to-axle housing bolt, the parking brake bracket must be removed after the nut.

4. Inspect and test the shock absorber, then replace them (if necessary).

To install:
1. Connect the shock absorber-to-frame nut/bolt (DO NOT tighten) and the shock absorber-to-axle nut/bolt.

NOTE: If installing the shock absorber onto the right side, be sure to install the parking brake bracket.

2. Observe the following torques:
● Shock absorber-to-frame nut: 75 ft. lbs.
● Shock absorber-to-frame bolt: 83 ft. lbs.
● Shock absorber-to-axle housing nut: 75 ft. lbs.
3. Lower the vehicle.

TESTING

Visually inspect the shock absorber. If there is evidence of leakage and the shock absorber is covered with oil, the shock is defective and should be replaced.

If there is no sign of excessive leakage (a small amount of weeping is normal) bounce the van at one corner by pressing down on the bumper and releasing it. When you have the van bouncing as much as you can, release the bumper. The van should stop bouncing after the first rebound. If the bouncing continues past the center point of the bounce more than once, the shock absorbers are worn and should be replaced.

Stabilizer Bar

REMOVAL AND INSTALLATION

1. Raise the vehicle and support with jackstands.
2. Remove the bolts and washers from the link brackets.
3. Remove the nuts, washers and clamps from the anchor block studs.
4. Remove the insulator from the stabilizer bar.

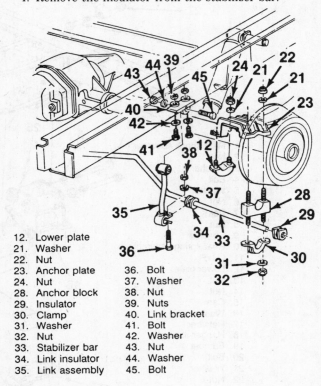

12. Lower plate	
21. Washer	
22. Nut	
23. Anchor plate	36. Bolt
24. Nut	37. Washer
28. Anchor block	38. Nut
29. Insulator	39. Nuts
30. Clamp	40. Link bracket
31. Washer	41. Bolt
32. Nut	42. Washer
33. Stabilizer bar	43. Nut
34. Link insulator	44. Washer
35. Link assembly	45. Bolt

Rear stabilizer bar

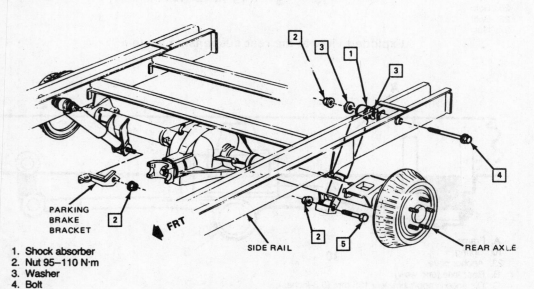

1. Shock absorber
2. Nut 95–110 N·m
3. Washer
4. Bolt
5. Bolt

Exploded view of the shock absorber assemblies

5. Remove the upper link nuts, washers and bolts from the link assembly.

6. Remove the link bracket.

To install:

1. Install the insulator to the bar.

2. Install the link assembly to the link insulator.

3. Install the link bolts, washers and nuts.

4. Install the link brackets to the link assembly.

5. Install the upper link nuts, washers and bolts.

6. Install the clamps over the insulator onto the anchor block studs.

7. Observe the following torques:

- Link bracket bolts: 25 ft. lbs.
- Lower link bolts: 12 ft. lbs.
- Upper link bolts: 33 ft. lbs.
- Cap nuts: 38 ft. lbs.

8. Install the rear wheels. Check all fasteners for proper torque.

9. Lower the vehicle and road test.

Rear Suspension Alignment

If the tire wear indicates that the rear springs may be mislocated or the axle housing may be bent, check the alignment as follows:

1. Position the rear of the vehicle on an alignment machine.

2. Compensate for the wheel runout; perform the same procedure as for checking the front wheel toe-in. The toe-out should be 0–$\frac{1}{16}$ in. (0–1.6mm).

NOTE: If the vehicle is backed onto an alignment machine, the toe-out will be read as the toe-in.

3. Check the camber reading, it should be 3°N–5°P.

4. If alignment operations are necessary, they may be performed by using frame straightening equipment or relocating the spring onto the axle housing without removing the axle housing from the vehicle.

STEERING

Troubleshooting the Steering Column

Problem	Cause	Solution
Will not lock	• Lockbolt spring broken or defective	• Replace lock bolt spring
High effort (required to turn ignition key and lock cylinder)	• Lock cylinder defective • Ignition switch defective • Rack preload spring broken or deformed • Burr on lock sector, lock rack, housing, support or remote rod coupling • Bent sector shaft • Defective lock rack • Remote rod bent, deformed • Ignition switch mounting bracket bent • Distorted coupling slot in lock rack (tilt column)	• Replace lock cylinder • Replace ignition switch • Replace preload spring • Remove burr • Replace shaft • Replace lock rack • Replace rod • Straighten or replace • Replace lock rack
Will stick in "start"	• Remote rod deformed • Ignition switch mounting bracket bent	• Straighten or replace • Straighten or replace

Troubleshooting the Steering Column (cont.)

Problem	Cause	Solution
Key cannot be removed in "off-lock"	• Ignition switch is not adjusted correctly • Defective lock cylinder	• Adjust switch • Replace lock cylinder
Lock cylinder can be removed without depressing retainer	• Lock cylinder with defective retainer • Burr over retainer slot in housing cover or on cylinder retainer	• Replace lock cylinder • Remove burr
High effort on lock cylinder between "off" and "off-lock"	• Distorted lock rack • Burr on tang of shift gate (automatic column) • Gearshift linkage not adjusted	• Replace lock rack • Remove burr • Adjust linkage
Noise in column	• One click when in "off-lock" position and the steering wheel is moved (all except automatic column) • Coupling bolts not tightened • Lack of grease on bearings or bearing surfaces • Upper shaft bearing worn or broken • Lower shaft bearing worn or broken • Column not correctly aligned • Coupling pulled apart • Broken coupling lower joint • Steering shaft snap ring not seated • Shroud loose on shift bowl. Housing loose on jacket—will be noticed with ignition in "off-lock" and when torque is applied to steering wheel.	• Normal—lock bolt is seating • Tighten pinch bolts • Lubricate with chassis grease • Replace bearing assembly • Replace bearing. Check shaft and replace if scored. • Align column • Replace coupling • Repair or replace joint and align column • Replace ring. Check for proper seating in groove. • Position shroud over lugs on shift bowl. Tighten mounting screws.
High steering shaft effort	• Column misaligned • Defective upper or lower bearing • Tight steering shaft universal joint • Flash on I.D. of shift tube at plastic joint (tilt column only) • Upper or lower bearing seized	• Align column • Replace as required • Repair or replace • Replace shift tube • Replace bearings
Lash in mounted column assembly	• Column mounting bracket bolts loose • Broken weld nuts on column jacket • Column capsule bracket sheared • Column bracket to column jacket mounting bolts loose • Loose lock shoes in housing (tilt column only) • Loose pivot pins (tilt column only)	• Tighten bolts • Replace column jacket • Replace bracket assembly • Tighten to specified torque • Replace shoes • Replace pivot pins and support

Troubleshooting the Steering Column (cont.)

Problem	Cause	Solution
Lash in mounted column assembly (cont.)	• Loose lock shoe pin (tilt column only) • Loose support screws (tilt column only)	• Replace pin and housing • Tighten screws
Housing loose (tilt column only)	• Excessive clearance between holes in support or housing and pivot pin diameters • Housing support-screws loose	• Replace pivot pins and support • Tighten screws
Steering wheel loose—every other tilt position (tilt column only)	• Loose fit between lock shoe and lock shoe pivot pin	• Replace lock shoes and pivot pin
Steering column not locking in any tilt position (tilt column only)	• Lock shoe seized on pivot pin • Lock shoe grooves have burrs or are filled with foreign material • Lock shoe springs weak or broken	• Replace lock shoes and pin • Clean or replace lock shoes • Replace springs
Noise when tilting column (tilt column only)	• Upper tilt bumpers worn • Tilt spring rubbing in housing	• Replace tilt bumper • Lubricate with chassis grease
One click when in "off-lock" position and the steering wheel is moved	• Seating of lock bolt	• None. Click is normal characteristic sound produced by lock bolt as it seats.
High shift effort (automatic and tilt column only)	• Column not correctly aligned • Lower bearing not aligned correctly • Lack of grease on seal or lower bearing areas	• Align column • Assemble correctly • Lubricate with chassis grease
Improper transmission shifting—automatic and tilt column only	• Sheared shift tube joint • Improper transmission gearshift linkage adjustment • Loose lower shift lever	• Replace shift tube • Adjust linkage • Replace shift tube

Troubleshooting the Ignition Switch

Problem	Cause	Solution
Ignition switch electrically inoperative	• Loose or defective switch connector • Feed wire open (fusible link) • Defective ignition switch	• Tighten or replace connector • Repair or replace • Replace ignition switch
Engine will not crank	• Ignition switch not adjusted properly	• Adjust switch
Ignition switch wil not actuate mechanically	• Defective ignition switch • Defective lock sector • Defective remote rod	• Replace switch • Replace lock sector • Replace remote rod
Ignition switch cannot be adjusted correctly	• Remote rod deformed	• Repair, straighten or replace

Troubleshooting the Turn Signal Switch

Problem	Cause	Solution
Turn signal will not cancel	• Loose switch mounting screws • Switch or anchor bosses broken • Broken, missing or out of position detent, or cancelling spring	• Tighten screws • Replace switch • Reposition springs or replace switch as required
Turn signal difficult to operate	• Turn signal lever loose • Switch yoke broken or distorted • Loose or misplaced springs • Foreign parts and/or materials in switch • Switch mounted loosely	• Tighten mounting screws • Replace switch • Reposition springs or replace switch • Remove foreign parts and/or material • Tighten mounting screws
Turn signal will not indicate lane change	• Broken lane change pressure pad or spring hanger • Broken, missing or misplaced lane change spring • Jammed wires	• Replace switch • Replace or reposition as required • Loosen mounting screws, reposition wires and retighten screws
Turn signal will not stay in turn position	• Foreign material or loose parts impeding movement of switch yoke • Defective switch	• Remove material and/or parts • Replace switch
Hazard switch cannot be pulled out	• Foreign material between hazard support cancelling leg and yoke	• Remove foreign material. No foreign material impeding function of hazard switch—replace turn signal switch.
No turn signal lights	• Inoperative turn signal flasher • Defective or blown fuse • Loose chassis to column harness connector • Disconnect column to chassis connector. Connect new switch to chassis and operate switch by hand. If vehicle lights now operate normally, signal switch is inoperative • If vehicle lights do not operate, check chassis wiring for opens, grounds, etc.	• Replace turn signal flasher • Replace fuse • Connect securely • Replace signal switch • Repair chassis wiring as required
Instrument panel turn indicator lights on but not flashing	• Burned out or damaged front or rear turn signal bulb • If vehicle lights do not operate, check light sockets for high resistance connections, the chassis wiring for opens, grounds, etc. • Inoperative flasher • Loose chassis to column harness connection	• Replace bulb • Repair chassis wiring as required • Replace flasher • Connect securely

Troubleshooting the Turn Signal Switch (cont.)

Problem	Cause	Solution
Instrument panel turn indicator lights on but not flashing	• Inoperative turn signal switch • To determine if turn signal switch is defective, substitute new switch into circuit and operate switch by hand. If the vehicle's lights operate normally, signal switch is inoperative.	• Replace turn signal switch • Replace turn signal switch
Stop light not on when turn indicated	• Loose column to chassis connection • Disconnect column to chassis connector. Connect new switch into system without removing old.	• Connect securely • Replace signal switch
Stop light not on when turn indicated (cont.)	Operate switch by hand. If brake lights work with switch in the turn position, signal switch is defective. • If brake lights do not work, check connector to stop light sockets for grounds, opens, etc.	• Repair connector to stop light circuits using service manual as guide
Turn indicator panel lights not flashing	• Burned out bulbs • High resistance to ground at bulb socket • Opens, ground in wiring harness from front turn signal bulb socket to indicator lights	• Replace bulbs • Replace socket • Locate and repair as required
Turn signal lights flash very slowly	• High resistance ground at light sockets • Incorrect capacity turn signal flasher or bulb • If flashing rate is still extremely slow, check chassis wiring harness from the connector to light sockets for high resistance • Loose chassis to column harness connection • Disconnect column to chassis connector. Connect new switch into system without removing old. Operate switch by hand. If flashing occurs at normal rate, the signal switch is defective.	• Repair high resistance grounds at light sockets • Replace turn signal flasher or bulb • Locate and repair as required • Connect securely • Replace turn signal switch
Hazard signal lights will not flash—turn signal functions normally	• Blow fuse • Inoperative hazard warning flasher • Loose chassis-to-column harness connection	• Replace fuse • Replace hazard warning flasher in fuse panel • Conect securely

Troubleshooting the Turn Signal Switch (cont.)

Problem	Cause	Solution
Hazard signal lights will not flash—turn signal functions normally	• Disconnect column to chassis connector. Connect new switch into system without removing old. Depress the hazard warning lights. If they now work normally, turn signal switch is defective.	• Replace turn signal switch
	• If lights do not flash, check wiring harness "K" lead for open between hazard flasher and connector. If open, fuse block is defective	• Repair or replace brown wire or connector as required

Troubleshooting the Manual Steering Gear

Problem	Cause	Solution
Hard or erratic steering	• Incorrect tire pressure	• Inflate tires to recommended pressures
	• Insufficient or incorrect lubrication	• Lubricate as required (refer to Maintenance Section)
	• Suspension, or steering linkage parts damaged or misaligned	• Repair or replace parts as necessary
	• Improper front wheel alignment	• Adjust incorrect wheel alignment angles
	• Incorrect steering gear adjustment	• Adjust steering gear
	• Sagging springs	• Replace springs
Play or looseness in steering	• Steering wheel loose	• Inspect shaft spines and repair as necessary. Tighten attaching nut and stake in place.
	• Steering linkage or attaching parts loose or worn	• Tighten, adjust, or replace faulty components
	• Pitman arm loose	• Inspect shaft splines and repair as necessary. Tighten attaching nut and stake in place
	• Steering gear attaching bolts loose	• Tighten bolts
	• Loose or worn wheel bearings	• Adjust or replace bearings
	• Steering gear adjustment incorrect or parts badly worn	• Adjust gear or replace defective parts
Wheel shimmy or tramp	• Improper tire pressure	• Inflate tires to recommended pressures
	• Wheels, tires, or brake rotors out-of-balance or out-of-round	• Inspect and replace or balance parts
	• Inoperative, worn, or loose shock absorbers or mounting parts	• Repair or replace shocks or mountings
	• Loose or worn steering or suspension parts	• Tighten or replace as necessary
	• Loose or worn wheel bearings	• Adjust or replace bearings
	• Incorrect steering gear adjustments	• Adjust steering gear
	• Incorrect front wheel alignment	• Correct front wheel alignment

Troubleshooting the Manual Steering Gear

Problem	Cause	Solution
Tire wear	• Improper tire pressure	• Inflate tires to recommended pressures
	• Failure to rotate tires	• Rotate tires
	• Brakes grabbing	• Adjust or repair brakes
	• Incorrect front wheel alignment	• Align incorrect angles
	• Broken or damaged steering and suspension parts	• Repair or replace defective parts
	• Wheel runout	• Replace faulty wheel
	• Excessive speed on turns	• Make driver aware of conditions
Vehicle leads to one side	• Improper tire pressures	• Inflate tires to recommended pressures
	• Front tires with uneven tread depth, wear pattern, or different cord design (i.e., one bias ply and one belted or radial tire on front wheels)	• Install tires of same cord construction and reasonably even tread depth, design, and wear pattern
	• Incorrect front wheel alignment	• Align incorrect angles
	• Brakes dragging	• Adjust or repair brakes
	• Pulling due to uneven tire construction	• Replace faulty tire

Troubleshooting the Power Steering Gear

Problem	Cause	Solution
Hissing noise in steering gear	• There is some noise in all power steering systems. One of the most common is a hissing sound most evident at standstill parking. There is no relationship between this noise and performance of the steering. Hiss may be expected when steering wheel is at end of travel or when slowly turning at standstill.	• Slight hiss is normal and in no way affects steering. Do not replace valve unless hiss is extremely objectionable. A replacement valve will also exhibit slight noise and is not always a cure. Investigate clearance around flexible coupling rivets. Be sure steering shaft and gear are aligned so flexible coupling rotates in a flat plane and is not distorted as shaft rotates. Any metal-to-metal contacts through flexible coupling will transmit valve hiss into passenger compartment through the steering column.
Rattle or chuckle noise in steering gear	• Gear loose on frame	• Check gear-to-frame mounting screws. Tighten screws to 88 N·m (65 foot pounds) torque.
	• Steering linkage looseness	• Check linkage pivot points for wear. Replace if necessary.
	• Pressure hose touching other parts of car	• Adjust hose position. Do not bend tubing by hand.
	• Loose pitman shaft over center adjustment	• Adjust to specifications

Troubleshooting the Power Steering Gear (cont.)

Problem	Cause	Solution
Rattle or chuckle noise in steering gear	NOTE: A slight rattle may occur on turns because of increased clearance off the "high point." This is normal and clearance must not be reduced below specified limits to eliminate this slight rattle. • Loose pitman arm	• Tighten pitman arm nut to specifications
Squawk noise in steering gear when turning or recovering from a turn	• Damper O-ring on valve spool cut	• Replace damper O-ring
Poor return of steering wheel to center	• Tires not properly inflated • Lack of lubrication in linkage and ball joints • Lower coupling flange rubbing against steering gear adjuster plug • Steering gear to column misalignment • Improper front wheel alignment • Steering linkage binding • Ball joints binding • Steering wheel rubbing against housing • Tight or frozen steering shaft bearings • Sticking or plugged valve spool • Steering gear adjustments over specifications • Kink in return hose	• Inflate to specified pressure • Lube linkage and ball joints • Loosen pinch bolt and assemble properly • Align steering column • Check and adjust as necessary • Replace pivots • Replace ball joints • Align housing • Replace bearings • Remove and clean or replace valve • Check adjustment with gear out of car. Adjust as required. • Replace hose
Car leads to one side or the other (keep in mind road condition and wind. Test car in both directions on flat road)	• Front end misaligned • Unbalanced steering gear valve NOTE: If this is cause, steering effort will be very light in direction of lead and normal or heavier in opposite direction	• Adjust to specifications • Replace valve
Momentary increase in effort when turning wheel fast to right or left	• Low oil level • Pump belt slipping • High internal leakage	• Add power steering fluid as required • Tighten or replace belt • Check pump pressure. (See pressure test)
Steering wheel surges or jerks when turning with engine running especially during parking	• Low oil level • Loose pump belt • Steering linkage hitting engine oil pan at full turn • Insufficient pump pressure • Pump flow control valve sticking	• Fill as required • Adjust tension to specification • Correct clearance • Check pump pressure. (See pressure test). Replace relief valve if defective. • Inspect for varnish or damage, replace if necessary

Troubleshooting the Power Steering Pump

Problem	Cause	Solution
Chirp noise in steering pump	• Loose belt	• Adjust belt tension to specification
Belt squeal (particularly noticeable at full wheel travel and stand still parking)	• Loose belt	• Adjust belt tension to specification
Growl noise in steering pump	• Excessive back pressure in hoses or steering gear caused by restriction	• Locate restriction and correct. Replace part if necessary.
Growl noise in steering pump (particularly noticeable at stand still parking)	• Scored pressure plates, thrust plate or rotor • Extreme wear of cam ring	• Replace parts and flush system • Replace parts
Groan noise in steering pump	• Low oil level • Air in the oil. Poor pressure hose connection.	• Fill reservoir to proper level • Tighten connector to specified torque. Bleed system by operating steering from right to left—full turn.
Rattle noise in steering pump	• Vanes not installed properly • Vanes sticking in rotor slots	• Install properly • Free up by removing burrs, varnish, or dirt
Swish noise in steering pump	• Defective flow control valve	• Replace part
Whine noise in steering pump	• Pump shaft bearing scored	• Replace housing and shaft. Flush system.
Hard steering or lack of assist	• Loose pump belt • Low oil level in reservoir NOTE: Low oil level will also result in excessive pump noise • Steering gear to column misalignment • Lower coupling flange rubbing against steering gear adjuster plug • Tires not properly inflated	• Adjust belt tension to specification • Fill to proper level. If excessively low, check all lines and joints for evidence of external leakage. Tighten loose connectors. • Align steering column • Loosen pinch bolt and assemble properly • Inflate to recommended pressure
Foaming milky power steering fluid, low fluid level and possible low pressure	• Air in the fluid, and loss of fluid due to internal pump leakage causing overflow	• Check for leaks and correct. Bleed system. Extremely cold temperatures will cause system aeriation should the oil level be low. If oil level is correct and pump still foams, remove pump from vehicle and separate reservoir from body. Check welsh plug and body for cracks. If plug is loose or body is cracked, replace body.

Troubleshooting the Power Steering Gear (cont.)

Problem	Cause	Solution
Excessive wheel kickback or loose steering	• Air in system	• Add oil to pump reservoir and bleed by operating steering. Check hose connectors for proper torque and adjust as required.
	• Steering gear loose on frame	• Tighten attaching screws to specified torque
	• Steering linkage joints worn enough to be loose	• Replace loose pivots
	• Worn poppet valve	• Replace poppet valve
	• Loose thrust bearing preload adjustment	• Adjust to specification with gear out of vehicle
	• Excessive overcenter lash	• Adjust to specification with gear out of car
Hard steering or lack of assist	• Loose pump belt	• Adjust belt tension to specification
	• Low oil level **NOTE:** Low oil level will also result in excessive pump noise	• Fill to proper level. If excessively low, check all lines and joints for evidence of external leakage. Tighten loose connectors.
	• Steering gear to column misalignment	• Align steering column
	• Lower coupling flange rubbing against steering gear adjuster plug	• Loosen pinch bolt and assemble properly
	• Tires not properly inflated	• Inflate to recommended pressure
Foamy milky power steering fluid, low fluid level and possible low pressure	• Air in the fluid, and loss of fluid due to internal pump leakage causing overflow	• Check for leak and correct. Bleed system. Extremely cold temperatures will cause system aeration should the oil level be low. If oil level is correct and pump still foams, remove pump from vehicle and separate reservoir from housing. Check welsh plug and housing for cracks. If plug is loose or housing is cracked, replace housing.
Low pressure due to steering pump	• Flow control valve stuck or inoperative	• Remove burrs or dirt or replace. Flush system.
	• Pressure plate not flat against cam ring	• Correct
Low pressure due to steering gear	• Pressure loss in cylinder due to worn piston ring or badly worn housing bore	• Remove gear from car for disassembly and inspection of ring and housing bore
	• Leakage at valve rings, valve body-to-worm seal	• Remove gear from car for disassembly and replace seals
Low pump pressure	• Flow control valve stuck or inoperative	• Remove burrs or dirt or replace. Flush system.
	• Pressure plate not flat against cam ring	• Correct

Troubleshooting the Power Steering Pump (cont.)

Problem	Cause	Solution
Momentary increase in effort when turning wheel fast to right or left	• Low oil level in pump • Pump belt slipping • High internal leakage	• Add power steering fluid as required • Tighten or replace belt • Check pump pressure. (See pressure test)
Steering wheel surges or jerks when turning with engine running especially during parking	• Low oil level • Loose pump belt • Steering linkage hitting engine oil pan at full turn • Insufficient pump pressure	• Fill as required • Adjust tension to specification • Correct clearance • Check pump pressure. (See pressure test). Replace flow control valve if defective.
Steering wheel surges or jerks when turning with engine running especially during parking (cont.)	• Sticking flow control valve	• Inspect for varnish or damage, replace if necessary
Excessive wheel kickback or loose steering	• Air in system	• Add oil to pump reservoir and bleed by operating steering. Check hose connectors for proper torque and adjust as required.
Low pump pressure	• Extreme wear of cam ring • Scored pressure plate, thrust plate, or rotor • Vanes not installed properly • Vanes sticking in rotor slots • Cracked or broken thrust or pressure plate	• Replace parts. Flush system. • Replace parts. Flush system. • Install properly • Freeup by removing burrs, varnish, or dirt • Replace part

The steering box (manual or power) consists of a recirculating balls, which transmits force from the worm gear to the sector gear. A relay type steering linkage is used with a pitman arm connected to one end of the relay rod. The relay rod is supported by two idler arms; the idler arms pivot on a support which is attached to the frame. The relay rod is connected to the steering arms by two adjustable tie rods. Most models are equipped with a collapsible steering column designed to collapse on impact, thereby reducing possible chest injuries during accidents. When making any repairs to the steering column or steering wheel, excessive pressure or force capable of collapsing the column must be avoided. The ignition lock, ignition switch and an anti-theft system are built into each column.

On the automatic transmission, the ignition key cannot be removed unless the shift lever is in the **PARK** position and the ignition switch in the Lock position. Placing the lock in the Lock position activates a rod within the column which locks the steering wheel and shift lever.

On the floor shift models, a back drive linkage between the floorshift and the column produces the same effect.

Steering Wheel

REMOVAL AND INSTALLATION

NOTE: The following procedure requires the use of the GM Steering Wheel Puller tool No. J–1859–03 or equivalent.

1. Disconnect the negative battery terminal from the battery.
2. Position the steering wheel so that it is in the horizontal position.
3. If equipped with a horn cap, pry the cap from the center of the steering wheel. If equipped with a steering wheel shroud, remove the screw from the rear of the steering wheel and remove the shroud.

NOTE: If the horn cap or shroud is equipped with an electrical connector, disconnect it.

4. Remove the steering wheel-to-steering shaft retainer (snapring) and nut.

NOTE: Since the steering column is designed to collapse upon impact, it is recommended NEVER to hammer on it.

5. Matchmark the relationship of the steering wheel to the steering shaft.

6. Using the GM Steering Wheel Puller tool No. J–1859–03 or equivalent, press the steering wheel from the steering column.

NOTE: Before installing the steering wheel, be sure that the combination control switch is in the Neutral position. DO NOT misalign the steering wheel more than 1 in. (25mm) from the horizontal centerline.

To install:

1. Install the steering wheel, align the matchmarks and push it onto the steering shaft splines, torque the steering wheel-to-steering shaft nut to 30 ft. lbs. (41 Nm).

2. Connect the horn wire and install the horn pad.

3. Connect the negative battery cable and check operation.

Combination Switch

The combination switch is a combination of the turn signal, the windshield wiper/washer, the dimmer and the cruise control switches.

REMOVAL AND INSTALLATION

NOTE: The following procedure requires the use of the GM Lock Plate Compressor tool No. J–23653 or equivalent.

1. Disconnect the negative (−) battery cable. Refer to the Steering Wheel, Removal and Installation procedures in this section and remove the steering wheel.

2. If necessary, remove the steering column-to-lower instrument panel cover. Disconnect the electrical harness connector from the steering column jacket (under the dash).

3. Using a screwdriver, insert into the slots between the steering shaft lock plate cover and the steering column housing, then pry upward to remove the cover from the lock plate.

4. Using the GM Lock Plate Compressor tool No. J–23653–A or equivalent, screw the center shaft onto the steering shaft (as far as it will go), then screw the center post nut clockwise until the lock plate is compressed.

5. Using a small pry bar, pry the snapring from the steering shaft slot.

NOTE: If the steering column is being disassembled on a bench, the steering shaft will slide out of the mast jacket when the snapring is removed.

6. Remove the GM Lock Plate Compressor tool No. J–23653 or equivalent, and the lock plate.

7. Remove the multi-function lever-to-switch screw and the lever.

8. To remove the hazard warning switch, press the knob inward and unscrew it.

9. Remove the combination switch assembly-to-steering column screws.

10. Lift the combination switch assembly from the steering column, then slide the electrical connector through the column housing and the protector.

NOTE: If the steering column is the tilting type, position the steering housing into the Low position.

11. To remove the harness cover, pull it toward the lower end of the column; be careful not to damage the wires.

12. To remove the wire protector, grab the protector's tab with a pair of pliers, then pull the protector downward, out of the steering column.

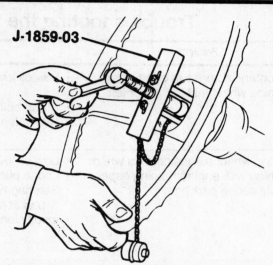

Removing the steering wheel from the steering column

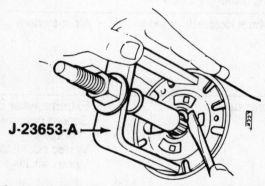

Compressing the locking plate on the steering column

NOTE: When assembling the steering column, use only fasteners of the correct length; overlength fasteners could prevent a portion of the assembly from compressing under impact.

To install:

1. Install the combination switch electrical connector, perform the following procedures:

a. On the non-tilt columns, be sure that the electrical connector is on the protector, then feed it and the cover down through the housing and under the mounting bracket.

b. On the tilt columns, feed the electrical connector down through the housing and under the mounting bracket, then install the cover onto the housing.

2. Install the clip the electrical connector to the clip on the jacket, the combination switch-to-steering column mounting screws, the lower instrument trim panel, the turn signal lever/screws and the hazard warning knob.

NOTE: With the multi-function lever installed, place it into the Neutral position. With the hazard warning knob installed, pull it Outward.

3. Onto the upper end of the steering shaft, install the washer, the upper bearing preload spring, the canceling cam, the lock plate and a new retaining ring (snapring). Using the GM Lock Plate Compressor tool No. J–23653 or equivalent, compress the

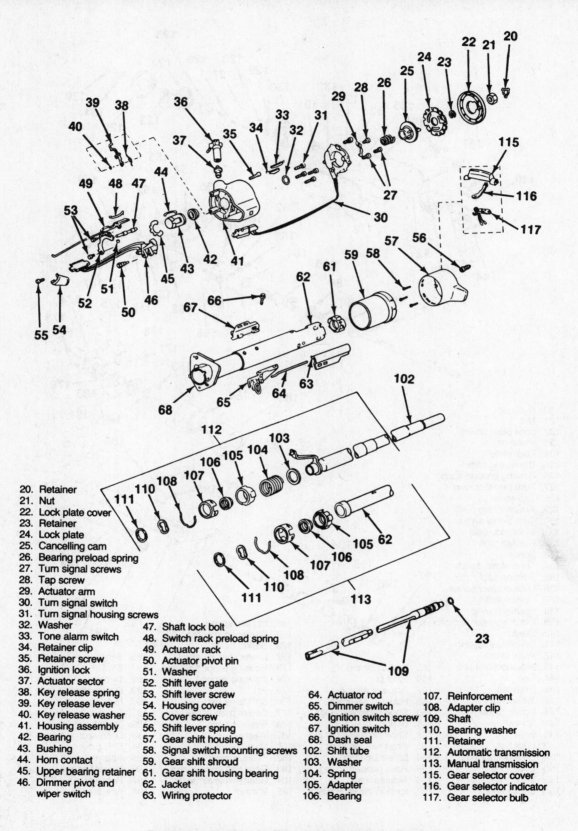

20. Retainer
21. Nut
22. Lock plate cover
23. Retainer
24. Lock plate
25. Cancelling cam
26. Bearing preload spring
27. Turn signal screws
28. Tap screw
29. Actuator arm
30. Turn signal switch
31. Turn signal housing screws
32. Washer
33. Tone alarm switch
34. Retainer clip
35. Retainer screw
36. Ignition lock
37. Actuator sector
38. Key release spring
39. Key release lever
40. Key release washer
41. Housing assembly
42. Bearing
43. Bushing
44. Horn contact
45. Upper bearing retainer
46. Dimmer pivot and
    wiper switch
47. Shaft lock bolt
48. Switch rack preload spring
49. Actuator rack
50. Actuator pivot pin
51. Washer
52. Shift lever gate
53. Shift lever screw
54. Housing cover
55. Cover screw
56. Shift lever spring
57. Gear shift housing
58. Signal switch mounting screws
59. Gear shift shroud
61. Gear shift housing bearing
62. Jacket
63. Wiring protector
64. Actuator rod
65. Dimmer switch
66. Ignition switch screw
67. Ignition switch
68. Dash seal
102. Shift tube
103. Washer
104. Spring
105. Adapter
106. Bearing
107. Reinforcement
108. Adapter clip
109. Shaft
110. Bearing washer
111. Retainer
112. Automatic transmission
113. Manual transmission
115. Gear selector cover
116. Gear selector indicator
117. Gear selector bulb

Exploded view of the standard steering column

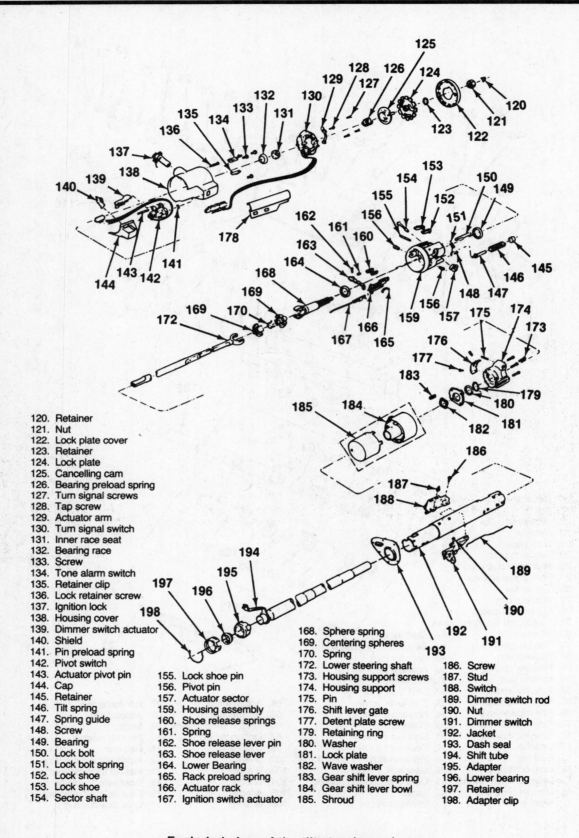

120. Retainer
121. Nut
122. Lock plate cover
123. Retainer
124. Lock plate
125. Cancelling cam
126. Bearing preload spring
127. Turn signal screws
128. Tap screw
129. Actuator arm
130. Turn signal switch
131. Inner race seat
132. Bearing race
133. Screw
134. Tone alarm switch
135. Retainer clip
136. Lock retainer screw
137. Ignition lock
138. Housing cover
139. Dimmer switch actuator
140. Shield
141. Pin preload spring
142. Pivot switch
143. Actuator pivot pin
144. Cap
145. Retainer
146. Tilt spring
147. Spring guide
148. Screw
149. Bearing
150. Lock bolt
151. Lock bolt spring
152. Lock shoe
153. Lock shoe
154. Sector shaft

155. Lock shoe pin
156. Pivot pin
157. Actuator sector
159. Housing assembly
160. Shoe release springs
161. Spring
162. Shoe release lever pin
163. Shoe release lever
164. Lower Bearing
165. Rack preload spring
166. Actuator rack
167. Ignition switch actuator

168. Sphere spring
169. Centering spheres
170. Spring
172. Lower steering shaft
173. Housing support screws
174. Housing support
175. Pin
176. Shift lever gate
177. Detent plate screw
179. Retaining ring
180. Washer
181. Lock plate
182. Wave washer
183. Gear shift lever spring
184. Gear shift lever bowl
185. Shroud

186. Screw
187. Stud
188. Switch
189. Dimmer switch rod
190. Nut
191. Dimmer switch
192. Jacket
193. Dash seal
194. Shift tube
195. Adapter
196. Lower bearing
197. Retainer
198. Adapter clip

Exploded view of the tilt steering column

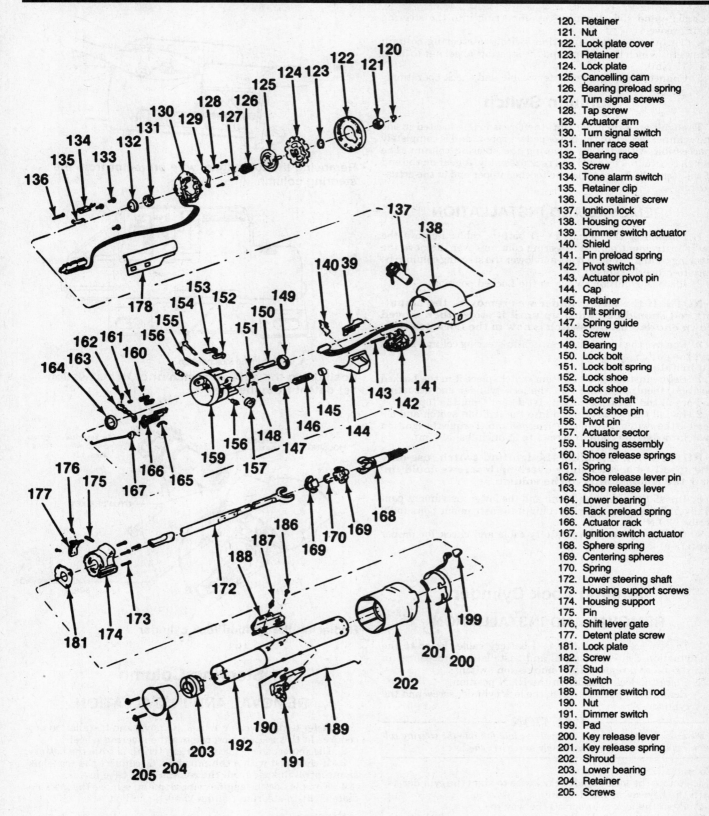

120. Retainer
121. Nut
122. Lock plate cover
123. Retainer
124. Lock plate
125. Cancelling cam
126. Bearing preload spring
127. Turn signal screws
128. Tap screw
129. Actuator arm
130. Turn signal switch
131. Inner race seat
132. Bearing race
133. Screw
134. Tone alarm switch
135. Retainer clip
136. Lock retainer screw
137. Ignition lock
138. Housing cover
139. Dimmer switch actuator
140. Shield
141. Pin preload spring
142. Pivot switch
143. Actuator pivot pin
144. Cap
145. Retainer
146. Tilt spring
147. Spring guide
148. Screw
149. Bearing
150. Lock bolt
151. Lock bolt spring
152. Lock shoe
153. Lock shoe
154. Sector shaft
155. Lock shoe pin
156. Pivot pin
157. Actuator sector
159. Housing assembly
160. Shoe release springs
161. Spring
162. Shoe release lever pin
163. Shoe release lever
164. Lower bearing
165. Rack preload spring
166. Actuator rack
167. Ignition switch actuator
168. Sphere spring
169. Centering spheres
170. Spring
172. Lower steering shaft
173. Housing support screws
174. Housing support
175. Pin
176. Shift lever gate
177. Detent plate screw
181. Lock plate
182. Screw
187. Stud
188. Switch
189. Dimmer switch rod
190. Nut
191. Dimmer switch
199. Pad
200. Key release lever
201. Key release spring
202. Shroud
203. Lower bearing
204. Retainer
205. Screws

Exploded view of the tilt steering column from the floor shift

lock plate and slide the new retaining ring into the steering shaft groove.

4. Torque the multi-function switch-to-steering column screws to 35 inch lbs. (4 Nm) and the steering wheel nut to 30 ft. lbs. (41 Nm).

5. Connect the negative battery cable and check operation.

Ignition Switch

The ignition switch, for anti-theft reasons, is located inside the channel section of the brake pedal support and is completely inaccessible without first lowering the steering column. The switch is actuated by a rod and rack assembly. A gear on the end of the lock cylinder engages the toothed upper end of the actuator rod.

REMOVAL AND INSTALLATION

1. Disconnect the negative (−) battery cable. Remove the lower instrument panel-to-steering column cover. Remove the steering column-to-dash bolts and lower the steering column; be sure to properly support it.

2. Place the ignition switch in the Locked position.

NOTE: If the lock cylinder was removed, the actuating rod should be pulled up until it stops, then moved down one detent; the switch is now in the Lock position.

3. Remove the two ignition switch-to-steering column screws and the switch assembly.

To install:

1. Before installing the ignition switch, place it in the Locked position, then make sure that the lock cylinder and actuating rod are in the Locked position (1st detent from the top).

2. Install the activating rod into the ignition switch and assemble the switch onto the steering column. Torque the ignition switch-to-steering column screws to 35 inch lbs. (4 Nm).

NOTE: When installing the ignition switch, use only the specified screws since overlength screws could impair the collapsibility of the column.

3. Install the steering column and the lower instrument panel cover. Torque the steering column-to-instrument bolts to 22 ft. lbs. (30 Nm).

4. Connect the negative battery cable and check for proper operation.

Ignition Lock Cylinder

REMOVAL AND INSTALLATION

1. Disconnect the negative (−) battery cable. Refer to the Combination Switch, Removal and Installation procedures in this section and remove the combination switch.

2. Place the lock cylinder in the **RUN** position.

3. Remove the buzzer switch, the lock cylinder screw and the lock cylinder.

── CAUTION ──

If the screw is dropped upon removal, it could fall into the steering column, requiring complete disassembly to retrieve the screw.

To install:

1. Rotate the lock cylinder clockwise to align the cylinder key with the keyway in the housing.

2. Push the lock cylinder all the way in.

3. Install the cylinder lock-to-housing screw. Tighten the screw to 14 inch lbs.

4. Connect the negative battery cable and check operation.

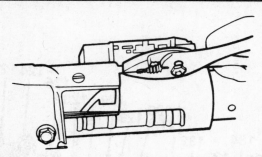

Removing the turn signal wire protector from the steering column

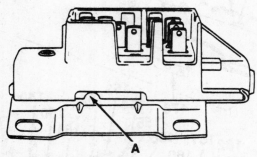

A. Switch in the lock position

Positioning the ignition switch prior to installation — 1st detent from the top

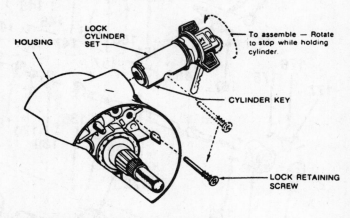

HOUSING — LOCK CYLINDER SET — To assemble — Rotate to stop while holding cylinder. — CYLINDER KEY — LOCK RETAINING SCREW

Replacing the ignition lock cylinder

Steering Column

REMOVAL AND INSTALLATION

1. Refer to the Steering Wheel, Removal and Installation procedures in this section and remove the steering wheel.

2. Disconnect the negative battery terminal from the battery.

3. If equipped with a column shift, disconnect the transmission control linkage from the column shift tube levers.

4. From inside the engine compartment, remove the intermediate shaft-to-steering column shaft pinch bolt.

NOTE: Before separating the intermediate shaft from the steering column shaft, mark the relationship of the two shafts.

5. Remove the lower instrument panel-to-steering column cover, the steering column bracket-to-dash nuts/bolts (support the steering column) and the steering column-to-firewall cover (if necessary).

6. From under the dash, disconnect the electrical harness connectors from the steering column.

NOTE: Some models are equipped with a back-up light switch and a neutral/start switch, be sure to disconnect the electrical connectors from them.

7. Remove the steering column from the vehicle.

NOTE: If equipped with a column shifter, rotate the steering column so that the shift lever clears the dash opening.

To install:

1. Align the matchmarks of the steering column shaft and the intermediate shaft, tighten the fasteners finger tight.

NOTE: Make sure that the Cardan joint (intermediate shaft) operating angle is between 34–39°.

2. Torque the intermediate shaft-to-steering column shaft pinch bolt to 30 ft. lbs. (41 Nm), the steering column bracket-to-dash nuts to 25 ft. lbs. (34 Nm) and the steering column-to-firewall screws to 7 ft. lbs. (10 Nm).

3. Reconnect the electrical harness-to-steering column connectors. Reinstall the steering wheel and the negative battery terminal.

NOTE: If equipped with steering column shifter, reconnect the transmission-to-steering column linkage.

Steering Linkage

The steering linkage consists of: a forward mounted linkage (parallelogram type), crimp nuts at the inner pivots, castellated nuts at the steering knuckle arm, a second idler arm and steering gear pitman arm-to-relay rod connecting rod to maintain proper geometry, and a steering damper (manual steering). Grease fittings are equipped with each joint, for durability.

REMOVAL AND INSTALLATION

Pitman Arm

NOTE: The following procedure requires the use of the GM Steering Linkage Puller tool No. J–24319–01 or equivalent, the GM Pitman Arm Remover tool No. J–6632 or equivalent, and the GM Steering Linkage Installer tool No. J–29193 (12mm) or J–29194 (14mm) or equivalent.

1. Raise and support the front of the vehicle on jackstands.

2. Disconnect the nut from the pitman arm ball joint stud.

3. Using the GM Steering Linkage Puller tool No. J–24319–01 or equivalent, separate the connecting rod from the pitman arm. Pull down on the connecting rod and separate it from the stud.

4. Remove the pitman arm-to-pitman shaft nut, mark the relationship the arm to the shaft. Using the GM Pitman Arm Remover tool No. J–6632 or equivalent, separate the pitman arm from the pitman shaft.

NOTE: When separating the pitman arm from the shaft, DO NOT use a hammer or apply heat to the arm.

To install:

1. Align the pitman arm-to-pitman shaft matchmark and the pitman shaft nut; torque the pitman arm-to-pitman shaft nut to 177–185 ft. lbs. (235–250 Nm).

2. Connect the pitman arm to the connecting rod ball stud (make sure that the seal is on the stud. Using the GM Steering

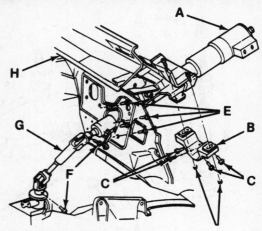

A. Steering column assembly
B. Bracket
C. 40 N·m (30 ft. lbs.)
D. Capsule nuts 34 N·m (25 ft. lbs.)
E. 9 N·m (7 ft. lbs.)
F. Pinch bolt 40 N·m (30 ft. lbs.)
G. Intermediate shaft assembly
H. Panel

Replacing the steering column

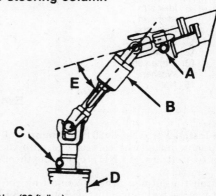

A. 40 N·m (30 ft. lbs.)
B. Intermediate shaft
C. 40 N·m (30 ft. lbs.)
D. Steering gear
E. 36–58° angle must not exceed 39 degrees maximum or 34 degrees minimum

View of the intermediate shaft with Carden joint

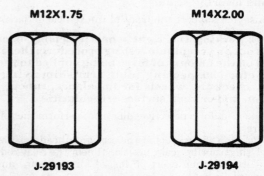

M12X1.75 M14X2.00

J-29193 J-29194

View of the special tools used to seat the pitman arm-to-pitman shaft tapers

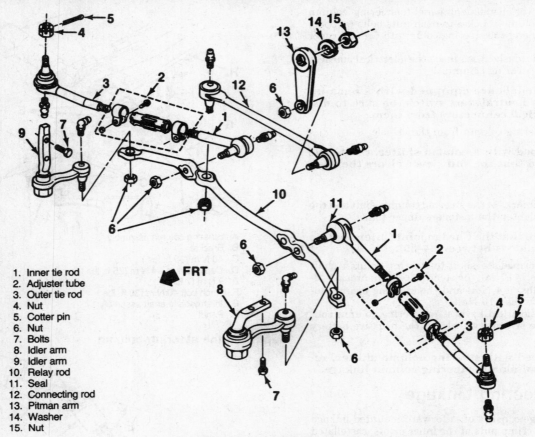

1. Inner tie rod
2. Adjuster tube
3. Outer tie rod
4. Nut
5. Cotter pin
6. Nut
7. Bolts
8. Idler arm
9. Idler arm
10. Relay rod
11. Seal
12. Connecting rod
13. Pitman arm
14. Washer
15. Nut

Exploded view of the steering linkage

Linkage Installer tool No. J–29193 (12mm) or J–29194 (14mm) or equivalent, install the correct one onto the ball stud and torque it to 40 ft. lbs. (54 Nm) to seat the tapers; after seating, remove the tool.

3. Install the pitman arm-to-connecting rod ball joint nut, then torque the ball joint nut to 66 ft. lbs. (89 Nm).

Idler Arm

NOTE: The following procedure requires the use of the GM Steering Linkage Puller tool No. J–24319–01 or equivalent, the GM Pitman Arm Remover tool No. J–6632 or equivalent, the GM Steering Linkage Installer tool No. J–29193 (12mm) or J–29194 (14mm) or equivalent, and a spring scale.

1. Raise and support the front of the vehicle on jackstands.

NOTE: Jerking the right wheel assembly back and forth is not an acceptable testing procedure; there is not control on the amount of force being applied to the idler arm. Before suspecting idler arm shimmying complaints, check the wheels for imbalance, runout, force variation and/or road surface irregularities.

2. To inspect for a defective idler arm, perform the following procedures:

a. Position the wheels in the straight ahead position.

b. Using a spring scale, position it near the relay rod end of the idler arm, then exert 25 lbs. of force upward and then downward.

c. Measure the distance between the upward and downward directions that the idler arm moves. The allowable de-

flection is 3mm for each direction; a total difference of 6mm. If the idler arm deflection is beyond the allowable limits, replace it.

3. Remove the idler arm-to-frame bolts and the idler arm-to-relay rod ball joint nut.

4. Using the GM Steering Linkage Puller tool No. J–24319–01 or equivalent, separate the relay rod from the ball joint stud.

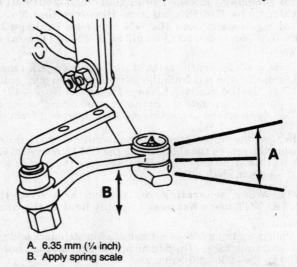

A. 6.35 mm (¼ inch)
B. Apply spring scale

Inspecting the idler arm movement

5. Inspect and/or replace (if necessary) the idler arm.

To install:

1. Install the idler arm-to-frame bolts and torque them to 37 ft. lbs. (50 Nm).

2. Connect the relay rod to the idler arm ball joint stud. Using the GM Steering Linkage Installer tool No. J–29193 (12mm) or J–29194 (14mm) or equivalent, seat (torque) the relay rod-to-idler arm ball joint stud to 40 ft. lbs. (54 Nm), then remove the tool.

3. Install the idler arm-to-relay rod stud nut and torque it to 66 ft. lbs. (89 Nm).

4. Lower the vehicle.

5. Have a qualified alignment technician align the front end.

Relay Rod

NOTE: The following procedure requires the use of the GM Steering Linkage Puller tool No. J–24319–01 or equivalent, and the GM Steering Linkage Installer tool No. J–29193 (12mm) or J–29194 (14mm) or equivalent.

1. Refer to the Tie Rod, Removal and Installation procedures in this section and disconnect the inner tie rod ends from the relay rod.

2. Remove the connecting rod stud-to-relay rod nut and the idler arm stud-to-relay rod nuts.

3. Using the GM Steering Linkage Puller tool No. J–24319–01 or equivalent, disconnect the connecting rod from the relay rod.

4. Using the GM Steering Linkage Puller tool No. J–24319–01 or equivalent, disconnect the relay rod from the idler arms, then remove the relay rod from the vehicle.

To install:

1. Clean and inspect the threads on the tie rod, the tie rod ends and the ball joints for damage, then replace them (if necessary). Inspect the ball joint seals for excessive wear, then replace them (if necessary).

2. Position the relay rod onto the idler arms (no mounting nuts). Using the GM Steering Linkage Installer tool No. J–29193 (12mm) or J–29194 (14mm) or equivalent, install them onto the idler arm studs and torque the idler arm-to-relay rod stud nuts to 40 ft. lbs. (54 Nm) to seat the tapers. Remove the installer tool, then install the mounting nuts and torque the idler arm-to-relay arm stud nuts to 66 ft. lbs. (89 Nm).

3. Position the connecting rod onto the relay rod (no mounting nut). Using the GM Steering Linkage Installer tool No. J–29193 (12mm) or J–29194 (14mm) or equivalent, install one onto the connecting rod stud and torque the connecting rod-to-relay rod stud to 40 ft. lbs. (54 Nm) to seat the taper. Remove the installer tool, then install the mounting nuts and torque the connecting rod-to-relay rod stud nuts to 66 ft. lbs. (89 Nm).

4. Position the inner tie rod ball joints onto the relay rod (no mounting nuts). Using the GM Steering Linkage Installer tool No. J–29193 (12mm) or J–29194 (14mm) or equivalent, install them onto the tie rod studs and torque the tie rod-to-relay rod stud nuts to 40 ft. lbs. (54 Nm) to seat the tapers. Remove the installer tool, then install the mounting nuts and torque the tie rod-to-relay rod stud nuts to 66 ft. lbs. (89 Nm).

5. Lower the vehicle and check the steering linkage performance.

6. Have a qualified alignment technician align the front end.

Connecting Rod

NOTE: The following procedure requires the use of the GM Steering Linkage Puller tool No. J–24319–01 or equivalent, and the GM Steering Linkage Installer tool No. J–29193 (12mm) or J–29194 (14mm) or equivalent.

1. Raise and support the front of the vehicle on jackstands.

2. Remove the connecting rod stud-to-relay rod nut and the connecting rod stud-to-pitman arm nut.

3. Using the GM Steering Linkage Puller tool No. J–24319–01 or equivalent, separate the connecting rod from the relay rod and the pitman arm, then remove the connecting rod from the vehicle.

4. Clean and inspect the ball joint threads for damage, then replace the rod (if necessary). Inspect the ball joint seals for excessive wear, then replace them (if necessary).

To install:

1. Position the connecting rod onto the relay rod and the pitman arm (no mounting nuts). Using the GM Steering Linkage Installer tool No. J–29193 (12mm) or J–29194 (14mm) or equivalent, install them onto the connecting rod studs and torque the connecting rod stud nuts to 40 ft. lbs. (54 Nm) to seat the tapers. Remove the installer tools, then install the mounting nuts and torque them to 66 ft. lbs. (89 Nm).

2. Lower the vehicle and check the steering linkage performance.

3. Have a qualified alignment technician align the front end.

Tie Rod

NOTE: The following procedure requires the use of the Steering Linkage Installer tool No. J–29193 (12mm) or J–29194 (14mm) or equivalent, and the GM Wheel Stud and Tie Rod Remover tool No. J–6627–A or equivalent.

1. Raise and support the front of the vehicle on jackstands.

2. Remove the cotter pin from the tie rod-to-steering knuckle stud.

3. Remove the tie rod-to-relay rod stud nut and the tie rod-to-steering knuckle stud nut.

NOTE: DO NOT attempt to separate the tie rod-to-steering knuckle joint using a wedge type tool for seal damage could result.

4. Using the GM Wheel Stud Remover tool No. J–6627–A or equivalent, separate the outer tie rod stud from the steering knuckle and the inner tie rod stud from the relay rod. Remove the tie rod from the vehicle.

5. If removing ONLY the tie rod end, perform the following procedures:

    a. Disconnect the defective ball joint end of the tie rod.

    b. Loosen the adjuster tube clamp bolt.

    c. Unscrew the tie rod end from the adjuster tube; count the number of turns necessary to remove the tie rod end.

    d. Clean, inspect and lubricate the adjuster tube threads.

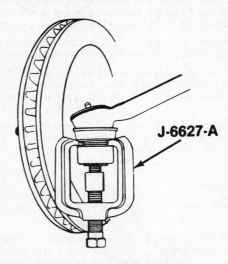

Separating the tie rod end ball joint stud

e. To install a new tie rod end, screw it into the adjuster tube using the same number of turns necessary to remove it.

f. Position the clamp bolts between the adjuster tube dimples (located at each end) and in the proper location (see illustration). Torque the adjuster tube clamp bolt 13 ft. lbs. (17 Nm).

To install:

1. Position the tie rod onto the steering knuckle and the relay rod. Using the Steering Linkage Installer tool No. J–29193 (12mm) or J–29194 (14mm) or equivalent, install them onto the studs and torque them to 40 ft. lbs. (54 Nm) to seat the tapers. After seating the tapers, remove the tools, install the mounting nuts and torque mounting nuts to 66 ft. lbs. (89 Nm).

2. At the tie rod-to-steering knuckle stud, tighten the nut until the castle nut slot aligns with the hole in the stud, then install a new cotter pin.

3. Lower the vehicle and check the steering linkage performance.

4. Have a qualified alignment technician align the front end.

Damper Assembly

The damper assembly is used to the remove steering wheel vibration and vehicle wonder; not all vehicles are equipped with it.

1. Raise and support the front of the vehicle on jackstands.

2. Remove the damper assembly-to-connecting rod cotter pin and nut.

3. Remove the damper assembly-to-bracket nut/bolt and remove the damper assembly from the vehicle.

To install:

1. If necessary, install a new damper assembly. Torque the damper assembly-to-bracket nut/bolt to 22 ft. lbs. (29 Nm) and the damper assembly-to-connecting rod nut to 41 ft. lbs. (56 Nm).

2. Align the castle nut slot with the hole in the ball joint stud and install a new cotter pin and bend over.

3. Have a qualified alignment technician align the front end.

Manual Steering Gear

The recirculating ball type manual steering gear is manufactured by Saginaw and is equipped with a mechanical ratio of 24:1.

ADJUSTMENTS

NOTE: The following procedure requires the use the GM Steering Linkage Puller tool No. J–6632 or equivalent, and a 0–50 inch lbs. (0–5.5 Nm) torque wrench.

1. Disconnect the negative battery terminal from the battery.

2. Raise and support the front of the vehicle on jackstands.

NOTE: Before adjustments are made to the steering gear, be sure to check the front end alignment, the shock absorbers, the wheel balance and the tire pressure.

3. Remove the pitman arm-to-pitman shaft nut and matchmark the pitman arm to the pitman shaft. Using the GM Steering Linkage Puller tool No. J–6632 or equivalent, remove the pitman arm from the pitman shaft.

4. Loosen the steering gear adjuster plug locknut and back-off the adjuster plug ¼ turn.

5. From the steering wheel, remove the horn cap or cover.

6. Gently, turn the steering wheel (in one direction) to the stop; then, turn it back ½ turn.

NOTE: When the steering linkage is disconnected from the steering gear, DO NOT turn the steering wheel hard against the stops for damage to the ball guides may result.

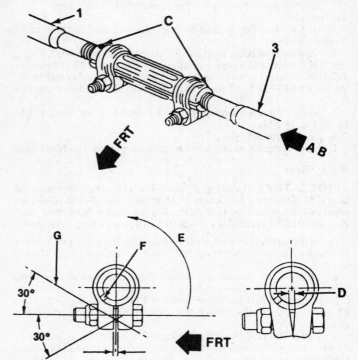

1. Inner tie rod
3. Outer tie rod
C. Clamp must be between and clear of dimples before torquing nut
D. Clamp ends must touch when nuts are torqued to specifications. But gap must be visible adjacent to adjuster tube
E. Rearward rotation
F. Adjuster tube slot
G. Center line of bolt

Proper orientation of the tie rod clamps and adjuster

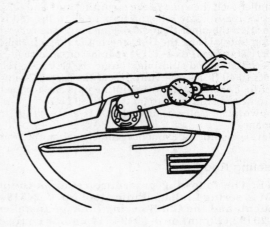

Using a dial torque wrench to measure the bearing drag

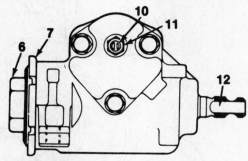

6. Adjuster plug
7. Nut
10. Adjuster screw
11. Jam nut
12. Wormshaft flat

View of the steering gear adjustment points

7. Using a torque wrench (0–50 inch lbs.), position it onto the steering wheel nut, then measure and record the bearing drag. To measure the bearing drag, use the torque wrench to rotate the steering wheel 90°.

8. Using a torque wrench (0–50 inch lbs.), tighten the adjuster plug (on the steering gear) to obtain a thrust bearing preload of 5–8 inch lbs. After the thrust bearing preload is obtained, torque the adjuster plug locknut to 25 ft. lbs. (34 Nm).

NOTE: If the steering gear feels lumpy (after adjustment), suspect damage to the bearings, probably due to the improper adjustment or severe impact.

9. To adjust the overcenter preload, perform the following procedures:

a. Turn the steering wheel, from one stop all the way to the other stop, counting the number of turns. Turn the steering wheel back exactly ½ way, to the center position.

b. Turn the overcenter adjusting screw clockwise, until the lash is removed between the ball nut and the pitman shaft sector teeth, then tighten the locknut.

c. Using a torque wrench (0–50 inch lbs.), check the highest force necessary to turn the steering wheel through the center position; the usable torque is 4–10 inch lbs.

d. If necessary, loosen the locknut and readjust the overcenter adjusting screw to obtain the proper torque. Retorque the locknut to 25 ft. lbs. (34 Nm) and recheck the steering wheel torque through the center of travel.

NOTE: If the maximum is too high, turn the overcenter adjuster screw counterclockwise, then torque the adjuster lock nut in the clockwise motion to achieve the proper torque.

10. To install, realign the pitman arm-to-pitman shaft, torque the pitman shaft nut to 177–185 ft. lbs. (240–250 Nm).

REMOVAL AND INSTALLATION

NOTE: The following procedure requires the use of the GM Pitman Arm Remover tool No. J–6632 or equivalent.

1. Disconnect the negative battery terminal from the battery.
2. Raise and support the front of the vehicle on jackstands. Position the wheel in the straight ahead direction.
3. Remove the intermediate shaft-to-steering gear pinch bolt.
4. Remove the pitman arm-to-pitman shaft nut, mark the relationship the arm to the shaft. Using the GM Pitman Arm Remover tool No. J–6632 or equivalent, separate the pitman arm from the pitman shaft.

NOTE: When separating the pitman arm from the shaft, DO NOT use a hammer or apply heat to the arm.

5. Remove the steering gear-to-frame bolts and the gear from the vehicle.

NOTE: When installing the steering gear, be sure that the intermediate shaft bottoms on the worm shaft, so that the pinch bolt passes through the undercut on the worm shaft. Check and/or adjust the alignment of the pitman arm-to-pitman shaft.

To install:

1. Align the matchmarks and install the steering gear. Torque the steering gear-to-frame bolts to 70 ft. lbs. (95 Nm).

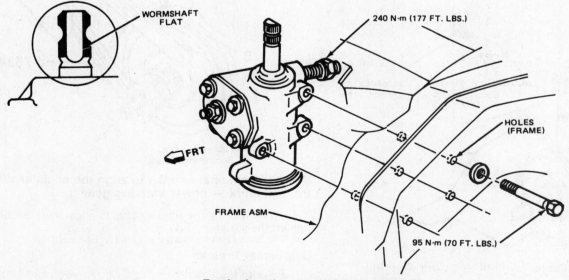

Replacing the manual steering gear

2. Install the pitman arm-to-shaft and torque the pitman arm-to-pitman shaft nut to 177–185 ft. lbs. (240–250 Nm).

3. Install the intermediate shaft and torque the bolt to 30 ft. lbs. (41 Nm).

Power Steering Gear

The recirculating ball type power steering gear is basically the same as the manual steering gear, except that it uses a mechanical advantage.

The power steering gear control valve directs the power steering fluid to either side of the rack piston. The steering rack converts the hydraulic pressure into mechanical force. Should the vehicle loose the hydraulic pressure, it can still be controlled mechanically.

ADJUSTMENTS

NOTE: To perform adjustments to the power steering gear, it is recommended to remove the power steering gear from the vehicle and place it in a vise. Before adjustments are performed to the system, be sure to check problems relating to hydraulic pressures and performance.

Worm Bearing Preload

NOTE: The following procedure requires the use of the GM Adjustable Spanner Wrench tool No. J–7624 or equivalent.

1. Refer to the Power Steering Gear, Removal and Installation procedures in this section, remove the steering gear from the vehicle and position it in a vise.

2. Using a hammer and a brass punch, drive the adjuster plug counterclockwise and remove it from the end of the steering gear.

3. Using the GM Adjustable Spanner Wrench tool No. J–7624 or equivalent, turn the adjuster plug inward, until it firmly bottoms in the housing with a torque of 20 ft. lbs. (27 Nm).

4. Using a scribing tool, place a matchmark (on the housing) next to the one of the spanner wrench holes in the adjuster plug.

5. Using a ruler, measure 13mm counterclockwise from the scribed mark (on the housing) and place another mark.

6. Using the GM Adjustable Spanner Wrench tool No. J–7624 or equivalent, turn the adjuster plug (counterclockwise) until the hole in the adjuster plug aligns with the 2nd scribed mark.

Removing the adjuster jam nut — power steering gear

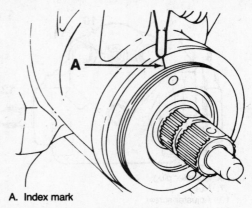

A. Index mark

Match-mark the power steering housing

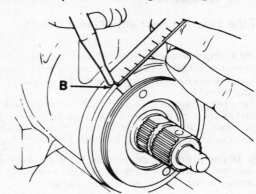

B. Second index mark

Remarking the power steering housing

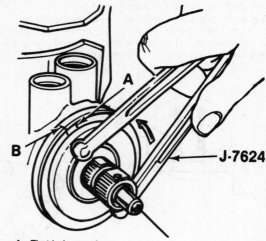

A. First index mark
B. Second index mark

Using the spanner wrench to align the adjuster with the 2nd mark — power steering gear

7. While holding the adjuster plug in alignment, install and tighten the adjuster plug nut.

8. Perform the overcenter preload adjustment.

Overcenter Preload

1. Refer to the Power Steering Gear, Removal and Installation procedures in this section, remove the steering gear from

the vehicle and position it in a vise.

2. Rotate the stud shaft from stop-to-stop and count the number of turns necessary.

3. Starting from one stop, turn the stub shaft back ½ the number of turns (center of the gear).

NOTE: With the stub gear centered, the flat on top of the shaft should face upward and be parallel with the side cover; the master spline on the pitman shaft should be in line with the adjuster screw.

4. Loosen the pitman shaft adjuster screw locknut and turn the adjuster screw counterclockwise until it is fully extended, then turn it clockwise one full turn.

5. Using a torque wrench (0–50 inch lbs.), position it onto the stub shaft, rotate it 45° (to each side) and record the highest drag measured near or on the center.

6. Turn the adjuster screw inward until the torque on the stub shaft is 6–10 inch lbs. (1.0–1.8 Nm) greater than the initial reading.

7. Install the adjuster screw jam nut and torque it to 20 ft. lbs. (27 Nm). Reinstall the power steering gear into the vehicle.

REMOVAL AND INSTALLATION

1. Refer to the Pitman Arm, Removal and Installation procedures in this section and disconnect the pitman arm from the power steering gear.

2. Position a fluid catch pan under the power steering gear.

3. At the power steering gear, disconnect and plug the pressure hoses; any excess fluid will be caught by the catch pan.

NOTE: Be sure to plug the pressure hoses and the openings of the power steering pump to keep dirt out of the system.

4. Remove the intermediate shaft-to-steering gear bolt. Matchmark the intermediate shaft-to-power steering gear and separate the shaft from the gear.

5. Remove the power steering gear-to-frame bolts, washers and the steering gear from the vehicle.

To install:

1. Install the steering gear and torque the power steering gear-to-frame bolts to 55 ft. lbs. (75 Nm), the intermediate shaft-to-power steering gear bolt to 30 ft. lbs. (41 Nm) and the pitman arm-to-pitman shaft nut to 177–185 ft. lbs. (240–250 Nm).

2. Connect the pressure hoses to the power steering gear.

3. Refill the power steering reservoir and bleed the power steering system.

4. Road test the vehicle.

Power Steering Pump

REMOVAL AND INSTALLATION

NOTE: The following procedure requires the use of the GM Puller tool No. J–29785–A or equivalent, and the GM Pulley Installer tool No. J–25033–B or equivalent.

1. Disconnect the negative (–) battery cable. Position a fluid catch pan under the power steering pump.

2. Remove the pressure hoses from the power steering pump and drain the excess fluid into the catch pan.

NOTE: On models equipped with a remote fluid reservoir, disconnect and plug the hose(s).

3. Loosen the power steering pump adjusting bolt, the washer and the pivot bolt, then remove the drive belt.

4. Using the GM Puller tool No. J–29785–A or equivalent, install it onto the power steering pump pulley. While holding the

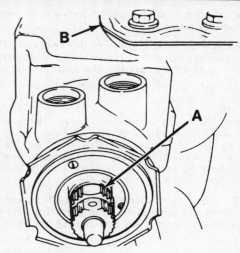

A. Stub shaft flat
B. Side cover

Aligning the stub shaft — power steering gear

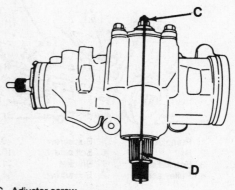

C. Adjuster screw
D. Master spline on the pitman shaft

Aligning the master spline on the pitman arm shaft — power steering

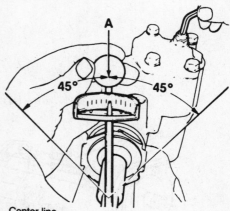

A. Center line

Checking the over-center rotational torque — power steering

tool body, turn the pilot bolt counterclockwise to press the drive pulley from the pump.

> **NOTE: When installing the puller tool onto the power steering pump pulley, be sure that the pilot bolt bottoms in the pump shaft by turning the head of the pilot bolt.**

5. Remove the power steering pump-to-bracket bolts and the pump from the vehicle.

To install:

1. Install the steering pump and torque the power steering pump-to-bracket bolts to 18 ft. lbs. (25 Nm).

2. Using the GM Pulley Installer tool No. J–25033–B or equivalent, press the drive pulley onto the power steering pump. While holding the tool body, turn the pilot bolt clockwise to press the drive pulley onto the pump.

> **NOTE: When installing the installer tool onto the power steering pump pulley, be sure that the pilot bolt bottoms in the pump shaft by turning the head of the pilot bolt.**

3. Hand tighten the pivot bolt, the adjusting bolt and the washer.

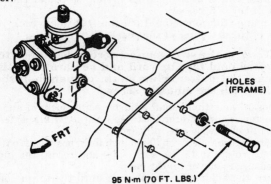

Replacing the power steering gear

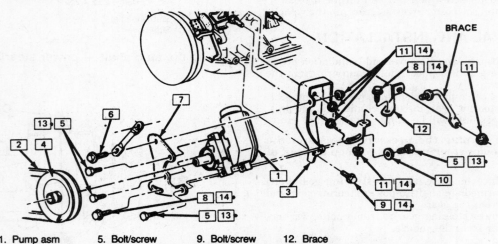

1. Pump asm	5. Bolt/screw	9. Bolt/screw	12. Brace
2. Belt	6. Bolt/screw	10. Washer	13. 25 N·m (18 ft. lbs.)
3. Bracket asm	7. Bracket	11. Nut	14. 50 N·m (37 ft. lbs.)
4. Pulley asm	8. Bolt/screw		

Exploded view of the power steering pump assembly — 2.5L engine

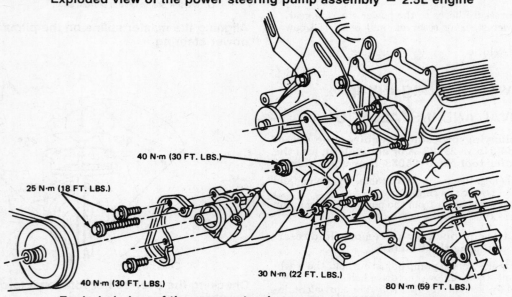

Exploded view of the power steering pump assembly — 4.3L engine

4. Install the drive belt and adjust the drive belt tension. Torque the mounting bolts and nut to 30 ft. lbs. (41 Nm). Install the pressure hoses (to the pump).

5. Refill the power steering reservoir and bleed the system.

6. Connect the negative battery cable and check operation

NOTE: Be sure to secure any hoses which may get in the way or rub other components.

7. Test drive the vehicle.

SYSTEM BLEEDING

1. Run the engine until the power steering fluid reaches normal operating temperature, approximately 170°F (76°C), then shut the engine Off. Remove the reservoir filler cap and check the oil level.

2. If the oil level is low, add power steering fluid to proper level and replace the filler cap. When adding or making a complete fluid change, always use GM No. 1050017 or equivalent, power steering fluid. DO NOT use transmission fluid.

3. Start the engine and turn the wheels in both directions (to the stops) several times. Stop the engine and add power steering fluid to the level indicated on the reservoir.

NOTE: Maintain the fluid level just above the internal pump casting. Fluid with air in it will have a light tan or milky appearance. This air must be eliminated from the fluid before normal steering action can be obtained.

4. Return the wheels to the center position and continue to run it for 2–3 minutes, then shut the engine Off.

5. Road test the vehicle to make sure the steering functions normally and is free from noise.

6. Allow the vehicle to stand for 2–3 hours, then recheck the power steering fluid.

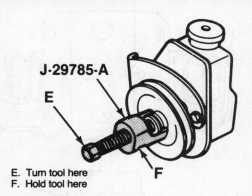

J-29785-A

E. Turn tool here
F. Hold tool here

Removing the power steering pump pulley

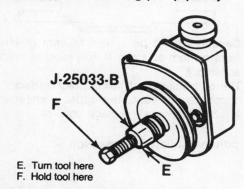

J-25033-B

E. Turn tool here
F. Hold tool here

Installing the power steering pump pulley

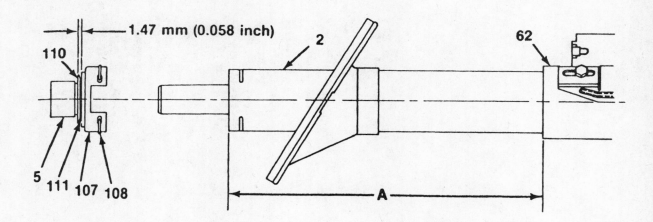

1.47 mm (0.058 inch)

A { Standard Column — Column Shift — 254.9 mm (10.03 inch)

2. Lower Column Jacket
5. Sleeve
62. Upper Column Jacket
107. Bearing Retainer
108. Clip
110. Bearing Preload Washer
111. Lower Spring Retainer

Steering column collapse inspection

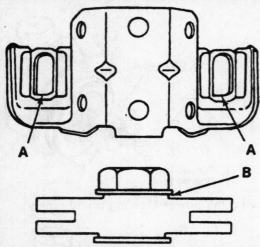

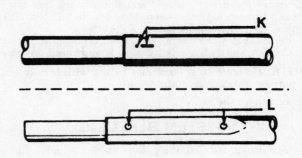

A. Capsules must be within 1.59mm (¹/₁₆-inch) from bottom of slots. If not, replace bracket assembly.

B. The bolt head must not contact surface "B." If contact is made, the capsule shear load will be increased – replace bracket.

Steering column collapse inspection

K. Inspect for sheared injected plastic in the shift tube.
L. Inspect for sheared injected plastic in the steering shaft.

Steering column collapse inspection

Brakes

BRAKE SYSTEM

These vans are equipped with independent front and rear brake systems. The systems consist of a power booster, a master cylinder, a combination valve, front disc and rear drum assemblies.

The 1989 models are equipped with rear wheel anti-lock brakes (RWAL). The system is designed to reduce the occurrence of rear wheel lockup during a severe brake application. A pressure regulator limits the amount of hydraulic line pressure to the rear brakes by the use of a control valve. The valve is controlled by a microcomputer which is tied in with the ECU (electronic control unit). The ECU is mounted next to the master cylinder.

The 1990 models could be ordered with 4-wheel anti-lock (4WAL) brakes as an option. The system is designed to reduce the occurrence of wheel lockup during a severe brake application. The system regulates hydraulic line pressure by the use of an electro-hydraulic control unit valve (EHCU) located under the master cylinder. An isolation valve maintains pressure to each wheel separately and the rear wheels combined.

The standard master cylinder, mounted on the left firewall or power booster, consists of 2 fluid reservoirs, a primary (rear) cylinder, a secondary (front) cylinder and springs. The reservoirs, being independent of one another, are contained within the same housing; fluid cannot pass from one to the other. The rear reservoir supplies fluid to the front brakes while the front reservoir supplies fluid to the rear brakes.

During standard operation, fluid drains from the reservoirs to the master cylinder. When the brake pedal is applied, fluid from the master cylinder is sent to the combination valve, mounted on the left front fender or frame side rail beneath the master cylinder. Here it is monitored and proportionally distributed to the front or rear brake systems. Should a loss of pressure occur in one system, the other system will provide enough braking pressure to stop the vehicle. Also, should a loss of pressure in one system occur, the differential warning switch, located on the combination valve, will turn ON the brake warning light, located on the dash board with standard brakes only.

As the fluid enters each brake caliper or wheel cylinder, the

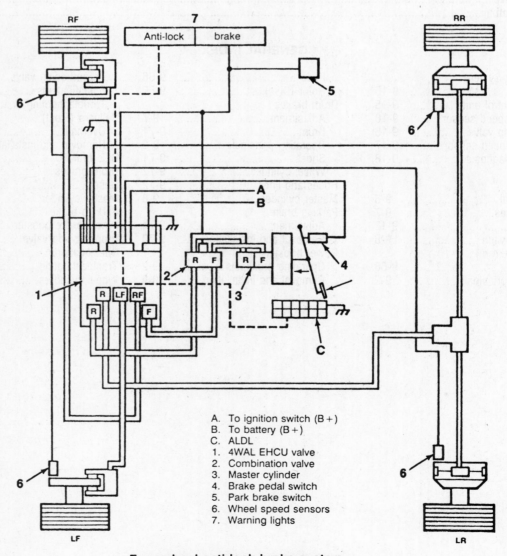

A. To ignition switch (B+)
B. To battery (B+)
C. ALDL
1. 4WAL EHCU valve
2. Combination valve
3. Master cylinder
4. Brake pedal switch
5. Park brake switch
6. Wheel speed sensors
7. Warning lights

Four wheel anti-lock brake system

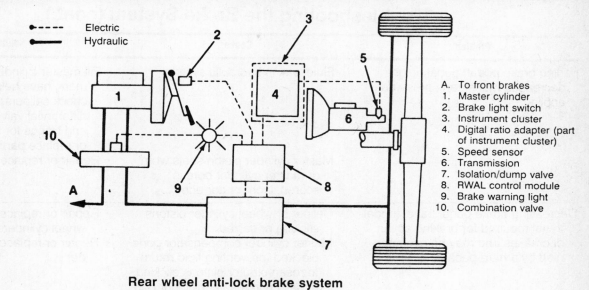

A. To front brakes
1. Master cylinder
2. Brake light switch
3. Instrument cluster
4. Digital ratio adapter (part of instrument cluster)
5. Speed sensor
6. Transmission
7. Isolation/dump valve
8. RWAL control module
9. Brake warning light
10. Combination valve

Rear wheel anti-lock brake system

Troubleshooting the Brake System

Problem	Cause	Solution
Low brake pedal (excessive pedal travel required for braking action.)	• Excessive clearance between rear linings and drums caused by inoperative automatic adjusters	• Make 10 to 15 alternate forward and reverse brake stops to adjust brakes. If brake pedal does not come up, repair or replace adjuster parts as necessary.
	• Worn rear brakelining	• Inspect and replace lining if worn beyond minimum thickness specification
	• Bent, distorted brakeshoes, front or rear	• Replace brakeshoes in axle sets
	• Air in hydraulic system	• Remove air from system. Refer to Brake Bleeding.
Low brake pedal (pedal may go to floor with steady pressure applied.)	• Fluid leak in hydraulic system	• Fill master cylinder to fill line; have helper apply brakes and check calipers, wheel cylinders, differential valve tubes, hoses and fittings for leaks. Repair or replace as necessary.
	• Air in hydraulic system	• Remove air from system. Refer to Brake Bleeding.
	• Incorrect or non-recommended brake fluid (fluid evaporates at below normal temp).	• Flush hydraulic system with clean brake fluid. Refill with correct-type fluid.
	• Master cylinder piston seals worn, or master cylinder bore is scored, worn or corroded	• Repair or replace master cylinder
Low brake pedal (pedal goes to floor on first application—o.k. on subsequent applications.)	• Disc brake pads sticking on abutment surfaces of anchor plate. Caused by a build-up of dirt, rust, or corrosion on abutment surfaces	• Clean abutment surfaces

Troubleshooting the Brake System (cont.)

Problem	Cause	Solution
Fading brake pedal (pedal height decreases with steady pressure applied.)	• Fluid leak in hydraulic system	• Fill master cylinder reservoirs to fill mark, have helper apply brakes, check calipers, wheel cylinders, differential valve, tubes, hoses, and fittings for fluid leaks. Repair or replace parts as necessary.
	• Master cylinder piston seals worn, or master cylinder bore is scored, worn or corroded	• Repair or replace master cylinder
Decreasing brake pedal travel (pedal travel required for braking action decreases and may be accompanied by a hard pedal.)	• Caliper or wheel cylinder pistons sticking or seized	• Repair or replace the calipers, or wheel cylinders
	• Master cylinder compensator ports blocked (preventing fluid return to reservoirs) or pistons sticking or seized in master cylinder bore	• Repair or replace the master cylinder
	• Power brake unit binding internally	• Test unit according to the following procedure: (a) Shift transmission into neutral and start engine (b) Increase engine speed to 1500 rpm, close throttle and fully depress brake pedal (c) Slow release brake pedal and stop engine (d) Have helper remove vacuum check valve and hose from power unit. Observe for backward movement of brake pedal. (e) If the pedal moves backward, the power unit has an internal bind—replace power unit
Grabbing brakes (severe reaction to brake pedal pressure.)	• Brakelining(s) contaminated by grease or brake fluid	• Determine and correct cause of contamination and replace brakeshoes in axle sets
	• Parking brake cables incorrectly adjusted or seized	• Adjust cables. Replace seized cables.
	• Incorrect brakelining or lining loose on brakeshoes	• Replace brakeshoes in axle sets
	• Caliper anchor plate bolts loose	• Tighten bolts
	• Rear brakeshoes binding on support plate ledges	• Clean and lubricate ledges. Replace support plate(s) if ledges are deeply grooved. Do not attempt to smooth ledges by grinding.
	• Incorrect or missing power brake reaction disc	• Install correct disc
	• Rear brake support plates loose	• Tighten mounting bolts

Troubleshooting the Brake System (cont.)

Problem	Cause	Solution
Spongy brake pedal (pedal has abnormally soft, springy, spongy feel when depressed.)	• Air in hydraulic system • Brakeshoes bent or distorted • Brakelining not yet seated with drums and rotors • Rear drum brakes not properly adjusted	• Remove air from system. Refer to Brake Bleeding. • Replace brakeshoes • Burnish brakes • Adjust brakes
Hard brake pedal (excessive pedal pressure required to stop vehicle. May be accompanied by brake fade.)	• Loose or leaking power brake unit vacuum hose • Incorrect or poor quality brakelining • Bent, broken, distorted brakeshoes • Calipers binding or dragging on mounting pins. Rear brakeshoes dragging on support plate. • Caliper, wheel cylinder, or master cylinder pistons sticking or seized • Power brake unit vacuum check valve malfunction • Power brake unit has internal bind	• Tighten connections or replace leaking hose • Replace with lining in axle sets • Replace brakeshoes • Replace mounting pins and bushings. Clean rust or burrs from rear brake support plate ledges and lubricate ledges with molydisulfide grease. **NOTE:** If ledges are deeply grooved or scored, do not attempt to sand or grind them smooth—replace support plate. • Repair or replace parts as necessary • Test valve according to the following procedure: (a) Start engine, increase engine speed to 1500 rpm, close throttle and immediately stop engine (b) Wait at least 90 seconds then depress brake pedal (c) If brakes are not vacuum assisted for 2 or more applications, check valve is faulty • Test unit according to the following procedure: (a) With engine stopped, apply brakes several times to exhaust all vacuum in system (b) Shift transmission into neutral, depress brake pedal and start engine (c) If pedal height decreases with foot pressure and less pressure is required to hold pedal in applied position, power unit vacuum system is operating normally. Test power unit. If power unit exhibits a bind condition, replace the power unit.

Troubleshooting the Brake System (cont.)

Problem	Cause	Solution
Hard brake pedal (excessive pedal pressure required to stop vehicle. May be accompanied by brake fade.)	• Master cylinder compensator ports (at bottom of reservoirs) blocked by dirt, scale, rust, or have small burrs (blocked ports prevent fluid return to reservoirs). • Brake hoses, tubes, fittings clogged or restricted • Brake fluid contaminated with improper fluids (motor oil, transmission fluid, causing rubber components to swell and stick in bores • Low engine vacuum	• Repair or replace master cylinder **CAUTION:** Do not attempt to clean blocked ports with wire, pencils, or similar implements. Use compressed air only. • Use compressed air to check or unclog parts. Replace any damaged parts. • Replace all rubber components, combination valve and hoses. Flush entire brake system with DOT 3 brake fluid or equivalent. • Adjust or repair engine
Dragging brakes (slow or incomplete release of brakes)	• Brake pedal binding at pivot • Power brake unit has internal bind • Parking brake cables incorrrectly adjusted or seized • Rear brakeshoe return springs weak or broken • Automatic adjusters malfunctioning • Caliper, wheel cylinder or master cylinder pistons sticking or seized • Master cylinder compensating ports blocked (fluid does not return to reservoirs).	• Loosen and lubricate • Inspect for internal bind. Replace unit if internal bind exists. • Adjust cables. Replace seized cables. • Replace return springs. Replace brakeshoe if necessary in axle sets. • Repair or replace adjuster parts as required • Repair or replace parts as necessary • Use compressed air to clear ports. Do not use wire, pencils, or similar objects to open blocked ports.
Vehicle moves to one side when brakes are applied	• Incorrect front tire pressure • Worn or damaged wheel bearings • Brakelining on one side contaminated • Brakeshoes on one side bent, distorted, or lining loose on shoe • Support plate bent or loose on one side • Brakelining not yet seated with drums or rotors • Caliper anchor plate loose on one side • Caliper piston sticking or seized • Brakelinings water soaked • Loose suspension component attaching or mounting bolts • Brake combination valve failure	• Inflate to recommended cold (reduced load) inflation pressure • Replace worn or damaged bearings • Determine and correct cause of contamination and replace brakelining in axle sets • Replace brakeshoes in axle sets • Tighten or replace support plate • Burnish brakelining • Tighten anchor plate bolts • Repair or replace caliper • Drive vehicle with brakes lightly applied to dry linings • Tighten suspension bolts. Replace worn suspension components. • Replace combination valve

Troubleshooting the Brake System (cont.)

Problem	Cause	Solution
Chatter or shudder when brakes are applied (pedal pulsation and roughness may also occur.)	• Brakeshoes distorted, bent, contaminated, or worn • Caliper anchor plate or support plate loose • Excessive thickness variation of rotor(s)	• Replace brakeshoes in axle sets • Tighten mounting bolts • Refinish or replace rotors in axle sets
Noisy brakes (squealing, clicking, scraping sound when brakes are applied.)	• Bent, broken, distorted brakeshoes • Excessive rust on outer edge of rotor braking surface	• Replace brakeshoes in axle sets • Remove rust
Noisy brakes (squealing, clicking, scraping sound when brakes are applied.) (cont.)	• Brakelining worn out—shoes contacting drum of rotor • Broken or loose holdown or return springs • Rough or dry drum brake support plate ledges • Cracked, grooved, or scored rotor(s) or drum(s) • Incorrect brakelining and/or shoes (front or rear).	• Replace brakeshoes and lining in axle sets. Refinish or replace drums or rotors. • Replace parts as necessary • Lubricate support plate ledges • Replace rotor(s) or drum(s). Replace brakeshoes and lining in axle sets if necessary. • Install specified shoe and lining assemblies
Pulsating brake pedal	• Out of round drums or excessive lateral runout in disc brake rotor(s)	• Refinish or replace drums, re-index rotors or replace

pistons are forced outward. The outward movement of the pistons force the brake pads against a round flat disc or the brake shoes against a round metal drum. The brake lining attached to the pads or shoes comes in contact with the revolving disc or drum, causing friction, which brings the wheel to a stop.

In time, the brake linings wear down. If not replaced, their metal support plates (bonded type) or rivet heads (riveted type) will come in contact with the disc or drum; damage to the disc or drum will occur. Never use brake pads or shoes with a lining thickness less than 0.8mm ($\frac{1}{32}$ in.).

Most manufacturers provide a wear sensor, a piece of spring steel, attached to the rear edge of the inner brake pad. When the pad wears to the replacement thickness, the sensor will produce a high pitched squeal.

Adjustments

REAR DRUM BRAKES

Normal adjustments of the rear drum brakes are automatic and are made during the reverse applications of the brakes. ONLY, if the lining has been renewed, should the following procedure be performed.

NOTE: The following procedure requires the use of the GM Brake Adjustment tool No. J–4735 or equivalent.

1. Raise and support the rear of the vehicle on jackstands.
2. Using a punch and a hammer, at the rear of the backing plate, knock out the lanced metal area near the star wheel assembly.

NOTE: When knocking out the lanced metal area from the backing plate, the wheels must be removed and all of the metal pieces discarded.

3. Using the GM Brake Adjustment tool No. J–4735 or equivalent, insert it into the slot and engage the lowest possible tooth on the star wheel. Move the end of the brake tool downward to move the star wheel upward and expand the adjusting screw. Repeat this operation until the brakes lock the wheel.
4. Insert a small screwdriver or piece of firm wire (coathanger wire) into the adjusting slot and push the automatic adjuster lever out and free of the star wheel on the adjusting screw.

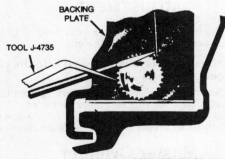

INSERT SMALL SCREWDRIVER OR AWL THROUGH BACKING PLATE SLOT AND HOLD ADJUSTER LEVER AWAY FROM SPROCKET BEFORE BACKING OFF BRAKE SHOE ADJUSTMENT

Adjusting the rear brake shoes

5. While holding the adjusting lever out of the way, engage the topmost tooth possible on the star wheel (with the brake tool). Move the end of the adjusting tool upward to move the adjusting screw star wheel downward and contact the adjusting screw. Back off the adjusting screw star wheel until the wheel spins freely with a minimum of drag. Keep track of the number of turns the star wheel is backed off.

6. Repeat this operation for the other side. When backing off the brakes on the other side, the adjusting lever must be backed off the same number of turns to prevent side-to-side brake pull.

NOTE: Backing off the star wheel 12 notches (clicks) is usually enough to eliminate brake drag.

7. Repeat this operation on the other side of the rear brake system.

8. After the brakes are adjusted, install a rubber hole cover into the backing plate slot. To complete the brake adjustment operation, make several stops while backing the vehicle to equalize the wheels.

9. Road test the vehicle.

BRAKE PEDAL TRAVEL

The brake pedal travel is the distance the pedal moves toward the floor from the fully released position. Inspection should be made with 90 lbs. pressure on the brake pedal, when the brake system is Cold. The brake pedal travel should be 114mm (4½ in.) for manual, or 89mm (3½ in.) for power.

NOTE: If equipped with power brakes, be sure to pump the brake pedal at least 3 times with the engine Off, before making the brake pedal check.

1. From under the dash, remove the pushrod-to-pedal clevis pin and separate the pushrod from the brake pedal.

2. Loosen the pushrod adjuster lock nut, then adjust the pushrod.

3. After the correct travel is established, reverse the removal procedure.

Brake Light Switch

REMOVAL AND INSTALLATION

1. Disconnect the negative battery terminal from the battery.
2. Disconnect the electrical connector from the brake light switch.
3. Turn the brake light switch retainer (to align the key with the bracket slot), then remove the switch with the retainer.
4. To install, reverse the removal procedures. Adjust the brake light switch.

ADJUSTMENT

1. Depress the brake pedal and press the brake light switch inward until it seats firmly against the clip.

NOTE: As the switch is being pushed into the clip, audible clicks can be heard.

2. Release the brake pedal, then pull it back against the pedal stop until the audible click can no longer be heard.

3. The brake light switch will operate when the pedal is depressed 13mm (0.53 in.) from the fully released position.

Master Cylinder

REMOVAL AND INSTALLATION

NOTE: The master cylinder removal and installation procedures are basically the same for all brake systems.

Always use flare nut wrenches to remove the hydraulic brake line. Damage to the fitting nut may occur if this procedure is not followed.

1. Disconnect the negative (−) battery cable. Apply the parking brakes or block the wheels.

2. Using a siphon, remove and discard some of the brake fluid from the master cylinder reservoirs.

3. Disconnect and plug the hydraulic lines from the master cylinder using flare nut wrenches only.

4. If equipped with a manual brake system, disconnect the pushrod from the brake pedal.

5. Remove the master cylinder-to-bracket (manual) or vacuum booster (power) nuts, then separate the combination valve/bracket from the master cylinder.

6. Remove the master cylinder, the gasket and the rubber boot from the vehicle.

To install:

1. Bench bleed the master cylinder and install the cylinder onto the vehicle. Torque the master cylinder mounting nuts to 28 ft. lbs. (38 Nm).

2. Connect the hydraulic lines and torque to 20 ft. lbs. (27 Nm).

3. Refill the master cylinder with clean brake fluid, bleed the brake system and check the brake pedal travel.

NOTE: If equipped with manual brakes, be sure to reconnect the pushrod to the brake pedal.

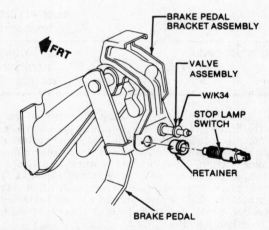

Exploded view of the brake light switch

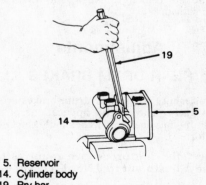

5. Reservoir
14. Cylinder body
19. Pry bar

Removing the reservoirs from the master cylinder

OVERHAUL

1. Refer to the Master Cylinder, Removal and Installation procedures in this Section and remove the master cylinder from the vehicle.

2. At the rear of the master cylinder, depress the primary piston and remove the lock ring.

3. Block the rear outlet hole on the master cylinder. Using compressed air, gently direct it into the front outlet hole to remove the primary and secondary pistons from the master cylinder. If compressed air is not available, use a hooked wire to pull out the secondary piston.

———— CAUTION ————

If using compressed air to remove the pistons from the master cylinder, DO NOT stand in front of the pistons, for too much air will cause the pistons to be fired from the master cylinder, causing bodily harm.

4. From the secondary piston, remove the spring retainer and the seals.

5. Using the mounting flange (ear) on the master cylinder, clamp it into a vise.

6. Using a medium pry bar, pry the reservoirs from the master cylinder. Remove the reservoir grommets.

NOTE: DO NOT attempt to remove the quick take-up valve from the master cylinder body; the valve is not serviceable separately.

7. Using denatured alcohol, clean and blow dry all of the master cylinder parts.

8. Inspect the master cylinder bore for corrosion or scratches; if damaged, replace the master cylinder with a new one.

To install:

9. Use new reservoir grommets (lubricated with silicone brake lube) and press them into the master cylinder body. Install new seals onto the primary and secondary pistons.

10. Position the reservoirs on flat, hard surfaces (block of wood), then press the master cylinder onto the reservoirs, using a rocking motion.

11. Using heavy duty brake fluid, meeting Dot 3 specifications, lubricate the primary and secondary pistons, then install them into the master cylinder. While depressing the primary piston, install the lock ring.

12. Install new diaphragms onto the reservoir covers.

13. Install the master cylinder onto the vehicle and torque the mounting bolts to 28 ft. lbs. (38 Nm). Bleed the system as outlined in this Section.

Power Brake Booster

The power brake booster is a tandem vacuum suspended unit, equipped with a single or dual function vacuum switch that activates a brake warning light should low booster vacuum be present. Under normal operation, vacuum is present on both sides of the diaphragms. When the brakes are applied, atmospheric air is admitted to one side of the diaphragms to provide power assistance.

REMOVAL AND INSTALLATION

1. Disconnect the negative (−) battery cable. Apply the parking brake or block the wheels.

2. Remove the master cylinder-to-power brake booster nuts and move the master cylinder out of the way; if necessary, support the master cylinder on a wire.

NOTE: When removing the master cylinder from the power brake booster, it is not necessary to disconnect the hydraulic lines.

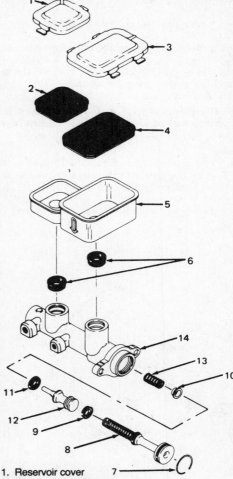

1. Reservoir cover
2. Reservoir diaphragm
3. Reservoir cover
4. Reservoir diaphragm
5. Reservoir
6. Reservoir grommet
7. Lock ring
8. Primary piston assembly
9. Secondary seal
10. Spring retainer
11. Primary seal
12. Secondary piston
13. Spring
14. Cylinder body

Exploded view of the master cylinder assembly

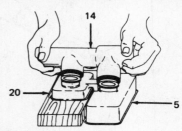

5. Reservoir
14. Cylinder body
20. Block

Installing the reservoirs onto the master cylinder

3. Disconnect the vacuum hose from the power brake booster.

4. From under the dash, disconnect the pushrod from the brake pedal.

5. From under the dash, remove the power brake booster-to-cowl nuts.

6. From the engine compartment, remove the power brake booster and the gasket from the vehicle.

NOTE: If equipped with anti-lock brakes, support the control valves out of the way while removing the brake booster.

To install:

1. Use a new gaskets and install the brake booster onto the firewall. Torque the power brake booster-to-cowl nuts and the master cylinder-to-power brake booster nuts to 28 ft. lbs. (38 Nm).

2. Start the engine and check the brake system operation.

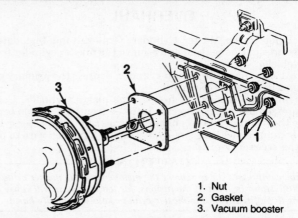

1. Nut
2. Gasket
3. Vacuum booster

Removing the power brake booster from the cowl

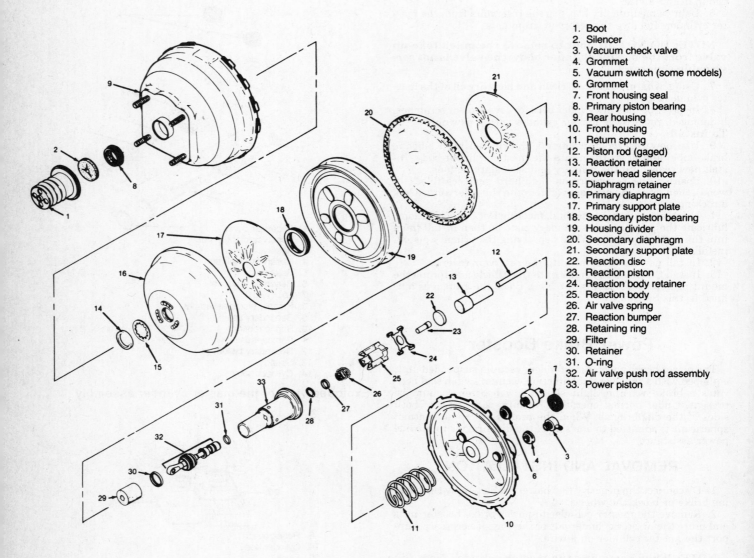

1. Boot
2. Silencer
3. Vacuum check valve
4. Grommet
5. Vacuum switch (some models)
6. Grommet
7. Front housing seal
8. Primary piston bearing
9. Rear housing
10. Front housing
11. Return spring
12. Piston rod (gaged)
13. Reaction retainer
14. Power head silencer
15. Diaphragm retainer
16. Primary diaphragm
17. Primary support plate
18. Secondary piston bearing
19. Housing divider
20. Secondary diaphragm
21. Secondary support plate
22. Reaction disc
23. Reaction piston
24. Reaction body retainer
25. Reaction body
26. Air valve spring
27. Reaction bumper
28. Retaining ring
29. Filter
30. Retainer
31. O-ring
32. Air valve push rod assembly
33. Power piston

Exploded view of the tandem power brake booster

Combination Valve

The standard combination valve is located in the engine compartment, directly under the master cylinder. It consists of 3 sections: the metering valve, the warning switch and the proportioning valve.

The metering section limits the pressure to the front disc brakes until a predetermined front input pressure is reached, enough to overcome the rear shoe retractor springs. Under 3 psi, there is no restriction of the inlet pressures; the pressures are allowed to equalize during the no brake period.

The proportioning section controls the outlet pressure to the rear brakes after a predetermined rear input pressure has been reached; this feature is provided for vehicles with light loads, to prevent rear wheel lock-up. The By-pass feature of this valve assures full system pressure to the rear brakes in the event of a front brake system malfunction. Also, full front pressure is retained if the rear system malfunctions.

The pressure differential warning switch is designed to constantly compare the front and the rear brake pressures; if one should malfunction, the warning light (on the dash) will turn On. The valve and switch are designed to lock On the warning position once the malfunction has occurred. The only way the light can be turned Off is to repair the malfunction and apply a brake line force of 450 psi.

REMOVAL AND INSTALLATION

Non-antilock

1. Disconnect and plug the hydraulic lines from the combination valve to prevent the loss of brake fluid or dirt from entering the system.
2. Disconnect the electrical connector from the combination valve.
3. Remove the combination valve-to-bracket nuts and the combination valve from the vehicle.

NOTE: The combination valve is not repairable and must be replaced as a complete assembly.

To install:
1. Use a new combination valve (if defective) and install.
2. Torque the combination valve-to-bracket nuts to 37 ft. lbs. (49 Nm).
3. Reconnect the electrical connector to the combination valve. Bleed the brake system.

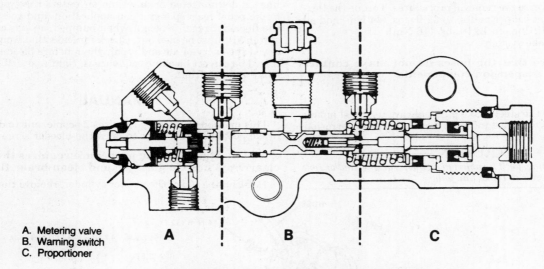

A. Metering valve
B. Warning switch
C. Proportioner

Cross-sectional view of the combination valve

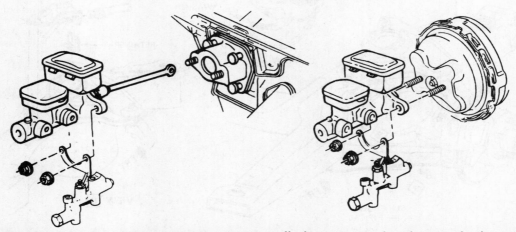

Removing the combination valve and the master cylinder — manual and power brake systems

Brake Pipes and Hoses

REMOVAL AND INSTALLATION

Flexible Hoses

Flexible hoses are installed between the frame-to-front calipers and the frame-to-rear differential.

1. Using a wire brush, clean the dirt and/or grease from both ends of the hose fittings.
2. Disconnect the steel pipes from the flexible hose.
3. To remove the brake hose from the front brake caliper or the rear differential, perform the following procedures:

   a. Remove the brake hose-to-frame bracket retaining clip.

   b. Remove the brake hose-to-brake caliper or differential junction block bolt.

   c. Remove the brake hose and the gaskets from the vehicle.

NOTE: After disconnecting the brake hose(s) from the fittings, be sure to plug the fittings to keep the fluid from discharging or dirt from entering the system.

4. Clean and inspect the brake hose(s) for cracking, chafing or road damage; replace the hose(s) if any signs are observed.

To install:

5. Using new flexible hose-to-caliper gaskets, install the flexible hose(s) and reverse the removal procedures. Torque the flexible hose(s)-to-front caliper bolt(s) to 32 ft. lbs. (44 Nm) and all other brake pipe fittings to 13 ft. lbs. (16 Nm).
6. Bleed the brake system.

NOTE: Be sure that the hoses do not make contact with any of the suspension components.

Steel Pipes

When replacing the steel brake pipes, always use steel piping which is designed to withstand high pressure, resist corrosion and is of the same size.

--- CAUTION ---

Never use copper tubing, for it is subject to fatigue, cracking, and/or corrosion, which will result in brake line failure.

NOTE: The following procedure requires the use of the GM Tube Cutter tool No. J–23533 or equivalent, and the GM Flaring tool No. J–23530 or equivalent.

1. Disconnect the steel brake pipe(s) from the flexible hose connections or the rear wheel cylinders; be sure to remove any retaining clips.
2. Remove the steel brake pipe from the vehicle.
3. Using new steel pipe (same size) and a tube cutter, cut the pipe to length; be sure to add 3mm (⅛ in.) for each flare.

NOTE: Be sure to install the correct pipe fittings onto the tube before forming any flares.

4. Using a double-flare tool, follow the instructions that come with the tool to form double flares on the ends of the pipes.
5. Using a small pipe bending tool, bend the pipe to match the contour of the pipe which was removed.
6. To install, reverse the removal procedures. Bleed the hydraulic system.

Bleeding

Non-antilock

The hydraulic brake system must be bled any time one of the lines is disconnected or any time air enters the system. If the brake pedal feels spongy upon application, and goes almost to the floor but regains height when pumped, air has entered the system. It must be bled out. Check for leaks that would have allowed the entry of air and repair them before bleeding the system. The correct bleeding sequence is; right rear, left rear, right front and left front.

MANUAL

This method of bleeding requires 2 people, one to depress the brake pedal and the other to open the bleeder screws.

NOTE: The following procedure requires the use of a clear vinyl hose, a glass jar and clean brake fluid.

1. Clean the top of the master cylinder, remove the cover and

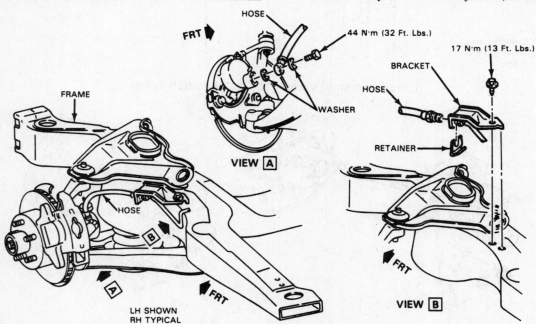

View of the front brake hose assemblies

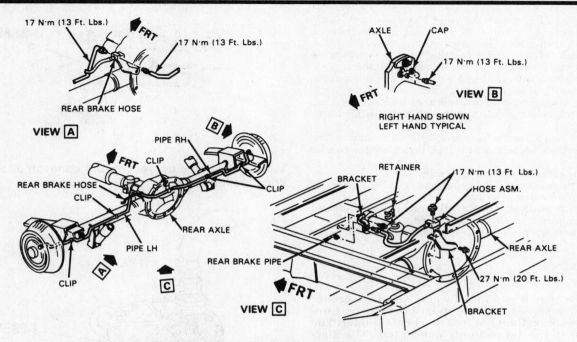

View of the rear brake hose and steel tube assemblies

fill the reservoirs with clean fluid. To prevent squirting fluid, replace the cover.

NOTE: On vehicles equipped with front disc brakes, it will be necessary to hold in the metering valve pin during the bleeding procedure. The metering valve is located beneath the master cylinder and the pin is situated under the rubber boot on the end of the valve housing. This may be tapped in or held by an assistant.

2. Fill the master cylinder with brake fluid.

3. Install a box end wrench onto the bleeder screw on the right rear wheel.

4. Attach a length of small diameter, clear vinyl tubing to the bleeder screw. Submerge the other end of the tubing in a glass jar partially filled with clean brake fluid. Make sure the tube fits on the bleeder screw snugly or you may be squirted with brake fluid when the bleeder screw is opened.

5. Have your assistant slowly depress the brake pedal. As this is done, open the bleeder screw ½ turn and allow the fluid to run through the tube. Close the bleeder screw, then return the brake pedal to its fully released position.

6. Repeat this procedure until no bubbles appear in the jar. Refill the master cylinder.

7. Repeat this procedure on the left rear, right front and the left front wheels, in that order. Periodically, refill the master cylinder so that it does not run dry.

8. If the brake warning light is On, depress the brake pedal firmly. If there is no air in the system, the light will go Off.

PRESSURE

NOTE: The following procedure requires the use of the GM Brake Bleeder Adapter tool No. J-29567 or equivalent, and the GM Combination Valve Depressor tool No. J-35856 or equivalent.

1. Using the GM Brake Bleeder Adapter tool No. J-29567 or equivalent, fill the pressure tank to at least ⅓ full of brake fluid. Using compressed air, charge the pressure tank to 20–25 psi., then install it onto the master cylinder.

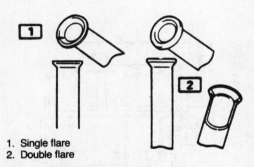

1. Single flare
2. Double flare

View of the single and double flare fittings

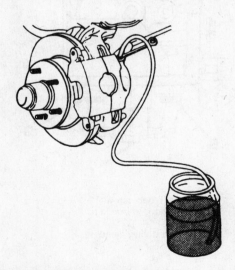

Installing a clear vinyl bleeder hose to the wheel caliper

2. Using the GM Combination Valve Depressor tool No. J–35856 or equivalent, install it onto the combination valve to hold the valve open during the bleeding operation.

3. Bleed each wheel cylinder or caliper in the following sequence: right rear, left rear, right front and left front.

4. Connect a hose from the bleeder tank to the adapter at the master cylinder, then open the tank valve.

5. Attach a clear vinyl hose to the brake bleeder screw, then immerse the opposite end into a container partially filled with clean brake fluid.

6. Open the bleeder screw ¾ turn and allow the fluid to flow until no air bubbles are seen in the fluid, then close the bleeder screw.

7. Repeat the bleeding process to each wheel.

8. Inspect the brake pedal for sponginess and if necessary, repeat the entire bleeding procedure.

9. Remove the depressor tool from the combination valve and the bleeder adapter from the master cylinder.

10. Refill the master cylinder to the proper level with brake fluid.

Anti-lock Brakes
EHCU Valve

NOTE: The rear wheel and 4-wheel anti-lock brakes are bled the same way as the standard brakes, pertaining to the master cylinder and each wheel cylinder. The difference is in the 4-wheel anti-lock system. The Electro-hydraulic Control Unit (EHCU) valve has to be bled after replacement only.

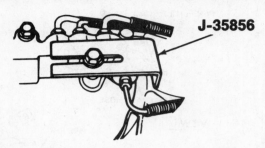

View of the valve depressor tool connected to the combination valve

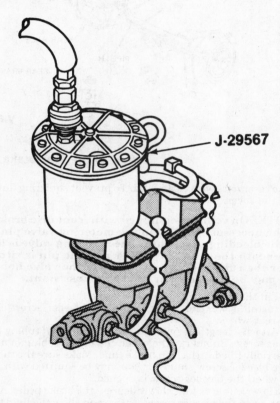

View of the bleeder adapter tool connected to the master cylinder reservoir

Use the 2 bleed screws on the EHCU valve for bleeding. There are also 2 bleeders on the front of the unit that look like normal brake bleeders. These are NOT the correct bleeders for bleeding the valve and they should not be turned.

1. Bleed the calipers and wheel cylinder first.

2. Install a valve depressor tool J–35856 onto the left high pressure accumulator bleed stem of the EHCU valve.

3. Slowly depress the brake pedal one time and hold. Loosen the left bleeder screw ¼ turn to purge the air from the EHCU valve.

4. Tighten the bleeder screw to 60 inch lbs. (7 Nm) and slowly release the pedal.

5. Wait 15 seconds, then repeat the sequence, purging the EHCU valve.

6. Repeat steps 2–5 at the right side of the EHCU valve.

7. Remove the valve depressor tool.

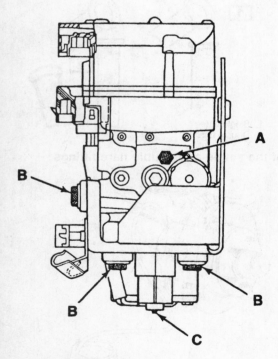

A. Internal bleed screw
B. EHCU valve-to-bracket bolts
C. Depress during bleeding

EHCU (electro-hydraulic control unit) bleeding — only after valve replacement

ANTI-LOCK BRAKES

EHCU Valve

REMOVAL AND INSTALLATION

4-Wheel Anti-lock

The EHCU valve is not serviceable. Replace the valve only when defective.

1. Disconnect the negative (−) battery cable.
2. Disconnect the intermediate steering shaft from the steering column as outlined in Section 8.
3. Disconnect the brake lines from the bottom of the combination valve.
4. Disconnect the electrical connectors from the master cylinder and EHCU.
5. Remove the master cylinder and combination valve as outlined earlier in this Section.
6. Disconnect the brake lines from the EHCU using a flare nut wrench.
7. Remove the bolts, nuts and EHCU from the vehicle.

To install:

1. Install the EHCU onto the bracket. Torque the 6 mounting bolts to 60 inch lbs. (7 Nm).
2. Connect the electrical connectors and hydraulic lines. Torque the line fittings to 16 ft. lbs. (25 Nm).
3. Install the master cylinder, combination valve and hydraulic lines.
4. Reconnect the intermediate steering shaft.
5. Bleed the system as outlined in the "Bleeding" procedures earlier in this Section. Also, bleed the EHCU as outlined in the "Anti-lock Brake" bleeding procedures in this Section.
6. Connect the negative battery cable, pump the brakes before road test and road test

Electronic Control Unit

REMOVAL AND INSTALLATION

Rear Wheel Anti-lock Brakes

The ECU is not serviceable. Replace the unit only when defective.

NOTE: Do not touch the electrical connections and pins or allow them to come in contact with brake fluid as this may damage the ECU.

1. Disconnect the negative (−) battery cable and ECU connectors.
2. Remove the ECU by prying the tab at the rear of the ECU and pull it toward the front of the vehicle.

To install:

1. Install the ECU by sliding the unit into the bracket until the tab locks into the hole.
2. Connect the electrical connectors and negative battery cable.

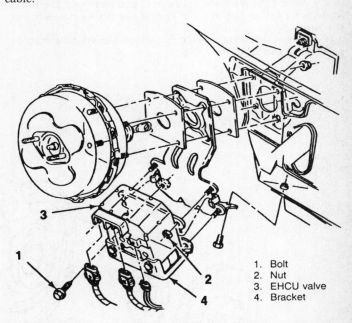

1. Bolt
2. Nut
3. EHCU valve
4. Bracket

EHCU valve and connectors — four wheel anti-lock brakes

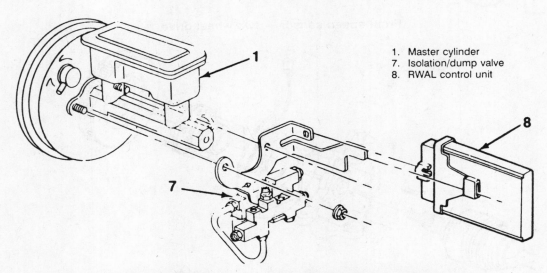

1. Master cylinder
7. Isolation/dump valve
8. RWAL control unit

Electronic control unit — rear wheel anti-lock brakes

Isolation/Dump Valve

REMOVAL AND INSTALLATION

Rear Wheel Anti-lock Brakes

The isolation/dump valve is not serviceable. Replace the unit only when defective.

1. Disconnect the negative (−) battery cable.
2. Disconnect the brake line fittings using a flare nut wrench.
3. Disconnect the bottom electrical connector from the ECU. Do not allow the isolation/dump valve to hang by the pigtail.
4. Remove the valve from the vehicle.

To install:

1. Install the valve and torque the bolts to 21 ft. lbs. (29 Nm).
2. Connect the electrical connectors and reconnect the brake lines using a flare nut wrench. Torque the fittings to 18 ft. lbs. (24 Nm).
3. Connect the negative battery cable and bleed the system as outlined in this Section.

Front Wheel Speed Sensor

REMOVAL AND INSTALLATION

2-Wheel Drive

1. Disconnect the negative (−) battery cable.
2. Raise the vehicle and support with jackstands. Remove the wheel and tire assembly.

— **CAUTION** —

Some brake pads contain asbestos, which has been determined to be a cancer causing agent. Never clean the brake surfaces with compressed air! Avoid inhaling any dust from any brake surface! When cleaning brake surfaces, use a commercially available brake cleaning fluid.

3. Remove the brake caliper, hub and rotor.
4. Disconnect the sensor electrical connector.
5. Remove the splash shield with the sensor from the steering knuckle.

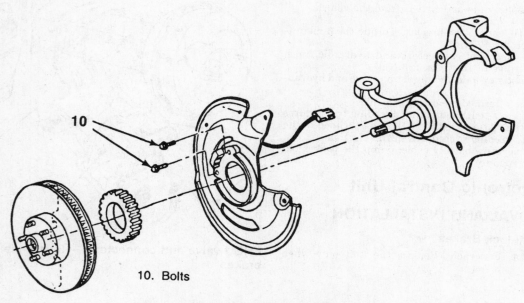

10. Bolts

Front speed sensor — two wheel drive

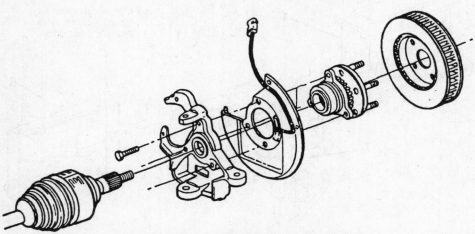

Front speed sensor — all wheel drive

To install:

1. Install the splash shield with the sensor onto the steering knuckle and torque the bolts to 11 ft. lbs. (15 Nm).
2. Connect the sensor wire.
3. Install the hub, rotor and caliper.
4. Install the front wheel and torque the lug nuts to 100 ft. lbs. (136 Nm).
5. Connect the negative battery cable and check operation.

4-Wheel Drive

1. Disconnect the negative (−) battery cable.
2. Raise the vehicle and support with jackstands. Remove the wheel and tire assembly.

------------------ **CAUTION** ------------------

Some brake pads contain asbestos, which has been determined to be a cancer causing agent. Never clean the brake surfaces with compressed air! Avoid inhaling any dust from any brake surface! When cleaning brake surfaces, use a commercially available brake cleaning fluid.

3. Remove the brake caliper and rotor.
4. Remove the hub and bearing assembly.
5. Disconnect the sensor electrical connector.
6. Remove the splash shield with the sensor from the steering knuckle.

To install:

1. Install the splash shield with the sensor onto the steering knuckle and torque the bolts to 11 ft. lbs. (15 Nm).
2. Connect the sensor wire.
3. Install the hub and bearing assembly.
4. Install the rotor and caliper.
5. Install the front wheel and torque the lug nuts to 100 ft. lbs. (136 Nm).
6. Connect the negative battery cable and check operation.

Rear Wheel Speed Sensor

REMOVAL AND INSTALLATION

1. Disconnect the negative (−) battery cable.
2. Raise the vehicle and support with jackstands.
3. Remove the rear wheels.

------------------ **CAUTION** ------------------

Some brake pads contain asbestos, which has been determined to be a cancer causing agent. Never clean the brake surfaces with compressed air! Avoid inhaling any dust from any brake surface! When cleaning brake surfaces, use a commercially available brake cleaning fluid.

4. Remove the brake drum and primary brake show.
5. Disconnect the sensor connector.
6. Remove the 2 bolts and sensor by pulling the wire through the hole in the backing plate.

To install:

1. Install the sensor, bolts and torque to 26 ft. lbs. (35 Nm).
2. Connect the electrical connector.
3. Install the primary shoe, brake drum and rear wheel. Torque the lug nuts to 100 ft. lbs. (136 Nm).
4. Connect the negative battery cable and check operation.

DIAGNOSIS

Rear Wheel Anti-lock Brakes

TROUBLE CODE IDENTIFICATION

The trouble codes are read by jumping the terminal **A** and terminal **H** of the ALDL (assembly line diagnostic link) with a jumper wire. Observe the flashing of the brake warning light. The terminals must be jumped for about 20 seconds before the code will begin to flash.

Count the number of short flashes starting from the long flash. Include the long flash as a count. Sometimes the first count sequence will be short, however, following counts will be accurate.

If there is more than one failure, only the first recognized code will be retained and flashed.

4-Wheel Anti-lock Brakes

TROUBLE CODE IDENTIFICATION

The trouble codes are read by jumping the terminal **A** and terminal **H** of the ALDL (assembly line diagnostic link) with a jumper wire. Observe the flashing of the ANTI-LOCK warning light. The terminals must be jumped for about 20 seconds before the code will begin to flash.

Count the number of short flashes starting from the long flash. Include the long flash as a count. Sometimes the first count sequence will be short, however, following counts will be accurate.

If there is more than one failure, only the first recognized code will be retained and flashed.

CLEARING TROUBLE CODES

The trouble codes may be cleared using a Tech I scan tool or by performing the following procedures.

1. Turn the ignition switch to the **RUN** position.
2. Use a jumper wire to ground the ALDL terminal **A** to **H** for 2 seconds.
3. Remove the jumper wire for 2 seconds.
4. Repeat the grounding and ungrounding 2 more times.
5. Check that the memory is cleared by making a diagnostic request.
6. Turn the ignition switch **OFF**.

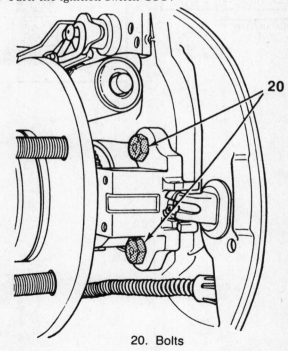

20. Bolts

Rear speed sensor — all anti-lock models

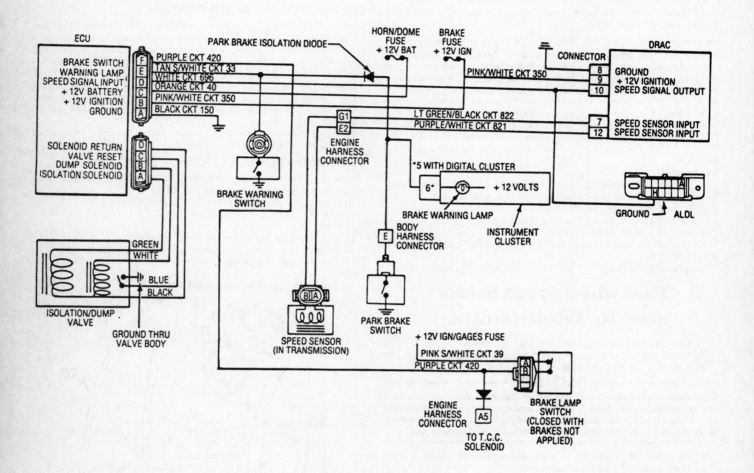

Rear wheel anti-lock wiring diagram

DIAGNOSTIC CIRCUIT CHECK

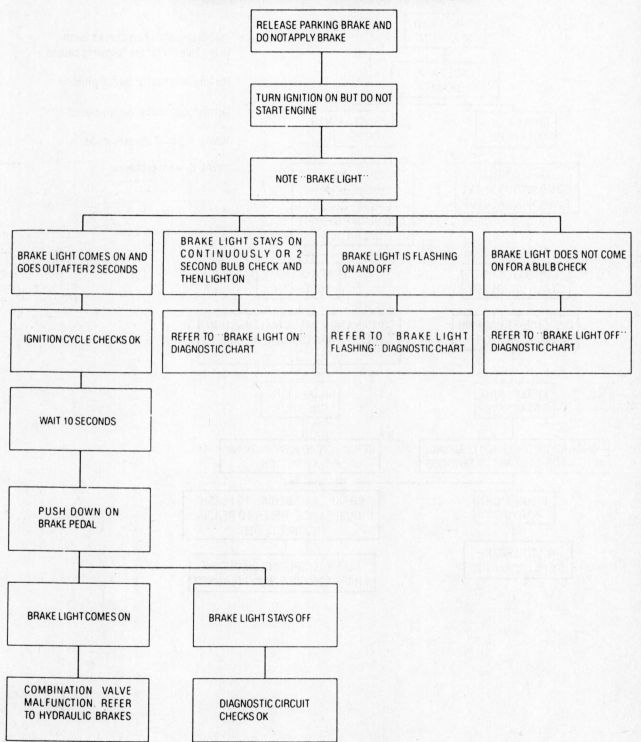

RELEASE PARKING BRAKE AND DO NOT APPLY BRAKE

TURN IGNITION ON BUT DO NOT START ENGINE

NOTE "BRAKE LIGHT"

BRAKE LIGHT COMES ON AND GOES OUT AFTER 2 SECONDS	BRAKE LIGHT STAYS ON CONTINUOUSLY OR 2 SECOND BULB CHECK AND THEN LIGHT ON	BRAKE LIGHT IS FLASHING ON AND OFF	BRAKE LIGHT DOES NOT COME ON FOR A BULB CHECK
IGNITION CYCLE CHECKS OK	REFER TO "BRAKE LIGHT ON" DIAGNOSTIC CHART	REFER TO "BRAKE LIGHT FLASHING" DIAGNOSTIC CHART	REFER TO "BRAKE LIGHT OFF" DIAGNOSTIC CHART

WAIT 10 SECONDS

PUSH DOWN ON BRAKE PEDAL

BRAKE LIGHT COMES ON

BRAKE LIGHT STAYS OFF

COMBINATION VALVE MALFUNCTION. REFER TO HYDRAULIC BRAKES

DIAGNOSTIC CIRCUIT CHECKS OK

BRAKE LIGHT ON — PART 1

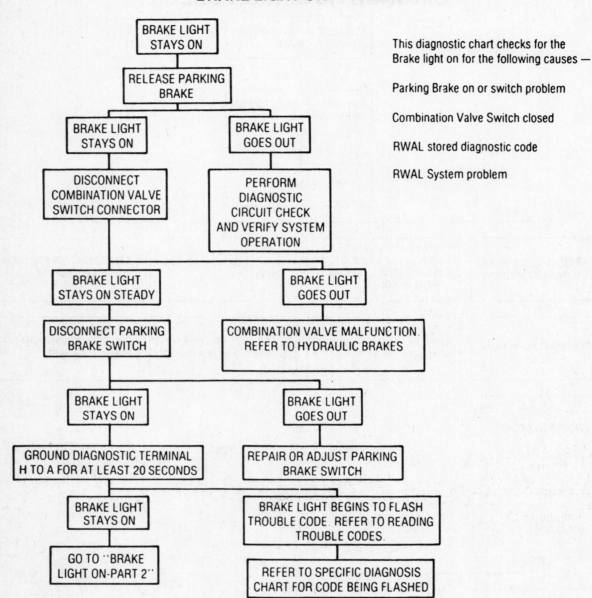

This diagnostic chart checks for the Brake light on for the following causes —

Parking Brake on or switch problem

Combination Valve Switch closed

RWAL stored diagnostic code

RWAL System problem

BRAKE LIGHT ON — PART 2

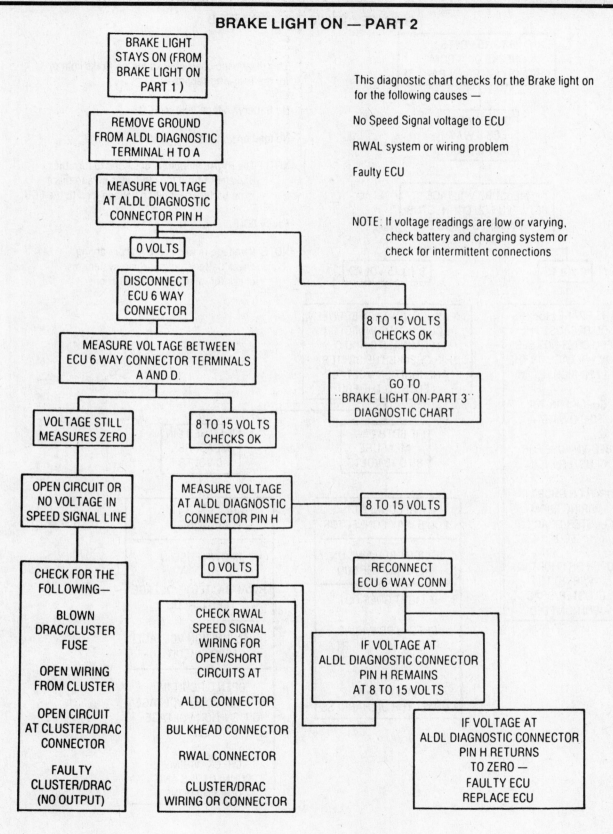

BRAKE LIGHT STAYS ON (FROM BRAKE LIGHT ON PART 1)

REMOVE GROUND FROM ALDL DIAGNOSTIC TERMINAL H TO A

MEASURE VOLTAGE AT ALDL DIAGNOSTIC CONNECTOR PIN H

0 VOLTS

DISCONNECT ECU 6 WAY CONNECTOR

MEASURE VOLTAGE BETWEEN ECU 6 WAY CONNECTOR TERMINALS A AND D.

VOLTAGE STILL MEASURES ZERO

8 TO 15 VOLTS CHECKS OK

OPEN CIRCUIT OR NO VOLTAGE IN SPEED SIGNAL LINE

MEASURE VOLTAGE AT ALDL DIAGNOSTIC CONNECTOR PIN H

8 TO 15 VOLTS

0 VOLTS

RECONNECT ECU 6 WAY CONN

CHECK FOR THE FOLLOWING—

BLOWN DRAC/CLUSTER FUSE

OPEN WIRING FROM CLUSTER

OPEN CIRCUIT AT CLUSTER/DRAC CONNECTOR

FAULTY CLUSTER/DRAC (NO OUTPUT)

CHECK RWAL SPEED SIGNAL WIRING FOR OPEN/SHORT CIRCUITS AT

ALDL CONNECTOR

BULKHEAD CONNECTOR

RWAL CONNECTOR

CLUSTER/DRAC WIRING OR CONNECTOR

IF VOLTAGE AT ALDL DIAGNOSTIC CONNECTOR PIN H REMAINS AT 8 TO 15 VOLTS

IF VOLTAGE AT ALDL DIAGNOSTIC CONNECTOR PIN H RETURNS TO ZERO — FAULTY ECU REPLACE ECU

8 TO 15 VOLTS CHECKS OK

GO TO "BRAKE LIGHT ON-PART 3" DIAGNOSTIC CHART

This diagnostic chart checks for the Brake light on for the following causes —

No Speed Signal voltage to ECU

RWAL system or wiring problem

Faulty ECU

NOTE: If voltage readings are low or varying, check battery and charging system or check for intermittent connections

BRAKE LIGHT ON — PART 3

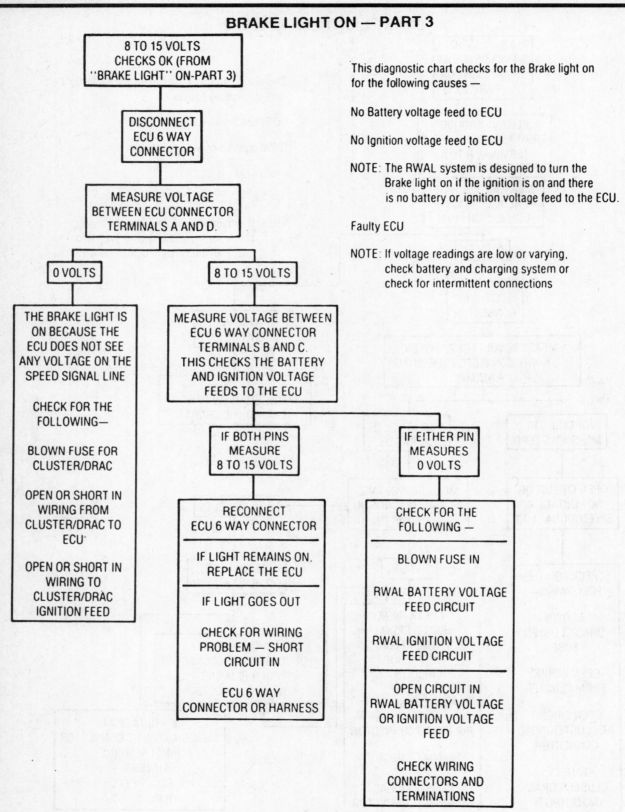

8 TO 15 VOLTS CHECKS OK (FROM ''BRAKE LIGHT'' ON-PART 3)

DISCONNECT ECU 6 WAY CONNECTOR

MEASURE VOLTAGE BETWEEN ECU CONNECTOR TERMINALS A AND D.

0 VOLTS

8 TO 15 VOLTS

THE BRAKE LIGHT IS ON BECAUSE THE ECU DOES NOT SEE ANY VOLTAGE ON THE SPEED SIGNAL LINE

CHECK FOR THE FOLLOWING—

BLOWN FUSE FOR CLUSTER/DRAC

OPEN OR SHORT IN WIRING FROM CLUSTER/DRAC TO ECU

OPEN OR SHORT IN WIRING TO CLUSTER/DRAC IGNITION FEED

MEASURE VOLTAGE BETWEEN ECU 6 WAY CONNECTOR TERMINALS B AND C. THIS CHECKS THE BATTERY AND IGNITION VOLTAGE FEEDS TO THE ECU

IF BOTH PINS MEASURE 8 TO 15 VOLTS

IF EITHER PIN MEASURES 0 VOLTS

RECONNECT ECU 6 WAY CONNECTOR

IF LIGHT REMAINS ON. REPLACE THE ECU

IF LIGHT GOES OUT

CHECK FOR WIRING PROBLEM — SHORT CIRCUIT IN

ECU 6 WAY CONNECTOR OR HARNESS

CHECK FOR THE FOLLOWING —

BLOWN FUSE IN

RWAL BATTERY VOLTAGE FEED CIRCUIT

RWAL IGNITION VOLTAGE FEED CIRCUIT

OPEN CIRCUIT IN RWAL BATTERY VOLTAGE OR IGNITION VOLTAGE FEED

CHECK WIRING CONNECTORS AND TERMINATIONS

This diagnostic chart checks for the Brake light on for the following causes —

No Battery voltage feed to ECU

No Ignition voltage feed to ECU

NOTE: The RWAL system is designed to turn the Brake light on if the ignition is on and there is no battery or ignition voltage feed to the ECU.

Faulty ECU

NOTE: If voltage readings are low or varying, check battery and charging system or check for intermittent connections

BRAKE LIGHT FLASHING

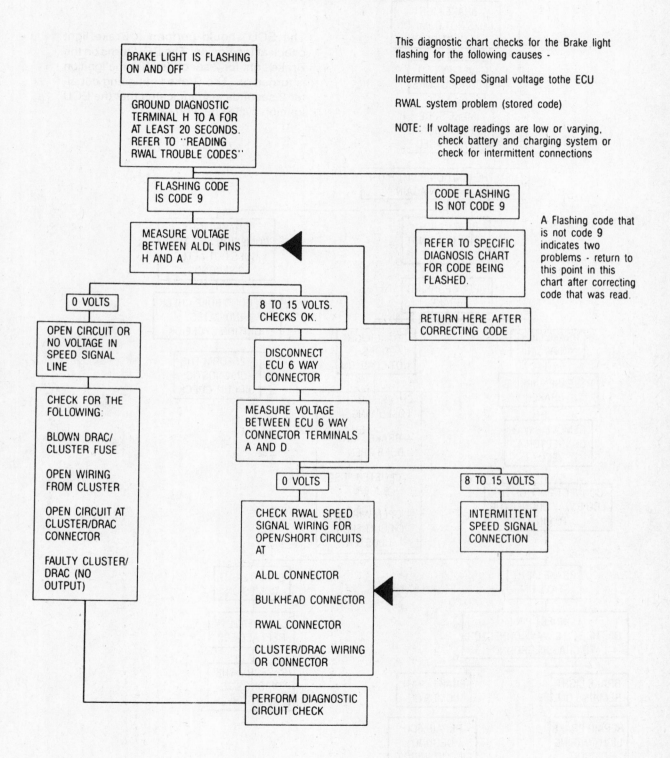

This diagnostic chart checks for the Brake light flashing for the following causes -

Intermittent Speed Signal voltage to the ECU

RWAL system problem (stored code)

NOTE: If voltage readings are low or varying, check battery and charging system or check for intermittent connections

BRAKE LIGHT IS FLASHING ON AND OFF

GROUND DIAGNOSTIC TERMINAL H TO A FOR AT LEAST 20 SECONDS. REFER TO "READING RWAL TROUBLE CODES"

FLASHING CODE IS CODE 9

CODE FLASHING IS NOT CODE 9

MEASURE VOLTAGE BETWEEN ALDL PINS H AND A

REFER TO SPECIFIC DIAGNOSIS CHART FOR CODE BEING FLASHED.

A Flashing code that is not code 9 indicates two problems - return to this point in this chart after correcting code that was read.

0 VOLTS

8 TO 15 VOLTS. CHECKS OK.

RETURN HERE AFTER CORRECTING CODE

OPEN CIRCUIT OR NO VOLTAGE IN SPEED SIGNAL LINE

DISCONNECT ECU 6 WAY CONNECTOR

CHECK FOR THE FOLLOWING:

BLOWN DRAC/ CLUSTER FUSE

OPEN WIRING FROM CLUSTER

OPEN CIRCUIT AT CLUSTER/DRAC CONNECTOR

FAULTY CLUSTER/ DRAC (NO OUTPUT)

MEASURE VOLTAGE BETWEEN ECU 6 WAY CONNECTOR TERMINALS A AND D

0 VOLTS

8 TO 15 VOLTS

CHECK RWAL SPEED SIGNAL WIRING FOR OPEN/SHORT CIRCUITS AT

ALDL CONNECTOR

BULKHEAD CONNECTOR

RWAL CONNECTOR

CLUSTER/DRAC WIRING OR CONNECTOR

INTERMITTENT SPEED SIGNAL CONNECTION

PERFORM DIAGNOSTIC CIRCUIT CHECK

BRAKE LIGHT OFF

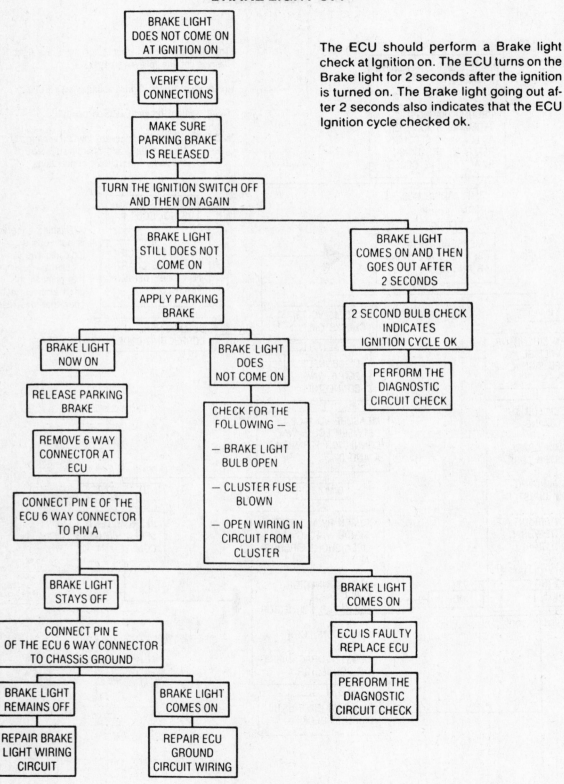

The ECU should perform a Brake light check at Ignition on. The ECU turns on the Brake light for 2 seconds after the ignition is turned on. The Brake light going out after 2 seconds also indicates that the ECU Ignition cycle checked ok.

BRAKE LIGHT DOES NOT COME ON AT IGNITION ON

VERIFY ECU CONNECTIONS

MAKE SURE PARKING BRAKE IS RELEASED

TURN THE IGNITION SWITCH OFF AND THEN ON AGAIN

BRAKE LIGHT STILL DOES NOT COME ON

BRAKE LIGHT COMES ON AND THEN GOES OUT AFTER 2 SECONDS

2 SECOND BULB CHECK INDICATES IGNITION CYCLE OK

PERFORM THE DIAGNOSTIC CIRCUIT CHECK

APPLY PARKING BRAKE

BRAKE LIGHT NOW ON

BRAKE LIGHT DOES NOT COME ON

RELEASE PARKING BRAKE

CHECK FOR THE FOLLOWING —
- **BRAKE LIGHT BULB OPEN**
- **CLUSTER FUSE BLOWN**
- **OPEN WIRING IN CIRCUIT FROM CLUSTER**

REMOVE 6 WAY CONNECTOR AT ECU

CONNECT PIN E OF THE ECU 6 WAY CONNECTOR TO PIN A

BRAKE LIGHT STAYS OFF

BRAKE LIGHT COMES ON

CONNECT PIN E OF THE ECU 6 WAY CONNECTOR TO CHASSIS GROUND

ECU IS FAULTY REPLACE ECU

BRAKE LIGHT REMAINS OFF

BRAKE LIGHT COMES ON

PERFORM THE DIAGNOSTIC CIRCUIT CHECK

REPAIR BRAKE LIGHT WIRING CIRCUIT

REPAIR ECU GROUND CIRCUIT WIRING

CODE 2
OPEN ISOLATION VALVE OR MALFUNCTIONING ECU

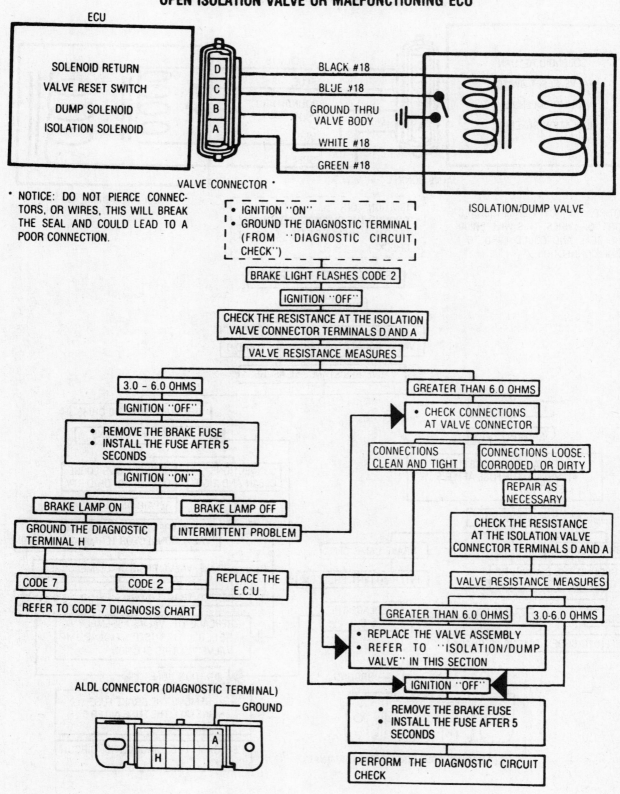

ECU

SOLENOID RETURN

VALVE RESET SWITCH

DUMP SOLENOID

ISOLATION SOLENOID

BLACK #18

BLUE #18

GROUND THRU VALVE BODY

WHITE #18

GREEN #18

VALVE CONNECTOR

ISOLATION/DUMP VALVE

* NOTICE: DO NOT PIERCE CONNECTORS, OR WIRES, THIS WILL BREAK THE SEAL AND COULD LEAD TO A POOR CONNECTION.

- IGNITION "ON"
- GROUND THE DIAGNOSTIC TERMINAL (FROM "DIAGNOSTIC CIRCUIT CHECK")

BRAKE LIGHT FLASHES CODE 2

IGNITION "OFF"

CHECK THE RESISTANCE AT THE ISOLATION VALVE CONNECTOR TERMINALS D AND A

VALVE RESISTANCE MEASURES

3.0 – 6.0 OHMS

IGNITION "OFF"

- REMOVE THE BRAKE FUSE
- INSTALL THE FUSE AFTER 5 SECONDS

IGNITION "ON"

BRAKE LAMP ON

BRAKE LAMP OFF

GROUND THE DIAGNOSTIC TERMINAL H

INTERMITTENT PROBLEM

CODE 7

CODE 2

REPLACE THE E.C.U.

REFER TO CODE 7 DIAGNOSIS CHART

GREATER THAN 6.0 OHMS

- CHECK CONNECTIONS AT VALVE CONNECTOR

CONNECTIONS CLEAN AND TIGHT

CONNECTIONS LOOSE, CORRODED, OR DIRTY

REPAIR AS NECESSARY

CHECK THE RESISTANCE AT THE ISOLATION VALVE CONNECTOR TERMINALS D AND A

VALVE RESISTANCE MEASURES

GREATER THAN 6.0 OHMS

3.0-6.0 OHMS

- REPLACE THE VALVE ASSEMBLY
- REFER TO "ISOLATION/DUMP VALVE" IN THIS SECTION

IGNITION "OFF"

- REMOVE THE BRAKE FUSE
- INSTALL THE FUSE AFTER 5 SECONDS

PERFORM THE DIAGNOSTIC CIRCUIT CHECK

ALDL CONNECTOR (DIAGNOSTIC TERMINAL)

GROUND

H

A

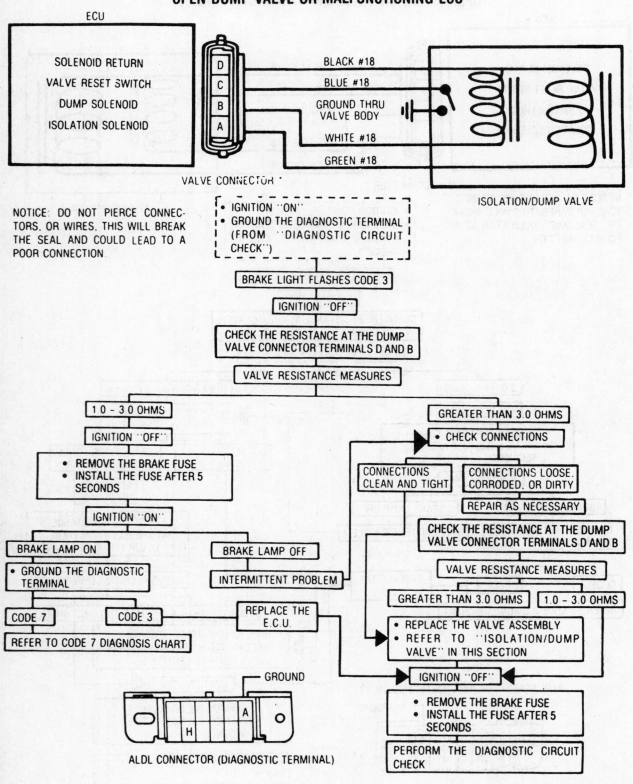

CODE 3
OPEN DUMP VALVE OR MALFUNCTIONING ECU

ECU

SOLENOID RETURN
VALVE RESET SWITCH
DUMP SOLENOID
ISOLATION SOLENOID

D
C
B
A

BLACK #18
BLUE #18
GROUND THRU VALVE BODY
WHITE #18
GREEN #18

VALVE CONNECTOR

ISOLATION/DUMP VALVE

NOTICE: DO NOT PIERCE CONNECTORS, OR WIRES. THIS WILL BREAK THE SEAL AND COULD LEAD TO A POOR CONNECTION.

- IGNITION "ON"
- GROUND THE DIAGNOSTIC TERMINAL (FROM "DIAGNOSTIC CIRCUIT CHECK")

BRAKE LIGHT FLASHES CODE 3

IGNITION "OFF"

CHECK THE RESISTANCE AT THE DUMP VALVE CONNECTOR TERMINALS D AND B

VALVE RESISTANCE MEASURES

1.0 – 3.0 OHMS

IGNITION "OFF"

- REMOVE THE BRAKE FUSE
- INSTALL THE FUSE AFTER 5 SECONDS

IGNITION "ON"

BRAKE LAMP ON

- GROUND THE DIAGNOSTIC TERMINAL

CODE 7

REFER TO CODE 7 DIAGNOSIS CHART

CODE 3

BRAKE LAMP OFF

INTERMITTENT PROBLEM

REPLACE THE E.C.U.

GREATER THAN 3.0 OHMS

- CHECK CONNECTIONS

CONNECTIONS CLEAN AND TIGHT

CONNECTIONS LOOSE, CORRODED, OR DIRTY

REPAIR AS NECESSARY

CHECK THE RESISTANCE AT THE DUMP VALVE CONNECTOR TERMINALS D AND B

VALVE RESISTANCE MEASURES

GREATER THAN 3.0 OHMS

1.0 – 3.0 OHMS

- REPLACE THE VALVE ASSEMBLY
- REFER TO "ISOLATION/DUMP VALVE" IN THIS SECTION

IGNITION "OFF"

- REMOVE THE BRAKE FUSE
- INSTALL THE FUSE AFTER 5 SECONDS

PERFORM THE DIAGNOSTIC CIRCUIT CHECK

GROUND

H   A

ALDL CONNECTOR (DIAGNOSTIC TERMINAL)

CODE 4
GROUNDED ANTI-LOCK VALVE SWITCH

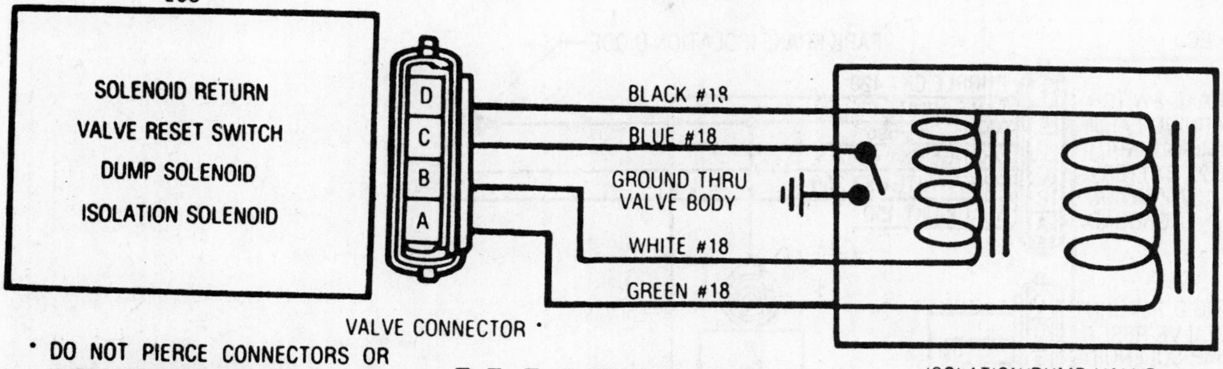

ECU

SOLENOID RETURN

VALVE RESET SWITCH

DUMP SOLENOID

ISOLATION SOLENOID

D
C
B
A

BLACK #18

BLUE #18

GROUND THRU VALVE BODY

WHITE #18

GREEN #18

VALVE CONNECTOR

ISOLATION/DUMP VALVE

• DO NOT PIERCE CONNECTORS OR WIRES. THIS WILL BREAK THE SEAL AND COULD LEAD TO A POOR CONNECTION.

- IGNITION "ON"
- GROUND THE DIAGNOSTIC TERMINAL (FROM "DIAGNOSTIC CIRCUIT CHECK")

BRAKE LIGHT FLASHES CODE 4

IGNITION "OFF"

- CHECK THE RESISTANCE BETWEEN VALVE RESET SWITCH TERMINAL C AND THE VALVE BODY.
- CHECK THE RESISTANCE BETWEEN TERMINAL C AND TERMINAL D

IF EITHER CHECK MEASURES LESS THAN 50,000 OHMS

IF BOTH CHECKS MEASURE GREATER THAN 50,000 OHMS

IGNITION "ON"

- REPLACE THE VALVE ASSEMBLY
- REFER TO "ISOLATION/DUMP VALVE" IN THIS SECTION

MEASURE VOLTAGE BETWEEN ECU PINS D AND C

0 VOLTS

4 VOLTS OR MORE

REPLACE THE VALVE ASSEMBLY

- REPLACE THE ECU
- REFER TO "ELECTRONIC CONTROL UNIT" IN THIS SECTION

IGNITION "OFF"

ALDL CONNECTOR (DIAGNOSTIC TERMINAL)

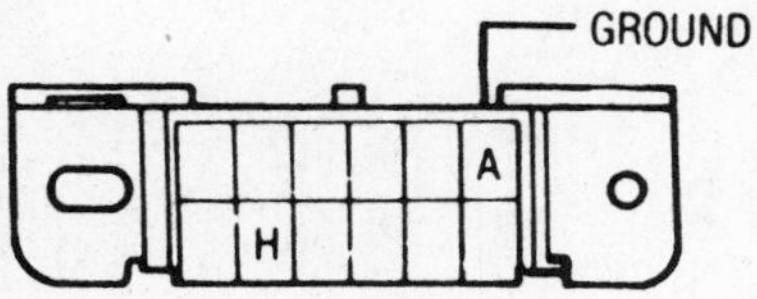

- REMOVE THE BRAKE FUSE
- INSTALL THE FUSE AFTER 5 SECONDS

PERFORM THE DIAGNOSTIC CIRCUIT CHECK

GROUND

H
A

CODE 5
EXCESSIVE ACTUATIONS OF THE DUMP VALVE DURING AN ANTILOCK STOP

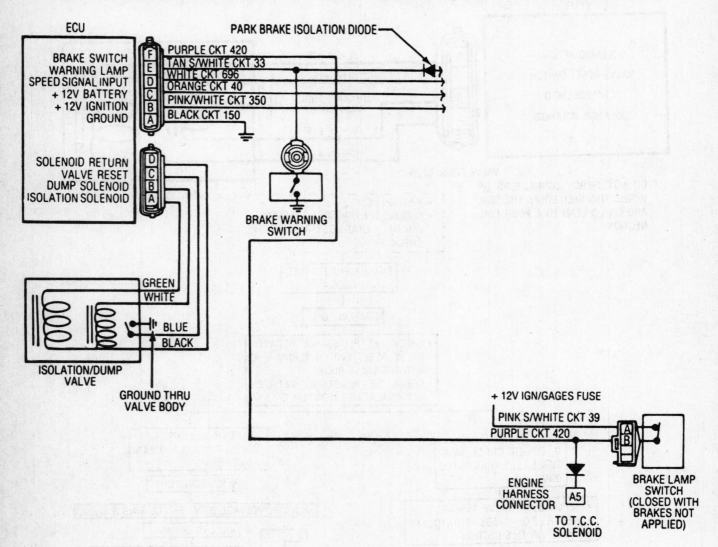

ECU

BRAKE SWITCH
WARNING LAMP
SPEED SIGNAL INPUT
+ 12V BATTERY
+ 12V IGNITION
GROUND

PURPLE CKT 420
TAN S/WHITE CKT 33
WHITE CKT 696
ORANGE CKT 40
PINK/WHITE CKT 350
BLACK CKT 150

PARK BRAKE ISOLATION DIODE

SOLENOID RETURN
VALVE RESET
DUMP SOLENOID
ISOLATION SOLENOID

BRAKE WARNING
SWITCH

GREEN
WHITE
BLUE
BLACK

ISOLATION/DUMP
VALVE

GROUND THRU
VALVE BODY

+ 12V IGN/GAGES FUSE
PINK S/WHITE CKT 39
PURPLE CKT 420

ENGINE
HARNESS
CONNECTOR

A5

TO T.C.C.
SOLENOID

BRAKE LAMP
SWITCH
(CLOSED WITH
BRAKES NOT
APPLIED)

CODE 5
EXCESSIVE ACTUATIONS OF THE DUMP VALVE
DURING AN ANTI-LOCK STOP

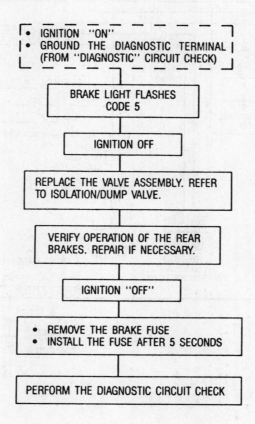

```
┌ ─ ─ ─ ─ ─ ─ ─ ─ ─ ─ ─ ─ ─ ─ ─ ─ ─ ┐
│ • IGNITION "ON"                    │
│ • GROUND THE DIAGNOSTIC TERMINAL   │
│   (FROM "DIAGNOSTIC" CIRCUIT CHECK)│
└ ─ ─ ─ ─ ─ ─ ─ ─ ─ ─ ─ ─ ─ ─ ─ ─ ─ ┘
                 │
┌────────────────────────────────┐
│      BRAKE LIGHT FLASHES        │
│           CODE 5                │
└────────────────────────────────┘
                 │
┌────────────────────────────────┐
│         IGNITION OFF            │
└────────────────────────────────┘
                 │
┌────────────────────────────────┐
│ REPLACE THE VALVE ASSEMBLY. REFER│
│ TO ISOLATION/DUMP VALVE.        │
└────────────────────────────────┘
                 │
┌────────────────────────────────┐
│ VERIFY OPERATION OF THE REAR    │
│ BRAKES. REPAIR IF NECESSARY.    │
└────────────────────────────────┘
                 │
┌────────────────────────────────┐
│        IGNITION "OFF"           │
└────────────────────────────────┘
                 │
┌────────────────────────────────┐
│ • REMOVE THE BRAKE FUSE         │
│ • INSTALL THE FUSE AFTER 5 SECONDS│
└────────────────────────────────┘
                 │
┌────────────────────────────────┐
│ PERFORM THE DIAGNOSTIC CIRCUIT CHECK│
└────────────────────────────────┘
```

ALDL CONNECTOR (DIAGNOSTIC TERMINAL)

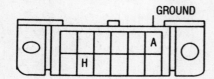

GROUND

CODE 6
ERRATIC SPEED SIGNAL

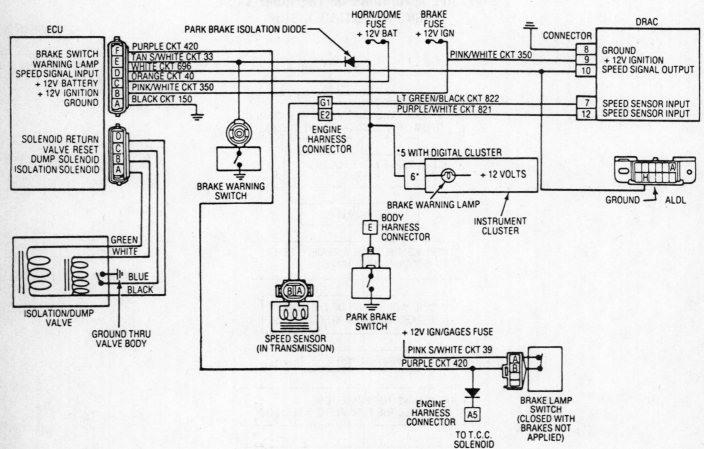

CODE 6
ERRATIC SPEED SIGNAL

- IGNITION "ON"
- GROUND THE DIAGNOSTIC TERMINAL FROM "DIAGNOSTIC CIRCUIT CHECK")

This diagnostic chart checks for the Brake light flashing a code 6 for the following causes:

Erratic Speed Signal to the ECU

Intermittent/erratic Speed signal connection

Faulty ECU

NOTE: If voltage readings are low or varying, check battery and charging system or check for intermittent connections.

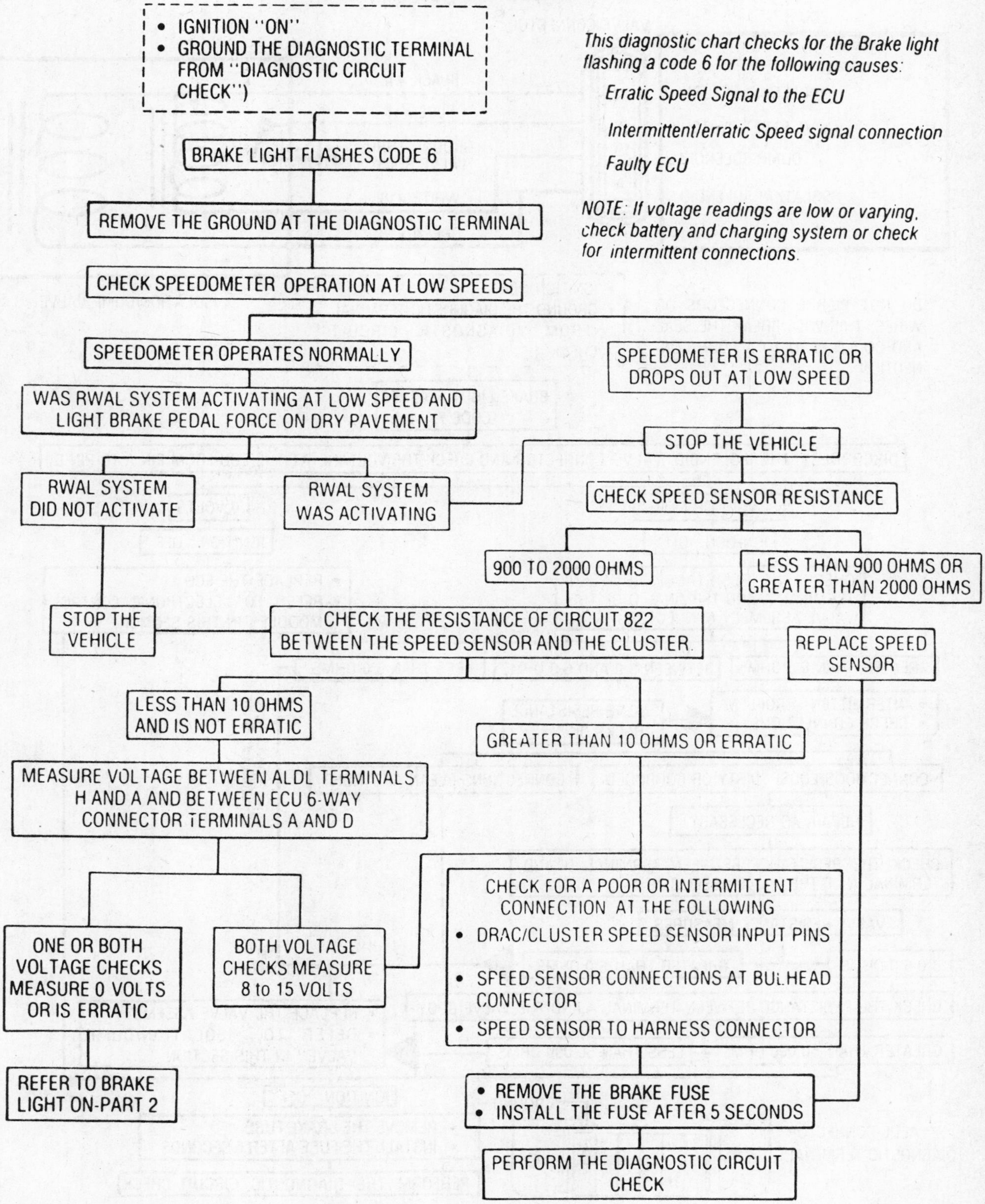

BRAKE LIGHT FLASHES CODE 6

REMOVE THE GROUND AT THE DIAGNOSTIC TERMINAL

CHECK SPEEDOMETER OPERATION AT LOW SPEEDS

SPEEDOMETER OPERATES NORMALLY

SPEEDOMETER IS ERRATIC OR DROPS OUT AT LOW SPEED

WAS RWAL SYSTEM ACTIVATING AT LOW SPEED AND LIGHT BRAKE PEDAL FORCE ON DRY PAVEMENT

STOP THE VEHICLE

RWAL SYSTEM DID NOT ACTIVATE

RWAL SYSTEM WAS ACTIVATING

CHECK SPEED SENSOR RESISTANCE

900 TO 2000 OHMS

LESS THAN 900 OHMS OR GREATER THAN 2000 OHMS

STOP THE VEHICLE

CHECK THE RESISTANCE OF CIRCUIT 822 BETWEEN THE SPEED SENSOR AND THE CLUSTER.

REPLACE SPEED SENSOR

LESS THAN 10 OHMS AND IS NOT ERRATIC

GREATER THAN 10 OHMS OR ERRATIC

MEASURE VOLTAGE BETWEEN ALDL TERMINALS H AND A AND BETWEEN ECU 6-WAY CONNECTOR TERMINALS A AND D

CHECK FOR A POOR OR INTERMITTENT CONNECTION AT THE FOLLOWING

- DRAC/CLUSTER SPEED SENSOR INPUT PINS
- SPEED SENSOR CONNECTIONS AT BULHEAD CONNECTOR
- SPEED SENSOR TO HARNESS CONNECTOR

ONE OR BOTH VOLTAGE CHECKS MEASURE 0 VOLTS OR IS ERRATIC

BOTH VOLTAGE CHECKS MEASURE 8 to 15 VOLTS

REFER TO BRAKE LIGHT ON-PART 2

- REMOVE THE BRAKE FUSE
- INSTALL THE FUSE AFTER 5 SECONDS

PERFORM THE DIAGNOSTIC CIRCUIT CHECK

CODE 7
SHORTED ISOLATION VALVE OR FAULTY ECU

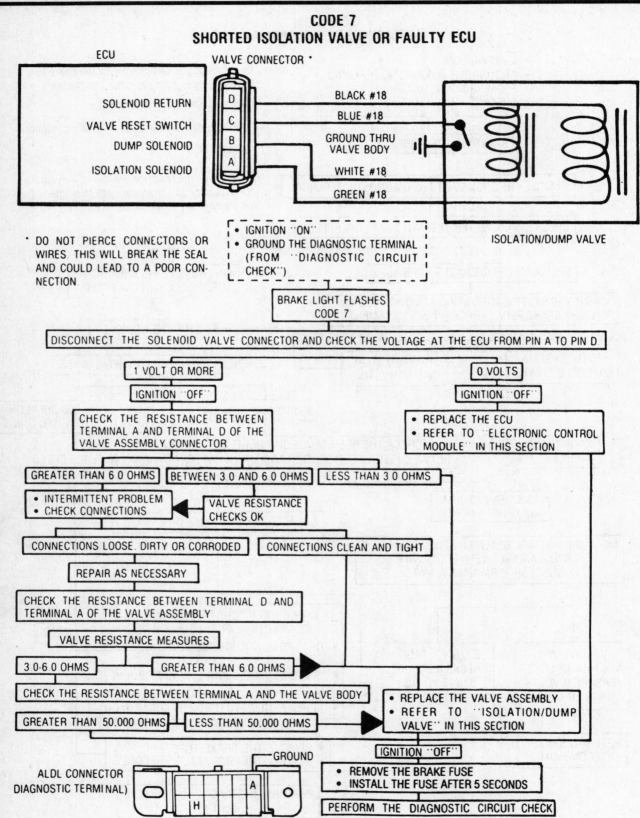

CODE 8
SHORTED DUMP VALVE OR FAULTY ECU

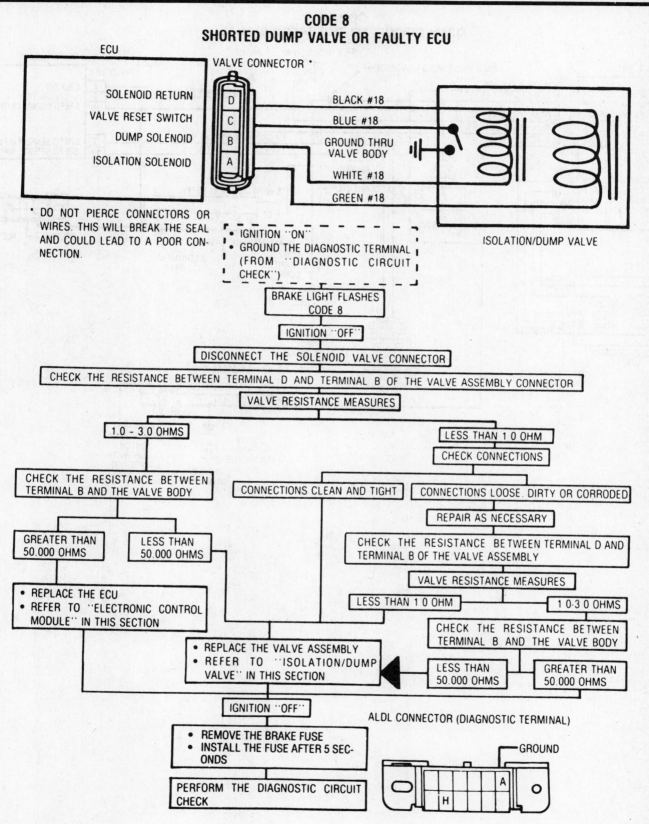

ECU

VALVE CONNECTOR *

SOLENOID RETURN

VALVE RESET SWITCH

DUMP SOLENOID

ISOLATION SOLENOID

D
C
B
A

BLACK #18

BLUE #18

GROUND THRU
VALVE BODY

WHITE #18

GREEN #18

ISOLATION/DUMP VALVE

* DO NOT PIERCE CONNECTORS OR WIRES. THIS WILL BREAK THE SEAL AND COULD LEAD TO A POOR CONNECTION.

- IGNITION "ON"
- GROUND THE DIAGNOSTIC TERMINAL (FROM "DIAGNOSTIC CIRCUIT CHECK")

BRAKE LIGHT FLASHES CODE 8

IGNITION "OFF"

DISCONNECT THE SOLENOID VALVE CONNECTOR

CHECK THE RESISTANCE BETWEEN TERMINAL D AND TERMINAL B OF THE VALVE ASSEMBLY CONNECTOR

VALVE RESISTANCE MEASURES

1.0 - 3.0 OHMS

LESS THAN 1 0 OHM

CHECK CONNECTIONS

CHECK THE RESISTANCE BETWEEN TERMINAL B AND THE VALVE BODY

CONNECTIONS CLEAN AND TIGHT

CONNECTIONS LOOSE, DIRTY OR CORRODED

GREATER THAN 50.000 OHMS

LESS THAN 50.000 OHMS

REPAIR AS NECESSARY

CHECK THE RESISTANCE BETWEEN TERMINAL D AND TERMINAL B OF THE VALVE ASSEMBLY

VALVE RESISTANCE MEASURES

- REPLACE THE ECU
- REFER TO "ELECTRONIC CONTROL MODULE" IN THIS SECTION

LESS THAN 1 0 OHM

1 0-3 0 OHMS

CHECK THE RESISTANCE BETWEEN TERMINAL B AND THE VALVE BODY

- REPLACE THE VALVE ASSEMBLY
- REFER TO "ISOLATION/DUMP VALVE" IN THIS SECTION

LESS THAN 50.000 OHMS

GREATER THAN 50.000 OHMS

IGNITION "OFF"

ALDL CONNECTOR (DIAGNOSTIC TERMINAL)

- REMOVE THE BRAKE FUSE
- INSTALL THE FUSE AFTER 5 SECONDS

GROUND

PERFORM THE DIAGNOSTIC CIRCUIT CHECK

H
A

CODE 9
OPEN CIRCUIT TO THE SPEED SIGNAL

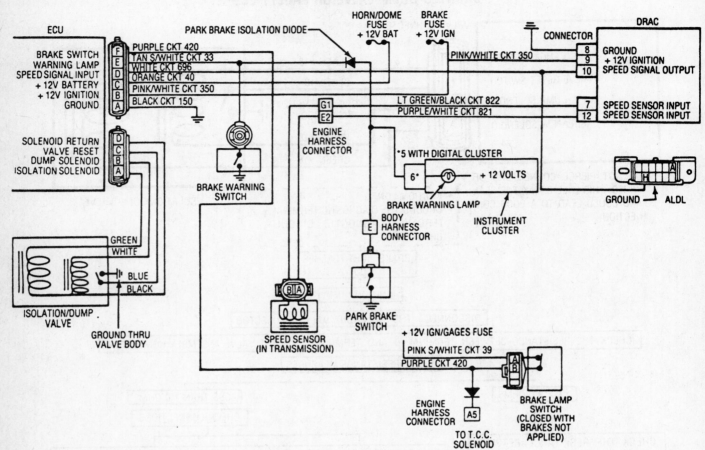

CODE 9
OPEN CIRCUIT TO THE SPEED SIGNAL

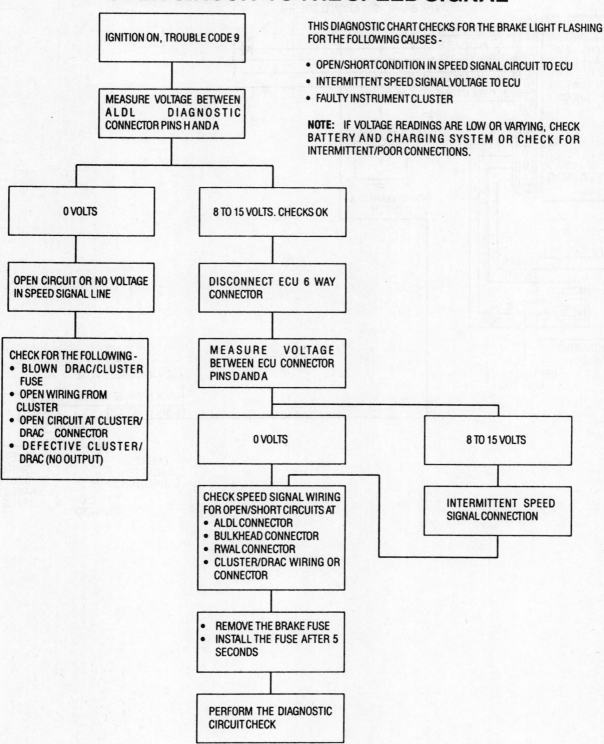

THIS DIAGNOSTIC CHART CHECKS FOR THE BRAKE LIGHT FLASHING FOR THE FOLLOWING CAUSES -

- OPEN/SHORT CONDITION IN SPEED SIGNAL CIRCUIT TO ECU
- INTERMITTENT SPEED SIGNAL VOLTAGE TO ECU
- FAULTY INSTRUMENT CLUSTER

NOTE: IF VOLTAGE READINGS ARE LOW OR VARYING, CHECK BATTERY AND CHARGING SYSTEM OR CHECK FOR INTERMITTENT/POOR CONNECTIONS.

IGNITION ON, TROUBLE CODE 9

MEASURE VOLTAGE BETWEEN ALDL DIAGNOSTIC CONNECTOR PINS H AND A

0 VOLTS

8 TO 15 VOLTS. CHECKS OK

OPEN CIRCUIT OR NO VOLTAGE IN SPEED SIGNAL LINE

DISCONNECT ECU 6 WAY CONNECTOR

CHECK FOR THE FOLLOWING -
- BLOWN DRAC/CLUSTER FUSE
- OPEN WIRING FROM CLUSTER
- OPEN CIRCUIT AT CLUSTER/ DRAC CONNECTOR
- DEFECTIVE CLUSTER/ DRAC (NO OUTPUT)

MEASURE VOLTAGE BETWEEN ECU CONNECTOR PINS D AND A

0 VOLTS

8 TO 15 VOLTS

CHECK SPEED SIGNAL WIRING FOR OPEN/SHORT CIRCUITS AT
- ALDL CONNECTOR
- BULKHEAD CONNECTOR
- RWAL CONNECTOR
- CLUSTER/DRAC WIRING OR CONNECTOR

INTERMITTENT SPEED SIGNAL CONNECTION

- REMOVE THE BRAKE FUSE
- INSTALL THE FUSE AFTER 5 SECONDS

PERFORM THE DIAGNOSTIC CIRCUIT CHECK

CODE 10
BRAKE LAMP SWITCH CIRCUIT

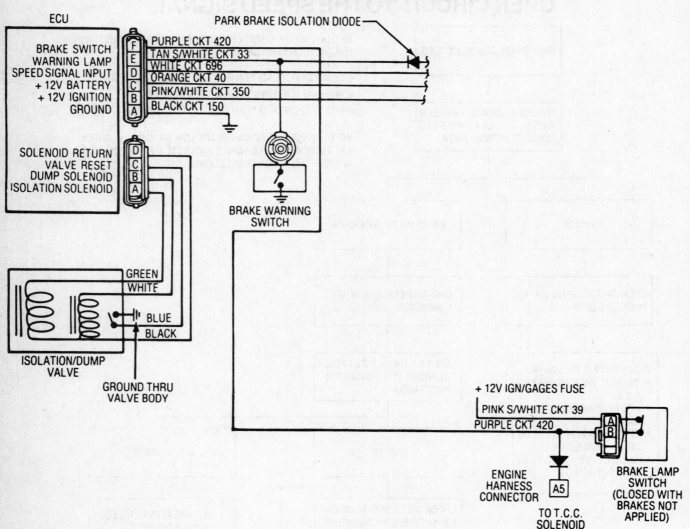

CODES 10-BRAKE LAMP SWITCH CIRCUIT*

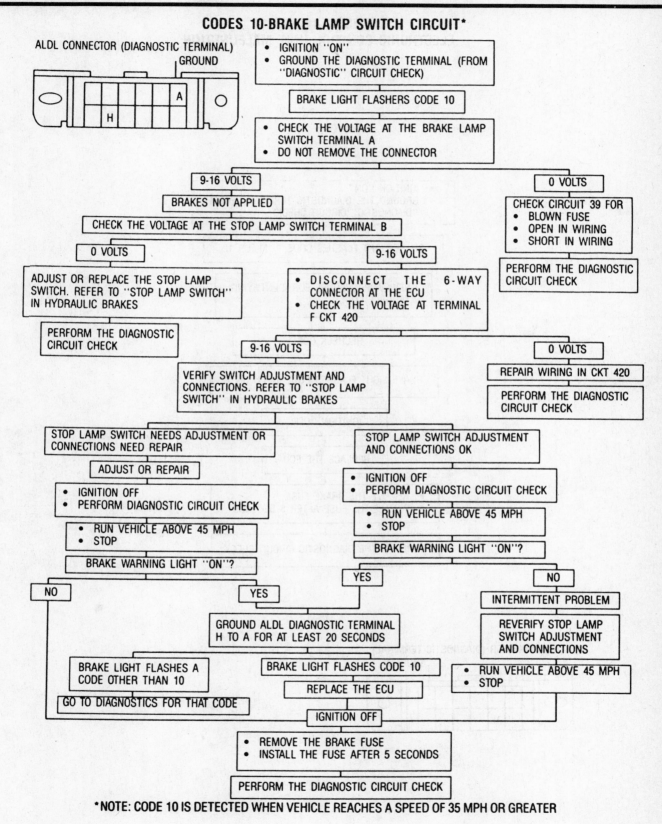

ALDL CONNECTOR (DIAGNOSTIC TERMINAL) GROUND

- IGNITION "ON"
- GROUND THE DIAGNOSTIC TERMINAL (FROM "DIAGNOSTIC" CIRCUIT CHECK)

BRAKE LIGHT FLASHERS CODE 10

- CHECK THE VOLTAGE AT THE BRAKE LAMP SWITCH TERMINAL A
- DO NOT REMOVE THE CONNECTOR

9-16 VOLTS

BRAKES NOT APPLIED

CHECK THE VOLTAGE AT THE STOP LAMP SWITCH TERMINAL B

0 VOLTS

ADJUST OR REPLACE THE STOP LAMP SWITCH. REFER TO "STOP LAMP SWITCH" IN HYDRAULIC BRAKES

PERFORM THE DIAGNOSTIC CIRCUIT CHECK

9-16 VOLTS

- DISCONNECT THE 6-WAY CONNECTOR AT THE ECU
- CHECK THE VOLTAGE AT TERMINAL F CKT 420

9-16 VOLTS

VERIFY SWITCH ADJUSTMENT AND CONNECTIONS. REFER TO "STOP LAMP SWITCH" IN HYDRAULIC BRAKES

STOP LAMP SWITCH NEEDS ADJUSTMENT OR CONNECTIONS NEED REPAIR

ADJUST OR REPAIR

- IGNITION OFF
- PERFORM DIAGNOSTIC CIRCUIT CHECK

- RUN VEHICLE ABOVE 45 MPH
- STOP

BRAKE WARNING LIGHT "ON"?

NO

YES

GROUND ALDL DIAGNOSTIC TERMINAL H TO A FOR AT LEAST 20 SECONDS

BRAKE LIGHT FLASHES A CODE OTHER THAN 10

GO TO DIAGNOSTICS FOR THAT CODE

BRAKE LIGHT FLASHES CODE 10

REPLACE THE ECU

IGNITION OFF

0 VOLTS

CHECK CIRCUIT 39 FOR
- BLOWN FUSE
- OPEN IN WIRING
- SHORT IN WIRING

PERFORM THE DIAGNOSTIC CIRCUIT CHECK

0 VOLTS

REPAIR WIRING IN CKT 420

PERFORM THE DIAGNOSTIC CIRCUIT CHECK

STOP LAMP SWITCH ADJUSTMENT AND CONNECTIONS OK

- IGNITION OFF
- PERFORM DIAGNOSTIC CIRCUIT CHECK

- RUN VEHICLE ABOVE 45 MPH
- STOP

BRAKE WARNING LIGHT "ON"?

YES

NO

INTERMITTENT PROBLEM

REVERIFY STOP LAMP SWITCH ADJUSTMENT AND CONNECTIONS

- RUN VEHICLE ABOVE 45 MPH
- STOP

- REMOVE THE BRAKE FUSE
- INSTALL THE FUSE AFTER 5 SECONDS

PERFORM THE DIAGNOSTIC CIRCUIT CHECK

*NOTE: CODE 10 IS DETECTED WHEN VEHICLE REACHES A SPEED OF 35 MPH OR GREATER

CODES 1, 11 AND 12
ELECTRONIC CONTROL UNIT MALFUNCTION

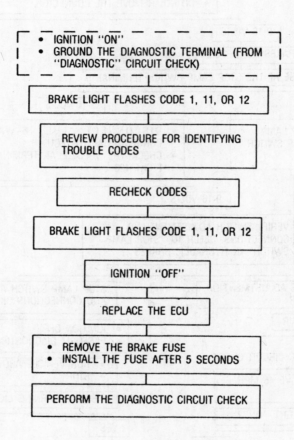

- IGNITION "ON"
- GROUND THE DIAGNOSTIC TERMINAL (FROM "DIAGNOSTIC" CIRCUIT CHECK)

BRAKE LIGHT FLASHES CODE 1, 11, OR 12

REVIEW PROCEDURE FOR IDENTIFYING TROUBLE CODES

RECHECK CODES

BRAKE LIGHT FLASHES CODE 1, 11, OR 12

IGNITION "OFF"

REPLACE THE ECU

- REMOVE THE BRAKE FUSE
- INSTALL THE FUSE AFTER 5 SECONDS

PERFORM THE DIAGNOSTIC CIRCUIT CHECK

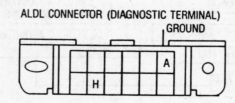

ALDL CONNECTOR (DIAGNOSTIC TERMINAL)
GROUND

CODE 13, 14, AND 15
ELECTRONIC CONTROL UNIT MALFUNCTION

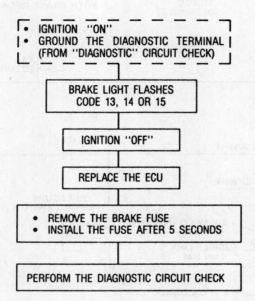

- IGNITION "ON"
- GROUND THE DIAGNOSTIC TERMINAL (FROM "DIAGNOSTIC" CIRCUIT CHECK)

BRAKE LIGHT FLASHES
CODE 13, 14 OR 15

IGNITION "OFF"

REPLACE THE ECU

- REMOVE THE BRAKE FUSE
- INSTALL THE FUSE AFTER 5 SECONDS

PERFORM THE DIAGNOSTIC CIRCUIT CHECK

ALDL CONNECTOR (DIAGNOSTIC TERMINAL)

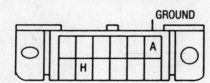

GROUND

A

H

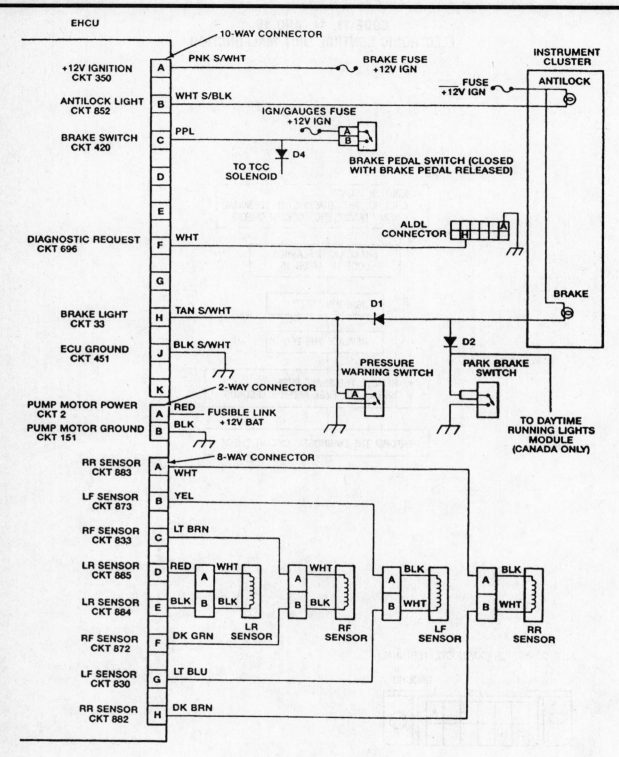

Four Wheel Antilock Wiring Diagram

DIAGNOSTIC CIRCUIT CHECK

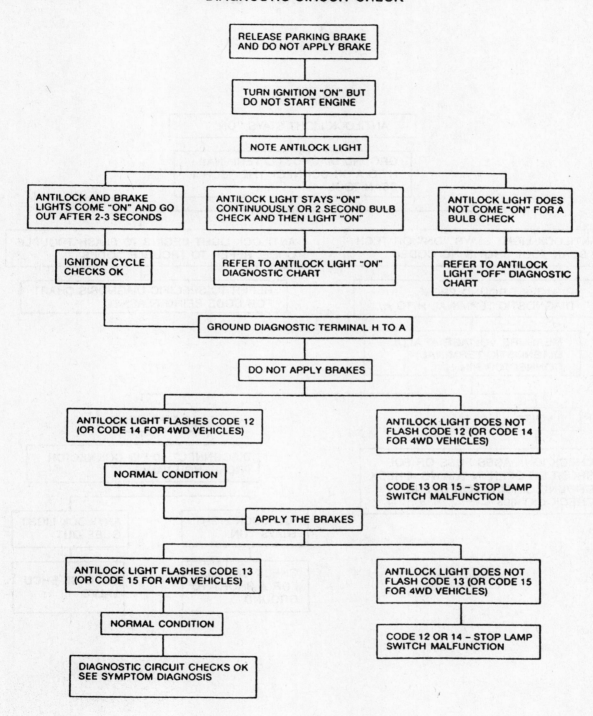

RELEASE PARKING BRAKE AND DO NOT APPLY BRAKE

TURN IGNITION "ON" BUT DO NOT START ENGINE

NOTE ANTILOCK LIGHT

ANTILOCK AND BRAKE LIGHTS COME "ON" AND GO OUT AFTER 2-3 SECONDS

ANTILOCK LIGHT STAYS "ON" CONTINUOUSLY OR 2 SECOND BULB CHECK AND THEN LIGHT "ON"

ANTILOCK LIGHT DOES NOT COME "ON" FOR A BULB CHECK

IGNITION CYCLE CHECKS OK

REFER TO ANTILOCK LIGHT "ON" DIAGNOSTIC CHART

REFER TO ANTILOCK LIGHT "OFF" DIAGNOSTIC CHART

GROUND DIAGNOSTIC TERMINAL H TO A

DO NOT APPLY BRAKES

ANTILOCK LIGHT FLASHES CODE 12 (OR CODE 14 FOR 4WD VEHICLES)

ANTILOCK LIGHT DOES NOT FLASH CODE 12 (OR CODE 14 FOR 4WD VEHICLES)

NORMAL CONDITION

CODE 13 OR 15 – STOP LAMP SWITCH MALFUNCTION

APPLY THE BRAKES

ANTILOCK LIGHT FLASHES CODE 13 (OR CODE 15 FOR 4WD VEHICLES)

ANTILOCK LIGHT DOES NOT FLASH CODE 13 (OR CODE 15 FOR 4WD VEHICLES)

NORMAL CONDITION

CODE 12 OR 14 – STOP LAMP SWITCH MALFUNCTION

DIAGNOSTIC CIRCUIT CHECKS OK SEE SYMPTOM DIAGNOSIS

ANTILOCK LIGHT "ON"

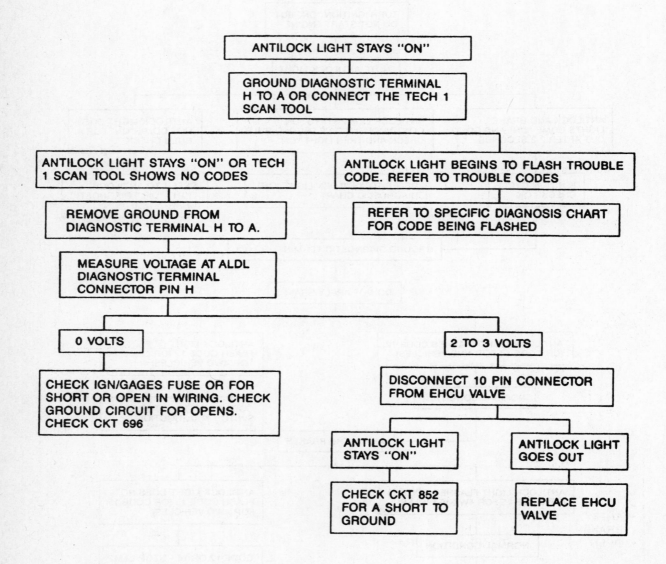

ANTILOCK LIGHT STAYS "ON"

GROUND DIAGNOSTIC TERMINAL H TO A OR CONNECT THE TECH 1 SCAN TOOL

ANTILOCK LIGHT STAYS "ON" OR TECH 1 SCAN TOOL SHOWS NO CODES

ANTILOCK LIGHT BEGINS TO FLASH TROUBLE CODE. REFER TO TROUBLE CODES

REMOVE GROUND FROM DIAGNOSTIC TERMINAL H TO A.

REFER TO SPECIFIC DIAGNOSIS CHART FOR CODE BEING FLASHED

MEASURE VOLTAGE AT ALDL DIAGNOSTIC TERMINAL CONNECTOR PIN H

0 VOLTS

2 TO 3 VOLTS

CHECK IGN/GAGES FUSE OR FOR SHORT OR OPEN IN WIRING. CHECK GROUND CIRCUIT FOR OPENS. CHECK CKT 696

DISCONNECT 10 PIN CONNECTOR FROM EHCU VALVE

ANTILOCK LIGHT STAYS "ON"

ANTILOCK LIGHT GOES OUT

CHECK CKT 852 FOR A SHORT TO GROUND

REPLACE EHCU VALVE

ANTILOCK LIGHT "OFF"

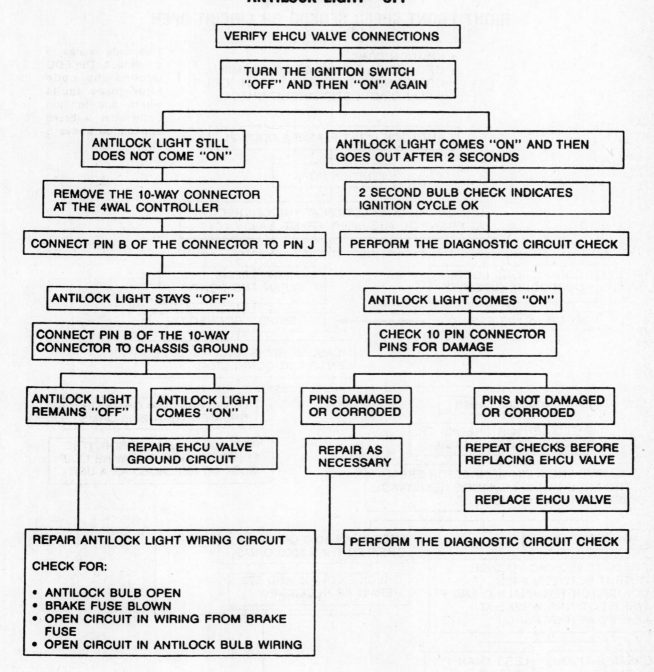

VERIFY EHCU VALVE CONNECTIONS

TURN THE IGNITION SWITCH "OFF" AND THEN "ON" AGAIN

ANTILOCK LIGHT STILL DOES NOT COME "ON"

ANTILOCK LIGHT COMES "ON" AND THEN GOES OUT AFTER 2 SECONDS

REMOVE THE 10-WAY CONNECTOR AT THE 4WAL CONTROLLER

2 SECOND BULB CHECK INDICATES IGNITION CYCLE OK

CONNECT PIN B OF THE CONNECTOR TO PIN J

PERFORM THE DIAGNOSTIC CIRCUIT CHECK

ANTILOCK LIGHT STAYS "OFF"

ANTILOCK LIGHT COMES "ON"

CONNECT PIN B OF THE 10-WAY CONNECTOR TO CHASSIS GROUND

CHECK 10 PIN CONNECTOR PINS FOR DAMAGE

ANTILOCK LIGHT REMAINS "OFF"

ANTILOCK LIGHT COMES "ON"

PINS DAMAGED OR CORRODED

PINS NOT DAMAGED OR CORRODED

REPAIR EHCU VALVE GROUND CIRCUIT

REPAIR AS NECESSARY

REPEAT CHECKS BEFORE REPLACING EHCU VALVE

REPLACE EHCU VALVE

PERFORM THE DIAGNOSTIC CIRCUIT CHECK

REPAIR ANTILOCK LIGHT WIRING CIRCUIT

CHECK FOR:

- ANTILOCK BULB OPEN
- BRAKE FUSE BLOWN
- OPEN CIRCUIT IN WIRING FROM BRAKE FUSE
- OPEN CIRCUIT IN ANTILOCK BULB WIRING

CODE 21
RIGHT FRONT SPEED SENSOR OR CIRCUIT OPEN

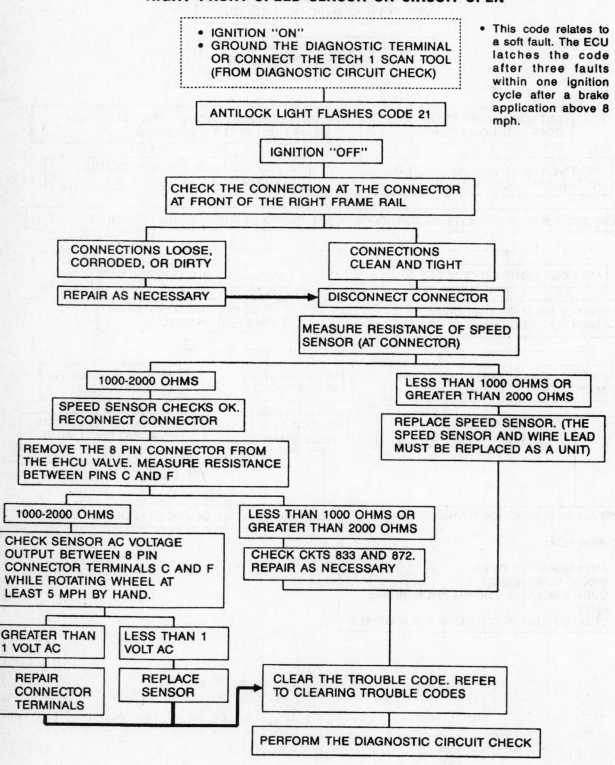

- IGNITION "ON"
- GROUND THE DIAGNOSTIC TERMINAL OR CONNECT THE TECH 1 SCAN TOOL (FROM DIAGNOSTIC CIRCUIT CHECK)

- This code relates to a soft fault. The ECU latches the code after three faults within one ignition cycle after a brake application above 8 mph.

ANTILOCK LIGHT FLASHES CODE 21

IGNITION "OFF"

CHECK THE CONNECTION AT THE CONNECTOR AT FRONT OF THE RIGHT FRAME RAIL

CONNECTIONS LOOSE, CORRODED, OR DIRTY

REPAIR AS NECESSARY

CONNECTIONS CLEAN AND TIGHT

DISCONNECT CONNECTOR

MEASURE RESISTANCE OF SPEED SENSOR (AT CONNECTOR)

1000-2000 OHMS

SPEED SENSOR CHECKS OK. RECONNECT CONNECTOR

LESS THAN 1000 OHMS OR GREATER THAN 2000 OHMS

REPLACE SPEED SENSOR. (THE SPEED SENSOR AND WIRE LEAD MUST BE REPLACED AS A UNIT)

REMOVE THE 8 PIN CONNECTOR FROM THE EHCU VALVE. MEASURE RESISTANCE BETWEEN PINS C AND F

1000-2000 OHMS

CHECK SENSOR AC VOLTAGE OUTPUT BETWEEN 8 PIN CONNECTOR TERMINALS C AND F WHILE ROTATING WHEEL AT LEAST 5 MPH BY HAND.

LESS THAN 1000 OHMS OR GREATER THAN 2000 OHMS

CHECK CKTS 833 AND 872. REPAIR AS NECESSARY

GREATER THAN 1 VOLT AC

LESS THAN 1 VOLT AC

REPAIR CONNECTOR TERMINALS

REPLACE SENSOR

CLEAR THE TROUBLE CODE. REFER TO CLEARING TROUBLE CODES

PERFORM THE DIAGNOSTIC CIRCUIT CHECK

CODE 22
MISSING RIGHT FRONT SPEED SIGNAL
(SET WITH VEHICLE IN MOTION)

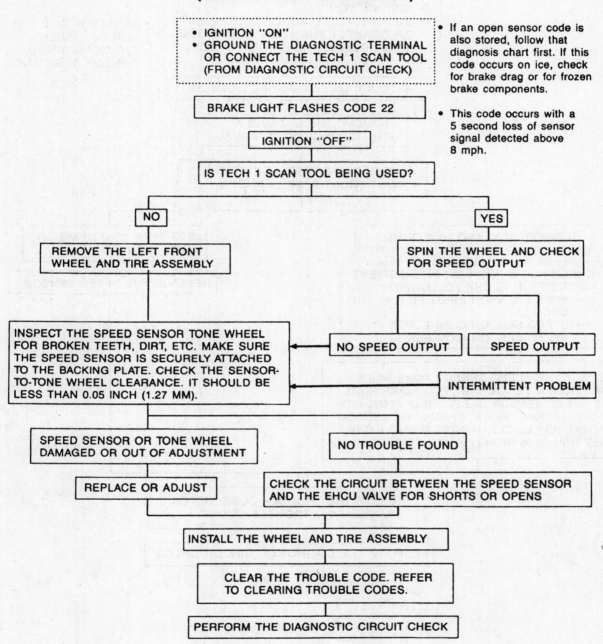

- IGNITION "ON"
- GROUND THE DIAGNOSTIC TERMINAL OR CONNECT THE TECH 1 SCAN TOOL (FROM DIAGNOSTIC CIRCUIT CHECK)

- If an open sensor code is also stored, follow that diagnosis chart first. If this code occurs on ice, check for brake drag or for frozen brake components.

- This code occurs with a 5 second loss of sensor signal detected above 8 mph.

BRAKE LIGHT FLASHES CODE 22

IGNITION "OFF"

IS TECH 1 SCAN TOOL BEING USED?

NO

YES

REMOVE THE LEFT FRONT WHEEL AND TIRE ASSEMBLY

SPIN THE WHEEL AND CHECK FOR SPEED OUTPUT

NO SPEED OUTPUT

SPEED OUTPUT

INSPECT THE SPEED SENSOR TONE WHEEL FOR BROKEN TEETH, DIRT, ETC. MAKE SURE THE SPEED SENSOR IS SECURELY ATTACHED TO THE BACKING PLATE. CHECK THE SENSOR-TO-TONE WHEEL CLEARANCE. IT SHOULD BE LESS THAN 0.05 INCH (1.27 MM).

INTERMITTENT PROBLEM

SPEED SENSOR OR TONE WHEEL DAMAGED OR OUT OF ADJUSTMENT

NO TROUBLE FOUND

REPLACE OR ADJUST

CHECK THE CIRCUIT BETWEEN THE SPEED SENSOR AND THE EHCU VALVE FOR SHORTS OR OPENS

INSTALL THE WHEEL AND TIRE ASSEMBLY

CLEAR THE TROUBLE CODE. REFER TO CLEARING TROUBLE CODES.

PERFORM THE DIAGNOSTIC CIRCUIT CHECK

CODE 23
ERRATIC RIGHT FRONT SPEED SENSOR

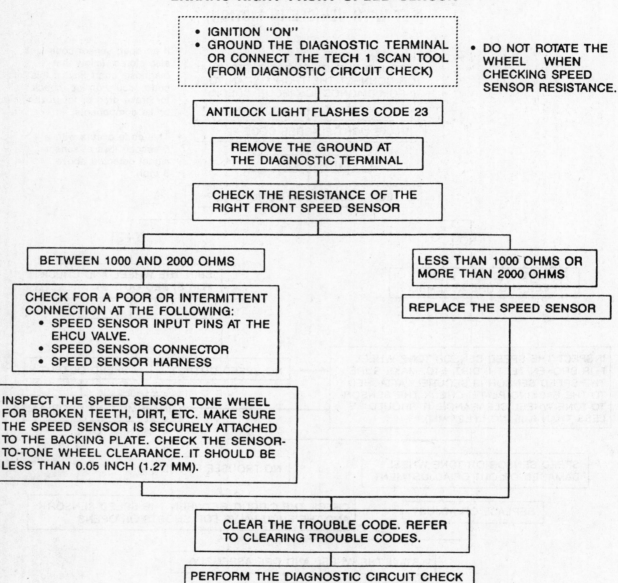

- IGNITION "ON"
- GROUND THE DIAGNOSTIC TERMINAL OR CONNECT THE TECH 1 SCAN TOOL (FROM DIAGNOSTIC CIRCUIT CHECK)

- DO NOT ROTATE THE WHEEL WHEN CHECKING SPEED SENSOR RESISTANCE.

ANTILOCK LIGHT FLASHES CODE 23

REMOVE THE GROUND AT THE DIAGNOSTIC TERMINAL

CHECK THE RESISTANCE OF THE RIGHT FRONT SPEED SENSOR

BETWEEN 1000 AND 2000 OHMS

LESS THAN 1000 OHMS OR MORE THAN 2000 OHMS

CHECK FOR A POOR OR INTERMITTENT CONNECTION AT THE FOLLOWING:
- SPEED SENSOR INPUT PINS AT THE EHCU VALVE.
- SPEED SENSOR CONNECTOR
- SPEED SENSOR HARNESS

REPLACE THE SPEED SENSOR

INSPECT THE SPEED SENSOR TONE WHEEL FOR BROKEN TEETH, DIRT, ETC. MAKE SURE THE SPEED SENSOR IS SECURELY ATTACHED TO THE BACKING PLATE. CHECK THE SENSOR-TO-TONE WHEEL CLEARANCE. IT SHOULD BE LESS THAN 0.05 INCH (1.27 MM).

CLEAR THE TROUBLE CODE. REFER TO CLEARING TROUBLE CODES.

PERFORM THE DIAGNOSTIC CIRCUIT CHECK

CODE 25
LEFT FRONT SPEED SENSOR OR CIRCUIT OPEN

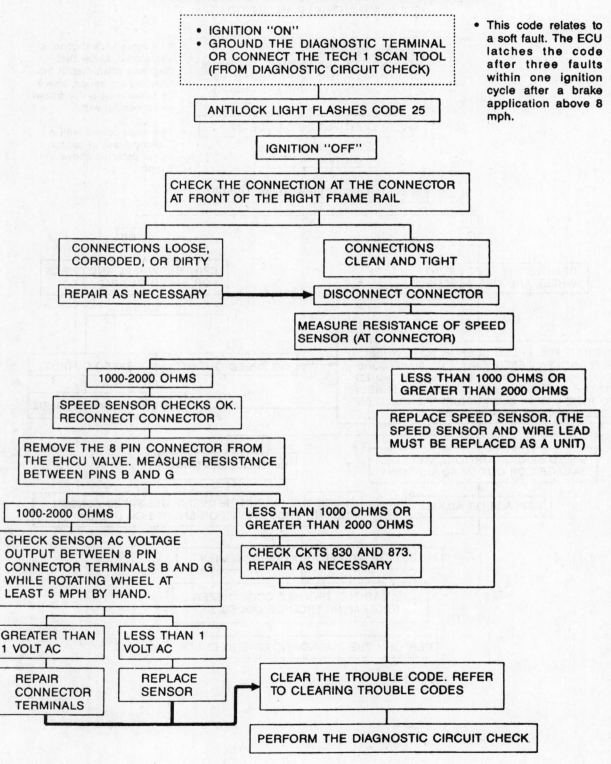

- IGNITION "ON"
- GROUND THE DIAGNOSTIC TERMINAL OR CONNECT THE TECH 1 SCAN TOOL (FROM DIAGNOSTIC CIRCUIT CHECK)

- This code relates to a soft fault. The ECU latches the code after three faults within one ignition cycle after a brake application above 8 mph.

ANTILOCK LIGHT FLASHES CODE 25

IGNITION "OFF"

CHECK THE CONNECTION AT THE CONNECTOR AT FRONT OF THE RIGHT FRAME RAIL

CONNECTIONS LOOSE, CORRODED, OR DIRTY

REPAIR AS NECESSARY

CONNECTIONS CLEAN AND TIGHT

DISCONNECT CONNECTOR

MEASURE RESISTANCE OF SPEED SENSOR (AT CONNECTOR)

1000-2000 OHMS

SPEED SENSOR CHECKS OK. RECONNECT CONNECTOR

LESS THAN 1000 OHMS OR GREATER THAN 2000 OHMS

REPLACE SPEED SENSOR. (THE SPEED SENSOR AND WIRE LEAD MUST BE REPLACED AS A UNIT)

REMOVE THE 8 PIN CONNECTOR FROM THE EHCU VALVE. MEASURE RESISTANCE BETWEEN PINS B AND G

1000-2000 OHMS

CHECK SENSOR AC VOLTAGE OUTPUT BETWEEN 8 PIN CONNECTOR TERMINALS B AND G WHILE ROTATING WHEEL AT LEAST 5 MPH BY HAND.

LESS THAN 1000 OHMS OR GREATER THAN 2000 OHMS

CHECK CKTS 830 AND 873. REPAIR AS NECESSARY

GREATER THAN 1 VOLT AC

LESS THAN 1 VOLT AC

REPAIR CONNECTOR TERMINALS

REPLACE SENSOR

CLEAR THE TROUBLE CODE. REFER TO CLEARING TROUBLE CODES

PERFORM THE DIAGNOSTIC CIRCUIT CHECK.

CODE 26
MISSING LEFT FRONT SPEED SIGNAL
(SET WITH VEHICLE IN MOTION)

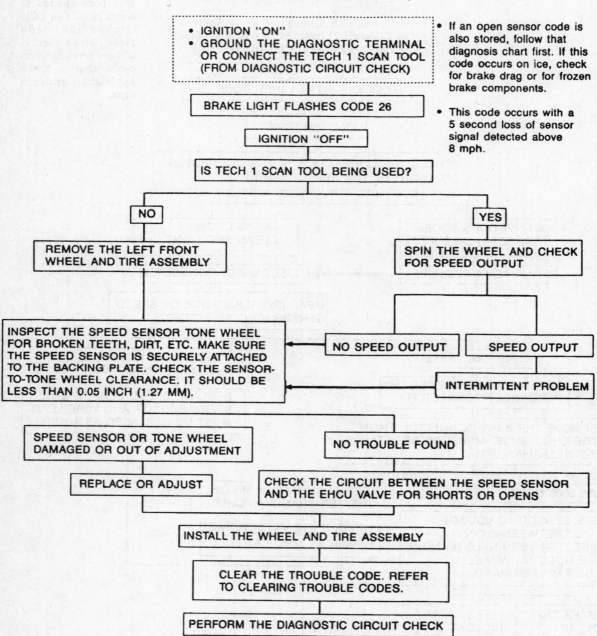

- IGNITION "ON"
- GROUND THE DIAGNOSTIC TERMINAL OR CONNECT THE TECH 1 SCAN TOOL (FROM DIAGNOSTIC CIRCUIT CHECK)

- If an open sensor code is also stored, follow that diagnosis chart first. If this code occurs on ice, check for brake drag or for frozen brake components.

- This code occurs with a 5 second loss of sensor signal detected above 8 mph.

BRAKE LIGHT FLASHES CODE 26

IGNITION "OFF"

IS TECH 1 SCAN TOOL BEING USED?

NO

YES

REMOVE THE LEFT FRONT WHEEL AND TIRE ASSEMBLY

SPIN THE WHEEL AND CHECK FOR SPEED OUTPUT

INSPECT THE SPEED SENSOR TONE WHEEL FOR BROKEN TEETH, DIRT, ETC. MAKE SURE THE SPEED SENSOR IS SECURELY ATTACHED TO THE BACKING PLATE. CHECK THE SENSOR-TO-TONE WHEEL CLEARANCE. IT SHOULD BE LESS THAN 0.05 INCH (1.27 MM).

NO SPEED OUTPUT

SPEED OUTPUT

INTERMITTENT PROBLEM

SPEED SENSOR OR TONE WHEEL DAMAGED OR OUT OF ADJUSTMENT

NO TROUBLE FOUND

REPLACE OR ADJUST

CHECK THE CIRCUIT BETWEEN THE SPEED SENSOR AND THE EHCU VALVE FOR SHORTS OR OPENS

INSTALL THE WHEEL AND TIRE ASSEMBLY

CLEAR THE TROUBLE CODE. REFER TO CLEARING TROUBLE CODES.

PERFORM THE DIAGNOSTIC CIRCUIT CHECK

CODE 27
ERRATIC LEFT FRONT SPEED SENSOR

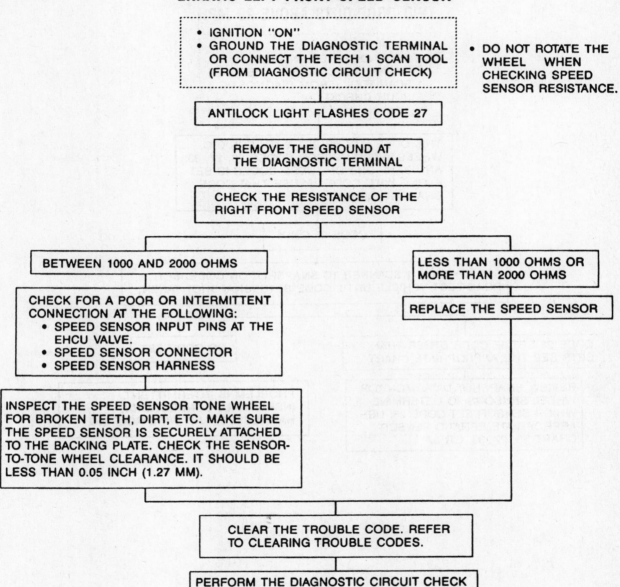

- IGNITION "ON"
- GROUND THE DIAGNOSTIC TERMINAL OR CONNECT THE TECH 1 SCAN TOOL (FROM DIAGNOSTIC CIRCUIT CHECK)

- DO NOT ROTATE THE WHEEL WHEN CHECKING SPEED SENSOR RESISTANCE.

ANTILOCK LIGHT FLASHES CODE 27

REMOVE THE GROUND AT THE DIAGNOSTIC TERMINAL

CHECK THE RESISTANCE OF THE RIGHT FRONT SPEED SENSOR

BETWEEN 1000 AND 2000 OHMS

LESS THAN 1000 OHMS OR MORE THAN 2000 OHMS

CHECK FOR A POOR OR INTERMITTENT CONNECTION AT THE FOLLOWING:
- SPEED SENSOR INPUT PINS AT THE EHCU VALVE.
- SPEED SENSOR CONNECTOR
- SPEED SENSOR HARNESS

REPLACE THE SPEED SENSOR

INSPECT THE SPEED SENSOR TONE WHEEL FOR BROKEN TEETH, DIRT, ETC. MAKE SURE THE SPEED SENSOR IS SECURELY ATTACHED TO THE BACKING PLATE. CHECK THE SENSOR-TO-TONE WHEEL CLEARANCE. IT SHOULD BE LESS THAN 0.05 INCH (1.27 MM).

CLEAR THE TROUBLE CODE. REFER TO CLEARING TROUBLE CODES.

PERFORM THE DIAGNOSTIC CIRCUIT CHECK

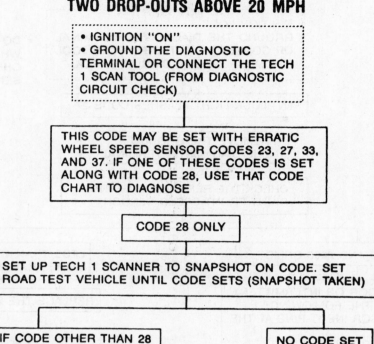

CODE 28
ERRATIC SPEED SENSOR SIGNAL
TWO DROP-OUTS ABOVE 20 MPH

• IGNITION "ON"
• GROUND THE DIAGNOSTIC
TERMINAL OR CONNECT THE TECH
1 SCAN TOOL (FROM DIAGNOSTIC
CIRCUIT CHECK)

THIS CODE MAY BE SET WITH ERRATIC
WHEEL SPEED SENSOR CODES 23, 27, 33,
AND 37. IF ONE OF THESE CODES IS SET
ALONG WITH CODE 28, USE THAT CODE
CHART TO DIAGNOSE

CODE 28 ONLY

SET UP TECH 1 SCANNER TO SNAPSHOT ON CODE. SET
ROAD TEST VEHICLE UNTIL CODE SETS (SNAPSHOT TAKEN)

CODE 28 SET. IF CODE OTHER THAN 28
SETS SEE THE APPROPRIATE CHART

NO CODE SET

REVIEW SNAPSHOT DATA. MONITOR
WHEEL SENSORS TO DETERMINE
WHICH SENSOR SET CODE 28. USE
APPROPRIATE ERRATIC SENSOR
CHART 23, 27, 33, OR 37

PROBLEM IS INTERMITTENT.
INSPECT ALL CONNECTIONS,
HARNESSES, AND WIRE ROUTING

CODE 29
SIMULTANEOUS DROP-OUT OF ALL FOUR SENSORS
AT SPEEDS ABOVE 8 MPH

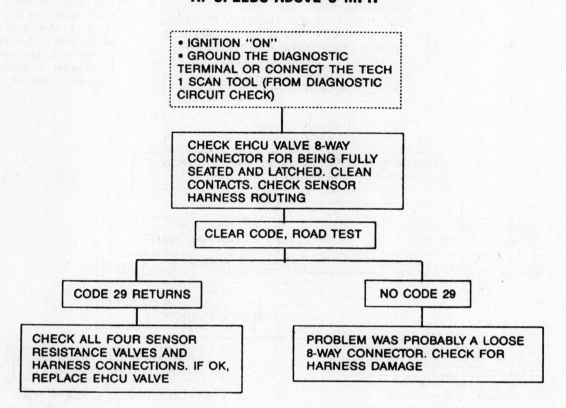

• IGNITION "ON"
• GROUND THE DIAGNOSTIC TERMINAL OR CONNECT THE TECH 1 SCAN TOOL (FROM DIAGNOSTIC CIRCUIT CHECK)

CHECK EHCU VALVE 8-WAY CONNECTOR FOR BEING FULLY SEATED AND LATCHED. CLEAN CONTACTS. CHECK SENSOR HARNESS ROUTING

CLEAR CODE, ROAD TEST

CODE 29 RETURNS

NO CODE 29

CHECK ALL FOUR SENSOR RESISTANCE VALVES AND HARNESS CONNECTIONS. IF OK, REPLACE EHCU VALVE

PROBLEM WAS PROBABLY A LOOSE 8-WAY CONNECTOR. CHECK FOR HARNESS DAMAGE

CODE 31
RIGHT REAR SPEED SENSOR OR CIRCUIT OPEN

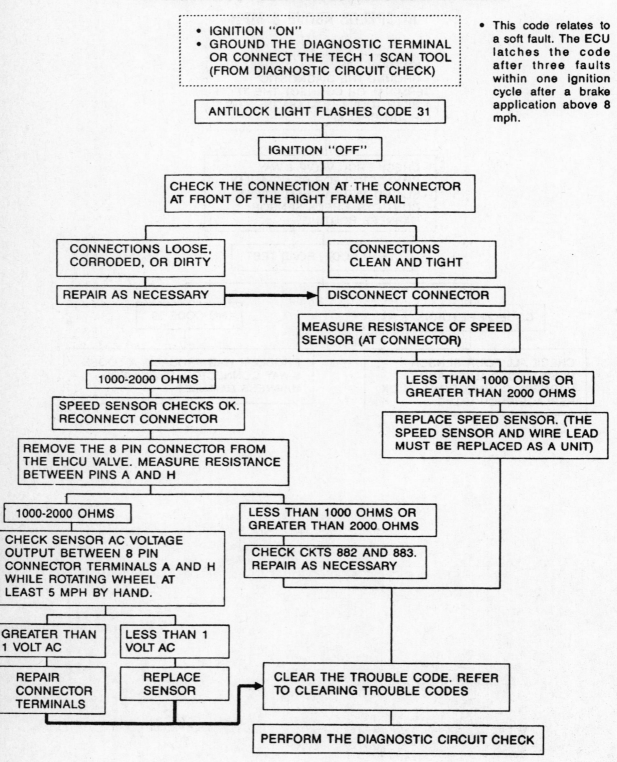

- IGNITION "ON"
- GROUND THE DIAGNOSTIC TERMINAL OR CONNECT THE TECH 1 SCAN TOOL (FROM DIAGNOSTIC CIRCUIT CHECK)

- This code relates to a soft fault. The ECU latches the code after three faults within one ignition cycle after a brake application above 8 mph.

ANTILOCK LIGHT FLASHES CODE 31

IGNITION "OFF"

CHECK THE CONNECTION AT THE CONNECTOR AT FRONT OF THE RIGHT FRAME RAIL

CONNECTIONS LOOSE, CORRODED, OR DIRTY

CONNECTIONS CLEAN AND TIGHT

REPAIR AS NECESSARY

DISCONNECT CONNECTOR

MEASURE RESISTANCE OF SPEED SENSOR (AT CONNECTOR)

1000-2000 OHMS

SPEED SENSOR CHECKS OK. RECONNECT CONNECTOR

LESS THAN 1000 OHMS OR GREATER THAN 2000 OHMS

REPLACE SPEED SENSOR. (THE SPEED SENSOR AND WIRE LEAD MUST BE REPLACED AS A UNIT)

REMOVE THE 8 PIN CONNECTOR FROM THE EHCU VALVE. MEASURE RESISTANCE BETWEEN PINS A AND H

1000-2000 OHMS

LESS THAN 1000 OHMS OR GREATER THAN 2000 OHMS

CHECK SENSOR AC VOLTAGE OUTPUT BETWEEN 8 PIN CONNECTOR TERMINALS A AND H WHILE ROTATING WHEEL AT LEAST 5 MPH BY HAND.

CHECK CKTS 882 AND 883. REPAIR AS NECESSARY

GREATER THAN 1 VOLT AC

LESS THAN 1 VOLT AC

REPAIR CONNECTOR TERMINALS

REPLACE SENSOR

CLEAR THE TROUBLE CODE. REFER TO CLEARING TROUBLE CODES

PERFORM THE DIAGNOSTIC CIRCUIT CHECK

CODE 32
MISSING RIGHT REAR SPEED SIGNAL (SET WITH VEHICLE IN MOTION)

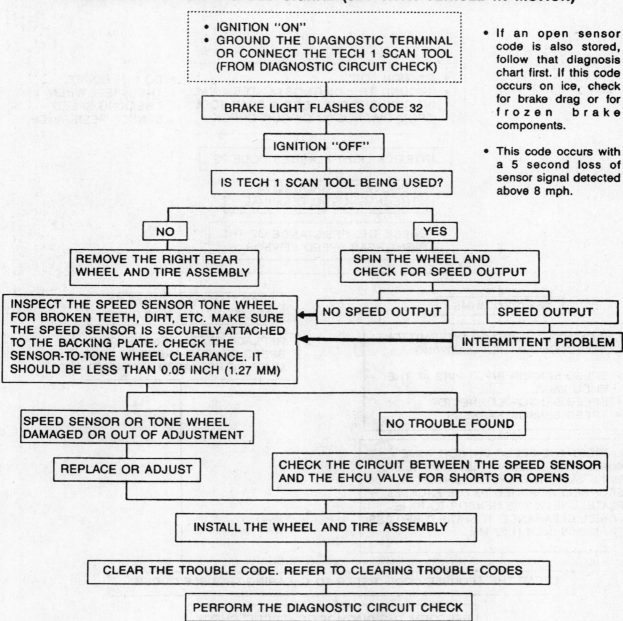

- IGNITION "ON"
- GROUND THE DIAGNOSTIC TERMINAL OR CONNECT THE TECH 1 SCAN TOOL (FROM DIAGNOSTIC CIRCUIT CHECK)

- If an open sensor code is also stored, follow that diagnosis chart first. If this code occurs on ice, check for brake drag or for frozen brake components.

- This code occurs with a 5 second loss of sensor signal detected above 8 mph.

BRAKE LIGHT FLASHES CODE 32

IGNITION "OFF"

IS TECH 1 SCAN TOOL BEING USED?

NO

YES

REMOVE THE RIGHT REAR WHEEL AND TIRE ASSEMBLY

SPIN THE WHEEL AND CHECK FOR SPEED OUTPUT

NO SPEED OUTPUT

SPEED OUTPUT

INTERMITTENT PROBLEM

INSPECT THE SPEED SENSOR TONE WHEEL FOR BROKEN TEETH, DIRT, ETC. MAKE SURE THE SPEED SENSOR IS SECURELY ATTACHED TO THE BACKING PLATE. CHECK THE SENSOR-TO-TONE WHEEL CLEARANCE. IT SHOULD BE LESS THAN 0.05 INCH (1.27 MM)

SPEED SENSOR OR TONE WHEEL DAMAGED OR OUT OF ADJUSTMENT

NO TROUBLE FOUND

REPLACE OR ADJUST

CHECK THE CIRCUIT BETWEEN THE SPEED SENSOR AND THE EHCU VALVE FOR SHORTS OR OPENS

INSTALL THE WHEEL AND TIRE ASSEMBLY

CLEAR THE TROUBLE CODE. REFER TO CLEARING TROUBLE CODES

PERFORM THE DIAGNOSTIC CIRCUIT CHECK

CODE 33
ERRATIC RIGHT REAR SPEED SENSOR

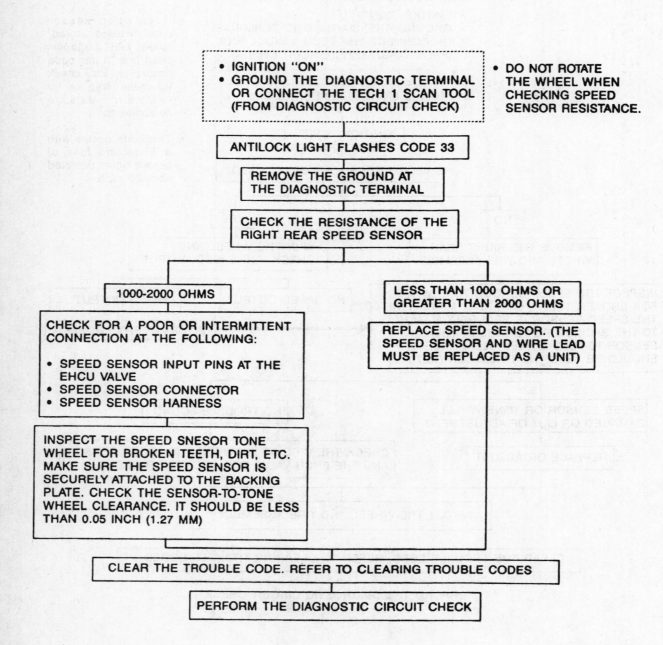

- IGNITION "ON"
- GROUND THE DIAGNOSTIC TERMINAL OR CONNECT THE TECH 1 SCAN TOOL (FROM DIAGNOSTIC CIRCUIT CHECK)

- DO NOT ROTATE THE WHEEL WHEN CHECKING SPEED SENSOR RESISTANCE.

ANTILOCK LIGHT FLASHES CODE 33

REMOVE THE GROUND AT THE DIAGNOSTIC TERMINAL

CHECK THE RESISTANCE OF THE RIGHT REAR SPEED SENSOR

1000-2000 OHMS

LESS THAN 1000 OHMS OR GREATER THAN 2000 OHMS

CHECK FOR A POOR OR INTERMITTENT CONNECTION AT THE FOLLOWING:

- SPEED SENSOR INPUT PINS AT THE EHCU VALVE
- SPEED SENSOR CONNECTOR
- SPEED SENSOR HARNESS

REPLACE SPEED SENSOR. (THE SPEED SENSOR AND WIRE LEAD MUST BE REPLACED AS A UNIT)

INSPECT THE SPEED SNESOR TONE WHEEL FOR BROKEN TEETH, DIRT, ETC. MAKE SURE THE SPEED SENSOR IS SECURELY ATTACHED TO THE BACKING PLATE. CHECK THE SENSOR-TO-TONE WHEEL CLEARANCE. IT SHOULD BE LESS THAN 0.05 INCH (1.27 MM)

CLEAR THE TROUBLE CODE. REFER TO CLEARING TROUBLE CODES

PERFORM THE DIAGNOSTIC CIRCUIT CHECK

CODE 35
LEFT REAR SPEED SENSOR OR CIRCUIT OPEN

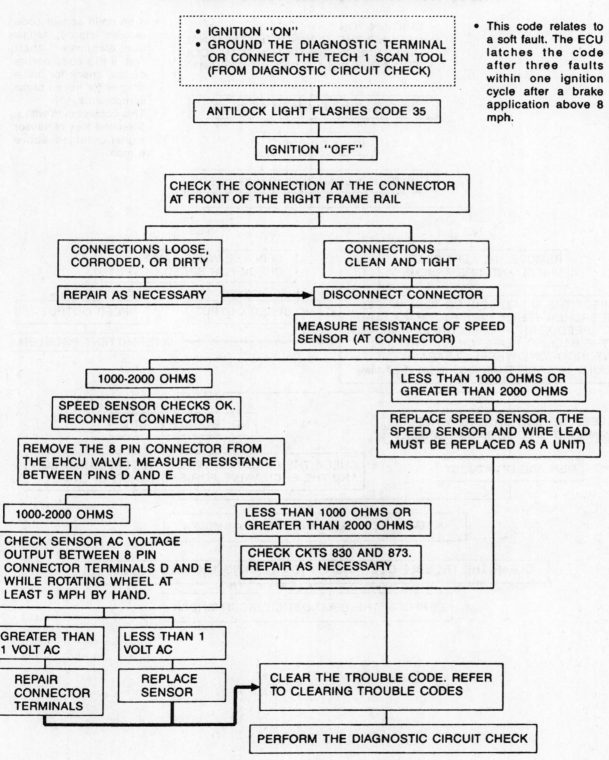

- This code relates to a soft fault. The ECU latches the code after three faults within one ignition cycle after a brake application above 8 mph.

- IGNITION "ON"
- GROUND THE DIAGNOSTIC TERMINAL OR CONNECT THE TECH 1 SCAN TOOL (FROM DIAGNOSTIC CIRCUIT CHECK)

ANTILOCK LIGHT FLASHES CODE 35

IGNITION "OFF"

CHECK THE CONNECTION AT THE CONNECTOR AT FRONT OF THE RIGHT FRAME RAIL

CONNECTIONS LOOSE, CORRODED, OR DIRTY

REPAIR AS NECESSARY

CONNECTIONS CLEAN AND TIGHT

DISCONNECT CONNECTOR

MEASURE RESISTANCE OF SPEED SENSOR (AT CONNECTOR)

1000-2000 OHMS

SPEED SENSOR CHECKS OK. RECONNECT CONNECTOR

LESS THAN 1000 OHMS OR GREATER THAN 2000 OHMS

REPLACE SPEED SENSOR. (THE SPEED SENSOR AND WIRE LEAD MUST BE REPLACED AS A UNIT)

REMOVE THE 8 PIN CONNECTOR FROM THE EHCU VALVE. MEASURE RESISTANCE BETWEEN PINS D AND E

1000-2000 OHMS

CHECK SENSOR AC VOLTAGE OUTPUT BETWEEN 8 PIN CONNECTOR TERMINALS D AND E WHILE ROTATING WHEEL AT LEAST 5 MPH BY HAND.

LESS THAN 1000 OHMS OR GREATER THAN 2000 OHMS

CHECK CKTS 830 AND 873. REPAIR AS NECESSARY

GREATER THAN 1 VOLT AC

LESS THAN 1 VOLT AC

REPAIR CONNECTOR TERMINALS

REPLACE SENSOR

CLEAR THE TROUBLE CODE. REFER TO CLEARING TROUBLE CODES

PERFORM THE DIAGNOSTIC CIRCUIT CHECK

CODE 36
MISSING LEFT REAR SPEED SIGNAL (SET WITH VEHICLE IN MOTION)

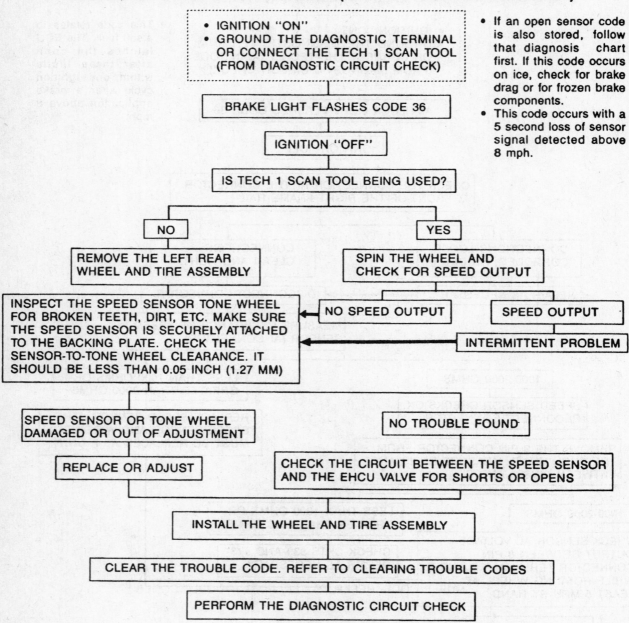

- IGNITION "ON"
- GROUND THE DIAGNOSTIC TERMINAL OR CONNECT THE TECH 1 SCAN TOOL (FROM DIAGNOSTIC CIRCUIT CHECK)

- If an open sensor code is also stored, follow that diagnosis chart first. If this code occurs on ice, check for brake drag or for frozen brake components.
- This code occurs with a 5 second loss of sensor signal detected above 8 mph.

BRAKE LIGHT FLASHES CODE 36

IGNITION "OFF"

IS TECH 1 SCAN TOOL BEING USED?

NO

YES

REMOVE THE LEFT REAR WHEEL AND TIRE ASSEMBLY

SPIN THE WHEEL AND CHECK FOR SPEED OUTPUT

NO SPEED OUTPUT

SPEED OUTPUT

INTERMITTENT PROBLEM

INSPECT THE SPEED SENSOR TONE WHEEL FOR BROKEN TEETH, DIRT, ETC. MAKE SURE THE SPEED SENSOR IS SECURELY ATTACHED TO THE BACKING PLATE. CHECK THE SENSOR-TO-TONE WHEEL CLEARANCE. IT SHOULD BE LESS THAN 0.05 INCH (1.27 MM)

SPEED SENSOR OR TONE WHEEL DAMAGED OR OUT OF ADJUSTMENT

NO TROUBLE FOUND

REPLACE OR ADJUST

CHECK THE CIRCUIT BETWEEN THE SPEED SENSOR AND THE EHCU VALVE FOR SHORTS OR OPENS

INSTALL THE WHEEL AND TIRE ASSEMBLY

CLEAR THE TROUBLE CODE. REFER TO CLEARING TROUBLE CODES

PERFORM THE DIAGNOSTIC CIRCUIT CHECK

CODE 37
ERRATIC LEFT REAR SPEED SENSOR

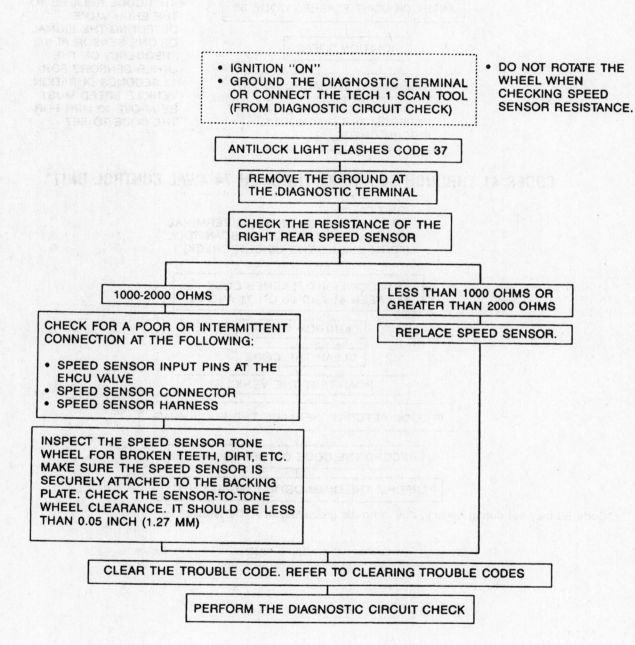

- IGNITION "ON"
- GROUND THE DIAGNOSTIC TERMINAL OR CONNECT THE TECH 1 SCAN TOOL (FROM DIAGNOSTIC CIRCUIT CHECK)

- DO NOT ROTATE THE WHEEL WHEN CHECKING SPEED SENSOR RESISTANCE.

ANTILOCK LIGHT FLASHES CODE 37

REMOVE THE GROUND AT THE DIAGNOSTIC TERMINAL

CHECK THE RESISTANCE OF THE RIGHT REAR SPEED SENSOR

1000-2000 OHMS

LESS THAN 1000 OHMS OR GREATER THAN 2000 OHMS

REPLACE SPEED SENSOR.

CHECK FOR A POOR OR INTERMITTENT CONNECTION AT THE FOLLOWING:

- SPEED SENSOR INPUT PINS AT THE EHCU VALVE
- SPEED SENSOR CONNECTOR
- SPEED SENSOR HARNESS

INSPECT THE SPEED SENSOR TONE WHEEL FOR BROKEN TEETH, DIRT, ETC. MAKE SURE THE SPEED SENSOR IS SECURELY ATTACHED TO THE BACKING PLATE. CHECK THE SENSOR-TO-TONE WHEEL CLEARANCE. IT SHOULD BE LESS THAN 0.05 INCH (1.27 MM)

CLEAR THE TROUBLE CODE. REFER TO CLEARING TROUBLE CODES

PERFORM THE DIAGNOSTIC CIRCUIT CHECK

CODE 38
WHEEL SPEED ERROR

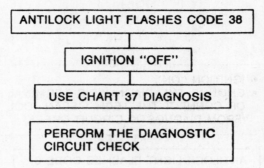

ANTILOCK LIGHT FLASHES CODE 38

IGNITION "OFF"

USE CHART 37 DIAGNOSIS

PERFORM THE DIAGNOSTIC CIRCUIT CHECK

- THIS CODE RELATES TO THE EHCU VALVE DETECTING THE SIGNAL OF ONE SENSOR AT 1/2 FREQUENCY OF THE OTHER SENSORS FOR 12 SECONDS DURATION. VEHICLE SPEED MUST BE ABOVE 12 MPH FOR THE CODE TO SET.

CODES 41 THROUGH 66 AND 71 THROUGH 74 4WAL CONTROL UNIT*

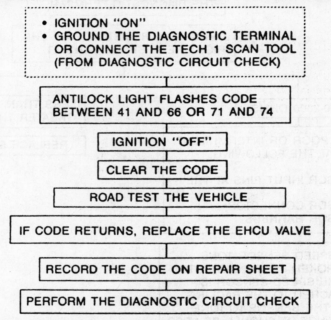

- IGNITION "ON"
- GROUND THE DIAGNOSTIC TERMINAL OR CONNECT THE TECH 1 SCAN TOOL (FROM DIAGNOSTIC CIRCUIT CHECK)

ANTILOCK LIGHT FLASHES CODE BETWEEN 41 AND 66 OR 71 AND 74

IGNITION "OFF"

CLEAR THE CODE

ROAD TEST THE VEHICLE

IF CODE RETURNS, REPLACE THE EHCU VALVE

RECORD THE CODE ON REPAIR SHEET

PERFORM THE DIAGNOSTIC CIRCUIT CHECK

*Code 65 may set during service, due to erratic grounding of ALDL terminal H.

CODE 67
OPEN MOTOR CIRCUIT OR SHORTED ECU OUTPUT

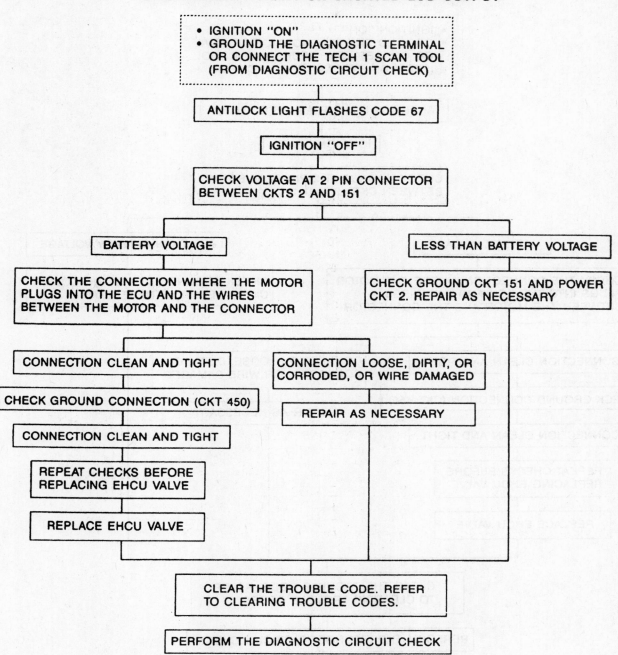

- IGNITION "ON"
- GROUND THE DIAGNOSTIC TERMINAL OR CONNECT THE TECH 1 SCAN TOOL (FROM DIAGNOSTIC CIRCUIT CHECK)

ANTILOCK LIGHT FLASHES CODE 67

IGNITION "OFF"

CHECK VOLTAGE AT 2 PIN CONNECTOR BETWEEN CKTS 2 AND 151

BATTERY VOLTAGE

LESS THAN BATTERY VOLTAGE

CHECK THE CONNECTION WHERE THE MOTOR PLUGS INTO THE ECU AND THE WIRES BETWEEN THE MOTOR AND THE CONNECTOR

CHECK GROUND CKT 151 AND POWER CKT 2. REPAIR AS NECESSARY

CONNECTION CLEAN AND TIGHT

CONNECTION LOOSE, DIRTY, OR CORRODED, OR WIRE DAMAGED

CHECK GROUND CONNECTION (CKT 450)

REPAIR AS NECESSARY

CONNECTION CLEAN AND TIGHT

REPEAT CHECKS BEFORE REPLACING EHCU VALVE

REPLACE EHCU VALVE

CLEAR THE TROUBLE CODE. REFER TO CLEARING TROUBLE CODES.

PERFORM THE DIAGNOSTIC CIRCUIT CHECK

CODE 68
LOCKED MOTOR OR SHORTED MOTOR CIRCUIT

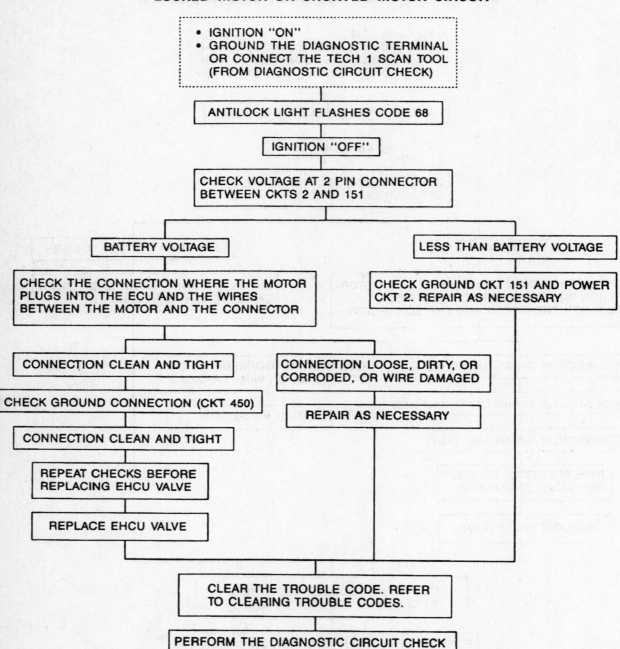

- IGNITION "ON"
- GROUND THE DIAGNOSTIC TERMINAL OR CONNECT THE TECH 1 SCAN TOOL (FROM DIAGNOSTIC CIRCUIT CHECK)

ANTILOCK LIGHT FLASHES CODE 68

IGNITION "OFF"

CHECK VOLTAGE AT 2 PIN CONNECTOR BETWEEN CKTS 2 AND 151

BATTERY VOLTAGE

LESS THAN BATTERY VOLTAGE

CHECK THE CONNECTION WHERE THE MOTOR PLUGS INTO THE ECU AND THE WIRES BETWEEN THE MOTOR AND THE CONNECTOR

CHECK GROUND CKT 151 AND POWER CKT 2. REPAIR AS NECESSARY

CONNECTION CLEAN AND TIGHT

CONNECTION LOOSE, DIRTY, OR CORRODED, OR WIRE DAMAGED

CHECK GROUND CONNECTION (CKT 450)

REPAIR AS NECESSARY

CONNECTION CLEAN AND TIGHT

REPEAT CHECKS BEFORE REPLACING EHCU VALVE

REPLACE EHCU VALVE

CLEAR THE TROUBLE CODE. REFER TO CLEARING TROUBLE CODES.

PERFORM THE DIAGNOSTIC CIRCUIT CHECK

CODE 85
OPEN ANTILOCK WARNING LAMP

- IGNITION "ON"
- GROUND THE DIAGNOSTIC TERMINAL OR CONNECT THE TECH 1 SCAN TOOL (FROM DIAGNOSTIC CIRCUIT CHECK)

BRAKE LIGHT FLASHES CODE 85

CHECK THE ANTILOCK BULB AND CKT 952 FOR OPENS. REPAIR AS NECESSARY.

CLEAR THE TROUBLE CODE. REFER TO CLEARING TROUBLE CODES.

PERFORM THE DIAGNOSTIC CIRCUIT CHECK

CODE 86
SHORTED ANTILOCK WARNING LAMP

- GROUND THE DIAGNOSTIC TERMINAL OR CONNECT THE TECH 1 SCAN TOOL (FROM DIAGNOSTIC CIRCUIT CHECK)

ANTILOCK LIGHT FLASHES CODE 86

IGNITION "OFF"

CHECK CKT 952 FOR A SHORT TO B+

CLEAR THE TROUBLE CODE. REFER TO CLEARING TROUBLE CODES.

PERFORM THE DIAGNOSTIC CIRCUIT CHECK

CODE 81
BRAKE SWITCH CIRCUIT SHORTED OR OPEN

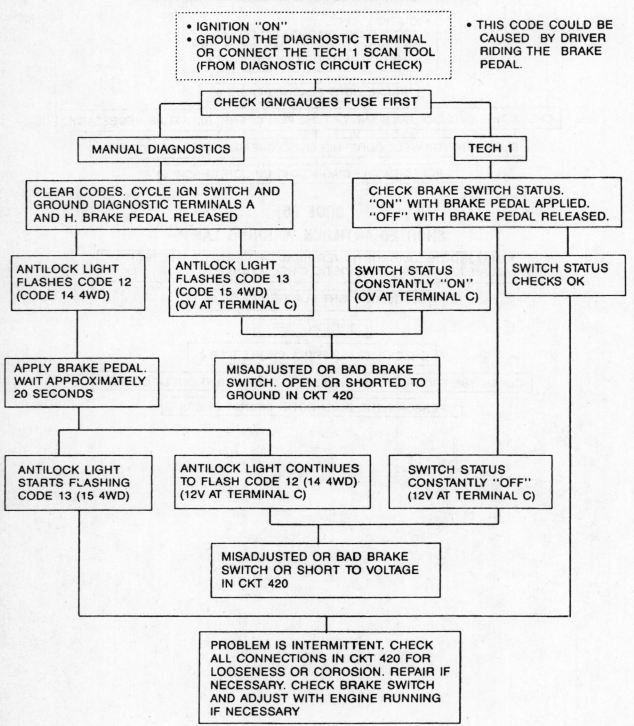

- IGNITION "ON"
- GROUND THE DIAGNOSTIC TERMINAL OR CONNECT THE TECH 1 SCAN TOOL (FROM DIAGNOSTIC CIRCUIT CHECK)

- THIS CODE COULD BE CAUSED BY DRIVER RIDING THE BRAKE PEDAL.

CHECK IGN/GAUGES FUSE FIRST

MANUAL DIAGNOSTICS

TECH 1

CLEAR CODES. CYCLE IGN SWITCH AND GROUND DIAGNOSTIC TERMINALS A AND H. BRAKE PEDAL RELEASED

CHECK BRAKE SWITCH STATUS. "ON" WITH BRAKE PEDAL APPLIED. "OFF" WITH BRAKE PEDAL RELEASED.

ANTILOCK LIGHT FLASHES CODE 12 (CODE 14 4WD)

ANTILOCK LIGHT FLASHES CODE 13 (CODE 15 4WD) (OV AT TERMINAL C)

SWITCH STATUS CONSTANTLY "ON" (OV AT TERMINAL C)

SWITCH STATUS CHECKS OK

APPLY BRAKE PEDAL. WAIT APPROXIMATELY 20 SECONDS

MISADJUSTED OR BAD BRAKE SWITCH. OPEN OR SHORTED TO GROUND IN CKT 420

ANTILOCK LIGHT STARTS FLASHING CODE 13 (15 4WD)

ANTILOCK LIGHT CONTINUES TO FLASH CODE 12 (14 4WD) (12V AT TERMINAL C)

SWITCH STATUS CONSTANTLY "OFF" (12V AT TERMINAL C)

MISADJUSTED OR BAD BRAKE SWITCH OR SHORT TO VOLTAGE IN CKT 420

PROBLEM IS INTERMITTENT. CHECK ALL CONNECTIONS IN CKT 420 FOR LOOSENESS OR COROSION. REPAIR IF NECESSARY. CHECK BRAKE SWITCH AND ADJUST WITH ENGINE RUNNING IF NECESSARY

CODES 68, 43, 44, 47, 48, 53, AND 54
LOSS OF POWER GROUND

- IGNITION "ON"
- GROUND THE DIAGNOSTIC TERMINAL OR CONNECT THE TECH 1 SCAN TOOL (FROM DIAGNOSTIC CIRCUIT CHECK)

ANTILOCK LIGHT FLASHES CODES 68, 43, 44, 47, 48, 53, AND 54

CHECK CKT 2 FOR OPENS AND LOOSE, DIRTY, OR CORRODED CONNECTIONS. REPAIR AS NECESSARY

CLEAR THE TROUBLE CODE. REFER TO CLEARING TROUBLE CODES

CODE 88
SHORTED BRAKE WARNING LAMP

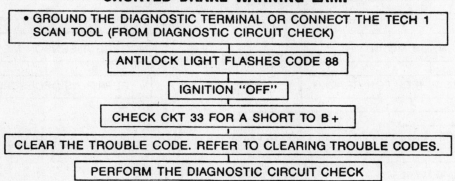

- GROUND THE DIAGNOSTIC TERMINAL OR CONNECT THE TECH 1 SCAN TOOL (FROM DIAGNOSTIC CIRCUIT CHECK)

ANTILOCK LIGHT FLASHES CODE 88

IGNITION "OFF"

CHECK CKT 33 FOR A SHORT TO B+

CLEAR THE TROUBLE CODE. REFER TO CLEARING TROUBLE CODES.

PERFORM THE DIAGNOSTIC CIRCUIT CHECK

BRAKE PEDAL PULSES
(NO CODE CONDITION)

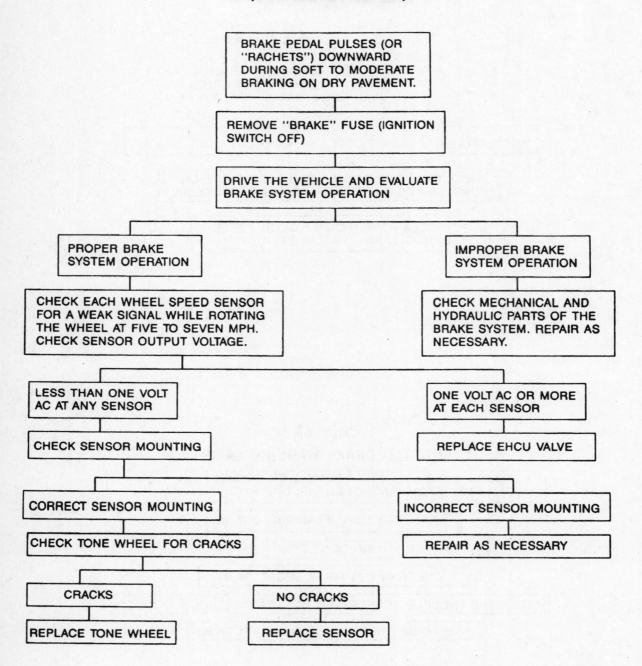

BRAKE PEDAL PULSES (OR "RACHETS") DOWNWARD DURING SOFT TO MODERATE BRAKING ON DRY PAVEMENT.

REMOVE "BRAKE" FUSE (IGNITION SWITCH OFF)

DRIVE THE VEHICLE AND EVALUATE BRAKE SYSTEM OPERATION

PROPER BRAKE SYSTEM OPERATION

IMPROPER BRAKE SYSTEM OPERATION

CHECK EACH WHEEL SPEED SENSOR FOR A WEAK SIGNAL WHILE ROTATING THE WHEEL AT FIVE TO SEVEN MPH. CHECK SENSOR OUTPUT VOLTAGE.

CHECK MECHANICAL AND HYDRAULIC PARTS OF THE BRAKE SYSTEM. REPAIR AS NECESSARY.

LESS THAN ONE VOLT AC AT ANY SENSOR

ONE VOLT AC OR MORE AT EACH SENSOR

CHECK SENSOR MOUNTING

REPLACE EHCU VALVE

CORRECT SENSOR MOUNTING

INCORRECT SENSOR MOUNTING

CHECK TONE WHEEL FOR CRACKS

REPAIR AS NECESSARY

CRACKS

NO CRACKS

REPLACE TONE WHEEL

REPLACE SENSOR

EXCESSIVE BRAKE PEDAL
TRAVEL OR SOFT PEDAL

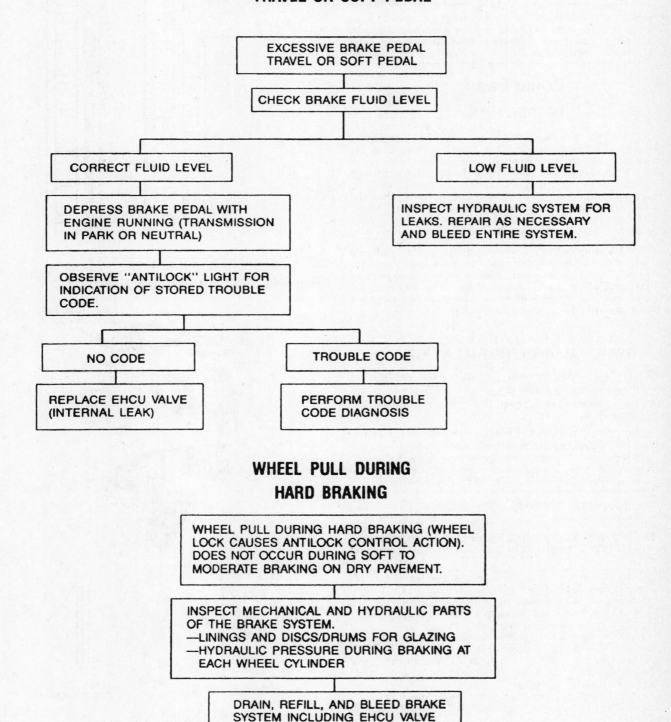

EXCESSIVE BRAKE PEDAL
TRAVEL OR SOFT PEDAL

CHECK BRAKE FLUID LEVEL

CORRECT FLUID LEVEL

LOW FLUID LEVEL

DEPRESS BRAKE PEDAL WITH
ENGINE RUNNING (TRANSMISSION
IN PARK OR NEUTRAL)

INSPECT HYDRAULIC SYSTEM FOR
LEAKS. REPAIR AS NECESSARY
AND BLEED ENTIRE SYSTEM.

OBSERVE "ANTILOCK" LIGHT FOR
INDICATION OF STORED TROUBLE
CODE.

NO CODE

TROUBLE CODE

REPLACE EHCU VALVE
(INTERNAL LEAK)

PERFORM TROUBLE
CODE DIAGNOSIS

WHEEL PULL DURING
HARD BRAKING

WHEEL PULL DURING HARD BRAKING (WHEEL
LOCK CAUSES ANTILOCK CONTROL ACTION).
DOES NOT OCCUR DURING SOFT TO
MODERATE BRAKING ON DRY PAVEMENT.

INSPECT MECHANICAL AND HYDRAULIC PARTS
OF THE BRAKE SYSTEM.
—LININGS AND DISCS/DRUMS FOR GLAZING
—HYDRAULIC PRESSURE DURING BRAKING AT
   EACH WHEEL CYLINDER

DRAIN, REFILL, AND BLEED BRAKE
SYSTEM INCLUDING EHCU VALVE

FRONT DISC BRAKES

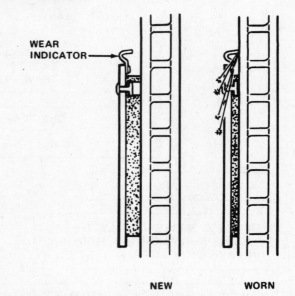

Front disc brake pad wear indicator

CAUTION

Brake shoes contain asbestos, which has been determined to be a cancer causing agent. Never clean the brake surfaces with compressed air! Avoid inhaling any dust from any brake surface! When cleaning brake surfaces, use a commercially available brake cleaning fluid.

Brake Pads

INSPECTION

Brake pads should be inspected once a year or at 7,500 miles (12,000 km), which ever occurs first. Check both ends of the outboard shoe, looking in at each end of the caliper; then check the lining thickness on the inboard shoe, looking down through the inspection hole. The lining should be more than 0.8mm ($\frac{1}{32}$ in.) thick above the rivet (so that the lining is thicker than the metal backing). Keep in mind that any applicable state inspection standards that are more stringent, take precedence. All 4 pads must be replaced if one shows excessive wear.

NOTE: All models have a wear indicator that makes a noise when the linings wear to a degree where replacement is necessary. The spring clip is an integral part of the inboard shoe and lining. When the brake pad reaches a certain degree of wear, the clip will contact the rotor and produce a warning noise.

REMOVAL AND INSTALLATION

NOTE: The following procedure requires the use of a C-clamp and channel lock pliers.

1. Siphon off about ⅔ of the brake fluid from the master cylinder reservoirs.

CAUTION

The insertion of thicker replacement pads will push the piston back into its bore and will cause a full master cylinder reservoir to overflow, possibly causing paint damage. In addition to siphoning off fluid, it would be wise to keep the reservoir cover on during pad replacement.

---

2. Raise and support the front of the vehicle on jackstands. Remove the wheels.

NOTE: When replacing the pads on just one wheel, uneven braking will result; always replace the pads on both wheels.

3. Install a C-clamp on the caliper so that the frame side of the clamp rests against the back of the caliper and so the screw end rests against the metal part (shoe) of the outboard pad.

4. Tighten the clamp until the caliper moves enough to bottom the piston in its bore. Remove the clamp.

5. Remove the 2 Allen head caliper mounting bolts enough to allow the caliper to be pulled off the disc.

6. Remove the inboard pad and loosen the outboard pad. Place the caliper where it will not strain the brake hose; it would be best to wire it out of the way.

7. Remove the pad support spring clip from the piston.

8. Remove the 2 bolt ear sleeves and the 4 rubber bushings from the ears.

9. Riveted style brake pads should be replaced when they are worn to within 0.8mm ($\frac{1}{32}$ in.) of the rivet heads; bonded style pads should be replaced when they are worn to no less than 0.8mm ($\frac{1}{32}$ in.) of the backing plate.

10. Check the inside of the caliper for leakage and the condition of the piston dust boot.

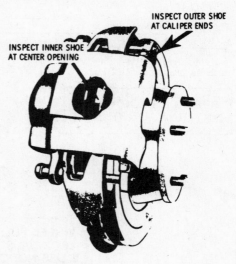

Disc brake pad inspection

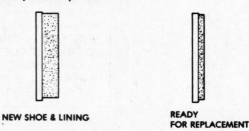

New and worn brake pads

To install:

1. Lubricate the 2 new sleeves and 4 bushings with a silicone spray.

2. Install the bushings in each caliper ear. Install the 2 sleeves in the 2 inboard ears.

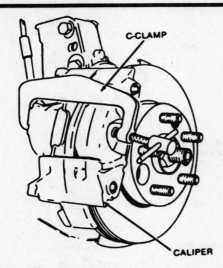

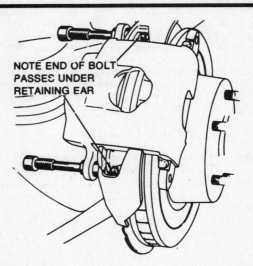

Install a C-clamp to retract the brake pads

Caliper bolts must go under the pad retaining ears

3. Install the pad support spring clip and the old pad into the center of the piston. You will then push this pad down to get the piston flat against the caliper. This part of the job is a hassle and requires an assistant. While the assistant holds the caliper and loosens the bleeder valve to relieve the pressure, obtain a medium pry bar and try to force the old pad inward, making the piston flush with the caliper surface. When it is flush, close the bleeder valve so that no air gets into the system.

NOTE: Make sure that the wear sensor is facing toward the rear of the caliper.

4. Place the outboard pad in the caliper with its top ears over the caliper ears and the bottom tab engaged in the caliper cutout.

5. After both pads are installed, lift the caliper and place the bottom edge of the outboard pad on the outer edge of the disc to make sure that there is no clearance between the tab on the bottom of the shoes and the caliper abutment.

6. Place the caliper over the disc, lining up the hole in the caliper ears with the hole in the mounting bracket. Make sure that the brake hose is not kinked.

7. Start the caliper-to-mounting bracket bolts through the sleeves in the inboard caliper ears and through the mounting bracket, making sure that the ends of the bolts pass under the retaining ears of the inboard shoe.

8. Push the mounting bolts through to engage the holes in the outboard shoes and the outboard caliper ears and then threading them into the mounting bracket.

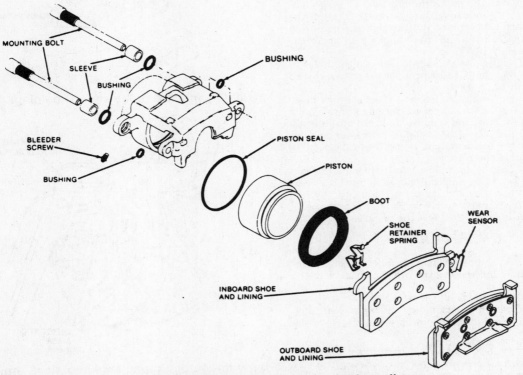

Exploded view of the front disc brake caliper

9. Torque the mounting bolts to 37 ft. lbs. (50 Nm). Pump the brake pedal to seat the linings against the rotors.

10. Using a pair of channel lock pliers, place them on the notch on the caliper housing, bend the caliper upper ears until no clearance exists between the shoe and the caliper housing.

11. Install the wheels, lower the vehicle and refill the master cylinder reservoirs with brake fluid. Pump the brake pedal to make sure that it is firm. If it is not, bleed the brakes.

Brake Caliper

REMOVAL AND INSTALLATION

1. Refer to the Brake Pads, Removal and Installation procedures in this Section and remove the brake caliper from the steering knuckle.

2. Disconnect the flexible brake hose-to-caliper bolt, discard the pressure fitting washers, then remove the brake caliper from the vehicle and place it on a work bench.

3. To inspect the caliper assembly, perform the following procedures:

    a. Check the inside of the caliper assembly for signs of leakage; if necessary, replace or rebuild the caliper.

    b. Check the mounting bolts and sleeves for signs of corrosion; if necessary, replace the bolts.

NOTE: If the mounting bolts have signs of corrosion, DO NOT attempt to polish away the corrosion.

To install:

1. Use new caliper bushing and sleeves, use Delco® Silicone Lube or equivalent to lubricate the mounting bolts and new brake pads (if necessary).

2. After both pads are installed, lift the caliper and place the bottom edge of the outboard pad on the outer edge of the disc to make sure that there is no clearance between the tab on the bottom of the shoes and the caliper abutment.

3. Place the caliper over the disc, lining up the hole in the caliper ears with the hole in the mounting bracket.

4. Start the caliper-to-mounting bracket bolts through the sleeves in the inboard caliper ears and through the mounting bracket, making sure that the ends of the bolts pass under the retaining ears of the inboard shoe.

5. Push the mounting bolts through to engage the holes in the outboard shoes and the outboard caliper ears, then thread them into the mounting bracket.

6. To complete the installation, use new flexible brake hose-to-caliper washers. Torque the caliper-to-steering knuckle bolts to 30–45 ft. lbs. (41–61 Nm) and the flexible brake hose-to-caliper bolt to 18–30 ft. lbs. (25–41 Nm). Refill the master cylinder reservoirs and bleed the brake system. Pump the brake pedal to seat the linings against the rotors.

7. Using a pair of channel lock pliers, place them on the caliper housing notch, bend the caliper upper ears until no clearance exists between the shoe and the caliper housing.

8. Install the wheels, lower the vehicle. Pump the brake pedal to make sure that it is firm. Road test the vehicle.

OVERHAUL

1. Refer to the Brake Caliper, Removal and Installation procedures in this Section and remove the brake caliper from the vehicle.

2. Remove the inlet fitting from the brake caliper.

3. Position the caliper on a work bench and place clean shop cloths in the caliper opening. Using compressed air, force the piston from its bore.

CAUTION

DO NOT apply too much air pressure to the bore, for the piston may jump out, causing damage to the piston and/or the operator.

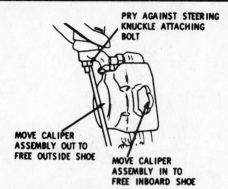

Compressing the caliper with a prybar

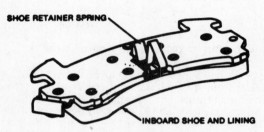

Proper retaining spring installation

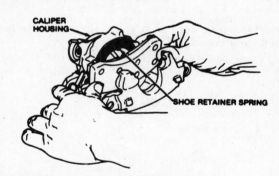

Install the inboard brake shoe and linings

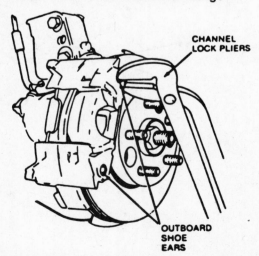

Bend the outboard pad ears into place with a large pair of slipjoint pliers

4. Remove and discard the piston boot and seal (with a plastic or wooden tool).

5. Clean all of the parts with non-mineral based solvent and blow dry with compressed air. Replace the rubber parts with those in the brake service kit.

6. Inspect the piston and the caliper bore for damage or corrosion. Replace the caliper and/or the piston (if necessary).

7. Remove the bleeder screw and it's rubber cap.

8. Inspect the guide pins for corrosion, replace them (if necessary). When installing the guide pins, coat them with silicone grease.

9. To install, perform the following procedures:

   a. Maintain the proper tolerances by referring to the following chart.

   b. Lubricate the piston, caliper and seal with clean brake fluid.

NOTE: When positioning the piston seal on the piston, it goes in the groove nearest the piston's flat end with the lap facing the largest end. If placement is correct, the seal lips will be in the groove and not extend over the groove's step.

   c. Replace the mounting bolts and torque to 22–25 ft. lbs. (30–34 Nm).

10. Bleed the brake system after installation and pump the pedal before moving the vehicle.

Brake Disc (Rotor)

The 2-wheel drive brake disc rotor and the wheel bearing hub assembly are designed from one piece of material; therefore, to remove the brake disc, remove the wheel bearing assembly.

The 4-wheel drive brake disc rotor is separate from the hub assembly and can be removed without removing the hub and bearings assembly. The hub and bearing assembly is non-serviceable and has to be replaced as a unit.

REMOVAL AND INSTALLATION

NOTE: For the 2-wheel drive model, refer to the Wheel Bearing, Removal, Packing and Installation procedures in Section 1 and replace the brake disc rotor.

INSPECTION

1. Raise and support the front of the vehicle on jackstands. Remove the wheels.

2. To check the disc runout, perform the following procedures:

   a. Using a dial indicator, secure and position it so that the button contacts the disc about 25mm (1 in.) from the outer edge.

   b. Rotate the disc. The lateral reading should not exceed 0.1mm (0.004 in.). If the reading is excessive, recondition or replace the disc.

3. To check the disc parallelism, perform the following procedures:

   a. Using a micrometer, check the disc thickness at 4 locations around the disc, at the same distance from the edge.

   b. The thickness should not vary more than 0.013mm (0.0005 in.). If the readings are excessive, recondition or replace the disc.

4. The surface finish must be relatively smooth to avoid pulling and erratic performance, also, to extend the lining life. Light rotor surface scoring of up to 0.38mm (0.015 in.) in depth, can be tolerated. If the scoring depths are excessive, refinish or replace the rotor.

Refinishing Brake Rotors

All brake rotors have a minimum thickness dimension cast

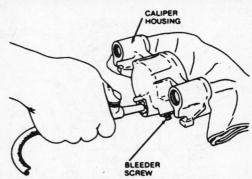

Use air pressure to remove the piston from the bore

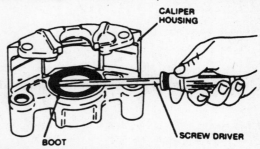

Remove the piston boot with an awl

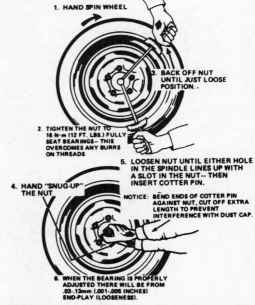

Wheel bearing adjustment — Two wheel drive

onto them. Do NOT use a brake rotor that will not meet minimum thickness specifications in the "Brake Specifications" chart at the end of this Section.

Accurate control of rotor tolerances is necessary for proper brake performance and safety. Machining of the rotor should be done by a qualified machine shop with the proper machining equipment.

The optimum speed for refinishing the rotor surface is a spindle speed of 200 rpm. Crossfeed for rough cutting should range from 0.25–0.15mm (0.010–0.006 in.) per revolution. The finish cuts should be made at crossfeeds no greater than 0.05mm (0.002 in.) per revolution.

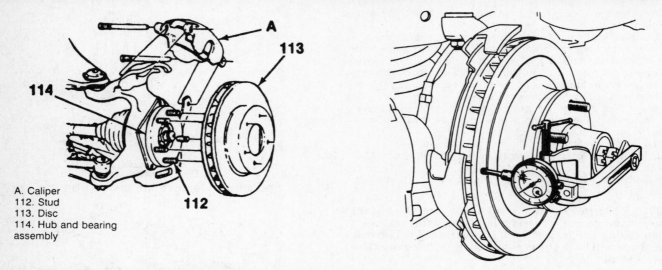

A. Caliper
112. Stud
113. Disc
114. Hub and bearing
assembly

Rotor, hub and bearing assembly — All wheel drive

Use a dial indicator to determine brake disc runout

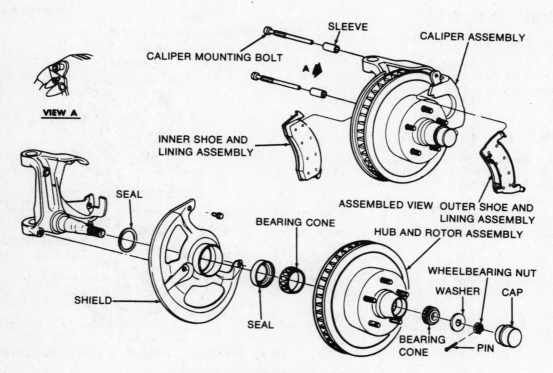

Exploded view of the disc brake assembly

REAR DRUM BRAKES

— CAUTION —

Brake shoes contain asbestos, which has been determined to be a cancer causing agent. Never clean the brake surfaces with compressed air! Avoid inhaling any dust from any brake surface! When cleaning brake surfaces, use a commercially available brake cleaning fluid.

Brake Drums

REMOVAL AND INSTALLATION

1. Raise and support the rear of the vehicle on jackstands.
2. Remove the wheel and tire assemblies.
3. Pull the brake drum off. It may by necessary to gently tap the rear edges of the drum to start it off the studs.
4. If extreme resistance to removal is encountered, it will be necessary to retract the adjusting screw. Remove the access hole cover from the backing plate and turn the adjuster to retract the linings away from the drum.
5. Install a replacement hole cover before reinstalling the drum.
6. Install the drums in the same position on the hub as removed.

NOTE: The rear wheel bearings are not adjustable, they are serviced by replacement ONLY. If necessary to replace the rear wheel bearings, refer to the Axle Shaft, Bearing and Seal, Removal and Installation procedures in Section 7 and follow the replacement procedures.

INSPECTION

1. Check the drums for any cracks, scores, grooves or an out-of-round condition; if it is cracked, replace it. Slight scores can be removed with fine emery cloth while extensive scoring requires turning the drum on a lathe.
2. Never have a drum turned more than 1.5mm (0.060 in.).

Brake Shoes

INSPECTION

Remove the drum and inspect the lining thickness of both brake shoes. The rear brake shoes should be replaced if the lining is less than 1.5mm ($\frac{1}{16}$ in.) at the lowest point (bonded linings) or above the rivet heads (riveted linings) on the brake shoe. However, these lining thickness measurements may disagree with your state inspections laws.

NOTE: Brake shoes should always be replaced in sets.

REMOVAL AND INSTALLATION

NOTE: The following procedure requires the use of the GM Brake Spring Pliers tool No. J–8057 or equivalent.

1. Raise and support the rear of the vehicle on jackstands.
2. Slacken the parking brake cable.

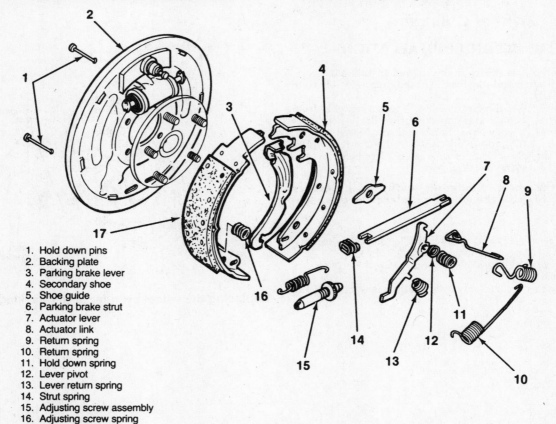

1. Hold down pins
2. Backing plate
3. Parking brake lever
4. Secondary shoe
5. Shoe guide
6. Parking brake strut
7. Actuator lever
8. Actuator link
9. Return spring
10. Return spring
11. Hold down spring
12. Lever pivot
13. Lever return spring
14. Strut spring
15. Adjusting screw assembly
16. Adjusting screw spring
17. Primary shoe

Exploded view of the rear brake assembly

3. Remove the rear wheels and the brake drum.

4. Using the GM Brake Spring Pliers tool No. J–8057 or equivalent, disconnect the brake shoe return springs, the actuator pullback spring, the holddown pins/springs and the actuator assembly.

NOTE: Special brake spring tools are available from the auto supply stores, which will ease the replacement of the spring and anchor pin, but the job may still be performed with common hand tools.

5. Disconnect the adjusting mechanism and spring, then remove the primary shoe. The primary shoe has a shorter lining than the secondary and is mounted at the front of the wheel.

6. Disconnect the parking brake lever from the secondary shoe and remove the shoe.

To install:

1. Clean and inspect all of the brake parts.

2. Check the wheel cylinders for seal condition and leaking.

3. If necessary, repack the wheel bearings and replace the oil seals.

4. Inspect the replacement shoes for nicks or burrs, lubricate the backing plate contact points, the brake cable, the levers and adjusting screws, then reassemble them.

5. Make sure that the right and left hand adjusting screws are not mixed. You can prevent this by working on one side at a time. This will also provide you with a reference for reassembly. The star wheel should be nearest to the secondary shoe when correctly installed.

6. Using lithium grease or equivalent, lubricate the shoe pads (on the backing plate) and the adjusting screw threads.

7. Install the springs and adjusters. When completed, make an initial adjustment as previously described.

Wheel Cylinders

REMOVAL AND INSTALLATION

1. Refer to the Brake Shoe, Removal and Installation procedures in this Section and remove the brake shoe assembly from the backing plate.

2. Clean away all of the dirt, crud and foreign material from around the wheel cylinder. It is important that dirt be kept away from the brake line when the cylinder is disconnected.

3. Disconnect and plug the inlet tube at the wheel cylinder.

4. Remove the wheel cylinder-to-backing plate bolts and the wheel cylinder from the backing plate.

NOTE: If the wheel cylinder is sticking, use a hammer and a punch to drive the wheel cylinder from the backing plate.

To install:

1. Install the wheel cylinder and bolts. Torque the wheel cylinder-to-backing plate bolts to 13 ft. lbs. (18 Nm).

2. Install the rear brake shoes and hardware as outlined earlier in this Section.

3. Bleed the rear brake system. Adjust the rear brake assembly.

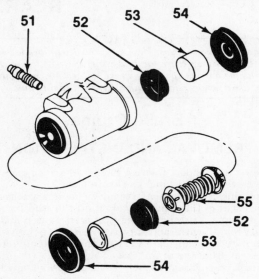

51. Bleeder valve
52. Seal
53. Piston
54. Boot
55. Spring assembly

Exploded view of the rear wheel cylinder

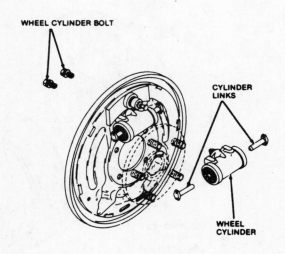

Replacing the wheel cylinder at the backing plate

PARKING BRAKE

Pedal Assembly

REMOVAL AND INSTALLATION

1. Disconnect the negative (–) battery cable.
2. Release the parking brake before removal.
3. Remove the instrument panel and dash assembly as outlined in Section 6.
4. Disconnect the release rod, and parking brake lamp switch.
5. Remove the bolts and disconnect the cable assembly.
6. Remove the pedal assembly from under the instrument panel.

To install:
1. Connect the cable assembly and install the pedal to the vehicle body.
2. Install the bolts and torque to 18 ft. lbs. (24 Nm).
3. Connect the switch and release rod.
4. Install the instrument panel and dash assembly.
5. Adjust the parking brake cable as outlined in this Section.
6. Connect the negative battery cable and check operation.

Front Cable

REMOVAL AND INSTALLATION

1. Raise and support the front of the vehicle on jackstands.

2. Under the left center of the vehicle, loosen the cable equalizer assembly.
3. Separate the front cable connector from the equalizer cable.
4. Remove the front cable retaining bolts and clips, then bend the retaining fingers.
5. Disconnect the front cable from the parking pedal assembly and the cable from the vehicle.

To install:
1. To install the front cable, attach a piece of wire to the cable, fish it through the cowl and connect it to the equalizer cable. Adjust the parking brake.
2. Lower the vehicle and check the parking brake operation.

Rear Cable

REMOVAL AND INSTALLATION

1. Raise and support the rear of the vehicle on jackstands.
2. Under the left center of the vehicle, loosen the cable equalizer assembly.
3. Separate the front cable connector from the equalizer cable.
4. Refer to the Brake Shoe, Removal and Installation procedures in this Section and remove the brake shoes.
5. At the backing plate, bend the cable retaining fingers.

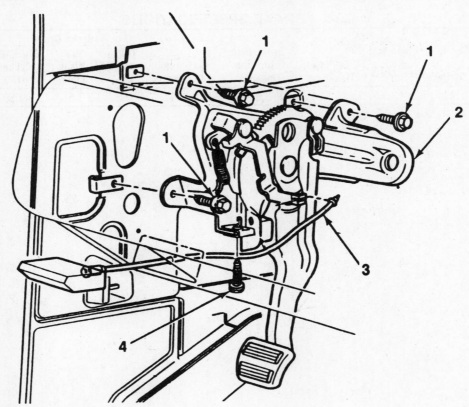

1. Bolt
2. Pedal assembly
3. Release rod
4. Bolt

Exploded view of the parking brake pedal assembly

6. Disconnect the rear cable(s) from the secondary brake shoe(s) and the cable(s) from the vehicle.

To install:

1. To install the rear cable(s), insert the cable through the backing plate and engage it with the secondary brake shoe.
2. Connect the cable to the equalizer cable.
3. Adjust the parking brake.

NOTE: **When installing the rear parking brake cables, make sure that the retaining fingers are completely through the backing plate.**

4. Lower the vehicle and check the parking brake operation.

ADJUSTMENT

NOTE: **Before adjusting the parking brakes, check the condition of the service brakes; replace any necessary parts.**

1. Block the front wheels.
2. Raise and support the rear of the vehicle on jackstands.
3. Under the left center of the vehicle, loosen the equalizer.
4. Position the parking brake pedal on the second click (2 ratchet clicks).
5. Turn the cable equalizer until the rear wheel drags (when turned by hand).
6. Tighten the equalizer lock nut.
7. Release the parking brake pedal, then test it; the correct adjustment should be 9–16 clicks.

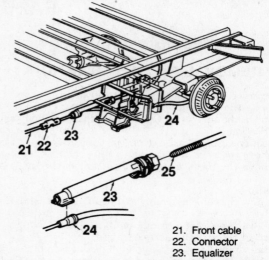

21. Front cable
22. Connector
23. Equalizer
24. Left rear cable
25. Right rear cable

Exploded view of the parking brake cable assembly

BRAKE SPECIFICATIONS

Years	Model	Master Cyl. Bore	Brake Disc			Brake Drum			Wheel Cyl. or Caliper Bore	
			Original Thickness	Minimum Thickness	Maximum Run-out	Orig. Inside Dia.	Max. Wear Limit	Maximum Machine O/S	Front	Rear
1985–90	All	NA	1.04	0.980	0.004	9.5	9.59	9.56	NA	NA

NA: Information Not Available

Body

QUICK REFERENCE INDEX

GENERAL INDEX

EXTERIOR

Front Doors

REMOVAL AND INSTALLATION

NOTE: The following procedure requires the use of the GM Door Hinge Spring Compressor tool No. J-28625-A or equivalent.

1. If equipped with power door components, perform the following procedures:
   a. Disconnect the negative battery cable from the battery.
   b. Refer to the "Door Panel, Removal and Installation" procedures in this Section and remove the door panel.
   c. Disconnect the electrical harness connector from the power door lock motor and/or the power window regulator.
   d. Remove the electrical harness from the door.

CAUTION

Before removing the hinge spring from the door, be sure to cover it (to keep it from flying); it could cause personal injury.

2. Using the GM Door Hinge Spring Compressor tool No. J-28625-A or equivalent, compress the door hinge spring and remove it.
3. To remove the door hinge pin clips, spread the clips and move them above the recess on the pin; when the pin is removed, the clip will ride on the pin and fall free of it.
4. Using a soft-head hammer and a pair of locking pliers, remove the lower pin from the door hinge; then, install a bolt (in the lower pin hole) to hold the door in place until the upper hinge pin is removed.
5. Remove the upper door hinge pin and support the door, then remove the bolt from the lower hinge pin hole and the door from the vehicle.

To install:
1. Position the door onto the hinges and insert a bolt through the lower hinge pin hole.
2. Using a new hinge pin clip, install the upper hinge pin.
3. Remove the bolt from the lower hinge pin hole. Using a new hinge pin, install it into the lower hinge pin holes.
4. Using the GM Door Hinge Spring Compressor tool No. J-28625-A or equivalent, compress the door hinge spring and install it into the door hinge.
5. If equipped with power door components, reconnect the electrical harness connector(s), install the door panel and the reconnect the negative battery terminal.

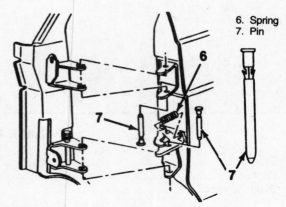

6. Spring
7. Pin

Replacing the door spring and the hinge pin

ADJUSTMENTS

Factory installed hinges are welded in place, so no adjustment of the system is necessary or recommended.

Front Door Hinges

NOTE: The following procedure requires the use of an ⅛ in. (3mm) drill bit, ½ in. (13mm) drill bit, a center punch, a cold chisel, a portable body grinder, a putty knife, a scribing tool.

REMOVAL AND INSTALLATION

1. Refer to the "Door, Removal and Installation" procedures in this Section and remove the door(s), then place the door on a padded workbench.
2. Using a putty knife, remove the sealant from the around the edge of the hinge.
3. Using a scribing tool, outline the position of the hinge(s) on the door and the body pillar.
4. Using a center punch, mark the center position of the hinge-to-door and the hinge-to-body pillar welds.
5. Using a ⅛ in. (3mm) drill bit, drill a pilot hole completely through each weld.

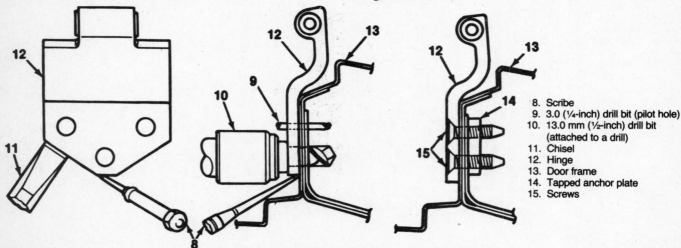

8. Scribe
9. 3.0 (¼-inch) drill bit (pilot hole)
10. 13.0 mm (½-inch) drill bit (attached to a drill)
11. Chisel
12. Hinge
13. Door frame
14. Tapped anchor plate
15. Screws

Installing replacement door hinges onto the vehicle

NOTE: When drilling the holes through the hinge welds, DO NOT drill through the door or the body pillar.

6. Using a ½ in. (13mm) drill bit, drill a hole through the hinge base, following the ⅛ in. (3mm) pilot hole.

7. Using a cold chisel and a hammer, separate the hinge from the door and/or the body pillar. Using a portable grinder, clean off any welds remaining on the door or the body pillar.

To install:

1. To fasten the replacement hinge(s) to the door and/or body pillar, perform the following procedures:

　a. Align the replacement hinge, with the scribe lines, previously made.

　b. Using a center punch and the new hinge as a template, mark the location of each bolt hole.

　c. Using a ½ in. (13mm) drill bit, drill holes (using the center marks) through the door and body pillar.

　d. If the upper body side hinge is to be replaced, remove the instrument panel fasteners, pull the panel outwards and support it.

2. Use medium body sealant (apply it to the hinge-to-door or body pillar surface), the hinge-to-door/body pillar bolts and tapped anchor plate.

3. Torque the hinge-to-door/body pillar bolts to 20 ft. lbs. (27 Nm).

4. Apply paint to the hinge and the surrounding area.

NOTE: If the instrument panel was removed, replace it.

ADJUSTMENT

NOTE: The ½ in. (13mm) drill hinge holes provide for some adjustment.

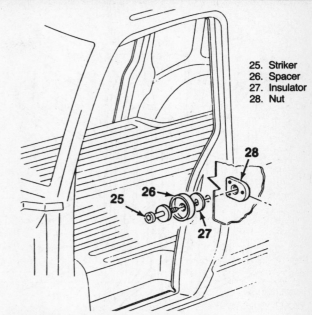

25. Striker
26. Spacer
27. Insulator
28. Nut

Exploded view of the front door striker

1. Loosen, adjust, then tighten the hinge-to-door/body pillar bolts; close the door, then check the door gap, it should be 4–6mm between the door and the door frame.

2. With the door closed, it should be flush, ± 1.0mm, with the body; if not, enlarge the striker hole.

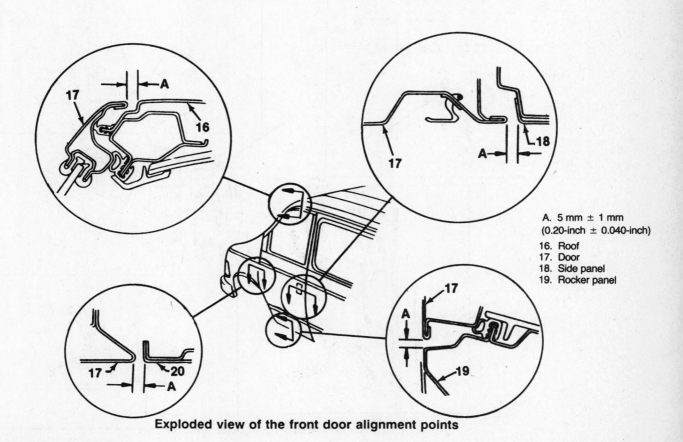

A. 5 mm ± 1 mm
(0.20-inch ± 0.040-inch)

16. Roof
17. Door
18. Side panel
19. Rocker panel

Exploded view of the front door alignment points

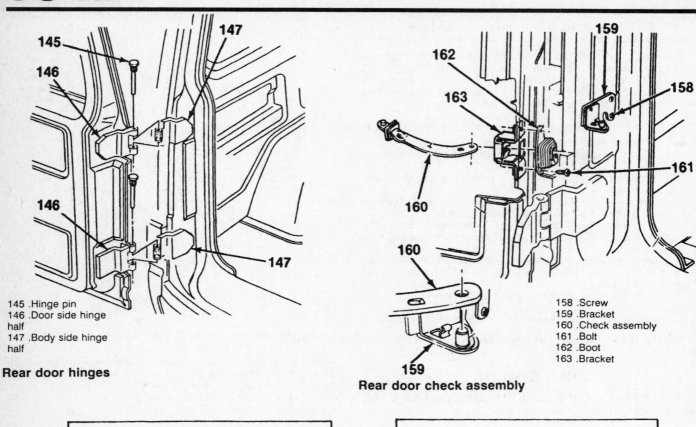

145 .Hinge pin
146 .Door side hinge half
147 .Body side hinge half

Rear door hinges

158 .Screw
159 .Bracket
160 .Check assembly
161 .Bolt
162 .Boot
163 .Bracket

Rear door check assembly

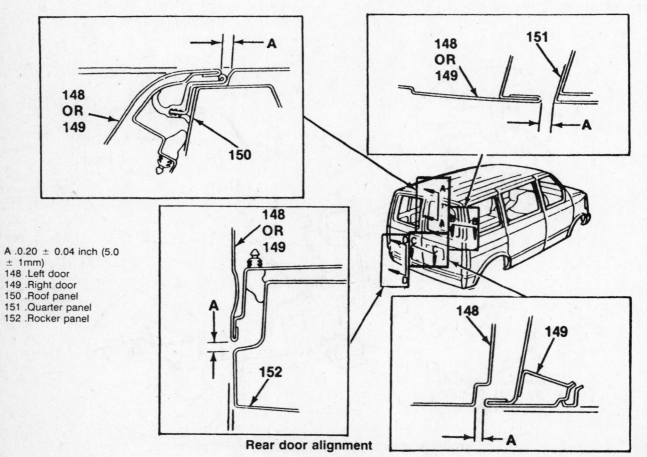

A .0.20 ± 0.04 inch (5.0 ± 1mm)
148 .Left door
149 .Right door
150 .Roof panel
151 .Quarter panel
152 .Rocker panel

Rear door alignment

Rear Doors

REMOVAL AND INSTALLATION

1. Disconnect the negative (−) battery cable.
2. Remove the door trim panel on the right door only.
3. Disconnect the wiring harness from the license plate lamp and power door lock, if so equipped. Remove the harness from the door.
4. Disconnect the check strap from the door frame.
5. Drive the hinge pins while an assistant holds the door in place.
6. Remove the door from the vehicle.

To install:
1. With an assistant, install the door onto the vehicle.
2. Drive the hinge pins through both hinge halves.
3. Connect the wiring harness, install the trim panel and connect the negative battery cable.

ADJUSTMENT

The original door hinges are welded in place, and adjustment is not recommended. However, with service bolt-on hinges, adjustment is possible.
1. Loosen the door striker.
2. Adjust the left door first and then the right.
3. Adjust the left door so that there is a 5.0mm gap between the door and the door frame at the top, bottom and side of the door.
4. Adjust the right door so that there is a 5.0mm gap between the door and the door frame at the top, bottom and side of the door.

Rear Door Check

REMOVAL AND INSTALLATION

1. Open the door and disconnect the check assembly from the bracket.
2. Remove the mounting bracket screws, bracket and door trim panel.
3. Remove the boot-to-bracket bolts and boot.
4. Remove the bracket and check assembly from the inside of the door.

To install:
1. Install the bracket and check assembly.
2. Install the boot and bolts.
3. Install the trim panel, mounting bracket and screws.
4. Connect the check to the bracket and check operation.

Sliding Door

REMOVAL AND INSTALLATION

1. Remove the track cover.
2. Using a marking tool, mark the alignment of the lower roller bracket-to-door position.
3. Remove the upper roller bracket-to-door screws, then the lower roller bracket-to-sliding door bolts.
4. Using an assistant, to support the sliding door, open the door and roll the center roller bracket off the end of the track.
5. **To install,** use an assistant to roll the center roller bracket onto the end of the track.
6. Align the lower roller bracket-to-door marks and install the mounting bolts. Torque all of the door roller bracket bolts to 20 ft. lbs. (27 Nm).

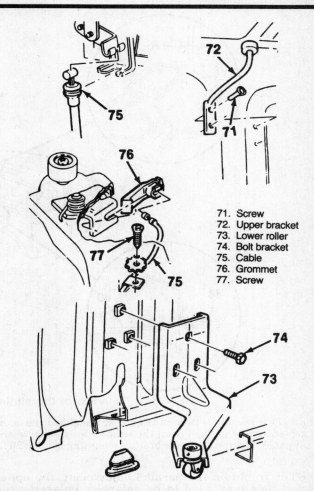

71. Screw
72. Upper bracket
73. Lower roller
74. Bolt bracket
75. Cable
76. Grommet
77. Screw

Exploded view of the upper/lower roller brackets and cable latch — sliding door

ADJUSTMENT

Although the sliding door is designed without any adjustment provisions, it is possible to rework certain portions of the system.
- Using the rear striker, at the center rear of the door, adjust the height and flushness.
- Using the lower roller bracket, adjust the parallel gap at the base of the door.
- To obtain flushness and vertical support, at the front of the door, adjust the door locator pins and sockets.
- To obtain proper gap and a level swing-in, at the rear of the door, adjust the center roller track fore and aft.
- Using Lubriplate® or equivalent, lubricate the roller track contact surfaces.
1. To obtain the height (up/down) and the flushness (in/out) movements, between the door and the rear quarter panel, enlarge the rear striker hole.

NOTE: When making the rear striker adjustments, DO NOT bend the striker to obtain the adjustment.

2. To obtain a parallel gap between the base of the door and the rocker panel, loosen the lower roller bracket bolts. Check

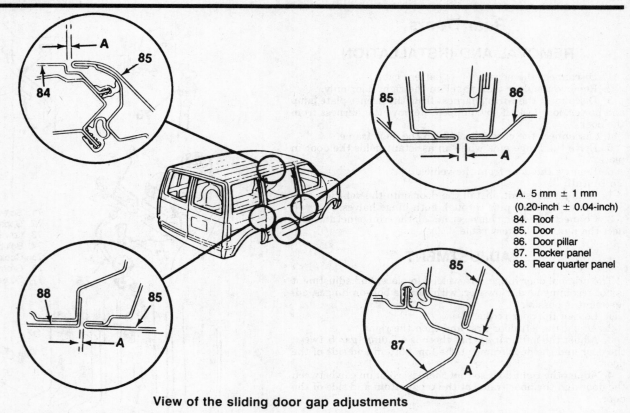

A. 5 mm ± 1 mm
(0.20-inch ± 0.04-inch)
84. Roof
85. Door
86. Door pillar
87. Rocker panel
88. Rear quarter panel

View of the sliding door gap adjustments

and/or adjust the gap between the quarter panel and the door; the gap should be parallel from the window area down to the rocker panel. Tighten the lower bracket mounting bolts to 20 ft. lbs.

NOTE: To obtain the parallel adjustment, the upper bracket hole may have to be enlarged; enlarging the hole may mean that the feature alignment of the door may have to be compromised.

3. To obtain flushness between the door and the rocker panel, adjust the lower locating pin so that its surface is in contact with the outer edges of the locator guide. If you are having trouble obtaining the flushness, perform the following procedures:

a. Using a rubber hammer, strike the locator pin (while in position) to bend the sheet metal slightly.

b. Using a portable grinder, remove some of the material from the top or bottom of the locator guide; DO NOT remove too much material that a hole is ground through the guide.

c. Readjust the door height at the lower roller bracket.

4. Adjust the upper locator pin until it is flush with the locator guide; the locator should rub the outer edge of the locator guide. If you are having trouble obtaining the adjustment, perform the following procedures:

a. Using a rubber hammer, strike the locator pin (while in position) to bend the sheet metal slightly.

b. Using a portable grinder, remove some of the material from the top or bottom of the locator guide; DO NOT remove too much material that a hole is ground through the guide.

5. To obtain equal gaps between the door, the quarter panel and the door pillar, perform the following procedures:

a. For access to the center roller track, remove the right rear tail light bezel, the interior trim from around the track and the track cover.

b. Inspect the track rollers; the bottom rollers should ride on the track base and the side roller should ride on the outer flange of the track.

c. Loosen the track fasteners and slide the track rearward until it comes in contact the center rollers, then center the

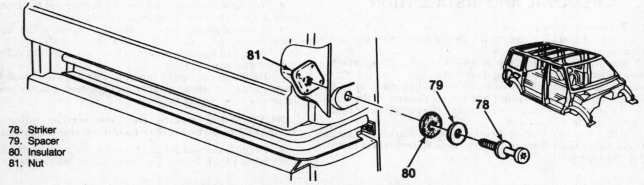

78. Striker
79. Spacer
80. Insulator
81. Nut

Exploded view of the door striker — sliding door

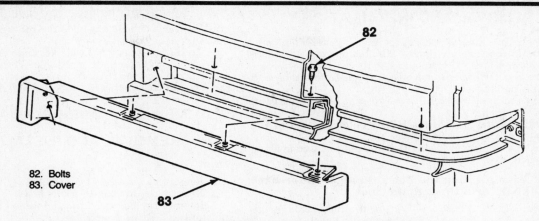

82. Bolts
83. Cover

Exploded view of the center roller track cover — sliding door

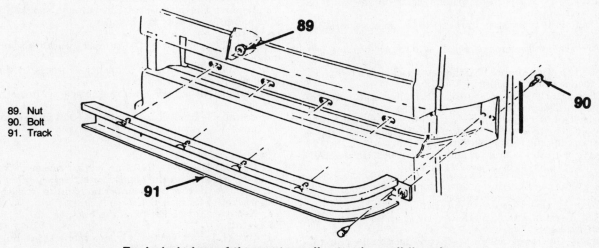

89. Nut
90. Bolt
91. Track

Exploded view of the center roller track — sliding door

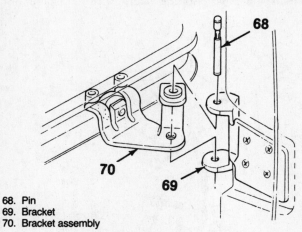

68. Pin
69. Bracket
70. Bracket assembly

Exploded view of the center roller bracket — sliding door

door in the opening. Tighten the track fasteners by starting with the one closest to the rear door striker.

d. Loosen the forward track fastener, then push the track up or down until the rear latch rolls onto the striker in a level position; if necessary, elongate the hole.

e. Install the track cover, the interior trim and the rear tail light bezel.

6. Adjust the upper roller bracket so that the roller runs in the middle of the track; it must not touch the upper or lower edge of the track. If necessary physically adjust it, remove it from the bracket and bend it at its base.

Roller Brackets

REMOVAL AND INSTALLATION

Upper

1. Remove the upper roller bracket trim.
2. Remove the front cap.
3. Remove the upper bracket-to-door screws and the bracket from the vehicle.
4. **To install,** position the bracket onto the vehicle. Torque the upper roller bracket-to-door screws to 20 ft. lbs. (27 Nm). Adjust the door gap, if necessary.

Center

NOTE: The following procedure requires the use of an ⅛ in. (3mm) drill bit, ½ in. (13mm) drill bit, a center punch, a cold chisel, a portable body grinder, a putty knife, a scribing tool.

REMOVAL AND INSTALLATION

1. Refer to the ''Sliding Door, Removal and Installation'' procedures in this Section and remove the sliding door, then place the door on a padded workbench.

2. Using a putty knife, remove the sealant from the around the edge of the bracket.

3. Using a scribing tool, outline the position of the bracket on the door.

4. Using a center punch, mark the center position of the bracket base welds.

5. Using a ⅛ in. (3mm) drill bit, drill a pilot hole completely through each weld.

NOTE: When drilling the holes through the bracket welds, DO NOT drill through the door.

6. Using a ½ in. (13mm) drill bit, drill a hole through the bracket base, following the ⅛ in. (3mm) pilot hole.

7. Using a cold chisel and a hammer, separate the bracket from the door. Using a portable grinder, clean off any welds remaining on the door.

8. To fasten the replacement bracket to the door, perform the following procedures:

   a. Align the replacement bracket, with the scribe lines, previously made.

   b. Using a center punch and the new bracket as a template, mark the location of each bolt hole.

   c. Using a ½ in. (13mm) drill bit, drill holes (using the center marks) through the door.

9. **To install**, use medium body sealant and apply it to the bracket-to-door surface, the bracket-to-door bolts and tapped anchor plate. Torque the bracket-to-door bolts to 20 ft. lbs. (27 Nm). Apply paint to the bracket and the surrounding area. Adjust the sliding door-to-body gap, if necessary.

Lower

1. Remove the lower striker from the door.

2. Using a scribing tool, mark the lower roller bracket-to-door position.

3. Remove the lower roller bracket-to-door bolts and the catch cable from the bracket.

4. Slide the door to the fully back position.

5. Remove the lower roller bracket-to-body fasteners, pull the bracket from the body and slide the roller bracket out through the rear of the track.

6. **To install**, position the striker and roller bracket onto the door and install the bolts and cable. Torque the lower roller bracket-to-door bolts to 20 ft. lbs. (27 Nm). Adjust the door-to-body gap, if necessary.

Bumpers

REMOVAL AND INSTALLATION

Front

1. Remove the brace-to-frame bolts.

2. Remove the bracket-to-frame bolts.

3. Remove the bumper from the vehicle with the help of an assistant.

4. Remove the brace-to-plate bolt and nuts, braces from the bumper and bumper-to-plate bolts.

5. Remove the plate from the bumper, bracket-to-bumper bolts and bracket from the bumper.

To install:

1. Install the bracket to the bumper, bracket-to-bumper nuts and bolts.

2. Install the bumper-to-plate bolts, braces to the bumper and brace-to-plate bolts and nuts.

3. Install the bumper onto the vehicle with the help of an assistant.

4. Install the bracket-to-frame bolts and torque to 40 ft. lbs. (55 Nm).

Rear

1. Remove the brace-to-frame bolts, bracket-to-frame bolts and the bumper from the vehicle with the help of an assistant.

2. Remove the brace-to-bumper nuts, brace from the bumper and bracket-to-bumper bolts.

3. Remove the bracket from the bumper.

To install:

1. Install the bracket to the bumper, bracket-to-bumper bolts and the brace to the bumper.

2. Install the bumper onto the vehicle with the help of an assistant.

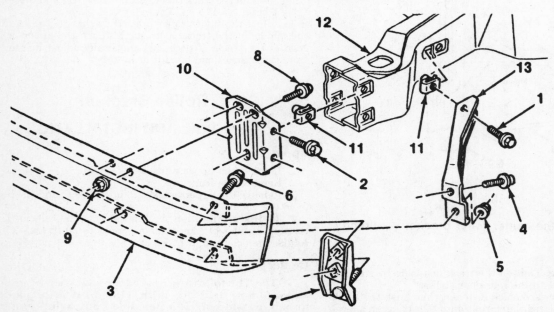

1. Bolt
2. Bolt
3. Bumper
4. Bolt
5. Nut
6. Bolt
7. Plate
8. Bolt
9. Nut
10. Bracket
11. Clip
12. Frame
13. Brace

Front bumper — two wheel drive

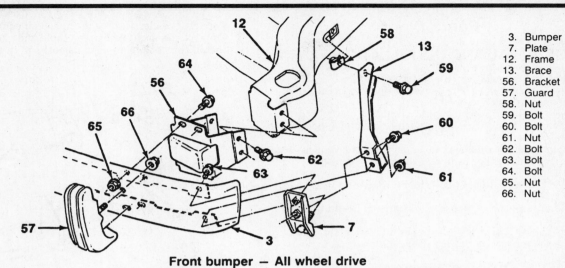

Front bumper — All wheel drive

3. Bumper
7. Plate
12. Frame
13. Brace
56. Bracket
57. Guard
58. Nut
59. Bolt
60. Bolt
61. Nut
62. Bolt
63. Bolt
64. Bolt
65. Nut
66. Nut

3. Install the bracket-to-frame bolts and nuts. Torque the fasteners to 26 ft. lbs. (35 Nm).

Grille

REMOVAL AND INSTALLATION

1. Remove the headlight bezel and front end panel-to-grille bolts.
2. Remove the grille-to-radiator support screws and the grille.

To install:

1. Install the grille and radiator support screws.
2. Install the front end panel-to-grille bolts and the headlight bezel.

19. Bolt
20. Bolt
21. Bolt
22. Bumper
23. Nut
24. Brace
25. Nut
26. Bolt
27. Bolt
28. Nut
29. Bracket

Rear bumper

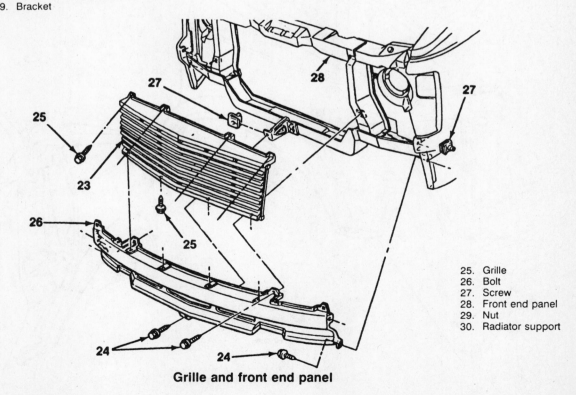

25. Grille
26. Bolt
27. Screw
28. Front end panel
29. Nut
30. Radiator support

Grille and front end panel

Fender

REMOVAL AND INSTALLATION

1. Disconnect the negative (−) battery cable.
2. Remove the headlight bezel, bumper and cowl vent grille.
3. Raise and support the hood.
4. Remove the hood-to-fender nut and bolt.
5. Remove the front wheelhouse extension and fender-to-body bolts.
6. With an assistant, remove the fender from the vehicle. Be careful not to damage the painted surfaces.

To install:
1. Install the fender-to-body bolts and torque to 18 ft. lbs. (25 Nm).
2. Install the front wheelhouse extension and hood-to-fender nuts and bolts.
3. Install the cowl vent grille, bumper and headlight bezel.
4. Connect the negative battery cable and align the fender.

Outside Mirrors

REMOVAL AND INSTALLATION

1. Disconnect the negative (−) battery cable.
2. Remove the door trim panel as outlined in this Section.
3. Disconnect the electrical connector, if so equipped.
4. Remove the retaining nuts and mirror assembly from the door.

To install:
1. Install the mirror and nuts to the door.

2. Connect the electrical connector, if so equipped.
3. Connect the negative battery cable and check operation.
4. Install the door trim panel as outlined in this Section.

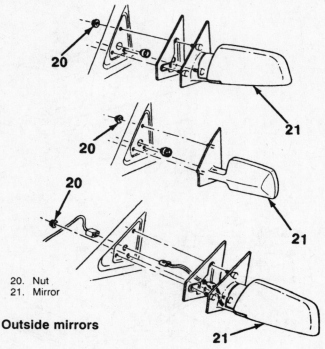

20. Nut
21. Mirror

Outside mirrors

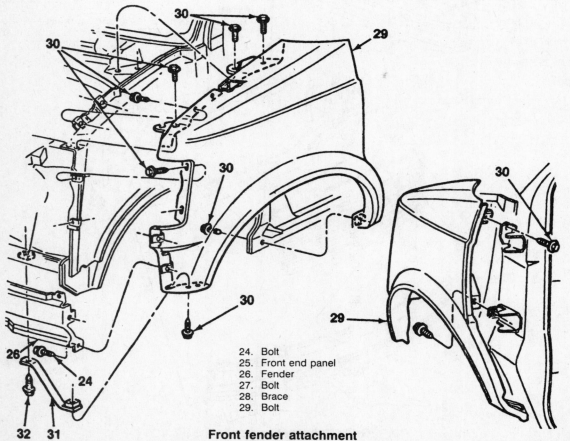

24. Bolt
25. Front end panel
26. Fender
27. Bolt
28. Brace
29. Bolt

Front fender attachment

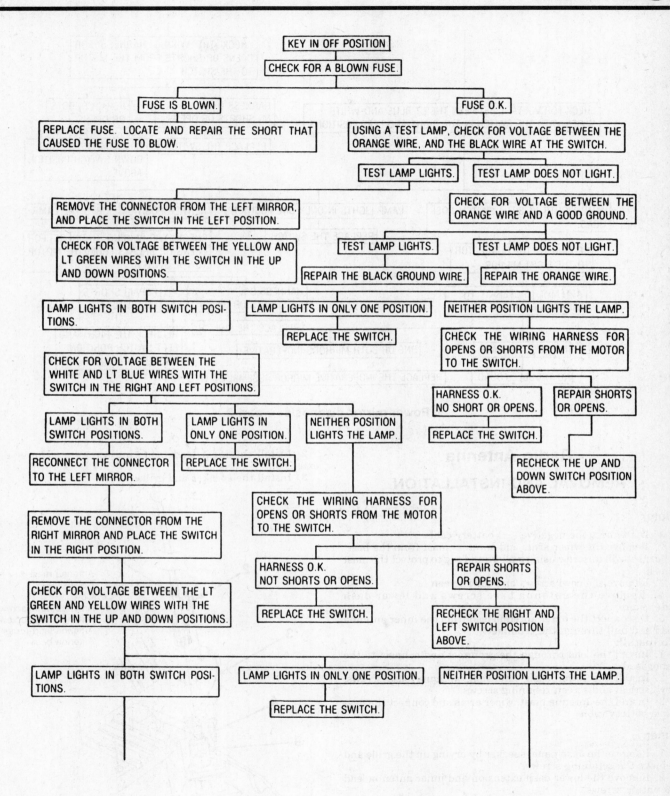

Power mirror diagnosis — part 1

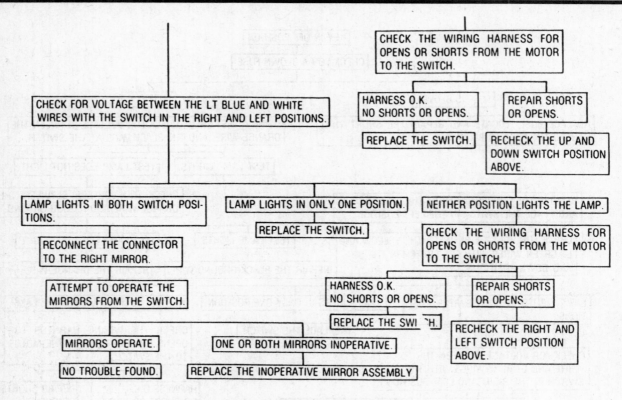

CHECK THE WIRING HARNESS FOR OPENS OR SHORTS FROM THE MOTOR TO THE SWITCH.

HARNESS O.K. NO SHORTS OR OPENS.

REPLACE THE SWITCH.

REPAIR SHORTS OR OPENS.

RECHECK THE UP AND DOWN SWITCH POSITION ABOVE.

CHECK FOR VOLTAGE BETWEEN THE LT BLUE AND WHITE WIRES WITH THE SWITCH IN THE RIGHT AND LEFT POSITIONS.

LAMP LIGHTS IN BOTH SWITCH POSITIONS.

LAMP LIGHTS IN ONLY ONE POSITION.

REPLACE THE SWITCH.

NEITHER POSITION LIGHTS THE LAMP.

CHECK THE WIRING HARNESS FOR OPENS OR SHORTS FROM THE MOTOR TO THE SWITCH.

RECONNECT THE CONNECTOR TO THE RIGHT MIRROR.

ATTEMPT TO OPERATE THE MIRRORS FROM THE SWITCH.

HARNESS O.K. NO SHORTS OR OPENS.

REPLACE THE SWITCH.

REPAIR SHORTS OR OPENS.

RECHECK THE RIGHT AND LEFT SWITCH POSITION ABOVE.

MIRRORS OPERATE.

NO TROUBLE FOUND.

ONE OR BOTH MIRRORS INOPERATIVE.

REPLACE THE INOPERATIVE MIRROR ASSEMBLY

Power mirror diagnosis — part 2

Radio Antenna

REMOVAL AND INSTALLATION

2. Install the inner lead mounting screws and lower dash extension.
3. Install the speaker and grille.

Outer

1. Disconnect the negative (−) battery cable.
2. Remove the wiper arms and antenna mast from the base. The mast will unscrew using a pliers and rag to protect the mast finish.
3. Remove the cowl screws and cowl screen.
4. Remove the antenna base screws and lower dash extension.
5. Disconnect the outer antenna lead from the inner antenna lead and pull through the grommet.

To install:
1. Install the lead through the grommet and connect to the inner lead.
2. Install the lower dash extension, antenna base screws, cowl screen and screen retaining screws.
3. Install the antenna mast, wiper arms and connect the negative battery cable.

Inner

1. Remove the dash panel speaker by prying up the grille and remove the retaining screws.
2. Remove the lower dash extension and inner antenna lead mounting screws.
3. Disconnect the antenna lead from the routing clips and radio receiver.

To install:
1. Install the antenna lead to the routing clips and radio receiver.

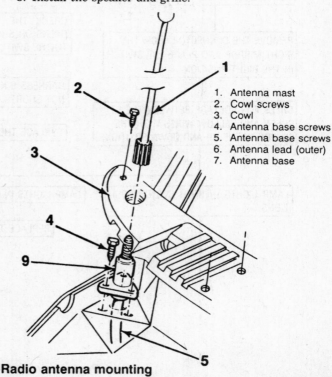

1. Antenna mast
2. Cowl screws
3. Cowl
4. Antenna base screws
5. Antenna base screws
6. Antenna lead (outer)
7. Antenna base

Radio antenna mounting

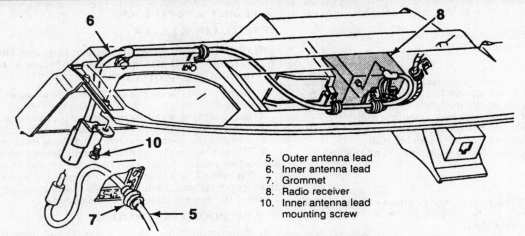

5. Outer antenna lead
6. Inner antenna lead
7. Grommet
8. Radio receiver
10. Inner antenna lead mounting screw

Antenna wire routing

Door Locks

REMOVAL AND INSTALLATION

Front Door Manual Locks

OUTSIDE HANDLE AND LOCK CYLINDER

1. Refer to the "Door Panel, Removal and Installation" procedures in this Section and remove the door panel.
2. Remove the outside handle-to-door nuts.

NOTE: Removing the soft plug at the edge of the door may provide additional room to access the bottom door handle nut.

3. Remove the outside handle-to-lock rod and the handle from the door.
4. Remove the lock rod from the lock cylinder, then the lock cylinder retainer, the gasket and the lock cylinder from the door.

To install:

1. Install the lock rod to the lock cylinder, then the lock cylinder retainer, the gasket and the lock cylinder to the door.

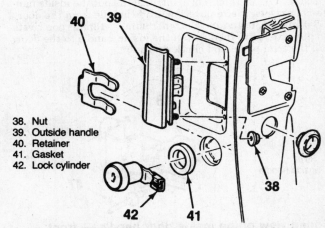

38. Nut
39. Outside handle
40. Retainer
41. Gasket
42. Lock cylinder

Exploded view of the outside handle and lock cylinder assembly — front door

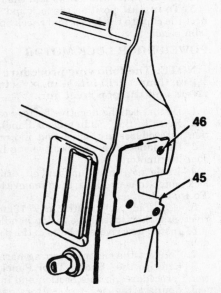

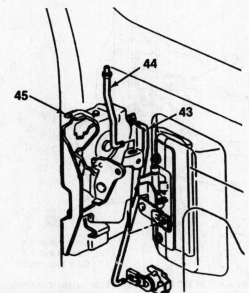

43. Lock cylinder rod
44. Outside handle rod
45. Lock assembly
46. Screw

View of the lock assembly — front door

2. Install the outside handle-to-lock rod and the handle to the door.

3. Install the outside handle-to-door nuts.

4. Install the door panel.

LOCK ASSEMBLY

1. Refer to the "Door Panel, Removal and Installation" procedures in this Section and remove the door panel.

2. Remove the outside handle-to-lock assembly rod.

3. Remove the lock cylinder-to-lock assembly rod.

4. Remove the inside handle-to-lock assembly rod.

5. Remove the inside lock-to-lock assembly rod.

6. Remove the lock assembly-to-door screws and the lock assembly from door.

INSIDE HANDLE

NOTE: The following procedure requires the use of a $^3/_{16}$ in. (5mm) drill bit, $\frac{1}{4}$ in. × $\frac{1}{2}$ in. (6mm × 13mm) pop rivets and the pop rivet gun.

1. Refer to the "Door Panel, Removal and Installation" procedures in this Section and remove the door panel.

2. Remove the inside handle-to-lock rod.

3. Using a $^3/_{16}$ in. (5mm) drill bit, drill the out the inside handle-to-door rivets, the remove the inside handle from the door.

4. **To install,** use $\frac{1}{4}$ in. × $\frac{1}{2}$ in. (6mm × 13mm) pop rivets and a pop rivet gun, then install the inside handle to the door. Install the trim panel and check operation.

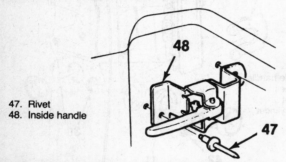

47. Rivet
48. Inside handle

Exploded view of the inside door handle — front door

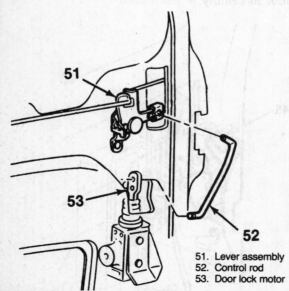

51. Lever assembly
52. Control rod
53. Door lock motor

Exploded view of the power door lock components — sliding door

Front Door w/Power Locks
REMOTE LOCK LEVER

NOTE: The following procedure requires the use of a $^3/_{16}$ in. (5mm) drill bit, $\frac{1}{4}$ in. × $\frac{1}{2}$ in. (6mm × 13mm) pop rivets and the pop rivet gun.

1. Refer to the "Door Panel, Removal and Installation" procedures in this Section and remove the door panel.

2. Remove the power door lock motor to remove the lever rod.

3. Remove the remote lever-to-lock assembly rod.

4. Remove the remote lever-to-inside lock lever rod.

5. Using a $^3/_{16}$ in. (5mm) drill bit, drill the out the inside handle-to-door rivets, the remove the inside handle from the door.

6. **To install,** use $\frac{1}{4}$ in. × $\frac{1}{2}$ in. (6mm × 13mm) pop rivets and a pop rivet gun, then install the inside handle to the door. Connect the remote lever-to-lock lever rod.

POWER DOOR LOCK MOTOR

1. Refer to the "Door Panel, Removal and Installation" procedures in this Section and remove the door panel.

2. Remove the power door lock motor to remove the lever rod.

3. Disconnect the electrical connector from the power door lock motor.

4. Remove the motor-to-door bolts and the motor from the door.

5. **To install,** position the motor to the door and install the mounting bolts. Reconnect the electrical connector and install the door trim panel.

Sliding Door
LOCK ASSEMBLY

1. Refer to the "Sliding Door Panel, Removal and Installation" procedures in this Section and remove the door panel.

2. To remove the upper control-to-lock rods, perform the following procedures:

    a. Using a small pry bar, pry the anchor clip out of the hole and push the clip away from the lever.

    b. Pull the rod and clip away from the lever.

3. To remove the remote control-to-locks rods from the remote control, perform the following procedures:

    a. Using a small pry bar, pry the anchor clip out of the hole and push the clip away from the lever.

    b. Pull the rod and clip away from the lever.

4. Remove the lock screws and the lock from the door.

5. **To install,** position the lock and screws to the door. Connect the clips to the levers and check operation. Install the door trim panel.

POWER DOOR LOCK MOTOR

NOTE: The following procedure requires the use of a $^3/_{16}$ in. (5mm) drill bit, $\frac{1}{4}$ in. × $\frac{1}{2}$ in. (6mm × 13mm) pop rivets and the pop rivet gun.

1. Disconnect the negative battery cable from the battery.

2. Refer to the "Sliding Door Panel, Removal and Installation" procedures in this Section and remove the door panel.

3. Disconnect the electrical wiring harness from the power door lock motor.

4. Using a $^3/_{16}$ in. (5mm) drill bit, drill the out the power door lock motor-to-door rivets, then remove the motor from the door.
To install:

5. Use $\frac{1}{4}$ in. × $\frac{1}{2}$ in. (6mm × 13mm) pop rivets and a pop rivet gun, then install the inside handle to the door.

6. Install new rivets or bolts to the power door lock motor-to-door.

7. Connect the electrical wiring harness.

8. Refer to the "Sliding Door Panel, Removal and Installation" procedures in this Section and install the door panel.

9. Connect the negative battery cable to the battery and check operation.

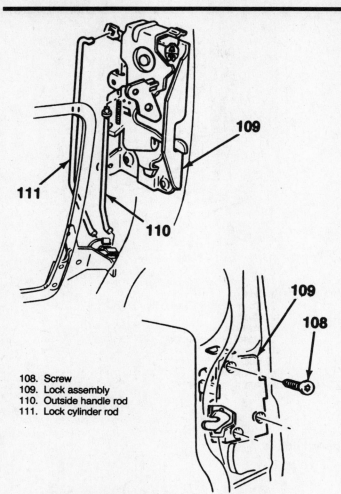

108. Screw
109. Lock assembly
110. Outside handle rod
111. Lock cylinder rod

View of the lock assembly — sliding door

Rear Door w/Manual Locks
OUTSIDE HANDLE AND LOCK CYLINDER

1. Refer to the "Door Panel, Removal and Installation" procedures in this Section and remove the door panel.
2. Remove the control rod from the outside handle by prying the clip anchor out of the hole and pushing the clip away from the lever. Then pull the rod and the clip away from the lever.
3. Remove the outside handle-to-lock nuts and remove the rod and the handle from the door.
4. Remove the license plate housing bolts, and the license plate housing.
5. Remove the door lock shield.
6. Remove the lock control rod from the lock cylinder by prying the clip anchor out of the hole and pushing the clip away from the lever. Then pull the rod and the clip away from the lever.
7. Remove the lock cylinder retainer, and the lock cylinder from the door.

To install:

1. Install the lock cylinder retainer, and the lock cylinder to the door.
2. Install the lock control rod to the lock cylinder.
3. Install the door lock shield.
4. Install the license plate housing assembly and bolts.
5. Install the outside handle-to-lock nuts and handle.
6. Install the control rod to the outside handle.
7. Refer to the "Door Panel, Removal and Installation" procedures in this Section and install the door panel.

LOCK ASSEMBLY

1. Refer to the "Door Panel, Removal and Installation" procedures in this Section and remove the door panel.
2. Remove the outside handle-to-lock assembly rod.
3. Remove the lock cylinder-to-lock assembly rod.
4. Remove the inside handle-to-lock assembly rod.
5. Remove the inside lock-to-lock assembly rod.
6. Remove the lock assembly-to-door screws and the lock assembly from door.

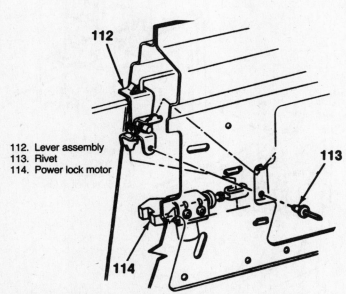

112. Lever assembly
113. Rivet
114. Power lock motor

Exploded view of the power door lock motor assembly — sliding door

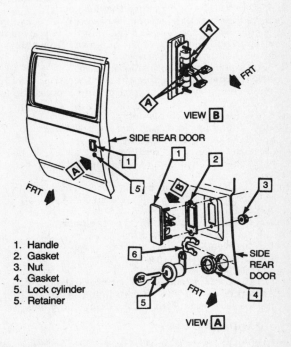

1. Handle
2. Gasket
3. Nut
4. Gasket
5. Lock cylinder
5. Retainer

Rear door lock cylinder removal

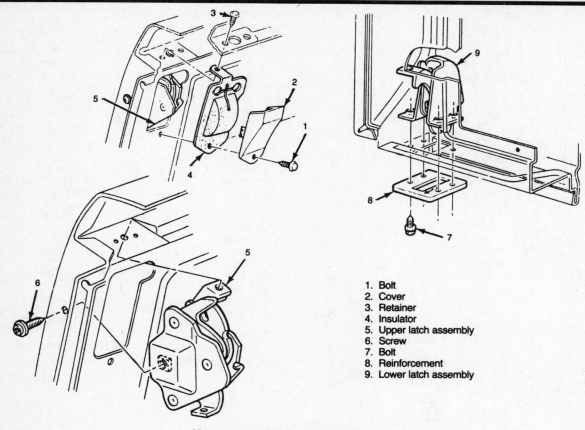

1. Bolt
2. Cover
3. Retainer
4. Insulator
5. Upper latch assembly
6. Screw
7. Bolt
8. Reinforcement
9. Lower latch assembly

Upper and lower door latches

UPPER AND LOWER LATCH REPLACEMENT

1. Refer to the "Door Panel, Removal and Installation" procedures in this Section and remove the door panel.
2. Remove the control rods from the remote control by prying the clip anchor out of the hole and pushing the clip away from the lever. Then pull the rod and the clip away from the lever.
3. Remove the upper latch screws.
4. Remove the upper latch insulator cover.
5. Pry the plastic nails holding the weatherstrip away from the door and remove the weatherstrip from around the latch area.
6. Remove the door latch insulator.
7. Remove the upper latch and rod from the door.
8. Remove the lower latch screws.
9. Remove the lower latch reinforcement plate.
10. Remove the lower latch and rod from the door.

To install:

1. Install the lower latch and rod to the door.
2. Install the lower latch reinforcement plate.
3. Install the lower latch screws.
4. Install the upper latch and rod to the door.
5. Install the door latch insulator.
6. Install the weatherstrip to the latch area.
7. Install the upper latch insulator cover.
8. Install the upper latch screws.
9. Install the control rods to the remote control.
10. Refer to the "Door Panel, Removal and Installation" procedures in this Section and install the door trim panel.

Rear Door w/Power

REMOTE LOCK LEVER

1. Refer to the "Door Panel, Removal and Installation" pro-

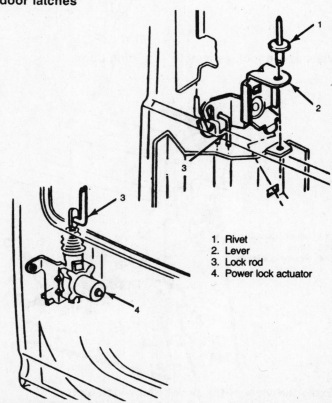

1. Rivet
2. Lever
3. Lock rod
4. Power lock actuator

Lock actuator components

cedures in this Section and remove the door panel.

2. Disconnect the negative battery cable and remove the actuator to lever rod.

3. Using a ³/₁₆ in. (5mm) drill bit, drill out the the head of the actuator-to-door rivets.

4. Remove the actuator from the door.

5. **To install**, use ¼ in. diameter bolt (½ in. long) with a spring washer and nut to attach the actuator to the door. Connect the lever rod to the actuator. Install the door trim panel and check operation.

POWER LOCK ACTUATOR

1. Refer to the "Door Panel, Removal and Installation" procedures in this Section and remove the door panel.

2. Remove the power door lock actuator to remove the lever rod.

3. Disconnect the electrical connector from the power door lock actuator.

4. Remove the actuator-to-door bolts and the actuator from the door.

5. **To install** position the actuator to the door and install the bolts. Connect the electrical connector and lever rod. Install the door trim panel and check operation.

Hood

REMOVAL AND INSTALLATION

1. Disconnect the negative (−) battery cable. Mark the area around the hinges to make installation easier. Tape or cover the painted areas around the hood for finish protection.

2. With an assistant, support the hood and remove the hinge to hood frame bolts.

3. Remove the hood from the van.

4. **To install**, with an assistant, position the hood onto the van and install the retaining bolts. Adjust the hood to the original position and torque the bolts to 20 ft. lbs. (27 Nm). Check alignment before slamming the hood.

Windshield

NOTE: Bonded windshields require special tools and special removal procedures to be removed without being broken. For this reason we recommend that you refer all removal and installation to a qualified technician.

────────── CAUTION ──────────
Always wear heavy gloves when handling glass to reduce the risk of injury!
────────────────────────────

When replacing a cracked windshield, it is important that the cause of the crack be determined and the condition corrected, before a new glass is installed.

The cause of the crack may be an obstruction or a high spot somewhere around the flange of the opening; cracking may not occur until pressure from the high spot or obstruction becomes particularly high due to winds, extremes of temperature, or rough terrain.

Suggestions of what to look for are described later in this Section under inspection.

REMOVAL

When a windshield is broken, the glass may have already have fallen or been removed from the weatherstrip. Often, however, it is necessary to remove a cracked or otherwise imperfect windshield that is still intact. In this case, it is a good practise to crisscross the glass with strips of masking tape before removing the it; this will help hold the glass together and minimize the risk of injury.

If a crack extends to the edge of the glass, mark the point where the crack meets the weather strip. (Use a piece of chalk and mark the point on the cab, next to the weatherstrip.) Later, when examining the flange of the opening for a cause of the crack start at the point marked.

The higher the temperature of the work area, the more pliable the weather strip will be. The more pliable the weather strip, the more easily the windshield can be removed.

Before removing the glass, cover the instrument panel, and the surrounding sheet metal with protective covering and remove the wiper arms.

There are two methods of windshield removal, depending on the method of windshield replacement chosen. When using the short method of installation, it is important to cut the glass from the urethane adhesive as close to the glass as possible. This is due to the fact that the urethane adhesive will be used to provide a base for the replacement windshield.

When using the extended method of windshield replacement, all the urethane adhesive must be removed from the pinchweld flange so, the process of cutting the window from the adhesive is less critical.

Special tool J–24402–A, Glass Sealant Remover Knife, or its equivalent is required to perform this procedure. To remove the windshield:

1. Place the protective covering around the area where the glass will be removed.

2. Remove the windshield wiper arms, and the interior garnish moldings.

3. Remove the exterior reveal moldings and the support molding from the urethane adhesive by prying one end of the molding from the adhesive. Pull the free end of the molding away from the windshield or the pinchweld flange until the molding is completely free of the windshield.

4. Using J–24402–A cut the windshield from the urethane adhesive. If the short method of glass replacement is to be used, keep the knife as close to the glass as possible in order to leave a base for the replacement glass.

5. With the help of an assistant, remove the glass.

6. If the original glass is to be reinstalled, place it on a protected bench or a holding or holding fixture. Remove any remaining adhesive with a razor blade or a sharp scraper. Any remaining traces of adhesive material can be removed with denatured alcohol or lacquer thinner.

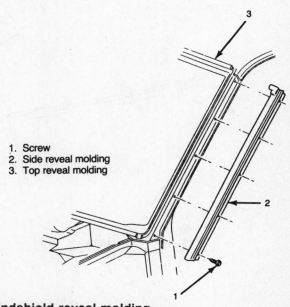

1. Screw
2. Side reveal molding
3. Top reveal molding

Windshield reveal molding

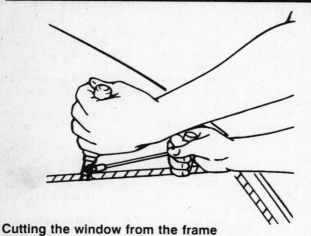

Cutting the window from the frame

NOTE: When cleaning windshield glass, avoid contacting the edge of the plastic laminate material (on the edge of the glass) with volatile cleaner. Contact may cause discoloration and deterioration of the plastic laminate. Do not use a petroleum based solvent such as gasoline or kerosene. The presence of oil will prevent the adhesion of new material.

INSPECTION

An inspection of the windshield opening, the weather strip, and the glass may reveal the cause of a broken windshield. This can help prevent future breakage. If there is no apparent cause of breakage, the weatherstrip should be removed from the flange of the opening and the flange inspected. Look for high weld or solder spots, hardened spot welds sealer, or any other obstruction or irregularity in the flange. Check the weatherstrip for irregularities or obstructions in it.

Check the windshield to be installed to make sure that it does not have any chipped edges. Chipped edges can be ground off, restoring a smooth edge to the glass, and minimizing concentrations of pressure that cause breakage. Remove no more than necessary, in an effort to maintain the original shape of the glass and the proper clearance between it and the flange of the opening.

INSTALLATION METHODS

There are two methods used for windshield replacement. The short method described previously in the removal procedure is used when the urethane adhesive can be used as a base for the new glass. This method would be used in the case of a cracked glass, if, no other service needs to be done to the windshield frame such as sheet metal or repainting work.

The extended method should be used when work must be done to the windshield frame such as straightening or repairing sheet metal or repainting the windshield frame. In this method all of the urethane adhesive must be removed from the pinchweld flange.

INSTALLATION

To replace a urethane adhered windshield, GM adhesive service kit No. 9636067 contains some of the materials needed, and must be used to insure the original integrity of the windshield design. Materials in this kit include:
1. One tube of adhesive material.
2. One dispensing nozzle.
3. Steel music wire.
4. Rubber cleaner.
5. Rubber Primer.
6. Pinchweld primer.
7. Blackout primer.
8. Filler strip (for use on windshield installations for vehicles equipped with embedded windshield antenna).
9. Primer applicators.

1. Top revel molding
2. Lower support
3. Spacer
4. Strip filler
5. Urethane adhesive
6. V.I.N. plate

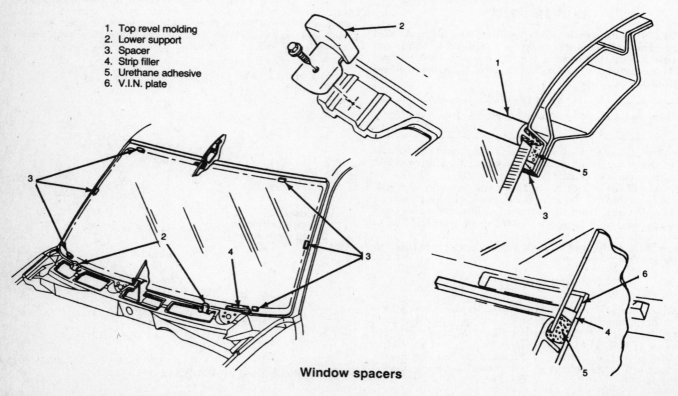

Window spacers

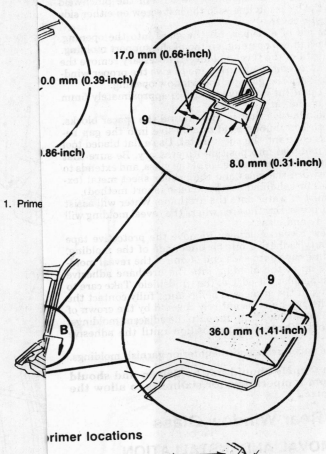

17.0 mm (0.66-inch)

0.0 mm (0.39-inch)

9

).86-inch)

8.0 mm (0.31-inch)

1. Prime

9

B

36.0 mm (1.41-inch)

rimer locations

Other materials are
which are not included
1. GM rubber lubric
2. Alcohol for cleanii
3. Adhesive dispensi
4. A commercial type
5. Two rubber suppo

Extended Method

1. Clean all metal sur
clean alcohol dampened
2. Apply the pinchwe
pinchweld area. Do not l
posed paint because dan
ty minutes for the prim
3. Follow the steps lis
der of the procedure.

Short Method

1. Install the suppor
from inside the vehicle.
ed at the bottom center
2. Thoroughly clean t
sive material will be ap
cloth. Allow the alcohol
3. Apply the clear glas
the windshield from the
the primer around the e
primer to cure for thirty
4. Apply the blackout
the clear primer. Allow t

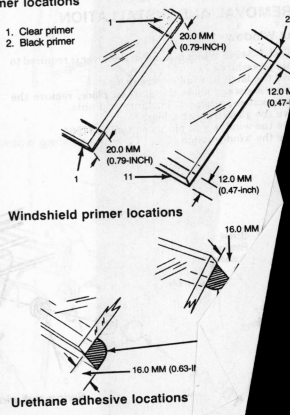

1. Clear primer
2. Black primer

1

2

20.0 MM
(0.79-INCH)

12.0 M
(0.47-

20.0 MM
(0.79-INCH)

1

11

12.0 MM
(0.47-inch)

Windshield primer locations

16.0 MM

16.0 MM (0.63-I

Urethane adhesive locations

5. Place two rubber blocks onto the base ~~ch~~ retainer screws.
flange. Place the blocks in line with the last sc ~~ring~~, bushings and nut.
of the cowl grille cover.

6. With the aid of a helper, lift the glass ~~ing~~, bushings and nut.
Center the glass in the opening, on top of the retainer screws.

7. Check the fit of the revel molding. If nece
glass and cut away additional urethane to give
shield height. Place the glass in the window

8. Cut the tip of the adhesive cartridge ap
from the end of the tip.

9. Apply the adhesive first in and around t
Apply a smooth continuous bead of adhesive
tween the glass edge and the sheet metal. Use
to paddle the material into position if necessa
the adhesive contacts the entire edge of the gla
fill the gap between the glass and the primer
tended method) or solidified urethane base (s

10. Spray a mist of water onto the urethane.
in the curing process. Dry the area where the re
contact the body and glass.

11. Install new reveal moldings. Remove the
covering the butyl adhesive on the underside
Push the molding caps onto each end of one of
ings. Press the lip of the molding into the u
while holding it against the edge of the windshi
at the molding in the corners. The lip must
hesive and the gap must be entirely covered
molding. Slide the molding caps onto the ad **latch**
tape to hold the molding in position un

tall the wiper arms and the interior g ~~h~~ modling

**The vehicle should not be driv
room temperature for six hou
cure.**

Rear Window Glass

VAL AND INSTALLAT

46 Window Roll Pin Remov
ire.
h to window screws.
ant holds the glass in pl
retainers, bushings and
s from the door.
low roll pin using tool J—
ow latch. **olding**

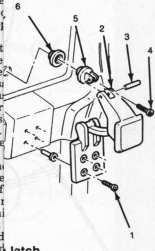

1. Screw
2. Latch
3. Pin
4. Screw
5. Bearing
6. Bushing
7. Nut

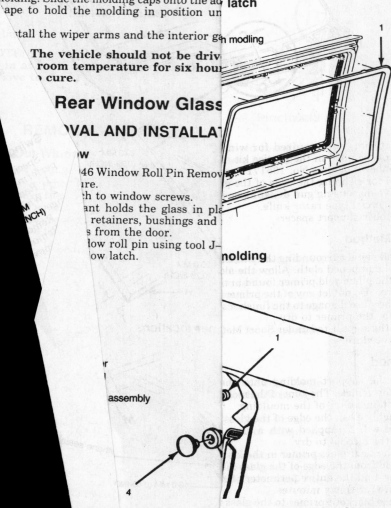

assembly

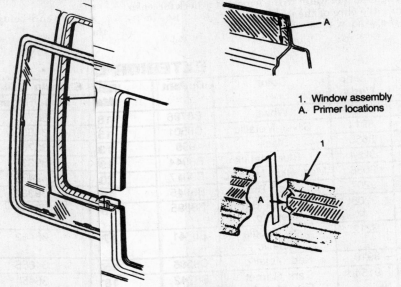

1. Window assembly
A. Primer locations

...ons for fixed windows

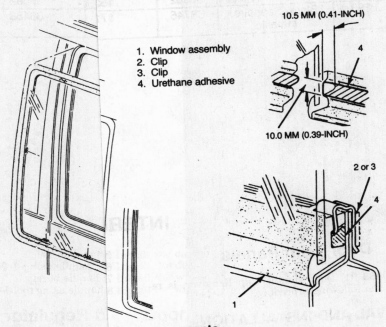

1. Window assembly
2. Clip
3. Clip
4. Urethane adhesive

10.5 MM (0.41-INCH)

10.0 MM (0.39-INCH)

2 or 3

...ndow components

3. Install the window latch.
4. Install the window roll pi...
5. Install the glass to the do...
6. While an assistant holds th...ge
to glass screws, retainers, bush...
7. Install the latch to windo...

Stationary Window

Special tool J–28628, Adhesi...a-
lent, is required to perform thi...
1. Remove the door garnish...
2. Remove the window moldi...
3. Remove the window retair...
4. Remove the window assem...ool

J–28628. Cut through the urethane adhesive f...
the vehicle.
5. Remove all the urethane from the pin...
To install:
1. Clean the pinchweld flange and the ...the fig-
with solvent and allow it to air dry. ...applying
2. Apply urethane adhesive primer t...
and the window assembly molding in t...high into
ure. Allow the primer to dry at least 3...
the adhesive.
3. Apply a triangle bead of uretha... flange.
the trough of the window assembl...
4. Install the window assembly...
5. Install the window assembl...

10–21

6. Apply a light mist of water to the window to chec̓r garnish molding.
and to enhance the cure of the urethane.
hane adhesive 6 hours to cure before moving
7. Install the window molding.

EX

GM Code	Fisher Code	Color	DuPzler	Martin Senor	Sherwin Williams Acme/Rogers
10	9225	White	B8015	36783	36783
15	8914	Silver Metallic	C85796	32-5452	34856
20	8555	Black	99700	30-5296	33756
27	9264	Lt. Blue Metallic	B89146	39337	39337
30	9086	Med. Blue Metallic	B90238	42478	42478
33	9207	Lt. Mesa Brown	B89152	39338	39338
34	9208	Light Mesa Brown Metallic	B88107	38145	38145
68	9212	Dark Saddle Metallic	B87001	36452	36452
75	8919	Red Metallic	C85804	32-5459	34855
77	9154	Dark Garnet Red Metallic	B87002	36454	36454
83	8915	Gunmetal Metallic	C85805	32-5467	35082
98	8863	Black Sapphire Metallic	B87003	36458	36458

Door Trim Panels

ntrol assembly handle bezel.
or lock assembly handle using J–9886–01.
Special tool J–9886–01, Door Handle Clip Remover
ndow regulator handle bezel.
`red to perform the following procedure.
ndow regulator handle using tool J–9886–01.

REMOVAL AND INSTALLATION

Glass and Regulator

`move the window regulator handle using tool J

VAL AND INSTALLATION

ove the window regulator handle bezel.
`ve the door lock assembly handle using J–98

—— CAUTION ——
`loves when handling glass to minimize the risk of

`ve the control assembly handle bezel.
`e the assist handle.
` the arm rest.
`he door trim outer panel screws and pull th
`he retainer.
`ass to the bottom of the door and remove the
` door trim inner panel screws and remo
2.
3.
`door channel run assembly.
4. `r trim inner panel and screws.

`or cover any sharp edges that could
` trim outer panel screws.
`s.
`est.
`handle.

`ss forward until the front roller is in line with
`ash channel.

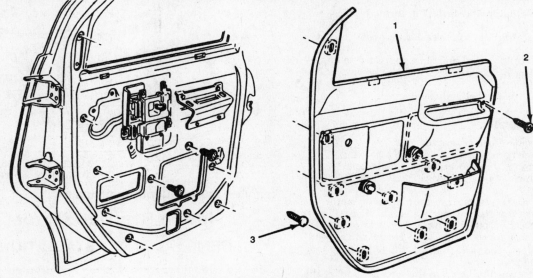

1. Trim panel
2. Screw
3. Retainer

Assist handle cover

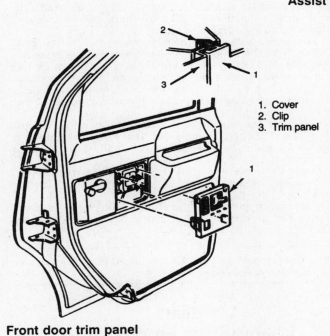

1. Cover
2. Clip
3. Trim panel

1. Glass
2. Sash
3. Regulator
4. Rivets

Front door trim panel

Window regulator components

4. Disengage the roller from the channel.
5. Push the window forward, then tilt it up until the rear roller is disengaged.
6. Place the window in a level position, and raise it straight up and out of the door.
To install:
1. Install the window into the door.
2. Push the window forward, then tilt it up until the rear roller is engaged.
3. Engage the roller to the channel.
4. Slide the glass forward until the front roller is in line with the notch in the sash channel.
5. Install the door channel run assembly.
6. Lower the glass to the bottom of the door and install the door trim panel.

Regulator

1. Raise the window and tape the glass in the full up position using cloth body tape.
2. Remove the door trim panel and the door panel, then, using a $^3/_{16}$ in. (5mm) drill bit, drill the head from the rivet.
3. Slide the regulator forward and then rearward to disengage the rear roller from the sash channel. Then disengage the lower roller from the regulator rail.
4. Disengage the forward roller from the sash channel at the notch in the sash channel.
5. Collapse the regulator and remove it through the access hole in the door.
6. Lubricate the regulator and the sash channel and regulator rails with Lubriplate® or its equivalent.

To install:

1. Collapse the regulator and install it through the access hole in the door.
2. Engage the forward roller to the sash channel at the notch in the sash channel.
3. Slide the regulator forward and then rearward to engage the rear roller to the sash channel. Then engage the lower roller to the regulator rail.
4. Install the door trim panel and the door panel.

Power Window Regulator

1. Remove the negative battery cable.
2. Remove the door trim panel.
3. Remove the armrest bracket and water deflector.
4. Raise the window and tape the glass in the full up position using cloth body tape.
5. Remove the wiring harness from the regulator motor.
6. Remove the regulator to door rivets, using a $\frac{3}{16}$ in. (5mm) drill bit to drill the heads from the rivets.
7. Slide the regulator forward and then rearward to disengage the rear roller from the sash channel. Then disengage the lower roller from the regulator rail.
8. Disengage the forward roller from the sash channel at the notch in the sash channel.
9. Collapse the regulator and remove it through the access hole in the door.

To install:

1. Lubricate the regulator and install through the access hole in the door.
2. Engage the forward roller to the sash channel at the notch in the sash channel.
3. Slide the regulator forward and then rearward to engage the rear roller to the sash channel. Then engage the lower roller to the regulator rail.
4. Install the regulator to door rivets, using $\frac{3}{16}$ in. (5mm) rivets.
5. Install the wiring harness to the regulator motor.
6. Remove the tape from the glass.
7. Install the armrest bracket and water deflector.
8. Install the door trim panel.
9. Connect the negative battery cable and check operation.

Electric Window Motor

REMOVAL AND INSTALLATION

1. Remove the power window regulator as described above.

───────── **CAUTION** ─────────

Step 2 MUST be performed if the regulator motor is to be removed from the regulator. The regulator lift arms are under pressure from the counterbalance spring and can cause serious injury if the motor is removed without locking the sector gear in position.

───────────────────────────────

2. Install a pan head sheet metal tapping screw through the sector gear and the backing plate at the hole provided to lock the sector gear into position. Then drill out the motor to regulator attaching rivets.
3. Remove the motor from the regulator.

To install:

1. Lubricate the motor drive gear and the regulator sector teeth. Install the motor to the regulator and check the mesh of the motor to the regulator.
2. Install rivets to the motor and the regulator.
3. Remove the sheet metal tapping screw.
4. Install the power window regulator.

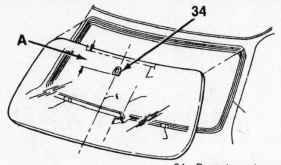

34. Rear view mirror support
A. 3.41 inches (86.75mm)

Rearview mirror support positioning

Inside Rearview Mirror

REMOVAL AND INSTALLATION

The rearview mirror is attached to a support which is secured to the windshield glass. A service replacement windshield glass has the support bonded to the glass assembly. To install a detached mirror support or install a new part, use the following procedures to complete the service.

1. Locate the support position at the center of the glass 86.75mm from the top of the glass to the top of the support.
2. Circle the location on the outside of the glass with a wax pencil or crayon. Draw a large circle around the support circle.
3. Clean the area within the circle with household cleaner and dry with a clean towel. Repeat the procedures using rubbing alcohol.
4. Sand the bonding surface of the support with fine grit (320–360) emery cloth or sandpaper. If the original support is being used, remove the old adhesive with rubbing alcohol and a clean towel.
5. Apply the adhesive as outlined in the kit instructions.
6. Position the support to the marked location with the rounded end UP.
7. Press the support to the glass for 30–60 seconds. Excessive adhesive can be removed after five minutes with rubbing alcohol.

───────── **CAUTION** ─────────

Do NOT apply excessive pressure to the windshield glass. The glass may break, causing personal injury!

───────────────────────────────

Seats

REMOVAL AND INSTALLATION

Front

1. Disconnect the negative (–) battery cable.
2. Remove the seat riser and floor nuts.
3. Disconnect the power seat wiring harness.
4. Remove the seat belt and guide from the floor studs.
5. Slide the seat forward and rearward to gain access to the seat bolts. Remove the seat from the vehicle with an assistant.
6. Remove the seat from the risers.

To install:

1. If removed, install the adjuster wire, seat riser nuts, bolts and riser.
2. Install the seat and connect the seat belt and guide to the floor studs.
3. Connect the power seat electrical connectors.
4. Torque the floor-to-riser nuts to 26 ft. lbs. (35 Nm).
5. Connect the negative battery cable and check operation.

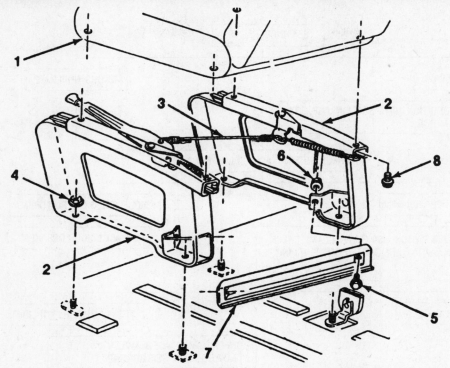

1. Seat
2. Seat riser and adjuster
3. Adjuster wire
4. Nut
5. Bolt
6. Nut
7. Spacer
8. Bolt

Front bucket seats — with manual adjuster

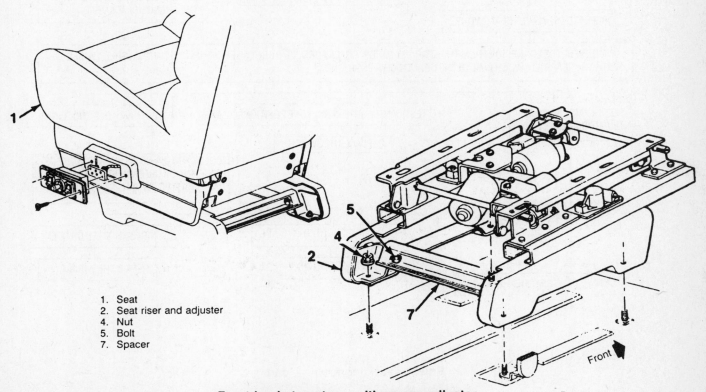

1. Seat
2. Seat riser and adjuster
4. Nut
5. Bolt
7. Spacer

Front bucket seats — with power adjuster

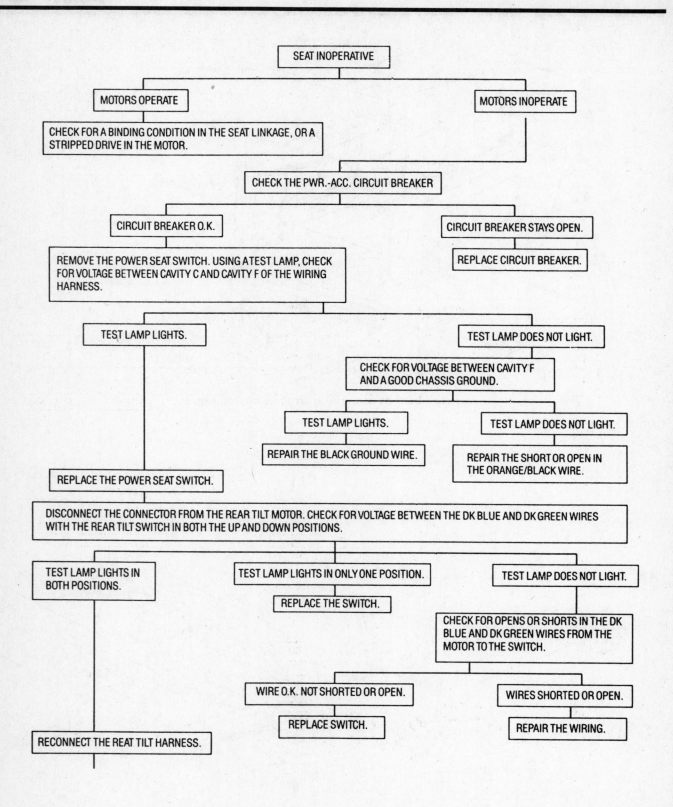

Power seat diagnosis — part 1

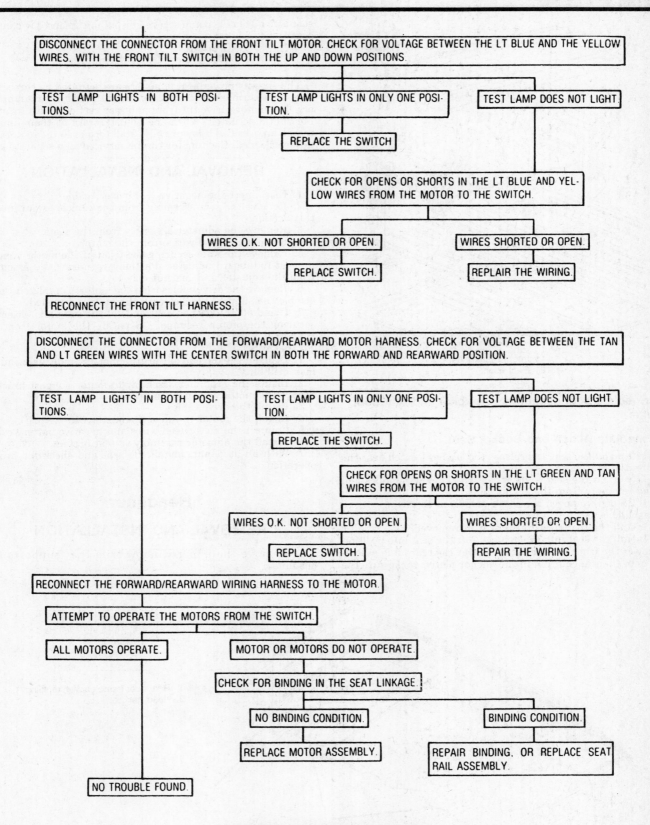

DISCONNECT THE CONNECTOR FROM THE FRONT TILT MOTOR. CHECK FOR VOLTAGE BETWEEN THE LT BLUE AND THE YELLOW WIRES. WITH THE FRONT TILT SWITCH IN BOTH THE UP AND DOWN POSITIONS.

TEST LAMP LIGHTS IN BOTH POSITIONS.

TEST LAMP LIGHTS IN ONLY ONE POSITION.

REPLACE THE SWITCH

TEST LAMP DOES NOT LIGHT.

CHECK FOR OPENS OR SHORTS IN THE LT BLUE AND YELLOW WIRES FROM THE MOTOR TO THE SWITCH.

WIRES O.K. NOT SHORTED OR OPEN.

REPLACE SWITCH.

WIRES SHORTED OR OPEN.

REPLAIR THE WIRING.

RECONNECT THE FRONT TILT HARNESS.

DISCONNECT THE CONNECTOR FROM THE FORWARD/REARWARD MOTOR HARNESS. CHECK FOR VOLTAGE BETWEEN THE TAN AND LT GREEN WIRES WITH THE CENTER SWITCH IN BOTH THE FORWARD AND REARWARD POSITION.

TEST LAMP LIGHTS IN BOTH POSITIONS.

TEST LAMP LIGHTS IN ONLY ONE POSITION.

REPLACE THE SWITCH.

TEST LAMP DOES NOT LIGHT.

CHECK FOR OPENS OR SHORTS IN THE LT GREEN AND TAN WIRES FROM THE MOTOR TO THE SWITCH.

WIRES O.K. NOT SHORTED OR OPEN.

REPLACE SWITCH.

WIRES SHORTED OR OPEN.

REPAIR THE WIRING.

RECONNECT THE FORWARD/REARWARD WIRING HARNESS TO THE MOTOR.

ATTEMPT TO OPERATE THE MOTORS FROM THE SWITCH.

ALL MOTORS OPERATE.

MOTOR OR MOTORS DO NOT OPERATE.

CHECK FOR BINDING IN THE SEAT LINKAGE.

NO BINDING CONDITION.

REPLACE MOTOR ASSEMBLY.

BINDING CONDITION.

REPAIR BINDING, OR REPLACE SEAT RAIL ASSEMBLY.

NO TROUBLE FOUND.

Power seat diagnosis — part 2

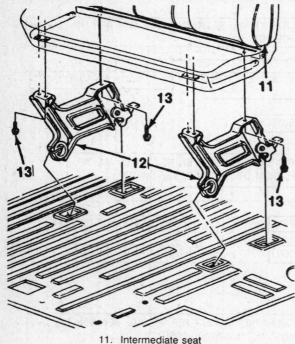

11. Intermediate seat
12. Seat riser
13. Bolt

Intermediate seat assembly — bucket and rear seat similar

Intermediate Bench and Bucket Seat

1. Lift up on the seat and release the latches located near the floor on the rear legs of the seat.
2. Lift up on the seat to disengage the latch assemblies and hooked retainers from the anchor pins.
3. If needed, removed the seat risers from the seat.

To install:

1. Install the seat riser to the seat, if removed.
2. Install the seat into the vehicle. Lift the seat into position and lower the front anchor plates. Lower the rear latch assemblies onto their anchor pin in the anchor plates. Make sure the seat is firmly latched and secured by pulling up and down on the seat.

Power Seat Motors

The six-way power seat adjusters are actuated by three 12V, reversible permanent magnet motors with built in circuit breakers. The motors drive the front and rear vertical gearnuts and a horizontal actuator. When the adjusters are at their limit of travel, an overload relay provides stall torque so the motors are not overloaded. Each motor can be serviced as a separate unit.

REMOVAL AND INSTALLATION

1. Disconnect the negative (−) battery cable.
2. Remove the seat assembly from the vehicle as outlined in this Section.
3. Remove the adjuster assembly from the seat.
4. Remove the feed wires from the motor.
5. Remove the nuts securing the front of the motor support bracket-to-inboard adjuster. Partially withdraw the assembly from the adjuster and gearnut drives.
6. Remove the drive cables from the motor. Completely disassemble the support bracket with the motors attached.
7. Grind off the peened over ends of the grommet assembly securing the motor-to-support. Separate the motor from the support.

To install:

1. Drill out the top end of the grommet assembly using an $^3/_{16}$ inch drill bit.
2. Install the grommet assembly-to-motor support bracket. Secure the motor with a $^3/_{16}$ in. rivet.
3. Install the drive cables.
4. Install the motor-to-inboard adjuster.
5. Connect the motor feed wires and negative battery cable.
6. Install the adjuster assembly-to-seat bottom.
7. With an assistant, install the seat and check for proper operation.

Headliner

REMOVAL AND INSTALLATION

1. Remove the upper window trim that supports the headliner.

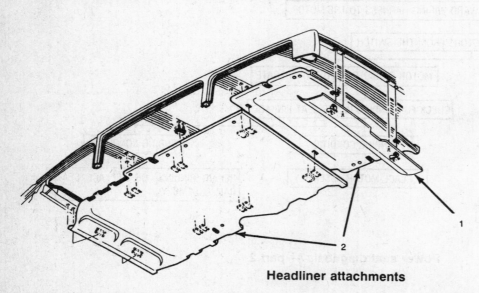

1. Rear door frame garnish molding
2. Headliner

Headliner attachments

2. Remove the sun visors and the door opening garnish moldings. Pull the headliner bow from the retainer (if equipped).
3. Remove the retainer bolts and the retainers.
4. Shift the headliner from side to side to disengage the headliner from the clips.
5. Remove the headliner from the vehicle.

To install:
1. Install the headliner to the vehicle.

2. Shift the headliner from side to side to engage the headliner to the clips.
3. Install the retainer bolts and the retainers.
4. Install the sun visors and the door opening garnish moldings.
5. Install the upper window trim that supports the headliner.

INTERIOR COLORS

NOTE: When two numbers are given, the top number indicates a 12 degree gloss paint. The bottom number is 5 degree gloss paint used only on the instrument panel.

GM Code	Fisher Code	Color	DuPont No.	Ditzler No.	Martin Senour	Sherwin Williams Acme/Rogers
12DN	7701	Graphite	C8345	33622	16905	32989
			—	33870	16963	33767
24CN	9059	Dark Blue	C8792	16323	32-36478	36478
			—	—	—	—
24EN	9541	Midnight Blue	C9006	16998	42600	42600
			—	16999	42599	42599
47CN	9104	Dark Red	C9007	73381	42602	42602
				73380	42601	42601
47DN	9253	Very Dark Red	C9008	73383	42604	42604
			—	73382	42603	42603
60BN	9205	Medium Cognac	C8808	26281	38394	38394
			—	—	38393	38393
60CN	9099	Dark Cognac	C8810	26284	38395	38395
			—	—	38392	38392
60DN	9252	Very Dark Cognac	C8819	26285	38396	38396
			—	—	38391	38391
82CN	8247	Medium Dark Gray	C8447	33665	16949	33714
			—	—	—	—
82DN	8595	Dark Gray	C8550	33824	17071	34602
				33874	17080	34611

How to Remove Stains from Fabric Interior

For best results, spots and stains should be removed as soon as possible. Never use gasoline, lacquer thinner, acetone, nail polish remover or bleach. Use a 3′ x 3″ piece of cheesecloth. Squeeze most of the liquid from the fabric and wipe the stained fabric from the outside of the stain toward the center with a lifting motion. Turn the cheesecloth as soon as one side becomes soiled. When using water to remove a stain, be sure to wash the entire section after the spot has been removed to avoid water stains. Encrusted spots can be broken up with a dull knife and vacuumed before removing the stain.

Type of Stain	How to Remove It
Surface spots	Brush the spots out with a small hand brush or use a commercial preparation such as K2R to lift the stain.
Mildew	Clean around the mildew with warm suds. Rinse in cold water and soak the mildew area in a solution of 1 part table salt and 2 parts water. Wash with upholstery cleaner.
Water stains	Water stains in fabric materials can be removed with a solution made from 1 cup of table salt dissolved in 1 quart of water. Vigorously scrub the solution into the stain and rinse with clear water. Water stains in nylon or other synthetic fabrics should be removed with a commercial type spot remover.

How to Remove Stains from Fabric Interior

Type of Stain	How to Remove It
Chewing gum, tar, crayons, shoe polish (greasy stains)	Do not use a cleaner that will soften gum or tar. Harden the deposit with an ice cube and scrape away as much as possible with a dull knife. Moisten the remainder with cleaning fluid and scrub clean.
Ice cream, candy	Most candy has a sugar base and can be removed with a cloth wrung out in warm water. Oily candy, after cleaning with warm water, should be cleaned with upholstery cleaner. Rinse with warm water and clean the remainder with cleaning fluid.
Wine, alcohol, egg, milk, soft drink (non-greasy stains)	Do not use soap. Scrub the stain with a cloth wrung out in warm water. Remove the remainder with cleaning fluid.
Grease, oil, lipstick, butter and related stains	Use a spot remover to avoid leaving a ring. Work from the outisde of the stain to the center and dry with a clean cloth when the spot is gone.
Headliners (cloth)	Mix a solution of warm water and foam upholstery cleaner to give thick suds. Use only foam—liquid may streak or spot. Clean the entire headliner in one operation using a circular motion with a natural sponge.
Headliner (vinyl)	Use a vinyl cleaner with a sponge and wipe clean with a dry cloth.
Seats and door panels	Mix 1 pint upholstery cleaner in 1 gallon of water. Do not soak the fabric around the buttons.
Leather or vinyl fabric	Use a multi-purpose cleaner full strength and a stiff brush. Let stand 2 minutes and scrub thoroughly. Wipe with a clean, soft rag.
Nylon or synthetic fabrics	For normal stains, use the same procedures you would for washing cloth upholstery. If the fabric is extremely dirty, use a multi-purpose cleaner full strength with a stiff scrub brush. Scrub thoroughly in all directions and wipe with a cotton towel or soft rag.

Glossary

AIR/FUEL RATIO: The ratio of air to gasoline by weight in the fuel mixture drawn into the engine.

AIR INJECTION: One method of reducing harmful exhaust emissions by injecting air into each of the exhaust ports of an engine. The fresh air entering the hot exhaust manifold causes any remaining fuel to be burned before it can exit the tailpipe.

ALTERNATOR: A device used for converting mechanical energy into electrical energy.

AMMETER: An instrument, calibrated in amperes, used to measure the flow of an electrical current in a circuit. Ammeters are always connected in series with the circuit being tested.

AMPERE: The rate of flow of electrical current present when one volt of electrical pressure is applied against one ohm of electrical resistance.

ANALOG COMPUTER: Any microprocessor that uses similar (analogous) electrical signals to make its calculations.

ARMATURE: A laminated, soft iron core wrapped by a wire that converts electrical energy to mechanical energy as in a motor or relay. When rotated in a magnetic field, it changes mechanical energy into electrical energy as in a generator.

ATMOSPHERIC PRESSURE: The pressure on the Earth's surface caused by the weight of the air in the atmosphere. At sea level, this pressure is 14.7 psi at 32°F (101 kPa at 0°C).

ATOMIZATION: The breaking down of a liquid into a fine mist that can be suspended in air.

AXIAL PLAY: Movement parallel to a shaft or bearing bore.

BACKFIRE: The sudden combustion of gases in the intake or exhaust system that results in a loud explosion.

BACKLASH: The clearance or play between two parts, such as meshed gears.

BACKPRESSURE: Restrictions in the exhaust system that slow the exit of exhaust gases from the combustion chamber.

BAKELITE: A heat resistant, plastic insulator material commonly used in printed circuit boards and transistorized components.

BALL BEARING: A bearing made up of hardened inner and outer races between which hardened steel balls roll.

BALLAST RESISTOR: A resistor in the primary ignition circuit that lowers voltage after the engine is started to reduce wear on ignition components.

BEARING: A friction reducing, supportive device usually located between a stationary part and a moving part.

BIMETAL TEMPERATURE SENSOR: Any sensor or switch made of two dissimilar types of metal that bend when heated or cooled due to the different expansion rates of the alloys. These types of sensors usually function as an on/off switch.

BLOWBY: Combustion gases, composed of water vapor and unburned fuel, that leak past the piston rings into the crankcase during normal engine operation. These gases are removed by the PCV system to prevent the buildup of harmful acids in the crankcase.

BRAKE PAD: A brake shoe and lining assembly used with disc brakes.

BRAKE SHOE: The backing for the brake lining. The term is, however, usually applied to the assembly of the brake backing and lining.

BUSHING: A liner, usually removable, for a bearing; an anti-friction liner used in place of a bearing.

BYPASS: System used to bypass ballast resistor during engine cranking to increase voltage supplied to the coil.

CALIPER: A hydraulically activated device in a disc brake system, which is mounted straddling the brake rotor (disc). The caliper contains at least one piston and two brake pads. Hydraulic pressure on the piston(s) forces the pads against the rotor.

CAMSHAFT: A shaft in the engine on which are the lobes (cams) which operate the valves. The camshaft is driven by the crankshaft, via a belt, chain or gears, at one half the crankshaft speed.

CAPACITOR: A device which stores an electrical charge.

CARBON MONOXIDE (CO): A colorless, odorless gas given off as a normal byproduct of combustion. It is poisonous and extremely dangerous in confined areas, building up slowly to toxic levels without warning if adequate ventilation is not available.

GLOSSARY

CARBURETOR: A device, usually mounted on the intake manifold of an engine, which mixes the air and fuel in the proper proportion to allow even combustion.

CATALYTIC CONVERTER: A device installed in the exhaust system, like a muffler, that converts harmful byproducts of combustion into carbon dioxide and water vapor by means of a heat-producing chemical reaction.

CENTRIFUGAL ADVANCE: A mechanical method of advancing the spark timing by using flyweights in the distributor that react to centrifugal force generated by the distributor shaft rotation.

CHECK VALVE: Any one-way valve installed to permit the flow of air, fuel or vacuum in one direction only.

CHOKE: A device, usually a moveable valve, placed in the intake path of a carburetor to restrict the flow of air.

CIRCUIT: Any unbroken path through which an electrical current can flow. Also used to describe fuel flow in some instances.

CIRCUIT BREAKER: A switch which protects an electrical circuit from overload by opening the circuit when the current flow exceeds a predetermined level. Some circuit breakers must be reset manually, while most reset automatically

COIL (IGNITION): A transformer in the ignition circuit which steps up the voltage provided to the spark plugs.

COMBINATION MANIFOLD: An assembly which includes both the intake and exhaust manifolds in one casting.

COMBINATION VALVE: A device used in some fuel systems that routes fuel vapors to a charcoal storage canister instead of venting them into the atmosphere. The valve relieves fuel tank pressure and allows fresh air into the tank as the fuel level drops to prevent a vapor lock situation.

COMPRESSION RATIO: The comparison of the total volume of the cylinder and combustion chamber with the piston at BDC and the piston at TDC.

CONDENSER: 1. An electrical device which acts to store an electrical charge, preventing voltage surges.
2. A radiator-like device in the air conditioning system in which refrigerant gas condenses into a liquid, giving off heat.

CONDUCTOR: Any material through which an electrical current can be transmitted easily.

CONTINUITY: Continuous or complete circuit. Can be checked with an ohmmeter.

COUNTERSHAFT: An intermediate shaft which is rotated by a mainshaft and transmits, in turn, that rotation to a working part.

CRANKCASE: The lower part of an engine in which the crankshaft and related parts operate.

CRANKSHAFT: The main driving shaft of an engine which receives reciprocating motion from the pistons and converts it to rotary motion.

CYLINDER: In an engine, the round hole in the engine block in which the piston(s) ride.

CYLINDER BLOCK: The main structural member of an engine in which is found the cylinders, crankshaft and other principal parts.

CYLINDER HEAD: The detachable portion of the engine, fastened, usually, to the top of the cylinder block, containing all or most of the combustion chambers. On overhead valve engines, it contains the valves and their operating parts. On overhead cam engines, it contains the camshaft as well.

DEAD CENTER: The extreme top or bottom of the piston stroke.

DETONATION: An unwanted explosion of the air/fuel mixture in the combustion chamber caused by excess heat and compression, advanced timing, or an overly lean mixture. Also referred to as "ping".

DIAPHRAGM: A thin, flexible wall separating two cavities, such as in a vacuum advance unit.

DIESELING: A condition in which hot spots in the combustion chamber cause the engine to run on after the key is turned off.

DIFFERENTIAL: A geared assembly which allows the transmission of motion between drive axles, giving one axle the ability to turn faster than the other.

DIODE: An electrical device that will allow current to flow in one direction only.

DISC BRAKE: A hydraulic braking assembly consisting of a brake disc, or rotor, mounted on an axle, and a caliper assembly containing, usually two brake pads which are activated by hydraulic pressure. The pads are forced against the sides of the disc, creating friction which slows the vehicle.

DISTRIBUTOR: A mechanically driven device on an engine which is responsible for electrically firing the spark plug at a predetermined point of the piston stroke.

DOWEL PIN: A pin, inserted in mating holes in two different parts allowing those parts to maintain a fixed relationship.

DRUM BRAKE: A braking system which consists of two brake shoes and one or two wheel cylinders, mounted on a fixed backing plate, and a brake drum, mounted on an axle, which revolves around the assembly. Hydraulic action applied to the wheel cylinders forces the shoes outward against the drum, creating friction, slowing the vehicle.

DWELL: The rate, measured in degrees of shaft rotation, at which an electrical circuit cycles on and off.

ELECTRONIC CONTROL UNIT (ECU): Ignition module, module, amplifier or igniter. See Module for definition.

ELECTRONIC IGNITION: A system in which the timing and firing of the spark plugs is controlled by an electronic control unit, usually called a module. These systems have no points or condenser.

ENDPLAY: The measured amount of axial movement in a shaft.

ENGINE: A device that converts heat into mechanical energy.

EXHAUST MANIFOLD: A set of cast passages or pipes which conduct exhaust gases from the engine.

FEELER GAUGE: A blade, usually metal, of precisely predetermined thickness, used to measure the clearance between two parts. These blades usually are available in sets of assorted thicknesses.

F-Head: An engine configuration in which the intake valves are in the cylinder head, while the camshaft and exhaust valves are located in the cylinder block. The camshaft operates the intake valves via lifters and pushrods, while it operates the exhaust valves directly.

FIRING ORDER: The order in which combustion occurs in the cylinders of an engine. Also the order in which spark is distributed to the plugs by the distributor.

FLATHEAD: An engine configuration in which the camshaft and all the valves are located in the cylinder block.

FLOODING: The presence of too much fuel in the intake manifold and combustion chamber which prevents the air/fuel mixture from firing, thereby causing a no-start situation.

FLYWHEEL: A disc shaped part bolted to the rear end of the crankshaft. Around the outer perimeter is affixed the ring gear. The starter drive engages the ring gear, turning the flywheel, which rotates the crankshaft, imparting the initial starting motion to the engine.

FOOT POUND (ft.lb. or sometimes, ft. lbs.): The amount of energy or work needed to raise an item weighing one pound, a distance of one foot.

FUSE: A protective device in a circuit which prevents circuit overload by breaking the circuit when a specific amperage is present. The device is constructed around a strip or wire of a lower amperage rating than the circuit it is designed to protect. When an amperage higher than that stamped on the fuse is present in the circuit, the strip or wire melts, opening the circuit.

GEAR RATIO: The ratio between the number of teeth on meshing gears.

GENERATOR: A device which converts mechanical energy into electrical energy.

HEAT RANGE: The measure of a spark plug's ability to dissipate heat from its firing end. The higher the heat range, the hotter the plug fires.

HUB: The center part of a wheel or gear.

HYDROCARBON (HC): Any chemical compound made up of hydrogen and carbon. A major pollutant formed by the engine as a byproduct of combustion.

HYDROMETER: An instrument used to measure the specific gravity of a solution.

INCH POUND (in.lb. or sometimes, in. lbs.): One twelfth of a foot pound.

INDUCTION: A means of transferring electrical energy in the form of a magnetic field. Principle used in the ignition coil to increase voltage.

INJECTION PUMP: A device, usually mechanically operated, which meters and delivers fuel under pressure to the fuel injector.

INJECTOR: A device which receives metered fuel under relatively low pressure and is activated to inject the fuel into the engine under relatively high pressure at a predetermined time.

INPUT SHAFT: The shaft to which torque is applied, usually carrying the driving gear or gears.

INTAKE MANIFOLD: A casting of passages or pipes used to conduct air or a fuel/air mixture to the cylinders.

JOURNAL: The bearing surface within which a shaft operates.

KEY: A small block usually fitted in a notch between a shaft and a hub to prevent slippage of the two parts.

MANIFOLD: A casting of passages or set of pipes which connect the cylinders to an inlet or outlet source.

MANIFOLD VACUUM: Low pressure in an engine intake manifold formed just below the throttle plates. Manifold vacuum is highest at idle and drops under acceleration.

GLOSSARY

MASTER CYLINDER: The primary fluid pressurizing device in a hydraulic system. In automotive use, it is found in brake and hydraulic clutch systems and is pedal activated, either directly or, in a power brake system, through the power booster.

MODULE: Electronic control unit, amplifier or igniter of solid state or integrated design which controls the current flow in the ignition primary circuit based on input from the pick-up coil. When the module opens the primary circuit, the high secondary voltage is induced in the coil.

NEEDLE BEARING: A bearing which consists of a number (usually a large number) of long, thin rollers.

OHM: (Ω) The unit used to measure the resistance of conductor to electrical flow. One ohm is the amount of resistance that limits current flow to one ampere in a circuit with one volt of pressure.

OHMMETER: An instrument used for measuring the resistance, in ohms, in an electrical circuit.

OUTPUT SHAFT: The shaft which transmits torque from a device, such as a transmission.

OVERDRIVE: A gear assembly which produces more shaft revolutions than that transmitted to it.

OVERHEAD CAMSHAFT (OHC): An engine configuration in which the camshaft is mounted on top of the cylinder head and operates the valve either directly or by means of rocker arms.

OVERHEAD VALVE (OHV): An engine configuration in which all of the valves are located in the cylinder head and the camshaft is located in the cylinder block. The camshaft operates the valves via lifters and pushrods.

OXIDES OF NITROGEN (NOx): Chemical compounds of nitrogen produced as a byproduct of combustion. They combine with hydrocarbons to produce smog.

OXYGEN SENSOR: Used with the feedback system to sense the presence of oxygen in the exhaust gas and signal the computer which can reference the voltage signal to an air/fuel ratio.

PINION: The smaller of two meshing gears.

PISTON RING: An open ended ring which fits into a groove on the outer diameter of the piston. Its chief function is to form a seal between the piston and cylinder wall. Most automotive pistons have three rings: two for compression sealing; one for oil sealing.

PRELOAD: A predetermined load placed on a bearing during assembly or by adjustment.

PRIMARY CIRCUIT: Is the low voltage side of the ignition system which consists of the ignition switch, ballast resistor or resistance wire, bypass, coil, electronic control unit and pick-up coil as well as the connecting wires and harnesses.

PRESS FIT: The mating of two parts under pressure, due to the inner diameter of one being smaller than the outer diameter of the other, or vice versa; an interference fit.

RACE: The surface on the inner or outer ring of a bearing on which the balls, needles or rollers move.

REGULATOR: A device which maintains the amperage and/or voltage levels of a circuit at predetermined values.

RELAY: A switch which automatically opens and/or closes a circuit.

RESISTANCE: The opposition to the flow of current through a circuit or electrical device, and is measured in ohms. Resistance is equal to the voltage divided by the amperage.

RESISTOR: A device, usually made of wire, which offers a preset amount of resistance in an electrical circuit.

RING GEAR: The name given to a ring-shaped gear attached to a differential case, or affixed to a flywheel or as part a planetary gear set.

ROLLER BEARING: A bearing made up of hardened inner and outer races between which hardened steel rollers move.

ROTOR: 1. The disc-shaped part of a disc brake assembly, upon which the brake pads bear; also called, brake disc.
 2. The device mounted atop the distributor shaft, which passes current to the distributor cap tower contacts.

SECONDARY CIRCUIT: The high voltage side of the ignition system, usually above 20,000 volts. The secondary includes the ignition coil, coil wire, distributor cap and rotor, spark plug wires and spark plugs.

SENDING UNIT: A mechanical, electrical, hydraulic or electromagnetic device which transmits information to a gauge.

SENSOR: Any device designed to measure engine operating conditions or ambient pressures and temperatures. Usually electronic in nature and designed to send a voltage signal to an on-board computer, some sensors may operate as a simple on/off switch or they may provide a variable voltage signal (like a potentiometer) as conditions or measured parameters change.

SHIM: Spacers of precise, predetermined thickness used between parts to establish a proper working relationship.

SLAVE CYLINDER: In automotive use, a device in the hydraulic clutch system which is activated by hydraulic force, disengaging the clutch.

SOLENOID: A coil used to produce a magnetic field, the effect of which is produce work.

SPARK PLUG: A device screwed into the combustion chamber of a spark ignition engine. The basic construction is a conductive core inside of a ceramic insulator, mounted in an outer conductive base. An electrical charge from the spark plug wire travels along the conductive core and jumps a preset air gap to a grounding point or points at the end of the conductive base. The resultant spark ignites the fuel/air mixture in the combustion chamber.

SPLINES: Ridges machined or cast onto the outer diameter of a shaft or inner diameter of a bore to enable parts to mate without rotation.

TACHOMETER: A device used to measure the rotary speed of an engine, shaft, gear, etc., usually in rotations per minute.

THERMOSTAT: A valve, located in the cooling system of an engine, which is closed when cold and opens gradually in response to engine heating, controlling the temperature of the coolant and rate of coolant flow.

TOP DEAD CENTER (TDC): The point at which the piston reaches the top of its travel on the compression stroke.

TORQUE: The twisting force applied to an object.

TORQUE CONVERTER: A turbine used to transmit power from a driving member to a driven member via hydraulic action, providing changes in drive ratio and torque. In automotive use, it links the driveplate at the rear of the engine to the automatic transmission.

TRANSDUCER: A device used to change a force into an electrical signal.

TRANSISTOR: A semi-conductor component which can be actuated by a small voltage to perform an electrical switching function.

TUNE-UP: A regular maintenance function, usually associated with the replacement and adjustment of parts and components in the electrical and fuel systems of a vehicle for the purpose of attaining optimum performance.

TURBOCHARGER: An exhaust driven pump which compresses intake air and forces it into the combustion chambers at higher than atmospheric pressures. The increased air pressure allows more fuel to be burned and results in increased horsepower being produced.

VACUUM ADVANCE: A device which advances the ignition timing in response to increased engine vacuum.

VACUUM GAUGE: An instrument used to measure the presence of vacuum in a chamber.

VALVE: A device which control the pressure, direction of flow or rate of flow of a liquid or gas.

VALVE CLEARANCE: The measured gap between the end of the valve stem and the rocker arm, cam lobe or follower that activates the valve.

VISCOSITY: The rating of a liquid's internal resistance to flow.

VOLTMETER: An instrument used for measuring electrical force in units called volts. Voltmeters are always connected parallel with the circuit being tested.

WHEEL CYLINDER: Found in the automotive drum brake assembly, it is a device, actuated by hydraulic pressure, which, through internal pistons, pushes the brake shoes outward against the drums.